Sexuality, Gender, and the Law

by

William N. Eskridge, Jr.
Professor of Law
Georgetown University Law Center

Nan D. Hunter
Associate Professor of Law
Brooklyn Law School

WESTBURY, NEW YORK
The Foundation Press, Inc.
1997

Library of Congress Cataloging-in-Publication Data

Eskridge, William N.

    Sexuality, gender, and the law / by William N. Eskridge, Jr. and
Nan D. Hunter.

       p.   cm. — (University casebook series)

    Includes index.

    ISBN 1–56662–461–4 (hard cover)

    1. Sex crimes—United States—Cases.   2. Sex and law—United
States—Cases.   3. Sex discrimination—Law and legislation—
United States—Cases.   I. Hunter, Nan D.   II. Title.   III. Series.

KF9325.A7E84   1997

342.73'087—dc21   97–7104

TEXT IS PRINTED ON 10% POST
CONSUMER RECYCLED PAPER

To Morgan Young and Abigail Thornhill
     — from WNEJr

To Lisa Duggan
     — from NDH

To the litigators and scholars who created this field
     — from both of us.

*

The final third of the book emphasizes sexuality and gender in daily life. Chapter 9 explores the increasing impact of these issues on family law, including the very definition of marriage. Chapter 10 turns to employment, delineating constitutional and statutory concepts as to pregnancy, sexual orientation, sexual harassment, and the presence of people with AIDS in the workplace. Chapter 11 takes up one of the key concepts in the field, consent, and seeks to problematize it by exploring issues associated not only with rape but also with prostitution, sex by and between minors, and sexual practices involving bondage or violence in which the participants freely engage. The final chapter explores a series of issues new even in this relatively new field: AIDS as a conflation of sexuality and disease, trans-gender or transsexual issues, and the regulation of gender normative dress.

To paraphrase Justice Blackmun's dissent in *Bowers v. Hardwick*, there are *many* "right" ways of teaching sexuality, gender, and the law. This text emphasizes doctrine, theory, and practice. Our six appendices include statutory provisions, a category of legal materials often overlooked or slighted in legal education, and we encourage readers to avail themselves of close analysis of those texts. We also draw heavily on nonlegal materials, but they are always, hopefully, linked to the law. In addition to notes following the major cases, we include several extended problems in each chapter, which can serve as the focus for class discussions or assignments. These are intended to probe current questions that are particularly difficult and to inspire lively debate among any group of students.

Although one can slice the field (or this text) in numerous ways, we view sexuality and gender in intellectual terms as so inextricably linked as to cast doubt on the ability to separate them completely and still attain a thorough understanding of either. As a taxonomic matter, we use "sex" to mean anatomic categories of males and females, "gender" to mean social characteristics associated with (and constituting) maleness and femaleness, and "sexuality" to mean social understandings of erotic desire. Of these three, we focus least on the first. One theme of the book is that debates over gender now lie at the heart of the most serious disputes over sex discrimination doctrine. Thus we concentrate on those aspects of discrimination "based on sex" that most clearly illustrate its linkages to gender—for example, the attempt by Virginia to preserve the Virginia Military Institute's training of young men in the ways of masculinity and the lively debate over employment policies related to pregnancy.

We consider "sexuality" in its broadest sense. One enterprise in these pages is the deconstruction and analysis of sexual identity, and we do not limit that to gay, lesbian, and bisexual identities. We explore how the law constructs homosexuality *and* heterosexuality in diacritical relationship to each other. We explicate at some length the law's impact on stigmatized sexualitites, but we also examine aspects of sexuality—such as pregnancy and rape—that help constitute social and legal understandings of heterosexuality. We use this approach to achieve two goals: to render visible the lives of lesbians and gay men, who are often invisible in the law, and at the same time to analyze the social meanings of heterosexuality, which is often un-questioned in the law.

One shortcoming that we must acknowledge is the insufficient depth to which this book examines the interrelationship between sexuality and race. We have, we hope, demonstrated some of the ways that sexuality is racial-ized and race is sexualized in American law. We realize, however, that the issue goes much deeper, to the point where, at least in the United States, meanings of race and sexuality are often mutually dependent. Developing the materials necessary to fully explore this proposition was simply beyond the abilities of the authors to do in the time allotted to produce this book. We invite our readers to join the scholarly project of helping fill that gap.

WILLIAM N. ESKRIDGE, JR.
Washington, D.C.

NAN D. HUNTER
New York, New York

ACKNOWLEDGMENTS

We gratefully acknowledge the help of many colleagues, students and other supporters. We want first to acknowledge the founders of the field. The practitioners who advocated on behalf of lesbians and gay men before it became respectable carved out protections from disparate strands of law, often before hostile courts. Their work made possible the body of law and theory which forms this book. Building on this effort (and often participating as well), a handful of scholars created the early sexuality and the law courses. We especially thank Rhonda Rivera of Ohio State, Don Knutson of the University of Southern California, Harlon Dalton of Yale, Arthur Leonard of New York Law School, and Thomas Stoddard of NYU for their work as pioneers.

Many colleagues and friends have contributed suggestions or comments about earlier versions of these materials or the ideas therein. We are particularly grateful to Mary Becker, Matt Coles, Jane Dolkart, Lisa Duggan, Chai Feldblum, Jeanne Goldberg, Ruth Harlow, Marcia Kuntz, Art Leonard, Michael Madow, Steve Pershing, Nancy Polikoff, Robert Raben, Bill Rubenstein, Jane Schacter, Elizabeth Schneider, Tim Westmoreland, Wendy Webster Williams, and Michele Zavos.

Numerous students have contributed to these materials, and in a variety of ways. Students in our sexuality, gender, and the law classes at Brooklyn, Georgetown, Harvard, and Yale stimulated our thinking about these issues generally and provided critical as well as supportive feedback for earlier versions of this book. Most valuable has been the research assistance provided by Kristen Bebelaar (Brooklyn, Class of 1996); Glenn Edwards (Yale, Class of 1997); Eden Fitzgibbons (Brooklyn, Class of 1997); Bonny Harbinger (Georgetown, Class of 1997); Mitsuka Herrera (Georgetown, Class of 1998); Ronnie Ann Himmel (Brooklyn, Class of 1994); Barnett McGowan (Georgetown, Class of 1997); Monica Marquez (Yale, Class of 1997); Jennifer Nash (Georgetown, Class of 1997); Mara Rosenthal (Georgetown, Class of 1998); and Jordan Young (Georgetown, Class of 1998). Professor Hunter would like to thank Georgetown for the research assistance furnished by its students while she was on leave from Brooklyn Law School and located in Washington.

We are grateful to our deans, David Trager and Joan Wexler of Brooklyn Law School and Judy Areen of the Georgetown University Law Center, for making available funds during the summers as well as during the school year that materially supported this project. Professor Eskridge is also grateful to the Simon Guggenheim Foundation for its grant which enabled him to do archival research that contributed to the project. Special thanks for technical support to Golda Lawrence and Rose Patti of Brooklyn Law School and to Mary Ann DeRosa and Karen Neal of the Georgetown University Law Center.

WNE, JR.
NDH

SUMMARY OF CONTENTS

INTRODUCTION v
ACKNOWLEDGMENTS ix
TABLE OF CASES xxxi
PREFACE ON CONSTITUTIONAL RIGHTS xxxix

CHAPTER 1 The Constitution and Sexuality 1

Sec.
1. The Right to Sexual Privacy 3
2. State Regulation of Sexual Practices—The Special Case of Sodomy .. 37
3. Other Constitutional Strategies for Challenging State Regulation of
   Sexuality and Gender 73

CHAPTER 2 Medicalization of Sex, Gender, and Sexuality 133

1. Doctors, Gender, and Sex: From the Sexologists to the Anti–Freudi-
   ans 136
2. Medicalization and American Law 153
3. Current Issues Involving Medicalization, Sexuality, Gender, and the
   Law 203

CHAPTER 3 Theories of Sexuality, Gender, and Law 227

1. Modern Theories of Sexuality 229
2. Postmodern Theories 262
3. The Role of Law in the Social Construction Process 306

CHAPTER 4 U.S. Military Exclusions and the Construction of Man-
   hood 319

1. Racial Exclusion and Segregation in the U.S. Armed Services 321
2. The Exclusion of Women From Combat 342
3. The Military's Exclusion of Lesbians, Gay Men, and Bisexuals 366

CHAPTER 5 Identity Speech in the Body Politic 409

1. Political Speech, Publication, and Association 411
2. Privacy and Sexual "Outing" 463
3. Hate Speech 491

CHAPTER 6 Sexual Speech 507

1. Sexual Speech and the First Amendment: A Dysfunctional Dyad ... 508
2. Feminist Theories of Sexual Speech and Its Regulation 533
3. Cutting Edge Issues of Sexual Speech Law 563

CHAPTER 7   Sexuality and Gender in Education 595

Sec.
1. Regulating Student Exploration and Expression of Sexuality 597
2. Academic Freedom and Issues of Gender and Sexuality 620
3. Legal Issues Arising Out of Public Sex Education 652

CHAPTER 8   Citizenship and Community in a Sexualized World 683

1. Accommodating Religion in a Sexualized World..................... 685
2. Citizens in Conflict: Anti–Civil Rights and Anti–Gay Initiatives...... 715
3. Sexuality and Citizenship in an International Setting 739

CHAPTER 9   Families We Choose 763

1. The Privatization of Family Law.................................. 765
2. The Expanding Right to Marry 795
3. Children in Families of Choice 827

CHAPTER 10   Sexuality and Gender in the Workplace 869

1. Exclusions From Government Employment......................... 876
2. The Statutory Ban Against Sex Discrimination 898
3. Current Issues in Workplace Discrimination....................... 938

CHAPTER 11   The Law's Construction of Consent 969

1. Forcible Sex.. 971
2. Sex by and With Minors...1021
3. Commercial Sex...1044

CHAPTER 12   The Body: New Frontiers 1063

1. AIDS: The Conflation of Sexuality and Disease 1065
2. Transgender Issues and the Law..................................1102
3. The Legal Regulation of Cross–Dressing 1129

APPENDICES

1. Individual Rights Provisions From the Amendments to the Constitution of the United States..1147
2. The District of Columbia Human Rights Act (Excerpts).............1151
3. Wisconsin Fair Employment Act (Experts) 1159
4. The Proposed Employment Non–Discrimination Act (ENDA) 1165
5. West Hollywood Domestic Partnership Ordinance 1171
6. Texas Sex Crime Statutes 1175

TOPICS INDEX...1187

TABLE OF CONTENTS

INTRODUCTION v
ACKNOWLEDGMENTS ix
TABLE OF CASES xxxi
PREFACE ON CONSTITUTIONAL RIGHTS xxxix
    1. Due Process xl
      A. Procedural Protections xl
      B. Vagueness xlii
      C. Substantive Due Process and the Right of Privacy xliii
    2. Equal Protection xlv
      A. The *Carolene Products* Formulation: Strict Scrutiny for
          Classifications Aimed at Marginalized Groups (Race, Il-
          legitimacy, Alienage) xlvi
      B. The New Equal Protection Model: Intermediate Scrutiny
          of Sex—and Sexual Orientation?—Classifications xlvii
      C. Fundamental Rights and Equal Protection xlix
    3. Freedom of Expression l
      A. "Low Value" Expression Receiving Less or No First
          Amendment Protection li
      B. The Forum Matters: Deference to State Regulation of
          Speech in Certain Contexts lii
      C. Nondiscrimination versus the First Amendment liii

CHAPTER 1 The Constitution and Sexuality 1

Sec.
1. The Right to Sexual Privacy 3
    A. The Birth of Privacy: The Contraception Cases 3
      New York v. Margaret Sanger 4
      The Early Birth Control Movement 5
      Paul and Pauline Poe et al. v. Abraham S. Ullman 10
      Estelle T. Griswold et al. v. Connecticut 13
      Notes on *Griswold* and the Right of Sexual Privacy 15
      Problem 1–1 Sex, Law and Public Policy 19
    B. The Expanding Right of Sexual Privacy 19
      Robert Eli Stanley v. State of Georgia 20
      Notes on *Stanley* and the Right of Privacy Outside of Marriage .. 21
      Robert H. Bork, Neutral Principles and Some First Amendment
          Problems 22
      Thomas S. Eisenstadt v. William R. Baird 24
      Notes on *Eisenstadt* and the Expanding Privacy Right 29

Sec.

1. The Right to Sexual Privacy—Continued

   C. The Right to Privacy and Abortion 30

      Jane Roe et al. v. Henry Wade 30

      Notes on *Roe* and the Right to Abortion 33

      *Reva Siegel, Reasoning From the Body: A Historical Perspective
        on Abortion Regulation and Questions of Equal Protection* ... 35

**2. State Regulation of Sexual Practices—The Special Case of
   Sodomy** 37

   Note on Sodomy Laws and the Vagueness Doctrine 39

   People v. Ronald Onofre et al. 40

   Note: How Private Is Privacy? 43

   Michael J. Bowers v. Michael Hardwick et al. 44

   Notes on *Hardwick, Onofre,* and the Right to Engage in Consensual
      Sodomy 53

   Problem 1–2 The Role of Morality 55

   Academic Reflections on *Hardwick* 56

      Anne B. Goldstein, History, Homosexuality and Political Values ... 56

      Janet E. Halley, Reasoning About Sodomy 57

      Jed Rubenfeld, The Right of Privacy 61

      Kendall Thomas, Corpus Juris (Hetero)sexualis 66

      Michael Sandel, Moral Argument and Liberal Toleration 71

**3. Other Constitutional Strategies for Challenging State Regu-
   lation of Sexuality and Gender** 73

   A. Sex Discrimination 73

      Sharon A. Frontiero and Joseph Frontiero v. Elliot L. Richardson ... 74

      Notes on the Cases and Arguments for Heightened Scrutiny for
        Classifications Based on Sex 78

      United States v. Virginia 81

      *Katherine M. Franke, The Central Mistake of Sex Discrimination
        Law: The Disaggregation of Sex From Gender* 90

      Notes on the VMI Case and the Aggregation of Sex and Gender ... 91

   B. Sexual Orientation Discrimination 92

      1. Is Anti–Gay Discrimination Rational? 92

      City of Cleburne v. Cleburne Living Center 92

      Roy Romer v. Richard G. Evans 93

      Notes on *Evans* and Its Implications for *Hardwick* 105

      Problem 1–3 Same Sex Sodomy Laws 108

      2. Should Sexual Orientation Be a Suspect Classification? 108

      Perry J. Watkins v. United States Army 109

      Notes on *Watkins* and the Level of Constitutional Scrutiny for
        Sexual Orientation Classifications 117

      Nan D. Hunter, Life After Hardwick 118

      3. Is Sexual Orientation Discrimination Sex Discrimination? 119

      Ninia Baehr and Genora Dancel et al. v. John C. Lewin 119

      *Andrew Koppelman, Why Discrimination Against Lesbians
        and Gay Men Is Sex Discrimination* 119

      Notes on Sexuality, Gender, and Sex Discrimination 122

Sec.

3. Other Constitutional Strategies for Challenging State Regulation of Sexuality and Gender—Continued

   C. Intimate Association _____ 124
      Robin Joy Shahar v. Michael Bowers _____ 124
      Notes on *Shahar* and Rights of Intimate Association_____ 131

CHAPTER 2 Medicalization of Sex, Gender, and Sexuality____ 133

1. Doctors, Gender, and Sex: From the Sexologists to the Anti–Freudians_____ 136
   A. The Early Sexologists _____ 136
   B. Freud and His Followers_____ 141
   C. The Post–Freudians _____ 145
     1. Kinsey, Hooker, and the Anti–Moralists_____ 145
     2. Chodorow and Other Feminist Critics of Freud _____ 148
     3. Szasz, Foucault, and the Anti–Clinicians_____ 151
     Problem 2–1 The Relationship Between Sodomy and Homosexuality_____ 152

2. Medicalization and American Law_____ 153
   A. Degeneracy and Feminized Vice, 1870–1920 _____ 153
     1. The Regulation of Prostitution _____ 153
       Problem 2–2 The Mann Act, "White Slavery," and Fornication: An Exercise in the Legal Process _____ 156
       Drew Caminetti and Maury Diggs v. United States _____ 158
       Notes on the Evolution of the White Slave Traffic Act _____ 160
     2. Gender Revolt _____ 162
     3. Suppressing Homosexuality _____ 166
       People v. Donald Friede _____ 168
       Sequel to Friede _____ 170
   B. The Sexual Psychopath, 1930s–1960s _____ 170
     1. Shifting Regulatory Concerns, circa 1930 _____ 170
       Problem 2–3 The District of Columbia Psychopath Law _____ 173
     2. The Post–World War II Anti-homosexual Campaign _____ 174
     3. Case Study: The Psychopathic Personality Exclusion in U.S. Immigration Law, 1952–1990 _____ 175
       *Report of the Public Health Service on the Medical Aspects of H.R. 2379*_____ 177
       Problem 2–4 Application of the Psychopathic Personality Exclusion _____ 178
       Clive Michael Boutilier v. Immigration & Naturalization Service _____ 179
       Notes on *Boutilier* and Evolving Psychiatric Opinion About Homosexuality as a Mental Disorder _____ 183
       Problem 2–5 What to Make of the New APA Stance? _____ 186
       Notes on the Post-*Boutilier* Evolution of the Immigration Exclusion of Lesbians and Gay Men _____ 186
       *Postscript: Immigration Exclusion of People With HIV*_____ 189

Sec.

2. **Medicalization and American Law**—Continued

    C. Medicalization, Abortion, and the Control of Women's Sexuality- 189

        Jane Hodgson, M.D., et al. v. Minnesota _____ 190

        Notes on Parental Notification Abortion Laws and Parental Control Over Their Daughters' Sexuality _____ 195

        Jane Hodgson, et al. v. Minnesota _____ 198

        Notes on the Supreme Court's Allowance of Parental Notification Statutes, With Bypasses _____ 199

        Planned Parenthood of Southeastern Pennsylvania v. Robert Casey _____ 201

3. **Current Issues Involving Medicalization, Sexuality, Gender, and the Law** _____ 203

    A. Science–Based Questions About the Assumption of Sex Binariness _____ 203

        John Money, Joan G. Hampson and John L. Hampson, An Examination of Some Basic Sexual Concepts: The Evidence of Human Hermaphroditism _____ 204

        Anthropological Note on the Cultural Construction of Sex and Gender _____ 209

        Problem 2–6 Hermaphrodites and Marriage _____ 211

    B. Transsexualism, Medicalization and Commodification _____ 212

    C. Hard–Wired Homosexuals? _____ 214

        1. Anatomic Studies _____ 214

        2. Hormonal Studies _____ 216

        3. Genetic Studies _____ 217

        Edward Stein, The Relevance of Scientific Research About Sexual Orientation to Lesbian and Gay Rights _____ 219

        Note on the Thesis That Hard–Wired Homosexuality Could Win Recognition of Gay Rights _____ 225

        Concluding Note on Ideology and Science _____ 226

CHAPTER 3 Theories of Sexuality, Gender, and Law _____ 227

1. **Modern Theories of Sexuality** _____ 229

    A. Natural Law Theories _____ 229

        John M. Finnis, Law, Morality, and "Sexual Orientation" _____ 230

        Notes on Finnis and the Implications of "the New Natural Law" for Sexuality and Law _____ 233

    B. Materialist or Economic Theories _____ 234

        John D'Emilio, Capitalism and Gay Identity _____ 235

        Note on Richard Posner's "Rational Choice" Theory of Sex _____ 238

        Richard A. Posner, Sex and Reason _____ 241

        Notes on Materialist Theories of Sexuality _____ 244

        John Stuart Mill, On Liberty _____ 246

        Note on Carol Rose's Feminist Economics and Her Defense of Polygamy _____ 248

Sec.

1. Modern Theories of Sexuality—Continued

  C. Feminist Theories _____ 248

    Note on Catharine MacKinnon's Theory of the Relationship of
      Patriarchy, Gender, and Sexuality _____ 249

    Gayle S. Rubin, Thinking Sex: Notes for a Radical Theory of the
      Politics of Sexuality _____ 250

    Note on MacKinnon's and Rubin's Theories of Sexuality _____ 259

2. Postmodern Theories _____ 262

  A. Sexuality as a Social Construction _____ 262

    1. Foucault's Critique of the Repressive Hypothesis _____ 263

    2. Systems of Power _____ 264

    3. Sexuality as a Discursive Production _____ 265

    Problem 3–1 Strategies for Challenging Discrimination _____ 267

    Janet E. Halley, Sexual Orientation and the Politics of Biology:
      A Critique of the Argument From Immutability _____ 267

  B. Feminism and Foucault _____ 271

    Problem 3–2 Law, Foucault, Feminism, Rape, Statutory Rape,
      and Incest _____ 274

    State v. Marvin K. Kaiser _____ 274

    Foucault v. Feminism in *Kaiser* _____ 277

    Judith Butler, Gender Trouble: Feminism and the Subversion of
      Identity _____ 280

    Price Waterhouse v. Ann B. Hopkins _____ 282

    Notes on *Hopkins* and Law's Invocation of Gender _____ 287

  C. Deconstructive Theory (Binarisms and the Double Bind) _____ 289

    Eve Kosofsky Sedgwick, The Epistemology of the Closet _____ 289

    Note on the "Double Bind" _____ 300

    Marjorie Rowland v. Mad River Local School District _____ 301

    Note on the Mad River Case and the Construction of Heterosex-
      uality _____ 304

3. The Role of Law in the Social Construction Process _____ 306

  A. Operations of Law _____ 306

    Ellen Ross and Rayna Rapp, Sex and Society: A Research Note
      From Social History and Anthropology _____ 306

    Problem 3–3 The Means of Production _____ 309

  B. Sexual Identity _____ 309

    Dennis R. Beller v. J. William Middendorf _____ 310

    Note on James Miller's Case and Law's (Occasional) Insistence
      on Sexual Closure _____ 313

    Note on Non–Judicial Mechanisms of Legal Power _____ 314

    Patricia Klein Lerner, Jailer Learns Gay Culture to Foil Straight
      Inmates _____ 314

  C. Rethinking Privacy _____ 316

    Jed Rubenfeld, The Right of Privacy _____ 316

    Note on Foucault, Privacy, and Rights Discourse _____ 317

CHAPTER 4 U.S. Military Exclusions and the Construction of Manhood 319

1. Racial Exclusion and Segregation in the U.S. Armed Services 321

Kenneth L. Karst, *The Pursuit of Manhood and the Desegregation of the Armed Forces* 321

Notes on the Legality of Racial Segregation in the U.S. Armed Forces (1940s) 331

Problem 4–1   Legal Considerations re Desegregating the Armed Forces, 1948 336

Executive Order 9981 338

Note on the Truman Order and the Process of Desegregating the Armed Forces 339

2. The Exclusion of Women From Combat 342

A. A History of Women in the Military, 1861–1971 342

B. Judicial Review of the Different Treatment of Women in the Armed Forces, 1971–81 346

Sharon A. Frontiero and Joseph Frontiero v. Elliot L. Richardson 346

Problem 4–2   Constitutional Issues for Women in the Military, Late 1970s 346

Bernard Rostker v. Robert L. Goldberg et al. 348

Note on *Rostker* 356

C. Women's Exclusion From Combat 357

Mady Wechsler Segal, The Argument for Female Combatants 359

Note on Congressional Response to the Demand for a Combat Role for Women 361

Problem 4–3   The Legality of Current Policy Excluding Women From Combat 364

3. The Military's Exclusion of Lesbians, Gay Men, and Bisexuals 366

A. Origins of the Gay and Lesbian Exclusion 366

B. The Gay and Lesbian Exclusion Under Legal Seige, 1976–94 372

Department of Defense Directive 1332.14 (1982) 372

Problem 4–4   Issues Under Directive 1332.14.1.H 373

Perry J. Watkins v. United States Army 374

Joseph Steffan v. William J. Perry 374

Notes on *Watkins* and *Steffan* and the "Old" Exclusion of Gays From the Armed Forces 382

Michelle M. Benecke and Kristin S. Dodge, Military Women in Nontraditional Fields: Casualties of the Armed Forces' War on Homosexuals 384

C. Don't Ask, Don't Tell, 1993–? 388

Policy Concerning Homosexuality in the Armed Forces: Hearings Before the Senate Committee on Armed Services 388

Note on the Aftermath of the Gays in the Military Hearings: Don't Ask, Don't Tell 396

Sec.
3. The Military's Exclusion of Lesbians, Gay Men, and Bisexuals—Continued

Department of Defense Directive Number 1332.14 Enlisted Administrative Separations (1993) ------------------------------ 400

Problem 4–5   Applications of Don't Ask, Don't Tell ---------------- 403

Lt. Paul Thomasson, USN v. William J. Perry ----------------------- 403

Lt. Col. Jane Able et al. v. United States ----------------------------- 404

Problem 4–6   Deference to Congressional Judgments Excluding or Segregating Citizens in the Armed Forces -------------------- 406

CHAPTER 5   Identity Speech in the Body Politic ------------------ 409

1. Political Speech, Publication, and Association -------------------- 411

One, Inc. v. Otto K. Olesen --- 411

Note on *One, Inc.* and Possible Goals of the First Amendment ------- 413

A. Rights of Association -- 415

Sol M. Stoumen v. George R. Reilly et al. ------------------------------ 416

Notes on the Black Cat Case: Gay Bars, Narrowing Interpretations, and Unconstitutional Conditions----------------------------- 417

Postscript on the Nine Lives of the Black Cat----------------------- 419

Gay Students Organization of the University of New Hampshire v. Thomas N. Bonner -- 420

Notes on *Bonner* and Current First Amendment Doctrine --------- 425

B. State Insistence Upon the Closet--- 426

National Gay Task Force v. Board of Education of the City of Oklahoma City --- 426

Notes on *Gay Task Force* and the Fading Boundary Between Sexual Speech and Political Speech -- 429

Joseph Acanfora, III v. Board of Education of Montgomery County --- 430

Marjorie Rowland v. Mad River Local School District -------------- 431

Gay Law Students Association et al. v. Pacific Telephone and Telegraph Co. -- 431

Note on *PT & T* and "Coming Out" as "Political" Activity --------- 433

David Cole and William N. Eskridge, Jr., From Hand–Holding to Sodomy: First Amendment Protection of Homosexual (Expressive) Conduct -- 434

Problem 5–1   Misconduct or Viewpoint? ------------------------------ 436

C. Identity and Viewpoint: The Clash of Nondiscrimination and First Amendment Norms-- 437

Kathryn Roberts v. United States Jaycees--------------------------------- 437

John J. ["Wacko"] Hurley v. Irish–American Gay, Lesbian and Bisexual Group of Boston-- 438

Note on *Hurley*, State Action, and the Speech–Identity Divide---- 441

Problem 5–2   Parades and Exclusions ------------------------------------ 443

Gay Rights Coalition of Georgetown University Law Center et al. v. Georgetown University --- 443

Sec.

1. Political Speech, Publication, and Association—Continued
  Notes on the Georgetown Case ------------------------------------ 453
  *Ronald W. Rosenberger v. Rector and Visitors of the University
    of Virginia* -- 455
  Note on *Rosenberger* and Religious–Based Identity Speech -------- 462
2. Privacy and Sexual "Outing" ---------------------------------- 463
  A. First Amendment Parameters ----------------------------------- 463
    The Florida Star v. B.J.F. ---------------------------------- 463
    Note on the Impact of *Florida Star* -------------------------- 470
    Problem 5–3 Balancing Interests in the Reporting of Rapes ----- 470
    Ellen Willis, Naming Names ---------------------------------- 471
  B. Invasion of Privacy -- 472
    Oliver W. Sipple v. The Chronicle Publishing Co. ------------ 472
    Notes on *Sipple* and the Continuum of the Closet ------------- 476
    Note on Outing -- 477
    Richard Rouilard, Comment ----------------------------------- 478
  C. Defamation --- 479
    Kathleen Hayes v. Roger W. Smith, Jr. and Samantha Smith ---- 479
    Janet Nazeri v. Missouri Valley College -------------------- 481
    Notes on Defamation Law and Issues of Sexuality -------------- 484
    Robert McCune v. Rose Neitzel ------------------------------ 485
    Note on Sexuality–Based Speech and Intentional Infliction of
      Emotional Distress --- 489
3. Hate Speech --- 491
  *Mari J. Matsuda, Public Response to Racist Speech: Considering the
    Victim's Story* --- 491
  Notes on Whether the First Amendment Protects Sexist and Homo-
    phobic Speech --- 493
  Notes on University Hate Speech Codes-------------------------- 495
  R.A.V. v. City of St. Paul ---------------------------------- 495
  Notes on *R.A.V.* and First Amendment Limits on Hate Speech Regu-
    lation -- 504
  Wisconsin v. Todd Mitchell ---------------------------------- 505

CHAPTER 6   Sexual Speech -------------------------------------- 507

**1. Sexual Speech and the First Amendment: A Dysfunctional
   Dyad** --- 508
  Samuel Roth v. United States and David S. Alberts v. California ----- 508
  Notes on *Roth* and the State's Power to Suppress "Obscenity" -------- 514
  Barnes v. Glen Theatre, Inc. -------------------------------- 519
  *David Cole, Playing by Pornography's Rules: The Regulation of Sex-
    ual Expression* --- 521
  Problem 6–1 Regulation of Child Pornography ------------------ 525
  New York v. Paul Ira Ferber --------------------------------- 526
  Note on Application of *Ferber* to Customers------------------- 531
  Problem 6–2 Child Porn Without Live Models ------------------- 532

Sec.

2. **Feminist Theories of Sexual Speech and Its Regulation** 533
   Problem 6–3   The Dworkin–MacKinnon Pornography Ordinances ... 533
   Catharine A. MacKinnon, Pornography, Civil Rights, and Speech 534
   Lisa Duggan, Nan D. Hunter, and Carole S. Vance, False Promises:
       Feminist Anti–Pornography Legislation ------------------------------- 542
   Notes on the Feminist Debate Over Pornography ------------------- 547
   American Booksellers Association, Inc. v. William H. Hudnut, III 549
   Regina v. Donald Victor Butler ----------------------------------- 555
   Notes on *Butler* versus *Hudnut* ------------------------------------ 561
   Note on Lesbian and Gay Pornography ------------------------------ 562

3. **Cutting Edge Issues of Sexual Speech Law** ----------------------- 563
   A. Intersections of Race and Sex ---------------------------------- 564
      Luke Records, Inc. et al. v. Nick Navarro ---------------------- 564
      Kimberlé Williams Crenshaw, Mapping the Margins: Intersec-
          tionality, Identity Politics, and Violence Against Women of
          Color --- 567
   B. Censorship of State–Subsidized Speech ------------------------ 573
      Karen Finley, John Fleck, Holly Hughes, Tim Miller, and the Na-
          tional Association of Artists' Organizations v. National En-
          dowment for the Arts -- 573
      Irving Rust v. Dr. Louis W. Sullivan --------------------------- 579
      Hilton Kramer, Is Art Above the Laws of Decency? ------------ 581
      Notes on Funding for Sexually Explicit Art --------------------- 582
   C. "Indecency" and Electronic Media ----------------------------- 583
      Note on the Supreme Court's Rulings on Indecent Speech in the
          Electronic Media --- 583
      Denver Area Educational Telecommunications Consortium v.
          Federal Communications Commission ------------------------- 585
      Notes on "Indecency" and New Media -------------------------- 593

CHAPTER 7   Sexuality and Gender in Education ------------------ 595

1. **Regulating Student Exploration and Expression of Sexuality** 597
   John F. Tinker v. Des Moines Independent Community School Dis-
       trict --- 597
   Aaron Fricke v. Richard B. Lynch --------------------------------- 598
   Rock Lobster Postscript --- 601
   Bethel School District No. 403 v. Matthew N. Fraser, a Minor and
       E.L. Fraser, Guardian Ad Litem --------------------------------- 602
   Notes on *Fraser* and the Rock Lobster Case ----------------------- 606
   Problem 7–1   Excluding Gay Clubs in Public High Schools ----------- 609
   Board of Education, Island Trees Union Free School District No. 26
       et al. v. Steven A. Pico --- 610
   Notes on *Pico* and Students' Right to Know ----------------------- 616
   Problem 7–2   Availability of Gay Publications in Public Libraries ... 618

Sec.

2. **Academic Freedom and Issues of Gender and Sexuality** ------- 620
   A. Academic Freedom and Silencing Classroom Discussion of Sexuality -- 620
      David O. Solmitz v. Maine School Administrative District No. 59 621
      Note on *Solmitz* and Institutional Control of Sexuality Discourse in the Classroom --- 624
      Joseph Acanfora, III v. Board of Education of Montgomery County -- 625
      Notes on *Acanfora* and the Double Bind Faced by Sexual Minorities in Teaching-- 627
      Problem 7–3   Other Sexuality–Based Limits on Teaching Personnel-- 629
   B. Title IX and Responsibilities of Educational Institutions to Prevent Sexual Harassment-- 630
      Dean Cohen v. San Bernardino Valley College ----------------------- 632
      Notes on the Balance Between Academic Freedom and Avoiding a Hostile Educational Environment------------------------------ 637
      James S. Nabozny v. Mary Podlesny ------------------------------- 638
      Debra Rowinsky, For Herself and as Next Friend of Her Minor Children, et al. v. Bryan Independent School District -------- 639
      Note on Title IX and Athletic Programs ------------------------------ 644
   C. Gender Equity and the Issue of Same–Sex Schools------------------ 644
      United States v. Virginia--- 647
      Note on the Impact on the VMI Case on the Legality of Same–Sex Educational Institutions ----------------------------------- 649
3. **Legal Issues Arising Out of Public Sex Education**---------------- 652
   A. Students' Rights to Sexuality Instruction That Is Factually Accurate -- 653
      Alabama Statutes § 16–40A–2, Minimum Contents to Be Included in Sex Education Program or Curriculum ---------------- 654
      Problem 7–4   Reconciling Alabama's Education Directives and Students' Need to Know About Sexuality ---------------------- 655
      Bettye Coleman et al. v. Caddo Parish School Board et al. --------- 656
   B. AIDS Education-- 662
      1. The Case for AIDS Education -------------------------------------- 662
      2. Educational Theory --- 663
      3. Legal Issues Raised by AIDS Education ---------------------------- 666
      Ignacia Alfonso et al. v. Joseph A. Fernandez et al.---------------- 666
      Notes on the Legality of Condom Distribution Programs and Parents' Constitutional Rights in Their Children's Upbringing-- 671
      Problem 7–5   AIDS Instruction as Sexual Harassment? -------- 673
   C. No Promo Homo Policies --- 673
      Arizona Revised Statutes § 15–716, Instruction on Acquired Immune Deficiency Syndrome -------------------------------------- 674
      Problem 7–6   State AIDS Education and the Policy Against Promoting Homosexuality --- 675

Sec.
3. Legal Issues Arising Out of Public Sex Education—Continued
Gay Men's Health Crisis et al. v. Dr. Louis Sullivan ----------------- 676
Note on Constitutional Challenges to "No Promo Homo" Policies 680

CHAPTER 8 Citizenship and Community in a Sexualized World -- 683

1. Accommodating Religion in a Sexualized World ------------------ 685
John Ware et al. v. Valley Stream High School District ----------------- 685
Problem 8–1 Rethinking AIDS Education in Light of Later Free Exercise Decisions and the Religious Freedom Restoration Act .. 693
Evelyn Smith v. Fair Employment and Housing Commission --------- 695
Gay Rights Coalition of Georgetown University Law Center v. Georgetown University -- 696
Notes on the Georgetown Case and the Accommodation of Free Exercise and Nondiscrimination Norms ----------------------------- 708
Robert M. Cover, The Supreme Court, 1982 Term—Foreword: Nomos and Narrative -- 709
Note on the Establishment Clause as a Limitation on State Endorsement of Religious Messages ----------------------------------- 713
2. Citizens in Conflict: Anti–Civil Rights and Anti–Gay Initiatives -- 715
A. Introduction to Direct Democracy ------------------------------- 715
St. Paul Citizens for Human Rights v. City Council of the City of St. Paul -- 716
Notes on *St. Paul Citizens* and the Limitations of Direct Democracy -- 719
B. Equal Protection Limits to Anti–Civil Rights Initiatives ----------- 723
Nellie Hunter v. Erickson --- 723
James et al. v. Anna Valtierra et al. ------------------------------- 723
Washington v. Seattle School District No. 1 ---------------------- 724
Problem 8–2 Initiatives Having Indirect Race–Based Effects ---- 725
C. The Constitutionality of Anti–Gay Initiatives------------------ 725
Richard G. Evans et al. v. Roy Romer et al. --------------------- 727
Roy Romer et al. v. Richard G. Evans et al. --------------------- 729
Notes on the Colorado Initiative Decisions and Equal Protection Limits on Direct Democracy ------------------------------------- 729
Problem 8–3 Anti-Gay Initiatives After *Romer* ------------------ 732
Jane S. Schacter, The Gay Civil Rights Debate in the States: Decoding the Discourse of Equivalents ----------------------------- 733
Note on the "Discourse of Equivalents" ------------------------- 738
3. Sexuality and Citizenship in an International Setting--------- 739
A. Sexuality and Citizenship------------------------------------- 739
Marie Posusta v. United States ----------------------------------- 740
Notes on *Posusta* and the Evolution of Naturalization Policy in the Era of *Griswold* -- 742
In re Petition of Natualization of Manuel Labady ----------------- 743

Sec.

3. Sexuality and Citizenship in an International Setting—Continued

Problem 8–4 Formulating a Coherent Approach to "Good Moral Character" -- 746

B. International Obligations and United States' Regulation of Sexuality -- 747

International Covenant on Civil and Political Rights ---------------- 748

Problem 8–5 Applying the ICCPR to American Sodomy Laws ---- 750

Nicholas Toonen v. Australia ------------------------------------- 751

Note on Transnational Deregulation of Consensual Same–Sex Intimacy --- 754

C. Gender, Sexuality, and Asylum ------------------------------------- 755

In re Fauziya Kasinga --- 756

Notes on *Kasinga* and Asylum for Gender Oppression ------------ 759

Problem 8–6 Asylum for Gay People? -------------------------------- 760

CHAPTER 9 Families We Choose ---------------------------------- 763

1. The Privatization of Family Law ------------------------------- 765

Jana B. Singer, The Privatization of Family Law ------------------ 765

Notes on Implications of Privatization for Sexuality and Gender ----- 770

Note on Feminist Critiques of Privatization --------------------------- 772

A. Surrogacy and Baby Selling -------------------------------------- 774

In the Matter of Baby M -- 775

Notes on Feminist and Gaylegal Defenses and Critiques of Surrogacy -- 778

B. Legal Recognition and Enforcement of Nonmarital Obligations and Benefits --- 781

Michelle Marvin v. Lee Marvin ---------------------------------- 781

Notes on *Marvin* and the Treatment of Families We Choose ------- 783

In re Adoption of Robert Paul P. ---------------------------------- 786

Miguel Braschi v. Stahl Associates Co. ---------------------------- 787

In re Alison D. v. Virginia M. ------------------------------------ 789

Note on the New York Court of Appeals' Approach[es] to Same–Sex Families --- 789

In re Guardianship of Sharon Kowalski -------------------------- 789

C. New Legal Forms for Recognizing Relationships: Domestic Partnership Laws -- 791

Problem 9–1 Legal Consequences of Domestic Partnership? ----- 792

Note on the Benefits and Obligations Conferred by Marriage and European Registered Partnerships ------------------------------ 793

2. The Expanding Right to Marry --------------------------------- 795

A. The Constitutional Right to Marry -------------------------------- 795

Richard and Mildred Loving v. Virginia -------------------------- 795

John F. Singer and Paul C. Barwick v. Lloyd Hara ---------------- 799

Note on Constitutional Arguments Allowing the State to Deny Same–Sex Marriage --- 803

Sec.

2. The Expanding Right to Marry—Continued

Thomas E. Zablocki v. Roger C. Redhail ---------------------------- 805

William R. Turner v. Leonard Safley ------------------------------ 806

Problem 9–2   Same-Sex Marriage in the District of Columbia? --- 807

B. The Same–Sex Marriage Debate ------------------------------------ 807

Ninia Baehr and Genora Dancel et al. v. John C. Lewin ------------ 807

Notes on the Hawaii Same–Sex Marriage Case and Interstate
Recognition of Same–Sex Marriages --------------------------- 813

Problem 9–3   The Defense of Marriage Act ----------------------- 816

*Paula L. Ettelbrick, Since When Is Marriage a Path to Libera-
tion?* --- 817

*Thomas B. Stoddard, Why Gay People Should Seek the Right to
Marry* -- 818

Notes on the Ettelbrick–Stoddard Debate ------------------------ 820

C. The Constitutionality of Other Restrictions on Marriage ---------- 822

1. Age Restrictions --- 822

2. Incest -- 823

Martin Richard Israel and Tammy Lee Bannon Israel v. Allen 823

Notes on the Difficulty of Defending Prohibitions Against Incestuous Marriages -- 823

3. Polygamy -- 824

George Reynolds v. United States ------------------------------ 824

Notes on Polygamy --- 825

3. Children in Families of Choice ------------------------------------ 827

A. State Decisions About the Placement of Children ---------------- 828

1. Sexuality, Race, and Child Custody ------------------------- 828

Virginia Whaley v. Robert Whaley ---------------------------- 828

Linda Sidoti Palmore v. Anthony J. Sidoti ------------------- 831

Note on the Implications of *Palmore v. Sidoti* --------------- 831

2. Sexual Orientation and Custody --------------------------- 832

Charles L. Conkel v. Kim D. Conkel ------------------------- 833

Note on Custody and Visitation Disputes Involving Lesbian,
Bisexual, and Gay Parents --------------------------------- 836

Pamela Kay Bottoms v. Sharon Lynne Bottoms ---------------- 838

Problem 9–4   The Constitution, Sharon Lynne Bottoms, and
the Virginia Supreme Court --------------------------------- 841

3. Sexual Orientation, Race, and Adoption ------------------- 841

In re Adoption of Charles B. ------------------------------- 841

Note on Sexual Orientation and Adoption --------------------- 843

Problem 9–5   Prohibiting "Homosexual" Adoption, Foster
Care, and Child Care --------------------------------------- 844

*Charlotte J. Patterson, Adoption of Minor Children by Lesbian
and Gay Adults* -- 846

Note on Race and Adoption ----------------------------------- 848

Sec.
3. Children in Families of Choice—Continued
    B. Issues Arising Out of Surrogacy and Artificial Insemination 848
        Marla J. Hollandsworth, Gay Men Creating Families Through
           Surro–Gay Arrangements: A Paradigm for Reproductive
           Freedom 849
        Note on the Constitutional Rights of Biological Fathers 853
        Michael H. v. Gerald D. 854
        In re Thomas S. v. Robin Y. 855
        Note on Robin Y.'s Arguments on Appeal 861
    C. Second–Parent Adoptions 861
        In re M.M.D. & B.H.M. 863
        Note on Race, Sexual Orientation, and Second–Parent Adoptions 866
        Problem 9–6 Second–Parent Adoptions in New York 868

CHAPTER 10 Sexuality and Gender in the Workplace 869

Rosemary Pringle, Sexuality at Work 870
1. Exclusions From Government Employment 876
    A. State Discrimination on the Basis of Sex 876
        Personnel Administrator of Massachusetts v. Helen Feeney 879
    B. State Discrimination on the Basis of Sexual Orientation 880
        David K. Johnson, Homosexual Citizens: Washington's Gay
           Community Confronts the Civil Service 880
        Clifford L. Norton v. John Macy et al. 886
        Notes on *Norton* and Its Insistence That the State Show a "Nex-
          us" Between Sexual Orientation and Job Requirements 890
        Problem 10–1 Civil Service Discrimination After *Norton* 892
        John Singer v. U.S. Civil Service Commission 892
        Postscripts to *Singer* and the Fall of the Civil Service Exclusion
          of "Immoral" Homosexuals 894
    C. State Discrimination on the Basis of Pregnancy 896
        Dwight Geduldig v. Carolyn Aiello 896
2. The Statutory Ban Against Sex Discrimination 898
    A. Pregnancy Discrimination Under Title VII 900
        Note on the Equal Treatment/Special Treatment Debate and the
          PDA's Application to Pregnancy–Based Protections 901
        California Federal Savings and Loan Association v. Mark Guer-
          ra 903
        Note on Subsequent Parental Leave Legislation 906
        Crystal Chambers v. Omaha Girls Club, Inc. 906
        Notes on *Chambers*, Title VII Disparate Impact Liability, and
          Role Model Arguments 911
        Problem 10–2 Pregnancy Discrimination to Protect the Fetus .. 913
    B. Gender and Sexual Orientation Discrimination Under Title VII . 913
        Robert DeSantis et al. v. Pacific Telephone & Telegraph Co., Inc.
          and Judy Lundin and Barbara Buckley v. Pacific Telephone
          & Telegraph Co. 914

Sec.
2. **The Statutory Ban Against Sex Discrimination—**Continued
    Price Waterhouse v. Ann B. Hopkins ------------------------- 917
    Note on *Hopkins* and Title VII's Application to Gender–Stereo-
        type Discrimination -- 917
    C. Sexual Harassment and Hostile Work Environment Under Title
        VII --- 919
        Lisa Ann Burns v. McGregor Electronic Industries, Inc. ----- 921
        Ernest Dillon v. Frank ----------------------------------- 926
        Mark McWilliams v. Fairfax County Board of Supervisors -------- 930
        Notes on *Burns, Dillon,* and *McWilliams* ------------------ 933
        Problem 10–3 The First Amendment and Hostile Workplace
          Rules --- 935
3. **Current Issues in Workplace Discrimination** ------------------ 938
    A. The Persistence of Gender: Sex–Segregated Jobs ----------- 938
        Equal Employment Opportunity Commission v. Sears, Roebuck
          & Co. --- 938
        Note on Gendered Job Preferences and Feminist "Difference"
          Theory -- 942
        Vicki Schultz, Telling Stories About Women and Work: Judicial
          Interpretations of Sex Segregation in the Workplace in Title
          VII Cases Raising the Lack of Interest Argument ------------ 943
        Note on Gender Ghettoes and the Law: Affirmative Action for
          Women in the Workplace? ------------------------------- 947
    B. Legal Bans Against Sexual Orientation Discrimination ----------- 948
        Problem 10–4 Drafting a Sexual Orientation Nondiscrimination
          Law --- 950
        Chad Leibert v. Transworld Systems, Inc. ------------------ 950
        Notes on Sexual Orientation Discrimination Claims----------- 953
        Mary K. Ross v. Denver Department of Health and Hospitals ------ 954
        Notes on Extending Employment Benefits to Domestic Partners 957
    C. AIDS in the Workplace ------------------------------------- 958
        1. Disability Discrimination: Constitutional Law------------- 958
        2. The Rehabilitation Act --------------------------------- 959
        3. The Americans With Disabilities Act --------------------- 961
          Problem 10–5 The ADA and Homosexuality --------------- 962
          Edwin C. Anderson v. Gus Mayer Boston Store of Delaware --- 963
          Note on the ADA and Health Benefits for People With AIDS-- 967

CHAPTER 11 The Law's Construction of Consent ----------- 969

1. **Forcible Sex**-- 971
    A. The Law of Rape--- 972
        State v. Edward Rusk ----------------------------------- 972
        Notes on *Rusk* and the Changing Law of Rape ------------- 979
        Problem 11–1 Defining Sexual Assault --------------------- 981
        Martha Chamallas, Consent, Equality, and the Legal Control of
          Sexual Conduct --- 982

Sec.

1. Forcible Sex—Continued

Notes on the Law's Movement Toward a Mutuality Approach 992

Thomas A. Neal and Jill LaGasse v. Mary Neal _____ 993

Problem 11–2   Should Rape Be a Hate Crime? _____ 994

B. Race and Double–Edged Constructions of "Force" _____ 995

McQuirter v. State _____ 998

Notes on the Racialization of Rape _____ 1000

Kimberlé Crenshaw, Whose Life Is It Anyway? _____ 1002

C. Sadomasochism: "Consensual Violence"? _____ 1003

Regina v. Anthony Brown et al. _____ 1003

Note on the "Spanner Case" _____ 1010

Problem 11–3   Sadomasochistic Practices and American Criminal Law _____ 1010

Bat-Ami Bar-On Feminism and Sadomasochism: Self Critical Notes _____ 1012

Pat Califia, Feminism and Sadomasochism _____ 1015

Notes on the Feminist SM Debate _____ 1019

2. Sex by and With Minors _____ 1021

A. Sex Between Minors _____ 1024

Michael M. v. Superior Court of Sonoma County _____ 1024

Notes on Stereotypes and Statutory Rape Laws _____ 1029

Problem 11–4   The Law and Children's Sexual Experiences _____ 1030

B. The Criminalization of Intergenerational Sex _____ 1030

Claudia Konker, Rethinking Child Sexual Abuse: An Anthropological Perspective _____ 1031

Notes on Normative Theories of Intergenerational Sex _____ 1034

C. Procedural Issues in Child Sex Cases _____ 1035

Marlene Lemmerman v. Benjamin Fealk _____ 1036

Maryland v. Sandra Ann Craig _____ 1037

Keith Jacobson v. United States _____ 1038

Notes on *Jacobson* and the Use of Sting Operations to Enforce Sex Laws _____ 1042

3. Commercial Sex _____ 1044

A. Anti–Prostitution Laws _____ 1044

The People v. Superior Court of Alameda County _____ 1046

Problem 11–5   Federal Constitutional Questions About Sexual Solicitation Laws _____ 1049

B. Should Prostitution Be Illegal? _____ 1050

Debra Satz, Markets in Women's Sexual Labor _____ 1051

Notes on Whether Prostitution Should Be Legal _____ 1055

C. Sexual Harassment in a Sexualized Workplace _____ 1057

Marjorie Lee Thoreson, a*k*a Anneka DiLorenzo v. Penthouse International, Ltd. and Robert C. Guccione _____ 1057

Problem 11–6   Sex Discrimination in a Sexualized Workplace: "Hooters" _____ 1062

CHAPTER 12 The Body: New Frontiers ------------------------------1063

1. AIDS: The Conflation of Sexuality and Disease------------------1065
    Problem 12–1 The Process of Classification ----------------------1065
    A. Theoretical Groundings --------------------------------------1066
        Linda Singer, Bodies—Pleasures—Powers----------------------1066
        Paula A. Treichler, AIDS, Homophobia and Biomedical Discourse: An Epidemic of Signification ------------------------1069
        Harlon L. Dalton, AIDS in Blackface ------------------------1074
        Notes on Social Meanings of AIDS----------------------------1078
        Note on AIDS and Metaphor ------------------------------1079
    B. Public Health Law --1080
        People v. Henrietta Adams and Peggy Madison----------------1080
        City of New York v. New Saint Mark's Baths------------------1086
        Notes on AIDS and Public Health Law------------------------1089
    C. Criminal and Civil Liability for Sexual Transmission --------------1090
        State of Oregon v. Timothy Alan Hinkhouse------------------1090
        Jane Doe and Infant Doe v. Earvin Johnson, Jr. --------------1092
        Notes on Legal Regulation of Sexually Transmitted Disease-------1099
        Note on Designing an Effective AIDS Policy ------------------1100
2. Transgender Issues and the Law------------------------------1102
    A. Sex Discrimination and Transsexual/Transgender Discrimination --1102
        Karen Frances Ulane v. Eastern Airlines, Inc. --------------1103
        Notes on the Meaning of "Sex Discrimination"----------------1106
        Problem 12–2 Employment Discrimination Against Transsexuals Under the District of Columbia Human Rights Act -------1109
    B. The Medicalization of Trans–Sexualism ----------------------1109
        Jane Doe v. United States Postal Service--------------------1109
        Note on the Application of Disability Discrimination Law ---------1111
        G.B. v. Jerome Lackner----------------------------------1112
        Note on Transsexuals' Right to Treatment Under Federal and State Law--1117
    C. Public Law Issues Relevant to Transgendered Persons-----------1117
        M.T. v. J.T. --1117
        In re Elaine Frances Ladrach ----------------------------1122
        Note on Transsexual Marriage and Child Custody Law-------------1124
        Dee Farmer v. Edward Brennan, Warden, et al. --------------1124
3. The Legal Regulation of Cross–Dressing----------------------1129
    Marjorie Garber, Vested Interests ------------------------------1129
    A. When Clothes Make a Man: A History of American Regulation of Cross–Dressing--1130
    B. The State's Interest in Gender Normative Dress ----------------1132
        People of the State of New York v. Mauricio Archibald ---------1132
        City of Chicago v. Wallace Wilson and Kim Kimberley ---------1135
        City of Columbus v. John H. Rogers ------------------------1137
        Notes on the Decline and Fall of Cross–Dressing Statutes---------1138

Sec.

3. The Legal Regulation of Cross–Dressing—Continued
　Problem 12–3　Context, Cross–Dressing, and Conduct Unbecoming _____1139
　C. Cross–Dressing on the Job and in the Family _____1140
　　Jane Doe v. Boeing Co. _____1140
　　Notes on Employment Nondiscrimination and Dress Codes ____1143
　　In re Karin T. v. Michael T. _____1144
　　Note on Rights of Cross–Dressing Parents _____1146

APPENDICES

1. Individual Rights Provisions From the Amendments to the Constitution of the United States _____1147
2. The District of Columbia Human Rights Act (Excerpts) _____1151
3. Wisconsin Fair Employment Act (Experts) _____1159
4. The Proposed Employment Non–Discrimination Act (ENDA) ____1165
5. West Hollywood Domestic Partnership Ordinance _____1171
6. Texas Sex Crime Statutes _____1175

TOPICS INDEX _____1187

TABLE OF CASES

Principal cases are in bold type. Non-principal cases are in roman type. References are to Pages.

A. v. City of New York, 1024
Able v. United States, 404, 406
A.C. v. C.B., 789, 836
Acanfora v. Board of Ed. of Montgomery County, 430, **625,** 627, 628, 629
Action for Children's Television v. F.C.C., 584
Adams v. Howerton, 803, 804
Adams, People v., 1080
Adamson v. California, 16
Adarand Constructors, Inc. v. Pena, 948
Adkins v. Children's Hospital of the District of Columbia, 878
Adoption of B.L.V.B., In re, 866
Adoption of Charles B., In re, 841, 846
Adoption of Evan, Matter of, 867
Adoption of Jessica N., Matter of, 868
Adoption of Robert Paul P., Matter of, 786, 868
Adoption of Tammy, 866
Adoption of Two Children by H.N.R., Matter of, 867
Alberts v. California, 508, 511
Alderson v. Alderson, 784
Alfonso v. Fernandez, 666, 671, 672
Alison D. v. Virginia M., 789, 861, 868
Allied Stores of Ohio, Inc. v. Bowers, 629
Amalgamated Food Emp. Union Local 590 v. Logan Valley Plaza, Inc., 442
American Booksellers Ass'n, Inc. v. Hudnut, 549, 561
American Civil Liberties Union v. Reno, 594
American Life League, Inc. v. Reno, 695
Anderson v. Celebrezze, 730
Anderson v. Gus Mayer Boston Store of Delaware, 963, 967
Andrews v. Drew Municipal Separate School Dist., 910, 913
Angel Lace M., In re, 867
Anonymous v. Anonymous, 836
Appeal in Pima County Juvenile Action B–10489, Matter of, 844
Arcara v. Cloud Books, Inc., 44
Archibald, People v., 1132, 1138, 1139
Arthur v. City of Toledo, Ohio, 725
Ashling, Matter of Marriage of, 836
Atlanta, City of v. McKinney, 792
Avery v. Homewood City Bd. of Ed., 910

Baby M, Matter of, 775, 778, 780, 861
Bachman, Commonwealth ex rel. v. Bradley, 832
Bacot, Succession of, 803
Baehr v. Lewin, 119, **807,** 813, 814, 815, 822
Baker v. Nelson, 803, 804
Baker v. Wade, 1089
B. (Anonymous) v. B. (Anonymous), 1146
Barnes v. Costle, 919
Barnes v. Glen Theatre, Inc., 519
Barnes v. Train, 919
Barretta v. Barretta, 18
Bauer, United States v., 695
Becker v. New York State Liquor Authority, 419
Beller v. Middendorf, 310
Bellotti v. Baird, 190, 194, 198, 199, 201
Bennett v. Clemens, 832
Berg v. Claytor, 372
Bethel School Dist. No. 403 v. Fraser, 602, 606, 607, 608, 609, 610, 620, 629, 654
Bezio v. Patenaude, 832, 836
Birdsall, In re Marriage of, 836, 837
Blackwell v. United States Dept. of Treasury, 1109, 1111
Blew v. Verta, 836, 837
Board of Educ., Island Trees Union Free School Dist. No. 26 v. Pico, 610, 616, 617, 618, 620, 629, 653, 654
Board of Educ. of Westside Community Schools v. Mergens By and Through Mergens, 609
Bob Jones University v. United States, 650, 708
Bonadio, Commonwealth v., 44
Bosley v. McLaughlin, Cal., 878
Bottoms v. Bottoms, 838, 846, 848, 862
Bougher v. University of Pittsburgh, 631
Boutilier v. Immigration and Naturalization Service, 179, 183, 184, 186, 187, 188, 732, 743
Bowen v. Roy, 693
Bowers v. Hardwick, 44, 53, 54, 55, 56, 61, 71, 106, 107, 108, 110, 117, 131, 152, 233, 260, 266, 383, 519, 520, 732, 750, 755, 827, 828, 854, 891, 896
Boyd v. Harding Academy of Memphis, Inc., 913

xxxi

Bradley, Commonwealth ex rel. Bachman v., 832

Bradwell v. Illinois, 876, 877

Brandenburg v. Ohio, 425

Braschi v. Stahl Associates Co., 131, 787, 788, 789, 861

Brockett v. Spokane Arcades, Inc., 518

Brown v. Board of Ed. of Topeka, Shawnee County, Kan., 732

Brown v. Hot, Sexy and Safer Productions, Inc., 673

Brown, People v., 836

Brown, Regina v., 1003, 1010, 1020

Bryant, United States v., 971

Brzonkala v. Virginia Polytechnic and State University, 995

Burdick v. Takushi, 730

Burns v. McGregor Electronic Industries, Inc., 921, 933, 934

Burton v. Wilmington Parking Authority, 442

Butcher v. Superior Court of Orange County, 785

Butler, Regina v., 555, 561

Buttino v. F.B.I., 892

Byrne, People v., 8

C. and D., In re Marriage of, 211

Califano v. Goldfarb, 80

California Federal Sav. and Loan Ass'n v. Guerra, 903

Callender v. Corbett, 803

Caminetti v. United States, 158, 161, 162, 1045

Campbell v. Sundquist, 38, 55

Cannon v. University of Chicago, 630

Care and Treatment of Hendricks, Matter of, 174

Carey v. Population Services, Intern., 29, 30, 672

Carlson v. Olson, 784

Carolene Products Co., United States v., 722, 723

Carroll v. Talman Federal Sav. and Loan Ass'n of Chicago, 1143

Case v. Unified School Dist. No. 233, p. 618

Casper v. Casper, 772

Castle v. Immigration and Naturalization Service, 747

Chambers v. Omaha Girls Club, Inc., 906, 911, 912, 950

Chang, Matter of, 760

Chaplinsky v. New Hampshire, 491, 508

Charpentier v. Charpentier, 836

Cheffer v. Reno, 695

Chicago, City of v. Wilson, 1135, 1138, 1139

Childers v. Dallas Police Dept., 895

Christensen v. State, 55

Christian v. Randall, 1124

Church of the Lukumi Babalu Aye, Inc. v. City of Hialeah, 693

Citizens for Parental Rights v. San Mateo County Bd. of Educ., 652, 671

Citizens for Responsible Behavior v. Superior Court (Riverside City Council), 733

City of (see name of city)

Clark, State v., 161

Clarke v. United States, 455

Cleburne, Tex., City of v. Cleburne Living Center, 92, 106, 383, 848, 959

Cleveland v. United States, 161, 162, 1045

Cleveland Bd. of Educ. v. LaFleur, 896

Cohen v. California, 517, 584

Cohen v. San Bernardino Valley College, 632, 681

Coker v. Georgia, 1001

Coleman v. Caddo Parish School Bd., 656, 681

Collier, State v., 1011

Collins v. Secretary of Com., 726

Columbus, City of v. Rogers, 1137, 1138, 1139

Commitment of J.N., Matter of, 868

Commonwealth v. _____ (see opposing party)

Commonwealth ex rel. v. _____ (see opposing party and relator)

Conkel v. Conkel, 833, 836, 837

Coon v. Joseph, 785

Corne v. Bausch & Lomb, Inc., 919

Cox v. Florida Dept. of Health and Rehabilitative Services, 844

Cox Broadcasting Corp. v. Cohn, 470

Craig v. Boren, 80, 356, 383, 1024, 1029, 1038

Crooke v. Gilden, 785

Cuevas v. Mills, 803

Cumming v. Richmond County Board of Ed., 335

Curran v. Mount Diablo Council of Boy Scouts of America, 913

Custody of H.S.H.–K., In re, 789

Custody of T.J., In re, 1124

Dallas, City of v. England, 55

Daly v. Daly, 1124

Dandridge v. Williams, 772

Davidson v. Aetna Life & Cas. Ins. Co., 1117

Davis v. Beason, 98

Davis v. Davis, 836

Davis v. Monroe County Bd. of Educ., 641

Davis, United States v., 1140

Dawson v. Delaware, 506

D.C. v. City of St. Louis, Mo., 1139

Dean v. District of Columbia, 803, 807, 867

Dennett, United States v., 6

Denver Area Educational Telecommunications Consortium, Inc. v. F.C.C., 585

DeSantis v. Pacific Tel. & Tel. Co., Inc., 914, 918

De Santo v. Barnsley, 803

D. H. v. J. H., 836

Dial Information Services Corp. of New York v. Thornburgh, 584, 585

Diehl, In re Marriage of, 837

Dillon v. Frank, 926, 933, 934

Dobre v. National R.R. Passenger Corp. (Amtrak), 1108, 1112
Dodgeon v. United Kingdom, 755
Doe v. Boeing Co., 1111, **1140,** 1144
Doe v. Doe, 995
Doe v. Duling, 55
Doe v. Irwin, 671, 672
Doe v. Johnson, 1092, 1100
Doe v. United States Postal Service, **1109,** 1111
Doe v. University of Michigan, 638
Dothard v. Rawlinson, 900
Dubbs v. C.I.A., 892
Dugan v. Dugan, 772

Edmonson v. Leesville Concrete Co., Inc., 442
Edye v. Robertson, 750
E.E.O.C. v. Sears, Roebuck & Co., **938,** 947, 948
E.E.O.C. v. Walden Book Co., Inc., 933
Eisenstadt v. Baird, 24, 29, 33, 37, 42, 854, 1100
Employment Div., Dept. of Human Resources of Oregon v. Smith, 693, 694, 695, 708
Epperson v. Arkansas., 621
Evans v. Romer, 629, **727,** 731, 732, 733, 738
Everson v. Board of Ed. of Ewing Tp., 713, 714

Farmer v. Brennan, 1124
Fauziya Kasinga, In re, 756, 759, 760
F. C. C. v. Pacifica Foundation, 517, 583, 584, 593
Finley v. National Endowment for the Arts, 573, 582
Flagg Bros., Inc. v. Brooks, 442
Fleuti v. Rosenberg, 179, 183
Franklin v. Gwinnett County Public Schools, 631, 632, 638
Fricke v. Lynch, 598, 607, 608
Friede, People v., 168, 170, 515
Frontiero v. Richardson, 346, 359, 879, 896

G.A. v. D.A., 837
Gajovski v. Gajovski, 803
Garrett v. Board of Educ. of School Dist. of City of Detroit, 649
Gay Law Students Ass'n v. Pacific Tel. & Tel. Co., 431, 433
Gaylord v. Tacoma School Dist. No. 10, p. 895
Gay Men's Health Crisis v. Sullivan, 792 F.Supp. 278, pp. **676,** 680, 681
Gay Men's Health Crisis v. Sullivan, 733 F.Supp. 619, p. 676
Gay Rights Coalition of Georgetown University Law Center v. Georgetown University, 509 F.2d 652, pp. 443, **696,** 708

Gay Rights Coalition of Georgetown University v. Georgetown University, 536 A.2d 1, pp. 453, 454, 462
Gay Students Organization of University of New Hampshire v. Bonner, 420, 425, 453, 454, 455, 462, 609
G. B. v. Lackner, 1112
Geduldig v. Aiello, 81, 896, 897, 900, 901
General Elec. Co. v. Gilbert, 900, 901
Gillespie–Linton v. Miles, 624, 785
Gitlow v. New York, 21, 37
Globe Communications Corp., State v., 470
Glover v. Eastern Nebraska Community Office of Retardation, 867 F.2d 461, p. 958
Glover v. Eastern Nebraska Community Office of Retardation, 686 F.Supp. 243, p. 959
Goesaert v. Cleary, 879
Goldman v. Weinberger, 356, 405, 693
Griggs v. Duke Power Co., 900, 911
Griswold v. Connecticut, 9, 13, 15, 16, 17, 18, 19, 20, 21, 22, 23, 30, 33, 37, 61, 233, 245, 518, 628, 742, 770, 854, 855, 1100
Grove City College v. Bell, 651
Guardianship of (see name of party)
Guerrero, United States v., 1140
Guinn v. United States, 335

H. v. D., 16, 854, 855
Haas v. Lewis, 785
Hadinger, State v., 794
Hamilton v. Schriro, 694
Hanke v. Safari Hair Adventure, 935
Harper v. Virginia State Bd. of Elections, 729
Harris v. Forklift Systems, Inc., 631
Harris v. McRae, 198, 260
Harvey v. Young Women's Christian Ass'n, 913
Hayes v. Smith, 479, 485
Hazelwood School Dist. v. Kuhlmeier, 607, 608, 609, 610, 617, 621, 625
Heller v. Doe by Doe, 377
Henry, State v., 515, 516
Henson v. City of Dundee, 919
Herring v. State, 39
Hershberger, State v., 694, 695
Hewitt v. Hewitt, 784
Hicklin, Regina v., 515
High Tech Gays v. Defense Indus. Sec. Clearance Office, 899
Hill v. I.N.S., 188
Hinds County School Bd., United States v., 646
Hinkhouse, State v., 1090, 1100
Hodgson v. Minnesota, 110 S.Ct. 2926, pp. 198, 672
Hodgson v. Minnesota, 648 F.Supp. 756, pp. **190,** 195, 196, 197, 198, 199, 200, 201, 202
Hoffman, In re, 442
Hoke v. United States, 157
Hoyt v. State of Fla., 184
Hudson View Properties v. Weiss, 788
Hunter v. Erickson, 723, 724, 725, 729

Hunter v. Fiumara, 485
Hurley v. Irish–American Gay, Lesbian and Bisexual Group of Boston, 438, 441, 443, 453
Hustler Magazine v. Falwell, 490, 517

Immerman v. Immerman, 832
In re (see name of party)
I.N.S. v. Cardoza–Fonseca, 756
I.N.S. v. Stevic, 755
International Union, United Auto., Aerospace and Agr. Implement Workers of America, UAW v. Johnson Controls, Inc., 913
Israel v. Allen, 823, 824

Jacob, Matter of, 868
Jacobson v. Jacobson, 803, 836
Jacobson v. United States, 1038, 1042
James v. Valtierra, 723, 729
Jane B., In re, 837
J.E.B. v. Alabama ex rel. T.B., 80
J.L.P.(H.) v. D.J.P., 837
Joachim v. AT & T Information Systems, 953
Johnson v. Calvert, 778
Johnson v. Transportation Agency, Santa Clara County, Cal., 948
Jones v. Daly, 784, 785
Jones v. Hallahan, 803, 804
J. S. & C., In re, 837

Kahn v. Shevin, 79
Kaiser, State v., 274, 277, 278, 279
Kapellas v. Kofman, 475
Karin T. v. Michael T., 1144
Katz v. United States, 21
Keegstra, Regina v., 557, 561
Keyes, People v., 532
Keyishian v. Board of Regents of University of State of N. Y., 620, 625
King v. Smith, 772
Kingsley Intern. Pictures Corp. v. Regents of University of State of N.Y., 79 S.Ct. 1362, p. 517
Kingsley Intern. Pictures Corp. v. Regents of University of N.Y., 175 N.Y.S.2d 39, p. 517
Kiyoshi Hirabayashi v. United States, 335
Kowalski, In re Guardianship of, 789, 790
Kramer v. Union Free Sch. Dist. No. 15, p. 727
Krizek v. Board of Educ. of Cicero–Stickney Tp. High School Dist. No. 201, Cook County, Ill., 625
Kulla v. McNulty, 789

Labady, In re Naturalization of Manuel, 743, 746
Ladrach, In re, 1122
Lanzetta v. New Jersey, 40
Laws v. Griep, 785
Lee, United States v., 693
Lee v. Weisman, 714

Leibert v. Transworld Systems, Inc., 950
Lemmerman v. Fealk, 1036, 1037
Lemon v. Kurtzman, 714
Lilly v. City of Minneapolis, 792, 957
Little Sisters Book and Art Emporium v. The Minister of Justice and Attorney General of Canada, 561
Lloyd Corp., Limited v. Tanner, 442
Logan v. Sears, Roebuck & Co., 490
Lonas v. State, 815
Longstaff, Matter of, 188, 189
Lopez, United States v., 995
Loving v. Virgina, 18, 122, 123, 494, 518, 732, **795,** 804, 805, 813, 814, 815, 817, 854, 855
Lovisi v. Slayton, 44
Lovisi v. Zahradnick, 44
Lugar v. Edmondson Oil Co., Inc., 442
Luke Records, Inc. v. Navarro, 564
Lyng v. Northwest Indian Cemetery Protective Ass'n, 693

Maffei v. Kolaeton Industry, Inc., 1108
Maher v. Roe, 198
Marriage of (see name of party)
Martinez v. Brown, 495
Marvin v. Marvin, 781, 783, 784, 785, 786, 789, 861
Maryland v. Craig, 1037
Massachusetts Bd. of Retirement v. Murgia, 92
Matlovich v. Secretary of the Air Force, 372
Matter of (see name of party)
Mayfield v. Mayfield, 1146
McCune v. Neitzel, 485, 489
McLaughlin v. Florida, 18
McQuirter v. State, 998, 1000
McWilliams v. Fairfax County Bd. of Supervisors, 930, 933, 934
Meinhold v. United States Dept. of Defense, 382, 383
Memoirs of Fanny Hill v. Massachusetts, 21
Meritor Sav. Bank, FSB v. Vinson, 631, 920
Meyer v. Nebraska, 9, 13, 24, 671
Michael M. v. Sonoma County Superior Court, 80, 981, 1023, **1024,** 1029, 1030, 1035
Miles v. Denver Public Schools, 624
Miller v. Bank of America, 919
Miller v. California, 517, 518, 526, 534, 549
Miller v. Rumsfield, 310
Miller's Estate, In re, 816
Minnesota ex rel. Pearson v. Probate Court of Ramsey County, 174
Mississippi University for Women v. Hogan, 80, 83, 87, 88, 645, 646, 647, 650
Missouri ex rel. Gaines v. Canada, 335
M.M.D., In re, 862, 868
Modinos v. Cyprus, 755
Morales, State v., 55
Morgan v. Virginia, 336
Morone v. Morone, 784
Morrison v. State Bd. of Educ., 628, 891
Mortenson's Estate, In re, 816

Moses, United States v., 1045

M. P. v. S. P., 836

M. T. v. J. T., 1117

M.T.S., State ex rel., 971

Mueller v. Allen, 714

Mueller, State v., 808

Muller v. State of Oregon, 878

Music v. Rachford, 789

Nabozny v. Podlesny, 638

Nancy S. v. Michele G., 789

National Ass'n for Advancement of Colored People v. Alabama, ex rel. Patterson, 415, 416, 418

National Gay Task Force v. Board of Educ. of City of Oklahoma City, 426, 429, 628, 681

Nazeri v. Missouri Valley College, 481, 485

Neal v. Neal, 993

Nemetz v. Immigration and Naturalization Service, 743

Newport News Shipbuilding and Dry Dock Co. v. E.E.O.C., 901

New York v. Ferber, 502, **526,** 531, 532, 534, 593

New York, City of v. New St. Mark's Baths, 1086

Nickerson v. Nickerson, 836

Norris v. Ireland, 755

North v. North, 837

Norton v. Macy, 886, 890, 891, 892, 895

Norwood v. Harrison, 650

O'Brien v. O'Brien, 772

O'Brien, United States v., 519, 520, 521, 936

O'Connor v. Board of Ed. of School Dist. 23, p. 644

O'Connor v. Sobol, 625

Olmstead v. United States, 8

One Book Entitled Ulysses by James Joyce, United States v., 516

One Eleven Wines & Liquors, Inc. v. Division of Alcoholic Beverage Control, 419

One, Incorporated v. Olesen, 78 S.Ct. 364, p. 413

One, Inc. v. Olesen, 241 F.2d 772, pp. **411,** 414, 415, 418, 425, 494

One Package, United States v., 6, 9, 18, 37, 39

Onofre, People v., 40, 44, 53

Opinion of the Justices, 845, 848

Orr v. Orr, 770

Owens v. Brown, 356, 357

P. v. S. and Cornwall County Council, 1107

Padula v. Webster, 891, 892

Palko v. Connecticut, 16

Palmore v. Sidoti, 831, 832, 836, 837, 848, 867

Papachristou v. City of Jacksonville, 162

Parish v. Minvielle, 816

Parrish v. Civil Service Commission of Alameda County, 772

People v. _____ (see opposing party)

Personnel Adm'r of Massachusetts v. Feeney, 80, 879, 911, 1050

Phillips v. Wisconsin Personnel Com'n, 958

Pickering v. Board of Ed. of Tp. High School Dist. 205, Will County, Illinois, 125, 620, 621

Pierce v. Society of the Sisters of the Holy Names of Jesus and Mary, 9, 13, 24, 671

Pinneke v. Preisser, 1117

Planned Parenthood Ass'n of Kansas City, Mo., Inc. v. Ashcroft, 194, 198

Planned Parenthood of Central Missouri v. Danforth, 190, 194

Planned Parenthood of Southeastern Pennsylvania v. Casey, 17, 34, 201, 202

Plessy v. Ferguson, 106, 107, 334, 335, 336, 454, 732

P.L.W. v. T.R.W., 1146

Poe v. Ullman, 9, **10,** 15, 17, 18, 33, 34

Ponton v. Newport News School Bd., 910

Porth v. Roman Catholic Diocese of Kalamazoo, 695

Post v. Oklahoma, 39, 55, 981

Posusta v. United States, 740, 742, 746

Price Waterhouse v. Hopkins, 282, 287, 288, **917,** 918, 921, 933, 1107

Prince v. Massachusetts, 672

PruneYard Shopping Center v. Robins, 452

Quick v. Donaldson Co., Inc., 933

Quilloin v. Walcott, 853, 854

Quong Wing v. Kirkendall, 878

R. v. Scythes, 561,

Radice v. New York, 878

Rankin v. McPherson, 635

R.A.V. v. City of St. Paul, Minn., 425, **495,** 504, 505, 506, 520, 530, 561, 936, 936

Red Lion Broadcasting Co. v. F. C. C., 583

Reed v. Reed, 34, 73, 80, 346, 896

Regina v. _____ (see opposing party)

Reitman v. Mulkey, 723, 724

Rendon v. United Airlines, 935

Renton, City of v. Playtime Theatres, Inc., 517, 520

Reynolds v. Sims, 729

Reynolds v. United States, 824, 825

Riley v. Garrett, 40

Roberts v. United States Jaycees, 80, 125, 416, 437, 443, 495

Robins v. Pruneyard Shopping Center, 442

Roe v. K–Mart Corp., 933

Roe v. Roe, 837

Roe v. Wade, 30, 33, 34, 35, 36, 37, 189, 194, 199, 201, 233, 245, 260, 419, 770, 855

Romer v. Evans, 93, 106, 108, 117, 131, 383, 384, 404, 405, 429, 504, 684, **729,** 832, 844, 848, 896, 949

Rose v. Locke, 40

Rosenberger v. University of Virginia, 419, **455,** 462, 504, 582, 624, 714

Ross v. Denver Dept. of Health and Hospitals, 954

Ross v. Midwest Communications, Inc., 477

Rostker v. Goldberg, 80, 88, **348,** 356, 357, 364, 365

Roth v. United States, 21, 413, **508,** 511, 514, 515, 516, 517, 518, 526

Rowinsky v. Bryan Independent School Dist., 639

Rowland v. Mad River Local School Dist., Montgomery County, Ohio, 301, 426, 431, 628, 896, 899

Rusk, State v., 972, 979, 980, 981, 992, 1019

Rust v. Sullivan, 419, 579, 582, 583

S v. S, 832, 836

Saal v. Middendorf, 310

Sable Communications of California, Inc. v. F.C.C., 584, 585

Sanger, People v., 5

Saunders, State v., 55

Sawatzky v. City of Oklahoma City, 44

Sawyer v. Bailey, 785

Schlesinger v. Ballard, 79

Schmid, State v., 442

Schochet v. State, 39, 55, 981

School Bd. of Nassau County, Fla. v. Arline, 960, 961, 1089

Schuster v. Schuster, 832, 836

Scott v. State, 814

Seminole Tribe of Florida v. Florida, 637

Shahar v. Bowers, 124, 895, 131

Shelley v. Kraemer, 336

Sherbert v. Verner, 693, 694, 695, 696

Sherman, City of v. Henry, 55, 1042

Singer v. Hara, 799, 803, 804, 813, 814

Singer v. United States Civil Service Com'n, 430, **892,** 894, 895

Sipple v. Chronicle Pub. Co., 472, 476, 477

Sipuel v. Board of Regents of University of Okl., 336

Skinner v. Railway Labor Executives' Ass'n, 1082

Skinner v. State of Okl. ex rel. Williamson, 9

Slayton v. State, 803

Smith v. Fair Employment and Housing Com'n (Phillips), 695, 723

S.N.E. v. R.L.B., 836

Solmitz v. Maine School Administrative Dist. No. 59, 621, 624, 681

Sommers v. Iowa Civil Rights Com'n, 1112

Sorrells v. United States, 1042

Sostock v. Reiss, 785

Stanley v. Illinois, 853

Stanley v. State of Georgia, 20, 21, 22, 517, 519, 520, 532, 854, 855, 1042

State v. _____ (see opposing party)

State, Dept. of Health and Rehabilitative Services v. Cox, 844

State of (see name of state)

Steffan v. Aspin, 375, 382, 383, 403

Steffan v. Perry, 374

Stoumen v. Reilly, 416, 418, 419, 425

Stowell, Commonwealth v., 55

St. Paul Citizens for Human Rights v. City Council of City of St. Paul, 716, 719, 721, 722

Stroman v. Williams, 836

Succession of (see name of party)

Superior Court of Alameda County, People v., 1046

Swanner v. Anchorage Equal Rights Com'n, 696

Sweezy v. New Hampshire, 620

Tenorio, In re, 760

The Charming Betsy, 751

The Florida Star v. B.J.F., 463, 464, 470

Thomas v. Sullivan, 816

Thomas S. v. Robin Y., 855

Thomasson v. Perry, 403

Thompson v. Aldredge, 39

Thompson v. Wisconsin Dept. of Public Instruction, 912

Thoreson v. Penthouse Intern., Ltd., 1057, 1062

Thornburgh v. American College of Obstetricians and Gynecologists, 34

333 East 53rd Street Associates v. Mann, 787

Tileston v. Ullman, 9

Tinker v. Des Moines Independent Community School Dist., 424, 597, 607, 609, 638

Toboso–Alfonso, Matter of, 761

Toll v. Moreno, 751

Toonen v. Australia, 751

Torosyan v. Boehringer Ingelheim Pharmaceuticals, Inc., 954

Toyosaburo Korematsu v. United States, 335, 336, 406, 690, 732

Tremblay v. Carter, 785

Turner v. Safley, 806, 813, 822

Turner Broadcasting System, Inc. v. F.C.C., 583

12 200–Foot Reels of Super 8mm. Film, United States v., 515

Tyson v. Tyson, 1037

Ulane v. Eastern Airlines, Inc., 1102, 1103, 1106, 1107, 1108

Underwood v. Archer Management Services, Inc., 1109

United States v. _____ (see opposing party)

Uplinger, People v., 44

UWM Post, Inc. v. Board of Regents of University of Wisconsin System, 638

Vallerga v. Department of Alcoholic Beverage Control, 419

Vandeventer v. Wabash Nat. Corp., 934, 935

Van Dyck v. Van Dyck, 803
Van Ooteghem v. Gray, 430
Virginia, United States v., 81, 91, 92, 364, 365, **647,** 1029
Vorchheimer v. School Dist. of Philadelphia, 646
Vuitch, United States v., 40

Wainwright v. Stone, 40
Walsh, State v., 55, 485
Ward v. Hickey, 625
Ware v. Valley Stream High School Dist., 685, 693, 694, 695, 708
Washington v. Davis, 880, 1050
Washington v. Seattle School Dist. No. 1, pp. 724, 729
Wasson, Commonwealth v., 38, 54
Waters v. Churchill, 131
Watkins v. United States Army, 875 F.2d 699, p. 383
Watkins v. United States Army, 847 F.2d 1329, pp. 106, **109,** 117, 118, **374,** 382
Webster v. Reproductive Health Services, 34
Weinberger v. Wiesenfeld, 79, 80
Weiss v. United States, 356
Whaley v. Whaley, 828, 832, 833, 837
Whorton v. Dillingham, 785

Wiarda, In re Marriage of, 836
Wilkins v. Zelichowski, 816
Williams, In re Marriage of, 836
Williams v. McNair, 650
Williams v. Rhodes, 729
Williams v. North Carolina, 65 S.Ct. 1092, p. 815
Williams v. North Carolina, 63 S.Ct. 207, p. 815
Willingham v. Macon Tel. Pub. Co., 1143
Wisconsin v. Mitchell, 405, 505, 506
Wisconsin v. Yoder, 693, 694, 695, 696
Wright v. Methodist Youth Services, Inc., 934
Wright v. State, 1001
Wyman v. James, 772

X–Citement Video, Inc., United States v., 532, 1042

Young v. American Mini Theatres, Inc., 516, 517

Zablocki v. Redhail, 805, 810, 813, 814, 822, 823, 824

*

PREFACE ON CONSTITUTIONAL RIGHTS

The Framers of the Constitution of 1789 believed that the main protection for the rights of the individual citizen were to be found in the Constitution's relentless division of powers among the states and federal government, the three branches of the federal government, and even within the legislative branch (the branch most feared) itself. But in 1791, as one of the deals made to get the Constitution ratified, they adopted a Bill of Rights that enumerated protections against federal intrusion into the lives of citizens. The Bill of Rights and other pertinent constitutional amendments are reproduced in Appendix 1 to this casebook. The due process clause of the Fourteenth Amendment has been interpreted to apply most of the individual rights of the first ten amendments to state governments as well.

The states have their own separate constitutions, which create individual rights against the states. This layer-cake arrangement tends to multiply rights.[a] On the one hand, if the U.S. Supreme Court declines to recognize a right under the U.S. Constitution, state high courts might still recognize a right under their state constitutions. (Note, too, that the federal or state legislatures can also enforce that right through ordinary legislation, as Congress sought to do with the Religious Freedom Restoration Act [Chapter 8, Section 1].) On the other hand, if the U.S. Supreme Court does recognize a federal constitutional right, state courts cannot derogate from that right, because of the supremacy clause (Article VI of the U.S. Constitution). Similarly, most of the time neither Congress nor the state legislatures can override individual rights recognized by the U.S. Supreme Court.

Constitutional law courses that cover issues of due process, equal protection, and free expression provide the student of *Sexuality, Gender, and the Law* with enough constitutional background to handle all the cases and issues in our book. This preface is written especially for students who have not studied the Constitution's individual rights jurisprudence or for students who are studying this book as their introduction to constitutional rights. We attempt to lay out the overall analytical framework for the three main areas relevant to our subject matter (due process, equal protection, free expression), explain the particular doctrines, and provide cross-references for these areas and doctrines in this casebook.[b]

[a] See William N. Eskridge, Jr. & John Ferejohn, "Virtual Logrolling: How the Court, Congress, and the States Multiply Rights," 68 *S. Cal. L. Rev.* 1545 (1995).

[b] Due process ideas, especially the right of privacy, are developed in Chapter 1, Sections 1 and 2; the due process right to marry is the focus of Chapter 9, Section 2. Equal protection

SECTION 1. DUE PROCESS

The Fifth and Fourteenth Amendments, the former applicable to the federal government and the latter to the states, protect citizens against deprivation of life, liberty, and property without "due process of law." The Supreme Court once said that the due process clause does not assure all procedural or substantive rights that seem fair, but only invalidates laws that violate "a principle of justice so rooted in the tradition and conscience of our people as to be ranked as fundamental." *Palko v. Connecticut*, 302 U.S. 319 (1937). Since the Warren Court (1954-69), however, the due process clause has been read in light of the general policy it embodies, that individual life, liberty, and property should not be at the mercy of arbitrary state intrusion. For our purposes, those protections have been particularly important in cases where the state is invoking the criminal law against people who violate America's sexual mores, including women desiring contraceptives or abortions, sodomites and homosexuals, prostitutes and other people soliciting sex, unmarried pregnant women, cross-dressers and transvestites, pornographers and purveyors of indecent materials, people who love those of another race or the same sex, polygamists, and so on.

A. Procedural Protections. At the most general level, the due process clause requires that the state cannot deprive anyone of liberty or property without giving that person prior notice, a meaningful right to be heard (usually before the deprivation occurs), and an impartial decisionmaker. See *Goldberg v. Kelly*, 397 U.S. 254 (1970) (welfare benefits); *Board of Regents v. Roth*, 408 U.S. 564 (1972) (state job). When a fundamental individual interest is involved, the state has to provide more procedural protections. For example, the state cannot preclude poor people from marrying or divorcing simply because they cannot afford the state filing fees, *Boddie v. Connecticut*, 401 U.S. 371 (1970), and cannot deprive a parent of her children without proof of the necessary grounds by "clear and convincing evidence," *Santosky v. Kramer*, 455 U.S. 745 (1982), or foreclose that parent's appeal of an order terminating parental rights because she cannot afford to pay for a transcript. *M.L.B. v. S.L.J.*, 117 S.Ct. 555 (1996). For these reasons, the state usually is not able to invoke traditional morality as the basis for breaking up homes of sexual nonconformists, although these protections do not prevent the state from siding with sexual conformists against nonconformists when two parents battle for child custody (Chapter 9, Section 3[A]).

---

doctrine is developed in Chapter 1, Section 3; Chapter 4's case study of the armed forces' construction of manhood compares and contrasts the doctrines of race (Section 1), sex (Section 2), and sexual orientation (Section 3) discrimination. First Amendment doctrines are developed in Chapters 5 and 6, starting with first principles (Chapter 5, Section 1) and exploring issues of association, identity speech, libel, hate speech and fighting words, and obscenity. Chapter 7 treats speech in the special forum of schools, and Chapter 8, Section 1 briefly examines the religion clauses of the First Amendment.

This Preface is not a comprehensive analysis of constitutional law or even the Bill of Rights. It borrows intellectually from Daniel A. Farber et al., *Cases and Materials on Constitutional Law: Themes for the Constitution's Third Century* (1993), to which the student is referred for more detailed treatment.

In Anglo-American society, deprivation of physical liberty is considered the greatest deprivation (short of a death sentence), and the procedural protections are correspondingly greater. By 1970, the Supreme Court had nationalized the rights of criminal defendants, by "incorporating" most of the criminal procedure protections of the Bill of Rights into the due process clause, which rendered them directly applicable to the states. Among the rights of criminal defendants that were so nationalized are the following:

- the right to be free of unreasonable searches and seizures (Fourth Amendment),[c]

- the right to be free of cruel and unusual punishment (Eighth Amendment),[d]

- the right not to incriminate onself (Fifth Amendment),[e]

- the right to counsel provided by the state if the defendant cannot afford one (Sixth Amendment),[f]

- the right not to be tried twice for the same offense (Fifth Amendment),[g] and

- the right to confront one's accusers (Sixth Amendment).[h]

These rights inure to the benefit of defendants charged with sex or gender crimes. For example, the state cannot search the apartment of suspected child molesters or rapists without probable cause and usually cannot convict without providing an opportunity for the accused to confront witnesses against him (see Chapter 11, Section 2[C]). Note that the same criminal procedure protections apply to sex crimes that have victims (rape, child molestation) as to those that are essentially victimless (consensual sodomy, prostitution).

Another important protection teased out of the due process clause in criminal cases has no analogue in the Bill of Rights: the entrapment defense. Enforcement of laws against prostitution, homosexual solicitation, and public lewdness (all of which are still on the books in many states) have usually been by "decoy police," undercover officers who lure defendants into committing a crime (Chapter 2, Section 2[A]). The U.S. Supreme Court has held that entrapment cannot be the basis for a criminal conviction if the defendant did not otherwise have a "predisposition" to commit the crime. Some states follow a more liberal rule, which invalidates any conviction where the police induce a "law-abiding" citizen to commit a crime. *E.g.*, *People v. Barazza*, 591 P.2d 947 (Cal. 1979). Today, undercover operations

---

[c] *Wolf v. Colorado*, 338 U.S. 25 (1949).

[d] *Robinson v. California*, 370 U.S. 660 (1962), which held that people could not be punished simply for their "status," in that case being an alcoholic.

[e] *Malloy v. Hogan*, 378 U.S. 1 (1964); *cf. Miranda v. Arizona*, 384 U.S. 436 (1965) (police must inform defendant of his or her right not to incriminate him or herself).

[f] *Gideon v. Wainwright*, 372 U.S. 335 (1963); *cf. Argersinger v. Hamlin*, U.S. (1974) (right to counsel applies even to misdemeanors resulting in incarceration of just a single day).

[g] *Benton v. Maryland*, 395 U.S. 784 (1969), overruling *Palko*.

[h] *California v. Green*, 399 U.S. 149 (1970).

tend to be more sophisticated "stings" against child pornographers, rings of prostitutes, and customers. *Jacobson v. United States*, 503 U.S. 540 (1992) (Chapter 11, Section 2[C]).

B. Vagueness. The Supreme Court has repeatedly invalidated, on due process "vagueness" grounds, statutes that are not sufficiently clear for citizens and police to know precisely what conduct is criminal.[i] In addition to the obvious constitutional policy of fair notice, the doctrine also implements two subtler constitutional policies. One is the policy against arbitrary enforcement of broad criminal laws against disfavored status groups. A vice of vague criminal laws is the large discretion they vest in law enforcement officials, and the concomitant danger that the discretion will not be applied neutrally. The most subtle policy underlying the vagueness doctrine lies in a need to weed out obsolescent crimes. Statutory commands, clear once upon a time, might grow muddier as time passes and the meaning conveyed to the original audience is lost upon new audiences. At some point, judges have an obligation to sweep such statutes off the books and insist that the legislature update their commands into something more intelligible to the average citizen.[j] A good many of the once-clear commands that grew muddier over time were statutory crimes targeting people or conduct considered deviant or even dangerous in the nineteenth century but not today.

All of these policies were important to the Court in *Papachristou v. Florida*, 405 U.S. 156 (1972), which invalidated a Jacksonville, Florida vagrancy ordinance making it a crime to be "vagabonds, or dissolute persons who go about begging, * * * lewd, wanton, and lascivious persons, * * * persons wandering or strolling around from place to place without any lawful purpose or object, habitual loafers, disorderly persons," and so forth. *Papachristou*-like arguments have been invoked by people challenging abortion statutes and sodomy laws (Chapter 1, Section 2); federal guidelines restricting "indecent" sexual speech in grants by the National Endowment for the Arts (Chapter 6, Section 3[B]), radio broadcasts (Chapter 6, Section 3[C]), and AIDS programs (Chapter 7, Section 3[C]); and laws criminalizing public appearance in attire not of one's own sex (Chapter 12, Section 3).

A corollary of the due process rule against vague criminal statutes is the rule of lenity, which requires that ambiguous criminal laws be interpreted narrowly (against the government and in favor of the accused).[k] White collar crime statutes, for example, regularly receive lenient constructions from federal and state courts. Interpreting or applying statutes targeting

---

[i] *United States v. Harriss*, 347 U.S. 612, 617 (1954) (due process requires that criminal laws "give a person of ordinary intelligence fair notice that his contemplated conduct is forbidden by the statute"); *Lanzetta v. New Jersey*, 306 U.S. 451 (1939); see Anthony Amsterdam, "The Void-For-Vagueness Doctrine in the Supreme Court," 109 *U. Pa. L. Rev.* 67 (1960) (student note).

[j] See Alexander Bickel, *The Least Dangerous Branch* (1962); Guido Calabresi, *The Common Law in the Age of Statutes* (1982).

[k] An exploration of the rule of lenity can be found in William N. Eskridge, Jr. & Philip P. Frickey, *Cases and Materials on Legislation: Statutes and the Creation of Public Policy* 652-75 (2d ed. 1995).

gender-benders, fornicators, and homosexuals, however, courts have usually ignored or slighted the rule of lenity. See *Caminetti v. United States*, 242 U.S. 470 (1917) (fornicators) (Chapter 2, Section 2[A][1]); *Boutilier v. INS*, 387 U.S. 117 (1967) (bisexuals) (Chapter 2, Section 2[B][3]); *Beller v. Middendorf*, 632 F.2d 788 (9th Cir. 1980) (occasional sodomite) (Chapter 3, Section 3[B]); *Steffan v. Perry*, 41 F.3d 677 (D.C. Cir. 1995) (gays in the military) (Chapter 4, Section 3[B][2]); *FCC v. Pacifica Found.*, 438 U.S. 726 (1978) (dirty words) (Chapter 6, Section 3[C]); *Regina v. Brown*, [1994] 1 AC 212, [1993] 2 All ER 75, [1993] 2 WLR 556 (U.K. House of Lords, 1993) (consensual sado-masochists) (Chapter 11, Section 1[C]). For an example where lenity has been shown, see *Mienhold v. Department of the Navy*, 34 F.2d 1469 (9th Cir. 1994) (gays in the military) (discussed in Chapter 4, Section 3[B][2]).

C. Substantive Due Process and the Right of Privacy. The Supreme Court has historically held that there is a "substantive" feature to the due process clause that empowers courts to strike down laws that are purely arbitrary or that unduly trench on people's "fundamental" rights. The nonarbitrariness requirement of the due process clause was the basis for judicial scrutiny of civil service exclusions of lesbian and gay employees, for example. See *Norton v. Macy*, 417 F.2d 1161 (D.C. Cir. 1969) (Chapter 10, Section 1[B]).

The right of privacy is the most relevant exemplar of the fundamental rights component of the due process jurisprudence. The right of privacy is the right people have to be free of state interference in the most fundamental decisions of human life and intimacy. Although ten states have explicit right of privacy clauses in their state constitutions,[1] it is not explicitly recognized in the U.S. Constitution. Nonetheless, early Supreme Court cases held that decisions about family and child-rearing involve fundamental rights protected by the due due process clause.[m]

Connecticut prohibited the use of birth control devices in 1879 and, with Massachusetts, remained the last bastion of such statutes in 1961. In that year, the Supreme Court used a procedural dodge to avoid a constitutional challenge to the law, but over a powerful dissent by Justice Harlan. *Poe v. Ullman*, 367 U.S. 497 (1961) (Harlan, J., dissenting) (Chapter 1, Section 1[A]). Harlan found in the due process clause's "principle of liberty" constitutional protection for the "most intimate details of the marital relation," including use of contraception. Four years later, the Supreme Court

---

[1] Article I, § 22 of the Alaska Constitution; Article II, § 8 of the Arizona Constitution; Article I, § 1 of the California Constitution; Article I, § 23 of the Florida Constitution; Article I, § 6 of the Hawaii Constitution; Article I, § 12 of the Illinois Constitution; Article I, § 5 of the Louisiana Constitution; Article II, § 10 of the Montana Constitution; Article I, § 10 of the South Carolina Constitution; and Article I, § 7 of the Washington Constitution.

[m] In *Meyer v. Nebraska*, 262 U.S. 390 (1923), the Court ruled that the "liberty" protected by the due process clause includes "not merely freedom from bodily restraint but also the right of the individual to contract, to engage in any of the common occupations of life, to acquire useful knowledge, to marry, to establish a home and bring up children." See also *Pierce v. Society of Sisters*, 268 U.S. 510 (1925) (state could not require children to attend public school).

struck down the Connecticut law in *Griswold v. Connecticut*, 381 U.S. 479 (1965) (Chapter 1, Section 1[A]). Speaking of the freedom of married couples to choose the terms of their sexual intimacy, Justice Douglas' majority opinion found a right to privacy in the shadows ("penumbras") of the First, Fourth, Fifth, and Ninth Amendments.

Subsequent moves by the Supreme Court applied *Griswold* in ways that expanded the breadth of the precedent. The Court's decision overturning abortion statutes in *Roe v. Wade*, 410 U.S. 113 (1973) (Chapter 1, Section 1[C]) confirmed that the right of privacy was not limited to married couples and suggested that this right entailed a freedom for women to control not just their bodies, but to enjoy sexual liberty previously unheard of. *Roe* also authoritatively established the right of privacy in the due process clause and formally abandoned *Griswold*'s experiment in penumbral reasoning. See also *Planned Parenthood v. Casey*, 112 S. Ct. 2791 (1992) (reaffirming the central holding of *Roe* and adopting the rationale of Harlan's *Poe* dissent). *Roe* has spawned a complicated jurisprudence evaluating various kinds of state laws placing various burdens on a woman's right to choose an abortion. *E.g., Hodgson v. Minnesota*, 497 U.S. 417 (1990) (Chapter 2, Section 2[C]) (allowing statutory requirement that minor female notify both parents or receive judicial approval before she can choose an abortion), followed in *Casey*.

In *Loving v. Virginia*, 388 U.S. 1 (1967) (Chapter 9, Section 2[A]), the Court recognized a fundamental right to marry as one ground for invalidating Virginia's law criminalizing miscegenation, or different-race marriages. The leading right to marry case is *Zablocki v. Redhail*, 434 U.S. 374 (1978) (Chapter 9, Section 2[A]), which struck down a Wisconsin law preventing remarriage by people in arrears on outstanding child and spouse support obligations. Notwithstanding the worthy state goal, the Court held that there were other ways of meeting it that did not deprive people of a fundamental constitutional right. Does the right to marry apply to same-sex couples (Chapter 9, Section 2[B])? Incestophiles and polygamists (Chapter 9, Section 2[C])?

In *Moore v. City of East Cleveland*, 431 U.S. 494 (1977), the Court struck down an ordinance limiting occupancy of any dwelling unit to members of the same "family," defined to include only "related" persons. Justice Powell's plurality opinion applied heightened scrutiny because the ordinance regulated "choices concerning family living arrangements," which in *Moore* involved a household consisting of a grandmother, son, and two grandsons from another child. "The Constitution prevents East Cleveland from standardizing its children—and its adults—by forcing all to live in certain narrowly defined family patterns." (A fifth Justice concurred in the result on the odd ground that the ordinance was a "taking" of property without just compensation.)

The right of privacy has also been a basis for challenging laws criminalizing consensual sodomy. New York struck down its consensual sodomy law in *People v. Onofre*, 415 N.E.2d 936 (N.Y. 1980) (Chapter 1, Section 2). The state court of appeals held that the right of privacy is not limited to marriage and procreation-based activities and is "a right of independence in making certain kinds of important decisions, with a concomitant right to conduct oneself in accordance with those decisions, undeterred by governmental restraint." The U.S. Supreme Court reached the opposite result in *Bowers v. Hardwick*, 478 U.S. 186 (1986) (Chapter 1, Section 2), which held that *Griswold, Roe*, and *Loving* were limited to situations of sexual intimacy involving marriage and possible pregnancy. Hence, their constitutional protections had no relevance for "homosexual sodomy," even if consensual. Some state courts after *Bowers* have interpreted their state constitutions to protect consensual homosexual as well as heterosexual intimacy,[n] and certain international tribunals have insisted that a meaningful right to privacy is inconsistent with criminalizing consensual homosexual sodomy (Chapter 8, Section 3[B]).

The most recent privacy issue to bedevil the courts involves the "right to die." The Court in *Cruzan v. Director, Missouri Dep't of Health*, 497 U.S. 261 (1990), assumed that a person has a due process liberty interest in refusing unwanted medical treatment but upheld state regulation in a case where the person was in a coma and therefore unable to make the choice herself. Only Justice Scalia, concurring in the judgment, challenged such a right. As this casebook goes to press, the Supreme Court is deliberating a pair of cases squarely presenting right to die issues where the persons desiring suicide are capable of choice. See *Washington v. Glucksberg*, No. 96–110; *Vacco v. Quill*, No. 95–1858, both argued January 8, 1997.

SECTION 2.   EQUAL PROTECTION

The Fourteenth Amendment also provides: "nor shall any State * * * deny to any person within its jurisdiction the equal protection of the laws." In the first case interpreting the equal protection clause, the Supreme Court "doubt[ed] very much whether any action of a state not directed by way of discrimination against the negroes as a class, or on account of their race, will ever be held to come within the purview of this provision." *Slaughter House Cases*, 83 U.S. 36 (1872).[o] Consistent with this dictum, the Supreme Court has regularly upheld state policies that rely on classifications such as income, height, emissions levels, public conduct and appearance, and the like upon a showing that the classifications have a *rational basis*: they are plausibly related to a legitimate state goal. The big question in equal protection law is when the Court should demand something more than a rational basis to support statutory classifications. An ancillary question is when a law does not even have a rational basis.

---

[n] See *Wasson v. Commonwealth*, 847 S.W.2d 487 (Ky. 1992); *Campbell v. Sundquist*, 926 S.W.2d 250 (Tenn. App. 1996). State constitutional arguments were also successful at the intermediate appellate level in challenging the Texas sodomy law in *City of Dallas v. England*, 846 S.W. 2d 957 (Tex. App. 1993) and *State v. Morales*, 826 S.W.2d 201 (Tex. App. 1992), *reversed on other grounds*, 869 S.W.2d 94 (Tex. 1994).

[o] Nonetheless, the Court applied the equal protection clause to invalidate local policies discriminating against Chinese Americans in *Yick Wo v. Hopkins*, 118 U.S. 376 (1886), and stated in *Strauder v. West Virginia*, 100 U.S. 303 (1879) that discrimination on the basis of ethnicity would also be scrutinized skeptically under the clause.

A. The Carolene Products Forumulation: Strict Scrutiny for Classifications Aimed at Marginalized Groups (Race, Illegitimacy, Alienage). The modern Court's classic equal protection analysis came in a case involving the constitutionality of a federal law prohibiting the interstate transportation of "filled milk." In *United States v. Carolene Products Co.*, 304 U.S. 144 (1938), the Court deferred to the legislative health rationale for the filled milk classification, even though the statute reeked of special interest (the milk lobby). Justice Stone's opinion famously suggested limits to such deference, stating in footnote 4 that the "presumption of constitutionality" might be rebutted in cases where statutes (1) violate the plain meaning of a specific constitutional prohibition such as those in the Bill of Rights; (2) close off the political process, as by restricting the right to vote, to organize politically, or to assemble; or (3) are "directed at particular religious * * * or national * * * or racial minorities" or reflect "prejudice against discrete or insular minorities * * * which tends seriously to curtail the operation of the political processes ordinarily to be relied upon the protect minorities."

Consistent with both the original focus of the Fourteenth Amendment and the *Carolene* formulation, the Supreme Court has departed from the rational basis test when evaluating race-based classifications. In *Korematsu v. United States*, 323 U.S. 214 (1944), where the Supreme Court notoriously upheld federal internment of Japanese Americans during World War II, the Court stated that "all legal restrictions which curtail the civil rights of a single racial group are immediately suspect" and "courts must subject them to the most rigid scrutiny." This idea was key in the post-World War II legal assault on racial apartheid. The first major apartheid-based policy to fall was the U.S. armed services' segregation of African Americans and other persons of color, which President Truman ended by executive order in 1948 (Chapter 4, Section 1).

Brown v. Board of Education, 347 U.S. 483 (1954), held that racial segregation of public schools violates the equal protection clause. In a companion case, *Bolling v. Sharpe*, 347 U.S. 497 (1954), the Court held for the first time that the federal government is also subject to equal protection limits, teased (or tortured, depending on your constitutional theory) out of the due process clause of the Fifth Amendment. *Loving v. Virginia*, 388 U.S. 1 (1967) (Chapter 9, Section 2[A]), noted above as the first due process right to marry case, ruled as its primary holding that the Virginia anti-miscegenation law violated the equal protection clause because it deployed an unsupported race-based classification: a black-white couple could not marry, whereas a similarly situated black-black or white-white couple could.

Cases involving race-based classifications have been the most dramatic occasions for judicial application of the equal protection clause to strike down state and federal laws, but *Carolene*'s concern with laws reflecting "prejudice against discrete or insular minorities" has been interpreted to subject other classifications to strict scrutiny. See *Graham v. Richardson*, 403 U.S. 365 (1971), which held that state (but not necessarily federal) rules based on alienage would be subjected to heightened scrutiny for *Carolene* reasons. In *Levy v. Louisiana*, 391 U.S. 68 (1968), the Court held that illegitimacy is also a *suspect classification*. Although the Court has been willing to uphold some illegitimacy classifications, heightened scrutiny and changing social mores have basically eliminated illegitimacy as a legal classification. Children born outside of marriage are now treated the same by the law as those born within marriage (Chapter 9, Section 1).

The large majority of classifications, of course, fall under the default rule of the rational basis approach. For example, the Court in *Massachusetts Bd. of Retirement v. Murgia*, 427 U.S. 307 (1976), held that age-based classifications such as mandatory retirement ages do not justify heightened scrutiny because old people have not been a discrete and insular minority disadvantaged in the political process. Similarly, the Court has held that neither wealth, *San Antonio Indep. School Dist. v. Rodriguez*, 411 U.S. 1 (1973), nor personal disability, *City of Cleburne v. Cleburne Living Center*, 473 U.S. 432 (1985) (Chapter 1, Section 3[B][1]), is a classification that triggers heightened scrutiny. *Cleburne* is significant, however, in the Court's invalidating a law discriminating against the disabled because its underlying animus against the disabled flunked even the rational basis test.

B. The New Equal Protection Model: Intermediate Scrutiny of Sex—and Sexual Orientation?—Classifications. Because women are not a "discrete and insular minority" but have been objects of legislation based on gender- or sex-based stereotypes, classifications based on sex posed a difficult problem for the *Carolene Products* formulation. The Supreme Court routinely upheld sex-based classifications as rational until *Reed v. Reed*, 404 U.S. 71 (1971). Apparently applying the rational basis test, the Court invalidated an Idaho statute preferring men over women as executors of estates. The next year Congress passed the Equal Rights Amendment, which would have made sex a suspect classification. While the ERA was in the process of state ratification, four Justices on the Court argued for strict scrutiny under the equal protection clause in *Frontiero v. Richardson*, 311 U.S. 677 (1973) (Chapter 1, Section 3[A] and Chapter 4, Section 2[B]).

The ERA was never ratified, but seventeen states have added ERAs to their state constitutions,[p] and the U.S. Supreme Court has inched toward making sex a suspect classification. In *Craig v. Boren*, 429 U.S. 190 (1976), the Court struck down a state law allowing 18 year old girls to buy low-alco-

---

[p] "Sex" is inserted into a broader equal protection clause in the Alaska Constitution, article I, § 3 ("sex" added 1972); Connecticut Constitution, article I, § 20 (added 1974); Hawaii Constitution, article I, § 5; Illinois Constitution, article I, § 17 (1970 revised constitution); Massachusetts Declaration of Rights, part I, article I (added 1976); Montana Constitution, article II, § 4 (1972 revised constitution); New Hampshire Constitution, part I, article 2 (added 1974); Texas Constitution, article I, § 3a (added 1972); Virginia Constitution, article I, § 11 (added 1970); Wyoming Constitution, article I, § 3 (1889 constitution). Following the ERA, other states have clauses specially protecting against sex discrimination, namely, Colorado Constitution, article II, § 29 (equal rights amendment added 1972); Illinois Constitution, article I, § 8 (1970 revised constitution); Maryland Declaration of Rights, article 46 (added 1972); New Mexico Constitution, article II, § 18 (added 1972); Pennsylvania Constitution, article I, § 28 (added 1971); Utah Constitution, article IV, § 1 (1896 constitution); Washington Constitution, article 31, § 1 (added 1972).

hol beer but requiring boys to be 21 years old. Writing for six members of the Court, Justice Brennan's opinion held that "classifications by gender must serve important governmental objectives and must be substantially related to achievement of those objectives." This verbal formulation is not as demanding as that the Court uses to scrutinize race-based classifications, and so it is considered "heightened" or "intermediate" rather than "strict" scrutiny. In *United States v. Virginia*, 116 S. Ct. 2264 (1996) (Chapter 1, Section 3[A]), Justice Ginsburg's opinion for six Justices held that sex-based classifications must be supported by a justification that is "exceedingly persuasive." Also, the "justification must be genuine, not hypothesized or invented post hoc in response to litigation. And it must not rely on overbroad generalizations about the different talents, capacities, or preferences of males and females."

The Supreme Court has applied, sometimes rather weakly sometimes quite strongly, *Craig*'s heightened scrutiny to sex-based classifications in military service (Chapter 4, Section 2), education (Chapter 7, Section 2), workplace rules (Chapter 10, Section 1[A]), and statutory rape law (Chapter 11, Section 2[A]), to name just a few areas covered in this book. A specific doctrinal issue bears emphasis at this point. Heightened equal protection scrutiny applies only to statutes or regulations that openly discriminate on the basis of sex *or* that can be shown to be motivated by a discriminatory purpose. Thus, the Supreme Court has not strictly scrutinized employment policies that disproportionately hurt women in the workforce. See *Geduldig v. Aiello*, 417 U.S. 484 (1974) (Chapter 10, Section 1[C]) (discrimination on the basis of pregnancy); *Personnel Administrator v. Feeney*, 442 U.S. 256 (1979) (Chapter 10, Section 1[A]) (discrimination in favor of military veterans). The rule is different, however, when one leaves the realm of protection under the Constitution. Congress has made both kinds of sex discrimination unlawful in Title VII of the Civil Rights Act of 1964, as amended (Chapter 10, Section 2).

In the most interesting application of a state ERA, the Hawaii Supreme Court held in *Baehr v. Lewin*, 852 P.2d 44 (Haw. 1993) (Chapter 9, Section 2[B]) that it is sex discrimination for the state to deny a marriage license to two women when a similarly situated man and woman would receive one. The analogy to *Loving* is striking (see Chapter 1, Section 3[B][3]): where *Loving* subjected laws prohibiting different-race marriage to heightened scrutiny because they denied marriage licenses based on the race of one of the partners, *Baehr* subjected laws prohibiting same-sex marriage to heightened scrutiny because they deny marriage licenses based on the sex of one of the partners. Contrast federal court decisions refusing to interpret Title VII's protection against workplace sex discrimination to protect gay people (Chapter 10, Section 2[B]) or to protect transsexuals (Chapter 12, Section 2) or transvestites (Chapter 12, Section 3).

Should sexual orientation itself be a classification that triggers heightened scrutiny? Judge Norris's opinion in *Watkins v. U.S. Army*, 847 F.2d 1329 (9th Cir. 1988), *vacated*, 872 F.2d 699 (9th Cir. en banc 1989) (Chapter 1, Section 3[B][2]), remains the leading analytical defense of that proposition along the lines of *Carolene Products* or *Frontiero*. The U.S. Supreme Court's opinion in *Romer v. Evans*, 116 S. Ct. 1620 (1996) (Chapter 1, Section 3[B][1]) invalidated an anti-gay initiative under the rational basis test. One question is whether *Evans*, like *Reed v. Reed,* might be a harbinger for future Courts to apply some kind of heightened scrutiny to sexual orientation classifications. The irrationality of these classifications is explored through the materials in Chapter 2, Section 2(B) and Section 3, and Chapter 10, Section 1(B). Are policies that discriminate on the basis of cross-dressing or gender dysphoria (a disconnect between biological sex and gender identity) irrational?

Classifications based upon sexual orientation remain common. They include state sodomy or solicitation laws that apply only to homosexual and not heterosexual sodomy or solicitation (Chapter 1, Section 2); the federal government's exclusion of bisexuals, lesbians, and gay men from the armed forces (Chapter 4, Section 3); local policies against allowing openly lesbian, gay, or bisexual people to be teachers (Chapter 5, Section 1[B]) or allowing gay clubs or informational publications in the public school system (Chapter 7, Sections 1 and 2[A]); state laws prohibiting the promulgation of positive information about homosexuality or requiring the inculcation of anti-homosexual viewpoints (Chapter 7, Section 3[A]); federal and state policies requiring that AIDS education be anti-homosexual (Chapter 7, Section 3[C]); state law exclusions of lesbian and gay couples from marriage, typically by implication but sometimes explicitly, as well as state statutes requiring state courts not to give full faith and credit to same-sex marriages recognized in other states (Chapter 9, Section 2); and state presumptions against adoption or child custody by lesbian, gay, or bisexual parents or putative parents (Chapter 9, Section 3[A]). Will these policies be suspect under *Romer v. Evans*?

C. Fundamental Rights and Equal Protection. Another gap in the *Carolene Products* formulation is that classifications affecting the state's distribution of "fundamental rights" are also susceptible to heightened scrutiny under the equal protection clause. This is the literal reading of the Court's opinion in *Brown v. Board of Education*, for example. The Supreme Court held segregated public schools unconstitutional, not because they were founded on a suspect classification (the typical reading of the opinion in retrospect), but because they affected children's access to the fundamental right to public education (an understanding of *Brown* inconsistent with *San Antonio Indep. School Dist. v. Rodriguez*). Compare also *Plyler v. Doe*, 457 U.S. 202 (1982), where the Court invalidated a state policy closing off public schools to the children of illegal immigrants.

The earliest Supreme Court procreation cases were equal protection rather than substantive due process cases. In *Buck v. Bell*, 274 U.S. 200 (1927) the Court upheld Virginia's policy of sterilizing mentally disabled citizens, a shocking result implicitly overruled in *Skinner v. Oklahoma*, 316 U.S. 535 (1942). The state law struck down in *Skinner* required sterilization of habitual criminals committing crimes of "moral turpitude" but not white collar crimes such as embezzlement. The Supreme Court held the legislative classification to a higher standard because the law dealt with one of "the basic civil rights of man," the right to marry and procreate. In *Eisenstadt v. Baird*, 405 U.S. 438 (1973) (Chapter 1, Section 1[B]), the Court struck down a Massachusetts law which criminalized the distribution of contraceptives to unmarried people. Justice Brennan's opinion held that *Griswold*'s fundamental right of privacy justified heightened equal protection scrutiny. *Zablocki v. Redhail*, a leading right to marry precedent, was treated by the Court as an equal protection case.

SECTION 3. FREEDOM OF EXPRESSION

The First Amendment on its face protects (1) free speech; (2) freedom of the press; (3) peaceful assembly; (4) the right to petition the government; (5) free exercise of religion; and (6) the right not to have a state-established religion. Although the First Amendment limits only Congress' power, the Supreme Court has held it to be one of the rights "incorporated" in the Fourteenth Amendment's due process clause and therefore applicable to the states as well. The Court has also recognized as instinct in the First Amendment a right of association, *NAACP v. Alabama*, 357 U.S. 449 (1958), which has been applied to protect the rights of gay men and lesbians to congregate in bars, to form clubs at public universities, and to form organizations (Chapter 5, Section 1[A]). Also the Court has extended the First Amendment's protection to "expressive conduct" such as draft card and flagburning, marches, and erotic dancing (Chapter 5, Section 1 and Chapter 6, Section 1).

The Supreme Court has applied the religion clauses with ambivalence (Chapter 8, Section 1) but has forcefully applied the speech, press, assembly, petition, and association rights to protect unpopular persons and groups, including sexual orientation minorities. Generally, it is unconstitutional for the state to censor individual or group expressive communications unless the state can prove that the speech regulation is the "least restrictive means" necessary to advance a compelling governmental interest.[q] Fatal to First Amendment inquiry is the state's regulation of speech because it offends others; the so-called heckler's veto is not allowed as a defense. Exemplary is *Cohen v. California*, 403 U.S. 15 (1971), where the Court disallowed state regulation of a young man whose bomber jacket bore the words "Fuck the draft." "If there is a bedrock principle underlying the First Amendment, it is that the Government may not prohibit the expression of an idea simply because society finds the idea itself offensive or disagreeable." *Texas v. Johnson*, 491 U.S. 397 (1989) (the flagburning case).

---

[q] In "expressive conduct" or symbolic speech cases, such as flagburning or nude dancing, the applicable test is that of *United States v. O'Brien*, 391 U.S. 367 (1968), which allowed state regulation of draft card burning. When pure speech is mixed with nonspeech, "a government regulation is sufficiently justified if it * * * furthers an important or substantial governmental interest; if the governmental interest is unrelated to the suppression of free expression; and if the incidental restriction on alleged First Amendment freedoms is no greater than is essential to the furtherance of that interest."

Generally, therefore, one might expect that the state would rarely be allowed to censor expression or expressive conduct, either before the fact (through a prior restraint, which is especially disfavored) or after the fact. One might be wrong, as that generalization is subject to a range of caveats relating to exceptions for certain types of expression, the circumstances of the expression, and some state justifications.

A. "Low Value" Expression Receiving Less or No First Amendment Protection. Certain kinds of expression are considered to be so low in value that the Court refuses to give them First Amendment protection. Consider the most important categories:

- *Obscenity.* Expression that is "obscene" is outside the protection of the First Amendment, the Court held in *Roth v. United States*, 354 U.S. 476 (1957) (Chapter 6, Section 1). As refined by subsequent decisions, expression is obscene only if it describes or depicts explicit sexual activity and (1) appeals mainly to people's prurient interest in sex, (2) is offensive to community standards, and (3) taken as a whole lacks serious literary, artistic, political, or scientific value. *Miller v. California*, 413 U.S. 15 (1973). Material presenting minority sexualities in a positive light was until recently considered obscene (Chapter 2, Section 2[A][3] and Chapter 5, Section 1).

- *Libel.* Expression that is false and injures other people is not protected, although the First Amendment does require that defamatory speech about "public figures" or private figures engaged in a "public event" is immune from lawsuits unless the victim can show that the publisher acted with "actual malice." *New York Times v. Sullivan*, 376 U.S. 254 (1964). Generally, speech that is true but embarrassing, such as publication of the name of a rape victim or "outing" someone as lesbian or gay, is immune from lawsuit. See *Florida Star v. B.F.J.*, 491 U.S. 524 (1989) and other cases in Chapter 5, Section 2.

- *Fighting Words and Inciteful Speech.* Speech that is directed toward the incitement of imminent lawless action and is likely to have that effect can be suppressed. This is a narrow exception to the First Amendment. *Brandenburg v. Ohio*, 395 U.S. 444 (1969) (*per curiam*) (overturning prosecution of a KKK group where racist and lawless advocacy was generalized and unlikely to produce imminent lawless actions). Possibly broader is the "fighting words" doctrine of *Chaplinsky v. New Hampshire*, 315 U.S. 568 (1942), which held outside the First Amendment abusive ephithets which are inherently likely to provoke a violent reaction.

Some kinds of expression were once outside the First Amendment but have eased their way into its protection, albeit at a lower level. The best example is *commercial speech* (such as advertising), which was once unprotected by the First Amendment; false or misleading commercial speech is still unprotected. Regulation of truthful commercial speech is now subjected to an intermediate scrutiny: its regulation must "directly advance" a "substantial" governmental interest and must be "not more extensive than is necessary to advance that interest." *Central Hudson Gas & Elec. Corp. v. Public Serv. Comm'n*, 447 U.S. 557 (1980).

B. The Forum Matters: Deference to State Regulation of Speech in Certain Contexts. Even the speech most important to the First Amendment is allowed to be regulated in "special" contexts for institutionalist reasons, such as:

- *The Military.* The Supreme Court defers in an exaggerated manner to decisions made within the military context. In *Goldman v. Weinberger*, 475 U.S. 503 (1986), for example, the Court allowed a military dress code to prohibit a rabbinical officer from wearing the yarmulke required by his religion. The Court allowed exclusion of women from the draft in *Rostker v. Goldberg*, 453 U.S. 57 (1981) (Chapter 4, Section 2). Thus far (1997), most appellate courts have held that the military can discharge a person for saying, "I am a lesbian" (Chapter 4, Section 3), or for engaging in private acts of sodomy (Chapter 3, Section 3[B]).

- *Public Employment.* Although public employees do not surrender their First Amendment rights and cannot be discharged for their public activities, *Pickering v. Board of Education*, 391 U.S. 563 (1968), the government has a wide berth to discharge or discipline employees for private remarks and behavior that disrupts the public service. *Connick v. Myers*, 461 U.S. 138 (1983), applied to gender-benders in *Rowland v. Mad River Local School Dist.*, 730 F.2d 444 (6th Cir.), *cert. denied*, 470 U.S. 1009 (1985) (Chapter 3, Section 2[C]), and *Singer v. U.S. Civil Serv. Comm'n*, 530 F.2d 247 (9th Cir. 1976), *vacated*, 429 U.S. 1034 (1977) (Chapter 10, Section 1[B]).

- *Schools.* Public schools cannot censor student speech on political matters, *Tinker v. Des Moines Indep. School Dist.*, 393 U.S. 503 (1969) (Chapter 7, Section 1), but can prevent students from certain kinds of sexual speech. *Bethel School Dist. v. Fraser*, 478 U.S. 675 (1986) (Chapter 7, Section 1). Also, schools can control the sexual speech of teachers and under the aegis of academic freedom might be able to control the instructional agenda (Chapter 7, Section 2[A]).

- *Prisons.* Although convicted felons do not lose all their constitutional rights, prisons are a totalizing institution, within which the Court allows substantial regulation of speech and other communications. Still, prisoners enjoy a constitutional right to marry, *Turner v. Safley*, 482 U.S. 78 (1987) (Chapter 9, Section 2[A]), and to be free from cruel and unusual punishment, including sexual assaults, *Farmer v. Brennan*, 114 S. Ct. 1970 (1994) (Chapter 12, Section 2).

- *Broadcast Media.* The Supreme Court has held that the state can impose greater regulations on the broadcast media than on the print media. *Red Lion Broadcasting Co. v. FCC*, 395 U.S. 367 (1969). The original justification, scarcity of radio and television frequencies, has been overtaken by technology, but this special treatment perists in the sexual speech arena because the broadcast media enter the home and are available for access by children. See *FCC v. Pacifica Foundation*,

438 U.S. 726 (1978) (Chapter 6, Section 3[C]), where the Court allowed the FCC to censor "seven dirty words" from the radio. As we go to press in 1997, the Court has not decided how to treat state regulation of cable television and the internet (Chapter 6, Section 3C]).

- *State-Funded Activities.* The state has some freedom to condition state programs on speech regulations that it could not prohibit in the private sector. *Rust v. Sullivan,* 500 U.S. 173 (1991) (Chapter 6, Section 3[B]). When the state creates a "public forum," however, it can limit the general subject matter of speech but cannot discriminate on the basis of viewpoint. *Rosenberger v. University of Virginia,* 115 S.Ct. 2510 (1995) (Chapter 8, Section 1). The distinction between a public forum and a state funding situation is often elusive, as litigation involving the National Endowment for the Arts (NEA) illustrates. See *NEA v. Finley,* 100 F.3d 671 (9th Cir. 1996) (Chapter 6, Section 3[B]).

Note that speech in forums which are basically the creations of the state can often be regulated. As the modern regulatory state has become pervasive in our lives, the First Amendment has shrunk in some ways as it has expanded in others.

C. Nondiscrimination versus the First Amendment. Free expression values can be sacrificed when the state seeks to advance equality values, which can be "compelling" or "substantial" state interests, so long as the regulation is the "least restrictive means" for meeting the state equality goal. A leading case is *Roberts v. Jaycees,* 468 U.S. 609 (1984) (Chapter 5, Section 1[C]), where the Supreme Court held that Minneapolis could require a private association to end its longstanding discrimination against women. The District of Columbia Court of Appeals held in *Gay Rights Coalition v. Georgetown University,* 536 A.2d 1 (D.C. 1987) (en banc) (Chapter 5, Section 1[C] and Chapter 8, Section 1), that the District's policy of equality for its lesbian, gay, and bisexual minority is a compelling interest justifying a requirement that a Roman Catholic university provide equal access and services to gay student groups. The court also held, however, that the District's Human Rights Act (Appendix 2 to this casebook) could not be interpreted to require Georgetown to "recognize" the gay groups; such required recognition would clash with both the free speech and free exercise of religion prongs of the First Amendment.

Roberts and, even more particularly, *Georgetown* might be revisited in light of later Supreme Court decisions calibrating the equality/expression balance. For example, *Hurley v. Irish-American Gay, Lesbian, and Bisexual Group of Boston,* 115 S.Ct. 2338 (1995) (Chapter 5, Section 1[C]) held that Massachusetts could not apply its public accommodations law to require a parade to include a gay, lesbian, and bisexual contingent. Significant to the outcome of the case is the *state action doctrine*: like the due process and equal protection clauses, the First Amendment applies only to the state or an enterprise embroiled with the state. *Hurley* made apparent that a state parade could not exclude lesbians and gays for the same reason that the state could not compel a private parade to include them: the state cannot edit for expressive content in either case.

Another area pitting equality against free expression is hate speech. Speech that insults people on the basis of their race, sex, or sexual orientation chills their own expression at the same time that it perpetuates social inequality. Most hate speech regulations adopted by municipalities and public universities have come under constitutional fire. In a striking opinion, Justice Scalia ruled in *R.A.V. v. St. Paul*, 505 U.S. 377 (1992) (Chapter 5, Section 3) that laws criminalizing certain actions because they were hate-inspired were unconstitutional. This was true, said the Court, even when the hateful activity amounted to "fighting words," which are outside normal First Amendment protection.

The most dramatic clash between expression and equality, for our purposes, involves sexually explicit speech. Some feminists maintain that pornography hurts women not only by perpetuating sexist stereotypes, but also by stimulating physical violence against women. American courts have rejected this argument as a justificaton for regulation of nonobscene pornography, *American Booksellers Ass'n v. Hudnut*, 771 F.2d 323 (7th Cir. 1985), aff'd mem., 475 U.S. 1001 (1986) (Chapter 6, Section 2), but Canada's high court has allowed similar regulation in *Regina v. Butler*, 89 D.L.R.4th 449 (Can. Sup. Ct. 1992) (Chapter 6, Section 2).

SEXUALITY, GENDER, AND THE LAW

*

CHAPTER 1

THE CONSTITUTION AND SEXUALITY

SECTION 1   The Right to Sexual Privacy

SECTION 2   State Regulation of Sexual Practices—The Special Case of Sodomy

SECTION 3   Other Constitutional Strategies for Challenging State Regulation of Sexuality and Gender

The regulation of sex in America is as old as Cotton Mather. From colonial times into this century, virtually all American state or colonial jurisdictions had laws criminalizing fornication (sex outside of marriage), adultery (sex by a married person with anyone other than her or his spouse), sodomy (anal and, later, oral sex), incest (sex with a close relative), seduction (sex with a minor woman), and rape (forcible vaginal sex). Many jurisdictions added laws criminalizing interracial sex, cohabitation, and marriage. In the late eighteenth and early nineteenth centuries, American jurisdictions adopted laws against "obscene" publications and "lewd" acts; these terms were generally not defined, but the common law made clear that they could be applied to anything explicitly sex-based.

The middle part of the nineteenth century (about 1840–80) witnessed the emergence of an intense interest in sex regulations targeting women's control of their bodies. Most states and cities adopted statutes not only criminalizing prostitution (a woman's agreement to engage in "promiscuous" sex, often but not necessarily in exchange for money), but also making it a crime to operate a "disorderly house," to solicit for prostitution, or to associate with a disorderly house or purveyors of prostitution. Laws against disorderly conduct and vagrancy were often extended or amended to cover prostitution and other forms of public sex. Shortly after cities and states began developing these anti-prostitution measures (generally, the 1850s through 1870s), they adopted laws prohibiting abortion and the sale or use of contraceptives. The federal Comstock Act of 1873 prohibited the inter-state transportation in contraceptives as part of its ban against obscene materials. Municipalities in this period adopted laws prohibiting the wear-ing of apparel of the opposite sex; such laws were used against women who "passed" as men in order to gain economic and social advantages.

The turn of the century (1880–1920) yielded yet another twist in American regulation of sex, as cities and states with large cities began to focus regulatory attention on sexual "inverts," later called "homosexuals." Sodomy laws were broadened in this period to include prohibitions of oral sex, often between consenting male "inverts." Disorderly conduct, lewd-ness, and cross dressing laws came to be applied to homosexuals with great vigor, and some jurisdictions adopted new laws targeting homosexual cruising, intercourse, and even literature.

The foregoing constitute the classic regime of sex regulation in the United States as of 1920. Almost all of the regulations reached conduct that was personal, intimate, consenting, and private between two individuals. After World War I and, even more so, World War II, American sexual practices became increasingly discordant with this classic regime. First heterosexual women and then lesbians and gay men turned to the Consti-tution as a basis for rethinking this regulatory regime.

THE RIGHT TO SEXUAL PRIVACY[a]

PART A.   THE BIRTH OF PRIVACY: THE CONTRACEPTION CASES

The articulation of a right to sexual privacy grew directly out of the birth control movement. Although the American campaign to empower women to avoid unwanted pregnancy originated in the provocative speeches and writings of radicals such as Emma Goldman, it was Margaret Sanger, more than any other individual, who transformed those ideas into a new social movement.

Margaret Higgins Sanger was born to a poor Irish family in Corning, New York in 1879. Convinced that her own mother's ill health and eventual death resulted from bearing eleven children, Sanger developed a fierce belief in women's right to sexual and reproductive autonomy. For her, the means to this end were legalized birth control and greater public candor about sexuality. A nurse before she became a reformer, Sanger attacked a social structure that denied information to women about even simple methods of birth control. Lacking the power to control pregnancy led to enormous hardships for women, ranging from the economic strain of large families to possible death or impaired health. And the only way then for women to prevent unwanted pregnancies was to be able to negotiate the terms of their sexual relations with men.

Sanger's first writings about sex education were published in *The Call*, a socialist newspaper. Sanger soon started her own magazine, *The Woman Rebel*, which led to a federal indictment in 1914 for sending indecent material through the mails. Sanger was charged under the Comstock law, a federal obscenity statute. Prosecutions for obscenity under federal or state law were then the primary legal tool used to suppress birth control

a. For a fuller sense of the context of the times, see the books upon which the historical commentary in this section is based: Constance M. Chen,*"The Sex Side of Life:" Mary Ware Dennett's Pioneering Battle for Birth Control and Sex Education* (1996); Ellen Chesler, *Woman of Valor: Margaret Sanger and the Birth Control Movement in America* (1992); David J. Garrow, *Liberty & Sexuality: The Right to Privacy and the Making of Roe v. Wade* (1994); Linda Gordon, *Woman's Body, Woman's Right: Birth Control in America* (1974); David M. Kennedy, *Birth Control in America* (1970); Carole R. McCann, *Birth Control Politics in the United States 1916–1945* (1994); Rosalind Pollack Petchesky, *Abortion and Woman's Choice: The State, Sexuality and Reproductive Freedom* (1984); Jessie M. Rodrique, "The Black Community and the Birth Control Movement," in *Passion and Power: Sexuality in History* (Kathy Peiss & Christina Simmons, eds., 1989); and Margaret Sanger, *An Autobiography* (1971 ed.). Page references in the text will be to these sources.

materials. While under indictment, Sanger wrote and disseminated *Family Limitation*, a pamphlet detailing birth control methods and encouraging women to seek their own gratification in heterosexual relations. At the time, other Socialist Party members were also being prosecuted and jailed under the federal Comstock law and analogous state obscenity statutes. In that environment, Sanger fled to Europe to avoid prosecution. There she worked with sexologist Havelock Ellis and other reformers, and visited the world's first birth control clinic in the Netherlands. Upon her return the following year, growing public sympathy for the birth control movement led the U.S. Attorney's office to drop charges against her. Sanger made plans to open the first birth control clinic in the United States.

New York v. Sanger

Margaret Sanger decided that birth control reform would come about more quickly by challenging the laws through the judiciary than by seeking legislative change. She saw her chance to test that approach with the New York obscenity law. Under one section of the statute, physicians could provide contraceptives to prevent or cure disease. The prevailing interpretation at the time was that this exception referred only to venereal disease and the distribution of condoms. "In that case, the intent was to protect the man. * * * I wanted the interpretation to be broadened into the intent to protect women from ill health as the result of excessive childbearing and, equally important, to have the right to control their own destinies." (Sanger 212.)

To test the law, Sanger opened the first birth control clinic in the United States in 1916 in Brooklyn, New York. She notified local press and police, and distributed announcements that read,

> Mothers! Can you afford to have a large family? Do you want any more children? If not, why do you have them? Do not kill, Do not take life, But Prevent. Safe, harmless information can be obtained of trained nurses. * * * All mothers welcome. (Sanger 216.)

After nine days of providing services, during which 464 women came for help, Sanger and her staff were arrested.

Sanger's trial drew enormous public attention, including a rally at Carnegie Hall. The courtroom was packed each day with press, clinic patients, and wealthy society women whom Sanger adroitly solicited to support birth control. Both the prosecution and the defense relied on former patients as witnesses. The District Attorney elicited testimony that each woman had met with Sanger at the clinic, having gone there to "have her stop the babies." Sanger's attorney asked them to describe the miscarriages, sickness, and poverty they endured.

Sanger was convicted, and served 30 days in a women's prison. The appeals court affirmed, interpreting the statute to permit physicians to treat disease but not to give "promiscuous advice to patients irrespective of their condition." It also ruled, however, that "disease" could be broadly defined as "any alteration in the state of body which caused or threatened pain or sickness." *People v. Sanger*, 118 N.E. 637, 638 (N.Y.1918), *appeal dismissed*, 251 U.S. 537 (1919) (*per curiam*). This interpretation extended "disease" far beyond venereal disease, to include pregnancy, thus achieving one of Sanger's goals. The *Sanger* case produced the first legal victory for the birth control movement, and the approach of using litigation to broaden the doctors' exception shaped legal and political strategy for decades. The decision fell far short, however, of Sanger's desire to make birth control available to women for economic and social reasons.

* * *

You ought to be ashamed, I said, to look so antique.
(And her only thirty-one.)
I can't help it, she said, pulling a long face.
It's them pills I took, to bring it off, she said.
(She's had five already, and nearly died of young George.)
The chemist said it would be all right, but I've never been the same.
You are a proper fool, I said.
Well, if Albert won't leave you alone, there it is, I said.
What you get married for if you don't want children?
    T.S. Eliot, *The Waste Land* (1922).

* * *

The Early Birth Control Movement

Sanger's experience in Europe had convinced her of the need for a singleminded, single-issue strategy, and she never wavered from that approach. She built the birth control movement from a combination of elements of the Socialist Party, radical unions such as the International Workers of the World (popularly known as the Wobblies), women's suffragists, civil libertarians, eugenicists, and the "free love" movement. She herself drew on the full spectrum of those views, advocating both "the joys of the flesh," and arguing that "more children from the fit, less from the unfit—that is the chief issue of the birth control movement." She fused radical tactics such as civil disobedience with a growing deradicalization of the substance of her arguments, while building a political organization independent of any other movement.

1.   Sanger's "Doctors Only" Strategy

Sanger believed that the tactical advantages of a "doctors only" strategy outweighed its shortcomings. Under her direction, the birth control movement used the language of "health" and medical authority to associate itself with the respectability of a conservative and male-dominated profession. Her primary coalition partners were physicians, joined by social welfare groups and some religious organizations. Building on the decision in the Brooklyn clinic case, birth controllers argued that any limitation—*e.g.*, to prevent disease—on the use of such devices should be jettisoned, to allow doctors the discretion to prescribe as they saw fit. As this strategy evolved, Sanger's lawyers developed the legal argument that restrictive laws abridged the right of physicians to practice medicine.

The "doctors only" strategy also had negative ramifications. It encouraged the pathologizing of contraception, and downplayed the social and economic needs of women. It reinforced an income barrier because, despite advances in the law, contraception was to be available to women only through the advice of a physician. (The only reliable form of women's contraception then was the diaphragm.) Restricting access through physician intermediaries also reassured those who feared that easier access would promote immorality (although access by men to condoms was commonplace). A third effect of medicalization was to dampen consciousness of birth control as a political issue.

Despite—or because of—its shortcomings, the "doctors only" argument worked as a legal strategy. In 1936, the Second Circuit ruled that Congress had not intended to bar importation of diaphragms by doctors because a physician's goal of promoting health or saving lives was not immoral and therefore not within the intent behind the Comstock law. *United States v. One Package*, 86 F.2d 737 (2d Cir.1936). At the federal level, *One Package* effectively removed all obstacles limiting private physicians' access to birth control information and supplies. Interpretation of state obscenity laws followed suit. By 1960, Massachusetts and Connecticut were the only states left with statutes that banned contraception without providing for a physician exception. After winning *One Package*, Sanger and her allies shifted the bulk of their activities from opposing restrictive laws to opening clinics and lobbying for the inclusion of birth control in public health programs.

2. The "Free Speech" Strategy

Mary Ware Dennett, a rival birth control advocate, opposed the concept of a "doctors only" exception because it left birth control information classified as obscene. Dennett attempted, to no avail, to get sponsors for a bill repealing the New York obscenity statute as it applied to contraception. Deciding instead to focus on federal legislation, Dennett formed a federal lobbying organization, the Voluntary Parenthood League. In 1923, Dennett finally persuaded Senator Cummins of Iowa to introduce her legislation by agreeing to a requirement of five physicians to certify the reliability of any contraceptive product protected by law. The legislation never made it to the floor of either chamber of Congress. Support for repeal eroded, and within a year Dennett's Voluntary Parenthood League closed. Later court decisions held that birth control information did not fall within the scope of obscene speech. In 1930, the Second Circuit reversed Dennett's own obscenity conviction, for having mailed copies of a sex education pamphlet she had written for her own two children. *United States v. Dennett*, 39 F.2d 564 (2d Cir.1930). The *Dennett* decision cleared the way for development of formal sex education curricula.

3. Race–Based Arguments, Pro and Con

Groups on all sides of the birth control issue invoked race-based arguments. Anti-birth controllers asserted that upper-class persons were more likely to use birth control, meaning that the "fit" stock would die off. They argued that birth control amounted to "race suicide," language that left ambiguous whether the reference was to the human race or to certain racial groups. Birth control proponents also capitalized on the fear that native stock was being replaced by immigrants, but argued that providing access to birth control for the poor would help reverse that trend. Opponents on the left asserted that the duty of women, especially in minority racial and ethnic groups, was to bear children.

The African–American community developed its own birth control organizations. In 1918, the Women's Political Association of Harlem included birth control as a topic in its lecture series. In 1919, W.E.B. DuBois published an essay arguing that a woman "must have the right of motherhood at her own discretion." Black community organizations started and supported birth control clinics throughout the United States. Debate about whether birth control was good for the community or destructive of its future was a common feature of the black press.

Official government actions were also divided. In the South, then the region of the United States where the majority of African Americans lived, racist policy manifested itself in divergent ways. Some state agencies offered contraceptive services to whites only. In other states, birth control was funded as a method of limiting African–American population growth.

African–American organizations balanced these pressures by creating new approaches to the issue. In 1941, the National Council of Negro Women became the first national women's organization to endorse birth control. Its resolution argued that birth control should be used to help families have *all* the children they could afford. Racial betterment, rather than individual freedom, was the predominant theme of birth control advocates within the African–American community.

4. Women's Sexuality

Divergent perspectives on women's sexuality split birth control advocates from feminism in the early twentieth century. The women's movement divided between the suffragist wing, which sought equality in public realms such as voting and employment, and maternalist or welfare feminism, which emphasized the special needs of mothers and young children. For both, sexual propriety was an important characteristic of the respectable woman.

Sanger and her allies deliberately sought to change the terms of the debate, which upset feminists in both camps. Sanger argued that good mothers had a right to heterosexual gratification: "a mutual and satisfied sexual act is of great benefit to the average woman." (McCann 37, quoting Sanger.) She began using the phrase "birth control" as a substitute for "voluntary motherhood," a slogan used to advocate the right of married women to abstain from sex. The very technology of diaphragms (then called pessaries) was controversial: not only did women control their usage, but they did not stop sexually transmitted diseases; their *only* function was to prevent conception. The claim for women's sexual freedom is evident in appellate briefs in the Brooklyn clinic prosecutions. Counsel argued that the law "denied [a woman] her absolute right of enjoyment of sexual relations unless the act be so conducted that pregnancy may be the result." *People v. Byrne*, 163 N.Y.S. 682, 686 (N.Y.Sup.Ct.1917). It was an argument that the court declined to consider.

The concepts of women's rights and of sexual pleasure in early birth control discourse ebbed and flowed with the tide of public opinion. In the late 1930s and 1940s, Planned Parenthood de-emphasized feminism and emphasized social planning, in part through its very name. The tide shifted back again when the "second wave" of feminism began in the late 1960s.

5. Birth Control as "Public Health"

In the Depression years of the 1930s, pressure mounted on government agencies to include birth control information in their services for the poor. Gradually and quietly, such policies were developed. As of 1935, for example, the Federal Emergency Relief Administration underwrote the cost of birth control services to the poor but would not admit it publicly. Sanger formed the Committee for Public Progress to pressure government agencies into full recognition of contraception as an integral part of public health. Two pieces of legislation were instrumental in this effort. Title V of the Social Security Act of 1938 granted millions of dollars to state maternal and child health services. The Venereal Disease Control Act in 1939 authorized federal dollars to be used for contraceptives for the traditional purpose of "fighting disease." Despite the legislation, however, implementation did not come easily. Only intervention by Eleanor Roosevelt eventually led officials of the Children's Bureau and the Public Health Service to support birth control programs openly.

During World War II, the executive branch changed its approach from passive approval to active initiation of birth control programs. Defense industries required the labor of women who would not be disabled by unwanted pregnancies. Birth control and women's health became national security interests. In the 1950s and 1960s, population growth became an international issue. In perhaps the movement's high-water mark of respectability, former Presidents Truman and Eisenhower became honorary co-chairs of the 1965 Planned Parenthood fundraising campaign. In 1970, Congress passed Title X of the Public Health Service Act, which provided federal funds to support family planning clinics.

6. The Claim to "Privacy"

The assertion that law should recognize a "right to privacy" originated in an 1890 law review essay by Samuel D. Warren and Louis D. Brandeis calling for "a general right to privacy for thoughts, emotions, and sensations," and focusing on tort law. After Brandeis was appointed to the Supreme Court, he advocated a "right to be let alone" from government intrusion in his dissent in *Olmstead v. United States*, 277 U.S. 438 (1928).

In two forerunners to modern privacy jurisprudence, the Court used the due process clause of the Fourteenth Amendment to strike down a law prohibiting the teaching of foreign languages in elementary schools, *Meyer v. Nebraska*, 262 U.S. 390 (1923), and a law requiring that all children attend public schools, *Pierce v. Society of Sisters*, 268 U.S. 510 (1925). Both decisions emphasized the rights of parents to control the education of their children and the limits on state power to indoctrinate, but neither referred to "privacy" as such. In *Meyer*, however, the Court described the "liberty" guaranteed by the due process clause as follows:

> Without doubt it denotes not merely freedom from bodily restraint, but also the right of the individual to contract, to engage in any of the common occupations of life, to acquire useful knowledge, to marry, establish a home and bring up children, to worship God according to the dictates of his own conscience, and, generally, to enjoy those privileges long recognized at common law as essential to the orderly pursuit of happiness by free men. (262 U.S. at 399.)

The procreative aspect of privacy was presaged in *Skinner v. Oklahoma*, 316 U.S. 535 (1942), in which the Court struck down a law that permitted forced sterilization of persons convicted three times of certain crimes, but not of other similar crimes. The defendant had been convicted of robbery; had his offense been embezzlement, he would not have been subject to the sterilization law. The Court held that "[m]arriage and procreation are fundamental to the very existence and survival of the race," *id.* at 541, and thus subjected the classification drawn by the statute to strict scrutiny under the equal protection clause.

Skinner

As Sanger and her allies grew pessimistic about repealing the hold-out anti-contraception laws in Massachusetts and Connecticut, they invoked decisions like these to challenge the constitutionality of those statutes. Appeals to read broad exceptions into the statutes (*i.e.*, to adopt a *One Package* interpretation of state law) or to overturn them entirely lost by narrow margins in the Massachusetts Supreme Court in 1938 and the Connecticut Supreme Court in 1940. The first birth control case to reach the Supreme Court was *Tileston v. Ullman*, 318 U.S. 44 (1943) (*per curiam*). The plaintiff in that case was a doctor who argued that the Connecticut statute prevented him from providing health- and life-saving medical advice to his patients. *Tileston* presented the Court with Sanger's doctor-oriented birth control strategy, but the Court skirted the substantive issue. The *per curiam* decision held that Tileston did not assert a harm personal to him and did not have standing to assert the rights of third parties, his patients.

In the next case, *Poe v. Ullman*, plaintiffs were married women who asserted that they were denied needed medical advice by the statute. This case reflected a fusion of Sanger's "doctors only" strategy with the privacy cases, and it seemed to meet the standing requirements of *Tileston*. The Supreme Court still refused to reach the issue. It finally did reach the merits in the third Connecticut contraception case that came before the Court, *Griswold v. Connecticut*, the next following case in the text. The victory in *Griswold* came nearly 50 years after Margaret Sanger served her 30–day prison sentence.

Paul and Pauline Poe et al. v. Abraham S. Ullman

United States Supreme Court, 1961.
367 U.S. 497, 81 S.Ct. 1752, 6 L.Ed.2d 989.

■ [MR. JUSTICE FRANKFURTER announced the judgment of the Court, holding that the lawsuit was not "ripe" for adjudication because the plaintiffs were not prevented from obtaining and using contraceptives. He relied on the availability of contraceptives in Connecticut drug stores and on his belief that only one person had been arrested under the 1879 law, and no one recently. We omit the majority and other opinions, because the opinion most important for future cases was that of Justice Harlan.]

■ MR. JUSTICE HARLAN, dissenting. [Justice Harlan began his argument by asserting that the due process clause safeguards more than procedural rights.]

Were due process merely a procedural safeguard it would fail to reach those situations where the deprivation of life, liberty or property was accomplished by legislation which by operating in the future could, given even the fairest possible procedure in application to individuals, nevertheless destroy the enjoyment of all three. Thus the guarantees of due process, though having their origin in Magna Carta's *per legem terrae* and considered as procedural safeguards "against executive usurpation and tyranny," have in this country "become bulwarks also against arbitrary legislation." * * *

Due process has not been reduced to any formula; its content cannot be determined by reference to any code. The best that can be said is that through the course of this Court's decisions it has represented the balance which our Nation, built upon postulates of respect for the liberty of the individual, has struck between that liberty and the demands of organized society. If the supplying of content to this Constitutional concept has of necessity been a rational process, it certainly has not been one where judges have felt free to roam where unguided speculation might take them. The balance of which I speak is the balance struck by this country, having regard to what history teaches are the traditions from which it developed as well as the traditions from which it broke. That tradition is a living thing. A decision of this Court which radically departs from it could not long survive, while a decision which builds on what has survived is likely to be sound. No formula could serve as a substitute, in this area, for judgment and restraint.

It is this outlook which has led the Court continuously to perceive distinctions in the imperative character of Constitutional provisions, since that character must be discerned from a particular provision's larger context. And inasmuch as this context is one not of words, but of history and purposes, the full scope of the liberty guaranteed by the Due Process Clause cannot be found in or limited by the precise terms of the specific guarantees elsewhere provided in the Constitution. This "liberty" is not a series of isolated points pricked out in terms of the taking of property; the freedom of speech, press, and religion; the right to keep and bear arms; the freedom from unreasonable searches and seizures; and so on. It is a rational continuum which, broadly speaking, includes a freedom from all substantial arbitrary impositions and purposeless restraints, and which also recognizes, what a reasonable and sensitive judgment must, that certain interests require particularly careful scrutiny of the state needs asserted to justify their abridgment.

* * * For it is the purposes of those guarantees and not their text, the reasons for their statement by the Framers and not the statement itself, which have led to their present status in the compendious notion of "liberty" embraced in the Fourteenth Amendment.

* * * Yet the very inclusion of the category of morality among state concerns indicates that society is not limited in its objects only to the physical well-being of the community, but has traditionally concerned itself with the moral soundness of its people as well. Indeed to attempt a line between public behavior and that which is purely consensual or solitary would be to withdraw from community concern a range of subjects with which every society in civilized times has found it necessary to deal. The laws regarding marriage which provide both when the sexual powers may be used and the legal and societal context in which children are born and brought up, as well as laws forbidding adultery, fornication and homosexual practices which express the negative of the proposition, confining sexuality to lawful marriage, form a pattern so deeply pressed into the substance of our social life that any Constitutional doctrine in this area must build upon that basis.

It is in this area of sexual morality, which contains many proscriptions of consensual behavior having little or no direct impact on others, that the State of Connecticut has expressed its moral judgment that all use of contraceptives is improper. Appellants cite an impressive list of authorities who, from a great variety of points of view, commend the considered use of contraceptives by married couples. What they do not emphasize is that not too long ago the current of opinion was very probably quite the opposite, and that even today the issue is not free of controversy. Certainly, Connecticut's judgment is no more demonstrably correct or incorrect than are the varieties of judgment, expressed in law, on marriage and divorce, on adult consensual homosexuality, abortion, and sterilization, or euthanasia and suicide. If we had a case before us which required us to decide simply, and in abstraction, whether the moral judgment implicit in the application of the present statute to married couples was a sound one, the very controversial nature of these questions would, I think, require us to hesitate long before concluding that the Constitution precluded Connecticut from choosing as it has among these various views.

* * * Precisely what is involved here is this: the State is asserting the right to enforce its moral judgment by intruding upon the most intimate details of the marital relation with the full power of the criminal law. Potentially, this could allow the deployment of all the incidental machinery of the criminal law, arrests, searches and seizures; inevitably, it must mean at the very least the lodging of criminal charges, a public trial, and

testimony as to the *corpus delicti*. Nor could any imaginable elaboration of presumptions, testimonial privileges, or other safeguards, alleviate the necessity for testimony as to the mode and manner of the married couples' sexual relations, or at least the opportunity for the accused to make denial of the charges. In sum, the statute allows the State to enquire into, prove and punish married people for the private use of their marital intimacy.

This, then, is the precise character of the enactment whose Constitutional measure we must take. The statute must pass a more rigorous Constitutional test than that going merely to the plausibility of its underlying rationale. This enactment involves what, by common understanding throughout the English-speaking world, must be granted to be a most fundamental aspect of "liberty," the privacy of the home in its most basic sense, and it is this which requires that the statute be subjected to "strict scrutiny." *Skinner*, 316 U.S. at 541. * * *

Of course, just as the requirement of a warrant is not inflexible in carrying out searches and seizures, so there are countervailing considerations at this more fundamental aspect of the right involved. "[T]he family * * * is not beyond regulation," *Prince v. Massachusetts*, [321 U.S. 158, 166 (1944)], and it would be an absurdity to suggest either that offenses may not be committed in the bosom of the family or that the home can be made a sanctuary for crime. The right of privacy most manifestly is not an absolute. Thus, I would not suggest that adultery, homosexuality, fornication and incest are immune from criminal enquiry, however privately practiced. So much has been explicitly recognized in acknowledging the State's rightful concern for its people's moral welfare. But not to discriminate between what is involved in this case and either the traditional offenses against good morals or crimes which, though they may be committed anywhere, happen to have been committed or concealed in the home, would entirely misconceive the argument that is being made.

Adultery, homosexuality and the like are sexual intimacies which the State forbids altogether, but the intimacy of husband and wife is necessarily an essential and accepted feature of the institution of marriage, an institution which the State not only must allow, but which always and in every age it has fostered and protected. It is one thing when the State exerts its power either to forbid extra-marital sexuality altogether, or to say who may marry, but it is quite another when, having acknowledged a marriage and the intimacies inherent in it, it undertakes to regulate by means of the criminal law the details of that intimacy.

In sum, even though the State has determined that the use of contraceptives is as iniquitous as any act of extra-marital sexual immorality, the intrusion of the whole machinery of the criminal law into the very heart of marital privacy, requiring husband and wife to render account before a criminal tribunal of their uses of that intimacy, is surely a very different thing indeed from punishing those who establish intimacies which the law has always forbidden and which can have no claim to social protection. * * *

Estelle T. Griswold et al. v. Connecticut

United States Supreme Court, 1965.
381 U.S. 479, 85 S.Ct. 1678, 14 L.Ed.2d 510.

■ JUSTICE DOUGLAS delivered the opinion of the Court [striking down the 1879 Connecticut law prohibiting the sale or use of contraceptives].

[W]e are met with a wide range of questions that implicate the Due Process Clause of the Fourteenth Amendment. * * * This law * * * operates directly on an intimate relation of husband and wife and their physician's role in one aspect of that relation.

The association of people is not mentioned in the Constitution nor in the Bill of Rights. The right to educate a child in a school of the parents' choice—whether public or private or parochial—is also not mentioned. Nor is the right to study any particular subject or any foreign language. Yet the First Amendment has been construed to include certain of those rights. [The Court then reviewed *Meyer v. Nebraska* and *Pierce v. Society of Sisters*, as well as First Amendment cases dealing with freedom of association.]

The foregoing cases suggest that specific guarantees in the Bill of Rights have penumbras, formed by emanations from those guarantees that help give them life and substance. Various guarantees create zones of privacy. The right of association contained in the penumbra of the First Amendment is one, as we have seen. The Third Amendment in its prohibition against the quartering of soldiers "in any house" in time of peace without the consent of the owner is another facet of that privacy. The Fourth Amendment explicitly affirms the "right of the people to be secure in their persons, houses, papers, and effects, against unreasonable searches and seizures." The Fifth Amendment in its Self–Incrimination Clause enables the citizen to create a zone of privacy which government may not force him to surrender to his detriment. The Ninth Amendment provides: "The enumeration in the Constitution, of certain rights, shall not be construed to deny or disparage others retained by the people."

The Fourth and Fifth Amendments were described in *Boyd v. United States*, 116 U.S. 616, 630, as protection against all governmental invasions "of the sanctity of a man's home and the privacies of life." We recently referred in *Mapp v. Ohio*, 367 U.S. 643, 656, to the Fourth Amendment as creating a "right to privacy, no less important than any other right carefully and particularly reserved to the people." * * *

The present case, then, concerns a relationship lying within the zone of privacy created by several fundamental constitutional guarantees. And it concerns a law which, in forbidding the use of contraceptives rather than regulating their manufacture or sale, seeks to achieve its goals by means having a maximum destructive impact upon that relationship. Such a law cannot stand in light of the familiar principle, so often applied by this Court, that a "governmental purpose to control or prevent activities constitutionally subject to state regulation may not be achieved by means which sweep unnecessarily broadly and thereby invade the area of protected freedoms." *NAACP v. Alabama*, 377 U.S. 288, 307. Would we allow the police to search the sacred precincts of marital bedrooms for telltale signs of the use of contraceptives? The very idea is repulsive to the notions of privacy surrounding the marriage relationship.

We deal with a right of privacy older than the Bill of Rights—older than our political parties, older than our school system. Marriage is a coming together for better or for worse, hopefully enduring, and intimate to the degree of being sacred. It is an association that promotes a way of life, not causes; a harmony in living, not political faiths; a bilateral loyalty, not commercial or social projects. Yet it is an association for as noble a purpose as any involved in our prior decisions. * * *

■ JUSTICE GOLDBERG, joined by CHIEF JUSTICE WARREN and JUSTICE BRENNAN, concurred.

* * * This Court, in a series of decisions, has held that the Fourteenth Amendment absorbs and applies to the States those specifics of the first eight amendments which express fundamental personal rights. The language and history of the Ninth Amendment reveal that the Framers of the Constitution believed that there are additional fundamental rights, protected from governmental infringement, which exist alongside those fundamental rights specifically mentioned in the first eight constitutional amendments.

[James Madison, the primary sponsor of the Ninth Amendment, justified including it at the end of the Bill of Rights for precisely this reason:]

It has been objected also against a bill of rights, that, by enumerating particular exceptions to the grant of power, it would disparage those rights which were not placed in that enumeration; and it might follow by implication, that those rights which were not singled out, were intended to be assigned into the hands of the General Government, and were consequently insecure. This is one of the most plausible arguments I have ever heard urged against the admission of a bill of rights into this system; but, I conceive, that it may be guarded against. I have attempted it, as gentlemen may see by turning to the last clause of the fourth resolution [the Ninth Amendment]. * * *

The Ninth Amendment simply shows the intent of the Constitution's authors that other fundamental personal rights should not be denied such protections or disparaged in any other way simply because they are not specifically listed in the first eight constitutional amendments. * * *

Finally, it should be said of the Court's holding today that it in no way interferes with a State's proper regulation of sexual promiscuity or misconduct. As my Brother Harlan so well stated in his dissenting opinion in *Poe v. Ullman*[:]

Adultery, homosexuality and the like are sexual intimacies which the State forbids ... but the intimacy of husband and wife is necessarily an essential and accepted feature of the institution of marriage, an institution which the State not only must allow, but which always in every age it has fostered and protected. * * *

■ [JUSTICE HARLAN concurred in the Court's opinion, based upon his dissenting opinion in *Poe v. Ullman*.]

■ JUSTICE WHITE, concurring in the judgment.

* * * [T]he statute is said to serve the State's policy against all forms of promiscuous or illicit sexual relationships, be they premarital or extra-marital, concededly a permissible and legitimate legislative goal.

Without taking issue with the premise that the fear of conception operates as a deterrent to such relationships in addition to the criminal proscriptions Connecticut has against such conduct, I wholly fail to see how the ban on the use of contraceptives by married couples in any way reinforces the State's ban on illicit sexual relationships. Connecticut does not bar the importation or possession of contraceptive devices; they are not considered contraband material under state law, and their availability in that State is not seriously disputed. The only way Connecticut seeks to limit or control the availability of such devices is through its general aiding and abetting statute whose operation in this context has been quite obviously ineffective and whose most serious use has been against birth-control clinics rendering advice to married, rather than unmarried, persons. * * *

■ [The dissenting opinions of JUSTICE BLACK and JUSTICE STEWART objected to the Court's creation of a constitutional right to "privacy" that is not moored in a firmer constitutional text. Although they found this an "uncommonly silly law" (Stewart), they found it violative of no provision of the Constitution.]

NOTES ON *GRISWOLD* AND THE RIGHT OF SEXUAL PRIVACY

1. *What Was the Best Constitutional Basis for the Result in* Griswold? In particular, which opinion best states a constitutional basis for a right of privacy? How do the jurisprudential approaches of Justices Douglas, Goldberg, and Harlan differ? All three approaches "create" a right that is not clearly instantiated in the Constitution's text. Douglas' penumbral theory is the most creative, for he implies an "underlying" constitutional right from the emanations of existing provisions. Goldberg's reliance on the Ninth Amendment is only slightly less creative. Although he relies on actual text in the Constitution, the Ninth Amendment seems like a residual "catch-all" provision. Harlan's invocation of the due process clause likewise relies on a specific provision but expands text that on its face refers only to process into a substantive provision with considerable constitutional bite.

Critics have accused the Court of becoming a "superlegislature" with this decision (see the Bork excerpt following these notes). Which approach (penumbras, Ninth Amendment, due process) best avoids this difficulty by tying the Court's decision to "principled" criteria that have a defensible connection to the Constitution?[b] Does Justice White avoid the specter of

b. One of the most ardent later critics of this reasoning, John Hart Ely, clerked for   Chief Justice Warren during the period when *Griswold* was before the Court, and reported-

Lochner by focusing on the irrationality of the means? Is a broader opinion necessary?

2. *Identifying "Fundamental" Rights (the Incorporation Controversy).* Probably the most controversial debate triggered by the Court in *Griswold* is by what process should the judiciary identify and recognize what has become known as a substantive due process right, an intrinsic component of "liberty" under the due process clause. It is especially difficult to derive guidance from this decision, because not only are there four separate opinions from a seven-person majority, but most of them focus on what Justice Harlan termed "the obnoxiously intrusive means" chosen by the state to effectuate its goals. A condition precedent to imposing close scrutiny on the means, however, is a finding that a "fundamental" due process right is abridged.

An important antecedent to this discussion is the debate within the Court over whether the due process clause of the Fourteenth Amendment "incorporates" the Bill of Rights (applicable by their terms to the federal government) and thereby renders them applicable to the states as well. Justice Benjamin Cardozo had written in 1937 that the due process clause incorporates rights that are "implicit in the concept of ordered liberty." *Palko v. Connecticut*, 302 U.S. 319 (1937). A majority of the Court adopted this approach and rejected Justice Black's theory that the due process clause simply incorporated the entire Bill of Rights and nothing else. See the debate in *Adamson v. California*, 332 U.S. 46 (1947) (a concurring opinion by Frankfurter favoring the "ordered liberty" formulation, countered by Justice Black's dissenting opinion favoring incorporation). In a few cases, like *Adamson*, the Court refused to find a Bill of Rights protection essential to ordered liberty, while in a few other cases, such as *Griswold*, the Court found essential to ordered liberty a protection not specifically found in the Bill of Rights.

Once the inquiry is phrased in due process, ordered liberty terms (as it came to be), a key issue is what the traditions of American liberty are. By what principles could a court discern the proper bounds of "tradition"? The Court confronted how tricky a term "tradition" is in *Michael H. v. Gerald D.*, 491 U.S. 110 (1989). In a controversial footnote, Justice Scalia wrote that the due process clause protects only the most specific form of tradition extant at the time of the adoption of the Fifth or Fourteenth Amendments. In that case, Justice Scalia identified the issue as the interests of a biological father never married to the mother, who was married to another man at the time of conception, rather than the more general interests of biological fathers or of parents. *Id.* at 127–28 n.6. His analysis produced a spirited rejoinder by Justice Brennan:

[Tradition] can be as malleable and as elusive as "liberty" itself. * * *
[O]ur task [should be] simply to identify a rule denying the asserted

ly persuaded Warren to join Goldberg's opinion because the Ninth Amendment provided a better limiting principle. One of the Goldberg clerks who had a hand in drafting the opinion was (now Justice) Stephen Breyer. (Garrow 248–250.)

interest and not to ask whether the basis for that rule—which is the true reflection of the values undergirding it—has changed too often or too recently to call the rule embodying that rationale a "tradition." *Id.* at 137, 140.

Justice Scalia's argument was rejected by the Court in dicta in *Planned Parenthood of Southeastern Pennsylvania v. Casey*, 505 U.S. 833, 847 (1992), but the Court did not engage the issue of the meaning of "tradition"; it wrote only that "[i]t is a promise of the Constitution that there is a realm of personal liberty which the government may not enter."

The plaintiffs in *Griswold* had argued that the Court should apply the obscenity test standard of "contemporary community values" for determining the boundaries of a state's legitimate interest in morality, a suggestion that no member of the Court adopted. Would that be workable as an alternative to analyzing "tradition"?

3. *Litigating and Adjudicating Sex.* Identify where the Justices' opinions describe the contours of the right of privacy: What language is used? Is the Court most interested in the locale (*i.e.*, the home? the bedroom)? Or the relationship (marriage)? Or sexuality? To the extent the Court anchors the decision on marriage, what is the Court's understanding of that institution?

Note that the Court employs numerous euphemisms referring to sexual relations. The opinion stops just short of holding that the right to sexual relations within marriage is a fundamental right. Indeed, explicitness may be part of the problem. Perhaps one reason *Griswold* is so frustratingly vague is that the Court could not bring itself to be sexually explicit. An alternative view is that the Court's conscious goal was to insure social stability and reinforce traditional family structures. *See* Thomas Grey, "Eros, Civilization and the Burger Court," 43 *L. & Contemp. Probs.* 83 (1980). What do you think: Is *Griswold* about marriage? sex? procreation?

The briefs in the case were more direct. The appellants' brief argued that "the inner core of the privacy right" lay in "the sanctity of the home and the intimacies of the sexual relationship in marriage." Counsel for appellants and for amicus Planned Parenthood in *Griswold* apparently drew on the language of the amicus brief filed by the American Civil Liberties Union (ACLU) in *Ullman*, which was the first brief to articulate a right of privacy for "sexual union and the right to bear and raise a family." The ACLU brief, written by Melvin Wulf and Ruth Emerson, argued that the Connecticut law forced married couples to choose between planning the size of their family and engaging in sexual intercourse, which "is no choice at all." In *Ullman*, the Planned Parenthood brief had centered on the rights of the doctors and on the potential medical harm caused by the statute.

In *Griswold*, counsel for Planned Parenthood dramatically altered their arguments, beginning their brief with a claim for "privacy," not mentioned in their *Ullman* brief, based on Harlan's dissent and the ACLU's earlier arguments. The *Griswold* brief refers repeatedly to sexual relations and the "sex drive," cites Kinsey's study on sexuality, and argues that restricting sexual intercourse to procreation is not a legitimate state purpose. It carefully links sexuality to marriage, however. The brief frames the privacy right as one to engage in marital sexual relations *and* to decide whether to have children. Given the one-way operation of the statute, that phrasing is euphemistic for having sexual relations and *not* having children, but it is framed as the right to decide, a conscience right. What strategic choices are embedded in this shift? Were they wise? How would you have structured these arguments?

4. *Marriage and Sex: Estoppel Against the State?* Are there other contexts in which the state recognizes a right to sexual relations in marriage? And indeed enforces it? "The point is that the state has undertaken to sponsor one institution that has at its core the love-sex relationship. That relationship demands liberty in the practice of the sexual act." Harry H. Wellington, "Common Law Rules and Constitutional Double Standards: Some Notes on Adjudication," 83 *Yale L.J.* 221, 292 (1973). The practical import of the Connecticut statute would be to force married couples to modify the frequency of intercourse in order to avoid pregnancy, a result which, according to Wellington, "smacks of fraud." *Id.* at 293. *Cf. Barretta v.* *Barretta*, 46 N.Y.S.2d 261 (Sup. Ct. Queens Cty. 1944) (denying request for separation by wife who had refused sexual relations with her husband unless he used contraceptives, on the ground that her refusal violated the marital contract and was contrary to public policy of the state).

During the same 1964 Term in which *Griswold* was argued, the Court also decided *McLaughlin v. Florida*, 379 U.S. 184 (1964). In *McLaughlin*, the Court struck down a Florida law forbidding interracial cohabitation because it violated equal protection. Florida defended the fornication provision as auxiliary to another section of the same statute that prohibited interracial marriage. The Court declined to examine whether the state's purpose of deterring interracial sexual relations was valid, but instead held that a race-neutral fornication law served that purpose as well as a race-specific one. Two terms later, the Court tackled the miscegenation issue head-on and ruled the Virginia law unconstitutional in *Loving v. Virginia*, 388 U.S. 1 (1967) (Chapter 9, Section 2[A]).

5. *"Safer Sex" for Women? The Forgotten Equality Argument.* In today's terms, we might refer to birth control as "safer sex" for heterosexual women. Is a sex discrimination claim possible on the facts of *Griswold*? If so what would it be? Why was its possibility not mentioned in either *Griswold* or *Poe*? See Section 3 for a discussion of sex discrimination law.

6. *The Public–Private Dynamic and the Role of Clinics.* The problem that the plaintiffs in both the Connecticut cases had in formulating a test case was that there had never been a prosecution against private doctors for violating the law, although their activities in prescribing contraceptives was well known. Nor had any but a few been prosecuted for purchasing condoms. What the law did succeed in doing, however, was to prevent the establishment of an openly operating birth control clinic in Connecticut after 1940, when the Connecticut courts upheld the statute and refused to import a *One Package* medical exception into its broad terms.

Note several ironies. The right recognized in *Griswold* purports to protect "private" sphere activities in the spirit of John Stuart Mill and Louis Brandeis. Because the contraceptive gendarmerie did not patrol bedrooms and contraceptives were available in drug stores, the private sphere (the marital bedroom) was essentially unregulated, leaving only the public sphere (birth control clinics) to actual regulation. But look again. The public sphere for men's access to condoms was not policed; only the clinics (which prescribed diaphragms and later pills for women) were. Most women in Connecticut found it hard to practice birth control (private sphere) without access to birth control clinics that could provide information (public sphere). A final look. The Roman Catholic Church, which had spearheaded political opposition to repealing anti-contraception laws, believed that the anti-procreation features of contraception (private sphere) had profound implications for marriage and religious community (public sphere). The availability of contraception, whether private or public, undermined the private as well as public (procreative) goals of marriage.

In short, the concept of "privacy" is easy to deconstruct. Does this ease of deconstruction vitiate the usefulness of the concept? Can it still serve any constitutional role, especially in light of the superlegislature concerns?

PROBLEM 1–1

SEX, LAW, AND PUBLIC POLICY

Imagine yourself to be a legal historian embarking on an analysis of the birth control movement. What were the critical turning points in the evolution of the law? Consider case law, legislation, and other embodiments of government policy. How did the doctrine generated at those points differ from the goals of the advocates? Note the irony in having a movement which sought to bring about an open discussion of sexuality culminate in a legal victory for "privacy." Whose point of view drove the process: the lawyers, or their clients such as Sanger? Was there a dialectic between the two?

Now, project yourself into the 1980s, as an AIDS activist. A scary new sexually transmitted disease is generating proposals for repressive laws. How do you frame your arguments on behalf of persons with this disease? Do you invoke medical expertise? Do you argue for sexual freedom? Privacy? Equality? Compare the role of AIDS lawyers in the 1980s to that of birth control lawyers in the 1920s. (For more analysis of AIDS as a social phenomenon, see Chapter 12, Section 1.)

PART B.   THE EXPANDING RIGHT OF SEXUAL PRIVACY

Many questions were left open in *Griswold*, including whether unmarried couples enjoyed the right to obtain contraceptives. The first case applying *Griswold*, however, arose in the context of obscenity law, the original situs for contraceptive regulation.

Robert Eli Stanley v. State of Georgia

United States Supreme Court, 1969.
394 U.S. 557, 89 S.Ct. 1243, 22 L.Ed.2d 542.

■ JUSTICE MARSHALL delivered the opinion for the Court [reversing a conviction for "possession of obscene matter" based on three reels of concededly obscene film found in the defendant's home].

* * * [The constitutional] right to receive information and ideas regardless of their social worth is fundamental to our free society. Moreover, in the context of this case—a prosecution for mere possession of printed or filmed matter in the privacy of a person's own home—that right takes on an added dimension. For also fundamental is the right to be free, except in very limited circumstances, from unwanted governmental intrusions into one's privacy.

> "The makers of our Constitution undertook to secure conditions favorable to the pursuit of happiness. They recognized the significance of man's spiritual nature, of his feelings and of his intellect. * * * They sought to protect Americans in their beliefs, their thoughts, their emotions and their sensations. They conferred, as against the government, the right to be let alone—the most comprehensive of rights and the right most valued by civilized man." *Olmstead v. United States*, 277 U.S. 438 (1928) (Brandeis, J., dissenting).

See *Griswold v. Connecticut.* * * *

* * * [I]n the face of these traditional notions of individual liberty, Georgia asserts the right to protect the individual's mind from the effects of obscenity. We are not certain that this argument amounts to anything more than the assertion that the State has the right to control the moral content of a person's thoughts. To some, this may be a noble purpose, but it is wholly inconsistent with the philosophy of the First Amendment. * * * Nor is it relevant that obscene materials in general, or the particular films before the Court, are arguably devoid of any ideological content. The line between the transmission of ideas and mere entertainment is much too elusive for this Court to draw, if indeed such a line can be drawn at all. Whatever the power of the state to control public dissemination of ideas inimical to the public morality, it cannot constitutionally premise legislation on the desirability of controlling a person's private thoughts. * * *

We hold that the First and Fourteenth Amendments prohibit making mere private possession of obscene material a crime. * * * [T]he States retain broad power to regulate obscenity; that power simply does not extend to mere possession by the individual in the privacy of his own home. * * *

■ [We omit JUSTICE BLACK's concurring opinion and JUSTICE STEWART's opinion concurring in the judgment.]

NOTES ON *STANLEY* AND THE RIGHT OF PRIVACY OUTSIDE OF MARRIAGE

1. *The Warren Court's Obscenity Revolution (Chapter 6).* The First Amendment provides that the federal government shall "make no law * * * abridging the freedom of speech, or of the press," and that prohibition has been applied to the states by selective incorporation in the due process clause of the Fourteenth Amendment. *Gitlow v. New York*, 268 U.S. 652 (1925). Since the late nineteenth century, both state and federal regulators had policed "obscene" publications; courts had generally backed up the censors, dismissing the First Amendment as irrelevant to publications that are obscene.

The Warren Court upheld this position in *Roth v. United States*, 354 U.S. 476 (1957) (Chapter 6, Section 1), but insisted that "obscenity" be defined more narrowly than state regulators did. In *Memoirs [of Fanny Hill] v. Massachusetts*, 383 U.S. 413 (1966), the Court held that to suppress material as obscene the state must show that the material appeals mainly to "prurient" tastes, is "patently offensive" to community standards, and is "utterly without redeeming social value." Virtually all state obscenity laws had to be rewritten or reinterpreted in order to meet the *Roth-Memoirs* test, and these substantive and other procedural requirements made state censorship extremely difficult. Hence it might be said that without these Warren Court decisions, it would have been very difficult for Mr. Stanley to have obtained obscene publications, either through the U.S. mails (*Roth*) or at the local porn shop (*Memoirs*). *Stanley* expands *Roth-Memoirs*, because it extends constitutional protection to possession of materials that are obscene and therefore beyond the First Amendment's normal rule.

2. *Oil (First Amendment) and Water (Privacy)? Another Constitutional Consideration (Fourth Amendment).* Note the ambiguity of Justice Marshall's reasoning. Did the Georgia police violate the First Amendment? Or the right to privacy (wherever that is located)? Do privacy and the First Amendment mix well in this case? What kind of privacy is at issue—certainly not marital rights or health rights or procreative decision-making. If it is the privacy interest in thoughts, emotions, and sensations which is implicated, how is that different in this context from First Amendment doctrine?

Related to this decision and to *Griswold* is a third important category of Warren Court decisions, the search and seizure cases under the Fourth Amendment (again applicable to the states as the Court selectively incorporated most of its features in the Fourteenth Amendment). In *Katz v. United States*, 389 U.S. 347 (1967), the Court held that the police could neither observe nor invade citizens' zones of privacy without obtaining a search warrant from a judicial officer. Justice Harlan's influential concurring opinion outlined an approach based upon the "reasonable expectations" of privacy held by citizens. State courts seized upon *Katz* to cordon off certain areas from police surveillance of sexual activity, protecting not just the bedroom but also the living room (where Mr. Stanley was apprehended), to secluded automobiles (a favorite sex hangout of the fifties), to closed toilet stalls (in many but not all states).

3. *Seclusion, Sex, and Judicial Activism.* Here again, the sequestered locus for the activity is crucial to the result, even more so than in *Griswold*, as becomes evident in later cases where birth control clinics, advertisements and other obviously public aspects of the contraception issue are protected from legal impediments, while at the same time laws are upheld that prohibit the sale or distribution of obscene materials, regardless of how discreetly done. Why the difference? See Chapter 6.

Note the line-drawing the Court is doing in *Stanley* as well as *Griswold*, and read the subsequent cases in light of this line-drawing. Robert Bork's early criticism of this line of cases reinvigorates Justice Black's dissent in *Griswold*. Consider Bork's critique in light of the subsequent decisions. Do they bear him out? Or sink his argument?[c]

[Handwritten margin note: location -privacy in home different than sale of obscene material]

Robert H. Bork, Neutral Principles and Some First Amendment Problems

47 *Indiana Law Journal* 1, 8–9 (1971).*

[In *Griswold*, Justice Douglas] performed a miracle of transsubstantiation. He called the first amendment's penumbra a protection of "privacy." He had no better reason to use the word "privacy" than that the individual is free within these zones, free to act in public as well as in private. None of these penumbral zones—from the first, third, fourth or fifth amendments, all of which he cited, along with the ninth—covered the case before him. One more leap was required. Justice Douglas asserted that these various "zones of privacy" created an independent right of privacy, a right not lying within the penumbra of any specific amendment. He did not disclose, however, how a series of specified rights combined to create a new and unspecified right.

The *Griswold* opinion fails every test of neutrality. The derivation of the principle was utterly specious, and so was its definition. In fact, we are left with no idea of what the principle really forbids. Derivation and definition are interrelated here. Justice Douglas called the amendments and their penumbras "zones of privacy," though of course they are not that at all. They protect both private and public behavior and so would more properly be labeled "zones of freedom." If we follow Justice Douglas in his next step, these zones would then add up to an independent right of freedom, which is to say, a general constitutional right to be free of legal coercion, a manifest impossibility in any imaginable society.

c. The article that follows was the key source of interrogation when Bork, then a judge, was being considered for the Supreme Court in 1987. Bork's criticisms of *Griswold* antagonized both the Senate Judiciary Committee and, according to the polls, a majority of the American people. His nomination failed.

Griswold, then, is an unprincipled decision, both in the way in which it derives a new constitutional right and in the way it defines that right, or rather fails to define it. We are left with no idea of the sweep of the right of privacy and hence no notion of the cases to which it may or may not be applied in the future. The truth is that the Court could not reach its result in *Griswold* through principle. The reason is obvious. Every clash between a minority claiming freedom and a majority claiming power to regulate involves a choice between the gratifications of the two groups. When the Constitution has not spoken, the Court will be able to find no scale, other than its own value preferences, upon which to weigh the respective claims to pleasure. Compare the facts in *Griswold* with a hypothetical suit by an electric utility company and one of its customers to void a smoke pollution ordinance as unconstitutional. The cases are identical.

In *Griswold* a husband and wife assert that they wish to have sexual relations without fear of unwanted children. The law impairs their sexual gratifications. The State can assert, and at one stage in that litigation did assert, that the majority finds the use of contraceptives immoral. Knowledge that it takes place and that the State makes no effort to inhibit it causes the majority anguish, impairs their gratifications.

The electrical company asserts that it wishes to produce electricity at low cost in order to reach a wide market and make profits. Its customer asserts that he wants a lower cost so that prices can be held low. The smoke pollution regulation impairs his and the company's stockholders' economic gratifications. The State can assert not only that the majority prefer clean air to lower prices, but also that the absence of the regulation impairs the majority's physical and aesthetic gratifications.

Neither case is covered specifically or by obvious implication in the Constitution. Unless we can distinguish forms of gratification, the only course for a principled Court is to let the majority have its way in both cases. It is clear that the Court cannot make the necessary distinction. There is no principled way to decide that one man's gratifications are more deserving of respect than another's or that one form of gratification is more worthy than another. Why is sexual gratification more worthy than moral gratification? Why is sexual gratification nobler than economic gratification? There is no way of deciding these matters other than by reference to some system of moral or ethical values that has no objective or intrinsic validity of its own and about which men can and do differ. Where the Constitution does not embody the moral or ethical choice, the judge has no basis other than his own values upon which to set aside the community judgment embodied in the statute. That, by definition, is an inadequate basis for judicial supremacy. The issue of the community's moral and ethical values, the issue of the degree of pain an activity causes, are matters concluded by the passage and enforcement of the laws in question. The judiciary has no role to play other than that of applying the statutes in a fair and impartial manner.

One of my colleagues refers to this conclusion, not without sarcasm, as the "Equal Gratification Clause." The phrase is apt, and I accept it, though not the sarcasm. Equality of human gratifications, where the document does not impose a hierarchy, is an essential part of constitutional doctrine because of the necessity that judges be principled. To be perfectly clear on the subject, I repeat that the principle is not applicable to legislatures. Legislation requires value choice and cannot be principled in the sense under discussion. Courts must accept any value choice the legislature makes unless it clearly runs contrary to a choice made in the framing of the Constitution.

It follows, of course, that broad areas of constitutional law ought to be reformulated. Most obviously, it follows that substantive due process, revived by the *Griswold* case, is and always has been an improper doctrine. Substantive due process requires the Court to say, without guidance from the Constitution, which liberties or gratifications may be infringed by majorities and which may not. This means that *Griswold's* antecedents were also wrongly decided, *e.g.*, *Meyer v. Nebraska*, which struck down a statute forbidding the teaching of subjects in any language other than English; *Pierce v. Society of Sisters*, which set aside a statute compelling all Oregon school children to attend public schools; *Adkins v. Children's Hospital*, which invalidated a statute of Congress authorizing a board to fix minimum wages for women and children in the District of Columbia; and *Lochner v. New York*, which voided a statute fixing maximum hours of work for bakers. With some of these cases I am in political agreement, and perhaps *Pierce's* result could be reached on acceptable grounds, but there is no justification for the Court's methods. In *Lochner*, Justice Peckham, defending liberty from what he conceived as a mere meddlesome interference, asked, "[A]re we all . . . at the mercy of legislative majorities?" The correct answer, where the Constitution does not speak, must be "yes."

* * *

Thomas S. Eisenstadt v. William R. Baird

United States Supreme Court, 1972.
405 U.S. 438, 92 S.Ct. 1029, 31 L.Ed.2d 349.

■ JUSTICE BRENNAN delivered the opinion of the Court.

Appellee William Baird was convicted * * * first, for exhibiting contraceptive articles in the course of delivering a lecture on contraception to a group of students at Boston University and, second, for giving a young woman a package of Emko vaginal foam at the close of his address. * * *

Massachusetts General Laws Ann., c. 272, § 21, under which Baird was convicted, provides a maximum five-year term of imprisonment for "whoever . . . gives away . . . any drug, medicine, instrument or article whatever for the prevention of conception," except as authorized in § 21A. Under § 21A, "(a) registered physician may administer to or prescribe for any married person drugs or articles intended for the prevention of pregnancy or conception. [And a] registered pharmacist actually engaged in the business of pharmacy may furnish such drugs or articles to any married person presenting a prescription from a registered physician." As interpreted by the State Supreme Judicial Court, these provisions make it a felony for anyone, other than a registered physician or pharmacist acting in accordance with the terms of § 21A, to dispense any article with the intention that it be used for the prevention of conception. The statutory scheme distinguishes among three distinct classes of distributees—first, married persons may obtain contraceptives to prevent pregnancy, but only from doctors or druggists on prescription; second, single persons may not obtain contraceptives from anyone to prevent pregnancy; and, third, married or single persons may obtain contraceptives from anyone to prevent, not pregnancy, but the spread of disease. This construction of state law is, of course, binding on us.

The legislative purposes that the statute is meant to serve are not altogether clear. In *Commonwealth v. Baird*, [247 N.E.2d 574, 578 (1969)], the Supreme Judicial Court noted only the State's interest in protecting the health of its citizens: "[T]he prohibition in § 21," the court declared, "is directly related to" the State's goal of "preventing the distribution of articles designed to prevent conception which may have undesirable, if not dangerous, physical consequences," In a subsequent decision, *Sturgis v. Attorney General*, 260 N.E.2d 687, 690 (1970), the court, however, found "a second and more compelling ground for upholding the statute"—namely, to protect morals through "regulating the private sexual lives of single persons." The Court of Appeals, for reasons that will appear, did not consider the promotion of health or the protection of morals through the deterrence of fornication to be the legislative aim. Instead, the court concluded that the statutory goal was to limit contraception in and of itself—a purpose that the court held conflicted "with fundamental human rights" under *Griswold*, where this Court struck down Connecticut's prohibition against the use of contraceptives as an unconstitutional infringement of the right of marital privacy.

We agree that the goals of deterring premarital sex and regulating the distribution of potentially harmful articles cannot reasonably be regarded as legislative aims of §§ 21 and 21A. And we hold that the statute, viewed as a prohibition on contraception *per se*, violates the rights of single persons under the Equal Protection Clause of the Fourteenth Amendment. * * *

* * * The question for our determination in this case is whether there is some ground of difference that rationally explains the different treatment accorded married and unmarried persons under Massachusetts General Laws Ann., c. 272, §§ 21 and 21A. For the reasons that follow, we conclude that no such ground exists.

First. Section 21 stems from Mass. Stat. 1879, c. 159, § 1, which prohibited without exception, distribution of articles intended to be used as contraceptives. In *Commonwealth v. Allison*, 116 N.E. 265, 266 (1917), the Massachusetts Supreme Judicial Court explained that the law's "plain purpose is to protect purity, to preserve chastity, to encourage continence and self restraint, to defend the sanctity of the home, and thus to engender in the State and nation a virile and virtuous race of men and women."

[Handwritten margin notes: "Equal Protection Clause- 14th Amend. # Is there a difference b/w married & unmarried persons that explains diff. policy?"]

Although the State clearly abandoned that purpose with the enactment of § 21A, at least insofar as the illicit sexual activities of married persons are concerned, the court reiterated in *Sturgis*, that the object of the legislation is to discourage premarital sexual intercourse. Conceding that the State could, consistently with the Equal Protection Clause, regard the problems of extramarital and premarital sexual relations as "[e]vils ... of different dimensions and proportions, requiring different remedies," *Williamson v. Lee Optical*, 348 U.S. 483, 489 (1955), we cannot agree that the deterrence of premarital sex may reasonably be regarded as the purpose of the Massachusetts law.

It would be plainly unreasonable to assume that Massachusetts has prescribed pregnancy and the birth of an unwanted child as punishment for fornication, which is a misdemeanor under Massachusetts General Laws Ann., c. 272, § 18. Aside from the scheme of values that assumption would attribute to the State, it is abundantly clear that the effect of the ban on distribution of contraceptives to unmarried persons has at best a marginal relation to the proffered objective. * * * §§ 21 and 21A do not at all regulate the distribution of contraceptives when they are to be used to prevent, not pregnancy, but the spread of disease. Nor, in making contraceptives available to married persons without regard to their intended use, does Massachusetts attempt to deter married persons from engaging in illicit sexual relations with unmarried persons. Even on the assumption that the fear of pregnancy operates as a deterrent to fornication, the Massachusetts statute is thus so riddled with exceptions that deterrence of premarital sex cannot reasonably be regarded as its aim.

Moreover, §§ 21 and 21A on their face have a dubious relation to the State's criminal prohibition on fornication. As the Court of Appeals explained, "fornication is a misdemeanor [in Massachusetts], entailing a thirty dollar fine, or three months in jail. Violation of the present statute is a felony, punishable by five years in prison. We find it hard to believe that the legislature adopted a statute carrying a five-year penalty for its possible, obviously by no means fully effective, deterrence of the commission of a ninety-day misdemeanor." Even conceding the legislature a full measure of discretion in fashioning means to prevent fornication, and recognizing that the State may seek to deter prohibited conduct by punishing more severely those who facilitate than those who actually engage in its commission, we, like the Court of Appeals, cannot believe that in this instance Massachusetts has chosen to expose the aider and abetter who simply *gives away* a contraceptive to *20* times the *90–day* sentence of the offender himself. The very terms of the State's criminal statutes, coupled with the *de minimis* effect of §§ 21 and 21A in deterring fornication, thus compel the conclusion that such deterrence cannot reasonably be taken as the purpose of the ban on distribution of contraceptives to unmarried persons.

Second. Section 21A was added to the Massachusetts General Laws by Stat. 1966, c. 265, §§ 1. The Supreme Judicial Court in *Baird* held that the purpose of the amendment was to serve the health needs of the community by regulating the distribution of potentially harmful articles. It is plain that

Massachusetts had no such purpose in mind before the enactment of § 21A. As the Court of Appeals remarked, "Consistent with the fact that the statute was contained in a chapter dealing with 'Crimes Against Chastity, Morality, Decency and Good Order,' it was cast only in terms of morals. A physician was forbidden to prescribe contraceptives even when needed for the protection of health." Nor did the Court of Appeals "believe that the legislature [in enacting § 21A] suddenly reversed its field and developed an interest in health. Rather, it merely made what it thought to be the precise accommodation necessary to escape the *Griswold* ruling."

Again, we must agree with the Court of Appeals. If health were the rationale of § 21A, the statute would be both discriminatory and overbroad. Dissenting in *Baird*, Justices Whittemore and Cutter stated that they saw "in § 21 and § 21A, read together, no public health purpose. If there is need to have physician prescribe (and a pharmacist dispense) contraceptives, that need is as great for unmarried persons as for married persons." * * *

Third. If the Massachusetts statute cannot be upheld as a deterrent to fornication or as a health measure, may it, nevertheless, be sustained simply as a prohibition on contraception? The Court of Appeals analysis "led inevitably to the conclusion that, so far as morals are concerned, it is contraceptives *per se* that are considered immoral—to the extent that *Griswold* will permit such a declaration." [The Court of Appeals upheld a fundamental right to contraceptive that the state cannot invade.] We need not, however, decide that important question in this case because, whatever the rights of the individual to access to contraceptives may be, the rights must be the same for the unmarried and the married alike.

If under *Griswold* the distribution of contraceptives to married persons cannot be prohibited, a ban on distribution to unmarried persons would be equally impermissible. It is true that in *Griswold* the right of privacy in question inhered in the marital relationship. Yet the marital couple is not an independent entity with a mind and heart of its own, but an association of two individuals each with a separate intellectual and emotional makeup. If the right of privacy means anything, it is the right of the *individual*, married or single, to be free from unwarranted governmental intrusion into matters so fundamentally affecting a person as the decision whether to bear or beget a child.

On the other hand, if *Griswold* is no bar to a prohibition on the distribution of contraceptives, the State could not, consistently with the Equal Protection Clause, outlaw distribution to unmarried but not to married persons. In each case the evil, as perceived by the State, would be identical, and the underinclusion would be invidious. Mr. Justice Jackson, concurring in *Railway Express Agency v. New York*, 336 U.S. 106, 112–13 (1949), made the point:

> * * * Conversely, nothing opens the door to arbitrary action so effectively as to allow those officials to pick and choose only a few to whom they will apply legislation and thus to escape the political retribution that might be visited upon them if larger numbers were affected.

Courts can take no better measure to assure that laws will be just than to require that laws be equal in operation. * * *

[T]he principle * * * has equal application to the legislation here. We hold that by providing dissimilar treatment for married and unmarried persons who are similarly situated, Massachusetts General Laws Ann., c. 272, §§ 21 and 21A, violate the Equal Protection Clause.

■ Mr. Justice Powell and Mr. Justice Rehnquist took no part in the consideration or decision of this case.

■ [We omit the concurring opinion of Mr. Justice Douglas. Mr. Justice White and Mr. Justice Blackmun concurred in the result, on the grounds that there was no evidence to suggest that medical supervision was necessary to protect health when the contraceptive being distributed was, as here, vaginal foam; nor was there record evidence as to the recipient's marital status.]

■ Mr. Chief Justice Burger, dissenting. * * *

Even if it were conclusively established once and for all that the product dispensed by appellee is not actually or potentially dangerous in the somatic sense, I would still be unable to agree that the restriction on dispensing it falls outside the State's power to regulate in the area of health. The choice of a means of birth control, although a highly personal matter, is also a health matter in a very real sense, and I see nothing arbitrary in a requirement of medical supervision. It is generally acknowledged that contraceptives vary in degree of effectiveness and potential harmfulness. There may be compelling health reasons for certain women to choose the most effective means of birth control available, no matter how harmless the less effective alternatives. Others might be advised not to use a highly effective means of contraception because of their peculiar susceptibility to an adverse side effect. Moreover, there may be information known to the medical profession that a particular brand of contraceptive is to be preferred or avoided, or that it has not been adequately tested. Nonetheless, the concurring opinion would hold, as a constitutional matter, that a State must allow someone without medical training the same power to distribute this medicinal substance as is enjoyed by a physician.

It is revealing, I think, that those portions of the majority and concurring opinions rejecting the statutory limitation on distributors rely on no particular provision of the Constitution. I see nothing in the Fourteenth Amendment or any other part of the Constitution that even vaguely suggests that these medicinal forms of contraceptives must be available in the open market. I do not challenge *Griswold v. Connecticut*, despite its tenuous moorings to the text of the Constitution, but I cannot view it as controlling authority for this case. The Court was there confronted with a statute flatly prohibiting the use of contraceptives, not one regulating their distribution. I simply cannot believe that the limitation on the class of lawful distributors has significantly impaired the right to use contraceptives in Massachusetts. By relying in *Griswold* in the present context, the Court has passed beyond the penumbras of the specific guarantees into the uncircumscribed area of personal predilections. * * *

NOTES ON *EISENSTADT* AND THE EXPANDING PRIVACY RIGHT

1. *What Was the State's Interest Underlying This Statute?* Justice Brennan's opinion for the seven-member Court (joined by only three other Justices) refused to accept either a morals or a health concern as the basis for the statute because he found both to be so imperfectly related to the impact of the law. In its brief and in oral argument, the state had claimed both justifications. Does this rationale hold up? What would the historical evidence suggest? Is Chief Justice Burger correct that the Court should defer to indications of a new, more scientific rationale?

Essentially the same questions regarding the legitimacy of the state's interest in using anti-contraceptive laws to discourage sexual activity arose in the context of a New York statute prohibiting distribution of contraceptives to persons younger than 16, except by a physician. *Carey v. Population Services International,* 431 U.S. 678 (1977). In *Carey,* four Justices joined a plurality opinion by Justice Brennan holding that minors have a privacy right that includes access to contraceptives, and that a state cannot impose restrictions on contraception for the purpose of deterring sexual activity by increasing the hazards of engaging in it. *Id.* at 694–95. Justice Stevens derided as "frivolous" the plurality's argument "that a minor has the constitutional right to put contraceptives to their intended use," but agreed with the plurality's result, because the state could not communicate its policy against teenage sexuality by imposing a risk of physical harm, regardless of whether minors had an underlying constitutional right. *Id.* at 713–716. Also concurring in the result, Justice Powell wrote that the state's interest in deterring such activity was sufficient to withstand review, although the New York statute failed because it infringed the rights of married teenagers and of parents. *Id.* at 703–08. Justice White did not reach the question of the propriety of the state's interest because he found that there was no indication that the statute actually had a deterrent effect. *Id.* at 702–703.

[handwritten margin note: Contraceptives for minors under 16]

2. *From Sex to Procreation in Three Easy Steps.* Justice Brennan found that the "real" state's interest was that the legislature had considered "contraceptives *per se*" to be immoral. In other words, he rejected the notion that the state's interest in morality was the instrumental one of deterring nonmarital sexual activities, but rather was the intrinsic immorality of preventing new life. Apply Brennan's over- and under-inclusiveness analyses to this rationale—how does it fare? This first step eliminated any need to scrutinize the sexual morality justification.

Both the plaintiffs and *amicus* Planned Parenthood had argued that even if the state could criminalize nonmarital sexual conduct, it could not penalize it by the less direct, but harsher, method of forcing individuals to risk pregnancy as a result. Such a means to that end, they argued, was arbitrary and capricious. Brennan sidestepped the question of what means could be utilized toward that end, however, by step two: finding that "whatever the rights of the individual to access to contraceptives may be, the rights must be the same for the unmarried and married alike.'' Thus, equal protection doctrine decides the case.

In step three, the Court returns, unnecessarily, to privacy. Brennan elaborated the holding with what is the most quoted portion of the opinion, the ''[i]f the right of privacy means anything'' sentence. At the end of that sentence, we have arrived at ''the right to decide whether to bear or beget a child.'' With marriage absent from the case, Brennan ignored those aspects of *Griswold* that focused on sexuality, and instead grounded this opinion solely in the decision-making aspects of procreation. By step three, the Court had substituted procreation for sexuality or sexual morality. Does that work? Is the conclusion supported by the cases Brennan cites? Is it a euphemistic cop-out or an artful dodge?

Note Justice Brennan's own summation of this line of cases in 1977:

> *Griswold* may no longer be read as holding only that a State may not prohibit a married couple's use of contraceptives. Read in light of its progeny, the teaching of *Griswold* is that the Constitution protects individual decisions in matters of childbearing from unjustified intrusion by the State.

Carey v. Population Services International, 431 U.S. 678, 687 (1977) (plurality opinion). In the same case, Brennan wrote that ''the Court has not definitively answered the difficult question whether and to what extent the Constitution prohibits state statutes regulating [private consensual sexual] behavior among adults.'' *Id.* at 695 n. 17.

3. *The Role of Doctors.* In an ironic turning of the tables, Chief Justice Burger would have used the fact that a non-physician distributed the contraceptive as grounds for upholding the restrictive statute. Planned Parenthood had argued in its *amicus* brief that the statutory requirement of a doctor's involvement, when the device carried no risk, violated the equal protection clause because as applied, it discriminated against the poor who could not afford physicians. The Planned Parenthood *amicus* brief also contained, for the first time since Margaret Sanger's early, more radical days, an explicit sex discrimination argument.

PART C.   THE RIGHT TO PRIVACY AND ABORTION

Beginning in the late 1960s, advocates began challenging state laws that restricted abortion. The case that reached the Supreme Court began with a ''women's liberation'' group at the University of Texas. (Garrow 389–95.)

Jane Roe et al. v. Henry Wade

United States Supreme Court, 1973.
410 U.S. 113, 93 S.Ct. 705, 35 L.Ed.2d 147.

■ MR. JUSTICE BLACKMUN delivered the opinion of the Court.

This [appeal presents] constitutional challenges to state criminal abortion legislation. The Texas statutes under attack here [which make procuring an abortion a crime except "by medical advice for the purpose of saving the life of the mother"] are typical of those that have been in effect in many states for approximately a century. * * *

* * * [The] restrictive criminal abortion laws in effect in a majority of States today are of relatively recent vintage. * * * [They] derive from statutory changes effected, for the most part, in the later half of the 19th century.

* * * [Abortion] was practiced in Greek times as well as in the Roman Era. * * * If abortion was prosecuted in some places, it seems to have been based on a concept of a violation of the father's right to his offspring. Ancient religion did not bar abortion. * * *

* * * [At] common law, abortion performed before "quickening"—the first recognizable movement of the fetus *in utero*, appearing usually from the 16th to the 18th week of pregnancy—was not an indictable offense. [Justice Blackmun explored the historiographical debates aver the precise common law position and concluded that it was not until the middle and late 19th century that the "quickening" distinction was abandoned and the degree of the offense and the penalties increased, both in England and in the American states.]

It is thus apparent that at common law, at the time of the adoption of our Constitution, and throughout the major portion of the 19th century, abortion was viewed with less disfavor than under most American statutes currently in effect. Phrasing it another way, a woman enjoyed a substantially broader right to terminate a pregnancy than she does in most States today. At least with respect to the early stage of pregnancy, and very possibly without such a limitation, the opportunity to make this choice was present in this country well into the 19th century. * * *

Three reasons have been advanced to explain historically the enactment of criminal abortion laws in the 19th century and to justify their continued existence.

It has been argued occasionally that these laws were the product of a Victorian social concern to discourage illicit sexual conduct. Texas, however, does not advance this justification in the present case, and it appears that no court or commentator has taken the argument seriously. * * *

A second reason is concerned with abortion as a medical procedure. When most criminal abortion laws were first enacted, the procedure was a hazardous one for the woman. Thus, it has been argued that a State's real concern in enacting a criminal abortion law was to protect the pregnant woman, that is, to restrain her from submitting to a procedure that placed her life in serious jeopardy.

Modern medical techniques have altered this situation. * * * Mortality rates for women undergoing early abortions [appear] to be as low as or lower than the rates for normal childbirth. * * * Of course, important state interests in the areas of health and medical standards do remain. The State has a legitimate interest in seeing to it that abortion, like any other medical procedure, is performed under circumstances that insure maximum safety for the patient. * * * Thus, the State retains a definite interest in protecting the woman's own health and safety when an abortion is proposed at a late stage of pregnancy.

The third reason is the State's interest—some phrase it in terms of duty—in protecting prenatal life. Some of the argument for this justification rests on the theory that a new human life is present from the moment of conception. * * * In assessing the State's interest, recognition may [also] be given to the less rigid claim that as long as at least *potential* life is involved, the state may assert interests beyond the protection of the pregnant woman * * *

The Constitution does not explicitly mention any right of privacy. [But] the Court has recognized that a right of personal privacy, or a guarantee of certain areas or zones of privacy, does exist under the Constitution. In varying contexts, the Court or individual Justices have, indeed, found at least the roots of that right in the First Amendment; in the Fourth and Fifth Amendments; in the penumbras of the Bill of Rights; or in the concept of liberty guaranteed by the first section of the Fourteenth Amendment. These decisions make it clear that only personal rights deemed "fundamental" or "implicit in the concept of ordered liberty," *Palko v. Connecticut*, 302 U.S. 319, 325 (1937), are included in this guarantee of personal privacy. They also make clear that the right has some extension to activities relating to marriage, *Loving*; procreation, *Skinner*; contraception, *Eisenstadt*; family relationships, *Prince*; and child rearing and education. *Pierce; Meyer*.

This right of privacy, whether it be founded in the Fourteenth Amendment's concept of personal liberty and restrictions upon state action, as we feel it is, or, as the District Court determined, in the Ninth Amendment's reservation of rights to the people, is broad enough to encompass a woman's decision whether or not to terminate her pregnancy. The detriment that the State would impose upon the pregnant woman by denying this choice altogether is apparent. Specific and direct harm medically diagnosable even in early pregnancy may be involved. Maternity, or additional offspring, may force upon the woman a distressful life and future. Psychological harm may be imminent. Mental and physical health may be taxed by child care. There is also the distress, for all concerned, associated with the unwanted child, and there is the problem of bringing a child into a family already unable, psychologically and otherwise, to care for it. In other cases, [the] additional difficulties and continuing stigma of unwed motherhood may be involved. All these are factors the woman and her responsible physician necessarily will consider in consultation.

On the basis of elements such as these, appellant and some *amici* argue that the woman's right is absolute and that she is entitled to terminate her pregnancy at whatever time, in whatever way, and for whatever reason she alone chooses. With this we do not agree. * * * The Court's decisions recognizing a right of privacy also acknowledge that some state regulation in areas protected by that right is appropriate. As noted above, a State may properly assert important interests in safeguarding health, in maintaining medical standards, and in protecting potential life. * * *

[Justice Blackmun set the "compelling" point, where the state can begin regulation, at approximately the end of the first trimester, when the fetus "quickens" in the old common law sense. During the first trimester the state cannot interfere with decisions by "the attending physician, in consultation with his patient." During the second trimester the state can set licensing and other medical regulations to protect the safety of the mother and to recognize the potential life.]

■ [We omit the separate concurring opinions of JUSTICES STEWART and DOUGLAS and of CHIEF JUSTICE BURGER. JUSTICES WHITE and REHNQUIST dissented in separate opinions.]

NOTES ON *ROE* AND THE RIGHT TO ABORTION

1. *Procreation as the Foundation.* With the Court's decision in *Roe*, the privacy line of cases became firmly grounded in the right to decide whether to bear a child. *Roe* also marks the apex of the medicalization of the law of reproductive decisionmaking, both in its consideration of medical history and in its vesting of the decision-making in "the woman and her responsible physician."

Note that although the *Griswold-Eisenstadt–Roe* line of cases is thought of as *in seriatim* building blocks, they may not have been so distinct in the minds of the Justices. *Eisenstadt* was argued before the Court on November 17 and 18, 1971; *Roe* was first argued less than a month later, on December 13. (*Roe* was put over for re-argument during the following term.) How might the pendency of *Roe* have affected the way the Court structured its decision in *Eisenstadt*?

2. *Finally a Home for the Right to Privacy.* After roosting in the penumbras of the Bill of Rights (the Douglas opinion in *Griswold*), the Ninth Amendment (the Goldberg concurrence), and even the equal protection clause (the Brennan opinion in *Eisenstadt*), the right to privacy finally found a constitutional home in the jurisprudential location where Justice Harlan's *Poe v. Ullman* opinion had identified it in the first place: the due process clause's protection of "liberty." Note that Justice Blackmun's opinion makes that placement *en passant*, without any analysis. Why would the Court have departed from the penumbral analysis of *Griswold*? Doesn't its grounding in the due process clause confirm Bork's *Lochner*-based critique?

Unlike *Griswold*, *Roe* has been extremely controversial as to its result and less controversial as to its derivation of the constitutional right.[b] After

b. Criticisms from liberals as well as conservatives include Archibald Cox, *The* *Role of the Supreme Court in American Government* 113–14 (1976); John Hart Ely, "The

a generation of political as well as academic criticism, the Court returned to both issues in *Planned Parenthood of Southeastern Pennsylvania v. Casey*, 505 U.S. 833 (1992). The "Joint Opinion" of Justices O'Connor, Kennedy, and Souter reaffirmed the holding in *Roe* that states could not prohibit abortion absent a compelling state interest, and explicitly grounded privacy jurisprudence in Justice Harlan's dissent in *Ullman*. 112 S. Ct. at 2806.

3. *The Missing Argument: Sex Discrimination. The Role of Sexuality?* Many commentators have opined that the abortion right would have been more strongly grounded in the Constitution and in social reality had it been based on a sex discrimination, rather than a privacy, argument.[c] In fact, a sex discrimination argument was made to the Court in *Roe* in an *amicus* brief filed by Nancy Stearns for the Center for Constitutional Rights. The CCR brief argued that abortion laws were a way to punish unmarried women for being heterosexually active. Another *amicus* brief, filed by Joan Bradford for the California Committee to Legalize Abortion, argued that forced childbearing was a form of involuntary servitude, prohibited under the Thirteenth Amendment. These arguments were made to a Court actively considering how to frame its equal protection analysis of classifications based on sex. A third case pending before the Court in the 1971 Term was *Reed v. Reed*, 404 U.S. 71 (1971), which marked the first time the Court struck down a sex-based classification as unconstitutional. *Reed* was argued on October 19, 1971 and decided quickly, on November 22 of the same year. (See Section 3 of this Chapter for an examination of constitutional protections against sex discrimination.)

In later abortion cases, the Court incorporated more of a women's rights analysis, although stopping short of an explicit equal protection holding. *See Thornburgh v. American College of Obstetricians & Gynecologists*, 476 U.S. 747, 772 (1986); *Webster v. Reproductive Health Services*, 492 U.S. 490, 557 (1989) (Blackmun, J., dissenting) ("millions of women, and their families, have ordered their lives around the right to reproductive choice, and [ ] this right has become vital to the full participation of women in the economic and political walks of American life"). In *Casey*, the Court held that in abortion cases, "the liberty of the woman is at stake in a sense unique to the human condition and so unique to the law," 112 S. Ct. at 2807, and Justice Blackmun's concurring and dissenting opinion briefly suggested a sex discrimination argument. On the other hand, *Casey* weakened the Court's earlier elaborations on *Roe* by holding that restrictive regulations (*e.g.*, waiting periods) would be permitted if they did not amount to an "undue burden." *Id.* at 2820.

Wages of Crying Wolf: A Comment on *Roe v. Wade*," 82 *Yale L.J.* 920 (1973); Richard Epstein, "Substantive Due Process by Any Other Name: The Abortion Cases," 1973 *Sup. Ct. Rev.* 159.

c. See, *e.g.*, Sylvia Law, "Rethinking Sex and the Constitution," 132 *U. Pa. L. Rev.*

955 (1984); Ruth Bader Ginsburg, "Some Thoughts on Autonomy and Equality in Relation to *Roe v. Wade*," 63 *N.C.L. Rev.* 375 (1985); Donald H. Regan, "Rewriting *Roe v. Wade*," 77 *Mich. L. Rev.* 1569, 1621–45 (1979).

Perhaps the one area in which issues of sexuality (as distinct from procreation) remain closest to the surface in contemporary abortion jurisprudence is the question of whether the state can intervene to regulate abortions for minor women in ways that it cannot for adult women. See Chapter 2, Section 2(C) for a discussion of parental notice and consent requirements imposed on adolescents seeking abortion. In many instances, these laws result in the first disclosure to parents of the teenager's sexual activity, as well as disclosure of her pregnancy. The Supreme Court in *Casey* reaffirmed the state's authority to restrict the privacy right in this way. Would there be a different result under an equal protection analysis?

[handwritten margin note: no social argument about sex discrimination in Roe v. Wade]

Reva Siegel, Reasoning From the Body: A Historical Perspective on Abortion Regulation and Questions of Equal Protection

44 *Stanford Law Review* 261, 276–77, 350–51 (1992).*

Roe thus holds that the state has an interest in potential life which becomes compelling at the point of viability. It defines this regulatory interest in potential life physiologically, without reference to the sorts of constitutional considerations that normally attend the use of state power against a citizen. In the Court's reasoning, facts concerning the physiological development of the unborn provide "logical and biological justifications" both limiting and legitimating state action directed against the pregnant woman. Because *Roe* analyzes an exercise of state power from a medical, rather than a social, point of view, it authorizes state action against the pregnant woman on the basis of physiological criteria, requiring no inquiry into the state's reasons for acting against the pregnant woman, or the impact of its actions on her. Indeed, *Roe* analyzes the state's interest in potential life as a benign exercise of state power for the protection of the unborn, and not as a coercive exercise of state power against pregnant women, often reasoning as if the state's interest in protecting potential life scarcely pertained to the pregnant woman herself. Thus, in the course of justifying its decision to protect the abortion decision as a right of privacy, the Court recognized an antagonistic state interest in restricting women's access to abortion on which it imposed temporal, but few principled, restraints.

To the extent that *Roe* relied upon physiological reasoning to define the state's interest in potential life, it unleashed a legal discourse of indeterminate content and scope—one legitimating boundless regulation of women's reproductive lives should the Court abandon the trimester framework that presently constrains it. In recognizing the state's interest in potential life, the Court ignored a simple social fact that should be of critical constitutional significance: When a state invokes an interest in potential life to justify fetal-protective regulation, the proposed use of public power concerns not merely the unborn, but women as well. Abortion-restrictive regulation is sex-based regulation, the use of public power to force women to bear children. Yet, the Court has never described the state's interest in protecting potential life as an interest in forcing women to bear children. *Roe's* physiological reasoning obscures that simple social fact. "[I]f one accepts the medical definitions of the developing young in the human uterus" as a sufficient, objective, and authoritative framework for evaluating the state's regulatory interest in abortion—as *Roe* did—state action compelling women to perform the work of motherhood can be justified without ever acknowledging that the state is enforcing a gender status role. In part, this is because analyzing abortion-restrictive regulation within physiological paradigms obscures its social logic, but also, and as importantly, it is because physiological reasons for regulating women's conduct are already laden with socio-political import: Facts about women's bodies have long served to justify regulation enforcing judgments about women's roles.

Abortion-restrictive regulation is state action compelling pregnancy and motherhood, and this simple fact cannot be evaded by invoking nature or a woman's choices to explain the situation in which the pregnant woman subject to abortion restrictions finds herself. A pregnant woman seeking an abortion has the practical capacity to terminate a pregnancy, which she would exercise but for the community's decision to prevent or deter her. If the community successfully effectuates its will, it is the state, and not nature, which is responsible for causing her to continue the pregnancy.
* * *

When abortion-restrictive regulation is analyzed as state action compelling motherhood, it presents equal protection concerns that *Roe's* physiological reasoning obscures.

State Regulation of Sexual Practices—The Special Case of Sodomy

The materials emphasized in Section 1 represent two categories of state and federal laws regulating sexual behavior. Whereas the foregoing laws directly regulated procreation (*Griswold, Eisenstadt, Roe*) and sexual expression (*One Package, Stanley*) in and outside of marriage, a third category of laws regulated sexual behavior outside of marriage. These laws have traditionally been the most extensive and include the following kinds of statutes:

- Fornication laws prohibiting sexual intercourse by unmarried (male-female) couples.
- Adultery laws prohibiting sexual intercourse where at least one of the (male-female) participants is married to another person.
- Sodomy or crime against nature laws prohibiting "unnatural" (anal or oral) intercourse between two persons.
- Indecent exposure, lewdness, or disorderly conduct statutes prohibiting lewd sexual behavior or its solicitation, usually in public or in the presence of offended people.
- Prostitution, disorderly house, and bawdy house laws prohibiting sexual intercourse or its solicitation for compensation (see Chapter 11).
- Rape and sexual abuse laws prohibiting unconsented sexual intercourse or sexual intercourse with children (see Chapter 11).

In most states, none of these laws—including rape and statutory rape prohibitions—applied to married couples, usually as a matter of law but sometimes only as a matter of practice. All of these laws were part of state criminal codes in the nineteenth century, and most can still be found in state codes (although some have been declared unconstitutional, they sometimes remain on the books for decades). For a history of these laws, with an emphasis on sodomy laws, see William N. Eskridge, Jr., *Gaylaw: Challenging the Apartheid of the Closet* chs. 1–4 (forthcoming 1998).

Many of these laws have become controversial, as challenges to state authority in this field have increased. The first repeal of a sodomy law occurred in Illinois in 1961, when that state adopted the Model Penal Code, which in effect decriminalized private consensual adultery, fornication, and sodomy. A number of states followed that model, and through the 1960s and 1970s modernized their criminal laws, in the process dropping or lightening their penalties for many consensual sexual practices.

A somewhat similar process occurred in England, where the publication in 1957 of *The Wolfenden Report* triggered a debate (most famously between Lord Patrick Devlin and Professor H.L.A. Hart) over the proper role of the state in regulating sexual conduct. *The Wolfenden Report* recommended the decriminalization of private consensual homosexual conduct and the continued criminalization, with increased penalties, of prostitution. (Adultery and fornication had previously been dropped from the British criminal code.) Parliament largely followed the *Wolfenden* recommendations, repealing the prohibition against consensual sodomy in 1967.

These contemporaneous cross-Atlantic developments generated an enormous amount of writing, most of it elaborating on and debating the principles first articulated by Jeremy Bentham and John Stuart Mill, who argued that the state had no legitimate right to intrude in individual conduct unless that conduct threatened to harm others. The questions that surfaced in the aftermath of the Model Penal Code and *Wolfenden* still dominate popular and legislative debate about the regulation of sex: When, if ever, does consensual sexual conduct harm others? How would you analyze adultery? Brother-sister incest? Polygamy? Do "secondary harms" count, and if so, for how much? Is the community's definition of morality a legitimate interest for the state to preserve? If so, by what means? Is there a principled method by which one can determine the scope and meaning of "morality" in the context of consensual sexual practices?

Starting in the mid–1970s and continuing through the 1980s, a counter trend developed in the United States: some states decriminalized sodomy between opposite sex partners, while enacting for the first time statutes that specified criminalization of homosexual sodomy. This specification was a new development, spurred perhaps by the growth and visibility of lesbian and gay communities and the resulting backlash. More recently, two more states have repealed orientation-neutral sodomy statutes—Nevada and the District of Columbia. This era of legislation resulted in seven statutes criminalizing only same-sex sodomy,[d] and eighteen with gender neutral criminal statutes.[e] Two of the gender neutral statutes have nonetheless

---

d. Ark. Code Ann. § 5–14–122 (Michie 1987); Kan. Stat. Ann. §§ 21–3501, 3505 (1988); Ky. Rev. Stat. 510.100; Mo. Ann. Stat. §§ 566.010, 090 (Vernon 1979 & Supp. 1993); Mont. Code Ann. §§ 45–2–101(20), 45–5–505 (1990); Tenn. Code Ann. § 39–13–510 (1991); Tex. Penal Code Ann. § 21.06. Courts in Kentucky and Tennessee have ruled those statutes unconstitutional. *Commonwealth v. Wasson*, 842 S.W.2d 487 (Ky.1992); *Campbell v. Sundquist*, 926 S.W.2d 250, (Tenn.App. 1996). A similar ruling by the Texas Court of Criminal Appeals was vacated on procedural (standing) grounds by the Texas Supreme Court.

e. Ala. Code §§ 13A–6–65(a)(3), 13A–6–60 (1982 & Supp. 1993); Ariz. Rev. Stat. Ann. §§ 13–1411, 13–1412 (1989); Fla. Stat. Ann. ch. 800.02 (Harrison 1991); Ga. Code Ann. § 16–6–2 (Michie 1992); Idaho Code § 18–6605 (1987); La. Rev. Stat. Ann. § 14:89 (West 1986); Md. Ann. Code art. 27, §§ 553–54 (1992); Mass. Gen. Laws. Ann. ch. 272, § 34 (West 1990); Mich. Comp. Laws Ann. §§ 750.158 (West 1991); Minn. Stat. Ann. § 609.293 (West 1987); Miss. Code Ann.

been interpreted to be inapplicable to consensual heterosexual sodomy.[f]

A threshold question in the sodomy case law is, exactly which practices does a sodomy statute forbid? Many of the early statutes were steeped in euphemisms such as "crime against nature." We turn first to the history of judicial interpretation of such phrases, and then to the leading case law—state and federal—on sodomy and the right of privacy.

NOTE ON SODOMY LAWS AND THE VAGUENESS DOCTRINE

The right to privacy is an innovation in due process jurisprudence. Much better established is the due process precept that criminal statutes must provide clear notice to the citizenry of their duties and of what conduct will entail criminal liability; correlatively, such statutes must also provide clear notice to police and prosecutors, who need to be restrained in their exercise of enforcement discretion. Two legal rules derive from this core due process precept. One is the rule of lenity: when a criminal statute is ambiguous as applied to particular conduct, ambiguities must be resolved against the state and in favor of the accused, lest the latter be convicted of a crime as to which he had no notice.[g] The rule of lenity justified narrowing the interpretation of the Comstock Act, such as the Second Circuit did in *One Package*, and has been used to limit the scope of state obscenity laws, to assure their conformity to constitutional standards as well as fair notice.

State courts construing sodomy and crime against nature laws have tended to interpret their laws narrowly in at least certain respects. For many years, for example, oral sex was not covered: the majority of state courts refused to interpret "crime against nature" or "carnal knowledge" or "sodomy" laws to include oral sex until the legislature broadened the statute.[h] The history of the Georgia sodomy law litigated in *Bowers v. Hardwick*, excerpted below, reveals a slightly different pattern. Although the Georgia Supreme Court had early on construed the state's "carnal knowledge" statute to include male fellatio, *Herring v. State*, 46 S.E. 876 (Ga.1904), the court refused to extend it to oral sex not involving penile penetration in *Thompson v. Aldredge*, 200 S.E. 799 (Ga.1939) (carnal knowledge law inapplicable to cunnilingus between two women), and again

§ 97–29–59 (1972); N.C. Gen. Stat. § 14–177 (1992); Okla. Stat. Ann. tit. 21, § 886 (West Supp. 1993); R.I. Gen. Laws § 11–10–1 (1981); S.C. Code Ann. § 16–15–120 (Law. Co-op. 1985); Utah Code Ann. § 76–5–403 (1990); Va. Code Ann. § 18.2–361 (Michie Supp. 1993). Also gender neutral is the Uniform Code of Military Justice, 10 U.S.C. § 925, art. 125 (1988).

f. See *Schochet v. State*, 580 A.2d 176 (Md.1990); *Post v. State*, 715 P.2d 1105 (Okl. Crim.App.), *cert. denied*, 479 U.S. 890 (1986). *Post* is analyzed in Larry Catá Backer, "Raping Sodomy and Sodomizing Rape: A Morali-

ty Tale About the Transformation of Modern Sodomy Jurisprudence," 21 *Am. J. Cr. L.* 37 (1993).

g. See William N. Eskridge, Jr. & Philip P. Frickey, *Legislation: Statutes and the Creation of Public Policy* ch. 8 (2d ed. 1994), for a comprehensive collection and analysis of the rule of lenity and other canons.

h. See Anne Goldstein, "History, Homosexuality, and Political Values: Searching for the Hidden Determinants of *Bowers v. Hardwick*," 97 *Yale L.J.* 1073 (1988), as well as Eskridge, *Gaylaw* chs. 1, 4.

in *Riley v. Garrett*, 133 S.E.2d 367 (Ga.1963) (inapplicable to cunnilingus between man and woman). The legislature overrode those decisions in 1968 Georgia Laws § 26–2002.

The other dimension of the notice feature of the due process clause requires invalidation of a criminal statute "which either forbids or requires the doing of an act in terms so vague that men of common intelligence must necessarily guess at its meaning and differ as to its application." *Lanzetta v. New Jersey*, 306 U.S. 451, 453 (1939). Void-for-vagueness challenges were sometimes brought against contraception and abortion statutes which spoke in general terms. For example, a federal district court struck down the District of Columbia abortion law on vagueness grounds in *United States v. Vuitch*, 305 F.Supp. 1032 (D.D.C.1969). The statute criminalized abortions unless "necessary for the preservation of the mother's life or health." Recall similar language in anti-contraception statutes. The district court said:

> The word "health" is not defined and in fact remains so vague in its interpretation and the practice under the act that there is no indication whether it includes varying degrees of mental as well as physical health. * * * The jury's acceptance or nonacceptance of an individual doctor's interpretation of the ambivalent and uncertain word "health" should not determine whether he stands convicted of a felony, facing ten years' imprisonment.

The United States Supreme Court reversed, but with a twist. *United States v. Vuitch*, 402 U.S. 62 (1971). The Court held that the government bore the burden of disproving the health defense. The Court further construed the health exception to include the woman's mental health. Under such narrowing constructions (the rule of lenity), the Court held that the statute was not unconstitutional for vagueness.

Several courts struck down sodomy laws as unconstitutionally vague in the 1970s, but the Supreme Court discouraged this strategy. In *Wainwright v. Stone*, 414 U.S. 21 (1973), the Court held that a generally worded sodomy law acquired sufficient specificity when it had been interpreted to apply to specific conduct by the state's highest court. In *Rose v. Locke*, 423 U.S. 48 (1975), summarily reversing 514 F.2d 570 (6th Cir.1975), the Court held that a law criminalizing "crimes against nature" was sufficiently precise to justify prosecution of a man for engaging in cunnilingus with a woman, because Tennessee courts had extended the law to cover fellatio of the male penis, the flip side of cunnilingus (the Court seemed to reason).

People v. Ronald Onofre et al.

New York Court of Appeals, 1980.
51 N.Y.2d 476, 434 N.Y.S.2d 947, 415 N.E.2d 936, *cert. denied sub nom.* New York v. Onofre, 451 U.S. 987 (1981).

■ JONES, JUDGE.

[The appeal consolidated several cases involving New York's 1965 law against "consensual sodomy," New York Penal Law § 130.38, which made it a misdemeanor to engage in "deviate sexual intercourse" (defined to include anal and oral but not vaginal sex) with another person. Ronald Onofre was convicted of having sex with his 17–year-old male lover at his home. Conde Peoples, III and Philip Goss were convicted for engaging in oral sex in an automobile parked in downtown Buffalo. Defendant Mary Sweat was convicted for having oral sex with a man in a parked truck, also in Buffalo. All defendants appealed their convictions and argued that the consensual sodomy statute was unconstitutional.]

The People are in no disagreement that a fundamental right of personal decision exists; the divergence of the parties focuses on what subjects fall within its protection, the People contending that it extends to only two aspects of sexual behavior—marital intimacy (by virtue of the Supreme Court's decision in *Griswold*) and procreative choice (by reason of *Eisenstadt* and *Roe v. Wade*). Such a stance fails however adequately to take into account the decision in *Stanley* and the explication of the right of privacy contained in the court's opinion in *Eisenstadt*. In *Stanley* the court found violative of the individual's right to be free from governmental interference in making important, protected decisions a statute which made criminal the possession of obscene matter within the privacy of the defendant's home. Although the material itself was entitled to no protection against government proscription (*Roth v. United States*, 354 U.S. 476 [1957]) the defendant's choice to seek sexual gratification by viewing it and the effectuation of that choice within the bastion of his home, removed from the public eye, was held to be blanketed by the constitutional right of privacy. That the right enunciated in *Griswold* to make decisions with respect to the consequence of sexual encounters and, necessarily, to have such encounters, was not limited to married couples was made clear by the language of the court in *Eisenstadt*. * * *

In light of these decisions, protecting under the cloak of the right of privacy individual decisions as to indulgence in acts of sexual intimacy by unmarried persons and as to satisfaction of sexual desires by resort to material condemned as obscene by community standards when done in a cloistered setting, no rational basis appears for excluding from the same protection decisions—such as those made by defendants before us—to seek sexual gratification from what at least once was commonly regarded as "deviant" conduct, so long as the decisions are voluntarily made by adults in a noncommercial, private setting. Nor is any such basis supplied by the claims advanced by the prosecution—that a prohibition against consensual sodomy will prevent physical harm which might otherwise befall the participants, will uphold public morality and will protect the institution of marriage. Commendable though these objectives clearly are, there is nothing on which to base a conclusion that they are achieved by [this statute]. No showing has been made, even in references tendered in the briefs, that physical injury is a common or even occasional consequence of the prohibited conduct, and there has been no demonstration either that this is a danger presently addressed by the statute or was one apprehended at the time the statutory section was enacted contemporaneously with the adoption of the new Penal Law in 1965. Indeed, the proposed comprehensive penal statute submitted to the Legislature by the Temporary Commission on Revision of the Penal Law and Criminal Code dropped all proscription against private acts of consensual sodomy. That the enactment of [this statute] was prompted by something other than fear for the physical safety of participants in consensual sodomy is suggested by the statement contained in the memorandum prepared by the chairman of the Temporary Commission: "It would appear that the Legislature's decision to restore the consensual sodomy offense was, as with adultery, based largely upon the premises that deletion thereof might ostensibly be construed as legislative approval of deviate conduct." (N.Y. Legis. Ann., 1965, pp. 51–52.)

Any purported justification for the consensual sodomy statute in terms of upholding public morality is belied by the position reflected in the *Eisenstadt* decision in which the court carefully distinguished between public dissemination of what might have been considered inimical to public morality and individual recourse to the same material out of the public arena and in the sanctum of the private home. There is a distinction between public and private morality and the private morality of an individual is not synonymous with nor necessarily will have effect on what is known as public morality. So here, the People have failed to demonstrate how government interference with the practice of personal choice in matters of intimate sexual behavior out of view of the public and with no commercial component will serve to advance the cause of public morality or do anything other than restrict individual conduct and impose a concept of private morality chosen by the State. * * *

In sum, there has been no showing of any threat, either to participants or the public in general, in consequence of the voluntary engagement by adults in private, discreet, sodomous conduct. Absent is the factor of commercialization with the attendant evils commonly attached to the retailing of sexual pleasures; absent the elements of force or of involvement of minors which might constitute compulsion of unwilling participants or of those too young to make an informed choice, and absent too intrusion on the sensibilities of members of the public, many of whom would be offended by being exposed to the intimacies of others. Personal feelings of distaste for the conduct sought to be proscribed by [this statute] and even disapproval by a majority of the populace, if that disapproval were to be assumed, may not substitute for the required demonstration of a valid basis for intrusion by the State in an area of important personal decision protected under the right of privacy drawn from the United States Constitution—areas, the number and definition of which have steadily grown but, as the Supreme Court has observed, the outer limits of which it has not yet marked. * * *

■ [JUDGE JASEN concurred in the result. He rejected the *Griswold* analysis but found that the law had no currently rational basis, much like Justice White's concurring opinion in *Griswold*.]

■ GABRIELLI, JUDGE [joined by COOKE, CHIEF JUDGE], dissenting. * * *

Under the analysis utilized by the majority, *all* private, consensual conduct would necessarily involve the exercise of a constitutionally protected "fundamental right" unless the conduct in question jeopardizes the physical health of the participant. In effect, the majority has held that a State statute regulating private conduct will not pass constitutional muster if it is not designed to prevent physical harm to the individual. Such an analysis, however, can only be based upon an unnecessarily restrictive view of the scope of the State's power to regulate the conduct of its citizens. In my view, the so-called "police powers" of the State must include the right of the State to regulate the moral conduct of its citizens and "to maintain a decent society." Indeed, without mentioning specific provisions, it is apparent that our State's penal code represents, in part, an expression of our society's collective view as to what is or is not morally acceptable conduct. And, although the Legislature may not exercise this power in a manner that would impair a constitutionally protected "fundamental right", it begs the question to suggest, as the majority has, that such a right is necessarily involved whenever the State seeks to regulate conduct pursuant only to its interest in the moral well-being of its citizenry. * * *

The "fundamental" rights recognized in *Griswold*, *Roe* and their progeny are clearly not a product of a belief on the part of the Supreme Court that modern values and changing standards of morality should be incorporated wholesale into the due process clause of the Fourteenth Amendment. To the contrary, the language of the Supreme Court decisions makes clear that the rights which have so far been recognized as part of our due process guarantee are those rights to make certain familial decisions which have been considered sacrosanct and immune from governmental intrusion throughout the history of western civilization. * * *

* * * [T]he fact remains that western man has never been free to pursue his own choice of sexual gratification without fear of State interference. Consequently, it simply cannot be said that such freedom is an integral part of our concept of ordered liberty as embodied in the due process clauses of the Fifth and Fourteenth Amendments.

In view of the continuous and unbroken history of anti-sodomy laws in the United States, the majority's decision to strike down New York's statute prohibiting consensual sodomy can only be regarded as an act of judicial legislation creating a "fundamental right" where none has heretofore existed. As such, today's decision represents a radical departure from cases such as *Griswold* and *Roe*, in which the Supreme Court merely swept aside State laws which impaired or prohibited entirely the free exercise of rights that traditionally had been recognized in western thought as being beyond the reach of government. * * *

NOTE: HOW PRIVATE IS PRIVACY?

One of the problems for the argument that sexuality is appropriately a matter of government concern only when it occurs in the public sphere is that it requires determining the criteria for the boundary between "private" and "public." Note that several of the defendants in the cases consolidated in *Onofre* were having sex in a car or truck parked in downtown Buffalo. Private or public? How would you resolve the following situations?

1. *Soliciting in public for private sex.* State courts have reached conflicting results on whether the law can criminalize public solicitation to engage in private, consensual sexual activity. Oklahoma courts upheld such a law, reasoning that "[p]rotecting citizens from solicitations for sexual acts is a legitimate governmental interest," regardless of whether those acts were criminal. *Sawatzky v. City of Oklahoma City*, 906 P.2d 785, 787 (Okl.Ct. Crim.App.1995), *cert. denied*, 116 S.Ct. 1544 (1996). The arrest resulted from a conversation between the defendant and an undercover police officer. On similar facts, the New York Court of Appeals invalidated New York's statute prohibiting solicitation to engage in consensual sodomy on the ground that the underlying conduct was permissible. *People v. Uplinger*, 447 N.E.2d 62 (N.Y.1983), *cert. dismissed as improvidently granted*, 467 U.S. 246 (1984).

2. *Consensual sex in a private location involving more than two persons.* When is even marital privacy waived? A married couple who invited a third person to join them for sex were later prosecuted for sodomy when photographs of the *ménage à trois* engaged in oral sex came to the attention of their teenage daughter's teacher. The Fourth Circuit upheld their conviction in *Lovisi v. Slayton*, 539 F.2d 349 (4th Cir.)(en banc), *cert. denied sub nom. Lovisi v. Zahradnick*, 429 U.S. 977 (1976), ruling that the couple's right of privacy had been waived by their invitation to the third party.

3. *Sexual acts in a commercial space open to the public, but sequestered except for those who knowingly enter.* Pennsylvania's consensual sodomy statute was ruled unconstitutional in a case involving the prosecution of two erotic dancers who performed oral sex on members of the audience. In *Commonwealth v. Bonadio*, 415 A.2d 47 (Pa.1980), the state supreme court held that the statute amounted to a morals regulation, not properly subject to police power because no one was harmed by the activity. By contrast, the U.S. Supreme Court has upheld a statute used to close an adult bookstore as a nuisance because it was used as the venue for sexual activities. *Arcara v. Cloud Books, Inc.*, 478 U.S. 697 (1986).

———

If you want to hear for yourself the oral argument that preceded the next decision, you can listen via the internet at http:// oyez.at.nwu.edu/oyez.html.

Michael J. Bowers v. Michael Hardwick et al.

United States Supreme Court, 1986.
478 U.S. 186, 106 S.Ct. 2841, 92 L.Ed.2d 140.

■ JUSTICE WHITE delivered the opinion of the Court.

In August 1982, respondent [Hardwick] was charged with violating the Georgia statute criminalizing sodomy[1] by committing that act with another adult male in the bedroom of respondent's home.[a] After a preliminary hearing, the District Attorney decided not to present the matter to the grand jury unless further evidence developed.

Respondent then brought suit in the Federal District Court, challenging the constitutionality of the statute insofar as it criminalized consensual sodomy. He asserted that he was a practicing homosexual, that the Georgia sodomy statute, as administered by the defendants, placed him in imminent danger of arrest, and that the statute for several reasons violates the Federal Constitution. The District Court granted the defendants' motion to dismiss for failure to state a claim * * *. [The Eleventh Circuit Court of Appeals reversed, and the Supreme Court reversed it in turn and reinstated the District Court judgment.]

This case does not require a judgment on whether laws against sodomy between consenting adults in general, or between homosexuals in particular, are wise or desirable. It raises no question about the right or propriety of state legislative decisions to repeal their laws that criminalize homosexual sodomy, or of state-court decisions invalidating those laws on state constitutional grounds. The issue presented is whether the Federal Constitution confers a fundamental right upon homosexuals to engage in sodomy and hence invalidates the laws of the many States that still make such conduct illegal and have done so for a very long time. The case also calls for some judgment about the limits of the Court's role in carrying out its constitutional mandate.

We first register our disagreement with the Court of Appeals and with respondent that the Court's prior cases have construed the Constitution to confer a right of privacy that extends to homosexual sodomy and for all intents and purposes have decided this case. The reach of this line of cases was sketched in *Carey v. Population Services International. Pierce* and *Meyer* were described as dealing with child rearing and education; *Prince*, with family relationships; *Skinner* with procreation; *Loving* with marriage; *Griswold* and *Eisenstadt* with contraception; and *Roe v. Wade* with abortion. The latter three cases were interpreted as construing the Due Process Clause of the Fourteenth Amendment to confer a fundamental individual right to decide whether or not to beget or bear a child.

---

1. Georgia Code Ann. § 16–6–2 (1984) provides, in pertinent part, as follows:

"(a) A person commits the offense of sodomy when he performs or submits to any sexual act involving the sex organs of one person and the mouth or anus of another. . . .

"(b) A person convicted of the offense of sodomy shall be punished by imprisonment for not less than one nor more than 20 years. . . ."

a. [Eds.] Michael Hardwick later told an interviewer that the police had come to his home to serve an expired arrest warrant, issued for drinking in public, by a police officer who saw him leaving a gay bar. Hardwick strongly suspected that this incident, and an unexplained physical assault shortly before his arrest, were engineered by police wanting to harass him for being gay. Peter Irons, "What Are You Doing in My Bedroom?," in *The Courage of Their Convictions* 392 (1988).

right to privacy doesn't extend to sodomy homosexual activity

Accepting the decisions in these cases and the above description of them, we think it evident that none of the rights announced in those cases bears any resemblance to the claimed constitutional right of homosexuals to engage in acts of sodomy that is asserted in this case. No connection between family, marriage, or procreation on the one hand and homosexual activity on the other has been demonstrated, either by the Court of Appeals or by respondent. Moreover, any claim that these cases nevertheless stand for the proposition that any kind of private sexual conduct between consenting adults is constitutionally insulated from state proscription is unsupportable. Indeed, the Court's opinion in *Carey* twice asserted that the privacy right, which the *Griswold* line of cases found to be one of the protections provided by the Due Process Clause, did not reach so far.

Precedent aside, however, respondent would have us announce, as the Court of Appeals did, a fundamental right to engage in homosexual sodomy. This we are quite unwilling to do. It is true that despite the language of the Due Process Clauses of the Fifth and Fourteenth Amendments, which appears to focus only on the processes by which life, liberty, or property is taken, the cases are legion in which those Clauses have been interpreted to have substantive content, subsuming rights that to a great extent are immune from federal or state regulation or proscription. Among such cases are those recognizing rights that have little or no textual support in the constitutional language. *Meyer*, *Prince*, and *Pierce* fall in this category, as do the privacy cases from *Griswold* to *Carey*.

Striving to assure itself and the public that announcing rights not readily identifiable in the Constitution's text involves much more than the imposition of the Justices' own choice of values on the States and the Federal Government, the Court has sought to identify the nature of the rights qualifying for heightened judicial protection. In *Palko v. Connecticut* it was said that this category includes those fundamental liberties that are "implicit in the concept of ordered liberty," such that "neither liberty nor justice would exist if [they] were sacrificed." A different description of fundamental liberties appeared in *Moore v. East Cleveland*, 431 U.S. 494, 503 (1977) (opinion of Powell, J.) where they are characterized as those liberties that are "deeply rooted in this Nation's history and tradition." *Id.* at 503.

It is obvious to us that neither of these formulations would extend a fundamental right to homosexuals to engage in acts of consensual sodomy. Proscriptions against that conduct have ancient roots. Sodomy was a criminal offense at common law and was forbidden by the laws of the original 13 States when they ratified the Bill of Rights. In 1868, when the Fourteenth Amendment was ratified, all but 5 of the 37 States in the Union had criminal sodomy laws. In fact, until 1961, all 50 States outlawed sodomy, and today, 24 States and the District of Columbia continue to provide criminal penalties for sodomy performed in private and between consenting adults. Against this background, to claim that a right to engage in such conduct is "deeply rooted in this Nation's history and tradition" or "implicit in the concept of ordered liberty" is, at best, facetious.

Nor are we inclined to take a more expansive view of our authority to discover new fundamental rights imbedded in the Due Process Clause. The Court is most vulnerable and comes nearest to illegitimacy when it deals with judge-made constitutional law having little or no cognizable roots in the language or design of the Constitution. That this is so was painfully demonstrated by the face-off between the Executive and the Court in the 1930s, which resulted in the repudiation of much of the substantive gloss that the Court had placed on the Due Process Clauses of the Fifth and Fourteenth Amendments. There should be, therefore, great resistance to expand the substantive reach of those Clauses, particularly if it requires redefining the category of rights deemed to be fundamental. Otherwise, the Judiciary necessarily takes to itself further authority to govern the country without express constitutional authority. The claimed right pressed on us today falls far short of overcoming this resistance.

Respondent, however, asserts that the result should be different where the homosexual conduct occurs in the privacy of the home. He relies on *Stanley*, where the Court held that the First Amendment prevents conviction for possessing and reading obscene material in the privacy of one's home: "If the First Amendment means anything, it means that a State has no business telling a man, sitting alone in his house, what books he may read or what films he may watch."

Stanley = 1st Amend. - not applicable to Hardwick

Stanley did protect conduct that would not have been protected outside the home, and it partially prevented the enforcement of state obscenity laws; but the decision was firmly grounded in the First Amendment. The right pressed upon us here has no similar support in the text of the Constitution, and it does not qualify for recognition under the prevailing principles for construing the Fourteenth Amendment. Its limits are also difficult to discern. Plainly enough, otherwise illegal conduct is not always immunized whenever it occurs in the home. Victimless crimes, such as the possession and use of illegal drugs, do not escape the law where they are committed at home. *Stanley* itself recognized that its holding offered no protection for the possession in the home of drugs, firearms, or stolen goods. And if respondent's submission is limited to the voluntary sexual conduct between consenting adults, it would be difficult, except by fiat, to limit the claimed right to homosexual conduct while leaving exposed to prosecution adultery, incest, and other sexual crimes even though they are committed in the home. We are unwilling to start down that road.

Even if the conduct at issue here is not a fundamental right, respondent asserts that there must be a rational basis for the law and that there is none in this case other than the presumed belief of a majority of the electorate in Georgia that homosexual sodomy is immoral and unacceptable. This is said to be an inadequate rationale to support the law. The law, however, is constantly based on notions of morality, and if all laws representing essentially moral choices are to be invalidated under the Due Process Clause, the courts will be very busy indeed. Even respondent makes no such claim, but insists that majority sentiments about the morality of homosexuality should be declared inadequate. We do not agree, and are unpersuaded that the sodomy laws of some 25 States should be invalidated on this basis.[8] * * *

■ CHIEF JUSTICE BURGER, concurring. * * *

As the Court notes, the proscriptions against sodomy have very "ancient roots." Decisions of individuals relating to homosexual conduct have been subject to state intervention throughout the history of Western Civilization. Condemnation of these practices is firmly rooted in Judeo–Christian moral and ethical standards. Homosexual sodomy was a capital crime under Roman law. During the English Reformation when powers of the ecclesiastical courts were transferred to the King's Courts, the first English statute criminalizing sodomy was passed. Blackstone described "the infamous crime against nature" as an offense of "deeper malignity" than rape, an heinous act "the very mention of which is a disgrace to human nature," and "a crime not fit to be named." The common law of England, including its prohibition of sodomy, became the received law of Georgia and the other Colonies. In 1816 the Georgia Legislature passed the statute at issue here, and that statute has been continuously in force in one form or another since that time. To hold that the act of homosexual sodomy is somehow protected as a fundamental right would be to cast aside millennia of moral teaching. * * *

■ JUSTICE POWELL, concurring.

I join the opinion of the Court. I agree with the Court that there is no fundamental right—i.e., no substantive right under the Due Process Clause—such as that claimed by respondent, and found to exist by the Court of Appeals. This is not to suggest, however, that respondent may not be protected by the Eighth Amendment of the Constitution. The Georgia statute at issue in this case authorizes a court to imprison a person for up to 20 years for a single private, consensual act of sodomy. In my view, a prison sentence for such conduct—certainly a sentence of long duration—would create a serious Eighth Amendment issue. Under the Georgia statute a single act of sodomy, even in the private setting of a home, is a felony comparable in terms of the possible sentence imposed to serious felonies such as aggravated battery, first-degree arson, and robbery.

In this case, however, respondent has not been tried, much less convicted and sentenced. Moreover, respondent has not raised the Eighth Amendment issue below. For these reasons this constitutional argument is not before us.

■ JUSTICE BLACKMUN, with whom JUSTICE BRENNAN, JUSTICE MARSHALL, and JUSTICE STEVENS join, dissenting.

This case is no more about "a fundamental right to engage in homosexual sodomy," as the Court purports to declare, than *Stanley* was about a fundamental right to watch obscene movies, or *Katz v. United States* was about a fundamental right to place interstate bets from a telephone booth.

---

8. Respondent does not defend the judgment below based on the Ninth Amendment, the Equal Protection Clause or the Eighth Amendment.

Rather, this case is about "the most comprehensive of rights and the right most valued by civilized men," namely, "the right to be let alone." *Olmstead* (Brandeis, J., dissenting). * * *

* * * I believe we must analyze respondent's claim in the light of the values that underlie the constitutional right to privacy. If that right means anything, it means that, before Georgia can prosecute its citizens for making choices about the most intimate aspects of their lives, it must do more than assert that the choice they have made is an "'abominable crime not fit to be named among Christians.'" *Herring v. State*, 46 S.E. 876, 882 (Ga.1904). * * *

[T]he Court's almost obsessive focus on homosexual activity is particularly hard to justify in light of the broad language Georgia has used. Unlike the Court, the Georgia Legislature has not proceeded on the assumption that homosexuals are so different from other citizens that their lives may be controlled in a way that would not be tolerated if it limited the choices of those other citizens. The sex or status of the persons who engage in the act is irrelevant as a matter of state law. * * * I therefore see no basis for the Court's decision to treat this case as an "as applied" challenge to § 16–6–2, or for Georgia's attempt, both in its brief and at oral argument, to defend § 16–6–2 solely on the grounds that it prohibits homosexual activity. * * *

* * * I disagree with the Court's refusal to consider whether § 16–6–2 runs afoul of the Eighth or Ninth Amendments or the Equal Protection Clause of the Fourteenth Amendment. * * * I believe that Hardwick has stated a cognizable claim that § 16–6–2 interferes with constitutionally protected interests in privacy and freedom of intimate association. But neither the Eighth Amendment nor the Equal Protection Clause is so clearly irrelevant that a claim resting on either provision should be peremptorily dismissed.[2] * * *

The Court concludes today that none of our prior cases dealing with various decisions that individuals are entitled to make free of governmental interference "bears any resemblance to the claimed constitutional right of homosexuals to engage in acts of sodomy that it asserted in this case." While it is true that these cases may be characterized by their connection to protection of the family, the Court's conclusion that they extend no further than this boundary ignores the warning in *Moore v. East Cleveland*, against "clos[ing] our eyes to the basic reasons why certain rights associated with the family have been accorded shelter under the Fourteenth

---

2. * * * With respect to the Equal Protection Clause's applicability to § 16–6–2, I note that Georgia's exclusive stress before this Court on its interest in prosecuting homosexual activity despite the gender-neutral terms of the statute may raise serious questions of discriminatory enforcement, questions that cannot be disposed of before this Court on a motion to dismiss. See *Yick Wo v. Hopkins*, 118 U.S. 356, 373–74 (1886). The legislature having decided that the sex of the participants is irrelevant to the legality of the acts, I do not see why the State can defend § 16–6–2 on the ground that individuals singled out for prosecution are of the same sex as their partners. Thus, under the circumstances of this case, a claim under the Equal Protection Clause may well be available without having to reach the more controversial question whether homosexuals are a suspect class. * * *

Amendment's Due Process Clause." We protect those rights not because they contribute, in some direct and material way, to the general public welfare, but because they form so central a part of an individual's life. "[T]he concept of privacy embodies the 'moral fact that a person belongs to himself and not others nor to society as whole.'" *Thornburgh v. American College of Obstetricians & Gynecologists* 476 U.S. 747, 777 n. 5 (1986) (Stevens, J., concurring), quoting Fried, "Correspondence," 6 *Phil. & Pub. Affairs* 288–289 (1977). And so we protect the decision whether to marry precisely because marriage "is an association that promotes a way of life, not causes; a harmony in living, not political faiths; a bilateral loyalty, not commercial or social projects." *Griswold.* We protect the decision whether to have a child because parenthood alters so dramatically an individual's self-definition, not because of demographic considerations or the Bible's command to be fruitful and multiply. And we protect the family because it contributes so powerfully to the happiness of individuals, not because of a preference for stereotypical households. The Court recognized in *Roberts [v. United States Jaycees,* 468 U.S. 609, 619 (1984)] that the "ability independently to define one's identity that is central to any concept of liberty" cannot truly be exercised in a vacuum; we all depend on the "emotional enrichment from close ties with others."

Only the most willful blindness could obscure the fact that sexual intimacy is "a sensitive, key relationship of human existence, central to family life, community welfare, and the development of human personality," *Paris Adult Theatre I v. Slaton,* 413 U.S. 49, 63 (1973). The fact that individuals define themselves in a significant way through their intimate sexual relationships with others suggests, in a Nation as diverse as ours, that there may be many "right" ways of conducting those relationships, and that much of the richness of a relationship will come from the freedom an individual has to *choose* the form and nature of these intensely personal bonds. See Karst, "The Freedom of Intimate Association," 89 *Yale L.J.* 624, 637 (1980). * * *

The central place that *Stanley* gives Justice Brandeis' dissent in *Olmstead,* a case raising *no* First Amendment claim, shows that *Stanley* rested as much on the Court's understanding of the Fourth Amendment as it did on the First. Indeed, in *Paris Adult Theatre I v. Slaton,* the Court suggested that reliance on the Fourth Amendment not only supported the Court's outcome in *Stanley* but actually was *necessary* to it: "If obscene material unprotected by the First Amendment in itself carried with it a 'penumbra' of constitutionally protected privacy, this Court would not have found it necessary to decide *Stanley* on the narrow basis of the 'privacy of the home,' which was hardly more than a reaffirmation that 'a man's home is his castle.'" *Id.,* 413 U.S. at 66. "The right of the people to be secure in their ... houses," expressly guaranteed by the Fourth Amendment, is perhaps the most "textual" of the various constitutional provisions that inform our understanding of the right to privacy, and thus I cannot agree with the Court's statement that "[t]he right pressed upon us here has no ... support in the text of the Constitution." Indeed, the right of an individual to conduct intimate relationships in the intimacy of his or her own home seems to me to be the heart of the Constitution's protection of privacy.

The Court's failure to comprehend the magnitude of the liberty interests at stake in this case leads it to slight the question whether petitioner, on behalf of the State, has justified Georgia's infringement on these interests. I believe that neither of the two general justifications for § 16–6–2 that petitioner has advanced warrants dismissing respondent's challenge for failure to state a claim.

First, petitioner asserts that the acts made criminal by the statute may have serious adverse consequences for "the general public health and welfare," such as spreading communicable diseases or fostering other criminal activity. Inasmuch as this case was dismissed by the District Court on the pleadings, it is not surprising that the record before us is barren of any evidence to support petitioner's claim. In light of the state of the record, I see no justification for the Court's attempt to equate the private, consensual sexual activity at issue here with the "possession in the home of drugs, firearms, or stolen goods," to which *Stanley* refused to extend its protection. None of the behavior so mentioned in *Stanley* can properly be viewed as "[v]ictimless": drugs and weapons are inherently dangerous, and for property to be "stolen," someone must have been wrongfully deprived of it. Nothing in the record before the Court provides any justification for finding the activity forbidden by § 16–6–2 to be physically dangerous, either to the persons engaged in it or to others.[4] * * *

The core of petitioner's defense of § 16–6–2, however, is that respondent and others who engage in the conduct prohibited by § 16–6–2 interfere with Georgia's exercise of the " 'right of the Nation and of the States to maintain a decent society,' " *Paris Adult Theatre I v. Slaton*, 413 U.S. at 59–60. Essentially, petitioner argues, and the Court agrees, that the fact that the acts described in § 16–6–2 "for hundreds of years, if not thousands, have been uniformly condemned as immoral" is a sufficient reason to permit a State to ban them today.

I cannot agree that either the length of time a majority has held its convictions or the passions with which it defends them can withdraw legislation from this Court's scrutiny. *Roe v. Wade*; *Loving v. Virginia*;

---

4. Although I do not think it necessary to decide today issues that are not even remotely before us, it does seem to me that a court could find simple, analytically sound distinctions between certain private, consensual sexual conduct, on the one hand, and adultery and incest (the only two vaguely specific "sexual crimes" to which the majority points), on the other. * * * [A] State might conclude that adultery is likely to injure third persons, in particular, spouses and children of persons who engage in extramari- tal affairs. With respect to incest, a court might well agree with respondent that the nature of familial relationships renders true consent to incestuous activity sufficiently problematical that a blanket prohibition of such activity is warranted. Notably, the Court makes no effort to explain why it has chosen to group private, consensual homosexual activity with adultery and incest rather than with private, consensual heterosexual activity by unmarried persons or, indeed, with oral or anal sex within marriage.

Brown v. Board of Education.[5] As Justice Jackson wrote so eloquently for the Court in *West Virginia Board of Education v. Barnette*, 319 U.S. 624, 641–42 (1943), "we apply the limitations of the Constitution with no fear that freedom to be intellectually and spiritually diverse or even contrary will disintegrate the social organization.... [F]reedom to differ is not limited to things that do not matter much. That would be a mere shadow of freedom. The test of its substance is the right to differ as to things that touch the heart of the existing order." It is precisely because the issue raised by this case touches the heart of what makes individuals what they are that we should be especially sensitive to the rights of those whose choices upset the majority. * * *

■ JUSTICE STEVENS, with whom JUSTICE BRENNAN and JUSTICE MARSHALL join, dissenting.

[This separate dissenting opinion argued, first, that Georgia's sodomy law, like most others, reached—and intended to reach—heterosexual as well as homosexual sodomy. Second, the law as broadly written criminalized some conduct that is clearly protected by the right of privacy. Even the state conceded that its sodomy law could not be constitutionally applied to private oral sex between a husband and wife. Third, since the law could not be constitutionally enforced as it was written, the state had the burden of justifying a selective application of the law, namely, against homosexuals.] Either the persons to whom Georgia seeks to apply its statute do not have the same interest in "liberty" that others have, or there must be a reason why the State may be permitted to apply a generally applicable law to certain persons that it does not apply to others.

The first possibility is plainly unacceptable. Although the meaning of the principle that "all men are created equal" is not always clear, it surely must mean that every free citizen has the same interest in "liberty" that the members of the majority share. From the standpoint of the individual, the homosexual and the heterosexual have the same interest in deciding how he will live his own life, and, more narrowly, how he will conduct himself in his personal and voluntary associations with his companions. State intrusion into the private conduct of either is equally burdensome.

---

5. The parallel between *Loving* and this case is almost uncanny. There, too, the State relied on a religious justification for its law. Compare 388 U.S., at 3 (quoting trial court's statement that "Almighty God created the races white, black, yellow, malay and red, and he placed them on separate continents.... The fact that he separated the races shows that he did not intend for the races to mix"), with Brief for Petitioner 20–21 (relying on the Old and New Testaments and the writings of St. Thomas Aquinas to show that "traditional Judeo–Christian values proscribe such conduct"). There, too, defenders of the challenged statute relied heavily on the fact that when the Fourteenth Amendment was ratified, most of the States had similar prohibitions. There, too, at the time the case came before the Court, many of the States still had criminal statutes concerning the conduct at issue. Yet the Court held, not only that the invidious racism of Virginia's law violated the Equal Protection Clause, but also that the law deprived the Lovings of due process by denying them the "freedom of choice to marry" that had "long been recognized as one of the vital personal rights essential to the orderly pursuit of happiness by free men."

The second possibility is similarly unacceptable. A policy of selective application must be supported by a neutral and legitimate interest— something more substantial than a habitual dislike for, or ignorance about, the disfavored group. Neither the State nor the Court has identified any such interest in this case. The Court has posited as a justification for the Georgia statute "the presumed belief of a majority of the electorate in Georgia that homosexual sodomy is immoral and unacceptable." But the Georgia electorate has expressed no such belief—instead, its representatives enacted a law that presumably reflects the belief that *all sodomy* is immoral and unacceptable. Unless the Court is prepared to conclude that such a law is constitutional, it may not rely on the work product of the Georgia Legislature to support its holding. For the Georgia statute does not single out homosexuals as a separate class meriting special disfavored treatment. * * *

NOTES ON *HARDWICK, ONOFRE,* AND THE RIGHT TO ENGAGE IN CONSENSUAL SODOMY

1. *Comparing* Hardwick *and* Onofre.   Consider two threshold points in reading *Hardwick* and *Onofre*.   First, what is the difference in substance between the two statutes before the courts? Answer: none—both prohibit oral and anal sex between any two persons.   Second, who were the plaintiffs in the two cases?   *Onofre* was actually three consolidated cases; two involved semi-public settings and one involved an accusation of heterosexual oral sex.   *Hardwick* began as a challenge by both Michael Hardwick and a married couple, but the latter were dismissed in the lower courts for lack of standing, a ruling that paved the way for the homosexuality-obsessed majority opinion.   How did the cast of characters affect the judicial response?

[handwritten margin note: Hardwick — homosexually based]

Next, develop a chart for the five major opinions in the two cases: the majority and dissent in *Onofre* and the majority and the two dissenting opinions in *Hardwick*.   Analyze each with regard to its doctrine, interpretation of precedent, proposed limiting principles on privacy (if any), and analysis of the proper role of morality in the law.   How does the dissent in *Onofre* compare to the opinion of the Court in *Hardwick?*   What is the difference between the two dissents in *Hardwick?*

2. *Judicial Discomfort and Justice Powell.* Justice Powell's original vote was reportedly with Justice Blackmun, which would have meant five votes to invalidate the Georgia statute, but Justice Powell changed his mind.[i] John Calvin Jeffries, Jr., Powell's biographer, writes that Powell agonized over his decision in the case and was aware of his ignorance about homosexuality. Jeffries, *Lewis F. Powell, Jr.* 313–30 (1993). At one point he engaged in a discussion of the matter with the "liberal" law clerk in his

i. Al Kamen, "Powell Changed Vote in Sodomy Case," *Wash. Post,* July 13 1986 at A1. In 1990, he told a student questioner at the NYU School of Law that he "probably made a mistake" in his vote in *Hardwick.* Ruth Marcus, "Powell Regrets Backing Sodomy Law," *Wash. Post,* Oct. 26, 1990, at A3.

chambers that term. The clerk tried to explain to the Justice that "homo-sexuals" are normal human beings who are part of the everyday environ-ment of virtually everyone. Justice Powell apparently found it hard to understand how this could be and confessed to the clerk that he had never met a "homosexual" that he knew of. The clerk, who was gay, bit his tongue.

3. *State Grounds for Sodomy Law Challenges.* In the aftermath of *Hard-wick*, litigators have sought to invalidate sodomy statutes on state constitu-tional grounds. In *Commonwealth of Kentucky v. Wasson*, 842 S.W.2d 487 (Ky.1992), a narrowly divided Kentucky Supreme Court ruled that its same-sex-only sodomy law violated the privacy guarantee of the state constitution, relying on a line of Kentucky constitutional case law establish-ing protection from surveillance for illegal alcohol (*id.* at 495–96):

> At the time *Campbell* [a decision striking down a law criminalizing the possession of intoxicating liquor] was decided, the use of alcohol was as much an incendiary moral issue as deviate sexual behavior in private between consenting adults is today. * * * The clear implication is that immorality in private which "does not operate to the detriment of others" is placed beyond the reach of state action by the guarantees of the Kentucky Constitution.

More remarkably, the court found that the sodomy law violated the equal protection guarantee of the Kentucky Constitution (*id.* at 501–02):

> To be treated equally by the law is a broader constitutional value than due process of law as discussed in the [*Hardwick*] case. We recognize it as such under the Kentucky Constitution, without regard to whether the United States Supreme Court continues to do so in federal consti-tutional jurisprudence. "Equal Justice Under Law" inscribed above the entrance to the United States Supreme Court, expresses the unique goal to which all humanity aspires. In Kentucky it is more than a mere aspiration. It is part of the "inherent and inalienable" rights protected by our Kentucky Constitution. Our protection against exercise of "arbitrary power over the . . . liberty . . . of freemen" by the General Assembly and our guarantee that all persons are entitled to "equal" treatment forbid a special act punishing the sexual preference of homosexuals. It matters not that the same act committed by persons of the same sex is more offensive to the majority because Section Two states such "power . . . exists nowhere in a republic, not even in the largest majority."

> The purpose of the present statute is not to protect the marital relationship against sexual activity outside of marriage, but only to punish one aspect of it while other activities similarly destructive of the marital relationship, if not more so, go unpunished. Sexual prefer-ence, and not the act committed, determines criminality, and is being punished. Simply because the majority, speaking through the General Assembly, finds one type of extramarital intercourse more offensive than another, does not provide a rational basis for criminalizing the sexual preference of homosexuals.

The Tennessee same-sex-only sodomy statute was found to violate that state's constitutional guarantee of privacy in *Campbell v. Sundquist*, 926 S.W.2d 250 (Tenn.App.1996). State constitutional arguments were also successful at the intermediate appellate level in challenging the Texas sodomy law in *City of Dallas v. England*, 846 S.W.2d 957 (Tex.App.1993) and *State v. Morales*, 826 S.W.2d 201 (Tex.App.1992), *reversed on other grounds*, 869 S.W.2d 941 (Tex.1994). On the other hand, two courts have ruled that their state constitution's protection of privacy extends no further than the federal right determined in *Hardwick*. *Christensen v. State*, 468 S.E.2d 188 (Ga.1996); *State v. Walsh*, 713 S.W.2d 508 (Mo.1986).

4. *Sodomy Laws as Applied to Heterosexual Conduct.* Given the gay-specific language of the Court in *Hardwick*, would the same result obtain if two (unmarried) heterosexuals engaged in oral or anal sex? Two state courts have ruled that gender-neutral sodomy laws do not apply to hetero-sexual sodomy. In *Schochet v. State*, 580 A.2d 176 (Md.1990), Maryland's highest court construed the statute—despite the absence of any limiting language in the statutory text—not to reach consensual, noncommercial, heterosexual activity between adults in private. In *Post v. State*, 715 P.2d 1105 (Okl.Crim.App.), *cert. denied,* 479 U.S. 890 (1986), the Oklahoma court in a pre-*Hardwick* decision invalidated the statute as applied to heterosexual acts using federal constitutional grounds; acting after its decision in *Hardwick*, the Supreme Court denied review without comment.

5. *Adultery and Fornication Laws.* No statute criminalizing adultery has been found unconstitutional as a violation of privacy rights. *See, e.g., Commonwealth v. Stowell*, 449 N.E.2d 357 (Mass.1983) (holding that the harmful impact of adultery on the marital relationship justified state prohibition). The Texas Supreme Court, relying heavily on *Hardwick*, ruled that denial of promotion to a police officer because he was engaged in adultery did not violate his right of privacy, even though adultery had been decriminalized. *City of Sherman v. Henry*, 928 S.W.2d 464 (Tex.1996). The record as to fornication laws, prohibiting sex when both partners are unmarried, is mixed. A challenge to the Virginia statute failed on standing grounds, because the court found no prospect of enforcement. *Doe v. Duling*, 782 F.2d 1202 (4th Cir.1986). The New Jersey Supreme Court, relying in part on state constitutional grounds, became the only court of last resort to invalidate a fornication statute on privacy grounds in *State v. Saunders*, 381 A.2d 333 (N.J.1977).

6. *Outside the United States.* The European Court of Human Rights has held that the right of privacy in the European Convention protects consensual homosexual sodomy, and an international tribunal reached the same result interpreting a human rights treaty which the U.S. has signed and ratified. These developments occurred after *Bowers v. Hardwick*. Do they provide a basis for overruling that decision? See Chapter 8, Section 3.

PROBLEM 1–2

THE ROLE OF MORALITY

What should the appropriate role of morality be in enacting legislation? Why shouldn't sincerely and widely held moral beliefs form the basis for a legitimate state interest? It is fine to argue that homosexuality causes no harm to others, but many Americans genuinely believe that it does cause serious social harm. Because so much discussion of morality in the law has centered on sexuality-related issues, it may be helpful to consider the problem in a different context.

Legislators in the State of Nature enact a statute prohibiting the consumption of meat within the state. The legislative history establishes that the law is intended to reflect the beliefs of Nature residents that killing animals for food consumption is repugnant to their moral beliefs. The American Carnivore Libertarian Union challenges the new statute as unconstitutional. What result? Can *Bowers v. Hardwick* be distinguished?

For two analyses that accept the validity of a concern with moral issues in legislating, but nonetheless favor decriminalization of sodomy, see the Sandel excerpt which follows and Chai R. Feldblum, "Sexual Orientation, Morality, and the Law: Devlin Revisited," 57 *U.Pitt.L.Rev.* 237 (1996).

ACADEMIC REFLECTIONS ON *HARDWICK*

Anne B. Goldstein, History, Homosexuality, and Political Values: Searching for the Hidden Determinants of *Bowers v. Hardwick*, 97 *Yale Law Journal* 1073, 1086–89 (1988).* The Court's opinion is bad history. "The majority bolstered its inferences about the framers' intentions with the claim that '[p]roscriptions against [homosexual sodomy] have ancient roots.' Although literally true, the statement is misleading in two ways. First, it oversimplifies and distorts a complex historical record; second, it misuses the relatively modern concept of 'homosexuality' to depict the past.

"Over the course of Western history, sexual practices between men, like other sexual practices, have been tolerated as well as condemned. In classical Greece and Rome, sexual practices between men were not uniformly condemned, and some were widely accepted; under Roman rule, even marriage between men was possible until at least 342 A.D. Sexual acts between men were also openly tolerated by both church and state during the early Middle Ages, and among the male social elite in eighteenth-century France. By ignoring ancient tolerance to focus selectively on ancient proscriptions, the majority distorted the historical record. This distortion enabled the majority to present its choice of proscription over tolerance as if it were merely fidelity to 'ancient roots,' and conformity with laws in force 'throughout the history of Western Civilization.'

"* * * All of the Justices seem to have assumed that 'homosexuality' has been an invariant reality, outside of history. In fact, however, like most ways of describing aspects of the human condition, 'homosexuality' is a cultural and historical artifact. No attitude toward 'homosexuals' or 'homosexuality' can really be identified before the mid-nineteenth century because the concept did not exist until then. Before the late 1800s, sexuality—whether tolerated or condemned—was something a person did, not what he or she was. Although both the behavior and the desires we now call 'homosexual' existed in earlier eras, our currently common assumption that persons who make love with others of their own sex are fundamentally different from the rest of humanity is only about one hundred years old.

"Even the word 'homosexual' is new. It was coined in the nineteenth century to express the new idea that a person's immanent and essential nature is revealed by the gender of his desired sex partner. The concept emerged around the time that sexuality began to seem a proper object of medical, as distinguished from clerical or judicial, concern. Before the invention of 'homosexuality,' sexual touchings between men were determined to be licit or illicit according to criteria that applied equally to heterosexual practices, such as the parts of the body involved, the relative status of the parties, and whether the sexual drama conformed to sex role stereotypes. Although illicit sexual acts were seen as sinful, immoral, criminal, or all three, before the 1870s illicit sexual acts between men were not seen as fundamentally different from, or necessarily worse than, illicit acts between a man and a woman.

"Thus, by referring to 'homosexual sodomy' in ancient times, in 1791, and even in 1868, White and Burger were inserting their modern understanding of 'homosexuality' anachronistically into systems of values organized on other principles, obscuring the relative novelty of the distinction between 'homosexuality' and 'heterosexuality' with a myth about its antiquity. * * *"

Goldstein also demonstrates that the "sodomy" Michael Hardwick was convicted of—oral sex—was not considered "sodomy" until the late nineteenth and early twentieth centuries (decades after the Fourteenth Amendment was ratified). In 1817, the English courts held that oral sex was not sodomy under the common law and its statutory complement; only anal sex was sodomy. Parliament created a new crime, "gross indecency" in 1885 to cover oral sex (it was this statute and not the sodomy law for which Oscar Wilde was convicted in 1895). Most American jurisdictions followed suit between 1885 and 1930, usually by new statutory enactments broadening state law beyond "sodomy" to include oral sex and other "perversions." Sometimes state courts expanded state statutes without legislative amendments, but this was exceptional.

Janet E. Halley, Reasoning About Sodomy: Act and Identity in and After Bowers v. Hardwick, 79 *Virginia Law Review* **1721, 1739–40, 1746–49, 1768–70, 1772 (1993).*** The Court's opinion creates a double bind that exploits the ambiguity of homosexuality and sodomy. "In the first volume of his *History of Sexuality*, Foucault claimed that the late nineteenth century saw 'a new specification of individuals':

As defined by the ancient civil or canonical codes, sodomy was a category of forbidden acts; their perpetrator was nothing more than the juridical subject of them. The nineteenth-century homosexual became a personage, a past, a case history, and a childhood, in addition to being a type of life, a life form, and a morphology, with an indiscreet anatomy and possibly a mysterious physiology. Nothing that went into his total composition was unaffected by his sexuality. It was everywhere present in him.... It was consubstantial with him, less as a habitual sin than as a singular nature[,] ... [and was] constituted ... less by a type of sexual relations than by a certain quality of sexual sensibility.... The sodomite had been a temporary aberration; the homosexual was now a species.

These celebrated lines do not explain what Foucault thought happened to sodomy after the great nineteenth-century shift from acts to sexualities. One reading, depending on the equation of sodomy with homosexual identity, assumes that sodomy (a regime of acts) was *transformed into* homosexuality (a regime of identities). Wherever this assumption operates, sodomy-the-act is thought to have been subsumed into homosexuality-the-identity; if sodomy nevertheless stubbornly reasserts its importance as a category of acts, the move is to save appearances by absorbing it into the newly invented personage of the homosexual.

"An alternative reading of Foucault's paragraph assumes less, and leaves in place a more complex and more adequate set of analytic categories for understanding the reasoning of sodomy. On this reading, the rhetoric of acts has not been evaporated or transformed; it has merely been displaced, set to one side and made slightly more difficult to discern by the rhetoric of identity. Thus sodomy—even sodomy between two people of the same sex or gender—is not necessarily the equivalent of acts or of identities; it is now unstably available for characterization as a species of act *and/or* as an indicator of sexual-orientation personality. * * *

"* * * As Justice White informed us,

The issue presented is whether the Federal Constitution confers a fundamental right *upon homosexuals* to engage in *sodomy* and hence invalidates the laws of the many States that still make *such conduct* illegal and have done so for a very long time.

What does the 'such' of 'such conduct' refer to? To sodomy generally? Or does it refer to sodomy as inflected by the homosexuals who do it? When Justice White invoked a historical argument to justify rejecting the fundamental rights claim framed in this way, he found that '[p]roscriptions against that conduct have ancient roots'—a conclusion that maintains a binocular vision of its object, hanging in delicate equipoise between act and identity.

"Are 'homosexuals' definitive of 'such conduct' or not? These formulations (and others appearing throughout Justice White's opinion for the majority and Chief Justice Burger's concurring opinion) keep the Court in suspense: it remains ready to answer yes or no. Sodomy can receive its definitive characteristic from the 'homosexuals' who do it, or can stand free of persons and be merely a 'bad act.' The majority Justices have enabled themselves to treat sodomy as a metonym for homosexual personhood—or not, as they wish. The question Justice White sets out to answer is thus apparently single but actually multiple: 'such conduct' represents not a purely act-based categorical system but an unstable hybrid one, in which identity and conduct simultaneously diverge and implicate one another. * * *

"A comparison of the Court's fundamental rights holding with its application of rational basis review reveals the advantages of the majority Justices' labile strategy by exposing the systematic ways in which acts and identities generate incoherence and instability. In his fundamental rights analysis, Justice White (cheered on by Chief Justice Burger) exploited the rhetoric of acts to make plausible his claim that sodomy has been, transhistorically and without surcease, the object of intense social disapprobation. In the rational basis holding, on the other hand, Justice White moved into a rhetoric of identities, holding that Georgia's sodomy statute rationally implements popular condemnation of *homosexuality*. Even within these distinct and opposed arguments, however, the two rhetorics are interlocked: that of acts implies and depends upon, even as it excludes, that of identities—and vice versa. The fundamental rights holding cannot actually constitute a coherent history of sodomy based on acts alone, for the acts that constitute sodomy are too various: Justice White achieves the appearance of coherence here only through persistent, implicit invocations of homosexual identity as the unifying theme of sodomy's prohibition. Conversely, his rational basis claim—that a facially neutral sodomy statute is reasonable because it makes a legitimate popular statement condemning homosexuality—is frontally incoherent. If the rational basis holding and its invocation of identity make sense at all, it is because they confer invisibility and immunity on a certain type of act. Indeed, heterosexual acts of sodomy are so thoroughly detached from the rhetoric of identity that those who do them are not even acknowledged as a class of persons.

"The result of these arrangements is a chiastic relationship shaped like this:

	Primary Rhetoric	Secondary Rhetoric
Fundamental Rights Holding	Acts	Identities
Rational Basis Holding	Identities	Acts

This diagram schematizes a double bind. In everyday language, you are in a double bind when you cannot win because your victorious opponent is willing to be a hypocrite and to 'damn you if you do and damn you if you don't.' More strictly examined, a double bind involves a systematic arrangement of symbolic systems with at least three characteristics. First, two conceptual systems (or "discourses") are matched in their opposition to one another; one is consistently understood to be not only different from but the logical alternative of the other. Second, the preferred discourse actually requires the submerged one to make it work. It is at this point that a naive

deconstructive claim is often made, that the secret inclusion of the nonpre-
ferred discourse as a prerequisite for the smooth operation of the express
one reveals the whole system to be fatally unstable. But third, that very
instability can be the source of suppleness and resilience, because the two
stacked discourses can be flipped: the one that was submerged and denied
can become express, and it in turn can be covertly supported by the one
that was preferred. The master of a double bind always has somewhere to
go. * * *

"It does not always have to be that way. The denied and submerged
element in a double bind provides a point for resistance. Several authors [of
other articles] in this volume recommend that pro-gay analysis directly
address the problem of acts—a focus that suggests a sense that acts must
be evaluated as a potential place from which to articulate the claims of gay
men, lesbians, and bisexuals as oppositional. To be sure, the dominant
group can at any moment make such resistance futile by flipping the
system. And where the dominant group is willing, as were the majority
Justices in *Hardwick*, to keep the paired dynamics of the double bind in
action simultaneously, the danger of such destabilization is perpetually
present, and imposes on the less powerful player a range of strategic
options in which fluidity will always be at least potentially valuable.* * *

"In its fundamental rights holding, the *Hardwick* Court pursues an
act-based approach that both distinguishes itself from and depends upon an
identity-based approach. The identity that does the work is that of the
homosexual, definitionally limited to the sodomy he or she does. In the
Hardwick decision's rational basis holding, a symmetrical but opposite
pattern appears: here, the explicit justification for refusing Michael Hardwick's claim is the rhetoric of identity; a rhetoric of acts actually underlies
that logic; and the implied actor is the *heterosexual sodomite* whose
invisibility is the linchpin of the whole argumentative structure.

"* * * Georgia's sodomy statute is said to arise from and be rationally
justified by 'majority sentiments about the morality of *homosexuality....*'
An attempt to justify a facially neutral sodomy statute by invoking the
immorality of *homosexuality* might be said to lack the minimum indicia of
reasoning. Tracing the interlocked meanings of this construction of acts for
homosexual and heterosexual identity, however, can make this passage
make sense of a grim kind. * * *

"* * * The view that sodomy is a category of acts undifferentiated by
identity, when viewed in light of Georgia's statute criminalizing all such
acts, creates unacceptable consequences for inhabitants of heterosexual
identity as the Court constructs them. *Heterosexual* acts are prohibited by
the Georgia sodomy statute and, notably, by virtually identical statutes in
force when the Justices rendered their decision not only in Washington
D.C., but also in Virginia and in Maryland, where presumably several of the
majority Justices spent their most intimate hours. By reasoning that the
Georgia statute plausibly supports an anti-homosexual morality, the Justices engage in masking their own status as potential sodomites *even if* they
never stray from the class of heterosexuals. Invisibility here is immunity;

and an important part of the rationality of sodomy is to interpellate a reasoning heterosexual who responds to this call—this 'Hey, you there!'—designating him or her as having a legitimate, state-sanctioned interest in seeking and maintaining immunity of this kind.

"As a conceptual matter, criticism of *Hardwick* isolates itself by posing the questions whether the Court's analysis is more fundamentally act-based or identity-based, and whether it can be better refuted from an act- or identity-based position. It is the unstable relationship between act and identity—not the preference of one to the other—that allows the Justices to exploit confusion about what sodomy is in ways that create opportunities for the exercise of homophobic power, and that create in particular the heterosexual subject position from which the opinion's reasoning issues. * * *

"Two benefits emerge from an emphasis on acts, one material and one symbolic. First, it can engage anti-homophobic heterosexuals, providing a place for them in gay, lesbian, bisexual, and queer movements and making possible a range of alliances capable of diversifying *heterosexual* identity by displaying its multiple relationships to sodomy-both cross-sex and same-sex. Second, it forces heterosexual identity to share some of the glaring light that shines, thanks to *Hardwick*'s privacy holding, on the profane homosexual bed, and exposing the immunity which invisibly gives heterosexuality its rationale. These goals are important enough that pro-gay advocates should pursue them even at the expense of a rigid-and, as it happens, also unsafe-loyalty to identities. * * *

Jed Rubenfeld, The Right of Privacy, 102 *Harvard Law Review* 737, 777–800 passim (1989).* The individualistic concept of privacy embedded in *Griswold* and in the *Hardwick* dissents is an imprisoning strategy. "Let us look carefully at personhood's stance on homosexuality. The personhood position, as we have seen, is that homosexual sex should receive constitutional protection because it is so essential to an individual's self-definition—to his identity. * * *

"There is, however, an ambiguity in the idea that homosexual sex is central to the identity of those who engage in it. Is homosexual sex said to be self-definitive simply because it is sex, or especially because it is homosexual sex? In fact, proponents of personhood appear to argue for the second proposition. One reason for this is that the first version of the argument would be quite difficult to sustain. To begin with, it would * * * be required to claim that prostitution, for example, is an exercise of one's constitutional rights. (Personhood could, of course, choose to defend this position.) Moreover, it simply seems implausible to assert that the act of sex on any given occasion is necessarily fundamental in defining the identity of the person engaging in it.

"* * * Prohibiting homosexual sex, personhood can say, violates the right to privacy because homosexual sex is for homosexuals 'expressive of innermost traits of being.' It 'touches the heart of what makes individuals what they are.' * * *

"Without doubt, personhood's arguments for homosexual rights are intended to show and to seek the highest degree of respect for those on behalf of whom they are made. Nevertheless, in the very concept of a homosexual identity there is something potentially disserving—if not disrespectful—to the cause advocated. There is something not altogether liberating. Those who engage in homosexual sex may or may not perceive themselves as bearing a 'homosexual identity.' Their homosexual relations may be a pleasure they take or an intimacy they value without constituting—at least qua homosexual relations—something definitive of their identity. At the heart of personhood's analysis is the reliance upon a sharply demarcated 'homosexual identity' to which a person is immediately consigned at the moment he seeks to engage in homosexual sex. For personhood, that is, homosexual relations are to be protected to the extent that they fundamentally define a species of person that is, by definition, to be strictly distinguished from the heterosexual. Persons may have homosexual sex only because they have elected to define themselves as 'homosexuals'— because homosexuality lies at 'the heart of . . . what they are.' Thus, even as it argues for homosexual rights, personhood becomes yet another turn of the screw that has pinned those who engage in homosexual sex into a fixed identity specified by their difference from 'heterosexuals.' * * *

"To put it another way, the idea of a 'homosexual identity' has its origin in precisely the kind of invidious classification described earlier. Homosexuality is first understood as a central, definitive element of a person's identity only from the viewpoint of its 'deviancy.' Indeed, there is from the outset an imbalance: within its own self-understanding, heterosexuality is merely normality, and the heterosexual must make some further, more particular decisions—pursuing certain kinds of partners or forms of sexual pleasure—before he will be said to have defined his identity according to sexual criteria. To the extent that heterosexuality does understand itself as definitive per se, it does so only in the face of and in contradistinction to a homosexuality already classified as abnormal and grotesque. By contrast, the mere act of being homosexual is seen as definitive in itself precisely because of its supposed abnormality, and it remains categorically definitive regardless of what sort of partners or sexual encounters the homosexual pursues. In defending homosexuality because of its supposedly self-definitive character, personhood reproduces the heterosexual view of homosexuality as a quality that, like some characterological virus, has invaded and fundamentally altered the nucleus of a person's identity.

"* * * Obviously, differences of sexuality, gender, and race exist among us. These are not, however, differences in *identity* until we make them so. Moreover, it is the desire to count oneself 'superior' to another, or even to count oneself 'normal,' that converts such differences into those specified identities in opposition to which we define ourselves. To protect the rights of 'the homosexual' would of course be a victory; doing so, however, because homosexuality is essential to a person's identity is no liberation, but simply the flip side of the same rigidification of sexual identities by which our society simultaneously inculcates sexual roles, normalizes sexual conduct, and vilifies 'faggots.'

"* * * We must reject the personhood thesis, then, not because the concept of 'self-definition' is analytically incoherent, nor because it is too 'individualistic,' but ultimately because it betrays privacy's—if not personhood's own—political aspirations. By conceiving of the conduct that it purports to protect as 'essential to the individual's identity,' personhood inadvertently reintroduces into privacy analysis the very premise of the invidious uses of state power it seeks to overcome.

"Perhaps the example of abortion can best serve to drive this point home. Personhood must defend the right to abortion on the ground that abortion is essential to the woman's self-definition. But underlying the idea that a woman is *defining her identity* by determining not to have a child is the very premise of those institutionalized sexual roles through which the subordination of women has for so long been maintained. Only if it were 'natural' for a woman to want to bear children—and unnatural if she did not—would it make sense to insist that the decision not to have a child at one given moment was centrally definitive of a woman's identity. Those of us who believe that a woman has a right to abort her pregnancy must defend the position on other grounds. The claim that an abortion is a fundamental act of self-definition is nothing other than a corollary to the insistence that motherhood, or at least the desire to be a mother, is the fundamental, inescapable, natural backdrop of womanhood against which every woman is defined.

"Women should be able to abort their pregnancies so that they may *avoid being forced into an identity*, not because they are defining their identities through the decision itself. Resisting an enforced identity is not the same as defining oneself. Therein lies the real flaw of the personhood account of privacy—and therein the core of the alternative view of privacy advanced in what follows.

"* * * Let us briefly revisit the past privacy cases. The purpose of this revisiting is twofold. We must first test the general principles suggested above against the actual decisions in order to assess their fit. In addition, we need to mix these general principles with concrete cases to give them more color and definition. If in the process we settle into some sort of 'reflective equilibrium'—we will have only ourselves to blame.

"* * * *Roe v. Wade* is probably the most important privacy case decided. Let us see whether our analysis can provide an adequate foundation for its result.

"In what way, if any, do laws against abortion effect a standardization? Do they operate in any way to confine, normalize, and functionalize identities? Even if this is so, do anti-abortion laws operate in this way any more than do other laws?

"The answer to these questions is a most emphatic yes. Considered solely in terms of their prohibition, anti-abortion laws are no more 'standardizing' than laws against murder. There can be nothing totalitarian, it might be said, in an injunction against the taking of life or of potential life. Considered, however, in productive rather than proscriptive terms, the picture looks quite different.

"Anti-abortion laws produce motherhood: they take diverse women with every variety of career, life-plan, and so on, and make mothers of them all. To be sure, motherhood is no unitary phenomenon that is experienced alike by all women. Nonetheless, it is difficult to imagine a state-enforced rule whose ramifications within the actual, everyday life of the actor are more far-reaching. For a period of months and quite possibly years, forced motherhood shapes women's occupations and preoccupations in the minutest detail it creates a perceived identity for women and confines them to it; and it gathers up a multiplicity of approaches to the problem of being a woman and reduces them all to the single norm of motherhood.

"The point at which the state is exerting its power in this context is important too, just as it was in *Pierce [v. Society of Sisters]*. Education involves the shaping of minds. If state-controlled education necessarily involves certain dangers, in *Pierce* these dangers were exacerbated precisely because the education at issue there involved minds as yet unshaped. The particular danger of state-controlled elementary education lies in the exertion of power in the *formation* of identity, thereby preceding and preempting resistance.

"Yet power need not be directed at the undeveloped mind to have this effect; it may also do so if directed at the fully-developed body. A person's life and identity may be shaped as forcefully through taking control over her body—as is done, for example, in some military or religious disciplines—as through the attempted control of her mind. Indeed, bodily control may be the more effective medium to the extent that thought cannot, as it were, meet such control head on, as it might when confronted by an idea that it is told to accept. The exertion of power over the body is in this respect comparable to the exertion of power over a child's mind: its effect can be *formative*, shaping identity at a point where intellectual resistance cannot meet it.

"Now, it is quite clear that *Roe v. Wade* had something to do with control over the body; indeed, it has become conventional to interpret *Roe* as resting at least in part on women's right to 'bodily integrity' or to 'control their own bodies.' This supposed right of bodily control, however, has been either poorly articulated or simply misunderstood. The right to control one's body cannot possibly be a right to do as one pleases with it even where the state can rationally identify harms being caused thereby; otherwise common law crimes or torts would be constitutionally immunized. Nor, however, should the bodily control theme in *Roe* be reduced to the woman's interest in deciding whether a certain surgical operation is to be performed upon her. In fact, anti-abortion laws produce a far more affirmative and pronounced bodily intervention: the compulsion to carry a fetus to term, to deliver the baby, and to care for the child in the first years of its life. All of these processes, in their real daily effects, involve without question the most intimate and strenuous exercises of the female body. The woman's body will be subjected to a continuous regimen of diet, exercise, medical examination, and possibly surgical procedures. Her most elemental biological and psychological impulses will be enlisted in the process. In these ways, anti-abortion laws exert power productively over a woman's body and, through the uses to which her body is put, forcefully reshape and redirect her life.

"A further point of similarity between *Pierce* and *Roe* should be noted. The danger of standardization that the Court noted in *Pierce* can in part be understood as the danger of treating individuals as mere instrumentalities of the state, rather than as citizens with independent minds who themselves constitute the state. Instrumentalization and the undermining of independence are also critically implicated in the abortion context. Women forced to bear children are compelled to devote both body and mind to their children. Many will, moreover, be thrown into positions of economic dependency from which it may be difficult ever to escape. Finally, all will be, by the act of reproduction itself, involuntarily drafted into the service of the state, the first requirement of which is the reproduction of its populace.

"Thus it is difficult to imagine a single proscription with a greater capacity to shape lives into singular, normalized, functional molds than the prohibition of abortions. Even if the propensity of anti-abortion laws to exert power over the body and to instrumentalize women is discounted, it remains the case that such laws radically and affirmatively redirect women's lives. Indeed it is difficult to conceive of a particular legal prohibition with a more total effect on the life and future of the one enjoined. It is no exaggeration to say that mandatory childbearing is a totalitarian intervention into a woman's life. With regard to the occupation and direction of lives, the positive ramifications of anti-abortion laws are unparalleled. Roe v. Wade was, in this view, correctly decided.

"* * * Finally, let us reconsider *Bowers v. Hardwick* in our new terms. * * * [L]aws against homosexual sex have an effect that most laws do not. They forceably channel certain individuals—supposing the law is obeyed— into a network of social institutions and relations that will occupy their lives to a substantial degree.

"Most fundamentally, the prohibition against homosexual sex channels individuals' sexual desires into *reproductive* outlets. Although the prohibition does not, like the law against abortions, produce as an imminent consequence compulsory child-bearing, it nonetheless forcibly directs individuals into the pathways of reproductive sexuality, rather than the socially 'unproductive' realm of homosexuality. These pathways are further guided, in our society, into particular institutional orbits, chief among which are the nuclear family and the constellation of practices surrounding a heterosexuality that is defined in conscious contradistinction to homosexuality. Indeed, it is difficult to separate our society's inculcation of a heterosexual identity from the simultaneous inculcation of a dichotomized complementarity of roles to be borne by men and women. Homosexual couples by necessity throw into question the allocation of specific functions—whether professional, personal, or emotional—between the sexes. It is this aspect of the ban on homosexuality—its central role in the maintenance of institutionalized sexual identities and normalized reproductive relations—that have made its affirmative or formative consequences, as well as the reaction against these consequences, so powerful a force in modern society."

Kendall Thomas, Corpus Juris (Hetero)sexualis: Doctrine, Discourse, and Desire in *Bowers v. Hardwick*, 1 *GLQ* 33 (1993).* Justice White's opinion is a rhetorical act of self-created heterosexual identity for the Court, but one whose rhetoric undermines the (hetero)self Justice White is trying to establish. "The decisive moment in the drama of heterosexual identification staged in the text of *Hardwick* occurs in a passage toward the end of the Court's explanation of its decision. Early on in the opinion he wrote for the majority, Justice White suggests that consideration of the issue presented in *Bowers v. Hardwick* will require something more than conventional constitutional analysis. This case, he opines, 'also calls for some judgment about the limits of the Court's role in carrying out its constitutional mandate'. * * * Justice White offers the following remarks about the likely institutional consequences of a judgment in Hardwick's favor.

[We are not] inclined to take a more expansive view of our authority to discover new fundamental rights imbedded in the Due Process Clause. The Court is most vulnerable and comes nearest to illegitimacy when it deals with judge-made constitutional law having little or no cognizable roots in the language or design of the Constitution. That this is so was painfully demonstrated by the face-off between the Executive and the Court in the 1930's, which resulted in the repudiation of much of the substantive gloss that the Court had placed on the Due Process Clauses of the Fourth and Fourteenth Amendments. There should be, therefore, great resistance to expand the substantive reach of those Clauses, particularly if it requires redefining the category of rights deemed to be fundamental. Otherwise, the Judiciary necessarily takes to itself further authority to govern the country without express constitutional authority. The claimed right pressed on us today falls far short of overcoming this resistance.

"This passage confronts us with a complex congeries of conflicting ideas and images. Conceptually speaking, the argument made here is a familiar one; indeed, it approaches orthodoxy. Justice White plainly fears that a decision upholding the 'claimed constitutional right of homosexuals to engage in acts of sodomy that is asserted in this case' would undermine the authority of the Court and erode the fragile foundations of judicial review. White's recollection of the 'face-off between the Executive and the Court in the 1930s' evokes the memory of the humiliations the Court suffered as a result of its 'substantive due process' decisions in *Lochner v. New York* and its progeny. In Justice White's view, judicial invalidation of the statute challenged in *Bowers v. Hardwick* on substantive due process grounds would threaten the delicate balance of power between the states and the federal government in general, and the Supreme Court in particular. Unlike the 1930s Court, Justice White and his colleagues are not 'inclined to take [an] expansive view of [their] authority to discover new fundamental rights imbedded in the Due Process Clause.' To do so, in Justice White's view, would be to render a constitutional judgment that would represent no more than the 'imposition of the Justices' own choice of values on the States'. * * *

"Reading this passage from *Hardwick*, one cannot help but note the brutal forcefulness of the figural strategies Justice White deploys to develop his argument against the claim 'pressed' on the Court by Michael Hardwick. Several points could be made about the 'ideological imagery'[a] in which Justice White's argument unfolds, but I will confine myself to two observations that will lead to my larger thesis. The first feature of this text that commands attention is the striking dissonance between the position of principled judicial self-restraint defended in *Bowers v. Hardwick* and the passionately unrestrained terms in which that defense is conducted. The radical discontinuity between Justice White's prudential narrative about the dangers of substantive due process doctrine and the overheated style (which I'll analyze in a moment) in which that narrative and its supposed lessons are cast seems odd—especially in an opinion which begins with a promise to confine its analytic scope to the narrow issue at hand, namely, 'whether the Federal Constitution confers a fundamental right upon homosexuals to engage in sodomy.' * * *

"A second and equally striking feature of this passage is its curiously apocalyptic tone. Adapting a concept made famous by the historian Richard Hofstadter, we might say that Justice White's language is an exemplary instance of the 'paranoid style' in American constitutional law. Justice White paints an ominous picture of the 'vulnerable' position in which the Court places itself: reliance on substantive due process doctrine to find rights which cannot be directly traced to the language of the Constitution would bring the Court to the brink of institutional 'illegitimacy.' Justice White speaks insistently of the need for vigilant 'resistance' to claims of constitutional right that might lead the Supreme Court to another 'face-off' of the kind it found itself in as a result of *Lochner*, a fight the Justices would almost certainly lose. Hardwick's claim of right 'falls far short' in its effort to 'overcom[e]' the Court's prudent unwillingness to 'start down' a jurisprudential 'road' whose unavoidable, ultimate destination would require judicial invalidation of statutes against 'adultery, incest and other sexual crimes'. In short, to extend the right of privacy to 'homosexual sodomy' would be to start down a primrose path of constitutional principle which can only lead to institutional perdition. The Court leaves little doubt that it is 'unwilling to start down that road.' * * *

a. [Eds.] Jay Feinman & Peter Gabel, "Contract Law as Ideology," in *The Politics of Law: A Progressive Critique* (David Kairys ed. 1990).

"What I am suggesting here is that the rhetorical register of Justice White's argument may be taken as a sign that the claimed right in *Bowers v. Hardwick* (and by extension, the individual in whose name that right has been asserted) provokes fears on the part of the Supreme Court which go far beyond the perceived threat to its judicial authority. The 'paranoid style' of *Bowers v. Hardwick* is a symptomatic figuration of a deeper and different anxiety. For the writer of this opinion, a decision in Hardwick's favor would somehow not only undermine the authority of the Court, but unman * * * the patriarchal (hetero)sexual ideologies and identities on which that authority ultimately rests. In *Hardwick*, the claimed right to commit 'homosexual sodomy' is thought (or not so much thought as fantasmatically represented) to be a threatened attack on patriarchal power.

"As White's reference to the shameful 'face-off' during the 1930s between Franklin Roosevelt and the Supreme Court suggests, the *Hardwick* case carries a traumatic force and engenders a sense of panic among the members of the Court which may fairly be described as the judicial equivalent of castration anxiety. The psychic pressures this trauma induces find displaced expression in the figural logic by which the *Hardwick* Court gives voice to (homo)phobic premises that the reigning protocols of constitutional doctrine do not permit the Court explicitly to acknowledge, but which emerge nonetheless from the discursive grounds of the decision. * * *

"* * * Remarkably, however, in *Bowers v. Hardwick* this predominant, traditional image of the Supreme Court Justice as Father undergoes a discursive sea-change, or should I say sex change. For the institutional subject-position figured in the text of Justice White's opinion begins to evoke, alongside the image of the Judge-as-Father, a vision of the Judge-as-Mother, in language whose logical entailments would lead the collective mind of the Court to uncomfortable conclusions. * * *

"* * * Justice White mobilizes maternal metaphor to generate a constellation of ideas and images which allow him to avoid the work of reasoned constitutional analysis and argument. Situating itself in the place and position of a woman (or, more precisely, within the cultural codes of femininity), the *Hardwick* Court seeks to persuade readers of its institutional chastity. Fidelity to the 'language [and] design' of the Law-of-the-(Founding)-(Father(s)) demands 'great resistance' to Hardwick's attempted seduction of the Court, and the 'illegitimacy' to which a betrayal of that law would lead. Since 'homosexual activity' bears 'no connection' to 'family, marriage, or procreation,' it cannot 'qualify for recognition' as a species of constitutional privacy. Since Michael Hardwick's asserted 'right to engage in homosexual sodomy' is 'not readily identifiable in the Constitution's text', judicial invalidation of Georgia's anti-sodomy law would represent an act of interpretive adultery, whose shameful outcome can only be the birth of a bastard right with no legitimate textual roots or claim to the Name-of-the-(Founding)-Father(s).

"What is the meaning of this discursive transformation of the institutional image of the Supreme Court in *Bowers v. Hardwick* from a subject-positionality of 'masculine' activity to 'feminine' (aggressive) passivity? The beginnings of an answer to this question may be found in Leo Bersani's essay, 'Is the Rectum a Grave?'[b] Bersani argues there that the regnant representation of the gay male homosexual in the homophobic American mind is that of 'a grown man, legs high in the air, unable to refuse the suicidal ecstacy of being a woman'. Drawing on the work of John Boswell and Michel Foucault, Bersani contends that this image is so terrifying in the patriarchal masculinist mind because it conjures up the sodomitical spectacle of a man in a passive (i.e., female) position, a position which, at least in the psychic economy of the male heterosexual, entails a horrifying abdication of power. For Bersani, the gay man's rectum is a 'grave in which the masculine ideal ... of proud subjectivity is buried'. Anal eroticism among men must therefore be repudiated (in psychoanalytic terms 'sublimated'), since it poses a threat to the phallic law of masculine heterosexuality. It is perhaps this image of male homosexuality that led Chief Justice Burger in his concurring opinion to note with apparent approval that Blackstone described sex between men 'as an offense of "deeper malignity" than rape.' The 'deeper malignity' of 'homosexual sodomy' lies in the fact that, unlike rape, sex between men represents an assault on the normative order of male heterosexuality—indeed, an abdication of masculine identity as such.

"In fact, however, in Justice White's text, the process of identification inscribed in the rhetorical operations by which the Court produces its ruling suggests that matters are considerably more complex than a simple misogynist aversion to the dangers that male homosexuality embodies for the masculinist heterosexual ideal. For *Hardwick* shows that the radical dis-identification with male homosexuality that Bersani takes to be basic to the fantasmatic structure of male heterosexuality is less fixed and more fluid than the terms of 'Is the Rectum a Grave?' suggest. What makes *Hardwick* so fascinating a text in the juridical archive of discursive heterosexual identification, and of the processes of homosexual differentiation by which heterosexual identity is secured, is its vertiginous instability: the opinion ricochets back and forth between masculine and feminine polarities. The Court's rhetorical contortions in *Hardwick* reveal the desperate lengths to which the paranoid judicial imagination is willing, at least figurally, to go in order to defend itself from a constitutional claim which 'gnaws at the roots of [the] male heterosexual identity'[c] that subtends the Court's institutional self-image.

"In order to deny Michael Hardwick's claim of constitutional privacy, the Father–Judges of the Supreme Court do not hesitate to abandon the paternal metaphor through which the Justices have traditionally represented the Court's role in our constitutional scheme, and the patrilineal

b. [Eds.] 43 *October* 197 (Winter 1987).

c. [Eds.] Jeffrey Weeks, *Sexuality and Its Discontents: Meanings, Myths and Modern Sexualities* 191 (1985).

identification from which a good measure of its cultural authority has historically derived. At the doctrinal level, the Court flatly rejects any connection between Hardwick's asserted right to commit homosexual sodomy and the heterosexual practices at issue in the Supreme Court's previous elaborations of the right to privacy. And yet, standing alone, the doctrinal disavowal of Hardwick's appeal to the privacy principle is not enough. The *Hardwick* Court's doctrinal pronouncements about the political 'limits' beyond which it refuses to go demand additional discursive reinforcement. The Court does not rest content with its summary rejection of Hardwick's 'facetious' claim of a constitutional right to commit what the Chief Justice (again quoting Blackstone) calls 'a heinous act "the very mention of which is a disgrace to human nature," and "a crime not fit to be named" '. The bonds between the law of normative male heterosexuality and American constitutional law are so close that the asserted right to commit 'homosexual sodomy' Michael Hardwick has 'pressed' on the Court provokes nothing less than a crisis of institutional representation. This panic finds displaced expression in the wild veering of subjective standpoint(s) from which the Court's analysis of Hardwick's claim is conducted. It is as if Justice White *needs* to go both ways, as it were: only a protean subject position can enable the *Hardwick* Court to manage the contradictions posed by its unwillingness to extend constitutional privacy jurisprudence to a case whose facts in many ways made it 'the most private of all [the] privacy cases'[d] Over and above the rule of the case, the potentially destabilizing effects of the issue posed in *Hardwick* seem to require this presumptively heterosexual Court to perform a radical act of rhetorical disidentification with the very *figure* of the male homosexual. Faced with a constitutional question that assaults its members' institutional and individual identities, the Supreme Court can only imagine or fear itself in a 'vulnerable,' unmanly, and perforce, effeminized position. If 'homosexual sodomy' is 'an offense of "deeper malignity" than rape,' the Supreme Court must meet its dangers with 'great,' indeed with 'utmost resistance.' This resistance is inscribed in the rhetorical politics of the *Hardwick* opinion itself. * * *

"* * * However, as I have argued, a careful reading of the text demonstrates that the language of the *Hardwick* opinion in fact undermines, and ultimately overtakes, the Court's putatively detached and disinterested logic. The figural unconscious of the text demonstrates that because of political commitments which he either cannot or will not acknowledge, Justice White is finally unable to follow through with his professed intention to avoid the dark domain of desire whither a serious judicial inquiry into the legal imposition of compulsory heterosexuality would lead the Court. Obviously, I mean to evoke the expansive understanding of 'desire' developed in the Freudian theory of the libido, for which the term refers to the full continuum of human emotions ranging

---

d.   [Eds.] Kendall Thomas, "Beyond the   1437 (1992).
Privacy Principle, 92 *Colum. L. Rev.* 1431,

from love to hatred. My point here is that in *Hardwick*, the voice of desire is 'imbedded' in the 'very delirium of metonymy'[e] by which the 'Court' (itself a metonymic figure) anxiously articulates its 'vulnerability' and mobilizes its power of 'resistance' to the claim 'pressed' by Michael Hardwick. By the end of the *Hardwick* opinion, the text has confessed with equal insistence the very interest in homosexuality that Justice White has so insistently disavowed: the rhetoric of *Bowers v. Hardwick* is shot through with the traces of the homophobic passion whose relevance the Court's decision has taken such great pain to deny. That passion eclipses the cool constitutional reason by which the Supreme Court claims to be bound, and belies Justice White's contention that the *Hardwick* decision has nothing to do with the 'imposition of the Justices' own choice of values' regarding the legal regulation of gay and lesbian sexuality."

Michael Sandel, Moral Argument and Liberal Toleration: Abortion and Homosexuality, 77 *California Law Review* **521, 535–38 (1989).*** Arguments from neutral principles and procedural protections miss the point; homosexual intimacy should be defended as a positively good thing. "Like Blackmun and Stevens, the appeals court [in *Hardwick*] constructed an analogy between privacy in marriage and privacy in homosexual relations. But unlike the Supreme Court dissenters, it did not rest the analogy on voluntarist grounds [the argument that government should be neutral among competing concepts of morality] alone. It argued instead that both practices may realize important human goods.

"The marital relationship is significant, wrote the court of appeals, not only because of its procreative purpose but also 'because of the unsurpassed opportunity for mutual support and self-expression that it provides.' It recalled the Supreme Court's observation in *Griswold* that '[m]arriage is a coming together for better or for worse, hopefully enduring, and intimate to the degree of being sacred.' And it went on to suggest that the qualities the Court so prized in *Griswold* could be present in homosexual unions as well: 'For some, the sexual activity in question here serves the same purpose as the intimacy of marriage.'

"Ironically, this way of extending privacy rights to homosexuals depends on an 'old-fashioned' reading of *Griswold* as protecting the human goods realized in marriage, a reading the Court has long since renounced in favor of an individualist reading. By drawing on the teleological dimension of *Griswold*, the substantive case for homosexual privacy offends the liberalism that insists on neutrality. It grounds the right of privacy on the good of the practice it would protect, and so fails to be neutral among conceptions of the good.

"The more frequently employed precedent for homosexual rights is not *Griswold* but *Stanley v. Georgia*, which upheld the right to possess obscene materials in the privacy of one's home. *Stanley* did not hold that the

---

e. [Eds.] Fredric Jameson, *Fables of Aggression: Wyndham Lewis, The Modernist as Fascist* 267 (1979).

obscene films found in the defendant's bedroom served a 'noble purpose,' only that he had a right to view them in private. The toleration *Stanley* defended was wholly independent of the value or importance of the thing being tolerated. * * *

"The problem with the neutral case for toleration is the opposite side of its appeal; it leaves wholly unchallenged the adverse views of homosexuality itself. Unless those views can be plausibly addressed, even a Court ruling in their favor is unlikely to win for homosexuals more than a thin and fragile toleration. A fuller respect would require, if not admiration, at least some appreciation of the lives homosexuals live. Such appreciation, however, is unlikely to be cultivated by a legal and political discourse conducted in terms of autonomy rights alone.

"The liberal may reply that autonomy arguments in court need not foreclose more substantive, affirmative arguments elsewhere; bracketing moral argument for constitutional purposes does not mean bracketing moral argument altogether. Once their freedom of choice in sexual practice is secured, homosexuals can seek, by argument and example, to win from their fellow citizens a deeper respect than autonomy can supply.

"The liberal reply, however, underestimates the extent to which constitutional discourse has come to constitute the terms of political discourse in American public life. While most at home in constitutional law, the main motifs of contemporary liberalism—rights as trumps, the neutral state, and the unencumbered self—figure with increasing prominence in our moral and political culture. Assumptions drawn from constitutional discourse increasingly set the terms of political debate in general.

"Admittedly, the tendency to bracket substantive moral questions makes it difficult to argue for toleration in the language of the good. Defining privacy rights by defending the practices privacy protects seems either reckless or quaint; reckless because it rests so much on moral argument, quaint because it recalls the traditional view that ties the case for privacy to the merits of the conduct privacy protects. But as the abortion and sodomy cases illustrate, the attempt to bracket moral questions faces difficulties of its own. They suggest the truth in the 'naive' view, that the justice or injustice of laws against abortion and homosexual sodomy may have something to do with the morality or immorality of these practices after all."

OTHER CONSTITUTIONAL STRATEGIES FOR CHALLENGING STATE REGULATION OF SEXUALITY AND GENDER

Reconsider the issues explored in Sections 1 and 2—contraception, abortion, and sodomy—from the perspective of equal protection theory. (Chapter 5 reconsiders these issues from the perspective of First Amendment free speech theory.) In the normal equal protection case, the Supreme Court will uphold any regulatory classification (such as good eyesight for getting a driver's license) so long as there is a "rational basis" for the classification: the legislature's goal (traffic safety) is a valid one, and its means (good sight) is rationally related to the achievement of that goal. The Court demands more of a regulation if it involves a "suspect" classification such as race, or involves a "fundamental" interest such as voting: the goal must be a "compelling" state interest such as national security, and the means must be narrowly tailored to meet that goal (the goal could not be achieved by a less restrictive alternative). Hence, "whites only" voting rules would be searchingly examined by the Supreme Court and would stand virtually no chance of being upheld. *Hardwick* is an example of ordinary rational basis review, but only in the context of a due process challenge. Neither *Hardwick* nor *Roe v. Wade* discussed equal protection challenges to the regulations of sexuality in those cases. Consider such arguments now.

PART A.   SEX DISCRIMINATION

American history is full of sex-based discriminations. Before 1920, women were generally excluded from voting, for example. This century has seen a gradual pruning of older sex-based discriminations, but mainly by legislatures and only recently by courts. See Barbara Allen Babcock, Ann E. Freedman, Susan Deller Ross, Wendy Webster Williams, Rhonda Copelon, Deborah L. Rhode, and Nadine Taub, *Sex Discrimination and the Law: History, Practice, and Theory* ch. 1 (1996) (comprehensive examination and analysis). Before 1971, the U.S. Supreme Court had never invalidated a statute because it discriminated against women or relied on a sex-based classification. The first decision to do so, *Reed v. Reed*, 404 U.S. 71 (1971), invalidated an Idaho statute preferring men over women as executors of estates. The next case involved the Court in a debate over whether sex-based classifications should be subjected to the same strict equal protection scrutiny as race-based classifications. Justice Brennan's plurality opinion made out a case for treating sex-based classifications as "suspect" ones, subject to the same strict scrutiny as race-based classifications.

Sharon A. Frontiero and Joseph Frontiero v. Elliot L. Richardson

United States Supreme Court, 1973.
411 U.S. 677, 93 S.Ct. 1764, 36 L.Ed.2d 583.

■ MR. JUSTICE BRENNAN announced the judgment of the Court in an opinion in which MR. JUSTICE DOUGLAS, MR. JUSTICE WHITE, and MR. JUSTICE MARSHALL join.

The question before us concerns the right of a female member of the uniformed services to claim her spouse as a "dependent" for the purposes of obtaining increased quarters allowances and medical and dental benefits under 37 U.S.C. §§ 401, 403, and 10 U.S.C. §§ 1072, 1076, on an equal footing with male members. Under these statutes, a serviceman may claim his wife as a "dependent" without regard to whether she is in fact dependent upon him for any part of her support. A servicewoman, on the other hand, may not claim her husband as a "dependent" under these programs unless he is in fact dependent upon her for over one-half of his support. Thus, the question for decision is whether this difference in treatment constitutes an unconstitutional discrimination against service-women in violation of the [Equal Protection component of the] Due Process Clause of the Fifth Amendment. * * *

Although the legislative history of these statutes [starting with the Integration Act] sheds virtually no light on the purposes underlying the differential treatment accorded male and female members, a majority of the three-judge District Court surmised that Congress might reasonably have concluded that, since the husband in our society is generally the "bread-winner" in the family—and the wife typically the "dependent" partner— "it would be more economical to require married female members claiming husbands to prove actual dependency than to extend the presumption of dependency to such members." Indeed, given the fact that approximately 99% of all members of the uniformed services are male, the District Court speculated that such differential treatment might conceivably lead to a "considerable saving of administrative expense and manpower."

At the outset, appellants contend that classifications based upon sex, like classifications based upon race, alienage, and national origin, are inherently suspect and must therefore be subjected to close judicial scruti-ny. We agree and, indeed, find at least implicit support for such an approach in our unanimous decision only last Term in *Reed*. * * *

The Court [in *Reed*] noted that the Idaho statute "provides that different treatment be accorded to the applicants on the basis of their sex; it thus establishes a classification subject to scrutiny under the Equal Protection Clause." Under "traditional" equal protection analysis, a legislative classification must be sustained unless it is "patently arbitrary" and bears no rational relationship to a legitimate governmental interest.

In an effort to meet this standard, appellee contended that the statutory scheme was a reasonable measure designed to reduce the workload on probate courts by eliminating one class of contests. Moreover, appellee argued that the mandatory preference for male applicants was in itself reasonable since "men (are) as a rule more conversant with business affairs than . . . women." Indeed, appellee maintained that "it is a matter of common knowledge, that women still are not engaged in politics, the professions, business or industry to the extent that men are." And the Idaho Supreme Court, in upholding the constitutionality of this statute, suggested that the Idaho Legislature might reasonably have "concluded that in general men are better qualified to act as an administrator than are women."

Despite these contentions, however, the Court held the statutory preference for male applicants unconstitutional. In reaching this result, the Court implicitly rejected appellee's apparently rational explanation of the statutory scheme, and concluded that, by ignoring the individual qualifications of particular applicants, the challenged statute provided "dissimilar treatment for men and women who are . . . similarly situated." The Court therefore held that, even though the State's interest in achieving administrative efficiency "is not without some legitimacy," "[t]o give a mandatory preference to members of either sex over members of the other, merely to accomplish the elimination of hearings on the merits, is to make the very kind of arbitrary legislative choice forbidden by the [Constitution][.]" This departure from "traditional" rational-basis analysis with respect to sex-based classifications is clearly justified.

There can be no doubt that our Nation has had a long and unfortunate history of sex discrimination. Traditionally, such discrimination was rationalized by an attitude of "romantic paternalism" which, in practical effect, put women, not on a pedestal, but in a cage. * * *

As a result of notions such as these, our statute books gradually became laden with gross, stereotyped distinctions between the sexes and, indeed, throughout much of the 19th century the position of women in our society was, in many respects, comparable to that of blacks under the pre-Civil War slave codes. Neither slaves nor women could hold office, serve on juries, or bring suit in their own names, and married women traditionally were denied the legal capacity to hold or convey property or to serve as legal guardians of their own children. And although blacks were guaranteed the right to vote in 1870, women were denied even that right * * * until adoption of the Nineteenth Amendment half a century later.

It is true, of course, that the position of women in America has improved markedly in recent decades. Nevertheless, it can hardly be doubted that, in part because of the high visibility of the sex characteristic, women still face pervasive, although at times more subtle, discrimination in our educational institutions, in the job market and, perhaps most conspicuously, in the political arena.

Moreover, since sex, like race and national origin, is an immutable characteristic determined solely by the accident of birth, the imposition of special disabilities upon the members of a particular sex because of their sex would seem to violate "the basic concept of our system that legal burdens should bear some relationship to individual responsibility...." *Weber v. Aetna Casualty & Surety Co.*, 406 U.S. 164, 175 (1972). And what differentiates sex from such non-suspect statuses as intelligence or physical disability, and aligns it with the recognized suspect criteria, is that the sex characteristic frequently bears no relation to ability to perform or contribute to society. As a result, statutory distinctions between the sexes often have the effect of invidiously relegating the entire class of females to inferior legal status without regard to the actual capabilities of its individual members.

We might also note that, over the past decade, Congress has itself manifested an increasing sensitivity to sex-based classifications. In Tit. VII of the Civil Rights Act of 1964, for example, Congress expressly declared that no employer, labor union, or other organization subject to the provisions of the Act shall discriminate against any individual on the basis of "race, color, religion, *sex*, or national origin." Similarly, the Equal Pay Act of 1963 provides that no employer covered by the Act "shall discriminate ... between employees on the basis of sex." And § 1 of the Equal Rights Amendment, passed by Congress on March 22, 1972, and submitted to the legislatures of the States for ratification, declares that "[e]quality of rights under the law shall not be denied or abridged by the United States or by any State on account of sex." Thus, Congress itself has concluded that classifications based upon sex are inherently invidious, and this conclusion of a coequal branch of Government is not without significance to the question presently under consideration.

With these considerations in mind, we can only conclude that classifications based upon sex, like classifications based upon race, alienage, or national origin, are inherently suspect, and must therefore be subjected to strict judicial scrutiny. Applying the analysis mandated by that stricter standard of review, it is clear that the statutory scheme now before us is constitutionally invalid.

The sole basis of the classification established in the challenged statutes is the sex of the individuals involved. * * * [A] female member of the uniformed services seeking to obtain housing and medical benefits for her spouse must prove his dependency in fact, whereas no such burden is imposed upon male members. In addition, the statutes operate so as to deny benefits to a female member, such as appellant Sharon Frontiero, who provides less than one-half of her spouse's support, while at the same time granting such benefits to a male member who likewise provides less than one-half of his spouse's support. Thus, to this extent at least, it may fairly be said that these statutes command "dissimilar treatment for men and women who are ... similarly situated." *Reed*.

Moreover, the Government concedes that the differential treatment accorded men and women under these statutes serves no purpose other than mere "administrative convenience." In essence, the Government maintains that, as an empirical matter, wives in our society frequently are dependent upon their husbands, while husbands rarely are dependent upon their wives. Thus, the Government argues that Congress might reasonably have concluded that it would be both cheaper and easier simply conclusively to presume that wives of male members are financially dependent upon their husbands, while burdening female members with the task of establishing dependency in fact.

The Government offers no concrete evidence, however, tending to support its view that such differential treatment in fact saves the Government any money. In order to satisfy the demands of strict judicial scrutiny, the Government must demonstrate, for example, that it is actually cheaper to grant increased benefits with respect to all male members, than it is to determine which male members are in fact entitled to such benefits and to grant increased benefits only to those members whose wives actually meet the dependency requirement. Here, however, there is substantial evidence that, if put to the test, many of the wives of male members would fail to qualify for benefits. And in light of the fact that the dependency determination with respect to the husbands of female members is presently made solely on the basis of affidavits rather than through the more costly hearing process, the Government's explanation of the statutory scheme is, to say the least, questionable.

In any case, our prior decisions make clear that, although efficacious administration of governmental programs is not without some importance, "the Constitution recognizes higher values than speed and efficiency." *Stanley v. Illinois*, 405 U.S. 645, 656 (1972). And when we enter the realm of "strict judicial scrutiny," there can be no doubt that "administrative convenience" is not a shibboleth, the mere recitation of which dictates constitutionality. On the contrary, any statutory scheme which draws a sharp line between the sexes, *solely* for the purpose of achieving administrative convenience, necessarily commands "dissimilar treatment for men and women who are ... similarly situated," and therefore involves the "very kind of arbitrary legislative choice forbidden by the [Constitution]...." *Reed*. We therefore conclude that, by according differential treatment to male and female members of the uniformed services for the sole purpose of achieving administrative convenience, the challenged statutes violate the Due Process Clause of the Fifth Amendment insofar as they require a female member to prove the dependency of her husband.

■ MR. JUSTICE STEWART concurs in the judgment, agreeing that the statutes before us work an invidious discrimination in violation of the Constitution. *Reed*.

■ [We omit the dissenting opinions of MR. JUSTICE REHNQUIST and the opinion of MR. JUSTICE POWELL (joined by THE CHIEF JUSTICE BURGER and MR. JUSTICE BLACKMUN) concurring in the judgment.]

NOTES ON THE CASES AND ARGUMENTS FOR HEIGHTENED SCRUTINY FOR CLASSIFICATIONS BASED ON SEX

1. *Should Sex–Based Classifications Trigger Heightened Scrutiny?* Because only a Court plurality (four out of nine) joined the Brennan opinion, *Frontiero* did not establish strict scrutiny for sex-based classifications, but it did present serious arguments for that proposition. A contrary position is that only race-based classifications should receive strict scrutiny.

(A) Original Intent. One might argue that the framers of the Fourteenth Amendment were only solicitous of protecting the rights of the former slaves. Even proponents of women's rights concede that "[b]oldly dynamic interpretation, departing radically from the original understanding, is required to tie to the fourteenth amendment's equal protection clause a command that government treat men and women as individuals equal in rights, responsibilities and opportunities." Ruth Bader Ginsburg, "Sexual Equality under the Fourteenth and Equal Rights Amendments," 1979 *Wash. U.L.Q.* 161.

An argument against Justice (then-Professor) Ginsburg's call for dynamic constitutional interpretation is that the appropriate mechanism for "updating" the Constitution is the amendment process outlined in Article V. Indeed, in 1972 Congress submitted the Equal Rights Amendment to the states. Section 1 said: "Equality of rights under the law shall not be denied or abridged by the United States or by any State on account of sex." Within months of its submission, the ERA was ratified by half of the 38 states needed for amendment of the Constitution, but then it became stalled by opposition. Defendants in the sex discrimination cases argued that it was inappropriate for the Court to "amend" the Constitution on its own, while the ERA was pending. Note that 18 states adopted ERAs to their state constitutions (see the list in our Preface on Constitutional Law). Should those state courts therefore be more willing to overturn sex-based classifications than the federal courts or the courts in other states?

(B) Discrete & Insular Minorities. Recall the *Carolene Products* idea that special constitutional protection might be extended to "discrete and insular minorities" subjected to systematic discrimination in the political process. Whereas African Americans are discrete and insular minorities, women are neither insular (wherever you find men in our society, you also find women) nor a minority. See Bruce Ackerman, "Beyond *Carolene Products*," 98 *Harv. L. Rev.* 713 (1985). John Hart Ely, *Democracy and Distrust: A Theory of Judicial Review* 164–70 (1980), argues that, although women have long been victims of laws that reflect invidious stereotypes, many of which were enacted in periods when women had no political representation (not getting the right to vote until 1920), women are today more than capable of being heard politically. But as you will see from

United States v. Virginia, the next following case, old stereotypes don't die easily or quickly. Also evident in that case, however, is the Court's continuing struggle with what the criteria for strict scrutiny should be.

(C) Immutability. In *Frontiero,* Justice Brennan used the argument that sex, like race, is immutable as one justification for applying the same degree of scrutiny to both sets of classifications. The immutability criterion is extremely problematic, however, for multiple reasons.

First, consider why immutability should make any difference at all. Most commonly, courts invoke the notion that because the individual has no control over her race or sex, she should not be penalized for it. That statement can only be true, however, if we believe that race and sex have no legitimate relationship to merit or qualification. There are many characteristics over which an individual may have no control—kleptomania, for example. If it could be shown that most shoplifters act out of an immutable compulsion, could they challenge discrimination against them in the criminal law? Unlikely. (Currently, there is an enormous debate over whether sexual orientation is partially innate, which has led to debates in the law over whether the immutability requirement for heightened scrutiny is met when anti-gay discrimination is challenged; see Chapter 2, Section 3[C] for a fuller discussion.) Conversely, there are characteristics over which an individual has total control, but which we would all agree should not be the basis for a penalty. Religious affiliation would be one example of that situation.

Second, are any of these characteristics really immutable? Chapter 2 presents extensive evidence against the proposition that sex (or gender) is unchangeable. Indeed, given the availability of transsexual surgery, one might argue that the only question is the extent to which an individual might elect to change sexes, i.e., by hormone treatment only or by full surgical change. Would race discrimination lose its suspect status if science perfected a method for alteration of skin color? Again, unlikely. Without medical intervention, stories of passing abound, both as to sex and as to race. Upon closer examination, the issue appears to be not immutability *per se* but whether the law should penalize a certain kind of difference.

2. *The Path to "Middle–Tier" (Intermediate) Scrutiny: The Oklahoma Beer Case.* As *Frontiero* resolved nothing doctrinally and the ERA continued to roil the political system, the Supreme Court decided cases on an ad hoc basis for several years. See *Kahn v. Shevin,* 416 U.S. 351 (1974) (upholding a state statute allowing widows, but not widowers, a small property tax exemption was upheld on the ground that, "[w]hether from overt discrimination or from the socialization process," such women faced more difficult barriers in the job market than widowers); *Schlesinger v. Ballard,* 419 U.S. 498 (1975) (upholding federal law giving male officers a shorter period in which to attain promotion or be discharged than female officers); *Weinberger v. Wiesenfeld,* 420 U.S. 636 (1975) (striking down a Social Security provision under which a surviving widow and minor children received benefits based on the earnings of the deceased husband and father, but under which only minor children received benefits if the mother died).

In *Craig v. Boren*, 429 U.S. 190 (1976), the Court evaluated a state law allowing 18 year old girls to buy low-alcohol beer but requiring boys to be 21 years old. Writing this time for six members of the Court, Justice Brennan's opinion fixed upon a formula for evaluating sex discrimination claims: "classifications by gender must serve important governmental objectives and must be substantially related to achievement of those objectives." This verbal formulation is not as demanding as the one the Court uses to scrutinize race-based classifications, and so it is considered "intermediate" rather than "strict" scrutiny. The statutory goal, traffic safety, was certainly "important," but the Court held the gender classification not "substantially related" to it. Although young males were more likely to be arrested for traffic offenses while drunk than young females, the Court did not find sex to be the key variable and openly doubted whether sale of 3.2% beer contributed much to drunkenness of either sex.

Equally important, *Craig* ruled that "archaic and overbroad" generalizations about the sexes could not be invoked to support a sex-based classification, confirming and expanding upon *Wiesenfeld*'s reasoning. Justice Brennan interpreted *Reed* as holding that "increasingly outdated misconceptions concerning the role of females in the home rather than in the 'marketplace and world of ideas' [must be] rejected," along with their accompanying statutory schemes. Because Oklahoma's beer-purchase law rested upon the stereotypes of " 'reckless' young men" and responsible young women, it was especially vulnerable to the new, tougher standard of review.

3. *After* Craig: *Intermediate Scrutiny in Action.* The Supreme Court has applied, sometimes rather weakly sometimes quite strongly, *Craig*'s heightened scrutiny to sex-based classifications. (Most of these decisions are excerpted in this casebook, but in other chapters.) The leading cases are *Califano v. Goldfarb*, 430 U.S. 199 (1977) (invalidating policy treating widowers differently from widows for purposes of federal old age, survivors, and disability benefits); *Personnel Administrator of Massachusetts v. Feeney*, 442 U.S. 256 (1979) (Chapter 10, Section 1[A]) (upholding state employment preference for veterans notwithstanding strong discriminatory effect upon female applicants); *Michael M. v. Sonoma County Superior Court*, 450 U.S. 464 (1981) (Chapter 11, Section 2[A]) (upholding statutory rape law applying only to sex with minor females); *Rostker v. Goldberg*, 453 U.S. 57 (1981) (Chapter 4, Section 2) (upholding exclusion of women from draft registration); *Mississippi Univ. for Women v. Hogan*, 458 U.S. 718 (1982) (invalidating state university's refusal to admit men to its nursing school); *Roberts v. U.S. Jaycees*, 468 U.S. 609, 619–20 (1984) (Chapter 5, Section 1[C]) (upholding municipality's law requiring civic association to admit women; burden on First Amendment right of association justified by compelling state interest in fighting sex discrimination); *J.E.B. v. Alabama ex rel. T.B.*, 511 U.S. 127 (1994) (invalidating state's use of sex-based peremptory challenges in jury selection).

Pregnancy and Sex Discrimination. One of the most contentious issues in the area of sex discrimination has been definitional: whether classifications based on pregnancy constitute classifications based on sex. The Court ruled that they don't, in *Geduldig v. Aiello*, 417 U.S. 484 (1974). Congress quickly amended Title VII of the 1964 Civil Rights Act to include pregnancy-based discrimination as a prohibited employment practice, but the Court's constitutional analysis stands unaltered. For an extensive discussion of pregnancy-based policies in the workplace, see Chapter 10, Section 2.

United States v. Virginia

United States Supreme Court, 1996.
518 U.S. ___, 116 S.Ct. 2264, 135 L.Ed.2d 735.

■ JUSTICE GINSBURG delivered the opinion of the Court.

[Virginia Military Institute (VMI) was the sole single-sex school among Virginia's public institutions of higher learning. VMI's distinctive mission was to produce "citizen-soldiers," men prepared for leadership in civilian life and in military service. Using an "adversative," or constantly challenging and doubting, method of training not available elsewhere in Virginia,[a] VMI endeavored to instill physical and mental discipline in its cadets and to impart to them a strong moral code. The adversative method has yielded a large number of civilian and military leaders in Virginia; VMI alumni have been unusually bonded to one another and to the school. Their school loyalty is legendary, and as a consequence VMI has had the largest per-student endowment of all undergraduate institutions in the Nation.

[The United States sued Virginia and VMI, alleging that VMI's exclusively male admission policy violated the equal protection clause. The District Court ruled in VMI's favor. The Fourth Circuit reversed and ordered Virginia to remedy the constitutional violation. In response, Virginia proposed a parallel program for women: Virginia Women's Institute for Leadership (VWIL), located at Mary Baldwin College, a private liberal arts school for women. In lieu of VMI's adversative method, the VWIL Task

---

a. [Eds.] According to the record in the case, the adversative model of education features "[p]hysical rigor, mental stress, absolute equality of treatment, absence of privacy, minute regulation of behavior, and indoctrination in desirable values." As one Commandant of Cadets described it, the adversative method "dissects the young student," and makes him aware of his "limits and capabilities," so that he knows "how far he can go with his anger, ... how much he can take under stress, ... exactly what he can do when he is physically exhausted." The cadets live in spartan barracks where surveillance is constant and privacy nonexistent; they wear uniforms, eat together in the mess hall, and regularly participate in drills. Freshmen students are exposed to the rat line, "an extreme form of the adversative model," comparable in intensity to Marine Corps boot camp. Extremely punishing if not torturing, the rat line bonds new cadets to their fellow sufferers and, when they have completed the 7–month experience, to their former tormentors. VMI also employs a hierarchical "class system" of privileges and responsibilities, a "dyke system" for assigning a senior class mentor to each entering class "rat," and a stringently enforced "honor code," which prescribes that a cadet "does not lie, cheat, steal nor tolerate those who do."

Force favored "a cooperative method which reinforces self-esteem." In addition to the standard bachelor of arts program offered at Mary Baldwin, VWIL students would take courses in leadership, complete an off-campus leadership externship, participate in community service projects, and assist in arranging a speaker series.

[The District Court found that Virginia's proposal satisfied the Constitution's equal protection requirement, and the Fourth Circuit affirmed. The appeals court deferentially reviewed Virginia's plan and determined that provision of single-sex educational options was a legitimate objective. Maintenance of single-sex programs, the court concluded, was essential to that objective. The court recognized, however, that its analysis risked bypassing equal protection scrutiny, so it fashioned an additional test, asking whether VMI and VWIL students would receive "substantively comparable" benefits. Although the Court of Appeals acknowledged that the VWIL degree lacked the historical benefit and prestige of a VMI degree, the court nevertheless found the educational opportunities at the two schools sufficiently comparable.]

* * * To summarize the Court's current directions for cases of official classification based on gender: Focusing on the differential treatment or denial of opportunity for which relief is sought, the reviewing court must determine whether the proffered justification is "exceedingly persuasive." The burden of justification is demanding and it rests entirely on the State. See *Mississippi Univ. for Women v. Hogan*, 458 U.S. 718, 724 (1982). The State must show "at least that the [challenged] classification serves 'important governmental objectives and that the discriminatory means employed' are 'substantially related to the achievement of those objectives.'" *Id*. The justification must be genuine, not hypothesized or invented *post hoc* in response to litigation. And it must not rely on overbroad generalizations about the different talents, capacities, or preferences of males and females.

The heightened review standard our precedent establishes does not make sex a proscribed classification. Supposed "inherent differences" are no longer accepted as a ground for race or national origin classifications. Physical differences between men and women, however, are enduring: "[T]he two sexes are not fungible; a community made up exclusively of one [sex] is different from a community composed of both." *Ballard v. United States*, 329 U.S. 187, 193 (1946).

"Inherent differences" between men and women, we have come to appreciate, remain cause for celebration, but not for denigration of the members of either sex or for artificial constraints on an individual's opportunity. Sex classifications may be used to compensate women "for particular economic disabilities [they have] suffered," *Califano v. Webster*, 430 U.S. 313, 320 (1977) (*per curiam*), to "promot[e] equal employment opportunity," see *California Federal Sav. & Loan Assn. v. Guerra*, 479 U.S. 272, 289 (1987), to advance full development of the talent and capacities of our Nation's people. But such classifications may not be used, as they once were, to create or perpetuate the legal, social, and economic inferiority of women.

Measuring the record in this case against the review standard just described, we conclude that Virginia has shown no "exceedingly persuasive justification" for excluding all women from the citizen-soldier training afforded by VMI. We therefore affirm the Fourth Circuit's initial judgment, which held that Virginia had violated the Fourteenth Amendment's Equal Protection Clause. Because the remedy proffered by Virginia—the Mary Baldwin VWIL program—does not cure the constitutional violation, i.e., it does not provide equal opportunity, we reverse the Fourth Circuit's final judgment in this case.

The Fourth Circuit initially held that Virginia had advanced no state policy by which it could justify, under equal protection principles, its determination "to afford VMI's unique type of program to men and not to women." Virginia challenges that "liability" ruling and asserts two justifications in defense of VMI's exclusion of women. First, the Commonwealth contends, "single-sex education provides important educational benefits," and the option of single-sex education contributes to "diversity in educational approaches." Second, the Commonwealth argues, "the unique VMI method of character development and leadership training," the school's adversative approach, would have to be modified were VMI to admit women. We consider these two justifications in turn.

Single-sex education affords pedagogical benefits to at least some students, Virginia emphasizes, and that reality is uncontested in this litigation. Similarly, it is not disputed that diversity among public educational institutions can serve the public good. But Virginia has not shown that VMI was established, or has been maintained, with a view to diversifying, by its categorical exclusion of women, educational opportunities within the State. In cases of this genre, our precedent instructs that "benign" justifications proffered in defense of categorical exclusions will not be accepted automatically; a tenable justification must describe actual state purposes, not rationalizations for actions in fact differently grounded. * * *

[Justice Ginsburg's review of the record of single-sex education in Virginia revealed that it originated in the state's belief that only men would benefit from higher education. Virginia persisted in that belief much longer than other states; its public university, the University of Virginia, did not admit female students until 1970. The only deliberative effort by the state to express its policy since 1970 was the report of the Virginia Commission on the University of the 21st Century, which found: "Because colleges and universities provide opportunities for students to develop values and learn from role models, it is extremely important that they deal with faculty, staff, and students without regard to sex, race, or ethnic origin." VMI's reexamination of its policy after *Mississippi University for Women* offered "no persuasive evidence" that diversity was the state's goal in maintaining VMI as a single-sex college. Justice Ginsburg then addressed the state's second justification: preserving the adversative method of education.]

* * * The District Court forecast from expert witness testimony, and the Court of Appeals accepted, that coeducation would materially affect "at least these three aspects of VMI's program—physical training, the absence

of privacy, and the adversative approach." And it is uncontested that women's admission would require accommodations, primarily in arranging housing assignments and physical training programs for female cadets. It is also undisputed, however, that "the VMI methodology could be used to educate women." The District Court even allowed that some women may prefer it to the methodology a women's college might pursue. "[S]ome women, at least, would want to attend [VMI] if they had the opportunity," the District Court recognized, and "some women," the expert testimony established, "are capable of all of the individual activities required of VMI cadets." * * *

In support of its initial judgment for Virginia, a judgment rejecting all equal protection objections presented by the United States, the District Court made "findings" on "gender-based developmental differences." These "findings" restate the opinions of Virginia's expert witnesses, opinions about typically male or typically female "tendencies." For example, "[m]ales tend to need an atmosphere of adversativeness," while "[f]emales tend to thrive in a cooperative atmosphere." "I'm not saying that some women don't do well under [the] adversative model," VMI's expert on educational institutions testified, "undoubtedly there are some [women] who do"; but educational experiences must be designed "around the rule," this expert maintained, and not "around the exception." * * *

It may be assumed, for purposes of this decision, that most women would not choose VMI's adversative method. As Fourth Circuit Judge Motz observed, however, in her dissent from the Court of Appeals' denial of rehearing en banc, it is also probable that "many men would not want to be educated in such an environment." (On that point, even our dissenting colleague might agree.) Education, to be sure, is not a "one size fits all" business. The issue, however, is not whether "women—or men—should be forced to attend VMI"; rather, the question is whether the State can constitutionally deny to women who have the will and capacity, the training and attendant opportunities that VMI uniquely affords.

The notion that admission of women would downgrade VMI's stature, destroy the adversative system and, with it, even the school, is a judgment hardly proved, a prediction hardly different from other "self-fulfilling prophec[ies]," see *Mississippi Univ. for Women*, routinely used to deny rights or opportunities. When women first sought admission to the bar and access to legal education, concerns of the same order were expressed. For example, in 1876, the Court of Common Pleas of Hennepin County, Minnesota, explained why women were thought ineligible for the practice of law. Women train and educate the young, the court said, which

> "forbids that they shall bestow that time (early and late) and labor, so essential in attaining to the eminence to which the true lawyer should ever aspire. It cannot therefore be said that the opposition of courts to the admission of females to practice ... is to any extent the outgrowth of ... 'old fogyism[.]' ... [I]t arises rather from a comprehension of the magnitude of the responsibilities connected with the successful practice of law, and a desire to *grade up* the profession." In re

Application of Martha Angle Dorsett to Be Admitted to Practice as Attorney and Counselor at Law (Minn. C.P. Hennepin Cty., 1876), in *The Syllabi*, Oct. 21, 1876, pp. 5, 6 (emphasis added).

A like fear, according to a 1925 report, accounted for Columbia Law School's resistance to women's admission, although

"[t]he faculty ... never maintained that women could not master legal learning.... No, its argument has been ... more practical. If women were admitted to the Columbia Law School, [the faculty] said, then the choicer, more manly and red-blooded graduates of our great universities would go to the Harvard Law School!" *The Nation*, Feb. 18, 1925, p. 173.

Medical faculties similarly resisted men and women as partners in the study of medicine. See R. Morantz–Sanchez, *Sympathy and Science: Women Physicians in American Medicine* 51–54, 250 (1985), More recently, women seeking careers in policing encountered resistance based on fears that their presence would "undermine male solidarity," see F. Heidensohn, *Women in Control?* 201 (1992); deprive male partners of adequate assistance, see id., at 184–185; and lead to sexual misconduct, see C. Milton et al., *Women in Policing* 32–33 (1974). Field studies did not confirm these fears. See *Women in Control? supra*, at 92–93; P. Bloch & D. Anderson, *Policewomen on Patrol: Final Report* (1974).

Women's successful entry into the federal military academies, and their participation in the Nation's military forces, indicate that Virginia's fears for the future of VMI may not be solidly grounded. The State's justification for excluding all women from "citizen-soldier" training for which some are qualified, in any event, cannot rank as "exceedingly persuasive," as we have explained and applied that standard. * * *

The State's misunderstanding and, in turn, the District Court's, is apparent from VMI's mission: to produce "citizen-soldiers," individuals

" 'imbued with love of learning, confident in the functions and attitudes of leadership, possessing a high sense of public service, advocates of the American democracy and free enterprise system, and ready ... to defend their country in time of national peril.' " 766 F. Supp., at 1425 (quoting Mission Study Committee of the VMI Board of Visitors, Report, May 16, 1986).

Surely that goal is great enough to accommodate women, who today count as citizens in our American democracy equal in stature to men. Just as surely, the State's great goal is not substantially advanced by women's categorical exclusion, in total disregard of their individual merit, from the State's premier "citizen-soldier" corps. Virginia, in sum, "has fallen far short of establishing the 'exceedingly persuasive justification,' " *Mississippi Univ. for Women*, that must be the solid base for any gender-defined classification. * * *

[Justice Ginsburg then turned to the remedial plan, whose constitutionality had been upheld in the lower courts. The Supreme Court's race discrimination precedents establish that the remedial decree must closely fit the constitutional violation; it must be shaped to place persons unconstitutionally denied an opportunity or advantage in "the position they would have occupied in the absence of [discrimination]." See *Milliken v. Bradley*, 433 U.S. 267, 280 (1977). Justice Ginsburg found that the establishment of the VWIL did not practically remedy the discrimination, in large part because the women's program was qualitatively different and quantitatively inferior to that retained for males at VMI. Tangible differences included fewer courses for VWIL students, less qualified faculty members, lower admissions standards for students, no comparable athletic facilities, a much smaller educational endowment, and incomplete access to VMI's impressive alumni network. Intangible differences included loss of the adversative method and the bonding it seems to achieve.] "[T]he most important aspects of the VMI educational experience occur in the barracks," the District Court found, yet Virginia deemed that core experience nonessential, indeed inappropriate, for training its female citizen-soldiers. * * *

Virginia maintains that these methodological differences are "justified pedagogically," based on "important differences between men and women in learning and developmental needs," "psychological and sociological differences" Virginia describes as "real" and "not stereotypes." The Task Force charged with developing the leadership program for women, drawn from the staff and faculty at Mary Baldwin College, "determined that a military model and, especially VMI's adversative method, would be wholly inappropriate for educating and training most women." The Commonwealth embraced the Task Force view, as did expert witnesses who testified for Virginia.

As earlier stated, generalizations about "the way women are," estimates of what is appropriate for *most women*, no longer justify denying opportunity to women whose talent and capacity place them outside the average description. Notably, Virginia never asserted that VMI's method of education suits *most men*. It is also revealing that Virginia accounted for its failure to make the VWIL experience "the entirely militaristic experience of VMI" on the ground that VWIL "is planned for women who do not necessarily expect to pursue military careers." By that reasoning, VMI's "entirely militaristic" program would be inappropriate for men in general or *as a group*, for "[o]nly about 15% of VMI cadets enter career military service." * * *

Virginia's VWIL solution is reminiscent of the remedy Texas proposed 50 years ago, in response to a state trial court's 1946 ruling that, given the equal protection guarantee, African Americans could not be denied a legal education at a state facility. See *Sweatt v. Painter*, 339 U.S. 629 (1950). Reluctant to admit African Americans to its flagship University of Texas Law School, the State set up a separate school for Herman [sic] Sweatt and other black law students. As originally opened, the new school had no independent faculty or library, and it lacked accreditation. Nevertheless, the state trial and appellate courts were satisfied that the new school offered Sweatt opportunities for the study of law "substantially equivalent to those offered by the State to white students at the University of Texas."

[The Supreme Court struck down the remedy on the ground that the tangible facilities and faculty of the new law school were distinctly inferior and that there was an even greater disparity in "those qualities which are incapable of objective measurement but which make for greatness" in a school, including "reputation of the faculty, experience of the administration, position and influence of the alumni, standing in the community, traditions and prestige."] Facing the marked differences reported in the *Sweatt* opinion, the Court unanimously ruled that Texas had not shown "substantial equality in the [separate] educational opportunities" the State offered. Accordingly, the Court held, the Equal Protection Clause required Texas to admit African Americans to the University of Texas Law School. In line with *Sweatt*, we rule here that Virginia has not shown substantial equality in the separate educational opportunities the State supports at VWIL and VMI. * * *

A prime part of the history of our Constitution * * * is the story of the extension of constitutional rights and protections to people once ignored or excluded. VMI's story continued as our comprehension of "We the People" expanded. There is no reason to believe that the admission of women capable of all the activities required of VMI cadets would destroy the Institute rather than enhance its capacity to serve the "more perfect Union." * * *

■ JUSTICE THOMAS took no part in the consideration of this case.

■ [CHIEF JUSTICE REHNQUIST concurred in the judgment. He maintained that the six-Justice Court had departed from the traditional test for evaluating sex-based classifications. The approach taken in earlier cases requires the state to offer only an "important government objective" that is "substantially related" to the sex-based classification. The Chief Justice believed that the Court's requirement of an "exceedingly persuasive justification" subtly alters the analysis. Chief Justice Rehnquist also objected to the Court's examination of Virginia's long history of excluding women from higher education on the basis of stereotypes about women's abilities and role. He maintained that the Court should only examine Virginia's justifications since *Mississippi University for Women*, decided in 1982, as it was only with that decision that states could have been on notice that single-sex institutions required any justification beyond tradition. Nonetheless, the Chief Justice found the Virginia had not offered a substantial justification borne out by the evidence in the case and agreed with the Court's judgment.]

■ JUSTICE SCALIA, dissenting. * * *

Much of the Court's opinion is devoted to deprecating the closed-mindedness of our forebears with regard to women's education, and even with regard to the treatment of women in areas that have nothing to do with education. Closed-minded they were—as every age is, including our own, with regard to matters it cannot guess, because it simply does not consider them debatable. The virtue of a democratic system with a First Amendment is that it readily enables the people, over time, to be persuaded that what they took for granted is not so, and to change their laws accordingly. That system is destroyed if the smug assurances of each age are removed from the democratic process and written into the Constitution. So to counterbalance the Court's criticism of our ancestors, let me say a word in their praise: they left us free to change. The same cannot be said of this most illiberal Court, which has embarked on a course of inscribing one after another of the current preferences of the society (and in some cases only the counter-majoritarian preferences of the society's law-trained elite) into our Basic Law. Today it enshrines the notion that no substantial educational value is to be served by an all-men's military academy—so that the decision by the people of Virginia to maintain such an institution denies equal protection to women who cannot attend that institution but can attend others. Since it is entirely clear that the Constitution of the United States—the old one—takes no sides in this educational debate, I dissent.

* * * [I]n my view the function of this Court is to *preserve* our society's values regarding (among other things) equal protection, not to *revise* them; to prevent backsliding from the degree of restriction the Constitution imposed upon democratic government, not to prescribe, on our own authority, progressively higher degrees. For that reason it is my view that, whatever abstract tests we may choose to devise, they cannot super-sede—and indeed ought to be crafted so as to reflect—those constant and unbroken national traditions that embody the people's understanding of ambiguous constitutional texts. More specifically, it is my view that "when a practice not expressly prohibited by the text of the Bill of Rights bears the endorsement of a long tradition of open, widespread, and unchallenged use that dates back to the beginning of the Republic, we have no proper basis for striking it down." *Rutan v. Republican Party of Ill.*, 497 U.S. 62, 95 (1990) (Scalia, J., dissenting). The same applies, *mutatis mutandis*, to a practice asserted to be in violation of the post-Civil War Fourteenth Amendment. * * *

[Justice Scalia then launched into a litany of criticisms: the Court was silently replacing the intermediate scrutiny standard traditionally applied in sex-discrimination cases with a strict scrutiny standard akin to that in race-discrimination cases; the Court's requirement that VMI must open its adversative method to women so long as there are any women who would benefit from it imported a least-restrictive-means requirement characteris-tic only of strict scrutiny and not of intermediate scrutiny as articulated in precedents such as *Mississippi University for Women* and, even more prominently, *Rostker v. Goldberg*; and the Court's approach destabilized equal protection law, and without any firm theoretical basis. With respect to his last criticism, Justice Scalia adverted to *Carolene Products*' justifica-tion for judicial review when "prejudice against discrete and insular minor-ities may be a special condition, which tends seriously to curtail the operation of those political processes ordinarily to be relied upon to protect minorities, and which may call for a correspondingly more searching judicial inquiry."]

It is hard to consider women a "discrete and insular minorit[y]" unable to employ the "political processes ordinarily to be relied upon," when they constitute a majority of the electorate. And the suggestion that they are incapable of exerting that political power smacks of the same paternalism that the Court so roundly condemns. Moreover, a long list of legislation proves the proposition false. See, e.g., Equal Pay Act of 1963, 29 U.S.C. § 206(d); Title VII of the Civil Rights Act of 1964, 42 U.S.C. § 2000e–2; Title IX of the Education Amendments of 1972, 20 U.S.C. § 1681; Women's Business Ownership Act of 1988, Pub. L. 100–533, 102 Stat. 2689; Violence Against Women Act of 1994, Pub. L. 103–322, Title IV, 108 Stat. 1902. * * *

* * * [B]esides its single-sex constitution, VMI is different from other colleges in another way. It employs a "distinctive educational method," sometimes referred to as the "adversative, or doubting, model of education." "Physical rigor, mental stress, absolute equality of treatment, absence of privacy, minute regulation of behavior, and indoctrination in desirable values are the salient attributes of the VMI educational experience." No one contends that this method is appropriate for all individuals; education is not a "one size fits all" business. Just as a State may wish to support junior colleges, vocational institutes, or a law school that emphasizes case practice instead of classroom study, so too a State's decision to maintain within its system one school that provides the adversative method is "substantially related" to its goal of good education. Moreover, it was uncontested that "if the state were to establish a women's VMI-type [*i.e.,* adversative] program, the program would attract an insufficient number of participants to make the program work"; and it was found by the District Court that if Virginia were to include women in VMI, the school "would eventually find it necessary to drop the adversative system altogether." Thus, Virginia's options were an adversative method that excludes women or no adversative method at all. * * *

* * * In an odd sort of way, it is precisely VMI's attachment to such old-fashioned concepts as manly "honor" that has made it, and the system it represents, the target of those who today succeed in abolishing public single-sex education. The record contains a booklet that all first-year VMI students (the so-called "rats") were required to keep in their possession at all times. Near the end there appears the following period-piece, entitled "The Code of a Gentleman":

> "Without a strict observance of the fundamental Code of Honor, no man, no matter how 'polished,' can be considered a gentleman. The honor of a gentleman demands the inviolability of his word, and the incorruptibility of his principles. He is the descendant of the knight, the crusader; he is the defender of the defenseless and the champion of justice ... or he is not a Gentleman.

> A Gentleman ...

> Does not discuss his family affairs in public or with acquaintances.

> Does not speak more than casually about his girl friend.

> Does not go to a lady's house if he is affected by alcohol. He is temperate in the use of alcohol.

Does not lose his temper; nor exhibit anger, fear, hate, embarrassment, ardor or hilarity in public.

Does not hail a lady from a club window.

A gentleman never discusses the merits or demerits of a lady.

Does not mention names exactly as he avoids the mention of what things cost.

Does not borrow money from a friend, except in dire need. Money borrowed is a debt of honor, and must be repaid as promptly as possible. Debts incurred by a deceased parent, brother, sister or grown child are assumed by honorable men as a debt of honor.

Does not display his wealth, money or possessions.

Does not put his manners on and off, whether in the club or in a ballroom. He treats people with courtesy, no matter what their social position may be.

Does not slap strangers on the back nor so much as lay a finger on a lady.

Does not 'lick the boots of those above' nor 'kick the face of those below him on the social ladder.'

Does not take advantage of another's helplessness or ignorance and assumes that no gentleman will take advantage of him.

A Gentleman respects the reserves of others, but demands that others respect those which are his.

A Gentleman can become what he wills to be . . ."

I do not know whether the men of VMI lived by this Code; perhaps not. But it is powerfully impressive that a public institution of higher education still in existence sought to have them do so. I do not think any of us, women included, will be better off for its destruction. * * *

Katherine M. Franke, The Central Mistake of Sex Discrimination Law: the Disaggregation of Sex From Gender

144 *University of Pennsylvania Law Review* 1–3 (1995).*

Contemporary sex discrimination jurisprudence accepts as one of its foundational premises the notion that sex and gender are two distinct aspects of human identity. That is, it assumes that the identities male and female are different from the characteristics masculine and feminine. Sex is regarded as a product of nature, while gender is understood as a function of culture. This disaggregation of sex from gender represents a central mistake of equality jurisprudence.

Antidiscrimination law is founded upon the idea that sex, conceived as biological difference, is prior to, less normative than, and more real than gender. Yet in every way that matters, sex bears an epiphenomenal relationship to gender; that is, under close examination, almost every claim with regard to sexual identity or sex discrimination can be shown to be grounded in normative gender rules and roles. Herein lies the mistake. In the name of avoiding "the grossest discrimination," that is, "treating things that are different as though they were exactly alike," sexual equality jurisprudence has uncritically accepted the validity of biological sexual differences. By accepting these biological differences, equality jurisprudence reifies as foundational *fact* that which is really an *effect* of normative gender ideology. This jurisprudential error not only produces obvious absurdities at the margin of gendered identity, but it also explains why sex discrimination laws have been relatively ineffective in dismantling profound sex segregation in the wage-labor market, in shattering "glass ceilings" that obstruct women's entrance into the upper echelons of corporate management, and in increasing women's wages, which remain a fraction of those paid men.

The targets of antidiscrimination law, therefore, should not be limited to the "gross, stereotyped distinctions between the sexes" but should also include the social processes that construct and make coherent the categories male and female. In many cases, biology operates as the excuse or cover for social practices that hierarchize individual members of the social category "man" over individual members of the social category "woman." In the end, biology or anatomy serve as metaphors for a kind of inferiority that characterizes society's view of women. * * *

NOTES ON THE VMI CASE AND THE AGGREGATION OF SEX AND GENDER

1. *Deconstructing VMI.* One can hardly imagine a more dramatic example of the "social processes that construct and make coherent the categor[y] male" than the adversative method at VMI. Yet the Court's decision sidesteps any attempt to engage in the more radical critique that Franke advocates. Indeed, Justice Ginsburg's comment that differences between male and female are to be "celebrated" makes one wonder about the function of that sentence. Was it part of the politics within the Court of building a majority? Is it meant to rebuff any attempt to examine the relationship between sex and gender? Does the success of using the traditional sex discrimination law model in the VMI case mean that a more radical approach is unwise or unnecessary?

2. *Sex Equality and Gender Equality.* The VMI decision is a model of formal sex equality doctrine: females should be given equal opportunity to do anything. In this case, women are being given an equal opportunity to become (socially) men. Is this an example of the radical potential of liberal feminism? Or is it shortsighted in its failure to question whether fostering manhood is a legitimate state interest? Note how Justice Scalia defines

what VMI seeks to achieve. What becomes gendered in this process—citizenship? honor? responsibility? How did the exclusively male VMI system construct gender for women?

As described in Chapter 4, Section 2(C), women are excluded from serving in ground combat positions in the U.S. armed forces. Consider Problem 4–3. Can the current policy survive *U.S. v. Virginia*?

3. *Sex, Gender, and the Private Sphere.* Most analyses of the relationship between sex and gender in the law occur in the context of statutory civil rights laws, especially Title VII. See cases and commentary in Chapter 10. Constitutional law operates only against the state. Should it make a difference whether one is challenging actions by the government or solely in the private sphere? Federal courts have repeatedly interpreted Title VII as resting upon highly conventional assumptions about sex binariness. To some extent, however, gender stereotypes that curtail the careers of ambitious women have been invalidated. (See Chapter 10, Section 2.) But courts have refused to apply Title VII's sex discrimination rules to prohibit discrimination based upon sexual orientation (Chapter 10, Section 2[B]), transsexualism (Chapter 12, Section 2), or cross-dressing (Chapter 12, Section 3). The evidence of legislative intent that curbs such statutory applications does not constrain their construction of the equal protection clause. Should courts interpret that clause to include some gender-bending and sexuality claims?

PART B.   SEXUAL ORIENTATION DISCRIMINATION

1.   IS ANTI-GAY DISCRIMINATION RATIONAL?

City of Cleburne v. Cleburne Living Center, 473 U.S. 432, 105 S.Ct. 3249, 87 L.Ed.2d 313 (1985). The Supreme Court considered a challenge to a zoning ordinance excluding homes for people with mental disabilities from a residential area. Justice White's opinion for the Court first considered whether disability-based classifications should be subjected to heightened scrutiny, as race, sex, and national origin classifications are. He pointed out that the Court has been stingy about which classifications trigger heightened scrutiny. Age-based classifications do not, for example; age is often a rational classification, and its invocation does not set off the same sorts of fire alarms (prejudice) that sex and race classifications do. See *Massachusetts Board of Retirement v. Murgia*, 427 U.S. 307 (1976).

"Against this background, we conclude for several reasons that the Court of Appeals erred in holding mental retardation a quasi-suspect classification calling for a more exacting standard of judicial review than is normally accorded economic and social legislation. First, it is undeniable, and it is not argued otherwise here, that those who are mentally retarded have a reduced ability to cope with and function in the everyday world. Nor are they all cut from the same pattern: as the testimony in this record indicates, they range from those whose disability is not immediately evident to those who must be constantly cared for. They are thus different, immutably so, in relevant respects, and the States' interest in dealing with and providing for them is plainly a legitimate one. * * *

"Second, the distinctive legislative response, both national and state, to the plight of those who are mentally retarded demonstrates not only that they have unique problems, but also that the lawmakers have been addressing their difficulties in a manner that belies a continuing antipathy or prejudice and a corresponding need for more intrusive oversight by the judiciary. * * *

"Third, the legislative response, which could hardly have occurred and survived without public support, negates any claim that the mentally retarded are politically powerless in the sense that they have no ability to attract the attention of the lawmakers. Any minority can be said to be powerless to assert direct control over the legislature, but if that were a criterion for higher level scrutiny by the courts, much economic and social legislation would now be suspect.

"Fourth, if the large and amorphous class of the mentally retarded were deemed quasi-suspect, it would be difficult to find a principled way to distinguish a variety of other groups who have perhaps immutable disabilities setting them off from others, who cannot themselves mandate the desired legislative responses, and who can claim some degree of prejudice from at least part of the public at large. * * *"

Although the Court did not subject the city's exclusionary zoning to strict scrutiny, the Court held that its policy lacked any rational basis. Essentially, the Court reasoned that the basis for the exclusion was social dislike of people with disabilities; state policy must be grounded upon something more than mere "prejudice" or dislike, the Court held. Four Justices would have applied strict scrutiny.

Roy Romer v. Richard G. Evans

United States Supreme Court, 1996.
___ U.S. ___ , 116 S.Ct. 1620, 134 L.Ed.2d 855.

■ JUSTICE KENNEDY delivered the opinion of the Court.

One century ago, the first Justice Harlan admonished this Court that the Constitution "neither knows nor tolerates classes among citizens." *Plessy v. Ferguson*, 163 U.S. 537, 559 (1896) (dissenting opinion). Unheeded then, those words now are understood to state a commitment to the law's neutrality where the rights of persons are at stake. The Equal Protection Clause enforces this principle and today requires us to hold invalid a provision of Colorado's Constitution.

The enactment challenged in this case is an amendment to the Constitution of the State of Colorado, adopted in a 1992 statewide referendum. The parties and the state courts refer to it as "Amendment 2," its designation when submitted to the voters. The impetus for the amendment and the contentious campaign that preceded its adoption came in large part from ordinances that had been passed in various Colorado municipalities.

For example, the cities of Aspen and Boulder and the City and County of Denver each had enacted ordinances which banned discrimination in many transactions and activities, including housing, employment, education, public accommodations, and health and welfare services. Denver Rev. Municipal Code, Art. IV §§ 28–91 to 28–116 (1991); Aspen Municipal Code § 13–98 (1977); Boulder Rev. Code §§ 12–1–1 to 12–1–11 (1987). What gave rise to the statewide controversy was the protection the ordinances afforded to persons discriminated against by reason of their sexual orientation. Amendment 2 repeals these ordinances to the extent they prohibit discrimination on the basis of "homosexual, lesbian or bisexual orientation, conduct, practices or relationships." Colo. Const., Art. II, § 30b.

Yet Amendment 2, in explicit terms, does more than repeal or rescind these provisions. It prohibits all legislative, executive or judicial action at any level of state or local government designed to protect the named class, a class we shall refer to as homosexual persons or gays and lesbians. The amendment reads:

"No Protected Status Based on Homosexual, Lesbian, or Bisexual Orientation. Neither the State of Colorado, through any of its branches or departments, nor any of its agencies, political subdivisions, municipalities or school districts, shall enact, adopt or enforce any statute, regulation, ordinance or policy whereby homosexual, lesbian or bisexual orientation, conduct, practices or relationships shall constitute or otherwise be the basis of or entitle any person or class of persons to have or claim any minority status, quota preferences, protected status or claim of discrimination. This Section of the Constitution shall be in all respects self-executing." *Ibid.* * * *

The State's principal argument in defense of Amendment 2 is that it puts gays and lesbians in the same position as all other persons. So, the State says, the measure does no more than deny homosexuals special rights. This reading of the amendment's language is implausible. We rely not upon our own interpretation of the amendment but upon the authoritative construction of Colorado's Supreme Court. The state court, deeming it unnecessary to determine the full extent of the amendment's reach, found it invalid even on a modest reading of its implications. The critical discussion of the amendment, set out in *Evans* I, is as follows:

"The immediate objective of Amendment 2 is, at a minimum, to repeal existing statutes, regulations, ordinances, and policies of state and local entities that barred discrimination based on sexual orientation. * * *

"The 'ultimate effect' of Amendment 2 is to prohibit any governmental entity from adopting similar, or more protective statutes, regulations, ordinances, or policies in the future unless the state constitution is first amended to permit such measures." 854 P.2d, at 1284–1285, and n. 26.

Sweeping and comprehensive is the change in legal status effected by this law. So much is evident from the ordinances that the Colorado

Supreme Court declared would be void by operation of Amendment 2. Homosexuals, by state decree, are put in a solitary class with respect to transactions and relations in both the private and governmental spheres. The amendment withdraws from homosexuals, but no others, specific legal protection from the injuries caused by discrimination, and it forbids reinstatement of these laws and policies.

The change that Amendment 2 works in the legal status of gays and lesbians in the private sphere is far-reaching, both on its own terms and when considered in light of the structure and operation of modern anti-discrimination laws. That structure is well illustrated by contemporary statutes and ordinances prohibiting discrimination by providers of public accommodations. "At common law, innkeepers, smiths, and others who 'made profession of a public employment,' were prohibited from refusing, without good reason, to serve a customer." *Hurley v. Irish–American Gay, Lesbian and Bisexual Group of Boston, Inc.*, 115 S. Ct. 2338, 2346 (1995). The duty was a general one and did not specify protection for particular groups. The common law rules, however, proved insufficient in many instances, and it was settled early that the Fourteenth Amendment did not give Congress a general power to prohibit discrimination in public accommodations, *Civil Rights Cases*, 109 U.S. 3, 25 (1883). In consequence, most States have chosen to counter discrimination by enacting detailed statutory schemes.

Colorado's state and municipal laws typify this emerging tradition of statutory protection and follow a consistent pattern. The laws first enumerate the persons or entities subject to a duty not to discriminate. The list goes well beyond the entities covered by the common law. The Boulder ordinance, for example, has a comprehensive definition of entities deemed places of "public accommodation." They include "any place of business engaged in any sales to the general public and any place that offers services, facilities, privileges, or advantages to the general public or that receives financial support through solicitation of the general public or through governmental subsidy of any kind." * * *

These statutes and ordinances also depart from the common law by enumerating the groups or persons within their ambit of protection. Enumeration is the essential device used to make the duty not to discriminate concrete and to provide guidance for those who must comply. In following this approach, Colorado's state and local governments have not limited anti-discrimination laws to groups that have so far been given the protection of heightened equal protection scrutiny under our cases. Rather, they set forth an extensive catalogue of traits which cannot be the basis for discrimination, including age, military status, marital status, pregnancy, parenthood, custody of a minor child, political affiliation, physical or mental disability of an individual or of his or her associates—and, in recent times, sexual orientation.

Amendment 2 bars homosexuals from securing protection against the injuries that these public-accommodations laws address. That in itself is a severe consequence, but there is more. Amendment 2, in addition, nullifies specific legal protections for this targeted class in all transactions in housing, sale of real estate, insurance, health and welfare services, private education, and employment.

Not confined to the private sphere, Amendment 2 also operates to repeal and forbid all laws or policies providing specific protection for gays or lesbians from discrimination by every level of Colorado government. The State Supreme Court cited two examples of protections in the governmental sphere that are now rescinded and may not be reintroduced. The first is Colorado Executive Order D0035 (1990), which forbids employment discrimination against "'all state employees, classified and exempt' on the basis of sexual orientation." Also repealed, and now forbidden, are "various provisions prohibiting discrimination based on sexual orientation at state colleges." The repeal of these measures and the prohibition against their future reenactment demonstrates that Amendment 2 has the same force and effect in Colorado's governmental sector as it does elsewhere and that it applies to policies as well as ordinary legislation.

Amendment 2's reach may not be limited to specific laws passed for the benefit of gays and lesbians. It is a fair, if not necessary, inference from the broad language of the amendment that it deprives gays and lesbians even of the protection of general laws and policies that prohibit arbitrary discrimination in governmental and private settings. At some point in the systematic administration of these laws, an official must determine whether homosexuality is an arbitrary and thus forbidden basis for decision. Yet a decision to that effect would itself amount to a policy prohibiting discrimination on the basis of homosexuality, and so would appear to be no more valid under Amendment 2 than the specific prohibitions against discrimination the state court held invalid.

If this consequence follows from Amendment 2, as its broad language suggests, it would compound the constitutional difficulties the law creates. The state court did not decide whether the amendment has this effect, however, and neither need we. In the course of rejecting the argument that Amendment 2 is intended to conserve resources to fight discrimination against suspect classes, the Colorado Supreme Court made the limited observation that the amendment is not intended to affect many anti-discrimination laws protecting non-suspect classes, *Evans II*, 882 P.2d at 1346, n.9. In our view that does not resolve the issue. In any event, even if, as we doubt, homosexuals could find some safe harbor in laws of general application, we cannot accept the view that Amendment 2's prohibition on specific legal protections does no more than deprive homosexuals of special rights. To the contrary, the amendment imposes a special disability upon those persons alone. Homosexuals are forbidden the safeguards that others enjoy or may seek without constraint. They can obtain specific protection against discrimination only by enlisting the citizenry of Colorado to amend the state constitution or perhaps, on the State's view, by trying to pass helpful laws of general applicability. This is so no matter how local or discrete the harm, no matter how public and widespread the injury. We find nothing special in the protections Amendment 2 withholds. These are protections taken for granted by most people either because they already have them or do not need them; these are protections against exclusion from an almost limitless number of transactions and endeavors that constitute ordinary civic life in a free society.

The Fourteenth Amendment's promise that no person shall be denied the equal protection of the laws must co-exist with the practical necessity that most legislation classifies for one purpose or another, with resulting disadvantage to various groups or persons. *Personnel Administrator of Mass. v. Feeney*, 442 U.S. 256, 271–72 (1979); *F.S. Royster Guano Co. v. Virginia*, 253 U.S. 412, 415 (1920). We have attempted to reconcile the principle with the reality by stating that, if a law neither burdens a fundamental right nor targets a suspect class, we will uphold the legislative classification so long as it bears a rational relation to some legitimate end. See, *e.g.*, *Heller v. Doe*, 509 U.S. 312 (1993).

Amendment 2 fails, indeed defies, even this conventional inquiry. First, the amendment has the peculiar property of imposing a broad and undifferentiated disability on a single named group, an exceptional and, as we shall explain, invalid form of legislation. Second, its sheer breadth is so discontinuous with the reasons offered for it that the amendment seems inexplicable by anything but animus toward the class that it affects; it lacks a rational relationship to legitimate state interests.

① *Amendment imposes broad & undifferentiated disability on a single named group*

Taking the first point, even in the ordinary equal protection case calling for the most deferential of standards, we insist on knowing the relation between the classification adopted and the object to be attained. The search for the link between classification and objective gives substance to the Equal Protection Clause; it provides guidance and discipline for the legislature, which is entitled to know what sorts of laws it can pass; and it marks the limits of our own authority. In the ordinary case, a law will be sustained if it can be said to advance a legitimate government interest, even if the law seems unwise or works to the disadvantage of a particular group, or if the rationale for it seems tenuous. See *New Orleans v. Dukes*, 427 U.S. 297 (1976) (tourism benefits justified classification favoring push-cart vendors of certain longevity); *Williamson v. Lee Optical of Okla., Inc.*, 348 U.S. 483 (1955) (assumed health concerns justified law favoring optometrists over opticians); *Railway Express Agency, Inc. v. New York*, 336 U.S. 106 (1949) (potential traffic hazards justified exemption of vehicles advertising the owner's products from general advertising ban); *Kotch v. Board of River Port Pilot Comm'rs for Port of New Orleans*, 330 U.S. 552 (1947) (licensing scheme that disfavored persons unrelated to current river boat pilots justified by possible efficiency and safety benefits of a closely knit pilotage system). The laws challenged in the cases just cited were narrow enough in scope and grounded in a sufficient factual context for us to ascertain that there existed some relation between the classification and the purpose it served. By requiring that the classification bear a rational relationship to an independent and legitimate legislative end, we ensure that classifications are not drawn for the purpose of disadvantaging the group burdened by the law.* * *

Amendment 2 confounds this normal process of judicial review. It is at once too narrow and too broad. It identifies persons by a single trait and then denies them protection across the board. The resulting disqualification of a class of persons from the right to seek specific protection from the law is unprecedented in our jurisprudence. The absence of precedent for Amendment 2 is itself instructive; "[d]iscriminations of an unusual character especially suggest careful consideration to determine whether they are obnoxious to the constitutional provision." *Louisville Gas & Elec. Co. v. Coleman*, 277 U.S. 32, 37–38 (1928).

It is not within our constitutional tradition to enact laws of this sort. Central both to the idea of the rule of law and to our own Constitution's guarantee of equal protection is the principle that government and each of its parts remain open on impartial terms to all who seek its assistance. "'Equal protection of the laws is not achieved through indiscriminate imposition of inequalities.'" *Sweatt v. Painter*, 339 U.S. 629, 635 (1950) (quoting *Shelley v. Kraemer*, 334 U.S. 1, 22 (1948)). Respect for this principle explains why laws singling out a certain class of citizens for disfavored legal status or general hardships are rare. A law declaring that in general it shall be more difficult for one group of citizens than for all others to seek aid from the government is itself a denial of equal protection of the laws in the most literal sense. "The guaranty of 'equal protection of the laws is a pledge of the protection of equal laws.'" *Skinner v. Oklahoma ex rel. Williamson*, 316 U.S. 535, 541 (1942) (quoting *Yick Wo v. Hopkins*, 118 U.S. 356, 369 (1886)).

[The Court next responded to the analogy argued by the dissent to *Davis v. Beason*, 133 U.S. 333 (1890), which upheld "an Idaho territorial statute denying Mormons, polygamists, and advocates of polygamy the right to vote and to hold office because, as the Court construed the statute, it 'simply excludes from the privilege of voting, or of holding any office of honor, trust or profit, those who have been convicted of certain offences, and those who advocate a practical resistance to the laws of the Territory and justify and approve the commission of crimes forbidden by it.'"] To the extent *Davis* held that persons advocating a certain practice may be denied the right to vote, it is no longer good law. *Brandenburg v. Ohio*, 395 U.S. 444 (1969) (per curiam). To the extent it held that the groups designated in the statute may be deprived of the right to vote because of their status, its ruling could not stand without surviving strict scrutiny, a most doubtful outcome. *Dunn v. Blumstein*, 405 U.S. 330, 337 (1972). To the extent *Davis* held that a convicted felon may be denied the right to vote, its holding is not implicated by our decision and is unexceptionable. See *Richardson v. Ramirez*, 418 U.S. 24 (1974).

A second and related point is that laws of the kind now before us raise the inevitable inference that the disadvantage imposed is born of animosity toward the class of persons affected. "[I]f the constitutional conception of 'equal protection of the laws' means anything, it must at the very least mean that a bare ... desire to harm a politically unpopular group cannot constitute a legitimate governmental interest." *Department of Agriculture v. Moreno*, 413 U.S. 528, 534 (1973). Even laws enacted for broad and ambitious purposes often can be explained by reference to legitimate public policies which justify the incidental disadvantages they impose on certain persons. Amendment 2, however, in making a general announcement that gays and lesbians shall not have any particular protections from the law, inflicts on them immediate, continuing, and real injuries that outrun and belie any legitimate justifications that may be claimed for it. We conclude that, in addition to the far-reaching deficiencies of Amendment 2 that we have noted, the principles it offends, in another sense, are conventional and venerable; a law must bear a rational relationship to a legitimate governmental purpose, *Kadrmas v. Dickinson Public Schools*, 487 U.S. 450, 462 (1988), and Amendment 2 does not.

The primary rationale the State offers for Amendment 2 is respect for other citizens' freedom of association, and in particular the liberties of landlords or employers who have personal or religious objections to homosexuality. Colorado also cites its interest in conserving resources to fight discrimination against other groups. The breadth of the Amendment is so far removed from these particular justifications that we find it impossible to credit them. We cannot say that Amendment 2 is directed to any identifiable legitimate purpose or discrete objective. It is a status-based enactment divorced from any factual context from which we could discern a relationship to legitimate state interests; it is a classification of persons undertaken for its own sake, something the Equal Protection Clause does not permit. "[C]lass legislation . . . [is] obnoxious to the prohibitions of the Fourteenth Amendment. . . ." *Civil Rights Cases*, 109 U.S., at 24.

We must conclude that Amendment 2 classifies homosexuals not to further a proper legislative end but to make them unequal to everyone else. This Colorado cannot do. A State cannot so deem a class of persons a stranger to its laws. Amendment 2 violates the Equal Protection Clause, and the judgment of the Supreme Court of Colorado is affirmed.

■ JUSTICE SCALIA, with whom THE CHIEF JUSTICE [REHNQUIST] and JUSTICE THOMAS join, dissenting.

The Court has mistaken a Kulturkampf for a fit of spite. The constitutional amendment before us here is not the manifestation of a " 'bare . . . desire to harm' " homosexuals, but is rather a modest attempt by seemingly tolerant Coloradans to preserve traditional sexual mores against the efforts of a politically powerful minority to revise those mores through use of the laws. That objective, and the means chosen to achieve it, are not only unimpeachable under any constitutional doctrine hitherto pronounced (hence the opinion's heavy reliance upon principles of righteousness rather than judicial holdings); they have been specifically approved by the Congress of the United States and by this Court.

In holding that homosexuality cannot be singled out for disfavorable treatment, the Court contradicts a decision, unchallenged here, pronounced only 10 years ago, see *Hardwick*, and places the prestige of this institution behind the proposition that opposition to homosexuality is as reprehensible as racial or religious bias. Whether it is or not is *precisely* the cultural debate that gave rise to the Colorado constitutional amendment (and to the preferential laws against which the amendment was directed). Since the Constitution of the United States says nothing about this subject, it is left to be resolved by normal democratic means, including the democratic adoption of provisions in state constitutions. This Court has no business imposing upon all Americans the resolution favored by the elite class from which the Members of this institution are selected, pronouncing that "animosity" toward homosexuality, is evil. I vigorously dissent.

Let me first discuss [the Court's rejection of] the State's arguments that Amendment 2 "puts gays and lesbians in the same position as all other persons," and "does no more than deny homosexuals special rights." The Court concludes that this reading of Amendment 2's language is "implausible" under the "authoritative construction" given Amendment 2 by the Supreme Court of Colorado.

[Justice Scalia quoted the decision below, of the Colorado Supreme Court, which construed Amendment 2 as follows: "[It] seeks only to prevent the adoption of antidiscrimination laws intended to protect gays, lesbians, and bisexuals."] The clear import of the Colorado court's conclusion that it is not affected is that "general laws and policies that prohibit arbitrary discrimination" would continue to prohibit discrimination on the basis of homosexual conduct as well. This analysis, which is fully in accord with (indeed, follows inescapably from) the text of the constitutional provision, lays to rest such horribles, raised in the course of oral argument, as the prospect that assaults upon homosexuals could not be prosecuted. The amendment prohibits *special treatment* of homosexuals, and nothing more. It would not affect, for example, a requirement of state law that pensions be paid to all retiring state employees with a certain length of service; homosexual employees, as well as others, would be entitled to that benefit. But it would prevent the State or any municipality from making death-benefit payments to the "life partner" of a homosexual when it does not make such payments to the long-time roommate of a nonhomosexual employee. Or again, it does not affect the requirement of the State's general insurance laws that customers be afforded coverage without discrimination unrelated to anticipated risk. Thus, homosexuals could not be denied coverage, or charged a greater premium, with respect to auto collision insurance; but neither the State nor any municipality could require that distinctive health insurance risks associated with homosexuality (if there are any) be ignored.

Despite all of its hand-wringing about the potential effect of Amendment 2 on general antidiscrimination laws, the Court's opinion ultimately does not dispute all this, but assumes it to be true. The only denial of equal treatment it contends homosexuals have suffered is this: They may not obtain *preferential* treatment without amending the state constitution. That is to say, the principle underlying the Court's opinion is that one who is accorded equal treatment under the laws, but cannot as readily as others obtain *preferential* treatment under the laws, has been denied equal protection of the laws. If merely stating this alleged "equal protection" violation does not suffice to refute it, our constitutional jurisprudence has achieved terminal silliness.

The central thesis of the Court's reasoning is that any group is denied equal protection when, to obtain advantage (or, presumably, to avoid disadvantage), it must have recourse to a more general and hence more difficult level of political decisionmaking than others. The world has never heard of such a principle, which is why the Court's opinion is so long on emotive utterance and so short on relevant legal citation. And it seems to me most unlikely that any multilevel democracy can function under such a principle. For *whenever* a disadvantage is imposed, or conferral of a benefit is prohibited, at one of the higher levels of democratic decisionmaking (*i.e.*, by the state legislature rather than local government, or by the people at large in the state constitution rather than the legislature), the affected group has (under this theory) been denied equal protection. * * *

I turn next to whether there was a legitimate rational basis for the substance of the constitutional amendment—for the prohibition of special protection for homosexuals. It is unsurprising that the Court avoids discussion of this question, since the answer is so obviously yes. The case most relevant to the issue before us today is not even mentioned in the Court's opinion: In *Bowers v. Hardwick*, we held that the Constitution does not prohibit what virtually all States had done from the founding of the Republic until very recent years—making homosexual conduct a crime. That holding is unassailable, except by those who think that the Constitution changes to suit current fashions. But in any event it is a given in the present case: Respondents' briefs did not urge overruling *Bowers*, and at oral argument respondents' counsel expressly disavowed any intent to seek such overruling. If it is constitutionally permissible for a State to make homosexual conduct criminal, surely it is constitutionally permissible for a State to enact other laws merely disfavoring homosexual conduct. * * * And *a fortiori* it is constitutionally permissible for a State to adopt a provision *not even* disfavoring homosexual conduct, but merely prohibiting all levels of state government from bestowing *special protections* upon homosexual conduct. Respondents (who, unlike the Court, cannot afford the luxury of ignoring inconvenient precedent) counter *Bowers* with the argument that a greater-includes-the-lesser rationale cannot justify Amendment 2's application to individuals who do not engage in homosexual acts, but are merely of homosexual "orientation." * * *

But assuming that, in Amendment 2, a person of homosexual "orientation" is someone who does not engage in homosexual conduct but merely has a tendency or desire to do so, *Bowers* still suffices to establish a rational basis for the provision. If it is rational to criminalize the conduct, surely it is rational to deny special favor and protection to those with a self-avowed tendency or desire to engage in the conduct. Indeed, where criminal sanctions are not involved, homosexual "orientation" is an acceptable stand-in for homosexual conduct. A State "does not violate the Equal Protection Clause merely because the classifications made by its laws are imperfect," *Dandridge v. Williams*, 397 U.S. 471, 485 (1970). Just as a policy barring the hiring of methadone users as transit employees does not violate equal protection simply because some methadone users pose no threat to passenger safety, see *New York City Transit Authority v. Beazer*, 440 U.S. 568 (1979), and just as a mandatory retirement age of 50 for police officers does not violate equal protection even though it prematurely ends the careers of many policemen over 50 who still have the capacity to do the job, see *Massachusetts Bd. of Retirement v. Murgia*, 427 U.S. 307 (1976) (per curiam), Amendment 2 is not constitutionally invalid simply because it could have been drawn more precisely so as to withdraw special antidiscrimination protections only from those of homosexual "orientation" who actually engage in homosexual conduct. * * *

The foregoing suffices to establish what the Court's failure to cite any case remotely in point would lead one to suspect: No principle set forth in the Constitution, nor even any imagined by this Court in the past 200 years, prohibits what Colorado has done here. But the case for Colorado is much stronger than that. What it has done is not only unprohibited, but eminently reasonable, with close, congressionally approved precedent in earlier constitutional practice.

First, as to its eminent reasonableness. The Court's opinion contains grim, disapproving hints that Coloradans have been guilty of "animus" or "animosity" toward homosexuality, as though that has been established as Unamerican. Of course it is our moral heritage that one should not hate any human being or class of human beings. But I had thought that one could consider certain conduct reprehensible—murder, for example, or polygamy, or cruelty to animals—and could exhibit even "animus" toward such conduct. Surely that is the only sort of "animus" at issue here: moral disapproval of homosexual conduct, the same sort of moral disapproval that produced the centuries-old criminal laws that we held constitutional in *Bowers*. The Colorado amendment does not, to speak entirely precisely, prohibit giving favored status to people who are *homosexuals*; they can be favored for many reasons—for example, because they are senior citizens or members of racial minorities. But it prohibits giving them favored status *because of their homosexual conduct*—that is, it prohibits favored status *for homosexuality*.

But though Coloradans are, as I say, *entitled* to be hostile toward homosexual conduct, the fact is that the degree of hostility reflected by Amendment 2 is the smallest conceivable. The Court's portrayal of Coloradans as a society fallen victim to pointless, hate-filled "gay-bashing" is so false as to be comical. Colorado not only is one of the 25 States that have repealed their antisodomy laws, but was among the first to do so. See 1971 Colo. Sess. Laws, ch. 121, § 1. But the society that eliminates criminal punishment for homosexual acts does not necessarily abandon the view that homosexuality is morally wrong and socially harmful; often, abolition simply reflects the view that enforcement of such criminal laws involves unseemly intrusion into the intimate lives of citizens. * * *

There is a problem, however, which arises when criminal sanction of homosexuality is eliminated but moral and social disapprobation of homosexuality is meant to be retained. The Court cannot be unaware of that problem; it is evident in many cities of the country, and occasionally bubbles to the surface of the news, in heated political disputes over such matters as the introduction into local schools of books teaching that homosexuality is an optional and fully acceptable "alternate life style." The problem (a problem, that is, for those who wish to retain social disapprobation of homosexuality) is that, because those who engage in homosexual conduct tend to reside in disproportionate numbers in certain communities, see Record, Exh. MMM, have high disposable income, see *ibid.*; App. 254 (affidavit of Prof. James Hunter), and of course care about homosexual-rights issues much more ardently than the public at large, they possess political power much greater than their numbers, both locally and state-wide. Quite understandably, they devote this political power to achieving not merely a grudging social toleration, but full social acceptance, of homosexuality. * * *

By the time Coloradans were asked to vote on Amendment 2, their exposure to homosexuals' quest for social endorsement was not limited to newspaper accounts of happenings in places such as New York, Los Angeles, San Francisco, and Key West. Three Colorado cities—Aspen, Boulder, and Denver—had enacted ordinances that listed "sexual orientation" as an impermissible ground for discrimination, equating the moral disapproval of homosexual conduct with racial and religious bigotry. The phenomenon had even appeared statewide: the Governor of Colorado had signed an executive order pronouncing that "in the State of Colorado we recognize the diversity in our pluralistic society and strive to bring an end to discrimination in any form," and directing state agency-heads to "ensure non-discrimination" in hiring and promotion based on, among other things, "sexual orientation." Executive Order No. D0035 (Dec. 10, 1990). I do not mean to be critical of these legislative successes; homosexuals are as entitled to use the legal system for reinforcement of their moral sentiments as are the rest of society. But they are subject to being countered by lawful, democratic countermeasures as well.

That is where Amendment 2 came in. It sought to counter both the geographic concentration and the disproportionate political power of homosexuals by (1) resolving the controversy at the statewide level, and (2) making the election a single-issue contest for both sides. It put directly, to all the citizens of the State, the question: Should homosexuality be given special protection? They answered no. The Court today asserts that this most democratic of procedures is unconstitutional. Lacking any cases to establish that facially absurd proposition, it simply asserts that it *must* be unconstitutional, because it has never happened before. * * * As I have noted above, this is proved false every time a state law prohibiting or disfavoring certain conduct is passed, because such a law prevents the adversely affected group—whether drug addicts, or smokers, or gun owners, or motorcyclists—from changing the policy thus established in "each of [the] parts" of the State. What the Court says is even demonstrably false at the constitutional level. The Eighteenth Amendment to the Federal Constitution, for example, deprived those who drank alcohol not only of the power to alter the policy of prohibition *locally* or through *state legislation*, but even of the power to alter it through *state constitutional amendment* or *federal legislation*. The Establishment Clause of the First Amendment prevents theocrats from having their way by converting their fellow citizens at the local, state, or federal statutory level; as does the Republican Form of Government Clause prevent monarchists.

But there is a much closer analogy, one that involves precisely the effort by the majority of citizens to preserve its view of sexual morality statewide, against the efforts of a geographically concentrated and politically powerful minority to undermine it. The constitutions of the States of Arizona, Idaho, New Mexico, Oklahoma, and Utah *to this day* contain provisions stating that polygamy is "forever prohibited." Polygamists, and those who have a polygamous "orientation," have been "singled out" by these provisions for much more severe treatment than merely denial of favored status; and that treatment can only be changed by achieving amendment of the state constitutions. The Court's disposition today suggests that these provisions are unconstitutional, and that polygamy must be permitted in these States on a state-legislated, or perhaps even local-option, basis—unless, of course, polygamists for some reason have fewer constitutional rights than homosexuals. * * *

I cannot say that this Court has explicitly approved any of these state constitutional provisions; but it has approved a territorial statutory provision that went even further, depriving polygamists of the ability even to achieve a constitutional amendment, by depriving them of the power to vote. In *Davis v. Beason*, 133 U.S. 333 (1890), Justice Field wrote for a unanimous Court:

> "In our judgment, § 501 of the Revised Statutes of Idaho Territory, which provides that 'no person ... who is a bigamist or polygamist or who teaches, advises, counsels, or encourages any person or persons to become bigamists or polygamists, or to commit any other crime defined by law, or to enter into what is known as plural or celestial marriage, or who is a member of any order, organization or association which teaches, advises, counsels, or encourages its members or devotees or any other persons to commit the crime of bigamy or polygamy, or any other crime defined by law ... is permitted to vote at any election, or to hold any position or office of honor, trust, or profit within this Territory,' *is not open to any constitutional or legal objection.*" *Id.*, at 346–347 (emphasis added).

To the extent, if any, that this opinion permits the imposition of adverse consequences upon mere abstract advocacy of polygamy, it has of course been overruled by later cases. See *Brandenburg v. Ohio*, 395 U.S. 444 (1969) (per curiam). But the proposition that polygamy can be criminalized, and those engaging in that crime deprived of the vote, remains good law. See *Richardson v. Ramirez*, 418 U.S. 24, 53 (1974). *Beason* rejected the argument that "such discrimination is a denial of the equal protection of the laws." Among the Justices joining in that rejection were the two whose views in other cases the Court today treats as equal-protection lodestars [Justices Harlan and Bradley]. * * *

* * * Has the Court concluded that the perceived social harm of polygamy is a "legitimate concern of government," and the perceived social harm of homosexuality is not?

I strongly suspect that the answer to the last question is yes, which leads me to the last point I wish to make: The Court today, announcing that Amendment 2 "defies ... conventional [constitutional] inquiry," and "confounds [the] normal process of judicial review," employs a constitutional theory heretofore unknown to frustrate Colorado's reasonable effort to preserve traditional American moral values. * * *

When the Court takes sides in the culture wars, it tends to be with the knights rather than the villeins—and more specifically with the Templars, reflecting the views and values of the lawyer class from which the Court's Members are drawn. How that class feels about homosexuality will be evident to anyone who wishes to interview job applicants at virtually any of the Nation's law schools. The interviewer may refuse to offer a job because the applicant is a Republican; because he is an adulterer; because he went to the wrong prep school or belongs to the wrong country club; because he eats snails; because he is a womanizer; because she wears real-animal fur; or even because he hates the Chicago Cubs. But if the interviewer should wish not to be an associate or partner of an applicant because he disapproves of the applicant's homosexuality, then he will have violated the pledge which the Association of American Law Schools requires all its member-schools to exact from job interviewers: "assurance of the employer's willingness" to hire homosexuals. This law-school view of what "prejudices" must be stamped out may be contrasted with the more plebeian attitudes that apparently still prevail in the United States Congress, which has been unresponsive to repeated attempts to extend to homosexuals the protections of federal civil rights laws, see, e.g., Employment Non–Discrimination Act of 1994, S. 2238, 103d Cong., 2d Sess. (1994); Civil Rights Amendments of 1975, H.R. 5452, 94th Cong., 1st Sess. (1975), and which took the pains to exclude them specifically from the Americans With Disabilities Act of 1990, see 42 U.S.C. § 12211(a) (1988 ed., Supp. V).

Today's opinion has no foundation in American constitutional law, and barely pretends to. The people of Colorado have adopted an entirely reasonable provision which does not even disfavor homosexuals in any substantive sense, but merely denies them preferential treatment. Amendment 2 is designed to prevent piecemeal deterioration of the sexual morality favored by a majority of Coloradans, and is not only an appropriate means to that legitimate end, but a means that Americans have employed before. Striking it down is an act, not of judicial judgment, but of political will. I dissent.

NOTES ON *EVANS* AND ITS IMPLICATIONS FOR *HARDWICK*

1. *What Is Not Settled or Disputed in This Case.* Although the three dissenting Justices sharply disagreed with the six-Justice Court, a number of important issues are not debated by any Justice. One is what level of scrutiny should be applied to sexual orientation classifications. All nine Justices applied the rational basis test, at least six of the Justices giving that test the same kind of "bite" it had in *Cleburne*. There is no discussion, one way or the other, as to whether sexual orientation classifications should ever receive the same sort of heightened scrutiny that sex classifications receive.

Another issue receiving no attention is the theory announced by the Colorado Supreme Court when it subjected Amendment 2 to heightened scrutiny (see Chapter 8, Section 2). The state court held that Amendment 2 deprived gay people (an "identifiable group") of a "fundamental right," namely, access to the political process. Unlike other groups, which could achieve their policy goals simply by procuring local ordinances or state legislation, gay people would have to resort to a constitutional amendment—an unfair disadvantage under the U.S. Constitution according to the Colorado Supreme Court. No U.S. Supreme Court Justice took this position.

Thirdly, there was no finding that the state interests asserted by Colorado were in any way improper or defective, only that the means used (i.e., the classification) did not fit the ends.

2. *The Implications for* Hardwick. After *Evans*, *Hardwick* still stands, but how long will it be left standing and what will its meaning be? We consider Justice Kennedy's opening citation to the dissent in *Plessy v. Ferguson* as almost a metaphorical citation to Justice Blackmun's dissent in *Hardwick*. If that subtextual reading is correct, it may signal that the current Court would have decided *Hardwick* in the opposite way, but it doesn't mean that the current Court will sacrifice *stare decisis* principles to overturn it. How might the Court cut back on *Hardwick* without overruling it? Consider that as you read the *Watkins* decision below, especially Judge Reinhardt's characterization of what *Hardwick* means. How will future courts read *Hardwick*? What do you think *Hardwick* stands for, post-*Evans*?

3. *A Focus on the Classification, Not the Class.* Justice Kennedy's focus on the "classification" (the basis of sexual orientation) contrasts with Justice Scalia's focus on the "class" (homosexuals). Although *Carolene Products* and Professor Ely's "representation-reinforcing" analysis of the equal protection clause make the discriminated-against class the focus, like Justice Scalia does, many scholars and civil rights attorneys, including Matthew Coles in the *Evans* litigation, believe that Justice Kennedy's is the better approach in the general run of cases. An advantage of this approach would be to escape the implicit issue of whether a particular group is sufficiently "deserving" or "victimized" to merit heightened scrutiny of an invidious classification. Can such an inquiry really be avoided? Which is more consistent with the sex discrimination cases such as VMI? Which focus makes the best sense for the body politic as a whole?

4. *Special Rights?* Justice Scalia depicted lesbians, gay men, and bisexuals as a group earning higher than average incomes and wielding political power much greater than their tiny numbers would suggest. The result is "special rights" legislation such as the Aspen, Boulder, and Denver ordinances prohibiting sexual orientation discrimination. Justice Kennedy rejected the "special rights" rhetoric and considered gays and lesbians a group beset by "special animus" which threatened to close them out of the Colorado political process. Is this view more realistic than the other?

Does it make a difference to you whether Justice Scalia is right when he says that "homosexuals" make more money than heterosexuals? For support, he cites to evidence in the record that is not based on rigorous statistical analysis of a random sample. As of 1996, the only econometrically rigorous analysis of comparative earning power is that of economist Lee Badgett, "The Wage Effects of Sexual Orientation Discrimination," 48 *Indus. & Labor Rels. Rev.* 726 (1995). Analyzing pooled data from a national random sample, the General Social Survey, Badgett found that bisexual and gay male workers earned between 11 and 27% less money than heterosexual workers with the same experience, education, occupation, marital status, and region of residence. Badgett found that lesbians and bisexual women earned less than heterosexual women, but the difference was not statistically significant.

As to the political power of gay people, is Justice Scalia's evidence persuasive? Thirty years ago, opponents of civil rights for people of color made the same argument, that blacks were gaining special rights from civil rights statutes protecting them against discrimination. Did African Americans then (or now) wield disproportionate political power because of their ability to procure civil rights protections? See Chapter 8, Section 2(B). Is it possible to compare the legal status of racial groups and sexual orientation groups?

5. *The Polygamy Analogy.* Justice Scalia invoked a slippery slope: if "homosexuals" cannot be disadvantaged in the political process, then surely polygamists cannot be either, and therefore anti-polygamist provisions in several state constitutions are invalid. There is an easy answer to this concern: while the state might police illegal "conduct" (polygamy under nineteenth century precedents, sodomy under *Hardwick*), it cannot exclude people who merely exhibit an orientation toward that conduct ("polygamosexuals," homosexuals). Note how Justice Scalia conflated "homosexual conduct" (an activity) and "homosexuality" (an orientation).

Justice Kennedy's invocation of *Plessy* took on an added meaning in this context. One key reason for racial segregation, upheld by the *Plessy* majority, was to prevent interracial sexuality and marriage, criminal offenses in the segregated states of the South. Justice Scalia insisted that the state ought to be able to disapprove and penalize people who in his opinion are prone to commit illegalities. Isn't that a justification for de jure racial segregation? Yet isn't Justice Harlan, the *Plessy* dissenter, considered the wise voice in that case? Isn't this kind of argument typically a surrogate for prejudice?

6. *Animus und Kulturkampf.* Consider the deeper quarrel. Justice Kennedy focused on gay people as citizens and, as such, entitled to respect; he characterized the state's penalty as inspired by "animus." Justice Scalia focused on the power of the state to treat different groups differently, unless its treatment invokes one of the classifications that triggered heightened scrutiny (race, ethnicity, sex, illegitimacy, and possibly alienage); he characterized the state's penalty as inspired by family values. The two opinions, at bottom, are speaking past one another. How is the law to determine when a state's interest is promoting morality (acceptable, at least under rational basis review) or animus (presumptively disqualifying)?

Note the violence of Justice Scalia's rhetoric. *Kulturkampf* is "culture war" conducted by the state to erase an unpopular minority. (The original *Kulturkampf* was Chancellor Bismarck's effort to domesticate the Roman Catholic Church in Germany.) One can read Justice Scalia's dissent as a rhetorical invitation for states to condone citizens who "declare war" on gay people, and Justice Kennedy's majority opinion to be an insistence that the courts should not permit *Kulturkampf*. Justice Scalia seems to consign gay people to a "state of nature" (the essence of *Kulturkampf* if you are a minority and there is a history of political and physical violence against you by citizens in the majority), while Justice Kennedy insisted that gay people be treated as part of the "social contract" under which the state exists to protect its citizens against violence and war. We believe Justice Scalia did not consciously intend his dissent to carry this meaning, but his militant language resonates with a particular force in a social context in which anti-gay hatred and even violence are common. See Gregory M. Herek & Kevin T. Berrill, editors, *Hate Crimes: Confronting Violence Against Lesbians and Gay Men* (1992).

PROBLEM 1–3

SAME–SEX SODOMY LAWS

As of 1997, seven states (five by statute, two by court decision) immunize consensual heterosexual sodomy but criminalize consensual homosexual sodomy. Is this rational? Would these statutes fall under the rationale of *Evans,* or would a heightened scrutiny standard be necessary for a successful challenge?

2.   SHOULD SEXUAL ORIENTATION BE A SUSPECT CLASSIFICATION?

One question bedeviling current lesbian and gay rights litigation is whether *Hardwick* forecloses heightened scrutiny of such classifications. Most of the cases in which this issue has arisen have involved military policies (and were decided prior to *Evans*), which are explored in detail in Chapter 4, Section 3. Because courts traditionally have deferred to military judgments, this context may have skewed the analysis somewhat in favor of preserving the policies. At least theoretically, however, identifying how to interpret *Hardwick* and what is the appropriate standard of review for equal protection purposes should be the same regardless of whether the issue arises in a military or civilian context.

Perry J. Watkins v. United States Army

United States Court of Appeals for the Ninth Circuit, 1988.
847 F.2d 1329, *vacated en banc,* 875 F.2d 699 (9th Cir.1989).

■ NORRIS, CIRCUIT JUDGE.

In August 1967, at the age of 19, Perry Watkins enlisted in the United States Army. In filling out the Army's pre-induction medical form, he candidly marked "yes" in response to a question whether he had homosexual tendencies. The Army nonetheless considered Watkins "qualified for admission" and inducted him into its ranks. Watkins served fourteen years in the Army, and became, in the words of his commanding officer, "one of our most respected and trusted soldiers."

Even though Watkins' homosexuality was always common knowledge, the Army has never claimed that his sexual orientation or behavior interfered in any way with military functions. To the contrary, an Army review board found "there is no evidence suggesting that his behavior has had either a degrading effect upon unit performance, morale or discipline, or upon his own job performance."

In 1981 the Army promulgated new regulations which mandated the disqualification of all homosexuals from the Army without regard to the length or quality of their military service. Pursuant to these new regulations, the Army notified Watkins that he would be discharged and denied reenlistment because of his homosexuality. In this federal court action, Watkins challenges the Army's actions and new regulations on various statutory and constitutional grounds. * * *

We conclude that these regulations, on their face, discriminate against homosexuals on the basis of their sexual orientation. Under the regulations any homosexual act or statement of homosexuality gives rise to a presumption of homosexual orientation, and anyone who fails to rebut that presumption is conclusively barred from Army service. In other words, the regulations target homosexual orientation itself. The homosexual acts and statements are merely relevant, and rebuttable, indicators of that orientation.

Under the Army's regulations, "homosexuality," not sexual conduct, is the operative trait for disqualification. For example, the regulations ban homosexuals who have done nothing more than acknowledge their homosexual orientation even in the absence of evidence that the persons ever engaged in any form of sexual conduct. * * * Since the regulations define a "homosexual" as "a person, regardless of sex, who desires bodily contact between persons of the same sex, actively undertaken or passively permitted, with the intent to obtain or give sexual gratification," a person can be deemed homosexual under the regulations without ever engaging in a homosexual act. Thus, no matter what statements a person has made, the ultimate evidentiary issue is whether he or she has a homosexual orientation. [The person who engages in "homosexual acts" is only separated from the service if the acts reveal a homosexual orientation; if the soldier can prove that he or she has a heterosexual orientation, the soldier can remain in the service notwithstanding homosexual activities.]

Before reaching the question of the level of scrutiny applicable to discrimination based on sexual orientation and the question whether the Army's regulations survive the applicable level of scrutiny, we first address the Army's argument that we are foreclosed by existing Supreme Court precedent from holding that the Army's regulations deny Watkins equal protection of the laws because they discriminate on the basis of homosexual orientation. The Army first argues that the Supreme Court's decision in *Bowers v. Hardwick*, forecloses Watkins' equal protection challenge to its regulations. The Court's holding was limited to this due process question. [See note 8 of the Court's opinion in *Hardwick*.]

The Army * * * argues that it would be "incongruous" to hold that its regulations deprive gays of equal protection of the laws when *Hardwick* holds that there is no constitutionally protected privacy right to engage in homosexual sodomy. We disagree. First, while *Hardwick* does indeed hold that the due process clause provides no substantive privacy protection for acts of private homosexual sodomy, nothing in *Hardwick* suggests that the state may penalize gays for their sexual orientation. *Cf. Robinson v. California*, 370 U.S. 660 (1962) (holding that state violated due process by criminalizing the status of narcotics addiction, even though the state could criminalize the use of the narcotics—conduct in which narcotics addicts by definition are prone to engage).

Second, although *Hardwick* held that the due process clause does not prevent states from criminalizing acts of homosexual sodomy, nothing in *Hardwick* actually holds that the state may make invidious distinctions when regulating sexual conduct. Unlike the Army's regulations, the Georgia sodomy statute at issue in *Hardwick* was neutral on its face, making anal and oral intercourse a criminal offense whether engaged in by partners of the same or opposite sex. In deciding a due process challenge to the Georgia statute as applied to homosexual sodomy, the *Hardwick* Court simply did not address either the question whether heterosexual sodomy also falls outside the scope of the right to privacy or the separate question whether homosexual but not heterosexual sodomy may be criminalized without violating the equal protection clause. We cannot read *Hardwick* as standing for the proposition that government may outlaw sodomy only when committed by a disfavored class of persons. Surely, for example, *Hardwick* cannot be read as a license for the government to outlaw sodomy only when committed by blacks. If government insists on regulating private sexual conduct between consenting adults, it must, at a minimum, do so evenhandedly—prohibiting all persons from engaging in the proscribed sexual acts rather than placing the burden of sexual restraint solely on a disfavored minority. * * *

We now address the merits of Watkins' claim that we must subject the Army's regulations to strict scrutiny because homosexuals constitute a suspect class under equal protection jurisprudence. The Supreme Court has identified several factors that guide our suspect class inquiry.

The first factor the Supreme Court generally considers is whether the group at issue has suffered a history of purposeful discrimination. As the Army concedes, it is indisputable that "homosexuals have historically been the object of pernicious and sustained hostility." * * *

The second factor that the Supreme Court considers in suspect class analysis is difficult to capsulize and may in fact represent a cluster of factors grouped around a central idea—whether the discrimination embodies a gross unfairness that is sufficiently inconsistent with the ideals of equal protection to term it invidious. Considering this additional factor makes sense. After all, discrimination exists against some groups because the animus is warranted—no one could seriously argue that burglars form a suspect class. In giving content to this concept of gross unfairness, the Court has considered (1) whether the disadvantaged class is defined by a trait that "frequently bears no relation to ability to perform or contribute to society;" (2) whether the class has been saddled with unique disabilities because of prejudice or inaccurate stereotypes; and (3) whether the trait defining the class is immutable. We consider these questions in turn.

Sexual orientation plainly has no relevance to a person's "ability to perform or contribute to society." Indeed, the Army makes no claim that homosexuality impairs a person's ability to perform military duties. Sergeant Watkins' exemplary record of military service stands as a testament to quite the opposite. Moreover, as the Army itself concluded, there is not a scintilla of evidence that Watkins' avowed homosexuality "had either a degrading effect upon unit performance, morale or discipline, or upon his own job performance."

This irrelevance of sexual orientation to the quality of a person's contribution to society also suggests that classifications based on sexual orientation reflect prejudice and inaccurate stereotypes—the second indicia of a classification's gross unfairness. We agree with Justice Brennan that "discrimination against homosexuals is 'likely ... to reflect deep-seated prejudice rather than ... rationality.'" The Army does not dispute the hard fact that homosexuals face enormous prejudice. Nor could it, for the Army justifies its regulations in part by asserting that straight soldiers despise and lack respect for homosexuals and that popular prejudice against homosexuals is so pervasive that their presence in the Army will discourage enlistment and tarnish the Army's public image. Instead, the Army suggests that the public opprobrium directed towards gays does not constitute prejudice in the pejorative sense of the word, but rather represents appropriate public disapproval of persons who engage in immoral behavior. The Army equates homosexuals with sodomists and justifies its regulations as simply reflecting a rational bias against a class of persons who engage in criminal acts of sodomy. In essence, the Army argues that homosexuals, like burglars, cannot form a suspect class because they are criminals.

The Army's argument, essentially adopted by the dissent, rests on two false premises. First, the class burdened by the regulations is defined by the sexual *orientation* of its members, not by their sexual conduct. To our knowledge, homosexual orientation itself has never been criminalized in this country. * * *

Second, little of the homosexual *conduct* covered by the regulations is criminal. The regulations reach many forms of homosexual conduct other than sodomy such as kissing, handholding, caressing, and hand-genital contact. Yet, sodomy is the only consensual adult sexual conduct that Congress has criminalized. * * *

Finally, we turn to immutability as an indicator of gross unfairness. The Supreme Court has never held that only classes with immutable traits can be deemed suspect. We nonetheless consider immutability because the Supreme Court has often focused on immutability, and has sometimes described the recognized suspect classes as having immutable traits, see, *e.g., Parham v. Hughes*, 441 U.S. 347 (1979) (describing race, national origin, alienage, illegitimacy, and gender as immutable).

Although the Supreme Court considers immutability relevant, it is clear that by "immutability" the Court has never meant strict immutability in the sense that members of the class must be physically unable to change or mask the trait defining their class. People can have operations to change their sex. Aliens can ordinarily become naturalized citizens. The status of illegitimate children can be changed. People can frequently hide their national origin by changing their customs, their names, or their associations. Lighter skinned blacks can sometimes "pass" for white, as can Latinos for Anglos, and some people can even change their racial appearance with pigment injections. At a minimum, then, the Supreme Court is willing to treat a trait as effectively immutable if changing it would involve great difficulty, such as requiring a major physical change or a traumatic change of identity. Reading the case law in a more capacious manner, "immutability" may describe those traits that are so central to a person's identity that it would be abhorrent for government to penalize a person for refusing to change them, regardless of how easy that change might be physically. Racial discrimination, for example, would not suddenly become constitutional if medical science developed an easy, cheap, and painless method of changing one's skin pigment.

Under either formulation, we have no trouble concluding that sexual orientation is immutable for the purposes of equal protection doctrine. Although the causes of homosexuality are not fully understood, scientific research indicates that we have little control over our sexual orientation and that, once acquired, our sexual orientation is largely impervious to change. Scientific proof aside, it seems appropriate to ask whether heterosexuals feel capable of changing *their* sexual orientation. Would heterosexuals living in a city that passed an ordinance banning those who engaged in or desired to engage in sex with persons of the *opposite* sex find it easy not only to abstain from heterosexual activity but also to shift the object of their sexual desires to persons of the same sex? It may be that some heterosexuals and homosexuals can change their sexual orientation through extensive therapy, neurosurgery or shock treatment. But the possibility of such a difficult and traumatic change does not make sexual orientation "mutable" for equal protection purposes. To express the same idea under the alternative formulation, we conclude that allowing the government to penalize the failure to change such a central aspect of individual and group identity would be abhorrent to the values animating the constitutional ideal of equal protection of the laws.

The final factor the Supreme Court considers in suspect class analysis is whether the group burdened by official discrimination lacks the political power necessary to obtain redress from the political branches of government. Courts understandably have been more reluctant to extend heightened protection under equal protection doctrine to groups fully capable of securing their rights through the political process. In evaluating whether a class is politically underrepresented, the Supreme Court has focused on whether the class is a "discrete and insular minority."

The Court has held, for example, that old age does not define a discrete and insular group because "it marks a stage that each of us will reach if we live out our normal span." By contrast, most of us are not likely to identify ourselves as homosexual at any time in our lives. Thus, many of us, including many elected officials, are likely to have difficulty understanding or empathizing with homosexuals. Most people have little exposure to gays, both because they rarely encounter gays and because the gays they do encounter may feel compelled to conceal their sexual orientation. In fact, the social, economic, and political pressures to conceal one's homosexuality commonly deter many gays from openly advocating pro-homosexual legislation, thus intensifying their inability to make effective use of the political process. * * *

Even when gays overcome this prejudice enough to participate openly in politics, the general animus towards homosexuality may render this participation wholly ineffective. Elected officials sensitive to public prejudice may refuse to support legislation that even appears to condone homosexuality. Indeed, the Army itself argues that its regulations are justified by the need to "maintain the public acceptability of military service," because "toleration of homosexual conduct ... might be understood as tacit approval" and "the existence of homosexual units might well be a source of ridicule and notoriety." These barriers to political power are underscored by the underrepresentation of avowed homosexuals in the decisionmaking bodies of government and the inability of homosexuals to prevent legislation hostile to their group interests. * * *

In sum, our analysis of the relevant factors in determining whether a given group should be considered a suspect class for the purposes of equal protection doctrine ineluctably leads us to the conclusion that homosexuals constitute such a suspect class. * * *

* * * [E]ven granting special deference to the policy choices of the military, we must reject many of the Army's asserted justifications [for the policy] because they illegitimately cater to private biases. For example, the Army argues that it has a valid interest in maintaining morale and discipline by avoiding hostilities and " 'tensions between known homosexuals and other members [of the armed services] who despise/detest homosex-

uality.' " The Army also expresses its " 'doubts concerning a homosexual officer's ability to command the respect and trust of the personnel he or she commands' " because many lower-ranked heterosexual soldiers despise and detest homosexuality. Finally, the Army argues that the presence of gays in its ranks "might well be a source of ridicule and notoriety, harmful to the Army's recruitment efforts" and to its public image.

These concerns strike a familiar chord. For much of our history, the military's fear of racial tension kept black soldiers separated from whites. As recently as World War II both the Army chief of staff and the Secretary of the Navy justified racial segregation in the ranks as necessary to maintain efficiency, discipline, and morale. Today, it is unthinkable that the judiciary would defer to the Army's prior "professional" judgment that black and white soldiers had to be segregated to avoid interracial tensions. Indeed, the Supreme Court has decisively rejected the notion that private prejudice against minorities can ever justify official discrimination, even when those private prejudices create real and legitimate problems. * * *

■ REINHARDT, J., dissenting.

With great reluctance, I have concluded that I am unable to concur in the majority opinion. Like the majority, I believe that homosexuals have been unfairly treated both historically and in the United States today. Were I free to apply my own view of the meaning of the Constitution and in that light to pass upon the validity of the Army's regulations, I too would conclude that the Army may not refuse to enlist homosexuals. I am bound, however, as a circuit judge to apply the Constitution as it has been interpreted by the Supreme Court and our own circuit, whether or not I agree with those interpretations. Because of this requirement, I am sometimes compelled to reach a result I believe to be contrary to the proper interpretation of constitutional principles. This is, regrettably, one of those times.

* * * *Bowers v. Hardwick* is the landmark case involving homosexual conduct. In *Hardwick*, the Supreme Court decided that homosexual sodomy is not protected by the right to privacy, and thus that the states are free to criminalize that conduct. Because *Hardwick* did not challenge the Georgia sodomy statute under the Equal Protection Clause, and neither party presented that issue in its briefs or at oral argument, the Court limited its holding to due process and properly refrained from reaching any direct conclusion regarding an equal protection challenge to the statute. However, the fact that *Hardwick* does not address the equal protection question directly does not mean that the case is not of substantial significance to such an inquiry. * * *

* * * The answer to the meaning of *Hardwick* is not difficult to find. There are only two choices: either *Hardwick* is about "sodomy", and heterosexual sodomy is as constitutionally unprotected as homosexual sodomy, or it is about "homosexuality", and there are some acts which are protected if done by heterosexuals but not if done by homosexuals. In applying the opinion to future cases our first effort must be to decide which of the two propositions *Hardwick* stands for. * * *

In my opinion, *Hardwick* must be read as standing precisely for the proposition the majority rejects. To put it simply, I believe that after *Hardwick* the government may outlaw homosexual sodomy even though it fails to regulate the private sexual conduct of heterosexuals. In *Hardwick* the Court took great care to make clear that it was saying only that homosexual sodomy is not constitutionally protected, and not that all sexual acts—both heterosexual and homosexual—that fall within the definition of sodomy can be prohibited.

The Georgia statute at issue in *Hardwick* on its face barred all acts of sodomy. The Court could simply have upheld the statute without even mentioning the word "homosexual". Instead it carefully crafted its opinion to proscribe and condemn only homosexual sodomy. While it can be argued that the Court was faced with only a homosexual sodomy case, under the majority's theory the fact that the particular act of sodomy was homosexual in nature is of no significance. According to the majority, the race and sexual preference of the defendant are equally irrelevant. The majority says: "Surely, for example, *Hardwick* cannot be read as a license to outlaw sodomy only when committed by blacks." Surely not. And surely, had *Hardwick* been black rather than a homosexual, the Court would not, throughout its opinion, have written about "black sodomy" or black sodomists. It would simply have written about sodomy. Here, however, from the Court's standpoint the crucial fact was that Hardwick was a homosexual. For that reason, throughout its opinion the Court wrote about "homosexual sodomy". * * *

* * * The anti-homosexual thrust of *Hardwick*, and the Court's willingness to condone anti-homosexual animus in the actions of the government, are clear. * * * Justice Blackmun characterized the decision as being "obsessively focus[ed] on homosexual activity", and "proceed[ing] on the assumption that homosexuals are so different from other citizens that their lives may be controlled in a way that would not be tolerated if it limited the choices of . . . other citizens." *Hardwick* (Blackmun, J., dissenting). Indeed, it is hard to find any basis in the Court's opinion for interpreting it the way the majority chooses: the Court says explicitly that the statute is justified by "majority sentiments about homosexuality", not by "majority sentiments about sodomy". * * *

* * * The majority opinion concludes that under the criteria established by equal protection case law, homosexuals must be treated as a suspect class. Were it not for *Hardwick*, I would agree, for in my opinion the group meets all the applicable criteria. However, after *Hardwick*, we are no longer free to reach that conclusion.

The majority opinion treats as a suspect class a group of persons whose defining characteristic is their desire, predisposition, or propensity to engage in conduct that the Supreme Court has held to be constitutionally unprotected, an act that the states can—and approximately half the states have—criminalized. Homosexuals are different from groups previously afforded protection under the equal protection clause in that homosexuals are defined by their conduct—or, at the least, by their desire to engage in certain conduct. With other groups, such as blacks or women, there is no connection between particular conduct and the definition of the group. When conduct that plays a central role in defining a group may be prohibited by the state, it cannot be asserted with any legitimacy that the group is specially protected by the Constitution.

Sodomy is an act basic to homosexuality. In the relevant state statutes, sodomy is usually defined broadly to include "any sexual act involving the sex organs of one person and the mouth or anus of another." The practices covered by this definition are, not surprisingly, the most common sexual practices of homosexuals. Specifically, oral sex is the primary form of homosexual activity. See A. Bell & M. Weinberg, *Homosexualities* 106–11, 327–30 (1978). When the Supreme Court declares that an act that is done by a vast majority of a group's members and is fundamental to their very nature can be criminalized and further states that the basis for such criminalization is "the presumed belief of a majority of the electorate ... that [the practice] is immoral and unacceptable," I do not think that we are free, whatever our personal views, to describe discriminatory treatment of the group as based on "unreasoning prejudice". Rather we are obligated to accept the Supreme Court's conclusion that what the majority of this panel calls "unreasoning prejudice" is instead a permissible societal moral judgment.

* * * The majority states that the equal protection clause requires the government (if it wishes to criminalize homosexual sodomy) to prohibit all persons from engaging in "the proscribed sexual acts". This analysis affords equal treatment only in the most superficial meaning of the term. Government actions, neutral on their face, can sometimes have distinctly unequal effects, and carry implicit statements of inequality. Laws against sodomy do not affect homosexuals and heterosexuals equally. Homosexuals are more heavily burdened by such legislation, even if we ignore the governmental tendency to prosecute general sodomy statutes selectively against them. Oral sex, a form of sodomy, is the primary form of sexual activity among homosexuals; however, sexual intercourse is the primary form of sexual activity among heterosexuals.[13] If homosexuals were in fact a suspect class, a statute criminalizing both heterosexual sodomy and homosexual sodomy would still not survive equal protection analysis. For the prohibition to be equal, the government would have to prohibit sexual intercourse—conduct as basic to heterosexuals as sodomy is to homosexuals. This, obviously, the government would not and could not do. Therefore, if equal protection rules apply (i.e. if homosexuals are a suspect class), a ban on homosexual sodomy could not stand no matter how the statute was drawn. *Hardwick* makes it plain that the contrary is true.

Finally, the "protection" of homosexual rights provided by the majority opinion is hollow indeed. The majority unwittingly denigrates the equal protection clause as well as the right to privacy. Until now, a "suspect

---

13. Oral sex, though practiced by a substantial majority of heterosexuals, is not the primary sexual activity for that group. See W. Masters, V. Johnson & R. Kolodny, Human Sexuality 388–92, 418–22 (2nd ed. 1985).

class" has been a group whose members were afforded special solicitude. That is patently not the case with respect to homosexuals. Many states deny that group the right to engage in their most fundamental form of sexual activity. A "life without any physical intimacy", is hardly the life contemplated for our citizens by the Declaration of Independence ("the pursuit of happiness") or, one would have thought, by the Constitution. While *Hardwick* may not wholly preclude the possibility of lawful physical intimacy for homosexuals, it drastically limits that right. To proclaim that under these circumstances homosexuals are afforded special protection by the Constitution would be hypocritical at best. * * *

NOTES ON *WATKINS* AND THE LEVEL OF CONSTITUTIONAL SCRUTINY FOR SEXUAL ORIENTATION CLASSIFICATIONS

1. *Doctrinal Differences.* Professor Cass Sunstein has argued that *Hardwick* should not foreclose applying heightened scrutiny review to sexual orientation classifications, because of the intrinsic differences between the due process and equal protection clauses:

> The Due Process Clause often looks backward; it is highly relevant to the Due Process issue whether an existing or time-honored convention, described at the appropriate level of generality, is violated by the practice under attack. By contrast, the Equal Protection Clause looks forward, serving to invalidate practices that were widespread at the time of its ratification and that were expected to endure. The two clauses therefore operate along different tracks.

Cass Sunstein, "Sexual Orientation and the Constitution: A Note on the Relationship Between Due Process and Equal Protection," 55 *U. Chi. L. Rev.* 1161, 1163 (1988). Is that a persuasive way to distinguish *Hardwick*? Review the discussion in our constitutional law Preface to this casebook for specific examples of due process and equal protection analysis. Do they support Sunstein's generalization? Note, too, that this generalization provides a way to reconcile *Hardwick* with *Evans*, thereby saving *Hardwick*.

2. *Status Protected, Conduct Not: Pyrrhic Victory?* As you noted from the case caption, this decision by a panel of Ninth Circuit judges was vacated *en banc*; the full Circuit ruled that Watkins was entitled to reinstatement based on an estoppel theory, grounded in the Army's repeated re-enlistment of him throughout his career, while knowing that he was gay. Had the panel decision stood, however, what would have been the ramifications of its sharp status-conduct distinction? Would its achievement have been limited to a "right" to self-identified celibacy? How would you apply the status-conduct distinction to heterosexuality? to bisexuality?

3. *The Box of Equal Protection Doctrine.* The following excerpt suggests that both views in *Watkins* are wrong, or at least insufficient: the conduct focus is too narrow, the identity approach too broad. Do you agree? Would a shift in focus from who is being classified, i.e. which are the critical, defining characteristics of this group, to an examination of the processes and criteria for classification help?

Nan D. Hunter, Life After *Hardwick*, 27 Harvard Civil Rights–Civil Liberties Law Review 531 (1992). "The illogic of the Reinhardt view * * * inheres in the effort to base a finding of intrinsic difference on precisely that which is similar. The acts at issue in *Hardwick*—i.e., sodomy as defined by the Georgia statute—are the very acts that the two groups share in common. If there are specific sexual practices that explain the difference between the two groups, it must be those practices that are missing from one group and present for the other. *That* conduct is procreative sexuality."

"* * * The status-centered view has the better legal argument; it is truer to the holding of *Hardwick*. It insists that the power of the state to prohibit certain conduct must be applied evenhandedly. It is more intellectually honest. If one imagines, for example, that *Hardwick* had been decided the other way, such that the privacy right covered acts including homosexual sodomy, there would not be automatic invalidation of sexual orientation classifications under an Equal Protection test. If we had won *Hardwick*, we would not automatically, *ipso facto*, win a challenge to the military's exclusion of lesbian and gay service members. The government would still be able to argue (I believe incorrectly) that it should be entitled to create a sexual orientation classification based on factors unrelated to whether particular conduct was criminal. The same distinction between privacy and equality holds in the opposite direction: Although we lost *Hardwick*, our claims under the Equal Protection Clause should not, *ipso facto*, be foreclosed."

"The weakness of the status-centered view is its erasure of all conduct and its focus solely on identity. Judges Canby and Norris [in *Watkins*] insist that the class of persons who consider themselves homosexual is not 'virtually identical' to those who engage in homosexual sodomy. They are boxed into this position by a need to distinguish *Hardwick*. * * * Although lesbian and gay sexual expression does encompass many more acts than oral or anal sex alone, the Canby–Norris argument is unpersuasive in its refusal to acknowledge the substantial overlap."

"What the status-centered view substitutes for sexual acts as the core meaning of homosexuality is a concept of identity that is just as 'fundamental' and essentializing as conduct is in the Reinhardt approach. Under the status-centered view, sexual orientation is 'a central character of individual and group identity,' 'a central and defining aspect' of every individual's personality. Citing the *amicus* brief filed by a gay rights advocacy group, Judges Canby and Norris assert that 'one is a homosexual or a heterosexual while playing bridge just as much as while engaging in sexual activity.'

"Both the conduct-centered and the status-centered views illustrate the ascendancy of an identity definition in the debate over the parameters of constitutional rights. The conduct-centered view holds that what a person does determines what she is; the status-centered view argues that her sexuality is so central to her identity that what she is exists independently of what she does. Both approaches would have the law institutionalize the category of sexual orientation, albeit with radically different rationales and opposite outcomes. The former would permit the state to use homosexual identity as the newest bullseye at which to aim repressive measures, while the latter would legitimate the same identity as the basis for an egalitarian demand."

3. IS SEXUAL ORIENTATION DISCRIMINATION SEX DISCRIMINATION?

Ninia Baehr and Genora Dancel et al. v. John C. Lewin

Hawaii Supreme Court, 1993.
74 Haw. 530, 852 P.2d 44.

[Excerpted in Chapter 9, Section 2.]

Andrew Koppelman, Why Discrimination Against Lesbians and Gay Men Is Sex Discrimination

69 *New York University Law Review* 197, 202, 218 (1994).*

The principal arguments for lesbian and gay rights are quite old. The privacy argument, that an individual has a right to do what she likes with her body so long as she doesn't harm others, and the oppressed class argument, that lesbians and gay men have suffered persecution and discrimination in much the same way blacks have, both have been made for centuries, and these are the arguments one most often encounters. But there is a third argument, one that was first developed at about the same time as the emergence of radical feminism in the 1970s, and which, though it is less familiar than the other two, may turn out to be the most insightful and persuasive of the three. This is the argument that in contemporary American society, discrimination against lesbians and gay men reinforces the hierarchy of males over females and thus is wrong because it oppresses women.

Both the privacy and oppressed class arguments face a common difficulty: neither takes account of any reason for the oppression of lesbians and gay men. Each of the arguments implicitly holds that there is no good reason for laws that discriminate against homosexuals. The privacy argument presupposes that there is no valid societal interest that justifies interference with (at least this kind of) sexual freedom—that homosexual sex acts are of legitimate concern only to the consenting adults who participate in them—and the oppressed class argument presupposes that discrimination on the basis of sexual orientation or behavior is as arbitrary and unfair as discrimination on the basis of race. In other words, each argument requires its proponent to carry the heavy burden of proving a negative: that no good reason exists for discriminating against lesbians and gay men. If an argument were available that shifted the burden of proof to the state to justify discrimination against lesbians and gays, this might be a more strategically promising alternative for gay rights advocates. The sex discrimination argument, I argue, has this strength.

The importance of identifying the reasons for discrimination against lesbians and gay men may be illustrated by one of the key disagreements between the majority and the dissenters in *Bowers v. Hardwick*, in which the Supreme Court upheld the constitutionality of a sodomy law against a challenge based on the right to privacy. The Justices disagreed about whether the sodomy prohibition was more like the incest prohibition, or whether it was more like the miscegenation prohibition, which the Court had invalidated in *Loving v. Virginia*. None of the opinions turned on the analogy, but their differing views with respect to it reveal much about their deeper disagreement. In the majority opinion, Justice White stressed the analogy with the incest taboo, which he evidently regarded as an ancient prohibition, the reasons for which are not clear, but which appears some- how so necessary to the functioning of civilized society that it should not be disturbed. Seeing no plausible distinction between the two prohibitions and assuming that it would be plainly unacceptable to invalidate the incest prohibition, the Court concluded that the sodomy prohibition must similar- ly be sustained.

Both dissenting opinions, on the other hand, stressed the analogy between sodomy laws and miscegenation laws. Justice Blackmun argued that *Loving* revealed the fallacy of the argument "that either the length of time a majority has held its convictions or the passions with which it defends them can withdraw legislation from this Court's scrutiny." In a footnote, he added that "The parallel between *Loving* and this case is almost uncanny": both of the challenged laws had religious justifications; both were similar to laws on the books when the fourteenth amendment was ratified; and in both instances, many states still maintained similar laws at the time the case was decided. * * *

Both dissenters' analogies to *Loving* are underdeveloped. The grava- men of *Loving's* objection to the miscegenation prohibition was that it was "designed to maintain White Supremacy." The *Hardwick* dissenters did not show that the sodomy prohibition had a similarly illicit purpose. * * *

The sex discrimination argument has recently taken on a new rele- vance. In May 1993, the Hawaii Supreme Court held in *Baehr v. Lewin* that a law restricting marriage to opposite-sex couples came within the scope of the prohibition on sex discrimination in the equal protection clause of the state constitution. Baehr may well turn out to be the most important gay rights decision since *Hardwick*. [See Chapter 9, Section 2 for an extensive analysis of the gay marriage cases.] * * * *Baehr* appears to be the first judicial opinion in the United States to hold that discrimination against same-sex couples is sex discrimination. * * *

In this Article, I argue that the taboo against homosexuality is not entirely irrational, but serves a function, and that that function is similar to the function served by the taboo against miscegenation. Both taboos police the boundary that separates the dominant from the dominated in a social hierarchy that rests on a condition of birth. In the same way that the prohibition of miscegenation preserved the polarities of race on which white supremacy rested, the prohibition of homosexuality preserves the polarities of gender on which rests the subordination of women.

* * * Sex-based classifications therefore have been upheld only when the Court has found that they reflected accurate empirical generalizations. Since it began subjecting sex-based classifications to heightened scrutiny, the Court has *never* upheld a sex-based classification resting on *normative* stereotypes about the proper roles of the sexes. Nor has the Court announced any exception to the prohibition of normative stereotyping in cases where the desire for role-typing takes the form of deep moral conviction. It could hardly do so without vitiating the principle altogether, since *all* sexual role-typing has traditionally been thought to possess such moral force.

Laws that discriminate against gays rest upon a normative stereotype: the bald conviction that certain behavior—for example, sex with women—is appropriate for members of one sex, but not for members of the other sex. Such laws therefore flatly violate the constitutional prohibition on sex discrimination as it has been interpreted by the Supreme Court. Since intermediate scrutiny of gender-based classifications is appropriate, and laws that discriminate against gays cannot withstand intermediate scrutiny, our legal argument is concluded. A court applying received doctrine should invalidate any statute that singles out gays for unequal treatment.

* * * Much of the connection between sexism and the homosexuality taboo lies in social meanings that are accessible to everyone. It should be clear from ordinary experience that the stigmatization of the homosexual has *something* to do with the homosexual's supposed deviance from traditional sex roles. "Our society," Joseph Pleck observes, "uses the male heterosexual-homosexual dichotomy as a central symbol for *all* the rankings of masculinity, for the division on *any* grounds between males who are 'real men' and have power and males who are not. Any kind of powerlessness or refusal to compete becomes imbued with the imagery of homosexuality." Similarly, the denunciation of feminism as tantamount to lesbianism is depressingly familiar. The connection between sexism and the homosexuality taboo has been extensively documented by psychologists and historians, and I shall shortly survey their work, but it should be obvious even without scholarly support.

Most Americans learn no later than high school that one of the nastier sanctions that one will suffer if one deviates from the behavior traditionally deemed appropriate for one's sex is the imputation of homosexuality. The two stigmas, sex-inappropriateness and homosexuality, are virtually interchangeable, and each is readily used as a metaphor for the other. There is nothing esoteric or sociologically abstract in the claim that the homosexuality taboo enforces traditional sex roles. Everyone knows that it is so. The recognition that in our society homosexuality is generally understood as a metaphor for failure to live up to the norms of one's gender resembles the recognition that segregation stigmatizes blacks, in that both are "matters of common notoriety, matters not so much for judicial notice as for the background knowledge of educated men who live in the world."

* * * Just as the hierarchy of whites over blacks is greatly strengthened by extreme differentiation of the races, so the hierarchy of males over females is greatly strengthened by extreme differentiation of the sexes. The element of both differentiations that promotes hierarchy is the idea that certain anatomical features *necessarily* entail certain social roles: one's status in society is obviously and unproblematically determined by the color of one's skin or the shape of one's reproductive organs. Blacks are supposed to defer to whites and obey whites' wishes because that is what blacks do. Women are supposed to defer to men and obey men's wishes because that is what women do.

The reification of socially constructed reality is always useful for the maintenance of that reality. But such reification takes on added urgency in modern Western civilization, with its radically egalitarian philosophy that manifests itself in, among other things, the fourteenth amendment of the U.S. Constitution. Thus the miscegenation taboo ultimately could not be justified in terms of its real purpose, and ended its days rationalized as a eugenic measure, on the basis of the shabbiest kind of pseudo-science. Where hierarchies based on birth are illegitimate, their survival is greatly enhanced by invisibility. Overt homosexuality is thus a greater danger to gender hierarchy in our society than it has been in other, more stable cultures. It threatens the hierarchy of the sexes because its existence suggests that even in a realm where a person's sex has been regarded as absolutely determinative, anatomy has less to do with destiny than one might have supposed. It is therefore unsurprising that, as we shall shortly see, the courts, which have enforced both of these putatively "natural" prohibitions, have struggled to conceal their socially constructed character.

The point of emphasizing this socially constructed character is not to argue that since social contexts—taken for granted meanings and habitual practices—can be revealed to be social constructions that restrict human possibilities, they ought to be smashed. Rather, the point is that *certain* meanings and practices operate in furtherance of morally indefensible ends. Where this is true, exposure of those meanings and practices as socially constructed deprives them of the invisibility provided by the appearance of "naturalness" and makes them subject to criticism. In order to survive, these systems of social construction have to lie.

NOTES ON SEXUALITY, GENDER, AND SEX DISCRIMINATION

1. *The Miscegenation Analogy.* Koppelman's article and prior work offer a formal complement to the functional argument that compulsory heterosexuality (Adrienne Rich's term) is an instrument of sexism. The "miscegenation analogy" was first offered by Professor Paul Freund as a reason to oppose the ERA: if sex discrimination were forbidden, he told Congress, then states would have to permit same-sex marriage. The reason was that *Loving v. Virginia* (Chapter 9, Section 2[A]) held that denying a black/

white couple a marriage license is race discrimination because the only variable—the classification—is the race of one partner (the black/black couple got a license). Exactly parallel is the state's denial of a marriage license to a woman/woman couple: it is sex discrimination because the only variable—the classification—is the sex of one partner (the woman/man couple got a license). You might want to read *Loving* at this point. Is there any persuasive answer to Koppelman's argument? It is not enough to point to its transvestic quality, dressing up gay rights arguments in women's rights garb.

2. *Sexual Orientation, Gender, Sex: One Big Conflation?* Summarizing an extensive analysis, Professor Francisco Valdes proposed this chart to illustrate the relationships discussed above:

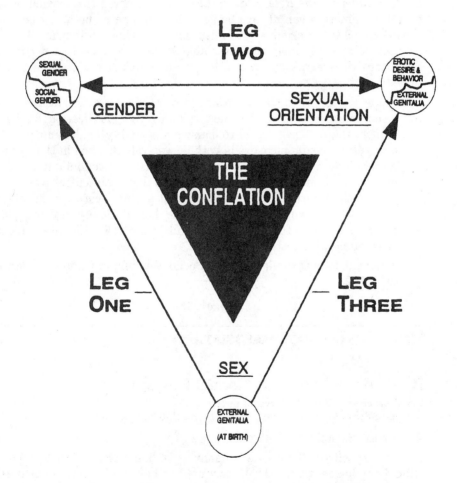

Francisco Valdes, "Queers, Sissies, Dykes, and Tomboys: Deconstructing the Conflation of 'Sex,' 'Gender,' and 'Sexual Orientation' in Euro–American Law and Society," 83 *Calif. L. Rev.* 1, 13 (1995). Valdes concludes:

> [S]exual orientation is at all times conflated with sex and/or gender: with sex under the third leg of the conflation and with gender under the second leg.* * *[U]nder the conflation, there is no such thing as discrimination *'based'* solely or exclusively on sexual orientation. * * * [I]t is possible to engage in sex and gender discrimination without simultaneously engaging in sexual orientation discrimination, but [] it is impossible to practice sexual orientation discrimination without also practicing sex and/or gender discrimination.

Id. at 16–17 (emphasis in the original). Using narratives about the lives of lesbians and gay men, Professor Marc Fajer makes a similar argument in "Can Two Real Men Eat Quiche Together? Storytelling, Gender–Role Stereotypes, and Legal Protections for Lesbians and Gay Men," 46 *U. Miami L. Rev.* 511 (1992).

3. *The Independent Role of Sexuality?* Do you agree that sexual orientation discrimination can always be subsumed in one or both of these other constructs? See the argument of anthropologist Gayle Rubin in Chapter 3, that sexuality is an independent variable. Professor Sylvia Law documented the extensive interrelationship of gender and sexual orientation, but cautioned:

> While the desire to privilege and reward gender-differentiated family structures provides the primary impetus and justification for heterosexism, the perceived need to constrain sexuality is also important. In our culture sexual pleasure is both pervasively invoked in the service of materialistic values and pervasively distrusted. Economic and political models built on assumptions of scarcity have difficulty dealing with valued experiences that are, in their nature, not scarce. A culture that rewards hard work and self-sacrifice has difficulty accommodating experiences of self-indulgence and fulfillment. A rationalist tradition has trouble with ecstasy and play.

Sylvia Law, "Homosexuality and the Social Meaning of Gender," 1988 *Wis. L. Rev.* 187, 235.

PART C.   INTIMATE ASSOCIATION

Robin Joy Shahar v. Michael Bowers

U.S. Court of Appeals for the Eleventh Circuit, 1995.
70 F.3d 1218, *vacated and rehearing en banc granted,* 78 F.3d 499 (1996).

■ GODBOLD, SENIOR CIRCUIT JUDGE:

The appellant Robin Joy Shahar is a homosexual female who was offered employment with the Department of Law of the State of Georgia to begin at a future date. She accepted the offer, but before the employment began she made known her plans to engage in a marriage ceremony with her female companion [Francine Greenfield]. The Attorney General of Georgia, who has ultimate responsibility for hiring and employment practices of the Department of Law, learned of her plans and, before the marriage ceremony took place, terminated the offer of employment.

[In September 1990, Attorney General Bowers offered Shahar a permanent position as a Department attorney to commence in the fall of 1991, and she accepted. On a departmental form filled out shortly after that, Shahar disclosed Greenfield as her "future spouse." In June 1991, the Attorney General himself learned that Shahar planned to marry another woman. The Attorney General wrote to Shahar on July 9, withdrawing the offer of employment. The letter said in part:

> This action has become necessary in light of information which has only recently come to my attention relating to a purported marriage between you and another woman. As the chief legal officer of this state inaction on my part would constitute tacit approval of this purported marriage and jeopardize the proper function of this office.

On July 28 a rabbi performed a Jewish marriage ceremony for the couple, conducted in a state park in South Carolina. Shahar sued Bowers soon thereafter. She alleged violations of her constitutional rights to intimate association, equal protection, expressive association, and free exercise of religion.

[The district court held that Shahar's relationship with her partner was within the "broad range of [constitutionally protected] human relationships" that *Roberts v. U.S. Jaycees*, 468 U.S. 609, 619–20 (1984) [Chapter 5, Section 1(C)], described as falling between familial relationships and associations such as large business enterprises. Applying the balancing test of *Pickering v. Board of Educ.*, 391 U.S. 563 (1968), the district court held that the defendant's concerns regarding Shahar's employment outweighed her interests in the intimate association with her female partner. The court therefore granted summary judgment for Bowers on all the association-based claims. It further ruled that there had been no equal protection violation because, even assuming sexual orientation discrimination requires heightened scrutiny, the Attorney General had not discriminated against Shahar based upon her sexual orientation; any discrimination was because of her open marriage to another woman.]

Shahar's position is that the district court correctly found that her intimate association was constitutionally protected but erred in applying the *Pickering* balancing test. The Attorney General's position is that the district court erred in finding that Shahar's association was constitutionally protected, but, if it was, the court correctly applied *Pickering* to find Shahar's associational interests were outweighed by the interests of the Attorney General. * * *

What Shahar claims is that she proposed to—and did—engage in a Jewish religious ceremony that is recognized as a marriage ceremony by the branch of Judaism to which she adheres; that this conferred upon her and her partner a religious-based status that is apart from and independent of civil marriage as provided by Georgia law; and that she can accept, describe, and hold out both the ceremonial event and the status created by it by using the term "marriage." In ¶ 1 of her amended complaint Shahar alleged that she was "fired" because of her participation "in a private religious ceremony of marriage." The rabbi performed a "Jewish marriage ceremony," ¶ 7, followed by "a weekend celebration of Jewish marriage," a "private religious marriage ceremony," ¶ 8. Plaintiff and her partner considered their "planned religious marriage" an important event, ¶ 9. Shahar has disclaimed any claim of "civil" or "legal" marriage pursuant to Georgia law. * * *

The intimate association Shahar asserts is not based upon false or sham assertions of religious belief, or hasty decision, or overnight conversion. She and her partner grew up in traditional Jewish families. Shahar attended Hebrew school from the third grade. She was bat mitzvahed at age 13 and continued in Hebrew school until she was confirmed at age 16. Greenfield grew up in a conservative, kosher, Jewish home. She went through Jewish training through high school, attended Jewish summer camps, and was involved in Jewish youth groups.

Shahar and Greenfield have been significant participants in the life of their synagogue, located in Atlanta. It is affiliated with the Reconstructionist Movement, one of several movements within Judaism. The synagogue serves gays, lesbians, and heterosexuals. The Reconstructionist Movement is regarded as liberal in some respects but is conservative in others. Shahar has led services at the synagogue and has given several sermons. She and Greenfield often attend together. The proposed ceremony was announced at a service of the synagogue. * * *

The evidence demonstrates without dispute that same-sex marriage is accepted within the Reconstructionist Movement of Judaism, that Shahar and her partner are committed to that belief, and that, in keeping with their Jewish principles, they carefully and thoughtfully prepared for marriage. * * *

The actual ceremony between Shahar and Greenfield occurred after her job commitment was terminated. But it is relevant to her claim that her association has religious basis and status. The ceremony was the culmination of a weekend of religious-centered activities. Approximately 150 family and friends were invited and approximately 100 attended. Events began Friday evening with the celebration of the Hebrew Sabbath, which extends from Friday evening to Saturday evening. The wedding occurred on Sunday. Essentially the ceremony followed a traditional ceremony for a heterosexual Jewish couple except for deletion of the terms "bride" and "groom." It took place beneath a traditional huppah, or canopy. The couple signed a traditional Kutubah, or written marriage contract. They exchanged rings in traditional fashion. The traditional glass was broken. The traditional seven blessings were given, done in Hebrew and in English. Rabbi Kleinbaum was dressed in traditional garb. She described the event as a "Jewish religious ceremony," as a "Jewish marriage," and as a "Jewish wedding."

The Attorney General states his position this way:

The Attorney General did not withdraw Shahar's offer of employment because of her association, religious or otherwise, with other homosexuals or her female partner, but rather because she invoked the civil and legal significance of being "married" to another woman. Shahar is still free to associate with her female partner, as well as other homosexuals, for religious and other purposes.

Brief, p. 35. But he did not submit substantial evidence tending to show that Shahar "invoked the civil and legal significance of being 'married' to another woman." Shahar and Greenfield have been companions for several years. They jointly own the house in which they live, but their joint ownership began several years before this case arose and, in any event, joint ownership is not limited to persons married pursuant to Georgia civil law. The couple benefit from an insurance rate (presumably on household or automobile insurance) lower than that available to single woman. But, under the undisputed evidence, Shahar talked to the insurance agent, explained that she was going to undergo a religious ceremony with her female partner, described and explained the ceremony, and asked if the company would consider giving them the rate available to married woman, and the company agreed to do so.

The intimate relationship between Shahar and her partner whom she planned to marry did not involve marriage in a civil, legal sense but it was inextricably entwined with Shahar's exercise of her religious beliefs. The court holds that the district court did not err in defining that intimate relationship as constitutionally protected. * * *

The court believes that the general standard of strict scrutiny is applicable to Shahar's intimate association claim and that the acts of the Attorney General must be deemed to infringe on Shahar's rights unless shown to be narrowly tailored to serve a compelling governmental interest. Shahar was not engaged in political commentary. Marriage in the conventional sense is an intimate association significant burdens on which are subject to strict scrutiny. *Zablocki v. Redhail*, 434 U.S. 374 (1978) [Chapter 9, Section 2(A)]. Though the religious-based marriage in which Shahar participated was not marriage in a civil, legal sense it was intimate and highly personal in the sense of affection, commitment, and permanency and, as we have spelled out, it was inextricably entwined with Shahar's exercise of her religious beliefs. Strong deference must be given to her interests and less to the employer's interest than in a *Pickering*-type case. * * *

■ KRAVITCH, CIRCUIT JUDGE, concurring in part and dissenting in part:

In my view, this case is not primarily about religion or expression or equal protection. Rather, the constitutional deprivation suffered by Shahar is the burdening of her First Amendment right of intimate association. In the public employment context, an employee's intimate association rights must be balanced against the government's legitimate concerns with the efficient functioning of its agencies. I therefore disagree with the majority's holding that strict scrutiny ought to be applied in this case. Nonetheless, utilizing a balancing test, I conclude that Shahar is entitled to constitutional protection.

Intimate associations involve "choices to enter into and maintain certain intimate human relationships." *Roberts v. United States Jaycees*, 468 U.S. 609, 617–18 (1984). Such choices "must be secured against undue intrusion by the State because of the role of such relationships in safeguarding the individual freedom that is central to our constitutional scheme." *Id.* In *Roberts*, the Supreme Court enumerated several characteristics typical of relationships entitled to constitutional protection as intimate associations: "relative smallness, a high degree of selectivity in decisions to begin and maintain the affiliation, and seclusion from others in critical aspects of the relationship." *Id.* at 620. Family relationships, which "by their nature, involve deep attachments and commitments to the necessarily few other individuals with whom one shares not only a special community of thoughts, experiences, and beliefs but also distinctively personal aspects of one's life," "exemplify"—but do not exhaust—this category of protected associations. * * *

A relationship that fits these descriptions is no less entitled to constitutional protection just because it is between individuals of the same sex.

This court has taken an expansive view of the right of intimate association under the First Amendment, protecting even dating relationships.

I agree with the district court and the majority that the relationship between Shahar and her partner qualifies as a constitutionally protected intimate association. The ceremony was to solemnize and celebrate a lifelong commitment between the two women, who share not only an emotional bond but, as the majority exhaustively describes, a religious faith. Even if Shahar and Greenfield were not religious, I would still find that their relationship involves the type of personal bond that characterizes a First Amendment intimate association. We protect such associations because "the 'ability independently to define one's identity that is central to any concept of liberty' cannot truly be exercised in a vacuum; we all depend on the 'emotional enrichment from close ties with others.' " *Bowers v. Hardwick*, 478 U.S. 186, 205 (1986) (Blackmun J., dissenting) (quoting *Roberts*, 468 U.S. at 618). Where intimacy and personal identity are so closely intertwined as in the relationship between Shahar and Greenfield, the core values of the intimate association right are at stake.

A public employee's freedom of association is burdened by adverse employment action if the protected association was a "substantial" or "motivating" factor in the employer's decision. *Mt. Healthy City School Dist. v. Doyle*, 429 U.S. 274, 287 (1977); *Hatcher v. Board of Pub. Educ.*, 809 F.2d 1546, 1558 (11th Cir.1987). Bowers argues that he withdraw Shahar's offer of employment only because she publicly "held herself out" as to be legally married, not because of the planned commitment ceremony or relationship per se, and therefore that Shahar's right to associate with her partner was not threatened. I agree with the district court, however, that Shahar's "conduct ('holding herself out' as about to marry another woman) is not sufficiently separate from her intimate association (marrying another woman) to allow a finding that this association was not burdened." *Shahar v. Bowers*, 836 F.Supp. 859, 863 (N.D.Ga.1993). * * *

The majority determines that because Shahar was involved in an intimate association akin to marriage and because the relationship was intertwined with religion, strict scrutiny should be applied. While I agree that heightened scrutiny is appropriate in cases where a public employee's First Amendment association rights have been burdened, it is also necessary to take into account the legitimate interests of government employers. These competing concerns lead me to a "balancing" analysis similar to both the test described in *Pickering v. Board of Educ.*, 391 U.S. 563 (1968), and strict scrutiny as it has been applied in public employment cases. * * *

The district court applied the *Pickering* balancing test to Shahar's intimate association claims. The court correctly noted that Bowers'

> asserted interests embody two over-arching concerns: (1) public credibility, specifically the need to avoid the appearance of endorsing conflicting interpretations of Georgia law, and (2) internal efficiency, specifically the need to employ attorneys who act with discretion, good judgement, and in a manner which does not conflict with the work of other Department attorneys.

Shahar, 836 F.Supp. at 864. Proceeding to find sufficient evidentiary support for Bower's articulated concerns, the district court concluded that "the unique circumstances of this case show that [Bower's] interests in the efficient operation of Department outweigh [Shahar's] interest in her intimate association with her female partner." *Id.* at 865. Absent from the district court's "balancing" discussion, however, is an explicit juxtaposition of Shahar's intimate association rights or any discussion of their countervailing weight.

The relationship celebrated through Shahar's and Greenfield's commitment ceremony is close to the core of the constitutional right to intimate association, for it exemplifies the characteristics determined by the Supreme Court to warrant special protection. In *Roberts,* the Court explained that between the poles of "family" relationships and large business enterprises "lies a broad range of human relationships that may make greater and lesser claims to constitutional protection from particular incursions by the State." [468 U.S.] at 618–22. Because Shahar's commitment ceremony and relationship with Greenfield fall close to the "family" end of this continuum, her intimate association rights weigh heavily on the balance.

On the other hand, Bowers is the chief legal officer of the state of Georgia, with responsibility for "seeing that State agencies" uphold the law and [for] upholding the law in general. Although Georgia does not have a statute which prohibits same-sex "marriages," and Shahar violated no law by planning and participating in the commitment ceremony with her partner, the state does not officially recognize such a union and would not authorize the issuance of a marriage license to a same-sex couple.

Bowers does not allege that Shahar's planned ceremony caused any actual disruption of the functioning of the Georgia Department of Law. Although we must consider a government employer's "reasonable predictions of disruption," the employer's assessment of harm should be discounted by the probability of its realization in order to weigh it fairly against an actual burden on an employee's constitutional rights. Certainly, the mere "subjective apprehension that [the employee's conduct] might have an adverse impact upon" the government agency will not outweigh such a burden.

Bowers first determined that Shahar's "holding herself out as 'married' to another woman . . . indicated a lack of discretion regarding the Department's public position on the proper application for the [Georgia] sodomy statute and Georgia's marriage laws." Shahar's pre-termination conduct, however, seems unrelated to the Department's legal positions. Second, Bowers characterized Shahar's representations about her commitment ceremony as "political conduct demonstrating that she did not believe in and was not going to uphold the laws regarding marriage and sodomy." But there is no evidence in the record to support such an inference; to the contrary, Shahar has never asserted any legal benefit from her marriage, and her commitment ceremony was far from a political demonstration or an act of civil disobedience. In any case, the Department has a rule against certain political activities, which Shahar had understood to preclude advocacy on behalf of, for instance, gay rights. Third, Bowers makes the general assertion that Shahar's presence in the Department would have a "disruptive" effect on her co-workers. Again, there is no evidence in support of this prediction in the record, and some evidence against: Shahar's summer clerkship with the Department appears to have been a success.

Bowers further contends that he was motivated to withdraw Shahar's job offer by the concern that the Department would be perceived by the public as disregarding Georgia law as it pertains to homosexual marriages (which are not recognized) and sodomy (which is illegal). Again, Shahar's commitment ceremony and relationship were not, before the inception of this case, thrust into the public domain. Even if members of the public were to become aware of and misunderstand the asserted status of the relationship between Shahar and her partner, it is questionable whether they would infer that the Department, by employing Shahar, was acquiescing in the legally legitimate status of the union. Shahar neither violated Georgia's laws pertaining to marriage nor attempted to avail herself of any legal rights or privileges reserved for legally married people. And there is no evidence that Shahar violated Georgia's sodomy law. Catering to private prejudice is not a legitimate government interest. * * *

Although the unique status of Bowers' office makes this a close case, I conclude that Shahar's constitutional interest in pursuing her intimate association outweighs any threat to the efficient operation of the Georgia Department of Law. * * *

Shahar's equal protection claim is based on the contention that Bowers withdrew her job offer, at least in part, because she is a homosexual.

Shahar argues that classifications based on sexual orientation should be subject to strict scrutiny under the Equal Protection Clause.

The facts of this case, however, do not support Shahar's contention that Bowers withdrew her offer because of her sexual orientation. Bowers asserted that he withdrew Shahar's job offer only because of conduct surrounding her commitment ceremony and relationship with her partner, not because of her status as a homosexual. The record establishes that the Department has neither a policy nor a proven practice of excluding homosexuals from employment, and that Bowers generally does not inquire into the sexual practices or preferences of applicants and employees. Furthermore, a number of Department employees, including at least two in management positions (but not, apparently, Bowers himself), were aware that Shahar was a lesbian when the offer of employment was extended. Although Shahar offers some indirect evidence of divergent attitudes in the Department towards homosexuals and heterosexuals, she has not shown that she was treated differently, for equal protection purposes, on the basis of sexual orientation. Her equal protection claim thus fails.

NOTES ON *SHAHAR* AND RIGHTS OF INTIMATE ASSOCIATION

1. *Another Means to Transcend* Hardwick? Recall that Justice Blackmun grounded his dissent in *Hardwick* not only on privacy but also on a right of intimate association. Blackmun, however, did no more than mention intimate association; he did not attempt to elaborate a theory underlying it. Associational rights derive from the First Amendment, on which the *Hardwick* court did not rule (Chapter 5, Section 1[A]); thus a fundamental rights claim based on intimate association survives that decision. What facts would be necessary to support this theory? Would an intimate association claim be viable in the context of prostitution? Adultery? Polygamy? Other sex crimes that we have studied?

2. *The Equal Protection Claim After* Evans? How can the judges deny that Bowers discriminated on the basis of sexual orientation, especially on a summary judgment motion? The real issue is whether *Evans* requires a closer scrutiny of state sexual orientation discrimination in public employment (not at issue in *Evans*). As the Eleventh Circuit's discussion illustrates, the Supreme Court has held that the state can consider third-party morale effects when an employee is being disciplined for engaging in conduct or speech protected by the First Amendment. See *Waters v. Churchill*, 511 U.S. 661 (1994). Should such a "heckler's veto" be allowed in Shahar's case?

3. *Families We Choose.* The analogy between committed same-sex partners and heterosexual marriages most often arises in the context of family law. It was especially strong in a case in which New York's highest court construed the term "family members" in a housing law to include a gay couple. *Braschi v. Stahl Assocs.*, 543 N.E.2d 49 (N.Y.1989). See Chapter 9, Section 1(B). Chapter 9 also explores whether it is constitutional for Georgia to refuse to recognize same-sex marriages. Under Koppelman's argument, the denial is also sex discrimination. Persuasive or not?

*

CHAPTER 2

MEDICALIZATION OF SEX, GENDER, AND SEXUALITY

SECTION 1   Doctors, Gender, and Sex: From the Sexologists to the Anti-Freudians

SECTION 2   Medicalization and American Law

SECTION 3   Current Issues Involving Medicalization, Sexuality, Gender, and the Law

Chapter 1 focused on *sexual activities* around which there is moral and legal debate: contraception, abortion, sodomy. Much western morality concerns itself with the legitimacy of these activities. Specifically, the Christian tradition problematized these activities because they defeat the primary goal of man-woman marriage, namely, procreation. This chapter focuses on *sexuality- or gender-based identities* around which there is moral and legal debate: the prostitute, the "homosexual," the "invert" (a mannish woman or an effeminate man). Specifically, the medical establishment problematized these statuses, because they represented at different points in time what was considered to be unhealthy sexual or gender development. There is a relationship between the old moral qualms about sex-based activities (e.g., sodomy) and the new medical qualms about identity (e.g, the homosexual).

The phenomenon we call "medicalization" helped produce the concept our culture calls "sexuality." By "sexuality" we mean something more than the biological act of sex; it refers to preferences and practices that culturally construct a sexual "identity." One's sexuality is not determined by the stark fact that one has sex with other human beings. Rather it is formed by what kind (sex, gender, age) of human beings attract one,[a] by the sexual practices one prefers to engage in with one's sexual choice,[b] and by which objects or human features one finds to be erotically stimulating.[c] Practiced and lived by the great mass of society or by smaller and more marginalized groups, these sexual scripts are part of the way Americans understand themselves and those around them.

We should distinguish concepts of "sexuality" from concepts of "gender." Gender we take to be what our culture considers to be the features or characteristics of the different sexes. "Masculine" and "feminine" are standard gender terms, though what our society considers "feminine" or "masculine" has not been stable even in the twentieth century.[d] Occupying conceptual terrain somewhere between sexuality and gender is the "transsexual." This is someone whose biological sex is incongruent with his or her gender (the "female trapped in a male body," for example). Last, many human beings do not have an unequivocal biological sex, either because they have unusual chromosomal patterns or because they have genitals of both sexes ("hermaphrodites").

The foregoing understandings of sexuality and gender have not always been part of western culture. In fact, they are relatively recent and reflect the vocabulary and evolving discourse of doctors and scientists, people retrospectively dubbed "sexologists." The first section of this chapter will introduce you to medical theories of sexuality and gender. These theories have served as the intellectual basis for much of the regulation as well as definition of sexuality in the twentieth century.

a. According to conventional usage, if one is attracted only to people of the same sex, one is "homosexual." If one is attracted only to people of the opposite sex, one is "heterosexual." If attracted to people of both sexes, one is "bisexual." The object of attraction can also be broken down by age or age differential. If one is predominantly attracted to prepubescent children of either sex, one is a "pedophile." A "hebephile" is someone sexually attracted to pubescent adolescents of either sex.

b. "Sodomists" prefer oral or anal sex to (or in addition to) penis-in-the-vagina sex. Some people simply prefer kissing to any kind of insertive sex. "Sadists" like the infliction of pain upon (or, for "bondage sadists," restraint of) the sexual object, typically a "masochist" who likes these activities. "Fantasists" enjoy such activities primarily in the context of a fantasy (e.g., cop arrests and molests lawbreaker) involving domination and submission.

c. A "fetishist" is stimulated by specific objects (such as hosiery) or body parts not usually assumed to be sexual (feet, for example). Leather fetishists, to be more targeted, are stimulated by leather apparatus or apparel. Rubber fetishists are turned on by rubber gear. Other people, "transvestites," are turned on by their own dressing in the clothing of the opposite sex.

d. For an amusing example, most people (especially parents) consider pink to be a "girl" color. When you see pink diapers, you think "girl" automatically; blue diapers trigger "boy" in your mind. In the early part of this century, pink was considered a highly "boy" color. See Marjorie Garber, *Vested Interests* (1991), for this and other interesting examples of the plasticity of gender codes.

That regulation will be illustrated by legal case studies in Section 2. These case studies will focus on turn-of-the-century regulation of prostitution, the mid-century craze of sexual psychopath statutes, and medical control of young women's (hetero)sexuality. Shifting discourses of sexuality provide a powerful lens through which to view these developments. We shall linger longest on immigration law as illustrating the operation of the concept of sexual pathology in the law, because its history encapsulates so much of the discursive history. The United States' early exclusion of prostitutes echoed medical and social hysteria about women's bodies and disease. Later, the focus of exclusion became "psychopathic personalities," a medical code word for "homosexuals and sex perverts." At present, immigration law has abandoned its interest in prostitutes and sexual psychopaths, in favor of an exclusion of people with HIV infection. Again, there is a hysterical concern about the link between sexuality and disease.

The last section of this chapter will introduce you to the cutting edge medical and scientific debates concerning sexuality and gender, an inquiry which will continue in Chapter 12. In this chapter, we introduce you to scientific evidence about the ambiguity of biological sex and the possible genetic component of sexual orientation. This evidence poses challenges for feminist and gaylesbian theorists of sexuality, and we invite you to consider its implications for law as well.

DOCTORS, GENDER, AND SEX: FROM THE SEXOLOGISTS TO THE ANTI-FREUDIANS[a]

From the early Middle Ages through the eighteenth century, the Judeo–Christian attitude toward sex dominated sexual discourse in the West. Like the Greeks and Romans, the Roman Catholic Church (and the main Protestant Churches as well) had no concept of "sexuality" as such but did have a comprehensive theory of and gender. According to the Church, the highest earthly goal of human beings was to enter into marriages through which children would be produced. Centering human welfare on marriage, the Church held that the only non-sinful form of sex was procreative sex between a husband and wife. Thus sex for pleasure between a husband and wife, adultery, masturbation, anal intercourse (sodomy), and oral sex were sinful acts. The dividing line that mattered was whether the form of sexuality in question was procreative or not. If it was non-procreative, then it was a sin. Conversely, the Church disapproved of practices that undermined the procreative potential of vaginal sex between a husband and a wife. Thus, contraception and abortion were ultimately disapproved by the Church. Recall the Church's intense effort to defend anti-contraception laws (Chapter 1, Section 1).

The natural law position still has resonance with many Americans (Chapter 3, Section 1[A]), but a competing perspective has supplemented and ultimately supplanted the natural law viewpoint: medical and psychoanalytic theories of human sexuality. This section introduces you to these theories and to their critics. The next section will trace the influence of these theories on the way the law has regulated sexuality.

PART A. THE EARLY SEXOLOGISTS[b]

Eighteenth century medicine reinforced the Christian attitudes toward sexuality. Physicians believed, consistent with Church doctrine, that sexual

---

a. An initial draft of this section was done by Barnett McGowan, Georgetown University Law Center Class of 1997. Jennifer Nash and Bonny Harbinger, also Class of 1997, edited and revised portions of the chapter.

b. This essay is derived from Vern L. Bullough, *Science in the Bedroom* (1994); Lillian Faderman, *Surpassing the Love of Men:*

activity was the cause of a variety of physical maladies. Early eighteenth century Dutch physician Herman Boerhave maintained that the cause of many physical maladies was the rash expenditure of semen. Thus masturbation and other forms of "excessive" sexual activity by a man would ultimately be physically debilitating. In the *Institutiones Medicae*, Boerhave wrote that ejaculation brought "on a lassitude, a feebleness, a weakening of motion, fits, wasting, dryness, fevers, aching of the cerebral membranes, obscuring of the senses, and above all the eyes, a decay of the spinal cord, a fatuity, and other like evils" (quoted in Bullough 19). Note the male bias of Boerhave's theory. Because women did not have semen, their health problems went unexplained.

Later in the century, French doctor S.A.D. Tissot argued that onanism led to the excessive loss of semen or vaginal discharges, which in turn led to a wide range of physically debilitating conditions. Tissot used "onanism" to refer to non-procreative sex activity such as masturbation, same-sex intercourse, oral and anal sex, and contraceptive use. Onanism affected both men and women. In men, the excessive loss of semen resulted in "(1) cloudiness of ideas and sometimes even madness; (2) a decay of bodily powers, resulting in coughs, fevers, and consumption (tuberculosis); (3) acute pains in the head, rheumatic pains and an aching numbness; (4) pimples of the face, suppurating blisters on the nose, breasts, and thighs, and painful itching; (5) . . . impotence, premature ejaculation, gonorrhea, priapism, and tumors in the bladders; and (6) . . . constipation, hemorrhoids, and so forth." Women suffered from the same problems due to the excessive loss of vaginal discharge, but in addition, they also suffered from "severe cramps, ulceration of the cervix, uterine tremors, incurable jaundice, and hysterical fits." (Quoted in Bullough 20–21.)

Both Boerhave and Tissot are representative of eighteenth century thought, especially in the way in which their theories rationalized already existing moral beliefs. Their medical theories, however, formed the social context of nineteenth century research on sexuality—"sexology" (Elizabeth Osgood Goodrich Willard's term). There were three new and defining features of nineteenth century sex research. To begin with, some of the researchers developed elaborate theories fixing and explaining gender differences between the sexes and the pathologies of sex. The most prominent pathology for most of the thinkers was "homosexuality." The idea itself was created as a distinct "orientation" fundamentally different from other forms of non-procreative sexuality. Finally, there were limited attempts to change attitudes regarding sexuality and ground sexology in non-moralistic approaches.

Karl von Westphal in 1871 described two cases of "contrary sexual feeling," similar to what Karl Maria Kertbey had the year before described

Romantic Friendship and Love Between Women from the Renaissance to the Present (1981); George Chauncey, Jr., "From Sexual Inversion to Homosexuality: Medicine and the Changing Conceptualization of Female Deviance," 58–59 *Salmagundi* 114 (Fall 1982–Winter 1983); William N. Eskridge, Jr., *Gaylaw: Challenging the Apartheid of the Closet* ch. 1 (forthcoming 1998).

as "homosexuality" (*Homosexualität*). Westphal's first case study involved a thirty-seven year old female servant who claimed to be profoundly disturbed by her love for a young girl. As a child she enjoyed playing boys' games and dressing in male clothing. The second case study was a man who liked to wear women's clothing and act the part of a woman. Westphal diagnosed both subjects as "congenital inverts," whose abnormalities were the product of a hereditary degeneration from normal male-female gender and sex characteristics. In short, the man had a feminine nature trapped in a man's body, and the woman had a masculine nature trapped in a woman's body. (Faderman 239–40.)

The first systematic theorizer of this new field of "sexuality" was Richard von Krafft–Ebing, whose *Psychopathia Sexualis* was published in 1882 and updated in a series of revised editions.[c] He started with strong assumptions about men's and women's different sexual instincts:

> Man has beyond doubt the stronger sexual appetite of the two. From the period of pubescence he is instinctively drawn towards woman. His love is sexual, and his choice is strongly prejudiced in favor of physical attractions. A mighty impulse of nature makes him aggressive and impetuous in his courtship. * * *
>
> Woman, however, if physically and mentally normal, and properly educated, has but little sensual desire. * * *
>
> Woman is wooed for her favour. She remains passive. Her sexual organisation demands it, and the dictates of good breeding come to her aid. (Krafft–Ebing 14.)

Krafft–Ebing posited that gender differences are profound. "The higher the anthropological development of the race, the stronger these contrasts between man and woman" (*id.* at 42).

Krafft–Ebing's main project was to catalogue sexual "pathologies," or dysfunctions. Many pathologies are physical in nature, but his *Psychopathia Sexualis* concentrated on the "cerebral" or "psychopathological" ones, especially "antipathic sexuality," or "homosexuality." Krafft–Ebing first distinguished between "perverse acts" and "perversion": some normal people engage in homosexual actions but without lasting consequence and are therefore "untainted." With "tainted" individuals, however, a congenital (hereditary) condition manifests itself. Krafft–Ebing categorized several stages of antipathic sexuality: what we would call *homosexual tendencies*, where the psychically and physically normal person nonetheless is attracted to those of her or his own sex and usually prefers to play a role appropriate to her or his sex (submissive female, insertive male); the *psychic invert*, who assumes the psychic characteristics of the opposite sex and prefers to play an inverted role in intercourse (the inverted male enjoys submission, the inverted female aggression); and the *physical invert*, whose physiology resembles that of the opposite sex and who can only play an inverted role in

c. The references and quotations in text will be to the authorized translation (by F.J. Rebman) of the twelfth German edition, *Psychopathia Sexualis, with Especial Reference to the Antipathic Sexual Instinct: A Medico–Forensic Study* (1931).

intercourse (Krafft–Ebing 54–55). He considered perversion to be a congenital condition which pathologically affects the entire person, yielding psychological neuroses or worse, "inversion" of gender characteristics (mannish women, effeminate men), and mental or physical "degeneration" (also *id.* at 382–83).

Krafft–Ebing's systematic treatment of a hot topic rendered it highly influential in scientific circles. Among those influenced by his approach was Havelock Ellis, whose widely read *Sexual Inversion* (1897), the first in his *Studies and the Psychology of Sex*, had fewer cut and dried generalizations than Krafft–Ebing's work did. Although Ellis was not certain whether homosexuality was congenital or acquired, his writing dealt mainly with Krafft–Ebing's "true invert" (essentially "the homosexual") and, like Krafft–Ebing, tended to view at least some sexual inverts as flipping gender roles as well. He had this to say about lesbians:

> The brusque, energetic movements, the attitude of the arms, the direct speech, the inflections of the voice, the masculine straight-forwardness and sense of honor * * * will often suggest the underlying psychic abnormality to a keen observer. In the habits not only is there frequently a pronounced taste for smoking cigarettes, often found in quite feminine women, but also a decided taste and tolerance for cigars. There is also a dislike and sometimes incapacity for needlework and other domestic occupations, while there is some capacity for athletics.

Ellis did not emphasize the gender inversion of homosexual men as much. He believed they were indistinguishable from other men but did evidence greater aptitude for drama and the arts.

Ellis's most important and ambivalent break with tradition and Krafft–Ebing regarded the sexuality of women. Throughout the eighteenth and nineteenth centuries, sex researchers assumed that women were asexual beings. A woman who enjoyed sex was believed to be ill or pathological. Ellis disputed this belief, maintaining that women are not only sexual beings, but are more sexual than men. He thought the sexual impulse is different in women because their impulse is more passive, more complex and less spontaneous, stronger after sexual relationships had been established. Ellis also claimed that women's threshold of excess is less easily reached and their sexual sphere is larger and more diffused, with more periodicity. Generally, Ellis thought there is greater variation in sexual response, both among women and within a single woman. Ellis believed that the difference is basically biological in nature. For the man, the sexual impulse is concentrated in the erect penis. Ellis rejected the idea that female sex is exclusively vaginal and argued that the sexual impulse for women is spread throughout the genital area, the breast, and even the womb. It is because women have a more diffuse erogenous region that they are more sexual, and that their sexuality is different.

Ellis' views about feminism are among his most interesting. Although he favored equal rights for women, Ellis opined that female homosexuality was increasing because of feminism. His reasoning was that the women's movement had led to "an increase in feminine criminality and feminine insanity . . . . . In connection with these we can scarcely be surprised to find an increase in homosexuality, which has always been regarded as belonging to an allied, if not the same, group of phenomena" (Ellis, *Sexual Inversion* 147–48). Moreover, women's ability to work outside the home enabled them to "find love where they find work," often love with other women. Statements such as these played into the hands of Anglo–American antifeminists, who ridiculed women's demands for equality in marriage and in the workplace and openly questioned the sexuality of the "new woman" of the nineteenth century.

American doctors found *Psychopathia Sexualis* intellectually congenial with their own experience with gender-bending women and men. Reflecting the views of many colleagues who had done case studies, Dr. George Beard wrote in 1884 that when one's "sex is perverted, they hate the opposite sex and love their own; men become women and women men, in their tastes, conduct, character, feelings and behavior."[d] The Americans were most fascinated with Krafft–Ebing's idea that any departure from strict binary gender roles (man = masculine, woman = feminine) represented a "degeneration" to more primitive forms. All vice and crime, maintained Dr. Frank Lydston in *The Diseases of Society* (1906), could be traced to "the degenerate classes," those "persons of low grade and development, physically and mentally, with a defective understanding of their true relations to the social system in which they live. * * * In them, vice, crime, and disease go hand in hand." (*Id.* at 37.) Prostitutes (with inordinate sexual desire) and sexual inverts (with inappropriate sex and gender roles) were two of the chief degenerate classes, and they contributed in urban areas to a dramatic surge in "perverted" sexual practices. Lydston believed in "evolutionary reversion," whereby the prostitute and invert abandon the inhibitions of civilization and revert to subhuman, animalistic desires. More alarmingly, degeneracy was thought to be a social disease that can be passed on to the next generation, both through heritable characteristics and the bad example set by degenerates to the young. As cures, Lydston and others of his era proposed bans on marriage by degenerates, eugenic castration, and sterilization.

The Americans' extension of Krafft–Ebing was explicitly racist as well as moralist. Dr. Lydston's 1906 book devoted an entire chapter to the so-called degenerated practices of racial minorities and nonwestern cultures. "Physical and moral degeneracy—the latter involving chiefly the higher and more frequently acquired attributes—with a distinct reversion of type is evident in the Southern negro. This physical and moral degeneracy and atavism is especially manifest in the direction of sexual proclivities," Lydston wrote. "The removal by his liberation of certain inhibitions placed upon the negro by slavery itself * * * has been especially effective as a causal factor of sexual crimes among the blacks of the South." (Lydston,

---

d. George M Beard, *Sexual Neurasthenia: Its Hygiene, Causes, Symptoms, and Treatment* (1884). This and other early medical discussions are collected in Jonathan Ned Katz, *Gay/Lesbian Almanac: A New Documentary* (1993).

Diseases 394–95.) Dr. Lydston spoke only of sexual assaults by African men upon Caucasian women. "When all inhibitions have been removed by sexual excitement, there is little difference, so far as the sense of personal responsibility is concerned, between the sexual furor of the degenerate human being, and that which prevails among the lower animals * * * . This is not confined to blacks, but is observed, although much less frequently, in some sexual criminals among the whites." (*Id.* at 396–97.) The hot climate of the South contributed to such reversion, the physician believed.

PART B.   FREUD AND HIS FOLLOWERS[e]

Sigmond Freud is the most famous of the sexologists. He, more than anyone else, is responsible for the shift in sexual discourse which began in the twentieth century. His most important contribution was to develop a comprehensive and dynamic theory which made sexuality a critical part of a person's identity. Where other sexologists asserted the existence of homosexuals and debated whether their condition was congenital, Freud posited a theory which explained people's normal as well as abnormal sexual development.

According to Freud, human children are sexually alert from a very early age and are bisexual in their sexuality. Children masturbate themselves from infancy and are typically attracted to their mothers. This is the famed "Oedipus complex" in which children desire their mother and are jealous of their father.[f] The great developmental struggle of childhood is the resolution of the Oedipus complex. In a "normal" sexual development, boys learn to escape their mother's embrace and to identify sexually with the once-hated father. Girls, on the other hand, learn that their mother is not their appropriate sexual object when they discover, to their dismay, that they do not have a penis. Recovering from this shock, girls learn to identify with their mothers and to accept sexual overtures from men, i.e. people with penises.

e. Our discussion of Sigmond Freud relies heavily on two of Freud's works, *Three Essays on Sexuality* (1905) (pages 135–243 of volume 7 of the standard edition of Freud's works, edited and translated by James Strachey), and *The Psychogenesis of a Case of Homosexuality in a Woman* (1920) (pages 147–72 of volume 18 of the standard edition). We also found Nathan G. Hale, Jr., *Freud and the Americans* (1971); Kenneth Lewes, *The Psychoanalytic Theory of Homosexuality* (1988), to be useful historical treatments of Freud.

f. The Greek myth of Oedipus inspired this nomenclature. Forewarned that his son will slay him, King Laius of Thebes orders his infant son, Oedipus, to be put to death. The servant charged with this duty has mercy and merely leaves Oedipus in the forest, where he survives and is raised by peasants. A grown [sexually potent] man, Oedipus departs for the big city. Along the road, he is treated rudely by a powerful man, whom he slays; the victim is his father, unknown to either. Oedipus later marries Jocasta, the king's widow and (still unknown to Oedipus) his own mother. When Oedipus learns what he has done, he puts out his eyes in an act of symbolic castration.

This theory of sexuality is not only dynamic, it is dramatic. Freud's happy ending—a well-integrated heterosexuality—depends upon boys' avoiding the fate of Oedipus (killing the father and cleaving to the mother) and girls' coming to identify with the mother and to accept her role in a future relationship. Like any dynamic, the movement from bisexual potential to "normal" heterosexuality is fraught with pitfalls, for almost anything can, and does, disrupt the normal development. When that happens, the individual develops in "perverse" ways, and her or his "perversion" could affect the entire personality.

Freud's most important contribution to sexology was to separate sexual "object" from sexual "aim." The "person from whom sexual attraction proceeds is the *sexual object* and the act toward which the instinct tends is the *sexual aim*" (*Three Essays* 135–36). According to Freud, the normal sexual object is an adult human of the opposite sex, with the normal sexual aim being vaginal intercourse. Any choice of a sexual object other than an adult human of the opposite sex is a perversion. Sexual activities which either "(a) extend, in an anatomical sense, beyond the regions of the body that are designed for sexual union, or (b) linger over the intermediate relations to the sexual object which should normally be traversed rapidly on the path towards the final sexual aim," were also perversions (*id.* at 150). Perverse sexual objects include members of the same sex, children, and animals. Perverse sexual aims include oral and anal intercourse, voyeurism, and sadomasochism.

Fetishism is another way in which a person could have a perverse object of sexual desire, according to Freud. In fetishism, some inappropriate body part (i.e., a foot) or some inanimate object related to the body (i.e., panties or stockings) becomes the sexual object. Fetishism begins as normal sexual desire. It is part of a normal sexual impulse for a person to be attracted to some features of his lover, or to feel sexual stimulation when he has some object of hers, when he cannot be with her. But when fixation on the body part or the object becomes necessary to satisfy the sexual impulse, this natural desire becomes a perversion. A fetish becomes pathological when the fixation "passes beyond the point of being merely a necessary condition attached to the sexual object and takes the place of the normal aim" (*Three Essays* 154). Freud's treatment of fetishism is illustrative of his "continuum" approach to sexual perversions, which linked the normal and the pathological.[g]

g. For Freud, kissing marked one of the boundaries between normal sexuality and perversion. The normal sexual aim is vaginal intercourse. However, couples usually kissed before having intercourse, and Freud recognized this as an intermediate act which heightened the pleasure of the ultimate sexual aim. Most people found kissing erotic, "in spite of the fact that the parts of the body involved do not form part of the sexual apparatus but constitute the entrance to the digestive tract" (*Three Essays* 150). Although kissing was part of a normal sex life, Freud observed that disgust kept most people from using the mouth for oral intercourse. This arbitrary division where disgust restricted the sexual impulse in normal people marked the point at which normal sexuality became extended into a perversion. Anal intercourse involved a similar arbitrary distinction.

Freud also broke new ground by recharacterizing the perceived link between perverse sexuality and illness. Sexual perversions are not themselves pathological, as Krafft–Ebing thought, but are the symptoms of neurosis. The theory is best understood by examining one of his case studies of a girl whose family brought her to Freud so that he might "cure" her of her inverse sexuality (*Homosexuality in a Woman* 147–60). The eighteen-year-old girl whom Freud examined had never shown interest in the affection of boys, but expressed considerable affection for members of her own sex. These feelings peaked with her attraction to a society woman ten years older. She became infatuated with this woman and pursued her ardently. The situation climaxed when the girl attempted suicide because the termination of the relationship seemed evident.

According to Freud, the girl's development was normal until her mother gave birth to a third brother when the girl was sixteen:

> It was just when the girl was experiencing the revival of her infantile Oedipus complex at puberty that she suffered her great disappointment. She became keenly conscious of the wish to have a child, and a male one; that what she desired was her *father's* child and an image of *him*, her consciousness was not allowed to know. And what happened next? It was not *she* who bore the child, but her unconsciously hated rival, her mother. Furiously resentful and embittered, she turned away from her father and men altogether. After this great reverse she forswore her womanhood and sought another goal for her libido. (*Homosexuality in a Woman* 157–58.)

The basic story is that stifled love for her father combined with the desire for the love of her mother, the desire to punish her father, and her sexual love of her oldest brother (a father figure), to disrupt her normal sexual development. As a result of these factors and some unexplained biological factors, the girl became an invert.

Regardless of the current cogency of Freud's analysis (the analysis in the previous paragraph is highly debatable), its revolutionary quality is clear. Freud was the first person to give a complex and seemingly scientific explanation of the cause of homosexuality. The apparent coherence between his theories and his analysis of his patients changed sexual discourse in a deep and pervasive way. But not in ways that Freud anticipated. Consistent with the above discussion, Freud in 1935 wrote his famous "Letter to an American Mother":

> I gather from your letter that your son is a homosexual. I am most impressed by the fact that you do not mention this term yourself in your information about him. May I question you, why you avoid it? Homosexuality is assuredly no advantage, but it is nothing to be ashamed of, no vice, no degradation, it cannot be classified as an illness; we consider it to be a variation of the sexual function produced by a certain arrest of sexual development. Many highly respectable individuals of ancient and modern times have been homosexuals, several of the greatest men among them (Plato, Michelangelo, Leonardo de Vince, etc.). It is a great injustice to persecute homosexuality as a

crime, and cruelty too. If you do not believe me, read the books of Havelock Ellis.

By asking me if I can help, you mean, I suppose, if I can abolish homosexuality and make normal heterosexuality take its place. The answer is, in a general way, we cannot promise to achieve it. In a certain number of cases we succeed in developing the blighted germs of heterosexual tendencies which are present in every homosexual, in the majority of cases it is no more possible. It is a question of the quality and the age of the individual. The result of treatment cannot be predicted.

What analysis can do for your son runs in a different line. If he is unhappy, neurotic, torn by conflicts, inhibited in his social life, analysis may bring him harmony, peace of mind, full efficiency whether he remains a homosexual or gets changed. * * *

Ironically, just as Freud was writing this celebrated letter, the psychoanalysts and psychiatrists in the United States were revising his theories in an entirely different direction.

The key figure was Sandor Rado, who rejected Freud's theory of human bisexuality and set forth a much less radical understanding of human sexuality in a series of articles written in the 1940s.[h] Reminiscent of Krafft–Ebing, Rado maintained that the sexes are an outcome of evolutionary differentiation of contrasting yet complementary reproductive systems, under which men and women are not ambiguous in the way Freud posited. Instead, men embody masculinity, and women femininity, and satisfactory relationships can only occur between masculine men and feminine women. Similarly, male-female mating is the only natural and healthy way to have sex. The social institution of marriage directs men and women in this natural direction, said Rado.

Some people, however, fall prey to a "schizophrenic disorganization" that overwhelms their natural heterosexuality and leads to a phobic turn to unnatural homosexuality. Other analysts, especially Irving Bieber, exploited Freud's drama of sexual development to maintain that homosexuality is caused by "pathologic" parent-child relationships, such as a boy's relationship to a smothering mother and distant father. The smothering mother conveys "demasculinizing and feminizing attitudes" to the helpless boy and inhibits "normal" male bonding between the boy and his offputting father and even other boys. Ultimately rejecting the mother's smothering and lacking a good male role model, the boy becomes a homosexual to avoid the "danger" of female control. But he will never know happiness, because he is immature and incapable of true intimacy. Unlike Freud, Rado and (even more) Bieber maintained that homosexual psychopathy can be cured in

h. The articles are collected in Rado, *Psychoanalysis of Behavior II* (1962). An "empirical" verification of his theory is Irving Bieber et al., *Homosexuality: A Psychoanalytic Study of Male Homosexuals* (1962). Carrying the torch for this theory even after it lost fashion is Charles Socarides, *Beyond Sexual Freedom* (1975), and *The Overt Homosexual* (1968).

therapy, by exposing these pathologic parental influences and showing the patient a way toward normal sexuality.

Also unlike Freud, Rado believed that homosexuals are mentally ill; allied thinkers termed homosexuality a species of the "psychopathic personality," the most severely disturbed personality state. American psychiatry in the 1940s and early 1950s rejected Freud and followed Rado on this point. The American Psychiatric Association's *Diagnostic and Statistical Manual, Mental Disorders (DSM–I),* developed in 1952 in cooperation with the Public Health Service, listed homosexuality and other "sexual deviations" with the most serious sociopathic personality disturbances. Those disturbances combined serious pathology with a lack of concern on the part of the patient. This trick explained how some homosexuals could consider themselves healthy and normal: part of their sickness was they didn't realize how sick they were! (Homosexuality lost its sociopathic classification in the 1968 second edition, *DSM-II,* but was still listed with other sexual deviations as a "mental disorder." We shall continue this historical drama in Section 2.)

Part C.   The Post-Freudians

It was not Freud but Rado who influenced the direction of American policy and the lives of thousands of people in this country. The orthodox views about gender and sexual orientation of the American Freudians were almost immediately challenged, and later on they were turned upside down entirely by thinkers who maintained that it was the doctors and not their patients who were deranged. Consider the following lines of critique that were developed after World War II.

1.   Kinsey, Hooker, and the Anti-Moralists

The categories and analysis of the American Freudians were generally consistent with traditional morality regarding sexuality and gender. Based on the empirical research like that of Magnus Hirschfeld, a German sexologist and open homosexual, rather than the theoretical models of Freud and his American followers, medical researchers after World War II directly challenged the Freudian categories and analysis. Their work was more empirically rigorous than that of the Freudians, and their conclusions rejected the traditional wisdom that had been backed up by American psychoanalysts.

Alfred C. Kinsey et al., *Sexual Behavior in the Human Male*, published in 1948, remains the most comprehensive empirical study of male sexuality in America. A taxonomical entomologist (bug expert) who made his scientific reputation in a definitive study of the gall wasp, Kinsey questioned the usefulness of taxonomy in thinking about human sexuality:

> Males do not represent two discrete populations, heterosexual and homosexual. The world is not to be divided into sheep and goats. * * *

It is a fundamental of taxonomy that nature rarely deals with discrete categories. Only the human mind invents categories and tries to force facts into separated pigeon-holes. The living world is a continuum in each and every one of its aspects. The sooner we learn this concerning human sexual behavior the sooner we shall reach a sound understanding of the realities of sex. (Kinsey, *Human Male* 639.)

The Kinsey approach eschewed preliminary categories and hypotheses and instead focused on comprehensive fact-gathering from the large but non-random sample of college students, prisoners, and Indianans swept into the giant study at his Institute for Sex Research.

The "facts" that Kinsey uncovered revolutionized Americans' thinking about sex. The facts were most dramatic in connection with homosexuality, which the Freudians depicted as biologically abnormal and psychologically poisonous:

- 37% of the male population had at least one overt homosexual experience to orgasm between the ages of 16 and 45, while another 13% react erotically to other males without having an experience to orgasm. This means that 50% of the male population had experienced significant homosexual erotic attraction during adulthood.

- 30% of the male population had had at least incidental homosexual experience or reactions (rating one or above on the Kinsey scale) over at least a three-year period between ages 16 and 55.

- 25% of the male population had had more than incidental experience (rating two or above) over at least a three-year period between the ages of 16 and 55.

- 18% of the male population had had at least as much homosexual as heterosexual experience (rating three or above) over at least a three-year period.

- 13% of the male population had had more homosexual than heterosexual experience (rating four or above) over at least a three-year period.

- 10% of the male population had been more or less exclusively homosexual (rating five or six) for at least a three-year period, with 8% being completely homosexual (rating six) for at least that period.

- 4% of the white male population was exclusively homosexual (rating six) for their entire adult lives. (Kinsey, *Human Male* 650–51, based upon the data in Tables 141–150 and Figures 162–170.)

Kinsey's findings regarding heterosexual activity were almost as surprising. Contrary to accepted American mores, Kinsey found that virtually all men masturbated, even after they were married; that many husbands had sexual affairs during their marriage, many of them without guilt (or discovery); and that married couples engaged in a range of sexual activities, including oral and anal sex as well as traditional vaginal sex. As a group, American men were kinkier than anybody had imagined.

Kinsey's *Report on Sexual Behavior in the Human Female,* published in 1953, reported significant but much lower homosexual attraction and activity among women.[i] His great contribution to study of women's sexuality was to establish beyond reasonable doubt that women are sexually active rather than passive "by nature." Consider some of the Kinsey findings:

- Nearly 50% of the sample had engaged in pre-marital intercourse, a considerable portion with their fiances in the year or two before marriage. Of women engaging in pre-marital coitus 53% had one partner, 34% had two to five partners, and 13% had six or more partners. At the time of Kinsey's studies, there were 35 states with statutes penalizing pre-marital coitus of adults as fornication. (Kinsey, *Human Female* 286, 325.)

- Among married couples, women tended to be more interested in intercourse later in the marriage, whereas men tended to be most interested early in the marriage. 75% of women experienced orgasm during their first year of marriage, but by the twentieth year 90% experienced orgasm. 9% of women had never had an orgasm, although Kinsey believed that all women are physiologically capable of responding to the point of orgasm. 14% of women in the sample regularly responded with multiple orgasms. (*Id.* at 374, 392.)

- 26% of women (in contrast to 50% of the male sample) had engaged in extra-marital coitus by the age of 40. Incidence of extra-marital intercourse in women was affected by religious background more than any other factor. The lowest incidence of extra-marital intercourse occurred in the most devoutly religious, and the highest among those least connected with any church activity. Most of the women's partners were married men of the same age. (*Id.* at 424–25.)

- By age 20, only 33% of women had masturbated, compared to 92% of their male contemporaries. 62% of women in the sample had masturbated at some point in their lives. Married women had derived about 10% of their total sexual outlet from masturbation. With women the percentage that masturbate increased up until middle age, whereas with men the percentage decreased after the teens.

- 37% of women had nocturnal sex dreams accompanied by orgasm, compared to 83% of men. The must common subject matter of female dreams accompanied by orgasm was coitus, the second was homosexual contact.

Like Kinsey, Evelyn Hooker was a scientist (a psychologist) drawn into sex research as a second career. She was critical of the generalizations made by psychiatrists based upon their experience with clinical patients—people who were almost by definition in great distress. To determine

---

i. Kinsey et al., *Sexual Behavior in the Human Female* 474–75 (1953), found that 28% of the women sampled had experienced significant erotic attraction to other women (compared with 50% of the male sample), and 13% had homosexual experiences to orgasm (compared with 37% of the male sample).

whether homosexuals really did have a distinct pathologic mental make-up, as Rado and his colleagues maintained, Hooker developed two samples matched in every way (IQ, income, age, sex, etc.) except for sexual orientation and tested the members of each sample by standard means (mainly the Rorschach). Independent judges blindly evaluated the results of the testing. The judges not only evaluated the homosexuals at a high level (i.e., they were psychologically functional) but could not discern any difference between the homosexual and heterosexual groups. Although they did not yield the popular interest of the Kinsey results, Hooker's published studies cast doubt on a generation's worth of generalizations about homosexuals and, indeed, exposed the work of Rado and other scholars as methodologically naive.[j]

2. CHODOROW AND OTHER FEMINIST CRITICS OF FREUD[k]

Since he first presented his research, Freud's analysis of women has been called into question both within and outside the discipline of psychoanalysis, and there has been considerable revision and challenge of Freud's theories. Feminists have called to attention the male bias in Freud's research—especially the priority Freud bestowed upon the male sexual organ and the centrality of castration theories to his analysis. Further, many feminist theorists suggest that heterosexuality may encode male dominance because it is tied to gender inequality and power differentials. Finally, there has been considerable recent reexamination of Freud's suppression of the seduction theory in light of increasing awareness of the high incidence of child sexual and physical abuse and violence against women that exists, not in the realm of fantasy, but rather, in very high numbers in actuality, with considerable implication for issues of female sexuality and gender.

In *Femininities, Masculinities, Sexualities: Freud and Beyond* (1994), Nancy Chodorow presents a feminist theory of psychoanalysis. Although Chodorow admires Freud's clinical accounts, his "forthright defense of hysterical women * * * his condemnation of the conditions leading to repression and hysteria in women [and] his toleration and understanding of variations in sexual object choice and sexual subjectivity," she finds his theory of femininity "extremely problematic." (*Id.* at 31.) Chodorow argues that what Freud's writings present is a treatment of woman in the male psyche-woman as object, not subject. For Freud "women, basically, are castrated men" (*id.* at 28). In contrast, Chodorow begins with woman as subject.

---

j. See Evelyn Hooker, "The Adjustment of the Overt Male Homosexual," 21 *J. Projective Techniques* 18 (1957), and "Male Homosexuality in the Rorschach," 22 *J. Projective Techniques* 33 (1958).

k. Our discussion draws from Nancy Chodorow, *Femininities, Masculinities, Sexualities* (1994), as well as Chodorow, *Feminism* and *Psychanalytic Theory* (1989); Dorothy Dinnerstein, *The Mermaid and the Minotaur* (1976). We also relied on Sandra Janoff, "The Influence of Legal Education on Moral Reasoning," 76 *Minn. L. Rev.* 193 (1991). The primary authors of this essay are Mara Rosenthal, Georgetown University Law Center, Class of 1998, and Jennifer Nash, Class of 1997.

Chodorow is most critical of Freud's focus on phallic sexuality in discussions of female sexuality. Female desire, for Freud, is focused on the missing penis; the girl's sexual desire is transferred to the desire for a baby, preferably a boy baby who brings the missing penis with him. Freud thus draws upon penis envy and the penis-baby equation to explain most of what he means by femininity. The centrality of penis envy in Freud's theories is profound.[1] As Chodorow puts it, the boy feels "horror of the mutilated creature or triumphant contempt for her" and the girl "begins to share the contempt felt by men for a sex which is the lesser in so important a respect." (*Femininities* 8.) Thus, in Freud's theory, both males and females develop a view of women as inferior.

Chodorow rejects Freud's negative description of female ego development and sets forth her own theory of how girls and boys develop differently. "Whereas Freud's masculine bias held that girls do not fully repress their conflicts between sexual identity and aggression and therefore have weaker ego boundaries, Chodorow explained that girls, mothered by women, experience preoedipal relationships which are less ego-threatening than those experienced by boys. Because women develop their gender identities within an ongoing, same-sex relationship, girls do not have to curtail their primary love. Male gender identity, on the other hand, requires an emotional separation from the mother and identification with the father. As a result, Chodorow postulate[s], the basic feminine sense of self is a sense of connectedness, whereas the basic masculine sense of self is a sense of separateness." (Janoff 200.)

In her own research, Chodorow argues that there is no monolithic "normal" sexuality but, rather, that there are many different sexualities. Researchers have focused and know much more about homosexuality and the so-called perversions than they do about taken-for-granted "normal" sexuality. Why shouldn't heterosexuality follow the same dynamic and developmental pathways as any other sexuality? If so, "clinically there is no normal heterosexuality." (*Femininities* 62.) Questioning the simplistic model of "one modal boy and one modal girl who develop into 'normal' heterosexuals, we find instead a wide variety of 'normal' heterosexualities just as we know that there are many homosexualities and many heterosexual perversions" (*id.* at 67). In place of the overgeneralized model of sexuality that has pervaded psychoanalytic writing since Freud, Chodorow suggests that "we treat all sexuality as problematic and to be accounted for" (*id.* at 69).

A feminist model of subjective sexuality and gender is rooted in culture, history, and early family development. Chodorow argues that biology cannot explain the content of either cultural fantasy or private eroticism or sexual orientation. Neither sexuality nor gender is an innate feature hardwired into an individual. Instead, an individual's sexuality and gender evolve from experiences in early childhood and family life and the

---

1. "She has seen it and knows that she is without it and wants to have it[;] she develops, like a scar, a sense of inferiority." Sigmund Freud, "Some Psychical Consequences of the Anatomical Distinction between the Sexes" (1925).

larger cultural meanings within which the family and individual are embedded. Thus, an individual's experience of family, including "engulfment, separateness, destruction, threat, love, hate," is mediated by the larger cultural context and socio-cultural meanings presented in, for example, the media.

Contemporary discussion of Freud's analysis of women must also focus on the controversy surrounding Freud's suppression of the seduction theory. The seduction theory refers to Freud's 1896 paper entitled "The Aetiology of Hysteria," in which he argued that female hysteria and many other female mental illnesses are caused by childhood sexual assault.[m] Freud subsequently revised this theory, on the ground that these childhood memories of sexual assault often were not real but rather fantasies concocted by his female patients.[n] It is now believed that Freud got it right the first time; surveys and statistics generated primarily since the 1970s indicate a tremendously high incidence of childhood physical and sexual abuse and violence against women. Researchers estimate that the incidence of child abuse may be as high as one in ten for boys and greater than one in three for girls.[o] This prevalence of sexual assault and violence against women has significant implications for female sexuality.

Although many women who are victims of sexual violence manage to "pass" and conduct successful lives and careers, research reveals a very high correlation between mental illness of women in clinical populations and a history of sexual abuse and violence against women. Studies indicate that up to 72% of psychiatric inpatients have histories of physical or sexual abuse or both.[p] Despite the availability of the data indicating the prevalence of patients with abuse histories in health care settings and the negative impact of abuse on women's health, health care providers have only recently begun to address these issues.[q]

---

m. The psychiatric establishment was shocked by Freud's theory and isolated Freud professionally. Ironically, Richard von Krafft–Ebing was the Chair at the Society for Psychiatry and Neurology in Vienna where Freud presented his paper. Kraft–Ebing denounced Freud's work as "a scientific fairytale." Max Schur, *Freud: Living and Dying* 104 (1972).

n. For a fascinating and controversial perspective on the history of Freud's development of the seduction theory and his subsequent revision of that theory see Jeffrey Moussaieff Masson, *The Assault on Truth: Freud's Suppression of the Seduction Theory* (1985).

o. Rose Peabody, *Strategies Responding to Hidden Abuse: A Role for Social Work in Reforming Mental Health Systems* (1991). Injury to women caused by domestic violence is higher than muggings, stranger rapes and car

accidents combined. D.G, "What's Love Got to Do with It?," *Ms.*, vol. 4, issue 2, at 37 (1994).

p. See, *e.g.*, Bryer et al., "Childhood Sexual and Physical Abuse as Factors in Adult Psychiatric Illness," 144 *Am. J. Psychiatry* 1426–30 (1987); Elaine Carmen et al., "Victims of Violence and Psychiatric Disorders," 141 *Am. J. Psychiatry* 378–83 (1984); Carmen & Rieker, "A Psychosocial Model of the Victim-to-Patient Process: Implications for Treatment," 12 *Psychiatric Clinics N. Am.* 431–43 (1989); Craine et al., "Prevalence of a History of Sexual Abuse among Female Psychiatric Patients in a State Hospital System," 39 *Hosp. & Community Psychiatry* 300–04 (1988); T. Mills et al., "Hospitalization Experiences of Victims of Abuse," 9 *Victimology* 436–49 (1984).

q. Carole Warshaw, "Violence and Women's Health: Old Models, New Chal-

Society has been slow to recognize sexual assault and violence against women as a powerful mechanism for subordinating women, and when there has been recognition it has been of female "victims" suffering at the hands of "pathological" brutes. Susan Stefan puts it this way:

> From Freud's Dora to Anita Hill, women's stories about sexual abuse and harassment have been disbelieved and discredited as hallucinations and delusions. This is a society where the victims of sexual violence are labeled as sick, and the perpetrators are, for the most part, less stigmatized and less labeled. * * * Freud asked, "What do women want?" * * * We want to stop having our survival strategies labeled as pathologies, and stop having our recognition that this society is a violent and dangerous place characterized as an adjustment difficulty. * * * We are aware of the harmful consequences of having "professionals" define and deal with our issues.[r]

Stefan argues that the medicalization of women's reactions to male violence leads to social assumptions that such violence is an aberration rather than the norm. For example, it was only in 1994 that the American Psychiatric Association in their classification of "rape trauma syndrome," deleted the terms that the trauma be "outside the range of usual human experience."[s] The extent to which doctors may have shifted the focus from sexual violence to pathological labeling of victims' responses to the violence illustrates how the process of "medicalization" itself can embody a male bias.

3.   SZASZ, FOUCAULT, AND THE ANTI-CLINICIANS

The critique of the empiricists was a deep but internal critique of the Freudians, to the effect that they were sloppy scientists. The critique of the feminists was an external critique, arguing that Freud and his followers were dressing up traditional gender attitudes in fancier jargon; this critique was generally limited to issues of gender. A third critique of the Freudians was initiated by Thomas Szasz, who reversed many of the psychoanalytical tropes to argue that it was the doctors and not their patients who were misreading reality.

Szasz distinguished between "real" illness such as measles or the flu, that had discernible causes and bad consequences for the individual, and "counterfeit" illnesses such as Freud's hysteria, which he described as myths concocted by strategic psychiatrists seeking power and prestige for themselves and their profession. In Judd Marmor's collection of essays on

lenges," in Human Resource Association of the Northeast, Proceedings of the Conference, *Dare to Vision: Shaping the National Agenda for Women, Abuse and Mental Health Services,* July 14–16, 1994, Arlington, Va., at 70 (1995).

r. Susan Stefan, "The Protection Racket–Violence against Women: Psychiatric Labeling and Law," in Human Resource Associ-

ation of the Northeast, Proceedings of the Conference, *Dare to Vision: Shaping the National Agenda for Women, Abuse and Mental Health Services,* July 14–16, 1994, Arlington, Va., at 29–30 (1995).

s. See Susan Stefan, "The Protection Racket: Rape Trauma Syndrome, Psychiatric Labeling, and Law," 88 *Nw. L. Rev.* 1271, 1275.

Sexual Inversion (1965), Szasz agreed that the biological desirability of procreation provides a descriptive case for heterosexuality, but not a normative argument that everybody must participate or that departures from heterosexuality are bad or even significant in the larger scheme of things. Szasz' *The Manufacture of Madness* (1970) went further, to compare modern psychiatry with the medieval inquisition: just as the Church used the rack to impose religious conformity and extinguish heresy, the psychiatrist used therapies including electroshock and drugs to impose sexual conformity and extinguish sexual deviation.

French philosopher Michel Foucault initiated a different and more fundamental critique. Although Freud presented himself as revolutionary, Foucault claimed that Freud was not significantly different than those whom he had criticized. Like his predecessors, Freud presented sexuality as an object to be discovered, tested, and (especially) treated. Foucault, in contrast, maintained that sexuality was itself constructed by the discourse of the sexologists and their bourgeois allies, and that repression only intensified the discourse of sexuality. For more on Foucault, see Chapter 3, Section 2(B).

PROBLEM 2–1

THE RELATIONSHIP BETWEEN SODOMY AND HOMOSEXUALITY

Reread *Bowers v. Hardwick* from Chapter 1. Think about the Justices' opinions—not just the result each opinion endorsed, but more particularly the reasoning and the metaphors or parallels deployed by each opinion. What insights do the following thinkers offer us about the opinions:

(a) Krafft–Ebing. See *Psychopathia Sexualis* 578–80.

(b) Freud. See "Letter to an American Mother." Contrast the views of Freud's American followers.

(c) Chodorow. See *Femininities*.

These thinkers might also offer descriptive insights. That is, rather than "causing" people to think about sexuality in a certain way, these thinkers might be products of underlying social and intellectual changes, and their thought might be a window into more general thinking about sodomy. If that is so, how would you expect middle-class society to be approaching the issue in 1880–1920 (Krafft–Ebing), 1920–60 (Freud's American followers), and 1970–present (Chodorow, perhaps also Szasz)? Where does Justice Byron White, the author of *Bowers v. Hardwick*, fit?

SECTION 2

MEDICALIZATION AND AMERICAN LAW

The partial displacement of religious or natural law discourse about *sex* by medicalized discourse about *sexuality* has had pervasive resonance in American law. We consider three different ones here: degeneracy and feminized vice, the sexual psychopath (especially the "homosexual"), and medical and parental control over young women's (hetero)sexuality. As you read these materials, consider the cogency of Carroll Smith–Rosenberg's theory that medicalization represented a way that middle class, professional male culture sought to preserve its power by controlling women's bodies.

PART A. DEGENERACY AND FEMINIZED VICE, 1870–1920

The Victorian era in the United States witnessed heightened concern with vice, especially as associated with "degraded" women.[a] The classic degraded woman was the prostitute, and prostitution was easily the primary focus of state concern, with reasons of hygiene and disease dominating the case for activist state regulation. Medicalization in this way reinforced the strictures of traditional morality, but in other ways medicalization pushed in different directions. It emphasized the view of women, not as receptacles or victims of vice, but as sexualized agents of vice. This view of women created a whole host of problems for society, which didn't like the new view, and the law, which struggled to incorporate it.

1. THE REGULATION OF PROSTITUTION[b]

St. Louis adopted a regulatory approach to prostitution in 1870, legalizing commercial sex by ordinance, licensing brothels for specified red

---

a. Particularly useful to us in the discussion that follows were Estelle B. Freedman, "'Uncontrolled Desires': The Response to the Sexual Psychopath, 1920–1960," 74 *J. Am. Hist.* 83 (1987); William E. Nelson, "Criminality and Sexual Morality in New York, 1920–1980," 5 *Yale J.L. & Humanities* 265 (1993).

b. Excellent studies of the regulation of prostitution and young women's sexuality in-

clude Ruth Rosen, *The Lost Sisterhood: Prostitution in America, 1900–1918* (1982), as well as Thomas Mackey, *Red Lights Out: A Legal History of Prostitution, Disorderly Houses, and Vice Districts, 1870–1917* (1987); David J. Pivar, *Purity Crusade: Sexual Morality and Social Control, 1868–1900* (1973); Leslie Fishbein, "Harlot or Heroine? Changing Views of Prostitution, 1870–1920," 43 *Historian* 28 (Nov. 1980).

light districts, and requiring periodic medical inspections of sex workers.[c] The reaction was overwhelmingly hostile. A "purity movement," including both women and men, urged that prostitution be suppressed rather than regulated. Purity reformers, especially women, rejected the double standard by which men could sow "wild oats" and women were supposed to remain chaste; the existence of prostitution was a threat to wives, not a safety valve as some claimed. And, most important, some of the purity reformers felt that the prostitute herself was a threat to traditional gender values, for she was a woman not only sexualized but entrepreneurial and public about a matter that the American Victorians were fervently private. Segments of the purity movement were strongly allied with the social hygiene movement, and in 1914 the American Vigilance Association (a leading purity group) and the leading hygiene group merged into the American Social Hygiene Association. The purity movement, substantially feminist in the 1870s, was thoroughly dominated by men by the 1910s.

At the same time that the Comstock Act of 1873 was being adopted to censor sexual obscenity and contraception (see Chapter 1, Section 1), American law rejected the St. Louis approach and turned on prostitutes with a vengeance. In cities as diverse as Richmond and San Francisco, Baltimore and New York, and even St. Louis (which abandoned its experiment), the police arrested hundreds of prostitutes a year, pursuant to municipal ordinances and state statutes banning disorderly houses, houses of ill fame, and immoral or lewd solicitation.[d] Ordinances and statutes were adopted in the 1880s and 1890s that added new enforcement weapons under the aegis of "lewd vagrancy" (*e.g.*, California) and "disorderly conduct" (*e.g.*, New York City). State enforcement of anti-prostitution laws was considerably abetted by the efforts of private groups, most prominently Anthony Comstock's Society for the Suppression of Vice. Comstock and his agent provocateurs roamed the streets and alleys of big cities, apprehending and intimidating prostitutes, their pimps or madames, and sometimes their customers.

Although Comstock himself was a defender of women's virtue in the old-fashioned moral sense, the next generation of progressive reformers emphasized disease as the key reason for regulating prostitution. New York's Committee of Fifteen prominent citizens noted that "the chief distinguishing feature of modern regulation is its endeavor to stamp out the diseases that everywhere attend vice." The Committee of Fifteen, *The Social Evil, with Special Reference to Conditions Existing in the City of New York* 21 (2d rev. ed. 1912, edited by Edwin R.A. Seligman). No fewer than 40 cities' vice commissions rejected the St. Louis experiment of regulating rather than suppressing prostitution. The Philadelphia Commis-

---

c. See John C. Burnham, "Medical Inspection of Prostitutes in America in the Nineteenth Century: The St. Louis Experiment and Its Sequel," 45 *Bull. Hist. Medicine* 203 (May 1971).

d. See Eskridge, "The Construction of the Homosexual: American Regulation of Same–Sex Intimacy, 1880–1946," *Iowa L. Rev.* (forthcoming 1997) (appendices for yearly arrests in Richmond, San Francisco, and St. Louis).

sion concluded that toleration "segregates a small minority of the sexually vicious, it can never isolate disease, and promotes rather than reduces clandestine prostitution," thereby "forcing families of the poor into evil association, * * * raising crime to the dignity of a business, * * * promoting the double standard of morality." Vice Comm'n of Philadelphia, *A Report of Existing Conditions* 19 (1913). Note how the purity campaign tended to demonize the prostitute herself, and how easily suppression dominated early feminist impulses toward actually helping the young women "forced" into that profession. (The purity movement, substantially feminist in the 1870s, was thoroughly dominated by prominent male citizens by 1910.)

Anti-vice committees were great categorizers, testers, and collectors of information. Consider the Massachusetts committee's conclusions from its study of 300 prostitutes:

> Nearly all come from families in adverse circumstances. Immorality, drunkenness and crime are usually a part of the early history. In 29% of the families the mother was obliged to work out of the home during the upbringing of the child. In 30% of the families, either one or both of parents had died or the family had been broken up by separation or divorce before the child was 12 years old. Only a few even pretended to come from normal, well-conducted homes, with a good father and mother who were able and willing properly to protect and bring up their children. * * *
>
> * * * [A] period of private immorality almost invariably preceded commercialized prostitution. The descent to prostitution as a rule was gradual. Only a few began prostitution immediately after beginning sex immorality, or deliberately and understandingly entered the life. * * *
>
> Of the 300 prostitutes examined, 154, or 51%, were actually feeble-minded. The well-known immoral tendencies and the suggestibility and social incapacity of the feeble-minded cause them to drift naturally into prostitution, and make them easy and willing victims of the pimp and the procurer. (*Report of the Commission for the Investigation of the White Slave Traffic, So Called* 42–43 [February 1914].)

Like New York's and Philadelphia's commissions, the Massachusetts Commission urged aggressive police action against organized vice, by closing down "places of prostitution and lewdness," prosecuting pimps and public prostitutes, and affording treatment for "feeble-minded" prostitutes.

Anti-prostitution campaigns were a staple of American municipal politics from 1870 through World War I. Although the federal government's powers were extremely circumscribed during this period, it too adopted such measures. The most obvious forum for federal regulation was immigration policy. The Act of March 3, 1875, § 3, 18 Stat. 477, forbade the "importation into the United States of women for the purposes of prostitution." Subsequent immigration statutes broadened that prohibition to include "persons suffering from a loathsome or a dangerous contagious disease," such as venereal diseases, Act of March 3, 1891, § 1, 26 Stat.

1084; "persons who have been convicted of a felony or other infamous crime or misdemeanor involving moral turpitude," *id.*; and "persons who procure or attempt to bring in prostitutes or women for the purpose of prostitution." Act of March 3, 1903, § 2, 32 Stat. 1213. All these prohibitions were carried forward by subsequent immigration laws, through the Immigration Act of 1917, Regulating the Immigration of Aliens to and Residence of Aliens in the United States, 39 Stat. 874.

PROBLEM 2–2

THE MANN ACT, "WHITE SLAVERY," AND FORNICATION: AN EXERCISE IN THE LEGAL PROCESS[e]

An important part of the anti-prostitution campaign was the progressives' war against "white slavery," a racket by which women and girls were involuntarily or unknowingly impressed into a life of prostitution, mainly for the profit of the pimps to whom they were sold. A series of muckraking news reports of international conspiracies to lure young women into white slavery yielded a feverish campaign for new statutes in 1907 and subsequent years. In 1909, Edwin Sims, the U.S. Attorney for Chicago, proclaimed (with virtually no evidence) that "the white slave traffic is a system operated by a syndicate which has its ramifications from the Atlantic seaboard to the Pacific Ocean, with 'clearing houses' or 'distribution centers' in nearly all the larger cities" (quoted in Langum 38). Sims worked with Representative James Mann to craft a federal statute to control the interstate features of this phenomenon.

With the immediate endorsement of President Taft and leading purity groups, the Mann bill sped through the federal legislative process. The House Commerce Committee reported the bill two weeks after it was introduced, with this explanation:

> The legislation is needed to put a stop to a villanous interstate and international traffic in women and girls. The legislation is not needed or intended as an aid to the States in the exercise of their police powers in the suppression or regulation of immorality in general. It does not attempt to regulate the practice of voluntary prostitution, but aims solely to prevent panderers and procurers from compelling thousands of women and girls against their will and desire to enter and continue in a life of prostitution. (House Report No. 47, 61st Cong., 2d Sess. 9–10 [1909].)

Representative Mann took the lead in defending his bill against charges that matters of morality should be left to the states. Relying on press accounts, Mann asserted that "the white-slave traffic, while not so extensive, is much more horrible than any black-slave traffic ever was in the history of the world." 45 *Congressional Record* 548 (1910). All the other speakers emphasized the same point. (Not only did the comparison slight

---

e. The factual information for this problem is taken from David J. Langum's   excellent *Crossing Over the Line: Legislating Morality and the Mann Act* (1994).

the horrors of the African slave trade, but it overstated the evidence of organized "white slavery.") At least one, Representative Gordon Russell of Texas, went further, contrasting the supporters of the bill as "men who reverence womanhood and who set a priceless value upon female purity," with opponents, "who hate God and scoff at innocence and laugh at female virtue." *Id.* at 821.

President Taft signed the Mann Act into law June 25, 1910. Section 2 made it a federal crime to transport a woman or girl in interstate or foreign commerce "for the purpose of prostitution or debauchery, or for any other immoral purpose, or with the intent and purpose to induce, entice, or compel such woman or girl to become a prostitute or to give herself up to debauchery, or to engage in any other immoral practice." The White Slave Traffic Act of 1910, § 2, 36 Stat. 825, codified at 18 U.S.C. § 2421. Section 3 prohibited any person from persuading or forcing, or assisting in either, a woman to travel in interstate or foreign commerce for the same prohibited purposes ("prostitution, debauchery or any other immoral purpose").

The U.S. Supreme Court upheld the constitutionality of the Mann Act pursuant to Congress' power to regulate interstate commerce, *Hoke v. United States*, 227 U.S. 308 (1913). This was relatively uncontroversial; more difficult was the question whether the statute applied to interstate transportation of women for "noncommercial" but nonetheless "immoral" purposes. In 1911, Attorney General George Wickersham opined that the statute did not cover such cases, but the Department of Justice generally deferred to local U.S. Attorneys, many of whom did prosecute such cases (Langum 65–68). In 1913, a false press report that Attorney General James MacReynolds directed that only the most flagrant commercial prosecutions could be filed, brought a firestorm of protest from churches, purity groups, and newspapers. Facing censure from the Senate, the Department of Justice issued a press statement that "no order to stop white slave prosecutions in cases not involving commercialism has been issued" (quoted in Langum 71). In 1914, 71% of the Mann Act convictions involved voluntary rather than coerced transportation of women for prostitution or other "immoral purposes," noncommercial cases accounted for 15% of the convictions, and cases that involved no prostitution or commercial consideration, no fraud, and no force constituted almost 10% of the convictions (Langum 75).

Whether the Mann Act allowed such prosecutions remained for the Supreme Court to determine. The test case involved the following scenario (Langum 97–112). Drew Caminetti and Maury Diggs were two young Sacramento playboys from prominent families (Caminetti's uncle was Commissioner of Immigration in the Wilson Administration). Although both were married, they entered into sexual affairs with young unmarried women, Lola Norris (age 19) and Marsha Warrington (age 20), respectively. Because all concerned were indiscreet, the affairs became public knowledge and generated enormous pressure on the two couples to break up. Mrs. Caminetti threatened to haul the women, who were both legal minors, before the Juvenile Court if they did not break off the affairs. The husbands were also in legal trouble, since adultery was a crime in California.

Rather than breaking off the affairs, the four slipped out of the city on the early morning train of March 10, 1913. The train arrived in Reno, Nevada later that morning, and the couples settled into a cottage at 235 Cheney Street. Sacramento was ablaze with the scandal, and arrest warrants were issued for the men, charging them with abandonment and contributing to the delinquency of minors. The Reno police arrested the men on March 14. The state actions were suspended when the U.S. Attorney for Northern California indicted the men for violating the Mann Act. The men were convicted of transporting women for "immoral purposes," namely, adultery and fornication. They appealed to the U.S. Supreme Court.

Drew Caminetti and Maury Diggs v. United States

United States Supreme Court, 1917.
242 U.S. 470, 37 S.Ct. 192, 61 L.Ed. 442.

■ MR. JUSTICE DAY delivered the opinion of the Court. * * *

It is contended that the act of Congress is intended to reach only "commercialized vice," or the traffic in women for gain, and that the conduct for which the several petitioners were indicted and convicted, however reprehensible in morals, is not within the purview of the statute when properly construed in the light of its history and the purposes intended to be accomplished by its enactment. In none of the cases [before the Court] was it charged or proved that the transportation was for gain or for the purpose of furnishing women for prostitution for hire, and it is insisted that, such being the case, the acts charged and proved, upon which conviction was had, do not come within the statute. * * *

* * * There is no ambiguity in the terms of this act. It is specifically made an offense to knowingly transport or cause to be transported, etc., in interstate commerce, any woman or girl for the purpose of prostitution or debauchery, or for "any other immoral purpose," or with the intent and purpose to induce any such woman or girl to become a prostitute or to give herself up to debauchery, or to engage in any other immoral practice.

Statutory words are uniformly presumed, unless the contrary appears, to be used in their ordinary and usual sense, and with the meaning commonly attributed to them. To cause a woman or girl to be transported for the purposes of debauchery, and for an immoral purpose, to wit, becoming a concubine or mistress, * * * would seem by the very statement of the facts to embrace transportation for purposes denounced by the act, and therefore fairly within its meaning. * * *

In *United States v. Bitty*, 208 U. S. 393 [1908], it was held that the act of Congress against the importation of alien women and girls for the purpose of prostitution "and any other immoral purpose" included the importation of an alien woman to live in concubinage with the person importing her. In that case this court said:

"* * * There can be no doubt as to what class was aimed at by the clause forbidding the importation of alien women for purposes of 'prostitution.' It refers to women who, for hire or without hire, offer their bodies to indiscriminate intercourse with men. The lives and example of such persons are in hostility to 'the idea of the family, as consisting in and springing from the union for life of one man and one woman in the holy estate of matrimony; the sure foundation of all that is stable and noble in our civilization; the best guaranty of that reverent morality which is the source of all beneficent progress in social and political improvement.' *Murphy v. Ramsey*, 114 U.S.... Now the addition in the last statute of the words, 'or for any other immoral purpose,' after the word 'prostitution,' must have been made for some practical object. Those added words show beyond question that Congress had in view the protection of society against another class of alien women other than those who might be brought here merely for purposes of 'prostitution.' In forbidding the importation of alien women 'for any other immoral purpose,' Congress evidently thought that there were purposes in connection with the importations of alien women which, as in the case of importations for prostitution, were to be deemed immoral. It may be admitted that, in accordance with the familiar rule of *ejusdem generis*, the immoral purpose referred to by the words 'any other immoral purpose' must be one of the same general class or kind as the particular purpose of 'prostitution' specified in the same clause of the statute. 2 Lewis' Sutherland Stat. Const. § 423, and authorities cited. But that rule cannot avail the accused in this case; for the immoral purpose charged in the indictment is of the same general class or kind as the one that controls in the importation of an alien woman for the purpose strictly of prostitution. The prostitute may, in the popular sense, be more degraded in character than the concubine, but the latter none the less must be held to lead an immoral life, if any regard whatever be had to the views that are almost universally held in this country as to the relations which may rightfully, from the standpoint of morality, exist between man and woman in the matter of sexual intercourse."

This definition of an immoral purpose was given prior to the enactment of the act now under consideration, and must be presumed to have been known to Congress when it enacted the law here involved. * * *

■ MR. JUSTICE MCREYNOLDS took no part in the consideration or decision of this case.

■ MR. JUSTICE MCKENNA, with whom concurred the CHIEF JUSTICE [WHITE] and MR. JUSTICE CLARKE, dissenting. * * *

* * * "Immoral" is a very comprehensive word. It means a dereliction of morals. In such sense it covers every form of vice, every form of conduct that is contrary to good order. It will hardly be contended that in this sweeping sense it is used in the statute. But, if not used in such sense, to

what is it limited and by what limited? If it be admitted that it is limited at all, that ends the imperative effect assigned to it in the opinion of the court. But not insisting quite on that, we ask again, By what is it limited? By its context, necessarily, and the purpose of the statute.

For the context I must refer to the statute; of the purpose of the statute Congress itself has given us illumination. It devotes a section to the declaration that the "Act shall be known and referred to as the 'White-slave traffic Act.' " * * * [T]here is no uncertainty as to the conduct it describes. It is commercialized vice, immoralities having a mercenary purpose, and this is confirmed by other circumstances.

The author of the bill was Mr. Mann, and in reporting it from the House Committee on Interstate and Foreign Commerce he declared for the Committee that it was not the purpose of the bill to interfere with or usurp in any way the police power of the States, and further, that it was not the intention of the bill to regulate prostitution or the places where prostitution or immorality was practised, which were said to be matters wholly within the power of the States, and over which the federal government had no jurisdiction. And further explaining the bill, it was said that the sections of the act had been "so drawn that they are limited to the cases in which there is an act of transportation in interstate commerce of women for the purposes of prostitution." And again:

> "The White Slave Trade. A material portion of the legislation suggested and proposed is necessary to meet conditions which have arisen within the past few years. The legislation is needed to put a stop to a villainous interstate and international traffic in women and girls. The legislation is not needed or intended as an aid to the states in the exercise of their police powers in the suppression or regulation of immorality in general. It does not attempt to regulate the practice of voluntary prostitution, but aims solely to prevent panderers and procurers from compelling thousands of women and girls against their will and desire to enter and continue in a life of prostitution." House Report No. 47, 61st Cong., 2d sess., pp. 9, 10. * * *

This being the purpose, the words of the statute should be construed to execute it, and they may be so construed even if their literal meaning be otherwise. [Justice McKenna discusses two recent cases where the Court did alter a statute's plain meaning to conform with the statutory purpose.]

NOTES ON THE EVOLUTION OF THE WHITE SLAVE TRAFFIC ACT

1. *The Broader Meaning of "Prostitution" Reflected in* Caminetti. Justice McKenna's charge is that the Court majority read its own moral values into the statute, displacing the statutory focus on involuntary prostitution; if you think like most people today, you probably are leaning toward the dissent, yes? But what is the principled basis for substituting a consent paradigm for a morality paradigm? Justice McKenna's best point is that there must be some limiting principle to "other immoral purposes," and the for-commercial-reasons principle seems most consistent with the legislative history. Justice Day could respond that his limiting principle, sexual looseness, is defensible.

"Prostitution," the Mann Act's core offense, was not a common law category. People we would consider prostitutes were regulated in the early and mid-nineteenth century pursuant to vagrancy, disorderly conduct, and public lewdness statutes; in the late nineteenth century cities and states added laws against lewd solicitation and inhabiting a disorderly house or house of ill fame. Few of the newer laws required commercial consideration, and a 1919 "model statute" defined prostitution "to include the offering or receiving of the body for sexual intercourse for hire, and shall also be construed to include the offering or receiving of the body for indiscriminate sexual intercourse without hire." (Quoted in Langum 124.) Most judges considered a woman a prostitute if she "invites or solicits by word or act. * * * Her avocation may be known from the manner in which she plays it, and not from pecuniary charges and compensation gained in any other manner." *State v. Clark*, 43 N.W. 273, 273 (Iowa 1889) (discussed in Langum 123). The Supreme Court's opinion in *Bitty* explicitly read "prostitution" in this broad way.

The point of Justice Day's opinion may have been that the Mann Act was aimed at precisely what occurred here: young women (minors) were being induced into a life of extramarital promiscuity. Justice McKenna would object that this is contrary to the intent of the statute's framers. Do you suppose Representative Mann was surprised by the Court's decision? Dismayed? See Langum 119 (quoting letter where Mann professed to be delighted by the decision).

2. *The Evolution of the White Slave Traffic Act and the Due Process Concerns That Raises.* Professor Langum's valuable study of the Mann Act found that most of the Mann Act prosecutions between 1917 and 1928 were noncommercial fornication cases; lots of people, including many women, went to jail for consensual adult intercourse (Langum 140–55). After 1928, juries stopped convicting defendants for simple intercourse, and prosecutors stopped bringing noncommercial cases unless there were an aggravating factor (*e.g.*, the woman was a minor or was tricked) or the defendant was someone the feds wanted to "get" for other reasons. Among the celebrity defendants the Department of Justice went after were black boxing champion Jack Johnson, leftwing movie star Charlie Chaplin, and gangster Jack Gebardi (Langum 175–97).

Some of the prosecutions got to the Supreme Court, the most interesting being one against fundamentalist Mormons who practiced polygamy. The FBI pounced when some of the wives were brought across state lines, and the Supreme Court affirmed the convictions in *Cleveland v. United States*, 329 U.S. 14 (1946). Justice Douglas' opinion for the Court pronounced polygamy "in the same genus as the other immoral practices covered by the Act." Justice Murphy in dissent argued that *Caminetti* should be overruled and noncommercial sex finally excluded from the White Slave Traffic Act, but Justice Douglas insisted upon *stare decisis*, the idea that the Court should rarely reconsider even wrongly decided precedents. Indeed, *Cleveland* is a leading citation for the rule that the Supreme Court should be even more reluctant to overrule its statutory precedents, because the onus should be on Congress to alter paths taken by the Court when it construes statutes. See Edward Levi, "An Introduction to Legal Reasoning," 15 *U. Chi. L. Rev.* 501, 524–38 (1948).

Consider the relevance of the due process rule against vague criminal statutes. The Supreme Court has been willing to invalidate criminal prohibitions that use vague terminology. See *Papachristou v. City of Jacksonville*, 405 U.S. 156 (1972), which struck down a vagrancy ordinance prohibiting "rogues and vagabonds * * * common night walkers * * * persons wandering or strolling around from place to place without any lawful purpose or object * * * persons neglecting all lawful business and habitually spending their time by frequenting houses of ill fame, gaming houses, or places where alcoholic beverages are sold or served." The opinion for the Court, by the same Justice Douglas who upheld and liberally applied "other immoral purposes" in *Cleveland*, emphasized the vices of vagueness: citizens do not necessarily know what the law expects of them, police and prosecutors are vested with excessive discretion, and respect for the law declines. Are these not the very problems afflicting the *Caminetti* construction of "other immoral purposes"? A related doctrine is that the Court will construe ambiguous penal statutes narrowly. Why was this "rule of lenity" not deployed in *Caminetti* or *Cleveland*? See also Chapter 1, Section 2.

3. *The New White Slave Traffic Act.* Congress revised the Mann Act, in minor ways in 1978 and more dramatically in 1986. It now criminalizes interstate transportation of "any individual * * * with intent that such individual engage in prostitution, or in any sexual activity for which any person can be charged with a criminal offense." Public Law No. 99–628, § 5(b)(1), 100 Stat. 3511 (1986), amending 18 U.S.C. § 2421. Under the new statute, would Caminetti be convicted? In some respects the "new" Mann Act is broader than the old. If a gay male couple crossed into a state prohibiting sodomy, they would appear to be guilty under the new federal law, where they were not in violation of the old law. The penalty for violation is up to five years in prison.

2.   GENDER REVOLT

Carroll Smith–Rosenberg's *Disorderly Conduct: Visions of Gender in Victorian America* part 3 (1985), lays out the now-classic framework for thinking about issues of sex, gender, and sexuality once bourgeois American women started to become economically and socially independent of men. At first, during the 1860s and 1870s, women assuming public roles did so in the spirit of "The Cult of True Womanhood" espoused in the earlier nineteenth century: woman is the nurturing conscience of man, the source of virtue and moderation in a world of selfish aggressive men. Women's clubs, temperance societies, soup kitchens, the Red Cross, and the like were examples of women's activism under the umbrella of traditional female virtue. At the same time, however, these women were also insisting upon political, social, and economic equality for themselves and their daughters.

"If the urban bourgeois matron of the 1860s and 1870s alarmed, her daughter frightened. The 1880s and 1890s saw the emergence of a novel social and political phenomenon—the New Woman. * * * I use the term [popularized by Henry James] to refer to a specific sociological and educational cohort of women born between the late 1850s and 1900. They represented the new demographic trends of later marriages for bourgeois women. Benefiting from bourgeois affluence, which endowed colleges for women, they were college-educated and professionally trained at a time when few men were. Few New Women married. * * * [T]he New Women, rejecting conventional female roles and asserting their right to a career, to a public voice, to visible power, laid claim to the rights and privileges customarily accorded bourgeois men." (*Disorderly Conduct* 176.) Jane Addams and Willa Cather were examples of New Women's first generation educated in the 1870s and 1880s and flourishing professionally in the generation before World War I. Gertrude Stein, Virginia Woolf, and Edna St. Vincent Millay represented the more aggressive and independent second generation of New Women, educated in the 1890s and coming into their own around the time of World War I. They openly defied gender conventions and insisted upon absolute political and social equality for themselves and other white, middle-class women.

Smith–Rosenberg examines the reactions, at first bemused but soon alarmed, of male culture to the New Woman. The main response was an effort to reassert control, not under the agency of traditional ideas, but through a transformation of expressive medical metaphors into strategies for social control—a process Smith–Rosenberg calls "the politicization of the body." Beginning in the Civil War period and intensifying after the war, doctors and medical experts were enlisted to reaffirm women's subordinate place in society, but in the new language of science rather than the old language of theology. The medical establishment readily supported laws prohibiting abortion and contraception, as ways to renormalize middle-class women around their traditional roles as mother and wife, but within the new scientific vocabulary of the era. Reva Siegel "Reasoning from the Body: A Historical Perspective on Abortion Regulation and Questions of Equal Protection," 44 *Stan. L. Rev.* 261 (1992), provides a detailed account of this medical, political, and legal struggle to regulate women's bodies once their souls were springing free.

"Whereas the troubled men of Jacksonian America chose a variety of sexual images to express their social concerns, mid-nineteenth century men turned increasingly to the sexually autonomous and gender-deviant woman. At first bourgeois men focused upon the bourgeois matron's declining birthrate. They molded the twin themes of birth control and abortion (always defining them as women's decisions) into condensed symbols of national danger and decay. Whether they appeared in race-suicide jeremiads or in anti-abortion propaganda, the women who practiced birth control and the aborting mother became metaphors for all that appeared 'unnatural' in small-town America. But by the opening decades of the twentieth century, in the wake of a successful anti-abortion campaign, the woman who simply restrained her motherhood no longer threatened male dominance and male order. * * * Bourgeois men turned, instead, to her metaphoric daughter—the New Woman. They seized upon the latter generation of New Women's overt sexuality and rejection of gender distinctions to construct the ultimate symbol of social disorder and of the 'unnatural'— the mannish lesbian. If her sexuality could be constrained and remolded, some men, at least, felt they would have demonstrated man's power to restrain disorder, to control change, to preserve male dominance." (*Disorderly Conduct* 180–81.)

"The medico-political campaign against abortion [1850s through 1880s] constituted the first effort at an alliance between the male medical leadership and bourgeois politicians. Having defeated and regulated their own women, bourgeois men then sought to control working-class women through state campaigns against the female prostitute [1870s through 1910s]. Only after both campaigns had succeeded did bourgeois men seek to control the bodies and the sexuality of other men." (*Disorderly Conduct* 181.) This theme in Smith–Rosenberg's theory is explored by Anthony Rotundo, *American Manhood* (1982), and George Chauncey, Jr., *Gay New York* (1994): medical creation of the "homosexual" (both female and male) contributed to the effort to reassert male control over women's bodies by reinforcing rigid gender lines around biological sex.

The image of degradation, or "degeneracy," associated with deviant women is dramatically displayed by the Alice Mitchell case,[f] which was widely reported in the news and medical media. Consider the description of the case in Krafft–Ebing's *Psychopathia Sexualis* 581–85:

> In January, 1892, Alice M[itchell], a young girl belonging to one of the best families of Memphis, Tennessee, U.S.A., killed in the public street of that town her girl friend, Freda W., also of the best society. She made several deep gashes in the neck of the girl with a razor.

> The trial elicited the following facts: * * *

> Alice was a nervous, irritable child, and very slow in physical development. She never enjoyed children's or girls' games. When she was four to five years old she took much pleasure in tormenting cats, suspending them by one leg.

> She preferred her younger brother and his games to her sisters; she vied with him in spinning tops, playing baseball and football, or shooting at targets, and in many silly pranks. She loved to climb trees and roofs, and was very clever in this sport. Above all things she loved to amuse herself in the stable among the mules. * * *

f. See Lisa Duggan, "The Trials of Alice Mitchell: Sensationalism, Sexology, and the Lesbian Subject in Turn-of-the-Century America," 18 *Signs* 791 (1993), for an excellent account and analysis of the Mitchell case.

When a child, she did not care for boys, and had no companions among them; later on she never cared for men, and had no lovers. She was quite indifferent towards the young men, even abrupt, and they looked upon her as being "cracked".

But "as far as she can remember" she had an extraordinary love for Freda W., a girl of her own age, daughter of a friend of the family. Freda was a tender and sweet girl; the love was mutual, but more violent on the part of Alice. It increased from year to year until it became a passion. A year previous to the catastrophe Freda's family moved away to another town. Alice was steeped in sorrow; a very tender love correspondence now ensued.

Twice Alice went to visit Freda's family, during which time the two girls, as witnesses attested, showed "disgusting tenderness" for each other. They were seen to swing together in a hammock by the hour, hugging and kissing each other—"they hugged and kissed *ad nauseum*". Alice was ashamed of doing this in public, but Freda upbraided her for this.

When Freda paid a visit in return, Alice made an attempt at killing her; she tried to pour laudanum down her throat whilst asleep. The attempt failed because Freda woke up in time.

Alice then took the poison herself before Freda, and was taken violently ill. The reason for the attempted murder and suicide was that Freda had shown some interest in two young men, and Alice declared she could not live without Freda's love, and again "she wanted to kill herself in order to find release from her tortures and make Freda free". After recovery they both resumed the amorous correspondence, even with more fervour than before.

Soon after this Alice proposed marriage to Freda. She sent her an engagement ring, and threatened death if she proved disloyal. They were to assume a false name and fly to St. Louis. Alice would wear men's clothes and earn a living for both; she would also grow a moustache, if Freda were to insist upon it, as she felt confident that by shaving frequently she could succeed in this.

Just before the attempted elopement the plot was discovered and prevented; the "engagement ring" was returned together with other love tokens to Alice's mother, and all intercourse between the two girls was stopped. * * *

[Alice] became emaciated, the face assumed an anxious expression, the eyes showed "a peculiar strange lustre". When she learned of an intended visit of Freda to Memphis she firmly resolved to kill her *if she could not possess* her. She stole a razor from her father and carefully concealed it. * * *

All attempts to see her or hear from her made by Alice during Freda's sojourn in Memphis failed. * * * On the very day, however, when Freda was leaving town and on her way to the steamboat Alice overtook her.

She felt mortally hurt because Freda, although walking alongside of the buggy in which she herself was riding, never spoke a word to her, but only gave her a glance now and then. She jumped from the vehicle and cut Freda with the razor. When Freda's sister tried to beat her off she became frantic and blindly cut deep gashes into the poor girl's neck, one reaching almost from ear to ear. Whilst everybody was busy about Freda she drove off furiously through the streets. When reaching home she immediately told her mother what had happened.
* * *

At moments, however, when her passionate love for Freda and her jealousy woke up, she yielded to boundless grief and emotion. *"Freda has broken her faith!"* "I have killed her because I loved her so!" The experts called in the case found her mental development on a level with that of a girl of thirteen or fourteen years. She comprehended that no children could have sprung from her "union" with Freda—but that a "marriage" between them would have been an absurdity she would not admit. She absolutely denied that sexual intercourse between the two (even mutual masturbation) ever took place. * * *

At the hearing on whether she was competent to stand trial, the prosecution and defense presented two different visions of Alice Mitchell: the former characterized her in the traditional language of vice and degradation, while the latter spoke in explicit medical terms of insanity and gender confusion (see Duggan). The jury found her insane; she was committed to an asylum. The Mitchell trial was widely reported by the popular press and was a sensation in the medical journals as well (where Krafft–Ebing came across it). Medical authorities seized upon the story as exemplary of "sexual inversion," one author dubbing Alice and Freda "sexual monsters." Alice Mitchell became the nightmare example of the New Woman: spoiled as well as independent, sexualized but perverted, and sexually deviant as well as gender-bending. Her case was connected with a new demon arising in bourgeois society: the "homosexual."

3. SUPPRESSING HOMOSEXUALITY[h]

Something of a hybrid between (or synthesis of) the lewd prostitute and the gender-bending cross dresser was the "sex pervert" or "homosexual," originally a medical category but destined to become an important legal category in the period after World War I. New York City, for the best documented example, treated male "degenerates" as a separate class of disorderly person in the 1910s; by statute in 1923, it was a crime in York City when "[a]ny person who with intent to provoke a breach of the peace, or whereby a breach of the peace may be occasioned * * * [f]requents or loiters about any public place soliciting men for the purpose of committing a crime against nature or other lewdness." New York Laws 1923, ch. 642, adding New York Penal Code § 722(8). Hundreds of men were arrested

---

h. The account that follows is taken from William N. Eskridge, Jr., *Gaylaw: Challenging the Apartheid of the Closet* ch. 1 (forthcoming 1998).

under this law each year in the 1920s, and more than 1000 per year during the depression.

Other municipalities did not develop a homosexuals-only arrest category, but it is apparent that ordinances and statutes enacted to control prostitution (solicitation, public lewdness, indecent exposure, vagrancy, disorderly conduct) could usually be applied to people engaged in open homosexual conduct or solicitation. Sodomy laws, which had traditionally been enforced mainly against the occasional aggressive male rapist or child molester, came to be enforced in a big way in American cities after the 1880s. Dozens and soon hundreds of men per year were arrested in New York City after 1890, most for consensual oral sex with other men or boys. "Fairies," inverted (effeminate) males offering oral sex to straight "trade," were the main objects of such enforcement.

The biggest sodomy mania arose out of an undercover sting operation (authorized ultimately by Undersecretary of Navy Franklin Roosevelt) targeting inverted sailors at Newport Naval Station during World War I.[i] Dozens of cross-dressing, oral sex-giving sailors were caught in the dragnet, among them Seaman David "Beckie" Goldstein, who was described this way by witness Gregory Cunningham:

> I know him to be a member of the coterie of so-called moral degenerates whose pastime and pleasure is given to lewd purposes. He is suspected of being a trafficker in the cocaine trade. There has been a number of fellows about the Naval Hospital of effeminate characters. I looked into the crowd to see what kind of fellows they were and found that they were perverts. * * * I was shown pictures of these fellows with so-called "seagoing" men, embracing each other and in compromising postures. * * *

Goldstein denied virtually none of this and other testimony against him, and he was convicted of sodomy and discharged dishonorably from the Navy, as were about two dozen others. Ironically, the decoy operation also came under Navy and, ultimately, congressional scrutiny, because the operatives who testified against Goldstein and the others actually accepted oral sex from them.

As American social and legal culture came to consider the "homosexual" as a recognizable and disgusting category of humanity, the Newport experience became the widely deployed rule, rather than a nervous exception. The armed forces' homosexual exclusion began in earnest in the wake of the Newport proceedings and subsequent scandal. At the same time homosexuals were being hunted by police and excluded by the government, they were also being censored by the Customs Service, state agencies, and even private watchdogs.

i. Excellent accounts of the proceedings can be found in Lawrence Murphy, *Perverts by Official Order: The Campaign Against Homosexuals by the United States Navy* (1988), and George Chauncey, Jr., "Christian Brotherhood or Sexual Perversion? Homosexual Identities and the Construction of Sexual Boundaries in the World War I Era," in *Hidden from History* 294.

The most dramatic early example of state censorship involved Radclyffe Hall's novel *The Well of Loneliness*. Like the protagonist of the novel, Stephen Gordon, a female invert, Hall wore her hair short and her suits well-tailored, carried a trim broad-shouldered frame, and excelled at upper crust sports such as fencing and riding. Viewing lesbianism as congenital, gender inverting, and ultimately unfulfilling, the novel tracks the theories of Ellis and Krafft–Ebing. In a climactic moment for the novel, Stephen discovers her sexual "truth"—her inversion—when she reads her father's marked copy of Krafft–Ebing's *Psychopathia Sexualis*.

The Well of Loneliness was a sensation from its publication in July 1928. Critics were scandalized by the novel's depiction of female inversion, a love that dared speak its name even less than male inversion. The Home Secretary, Sir William Joynson–Hicks, bullied Hall's English publisher into withdrawing the book before a single copy had been sold. Authors ranging from the bisexual Virginia Woolf to the closeted E.M. Forster protested this action, but an obscenity trial in November 1928 before Sir Chartres Biron resulted in a verdict that the Obscene Publications Act of 1857 precluded publication in England (until 1949).

The reaction in America was no less hysterical. The Customs Service seized copies of the book in 1928 and declared it "obscene" (a judgment reconsidered in 1929). After Hall's original publisher abandoned publication, Covici Friede tried to publish the book domestically but was blocked by the New York censors. The publisher sought an injunction.

People v. Donald Friede

New York City Magistrate's Court, Borough of Manhattan, 1929.
133 Misc. 611, 233 N.Y.S. 565.

■ BUSHEL, CITY MAGISTRATE. * * *

Section 1141 of the Penal Law provides: "A person who sells * * * or has in his possession with intent to sell, * * * any obscene, lewd, lascivious, filthy, indecent or disgusting book * * * is guilty of a misdemeanor." The defendants contend that as a matter of law "The Well of Loneliness" is not obscene, lewd, lascivious, filthy or disgusting within the meaning of the statute * * *.

The book here involved is a novel dealing with the childhood and early womanhood of a female invert [Stephen Gordon]. In broad outline the story shows how these unnatural tendencies manifested themselves from early childhood; the queer attraction of the child to the maid in the household, her affairs with one Angela Crossby, a normally sexed, but unhappily married, woman, causing further dissension between the latter and her husband, her jealousy of another man who later debauched this married woman, and her despair, in being supplanted by him in Angela's affections, are vividly portrayed. The book culminates with an extended elaboration upon her intimate relations with a normal young girl, who becomes a helpless subject of her perverted influence and passion, and pictures the struggle for this girl's affections between this invert and a man from whose normal advances she herself had previously recoiled, because of her own perverted nature. Her sex experiences are set forth in some detail and also her visits to various resorts frequented by male and female inverts.

The author has treated these incidents not without some restraint; nor is it disputed that the book has literary merit. To quote the people's brief: "It is a well-written, carefully constructed piece of fiction," and "contains no unclean words." Yet the narrative does not veer from its central theme, and the emotional and literary setting in which they are found give the incidents described therein great force and poignancy. The unnatural and depraved relationships portrayed are sought to be idealized and extolled. The characters in the book who indulge in these vices are described in attractive terms, and it is maintained throughout that they be accepted on the same plane as persons normally constituted, and that their perverse and inverted love is as worthy as the affection between normal beings and should be considered just as sacred by society.

The book can have no moral value, since it seeks to justify the right of a pervert to prey upon normal members of a community, and to uphold such relationship as noble and lofty. Although it pleads for tolerance on the part of society of those possessed of and inflicted with perverted traits and tendencies, it does not argue for repression or moderation of insidious impulses. An idea of the moral tone which the book assumes may be gained from the attitude taken by its principal character towards her mother, pictured as a hard, cruel and pitiless woman, because of the abhorrence she displays to unnatural lust, and to whom, because of that reaction, the former says: "But what I will never forgive is your daring to try and make me ashamed of my love. I'm not ashamed of it; there's no shame in me."

The theme of the novel is not only antisocial and offensive to public morals and decency, but the method in which it is developed, in its highly emotional way attracting and focusing attention upon perverted ideas and unnatural vices, and seeking to justify and idealize them, is strongly calculated to corrupt and debase those members of the community who would be susceptible to its immoral influence.

Although the book in evidence is prefaced by a laudatory commentary by Havelock Ellis, yet it is he who, in his scientific treatise on the subject, states: "We are bound to protect the helpless members of society against the invert." Havelock Ellis, *Studies in the Psychology of Sex*, vol. 2, p. 356. The court is charged with that precise duty here. The test of an obscene book laid down in *Regina v. Hicklin*, L.R. 3 Q.B. 360, 369, * * * is "whether the tendency of the matter charged as obscenity is to deprave or corrupt those whose minds are open to such immoral influences, and who might come into contact with it." * * *

Its application and soundness are assailed by learned counsel for the defendants, who argue that it seeks to gauge the mental and moral capacity of the community by that of its dullest-witted and most fallible members. This contention overlooks the fact that those who are subject to perverted influences, and in whom that abnormality may be called into activity, and who might be aroused to lustful and lecherous practices are not limited to the young and immature, the moron, the mentally weak, or the intellectually impoverished, but may be found among those of mature age and of high intellectual development and professional attainment.

* * * [The Legislature] has imposed upon the courts the duty of protecting the weaker members of society from corrupt, depraving, and lecherous influences, although exerted through the guise and medium of literature, drama, or art. The public policy so declared was reaffirmed by the Legislature by its recent amendment to the Penal Law (section 1140a), making it a misdemeanor to prepare, advertise, or present any drama, play, etc., dealing with the subject of sex degeneracy or sex perversion. Laws 1927, c. 690. * * *

SEQUEL TO *FRIEDE*

Magistrate Bushel's opinion was overturned by the New York Supreme Court, in an unreported opinion. See Patricia A. Cain, "Litigating for Lesbian and Gay Rights: A Legal History," 79 *Va. L. Rev.* 1551, 1157 n.37 (1993). Chapter 6 explores the First Amendment issues of state censorship of "obscenity" that are raised in *Friede*. Note that the judge in this decision treats the issue as quasi-medical, the book as a glorification of pathological degeneracy. The novel itself narrates a butch lesbian's affair with her feminine lover (the latter described in the opinion as "normal"). Was the court worried about contagion?

PART B.   THE SEXUAL PSYCHOPATH, 1930s-1960s[j]

1.   SHIFTING REGULATORY CONCERNS, CIRCA 1930

By 1930, American anxieties about sexuality, and the concomitant medicalization, were shifting from the desire to suppress prostitution and women's sexuality, to the desire to control men's sexuality, especially as directed against children. As Estelle Freedman has argued, popular anxiety and regulatory emphasis shifted from maintaining female purity toward controlling male violence.[k] The Victorian ideal of innate female purity was somewhat obsolete by the 1920s. Freudian ideas as well as bohemian lifestyles had contributed to a new urban sexual order. Acceptance of birth

---

j. The discussion in Part B is digested from William N. Eskridge, Jr., *Gaylaw: Challenging the Apartheid of the Closet* Chs. 1–2 (forthcoming 1998).

k. "The transformation of the psychopath into a violent, male, sexual criminal occurred gradually as a result of three convergent trends. First, as courts and prisons became important arenas into which American psychiatry expanded beyond its earlier base in state mental hospitals, the recently established specialization of forensic psychiatry sought new explanations for criminal behavior. Second, the social stresses of the depression drew attention to the problems of male deviance. Third, the scientific study of sexuality became respectable, and the influence of psychoanalytic theories on American psychiatry during the 1930s provided an intellectual base for a sexual theory of crime." Estelle Freedman, " 'Uncontrolled Desires': The Response to the Sexual Psychopath, 1920–1980," 74 *J. Am. Hist.* 83, 88 (1987).

control, sex outside of marriage, and female sexual desire diminished the power of ideals of female purity to regulate sexual activity. By the 1930s, calls to eliminate prostitution were disregarded; New York's famous Committee of Fifteen disbanded for lack of interest.

Freudian and other psychoanalytic theories framed but did not predetermine the contours of this shift. If Freud was right that sexualized children engage in a developmental process leading toward "normal" sexual maturity, adult interaction with children must be viewed with greater care. Freudian theory clearly supported increased concern about childhood sexuality but was more equivocal about two other features of American thought: the great danger of male aggression and, particularly, of the homosexual pervert. Following Havelock Ellis, Freud emphasized the sexuality of women as much as men, but his American followers neglected women's sexuality and focused on the stereotypical aggressive male, especially the male untamed by a civilizing (domesticating) marriage to a woman.

The favored American terminology for the sex offender was the "psychopath," namely a man who could not control his sexual impulses and preyed on others. The homosexual man was the quintessential psychopath, for he was by Freudian definition a man whose sexual development had been derailed, rendering him intrinsically perverted. Freud rejected Krafft-Ebing's concept that a male invert was basically womanish; his American followers conceptualized the male homosexual as aggressive. Accordingly, many American Freudians created a new fixation: the predatory male homosexual, who recruited little boys as sexual partners, because he was uninhibited by social pressures or domesticating females and was too sick even to find mature male companionship. Oddly, the American Freudians also construed the lesbian as predatory, as her mannishness carried with it male sexual aggressiveness. The "vampire lesbian" has been a stereotype invoked in popular literature, press, and even movies throughout the century. This Americanized version of Freud saturated both popular and legal culture.

It was ironic that the American Freudians, who belittled the reality of early childhood abuse and violence against women, did not hesitate to accept the reality of sexual abuse against children when it could be used to attack the adult homosexual—the supposed sexual deviant in the new psychiatric categorization of sexual disorders. This selective deployment of the phenomenon of child sexual abuse denied any real possibility of addressing and stopping the sexual abuse of children (primarily females), while at the same time using the phenomenon to harass and persecute homosexuals (primarily males). By categorizing child sexual abuse as deviant behavior perpetrated primarily by this new category of sexual "deviant," the altogether too common phenomena of child sexual abuse within the "normal" family structure was ignored. (Even in the 1930s and 1940s, the evidence suggested that the dominant pattern of child abuse was of female children by adult males, usually family members.)

Also ironic in light of the public hysteria, the demonized sex offender in the 1930s was often able to obtain a favorable plea bargain or a lenient sentence, allowing the offender to abuse still others. In response to this perceived leniency, first judges and then legislators experimented with new correctional approaches to the sexual psychopath. Most realized that longer prison sentences were not the solution, especially for the homosexual offender. What could be better designed to reinforcing rather than ameliorating homosexual tendencies than same-sex prisons, which everyone knew were rife with sodomy? A better response was to introduce some kind of rehabilitation into the state response to sexual offenders. The typical approach was for prosecutors to condition a plea bargain, judges to condition probation, and other authorities to condition parole on the defendant's agreement to accept psychiatric counseling, hospitalization, or castration. To "rehabilitate" sex offenders, hospitals administered lobotomies (2000 were performed on sex offenders between 1938 and 1946), massive injections of male hormones, electrical shock and other aversion therapy.

Notwithstanding the unproven results of these ad hoc measures, one state legislature after another expanded upon them in a series of "sexual psychopath" laws. The first laws were enacted in Michigan, Illinois, Minnesota, and California in the late 1930s. The Illinois law applied to "persons suffering from a mental disorder * * * coupled with criminal propensities to the commission of sex offenses." Ill. Rev. Stat. ch. 38, § 820. If a person charged with a criminal offense were thought to be a "criminal sexual psychopathic person," the Attorney General was authorized to petition the court for a jury trial on that subject. At trial, expert psychiatric evidence as well as the defendant's prior acts and any habitual behavior could be introduced into evidence. *Id.* §§ 823–824. If adjudged psychopathic, the person would be delivered to the Department of Public Safety for treatment "until fully and permanently recovered from such psychopathy." *Id.* § 824. In the first ten years of its operation, the only known case of psychopathic recovery involved a 30–year-old hairdresser who had been charged with committing oral sex with a 16–year-old boy. Because he admitted oral sex on other occasions, he was committed as a sexual psychopath but released four years later after the authorities pronounced him recovered. Only then was he tried for sodomy (and placed on probation when he pled guilty).[1]

Twenty-six state legislatures (including all the big-city states) and Congress, for the District of Columbia, adopted sexual psychopath laws between 1935 and 1960.[m] The statutes essentially sought to transfer authority over sex offenders from courts to psychiatrists. A man accused of sex crimes such as rape, sodomy, child molestation, and indecent exposure—if diagnosed as a "sexual psychopath"—could receive an indeterminate sentence to a psychiatric institution. The implied purpose of the

---

l. See William H. Haines et al., "Commitments Under the Criminal Sexual Psychopath Law in the Criminal Court of Cook County, Illinois," *Proc. Am. Psych. Ass'n* 420, 422–23 (1949).

m. The laws are collected, described, and analyzed in Alan A. Swanson, "Sexual Psychopath Statutes: Summary and Analysis," 21 *Cr. L. Comments & Abstracts* 215 (1960).

sexual psychopath statutes was to protect society and to rehabilitate the offender. Although psychiatrists in their writings had contributed to this stereotype and to the belief that homosexuality could be cured, they were generally skeptical and often hostile to the statutes that were actually enacted. The consensus view that emerged in the 1950s was that few people were actually processed through these statutes, that the people so processed were not the serious sex criminals, and that no real treatment or rehabilitation was actually provided.

PROBLEM 2–3

THE DISTRICT OF COLUMBIA PSYCHOPATH LAW

The Washington D.C. Sexual Psychopath Statute was enacted in 1951 and few changes have been made since. Under the D.C. law, "'sexual psychopath' means a person, not insane, who by a course of repeated misconduct in sexual matters has evidenced such lack of power to control his or her sexual impulses as to be dangerous to other persons because he or she is likely to attack or otherwise inflict injury, loss, pain, or other evil on the objects of his or her desire." D.C. Code § 22–3503. The court or the United States Attorney for the District of Columbia has discretion in bringing the initial proceedings. There is jurisdiction whether or not there has been a criminal charge or a conviction. Once a charge is filed, § 22–3506 requires:

(a) * * * [S]uch court shall appoint 2 qualified psychiatrists to make a personal examination of the patient. The patient shall be required to answer questions asked by the psychiatrists under penalty of contempt of court. Each psychiatrist shall file a written report of the examination, which shall include a statement of his or her conclusion as to whether the patient is a sexual psychopath.

(b) The counsel for the patient shall have the right to inspect the reports of the examination of the patient. No such report and no evidence resulting from the personal examination of the patient shall be admissible against him or her in any judicial proceeding except a proceeding * * * to determine whether the patient is a sexual psychopath.

After psychiatric examinations have been made, and findings reported to the court, the sexual psychopathy hearing is held. The hearing is heard by the court unless the defendant exercises his right to a jury. The defendant has rights of appeal and counsel. At the hearing, evidence of past crimes may be admitted.

"If the patient is determined to be a sexual psychopath, the court shall commit him or her to an institution to be confined there until released ... from confinement when an appropriate supervisory official finds that he or she has sufficiently recovered so as to not be dangerous to other persons, provided if the person to be released be one charged with crime or undergoing sentence therefor, that official shall give notice thereof to the judge of the criminal court and deliver him or her to the court in obedience to proper precept." D.C. Code § 22–3508. If the defendant was charged with a crime then he must face criminal proceedings upon discharge. If he was not charged with a crime then his release may be complete or he may be subject to parole.

What constitutional challenges can plausibly be made to this law on its face? Are they likely to have persuaded a typical judge in the 1950s? See *Minnesota ex rel. Pearson v. Probate Court*, 309 U.S. 270 (1940). Today, such laws are used to incarcerate accused "child molesters" for indeterminate sentences. What constitutional protections should be available for that class of persons? See *Matter of Care and Treatment of Leroy Hendricks*, 912 P.2d 129 (Kan.1996), *petition for cert. granted*, 116 S.Ct. 2522 (1996).

2. THE POST-WORLD WAR II ANTI-HOMOSEXUAL CAMPAIGN

In addition to the sexual psychopath laws, state action in the postwar era sought to erase the existence of homosexuals in America; one of us has set forth the legal mechanisms of this terror elsewhere,[n] and Chapter 4 recounts the evolution of the military exclusion of lesbians, gay men, and bisexuals. The phenomenon we are calling "medicalization" worked in complicated ways.

On the one hand, medical personnel provided neutral reasons for ferreting out homosexuals "for their own good," and the anti-homosexual hysteria used the medical ideas as secular justifications for what seem in retrospect extreme measures. Representative was the Senate Investigating Committee's December 1950 report on "Employment of Homosexuals and Other Sex Perverts in Government." The report made out the case against having "homosexuals and other sex perverts" in the government. "The social stigma attached to sex perversion is so great that many perverts go to great lengths to conceal their perverted tendencies," making them easy prey for "gangs of blackmailers" (p. 3). Also, "those who engage in overt acts of perversion lack the emotional stability of normal persons," and "indulgence in acts of sex perversion weakens the moral fiber of an individual to a degree that he is not suitable for a position of responsibility." Finally, "perverts will frequently attempt to entice normal individuals to engage in perverted practices. This is particularly true in the case of young and impressionable people who might come under the influence of a pervert. * * * One homosexual can pollute an entire office. Another point to be considered * * * is his tendency to gather other perverts about him." These reasons, a jumble of medical and moral judgments, were the basis for thousands of suspected homosexuals to be cashiered out of the federal civil service during the 1950s.[o]

n. William N. Eskridge, Jr., "Privacy Jurisprudence and the Apartheid of the Closet, 1946–1961," *Fla. St. U.L. Rev.* (forthcoming 1997).

o. In 1951, for example, the State Department fired 119 employees as homosexu-

als, and only 35 as security risks; the figures were 134 (homosexuals) and 70 (security risks) in 1952. The Eisenhower Administration was prepared to be even more aggressive than the Truman Administration. In April 1953, Eisenhower issued Executive Order

The publicity given the federal witch hunt beginning in 1950 stimulated many more state witch hunts. In light of the homosexual's perceived preying on children, it is hardly surprising that the most intense attention was focused on school teachers. Beginning in 1956, Florida state Senator Charley Johns chaired a series of interim committees investigating suspected homosexuals and other subversives, with a focus on teachers. Between 1959 and 1964, when the final investigating committee issued its report, 54 Floridians lost their teaching certificates on grounds of alleged immorality, with 83 still being processed through the system when the report was issued. Florida Legislative Investigating Committee, *Homosexuality and Citizenship in Florida* 12–13 (1964). The *in terrorem* effect of the investigations was even greater. Teachers and other state employees fell under suspicion when they were spotted at places investigators considered homosexual hangouts or when they were named by other suspected homosexuals. Once suspected, teachers and other employees were subjected to closed-door questioning about their sexuality. The committee justified its wide-ranging investigations because of the aggressive homosexual menace. "The homosexual's goal and part of the satisfaction is to 'bring over' the young person, to hook him for homosexuality. Whether it be with youth or older individuals, homosexuality is unique among the sexual assaults considered by our laws in that the person affected by the practicing homosexual is first a victim, then an accomplice, and finally himself a perpetrator of homosexual acts" (p. 10).

On the other hand, the medical approach to homosexuality was rehabilitative, and many psychiatrists vigorously opposed the punitive measures of the McCarthy period. Medical experts were the leading critics of sexual psychopath laws, of the application of sodomy laws to consensual conduct, and of employment discriminations against homosexuals. Even doctors who considered homosexuals mentally ill believed, with Krafft–Ebing and Ellis from the turn of the century, that mental illness could be dealt with medically and should not be the object of penal sanctions. Dr. Alfred Kinsey relentlessly criticized any law that penalized homosexuals, and he did so at a time when the ACLU endorsed criminal and civil penalties against homosexuals; he also paid a price, as his Institute lost funding in retaliation against his prohomosexual stands. Dr. Evelyn Hooker spoke against such laws, and also befriended homophile groups, encouraging them to resist public disapproval. Dr. Charles Bowman was the chief force behind Illinois' repeal of its sodomy law in 1961. Numerous others spoke out as well.

3.   CASE STUDY: THE PSYCHOPATHIC PERSONALITY EXCLUSION IN U.S. IMMIGRATION LAW, 1952–1990

Long before World War II, doctors were important players in national immigration policy. The Act of March 3, 1891, 26 Stat. 1084, excluded

---

10405, which added "sexual perversion" as a ground for investigation and exclusion under the federal loyalty-security program, designed in the Truman Administration to weed out subversives from government. In the next two years, more than 800 federal employees resigned or were terminated because they had "files contain[ing] information indicating sex perversion."

aliens who were "idiots, insane persons, * * * persons suffering from a loathsome or a dangerous contagious disease." Section 8 of the Act required a medical examination of each entering alien by "surgeons of a Marine Hospital Service" or other competent civil surgeon to assure exclusion of such unwelcome aliens. From that point onward, the immigration laws always included important roles for medics. The Immigration Act of 1917, 39 Stat. 874, excluded all medical categories created by earlier statutes as well as "persons of constitutional psychopathic inferiority," a catch-all provision that was sometimes used to exclude sexual inverts. Enforcement of that and the other medical exclusions was vested in the recently established United States Public Health Service (PHS).

The 1917 Act remained the keystone immigration law until its massive overhaul in the early 1950's. Policymakers drew on the experiences of the military during World War II in refining a medical model of the psychopathic homosexual.[p] Section 212(a) of the Immigration and Nationality (McCarran–Walter) Act of 1952 contained a grab bag of exclusions to prevent "undesirable" people from entering the United States. The statute excluded every category of individual excluded by the 1917 Act, and many others besides. Among the categories of people excluded were paupers, stowaways, Communists, and persons convicted of crimes involving "moral turpitude."

The first seven exclusions (§ 212(a)(1)-(7)) were "medical" exclusions to be enforced by the PHS in coordination with the Immigration and Naturalization Service (INS); the function of the medical exclusions was to prevent people from coming into the United States who had severe medical problems. The deliberating committees of Congress were generally happy with the categories of excluded people found in the 1917 Act, with these exceptions:

> The subcommittee [of the Senate Judiciary Committee] believes * * * that the purpose of the provision against "persons with constitutional psychopathic inferiority" will be more adequately served by changing that term to "persons afflicted with psychopathic personality," and that the classes of mentally defectives should be enlarged to include homosexuals and other sex perverts. (Senate Report No. 1515, 31st Congress, 2d Session 345 [1950].)

Senator Patrick McCarran, the chair of the Senate Judiciary Committee, sponsored an immigration reform bill that added these two new categories (plus much more). The House bill, sponsored by Representative Walter, had the same provision. Hence, the original version of § 212(a)(4) excluded both "persons afflicted with psychopathic personality" and "sex perverts and homosexuals," the latter being precisely the category of people who in

---

p. For an excellent description of the evolution of the military's policy, see Allan Bérubé, *Coming Out Under Fire: The History of Gay Men and Women in World War Two* (1990).

1947–52 were being hounded out of the U.S civil service. Nonetheless, the PHS suggested that § 212(a)(4) be revised to exclude people "afflicted with psychopathic personality" alone. The following memorandum summarizes the PHS position, which the Judiciary Committees followed when they revised the bill. Congress adopted the bill as revised.

REPORT OF THE PUBLIC HEALTH SERVICE ON THE MEDICAL ASPECTS OF H.R. 2379, A BILL TO REVISE THE LAWS RELATING TO IMMIGRATION, NATURALIZATION, AND NATIONALITY, AND FOR OTHER PURPOSES[q]

It is recommended that the following classes of aliens shall be ineligible to receive visas and shall be excluded from admission into the United States:

1. Aliens who are idiots, imbeciles, or morons.

2. Aliens who are insane.

3. Aliens who have had one or more attacks of insanity.

4. Aliens afflicted with psychopathic personality, epilepsy, or a mental defect.

5. Aliens who are narcotic drug addicts or chronic alcoholics.

6. Aliens who are afflicted with tuberculosis in any form, or with leprosy or any other dangerous contagious disease.

7. Aliens certified by the examining surgeon as having a physical defect, disease, or disability, when determined by the consular or immigration officer to be of such a nature that it may affect the ability of the alien to earn a living. * * *

Psychopathic personality.—Some comments should be expressed regarding the term "psychopathic personality." Although the term "psychopathic personality," used in classifying certain types of mental disorders, is vague and indefinite no more appropriate expression can be suggested at this time. The conditions classified within the group of psychopathic personalities are in effect, disorders of the personality. They are characterized by developmental defects or pathological trends in the personality structure manifest by lifelong patterns of action or behavior, rather than by mental or emotional symptoms. Individuals with such a disorder may manifest a disturbance of intrinsic personality patterns, exaggerated personality trends, or are persons ill primarily in terms of society and the prevailing culture. The latter or sociopathic reactions are frequently symp-

q. This Report was submitted to the House Committee on the Judiciary and is appended to House Report No. 1365, 82d Cong., 2d Sess. 46–47 (1952).

tomatic of a severe underlying neurosis or psychosis and frequently include those groups of individuals suffering from addiction or sexual deviation. Until a more definitive expression can be devised, the term "psychopathic personality" should be retained. * * *

Sexual perverts.—The language of the [McCarran] bill lists sexual perverts or homosexual persons as among those aliens to be excluded from admission to the United States. In some instances considerable difficulty may be encountered in substantiating a diagnosis of homosexuality or sexual perversion. In other instances where the action and behavior of the person is more obvious, as might be noted in the manner of dress (so-called transvestism or fetishism), the condition may be more easily substantiated. Ordinarily, a history of homosexuality must be obtained from the individual, which he may successfully cover up. Some psychological tests may be helpful in uncovering homosexuality of which the individual, himself, may be unaware. At the present time there are no reliable laboratory tests which would be helpful in making a diagnosis. The detection of persons with more obvious sexual perversion is relatively simple. Considerably more difficulty may be encountered in uncovering the homosexual person. Ordinarily, persons suffering from disturbances in sexuality are included within the classification of "psychopathic personality with pathologic sexuality." This classification will specify such types of pathologic behavior as homosexuality or sexual perversion which includes sexual sadism, fetishism, transvestism, pedophilia, etc. In those instances where the disturbance in sexuality may be difficult to uncover, a more obvious disturbance in personality may be encountered which would warrant a classification of psychopathic personality or mental defect.

PROBLEM 2–4

APPLICATION OF THE PSYCHOPATHIC PERSONALITY EXCLUSION

(A) You are the PHS General Counsel in 1965 and are confronted with the case of Clive Michael Boutilier, a Canadian national, first admitted to this country in 1955. In 1963 he applied for citizenship and submitted to the Naturalization Examiner an affidavit in which he admitted that he was arrested in New York in October 1959 on a charge of sodomy, which was later reduced to simple assault and thereafter dismissed on default of the complainant. In 1964, Boutilier submitted another affidavit. It described both homosexual and heterosexual experiences before his entry into the United States. During the eight and one-half years immediately subsequent to his entry, and up to the time of his second statement, Boutilier had homosexual relations on an average of three or four times a year. Since 1959, he has shared an apartment with a man who is his lover. Boutilier's personal affidavit says that since 1950 he has engaged in homosexual sodomy an average of three to four times per year but that he considers himself a "bisexual." An affidavit from Professor of Psychiatry Montague Ullman states that the doctor examined Boutilier and his records and concludes: "The patient has sexual interest in girls and has intercourse with them on a number of occasions. * * * His sexual structure still appears fluid and immature so that he moves from homosexual to heterosexual interests as well as abstinence with almost equal facility." Your agency (PHS) must decide whether to certify Mr. Boutilier as "afflicted with psychopathic personality." Does it sound like he qualifies?

(B) How would you weigh the evidence offered by Alfred Kinsey's studies of sexuality in men and women? Evelyn Hooker's empirical studies which found no correlation between pathology and homosexuality? Assume there are affidavits from both Hooker and the Kinsey Institute (Kinsey died in 1956) attesting that there is no intrinsic connection between homosexuality and psychopathic personality. On the other side of the ledger, critics have complained that the Kinsey study relied on unrepresentative (not statistically random) samples of Americans. Irving Bieber and an impressive list of colleagues have just (1962) published their book on homosexuality. It argues from the authors' clinical experience that homosexuality does have a connection with mental defect.

(C) Consider also the law and PHS practice. Since the early 1950s, your agency has routinely issued a Class "A" certificate to exclude anyone who admits to being a homosexual or to committing acts of homosexual sodomy. The Ninth Circuit in *Fleuti v. Rosenberg*, 302 F.2d 652, 657–658 (9th Cir.1962), *vacated and remanded on other grounds,* 374 U.S. 449 (1963), held that the term "psychopathic personality" was too vague to be constitutionally applied to "homosexuals" generally. The court explicitly relied on medical studies and experts skeptical of the precision or usefulness of the old term "psychopathic personality." At the urging of the PHS and INS, Congress has just amended § 212(a)(4) to override *Fleuti*, rewriting that part of the statute to exclude aliens "afflicted with psychopathic personality, or *sexual deviation*, or a mental defect." Act of Oct. 3, 1965, Public Law No. 89–236, § 15(b), 79 Stat. 911, 919 (new language emphasized). This amendment cannot apply retroactively to Boutilier, however. Considering all this information, what is your professional opinion as to Boutilier's certification?

Clive Michael Boutilier v. Immigration & Naturalization Service

United States Supreme Court, 1967.
387 U.S. 118, 87 S.Ct. 1563, 18 L.Ed.2d 661.

■ MR. JUSTICE CLARK delivered the opinion of the Court.

[Part I states the facts of the case, which are the same as those in Problem 2–4(A). Justice Clark then turned to Boutilier's argument that he was not "afflicted with psychopathic personality" under the statute and, if so, not consistently with the Constitution.]

The legislative history of the Act indicates beyond a shadow of a doubt that the Congress intended the phrase "psychopathic personality" to include homosexuals such as petitioner.

Prior to the 1952 Act the immigration law excluded "persons of constitutional psychopathic inferiority." 39 Stat. 875, as amended, 8 U.S.C. § 136(a) (1946 ed.). Beginning in 1950, a subcommittee of the Senate Committee on the Judiciary conducted a comprehensive study of the immigration laws and in its report found "that the purpose of the provision against 'persons with constitutional psychopathic inferiority' will be more adequately served by changing that term to 'persons afflicted with psychopathic personality,' and that the classes of mentally defectives should be enlarged to include homosexuals and other sex perverts." S. Rep. No. 1515, 81st Cong., 2d Sess., p. 345. The resulting legislation was first introduced as S. 3455 and used the new phrase "psychopathic personality." The bill, however, contained an additional clause providing for the exclusion of aliens "who are homosexuals or sex perverts." As the legislation progressed (now S. 2550 in the 82d Congress), however, it omitted the latter clause "who are homosexuals or sex perverts" and used only the phrase "psychopathic personality." The omission is explained by the Judiciary Committee Report on the bill:

> "The provisio(n) of S. 716 [one of the earlier bills not enacted] which specifically excluded homosexuals and sex perverts as a separate excludable class does not appear in the instant bill. The Public Health Service has advised that the provision for the exclusion of aliens afflicted with psychopathic personality or a mental defect which appears in the instant bill is sufficiently broad to provide for the exclusion of homosexuals and sex perverts. *This change of nomenclature is not to be construed in any way as modifying the intent to exclude all aliens who are sexual deviates.*" (Emphasis supplied.) S.Rep. No. 1137, 82d Cong., 2d Sess., p. 9.

Likewise a House bill, H.R. 5678, adopted the position of the Public Health Service that the phrase "psychopathic personality" excluded from entry homosexuals and sex perverts. The report that accompanied the bill shows clearly that the House Judiciary Committee adopted the recommendation of the Public Health Service that "psychopathic personality" should be used in the Act as a phrase that would exclude from admission homosexuals and sex perverts. H.R. Rep. No. 1365, 82d Cong., 2d Sess. It quoted at length, and specifically adopted, the Public Health Service report which recommended that the term "psychopathic personality" be used to "specify such types of pathologic behavior as homosexuality or sexual perversion." We, therefore, conclude that the Congress used the phrase "psychopathic personality" not in the clinical sense, but to effectuate its purpose to exclude from entry all homosexuals and other sex perverts.

Petitioner stresses that only persons *afflicted* with psychopathic personality are excludable. This, he says, is "a condition, physical or psychiatric, which may be manifested in different ways, including sexual behavior." Petitioner's contention must fall by his own admissions. For over six years prior to his entry petitioner admittedly followed a continued course of homosexual conduct. The Public Health Service doctors found and certified that at the time of his entry petitioner "was afflicted with a class A condition, namely, psychopathic personality, sexual deviate...." * * * Having substantial support in the record, we do not now disturb that finding, especially since petitioner admitted being a homosexual at the time of his entry. The existence of this condition over a continuous and uninterrupted period prior to and at the time of petitioner's entry clearly supports the ultimate finding upon which the order of deportation was based.

[Justice Clark rejected Boutilier's due process arguments, that the exclusion was vague and provided him with "no [sufficient] warning" when he entered the United States in 1955.] Therefore, he argues, he was unaware of the fact that homosexual conduct engaged in after entry could lead to his deportation. We do not believe that petitioner's post-entry conduct is the basis for his deportation order. At the time of his first entry he had continuously been afflicted with homosexuality for over six years. To us the statute is clear. It fixes "the time of entry" as the crucial date and the record shows that the findings of the Public Health Service doctors and the Special Inquiry Officer all were based on that date. We find no indication that the post-entry evidence was of any consequence in the ultimate decision of the doctors, the hearing officer or the court. Indeed, the proof was uncontradicted as to petitioner's characteristic at the time of entry and this brought him within the excludable class. A standard applicable solely to time of entry could hardly be vague as to post-entry conduct. * * *

■ MR. JUSTICE BRENNAN dissents for the reasons stated by Judge Moore of the Court of Appeals, 363 F.2d 488, 496–499.

■ MR. JUSTICE DOUGLAS, with whom MR. JUSTICE FORTAS concurs, dissenting.

The term "psychopathic personality" is a treacherous one like "communist" or in an earlier day "Bolshevik." A label of this kind when freely used may mean only an unpopular person. It is much too vague by constitutional standards for the imposition of penalties or punishment. * * *

Many experts think that it is a meaningless designation. "Not yet is there any common agreement * * * as to classification or * * * etiology." Noyes, *Modern Clinical Psychiatry* 410 (3d ed. 1948). "The only conclusion that seems warrantable is that, at some time or other and by some reputable authority, the term psychopathic personality has been used to designate every conceivable type of abnormal character." Curran & Mallinson, Psychopathic Personality, 90 *J. Mental Sci.* 266, 278. See also Guttmacher, Diagnosis and Etiology of Psychopathic Personalities as Perceived in Our Time, in *Current Problems in Psychiatric Diagnosis* 139, 154 (Hoch & Zubin ed. 1953); Tappan, Sexual Offences and the Treatment of Sexual Offenders in the United States, in *Sexual Offences* 500, 507 (Radzinowicz ed. 1957). It is much too treacherously vague a term to allow the high penalty of deportation to turn on it.

When it comes to sex, the problem is complex. Those "who fail to reach sexual maturity (hetero-sexuality), and who remain at a narcissistic or homosexual stage" are the products "of heredity, of glandular dysfunction, (or) of environmental circumstances." Henderson, Psychopathic Constitution and Criminal Behaviour, in *Mental Abnormality and Crime* 105, 114 (Radzinowicz & Turner ed. 1949).

The homosexual is one, who by some freak, is the product of an arrested development:

"All people have originally bisexual tendencies which are more or less developed and which in the course of time normally deviate either in the direction of male or female. This may indicate that a trace of homosexuality, no matter how weak it may be, exists in every human being. It is present in the adolescent stage, where there is a considerable amount of undifferentiated sexuality." Abrahamsen, *Crime and the Human Mind* 117 (1944).

Many homosexuals become involved in violations of laws; many do not. Kinsey reported: * * *

"It is unwarranted to believe that particular types of sexual behavior are always expressions of psychoses or neuroses. In actuality, they are more often expressions of what is biologically basic in mammalian and anthropoid behavior, and of a deliberate disregard for social convention. Many of the socially and intellectually most significant persons in our histories, successful scientists, educators, physicians, clergymen, business men, and persons of high position in governmental affairs, have socially taboo items in their sexual histories, and among them they have accepted nearly the whole range of so-called sexual abnormalities. Among the socially most successful and personally best adjusted persons who have contributed to the present study, there are some whose rates of outlet are as high as those in any case labelled nymphomania or satyriasis in the literature, or recognized as such in the clinic." Kinsey, *Sexual Behavior in the Human Male* 201–202 (1948).

It is common knowledge that in this century homosexuals have risen high in our own public service—both in Congress and in the Executive Branch—and have served with distinction. It is therefore not credible that Congress wanted to deport everyone and anyone who was a sexual deviate, no matter how blameless his social conduct had been nor how creative his work nor how valuable his contribution to society. I agree with Judge Moore, dissenting below, that the legislative history should not be read as imputing to Congress a purpose to classify under the heading 'psychopathic personality' every person who had ever had a homosexual experience:

"Professor Kinsey estimated that 'at least 37 per cent' of the American male population has at least one homosexual experience, defined in terms of physical contact to the point of orgasm, between the beginning of adolescence and old age. Kinsey, Pomeroy & Martin, *Sexual Behavior in the Human Male* 623 (1948). Earlier estimates had ranged from one per cent to 100 per cent. *Id.*, at 616–622. The sponsors of Britain's current reform bill on homosexuality have indicated that one male in 25 is a homosexual in Britain. To label a group so large 'excludable aliens' would be tantamount to saying that Sappho, Leonardo da Vinci, Michelangelo, Andre Gide, and perhaps even Shakespeare, were they to come to life again, would be deemed unfit to visit our shores. Indeed, so broad a definition might well comprise more than a few members of legislative bodies." 2 Cir., 363 F.2d 488, 497–498 [Moore, J., dissenting]. * * *

If we are to hold, as the Court apparently does, that any acts of homosexuality suffice to deport the alien, whether or not they are part of a fabric of antisocial behavior, then we face a serious question of due process. By that construction a person is judged by a standard that is almost incapable of definition. I have already quoted from clinical experts to show what a wide range the term "psychopathic personality" has. * * *

Deportation is the equivalent to banishment or exile. Though technically not criminal, it practically may be. The penalty is so severe that we have extended to the resident alien the protection of due process. Even apart from deportation cases, we look with suspicion at those delegations of power so broad as to allow the administrative staff the power to formulate the fundamental policy. * * * We deal here also with an aspect of "liberty" and the requirements of due process. They demand that the standard be sufficiently clear as to forewarn those who may otherwise be entrapped and to provide full opportunity to conform. "Psychopathic personality" is so broad and vague as to be hardly more than an epithet. * * *

[Even if the statute were not unconstitutionally vague, it could not properly be applied to Boutilier, in light of the record before the Court, Justice Douglas argued in conclusion. Occasional acts, even if considered "perverted," did not meet the statutory requirement that Boutilier be "afflicted" with psychopathy.]

NOTES ON *BOUTILIER* AND EVOLVING PSYCHIATRIC OPINION ABOUT HOMOSEXUALITY AS A MENTAL DISORDER

1. *The Legal Arguments, pro and con.* The main legal argument for Boutilier is the one accepted by the Ninth Circuit in *Fleuti* and elaborated by Justice Douglas: § 212(a)(4) should be interpreted to avoid the due process (notice, vagueness) problems with relying on the term "psychopathic personality" to reach "homosexuals." But consider: (a) The legislative history makes clear that "psychopathic personality" was a code word for "homosexual," and the psychiatric community in post-World War II America used the term similarly (see *DSM–I*). (b) If the legislative history was not clear, wasn't the PHS sufficiently clear? As the agency to which Congress had delegated statutory authority, the PHS had substantial discretion, which it exercised to exclude homosexual immigrants. (c) Congress had cleared up this sort of vagueness with the 1965 amendment adding "sexual deviation" to § 212(a)(4) (overriding *Fleuti*). Although the

1965 amendment did not apply to Boutilier, for post–1965 aliens the statute would appear sufficiently clear, yes?

On the other hand, what about the following responses: (a) The legislative history establishes that Congress *rejected* McCarran's proposed language flatly excluding "sex perverts and homosexuals." The PHS's position was that "psychopathic personality" would soak up *most* homosexuals—but not *all* of them, and none of them unless they met a profile of pathology. The only evidence in the Boutilier record was the medical affidavits submitted by Boutilier; those doctors all testified that he was not psychopathic. (b) Whatever medical support there was in 1952 for the view that most homosexuals are psychopathic was being overtaken by subsequent medical evidence, especially Hooker's studies. The *Boutilier* majority reads like pages out of Krafft–Ebing, who was sorely outdated by 1967, while the dissent resonates well with the reputable authorities: Freud, Kinsey, Hooker. (c) Was Boutilier a "homosexual" or, in Krafft–Ebing's terminology, a "true invert"? Wasn't he more like a "bisexual" (an "untrue invert"?), someone attracted to people of both sexes? Was the McCarran–Walter Act aimed at excluding bisexuals? If not, why should the PHS and the Court go out of their way to drag bisexuals into the statutory exclusion?

Notice, finally, Justice Douglas' scholarly use of then-current science. The majority gave no answers to any of his science-based arguments. Did Justice Clark have any answers to give? Was Justice Douglas' science relevant to the case?

2. *The Warren Court and Sexuality.* An irony of *Boutilier* is that the "liberal" Warren Court went out of its way to interpret the spongiest statutory term in the most broadly anti-homosexual way. Note that liberal Chief Justice Earl Warren and Justice Hugo Black voted with the majority, and future liberal Justice Thurgood Marshall was the Solicitor General who defended the position taken by the liberal administration of President Lyndon Johnson.

This much is apparent: liberals as well as conservatives agreed that homosexuals were mentally ill. The Krafft–Ebing, Rado understanding of homosexuality trumped the Kinsey, Hooker understanding. Consider why this might be, a theme renewed in Chapter 3. Note, further, that the Warren Court was not friendly to women's equality, either. Its only major sex discrimination decision upheld Florida's practice of allowing women but not men to escape jury service. *Hoyt v. Florida*, 368 U.S. 57 (1961). On the other hand, two important lines of Warren Court decisions contributed to liberty in the realm of sexuality: its privacy decisions (Chapter 1), its first amendment obscenity cases (Chapter 6), and perhaps most important its criminal procedure decisions. See generally William N. Eskridge, Jr., *Gaylaw: Challenging the Apartheid of the Closet* ch. 3 (forthcoming 1998).

3. *It All Changes with Stonewall (1969): Homosexuals Declare War on the Psychiatrists.* When the Supreme Court decided *Boutilier* in 1967, few people in the United States were openly gay or lesbian. With the McCarthy terror still fresh and state policies still openly discriminatory, homosexuals resided in their respective closets and retained a collective anonymity. This changed, literally overnight, on the night of June 26, 1969. On that date, New York City police raiding the Stonewall Inn in Greenwich Village triggered physical, indeed violent, resistance by drag queens, fags, and dykes. The following two evenings of rioting, breathlessly reported in *The Village Voice*, touched thousands of gay people. In the next several months, thousands of people "came out" of their closets, formed scores of gay liberation groups, and proclaimed their own civil rights movement. Permanent organizations took shape over the next year, and the gay rights movement developed an agenda. Prominent on the agenda was demedicalization of homosexuality—removal of its classification as a disease.

In 1970, the first spring after Stonewall, gay activists confronted their tormenters at the American Psychiatric Association's (APA) annual convention in San Francisco.[r] They wanted to remove the characterization of homosexuality as a psychiatric disorder from the APA's diagnostic manual, the *DSM–II*. Irving Bieber, then the leading anti-gay psychiatrist, was laughed off the stage by gay protesters. "I've read your book, Dr. Bieber," yelled one protester, "and if that book talked about black people the way it talks about homosexuals, you'd be drawn and quartered and you'd deserve it." A paper on electroshock treatment for sexual deviation met with shouts of "torture" and "Where did you take your residency, Auschwitz?" The crowd erupted in pandemonium at the conclusion of the paper, with much carrying on by the audience.

Dr. Kent Robinson, a psychiatrist, believed that the protesters' claims had possible merit and negotiated a panel at the 1971 APA convention which would include gay representatives. Robinson contacted gay activist Frank Kameny to organize the panel. Despite securing an official panel at the 1971 convention in Washington D.C., the activists did not want to appear mollified by the limited participation, and continued to organize street protests. On May 3, 1971, gay activists stormed the stately Convocation of Fellows at the APA Convention, and Kameny seized the microphone to deliver a diatribe against the profession: "Psychiatry is the enemy incarnate. Psychiatry has waged a relentless war of extermination against us. You may take this as a declaration of war against you." Gay activists later went on to conduct their panel. At the end of the convention, Kameny and his fellow panelists demanded that the APA revise its diagnostic manual to delete references to homosexuality as a psychiatric disorder.

Two years later, after continued pressure from gay activists as well as from inside the profession, including declarations by gay psychiatrists, and after a thorough review of the medical literature (including the work of Kinsey, Hooker, and Marmor), the APA's Nomenclature Committee was poised to accept the change. Bieber and Charles Socarides organized an Ad Hoc Committee Against the Deletion of Homosexuality and mobilized

---

r. The following account is drawn from Ronald Bayer, *Homosexuality and American Psychiatry: The Politics of Diagnosis* (1987); Gary Alinder, "Gay Liberation Meets the Shrinks," in *Out of the Closets: Voices of Gay Liberation* 141 (Karla Jay & Allen Young eds., 1972).

psychoanalysts to protest any caving in to gay pressure (as they would understand the matter). The proposal to delete homosexuality as a psychiatric disorder was presented and discussed at the 1973 APA Convention, where it received strong support. On December 15, 1973, the Committee voted to drop homosexuality's classification as a disease in *DSM-II*. Even the stuffy *New York Times* recognized the significance of this move; its headline read, "Psychiatrists in a Shift, Declare Homosexuality No Mental Illness."

The Nomenclature Committee's decision survived an unprecedented "referendum" (a vote among APA members) instigated by the Ad Hoc Committee. When the new *DSM-III* was issued later in the 1970s, homosexuality as an illness was a nonissue, but the manual did include the category "ego-dystonic homosexuality" as a diagnostic category. It was defined as "[a] desire to acquire or increase heterosexual arousal so that heterosexual relations can be initiated or maintained and a sustained pattern of overt homosexual arousal that the individual explicitly complains is unwanted as a source of distress." Although the category was undoubtedly strange, gay activists were mum, lest any protest trigger renewed debate over the 1973 deletion.

PROBLEM 2–5

WHAT TO MAKE OF THE NEW APA STANCE?

You are a lawyer for the National Gay Task Force (NGTF) formed in 1973 to lobby in Washington, D.C. on gay and lesbian rights' issues. After the dust settles on the APA's new stance regarding homosexuality, the NGTF decides to push for administrative change in the immigration exclusion described above. A meeting is arranged with officials of the INS and PHS. The announced goal of NGTF is to end the exclusion of gay, lesbian, and bisexual immigrants.

Devise a strategy for the NGTF to follow, including: What preliminary contacts should be made (perhaps even before the meeting is set up)? What legal arguments should NGTF make for the INS' or PHS' authority to end the exclusion? How do you deal with *Boutilier*, a binding Supreme Court precedent? What fall-back position, if any, should the NGTF be prepared to accept (perhaps down the road)? This exercise will be most useful if you write down your thoughts now, and then read the following Notes.

NOTES ON THE POST-*BOUTILIER* EVOLUTION OF THE IMMIGRATION EXCLUSION OF LESBIANS AND GAY MEN[s]

On July 17, 1974, Dr. John Spiegel, President of the American Psychiatric Association (APA), wrote the INS, informing the agency of the APA's official action "delisting" homosexuality as a sexual "deviance." Dr. Spiegel

---

s. This note is drawn from William N. Eskridge, Jr., *Gaylaw: Challenging the Apar-* *theid of the Closet* ch. 3 (forthcoming 1998).

further urged the INS to "use your statutory powers of discretion to refrain from the exclusion, deportation or refusal of citizenship to homosexual aliens." The INS General Counsel responded, first, with *Boutilier* as binding precedent on his agency and, second, with the assertion that "homosexuals" must in any event be denied citizenship on the ground that they lack the "good moral character" required by 8 U.S.C. § 1427(a). The Menninger Foundation wrote the INS "congratulating" it and criticizing the APA. "Soon homosexuals will want to 'marry,' have control of children, advocate their way of life as being normal to young people and so on." The matter was not reopened during the Nixon–Ford Administration.

At the beginning of the Carter Administration (in 1977), Department of Justice and White House officials met with ACLU and National Gay Task Force (NGTF) leaders to discuss the latter's petition for the INS to change its policy. We don't know exactly what went on at that meeting, but the upshot of pressure like this was that the PHS—not the INS—took the lead. There were rumblings of discontent at the PHS as early as November 1977, and in August 1979 the PHS announced that it would no longer carry out examinations or issue certificates to exclude gay men, bisexuals, and lesbians pursuant to § 212(a)(4). Memorandum from Surgeon General Julius Richmond to William H. Foege, Director Center for Disease Control (Aug. 2, 1979), reprinted in 56 *Interpreter Releases* 387 (1979). Invoking the 1974 edition of *DSM–II* and the forthcoming 1979 edition of *DSM–III*, the Surgeon General justified the change as reflecting "current and generally accepted canons of medical practice with respect to homosexuality. * * * [T]his change in the policy of the PHS with respect to the physical and mental examination of aliens has been made to reflect the most current judgments of health professionals on this subject."

Enforcement of § 212(a)(4) was built around the PHS, which was charged with examining immigrants for physical and mental defects, see 8 U.S.C. §§ 1222, 1224 (1988), and a PHS certificate was required for the INS to exclude an immigrant because of one of the "medical" exclusions. *Id.* § 1226(d) (if the PHS certifies that an immigrant "is afflicted with ... any mental disease, defect, or disability" excludable under § 212(a)(1)-(5), the INS decision to exclude "shall be based *solely* upon such certification" (emphasis added)). Contrast *id.* § 1225(a) ("inspection, other than the physical or mental examination" shall be done by INS). When the PHS refused to participate in the exclusion, for professional reasons, the statutory scheme was thrown into turmoil. The INS immediately suspended exclusions of "homosexuals" and alerted Congress to its dilemma. It also sought a legal opinion from the Office of Legal Counsel of the Department of Justice (OLC). How should the OLC advise? See OLC Memorandum No. 79–85, December 10, 1979.

As it turned out, the OLC insisted that *Boutilier* was still binding on the INS. In response to the OLC memorandum, the INS in September 1980 rescinded its suspension order and instructed agents to follow these procedures:

Primary Inspection—An alien shall not be asked any questions concerning his or her sexual preference during primary inspection.

Referral to Secondary Inspection—An alien shall be referred to secondary inspection for examination as to homosexuality only under the following circumstances: (1) When an alien makes an unsolicited, unambiguous oral or written admission of homosexuality. Buttons, literature or other materials referring to "gay rights" or describing or supporting homosexuality shall not be considered unambiguous admissions of homosexuality. (2) When a third party who presents him or herself for inspection voluntarily states, without prompting or prior questions, that an alien who arrived in the United States at the same time and is then being processed for admission is a homosexual. * * *

Secondary Inspection—An alien referred to secondary inspection for examination as to homosexuality shall be questioned privately. Inspectors must perform their duties in a professional manner and not allow personal beliefs to taint the inspection of the alien. An alien referred under paragraph 4 shall be asked *only* whether he or she is homosexual. If the answer is "no", the alien shall not be detained for further examination as to homosexuality. If the answer is "yes", the alien shall be asked to sign a statement to that effect. * * *

During the 1980s, the INS enforced the exclusion occasionally; more important, some gay immigrants made admissions in order to bring test cases. The big one was *Lesbian/Gay Freedom Day Committee, Inc. v. INS*, which challenged the INS' exclusion of Carl Hill. The Ninth Circuit in *Hill v. INS*, 714 F.2d 1470 (9th Cir.1983), interpreted the immigration law not to permit the INS to exclude gay men and lesbians without the cooperation of the PHS. At about the same time, the Fifth Circuit permitted the INS to enforce the exclusion without the PHS' cooperation, in *In re Longstaff*, 716 F.2d 1439 (5th Cir.1983), *cert. denied*, 467 U.S. 1219 (1984).

At this point, the government had many options. What ended up happening was the following: (1) The INS did not ask for an appeal of its loss in *Hill* and agreed to follow it, but only within the Ninth Circuit; it followed its earlier policy in all the other circuits. It is not unusual for agencies to "nonacquiesce" in a court decision and follow it only in the circuit where it is issued. (2) The PHS in June 1984 agreed to issue a certificate for "self-proclaimed homosexual aliens presented by the U.S. Immigration and Naturalization Service"—but only in the Ninth Circuit. Elsewhere in the country, the PHS would refuse to have anything to do with "homosexuals." (3) The INS, in turn, adopted the policy of telling "self-proclaimed homosexual aliens" that they could apply for a "waiver of excludability" which would defer action excluding them for the duration of their stay in the United States. Moreover, the alien could apply for the waiver before the alien came to the United States, and the suggestion was that such waivers would be routinely granted. What happened to *Boutilier*?

When Congress turned to revising the 1952 Act's exclusions, Representative Barney Frank was one of the main players. He and others insisted upon revamping the exclusions entirely (omitting the deviation/psychopathic personality exclusion altogether). Senator Alan Simpson specifically stated on the floor of the Senate that the revision would override *Longstaff* and revoke the historical policy of excluding "homosexuals." With very little controversy, the bill was enacted as the Immigration Act of 1990, Pub. L. No. 101–649, § 601, 104 Stat. 4978, 5067.

POSTSCRIPT: IMMIGRATION EXCLUSION OF PEOPLE WITH HIV

Just as the exclusion of gay people was being polished off, a new exclusion was inserted. Senator Jesse Helms in 1987 sponsored an appropriations rider that directed Health and Human Services (HHS) to list AIDS (later, "HIV infection") as one of the infectious diseases for which noncitizens could be excluded from entering the United States. The 1990 Act, which repealed the gay exclusion, also appeared to reverse the Helms Amendment, for it gave HHS discretion to determine "communicable diseases of a public health significance" which would trigger the new shorter list of immigration exclusions. 8 U.S.C. § 1182(a)(1)(A)(1).

In 1993, HHS Secretary Donna Shalala proposed regulations that would have removed HIV infection from the list of "communicable diseases" requiring exclusion. Congressional reaction impelled Shalala to back away from the proposed regulations. The HIV infection ban remains in effect (as of 1997). To the extent HIV infection is associated with gay and bisexual men, the HIV infection exclusion becomes a partial replacement for the gay exclusion—a striking example of the medicalization of American anxieties about sexuality. Chapter 12, Section 1 contains a more thorough consideration of sexuality issues presented by HIV and AIDS.

PART C.   MEDICALIZATION, ABORTION, AND THE CONTROL OF WOMEN'S SEXUALITY[t]

In *Roe v. Wade* [Chapter 1, Section 2], the Supreme Court held that women have a qualified constitutional right to abortion; that constitutional right was justified in Justice Blackmun's opinion by reference to medical standards, and *Roe*'s famous trimester regulatory framework was based upon then-current medical technology regarding viability of the fetus outside the womb. From the beginning, therefore, medicalization has been important for abortion law. Many feminists, such as Justice Ruth Bader Ginsburg and Professor Reva Siegel (Chapter 1, Section 2), have criticized *Roe*'s approach for clouding the issue of women's choice and women's equality with a medicalized gloss. State regulators, on the other hand, maintain that *Roe* is too restrictive.

---

t.   Mara Rosenthal, Georgetown University Law Center, Class of 1998, is the primary author (especially of the notes) and editor of the materials in this part.

At the center of recent debate over the choice/life debate have been laws requiring women to notify or seek consent from their parents or their husbands before they obtain abortions. Social scientists, clinical psychologists, and other medical experts have played major roles in litigation over these statutes. On the whole, they have been important voices opposed to parental/husband notification/consent statutes. Social science evidence tends to show that such statutes do not serve the "better communications" purposes they purport to serve and, instead, constitute substantial burdens on women's (especially minor women's) right to choose.

The Supreme Court in *Planned Parenthood of Central Missouri v. Danforth*, 428 U.S. 52 (1976), held that the state cannot require parental consent as a condition of a minor's obtaining an abortion in the first trimester. In *Bellotti v. Baird*, 443 U.S. 622 (1979) (*Bellotti II*), eight Justices voted to strike down a law requiring either parental consent to a minor's abortion or parental notification plus judicial approval. Writing for four Justices, Justice Powell stated that the statute could have passed muster if it had allowed the "judicial bypass" without parental notification. Writing for four other Justices, Justice Stevens found the law unconstitutional because third parties—either parents or a judge—held absolute veto power over a minor's fundamental right to an abortion. Writing only for himself, Justice White believed the law constitutional. The Powell opinion in *Bellotti II* spurred state legislation codifying his dicta outlining statutory schemes that he thought would pass muster.

Jane Hodgson, M.D., et. al. v. Minnesota

U.S. District Court for the District of Minnesota, 1986.
648 F.Supp. 756.

■ ALSOP, CHIEF JUDGE. * * *

[Plaintiffs are licensed physicians engaged in the practice of obstetrics and gynecology, including the performing of abortions; clinics providing birth control, abortions and related medical services to its patients including unemancipated minor women under the age of 18; unemancipated minors pregnant at the commencement of this action representing a class composed of pregnant minors who assert that they are mature and that notification of one or both of their parents would not be in their best interests; and the mother of plaintiff Ellen Z. who asserts that notification of Ellen Z's father of Ellen Z's desire to have an abortion would not have been in Ellen Z.'s best interests.]

[In 1981, Minnesota enacted § 144.343(2)-(7). Subdivision 2 requires physicians or their agents to attempt with reasonable diligence to notify the parents, of an unemancipated minor under the age of 18, at least 48 hours before performing an abortion. Subdivision 3 defines "parent" as both parents if both are living, one parent if only one is living or if the second one cannot be located through reasonably diligent effort, or the guardian or conservator if the pregnant woman has one. Subdivision 4 provides that the statutory notice requirement does not apply when the parents have consented to the abortion, when prompt action is needed to preserve the life of the minor, or when the minor reports that she is a victim of sexual or physical abuse or neglect. Subdivision 6 of the statute provides that if subdivision 2 is ever enjoined by judicial order, then the same notice requirement shall be effective together with an optional procedure whereby an unemancipated minor may obtain a court order permitting an abortion without notice to her parents upon a showing that she is mature and capable of giving informed consent to an abortion or, if she is not mature, that an abortion without notice to her parents nevertheless would be in her best interests.]

The experience of going to court for a judicial authorization produces fear and tension in many minors. Minors are apprehensive about the prospect of facing an authority figure who holds in his hands the power to veto their decision to proceed without notifying one or both parents. Many minors are angry and resentful at being required to justify their decision before complete strangers. Despite the confidentiality of the proceeding, many minors resent having to reveal intimate details of their personal and family lives to these strangers. Finally, minors are left feeling guilty and ashamed about their lifestyle and their decision to terminate their pregnancy. Some mature minors and some minors in whose best interests it is to proceed without notifying their parents are so daunted by the judicial proceeding that they forego the bypass option and either notify their parents or carry to term.

Some minors are so upset by the bypass proceeding that they consider it more difficult than the medical procedure itself. Indeed, the anxiety resulting from the bypass proceeding may linger until the time of the medical procedure and thus render the latter more difficult than necessary.
* * *

A minor who chooses not to go to court to avoid notifying her parents must notify both parents, if they are living, unless the second one cannot be located through reasonably diligent effort. The statute makes no exception for a non-custodial parent who is divorced or separated from the custodial parent, or for a parent who never married the custodial parent. No exception is made in the case of a parent, custodial or not, whom the minor considers likely to react abusively to notification, unless the minor is willing to declare that she is a victim of sexual or physical abuse. * * *

In practice, the requirement that the minor notify both parents, if living, affects many minors in single parent homes who have voluntarily notified the custodial parent. No exception is made, for example, in the case of a non-custodial parent who for years has exhibited no interest in the minor's development. No exception is made for parents likely to react with psychological, sexual or physical violence toward either the minor or the custodial parent. Minors in such circumstances must notify the non-custodial parent, or else go to court for authorization to proceed without notifying the non-custodial parent. Notification of an abusive or even a disinterested absent parent may reintroduce that parent's disruptive or unhelpful participation into the family at a time of acute stress. Alternatively, going to court to seek authorization introduces a traumatic distraction into the family relationship at a stressful juncture. The emotional trauma attending either option tends to interfere with and burden the parent-child communication the minor voluntarily initiated with the custodial parent.

The two parent notification requirement also affects minors in two parent homes who voluntarily have consulted with one parent but not with the other out of fear of psychological, sexual, or physical abuse toward either the minor or the notified parent. Here, too, the minor must choose either to notify the second parent or to endure the court bypass procedure. Once again, the emotional trauma attending either option tends to interfere with and burden the parent-child communication the minor voluntarily initiated with the custodial parent. * * *

The Minnesota legislature had several purposes in mind when it amended Minn.Stat. § 144.343 in 1981. The primary purpose was to protect the well-being of minors by encouraging minors to discuss with their parents the decision whether to terminate their pregnancies. Encouraging such discussion was intended to achieve several salutary results. Parents can provide emotional support and guidance and thus forestall irrational and emotional decision-making. Parents can also provide information concerning the minor's medical history of which the minor may not be aware. Parents can also supervise post-abortion care. In addition, parents can support the minor's psychological well-being and thus mitigate adverse psychological sequelae that may attend the abortion procedure.

The court finds that a desire to deter and dissuade minors from choosing to terminate their pregnancies also motivated the legislature. Testimony before a legislative committee considering the proposed notification requirement indicated that influential supporters of the measure hoped it "would save lives" by influencing minors to carry their pregnancies to term rather than aborting. * * *

The court heard testimony of judges who collectively have adjudicated over 90 percent of the parental notification petitions filed since August 1, 1981. None of these judges, on direct or cross examination, identified a positive effect of the law. * * *

Honorable William Sweeney testified, "* * * What I have come to believe ... [is] that really the judicial function is merely a rubber stamp. * * * The young women I have seen have been very mature and capable of giving the required consent."

He further testified that "the level of apprehension that I have seen contrasted with even the orders for protection, which is a very intense situation, very volatile, and the custody questions, is that the level of apprehension is twice what I normally see in court.... You see all the typical things that you would see with somebody under incredible amounts of stress, answering monosyllabically, tone of voice, tenor of voice, shaky, wringing of hands, you know, one young lady had her—her hands were turning blue and it was warm in my office...." * * *

On the basis of her experience, [counselor] Tina Welsh concludes that the law has not benefited intra-family communication. A minor's unplanned pregnancy is a crisis which is not conducive to an attempt to build good family communications. Ms. Welsh does not believe that the law helps teenagers make a better decision about whether to have an abortion or continue the pregnancy. Requiring a minor to tell either her parents or a judge about her pregnancy and the reasons she wants an abortion makes no beneficial contribution to the minor's decision.

The public defenders who participate in bypass proceedings believe that the law serves no beneficial purpose. Its sole function, in their view, is to create a hurdle and impose additional stress upon the young women. Similarly, the guardians ad litem do not perceive a beneficial purpose to their participation in the process. * * *

Minnesota courts have denied only an infinitesimal proportion of the petitions brought since 1981. This fact indicates that in Minnesota immature, non-best interest minors rarely seek judicial authorization to terminate their pregnancies without parental involvement. Such minors either inform their parents, obtain an abortion outside Minnesota, or carry the pregnancy to term.

Dr. Gary B. Melton suggested two partial explanations for this phenomenon. First, comparisons of personality functioning between adolescents who abort and those who carry to term generally show more adaptive, healthier functioning in the former group. Adaptation, in turn, marks a level of psychological and emotional development colloquially referred to as "maturity." Second, a minor's desire to maintain a measure of privacy of information about her personal matters is an important indication of individuation, a principal developmental task of adolescence. * * * [W]hile there may be "no logical relationship between the capacity to become pregnant and the capacity for mature judgment concerning the wisdom of an abortion," *H.L. v. Matheson*, 450 U.S. 398, 408 (1981), * * * some relationship does exist between the decision to abort in privacy and the capacity for mature judgment concerning the wisdom of this decision. Consequently, a regulation that affects only minors who have elected to terminate their pregnancies and to do so in privacy tends inevitably to reach only mature minors and immature minors driven to this choice by their own best interests. Such a regulation will fail to further the State's interest in protecting immature, non-best interest minors. * * *

Defendants offered the court no persuasive testimony upon which to base a finding that Minnesota's parental notification law enhances parent-child communications, or improves family relations generally. * * *

Five weeks of trial have produced no factual basis upon which the court can find that Minn.Stat. § 144.343(2)-(7) on the whole furthers in any meaningful way the State's interest in protecting pregnant minors or assuring family integrity. * * *

The effect of compelling an adolescent to share information about her pregnancy and abortion decision with both parents in a divorced or separated situation can be harmful. The non-custodial parent often will reintegrate with the family in a disruptive manner. The adolescent may be perplexed as to why the non-custodial parent should become an important factor in her life at this point, especially when the parent previously has paid her little attention and offered little support. Moreover, the testimony revealed no instances in which beneficial relations between a minor and an absent parent were reestablished following required notification. * * *

[The *Roe v. Wade* right of women to control their bodies, including the right to abortion, protects minors as well as adults, but the state has somewhat broader authority to regulate abortions by minors. See *Danforth*.]

As immature minors often lack the ability to make fully informed choices that take account of both immediate and long-range consequences, a State reasonably may determine that parental consultation often is desirable and in the best interests of the minor. *Bellotti II*, 443 U.S. at 640. Therefore, a State's interest in protecting immature minors will sustain the requirement of consent, either parental or judicial. But even the State's interest in encouraging parental involvement in their minor children's decision to have an abortion must give way to the constitutional right of a mature minor or an immature minor whose best interests are contrary to parental involvement. * * *

Without the judicial bypass option of subdivision 6, Minn. Stat. § 144.343(2) would unduly burden the exercise by minors of the right to seek an abortion. There are parents who would obstruct, and perhaps altogether prevent, the minor's efforts to exercise this right. *Bellotti II*, 443 U.S. at 647. Young, pregnant minors, especially those living at home, are particularly vulnerable to their parents' efforts to obstruct an abortion. The interests of the State, and of these parents, must give way to the constitutional right of a mature minor or of an immature minor whose best interests are contrary to parental involvement. * * * Therefore, the court concludes that it must permanently enjoin defendants from enforcing Minn. Stat. § 144.343(2) as unmodified by subdivision 6. * * *

[*Planned Parenthood Ass'n of Kansas City, Mo., Inc. v. Ashcroft*, 462 U.S. 476 (1983), held that a judicial bypass can save an otherwise unconstitutional parental consent statute so long as it contains certain protections for the minor's right to choose. Judge Alsop found that the judicial bypass procedure created by Minn.Stat. § 144.343(6) complied with the procedural requirements set forth in *Bellotti II* and approved in *Ashcroft*.]

Subdivision 3 of Minnesota Statute § 144.343 identifies the individuals entitled to notification as "both parents * * *." * * * The court finds that this requirement places a significant burden upon pregnant minors who do not live with both parents. Particularly in these cases, notification of an abusive, or even a disinterested, absent parent has the effect of reintroducing that parent's disruptive or unhelpful participation into the family at a time of acute stress. Similarly, the two parent notification requirement places a significant obstacle in the path of minors in two parent homes who voluntarily have consulted with one parent but not with the other out of fear of psychological, sexual, or physical abuse toward either the minor or the notified parent. In either case, the alternative of going to court to seek authorization to proceed without notifying the second parent introduces a traumatic distraction into her relationship with the parent whom the minor has notified. The anxiety attending either option tends to interfere with and burden the parent-child communication the minor voluntarily initiated with the custodial parent. * * *

This court concludes, however, that a regulation requiring notification of both parents even when the nuclear family unit either has broken apart or never formed is not reasonably designed to further the State's interest in protecting pregnant minors.

To the contrary, the court finds that the regulation adversely affects communication voluntarily initiated with one parent in a large number of cases. * * * Thus the court concludes that this requirement fails to further the State's interest. * * * [T]he court must enjoin defendants from enforcing the two parent notification requirement of Minn.Stat. § 144.343. * * *

The language of subdivision 3 defining "parent" as "both parents * * *" is inseparably intertwined within Minn.Stat. § 144.343(2)-(7). The Minnesota legislature would not have enacted a statute requiring notification of a minor's parents prior to the abortion without identifying the individuals entitled to such notice. More importantly, the remainder of the statute cannot be given effect without the offending language. *See* Minn. Stat. § 144.343(7).

In addition, this court is ill-situated to determine what alternative definition the legislature would employ to remedy the constitutional infirmity identified in this decision. * * * Therefore, the definition of parent contained in Minn.Stat. § 144.343(3) is not severable from the remainder of the statute. The court must enjoin defendants from enforcing Minn.Stat. § 144.343(2)-(7) in its entirety.

NOTES ON PARENTAL NOTIFICATION ABORTION LAWS AND PARENTAL CONTROL OVER THEIR DAUGHTERS' SEXUALITY

1. *ProFamily or ProFather?* Couched in terms of family values, the parental notification statutes have been promulgated by the same groups that have stated that their goal is to recriminalize abortion. The legislative history of the Minnesota statute indicates that supporters of the measure employed the parental notification and bypass laws to erect obstacles to women seeking abortions. State Senator Menning, one of the Act's most outspoken proponents, stated on the Senate floor that the statute would "save lives" by influencing minors not to abort. Brief for Cross–Respondents William Z. Petelovitch et al., Part II(B), *Hodgson v. Minnesota*, 497 U.S. 417 (Nos. 88–1125 and 88–1309). Studies assessing the impact of parental notification statutes on teenage birth rates indicate that the statutes do have the effect of decreasing abortion rates and increasing the birthrate of babies to teenagers.

Consider the contention that the two-parent notification requirement is an attempt to place control of minor women's sexuality in the hands of men. Studies indicate that those teenagers who communicate with a parent about sexuality and pregnancy are far more likely to confer with a mother than a father. Rosalind Petchesky concludes that "a requirement that both parents be informed affirms paternal authority and power over young women's sexual lives. In the concrete reality of many family situations, this may amount to undermining the mothers of teenage daughters, including their custody rights" *Abortion and Woman's Choice: The State, Sexuality and Reproductive Freedom* 307 (1990). Thus, two-parent notification laws may serve to bolster male authority and control of women's sexuality while at the same time potentially undermining mother-daughter relations.

2. *Statutes Giving Minors Decisionmaking Authority for Themselves and Their Children.* Many states give mature minors the right to consent to various medical treatments without parental consent, including mental health services, treatment for sexually transmitted diseases, drug and/or alcohol treatment and surgery related to childbirth. Brief for Amici Curiae American Psychological Association et al., Part II, *Hodgson.* Statutory "maturity" has been accorded minors who are married, active in the armed forces, living independently, etc. Ironically, should they have a child, minors are automatically granted the authority to make health care decisions for themselves and their child! How can this be reconciled with the lack of authority afforded to minors to make decisions regarding pregnancy?

3. *The Parental Notification/Judicial Bypass Process: A Codification of Socially Imposed Female Gender Categories.* The legal structure established by statutes such as the Minnesota parental notification law defines socially appropriate notions of female sexuality and gender. The law sets up one conflict between (sexually immature) *child* versus (sexually mature) *woman*, and a second conflict within the category of mature sexually active woman between *mother* and *criminal*. Thus, the law asserts that the minor is not a woman but a child who is subsumed under parental authority and must seek parental notice to proceed with the termination of a pregnancy. Alternatively, as a mature sexually active woman, the law provides only two options. The woman may carry the pregnancy to term with no social restriction, thus signaling society's sanction of the category of sexually active woman as mother. In contrast, should she desire to terminate the pregnancy then she must go to court, signaling the sexually active non-mother as criminal.

The association of the judicial bypass process with the notion of criminality is evident to teenagers. Thus, "some teenagers feel that they don't belong in the court system, that they are ashamed, embarrassed and somehow that they are being punished for the situation they are in. I had a teenager tell me last week when I was describing to her the location of the building, when I said the Juvenile Justice Center she said I feel like a criminal and I think that is pretty typical of the reaction that the kids have when they find out they have to go to court. They see court as a place for teenagers who have done something wrong." Trial Testimony Excerpts of Susanne Smith, Supervisor of Guardian Ad Litem Program in Hennepin County, Joint Appendix, Part 1, *Hodgson*. Indeed, testimony at trial showed that sometimes parents have been informed but refuse to sign the notification papers so that the girl is forced to go through the court system as a form of punishment. Trial Testimony Excerpts of Susan Stacy, Administrative Assistant in Guardian Ad Litem Office of Hennepin County. in Joint Appendix, Part 2, *Hodgson*. Thus, the parental notification/judicial bypass statutes send a strong message to young women. Either you are a child or a mature woman. If you are a mature woman who is sexually active you have two choices: mother or criminal.

4. *Uncloseting Teenage Sexuality.* Parental notification of a daughter's desire to have an abortion may represent a threefold jolt to a parent. The parent is notified that: (1) the daughter is sexually active, (2) she is pregnant, and (3) she desires an abortion. For many parents, this notice may be the first time they acknowledge that their daughter is sexually active. Thus, abortion becomes the public sign of a young woman's sexuality. See Petschesky, *Abortion and Woman's Choice* 209–22. Abortion decisions require young women to negotiate relations with those around them, including parents and boyfriends. The way in which a pregnancy is handled can represent a critical struggle for power and control between young women and their world.

Research in social and personality development indicates that by middle adolescence, teenagers have the ability to reason about moral dilemmas and interpersonal problems on a par with adults and that they have the intellectual and social capacities specifically outlined in the law as necessary for understanding treatment alternatives, considering risks and benefits and giving legally competent consent. By middle adolescence most teenagers develop an adult identity and understanding of self. Furthermore, the majority of teenagers do not repudiate parental values but, rather, incorporate those values as they search for their autonomy. APA Brief, Part II(B), *Hodgson*.

Studies show that parents are rarely significant sources of sex education for their children.[u] Is this distance between parents and teenagers in matters of sexuality healthy? Hodgson and the other plaintiffs thought so, Minnesota thought not. Which side is right?

5. *Abortion and Teenage Psychology.* According to the American Psychiatric Association (APA), abortion not only carries a low risk of negative psychological consequences for adolescents, but the psychological consequences of abortion for adolescents are usually positive, with significant

---

u. Rozema, "Defensive Communication Climate as a Barrier to Sex Education in the Home," 35 *Fam. Relations* 532 (1986); Bennet & Dickinson, "Student–Parent Involvement in Sex, Birth Control and Venereal Disease Education," 16 *J. Sex Research* 114, 115 (1980), as well as other sources in APA Brief, Part I(C), *Hodgson*. Many studies indicate that sex is an area of conflict that does not lend itself to open and honest communication between parents and teenagers. E.g., Marsman & Herold, "Attitudes Toward Sex Education and Values in Sex Education," 35 *Fam. Relations* 357 (1986).

lessening of anxiety and increased feelings of well-being. The primary response following abortion is generally overwhelming relief. APA Brief, Part II(B), *Hodgson*. An abortion removes serious potential constraints on the minor's life and future. After an abortion, the adolescent can resume her normal life and activities in school, at home, and with peers. In contrast, teenage mothers are significantly more likely to cut their education short, to hold low-paying jobs, to be single parents, and to end up on welfare. They are also more likely to have repeat pregnancies and for those who marry to legitimate the birth, they are more likely to experience marital instability. The data support the position that abortion is more psychologically benign than carrying to term for almost all adolescents. *Id.* Three major reviews of the psychological and psychiatric research confirm that for the majority of women who undergo an abortion, there are no long-term negative emotional effects.[v]

6. *Supreme Court Precedent and Judicial Bypass.* As Judge Alsop realized, Supreme Court dicta in *Bellotti II* and *Ashcroft* had accepted two-parent *consent* requirement for minors, so long as there was a sufficient judicial bypass for minors who are mature enough to make the decision. The factual situation, as Judge Alsop saw it, indicated that those precedents approved a regulation that places an undue burden on the minor woman's right to choose. Notice how Judge Alsop reconciled his disagreement with precedent and the facts of the matter as he saw them.

The judicial bypass procedure may be a privilege only for those teenagers fortunate enough to be able to afford to take the time and make the arrangements to go through the process. The teenagers who go through the judicial bypass process "are very much nonminority, they are very much white and they are very much middle class." Trial Testimony Excerpts of David Knutson, Attorney with Hennepin County Public Defender's Office, in Joint Appendix, part 2, *Hodgson*. The bypass procedure may also intimidate those teenagers who are less privileged and have not grown to view the legal establishment as supportive of their world. Do these concerns undermine the precedential force of *Bellotti II*?

Note that the Supreme Court has held that states can refuse to fund abortions in their Medicaid programs for the poor. See *Harris v. McRae*, 448 U.S. 297 (1980); *Maher v. Roe*, 432 U.S. 464 (1977). In this vein, the bypass procedure might be a rational screening device because it "takes a kind of forthright courageous youngster to travel two or three hundred miles, to come to a court in an alien city to get permission." Trial Testimony Excerpts by Judge Allen Oleisky, Juvenile Division Judge of Hennepin County, in Joint Appendix, part 2, *Hodgson*.

Jane Hodgson, et al. v. Minnesota, et al., 497 U.S. 417, 110 S.Ct. 2926, 111 L.Ed.2d 344 (1990). On appeal of Judge Alsop's injunction, a

v. Marecek, "Consequences of Adolescent Childbearing and Abortion," in *Adolescent Abortion: Psychological and Legal Issues* 96 (G. Melton ed. 1986); Adler & Dolcini, "Psychological Issues in Abortions for Adolescents," in *Adolescent Abortion: Psychological and Legal Issues* 74 (F. Melton ed. 1986); Shusterm, "The Psychological Factors of the Abortion Experience: A Critical Review," 1 *Psychol. Women Q.* 79 (1976).

majority of the Supreme Court held that the two-parent notice requirement contained in subsection 2 was unconstitutional but that the judicial bypass in subsection 6 saved the statute's constitutionality. Justice Kennedy's opinion for the Court emphasized that Minnesota was simply following the roadmap laid out by Justice Powell's plurality opinion in *Bellotti II.* "Justice Powell's considered reasoning, coupled with the dissenting views of Justice White, was intended to set forth the dispositive principles of law for deciding the constitutionality of parental consent laws. The Court has relied upon these principles in deciding the constitutionality of laws requiring notice or the consent of one parent, see *Akron v. Akron Center for Reproductive Health, Inc.,* 462 U.S., at 439–442 (1983) (consent); *Ohio v. Akron Center for Reproductive Health,* 497 U.S. 502, 511–514 (1990) (notice). As *Bellotti II* dealt with the far more demanding requirement of two-parent consent, and approved of such a requirement when coupled with a judicial bypass alternative, I must conclude that these same principles validate a two-parent notice requirement when coupled with a judicial bypass alternative."

Writing for four dissenting Justices, Justice Stevens argued that *Bellotti II* had no holding on this issue; Justice Powell's guidelines were only advisory. Also, allowing a judicial bypass—assured not to be used by many minors—to save the constitutionality of a two-parent notification scheme was inconsistent with the Court's refusal to allow states to burden even a minor's *Roe v. Wade* right to choice.

NOTES ON THE SUPREME COURT'S ALLOWANCE OF PARENTAL NOTIFICATION STATUTES, WITH BYPASSES

1. *Was* Bellotti II *Binding on the Issue in* Hodgson? What should be the precedential effect of Justice Powell's blueprint for states? Justice Powell spoke only for four Justices; the other Justices in *Bellotti II* either thought that two-parent consent statutes were constitutional without the Powell roadmap (Justice White) or were unconstitutional even with the Powell roadmap (the Stevens group). By counting votes the states could tell that a two-parent consent requirement *plus* judicial bypass would be likely to get five votes of the *Bellotti II* Court, but does that kind of vote-counting constitute a "holding" of the Court binding on future Courts?

One problem with treating policy roadmaps like Powell's as the holding of the Court is that such roadmaps are not tested in concrete Article III settings, with factual disputes and legal briefing by adversarial parties. *Hodgson* in fact represented the first case where there were facts to assess the implementation of two-parent notification/judicial bypass statutes. (In the first *Akron* case, the Court applied *Bellotti II* to a one-parent consent law.) Yet Justice Kennedy and the majority ignored Judge Alsop's findings illustrating that the statute not only furthered no state interests but rather interfered with those aims. The Supreme Court is required to defer to the trial court's findings of fact unless "clearly erroneous." Should the Court have used the case to reconsider rather than follow Justice Powell's blueprint?

2. *Are Two–Parent Consent Statutes More Intrusive Than Two–Parent Notification Statutes?* Invoking the old saying that the greater includes the lesser, Justice Kennedy argued that if consent statutes coupled with judicial bypass provisions have been upheld, then the "less demanding" notice statutes coupled with judicial bypass provisions should also be upheld. Although notification requirements do not give parents the legal authority to veto a daughter's abortion decision, as a practical matter the parents usually have veto power. Unemancipated minors are financially dependent on their parents and have numerous legal constraints imposed upon them. Parents also have considerable leeway, under the law, to punish their children. Thus, in practice, minors often have little choice but to comply with their parents' directives.

It is recognition of this vulnerability that has led courts to require confidentiality in the judicial bypass proceeding. For example, Dr. Hodgson testified about an incident in which a mother removed her 15–year-old daughter from school and kept her locked in the house to stop her from having an abortion. Brief for Cross–Respondents William Z. Petelovitch et al, Part I(B), *Hodgson*. One judge testified that 5% of the minors that came before him stated that their parents would force them to keep the child, 21% stated that their parents would force them to leave home. *Id*. Thus, in practice, the distinction between notice and consent statutes may be overstated.

As Judge Dembitz of New York State Family Court has observed, parents "who have opposed their unmarried daughters' efforts to secure abortions variously have expressed a vengeful desire to punish the daughter for her sexual activity by making her suffer the unwanted child, a fervor to impose a religious conviction the mother has failed to instill in her daughter, a hope of caring for her daughter's baby as her own because of an inability or unwillingness to bear another child herself, a defensive or resentful attitude because [the mother of the pregnant minor] bore illegitimate children without seeking or being able to secure an abortion, or a general distaste for abortion. None of these parental reasons for objecting relates to the daughter's well-being—only that of the mother." Nanette Dembitz, "The Supreme Court and a Minor's Abortion Decision," 80 *Colum. L. Rev.* 1251, 1255 (1980).

3. *Variation in Parental Notification Statutes.* As of 1990, Minnesota had the most intrusive parental notification statute in the country. Of the 38 states that then required parental participation in the minor's decision to terminate her pregnancy, 27 required participation of only one parent; three other states were ambiguous. The seven states (other than Minnesota) requiring notification of both parents had more loopholes than Minnesota.[w] Minnesota's extremism, coupled with the apparent legislative motiva-

---

w. Arkansas required an unmarried minor to notify both parents but provided exceptions where the second parent "cannot be located through reasonably diligent effort,"

tion to burden a minor woman's right to choose, troubled Judge Alsop. Should this have given the Supreme Court greater pause?

Planned Parenthood of Southeastern Pennsylvania v. Robert Casey, 505 U.S. 833, 112 S.Ct. 2791, 120 L.Ed.2d 674 (1992). The Supreme Court reaffirmed *Roe*'s "essential" holding that a woman has a fundamental right to choose an abortion, but the joint opinion of Justices O'Connor, Kennedy, and Souter took a relatively expansive view of the circumstances under which the state could regulate the right to choose. Joined by four Justices who would have overruled *Roe*, the authors of the joint opinion upheld all but the spousal consent provisions of Pennsylvania's regulatory scheme. Joined by Justices Blackmun and Stevens, who interpreted *Roe* more liberally, the joint opinion struck down the spousal consent provision as an "undue burden" (Justice O'Connor's test) on a woman's right to choose.

The joint opinion reaffirmed *Hodgson*'s reading of *Bellotti II*, "that a State may require a minor seeking an abortion to obtain the consent of a parent or guardian, provided that there is an adequate judicial bypass procedure." Accordingly, the Court upheld Pennsylvania's one-parent consent requirement, with a bypass. In reaching its decision striking down the constitutionality of spousal notice provisions, the Court stressed the high incidence of domestic violence against women, well more than one out of eight women according to a recent AMA survey.[x] From this and other evidence, the Court reasoned that in our society the husband was so likely to have such unwarranted power over his wife and her right to choose, that it was justified in denying his right to notice. This evidence suggested to

or a parent's "whereabouts are unknown," the parent has not been in contact with the minor's custodial parent or the minor for at least one year, or the parent is guilty of sexual abuse. Ark.Code Ann. §§ 20–16–802, 20–16–808 (Supp.1989). Delaware required the consent only of parents who are residing in the same household; if the minor is not living with both of her parents, the consent of one parent is sufficient. Del.Code.Ann., Tit. 24, § 1790(b)(3) (1987). Illinois law did not require the consent of a parent who has deserted the family or is not available. Ill. Rev.Stat., ch. 38, para. 81–54(3) (1989). Kentucky required an unmarried minor to obtain the consent of a legal guardian or "both parents, if available," but provided that if both parents are not available, the consent of the available parent shall suffice. Ky. Rev. Stat. Ann. §§ 311.732(2)(a), (b) (Michie 1990). Under Massachusetts law, an unmarried minor needed to obtain the consent of only one parent if the other parent "is unavailable to the physician within a reasonable time and in a reasonable manner," or if the parents are divorced and the other parent does not have custody. Mass. Gen. Laws § 112, § 12S (1988). Mississippi required only the consent of the parent with primary custody, care, and control of the minor if the parents are divorced or unmarried and living apart and, in all other cases, the consent of only one parent if the other parent is not available in a reasonable time or manner. Miss. Code Ann. § 41–41–53(2) (Supp.1989). North Dakota required only the consent of the custodial parent, if the parents are separated and divorced, or the legal guardian, if the minor is subject to guardianship. N.D.Cent.Code § 14–02.1–03.1 (1981).

x. According to the AMA, "[r]esearchers on family violence agree that the true incidence of partner violence is probably double the above estimates; or four million severely assaulted women per year. Studies suggest that from one-fifth to one-third of all women will be physically assaulted by a partner or ex-partner during their lifetime." AMA Council on Scientific Affairs, *Violence Against Women* 7 (1991). In families where wife-beating takes place child abuse is often present as well. *Id.* at 12.

the authors of the Joint Opinion (Justices O'Connor, Kennedy, and Souter) that spousal notice was an "undue burden" (the *Casey* test) on a woman's right to choose.

Given the findings of fact in *Hodgson* indicating the lack of benefit, and indeed potential harm, that minors may receive from forced consultation with their parents, the psychological and financial dependence of minors on their parents and the District Court's own findings in *Planned Parenthood* that "in a domestic abuse situation, it is common for the battering husband to also abuse the children," how can one reconcile the contrasting Supreme Court positions on spousal as opposed to parental notice?

CURRENT ISSUES INVOLVING MEDICALIZATION, SEXUALITY, GENDER, AND THE LAW

The immigration example, in particular, might leave you with the impression that "medicalization" of sexuality and gender has been a disaster, or at least unprogressive. Such an impression, though, might be an overreaction in light of the role of social scientists in the litigation of reproductive rights and gay rights cases. In addition, apart from whatever insights Freud or Kinsey or Hooker might still offer the thoughtful student, one can argue that more recent medical researchers have provided challenging theories and practical medicine that expand our sexual or gender horizons. Or have they simply repeated the arrogance of the past, with false theories and exploitive practices? You decide.

PART A. SCIENCE-BASED QUESTIONS ABOUT THE ASSUMPTION OF SEX BINARINESS

Socially, we assume that there are two sexes (male and female), each paired up with specific biological features: chromosomes (women XX, men XY), genitalia (women vaginas, men penises), internal organs (women ovaries, men testes), and hormones (women estrogen, men androgen). As a matter of science, these assumptions are oversimple, and perhaps wrong.

Not everyone has XX or XY chromosomal patterns. See John Money, *Venuses Penuses: Sexology, Sexosophy and Exigency Theory* ch. 6 (1986). People with Turner's syndrome have only 45 chromosomes rather than 46, with only one X chromosome. Such people are usually raised as women but do not have ovaries. People with Klinefelter's syndrome have XXY chromosomes. Such people are usually raised as men but have very small testicles and eunuchoid body types; they are usually reproductively sterile. People with XYY chromosomal patterns are usually raised as boys; the primary symptoms are psychological nervousness.

Moreover, many people with XX or XY chromosomes do not unambiguously display female or male sex characteristics, respectively. Anne Fausto–Sterling, "The Five Sexes: Why Male and Female Are Not Enough," *The Sciences*, March/April 1993, at 20–24, calls these people "intersexual" and divides them into the following groups. "True hermaphrodites" possess

203

both a testis and an ovary and usually have ambiguous external genitalia, often a small penis as well as a vagina. "Male pseudohermaphrodites" have testes and some manifestations of female genitalia but no ovaries. "Female pseudohermaphrodites" have ovaries and some manifestations of male genitalia but no testes. She and the Johns Hopkins researchers think that as many as 4% of human births are intersexual.

As Fausto–Sterling points out, none of this is new. Intersexuals have been known throughout human history. Perhaps surprisingly, research in this area is hardly new either. Consider an early classic study, whose conclusions have not (to our knowledge) been challenged and which is now considered conventional wisdom among scientists.

John Money, Joan G. Hampson and John L. Hampson, An Examination of Some Basic Sexual Concepts: The Evidence of Human Hermaphroditism

97 *Bulletin of the Johns Hopkins Hospital* 301, 301–10 (1955).*

Despite advancements of knowledge in embryology and endocrinology, most people have continued to make an absolute dichotomy between male and female—a dichotomy as seemingly axiomatic as the distinction of day from night, black from white. In psychology and psychiatry, this dichotomy is represented in the conception of predominant masculinity or femininity of the sexual instinct or drive. * * *

In an endeavor to ascertain if new and additional information relevant to psychologic theory of sexuality might be obtained from the study of hermaphroditism, the authors have, for the past four years, systematically been making psychologic studies of hermaphroditic patients. * * *

The sexual incongruities which occur in hermaphroditism involve divers contradictions, singly or in combination, between six variables of sex. These six variables are:

1. Assigned sex and sex of rearing;
2. External genital morphology;
3. Internal accessory reproductive structures;
4. Hormonal sex and secondary sexual characteristics;
5. Gonadal sex;
6. Chromosomal sex.

Patients showing various combinations and permutations of these six sexual variables may be appraised with respect to a seventh variable:

7. Gender role and orientation as male or female, established while growing up.

Thus one is enabled to ascertain something of the relative importance of each of the six variables in relation to the seventh.

Patients in whom ambisexual contradictions exist include seven subgroups in the traditional diagnostic category of hermaphroditism and a group traditionally diagnosed as ovarian agenesis but now more accurately named gonadal agenesis, or dysgenesis, since the chromosomal pattern is male. We have studied 76 patients in all.

CHROMOSOMAL SEX

[The authors identify 19 cases where the chromosomes (men are supposed to have XY, women XX) and the rearing were contradictory.[a]] In every instance, the person established a gender role and orientation consistent with assigned sex and rearing, and inconsistent with chromosomal sex. Thus, it is convincingly clear that gender role and orientation as male or female evidenced itself independently of chromosomal sex, but in close conformity with assigned sex and rearing.

GONADAL SEX

Among the 76 patients, there were 20 in whom a contradiction was found between gonadal sex [i.e., the existence of ovaries for women and testicles for men] and the sex of assignment and rearing.[b] All but 3 of these 20 disclosed themselves in a gender role fully concordant with their rearing. Gonadal structure per se proved a most unreliable prognosticator of a person's gender role and orientation as man or woman, boy or girl. By contrast, assigned sex and rearing proved a most reliable one.

HORMOMAL SEX

To consider now the relationship between hormonal sex and gender role: hormonal sex must be distinguished from gonadal structure, for ovaries do not always make estrogens [the female sex hormones], nor testicles androgens [male sex hormones]. The ovaries of hyperadrenocortical female pseudohermaphrodite are inert, and though their adrenals produce an excess of estrogens as well as of androgens, androgenic activity dominates and the body is excessively virilized. The testes of male pseudo-

---

a. In 14 cases ("dysgenesis" and "simulant female" cases), the chromosomes were male, but external genitals appeared female and the child was raised as a female. In 4 cases ("cryptorchid male hypospodiac"), the chromosomes were male, the external genitals showed features of both male and female, and the child was raised as a female. In 1 case ("true hermaphroditism"), the chromosomes were female, the external genitals showed features of both male and female, and the child was raised as a male.

b. In 6 cases ("female with phallus and ovogenesis" and "hyperandrencortical fe-

male"), the gonads and chromosomes were female, the external genitals were ambiguous, and the child was raised as a male. In 6 cases, the gonads were male and the external genitals were either ambiguous ("male with unarrested mullierian differentiation") or female ("simulant female"), and the child was raised as a female. In 8 cases ("cryptorchid male hypospodiac" and "simulant female"), the gonads and chromosomes were male, the genitals were ambiguous, and the child was raised as a female.

hermaphrodites of the simulant female variety produce estrogens which feminize the body. * * *

Of the 27 people whose hormonal functioning and secondary sexual body morphology contradicted their assigned sex and rearing, only four became ambivalent with respect to gender role as male or female.[c] All four had been reared as girls. One, acting on his own initiative, began living as a man from the age of sixteen onward. The other three, while living as women, showed some degree of bisexual inclination. These four patients do not, in themselves, offer any convincing evidence of hormonal sex as a causal agent in the establishment of maleness or femaleness of gender role: the patient who lived as a man declined testosterone substitution treatment after surgical castration for malignancy, and the three who lived as women had been thoroughly feminized on estrogen substitution treatment. Moreover, the other 23 of the 27 patients established a gender role consistent with their assigned sex and rearing, despite the embarrassment and worry occasioned by hormonal contradictions. Like gonadal sex, hormonal sex per se proved a most unreliable prognosticator of a person's gender role and orientation as man or woman, boy or girl.

INTERNAL ACCESSORY ORGANS

Since the uterus is the organ of menstruation, and the prostate the major organ of seminal fluid secretion, it is necessary to compare maleness or femaleness of gender role with internal reproductive equipment. There were 17 cases in whom assigned sex and rearing was inconsistent with predominant male or female structures internally. Gender role agreed with rearing in 14 of these 17. The three remaining were the same three individuals as deviated in [the hormonal and gonadal mismatches]. * * *

EXTERNAL GENITAL APPEARANCE

It goes without saying that the external genitals are the sign from which parents and others take their cue in assigning a sexual status to a neonate [i.e., newborn child] and in rearing him thereafter, and the sign, above all others, which gives a growing child assuredness of his or her gender. Nonetheless, it is possible for an hermaphrodite to establish a gender role fully concordant with assigned sex and rearing, despite a paradoxical appearance of the external genitals.

There were 23 among our 76 patients who, at the time they were studied, had lived for more than two-thirds of their lives with a contradiction between external genital morphology and assigned sex.[d] For one

---

c. In 23 cases, the people had male hormones but were reared as females, with 19 fully identifying as women notwithstanding contrary signals from their bodies. The four ambiguous cases included three cryporchid male phypospodiacs and one hyperandrenocortical female. In three cases, people with female hormones were raised as males and so identified. In one case of true hermaphroditism, there were both male and female hormones, and the patient was reared and self-identified as a male.

d. In 15 cases ("hyperadrenocortical female"), the genitals were male but the chromosomes, gonads, hormones, and sex of rearing were female. In two cases ("male with unarrested mullerian differentiation"), the

reason or another, they did not receive surgical correction of their genital deformity in infancy, but lived with a contradictory genital appearance for at least five and for as many as 47 years. In all but one instance, the person had succeeded in coming to terms with his, or her, anomaly and had a gender role and orientation wholly consistent with assigned sex and rearing.

It is not contended that these people encountered no difficulties in their lives. On the contrary, there was considerable evidence that visible genital anomalies occasioned much anguish and distress. Distress was greatest in those patients whose external genital morphology flagrantly contradicted, without hope of surgical correction, the sex in which they had grown up and established, indelibly, their gender role and orientation as boy or girl, man or woman. Distress was also quite marked in patients who had been left in perplexed confusion about the sex to which they belonged, in consequence either of parental or medical indecision, or of insinuations from age-mates that they were half boy, half girl. Uniformly, the patients were psychologically benefited by corrective plastic surgery, when it was possible, to rehabilitate them in the sex of assignment and rearing. Only one patient failed to take advantage of plastic surgery. Instructively enough, he was the person who, on his own initiative, changed his birth certificate and began living as a man from the age of sixteen onward. He was unable to summon up enough courage to have his genitals masculinized.

It is relevant to note in passing that psychotic symptoms in all of the patients were conspicuous by their absence. In remarkably few instances, evidence of neurotic symptomatology was apparent. In some, but by no means all patients, feelings of bashfulness, shame and oddity were to the fore, and they had great initial diffidence in talking about themselves.

ASSIGNED SEX AND REARING

Chromosomal sex, gonadal sex, hormonal sex, internal accessory reproductive organs and external genital morphology—each of these five variables of sex has passed successively in review and has been compared first with assigned sex and rearing and, second, with the gender role and orientation as boy or girl, man or woman, which the person established while growing up. In only four cases among 76 was any inconsistency between rearing and gender role observed, despite the many inconsistencies between these two and the other five variables of sex.

Evidently there is a very close connection between, on the one hand, the sex to which an individual is assigned, and thenceforth reassigned in a myriad subtle ways in the course of being reared day by day, and, on the

genitals and gonads were male, the chromosomes were undetermined, and the child was reared as a female. In five cases ("cryptorchid male hypospodiac"), the chromosomes and gonads were male, but the genitals and sex assigned during rearing were inconsistent (2 female-male, 3 male-female). In one case ("cryptorchid male hypospodiac with breasts"), the genitals were female, but everything else was male.

other hand, the establishment of gender role and orientation as male or female.

GENDER ROLE AND ORIENTATION

In the light of hermaphroditic evidence, it is no longer possible to attribute psychologic maleness or femaleness to chromosomal, gonadal or hormonal origins, nor to morphological sex differences of either the internal accessory reproductive organs or the external genitalia. Conceivably, of course, instinctive masculinity or femininity may be attributed to some other innate bodily origin. For example, Krafft–Ebing among others has suggested special brain centers. There is, however, no support for such a conjecture when, as may happen in hermaphroditism, among individuals of identical diagnosis, some have been reared as boys, some as girls. * * *

From the sum total of hermaphroditic evidence, the conclusion that emerges is that sexual behavior and orientation as male or female does not have an innate, instinctive basis.

In place of a theory of instinctive masculinity or femininity which is innate, the evidence of hermaphroditism lends support to a conception that, psychologically, sexuality is undifferentiated at birth and that it becomes differentiated as masculine or feminine in the course of the various experiences of growing up.

Those who find the concept of instinct or drive congenial may choose to say that there is a sexual instinct or drive that is undifferentiated and genderless at birth. In that case, sexual drive is neither male nor female to begin with, and it can be assumed to have no other somatic anchorage than in the erotically sensitive areas of the body. So limited, sexual drive becomes a special example of a kinaesthetic or haptic drive—an urge to touch and be touched, an urge for bodily contact.

Those who find the concept of drive uncongenial may choose simply to say that in the human species there are erotically sensitive areas of the body, especially the genital organs, and that these areas are sometimes stimulated and used by oneself or another person. In the course of growing up, a person's sexual organ sensations become associated with a gender role and orientation as male or female which becomes established through innumerable experiences encountered and transacted.

Our studies of hermaphroditism have pointed very strongly to the significance of life experiences encountered and transacted in the establishment of gender role and orientation. This statement is not an endorsement of a simple-minded theory of social and environmental determinism. Experiences are transacted as well as encountered—conjunction of the two terms is imperative—and encounters do not automatically dictate predictable transactions. There is ample place for novelty and the unexpected in cerebral and cognitional processes in human beings.

Novelty and unexpectedness notwithstanding, cerebral and cognitional processes are not infinitely modifiable. The observation that gender role is established in the course of growing up should not lead one to the hasty conclusion that gender role is easily modifiable. Quite the contrary! The evidence from examples of change or reassignment of sex in hermaphroditism, not to be presented here in detail, indicates that gender role becomes not only established, but also indelibly imprinted. Though gender imprinting begins by the first birthday, the critical period is reached by about the age of eighteen months. By the age of two and one-half years, gender role is already well established.

One may liken the establishment of a gender role through encounters and transactions to the establishment of a native language. Once imprinted, a person's native language may fall into disuse and be supplanted by another, but is never entirely eradicated. So also a gender role may be changed or, resembling native bilingualism, may be ambiguous, but it may also become so indelibly engraved that not even flagrant contradictions of body functioning and morphology may displace it.

ANTHROPOLOGICAL NOTE ON THE CULTURAL CONSTRUCTION OF SEX AND GENDER[e]

The punch line of the Johns Hopkins study is that one's "sex" is as much a cultural as a biological creation, just as "gender" has long been assumed to be. Cross-cultural and anthropological studies provide parallel evidence of this effect, indicating that human societies culturally categorize sex, gender, and sexuality in myriad different ways. Not all societies reduce sex to a simple dichotomy between two categories (i.e. the western distinction of "male" v. "female") or believe that biological features such as the reproductive organs define an individual's social and behavioral sex or gender.[f]

With regard to female gender characterizations, for example, the woman's childbearing role has been repeatedly singled out by western feminists as limiting the range of female activities. This goes against much ethnographic evidence. In the West, birth control and abortion practices have commonly been utilized to provide women with control over the childbearing role. But there is ethnographic evidence illustrating that in other societies, pregnancy is not considered debilitating and interferes only minimally, if at all, in societal activities. The fact that childbearing is associated with western women's present oppression does not mean this is the case in other social systems. Women's highly visible kinship function—bearing children—is surprisingly underrated, even ignored, in definitions of womanhood in a wide range of societies.[g] (Childrearing practices also vary

e. Anthropologist Mara Rosenthal, Georgetown University Law Center, Class of 1998, is the primary author of this note.

f. See the excellent collection of essays in *The Many Faces of Homosexuality: Anthropological Approaches to Homosexual Behavior* (Evelyn Blackwood ed. 1986), especially the essays by Evelyn Blackwood (survey of an-

thropology literature on role of women and sexual deviation), Serena Nanda (on Indian "Hijras"), Charles Callender and Lee Kochems (on Native American "berdaches"), and Walter Williams (same).

g. See Eleanor Burke Leacock's work, especially *Visibility and Power: Essays on Women in Society and Development* (1986);

greatly among cultures. It is important not to equate childbearing, a biological role relegated to some women, with childrearing, a social role in which women and men both can and have participated).

Cultures also manifest different mores regarding acceptable sexual or marital partners. Even in western culture, there has been variability as to who is considered an appropriate sexual partner. Church rules as to the appropriate distance between marriageable cousins have changed through time (*e.g.*, prohibiting marriage to a relative of the seventh degree prior to the thirteenth century, but to the fourth degree thereafter). Elsewhere, marriageable partners include not just cousins but other close relatives. In some cultures, marriage of cousins (of any degree) that are descended from the male line's brothers or the female line's sisters is viewed as an unnatural act of incest. Variation cross-culturally in the classification of kin groups and the categorization of appropriate marriage partners is abundant.

Not only appropriate sexual partners but also appropriate sexual practices vary cross-culturally. For example, in the south central lowlands of New Guinea and elsewhere in Melanesia, just as in ancient Greece, young men are initiated into full manhood through erotic connections with older men.[h] Unlike the more abstract Greeks, however, the New Guineans understand manhood to be a physical substance that is literally transmitted in the semen. Thus, a systematic method of transmitting the male substance from man to boy through the anus is socially prescribed. Amongst these tribes, a man did not fully become a man unless he had intercourse with another man. This contrasts with western notions where a man who has homosexual intercourse is perceived as becoming, in some respects, a woman.

Not only do appropriate sexual partners and normal sexual practices vary cross-culturally, but in many cultures the sexes are not limited to only two. Thus, many other cultures have what anthropologists call "supernumerary" genders. The supernumerary genders include, for example, the phenomenon of the *berdache*, a Native American term alternatively translated as "part-man, part woman" or "not-man, not-woman."[i] The *berdache* were found throughout the Plateau, Plains, Southwest, Prairie and Southwestern parts of the United States, as well as in Central America. The great American anthropologist Alfred Kroeber considered the phenomenon of the *berdache* so prevalent amongst native North American Indian tribes that it should be presumed to have been present, unless proven otherwise.

Women's Work: Development and the Division of Labor by Gender (1986); and *Myths of Male Dominance: Collected Articles on Women Cross-Culturally* (1981).

h. See Gilbert Herdt, *Guardians of the Flutes* (1981); *Ritualized Homosexuality in Melanesia* (Gilbert H. Herdt ed. 1984).

i. On the *berdache*, see Walter L. Williams, *The Spirit and the Flesh: Sexual Diversity in American Indian Culture* (1986);

Evelyn Blackwood, "Sexuality and Gender in Certain Native American Tribes: The Case of Cross–Gender Females," 10 *Signs* 27 (1984); Harriet Whitehead, "The Bow and the Burden Strap: A New Look at Institutionalized Homosexuality in Native North America," in *Sexual Meanings: The Cultural Construction of Gender and Sexuality* 80 (Sherry B. Ortner & Harriet Whitehead eds. 1981).

Berdache were accepted and respected within their tribes and were often noted for having special abilities as a matchmaker, magician, healer or ritual specialist. For example, amongst the Navaho, the *nadle* was commonly promoted as the head of a household and it was believed that his presence as leader of the family would bring wealth and prestige. Westerners usually considered *berdache* to be gender-benders or cross dressers, but Native Americans viewed them as a third sex with unique characteristics specific to their category.

Other examples of supernumerary genders include the division of what westerners call a single category, "woman," into at least four different "genders" amongst the Northern Piegan Indian tribes who had the *ninaki ninawki ninauposkitzpxpe* (translated as "manly-hearts or" "warrior women"), the *matsaps* (translated as "crazy-women"), the *ninaki* (translated as the "sits-beside-me-wife") and the "sun dance" women. Such examples are just a few of the many ethnographically documented descriptions of sex and gender variability indicating but a small portion of the vast range of sexualities and genders that have been identified cross-culturally.

Seeing gender and sexuality as cultural symbols liberates researchers from constraining naturalistic assumptions and opens up the study of sexuality and gender to a range of analytical questions that would otherwise not be asked. Consider the following legal problem as an opportunity to rethink assumptions.

PROBLEM 2–6

HERMAPHRODITES AND MARRIAGE

At the end of the Johns Hopkins study excerpt, Money and his colleagues describe a case study. The person had been reared as a male, even though his genitals were ambiguous; he had a small hypospadiac penis and a vestigial scrotum. During adolescence, his penis failed to become larger, and his body developed in a female direction (his breasts began to enlarge, for example). A medical examination at that time revealed the person had female internal organs (uterus, fallopian tubes, etc.) and hormones and presumably chromosomes as well. Because the child had been reared as a male, the parents had the female internal organs removed and male hormones introduced through regular therapy. At age 23, the person on his own decided to have plastic surgery in order to enlarge and straighten his penis; the person was conventionally masculine with slightly enlarged breasts but a deep voice, tall stature, facial hair, and male pubic hair. This person completely identified as a male and married a woman after the plastic surgery.

In Money's case study, the marriage was a happy one and was never the occasion for any legal scrutiny. Consider the following inquiries that have arisen in other contexts, *e.g., In re Marriage of C. and D. (Falsely Called C.),* 35 F.L.R. 340 (Family Court of Australia, Brisbane, 1979):

(A) The person does not tell his wife about the prior history, or provides a very generalized description. The wife discovers her husband's medical history and sues to have the marriage nullified. In the jurisdiction in question (as in most western jurisdictions), a marriage is *voidable* and can be nullified at the request of one of the parties if the consent of that party to the marriage was obtained "by fraud" *or* if the parties are unable to "consummate" the marriage. Will a typical judge in the United States grant this request? What are the odds?

(B) The husband and wife are happily married and there has been full disclosure. The husband dies without a will, and the wife stands to inherit a tidy sum of money, because the law of their jurisdiction provides that the spouse shall inherit everything in these circumstances. The husband's sister (the next of kin if there were no spouse) sues to inherit, on the ground that the marriage was *void* and never should have been recognized by the state. Her argument is that state law requires marriage between a *man* and a *woman*. The decedent was female according to the chromosomes, the internal gonads, and the hormones; the genitalia were at best ambiguous, and the other "male" features were phony. Assume that the sister is right that state law only recognizes male-female marriages and, further, that a marriage that violates this commandment was void from the beginning. What are the odds that the sister will prevail?

(C) Assume that in both (A) and (B) courts in the jurisdiction refuse to recognize a valid marriage. The next case to come before the courts involves someone just like the hermaphroditic person described in the Money case study—except that he wants to marry a man. What are the odds that the courts will allow him to do that?

PART B.   TRANSSEXUALISM, MEDICALIZATION AND COMMODIFICATION

Transsexuals (or transgendered persons) are a product of sex and gender binarism, for they are people who believe that their (male/female) biological sex does not meet their (female/male) gender. Our materials on transsexuals are concentrated in Chapter 12, Section 2, which you might choose to explore at this point. Issues of medicalization are critically important for transsexuals, in part because of the debate over whether this phenomenon is a psychological disability and in part because of the availability of sex-reassignment surgery as a way to meet the needs of transsexuals to realign their sex and gender. Indeed, most of the basic techniques for reassignment surgery were originally developed to help hermaphrodites or intersexuals match up their sex-of-rearing with their sex-of-genitalia in a more satisfying, culture-conforming way.

Most of the legal and normative issues relating to transsexuals are analyzed in Chapter 12, but one issue is particularly appropriate here: the use of medicine as a source of legitimization and of a claim for rights.

As is also the case with birth control, abortion, and AIDS advocates, transsexual persons have not been merely passive patients in this process. Medicalization is not simply a one-way street, of doctors imposing categories on patients. Bernice Hausman asserts that transsexuals themselves have adapted, modified, and re-articulated medical pronouncements:

> [T]he demand for sex change became the most significant symptom of transsexualism, its irrefutable sign. * * * By demanding sex change, transsexuals distinguished themselves from transvestite and homosexual subjects * * * The ways transsexuals understood themselves from the 1950s through the 1960s shifted as the diagnostic discourses concerning transvestism and homosexuality and their relationship to transsexualism changed, and it is through finely articulated differences in behavior, sensibility, and etiology that transsexuals were able, in dialogue with clinicians, to demand separate consideration in the form of different treatment protocols, practices, and therapeutic goals.

Bernice L. Hausman, *Changing Sex: Transsexualism, Technology, and the Idea of Gender* 111 (1995). These interactive dynamics have substantially created or constructed the meaning of transsexualism.

An earlier line of critique of the ramifications of medicalizing gender was made by sociologists Dwight Billings and Thomas Urban, "The Socio–Medical Construction of Transsexualism: An Interpretation and Critique," 29 *Soc. Probs.* 266, 276–77 (1982):

> Transsexual therapy, legitimated by the terminology of disease, pushes patients toward an alluring world of artificial vaginas and penises rather than toward self-understanding and sexual politics. * * *

> Critical theorists claim that the illusions of consumerism can be as pathological for individuals as the neuroses and psychoses symptomatic of the earlier period of capitalist industrial production. Today, in late-capitalist consumer culture, frenzied rituals of buying contradict the puritanical self-denial characteristic of the nineteenth century. We express our identity as much by the things we buy as the work we do. Commodities promise escape from alienation and the fulfillment of our needs. Critics compare the temporary solace of consumer spending with the transitory euphoria of a drug-induced trance. Similarly, transsexuals are in danger of becoming surgical junkies, as they strive for an idealized sexuality via surgical commodities. This is what physicians refer to as a "poly-surgical attitude" among post-operative patients. Male-to-female patients especially are caught up in an escalating series of cosmetic operations * * * to more closely approximate ideal female form. They routinely demand breast implants and operations to reduce the size of the Adam's apple. * * *

What long-term costs, if any, are there to the strategy of medicalization? Are they significant enough to forego making legal arguments grounded on that approach? Is transsexual surgery different in kind or only in degree from our broader cultural consumerism of gender and sexuality fantasies?

PART C.   HARD-WIRED HOMOSEXUALS?

The 1990s has witnessed a boom in research which claims to find evidence of a biological basis for sexual orientation. These studies follow three nonmutually exclusive lines: anatomic, hormonal, and genetic influences.[j] The following survey does not treat "sociobiological" theories of evolution-driven homosexuality, and the interested reader can consult the sources in the margin for such theories and their critiques.[k]

1.   ANATOMIC STUDIES

Anatomic studies share the common hypothesis that there are physical differences in the brain structures of gays and straights, and that these differences cause the difference in sexual orientation. The idea has its roots in the findings, first in laboratory rats then in humans, that certain areas of the brain differ in size between males and females. The most influential of these studies, done by Roger Gorski of UCLA and his colleagues, found a nucleus of cells in the hypothalamus of rat brains (which he dubbed the Sexually Dimorphic Nucleus, or SDN) which was several times larger in males than in females.[l] Moreover, the location of the SDN was in an area known to be connected to sexual behavior in rats. (No structure analogous to the SDN has been found, however, in mammals closer to man, like monkeys.) Following this discovery, Gorski and others at UCLA determined that an area of the human hypothalamus also differed in size between men and women; the male hypothalamus is larger.

The fact that men and women differ in the size of brain areas thought to be connected with sexual behavior, coupled with the cultural assumption that gay men have "female" brains and lesbians have "male" brains, led to the hypothesis that the hypothalamus might be different between gays and straights. This is precisely what neuroanatomist Simon LeVay of the Salk

j. Glenn Edwards, Yale Law School Class of 1997, wrote the initial draft of the expository material that follows.

k. The leading texts, which include analyses of homosexuality, are Edward O. Wilson, *Sociobiology: The New Synthesis* (1975), and *On Human Nature* (1978). Sympathetic accounts of sociobiological theory applied to homosexuality are Richard A. Posner, *Sex and Reason* (1992), and Michael Ruse, *Homosexuality: A Philosophical Inquiry* ch. 6 (1988). Critiques of sociobiology as applied to issues of gender and sexual orientation include Frances Dahlberg, *Woman the Gatherer* (1981) (rejecting Wilson's "men hunters, women breeders" stereotypes as lacking a

basis in sociobiological history); Paul Bloom & Edward Stein, "Reasoning Why," 60 *Am. Scholar* 315–20 (1990) (philosophical critique of sociobiological theories of homosexuality); Gillian Hadfield, "Flirting with Science: Richard Posner on the Bioeconomics of Sexual Man," 106 *Harv. L. Rev.* 479 (1992) (scathing review of *Sex and Reason*); Douglas Futuyama, "Sexual Orientation, Sociobiology and Evolution," 9 *J. Homosexuality* 157–68 (1983–84).

l. R.A. Gorski et al., "Evidence for a Morphological Sex Difference within the Medical Preoptic Area of the Rat Brain," 193 *J. Comp. Neurology* 529 (1980).

Institute in San Diego claimed to have found.[m] Le Vay obtained brain samples from autopsies of 41 subjects whose sexual orientation was presumed from their medical histories: 19 gay and bisexual men who had died of complications associated with AIDS, 16 presumably heterosexual men (6 of whom died of AIDS complications), and 6 presumably heterosexual women. LeVay examined the hypothalamus from each of the samples for differences in structure. He found that there was a small nucleus of cells, known as the third interstitial nucleus of the anterior hypothalamus (INAH–3), which was twice as large in the heterosexual men as in either the women *or* the gay and bisexual men. "The discovery that a nucleus differs in size between heterosexual and homosexual men illustrates that sexual orientation in humans is amenable to study at the biological level, and this discovery opens the door to studies of neurotransmitters or receptors that might be involved in regulating this aspect of personality," Le Vay concluded. Note an immediate paradox, however. The INAH–3 had been associated in earlier studies *not* with heterosexuality, but with "male-typical sexual behavior" in rats, specifically with mounting and insertive intercourse. Is this discovery about sexual orientation at all? Gay men certainly engage in insertive intercourse.

Le Vay's own article urged caution in interpreting his findings. Presumably gay male brains were accessible due to AIDS, but Le Vay's sample indicates nothing about lesbians and may be skewed in its sample of gay men. HIV infection and the complications associated with AIDS sometimes affect the brain and may have effects on the hypothalamus, as Le Vay has discreetly conceded. Other critics claim that the small sample size, the wide range of INAH–3 sizes found even within a group of similar sexual orientation, and the difficulty in accurately determining the subjects' sexual orientation from only their medical history limit or negate the value of Le Vay's study. All agree that, even if there is the claimed correlation, *correlation* says nothing about *causation*. The brain difference, for example, might be caused by the sexual orientation, not vice-versa.

In *The Sexual Brain* (1993), Le Vay broadens his discussion into a general theory of how brain structure affects gender as well as sexual orientation. Le Vay starts with a general proposition, that "the scientific evidence presently available points to a strong influence of nature, and only a modest influence of nurture" on human sexual development. Provocatively, Le Vay maintains that at least some gender differences are attributable to differences in male and female brain structures. He specifically adverts to women's lesser aggression, lower sex drive, poorer visuospatial skills, higher language skills, and greater interest in sharing feelings as having possible roots in biology. This understanding is related to the most prominent theories of "sociobiology" but strongly at odds with other biological theory and field work involving primates, Meredith F. Small, *Female Choices: Sexual Behavior of Female Primates* (1993), and human beings,

---

m. Simon Le Vay, "A Difference in Hypothalamic Structure Between Heterosexual and Homosexual Men," 253 *Science* 1034 (1991), elaborated and expanded in Le Vay, *The Sexual Brain* (1993).

Anne Fausto–Sterling, *Myths of Gender: Biological Theories About Women and Men* (1992). Compare Le Vay's biological theory with that of Krafft–Ebing at the turn of the century.

2.   HORMONAL STUDIES

These studies are similar to the anatomic studies in that the underlying hypothesis for sexual orientation assumes that gay men's brains are somehow feminized, and lesbian brains are masculinized. However, the suspected culprits are hormones, not brain structure. It is now standard medical wisdom that hormones affect or determine whether a fetus develops male or female genitalia. Do hormones also regulate a sexual dimorphism (i.e., different structural features for men and women) in the human brain? If so, could differences in sexual orientation be explained as the failure of hormones to accomplish that task completely in homosexuals?

The first attempts to answer these questions came up empty. Studies of adult men found no difference in hormone levels between gays and straights. Attention then turned to pre- and neo-natal environments, the hypothesis being that sexual orientation is formed early in life and is not influenced by later hormonal changes. Indirect support for this hypothesis could be found in studies which suggested a high degree of childhood gender nonconformity (CGN)—i.e., "effeminate" behavior in boys, "tomboyish" behavior in girls—was recalled by adult gays and lesbians. One explanation of this finding is that CGN, rather than causing later homosexuality in adults, was actually a *manifestation* of an already locked-in sexual orientation. Other explanations were readily available, of course. Because they are less invested in traditional gender roles, lesbians and gay men might be more likely to recall their own gender nonconformity as children. Such retrospective reordering is common among human beings.

Some recent studies reflect more substantial empirical support for a finding that pre- and neo-natal hormones correlate to sexual development. Most of the early evidence came from studies of people affected by endocrine aberrations involving variation in fetal production or utilization of androgens. For example, John Money's *Gay, Straight, and In–Between: The Sexology of Sexual Orientation* (1988), argued that prenatal exposure to androgens facilitates the development of erotic attraction to females, whether the recipient of the androgens is male or female. Conversely, nonexposure or nonresponsiveness to androgens may facilitate erotic attraction to men.

Heino Meyer–Bahlburg and his colleagues at Columbia University asked the next question: Does exposure to estrogen facilitate erotic attraction to women?[n] To answer this question, they assembled two samples: one of women having a prenatal exposure to DES (diethylstilbestrol), a nonsteroidal synthetic estrogen, and another of women not so exposed (the control group). Both groups were part of a longterm psychiatric study, and various

---

n. See Heino F.L. Meyer–Bahlburg et al., "Prenatal Estrogens and the Development of Homosexual Orientation," 31 *Developmental Psychology* 12 (1995).

features of sexual orientation were exposed through systematic interviews. The researchers found that the DES group had significantly higher Kinsey scores, that is, greater bisexual or homosexual preference and behavior. The conclusions were tentative, however. The researchers admitted the possibility of other variables, noted that most of the DES group were heterosexual, and expressed doubt that any single factor causes lesbianism. Their "working hypothesis" was that "multiple developmental pathways * * * lead to a homosexual or heterosexual orientation, involving the dynamic interplay of both biological and social variables that interact with each other throughout a person's life course."

3. GENETIC STUDIES

Genetic theories represent the ultimate determinist view, namely, that all traits—including complex personality traits—are preprogrammed genetically. Although few (and perhaps no) scientists take such an extreme view, the idea that there is at least *some* genetic component to all traits does have its proponents. The difficulty in testing such theories lies in the fact that genetic evidence must generally be gathered indirectly, from studies of family histories, and it is difficult to tease apart the intertwined effects of shared genetic material and shared rearing environment, particularly where a trait as complex as sexual orientation is concerned.

Studies of twins and adopted siblings have been particular favorites of researchers looking for genetic influence in sexual orientation.[o] Since identical twins theoretically share all of their genes, and fraternal twins only one-half, one would expect that a genetically-influenced trait would show up significantly more often in the former than the latter. This was the result found in studies of both female and male twins by J. Michael Bailey and Richard Pillard. In Bailey and Pillard's 1991 study,[p] subjects were recruited through advertisements in gay publications for gay or bisexual men over eighteen who had male siblings. Based upon reports of their own and their siblings' sexual orientation (checked with the latter where possible), Bailey and Pillard found that identical twin brothers were concordant for sexual orientation (i.e., if one brother was gay, so was the other) 52% of the time, as compared to 22% for fraternal twins, 9% for nontwin brothers and 11% for adoptive brothers.

---

o. Early studies were F.J. Kallmnann, "Comparative Twin Study on the Genetic Aspects of Male Homosexuality," 115 *J. Nervous Mental Disease* 283 (1952); F.J. Kallmann, "Twin and Sibship Study of Overt Male Homosexuality," 4 *Am. J. Human Genetics* 136 (1952); E.D. Eckert et al., "Homosexuality in Monozygotic Twins Reared Apart," 148 *Brit. J. Psychiatry* 421 (1986);

N.J. Buhrich et al., "Sexual Orientation, Sexual Identity, and Sex–Dimorphic Behaviors in Male Twins," 21 *Behavioral Genetics* 75 (1991).

p. Bailey and Pillard, "A Genetic Study of Male Sexual Orientation," 48 *Archives General Psychiatry* 1089 (1991).

	Homosexual Twins (Total No.)	Percentage of Total
Identical Twins	29 (56)	52%
Fraternal Twins	12 (54)	22%
Adoptive Brothers	6 (57)	11%
Biological Nontwin Brothers	13 (142)	9%

In 1993, Bailey, Pillard, and colleagues,[q] used the same methodology for lesbians and found very similar results: 71% of the identical twins were concordant for sexual orientation, as compared to 37% of the fraternal twins, 14% of the nontwin sisters and 33% of the adoptive sisters.

	Homosexual Twins (Total No.)	Percentage of Total
Identical Twins	34 (48)	71%
Fraternal Twins	6 (16)	37%
Adoptive Sisters	2 (6)	33%
Biological Nontwin Sisters	10 (73)	14%

As of early 1997, there have not been other large, or medium, scale studies of lesbians and their twins that might replicate this result.

A few points stand out from the twins studies. First, it is clear that sexual orientation cannot be *purely* genetic, because then the expected concordance rate for identical twins would be near 100%. Instead, the range of heritability estimates from these studies is from 30–70%. Second, the data are not completely consistent: the non-twin brothers should have a concordance rate equal to the fraternal twins, not the adoptive brothers, because, like fraternal twins, non-twin brothers share one-half of their genes, whereas adoptive brothers share no greater proportion than that shared by the population as a whole. In defense of their thesis, Bailey and Pillard point out that an earlier study found a concordance rate of 22% in non-twin brothers (which would fit perfectly with a genetic theory); they posit that their 9% is an artifact of random sampling variation. Critics have suggested that an equally plausible explanation is that since the fraternal twins presumably share more environmental factors than the non-twin brothers, but have the same amount of shared genetic material, the different concordance rates suggest environment, not genetics, as the key factor in sexual orientation.

The genetic thesis got perhaps its strongest, or at least best-publicized, support from a study by Dean Hamer and his colleagues in 1993.[r] The authors, researchers at the National Cancer Institute of the National Institutes of Health (NIH), claimed to have found a location on the X chromosome (Xq28, to be precise) where a "gay gene" would likely be found. The study concentrated on pairs of brothers in which both were gay,

q. Bailey et al., "Heritable Factors Influence Sexual Orientation in Women," 50 *Archives Gen. Psychiatry* 217 (1993).

r. Dean H. Hamer et al., "A Linkage Between DNA Markers on the X Chromosome and Male Sexual Orientation," 261 *Science* 321–27 (1993), elaborated in Dean Hamer & Peter Copeland, *The Science of Desire: The Search for the Gay Gene and the Biology of Behavior* (1994).

reasoning that if being gay was genetic, then families with pairs of gay brothers would be more "loaded" with the gay gene than others and would be the best place to look. The NIH group first found that among these families, the maternal uncles and male cousins were more likely to be gay than the general population or the paternal relatives; this pattern suggests a trait linked to the X chromosome, which men get from their mother but not their father. They then examined 40 pairs of gay brothers, and found that 33 of them shared the same markers in the Xq28 region of the X chromosome, a result significantly higher than the 50% one would expect from random distribution. Based on this data, the NIH group concluded (cautiously) that "at least one subtype of male sexual orientation is genetically influenced."

This NIH study has been criticized on a number of fronts.[s] To begin with, the study did not look to see if the "gay markers" were actually present in the heterosexual relatives as well; if they are, this would of course weaken the case for a genetic basis for homosexuality. The study has also been criticized for using a low estimate of the "base rate" of homosexuality in the general population—2% versus the generally quoted rates of 4 to 10% from other studies. (The higher the base rate used, the less significant the findings.) In defense, Hamer points out that the NIH group used an unusually strict definition of "gay," which could account for the lower base rate they found, and further that even at 4% the findings are statistically significant.

Edward Stein, The Relevance of Scientific Research About Sexual Orientation to Lesbian and Gay Rights

In *Gay Ethics: Controversies in Outing, Civil Rights, and Sexual Science* 271, 277–83, 290–91. Timothy Murphy, editor, 1994.*

People who think discovering a cause for homosexuality has good moral and political implications for lesbian and gay rights have various arguments in mind for their view. All of these arguments seem to have the same general structure. They begin with the claim that homosexuality has a genetic, biological, or hormonal basis. They then link this claim in a conditional to some fact they claim would follow, such as "If homosexuality is genetic, then being a lesbian or gay man is not a psychological disorder." They then make the consequent of this conditional the antecedent of a

---

s. Among the best critiques of Hamer's, as well as Le Vay's, "gay science" are William Byne & Bruce Parsons, "Human Sexual Orientation: The Biologic Theories Reappraised," 50 *Arch. Gen. Psychiatry* 228 (March 1993); Anne Fausto–Sterling & Evan Balaban, Letter on "Genetics and Male Sexual Orientation," 261 *Science* 1257 (1993); Janet E. Halley, "Sexual Orientation and the Politics of Biology: A Critique of the Argument from Immutability," 46 *Stan. L. Rev.*

503 (1994); Daniel J. Kevles, "The X Factor: The Battle over the Ramifications of a Gay Gene," *New Yorker*, Apr. 3, 1995, at 85–90. For a fascinating dialogue between a leading fan of gay science and a critic, see Edward Stein (the critic), "Evidence for Queer Genes: An Interview with Richard Pillard," 1 *GLQ* 93–110 (1993).

* Copyrighted © The Haworth Press. Reprinted with permission.

conditional that has the consequent that lesbians and gay men deserve rights, recognition, and protection against discrimination, such as "If being lesbian or gay is not a psychological disorder, then lesbians and gay men deserve rights, recognition, and protection against discrimination." In its schematic form, the argument is as follows:

(1) Homosexuality has a biological basis.

(2) If homosexuality is biological, then _____ .

(3) If _____ , then lesbian and gay men deserve rights, recognition, and protection against discrimination.

(4) Therefore, lesbians and gay men deserve rights, recognition, and protection against discrimination.

The different versions of the argument result from different ways of filling in the blanks. * * *

Protected Group Status

One way to fill in the blank in the above argument involves the notion of protected groups. In the United States, various categories of people are singled out as warranting special protection against discrimination. So, for example, race, sex, gender, religious affiliation, age, disability, nationality, and ethnic status are in various contexts singled out as protected categories. If sexual orientation deserves to be a "special status" category, then this might entail that lesbians and gay men deserve rights. Some people have argued that establishing a genetic basis for homosexuality will entail that sexual orientation should count as a protected category. The specific argument is as follows:

(1) Homosexuality has a biological basis.

(2a) If homosexuality has a biological basis, then sexual orientation should be a protected category.

(3a) If sexual orientation is a protected category, then lesbians and gay men deserve rights, recognition, and protection against discrimination.

(4) Therefore, lesbians and gay men deserve rights, recognition, and protection against discrimination.

But why should we believe premise (2a)? There are, in fact, several reasons for doubting its truth. First, just because a category has a biological basis does not thereby entail that members of it deserve protected status; there are many categories with a biological basis that are not thought to be morally relevant categories, much less to be categories that warrant protected status. For example, hair color has a biological basis but people with a particular hair color do not constitute a protected category. Being a biologically-based category is thus not a *sufficient* condition for being a category that deserves protected status. It is worth noting that being biologically based is not a *necessary* condition either. For example, being of a certain religious affiliation or nationality are not biologically based but they constitute protected categories.

A friend of the "protected group" argument for lesbian and gay rights might respond to the hair-color example by pointing out that *if* people were unjustifiably discriminated against on the basis of hair color, then hair color *should* be a protected category and it should be *because* it is genetically based. Behind this response is the notion that being biologically based is not enough to make a category a protected one; there must be some *further* requirement, perhaps that the category is the basis for unjustified discrimination. While there does seem to be something right about it, the further requirement that there be "unjustified discrimination" against members of a category for that category to warrant special protection is not necessarily connected to the "biologically based" requirement. Any category that is the basis for unjustified discrimination—whether biologically based or not— seems a plausible candidate for a protected category. This very fact—that whether or not the category is biologically based seems to have nothing to do with whether the category should be a protected one—suggests that there is no interesting connection between the causes of sexual orientation and whether sexual orientation should be a protected category. Premise (2a) is thereby undermined.

This consideration against (2a) aside, there is a further problem with the protected category argument for lesbian and gay rights. Even if being gay or lesbian is biologically based, so much of what is crucial about being a bisexual, a lesbian, or a gay man would not be biologically based, and hence would not be protected by the argument with premises (2a) and (3a). For example, even if homosexuality is biologically based, actually engaging in homosexual acts, actually identifying as lesbian or gay, and so on, are choices, choices that each lesbian or gay man might well not have made (that is, he or she could have decided to be abstinent and closeted). Someone who was convinced that lesbians and gay men deserve rights only because homosexuality is biologically based believes people should not be discriminated against on the basis of their biological features and on these alone. For example, if I were convinced by the protected-status argument, I would think that people who had homoerotic desires should not be discriminated against on the basis of their having these desires. This is perfectly compatible, however, with my thinking that people who engage in same-sex sexual acts *are* appropriate targets of discrimination, criminal penalties, and the like. A friend of the biological argument for lesbian and gay rights might try to respond to this criticism by attempting to make a connection between being protected against discrimination because one's desire is biologically based and being protected against discrimination on the basis of behaviors that stem from biologically-based desire. Without a detailed story of how it could be made, this connection seems implausible. Even if premises (1) and (2a) of the protected-status argument are true (and I have given some reason to doubt [2a]), there are further reasons to doubt premise (3a); even if sexual orientation is a protected category, lesbian and gay rights (in any non-trivial sense of the term "rights") do not follow.

This objection to the protected status argument seems to constitute an objection to all versions of the general argument with the biological basis of homosexuality as a premise and with the claim that lesbians and gay men deserve rights as the conclusion. Arguments of this form seem limited to showing that gay men and lesbians deserve rights only with respect to those attributes lesbians and gay men have in virtue of their particular biological constitution. Whether this objection applies to the other versions of the biological argument for lesbian and gay rights will be considered below. The conclusion of this subsection is thus two-fold: (1) being biologically based is neither a necessary nor a sufficient condition for establishing protected group status, and (2) biology seems to be infertile ground on which to plant an argument for lesbian and gay rights because behaviors not just desires are relevant to lesbian and gay rights.

Determinism

Another argument for lesbian and gay rights of the same general structure as the one discussed above involves determinism, the thesis that sexual orientation is not a choice. The idea behind this particular argument is that if homosexuality has a biological basis, then sexual orientation is not a choice, but if sexual orientation is not a choice, then one can hardly be punished for or discriminated against on the basis of sexual orientation. The argument goes on as follows:

(1) Homosexuality has a biological basis.

(2b) If homosexuality has a biological basis, then sexual orientation is not a choice.

(3b) If sexual orientation is not a choice, then lesbians and gay men deserve rights, recognition, and protection against discrimination.

(4) Therefore, lesbians and gay men deserve rights, recognition, and protection against discrimination.

This argument suffers from one of the problems I discussed above with respect to the protected status argument; the biological basis of homosexuality at most establishes that lesbians and gay men do not have a choice with respect to their homoerotic desires, but it leaves open that they have a choice with respect to their behavior, their public identification of their sexual orientation, and the like. If lesbians and gay men deserve rights with request to virtue of the truth of determinism about sexual orientation, then it would still be permissible to discriminate against people on the basis of things about which they do have a choice, such as sexual behavior and public sexual identity. In other words, it is consistent with determinism about sexual orientation that lesbians and gay men are discriminated against in virtue of, for example, engaging in same-sex sexual acts. This is to say that premise (3b) is false.

As an analogy, consider alcoholism. Suppose, as seems to be the case, that a predisposition for alcoholism is congenital. The truth of this claim might make it morally unacceptable to discriminate against someone because she is disposed to become an alcoholic. This, however, would *not* make it morally unacceptable to discriminate against someone who actually is an "active" alcoholic, that is, who gets drunk on a regular basis. Regardless of the biological basis of alcoholism, it is morally acceptable to decide not to live with someone, or not to hire her, because she is frequently under the influence of alcohol, a fact that affects her ability to behave responsibly. The point of the analogy is that even if the *disposition* to engage in a behavior is not a choice, actually engaging in that behavior may be a choice and, thus, discrimination on the basis of whether someone actually engages in such a behavior might be acceptable. Further, even if (contrary to fact) being an "active" alcoholic were biologically determined, it would *still* be acceptable to discriminate on the basis of being an active alcoholic. If this were the case, it would be wrong to *blame* someone for being an active alcoholic (since nothing she could do would, by stipulation, prevent her from drinking to excess), but this does not make it wrong to discriminate on that basis. Just because I cannot be blamed for a behavior does not mean that I get any rights in virtue of my behavior or that it is morally wrong to discriminate against me in virtue of it. Even if an active alcoholic is not to be blamed for her condition, she does not deserve special rights or protection on the mere basis of her status as an alcoholic.

The analogy to alcoholism shows two things. First, it makes clear that the lack of choice about falling into a natural human kind does not guarantee that people who fit that kind deserve rights, protection against discrimination, and the like merely on the basis of doing so. This objection counts against premise (3b) of the determinism argument for lesbian and gay rights. Second, the analogy make clear why (3b) seems appealing at first glance. If a person has no choice whether or not she falls into a particular human kind, then she should not be blamed for fitting that kind. Freedom from blame does not, however, entail freedom from discrimination or the receipt of special rights. Friends of the determinism argument for lesbian and gay rights seem to miss this point. Premise (3b) seems plausible only if you think that the absence of blame entails rights beyond the right not to be punished. The absence of blame does not have this implication. The lack of choice about one's sexual orientation does not provide grounds for lesbian and gay rights; (3b) is thus false, and the determinism argument for lesbian and gay rights fails.

The objection to the determinism argument for lesbian and gay rights is that the lack of choice about one's sexual orientation does not in itself provide grounds for lesbian and gay rights, that is, (3b) is false. First (3b) is false because the lack of choice about one's sexual desires fails to include much of what should be protected under the rubric of lesbian and gay rights. So, for example, even if my desire to have sex with other men was determined biologically—and thus not a choice and thus the basis for lesbian and gay rights, protection against discrimination, and the like—my decision to actually engage in sexual acts with other men would still *not* be determined biologically, and would be a choice, and thus would not be the basis for lesbian and gay rights, protection against discrimination, and the like. Second, even if (contrary to fact) all facets of being lesbian or gay (that is, engaging in same-sex sexual acts or identifying oneself as lesbian or gay) were biologically determined (3b) would still be false. Determinism about all facets of sexual orientation would show the absence of blame for all facets of sexual orientation, but this would not in turn entail lesbian and gay rights, since the lack of blame is not grounds for positive rights. The determinism argument for lesbian and gay rights thus fails.

Naturalness

[Stein considers the argument that the "naturalness" of homosexuality (it occurs in nature or it serves an evolutionary function) supports lesbian and gay rights. He deploys the same analytical structure as above, but with many variations to match the different ways "natural" can be used. The scientific evidence is very muddy as to whether or not homosexuality or same-sex behavior occurs among other animal species or serves evolutionary functions, to take a few uses of the term "natural." Even if natural occurrence could be established, it is not clear that such fact alone has normative significance for the future of human society. (Eds. By the way, this last point could be made for heterosexuality as well. With the availability of artificial insemination and in vitro fertilization, the evolutionary or natural uses of heterosexual sex for procreation are no longer necessary for the perpetuation of the human race.)]

Summary of Biological Arguments for Lesbian and Gay Rights

Many friends of lesbian and gay rights have claimed that scientific evidence for a genetic, hormonal, or biological basis for sexual orientation would be good news for lesbian and gay rights. The general idea behind this argument is to connect the existence of a biological basis for sexual orientation to lesbian and gay rights through something like the following schematic argument:

(1) Homosexuality has a biological basis.

(2) If homosexuality is biological, then _____ .

(3) If _____, then lesbians and gay men deserve rights, recognition, and protection against discrimination.

(4) Therefore, lesbians and gay men deserve rights, recognition, and protection against discrimination.

I have considered above several possible ways of filling in the blanks of this argument and found all of them inadequate with respect to producing valid arguments. The general problem is to find some claim that will bridge the gap between the empirical claim (homosexuality has a biological basis) and the normative one (lesbians and gay men deserve rights). If the blank is filled in with an empirical claim, then (2) might be plausible but (3) will not be (this was the case when the blank was filled in with "homosexuality is natural in the sense of not being man-made."). If the blank is filled in with a normative claim, then (3) might be plausible but (2) would not be. A related problem is that even if the premises are true, the attributes lesbians and gay men have and the behaviors (if any) in which they necessarily engage in virtue of the (supposed) biological basis of their sexual orientation are all that will be protected under this argument. At best, this will include homoerotic desires and dispositions to engage in same-sex sexual acts, a rather narrow range with respect to what we typically mean when we talk of lesbian and gay rights.

[Stein concludes that any argument for lesbian and gay rights must be either *normative* or *political*. That is, it must maintain that lesbian and gay rights are good for society, or at least neutral. Or it must show that lesbians and gay men are a group that must be accommodated in our pluralist system.]

NOTE ON THE THESIS THAT HARD–WIRED HOMOSEXUALITY COULD WIN RECOGNITION OF GAY RIGHTS

Polls show that many Americans (gay and straight) believe that homosexuals probably are hard-wired. Moreover, the typical political alignment on this issue is that the pro-gay voice makes the argument that sexual orientation is biologically determined, and the anti-gay voice claims that it is not. Consider several points that may help explain the political dynamics of the debate.

1. *The State Impotence Argument.* If sexual orientation is substantially determined by hormones, genes, or very early experience, there is very little society or the family can do to affect a child's sexual orientation. If that is so, it undermines a chief motivation for anti-homosexual laws, which aim to "discourage" people, especially children, from becoming homosexual. It also removes a great heterofear, that "predatory" homosexuals will "convert" heterosexual children into homosexual adults. This heterofear, which may seem silly to some of you, in fact has a distinguished scientific pedigree, especially the American Freudians. Although Freud himself believed that heterosexuality could not be programmed or dictated by parents or the state, his theory that homosexuality is the result of the derailment of normal sexual development has suggested to simpler minds that parents, teachers, and agencies of the state could somehow direct sexual orientation in approved directions.

More broadly, the assurance that sexual orientation is set by a very early age reinforces a notion of easy categories: we are all one or the other. Not only can lesbians and gay men not avoid their homosexuality, but heterosexuals are safely locked into their orientation. Thus it provides a sense of security, even if false. Is this advantageous to equality proponents? How do bisexuals fit into this model?

The state impotence argument is not all-purpose: it applies better to state policies seeking to mold the citizenry—especially laws requiring schools to teach that homosexuality is bad or prohibiting officials from relaying accurate information about sexual orientation—than to state policies that shield heterosexuals from confronting situations that repel them—especially the military's exclusion of bisexuals, gay men, and lesbians because they assertedly ruin morale and unit cohesion. How does this argument relate to the issue of sodomy? Gay marriage?

2. *Gays Are Here to Stay Arguments.* If homosexual attraction is hard-wired, not only will anti-homosexual policies fail to eradicate homosexuality, they will be doomed to expensive failure. Sodomy laws will not stop homosexuals (and heterosexuals) from committing sodomy, obscenity laws will not eradicate the market for depictions of homosexual sex, and anti-gay educational policies will not keep homosexual folklore out of the schoolyard. So these laws begin to look like pointless wastes of money, and, one might speculate, their widespread evasion generates disrespect for the law generally.

More important, the hard-wired argument combines with Stonewall (and the coming out of a generation of gay people) to suggest a powerful political point. Gays will always be within our society. Because they are randomly distributed, gays will always be part of all sectors and classes of society. For the state to declare war on part of itself is suicidal, and the best conservative strategy is to accommodate such a group once it is out of the closet. Although the scientific evidence is not necessary for this sort of argument to work, it may contribute to such an argument by discouraging people from thinking that the state can eradicate this particular group. *Query:* If there is a gay gene and people could predetermine and abort gay fetuses, might there be a private genocide? What role would or could law play to permit or forestall such a reaction?

3. *The Sexual Orientation-Sex Discrimination Argument.* Note how the new "gay science" provides links between sex and sexual orientation. If true, do such links support Andrew Koppelman's thesis that sexual orientation discrimination is a species of sex discrimination (Chapter 1, Section 3[B])? Or do they track gender rather than sex?

CONCLUDING NOTE ON IDEOLOGY AND SCIENCE

Set aside the Stein criticism that the new gay science does not logically contribute to gay rights, and the further criticism that the new gay science is not yet rigorous enough to justify any conclusions about sexual orientation's origins. Return to a central idea of our introductory essay on sexology: science typically follows rather than leads public opinion, and the corollary that scientific research itself is organized around categories driven by cultural assumptions more than by neutrality or objectivity.

Are there ideological biases in the new gay science that render it particularly dangerous for feminists or gay rights theorists? See Janet Halley, "Sexual Orientation and the Politics of Biology: A Critique of the Argument from Immutability," 46 *Stan. L. Rev.* 503 (1994).

CHAPTER 3

THEORIES OF SEXUALITY, GENDER, AND LAW

SECTION 1   Modern Theories of Sexuality

SECTION 2   Postmodern Theories

SECTION 3   The Role of Law in the Social Construction Process

One reason that our society finds it so difficult to resolve issues related to sexuality is that we disagree so fundamentally about even what it is we are talking about. Three irreconcilable models form the bases for most contemporary thinking about sexuality:

- Sexuality as a *natural force* grounded in universals, which society has the moral and ethical obligation to encourage in its healthy manifestations and discourage in its distorted forms.

- Sexuality as a *biological force* grounded in the individual body or psyche, usually described as a "sex drive," which society, usually with great futility, seeks to constrain.

- Sexuality as a *social force*, the product of the complex interaction of the particularities of the cultural and historical eras in which we live and the patterns of socialization that we experience.

Most debate in the legal arena still is limited to the first and second of these models. Indeed, Chapter 2 is devoted to an analysis of the emergence of the biological model and the interaction between that concept and the growing authority of the medical profession. It is the third model, however, which is producing most of the current scholarship on theories of sexuality, and it is on variants of this approach that we focus this chapter.

Section 1 offers a sampler of modern theories. It begins with a contemporary, nonsectarian argument of natural law theory (that of John Finnis), which maintains that procreative marital sex is the norm most natural and productive for human beings; deviations from that norm are both unnatural and unproductive. Materialist theories of sexuality, in contrast, take a broader view of the functions of sex and gender. John D'Emilio argues that sexuality and gender are products of changing social and economic conditions; Richard Posner emphasizes the evolving role of women. The most recent significant theories of gender and sexuality are feminist theories, which view the matter from the perspective or interests of women. There is a broad range of feminist theories—from the highly regulatory theory of Catharine MacKinnon to the "pro-sex" theory of Gayle Rubin.

Section 2 introduces what we have grouped together as "postmodern" theories, those that view sexuality and gender as social constructions related to complex discursive systems. For example, medicine and law generate specific discourses, or systems of understanding, that in turn profoundly shape broader social meanings. Postmodern scholars pay special attention to how discourse (a system consisting of texts, beliefs, and/or actions) functions both to organize social practices and to constitute our individual understandings and experiences of, for example, gender and sexuality. (Note that there is some overlap with the writers in Section 1 as well, since D'Emilio and Rubin, for example, would properly be characterized as social constructionists.) In general, though, the materials in Section 2 tend to differ from those in Section 1 in that they describe sexuality and gender as driven by forces more diverse and dispersed than either patriarchy (feminism) or the market or capitalism (economic theory). Michel Foucault is often viewed as the primary expositor of this school of thought. Judith Butler's work builds on Foucault's, adding a more explicitly feminist approach. Eve Kosofsky Sedgwick shows how our tropes of sexuality, prominently the homosexual/heterosexual dichotomy, reveal the complex interdependence of identities that other theories treat as disparate.

As you read these materials, think about how well each theory explains the phenomena in Chapters 1 and 2—the regulation of contraception, abortion, and same-sex intimacy. What normative edge does each theory have, if any? What is the role of law? Section 3 then challenges you to think about how law contributes to constructions of sexuality and gender.

MODERN THEORIES OF SEXUALITY

By "modern" theories of sexuality, we mean theories that eschew religion as a starting point, and seek to locate sexuality as part of a broader philosophy. "Scientific" theories of sexuality developed by Freud, Krafft–Ebing, and Kinsey (Chapter 2, Section 1) are *positive* or *descriptive* theories; they aspire to tell us what sexuality is, and how it works. The economic theories in this section (D'Emilio; Posner) tend to present themselves as positive theories but also have a *normative* or *prescriptive* component as well; they suggest how sexuality ought to be treated. More explicitly normative theories are the natural law theory (Finnis) with which we start this section, and the feminist theories (MacKinnon; Rubin) that close the section. Notice that similar starting premises, whether it is economics or feminism, do not dictate similar conclusions. MacKinnon and Rubin disagree as sharply as Posner and MacKinnon would.

PART A. NATURAL LAW THEORIES

We start with a theory of sex as old as Aristotle: natural law theory. Such theory posits human beings' "natural" or "universal" needs or constitution and argues for certain rules or strictures that best meet those needs or best fit that constitution. A natural law argument proceeds in this way: (1) The "order of nature" (human nature however conceptualized) is thus and so. (2) This practice is inconsistent with or undermines the order of nature. (3) This practice is therefore wrong ("unnatural").

Roman Catholic theology, epitomized in St. Augustine's *De Bono Conjugali* and St. Thomas Aquinas' *Summa Theologica*, is the best known natural law theory and finds expression in many accomplished works.[a] The views expressed in these works are by no means unique to Catholic theologians, however; they are shared by religious thinkers of many denominations and by thinkers who do not begin with a religious perspective. Oxford philosopher John Finnis, for example, maintains that the key precepts held by Roman Catholic natural law thinkers on issues of sex and sexuality are consistent with those advanced by ancient philosophers Plato, Aristotle, Plutarch, and others.

a. E.g., 2 Germain Grisez, *Living a Christian Life* (1983).

Finnis is, we think, representative of what Stephen Macedo refers to as "the new natural law,"[b] an effort to develop a systematic conservative philosophy of sexuality that is both consistent with and unconstrained by Christian religious precepts. The following excerpt is taken from Finnis' article on homosexuality, but we have chosen passages that lay out his general theory. The excerpt begins right after Finnis has discussed the theories of Plato, Aristotle, and other classical thinkers.

John M. Finnis, Law, Morality, and "Sexual Orientation"

69 *Notre Dame Law Review* 1049, 1063–69 (1994).*

Plato's mature concern, in the *Laws*, for familiarity, affection and love between spouses in a chastely exclusive marriage, Aristotle's representation [in *Nichomachean Ethics*] of marriage as an intrinsically desirable friendship between quasi-equals, and as a state of life even more natural to human beings than political life, and Musonius Rufus's conception [in *Discourses*] of the inseparable bonds of marriage, all find expression in Plutarch's celebration of marriage—as a union not of mere instinct but of reasonable love, and not merely for procreation but for mutual help, goodwill and cooperation for their own sake [*Life of Solon* and *Erotikos*]. * * * Genital intercourse between spouses enables them to actualize and experience (and in that sense express) their marriage itself, as a single reality with two blessings (children and mutual affection). Non-marital intercourse, especially but not only homosexual, has no such point and therefore is unacceptable.

The core of this argument can be clarified by comparing it with Saint Augustine's treatment of marriage in his *De Bono Coniugali*. The good of marital communion is here an instrumental good, in the service of the procreation and education of children so that the intrinsic, non-instrumental good of friendship will be promoted and realized by the propagation of the human race, and the intrinsic good of inner integration be promoted and realized by the "remedying" of the disordered desires of concupiscence. Now, when considering sterile marriages, Augustine had identified a further good of marriage, the natural *societas* (companionship) of the two sexes. Had he truly integrated this into his synthesis, he would have recognized that in sterile and fertile marriages alike, the communion, companionship, *societas* and *amicitia* of the spouses—their being married—*is* the very good of marriage, and is an intrinsic, basic human good, not

b. Stephen Macedo, "Homosexuality and the Conservative Mind," 84 *Geo. L.J.* 261 (1995). Among the exemplars of new natural law are John M. Finnis, *Natural Law and Natural Rights* (1980); Grisez, *Christian Life*, supra; Roger Scruton, *Sexual Desire* (1986); Robert P. George, "A Defense of the New Classical Natural Law Theory," 41 *Am. J. Juris.* (1996); Harvey C. Mansfield, "Saving Liberalism from the Liberals," *Harv. Crimson*, Nov. 8, 1993, p. 2; "The Homosexual Movement: A Response by the Ramsey Colloquium," *First Things*, Mar. 1994, p.16. These different theorists have different approaches to the issues, of course, and no one theorist can represent "the" natural law approach.

merely instrumental to any other good. And this communion of married life, this integral amalgamation of the lives of the two persons (as Plutarch put it before John Paul II), has as its intrinsic elements, as essential *parts* of one and the same good, the goods and ends to which the theological tradition, following Augustine, for a long time subordinated that communion. It took a long and gradual process of development of doctrine, through the Catechism of the Council of Trent, the teachings of Pius XI and Pius XII, and eventually those of Vatican II—a process brilliantly illuminated by Germain Grisez—to bring the tradition to the position that procreation and children are neither the *end* (whether primary or secondary) to which marriage is instrumental (as Augustine taught), nor instrumental to the good of the spouses (as much secular and "liberal Christian" thought supposes), but rather: Parenthood and children and family are the intrinsic fulfillment of a communion which, because it is not merely instrumental, can exist and fulfill the spouses even if procreation happens to be impossible for them.

Now if, as the recent encyclical on the foundations of morality, *Veritatis Splendor*, teaches, "the communion of persons in marriage" which is violated by every act of adultery is itself a "fundamental human good," there fall into place not only the elements of the classic philosophical judgments on non-marital sexual conduct but also the similar judgments reached about such conduct by decent people who cannot articulate explanatory premises for those judgments, which they reach rather by an insight into what is and is not *consistent with* realities whose goodness they experience and understand at least sufficiently to will and choose. In particular, there fall into place the elements of an answer to the question: Why cannot non-marital friendship be promoted and expressed by sexual acts? Why is the attempt to express affection by orgasmic non-marital sex the pursuit of an illusion? Why did Plato and Socrates, Xenophon, Aristotle, Musonius Rufus, and Plutarch, right at the heart of their reflections on the homoerotic culture around them, make the very deliberate and careful judgment that homosexual *conduct* (and indeed all extra-marital sexual gratification) is radically incapable of participating in, actualizing, the common good of friendship?

Implicit in the philosophical and common-sense rejection of extra-marital sex is the answer: The union of the reproductive organs of husband and wife really unites them biologically (and their biological reality is part of, not merely an instrument of, their *personal* reality); reproduction is one function and so, in respect of that function, the spouses are indeed one reality, and their sexual union therefore can *actualize* and allow them to *experience* their *real common good——their marriage* with the two goods, parenthood and friendship, which (leaving aside the order of grace) are the parts of its wholeness as an intelligible common good even if, independent of what the spouses will, their capacity for biological parenthood will not be fulfilled by that act of genital union. But the common good of friends who are not and cannot be married (for example, man and man, man and boy, woman and woman) has nothing to do with their having children by each other, and their reproductive organs cannot make them a biological (and therefore personal) unit. So their sexual acts together cannot do what they may hope and imagine. Because their activation of one or even each of their reproductive organs cannot be an actualizing and experiencing of the *marital* good—as marital intercourse (intercourse between spouses in a marital way) can, even between spouses who *happen* to be sterile—it can do no more than provide each partner with an individual gratification. For want of a *common good* that could be actualized and experienced *by and in this bodily union*, that conduct involves the partners in treating their bodies as instruments to be used in the service of their consciously experiencing selves; their choice to engage in such conduct thus disintegrates each of them precisely as acting persons.

Reality is known in judgment, not in emotion, and *in reality*, whatever the generous hopes and dreams and thoughts of *giving* with which some same-sex partners may surround their sexual acts, those acts cannot express or do more than is expressed or done if two strangers engage in such activity to give each other pleasure, or a prostitute pleasures a client to give him pleasure in return for money, or (say) a man masturbates to give himself pleasure and a fantasy of more human relationships after a gruelling day on the assembly line. This is, I believe, the substance of Plato's judgment—at that moment in the *Gorgias* which is also decisive for the moral and political philosophical critique of hedonism——that there is no important distinction in essential moral worthlessness between solitary masturbation, being sodomized as a prostitute, and being sodomized for the pleasure of it. Sexual acts cannot *in reality* be self-giving unless they are acts by which a man and a woman actualize and experience sexually the real giving of themselves to each other—in biological, affective and volitional union in mutual commitment, both openended and exclusive—which like Plato and Aristotle and most peoples we call marriage.

In short, sexual acts are not unitive in their significance unless they are marital (actualizing the all-level unity of marriage) and (since the common good of marriage has two aspects) they are not marital unless they have not only the generosity of acts of friendship but also the procreative significance, not necessarily of being intended to generate or capable in the circumstances of generating but at least of being, as human conduct, acts of the reproductive kind—actualizations, so far as the spouses then and there can, of the reproductive function in which they are biologically and thus personally one. * * *

Does this account seek to "make moral judgments based on natural facts"? Yes and no. No, in the sense that it does not seek to infer normative conclusions or theses from non-normative (natural-fact) premises. Nor does it appeal to any norm of the form "Respect natural facts or natural functions." But yes, it does apply the relevant practical reasons (especially that marriage and inner integrity are basic human goods) and moral principles (especially that one may never *intend* to destroy, damage, impede, or violate any basic human good, or prefer an illusory instantiation of a basic human good to a real instantiation of that or some other human good) to facts about the human personal organism.

NOTES ON FINNIS AND THE IMPLICATIONS OF "THE NEW NATURAL LAW" FOR SEXUALITY AND LAW

1. *Implications of Natural Law for the Right to Privacy.* Natural law theory valorizes procreative sex within a companionate male-female marriage. For these theorists, sexuality is among the greatest human wonders, but to preserve its wonder the exercise of sexuality must be carefully conserved. Accordingly, sex that is not procreative (fornication, sodomy, contraception) or that is outside marriage (adultery, bigamy) is not good. The consequence of natural law thinking is skepticism about the right to privacy. The abortion right is most inconsistent with natural law premises, which maintain that the fetus is a human life. Natural law, therefore, would not be receptive to *Griswold* and would be most hostile to *Roe v. Wade*. One would expect natural law thinking to support the result in *Bowers v. Hardwick*, allowing states to criminalize "homosexual sodomy." In a portion of the article we omitted, Finnis expresses skepticism about state sodomy laws that regulate private conduct, but for practical reasons: there are more important immoralities for the state to prosecute.

Note also the implications of natural law theory for the right to marry (Chapter 9). Natural law would seem hostile to same-sex marriage, but for the same reasons ought to oppose other marriages that do not seek procreation. Should sterile couples be able to marry? Couples that decide not to have children and use contraception and abortion as methods of procreation avoidance? Is there any principled way for the natural lawyer to oppose gay marriage yet allow the marriage of a sterile couple?

2. *Unity versus Procreation versus Utility as the Goal of Sex and Marriage. The Relevance of Natural Law?* In our urban society, sex for procreation is decidedly the exception; avoidance of procreation is the overwhelming desideratum in most instances. With much luxury time, modern Americans engage in sex primarily for pleasure (utility) and for closeness to another person (unity). *Griswold* is a reflection of how America's normative culture has decisively rejected natural law premises, that sex is only for procreation or potential procreation. In a world of *Griswold*, is there any relevance for natural law thinking? See Stephen Macedo, "Homosexuality and the Conservative Mind," 84 *Geo. L.J.* 261 (1995), and the response to his article by Robert George & Gerard Bradley, "Marriage and the Liberal Imagination," 84 *Geo.L.J.* 301 (1995).

One response is that the Roman Catholic Church and many fundamentalist Protestants accept natural law precepts as a matter of faith. What Finnis has to say is greatly relevant for those faithful. Note, however, that Finnis does not rest upon Catholic doctrine, though he invokes it as support. (Several of the natural law academics are not openly religious.) His position is that the broad sweep of human thinking—from Aristotle to Pope John Paul II—repeatedly returns to natural law premises about what is good for human beings. We might temporarily think that *Griswold* is the final word, but history will teach us better over the longer term.

3. *What Is Wrong with Nonprocreative Sex?* Michael J. Perry, "The Morality of Homosexual Conduct: A Response to John Finnis," 1 *Notre Dame J.L. Ethics & Pub. Pol'y* 41 (1995), takes Finnis to task for his distinction between good procreative sex and bad nonprocreative sex. Even St. Augustine believed that sterile couples (incapable of procreation) ought to be able to marry, because marriage involves a *unitive* as well as *procreative* good. Finnis does not disagree, but argues that the sterile couple can still have moral sex, because in their case the unitive goal is consistent, at least generally (even if not in their case), with the procreative goal. For the lesbian or gay couple, the unitive and procreative goals can never be consistent, and so their sex is immoral. Perry objects that the "communion" Finnis insists upon is just as possible for lesbian and gay couples and that Finnis' distinction between sterile different-sex couples and same-sex couples is either an incorrect humanism or a wacky biological formalism. How should Finnis respond?

PART B.   MATERIALIST OR ECONOMIC THEORIES

Materialist theories assume that people respond to economic stimuli and that patterns of economic and social change decisively contribute to the evolution of understandings about sex, gender, and sexuality. An economic analysis, for example, typically makes much of urbanization. Where the economy is arranged around subsistence farming, procreation is likely to be central to sexual relations, simply to produce the required labor force. In that setting, one would expect little sexual experimentation (for that is a luxury good). In a society that is urbanized, sex will be less organized around procreation, and women will be able to invest their time and labor in other economic and luxury activities; cities will be centers for experimentation and producers of variety; there will be a widening rural-urban cultural divide, as those with minority sexual tastes gravitate from the farm to the big city. And so on.

The excerpts that follow assume the importance of urbanization and speculate about how economic changes stimulated changes in household and family structure and how these changes, in turn, contributed to the evolution of attitudes about sex and sexuality. The first (D'Emilio) excerpt offers a history of homosexual subcultures as part of the history of capitalism, while the second (Posner) offers a history of 2000 years of women's status as correlated with important shifts in thinking about gender and sexuality. In between the two excerpts, we pose a note summarizing Posner's "rational choice" theory of sexuality, which helps set the stage for his history and which shows some connection with D'Emilio's theory.

As you read these essays, consider how each author would explain phenomena noted in Chapters 1 and 2, such as (1) the increased prominence of public prostitution and cross-dressing in late nineteenth century America and urban campaigns to suppress it, (2) the birth control movement and later the abortion movement in the twentieth century, and (3) the women's liberation and gay liberation movements after World War II.

John D'Emilio, Capitalism and Gay Identity

In *Powers of Desire: The Politics of Sexuality* 100, 102–06, 108–09.
Ann Snitow et al., Editors, 1983.*

* * * Under capitalism, workers are "free" laborers in two ways. We have the freedom to look for a job. We own our ability to work and have the freedom to sell our labor power for wages to anyone willing to buy it. We are also freed from the ownership of anything except our labor power. Most of us do not own the land or the tools that produce what we need, but rather have to work for a living in order to survive. So, if we are free to sell our labor power in the positive sense, we are also freed, in the negative sense, from any other alternative. This dialectic—the constant interplay between exploitation and some measure of autonomy—informs all of the history of those who have lived under capitalism. * * *

The expansion of capital and the spread of wage labor have effected a profound transformation in the structure and functions of the nuclear family, the ideology of family life, and the meaning of heterosexual relations. It is these changes in the family that are most directly linked to the appearance of a collective gay life.

The white colonists in seventeenth-century New England established villages structured around a household economy, composed of family units that were basically self-sufficient, independent, and patriarchal. Men, women, and children farmed land owned by the male head of household. Although there was division of labor between men and women, the family was truly an interdependent unit of production: the survival of each member depended on the cooperation of all. The home was a workplace where women processed raw farm products into food for daily consumption, where they made clothing, soap, and candles, and where husbands, wives, and children worked together to produce the goods they consumed.

By the nineteenth century, this system of household production was in decline. In the Northeast, as merchant capitalists invested the money accumulated through trade in the production of goods, wage labor became more common. Men and women were drawn out of the largely self-sufficient household economy of the colonial era into a capitalist system of free labor. For women in the nineteenth century, working for wages rarely lasted beyond marriage; for men, it became a permanent condition.

The family was thus no longer an independent unit of production. But although no longer independent, the family was still interdependent. Because capitalism had not expanded very far, because it had not yet taken over—or socialized—the production of consumer goods, women still performed necessary productive labor in the home. Many families no longer produced grain, but wives still baked into bread the flour they bought with their husbands' wages; or, when they purchased yarn or cloth, they still made clothing for their families. By the mid–1800s, capitalism had destroyed the economic self-sufficiency of many families, but not the mutual dependence of the members. * * *

* * * By the 1920s among the white middle class, the ideology surrounding the family described it as the means through which men and women formed satisfying, mutually enhancing relationships and created an environment that nurtured children. The family became the setting for a "personal life," sharply distinguished and disconnected from the public world of work and production.

The meaning of heterosexual relations also changed. In colonial New England, the birthrate averaged over seven children per woman of childbearing age. Men and women needed the labor of children. Producing offspring was as necessary for survival as producing grain. Sex was harnessed to procreation. The Puritans did not celebrate *hetero*sexuality but rather marriage; they condemned *all* sexual expression outside the marriage bond and did not differentiate sharply between sodomy and heterosexual fornication.

By the 1970s, however, the birthrate had dropped to under two. With the exception of the post-World War II baby boom, the decline has been continuous for two centuries, paralleling the spread of capitalist relations of production. It occurred even when access to contraceptive devices and abortion was systematically curtailed. The decline has included every segment of the population—urban and rural families, blacks and whites, ethnics and WASPs, the middle class and the working class.

As wage labor spread and production became socialized, then, it became possible to release sexuality from the "imperative" to procreate. Ideologically, heterosexual expression came to be a means of establishing intimacy, promoting happiness, and experiencing pleasure. In divesting the household of its economic independence and fostering the separation of sexuality from procreation, capitalism has created conditions that allow some men and women to organize a personal life around their erotic/emotional attraction to their own sex. It has made possible the formation of urban communities of lesbians and gay men and, more recently, of a politics based on a sexual identity.

Evidence from colonial New England court records and church sermons indicates that male and female homosexual behavior existed in the seventeenth century. Homosexual *behavior*, however, is different from homosexual *identity*. There was, quite simply, no "social space" in the colonial system of production that allowed men and women to be gay. Survival was structured around participation in a nuclear family. There were certain homosexual acts—sodomy among men, "lewdness" among women—in which individuals engaged, but family was so pervasive that colonial society lacked even the category of homosexual or lesbian to describe a person. It is quite possible that some men and women experienced a stronger attraction to their own sex than to the opposite sex—in fact, some colonial court cases refer to men who persisted in their "unnatural" attractions—but one could not fashion out of that preference a way of life. Colonial Massachusetts even had laws prohibiting unmarried adults from living outside family units.

By the second half of the nineteenth century, this situation was noticeably changing as the capitalist system of free labor took hold. Only when *individuals* began to make their living through wage labor, instead of as parts of an interdependent family unit, was it possible for homosexual desire to coalesce into a personal identity—an identity based on the ability to remain outside the heterosexual family and to construct a personal life based on attraction to one's own sex. By the end of the century, a class of men and women existed who recognized their erotic interest in their own sex, saw it as a trait that set them apart from the majority, and sought others like themselves. * * *

[As a consequence of these economics-driven changes, communities of gay people formed in major cities; bathhouses, bars, parks became meeting places for women and, especially, men attracted to those of the same sex. Medical theories of "homosexuality" were, according to D'Emilio, "an ideological response to a new way of organizing one's personal life."]

These new forms of gay identity and patterns of group life also reflected the differentiation of people according to gender, race, and class that is so pervasive in capitalist societies. Among whites, for instance, gay men have traditionally been more visible than lesbians. This partly stems from the division between the public male sphere and the private female sphere. Streets, parks, and bars, especially at night, were "male space." Yet the greater visibility of white gay men also reflected their larger numbers. The Kinsey studies of the 1940s and 1950s found significantly more men than women with predominantly homosexual histories, a situation caused, I would argue, by the fact that capitalism had drawn far more men than women into the labor force, and at higher wages. Men could more easily construct a personal life independent of attachments to the opposite sex, whereas women were more likely to remain economically dependent on men. Kinsey also found a strong positive correlation between years of schooling and lesbian activity. College-educated white women, far more able than their working-class sisters to support themselves, could survive more easily without intimate relationships with men.* * *

[The material foundation for an organized "gay community" was actualized by World War II and by the McCarthy era persecutions. The war "disrupted traditional patterns of gender relations and sexuality, and temporarily created a new erotic situation conducive to homosexual expression" for the millions of men and women it placed in intense homosocial settings. Many formed intimate relationships with one another and carried over those patterns into civilian life. The postwar witch hunts placed their feelings under seige and solidified a core of resistance that broke into the open in the 1960s; the Stonewall riots of June 1969 were the signal event for "gay liberation." Nonetheless, a "profamily" backlash against gay liberation developed in the 1970s.]

* * * How is it that capitalism, whose structure made possible the emergence of a gay identity and the creation of urban gay communities, appears unable to accept gay men and lesbians in its midst? Why do heterosexism and homophobia appear so resistant to assault?

The answers, I think, can be found in the contradictory relationship of capitalism to the family. On the one hand, as I argued earlier, capitalism has gradually undermined the material basis of the nuclear family by taking away the economic functions that cemented the ties between family members. As more adults have been drawn into the free labor system, and as capital has expanded its sphere until it produces as commodities most goods and services we need for our survival, the forces that propelled men and women into families and kept them there have weakened. On the other hand, the ideology of capitalist society has enshrined the family as the source of love, affection, and emotional security, the place where our need for stable, intimate human relationships is satisfied.

This elevation of the nuclear family to preeminence in the sphere of personal life is not accidental. Every society needs structures for reproduction and childrearing, but the possibilities are not limited to the nuclear family. Yet the privatized family fits well with capitalist relations of production. Capitalism has socialized production while maintaining that the products of socialized labor belong to the owners of private property. In many ways, childrearing has also been progressively socialized over the last two centuries, with schools, the media, peer groups, and employers taking over functions that once belonged to parents. Nevertheless, capitalist society maintains that reproduction and childrearing are private tasks, that children "belong" to parents, who exercise the rights of ownership. Ideologically, capitalism drives people into heterosexual families: each generation comes of age having internalized a heterosexist model of intimacy and personal relationships. Materially, capitalism weakens the bonds that once kept families together so that their members experience a growing instability in the place they come to expect happiness and emotional security. Thus, while capitalism has knocked the material foundation away from family life, lesbians, gay men, and heterosexual feminists have become the scapegoats for the social instability of the system.* * *

NOTE ON RICHARD POSNER'S "RATIONAL CHOICE" THEORY OF SEX

Richard Posner's *Sex and Reason* 111–80 (1992) propounds an eclectic but generally economic theory of sex. In this calculus, people's general sexual appetites are treated as exogenous variables, but their actual sexual practices are driven by their personal "cost-benefit" calculation. Specifically, one's sexual behavior is a function of the benefits and costs of different forms of sexual activity and the possibility of substituting one sexual practice for another.

According to Posner, there are three benefits of sex: procreative, hedonistic (pleasure), and sociable (*Sex and Reason* 111–12). One's various sexual activities will be determined in part by one's purposes and one's non-volitional preferences. For example, vaginal intercourse between a man and a woman is the primary sexual activity meeting the goal of procreation, but it is not the only activity that can meet the goal of sociability (and indeed may be disfavored unless reliable means of contraception are available), and it may be inferior to masturbation as a means of gratification, especially if one is not predominantly heterosexual. Posner assumes that humans have different sexual preferences, generally heterosexual or weakly bisexual, with a tiny minority (2–5% men, 1% women) "real homosexual[s]" (*id.* at 294–95).

The costs of sex also fall into three categories: various personal risks or "taxes" associated with different kinds of sex (*e.g.*, children with noncontraceptive vaginal sex, disease with promiscuous sex), social or legal disapproval, and search costs (*id.* at 115–15, 119–26). One reason that solitary masturbation is such a popular sexual activity is that it meets one widely shared purpose of sex (pleasure), with nominal search costs, no risk of unwanted children or disease, and ease of concealment (thereby avoiding social disapproval).

In Posner's calculus, the balance of benefits and costs will determine the relative frequency of different sexual practices (*id.* at 116). His concept of "substitution" of one practice for another renders his analysis particularly dynamic: when the cost of a particular sexual activity increases, humans will tend to reduce their level of that activity but will also tend to substitute previously less desirable activities (*id.* at 114–19). This is the reason that homosexual behavior is common in prisons. Even strongly heterosexual men will be likely to have intercourse with other men, because the search costs for a female partner are quite high (infinite in some prisons) and for gratification inmates will tend to substitute sex with other inmates.

Like most economic analysis, Posner's calculus of sexuality is reductionist, especially in its acceptance of male sexual aggressiveness and female sexual passivity as *a priori* biological truths,[a] but it nonetheless generates some interesting predictions about the dynamics of modern sexuality and efforts to regulate it. For instance, consider the argument that the spread of AIDS through unprotected anal intercourse is a modern justification for sodomy laws. Posner's analysis undercuts such arguments. He notes that the sexual marketplace is already responding to the problem by substituting safe for unsafe sexual conduct, as people adjust their

---

a. For examples, *Sex and Reason* (1) never sets forth a precise idea of what "sex" is and seems to assume that sex occurs only when there is orgasm, (2) neglects the benefits of sex relating to self-expression and assertion of power, and (3) takes no account of sexuality as an unequal power system between men and women. Note, however, that economic models often generate useful conclusions from similarly reductionist assumptions. See Daniel A. Farber & Philip P. Frickey, "Positive Political Theory in the Nineties," 80 *Geo. L.J.* 457, 466–68 (1992).

behavior to avoid the dire consequences of the disease.[b] Thus, the incidence of AIDS has dramatically changed the sexual practices of bisexual and gay men strongly away from unprotected anal intercourse toward intercourse with a condom (which is safer but not perfectly safe), oral intercourse (likewise), and mutual masturbation (which is safe) or abstinence (ditto).[c] As AIDS becomes more salient in the heterosexual population, the practices of predominantly heterosexual men and women are changing as well.[d]

Pursuant to this economic analysis, the best way for the government to fight the spread of AIDS would be through public education about the relative safety of different sexual practices. Since AIDS is often, and increasingly, spread by intravenous drug users' sharing of contaminated needles and then by heterosexual intercourse to the drug users' sexual partners, economic analysis would also be receptive to strategies such as the distribution of latex condoms to the general population and of clean needles to those addicted to intravenous drugs.[e] Sodomy laws can contribute little if anything to preventing the spread of AIDS, in part because they regulate conduct that is safe as well as unsafe. Even if sodomy laws reduced the overall incidence of unsafe sexual behavior (which seems doubtful), they create other incentives which contribute to rather than retard the spread of AIDS. By rendering a variety of sexual practices illegal, sodomy laws probably impede the flow of useful information about sex to the public,[f] and certainly impede the accurate reporting of AIDS cases and the tracing of the patients' sexual partners to inform them of their risks. Citing statistics from Sweden as an example, Posner argues that "[a] climate of sexual tolerance may actually retard rather than promote the spread of venereal diseases in general and AIDS in particular" (*Sex and Reason* 165).

A striking corollary of this sort of sexual calculus is that cultural

---

b. This theme is developed in greater detail in Tomas J. Philipson & Richard A. Posner, *Private Choices and Public Health: The AIDS Epidemic in an Economic Perspective* (1993), reviewed from a rational choice perspective in William N. Eskridge, Jr. & Brian D. Weimer, "The Economics Epidemic in an AIDS Perspective," 61 *U. Chi. L. Rev.* 733 (1994).

c. *See* J.L. Denser, *AIDS and the Heterosexual* 21–22 (1991) (safer sex practices in San Francisco stabilized percentage of population infected, 1982–88); David E. Kanouse et al., *Response to the AIDS Epidemic: A Survey of Homosexual and Bisexual Men in Los Angeles County* ix, # 44 (Rand 1991) (eight out of nine gay and bisexual men had made changes in sexual practices as a result of AIDS); Marshall H. Becker & Jill G. Joseph, "AIDS and Behavioral Change to Reduce Risk: A Review," 78 *Am. J. Pub. Health* 394 (1988); Donald E. Riesenberg, "AIDS-

Prompted Behavior Changes Reported," 255 *J. Am. Med. Ass'n* 171 (1986).

d. *See, e.g.*, David E. Kanouse et al., *AIDS-Related Knowledge, Attitudes, Beliefs, and Behaviors in Los Angeles County* (Rand 1991) (Table 18) (three out of ten heterosexuals made changes in sexual practices in response to AIDS).

e. See Lawrence O. Gostin et al., "Prevention of HIV/AIDS Among Injecting Drug Users," *J. Am. Med. Ass'n* (Dec. 1996).

f. When public health authorities want to distribute sexually explicit information about unsafe sex, they are routinely confronted with the argument that the government should not advertise or educate the public about conduct that is illegal. See Steve Brewer, "AIDS Seen as Real Threat in Crowded Jails of California," *Los Angeles Times*, July 5, 1987, at 3, col. 4.

context, perhaps more than biology,[g] must play a critical role in both the benefits and costs of sex,[h] and hence strongly affects the incidence of different kinds of sexual activity. Posner appreciates this and spends much of *Sex and Reason* tracing the different attitudes toward sex taken by different societies over time. His account follows.

Richard A. Posner, Sex and Reason

146–47, 157–59, 174–78 (1992).*

Among the citizen population in the Athens of Plato and Aristotle boys and girls were reared separately * * *. Polygamy was forbidden but flourished informally as the concubinage practiced by married men. * * * [G]irls married young and the husband usually was considerably older than the wife. As a result of this age difference, the low average marriage age for girls (about 16), the prevalence of arranged marriage, the practice of sequestering women, and the difference in educational attainments between the spouses, marriage was not companionate. Spouses were not good friends, united by bonds of love and trust and by shared interests, values, and experiences. * * *

In a culture in which marriage is not companionate, men will seek affective ties outside the home, either with other men of their own class or with women who, if not themselves of that class, specialize in providing companionship for them. Sex will sometimes, perhaps often, be used to cement these relationships; hence the homosexual relationships with citizen youths and the heterosexual relationships with tony courtesans. * * *

[When marriages are noncompanionate, the] wife does not expect the husband to be an intimate, to be faithful, to be attentive, and so forth; financial support and occasional intercourse are all that is expected; * * * most homosexual men are capable of vaginal intercourse, although they do not find it highly pleasurable or emotionally satisfying. The fact that it was so easy to be a successful married man in ancient Greece and chase young

---

g. Chapter 4 on "The Biology of Sex" (pp. 85–110) explicates a sociobiological theory of sex, which Posner recognizes is quite controversial. See Michael Ruse, *Homosexuality: A Philosophical Inquiry* 130–49 (1988). Posner claims that little if any of his analysis of sexual behavior would be affected if sociobiology were completely wrong (*Sex and Reason* 110), a claim criticized in Gillian Hadfield, "Flirting with Science: Richard Posner on the Bioeconomics of Sexual Man," 106 *Harv. L. Rev.* 479 (1992), and William N. Eskridge, Jr., "A Social Constructionist Critique of Posner's *Sex and Reason*: Steps Toward a Gaylegal Agenda," 102 *Yale L.J.* 333 (1992).

h. Of the three benefits of sex, one (sociability) is clearly linked to cultural attitudes, a second (hedonistic, especially the aesthetic feature) is partly linked, and the third (procreation) is biological in nature but dependent upon culture and context as to whether or to what extent it is a benefit. Of the three costs of sex, one (disapproval) is nothing but cultural attitudes, another (search costs) is heavily dependent upon such attitudes, and the third (taxes) is biological in nature but dependent upon culture and context as to whether or to what extent it is a benefit (a desired child is a benefit of man-woman vaginal sex, an unwanted child a tax).

men on the side made homosexuals seem less different from heterosexuals than in cultures of companionate marriage, such as our own. So much less different, indeed, as rarely to be remarked, in much the same way that we do not much remark left-handedness, because it has no significance for a person's social role. Prostitution was similarly unproblematic, since it did not threaten any essential feature of the marital relationship.* * *

[Posner speculates that young bachelors, especially the essentially heterosexual ones, would find young boys to be frequently the "best" substitute for women. Hence pederasty was common, because the "tastes" of opportunist homosexuals (heterosexuals who in a pinch are willing to engage in same-sex intimacy) will set the tone for the culture as a whole. Posner labels the Greek–Roman period of noncompanionate marriage as "Stage 1" in the evolution of sexual attitudes in the West. "Stage 2" began during the Roman Empire and early Christian eras of Western history and was marked primarily by the acceptance of companionate marriage.]

Companionate marriage * * * created pressure for the emergence of an overt homosexual subculture, which in turn created a sense of the homosexuual as profoundly different from the heterosexual, a perception that invites hostility and discrimination. A traditional charge against homosexuals is that they are selfish, narcissistic, because unwilling to make the effort required to establish an intimate relationship with a woman. Such a charge would have little resonance in a society of noncompanionate marriage * * *. In this and other ways, noncompanionate marriage fosters tolerant attitudes—even outright obliviousness—toward homosexuality. Today, the culture that most celebrates companionate marriage, in succession to England, is the United States; and it may be the Western nation least tolerant of homosexuals.

Homosexual activity is more likely to be punished in a society of companionate marriage than in one of noncompanionate marriage not only because it is more anomalous in the former but also because it is more threatening. Even the predominantly heterosexual married man may be tempted at times by the pretty boy. The more society insists on male sexual restraint, the more concerned it will be with any form of nonmarital sexual activity. * * *

Companionate marriage fosters puritanical attitudes generally, so we should not be surprised by the puritanical strain in the Anglo–American sexual culture. A husband's adultery becomes for the first time offensive, because it undermines love and trust and reduces the amount of time that he spends with his wife, which are elements of companionate but not of noncompanionate marriage. The patronizing of prostitutes by married men is a form of adultery, and so also becomes offensive. * * *

Christian sex ethics are related, via companionate marriage, to the status of women. If that status is very low—if women are deemed simple breeders and drudges, uneducated and uneducable—they will not seem fit to participate with men in a relationship, such as companionate marriage, that is built on love and trust. Christianity tried to raise the status of women above its level in the pagan societies of Greece and Rome. It did this in a number of ways. One—a particularly sharp break with the pagan past—was the forbidding of infanticide, which had been directed mainly at female infants. * * * Another was the forbidding of divorce, which in Greek and Roman society had usually been divorce at the whim of the husband, and involved no alimony, resulting in the creation of a mass of destitute abandoned women. * * *

The first two [stages in the evolution of sexual morality] are strongly family oriented rather than market oriented, and considerations of secure paternity are foremost. But if a woman's role is further enlarged to include market employment, then while such marriages as there are will be companionate, there will be fewer marriages; other forms of sexual relationship will no longer seem quite so abnormal; and policies designed to foster premarital virginity and marital chastity for the sake of companionate marriage will lose much of their point. This process of role enlargement, which ushers in stage 3 in the evolution of sexual morality, has progressed further in Sweden than in any other country. Almost three-fourths of Swedish women are employed outside the home, compared to fewer than 60 percent of American women, and the average wage of Swedish women is 90 percent of the average male wage, a third higher than in the United States.

In stage 3, as in stage 1, and in contrast to stage 2, men enjoy almost complete sexual license. The difference between stages 1 and 3 is that in the latter, but not in the former, women do too. Therefore * * * the sexually conservative retrenchment of the Victorian era should be associated with a reduction in the amount of female employment outside the home. It is.

The loosening grip of Christianity in sexually liberal societies such as Sweden may thus be not the cause of these societies' sexual liberality but the consequence. * * *

The underlying causes of the transition from stage 2 to stage 3 in the evolution of sexual morality are fairly plain. They are the decline in infant mortality, the decline in women's mortality in childbirth, the improvement in methods of contraception, and the growth of light employment, all factors working together to reduce the benefits and increase the costs (both private and social) of keeping women in the home. The underlying causes of the transition from stage 1 to stage 2—from woman as simple breeder to woman as child rearer and husband's companion—are more obscure. One possibility is the decline of slavery, an institution which by the end of Charlemagne's reign had largely disappeared from western Europe, gave wives a bigger role in their husbands' households * * *, or in other words increased the costs of confining them in the extraordinarily limited role * * * that they had played in a slave society. * * *

[It is clear] that Roman wives were less sequestered than Greek wives; that they were sexually freer; and that companionate marriage made progress during the empire, paving the way for the Christian embrace of the institution. Here are two other possible explanations: First, the ages of the spouses at marriage were generally closer in Roman than in Greek society. This would have facilitated companionate marriage, placing pressure on sequestration. Second, Rome at its height was a wealthier society than Greece of the fifth and fourth centuries B.C., and it is about wealthy Roman women that we have the most information. A man who dowers his daughter generously wants to make sure * * * that the daughter's husband will not squander or make off with her dowry[.] * * *

I have emphasized the impact of changes in the occupational role of women on women's sexual freedom, but there is an impact on men's sexual freedom too. * * * To begin with, there have to be male partners for the (heterosexual) newly emancipated women, and so the cost of nonmarital sex to men falls. A subtler point is that the reduction in the gains of marriage that is a by-product of female emancipation is experienced by men as well as by women, so men have less incentive to avoid extramarital sexual activity, which might endanger the marriage. If, as I believe, conventional sexual morality is a function of companionate marriage, forces that weaken the marital bond or reduce the (companionate) marriage rate will foster departures from the conventional morality. In their different ways, neither ancient Athens nor modern Sweden was (is) a society dominated by a norm of companionate marriage: Athens because a rival norm, noncompanionate marriage, held sway; Sweden because the marriage rate is so low and the gains from marriage so limited.

* * * [T]he relationship among the key variables—the occupational status of women, the strength of companionate marriage as an organizing principle of male-female relations, and the degree of sexual freedom in the society—seems clear. This is true even with respect to tolerance for male homosexuality * * * Greater female independence reduces the marriage rate, and by doing so makes homosexuality less anomalous: with fewer marriages, the group least likely to marry does not stand out as much. Take women's interests next. Women do not want male homosexuals to be forced into the marriage market, where they will waste women's time and occasionally deceive them into an unrewarding marriage. And women recognize that hostility to homosexuality is bound up with a general hostility to nonmarital sex and hence threatens the sexual freedom of heterosexual as well as homosexual women. To the extent, moreover, that Christian sexual morality is regarded as a package, a breakdown in some of the components, such as the prohibition against contraception, abortion, and fornication, may undermine the remaining ones. Finally, women want to be free to form lesbian relationships if they like, and what is sauce of the goose is sauce for the gander [sic].

NOTES ON MATERIALIST THEORIES OF SEXUALITY

1. *The Non–European History D'Emilio and Posner Neglect.* Posner's account purports to be an all-explanatory theory, but is Eurocentric. Even assuming its validity, consider what is missing: the history of gendered balance of power arrangements in domestic life and the impact of those on sexual behaviors and meanings in other, non-Christian and non-European cultures. D'Emilio's analysis of the emergence of homosexual communities specifically focuses on the United States but does not address racial differences. Tomás Almaguer points out that early gay communities were forged primarily by white gay men, at a time when white ethnic categories—such as Irish, Italian, or Jewish—were becoming less significant in the U.S., thus further facilitating the emergence of a gay identity for whites. He develops the following contrast:

> Chicanos, on the other hand, have never occupied the social space where a gay or lesbian identity can readily become a primary basis of self-identity. This is due, in part, to their structural position at the subordinate ends of both the class and racial hierarchies, and in a context where ethnicity remains a primary basis of group identity and survival. Moreover, Chicano family life requires allegiance to patriarchal gender relations and to a system of sexual meanings that directly militate against the emergence of this alternative basis of self-identity. Furthermore, factors such as gender, geographical settlement, age, nativity, language usage and degree of cultural assimilation further prevent, or at least complicate, the acceptance of a gay or lesbian identity by Chicanos or Chicanas respectively. They are not as free as individuals situated elsewhere in the social structure to redefine their sexual identity in ways that contravene the imperatives of minority family life and its traditional gender expectations. How they come to define their sexual identities as gay, straight, bisexual or, in Mexican/Latin–American terms, as an *activo, pasivo,* or *macho marica,* therefore, is not a straightforward or unmediated process. * * *

Tomás Almaguer, "Chicano Men: A Cartography of Homosexual Identity and Behavior," in *The Lesbian and Gay Studies Reader* 255, 264 (Henry Abelove et al., eds., 1993).

2. *The Role of Patriarchy?* The changing role of women in western history is key to both Posner and D'Emilio, albeit in different ways. Posner ignores gendered power differentials, the ways in which social and legal rules are set up to advantage men and limit women's options. One could tell a materialist story solely from the perspective of women. One such account is Carroll Smith–Rosenberg's *Disorderly Conduct* (1986) (Chapter 2, Section 2[A]). Smith–Rosenberg traces the history of contraception and abortion laws as patriarchy's response to the "New Woman" of the late nineteenth and early twentieth centuries. Alarmed by educated women who lived their lives undependent upon men, antifeminist backlash sought to control women's bodies by limiting their access to contraceptives and abortions. *Griswold* and *Roe v. Wade,* therefore, can be read as a long-delayed recognition of women's rights to control their bodies. Such legal milestones would have been impossible if women did not exercise considerable political power in the United States, or if male opinion had not shifted on these issues.

3. *Normative Implications of Materialist Theories?* D'Emilio and Posner describe somewhat different phenomena, but neither insists that the evolution of attitudes has been normatively the best evolution. What kind of normative yardstick can be developed from economic theory? There are several different candidates.

(A) No Implications. The role of economic theory is simply to describe positive developments. This is useful, because it helps us to see where we are today and to discern the limits of future change. Indeed, economic theory might be strongly read for the proposition that most if not all efforts at normative "improvement" will be swallowed up by the larger economic and social forces. Posner's economic analysis in particular lends itself toward a status quo-oriented pragmatism which envisions change only incrementally.

(B) Marxist. D'Emilio suggests that economic forces do not necessarily lead in one direction and may instead create contradictions that call for normative interventions. Capitalism, for example, both reinforces the heterosexual norm (the happy bourgeois family) and establishes conditions for undermining that norm (the liberated woman, the homosexual). There is much that is up for grabs, and different economic theories push in different directions. Marxist feminist theory, which animates D'Emilio's account, might support a radical egalitarian norm, in which the state promotes norms based upon equality: women have equal rights with men inside and outside the household, and sexual orientation minorities are no longer oppressed.

(C) Libertarian. Elsewhere in his book, Posner suggests a libertarian baseline for determining state policy for issues of sexuality (his actual prescriptions are more pragmatic than libertarian, however). He explicitly invokes chapter 4 of Mill's *On Liberty*, which follows below.

John Stuart Mill, On Liberty

Chapter 4 (1857).

* * * [E]very one who receives the protection of society owes a return for the benefit, and the fact of living in society renders it indispensable that each should be bound to observe a certain line of conduct towards the rest. This conduct consists, first, in not injuring the interests of one another, or rather certain interests, which, either by express legal provision or by tacit understanding, ought to be considered as rights; and secondly, in each person's bearing his share (to be fixed on some equitable principle) of the labors and sacrifices incurred for defending the society or its members from injury and molestation. * * * As soon as any part of a person's conduct affects prejudicially the interests of others, society has jurisdiction over it, and the question whether the general welfare will or will not be promoted by interfering with it, becomes open to discussion. But there is no room for entertaining any such questions when a person's conduct affects the interests of no persons besides himself, or needs not affect them unless they like (all the persons concerned being of full age, and the ordinary amount of understanding). In all such cases there should be perfect freedom, legal and social, to do the action and stand the consequences.

It would be a great misunderstanding of this doctrine to suppose that it is one of selfish indifference, which pretends that human beings have no business with each other's conduct in life, and that they should not concern themselves about the well-doing or well-being of one another, unless their own interest is involved. Instead of any diminution, there is need of a great increase of disinterested exertion to promote the good of others. But disinterested benevolence can find other instruments to persuade people to their good, than whips and scourges, either of the literal or metaphorical sort. * * * [N]either one person nor any number of persons, is warranted in saying to another human creature of ripe years, that he shall not do with his life for his own benefit what he chooses to do with it. He is the person most interested in his own well-being * * *. The interference of society to overrule his judgment and purposes in what only regards himself, must be grounded on general presumptions; which may be altogether wrong, and even if right, are as likely as not to be misapplied to individual cases, by persons no better acquainted with the circumstances of such cases than those who look at them merely from without. In this department, therefore, of human affairs, individuality has its proper field of action. * * *

* * * There are many who consider as an injury to themselves any conduct which they have a distaste for, and resent it as an outrage to their feelings; as a religious bigot, when charged with disregarding the religious feelings of others, has been known to retort that they disregard his feelings, by persisting in their abominable worship or creed. But there is no parity between the feeling of a person for his own opinion, and the feeling of another who is offended at his holding it; no more than between the desire of a thief to take a purse, and the desire of the right owner to keep it. And a person's taste is as much his own peculiar concern as his opinion or his purse. It is easy for any one to imagine an ideal public, which leaves the freedom and choice of individuals in all uncertain matters undisturbed, and only requires them to abstain from modes of conduct which universal experience has condemned. But where has there been seen a public which set any limit to its censorship? [O]r when does the public trouble itself about universal experience? In its interferences with personal conduct it is seldom thinking of anything but the enormity of acting or feeling different-ly from itself; and this standard of judgment, thinly disguised, is held up to mankind as the dictate of religion and philosophy, by nine-tenths of all moralists and speculative writers. * * *

[Mill follows with examples of legislation implementing what we today would call "nosy preferences"—the establishment of state religions, sabba-tarian laws, prohibition of the sale or consumption of alcohol. He closes with the hysterical reaction in America to Mormons.] The article of the Mormonite doctrine that is the chief provocative to the antipathy which thus breaks through the ordinary restraints of religious tolerance, is its sanction of polygamy * * *. No one has a deeper disapprobation than I have of this Mormon institution; both for other reasons, and because, far from being in any way countenanced by the principle of liberty, it it a direct infraction of that principle, being a mere riveting of the chains of one-half of the community, and an emancipation of the other from reciprocal obligations towards them. Still, it must be remembered that this relation is as much voluntary on the part of the women concerned in it, and who may be deemed the sufferers by it, as is the case with any other form of the marriage institution * * *. Other countries are not asked to recognize such unions, or release any portion of their inhabitants from their own laws on the score of Mormonite opinions. But when the dissentients * * * have left the countries to which their doctrines were unacceptable, and established themselves in a remote corner of the earth [Utah], which they have been the first to render habitable to human beings; it is difficult to see on what principles but those of tyranny they can be prevented from living there under what laws they please, provided they commit no aggression on other nations, and allow perfect freedom of departure to those who are dissatisfied with their ways. * * *

NOTE ON CAROL ROSE'S FEMINIST ECONOMICS AND HER DEFENSE OF POLYGAMY

Carol Rose's essay on "Women and Property: Gaining and Losing Ground," in *Property and Persuasion* 233–63 (1994), sets forth what might be called a rational choice explanation of patriarchy. If one assumes that women are more "cooperative" than men (readier to form relationships), it follows that Louise will be more willing to enter into relationships—commercial as well as personal—and less inclined to exit them than Sam will. Both might benefit from the relationship, but Sam will tend to benefit more. Because his demand for the relationship is more "inelastic" (he can take it or leave it), he will ask for, and Louise will be prone to accept, a greater share. Rose maintains that this game dynamic is just as applicable to an entrepreneurial partnership as to a marriage relationship. (Rose also says this dynamic works even if women are only perceived to be more cooperative, an assumption more easily defended.)

What are the implications of Rose's model for legal issues such as polygamy? (See Chapter 9, Section 2[C] for Rose's views.) For feminist theory?

PART C. FEMINIST THEORIES

Law and philosophy have traditionally been written only by men, and one would expect law and philosophy to reflect men's perspective and interests. In a society where women are equal citizens, at least formally, and should be equal citizens normatively, this state of affairs seems slanted. Feminist theories start from the perspective of women.

NOTE ON CATHARINE MACKINNON'S THEORY OF THE RELATIONSHIP OF PATRIARCHY, GENDER, AND SEXUALITY[i]

One of the leading feminist theorists of sexuality, gender and law has been Catharine MacKinnon. MacKinnon's early work was instrumental in helping to win recognition of sexual harassment as a form of sex discrimination prohibited by Title VII.[j] She has also been extremely prolific as a theorist. Writing in the early 1980s (at roughly the same time that D'Emilio wrote the essay excerpted above and that Gayle Rubin wrote the article that follows), MacKinnon articulated a claim that sexuality is central, not just to women's lives, but to the theory of feminism: "[s]exuality is to feminism what work is to Marxism: that which is most one's own, yet most taken away." ("Feminism, Marxism" 515.) Women's sexuality, she said, has been systematically expropriated by men in the same way that capital systematically expropriates the labor of workers. She analogized heterosexuality as a structuring system to class as a structuring system, and described both Marxism and feminism as "theories of power and its distribution: inequality." (*Id.*)

More radically, however, MacKinnon has identified sexuality as "the primary sphere" of male power. She has consistently argued that it is within the realm of sexuality that women's oppression is most fundamentally constructed. The experience of (hetero)sexuality is the locus for multiple forms of coercion and abnegation of the female sense of self, much less agency. "The substantive principle governing the authentic politics of women's personal lives is pervasive powerlessness to men, express and reconstituted daily *as* sexuality. To say that the personal is political means that gender as a division of power is discoverable and verifiable through women's intimate experience of sexual objectification, which is definitive of and synonymous with women's lives as gender female. * * * Sexual objectification is the primary process of the subjection of women. It unites act with word, construction with expression, perception with enforcement, myth with reality. Man fucks woman; subject verb object." (*Id.* at 535, 541.)

For MacKinnon, gender, or the social roles women and men are pressured to play, do not shape sexuality. It is the other way around: sexuality determines gender.

> If the literature on sex roles and the investigations of particular issues are read in light of each other, each element of the female *gender* stereotype is revealed as, in fact, sexual. Vulnerability means the appearance/reality of easy sexual access; passivity means receptivity and disabled resistance, enforced by trained physical weakness; softness means pregnability by something hard. * * *

---

i. This section draws on two of MacKinnon's works that focus most directly on the relationship between sexuality and gender: "Feminism, Marxism, Method, and the State: An Agenda for Theory," 7 *Signs* 515 (1982) and *Feminism Unmodified: Discourses on Life and Law* (1987).

j. See Catharine A. MacKinnon, *Sexual Harassment of Working Women* (1979).

Sexuality, then, is a form of power. Gender, as socially constructed, embodies it, not the reverse. Women and men are divided by gender, made into the sexes as we know them, by the social requirements of heterosexuality, which institutionalizes male sexual dominance and female sexual submission. If this is true, sexuality is the linchpin of gender inequality.

(*Id.* at 530, 533).

Although MacKinnon initiates her investigation from the perspective of women, she argues that sexuality constitutes manhood as well as womanhood. "[O]ur rapists * * *, serial murderers * * * and child molesters * * * enjoy their acts sexually and as men, to be redundant. It is sex *for them*. * * * When acts of dominance and submission, up to and including acts of violence, are experienced as sexually arousing, as sex itself, that is what they are." She thus describes gender as "the congealed form of the sexualization of inequality between men and women." (*Feminism Unmodified* 6.)

MacKinnon's view that (hetero)sexuality forms the central core and formative engine of gender oppression is the logic underlying various of her other controversial views. We take up the debate over pornography at length in Chapter 6. MacKinnon has also been highly critical of abortion rights and birth control advocacy for "remov[ing] the one remaining legitimized reason that women have had for refusing sex besides the headache." (*Id.* at 99.) MacKinnon supports recognition of a woman's right to have an abortion, but argues that "reproductive freedom" struggles have concerned not merely decisions about reproduction but about the norms and customs of intercourse. Where feminists like Sanger emphasized a woman's right to enjoy herself heterosexually, MacKinnon stresses the absence of recognition for a woman's right to refuse sexual activity. Moreover, MacKinnon is skeptical of the concept of consent: "[i]f sex is ordinarily accepted as something men do *to* women, the better question [than the proper definition of rape] would be whether consent is a meaningful concept." ("Feminism, Marxism" 532.)

Gayle S. Rubin, Thinking Sex: Notes for a Radical Theory of the Politics of Sexuality

In *Pleasure and Danger: Exploring Female Sexuality* 11–16, 31–34.
Carole Vance, Editor, 1984.*

The new scholarship on sex has brought a welcome insistence that sexual terms be restricted to their proper historical and social contexts, and a cautionary scepticism towards sweeping generalizations. But it is important to be able to indicate groupings of erotic behavior and general trends within erotic discourse. In addition to sexual essentialism, there are at least five other ideological formations whose grip on sexual thought is so strong that to fail to discuss them is to remain enmeshed within them. These are sex negativity, the fallacy of misplaced scale, the hierarchical valuation of sex acts, the domino theory of sexual peril, and the lack of a concept of benign sexual variation.

Of these five, the most important is sex negativity. Western cultures generally consider sex to be a dangerous, destructive, negative force. Most Christian tradition, following Paul, holds that sex is inherently sinful. It may be redeemed if performed within marriage for procreative purposes and if the pleasurable aspects are not enjoyed too much. In turn, this idea rests on the assumption that the genitalia are an intrinsically inferior part of the body, much lower and less holy than the mind, the "soul," the "heart," or even the upper part of the digestive system (the status of the excretory organs is close to that of the genitalia). Such notions have by now acquired a life of their own and no longer depend solely on religion for their perseverance.

This culture always treats sex with suspicion. It construes and judges almost any sexual practice in terms of its worst possible expression. Sex is presumed guilty until proven innocent. Virtually all erotic behavior is considered bad unless a specific reason to exempt it has been established. The most acceptable excuses are marriage, reproduction, and love. Sometimes scientific curiosity, aesthetic experience, or a long-term intimate relationship may serve. But the exercise of erotic capacity, intelligence, curiosity, or creativity all require pretexts that are unnecessary for other pleasures, such as the enjoyment of food, fiction, or astronomy.

What I call the fallacy of misplaced scale is a corollary of sex negativity. Susan Sontag once commented that since Christianity focused "on sexual behavior as the root of virtue, everything pertaining to sex has been a 'special case' in our culture." Sex law has incorporated the religious attitude that heretical sex is an especially heinous sin that deserves the harshest punishments. Throughout much of European and American history, a single act of consensual anal penetration was grounds for execution. In some states, sodomy still carries twenty-year prison sentences. Outside the law, sex is also a marked category. Small differences in value or behavior are often experienced as cosmic threats. Although people can be intolerant, silly, or pushy about what constitutes proper diet, differences in menu rarely provoke the kinds of rage, anxiety, and sheer terror that routinely accompany differences in erotic taste. Sexual acts are burdened with an excess of significance.

Modern Western societies appraise sex acts according to a hierarchical system of sexual value. Marital, reproductive heterosexuals are alone at the top of the erotic pyramid. Clamoring below are unmarried monogamous heterosexuals in couples, followed by most other heterosexuals. Solitary sex floats ambiguously. The powerful nineteenth-century stigma on masturbation lingers in less potent, modified forms, such as the idea that masturbation is an inferior substitute for partnered encounters. Stable, long-term lesbian and gay male couples are verging on respectability, but bar dykes and promiscuous gay men are hovering just above the groups at the very bottom of the pyramid. The most despised sexual castes currently include transsexuals, transvestites, fetishists, sadomasochists, sex workers such as prostitutes and porn models, and the lowliest of all, those whose eroticism transgresses generational boundaries.

Individuals whose behavior stands high in this hierarchy are rewarded with certified mental health, respectability, legality, social and physical mobility, institutional support, and material benefits. As sexual behaviors or occupations fall lower on the scale, the individuals who practice them are subjected to a presumption of mental illness, disreputability, criminality, restricted social and physical mobility, loss of institutional support, and economic sanctions.

Extreme and punitive stigma maintains some sexual behaviors as low status and is an effective sanction against chose who engage in them. The intensity of this stigma is rooted in Western religious traditions. But most of its contemporary content derives from medical and psychiatric opprobrium.

The old religious taboos were primarily based on kinship forms of social organization. They were meant to deter inappropriate unions and to provide proper kin. Sex laws derived from Biblical pronouncements were aimed at preventing the acquisition of the wrong kinds of affinal partners: consanguineous kin (incest), the same gender (homosexuality), or the wrong species (bestiality). When medicine and psychiatry acquired extensive powers over sexuality, they were less concerned with unsuitable mates than with unfit forms of desire. If taboos against incest best characterized kinship systems of sexual organization, then the shift to an emphasis on taboos against masturbation was more apposite to the newer systems organized around qualities of erotic experience.

Medicine and psychiatry multiplied the categories of sexual misconduct. The section on psychosexual disorders in the *Diagnostic and Statistical Manual of Mental and Physical Disorders (DSM)* of the American Psychiatric Association (APA) is a fairly reliable map of the current moral hierarchy of sexual activities. The APA list is much more elaborate than the traditional condemnations of whoring, sodomy, and adultery. The most recent edition, *DSM-III*, removed homosexuality from the roster of mental disorders after a long political struggle. But fetishism, sadism, masochism, transsexuality, transvestism, exhibitionism, voyeurism, and pedophilia are quite firmly entrenched as psychological malfunctions. Books are still being written about the genesis, etiology, treatment, and cure of these assorted "pathologies."

Psychiatric condemnation of sexual behaviors invokes concepts of mental and emotional inferiority rather than categories of sexual sin. Low-status sex practices are vilified as mental diseases or symptoms of defective personality integration. In addition, psychological terms conflate difficulties of psycho-dynamic functioning with modes of erotic conduct. They equate sexual masochism with self-destructive personality patterns, sexual sadism with emotional aggression, and homoeroticism with immaturity. These terminological muddles have become powerful stereotypes that are indiscriminately applied to individuals on the basis of their sexual orientations.

Popular culture is permeated with ideas that erotic variety is dangerous, unhealthy, depraved, and a menace to everything from small children to national security. Popular sexual ideology is a noxious stew made up of ideas of sexual sin, concepts of psychological inferiority, anti-communism, mob hysteria, accusations of witchcraft, and xenophobia. The mass media nourish these attitudes with relentless propaganda. I would call this system

The charmed circle:

Good, Normal, Natural, Blessed Sexuality

Heterosexual
Married
Monogamous
Procreative
Non-commercial
In pairs
In a relationship
Same generation
In private
No pornography
Bodies only
Vanilla

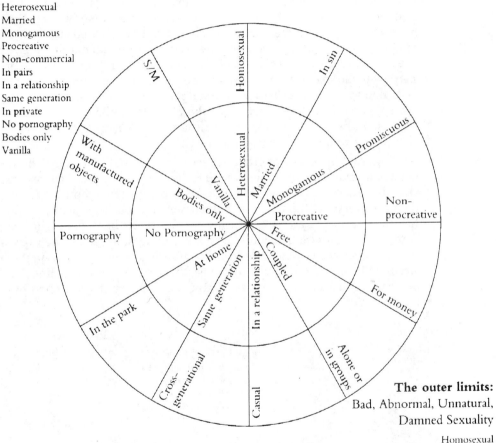

The outer limits:

Bad, Abnormal, Unnatural,
Damned Sexuality

Homosexual
Unmarried
Promiscuous
Non-procreative
Commercial
Alone or in groups
Casual
Cross-generational
In public
Pornography
With manufactured objects
Sadomasochistic

of erotic stigma the last socially respectable form of prejudice if the old forms did not show such obstinate vitality, and new ones did not continually become apparent.

All these hierarchies of sexual value—religious, psychiatric, and popular—function in much the same ways as do ideological systems of racism, ethnocentrism, and religious chauvinism. They rationalize the well-being of the sexually privileged and the adversity of the sexual rabble.

Figure 1 diagrams a general version of the sexual value system. According to this system, sexuality that is "good," "normal," and "natural" should ideally be heterosexual, marital, monogamous, reproductive, and non-commercial. It should be coupled, relational, within the same generation, and occur at home. It should not involve pornography, fetish objects, sex toys of any sort, or roles other than male and female. Any sex that violates these rules is "bad," "abnormal," or "unnatural." Bad sex may be homosexual, unmarried, promiscuous, non-procreative, or commercial. It may be masturbatory or take place at orgies, may be casual, may cross generational lines, and may take place in "public," or at least in the bushes or the baths. It may involve the use of pornography, fetish objects, sex toys, or unusual roles (see Figure 1).

Figure 2 diagrams another aspect of the sexual hierarchy: the need to draw and maintain an imaginary line between good and bad sex. Most of the discourses on sex, be they religious, psychiatric, popular, or political, delimit a very small portion of human sexual capacity as sanctifiable, safe, healthy, mature, legal, or politically correct. The "line" distinguishes these from all other erotic behaviors, which are understood to be the work of the devil, dangerous, psychopathological, infantile, or politically reprehensible. Arguments are then conducted over "where to draw the line," and to determine what other activities, if any, may be permitted to cross over into acceptability.

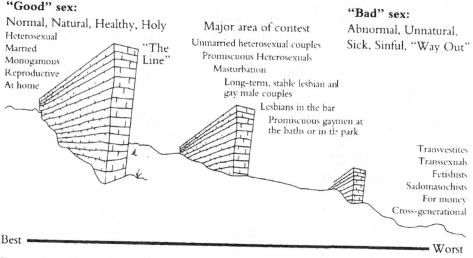

"Good" sex:
Normal, Natural, Healthy, Holy
Heterosexual
Married
Monogamous
Reproductive
At home

"The Line"

Major area of contest
Unmarried heterosexual couples
Promiscuous Heterosexuals
Masturbation
Long-term, stable lesbian and gay male couples
Lesbians in the bar
Promiscuous gaymen at the baths or in the park

"Bad" sex:
Abnormal, Unnatural, Sick, Sinful, "Way Out"

Transvestites
Transsexuals
Fetishists
Sadomasochists
For money
Cross-generational

Best ————————————————————— Worst

FIGURE 2.   The sex hierarchy: the struggle over where to draw the line

All these models assume a domino theory of sexual peril. The line appears to stand between sexual order and chaos. It expresses the fear that if anything is permitted to cross this erotic DMZ, the barrier against scary sex will crumble and something unspeakable will skitter across.

Most systems of sexual judgment—religious, psychological, feminist, or socialist—attempt to determine on which side of the line a particular act falls. Only sex acts on the good side of the line are accorded moral complexity. For instance, heterosexual encounters may be sublime or disgusting, free or forced, healing or destructive, romantic or mercenary. As long as it does not violate other rules, heterosexuality is acknowledged to exhibit the full range of human experience. In contrast, all sex acts on the bad side of the line are considered utterly repulsive and devoid of all emotional nuance. The further from the line a sex act is, the more it is depicted as a uniformly bad experience.

As a result of the sex conflicts of the last decade, some behavior near the border is inching across it. Unmarried couples living together, masturbation, and some forms of homosexuality are moving in the direction of respectability (see Figure 2). Most homosexuality is still on the bad side of the line. But if it is coupled and monogamous, the society is beginning to recognize that it includes the full range of human interaction. Promiscuous homosexuality, sadomasochism, fetishism, transsexuality, and cross-generational encounters are still viewed as unmodulated horrors incapable of involving affection, love, free choice, kindness, or transcendence.

This kind of sexual morality has more in common with ideologies of racism than with true ethics. It grants virtue to the dominant groups, and relegates vice to the underprivileged. A democratic morality should judge sexual acts by the way partners treat one another, the level of mutual consideration, the presence or absence of coercion, and the quantity and quality of the pleasures they provide. Whether sex acts are gay or straight, coupled or in groups, naked or in underwear, commercial or free, with or without video, should not be ethical concerns.

It is difficult to develop a pluralistic sexual ethics without a concept of benign sexual variation. Variation is a fundamental property of all life, from the simplest biological organisms to the most complex human social formations. Yet sexuality is supposed to conform to a single standard. One of the most tenacious ideas about sex is that there is one best way to do it, and that everyone should do it that way.

Most people find it difficult to grasp that whatever they like to do sexually will be thoroughly repulsive to someone else, and that whatever repels them sexually will be the most treasured delight of someone, somewhere. One need not like or perform a particular sex act in order to recognize that someone else will, and that this difference does not indicate a lack of good taste, mental health, or intelligence in either party. Most people mistake their sexual preferences for a universal system that will or should work for everyone.

This notion of a single ideal sexuality characterizes most systems of thought about sex. For religion, the ideal is procreative marriage. For psychology, it is mature heterosexuality. Although its content varies, the format of a single sexual standard is continually reconstituted within other rhetorical frameworks, including feminism and socialism. It is just as objectionable to insist that everyone should be lesbian, nonmonogamous, or kinky, as to believe that everyone should be heterosexual, married, or vanilla—though the latter set of opinions are backed by considerably more coercive power than the former.

Progressives who would be ashamed to display cultural chauvinism in other areas routinely exhibit it towards sexual differences. We have learned to cherish different cultures as unique expressions of human inventiveness rather than as the inferior or disgusting habits of savages. We need a similarly anthropological understanding of different sexual cultures.

Empirical sex research is the one field that does incorporate a positive concept of sexual variation. Alfred Kinsey approached the study of sex with the same uninhibited curiosity he had previously applied to examining a species of wasp. His scientific detachment gave his work a refreshing neutrality that enraged moralists and caused immense controversy. Among Kinsey's successors, John Gagnon and William Simon have pioneered the application of sociological understandings to erotic variety. * * *

[A] great deal of sex law does not distinguish between consensual and coercive behavior. Only rape law contains such a distinction. Rape law is based upon the assumption, correct in my view, that heterosexual activity may be freely chosen or forcibly coerced. One has the legal right to engage in heterosexual behavior as long as it does not fall under the purview of other statutes and as long as it is agreeable to both parties.

This is not the case for most other sexual acts. Sodomy laws, as I mentioned above, are based on the assumption that the forbidden acts are an "abominable and detestable crime against nature." Criminality is intrinsic to the acts themselves, no matter what the desires of the participants. "Unlike rape, sodomy or an unnatural or perverted sexual act may be committed between two persons both of whom consent, and, regardless of which is the aggressor, both may be prosecuted." Before the consenting adults statute was passed in California in 1976, lesbian lovers could have been prosecuted for committing oral copulation. If both participants were capable of consent, both were equally guilty.

Adult incest statutes operate in a similar fashion. Contrary to popular mythology, the incest statutes have little to do with protecting children from rape by close relatives. The incest statutes themselves prohibit marriage or sexual intercourse between adults who are closely related. Prosecutions are rare, but two were reported recently. In 1979, a 19–year-old Marine met his 42–year-old mother, from whom he had been separated at birth. The two fell in love and got married. They were charged and found guilty of incest, which under Virginia law carries a maximum ten-year sentence. During their trial, the Marine testified, "I love her very much. I feel that two people who love each other should be able to live together." In another case, a brother and sister who had been raised separately met and decided to get married. They were arrested and pleaded guilty to felony incest in return for probation. A condition of probation was that they not live together as husband and wife. Had they not accepted, they would have faced twenty years in prison.

In a famous S/M case, a man was convicted of aggravated assault for a whipping administered in an S/M scene. There was no complaining victim. The session had been filmed and he was prosecuted on the basis of the film. The man appealed his conviction by arguing that he had been involved in a consensual sexual encounter and had assaulted no one. In rejecting his appeal, the court ruled that one may not consent to an assault or battery "except in a situation involving ordinary physical contact or blows incident to sports such as football, loosing, or wrestling." The court went on to note that the "consent of a person without legal capacity to give consent, such as a child or insane person, is ineffective," and that "It is a matter of common knowledge that a normal person in full possession of his mental faculties does not freely consent to the use, upon himself, of force likely to produce great bodily injury."[84] Therefore, anyone who would consent to a whipping would be presumed *non compos mentis* and legally incapable of consenting. S/M sex generally involves a much lower level of force than the average football game, and results in far fewer injuries than most sports. But the court ruled that football players are sane, whereas masochists are not.

Sodomy laws, adult incest laws, and legal interpretations such as the one above clearly interfere with consensual behavior and impose criminal penalties on it. Within the law, consent is a privilege enjoyed only by those who engage in the highest-status sexual behavior. Those who enjoy low-status sexual behavior do not have the legal right to engage in it. In addition, economic sanctions, family pressures, erotic stigma, social discrimination, negative ideology, and the paucity of information about erotic behavior, all serve to make it difficult for people to make unconventional sexual choices. There certainly are structural constraints that impede free sexual choice, but they hardly operate to coerce anyone into being a pervert. On the contrary, they operate to coerce everyone toward normality.

The "brainwash theory" explains erotic diversity by assuming that some sexual acts are so disgusting that no one would willingly perform them. Therefore, the reasoning goes, anyone who does so must have been forced or fooled. Even constructivist sexual theory has been pressed into the service of explaining away why otherwise rational individuals might engage in variant sexual behavior. Another position that is not yet fully formed uses the ideas of [Michel] Foucault and [Jeffrey] Weeks to imply that the "perversions" are an especially unsavory or problematic aspect of the construction of modern sexuality. This is yet another version of the notion that sexual dissidents are victims of the subtle machinations of the

84. *People v. Samuels*, 58 Cal. Rptr. 439, 447 (Cal.App.1967).

social system. Weeks and Foucault would not accept such an interpretation, since they consider all sexuality to be constructed, the conventional no less than the deviant.

Psychology is the last resort of those who refuse to acknowledge that sexual dissidents are as conscious and free as any other group of sexual actors. If deviants are not responding to the manipulations of the social system, then perhaps the source of their incomprehensible choices can be found in a bad childhood, unsuccessful socialization, or inadequate identity formation. In her essay on erotic domination, Jessica Benjamin draws upon psychoanalysis and philosophy to explain why what she calls "sadomaso-chism" is alienated, distorted, unsatisfactory, numb, purposeless, and an attempt to "relieve an original effort to differentiation that failed." This essay substitutes a psychophilosophical inferiority for the more usual means of devaluing dissident eroticism. One reviewer has already construed Benjamin's argument as showing that sadomasochism is merely an "obses-sive replay of the infant power struggle."

The position which defends the political rights of perverts but which seeks to understand their "alienated" sexuality is certainly preferable to the WAP-style bloodbaths. But for the most part, the sexual moderates have not confronted their discomfort with erotic choices that differ from their own. Erotic chauvinism cannot be redeemed by tarting it up in Marxist drag, sophisticated constructivist theory, or retropsychobabble.

Whichever feminist position on sexuality—right, left, or center—even-tually attains dominance, the existence of such a rich discussion is evidence that the feminist movement will always be a source of interesting thought about sex. Nevertheless, I want to challenge the assumption that feminism is or should be the privileged site of a theory of sexuality. Feminism is the theory of gender oppression. To assume automatically that this makes it the theory of sexual oppression is to fail to distinguish between gender, on the one hand, and erotic desire, on the other.

In the English language, the word "sex" has two very different meanings. It means gender and gender identity, as in "the female sex" or "the male sex." But sex also refers to sexual activity, lust, intercourse, and arousal, as in "to have sex." This semantic merging reflects a cultural assumption that sexuality is reducible to sexual intercourse and that it is a function of the relations between women and men. The cultural fusion of gender with sexuality has given rise to the idea that a theory of sexuality may be derived directly out of a theory of gender. * * *

Catherine MacKinnon has made the most explicit theoretical attempt to subsume sexuality under feminist thought. According to MacKinnon, "Sexuality is to feminism what work is to marxism ... the molding, direction, and expression of sexuality organizes society into two sexes, women and men." This analytic strategy in turn rests on a decision to "use sex and gender relatively interchangeably." It is this definitional fusion that I want to challenge.*

---

* MacKinnon's published oeuvre has also burgeoned: Catherine A. MacKinnon, *Toward* *a Feminist Theory of the State,* Cambridge, Mass., Harvard University Press, 1989; Cath-

There is an instructive analogy in the history of the differentiation of contemporary feminist thought from Marxism. Marxism is probably the most supple and powerful conceptual system extant for analyzing social inequality. But attempts to make Marxism the sole explanatory system for all social inequalities have been dismal exercises. Marxism is most successful in the areas of social life for which it was originally developed—class relations under capitalism.

In the early days of the contemporary women's movement, a theoretical conflict took place over the applicability of Marxism to gender statification. Since Marxist theory is relatively powerful, it does in fact detect important and interesting aspects of gender oppression. It works best for those issues of gender most closely related to issues of class and the organization of labor. The issues more specific to the social structure of gender were not amenable to Marxist analysis.

The relationship between feminism and a radical theory of sexual oppression is similar. Feminist conceptual tools were developed to detect and analyze gender-based hierarchies. To the extent that these overlap with erotic stratifications, feminist theory has some explanatory power. But as issues become less those of gender and more those of sexuality, feminist analysis becomes misleading and often irrelevant. Feminist thought simply lacks angles of vision which can fully encompass the social organization of sexuality. The criteria of relevance in feminist thought do not allow it to see or assess critical power relations in the area of sexuality.

In the long run, feminism's critique of gender hierarchy must be incorporated into a radical theory of sex, and the critique of sexual oppression should enrich feminism. But an autonomous theory and politics specific to sexuality must be developed.

It is a mistake to substitute feminism for Marxism as the last word in social theory. Feminism is no more capable than Marxism of being the ultimate and complete account of all social inequality. Nor is feminism the residual theory which can take care of everything to which Marx did not attend. These critical tools were fashioned to handle very specific areas of social activity. Other areas of social life, their forms of power, and their characteristic modes of oppression, need their own conceptual implements. In this essay, I have argued for theoretical as well as sexual pluralism.

NOTE ON MACKINNON'S AND RUBIN'S THEORIES OF SEXUALITY

1. *The Chicken or Egg Problem.* The major theoretical point in dispute between MacKinnon and Rubin is the nature of the relationship between sexuality and gender. In MacKinnon's view, the two are seemingly inseparable: the sexual dominance of (most) women by (most) men constitutes the meaning of gender. In her view, gender inequality has a sexual dynamic

erine A. MacKinnon, *Feminism Unmodified: Discourses on Life and Law,* Cambridge, Mass., Harvard University Press, 1987.

which sustains it more powerfully than do, *e.g.*, economic institutions. Rubin, on the other hand, argues that sexuality is analytically independent of gender. Rubin asserts the need for developing theories specifically of sexuality, comparable to our theories of the marketplace or of the state.

The sex/gender/sexual orientation relationship in law is analyzed at length in Francisco Valdes, "Queers, Sissies, Dykes and Tomboys: Deconstructing the Conflation of 'Sex,' 'Gender,' and 'Sexual Orientation' in Euro–American Law and Society," 83 *Cal. L. Rev.* 1 (1995). Valdes posits a triangular structure, in which the three points are sex, gender, and sexual orientation. Because they are arranged in a triangle, each point is linked to both of the other two (see his diagram in Chapter 1, Section 3). Valdes argues that social thought and legal doctrine conflate, or blur, these three distinct concepts into each other and into what is often a confused stew of conventional wisdom. According to Valdez, "there is no such thing as discrimination 'based' only on any single endpoint. In fact, all acts and strains of discrimination always occur, or are situated, within one (or more) of the legs linking the endpoints" of sex, gender, and sexual orientation. *Id.* at 17. Each act of discrimination, therefore, always involves two or more of the three (sex, gender, sexual orientation). How does this insight cut in the Rubin–MacKinnon debate?

2. *The Role of the State.* What are the implications of these two approaches for legal doctrine? For example, how would MacKinnon and Rubin analyze the cases and issues in Chapter 1, such as *Roe v. Wade? Bowers v. Hardwick?* Much feminist theory reaches beyond the libertarian premises of the privacy doctrine and asserts a positive role for the state. Indeed, the right to be left alone has traditionally been a privacy deployed by men to beat and rape their wives, avoid responsibility for children, and harass female employees. Just as the Marxist state actively seeks to remold society toward class equality, so the feminist state might seek to counteract private violence against women with public intervention and education. Thus, it is not enough for the state to permit women to choose abortion; the state should also enable indigent women to afford such procedures in a safe environment. This is a position the Supreme Court has rejected. *Harris v. McRae*, 448 U.S. 297 (1980).

The challenge of the positive state is the productive deployment of state power, in particular the regulation of sexuality in nonhysterical ways. Consider two examples: laws against prostitution (Chapter 11, Section 3) and the White Slave Traffic Act of 1910 (Mann Act) (Chapter 2, Section 2[A]). How would MacKinnon and Rubin analyze those uses of state power?

3. *Compulsory Heterosexuality.* Many feminists maintain that heterosexuality is one way patriarchy controls women's sexuality. The leading author for this proposition is Adrienne Rich, "Compulsory Heterosexuality and Lesbian Existence," in *Blood, Bread, and Poetry: Selected Prose, 1979–1985*, at 23–75 (1986) (originally published in *Signs*, 1978). An open lesbian, Rich argued that society's insistence that women be heterosexual is a primary "beachhead of male dominance." A necessary corrective is the many facets of "lesbian existence," from supportive female friendships to romantic commitment to another woman. She concluded her essay with a denunciation of compulsory heterosexuality as a "profound falseness," a "lie" that "distorts our lives." Rich considers heterosexual "propaganda"— the erasure of the possibility of lesbian life—to be as invidious as it is pervasive, for it makes life as a woman inconceivable without men. Some feminists believe Rich overstates her case against compulsory heterosexuality, but most feminists believe that all women profit from lesbian experience.

Recall Sylvia Law's and Andrew Koppelman's argument that sexual orientation discrimination is a form of sex discrimination. How does Rich's concept of compulsory heterosexuality play into their argument? Under Rich's theory, does society's stigmatization of *gay men* undermine the possibility of *women's* liberation?

SECTION 2

POSTMODERN THEORIES

Section 2 presents a selection of theories that we have categorized for the sake of simplicity as "postmodern." The meaning of this now widely-used term is contested, but we use it to denote a variety of overlapping theoretical approaches: social constructionist, Foucauldian, poststructuralist, recent feminist theory, and what has become known as queer theory. Postmodern theories have revolutionized how we understand sexuality and gender.

PART A. SEXUALITY AS A SOCIAL CONSTRUCTION[a]

Interpreting the Kinsey data, Mary McIntosh, "The Homosexual Role," 16 Soc. Prob. 182 (1968), reprinted in *Forms of Desire: Sexual Orientation and the Homosexual Role* 25 (Edward Stein ed. 1990), asked, Why is it that "sexual orientation" is considered such an important object of study? She maintained that sexual orientation is a role created by society, and indeed created for socially regulatory purposes. McIntosh challenged the sexologists not as bad scientists (that was Kinsey's and Hooker's critique), but as bit players in a larger cultural drama of which they were but dimly aware.

McIntosh said that there is no transhistorical phenomenon that can be called "homosexuality." Much has been made in the last generation of her suggestive point. Michel Foucault's three-volume *History of Sexuality* (published in English 1978, 1985, 1986) developed this idea interestingly (without any attribution to McIntosh, however), arguing that "sexuality" per se was unknown in the ancient world and was the consequence of a confessional dialectic that has grown ever more intense in the modern world. Volume one of the *History* (the *Introduction*) treats the early modern and modern periods and maintains that "sexuality" itself is a consequence of an ongoing and increasingly focused attention to the body by priests, doctors, psychiatrists, and bureaucrats. Foucault explores the archaeology of sexual-

a. The account of Foucault draws mainly from his *Introduction*, volume one of *History of Sexuality* (Robert Hurley trans. 1978), and from his essay "Afterword: The Subject and the Power," in *Beyond Structuralism and Hermeneutics* (Hubert L. Dreyfuss & Paul Rabinow eds., 1982). Particularly useful secondary sources are Vikki Bell, *Interrogat-* *ing Incest: Feminism, Foucault and the Law* (1993); Celia Kitzinger, *The Social Construction of Lesbianism* (1987); David Macey, *The Lives of Michel Foucault* (1995). Barnett McGowan (Georgetown University Law Center, Class of 1997) researched and helped draft the essay that follows.

ity (its genealogy as an idea) through several interrelated inquiries and critiques.

1. FOUCAULT'S CRITIQUE OF THE REPRESSIVE HYPOTHESIS

One of Foucault's central and most provocative insights was to challenge the conventional wisdom that the relationship between power and sex is one of repression. It is a staple of popular thinking that uptight or religious societies repressed sex, and that in the last several decades, sexual rebels have sought liberation from these edicts. Not so, said Foucault. He perceived a very different history.

Foucault started with the seventeenth-century Christian practice of the confessional. A traditional view might see the confessional only as a moment when the church exercises its power over the penitent, who is required to divulge any sins against ecclesiastical proscriptions. Foucault, however, describes the confessional as the practice that "prescribed as a fundamental duty the task of passing everything having to do with sex through the endless mill of speech." (*Introduction* 21.) This method of transforming sex into discourse became "a rule for everyone" and thus a prime example of what Foucault calls "an incitement" to talk about sex. "This is the essential thing: that Western man has been drawn for three centuries to the task of telling everything concerning his sex" (*id.* at 23). Thus, while laws and customs may have formally prohibited certain sexual behaviors and effectively limited sexual speech in many situations (between parent and child, for example), "at the level of discourses and their domains .. the opposite phenomenon occurred[:] ... a proliferation of discourses concerned with sex" (*id.* at 18).

The technique of generating "confessional" speech or sex-talk was later reinforced and expanded by mechanisms of power other than the church. Beginning in the eighteenth century, governments started to understand that they were dealing not just with subjects or citizens, but with a "population." At the heart of the issue of population was sex. Thus agencies of the state developed an interest in birth rates, age of marriage, illegitimacy and procreative practices. In short, sexual conduct began to be understood as having a direct relationship to the wealth and security of nations. "It was essential that the state know what was happening with its citizens' sex, and the use they made of it, but also that each individual be capable of controlling the use he made of it. Between the state and the individual, sex became an issue, and a public issue no less; a whole web of discourses, special knowledges, analyses and injunctions settled upon it." (*Id.* at 26.)

Foucault cites the (French) school system of the 1700s as an example of an institutional system in which, on the surface, sex was eradicated but where, *sub rosa,* it was a driving force. "The space for classes, the shape of the tables, the planning of the recreation lessons, the distribution of the dormitories (with or without partitions, with or without curtains), the rules for monitoring bedtime and sleep periods—all this referred, in the most prolix manner, to the sexuality of children" (*Introduction* 28).[1]   It was deemed of paramount importance to monitor the children (boys) for any signs of sexuality, and to take all possible precautions to prevent masturbation.   Because of the perceived dangers of masturbation (onanism), "devices of surveillance were installed; traps were laid for compelling admissions; inexhaustible and corrective discourses were imposed; parents and teachers were alerted, and left with the suspicion that all children were guilty, and with the fear of being themselves at fault if their suspicions were not sufficiently strong; they were kept in readiness in the face of this recurrent danger; their conduct was prescribed and their pedagogy recodified; an entire medico-sexual regime took hold of the family milieu" (*id.* at 42).

In the nineteenth century, medical discourse became the primary arena in which sexuality was penalized and stigmatized, yet also simultaneously incited, monitored, and commented upon.   In a critical development, the mode of the confessional was medicalized, and in turn reconceptualized as therapeutic.   Recall that modern sexology acquired its professional status during the Victorian period.   Officially, Victorians adhered to the "triple edict of taboo, nonexistence and silence" about sex. (*id.* at 3)   But, as we saw in Chapter 2, that era also witnessed an unprecedented explosion of detailed examination, analysis, and speculation about these supposedly taboo topics.

In sum, Foucault interpreted the history of sexuality not as a simple story of the repression of sex, but as a much more complicated process "that spreads [sex] over the surface of things and bodies, arouses it, draws it out and bids it speak, implants it in reality and enjoins it to tell the truth." (*id.* at 72).

2.   SYSTEMS OF POWER

This is interesting, you may be thinking, but what about all those repressive laws?   Foucault saw power systems as more complex than law, and rejected the underlying assumptions of a law-centered view of the world.   He critiqued the precepts of what he called "juridico-discursive power" as naive.   Power is not simply the state, he wrote, but resides in a multiplicity of interconnecting (and sometimes contradictory) systems.   For example, he believed that the educational, religious, and medical systems exercised far greater power with respect to sexuality than did the law.

---

1.   *Règlement de police pour les lycées* (1809) (quoted in *Introduction* 28 n. 12) sets forth a regime that Foucault maintains was primarily geared toward preventing masturbation:

art. 67: "There shall always be, during class and study hours, an instructor watching the exterior, so as to prevent students who have gone out to relieve themselves from stopping and congregating.

art. 68: "After the evening prayer, the students will be conducted back to the dormitory, where the schoolmasters will put them to bed at once.

art. 69: "The masters will not retire except after having made certain that every student is in bed.

art. 70: "The beds shall be separated by partitions two meters in height.   The dormitories shall be illuminated during the night."

Where others might see a social/sexual structure dichotomized as freedom and repression or the individual versus the state, Foucault saw "a veritable 'technology' of sex" with multiple and conflicting players and effects. (*Introduction* 90.)

In general, Foucault understood power as a complex web.

It seems to me that power must be understood in the first instance as the multiplicity of force relations immanent in the sphere in which they operate and which constitute their own organization; as the process which, through ceaseless struggles and confrontations, transforms, strengthens, or reverses them; as the support which these force relations find in one another, thus forming a chain or a system, or on the contrary, the disjunctions and contradictions, which isolate them from one another; and lastly, as the strategies in which they take effect, whose general design or institutional crystallization is embodied in the state apparatus, in the formulation of the law, in the various social hegemonies. * * * [P]ower is not an institution, and not a structure; neither is it a certain strength we are endowed with; it is the name that one attributes to a complex strategical situation in a particular society. (*Id.* at 92–93.)

In short, power comes from everywhere (not simply from the top down). Systems of power relations ("force relations") enable and produce specific discourses, such as the discourses on sex. Discourses, or systems of understanding and practice, implement power relations, but also create points of resistance. "Discourse transmits and produces power; it reinforces it, but also undermines and exposes it, renders it fragile and makes it possible to thwart it." (*Id.* at 101.) A hegemonic (or dominant) discourse that presents homosexuality as an illness, for example, not only propagates that idea, but also can incite reaction, rebuttal, and rebellion.

Key to Foucault's theory is the belief that the operation of power is not simply prohibitory or negative. Power systems *produce* sexuality as well as prohibit it.

3. SEXUALITY AS A DISCURSIVE PRODUCTION

As the "discursive explosion" regarding sex continued through the eighteenth and nineteenth centuries, its subjects (and objects) began to jell. Foucault perceived a gradual organization of power-knowledge around four subjects: the "hysterization" of women's bodies (in which women's bodies were analyzed "as being thoroughly saturated with sexuality"); a "pedagogization" of children's sex; "a socialization of procreative sex"; and "a psychiatrization of perverse pleasure." (*Introduction* at 104–105.) What occurred was nothing less than

the very production of sexuality. Sexuality must not be thought of as a kind of natural given which power tries to hold in check, or as an obscure domain which knowledge tries gradually to uncover. It is the name that can be given to a historical construct: not a furtive reality that is difficult to grasp, but a great surface network in which the stimulation of bodies, the intensification of pleasures, the incitement to discourse, the formation of special knowledges, the strengthening of controls and resistances, are linked to one another, in accordance with a few major strategies of knowledge and power. (*Id.* at 105–06.)

In other words, the very same regulatory discourse that is conventionally described as repressive actually *produced* what we understand as "sexuality."

One specific example of this was the production of (the idea of) homosexuality. In analyzing the sexologists' study of "perverse pleasures" and what Foucault called "peripheral sexualities," he made his now famous observation dating the invention of homosexuality (as distinct from same-sex sexual practices) as a nineteenth century event:

> This new persecution of the peripheral sexualities entailed an *incorporation of perversions* and a new *specification of individuals*. As defined by the ancient civil or canonical codes, sodomy was a category of forbidden acts; their perpetrator was nothing more than the juridical subject of them. The nineteenth-century homosexual became a personage, a past, a case history, and a childhood. * * * Nothing that went into his total composition was unaffected by his sexuality. * * * The sodomite had been a temporary aberration; the homosexual was now a species. (*Id.* at 42–43, emphasis in the original.)

Recall the criticisms we examined of the *Hardwick* decision (Chapter 1, Section 2), especially of the extent to which Justice White conflated homosexuality with sodomy. Consider also that some of the arguments advocating equality for gay people are framed in terms suggestive of a view of the homosexual as a distinct type of person. We tend to think of the *Hardwick* decision and a gay rights argument as extreme opposites. Foucault, himself a gay man, might critique both, however, as representing simply the flip sides of a coin, both equally trapped inside one discursive system.

We hope this discussion gives you some understanding of the very complicated way in which sexual discourse operates, as well as the larger context in which Foucault comprehends this system. A further and important feature of that larger context is Foucault's tentative theory of sexuality as a dynamic system, and its implications for the future.

Before *sexuality* became an important system, *alliance* was the primary system for understanding and organizing households (in rural, nonwestern societies alliance is still typically the primary organizational system). In contrast to sexuality, a new and destabilizing system, alliance was a longstanding and homeostatic system: its mechanism was to establish ties of blood and marriage, and its goal was to protect and reproduce the traditional patriarchal family (*Introduction* 105–06). The modern era may be characterized by the eclipse of the regime of alliance and its gradual supplantation by the regime of sexuality.

The family is the situs of this transition, and now its battleground. Premodern society viewed the family as the fundamental unit of society, and individuals were formed in the shadow of family ties. One's identity was framed in relation to one's parents, one's spouse, and kinship group. Where families had earlier left children to their own devices in exploring genitals and gender, bourgeois families of the early modern era became highly attentive to children's masturbation and so forth. The attention showered on this matter not only sexualized certain body parts, but also sexualized the family itself. Thus the family, the apex of alliance, became the birthplace of sexuality, which now often overshadows alliance as the basis of individual identity.

The discourse of sexuality has hardly abated in western culture, and Foucault saw its productiveness only multiplying in the future. Traditional ties of family and kinship will be evermore overtaken by ties of pleasure and corporality. Foucault believed that the future would dissolve many of the boundaries that we cleave to insistently now (such as the significance of sexual orientation) and would multiply the categories of pleasure. In his most visionary moment, he predicted "nothing less than a transgression of laws, a lifting of prohibitions, an irruption of speech, a reinstating of pleasure within reality, and a whole new economy in the mechanisms of power will be required." (*Introduction* 5.)

PROBLEM 3–1

STRATEGIES FOR CHALLENGING DISCRIMINATION

Consider the insights of Foucauldian theories for the following issues: sodomy and abortion laws (Chapter 1); immigration law's former exclusion of prostitutes and homosexuals and its current exclusion of people with AIDS (Chapter 2); the exclusion of women from combat and the barring of lesbians, gay men, and bisexuals from service in the armed forces (Chapter 4); laws protecting against sex and sexual orientation discrimination in the workplace (Chapter 10) and anti-gay initiatives repealing some of those laws (Chapter 8); and the desirability of same-sex marriage (Chapter 9). Choose any issue and think about what strategy would be most useful for challenging existing norms. Refine your answer in light of, or response to, the following essay.

Janet E. Halley, Sexual Orientation and the Politics of Biology: A Critique of the Argument From Immutability

46 *Stanford Law Review* 503, 556–60, 563–65 (1994).*

Essentialisms differ in the depth or "thickness" of their causality: Weak essentialism merely claims that some entity (here, homosexuality) is an "irreducible, unchanging [in the Aristotelian sense] and therefore

* Copyright © 1994 by the Board of Trustees of the Leland Stanford Junior University. Reprinted by permission.

constitutive" characteristic, while strong essentialism gives that definitional core not only a cause but a cause in nature. * * *

Different versions of constructivism differ in the depth or thickness of the thing they claim is caused by socially and historically contingent circumstances and activities. In a wonderfully clear essay differentiating constructivisms in the study of human sexuality, Carole S. Vance ["Social Construction Theory: Problems in the History of Sexuality," in *Homosexuality, Which Homosexuality?* 13, 21 (Dennis Altman et al. eds. 1989)] argues that constructivists "differ in their willingness to imagine *what* was constructed." * * * Vance discerns five different forms of constructivism, each with a more expansive claim as to what is constructed than the last. The following paragraphs further explicate Vance's essentialism/constructivism spectrum.

Social meanings constructivism. This approach regards sexual object choice as fixed. The categories homosexual and heterosexual are good descriptions of all human beings, cross-culturally and transhistorically. Sexual object choice in turn dictates certain patterns of behavior, which also, therefore, appear in all human societies without alteration in their form. But different cultures and historical contexts give these differences in object choice and the attendant range of activities different social and experiential meanings. Activities that are thought normal in one setting are taboo or criminalized in another. Thus, in one culture it might be a sign of maternal affection for a mother to kiss her infant son's penis, while in another the same act would be deemed child abuse. In the former culture, this act would make a woman feel like a good mother; in the latter, like a transgressor. This shift in levels of social approval might mean that in the first culture a lot of women fellate their sons, but some in the second, who really relish this ritual, would be tempted to do it even at the cost of sanctions. The behavioral raw material underlying that difference in valuation does not vary: A person who would enjoy this act in the first culture would enjoy it in the second because she comes hardwired for female/male fellatio (of a particular kind).

Behavioral constructivism. This approach [also] regards sexual object choice as fixed across cultures and historical eras. In the most common version of this approach, some people are predominantly disposed to have sex with people of their own sex; some are predominantly disposed to have sex with people of the so-called opposite sex. That much is determined by nature. But the behavioral patterns available for satisfying these predispositions vary across time and place. *A fortiori*, the meanings attributed to sexual variety differ, as do the feelings they arouse. * * *

Behavioral constructivism as Vance configures it is rather specific about what aspect of sexuality remains essential: gender-of-object-choice. A weaker form of behavioral constructivism is distinguishable, however, in which some *object* is intrinsically and inherently preferred, but it is not necessarily congruent with sex or gender or even a particular kind of person.

Weak behavioral constructivism acknowledges the powerful reality of sexual-orientation categories as we know them, but posits that some *other* form or forms of human variance are primary. It thus challenges us to imagine *beyond* the sexual-orientation categories homo- and heterosexual. Eve Kosofsky Sedgwick provides a suggestive list of object choices that might definitively distinguish people, but that our culture either ignores or sorts only roughly into categories differentiated by gender-of-object-choice:

- Some people spend a lot of time thinking about sex, others little.

- Some people like to have a lot of sex, others little or none.

- Many people have their richest mental/emotional involvement with sexual acts that they don't do, or even don't *want* to do.

- For some people, it is important that sex be embedded in contexts resonant with meaning, narrative, and connectedness with other aspects of their life; for other people, it is important that they not be; to others it doesn't occur that they might be. * * *

Gender-of-object-choice constructivism. In this approach, sexuality—the capacity for a coherent, patterned organization of sex drive or sexual appetite—is predetermined and invariant, but sexual object choice, the associated behavioral forms, and their social and experiential meanings remain available for social adaptation. At this point constructivism abandons the assumption that the terms "homosexual" and "heterosexual" necessarily describe human sexual predispositions. Though this category is conceptually open, most historians of sexuality who pursue constructivism of a more thoroughgoing kind than behavioral constructivism develop the stronger constructivist hypothesis which I dub sexuality constructivism.

Sexuality constructivism. This approach, inaugurated by Foucault's *History of Sexuality, Vol. I*, but declining to extend constructivism as far as he did in that work, distinguishes between a raw physical capacity for erotic pleasure and the organization of that capacity into a coherent, patterned element of the self. The former is part of being human, but the latter is the product of complex historical contingencies which, once in place, are as inescapable as the capacity for orgasm. Object choice, behavioral repertoire, social meaning, and sexual emotion all fall within the domain of sexuality, and are produced by its means. * * *

[David] Halperin [*One Hundred Years of Homosexuality*] states that, "[u]nlike sex, which is a natural fact, sexuality is a cultural production: It represents the *appropriation* of the human body and of its erogenous zones by an ideological discourse." Sexuality is relatively autonomous from gender, and "[t]hat is precisely what makes sexuality alien to the spirit of ancient Mediterranean cultures," where "sexual typologies generally derived their criteria for categorizing people not from sex but from gender." Halperin does not question that "there really are, nowadays, homosexual and heterosexual people . . . : they really do desire what they do, and that is a *fact* about them." But this is a weak essentialist form produced by social rather than natural causes.

Sex constructivism. This may be the most thorough view of constructivism in the area of sexuality yet articulated. It assumes that the sheer recognition of certain bodily sensations *as sexual* is constructed. This is not merely to say, for instance, that living in a culture that "implants" "sex drive" would be a different thing than living in a culture in which sex originates in an "appetite." It is to insist that culture supplies the very terms for understanding bodily sex, in or between persons, as distinct from other modes of physical configuration, action, or sensation. * * * The equivalent of "sex constructivism" in the study of gender is, perhaps, Monique Wittig's response to the question whether she had a vagina, that she did not. * * *

[Halley's interesting conceptual exercise also has a practical punch line. In litigating the validity of laws that discriminate on the basis of sexual orientation, Halley urges that pro-gay essentialists and pro-gay constructivists settle on a strategy whose stance is behavioral constructivist, assuming that object choice may be essential and indeed biological, and that the related behavior and its meanings belong to the domain of culture. This stance would provide common ground where each side would give up little conceptual ground that it did not have to forfeit in any event. Pro-gay essentialists, such as scientists Richard Pillard and Dean Hamer, concede that even the most ambitious reading of the "hard-wired homosexuals" science (Chapter 2, Section 3) does not support a strong essentialist position. Few pro-gay constructivists go as far as Halperin or Foucault, and no one denies that in the short term there is much that is experienced as hard-wired.]

Indeed, at the threshold of suspect class analysis, strong essentialist models of sexual-orientation identity are a positive impediment. Several federal courts have held that *Hardwick* forecloses heightened scrutiny because criminalizable "sodomy *defines the class*" for which protection is sought. Though litigators have the option of attacking *Hardwick* directly, it is most likely that they will prefer in equal protection cases to "litigate around" it. Litigators can refute the extension of *Hardwick* by attacking its legal premise, that due process precedents apply to equal protection cases. And they can attack its definition of the class.

To make the latter argument, constructivists and essentialists alike should shed unnecessary definitional claims that undermine the distinction between sodomy and the class of homosexuals. Social meanings constructivism, which installs a predetermined behavioral repertoire in its natural categories "homosexual" and "heterosexual," actually *supports* the extension of *Hardwick*. *A fortiori*, unmediated strong essentialism does the same: It posits the same unbroken equation between homosexuals and their behavioral repertoire that disables social meanings constructivism. Behavioral constructivism will work only if it acknowledges that, in our culture, many elements of sexual-orientation identity operate in tandem with and independently of behavior to constitute and to populate the classification homosexual.

The constructivist view that sexual orientation is mutable because of slippages and rearrangements of desire, fantasy, behavior, private identity, and public identity is possibly the strongest refutation of a definition of homosexuality that makes sodomy its essence. Essentialists should be able to agree with this view as long as it falls short of its outermost reach, that *no one's* subjective sexual orientation accurately reflects the gender-of-object- choice entertained by his or her desire and fantasy. Unlike pro-gay essentialist uses of the argument from immutability, which at least theoretically exclude some gay men, lesbians, and bisexuals from the protected zone of heightened scrutiny, a pro-gay argument that distinguishes *Hardwick* by emphasizing the variety of gay, lesbian, bisexual, and queer identities embraces the most unwavering class member too.

Behavioral constructivism is also rich in representational resources for building positive arguments that heightened scrutiny is warranted. On a process-based analysis, behavioral constructivism allows advocates to focus on identity dynamics where they pinch: at the closet door. The process-based argument emphasizes that the volatilities and fixities of public identity make it exceedingly difficult for gay men, lesbians, bisexuals, and their friends to enter fully into political debate. Too many gay men, lesbians, and bisexuals remain silent so that they can keep their jobs; too many sympathetic heterosexuals remain silent so that no one will suppose they are queer. Social-meanings constructivism, because it assumes that public identity univocally and transparently reflects intrinsic sexual orientation, lacks the conceptual apparatus to describe these political impediments. Behavioral constructivism, because it is hospitable to the claim that public homosexual identity is affected by cultural forces, can support the further claim that the resulting social patterns deprive pro-gay advocates of unimpeded access to the political process.

PART B.   FEMINISM AND FOUCAULT[c]

Many American scholars have taken an interest in Foucault's work. The feminist treatment of Foucault has proven to be the most intellectually lively. Foucault's analysis of power relations simultaneously criticizes the feminist emancipation agenda, while providing fresh tools for the critical evaluation of patriarchy. The relationship between Foucault and feminism has not been one way. Feminists have presented some powerful challenges to Foucault's theory on sex, power, and truth, making it less contradictory

---

c. The works most helpful to us in this regard include Vikki Bell, *Interrogating Incest: Feminism, Foucault and the Law* (1993); Judith Butler, *Gender Trouble: Feminism and the Subversion of Identity* (1990); Susan Hekman, *Gender and Knowledge: Elements of a Postmodern Feminism* (1990); Carol Smart, *Feminism and the Power of Law* (1989); Ann Snitow et al., *Powers of Desire:* *The Politics of Sexuality* (1984); Biddy Martin, "Feminism, Criticism and Foucault," and other essays in *Feminism and Foucault: Reflections on Resistance* (Irene Diamond & Lee Quinby eds., 1988); Nancy Hartsock, "Foucault on Power: A Theory for Women?" in *Feminism/Postmodernism* (Linda J. Nicholson ed., 1990).

for the effort. Consider the following lines of dialogue between feminism and Foucault.

To begin with, there is much that Foucault and leading feminist theories have in common, for both lines of thought are critical of the traditional wisdom about sex and sexuality. Foucault provides feminism another vocabulary for situating and problematizing the sexologists' work. Most of the sexologists, Krafft–Ebing and Freud in particular, have insisted that women's sexual pleasure is tied to the male penis. Both feminists and Foucault critique this claim as deriving from any "natural science" and insist that the thought must be linked with other power relations, such as the traditional subordination of women to men in western society. For Foucault as for most feminists, there is nothing unnatural about sex between two women, and the hysteria it creates in men is related to threats those men see to their power, specifically, their monopoly on female sexuality.

Foucault's thought is not very helpful, however, in ignoring the *gendering aspects of sexuality*. As Vikki Bell puts it,

> Foucault's central interest is with the production of the concept of sexuality and categories of sexuality ('homosexual', 'heterosexual', 'paedophiliac', etc.) through knowledge/power networks. By contrast, feminists are more interested in those knowledges which create a differential relationship between men and women, or that act against women as a group. Knowledges which suggest that women need men in order to experience sexual satisfaction, which situate lesbianism as a deviant sexual choice, which depict masculine sexuality as inherently predatory, have been considered by feminists not simply as powerful knowledges that constrain all individuals, but as powerful knowledges that differentially constrain women. Crucially, the central concern of feminism is the way in which these ways of understanding sexuality have operated to make women subordinate to men as individuals and as a group.
>
> The major feminist criticism of Foucault's thesis on sexuality therefore is that he fails to consider what one might term the *gendering* aspects of sexuality. * * * What he fails to do is consider how the strategies of sexuality affect the relationship *between* men and women as gendered individuals. (Bell 26–27.)

Foucault does not view the operation of power as so consistently oppressing one group as feminist theorists do. Recall Catharine MacKinnon's argument that the social construction of male and female sexuality is the key to gender oppression.

Foucault, in turn, poses a critique of early feminist theory, namely, its too-simple understanding of power and its naive belief in truth. To the extent that some feminists believe that "patriarchy" unifies traditional power structures and that the feminist project is to overthrow patriarchy and thereby to liberate women's own true selves, Foucault would dissent. He argues that feminists have no better access to "truth" than the

Victorians and that the feminist emancipatory project is merely the flip side of traditional views that sex is essential and univocal. In short, feminist resistance to the Victorians is trapped in basically the same vocabulary.

A different strain in early feminist thought, however, was grounded in radical challenges to the very sorts of fixed identity categories that Foucault found wanting. According to him,

> [T]he real strength of the women's liberation movements is not that of having laid claim to the specificity of their sexuality and the rights pertaining to it, but that they have actually departed from the discourse conducted within the apparatuses of sexuality. Ultimately, it is a veritable movement of de-sexualisation, a displacement effected in relation to the sexual centering of the problem, formulating the demand for forms of culture, discourse, language and so on, which are no longer part of that rigid assignation and pinning-down to their sex which they had initially in some sense been politically obliged to accept in order to make themselves heard.

Michel Foucault, *Power/Knowledge: Selected Interviews and Other Writings* 219–20 (Colin Gordon, ed., 1980). Note how Foucault's analysis mixes concepts of sex, sexuality, and, implicitly, gender.

Consider Judith Butler's elaboration. Sex for the Victorians was univocal insofar as there was a simple identity between a person and her sex— "one is one's sex" (Butler 94). The Victorians argued that sex was the "continuous cause and signification of bodily pleasures." Thus sex was biological and not social. This view produced a distorted understanding of sex, by essentializing it. For the social constructionist, sex is not a cause, but rather an effect of "an open and complex historical system of discourse and power." Sex is social, not biological; and feminism misses this by taking sex as the starting point of its analysis. By accepting sex as the root cause of female domination, some feminist theory fails to grasp that sex is merely an effect of female domination. Some feminists too quickly agree with the patriarch that sex is the reason men dominate women, for she or he should see that men dominate women through the creation of sex. By accepting this effect as a cause, feminism legitimates the regulatory strategy of patriarchy, and is thus self-defeating.[d] (*Id.* at 94–95.)

A Foucauldian approach emphasizes a more complex understanding of power. Some feminist thought, especially in the early stages, seemed to operate under traditional views about power—what Foucault calls the *juridical* (or legal) model of power: power acts in negative (prohibitory) ways, repressing the illicit; power flows from a central hierarchical source; hence power can be overthrown by the powerless. If, as Foucault imagines, power is "omnipresent," productive rather than prohibitory, and normaliz-

---

d. Recall the Johns Hopkins studies of heterogeneity of sex-markers in some people (Chapter 2, Section 3), which might be read in support of Butler's notion that the designation of sex (It's a boy!) is itself a discourse and not a starting point.

ing rather than repressive, the feminist target (patriarchy) becomes more elusive and the role of the state (protect women against patriarchy) more ambiguous.

Butler's expansion of Foucault might be said to undermine the feminist agenda, basically by removing its subject. However theoretically attractive such a stance might be, its effect might be politically enervating. On the other hand, as Susan Hekman has argued, "the assumption that political action, to be valid, must be founded in absolute values is precisely the assumption that Foucault is challenging" (Hekman 180). The current situation of women is an "unstable truth" that can be the basis for political action and resistance, even if centuries from now our descendants might wonder why we became so anxious about gender as well as sexuality (recall the delphic conclusion of volume one of the *History of Sexuality*). Feminism might be viewed as a resistance discourse, which even if unstable is useful for an often silenced group to be heard (Bell 55–56). As Biddy Martin puts it,

> Our task is to deconstruct, to undo our own meanings and categories, the identities and the positions from which we intervene at any given point so as not to close the question of woman and discourse around new certainties and absolutes. We cannot afford to refuse to take a political stance 'which pins us to our sex' for the sake of abstract theoretical correctness, but we can refuse to be content with fixed identities or to universalize ourselves as revolutionary subjects. (Martin 16.)

PROBLEM 3–2

LAW, FOUCAULT, FEMINISM, RAPE, STATUTORY RAPE, AND INCEST

The criminal codes in virtually all the United States prohibit each of the following three situses of sex: rape (sexual assault), coercive sex against the will of one of the partners; statutory rape, where one of the partners is under the age of consent; and incest, where the partners are closely related. Consider the following case which involves all three of these issues, and consider further how this case illustrates the particular ways our culture has constructed sex and sexuality. Note that the defendant was charged with only one offense (incest), even though the facts also support a charge of rape.

State v. Marvin K. Kaiser

Washington Court of Appeals, 1983.
34 Wash. App. 559, 663 P.2d 839.

■ MUNSON, ACTING CHIEF JUDGE.

Marvin K. Kaiser appeals his incest conviction, RCW 9A.64.020.[1] He contends the trial court erred in admitting his confession, the evidence was insufficient, improper evidence was admitted at trial, and the incest statute denied him equal protection. We affirm.

Mr. Kaiser was charged with having committed incest with his 16–year-old stepdaughter. On May 13 and 14, Mr. Kaiser met with a police detective to informally discuss the accusation. On May 15, 1981, Mr. Kaiser was advised of his rights as required by *Miranda v. Arizona*, 384 U.S. 436 (1966), and progeny. He indicated he wished to speak to an attorney. The questioning stopped; the detective made immediate arrangements for Mr. Kaiser to meet with a public defender who was present at the jail. Mr. Kaiser and the public defender discussed the charge for 20 to 25 minutes. Mr. Kaiser stated the public defender told him the crime was a felony and advised him not to make a statement.

Mr. Kaiser returned to the detective and decided to make a statement. The detective gave him the *Miranda* warnings from a printed form which Mr. Kaiser initialed and signed. The detective then taped an oral confession from Mr. Kaiser which also began with a waiver of all *Miranda* rights. Mr. Kaiser stated he entered the stepdaughter's bed against her will, disrobed her, engaged in full intercourse for a brief time, realized he had erred, and left. At the end of the statement, Mr. Kaiser signified the statement was true, he understood his *Miranda* rights and waived them, and no promises had been made. [The trial judge held that the confession was voluntary and therefore admissible against Kaiser, a finding the appeals court affirmed.]
* * *

At the subsequent nonjury trial, the stepdaughter testified Mr. Kaiser had engaged in sexual intercourse against her wishes. She was asked whether her stepfather put his penis into her vagina. She replied that he had and that she knew this because of the pain. On cross examination, she was asked whether there was penetration. She replied, "I can't be sure."

Mr. Kaiser denied the event all together. He again explained the false statement was given to the detective to protect the family from publicity.

The stepdaughter's boyfriend testified she told him the following day that she had been raped by her stepfather. The boyfriend indicated she was distraught and cried for over an hour and a half before telling him; they later reported the incident to school officials.

The detective who received Mr. Kaiser's statement was asked by Mr. Kaiser's counsel whether he had recorded in any statement by the step-daughter anything which showed penetration had occurred. From her

---

1. Former RCW 9A.64.020:

    "(1) A person is guilty of incest if he engages in sexual intercourse with a person whom he knows to be related to him, either legitimately or illegitimately, as an ancestor, descendant, brother, or sister of either the whole or the half blood.

    "(2) *As used in this section, 'descendant' includes stepchildren and adopted children under eighteen years of age.*" (Italics ours.)

statement, the detective testified she had told him Mr. Kaiser inserted his penis in her vagina. The detective testified he explained the terms to her prior to the statement and she stated she understood them.

The trial court found Mr. Kaiser guilty of incest, reasoning that where the stepdaughter's testimony was equivocal the confession was not. Because the trial court could not accept Mr. Kaiser's stated reasons for making a false statement, the court accepted the statement over the in-court testimony. The court found the stepdaughter's version to be more credible. * * *

Mr. Kaiser * * * contends the stepdaughter's answer on cross examination raised a reasonable doubt. Her testimony was not as equivocal as first appears. On direct, she gave no doubt penetration had occurred. She may not have known the meaning of the word "penetration" because there is a question of whether she knew the meaning of the word "erection". This confusion was not clarified.

Even if a doubt remained after her testimony, Mr. Kaiser's statement and the testimony of both the boyfriend and the detective bolstered her credibility. Although Mr. Kaiser's statement differed from the stepdaughter's testimony in the degree of violence, it essentially agreed on the specific act of intercourse. * * *

Mr. Kaiser finally contends the incest statute denies him equal protection of the law. His argument appears to be twofold: (1) because the "object of the statute was obviously to prevent a procreation of children which may be affected by the relationship of the parties who are closer than second cousins," the inclusion of stepchildren bears no rational relationship to a legitimate governmental objective; and (2) nonconsensual intercourse is punished until age 16 under the statutory rape statutes[2]; equal protection is denied under the incest statute because even consensual intercourse is forbidden to age 18.

Historically, incest was prohibited by ecclesiastical canon; now, it is prohibited by statute. The statutory schemes differ; some states prevent illicit intercourse by consanguinity while others also include relation by affinity. R. Perkins, *Criminal Law*, ch. 5, § 1(c), at 383–84 (2d ed. 1969); M. Barnes, *Clark & Marshall on Crimes* § 11.05, at 770 (7th ed. 1967); 2 C. Torcia, *Wharton on Criminal Law* § 245, at 403–04 (14th ed. 1979).

Prevention of mutated birth is only one reason for these statutes. The crime is also punished to promote and protect family harmony, to protect children from the abuse of parental authority, and because society cannot function in an orderly manner when age distinctions, generations, sentiments and roles in families are in conflict. *Clark & Marshall, supra* at 770; 2 C. Torcia, *Wharton on Criminal Law* § 242, at 400 (14th ed. 1979). Thus, the statute bears a rational relation to a legitimate governmental objective.

---

2.   RCW 9A.44.090(1):

"(1) A person over eighteen years of age is guilty of statutory rape in the third degree when such person engages in sexual intercourse with another person, not married to the perpetrator, who is fourteen years of age or older but less than sixteen years old."

The legislation bears a reasonable and substantial relationship to the health, safety, morals or welfare of the public. We hold the statute is therefore constitutional.

Mr. Kaiser notes consensual intercourse is not punishable after a female reaches age 16 except under the incest statute where even consensual intercourse is forbidden to age 18. He then asserts: "Had the defendant chosen merely to live with the mother of Connie, he would have incurred no penalties because of his act of intercourse with the child, ..." Disregarding the fact that this intercourse was not consensual, and was therefore punishable as third degree rape, such a distinction would deny equal protection only if Mr. Kaiser could show the Legislature did not have a legitimate interest in discriminating between such individuals. As noted earlier, incest is a crime which affects the individuals, society, and, to a degree greater than other crimes, the family. The additional 2 years can be seen as an important protection for the family. The State has a legitimate interest in protecting children from parental abuse for an additional 2 years. Whether by consanguinity or affinity, parents have tremendous emotional and material leverage, even after a child reaches 16, which may not exist outside the home. The distinction is reasonable.

Mr. Kaiser's conviction is affirmed.

FOUCAULT v. FEMINISM IN *KAISER*

Segregate for a moment the (glaring) issue of rape, and consider separating the three issues presented in this case.

1. The Incest Issue. Incest is the tension point of Foucault's overlapping systems of individual identity: it is the key taboo in the system of kinship alliance, but the system of sexuality inspires and generates it as part of the family dynamics which literally inculcate sexuality. "[Incest] is manifested as a thing that is strictly forbidden in the family insofar as the latter functions as a deployment of alliance; but it is also a thing that is continually demanded in order for the family to be a hotbed of sexual incitement." (Foucault, *Introduction* 109.) Thus the incest taboo is not at all the old-fashioned idea moderns make it out to be—its intensity is owed to its central spot in both regimes, of sexuality and alliance. Note, for example, the centrality of the incest taboo for psychoanalysis; Freud is best known for his metaphorical statement of the relationship between family and sexuality—the Oedipus complex.

Consider the implications of Foucault's thought for *Kaiser* and for feminism. Foucault's theory of sexuality provides an interesting defense (only to incest, not to rape) and a fascinating problem with *Kaiser*. By making incest illegal, the state is announcing the convergence between the old regime of alliance and the new regime of sexuality: both are threatened by incest, and their coinciding concerns give incest prohibitions their particular power. On the other hand, criminalizing incest, and making it the occasion for the drama of a court proceeding, ought to intensify the family as a situs for sexuality.

In *Kaiser*, the incest is between a father and a (step)daughter. This is the typical scenario, and its typicality has generated enormous feminist interest. Feminists have encouraged women and girls to tell their stories of family (father) abuse and have encouraged mothers and prosecutors to punish men (fathers) who have sex with daughters and stepdaughters. Foucault would question this strategy. Does it not yield the same sort of discourse that produces rather than suppresses sexuality? Is it possible that prohibitory laws make incest "sexy" for men like Marvin Kaiser? How would feminist theorists answer this charge? See Vikki Bell, *Interrogating Incest: Feminism, Foucault and the Law* ch. 4 (1993), for an excellent discussion.

It has been argued by feminist writers that the incest taboo is not quite the taboo that Foucault makes it out to be. Although the taboo seems to be a genuine deterrent to mother-son sex, fathers apparently have sex often with daughters and stepdaughters. Judith Lewis Herman & Lisa Hirschman, *Father-Daughter Incest* (1981). Some feminist writers have conceptualized the asymmetrical incest taboo as reflecting the system by which men dominate women: the mother relinquishes her sexual feelings for the son, who enters into the father's world, while the father remains free to initiate the daughter into a sexualized world where men call the shots. Elizabeth Ward, *Father-Daughter Rape* (1984). These feminists, therefore, understand incest differently from Foucault: incest is important to the system of alliance, not just of family and kinship ties, but of a household which is dominated by men and whose denizens are sexually available to the paterfamilias.

Bell believes that "the incest prohibition functions by making people consider the reaction their behaviour would receive. The imagined reaction may be somebody's reaction in particular, people's reaction in general, or the law's response. * * * On the other hand, MacKinnon's argument that the prohibition or illegality of acts can be 'part of their excitement potential' suggests that the 'prohibition of incest' as a discursive phenomenon may also be involved in the *commission* of incest." (Bell 122.) Within this understanding, what role does *Kaiser*—the prosecution and a court decision affirming a conviction—play in the drama of the incest taboo?

2. *The Sex-with-Children Issue.* In 1978, Foucault, Guy Hocquenghem, and Jean Danet proposed that consensual sex between adults and children be legalized. See Foucault, *Politics, Philosophy, Culture: Interviews and Other Writings, 1977–1984* (Lawrence D. Kritzman ed. 1988). Their argument was that existing laws contributed to the child's fragile sexuality by setting it off limits, and deprives the child of the chance to explore her or his desires. Conversely, by creating and focusing on a special breed of criminal, the "child molester," the law is sexualizing a certain line and implicitly inviting people to cross over it—in derogation of the policy of protecting children. The three thinkers challenge the naturalness of the categories thus created ("vulnerable child," "child molester") and urge that the policy be abandoned.

Feminist theory has contributed importantly to the regulation of child abuse, and feminist discourse therefore is directly called into question by Foucault, Hocquenghem, and Danet. Feminist theory has tended to see all sex with children as akin to rape. "Adult-child sex is wrong because the fundamental conditions of consent cannot prevail in the relationship between an adult and a child." Emily Driver, "Introduction" to *Child Sexual Abuse: Feminist Perspectives* 5 (1989). If, as some feminists believe, there is a power disparity in all heterosexual relations, how much weight should be given to differences in age? Should relations between and adult woman and an underage male be treated the same or differently than relations between an adult man and an underage woman? (See Chapter 11 for further discussion.)

Vikki Bell believes that the Foucault critique is much more cogent than his prescription (Bell 154–60). Once he descends into the realm of policy prescription, Foucault falls victim to all the questionable intellectual moves he criticized in *History of Sexuality*: giving too much credit to law as a directive force and ignoring the greater importance of other social forces, idealizing "freedom" as the absence of legal prohibition, and neglecting the impossible question of what "consent" even is. More important, Bell worries that the introduction of a consent defense into adult-child sex will create new and painful discursive possibilities. Testimony in ordinary abuse cases is traumatic enough for the child, and testimony by adult women (subject to vicious cross-examination to establish consent or acquiescence) is traumatic enough for women; consider the double trauma for a child pressed on issues of consent, invitation, and acquiescence. As Bell reminds the Foucauldians, sometimes lines cut off discourse.

3.   *The Rape Issue.* Foucault was no defender of coerced sex, but he found perplexing the way in which rape laws privilege specific zones of the body. If Kaiser had struck his stepdaughter and knocked her teeth loose, he would be in much less legal trouble than if he had intercourse with her. One is assault, the other is sexual assault, which carries a much higher penalty. Foucault found such disparities ridiculous, for they gave too much significance to one orifice. See Foucault, *Politics, Philosophy, Culture* 201–02. Foucault resisted the way in which the deployment of sexuality—the way in which our sexuality is tied up with our identity—is so imperial in our laws as well as our lives.

Moreover, the higher penalty rests upon some fine distinctions. As *Kaiser* suggested, if there had been no "penetration" of the penis into the vagina, there would have been no rape (or statutory rape or incest). Apparently under Washington law, if Kaiser had forced his finger into his stepdaughter's vagina, he would not have been guilty of rape (other states do regulate this as sex, however). Foucault finds this just as ridiculous as before. "Sex" is not limited to penis-in-vagina, for it includes a panoply of pleasure-seeking touches. Foucault would both narrow sexuality's imperialism and expand what we mean by sexual pleasure.

Feminists tend to be more favorably impressed with this latter point than the former. See especially Monique Plaza, "Our Costs and Their

Benefits," 4 *m/f* 31–32 (1980). While feminists do tend to see rape as violence and not just sex, they see it as an especially harmful kind of violence, contrary to Foucault. What he missed is the political dimension of rape's violence: each rape is an assault against womanhood as well as woman, a marker for man's collective power to use and even erase woman. Like Bell, Plaza argues that Foucault neglects the insights of his own earlier work, namely, the social features of actions. A man punching another man is assault of a different nature than a man forcing his penis into a woman or even (Plaza agrees) punching a woman. The latter is more serious because of the other relations of power involved in man's hurting woman.

Judith Butler, Gender Trouble: Feminism and the Subversion of Identity

6–7, 22–23, 24–25 (1990).*

Although the unproblematic unity of "women" is often invoked to construct a solidarity of identity, a split is introduced in the feminist subject by the distinction between sex and gender. Originally intended to dispute the biology-is-destiny formulation, the distinction between sex and gender serves the argument that whatever biological intractability sex appears to have, gender is culturally constructed: hence, gender is neither the causal result of sex nor as seemingly fixed as sex. The unity of the subject is thus already potentially contested by the distinction that permits of gender as a multiple interpretation of sex.

If gender is the cultural meanings that the sexed body assumes, then a gender cannot be said to follow from a sex in any one way. Taken to its logical limit, the sex/gender distinction suggests a radical discontinuity between sexed bodies and culturally constructed genders. Assuming for the moment the stability of binary sex, it does not follow that the construction of "men" will accrue exclusively to the bodies of males or that "women" will interpret only female bodies. Further, even if the sexes appear to be unproblematically binary in their morphology and constitution (which will become a question), there is no reason to assume that genders ought to remain as two. * * * When the constructed status of gender is theorized as radically independent of sex, gender itself becomes a free-floating artifice, with the consequence that *man* and *masculine* might just as easily signify a female body as a male one, and *woman* and *feminine* a male body as easily as a female one.

* * * And what is "sex" anyway? Is it natural, anatomical, chromosomal, or hormonal, and how is a feminist critic to assess the scientific discourses which purport to establish such "facts" for us? * * * Is there a history of how the duality of sex was established, a genealogy that might expose the binary opinions as a variable construction? Are the ostensibly binary facts of sex discursively produced by various scientific discourses in

the service of other political and social interests? If the immutable character of sex is contested, perhaps this construct called "sex" is as culturally constructed as gender; indeed, perhaps it was always already gender, with the consequence that the distinction between sex and gender turns out to be no distinction at all.

It would make no sense, then, to define gender as the cultural interpretation of sex, if sex itself is a gendered category. Gender ought not to be conceived merely as the cultural inscription of meaning on a pregiven sex (a juridical conception); gender must also designate the very apparatus of production whereby the sexes themselves are established. As a result, gender is not to culture as sex is to nature; gender is also the discursive/cultural means by which "sexed nature" or "a natural sex" is produced and established as "prediscursive," prior to culture, a politically neutral surface *on which* culture acts. * * *

Gender can denote a *unity* of experience, of sex, of gender, and desire, only when sex can be understood in some sense to necessitate gender—where gender is a psychic and/or cultural designation of the self—and desire—where desire is heterosexual and therefore differentiates itself through an oppositional relation to that other gender it desires. The internal coherence or unity of either gender, man or woman, thereby requires both a stable and oppositional heterosexuality. That institutional heterosexuality both requires and produces the univocity of each of the gendered terms that constitute the limit of gendered possibilities within an oppositional, binary gender system. This conception of gender presupposes not only a causal relation among sex, gender, and desire, but suggests as well that desire reflects or expresses gender and that gender reflects or expresses desire. The metaphysical unity of the three is assumed to be truly known and expressed in a differentiating desire for an oppositional gender—that is, in a form of oppositional heterosexuality. Whether as a naturalistic paradigm which establishes a causal continuity among sex, gender, and desire, or as an authentic-expressive paradigm in which some true self is said to be revealed simultaneously or successively in sex, gender, and desire, here "the old dream of symmetry," as [Luce] Irigaray has called it, is presupposed, reified, and rationalized.

This rough sketch of gender gives us a clue to understanding the political reasons for the substantializing view of gender. The institution of a compulsory and naturalized heterosexuality requires and regulates gender as a binary relation in which the masculine term is differentiated from the feminine term, and this differentiation is accomplished through the practices of heterosexual desire. The act of differentiating the two oppositional moments of the binary results in a consolidation of each term, the respective internal coherence of sex, gender, and desire. * * *

In this sense, *gender* is not a noun, but neither is it a set of free-floating attributes, for we have seen that the substantive effect of gender is performatively produced and compelled by the regulatory practices of gender coherence. Hence * * * gender proves to be performative—that is, constituting the identity it is purported to be. In this sense, gender is always a doing, though not a doing by a subject who might be said to preexist the deed. * * * There is no gender identity behind the expressions of gender; that identity is performatively constituted by the very "expressions" that are said to be its results.

Price Waterhouse v. Ann B. Hopkins

United States Supreme Court, 1989.
490 U.S. 228, 109 S.Ct. 1775, 104 L.Ed.2d 268.

■ BRENNAN, J., announced the judgment of the Court and delivered an opinion in which JUSTICE MARSHALL, JUSTICE BLACKMUN, and JUSTICE STEVENS join.

Ann Hopkins was a senior manager in an office of Price Waterhouse when she was proposed for partnership in 1982. She was neither offered nor denied admission to the partnership; instead, her candidacy was held for reconsideration the following year. When the partners in her office later refused to repropose her for partnership, she sued Price Waterhouse under Title VII, * * * charging that the firm had discriminated against her on the basis of sex in its decisions regarding partnership. Judge Gesell in the Federal District Court for the District of Columbia ruled in her favor on the question of liability, * * * and the Court of Appeals for the District of Columbia Circuit affirmed. * * * We granted certiorari to resolve a conflict among the Courts of Appeals concerning the respective burdens of proof of a defendant and plaintiff in a suit under Title VII when it has been shown that an employment decision resulted from a mixture of legitimate and illegitimate motives. * * *

Ann Hopkins had worked at Price Waterhouse's Office of Government Services in Washington, D.C., for five years when the partners in that office proposed her as a candidate for partnership. Of the 662 partners at the firm at that time, 7 were women. Of the 88 persons proposed for partnership that year, only 1—Hopkins—was a woman. Forty-seven of these candidates were admitted to the partnership, 21 were rejected, and 20—including Hopkins—were "held" for reconsideration the following year. Thirteen of the 32 partners who had submitted comments on Hopkins supported her bid for partnership. Three partners recommended that her candidacy be placed on hold, eight stated that they did not have an informed opinion about her, and eight recommended that she be denied partnership.

In a jointly prepared statement supporting her candidacy, the partners in Hopkins' office showcased her successful 2–year effort to secure a $25 million contract with the Department of State, labeling it "an outstanding performance" and one that Hopkins carried out "virtually at the partner level." Despite Price Waterhouse's attempt at trial to minimize her contribution to this project, Judge Gesell specifically found that Hopkins had "played a key role in Price Waterhouse's successful effort to win a multi-million dollar contract with the Department of State." Indeed, he went on, "[n]one of the other partnership candidates at Price Waterhouse that year had a comparable record in terms of successfully securing major contracts for the partnership."

The partners in Hopkins' office praised her character as well as her accomplishments, describing her in their joint statement as "an outstanding professional" who had a "deft touch," a "strong character, independence and integrity." Clients appear to have agreed with these assessments. At trial, one official from the State Department described her as "extremely competent, intelligent," "strong and forthright, very productive, energetic and creative." Another high-ranking official praised Hopkins' decisiveness, broadmindedness, and "intellectual clarity"; she was, in his words, "a stimulating conversationalist." Evaluations such as these led Judge Gesell to conclude that Hopkins "had no difficulty dealing with clients and her clients appear to have been very pleased with her work" and that she "was generally viewed as a highly competent project leader who worked long hours, pushed vigorously to meet deadlines and demanded much from the multidisciplinary staffs with which she worked."

On too many occasions, however, Hopkins' aggressiveness apparently spilled over into abrasiveness. Staff members seem to have borne the brunt of Hopkins' brusqueness. Long before her bid for partnership, partners evaluating her work had counseled her to improve her relations with staff members. Although later evaluations indicate an improvement, Hopkins' perceived shortcomings in this important area eventually doomed her bid for partnership. Virtually all of the partners' negative remarks about Hopkins—even those of partners supporting her—had to do with her "interpersonal skills." Both "[s]upporters and opponents of her candidacy," stressed Judge Gesell, "indicated that she was sometimes overly aggressive, unduly harsh, difficult to work with and impatient with staff."

There were clear signs, though, that some of the partners reacted negatively to Hopkins' personality because she was a woman. One partner described her as "macho"; another suggested that she "overcompensated for being a woman"; a third advised her to take "a course at charm school." Several partners criticized her use of profanity; in response, one partner suggested that those partners objected to her swearing only "because it's a lady using foul language." Another supporter explained that Hopkins "ha[d] matured from a tough-talking somewhat masculine hardnosed mgr to an authoritative, formidable, but much more appealing lady ptr candidate." But it was the man who, as Judge Gesell found, bore responsibility for explaining to Hopkins the reasons for the Policy Board's decision to place her candidacy on hold who delivered the *coup de grace*: in order to improve her chances for partnership, Thomas Beyer advised, Hopkins should "walk more femininely, talk more femininely, dress more femininely, wear make-up, have her hair styled, and wear jewelry."

Dr. Susan Fiske, a social psychologist and Associate Professor of Psychology at Carnegie–Mellon University, testified at trial that the partnership selection process at Price Waterhouse was likely influenced by sex stereotyping. Her testimony focused not only on the overtly sex-based comments of partners but also on gender-neutral remarks, made by partners who knew Hopkins only slightly, that were intensely critical of her. One partner, for example, baldly stated that Hopkins was "universally disliked" by staff and another described her as "consistently annoying and irritating"; yet these were people who had had very little contact with Hopkins. According to Fiske, Hopkins' uniqueness (as the only woman in the pool of candidates) and the subjectivity of the evaluations made it likely that sharply critical remarks such as these were the product of sex stereotyping—although Fiske admitted that she could not say with certainty whether any particular comment was the result of stereotyping. Fiske based her opinion on a review of the submitted comments, explaining that it was commonly accepted practice for social psychologists to reach this kind of conclusion without having met any of the people involved in the decisionmaking process.

In previous years, other female candidates for partnership also had been evaluated in sex-based terms. As a general matter, Judge Gesell concluded, "[c]andidates were viewed favorably if partners believed they maintained their femin[in]ity while becoming effective professional managers"; in this environment, "[t]o be identified as a 'women's lib[b]er' was regarded as [a] negative comment." In fact, the judge found that in previous years "[o]ne partner repeatedly commented that he could not consider any woman seriously as a partnership candidate and believed that women were not even capable of functioning as senior managers—yet the firm took no action to discourage his comments and recorded his vote in the overall summary of the evaluations."

Judge Gesell found that Price Waterhouse legitimately emphasized interpersonal skills in its partnership decisions, and also found that the firm had not fabricated its complaints about Hopkins' interpersonal skills as a pretext for discrimination. Moreover, he concluded, the firm did not give decisive emphasis to such traits only because Hopkins was a woman; although there were male candidates who lacked these skills but who were admitted to partnership, the judge found that these candidates possessed other, positive traits that Hopkins lacked.

The judge went on to decide, however, that some of the partners' remarks about Hopkins stemmed from an impermissibly cabined view of the proper behavior of women, and that Price Waterhouse had done nothing to disavow reliance on such comments. He held that Price Waterhouse had unlawfully discriminated against Hopkins on the basis of sex by consciously giving credence and effect to partners' comments that resulted from sex stereotyping. Noting that Price Waterhouse could avoid equitable relief by proving by clear and convincing evidence that it would have placed Hopkins' candidacy on hold even absent this discrimination, the judge decided that the firm had not carried this heavy burden.

The Court of Appeals affirmed the District Court's ultimate conclusion, but departed from its analysis in one particular: it held that even if a plaintiff proves that discrimination played a role in an employment decision, the defendant will not be found liable if it proves, by clear and convincing evidence, that it would have made the same decision in the absence of discrimination. * * * Under this approach, an employer is not deemed to have violated Title VII if it proves that it would have made the same decision in the absence of an impermissible motive, whereas under the District Court's approach, the employer's proof in that respect only avoids equitable relief. We decide today that the Court of Appeals had the better approach, but that both courts erred in requiring the employer to make its proof by clear and convincing evidence.* * *

The District Court found that sex stereotyping "was permitted to play a part" in the evaluation of Hopkins as a candidate for partnership. Price Waterhouse disputes both that stereotyping occurred and that it played any part in the decision to place Hopkins' candidacy on hold. In the firm's view, in other words, the District Court's factual conclusions are clearly erroneous. We do not agree. * * *

[Justice Brennan defended the trial court's reliance on Dr. Fiske's expert opinion about sex stereotyping.] Indeed, we are tempted to say that Dr. Fiske's expert testimony was merely icing on Hopkins' cake. It takes no special training to discern sex stereotyping in a description of an aggressive female employee as requiring "a course at charm school." Nor, turning to Thomas Beyer's memorable advice to Hopkins, does it require expertise in psychology to know that, if an employee's flawed "interpersonal skills" can be corrected by a soft-hued suit or a new shade of lipstick, perhaps it is the employee's sex and not her interpersonal skills that has drawn the criticism.

Price Waterhouse also charges that Hopkins produced no evidence that sex stereotyping played a role in the decision to place her candidacy on hold. As we have stressed, however, Hopkins showed that the partnership solicited evaluations from all of the firm's partners; that it generally relied very heavily on such evaluations in making its decision; that some of the partners' comments were the product of stereotyping; and that the firm in no way disclaimed reliance on those particular comments, either in Hopkins' case or in the past. Certainly a plausible—and, one might say, inevitable—conclusion to draw from this set of circumstances is that the Policy Board in making its decision did in fact take into account all of the partners' comments, including the comments that were motivated by stereotypical notions about women's proper deportment.* * *

Nor is the finding that sex stereotyping played a part in the Policy Board's decision undermined by the fact that many of the suspect comments were made by supporters rather than detractors of Hopkins. A negative comment, even when made in the context of a generally favorable review, nevertheless may influence the decisionmaker to think less highly of the candidate; the Policy Board, in fact, did not simply tally the "yeses" and "noes" regarding a candidate, but carefully reviewed the content of the submitted comments. The additional suggestion that the comments were made by "persons outside the decisionmaking chain" * * *—and therefore could not have harmed Hopkins—simply ignores the critical role that partners' comments played in the Policy Board's partnership decisions.

Price Waterhouse appears to think that we cannot affirm the factual findings of the trial court without deciding that, instead of being overbearing and aggressive and curt, Hopkins is, in fact, kind and considerate and patient. If this is indeed its impression, petitioner misunderstands the theory on which Hopkins prevailed. The District Judge acknowledged that Hopkins' conduct justified complaints about her behavior as a senior manager. But he also concluded that the reactions of at least some of the partners were reactions to her as a *woman* manager. Where an evaluation is based on a subjective assessment of a person's strengths and weaknesses, it is simply not true that each evaluator will focus on, or even mention, the same weaknesses. Thus, even if we knew that Hopkins had "personality problems," this would not tell us that the partners who cast their evaluations of Hopkins in sex-based terms would have criticized her as sharply (or criticized her at all) if she had been a man. It is not our job to review the evidence and decide that the negative reactions to Hopkins were based on reality; our perception of Hopkins' character is irrelevant. We sit not to determine whether Ms. Hopkins is nice, but to decide whether the partners reacted negatively to her personality because she is a woman.

We hold that when a plaintiff in a Title VII case proves that her gender played a motivating part in an employment decision, the defendant may avoid a finding of liability only by proving by a preponderance of the evidence that it would have made the same decision even if it had not taken the plaintiff's gender into account. Because the courts below erred by deciding that the defendant must make this proof by clear and convincing evidence, we reverse the Court of Appeals' judgment against Price Waterhouse on liability and remand the case to that court for further proceedings.

■ [JUSTICE WHITE concurred only in the judgment. His analysis was relatively simple. *Mt. Healthy City School District Bd. of Educ. v. Doyle*, 429 U.S. 274 (1977), held that a public employee complaining of discharge in violation of his First Amendment rights had the burden of proving that constitutionally protected conduct was a "substantial factor" in the discharge decision. Justice White believed that the *Mt. Healthy* standard could be applied to Title VII cases without violence to the Court's precedents.]

■ [JUSTICE O'CONNOR also concurred only in the judgment. Like the plurality, she agreed to shift the burden of persuasion to employers once a Title VII plaintiff established that impermissible (sex) considerations were a "substantial factor" in an employment decision. Like the dissenters, she believed that this move was itself a "change in direction from some of our prior precedents" and sought to justify that change.]

■ JUSTICE KENNEDY, with whom THE CHIEF JUSTICE [REHNQUIST] and JUSTICE SCALIA join, dissenting.* * *

The ultimate question in every individual disparate-treatment case is whether discrimination caused the particular decision at issue. Some of the plurality's comments with respect to the District Court's findings in this case, however, are potentially misleading. As the plurality notes, the District Court based its liability determination on expert evidence that some evaluations of respondent Hopkins were based on unconscious sex stereotypes,[5] and on the fact that Price Waterhouse failed to disclaim reliance on these comments when it conducted the partnership review. The District Court also based liability on Price Waterhouse's failure to "make partners sensitive to the dangers [of stereotyping], to discourage comments tainted by sexism, or to investigate comments to determine whether they were influenced by stereotypes." * * *

Although the District Court's version of Title VII liability is improper under any of today's opinions, I think it important to stress that Title VII creates no independent cause of action for sex stereotyping. Evidence of use by decisionmakers of sex stereotypes is, of course, quite relevant to the question of discriminatory intent. The ultimate question, however, is whether discrimination caused the plaintiff's harm. Our cases do not support the suggestion that failure to "disclaim reliance" on stereotypical comments itself violates Title VII. Neither do they support creation of a "duty to sensitize." As the dissenting judge in the Court of Appeals observed, acceptance of such theories would turn Title VII "from a prohibition of discriminatory conduct into an engine for rooting out sexist thoughts." * * *

The language of Title VII and our well-considered precedents require this plaintiff to establish that the decision to place her candidacy on hold was made "because of" sex. Here the District Court found that the "comments of the individual partners and the expert evidence of Dr. Fiske do not prove an intentional discriminatory motive or purpose," * * * and that "[b]ecause plaintiff has considerable problems dealing with staff and peers, the Court cannot say that she would have been elected to partnership if the Policy Board's decision had not been tainted by sexually based evaluations," * * * Hopkins thus failed to meet the requisite standard of proof after a full trial. I would remand the case for entry of judgment in favor of Price Waterhouse.

NOTES ON *HOPKINS* AND LAW'S INVOCATION OF GENDER

1. *The Relationship Between Gender and Sex. Hopkins* might be criticized, as the dissent seems to do, for expanding a statutory ban on sex discrimination to include gender discrimination as well. (Title VII only prohibits

---

5. The plaintiff who engages the services of Dr. Susan Fiske should have no trouble showing that sex discrimination played a part in any decision. Price Waterhouse chose not to object to Fiske's testimony, and at this late stage we are constrained to accept it, but I think the plurality's enthusiasm for Fiske's conclusions unwarranted. Fiske purported to discern stereotyping in comments that were gender neutral—e.g., "overbearing and abrasive"—without any knowledge of the comments' basis in reality and without having met the speaker or subject. "To an expert of Dr. Fiske's qualifications, it seems plain that no woman could *be* overbearing, arrogant, or abrasive: any observations to that effect would necessarily be discounted as the product of stereotyping. If analysis like this is to prevail in federal courts, no employer can base any adverse action as to a woman on such attributes." 825 F.2d 458, 477 (1987) (Williams, J., dissenting). Today's opinions cannot be read as requiring factfinders to credit testimony based on this type of analysis.

employment decisions "because of" the employee's "sex.") It appears that Ann Hopkins was discriminated against because she was perceived as a "mannish" woman: her gender did not match her sex. Judith Butler's theory that sex and gender always work together provides some useful ways of thinking about this charge. The dissent insists on disaggregating gender from sex and only focusing on the latter; the plurality insists upon their interconnection. Butler seems to suggest that sex cannot be coherently understood without gender, as well as vice versa.

After *Hopkins*, it appears that two slightly different kinds of discrimination are remedied by Title VII: Price Waterhouse passed over Hopkins *either* because some partners didn't think women were capable of doing the job *or* because some partners were offended that this woman, however qualified, wasn't feminine enough for their tastes. In some ways, the second kind of discrimination (the kind Hopkins suffered) is more malignant, because it is so divorced from business necessity. Both kinds of discrimination are aimed at "gender stereotyping," either at the general level (women cannot do this job) or the specific (this woman can do the job, but she offends my sense of what a woman is). Can *Hopkins*, and Title VII, be read to create "an engine for rooting out sexist thoughts"? Should it?

Relatedly, the majority surely suspected that "abrasiveness" in male candidates was not disqualifying, as it was for Hopkins and probably other female candidates as well. (Is it conceivable that the voting partnership of Price Waterhouse did not contain a boatload of "abrasive" men?) The dissent might object that this "suspicion" is a wild use of judicial notice, without explicit support in the record. Should the remand have included inquiry into this issue? Or is it too obvious for inquiry?

2. *Burdens of Proof in Title VII.* In law, burdens of proof are often more important than the substantive rule. A key issue in the case was the district court's finding that other factors contributed to Hopkins' denial of partnership; the majority and dissent disagree about how to treat this "mixed motive" case. If Hopkins was not just "macho" but "abrasive," should the decision to deny her partnership be overturned? (Consider this question from the point of view of the office secretaries, who probably bore the brunt of Hopkins' testiness.) This divided the Justices in 1989. Congress overrode all nine Justices in the Civil Rights Act of 1991, codified at 42 U.S.C. § 703(m), which allows a finding of discrimination if the inadmissible criterion (sex, or gender) substantially contributed to the adverse employment decision.

3. *Sex, Gender, and Sexual Orientation.* Does *Hopkins* create a claim for relief by "effeminate" men for job discrimination because they don't conform to gender stereotypes? If the mannish woman and the effeminate man can sue because the employer penalizes them for not conforming to gender stereotypes, can the lesbian or the gay man sue because she or he does not conform to the stereotypes that all women "need" men and that a man is not a "man" unless he has sex with women? Remember that this is an issue of statutory interpretation (Title VII of the Civil Rights Act of 1964), not constitutional law (the equal protection clause). Does that make a difference? (See Chapter 10, Section 2[B], for exploration of this and other Title VII issues.)

How would Judith Butler analyze the argument (Chapter 1, Section 3[B][3]) that sexual orientation discrimination is a species of sex discrimination?

PART C.   DECONSTRUCTIVE THEORY (BINARISMS AND THE DOUBLE BIND)

Eve Sedgwick, the focus of this part, is a feminist theorist, so she would have been appropriate for inclusion earlier. She is also a self-styled "queer theorist," as she examines issues from the perspective of queers, whom one might characterize as a variety of sexual outsiders. We decided to include Sedgwick in the postmodern section, and to use the label "deconstructive," because her mode of reasoning shows how ordinary, "normal" metaphors and customs of compulsory heterosexuality incorporate and depend upon the thing they deny (homosexuality). This methodology is like Jacques Derrida's deployment of deconstruction. As you will see, Sedgwick develops a unique method all her own, and it is inspiring a lot of analytical spin offs.

Eve Kosofsky Sedgwick, The Epistemology of the Closet

67–68, 71–76, 78–90 (1990).*

The epistemology of the closet is not a dated subject or a superseded regime of knowing. While the events of June, 1969, and later vitally reinvigorated many people's sense of the potency, magnetism, and promise of gay self-disclosure, nevertheless the reign of the telling secret was scarcely overturned with Stonewall. * * * As D.A. Miller points out in an aegis-creating essay, secrecy can function as

> the subjective practice in which the oppositions of private/public, inside/outside, subject/object are established, and the sanctity of their first term kept inviolate. And the phenomenon of the "open secret" does not, as one might think, bring about the collapse of those binarisms and their ideological effects, but rather attests to their fantasmatic recovery.[1]

Even at an individual level, there are remarkably few of even the most openly gay people who are not deliberately in the closet with someone personally or economically or institutionally important to them. Furthermore, the deadly elasticity of heterosexist presumption means that, like Wendy in *Peter Pan,* people find new walls springing up around them even

1. D.A. Miller, "Secret Subjects, Open Secrets, "in his *The Novel and the Police,* p. 207.

as they drowse: every encounter with a new classful of students, to say nothing of a new boss, social worker, loan officer, landlord, doctor, erects new closets whose fraught and characteristic laws of optics and physics exact from at least gay people new surveys, new calculations, new draughts and requisitions of secrecy or disclosure. Even an out gay person deals daily with interlocutors about whom she doesn't know whether they know or not; it is equally difficult to guess for any given interlocutor whether, if they did know, the knowledge would seem very important. Nor—at the most basic level—is it unaccountable that someone who wanted a job, custody or visiting rights, insurance, protection from violence, from "therapy," from distorting stereotype, from insulting scrutiny, from simple insult, from forcible interpretation of their bodily product, could deliberately choose to remain in or to reenter the closet in some or all segments of their life. The gay closet is not a feature only of the lives of gay people. But for many gay people it is still the fundamental feature of social life; and there can be few gay people, however courageous and forthright by habit, however fortunate in the support of their immediate communities, in whose lives the closet is not still a shaping presence. * * *

The closet is the defining structure for gay oppression in this century. The legal couching, by civil liberties lawyers, of *Bowers v. Hardwick* as an issue in the first place of a Constitutional right to privacy, and the liberal focus in the aftermath of that decision on the image of the *bedroom invaded by policemen*—"Letting the Cops Back into Michael Hardwick's Bedroom," the *Native* headlined[4]—as though political empowerment were a matter of getting the cops back on the street where they belong and sexuality back into the impermeable space where *it* belongs, are among other things extensions of, and testimony to the power of, the image of the closet. * * *

I recently heard someone on National Public Radio refer to the sixties as the decade when Black people came out of the closet. For that matter, I recently gave an MLA talk purporting to explain how it's possible to come out of the closet as a fat woman. The apparent floating-free from its gay origins of that phrase "coming out of the closet" in recent usage might suggest that the trope of the closet is so close to the heart of some modern preoccupations that it could be, or has been, evacuated of its historical gay specificity. But I hypothesize that exactly the opposite is true. I think that a whole cluster of the most crucial sites for the contestation of meaning in twentieth-century Western culture are consequentially and quite indelibly marked with the historical specificity of homosocial/homosexual definition, notably but not exclusively male, from around the turn of the century.[6]

4. *New York Native,* no. 169 (July 14, 1986): 11.

6. A reminder that "the closet" retains (at least the chronic potential of) its gay semantic specification: a media flap in June, 1989, when a Republican National Committee memo calling for House Majority Leader Thomas Foley to "come out of the liberal closet" and comparing his voting record with that of an openly gay Congressman, Barney Frank, was widely perceived (and condemned) as insinuating that Foley himself is gay. The committee's misjudgment about whether it could maintain deniability for the

Among those sites are, as I have indicated, the pairings secrecy/ disclosure and private/public. Along with and sometimes through these epistemologically charged pairings, condensed in the figures of "the closet" and "coming out," this very specific crisis of definition has then ineffaceably marked other pairings as basic to modern cultural organization as masculine/feminine, majority/minority, innocence/initiation, natural/artificial, new/old, growth/decadence, urbane/provincial, health/illness, same/different, cognition/paranoia, art/kitsch, sincerity/sentimentality, and voluntarity/addiction. So permeative has the suffusing stain of homo/heterosexual crisis been that to discuss any of these indices in any context, in the absence of an antihomophobic analysis, must perhaps be to perpetuate unknowingly compulsions implicit in each.

For any modern question of sexuality, knowledge/ignorance is more than merely one in a metonymic chain of such binarisms. The process, narrowly bordered at first in European culture but sharply broadened and accelerated after the late eighteenth century, by which "knowledge" and "sex" become conceptually inseparable from one another—so that knowledge means in the first place sexual knowledge; ignorance, sexual ignorance; and epistemological pressure of any sort seems a force increasingly saturated with sexual impulsion—was sketched in Volume I of Foucault's *History of Sexuality*. In a sense, this was a process, protracted almost to retardation, of exfoliating the biblical genesis by which what we now know as sexuality is fruit—apparently the only fruit—to be plucked from the tree of knowledge. Cognition itself, sexuality itself, and transgression itself have always been ready in Western culture to be magnetized into an unyielding though not an unfissured alignment with one another, and the period initiated by Romanticism accomplished this disposition through a remarkably broad confluence of different languages and institutions.

In some texts, such as Diderot's *La Religieuse,* that were influential early in this process, the desire that represents sexuality per se, and hence sexual knowledge and knowledge per se, is a same-sex desire. This possibility, however, was repressed with increasing energy, and hence increasing visibility, as the nineteenth-century culture of the individual proceeded to elaborate a version of knowledge/sexuality increasingly structured by its pointed cognitive *refusal* of sexuality between women, between men. The gradually reifying effect of this refusal meant that by the end of the nineteenth century, when it had become fully current—as obvious to Queen Victoria as to Freud—that knowledge meant sexual knowledge, and secrets sexual secrets, there had in fact developed one particular sexuality that was distinctively constituted *as* secrecy: the perfect object for the by now insatiably exacerbated epistemological/sexual anxiety of the turn-of-the-century subject. Again, it was a long chain of originally scriptural identifications of a sexuality with a particular cognitive positioning (in this case, St. Paul's routinely reproduced and reworked denomination of sodomy as

insinuation is an interesting index to how   this locution may be perceived to be.
unpredictably full or empty of gay specificity

the crime whose name is not to be uttered, hence whose accessibility to knowledge is uniquely preterited) that culminated in Lord Alfred Douglas's epochal public utterance, in 1894, "*I am* the Love that dare not speak its name."[9] In such texts as *Billy Budd* and *Dorian Gray* and through their influence, the subject—the thematics—of knowledge and ignorance themselves, of innocence and initiation, of secrecy and disclosure, became not contingently but integrally infused with one particular object of cognition: no longer sexuality as a whole but even more specifically, now, the homosexual topic. And the condensation of the world of possibilities surrounding same-sex sexuality—including, shall we say, both gay desires and the most rabid phobias against them—the condensation of this plurality to *the homosexual topic* that now formed the accusative case of modern processes of personal knowing, was not the least infliction of the turn-of-the-century crisis of sexual definition. * * *

That train of painful imaginings was fraught with the epistemological distinctiveness of gay identity and gay situation in our culture. Vibrantly resonant as the image of the closet is for many modern oppressions, it is indicative for homophobia in a way it cannot be for other oppressions. Racism, for instance, is based on a stigma that is visible in all but exceptional cases (cases that are neither rare nor irrelevant, but that delineate the outlines rather than coloring the center of racial experience); so are the oppressions based on gender, age, size, physical handicap. Ethnic/cultural/religious oppressions such as anti-Semitism are more analogous in that the stigmatized individual has at least notionally some discretion—although, importantly, it is never to be taken for granted how much—over other people's knowledge of her or his membership in the group: one could "come out as" a Jew or Gypsy, in a heterogeneous urbanized society, much more intelligibly than one could typically "come out as," say, female, Black, old, a wheelchair user, or fat. A (for instance) Jewish or Gypsy identity, and hence a Jewish or Gypsy secrecy or closet, would nonetheless differ again from the distinctive gay versions of these things in its clear ancestral linearity and answerability, in the roots (however tortuous and ambivalent) of cultural identification through each individual's originary culture of (at a minimum) the family.

Proust, in fact, insistently suggests as a sort of limit-case of one kind of coming out precisely the drama of Jewish self-identification, embodied in the Book of Esther and in Racine's recasting of it that is quoted throughout the "Sodom and Gomorrah" books of *A la recherche*. The story of Esther seems a model for a certain simplified but highly potent imagining of coming out and its transformative potential. In concealing her Judaism from her husband, King Assuérus (Ahasuerus), Esther the Queen feels she is concealing, simply, her identity: "The King is to this day unaware who I am."[10] Esther's deception is made necessary by the powerful ideology that

---

9. Lord Alfred Douglas, "Two Loves," *The Chameleon* 1 (1894): 28 (emphasis added).

10. Jean Racine, *Esther*, ed. H. R. Roach (London: George G. Harrap, 1949), line 89; my translation. Further citations of

makes Assuérus categorize her people as unclean ("cette source impure" [1039]) and an abomination against nature ("Il nous croit en horreur à toute la nature" [174]). The sincere, relatively abstract Jew-hatred of this fuddled but omnipotent king undergoes constant stimulation from the grandiose cynicism of his advisor Aman (Haman), who dreams of an entire planet exemplarily cleansed of the perverse element.

> I want it said one day in awestruck centuries:
>
> "There once used to be Jews, there was an insolent race;
>
> widespread, they used to cover the whole face of the earth;
>
> a single one dared draw on himself the wrath of Aman,
>
> at once they disappeared, every one, from the earth."

The king acquiesces in Aman's genocidal plot, and Esther is told by her cousin, guardian, and Jewish conscience Mardochée (Mordecai) that the time for her revelation has come; at this moment the particular operation of suspense around her would be recognizable to any gay person who has inched toward coming out to homophobic parents. "And if I perish, I perish," she says in the Bible (Esther 4:16). That the avowal of her secret identity will have an immense potency is clear, is the premise of the story. All that remains to be seen is whether under its explosive pressure the king's "political" animus against her kind will demolish his "personal" love for her, or vice versa: will he declare her as good as, or better, dead? Or will he soon be found at a neighborhood bookstore, hoping not to be recognized by the salesperson who is ringing up his copy of *Loving Someone Jewish?*

The biblical story and Racinian play, bearable to read in their balance of the holocaustal with the intimate only because one knows how the story will end,[11] are enactments of a particular dream or fantasy of coming out. Esther's eloquence, in the event, is resisted by only five lines of her husband's demurral or shock: essentially at the instant she names herself, both her ruler and Aman see that the anti-Semites are lost *("AMAN, tout bas:* Je tremble" [1033]). Revelation of identity in the space of intimate love effortlessly overturns an entire public systematics of the natural and the unnatural, the pure and the impure. The peculiar strike that the story makes to the heart is that Esther's small, individual ability to risk losing the love and countenance of her master has the power to save not only her own space in life but her people. * * *

There is no question that to fixate, as I have done, on the scenario sketched here more than flirts with sentimentality. This is true for quite explicable reasons. First, we have too much cause to know how limited a leverage any individual revelation can exercise over collectively scaled and

---

this play will be noted by line number in the text.

11. It is worth remembering, of course, that the biblical story still ends with mass slaughter: while Racine's king *revokes* his orders (1197), the biblical king *reverses* his (Esther 8:5), licensing the Jews' killing of "seventy and five thousand" (9:16) of their enemies, including children and women (8:11).

institutionally embodied oppressions.* * * [Other, deeper distinctions are then suggested in detail:]

1. Although neither the Bible nor Racine indicates in what, if any, religious behaviors or beliefs Esther's Jewish identity may be manifested, *there is no suggestion that that identity might be a debatable, a porous, a mutable fact about her.* "Esther, my lord, had a Jew for her father" (1033)—ergo, Esther is a Jew. Taken aback though he is by this announcement, Assuérus does not suggest that Esther is going through a phase, or is just angry at Gentiles, or could change if she only loved him enough to get counseling. Nor do such undermining possibilities occur to Esther. The Jewish identity in this play—whatever it may consist of in real life in a given historical context—has a solidity whose very unequivocalness grounds the story of Esther's equivocation and her subsequent self-disclosure. In the processes of gay self-disclosure, by contrast, in a twentieth-century context, questions of authority and evidence can be the first to arise. "How do you know you're really gay? Why be in such a hurry to jump to conclusions? After all, what you're saying is only based on a few feelings, not real actions *[or alternatively:* on a few actions, not necessarily your real feelings]; hadn't you better talk to a therapist and find out?" Such responses—and their occurrence in the people come out to can seem a belated echo of their occurrence in the person coming out—reveal how problematical at present is the very concept of gay identity, as well as how intensely it is resisted and how far authority over its definition has been distanced from the gay subject her- or himself.

2. *Esther expects Assuérus to be altogether surprised by her self-disclosure; and he is.* Her confident sense of control over other people's knowledge about her is in contrast to the radical uncertainty closeted gay people are likely to feel about who is in control of information about their sexual identity. This has something to do with a realism about secrets that is greater in most people's lives than it is in Bible stories; but it has much more to do with complications in the notion of gay identity, so that no one person can take control over all the multiple, often contradictory codes by which information about sexual identity and activity can seem to be conveyed. In many, if not most, relationships, coming out is a matter of crystallizing intuitions or convictions that had been in the air for a while already and had already established their own power-circuits of silent contempt, silent blackmail, silent glamorization, silent complicity. After all, the position of those who think they *know something about one that one may not know oneself* is an excited and empowered one—whether what they think one doesn't know is that one somehow *is* homosexual, or merely that one's supposed secret is known to them. The glass closet can license insult ("I'd never have said those things if I'd *known* you were gay!"—yeah, sure); it can also license far warmer relations, but (and) relations whose potential for exploitiveness is built into the optics of the asymmetrical, the specularized, and the inexplicit. There are sunny and apparently simplifying versions of coming out under these circumstances: a woman painfully decides to tell her mother that she's a lesbian, and her mother responds, "Yeah, I sort of thought you might be when you and Joan started sleeping

together ten years ago.'' More often this fact makes the closet and its exits not more but less straightforward, however; not, often, more equable, but more volatile or even violent. Living in and hence coming out of the closet are never matters of the purely hermetic; the personal and political geographies to be surveyed here are instead the more imponderable and convulsive ones of the open secret.

3. *Esther worries that her revelation might destroy her or fail to help her people, but it does not seem to her likely to damage Assuérus, and it does not indeed damage him.* When gay people in a homophobic society come out, on the other hand, perhaps especially to parents or spouses, it is with the consciousness of a potential for serious injury that is likely to go in both directions. The pathogenic secret itself, even, can circulate contagiously *as a secret*: a mother says that her adult child's coming out of the closet with her has plunged her, in turn, into the closet in her conservative community. In fantasy, though not in fantasy only, against the fear of being killed or wished dead by (say) one's parents in such a revelation there is apt to recoil the often more intensely imagined possibility of its killing *them*. There is no guarantee that being under threat from a double-edged weapon is a more powerful position than getting the ordinary axe, but it is certain to be more destabilizing.

4. The inert substance of *Assuérus seems to have no definitional involvement with the religious/ethnic identity of Esther.* He sees neither himself nor their relationship differently when he sees that she is different from what he had thought her. The double-edged potential for injury in the scene of gay coming out, by contrast, results partly from the fact that the erotic identity of the person who receives the disclosure is apt also to be implicated in, hence perturbed by it. This is true first and generally because erotic identity, of all things, is never to be circumscribed simply as itself, can never not be relational, is never to be perceived or known by anyone outside of a structure of transference and countertransference. Second and specifically it is true because the incoherences and contradictions of homosexual identity in twentieth-century culture are responsive to and hence evocative of the incoherences and contradictions of compulsory heterosexuality.

5. *There is no suggestion that Assuérus might himself be a Jew in disguise.* But it is entirely within the experience of gay people to find that a homophobic figure in power has, if anything, a disproportionate likelihood of being gay and closeted. * * *

6. *Esther knows who her people are and has an immediate answerability to them.* Unlike gay people, who seldom grow up in gay families; who are exposed to their culture's, if not their parents', high ambient homophobia long before either they or those who care for them know that they are among those who most urgently need to define themselves against it; who have with difficulty and always belatedly to patch together from fragments a community, a usable heritage, a politics of survival or resistance; unlike these, Esther has intact and to hand the identity and history and commit-

ments she was brought up in, personified and legitimated in a visible figure of authority, her guardian Mardochée. * * *

Each of these complicating possibilities stems at least partly from the plurality and the cumulative incoherence of modern ways of conceptualizing same-sex desire and, hence, gay identity; an incoherence that answers, too, to the incoherence with which *hetero*sexual desire and identity are conceptualized. * * *

For surely, if paradoxically, it is the paranoid insistence with which the definitional barriers between "the homosexual" (minority) and "the heterosexual" (majority) are fortified, in this century, by nonhomosexuals, and especially by men against men, that most saps one's ability to believe in "the homosexual" as an unproblematically discrete category of persons. Even the homophobic fifties folk wisdom of *Tea and Sympathy* detects that the man who most electrifies those barriers is the one whose own current is at most intermittently direct. It was in the period of the so-called "invention of the 'homosexual'" that Freud gave psychological texture and credibility to a countervalent, universalizing mapping of this territory, based on the supposed protean mobility of sexual desire and on the potential bisexuality of every human creature; a mapping that implies no presumption that one's sexual penchant will always incline toward persons of a single gender, and that offers, additionally, a richly denaturalizing description of the psychological motives and mechanisms of male paranoid, projective homophobic definition and enforcement. Freud's antiminoritizing account only gained, moreover, in influence by being articulated through a developmental narrative in which heterosexist and masculinist ethical sanctions found ready camouflage. If the new common wisdom that hotly overt homophobes are men who are "insecure about their masculinity" supplements the implausible, necessary illusion that there could be a *secure* version of masculinity (known, presumably, by the coolness of its homophobic enforcement) and a stable, intelligible way for men to feel about other men in modern heterosexual capitalist patriarchy, what tighter turn could there be to the screw of an already off-center, always at fault, endlessly blackmailable male identity ready to be manipulated into any labor of channeled violence?

It remained for work emerging from the later feminist and gay movements to begin to clarify why the male paranoid project had become so urgent in the maintenance of gender subordination; and it remained for a stunningly efficacious coup of feminist redefinition to transform lesbianism, in a predominant view, from a matter of female virilization to one of woman-identification.[18] * * * Most moderately to well-educated Western people in this century seem to share a similar understanding of homosexual definition, independent of whether they themselves are gay or straight, homophobic or antihomophobic. That understanding is close to what Proust's probably was, what for that matter mine is and probably yours.

---

18. See, for example, Radicalesbians, "The Woman Identified Woman," reprinted in Anne Koedt, Ellen Levine, and Anita Rapone, eds., *Radical Feminism* (New York: Quadrangle, 1973), pp. 240–45; and Rich, "Compulsory Heterosexuality."

That is to say, it is organized around a radical and irreducible incoherence. It holds the minoritizing view that there is a distinct population of persons who "really are" gay; at the same time, it holds the universalizing views that sexual desire is an unpredictably powerful solvent of stable identities; that apparently heterosexual persons and object choices are strongly marked by same-sex influences and desires, and vice versa for apparently homosexual ones; and that at least male heterosexual identity and modern masculinist culture may require for their maintenance the scapegoating crystallization of a same-sex male desire that is widespread and in the first place internal.

It has been the project of many, many writers and thinkers of many different kinds to adjudicate between the minoritizing and universalizing views of sexual definition and to resolve this conceptual incoherence. * * * A perfect example of this potent incoherence was the anomalous legal situation of gay people and acts in this country after one recent legal ruling. The Supreme Court in *Bowers v. Hardwick* [Chapter 1, Section 2] notoriously left the individual states free to prohibit any *acts* they wish to define as "sodomy," by whomsoever performed, with no fear at all of impinging on any rights, and particularly privacy rights, safeguarded by the Constitution; yet only shortly thereafter a panel of the Ninth Circuit Court of Appeals ruled (in *Sergeant Perry J. Watkins v. United States Army* [Chapter 1, Section 3]) that homosexual *persons,* as a particular kind of person, *are* entitled to Constitutional protections under the Equal Protection clause. To be gay in this system is to come under the radically overlapping aegises of a universalizing discourse of acts and a minoritizing discourse of persons. Just at the moment, at least within the discourse of law, the former of these prohibits what the latter of them protects; but in the concurrent public-health constructions related to AIDS, for instance, it is far from clear that a minoritizing discourse of persons ("risk groups") is not even more oppressive than the competing, universalizing discourse of acts ("safer sex"). In the double binds implicit in the space overlapped by the two, at any rate, every matter of definitional control is fraught with consequence.

The energy-expensive but apparently static clinch between minoritizing and universalizing views of *homo/heterosexual definition* is not, either, the only major conceptual siege under which modern homosexual and heterosexist fates are enacted. The second one, as important as the first and intimately entangled with it, has to do with defining the relation to gender of homosexual persons and same-sex desires. (It was in this conceptual register that the radical-feminist reframing of lesbianism as woman-identification was such a powerful move.) Enduringly since at least the turn of the century, there have presided two contradictory *tropes of gender* through which same-sex desire could be understood. On the one hand there was, and there persists, differently coded (in the homophobic folklore and science surrounding those "sissy boys" and their mannish sisters, but also in the heart and guts of much living gay and lesbian culture), the trope of inversion, *anima muliebris in corpore virili inclusa*— "a woman's soul trapped in a man's body"—and vice versa. As such writers as Christopher

Craft have made dear, one vital impulse of this trope is the preservation of an essential *heterosexuality* within desire itself, through a particular reading of the homosexuality of persons: desire, in this view, by definition subsists in the current that runs between one male self and one female self, in whatever sex of bodies these selves may be manifested.[22] * * *

Charged as it may be with value, the persistence of the inversion trope has been yoked, however, to that of its contradictory counterpart, the trope of gender separatism. Under this latter view, far from its being of the essence of desire to cross boundaries of gender, it is instead the most natural thing in the world that people of the same gender, people grouped together under the single most determinative diacritical mark of social organization, people whose economic, institutional, emotional, physical needs and knowledges may have so much in common, should bond together also on the axis of sexual desire. As the substitution of the phrase "woman-identified woman" for "lesbian" suggests, as indeed does the concept of the continuum of male or female homosocial desire, this trope tends to reassimilate to one another identification and desire, where inversion models, by contrast, depend on their distinctness. Gender-separatist models would thus place the woman-loving woman and the man-loving man each at the "natural" defining center of their own gender, again in contrast to inversion models that locate gay people—whether biologically or culturally—at the threshold between genders (see Figure 2).

	Separatist:	Integrative:
Homo/hetero *sexual* definition:	*Minoritizing*, e.g., gay identity, essentialist, third-sex models, civil rights models	*Universalizing*, e.g., bisexual potential, "social constructionist," "sodomy" models, "lesbian continuum"
Gender definition:	*Gender separatist*, e.g., homosocial continuum, lesbian separatist, manhood-initiation models	*Inversion/liminality/transitivity*, e.g., cross-sex, androgyny, gay/lesbian solidarity models

Figure 2.   Models of Gay/Straight Definition in Terms of Overlapping Sexuality and Gender

The immanence of each of these models throughout the history of modern gay definition is clear from the early split in the German homosexual rights movement between Magnus Hirschfeld, founder (in 1897) of the Scientific–Humanitarian Committee, a believer in the "third sex" who posited, in Don Mager's paraphrase, "an exact equation ... between cross-gender behaviors and homosexual desire"; and Benedict Friedländer, co-founder (in 1902) of the Community of the Special, who concluded to the contrary "that homosexuality was the highest, most perfect evolutionary

---

22. Christopher Craft, "'Kiss Me with Those Red Lips': Gender and Inversion in   Bram Stoker's *Dracula*," *Representations*, no. 8 (Fall 1984): 107–34, esp. 114.

stage of gender differentiation."[23] As James Steakley explains, "the true *typus inversus*," according to this latter argument, "as distinct from the effeminate homosexual, was seen as the founder of patriarchal society and ranked above the heterosexual in terms of his capacity for leadership and heroism."

Like the dynamic impasse between minoritizing and universalizing views of homosexual definition, that between transitive and separatist tropes of homosexual gender has its own complicated history, an especially crucial one for any understanding of modern gender asymmetry, oppression, and resistance. One thing that does emerge with clarity from this complex and contradictory map of sexual and gender definition is that the possible grounds to be found there for alliance and cross-identification among various groups will also be plural. To take the issue of gender definition alone: under a gender-separatist topos, lesbians have looked for identifications and alliances among women in general, including straight women (as in Adrienne Rich's "lesbian continuum" model); and gay men, as in Friedländer's model—or more recent "male liberation" models—of masculinity, might look for them among men in general, including straight men. "The erotic and social presumption of women is our enemy," Friedländer wrote in his "Seven Theses on Homosexuality" (1908). Under a topos of gender inversion or liminality, in contrast, gay men have looked to identify with straight women (on the grounds that they are also "feminine" or also desire men), or with lesbians (on the grounds that they occupy a similarly liminal position); while lesbians have analogously looked to identify with gay men or, though this latter identification has not been strong since second-wave feminism, with straight men. (Of course, the political outcomes of all these trajectories of potential identification have been radically, often violently, shaped by differential historical forces, notably homophobia and sexism.) Note, however, that this schematization over "the issue of gender definition alone" also does impinge on the issue of homo/heterosexual definition, as well, and in an unexpectedly chiasmic way. Gender-*separatist* models like Rich's or Friedländer's seem to tend toward *universalizing* understandings of homo/heterosexual potential. To the degree that gender-integrative inversion or liminality models, such as Hirschfeld's "third-sex" model, suggest an alliance or identity between lesbians and gay men, on the other hand, they tend toward gay-*separatist*, minoritizing models of specifically gay identity and politics. Steakley makes a useful series of comparisons between Hirschfeld's Scientific–Humanitarian Committee and Friedländer's Community of the Special: "Within the homosexual emancipation movement there was a deep factionalization between the Committee and the Community.... [T]he Committee was an organization of men and women, whereas the Community was exclusively male.... The Committee called homosexuals a third sex in an effort to win

23. Don Mager, "Gay Theories of Gender Role Deviance," *SubStance* 46 (1985): 32–48; quoted from 35–36. His sources here are John Lauritsen and David Thorstad, *The Early Homosexual Rights Movement* (New York: Times Change Press, 1974), and James D. Steakley, *The Homosexual Emancipation Movement in Germany* (New York: Arno Press, 1975).

the basic rights accorded the other two; the Community scorned this as a beggarly plea for mercy and touted the notion of supervirile bisexuality." These crossings are quite contingent, however; Freud's universalizing understanding of sexual definition seems to go with an integrative, inversion model of gender definition, for instance. And, more broadly, the routes to be taken across this misleadingly symmetrical map are fractured in a particular historical situation by the profound asymmetries of gender oppression and heterosexist oppression.

Like the effect of the minoritizing/universalizing impasse, in short, that of the impasse of gender definition must be seen first of all in the creation of a field of intractable, highly structured discursive incoherence at a crucial node of social organization, in this case the node at which *any* gender is discriminated. I have no optimism at all about the availability of a standpoint of thought from which either question could be intelligibly, never mind efficaciously, adjudicated, given that the same yoking of contradictions has presided over all the thought on the subject, and all its violent and pregnant modern history, that has gone to form our own thought. Instead, the more promising project would seem to be a study of the incoherent dispensation itself, the indisseverable girdle of incongruities under whose discomfiting span, for most of a century, have unfolded both the most generative and the most murderous plots of our culture.

NOTE ON THE "DOUBLE BIND"

An important concept in Sedgwick's work is the "double bind." The double bind exploits the way in which discourse about gender can always be conceived as either sharply binary or nuanced in a continuum, and discourse about deviant sexuality can always be conceived as either universalizing or minoritizing. Any underlying agenda can be achieved by one's choice of conceptual alternatives. The different ways Ann Hopkins's dilemma was conceptualized exemplifies the relationship of legal theory to feminist theory to queer theory through a series of double binds.

One double bind was constructed by the employer and the dissenting Justices. Ann Hopkins was a macho woman who was making it in a macho male environment. Aggressiveness was a requisite to be successful at Price Waterhouse (integrative), but a disability if one were a woman (separatist). So Hopkins would not have had the economic push to make partner if she weren't aggressive, but her aggressiveness turned off many male partners because they thought it unfeminine. Damned if you are, damned if you aren't. Note that the partners' willingness to do whatever it took to penalize Hopkins demands some kind of explanation.

The Supreme Court majority saw the explanation as old-fashioned sexism (see its fascination with the partners' good ole boy remarks about charm school, etc.). The Court rejected this double bind as inconsistent with Title VII's commitment to women's equal position in the workplace, and perhaps to disavowing gender stereotypes as the basis for workplace decisions. But there is another possible explanation: homophobia. By ignoring this explanation, the Court created a new double bind for Hopkins, centering on the closet. Thus, the underlying reason for Price Waterhouse's action, fear of lesbians, may have been legally admissible, and it was the made-up pretext (the abrasive woman) that got them into legal trouble. This put Price Waterhouse in the double bind.

Consider how the following case illustrates the double bind.

Marjorie Rowland v. Mad River Local School District

U.S. Court of Appeals for the Sixth Circuit, 1984.
730 F.2d 444, *cert. denied*, 470 U.S. 1009 (1985).

■ LIVELY, Chief Judge:

The school district appeals from a judgment in favor of a non-tenured guidance counselor who was suspended, then transferred and finally not rehired at the end of her one-year appointment. The question presented is whether these actions deprived the plaintiff of her right to freedom of speech under the First Amendment or to equal protection of the law under the Fourteenth Amendment to the Constitution. We conclude that under the facts of this case neither constitutional deprivation occurred, and reverse the judgment of the district court.

The plaintiff began working as a vocational guidance counselor at Stebbins High School in Montgomery County, Ohio in August 1974 under a limited one-year contract. A short time later she told a secretary in an office she shared with other vocational education personnel that two of the students she was counseling were homosexual. During the same period in the fall of 1974 the plaintiff told the same secretary that she, the plaintiff, was bisexual and that she had a female lover. She also informed the assistant principal of the school and several teachers who were personal friends that she was bisexual. In December the plaintiff had a meeting with the principal of Stebbins, the defendant DiNino, and he suggested that she resign. The plaintiff refused to resign and then told several other Stebbins teachers that she had been asked to resign because she was bisexual, and sought their support. Following another meeting with DiNino, the defendant Hopper who was superintendent of the district, and the district's attorney, the plaintiff again refused to resign. Plaintiff's attorney also attended this meeting.

Following the second refusal to resign the plaintiff was suspended with full pay for the remainder of the contract year. She then filed the first of two actions in the district court. When the district court entered a preliminary injunction against her suspension, plaintiff was reassigned to a position involving development of a career education curriculum. This was a position with no student contact. In March 1975 DiNino recommended that the contract of the plaintiff, along with those of several other Stebbins teachers, not be renewed. Superintendent Hopper concurred, and the plaintiff was informed of the recommendation. At a regular meeting of the school board the recommendation to not renew Rowland's contract was unanimously adopted without independent investigation. The plaintiff filed a second action in the district court charging that the reassignment and failure to renew her contract violated a number of her constitutional rights. The defendants in both actions were the school district, the president and members of the board of the district, the superintendent of the district and the principal of Stebbins High. * * *

The magistrate determined to submit the issues, as he perceived them, to the jury in the form of a series of "special verdicts." Though all parties submitted extensive proposed instructions, the magistrate gave none of them, concluding that the alternative to special verdicts would be "a short course on the Constitution." In special verdicts 1 through 3 the jury found that neither plaintiff's disclosure to the secretary of her love for another woman, nor her statements to the assistant principal and to other teachers concerning her bisexuality interfered with the proper performance of anyone's duties or with the operation of the school generally. In the same verdicts the jury found that the decision to suspend the plaintiff was motivated at least in part by these statements regarding her bisexuality. In special verdict 4 the jury found that the decisions to transfer and to not renew her contract were not motivated even in part by the fact that plaintiff had filed a law suit regarding her suspension.

In special verdict 5 the jury found that in suspending and transferring her the defendants treated the plaintiff differently from similarly situated employees "because she was homosexual/bisexual." The jury also found that DiNino and Hopper treated her differently from similarly situated employees in recommending that plaintiff's contract not be renewed, but that the board of education did not treat her differently in voting not to renew Ms. Rowland's contract. In the same special verdict the jury found that at the time of her suspension the plaintiff was not performing as a vocational guidance counselor in a satisfactory manner "because she revealed to Mrs. Monell [the secretary] the sexual orientation of two students when it was not necessary to do so."

In special verdict 6 the jury found that defendants DiNino and Hopper acted in good faith in all their actions regarding plaintiff and in special verdict 7 that the board of education acted for no other reason than the recommendation of the defendant Hopper in voting not to renew Ms. Rowland's contract. In special verdict 8 the jury found that if plaintiff "had not been bisexual and if she had not told Mrs. Monell, the secretary, of her sexual preference," she would not have been suspended or transferred and the board of education would not have failed to renew her contract "anyway for other reasons."

On the basis of the special verdicts the magistrate entered an order finding in favor of the school board members in their individual capacities, and in favor of the defendants DiNino and Hopper "on all issues in the complaint" because they acted in good faith. However, he found in favor of the plaintiff and against the school district for the suspension and transfer of plaintiff "in violation of her rights to equal protection of the law and free speech" and for nonrenewal of her contract "in violation of her right to free speech." The jury then awarded damages of $13,500 for personal humiliation, mental anguish and suffering proximately caused by plaintiff's suspension, no damages for her transfer, and damages of $26,947 for loss of earnings proximately caused by nonrenewal of her contract. The jury found that plaintiff had suffered no loss of reputation or standing in the community and no personal humiliation, mental anguish or suffering as the result of the failure to renew her contract. * * *

The district court awarded damages against the school district on two theories: (1) That the school district violated plaintiff's Fourteenth Amendment right to equal protection of the law by suspending her because she is bisexual or homosexual; and (2) That the school district violated plaintiff's First Amendment right to freedom of speech by not renewing her one-year contract because she told Mrs. Monell, the secretary, Mr. Goheen, the assistant principal, and other teachers of her bisexuality. We conclude that the record does not support a finding that plaintiff established either constitutional violation. * * *

[The Court of Appeals found that Rowland had no claim as a matter of law under the First Amendment because her speech did not concern "a matter of public concern." The court then ruled that she had no equal protection claim because there was evidence of unsatisfactory job performance in her disclosure that two students were homosexual and because the jury found she was fired for the combined reason of being bisexual and speaking about it, and the latter was a permissible basis for termination. (See Chapter 6 for an analysis of the legal doctrine in this case.)]

The dissent's gratuitous statement that the majority treats this case as one involving a sick person is totally wrong. It is true that plaintiff has attempted to make homosexual rights the issue in this case. However, her personal sexual orientation is not a matter of public concern, and we have decided the First Amendment issue on the basis of the latest Supreme Court treatment of legally similar claims. And, as we have pointed out, the plaintiff sought to prevail on her equal protection claim without any showing that heterosexual school employees in situations similar to hers have been, or would be, treated differently for making their personal sexual preferences the topic of comment and discussion in the high school community. Again, this is nothing more than the required analysis of an equal protection claim.

■ GEORGE CLIFTON EDWARDS, JR., CIRCUIT JUDGE, dissenting.* * *

This school teacher has been deprived of her job solely because she let it be known to some colleagues and, through them, to her administrative superiors that her sexual preference was for another woman. * * *

This record presents a clear cut issue as to whether a citizen's mere statement of a homosexual preference may be punished by job loss by the joint decision of a school superintendent, a public school principal and assistant principal, and the school board, as a matter of institutional policy. I find no language in the Constitution of the United States which excludes citizens who are bisexual or homosexual from its protection, and particularly of the protection of the first and fourteenth amendments thereto. The Constitution protects all citizens of the United States; no language therein excludes the homosexual minority. Like all citizens, homosexuals are protected in these great rights, certainly to the extent of being homosexual and stating their sexual preference in a factual manner where there is no invasion of any other person's rights. * * *

My colleague's opinion seems to me to treat this case, *sub silento*, as if it involved only a single person and a sick one at that—in short, that plaintiff's admission of homosexual status was sufficient in itself to justify her termination. To the contrary, this record does not disclose that she is subject to mental illness; nor is she alone.

Careful studies of homosexuality have now established two facts of which the courts should be aware and should take judicial notice. The first is that homosexuality is not a mental disease, like insanity or a psychopathic personality. The second is the extent of homosexuality in the United States. [The dissent then quotes at length from the 1979 Surgeon General's opinion stating that "homosexuality per se will no longer be considered a 'mental disease or defect'" (excerpted in Chapter 2, Section 2[C]) and from a summary of Kinsey's work, stating "On the basis of these various studies it is fair to conclude, conservatively, that the incidence of more or less exclusively homosexual behavior in Western culture ranges from 5 to 10 percent for adult males and from 3 to 5 percent for adult females. If bisexual behavior is included, the incidence may well be twice these figures. It is clear, therefore, that the propensity for homosexual reactivity is a widespread one even in societies such as ours which strongly discourage it."]

NOTE ON THE MAD RIVER CASE AND THE CONSTRUCTION OF HETEROSEXUALITY

As the caption to the case indicates, the Supreme Court refused to take certiorari. Justice Brennan wrote an opinion, joined by Justice Marshall, dissenting from the denial of certiorari. He made several telling points. Justice Brennan wondered whether even the most confidential communication of bisexuality does not trigger the "public issue" protections of the First Amendment, because homosexuality and bisexuality were so controversial in southern Ohio. "The fact of petitioner's bisexuality, once spoken, necessarily and ineluctably involved her in that [public] debate." More telling, Justice Brennan suggested how Rowland's "First Amendment and equal protection claims may be seen to converge, because it is realistically impossible to separate her spoken statements from her status." 470 U.S. at 1016 n.11 (Brennan, J., dissenting from denial of certiorari).

Janet Halley, "The Construction of Heterosexuality," in *Fear of a Queer Planet: Queer Politics and Social Theory* 84–85 (Michael Warner ed., 1993), extends Justice Brennan's reading of Marjorie Rowland's case. "Both Rowland and the town of Mad River were engaged in a diacritical struggle—one in which the self-definition of both players was at stake. This should make visible what otherwise should remain hidden—Rowland's discursive exertions were made in interaction with a class of heterosexuals *also in the process of self-constitution*." Halley also says: "Mad River as a political entity emerges from the Rowland controversy *heterosexual*, but heterosexual only because it silences those—not only Rowland the guidance counsellor but also the possibly homosexual students she was counseling— who would even quietly question orientation orthodoxy. The price of citizenship in Mad River is silence about deviant sexuality, an insistence upon unknowing, a regimen of the closet."

THE ROLE OF LAW IN THE SOCIAL CONSTRUCTION PROCESS

We now turn to the question of how the legal system functions in the large and somewhat amorphous process of social construction. The conventional view is that legal regulation of sexuality used to be, in the colonial or Victorian eras for example, extremely repressive and that it has grown progressively less so. This is a common "march of progress" description often applied to the decriminalization of sodomy and of abortion. Foucault argues just the opposite: prior to the late nineteenth century, there were relatively few (albeit draconian) proscriptions, which have now been replaced by increasingly detailed, medicalized, specified regulatory regimes. In a state where sodomy has been decriminalized and a civil rights law including sexual orientation has been enacted, Foucault would see an expansion of force relations and systems of surveillance in, for example, the declarations or denials of sexual orientation in litigation or the establishment of an equal opportunity office to police the anti-discrimination law.

PART A.   OPERATIONS OF LAW

Ellen Ross and Rayna Rapp are anthropologists who start with the assumption that sexuality is socially constructed and then pose the questions, How does society shape sexuality? How do family contexts, religious ideologies, community norms, and political policies interact in the formation of sexual experience? What role does law play? Ross and Rapp resist the psychoanalytic approach which maintains that sexuality is constructed entirely within the family, and they insist that larger social and legal context help shape sexuality over the years.

Ellen Ross and Rayna Rapp, Sex and Society: A Research Note From Social History and Anthropology

In *Powers of Desire: The Politics of Sexuality* 51, 62–64, 67–68.
Ann Snitow et al., editors, 1985.*

Legal systems provide a material background against which sexual relations are played out, whether they affect sexuality directly (e.g., legitimacy clauses, the outlawing of abortion, and sex codes defining prostitution) or at a distance (e.g., welfare and the responsibilities of fathers). Laws defining paternity, for example, are important in setting up the context in which sexuality occurs. The effect does not necessarily result from forcing fathers to support their illegitimate children. Few women in England, either before or after the 1834 Bastardy Clauses undermined putative fathers' legal obligations, seem to have applied for child support, and we know too well how few divorced fathers in contemporary America pay child support consistently over the years. Rather, as such laws become known, they help to establish an atmosphere that changes the sexual balance of power. The commissioners investigating the causes of the "Rebecca Riots" in 1844 were convinced that this is what happened in southern Wales. Traditional marriage and courtship patterns in England had condoned premarital pregnancies, and eighteenth-century legislation made it relatively easy for mothers of bastards to collect regular support payments. The Bastardy Clauses to the 1834 Poor Law Amendment Act assigned financial responsibility solely to the mothers (or their parishes). Now, courting men seemed to feel a new license to avoid marriage. "It is a bad time for the girls, Sir," a woman reported to a Haverfordwest Poor Law Guardian who testified before the Commission. "The boys have their own way." The Bastardy Clauses were probably among the factors that influenced a shift in popular sexual culture: an earlier tradition of lively female sexual assertiveness as traced in folk ballads and tales gave way to a more prudish, cautious image of womanhood by the 1860s. Such a transformation appears quite rational in light of the shifting legal environment. What Flandrin calls the "legal disarming of women vis-à-vis their seducers" took place earlier and more thoroughly in France. In the seventeenth century it was legally possible for a seducer, unless he married the woman, to be charged with rape if the woman was under twenty-five. As the penalty for rape was death, many seducers charged in court no doubt preferred marriage. The Civil Code of 1804, however, forbade searching for putative fathers and made unmarried women solely responsible for their children.

Throughout Europe and America, the mid- to late-nineteenth century witnessed a hardening of legal definitions of sexual outcasts, as sexual behavior came under increasing state and cultural surveillance. It is from this period that many of the sex and vice codes still prevalent in Western societies can be dated. In England, a series of Contagious Disease Acts passed from 1864 on to control venereal disease in the army and navy by registering prostitutes had the effect of stigmatizing the women and isolating them from the working-class neighborhoods in which they lived and worked. Although a campaign to repeal the acts was ultimately successful, its social purity orientation led to still further sexually restrictive legislation. The Criminal Law Amendment Act, an omnibus crime bill passed in 1885, raised the age of consent for girls from thirteen to sixteen in response to a movement to "save" working-class girls from the perceived evils of "white slavery" and aristocratic male lust. The newly increased powers of the police were turned not on the wealthy buyers of sex, but on its poorer sellers. Lodging-house keepers were commonly prosecuted as brothel keepers, and prostitutes were often uprooted and cast out from their neighborhoods. Forced to find new lodging in areas of cities more specialized in vice, they became increasingly dependant on male pimps once community support, or at least toleration, of their occupation was shattered by legal prosecution.

In the Labouchere Amendment to the same 1885 act, all forms of sexual activity between men (with consent, in private as well as in public) were subject to prosecution. This represents a dramatic extension of the definition of male homosexuality (and its condemnation) beyond the "abominations of buggery" clauses promulgated under Henry VIII and remaining in force in the centuries that followed. The Labouchere Amendment was followed in 1898 by the Vagrancy Act, which turned police attention to homosexual solicitation. Anti-homosexual legislation was passed in an atmosphere of a purity campaign that viewed homosexuality as a vice of the rich visited on the poor. But the effects of the legislation were turned against working-class homosexuals, who were most likely to be tried, while wealthier men were often able to buy their way out of public notice and prosecution. * * *

* * * [C]ontemporary culture tempts us to reify sex as a thing-in-itself. The modern perception of sex is an ideological reflection of real changes that have occurred in the contexts of daily life within which sexuality is embedded. The separation, with industrial capitalism, of family life from work, of consumption from production, of leisure from labor, of personal life from political life, has completely reorganized the context in which we experience sexuality. These polarities are grossly distorted and miscast as antimonies in modern ideological formulations, but their seeming separation creates an ideological space called "personal life," one defining characteristic of which is sexual identity. Modern consciousness permits, as earlier systems of thought did not, the positing of "sex" for perhaps the first time as having an "independent" existence. * * * [A] common American complaint is that families are losing control over their children's sexual education and behavior, challenged by public schools, the mass media, and state policies (which grant sex education and abortions to teenagers, even without parental consent). The power of families and communities to determine sexual experience has indeed sharply diminished in the past two centuries, allegedly allowing for individual sexual "liberation."

Although the movement toward self-conscious sexuality has been hailed by modernists as liberatory, it is important to remember that sexuality in contemporary times is not simply released or free-floating. It continues to be socially structured, but we would argue that the dominant power to define and regulate sexuality has been shifting toward the group of what we have labeled large-scale social and economic forces, the most salient of which is perhaps the state. States now organize many of the reproductive relations that were once embedded in smaller scale contexts. Sexuality thus enters the "social contract," connecting the individual citizen and the state. In the process, an ideological space is created that allows us to "see" sex as a defining characteristic of the individual person, "released" from the traditional restraints of family and community. The rise of the two great ethnosciences of sexual and personal liberation—sexology and psychoanalysis—have accompanied this transformation, attempting to explain and justify it.

But the ideology of sexual freedom and the right to individual self-expression have come increasingly into conflict with both state hegemony and the residual powers of more traditional contexts such as family and community control. Today, abortion, sterilization abuse, sex education, homosexual rights, and welfare and family policies are explosive political issues in the United States and much of Western Europe. For as states claim a greater and greater interest in the structuring of sexuality, sexual struggles increasingly become part of public, consciously defined politics.
* * *

PROBLEM 3–3

THE MEANS OF PRODUCTION

Building on Foucault's insight that law produces as well as prohibits what it regulates, and supplementing the specific examples given by Ross and Rapp, pick one of the following kinds of sexual behavior and list the ways in which law shapes the frequency and meaning of that behavior *other than* by direct prohibition:

- Procreative sex outside of marriage

- Bisexuality

- Interracial sex

- Sexual assault

Note the sources of law which are relevant, including family law, tort law, and administrative law. Consider also the potential impact of the absence of law on certain points. Compare your examples to direct prohibition by criminal statutes. Which do you think have the most powerful impact on human behavior? Are there behaviors which have been functionally decriminalized even if a ban remains in effect? Conversely, are some behaviors functionally criminal, even if there is no direct prohibition?

PART B.   SEXUAL IDENTITY

In light of the Ross and Rapp essay, reconsider Marjorie Rowland's case and consider the case of James Miller that follows. Think about these questions in connection with these decisions:

- How is an identity being produced by this process?

- What is the impact on that production of the likely litigation strategy decisions made by counsel for both sides in this case?

- What do these cases tell us about what *the law* means by the terms homosexual, heterosexual, bisexual?

At the overall social level, i.e. at the level of abstraction in the Ross and Rapp article, what are the impacts produced by the processes described in these cases?

Dennis R. Beller v. J. William Middendorf
James Lee Miller v. Donald H. Rumsfield
Mary Roseann Saal v. J. William Middendorf

U.S. Court of Appeals for the Ninth Circuit, 1980.
632 F.2d 788, *cert. denied*, 454 U.S. 855 (1981).

■ [Anthony] Kennedy, Circuit Judge:

Although the factual and procedural settings of these three consolidated appeals differ, the broad outlines are similar: an enlisted person in the Navy, with an otherwise fine performance record, admitted engaging in homosexual acts, conduct prohibited by Navy regulations. Following proceedings before an administrative discharge board and review by the Secretary of the Navy, each was ordered discharged. Plaintiffs raise constitutional challenges to the Navy's regulations and proceedings. * * *

Plaintiff James Miller, currently a Yeoman Second Class, enlisted in the Navy in February, 1965. He had reenlisted twice, the most recent reenlistment being in 1972 for a period of six years. As a result of an unrelated incident, a Naval Investigative Service (NIS) inquiry began in 1975, and in an interview with the NIS investigator, after being advised of his rights, plaintiff admitted that he had participated recently in homosexual acts with two Taiwanese natives while he was stationed in Taiwan. Pursuant to orders issued prior to the institution of the NIS investigation, plaintiff was transferred to the USS ORISKANY at Alameda, California. He served on board for over one year and was given a Secret clearance by his commander, who had knowledge of the NIS investigation.

On April 12, 1976, a hearing board was convened to consider Miller's discharge for homosexuality. The board heard testimony from the NIS investigator, several witnesses as to Miller's good character and service in the Navy, and Miller on his own behalf. It found that plaintiff had admitted to committing homosexual acts during his assignment in Taiwan, but nevertheless recommended, by vote of two to one, that plaintiff be retained in the Navy. The dissenting member of the board voted that plaintiff be administratively discharged under honorable conditions.

Plaintiff was subsequently examined by the Senior Medical Officer who found that despite plaintiff's admitted homosexual episodes, he did not appear to be "a homosexual," and that he found no evidence of psychosis or neurosis. The medical officer recommended retention. The convening authority, the Commanding Officer of the USS ORISKANY, then forwarded the board proceedings to the Chief of Naval Personnel and recommended that plaintiff be retained in the Navy.

The Assistant Director of the Enlisted Performance Division recommended that plaintiff be separated with a General Discharge under honorable conditions by reason of misconduct, for his admitted participation in in-service homosexual acts. That recommendation was approved by the Assistant Secretary of the Navy and plaintiff was then scheduled for separation on June 23, 1976.

On that date, Miller brought suit in the district court, asking that his discharge be restrained and in the alternative that he be given not less than an honorable discharge. The Chief of Naval Personnel subsequently ordered Miller separated with an honorable discharge, but this discharge was stayed by the district court until, relying largely on its decision in *Beller*, it granted summary judgment for the Navy. This court, however, stayed Miller's discharge pending disposition of this appeal. Miller has been retained in the Navy pursuant to this court's order. He currently works for the Commanding Officer, Enlisted Personnel, Treasure Island. His commanding officer there requested that the Navy retain him.

Miller has tried to reenlist; the Navy denied his application. * * *

To evaluate the constitutionality of the Navy's conduct, it is necessary to determine what the Navy's policy regarding discharge of homosexuals really is. The policy of the Secretary which was applied to the plaintiffs begins: "Members involved in homosexuality are military liabilities who cannot be tolerated in a military organization.... Their prompt separation is essential." Inst. 1900.9A. We conclude that this instruction and the applicable regulations make discharge of known homosexuals mandatory, subject only to a kind of executive discretion vested in the Secretary which is unrelated to the fitness of any particular individual.[9] * * *

9. Since these lawsuits were initiated, the Navy has issued a new set of instructions and regulations governing the discharge of homosexuals. These regulations provide for limited retention of homosexuals. They state in part:

> A homosexual act is bodily contact with a person of the same sex with the intent of obtaining or giving sexual gratification.

> Any member who solicits, attempts, or engages in homosexual acts shall normally be separated from the naval service. The presence of such a member in a military environment seriously impairs combat readiness, efficiency, security and morale.

> A member who has solicited, attempted, or engaged in a homosexual act on a single occasion and who does not profess or demonstrate proclivity to repeat such an act may be considered for retention in the light of all relevant circumstances. Retention is to be permitted only if the aforesaid conduct is not likely to present any adverse impact either upon the member's continued performance of military duties or upon the readiness, efficiency, or morale of the unit to which the member is assigned either at the time of the conduct or at the time of processing according to the alternatives set forth herein.

SECNAV Instruction 1900.9C. The Navy has taken the position in writing that these regu-

The Secretary's policy regarding homosexuals states:

> Members involved in homosexuality are military liabilities who cannot be tolerated in a military organization. In developing and documenting cases involving homosexual conduct, commanding officers should be keenly aware that members involved in homosexual acts are security and reliability risks who discredit themselves and the naval service by their homosexual conduct. Their prompt separation is essential.

SECNAVINST 1900.9A. The Navy's Personnel Manual prescribes several grounds on which enlisted persons "may be separated by reason of misconduct." BUPERSMAN § 3420185. Homosexual acts, various sexual offenses, and sale or trafficking in drugs are the only categories where the regulations provide, "Processing for discharge is mandatory." The regulations governing other grounds for discharge by reason of misconduct permit various ways for a member to rehabilitate himself or to demonstrate that because of other reasons he should be retained. The regulations also provide that members may be discharged by reason of unfitness on similar grounds, and the plaintiffs here were discharged under the unfitness regulations. Homosexual acts (and conduct labelled "sexual perversion") are singled out with the directive, "Processing for discharge is mandatory," while some form of individual consideration or rehabilitation is provided for in connection with other grounds. The category for homosexual acts explicitly refers to INST. 1900.9 as an expression of the controlling policy.

The district courts in *Saal* and *Martinez v. Brown*, 449 F. Supp. 207 (N.D.Cal.1978), concluded the regulations required discharge of a person found to be homosexual. Both courts noted that the Navy was given the opportunity to demonstrate that it retains some known homosexuals and to articulate the factors which influence the Secretary's decision in such cases. The Secretary in these cases was either unable or unwilling to do so. Other indications in the records of the cases before us support the conclusion that "as applied, the regulations require the mandatory discharge of those found

lations do not apply retroactively to the plaintiffs in this case.

* * * Both Beller and Saal [the other plaintiffs challenging their discharges] have admitted to homosexual acts with various persons. The threshold criteria for discretionary retention under the new regulation are "a homosexual act" "on a single occasion"; the two criteria are conjunctive. The case of Miller is closer but no less clear. He has at various times denied being homosexual and expressed regret or repugnance at his acts. Nevertheless, no part of the record in his case, either alone or in combination with any

other part, suggests the possibility of our remanding his case for consideration under SECNAVINST 1900.9C. Miller does not himself appear to have suggested that he met the criteria of 1900.9C. If we were to ignore all but the record evidence most favorable to Miller, application of 1900.9C to Miller would still be prevented by his admission at his hearing to at least two homosexual acts on two separate occasions:

> I had had an experience once before ... then these two boys came along and we just had the experiences.

Record at 38.

to be homosexuals or to have engaged in homosexual conduct." *Martinez, supra*, 449 F. Supp. at 212.[13] * * *

NOTE ON JAMES MILLER'S CASE AND LAW'S (OCCASIONAL) INSISTENCE ON SEXUAL CLOSURE

Unlike Marjorie Rowland, James Miller does not clearly present his sexual orientation to the authorities, and the authorities don't quite know what to do with him. "He has at various times denied being homosexual and expressed regret or repugnance at his acts," said Judge, now Justice, Kennedy from the record. Most of the Navy authorities handling Miller's case were willing to keep him in the Navy; he "did not appear to be 'a homosexual,'" was the medical officer's justification. But the Navy review board decided that acts were enough and discharged him. Judge Kennedy's opinion does not know at all what to make of Miller but seems satisfied to wash its hands of the man and go along with the official story.

"The contrast with Marjorie Rowland * * * is instructive. While Rowland powerfully intervened in a public debate over homosexuality upon describing herself, in two ostensibly private conversations, as bisexual, Miller was drawn into that debate, and given a location in it, without consolidating the authority to describe himself. Instead, even as Miller claimed to expel himself from the class of homosexuals and to constitute himself as heterosexual, he was expelled from the class of heterosexuals and constituted as homosexual by an act of definitional power over which he had no control. That is, the disintegration of his authority to name himself indicates not merely Miller's unwillingness to be excluded from the Navy or his bafflement at the moralized binarism in which he was required to find a place; it also indicates that the class of heterosexuals gains at the moment of this exclusion what Miller has lost, the epistemological authority to know and to designate what (and who) a homosexual is." Halley, "Construction of Heterosexuality," 87–88.

Query. The provision quoted in footnote 9 that admits of the possibility of non-homosexuals engaging in homosexual sex (at least once) continues in modified form today. (See Chapter 4, Section 3.) How does it operate to constitute what is heterosexual sex?

---

13. * * * In response to an interrogatory from Miller, the Navy had an opportunity in the district court to demonstrate that in the past it exercised discretion to retain enlisted persons found to be homosexuals. The Navy instead claimed that Miller's question was ambiguous, and summary judgment was entered before the Navy responded to Miller's more precisely worded question:

> Interrogatory No. 30: If, as the Navy and the Secretary of Defense represented to the United States Court of Appeals for the Seventh Circuit in [an earlier case], the discharge or separation from the Navy is not mandatory, how many exceptions have been made over the past five years? In other words, how many members of the Navy, identified as "homosexuals" have been retained in the Navy?

> Answer No. 30: The use of the term "identified" makes this question impossible to answer. The term is imprecise. More information is needed. * * *

NOTE ON NON-JUDICIAL MECHANISMS OF LEGAL POWER

Lest we fall into the trap of believing that judicial opinions are the sole or even primary means by which the law extends its reach throughout the constitutive dynamics of a society, we suggest that you pause here and read carefully the texts of the various statutes reproduced in the appendices to this book. How do they define sexual identities? What are the implications of these statutory definitions? Imagine, for example, that you are drafting a complaint to allege discrimination based on one of the state or local civil rights laws or the proposed federal statute (the Employment Non-Discrimination Act)? What will you allege as the elements of your cause of action? Which kinds of facts will be most relevant? What defenses will your opposing counsel investigate and perhaps rely on? How will such civil rights lawsuits function to construct (reify?) sexual identities, regardless of who wins?

Although lawyers tend to think that the law is "made" once a case is decided, we should remember that judicial decisions continue to reverberate in their implementation, not just in their authority as precedent. Consider the following postscript to a prisoner rights suit:

Patricia Klein Lerner, Jailer Learns Gay Culture to Foil Straight Inmates

Los Angeles Times, December 27, 1990.

Each weekday morning, Los Angeles County Sheriff's Deputy Ernest Cobarrubias sits at his desk at the Hall of Justice Jail, with a pocket guide to gay bars at his side.

One by one, inmates are led into the room, which doubles as the jail barbershop.

"When did you last have sex with a woman?" Cobarrubias asks, facing the inmate from across the desk.

"What gay bars and bathhouses do you go to?"

"How long have you been gay?"

The questions may sound impertinent and overly personal, but Cobarrubias isn't just being nosy.

As the senior deputy in charge of classifying prisoners at the Hall of Justice Jail, part of Cobarrubias' job is to protect the jail's 350 or so homosexual inmates, who are segregated from the overall inmate population.

Neo-Nazis, gang members, skinheads, satanists and so-called "homophobes" have been known to feign homosexuality in an attempt to serve their time in the homosexual ward of the jail, atop Sheriff's Department headquarters downtown, authorities said.

Some of the phonies seek to prey on the homosexual inmates while others are merely trying to escape the tension, violence and overcrowded conditions of the main County Jail on nearby Bauchet Street, Cobarrubias said.

It's Cobarrubias' job to spot the fakes and send them back to the main jail.

In eight years on the job, Cobarrubias has become an expert on gay culture. The 40–year-old married father of two can detail the names and locales of dozens of gay bars and knows which gay magazines feature intellectual commentary and which ones offer little more than nude pictures of men.

Three mornings a week, Cobarrubias is assisted by David Glascock, 50, a gay community activist who monitors the screening process and the jail's treatment of homosexuals for the American Civil Liberties Union. * * *

Some inmates pretending to be homosexual have talked to other inmates and are ready with the name of a gay bar or two. But the questioning gets tougher.

"What's the cover charge? Where is it? How is it decorated?" Cobarrubias asks. * * *

Sometimes—maybe one case in 100, Cobarrubias estimates—a non-homosexual inmate slips through, usually after being coached. The mistake usually comes to light quickly because an inmate starts preying on other inmates or receives visits from a girlfriend or other inmates turn him in. Rarely—maybe five times in eight years, Cobarrubias said—has an inmate seriously beaten a homosexual inmate before being discovered.

Other jails have systems for segregating homosexual prisoners but Los Angeles' efforts are probably the most thorough, said John Hagar, a former ACLU attorney who helped work out a settlement in a 1983 ACLU lawsuit accusing the Sheriff's Department of unfairly denying homosexual inmates privileges available to other inmates. * * *

Glascock, 50, was brought in to the program to help teach Cobarrubias how to identify homosexual inmates. At first, he was a volunteer. Now his salary is paid by the county as part of the settlement of the ACLU suit.

Glascock has been concerned about the treatment of homosexuals by law enforcement officials since he was 19 years old and went to jail in Wisconsin for having sex with minors—two teen-age male prostitutes.

Cobarrubias had no particular past experience with homosexuals. A native of East Los Angeles, he spent five years as a social worker for the Department of Social Services before joining the Sheriff's Department in 1974, working as a patrol officer and bailiff.

The duty of weeding out fake gays fell to him because he was in charge of deciding where to place incoming prisoners at the Hall of Justice Jail. Other inmates housed there include juveniles, informants and "softs," prisoners who deputies believe would be in danger at the main jail.

Cross dressers—men who wear feminine clothes and makeup and even some who may have undergone sex change operations—are housed away from other gay inmates in a separate module to cut down on problems and disease, officials said.

Sometimes Cobarrubias will allow a non-homosexual inmate to stay at the jail if he believes the person has a genuine and well-founded fear of serving time in the main jail.

Conditions at the Hall of Justice Jail are better in many respects than in the main jail, Cobarrubias said. Televisions and telephones are on every row. The atmosphere is more relaxed and it is less crowded. The Hall of Justice Jail has 60 fewer prisoners than the 1,800 for which it was designed. The County Jail, designed for 5,276 inmates, has 6,482, Sheriff's Deputy Patrick Hunter said.

Cobarrubias' unusual assignment has prompted ribbing, some of it cruel, from fellow deputies who have called him the "homosexual deputy" or accused him of being bisexual.

"I'm sure they think I'm gay or it's at least crossed their minds," Cobarrubias said. "But once they sit down and talk to me, they know where I'm coming from. I'm just heterosexual, doing a job assigned me by the department."

PART C.   RETHINKING PRIVACY

How would a Foucauldian approach the problems imbedded in privacy doctrine that we identified in Chapter 1? Consider the following analysis.

Jed Rubenfeld, The Right of Privacy

102 *Harvard Law Review* 737, 783–84, 800 (1989).*

* * * The methodology heretofore universal in privacy analysis has begun with the question, "What is the state trying to forbid?" The proscribed conduct is then delineated and its significance tested through a pre-established conceptual apparatus: for its role in "the concept of ordered liberty," its status as a "fundamental" right, its importance to one's identity, or for any other criterion of fundamentality upon which a court can settle. Suppose instead we began by asking not what is being *prohibited*, but what is being *produced*. Suppose we looked not to the negative aspect of the law—the interdiction by which it formally expresses itself—but at its positive aspect: the real effects that conformity with the law produces at the level of everyday lives and social practices. * * *

* * * There *is* something fundamental at stake in the privacy decisions, but it is not the proscribed conduct, nor even the freedom of decision—it is not what is being taken away.

The distinctive and singular characteristic of the laws against which the right to privacy has been applied lies in their *productive* or *affirmative* consequences. There are perhaps no legal proscriptions with more profound, more extensive, or more persistent affirmative effects on individual lives than the laws struck down as violations of the right to privacy. Anti-abortion laws, anti-miscegenation laws, and compulsory education laws all involve the forcing of lives into well-defined and highly confined institutional layers. At the simplest, most quotidian level, such laws tend to *take over* the lives of the persons involved: they occupy and preoccupy. They affirmatively and very substantially shape a person's life; they direct a life's development along a particular avenue. These laws do not simply proscribe one act or remove one liberty; they inform the totality of a person's life.

The principle of the right to privacy is not the freedom to do certain, particular acts determined to be fundamental through some ever-progressing normative lens. It is the fundamental freedom not to have one's life too totally determined by a progressively more normalizing state. * * *

The danger, then, is a particular kind of creeping totalitarianism, an unarmed *occupation* of individuals' lives. That is the danger of which Foucault as well as the right to privacy is warning us: a society standardized and normalized, in which lives are too substantially or too rigidly directed. That is the threat posed by state power in our century. * * *

Most fundamentally, the prohibition against homosexual sex channels individuals' sexual desires into *reproductive* outlets. Although the prohibition does not, like the law against abortions, produce as an imminent consequence compulsory child-bearing, it nonetheless forcibly directs individuals into the pathways of reproductive sexuality, rather than the socially "unproductive" realm of homosexuality. These pathways are further guided, in our society, into particular institutional orbits, chief among which are the nuclear family and the constellation of practices surrounding a heterosexuality that is defined in conscious contradistinction to homosexuality. Indeed, it is difficult to separate our society's inculcation of a heterosexual identity from the simultaneous inculcation of a dichotomized complementarity of roles to be borne by men and women. Homosexual couples by necessity throw into question the allocation of specific functions—whether professional, personal, or emotional—between the sexes. It is this aspect of the ban on homosexuality—its central role in the maintenance of institutionalized sexual identities and normalized reproductive relations—that have made its *affirmative* or *formative* consequences, as well as the reaction against these consequences, so powerful a force in modern society. * * *

NOTE ON FOUCAULT, PRIVACY, AND RIGHTS DISCOURSE

A major point of agreement between feminism and Foucault is the recognition that sexuality functions as a power system ("the personal is political") and that it operates at multiple sites of power and resistance. Thus, for example, contested issues within a family, within a school or university, or within a profession are viewed as being just as much "politics" as an election or a policy protest. Does Rubenfeld's elaboration of a privacy doctrine undercut that proposition, by implicitly validating an anti-totalitarian defense only against the state?

Where does Foucauldian analysis leave the discourse of rights? Is the concept of an autonomous individual with a claim to a coherent, timeless body of rights obsolete and naive? If so, is paralysis the only outcome? For an analysis of the complexities of the dynamic between rights discourse and political organizing from a Marxist-feminist viewpoint, see Elizabeth M. Schneider, "The Dialectic of Rights and Politics: Perspectives from the Women's Movement," 61 *N.Y.U. L. Rev.* 589 (1986).

If Foucault and Rubenfeld are correct that law produces as well as restricts behaviors, should litigators use privacy doctrine in seeking intervention, and not just withdrawal, by the state? At least one scholar believes so:

> Rather than ask how individuals can be shielded from the exercise of state power, we should ask how state power might be invoked to restructure aspects of personal life in order to eliminate distorting factors in people's own interactions and personal decisionmaking.

Stephen J. Schnably, "Beyond *Griswold*: Foucauldian and Republican Approaches to Privacy," 23 *Conn. L. Rev.* 861, 870 (1991). The author goes on to conclude that the state should set the proper context for abortion counseling not merely by mandating that high quality, personalized counseling be made available, but also by providing funding for abortions and for day care, so that a woman's decision can be truly uncoerced. *Id.* at 940–41. How would a Foucauldian Constitution be structured?

U.S. MILITARY EXCLUSIONS AND THE CONSTRUCTION OF MANHOOD

SECTION 1   Racial Exclusion and Segregation in the the U.S. Armed Services

SECTION 2   The Exclusion of Women From Combat

SECTION 3   The Military's Exclusion of Lesbian, Gay Men, and Bisexuals

No government institution has been more important in American history or more indicative of American attitudes about sexuality and gender than the U.S. armed forces. Yet despite the military's central role, service in the armed forces has been a selective obligation of citizenship: only a minority of American citizens have ever been eligible for full military duty. The main exclusions have been ones that relate in some way or another to sexuality and gender: the exclusion and later segregation of people of color in the armed forces, a policy that ended in the 1950s (Section 1); the traditional exclusion of women from service and currently from combat positions, a policy under heavy fire for the last 20 years and perhaps on its way out in the 1990s (Section 2); and the current exclusion of lesbians, gay men, and bisexuals and still a robust policy as encoded in the famous "don't ask, don't tell" policy (Section 3). Although each has had multiple

319

meanings, one function they all share is policing the social understanding of "manhood."

A parallel project in this chapter will be to deepen the inquiry into equal protection law initiated in Chapter 1. The military's exclusions have focused on three classic discriminatory classifications: race, sex, and sexual orientation. Should the military, or any other branch of government, be able to classify and exclude along these lines without compelling justification? For most of our constitutional history, the answer has been "yes." Recently, race has become a "suspect" classification, and sex a "quasi-suspect" one if not a suspect one. As Chapter 1 indicated, sexual orientation is not (yet?) a suspect classification requiring "strict scrutiny." What should be its status? Do the reasons for scrutinizing race and sex classifications apply to sexual orientation? In addition, there are serious First Amendment problems with the current military exclusion of open gays and lesbians.

Finally, this chapter will offer different angles on how "manhood" or "masculinity" is understood and valued in our society. Chapter 2 offered some alternatives to manhood: the New Woman of the nineteenth century, the lesbian and male homosexual of the early twentieth century, and the transgendered person of the later twentieth century. Yet these alternatives remain marginal, even if less so than before, and the touchstone of sexuality and citizenship remains "the man." What does this mean? What is "manhood," and how does it relate to conceptions of citizenship? An excellent work of background history is Anthony Rotundo, *American Manhood: Transformations in Masculinity from the Revolution to the Modern Era* (1993), but form your own ideas as you read the following materials.

RACIAL EXCLUSION AND SEGREGATION IN THE U.S. ARMED SERVICES

Kenneth L. Karst, The Pursuit of Manhood and the Desegregation of the Armed Forces

38 *UCLA Law Review* 499–501, 502–08, 510–20 (1991).*

The statute of the Minuteman stands at the edge of they Lexington Battle Green as a reminder of the American tradition of the citizen soldier. From the Revolution onward, a great many Americans have believed that a citizen has the responsibility, in time of need, to serve in the armed forces. The same association of ideas also works in the other direction: when we amended the Constitution to lower the voting age to eighteen, one prominent slogan was, "If they're old enough to fight, they're old enough to vote." In the United States, as in Europe, citizenship and eligibility for military service have gone hand in hand. [Except that African Americans, women, and gays have been excluded or segregated for most of American history. Karst maintains that the three exclusions or segregations share a unifying theme.]

That unifying theme is the pursuit of manhood. Manhood, of course, has no existence except as it is expressed and perceived. The pursuit of manhood is an expressive undertaking, a series of dramatic performances. Masculinity is traditionally defined around the idea of power; the armed forces are the nation's preeminent symbol of power; and, not incidentally, "the Marines are looking for a few good men." The symbolism is not a side effect; it is the main point. From the colonial era to the middle of this century, our armed forces have alternately excluded and segregated blacks in the pursuit of manhood, and today's forms of exclusion and segregation are similarly grounded in the symbolism of masculine power. * * *

I. THE PROBLEM OF MANHOOD AND THE IDEOLOGY
OF MASCULINITY

The connections between military service and citizenship were well understood during the Civil War. Immediately after the first shots at Fort Sumter, black citizens began to volunteer for service in the Union Army

---

* Originally published in the *UCLA Law Review*. Copyright © 1991, The Regents of the University of California. All Rights Reserved. Reprinted by permission.

and the militia. At first these efforts were rebuffed. By law Congress had limited membership in the militia to whites, and the Lincoln administration, still wooing the border states, feared that admitting blacks to the Army would send the signal that the Union's aim was not merely the preservation of the Union, but the abolition of slavery. Furthermore, some generals "feared that the presence of black soldiers in the army would create disharmony and drive away white volunteers." Working-class whites in Northern cities threatened violence to blacks who were proposing to organize military companies. To men at high and low levels in white society, black manhood suggested a new and disquieting form of rivalry, and so the Union cause had to be "a white man's war."

The issue of full citizenship for black people was never far below the surface of the question of black participation in the Army and the militia. Both slavery and lesser forms of racial discrimination were premised on an assumption, sometimes explicit and sometimes unspoken, that denied manhood—in the full sense of competence to be citizens—to black men. Then, as now, a citizen was a respected and responsible participant in society, and especially in society's decisions. "Manhood suffrage," a term commonly used in the era of Andrew Jackson, was not a slogan of universality; it excluded women and tribal Indians, and even in the North it typically excluded black men. Whites sometimes referred to black men as "degraded"; as George Fredrickson has remarked, the use of this term suggested "that there was some ideal of manhood from which the Negro had fallen or to which he might be raised."[11]

In fact there was, and still is, an ideal of manhood. Historically the ideal, like the word itself, has embraced at least two meanings: masculinity and eligibility for equal citizenship. For most of our national history these meanings have been intertwined; a competence identified with masculinity has seemed a condition of full citizenship, and active participation in the community's public life has offered men reassurance of their masculinity. Because it is an abstract ideal, a construct of the mind, manhood in the sense of masculinity is in some measure unattainable; it can be pursued, but never wholly achieved. Yet, the achievement of manhood is seen by most men as essential to their identities. In combination, these elements are a recipe for anxiety. So, manhood is not just an ideal; it is also a problem. The problem begins early, when a little boy must seek his gender identity by separating himself from his mother and from the softness, domesticity, and nurturing she represents.[13] I use the term "represents"

11. [George M.] Fredrickson, *The Black Image in the White Mind: The Debate on Afro–American Character and Destiny, 1817–1914,* at 5 (1971).

13. The extensive modern literature on this subject begins in Nancy Chodorow's Freudian study, *The Reproduction of Mothering: Psychoanalysis and the Sociology of Gender* (1978). See [Jessica] Benjamin, *The Bonds of Love: Psychoanalysis, Feminism,* and the Problem of Domination (1988); [Nancy] Chodorow, *Feminism and Psychoanalytic Theory* 23–44 (1990); [Dorothy] Dinnerstein, *The Mermaid and the Minotaur: Sexual Arrangements and Human Malaise* (1976). Robert Stoller, a psychiatrist, suggests that the creation of masculinity out of the "protofemininity" of symbiosis with the mother leaves behind a permanent residue: "a vigilance, a fear of the pull of the symbiosis.... One

advisedly; gender, unlike sex, is not found in nature, but created and understood through representation, the playing of roles labeled "masculine" or "feminine."

Thus, masculinity begins in escape—the perceived need to separate from a feminine identity. The main demands for positive achievement of masculinity arise outside the home, and those demands reinforce the boy's need to be what his mother is not. In the hierarchical and rigorously competitive society of other boys, one categorical imperative outranks all the others: don't be a girl. Femininity is a "negative identity," a part of the self that must be repressed. The manhood pursued through male rivalry is more than maturity, more than adulthood; it also includes a set of qualities customarily defined as masculine. Although masculinity is defined against its polar opposite, the identification with competence and power in a male-dominated world has made it seem to be society's norm for being fully human. Femininity is seen, not merely as deviance from the norm, but as a fundamental flaw—a failure, at the deepest level, to qualify. Pondering this reality, Simone de Beauvoir described the traditional form of femininity as "mutilation."[15]

We are all consumers of images of manhood. According to these images a man is supposed to be: active; assertive; confident; decisive; ready to lead; strong; courageous; morally capable of violence; independent; competitive; practical; successful in achieving goals; emotionally detached; cool in the face of danger or crisis; blunt in expression; sexually aggressive and yet protective toward women. "Proving yourself" as a man can take many forms, but all of them are expressive, and all are variations on the theme of power.

When Henry Kissinger said, "Power is the ultimate aphrodisiac," perhaps the wish was father to the thought. Surely his pronouncement on the causal link between power and sex is only part of the story. If power is sexy, sex is also power. When men fear women and seek to dominate them, one reason is that they have learned to identify male sexuality with conquest. In another perspective, however, we can see the subordination of women as part of men's nervous efforts to repress the "feminine" in themselves, to keep their manhood visible to other men. The deepest fear of all, embedded in a never-ending drama of male rivalry, is the fear of being dominated by other men, humiliated for not measuring up to the manly ideal. * * *

The heart of the ideology of masculinity is the belief that power rightfully belongs to the masculine—that is, to those who display the traits traditionally called masculine. This belief has two corollaries. The first is

---

must maintain one's distance from women or be irreparably infected with femininity". [Robert] Stoller, *Presentations of Gender* 18 (1985).

15. [Simone] De Beauvoir, *The Second Sex* 682 (1968). The "traditional" model here evoked is, in the United States, mainly a model for white women. Black women are often seen as strong and active. See generally [Kimberlé] Crenshaw, "Demarginalizing the Intersection of Race and Sex: A Black Feminist Critique of Antidiscrimination Doctrine, Feminist Theory and Antiracist Politics," 1989 *U. Chi. L. Forum* 139.

that the gender line must be clearly drawn, and the second is that power is rightfully distributed among the masculine in proportion to their masculinity, as determined not merely by their physical stature or aggressiveness, but more generally by their ability to dominate and to avoid being dominated. Both parts of the ideology contribute to the subordination of groups. This function is easy to see in efforts to express the gender line in sharp definition; the ideology of masculinity will be effective in assigning power only if those who are masculine are clearly identified. The second corollary of the ideology highlights the centrality of male rivalry. By making anxiety into an everyday fact of life, it leads nervous men to seek reassurances of their masculinity through group rituals that express domination over other groups. In combination these two beliefs purport to justify power by tautology, to ground the legitimacy of domination in domination itself.

In our country's history, the male-rivalry strand of the ideology of masculinity is repeatedly visible in the readiness of white men, and especially poor white men, to exclude black men from equal citizenship. During the Civil War the white men in the Northeast who were most visibly offended by the sight of blacks in uniform were recent immigrants from Ireland. Because they occupied the bottom of the employment ladder, they had little in the way of traditional masculine achievement to bolster their sense of self-worth. For the same reason they had much to fear from the competition of black laborers. Those fears modulated into opposition to the war when it became clear that the Union was fighting for emancipation, which would greatly increase their rivals' numbers. Anxiety was sparked into violence in 1863 when the immigrants faced the choice of registration for the military draft or deportation. The Draft Riots in New York were in major part race riots, with hundreds of black people killed, dozens of them lynched in public. The Northern whites most bent on denying black men a traditional way of expressing manhood were those most in need of affirming their own.

Since the mid-nineteenth century the main path to manhood for American males has been the competitive pursuit of individual achievement in work and in other sectors of the community's public life. But changes in modes of work—notably the rise of large-scale industry and increased bureaucratization—have reduced many men's individual opportunities to exercise independence, take risks, seek to master other men, and otherwise behave in ways traditionally seen as manly. The same changes have also reduced individual men's sense of control over their own fates. As playwrights and novelists remind us, a man's apprehensions about failure and his anxiety about masculine identity are two perspectives on the same fear.

A man who finds the path of individual achievement to be rough going may try to express his power by engaging in private violence such as rape or wife-battering. Alternatively, he may attach himself to a group that pursues power through domination of members of other groups. An ugly example from overseas is instructive. In Germany between the wars, the Nazi movement found its greatest acceptance among men who saw themselves falling out of the middle class and who were searching in desperation for ways to reassert their worth as men and their status as citizens. Today's analogues in thuggery, from British football hooligans to American skinheads, are also searching for symbols of power. As individuals they seek to avoid the sense of humiliation by joining in groups to act out their squalid little dramas of domination.

It is easy to scorn the losers who seek to express their manhood by wearing swastikas or boots with metal toes. It is less convenient for us— and here I mean men who are more fortunate—to recognize that the losers' fears are our fears in exaggerated form; that their behavior expresses feelings akin to those lurking in the shadows of our minds; that our own behavior, though by more genteel means, often contributes to group subordination. One standard mode of repression of our negative identities is to project them onto other people, and especially onto members of groups that have been subordinated. The process works so well that it becomes second nature to see those people not as persons, but as the abstractions we have projected upon them. Each abstraction is a mask, and it bears a label: blackness, for example, or femininity, or homosexuality. To a great many white heterosexual men these masks of the Other are frightening; when we police the color line and the gender line in the world around us, we are policing the same line in our own minds, defending our senses of self. The fear of members of subordinated groups is more than a fear of competition, or even retaliation. No spectre is more terrifying than our own negative identity.[30] * * *

II.   MALE RIVALRY AND THE DOUBLE BATTLE OF BLACK SOLDIERS

Frederick Douglass saw black men in the Civil War as fighting a "double battle": for the Union but also for equality, against the slave power but also against racism.[37] Black soldiers—and sailors and airmen and marines—have always had to fight the same double battle, in war as in peacetime. Today's Army is rightly called a success story, and yet even there muted forms of racial discrimination persist; the other services have considerably farther to go in eliminating racism's effects. Like every story focused on black Americans as a group, this one begins with slavery. The

---

30. To say that a negative identity must be repressed is not to say that a white man fears becoming female or gay or black; the fear is that he will be perceived as being "effeminate" or gay or socially black. As Joel Williamson says:

> White America, in its stubborn and residual racial egotism, resists the realization of how very deeply and irreversibly black it is, and has been. The struggle against that awareness, the rage against the realization of their blackness and its legitimacy is the struggle of white people in race relations. To recognize and respect the blackness that is already within themselves would be to recognize

and respect the blackness that is within the nation, and, to surrender the uses, physical and psychological, that they have learned to make of blacks as a separate people.

[Joel] Williamson, *The Crucible of Race: Black–White Relations in the American South Since Emancipation* 522 (1984). This thoughtful passage would also make good sense if we were to substitute "male" or "heterosexual" for "white," and substitute "feminine" or "gay" for "black."

37. [David W.] Blight, *Frederick Douglass' Civil War: Keeping Faith in Jubilee* 163–64 (1989).

story's persistent themes, from the earliest beginnings, are the associations linking race and sex and violence. All these associations are grounded in the ideology of masculinity, and many of them have been engraved in law.

A. *Race, Sex, and the Roots of White Male Anxiety*

In the eyes of Englishmen in the era of colonization, slavery implied something less than humanity, a status akin to that of a beast. This assumption was part of a logic that was circular; to complete the circle of justification, the defenders of black slavery argued that blacks were not fully human. Beneath the surface of these apologies lay both male rivalry and anxieties about self-definition. African men were thought by Europeans to be especially libidinous; it was easy for white men to project their own desires onto blacks, and to connect the need for control over blacks with the need to control themselves. This association was intensified in the American colonies as many white slaveholders came to exercise sexual privileges over female slaves; if white men's fears of slave revolts came to be associated with fears of black men's supposed sexual aggressiveness, no doubt one reason was the fear of retaliation.

Even in the North, the perception of black men as threatening had roots in the fears of violent slave insurrections that had gripped the white South ever since Nat Turner's revolt in 1831. Those southern fears found a military expression. John Hope Franklin has written of "the militant South," an amalgam of martial spirit and gentlemanly chivalry that lives even today.[43] In the slave states the militia was composed of all adult white males. It served as a focal point for local social life in white communities, but its main function was to enforce the rigid discipline of slavery's caste system. Typically it was organized into "the patrol," a nightly sweep of the streets and highways by groups of mounted militiamen. By their actions the patrol showed that whites were whistling in the dark when they assured each other that black men were docile, even cowardly. The patrol routinely searched slaves' houses and persons for weapons or stolen property. They arrested any black person outside his or her plantation without a pass, and dispersed meetings of blacks. They dispensed summary justice, punishing transgressions as they found them, then and there. The patrol's main mission, of course, was not punishment but intimidation. Being called "Cap'n" and riding the "beat" at night also promoted the riders' masculine self-images, and surely that result was not just a by-product of the enterprise. The patrol publicly symbolized both white male power and the social gulf between citizens and slaves.

Given this historical example, it was no wonder that the black men who volunteered to serve the Union in 1861 associated manhood and citizenship. Understandably, they believed that military service would allow them to be seen as men, as citizens. Once Northern blacks put on the uniform, they believed, it would be hard to deny them the vote. If Southern blacks were freed to serve as Union soldiers, the war would become a war to end slavery. Developments like these were just the recognitions of black

---

43. See [John Hope] Franklin, *The Militant South, 1800–1861* (1956) * * *.

manhood that many white men (especially working class whites) feared and that Frederick Douglass and other black leaders hoped for. As it happened, these recognitions came to pass—but only for a season.

By the end of 1862 the enlistment of black soldiers could be seen to serve a clear military need, even if President Lincoln and Secretary of War Stanton did insist on placing white officers in command of black regiments, and Congress did peg the pay of black soldiers below that of whites. The Union had suffered some important losses in the field, white enlistments had fallen, and large numbers of slaves had begun to cross the lines seeking freedom. The Emancipation Proclamation of 1863 not only provided a legal foundation for a social upheaval already begun, but converted a war to save the Union into a crusade for liberation. By war's end almost 200,000 black men had served in the federal services, including about a quarter of the entire Navy; counting blacks who served in other capacities—cooks and carpenters, laborers and laundresses, servants and spies—one estimate places the total number of blacks who served the Union armed forces at nearly 390,000. At first these troops were used almost entirely in support functions that mainly involved manual labor. Eventually, however, black soldiers were employed in combat, and some 37,000 were killed. In 1863 black regiments showed particular heroism at Port Hudson, at Milliken's Bend, and, as the movie *Glory* dramatized, at Fort Wagner.

The moment was ripe for a triumphant ending in which the wartime sacrifices of black men vindicated the claims of black people to full citizenship. Seventy years later, W. E. B. DuBois said it was the fact that the black man "rose and fought and killed" that enabled whites to proclaim him "a man and a brother. . . . Nothing else made Negro citizenship conceivable, but the record of the Negro soldier as a fighter."[55] After the war three constitutional amendments and a package of Reconstruction civil rights acts not only abolished slavery, but promised black Americans equal citizenship, including the equal right to vote. Yet, formal citizenship was one thing, brotherhood quite another. * * * Black war veterans and black people generally learned that formal equality before the law could exist alongside the gravest sort of inequalities in fact. By the end of the century, racial discrimination remained a routine part of black people's experience in the North and West while the South had descended into the systematic racial subordination called Jim Crow.

A major motivating factor behind the Jim Crow segregation laws and the myriad social practices they reinforced was the pursuit of manhood among white men. As in the days of slavery, this pursuit translated into a need to deny, to repress, the manhood of black men. For "the militant South"—that is, for southern white men as a group—the humiliation of military defeat was compounded during twelve years of occupation by the Union army. By the late 1880s a sharp economic decline threatened the "family provider" function of large numbers of lower class white men, many of whom responded violently, removing black tenants from competi-

55. [William E.B.] Dubois, *Black Reconstruction in America* 104 (1935).

tion by driving them off desirable farm land. As economic recession deepened into depression, white violence against blacks intensified, taking new and more murderous forms. In the ensuing decades southern white lynch mobs and rioters would take thousands of black lives.

The problem of manhood was central in generating this violence. In the South, white men were supposed to be not only the providers for but the protectors of women. Then as now, the fears of losing, of not measuring up to the manly ideal, could turn men toward group action aimed at group domination. The rivalry of black men was seen in terms that were not just economic; it threatened a social status that had previously been awarded for whiteness alone. And if the day-to-day demonstrations of competence by liberated black men posed a problem for white male self-esteem, the abstraction of black manhood was frightening. This objectification originated in fear and grew on fear.

The political and social arrangements during the Reconstruction years and in the succeeding decade also threatened white Southern manhood by subjecting male-female relations to considerable strain. For the upper classes, the old chivalry was in tatters. But Southern white men of all stations in life shared a deeper anxiety about their ability to protect the women around them. At all levels of white society men had long exaggerated the sense that they were sexual aggressors. Not uncommonly they had been taught to believe that their sexuality was an animal urge that must be kept under strict control. Such a belief was heightened by the prevailing view of white women as symbols of purity who were anything but sexual beings. In this abstract, dehumanizing construction of womanhood, sex was at once a duty and a violation. For white men these beliefs were the seedbed for tension and guilt; they also translated readily into a nightmare of male rivalry.

When the anxiety about man-as-provider fused together with anxieties centered on sexuality, the combination was explosive. The abstract image of pure Southern womanhood became identified with a vision of white supremacy. The white woman, as the "perpetuator of [white] superiority's legitimate line," had to be kept remote from any sexual approach of the black man. The abstraction of black manhood was transformed into "the specific image of the black beast rapist." Anxious in the pursuit of manhood, a white man who joined a lynch mob could find three kinds of reassurance. He symbolically repressed the beast in himself; he found a sense of power in a ritual that expressed group domination; and he satisfied himself, in the safety of the crowd, that he was man enough to protect the women. Although only about one-third of all the lynchings of black men grew out of charges of rape, it was black-white rape that most whites specified as a justification of lynching in general. The explanation is plain: The image of black-white rape symbolized white men's self-doubt at the most primitive level.

B. *The Double Battle in the 20th Century*

Even before World War I began, black leaders were calling for the Army to establish new black regiments and to train blacks to serve as officers. At the close of the Civil War, Congress for the first time had made four black regiments part of the Regular Army. Although they saw combat in the Indian wars and the Spanish–American War, black soldiers continued to be subjected to discrimination by the civilian populations near their garrisons. When the United States entered the war in 1917, W.E.B. DuBois, like Frederick Douglass before him, argued that blacks should not "bargain with our loyalty," but should close ranks with their fellow citizens, all the while asserting their rightful claims to equal citizenship: the vote; equal educational opportunity; an end to lynchings and segregation. For the cause of racial equality, he argued, "We want victory . . . but it must not be cheap bargaining, it must be clean and glorious, won by our manliness. . . ."[67]

The experience of black soldiers in Europe fell far short of these high hopes. All of them served in segregated units that quickly became a "dumping ground" for ineffective officers. Most black draftees were assigned to labor units. Once in Europe, most blacks were placed under French command—perhaps because the officer corps of the United States Army largely shared the racial attitudes of the white South. When some black combat units performed unsatisfactorily, as some white units also had done, a few generals reacted by pronouncing black soldiers unfit for combat—despite contrary evidence from other black units. When they returned home, black veterans encountered the same old racial discrimination in a new and virulent form. In the South, their very presence, as living symbols of black manhood, challenged the Jim Crow system at its psychic foundations. The result was a new wave of racial violence, including the lynching of black veterans in their Army uniforms.

After the war the Navy stopped enlisting blacks for general service, relegating black enlisted men to work as stewards. The Army explicitly reaffirmed its policy of racial segregation, and kept blacks ineligible for service as airplane pilots or radio signalmen. As another world war approached, black leaders had good reason for announcing that they would resist efforts to restrict black troops to labor units. * * *

More than 1,000,000 black men and about 4,000 black women served in the [armed] forces during [World War II]. Some 900,000 of the men served in the Army, about three-quarters of them in menial jobs such as "road building, stevedoring, laundry, and fumigating." Even the training of blacks for combat was exceptional; and in 1942, when someone suggested to General George Marshall, the Army Chief of Staff, that black troops be sent to fight in North Africa, he responded that the commanders there would object. As in the Civil War and World War I, blacks had to "fight for the right to fight." On this front, despite a steady drumbeat of criticism from black newspapers and black leaders, the services mostly resisted change.

---

67. [William E.B.] Dubois, *The Crisis Writings* 259 (1972). DuBois's writings on World War I are collected in *id.* at 255–73.

Occasionally, however, those who were agitating for a racially inclusive military force could win a small victory. In 1942 the Navy announced that it would no longer limit black enlistees to messmen's duties, but would allow blacks to volunteer for general service—which, in this case, meant other support duties. By the end of the war, black enlistees constituted about four percent of the Navy and two and a half percent of the Marine Corps. Segregation remained the rule, however; given the problems of separation on shipboard, in 1944 the Navy established two ships with all-black crews. Soon thereafter a new Secretary of the Navy ordered integration of the crews on twenty-five auxiliary ships.

Around the same time the Army, which had not placed black combat troops in the line, was ordered to do so by a War Department that was reacting to political criticism. In Europe, when infantrymen became scarce, the Army inserted some black platoons into larger combat units. In the Army Air Force the black pilots of the segregated ninety-ninth Pursuit Squadron performed well. Even so, Army officials sought to minimize publicity about the achievements of black soldiers, to avoid blurring the Army's public image.

As the Navy's preposterous deployment of separate-but-equal vessels illustrated, the services' segregation policy was costly. New and separate units had to be organized and staffed, and separate training facilities had to be built; given the disparity in educational opportunities for blacks and whites before they entered the service, segregation prevented the most effective training and assignment of black soldiers and sailors. The main costs of segregation, however, lay in another dimension of human experience, one in which the problem of manhood was central. In 1941, before the attack on Pearl Harbor, William H. Hastie, an aide to Secretary of War Henry L. Stimson (and later the first black judge of the United States Court of Appeals), had written to his boss, criticizing the segregation of the Army in the strongest terms:

> The traditional mores of the South have been widely accepted and adopted by the Army as the basis of policy and practice affecting the Negro soldier.... This philosophy is not working.... In tactical units of the Army, the Negro is taught to be a fighting man[,] ... a soldier. It is impossible to create a dual personality which will be on the one hand a fighting man toward the foreign enemy, and on the other, a craven who will accept treatment as less than a man at home. One hears with increasing frequency from colored soldiers the sentiment that since they have been called to fight they might just as well do their fighting here and now.

General Marshall, asked to respond, had said that segregation was an established American custom, that "the level of intelligence and occupational skill of the Negro population is considerably below that of the white," and that "experiments within the Army in the solution of social problems are fraught with danger to efficiency, discipline, and morale."[77]

---

77. The Hastie and Marshall quotations can be found in [Richard M.] Dalfiume, *Desegregation of the U.S. Armed Forces* 61, 45–47 (1989); [Richard O. Hope, *Racial Strife*

The connection between this assessment and the historic anxieties of white men about the rivalry of black males is not hard to see. Marshall's unstated assumption was that white soldiers would lack confidence in blacks and be hostile to them, for they defined black men in general as incompetent and cowardly. Furthermore, integrating the Army would eventually result in placing black men in some positions of leadership; white soldiers would not accept this inversion of the historic racial definition of authority. Like all the Army's top leaders, Marshall had served in World War I and remembered the old accusations against black troops. But his assumption about the effect of integration on white attitudes proved mistaken. At the end of the war the Army took a survey of white soldiers who had served in combat alongside black platoons. At first, they said, they were resentful. But three-quarters of them said "their regard for the Negro had risen" as a result of the experience.[78] By doing their jobs well, black soldiers expressed their competence and so, in this limited way, performed functions of education and persuasion. * * *

NOTES ON THE LEGALITY OF RACIAL SEGREGATION IN THE U.S. ARMED FORCES (1940s)[a]

Although there were limited experiments with desegregated units near the end of World War II, the armed forces remained officially segregated through the end of the war. The Karst thesis suggests that desegregation would be very hard to accomplish in fact. Consider the following further context:

1. *The Uniform Resistance of the Top Brass to Desegregation.* Virtually all the nation's military leaders in the 1940s were opposed to racial integration. The military's top brass during World War II not only refused to integrate their armed forces, but were also reluctant to assign responsible duties to black units because of their "general consensus of opinion that colored units are inferior to the performance of white troops, except for service duties, * * * due to the inherent psychology of the colored race and their need for leadership" [Memo from General R.W. Crawford to General Eisenhower, 4/2/42, quoted in Dalfiume 60]. All the branches of the armed services in the 1940s concentrated African Americans in "service" branches because of the "general assumption within the armed forces that Negroes could perform only unskilled jobs and that they were particularly suited for

in the U.S. Military] 14–15 (1979); George Ware, *William Hastie: Grace Under Pressure* 99 (1984).

78. [Hope, *Racial Strife* 25]. On the effects of racial integration in diminishing racial prejudice, see *Social Research and the Desegregation of the U.S. Army* 132–34 ([Leo] Bogart ed. 1969).

a. The sources for this note are Richard M. Dalfiume, *Desegregation of the U.S.*

Armed Forces (1969); Ulysees Lee, *The United States Army in World War II, Special Studies: The Employment of Negro Troops* (1966); Morris J. MacGregor, Jr., *Integration of the Armed Forces, 1940–1965* chs. 2–3 (1981); Bernard C. Nalty, *Strength for the Fight: A History of Black Americans in the Military* (1986); *Blacks in the Military: Essential Documents* (Bernard C. Nalty & Morris J. MacGregor, Jr. eds. 1981).

labor units" [Dalfiume 61]. Recall General George Marshall's comment, quoted in the Karst article.

"The racist belief that the Negro was a natural coward was the real objection to integration by many in the Army" in 1949 [Dalfiume 188–89].[b] Lieutenant General Edward Almond wrote in 1971 that integration "weakens" the "efficiency" of the armed forces. "There is no question in my mind of the inherent difference in races. This is not racism—it is common sense and understanding. Those who ignore these differences merely interfere with the combat effectiveness of battle units." [Almond Letter, quoted in MacGregor 441.] The Army during World War II backed up such assertions by reference to polls taken in 1942 showing upwards of 90% of the white soldiers supported segregated units, as did 30–40% of the black soldiers [MacGregor 40]. Similar evidence exists for the Navy. In 1940, Admiral W.R. Sexton wrote to the Secretary of the Navy that if "colored men" served in the Navy, "teamwork, harmony, and ship efficiency [would be] seriously handicapped" because of the attitudes of white sailors [*Blacks in the Military* 135].

2. *The Attitudes of Black and White Soldiers During World War II.* Why were attitudes so sour? Theoreticians such as Karst maintain that a large and maybe preponderant part of the tension between the races was sexual in nature.[c] Quite by accident, we found internal military documents providing first-hand evidence regarding this thesis.[d] Even though U.S. forces in Europe were racially segregated during World War II (except for a few experiments), strong racial tensions existed and sometimes blew up in public, with many documented race-based fights and brawls documented in countries where Americans were stationed, especially England. What the Army called "the Negro problem" derived in large part from strongly hostile white animosity to people of color. In a 1942 survey, the Army found big problems at the two camps it surveyed which had significant percentages of African Americans. One-third of the soldiers in one of the camps emphasized "the Negro problem" in their morale surveys. The report reprinted the two most "extreme" statements:

b. The Army made this argument in 1949: "The soldier on the battlefield deserves to have, and must have, utmost confidence in his fellow soldiers. They must eat together, sleep together, and all too frequently die together. There can be no friction in their every-day living that might bring on failure in battle. A chain is as strong as its weakest link, and this is true of the Army unit on the battlefield." Quoted in Dalfiume 189 n.38.

c. See also Herbert Hovenkamp, "Social Science and Segregation Before *Brown*," 1985 *Duke L.J.* 624, which demonstrates from legal and scientific sources of the period 1850–1930 that a key reason for separation of the races was hysteria about interracial sex and marriage.

d. In gathering materials for another book project at the National Archives (Suitland, Maryland), we came across Army morale records that are based upon the Army's interviews with soldiers and, more interestingly, its reading the soldiers' mail to their lovers and families. The documents quoted in text can all be found in Record Group 338, Records of U.S. Army Commands, 1942 ff, European Theatre, Adjutant General's Section, Administrative Branch, Classified General Correspondence, 1942–44, 1945, Decimal File 250.1.

[One survey response:] Negro troops have the girls come down to camp and call for them. If anything will make a Southern's Blood run hot it is to see this happen. Things around this camp is getting pretty hot about these negro troops and white [English] girls. If it keeps on going as it is we will have a nice negro lynching down here and then things will be better.

[A different response:] The Negro problem has been very poorly handled here. In my outfit it is now "the thing to hate" the negros. Every effort must be made to show the white soldiers that the negro soldiers are just members of our own army, fighting for the same "freedoms". Actually what is taking place in our army today is nothing more disgraceful than what Hitler is doing to minorities in Germany. I joined the American Army to fight against the persecution of minorities. I resent that our army actually practices the same type of persecution.

[G–1 Section, European Theatre of Operations, "Survey of Soldier Opinion, European Theatre of Operations, September 14–26, 1942."]

Army censors read the mail of American soldiers stationed in Europe and reported on the racial concerns discussed in the letters home. African–American soldiers often reported loneliness in wholly white surroundings but sometimes also reported their surprise that the English were "swell" to them. The English women in particular were wild for men of color (the African Americans were frequently called "Indians" by the English). Some of the soldiers dated English women, and this raised the hackles of white soldiers to no end. Illustrative of the many letters are the following:

[A black T/5 wrote:] Nowhere to go except to a show. I am not going to town at night. It is too dangerous. Our white soldiers make our life miserable and I do not want to come into a fight. In case that something should happen the colored fellow so and so would not get any justice.

[A white private wrote:] I have seen nice looking white girls going with a coon. They think they are hot stuff. The girls here are so dumb it's pitiful. Wait till Georgia gets these *educated* negroes back there again.

[A white corporal wrote:] Already we have found a little trouble here for ourselves. It seems that several outfits of colored troops preceded us over here and have succeeded pretty well in salting away the local feminine pulchritude, what little there is of it. They have the natives convinced that they are 'full blooded American Indians' and the girls really go for them in preference to the white boys, a fact that irks the boys no end, especially those of the outfit from the south. No doubt there will be some bloodshed in the near future.

[Base Postal Censor Morale Reports, September 1942, quoting from soldiers' mail.] These are only a few of the many comments picked up by military censors.

It was reported, also in 1942, that white officers in charge of a black unit stationed in Pennsylvania issued the following order: "any association between the colored soldiers and white women, whether voluntary or not, would be considered rape." The punishment for this offense was the death penalty. [Dalfiume 69.]

3. *The Constitutional Status of Racial Segregation, 1940s.* When the Fourteenth Amendment to the Constitution was adopted in 1868, African Americans had served in the U.S. armed forces only in segregated units, and virtually all other institutions of public life also enforced some degree of segregation. When a challenge to Southern "Jim Crow" segregation reached the Supreme Court in 1896, the Court upheld the policy against equal protection challenge. Justice Henry Billings Brown's opinion in *Plessy v. Ferguson*, 163 U.S. 537 (1896), justified the obvious racial classification in this way:

> The object of the amendment was undoubtedly to enforce the absolute equality of the two races before the laws, but, in the nature of things, it could not have been intended to abolish distinctions based upon color, or to enforce social, as distinguished from political, equality, or a commingling of the two races upon terms unsatisfactory to either. Laws permitting, or even requiring, their separation, in places where they are liable to be brought into contact do not necessarily imply the inferiority of either race to the other, and have been generally, if not universally, recognized as within the competency of the state legislatures in the exercise of their police power. The most common instance of this is connected with establishment of separate schools for white and colored children, which have been held to be a valid exercise of the legislative power even by courts of States where the political rights of the colored race have been longest and most earnestly enforced. * * *

> So far, then, as a conflict with the Fourteenth Amendment is concerned, the case reduces itself to the question whether the statute of Louisiana [requiring segregation in public transportation] is a reasonable regulation, and with respect to this there must necessarily be a large discretion on the part of the legislature. In determining the question of reasonableness it is at liberty to act with reference to the established usages, customs, and traditions of the people, and with a view to the promotion of their comfort, and the preservation of the public peace and good order. * * * *Id.* at 544–550.

The Court also rejected Plessy's argument that the forced segregation stamped blacks with a "badge of inferiority." "If this be so, it is not by reason of anything found in the act, but solely because the colored race chooses to put that construction upon it." *Id.* at 551.

Justice John Marshall Harlan, the only dissenting Justice, denounced this characterization. "Every one knows that the statute in question had its origin in the purpose, not so much to exclude white persons from railroad cars occupied by blacks, as to exclude colored people from coaches occupied by or assigned to white persons." *Id.* at 557. In his eyes, the law was an effort to perpetuate a racial "caste" system, "a badge of servitude wholly inconsistent with the civil freedom and the equality before the law established by the [Reconstruction Amendments]." Justice Harlan lamented that abandoning that central goal of the Reconstruction Amendments was fraught with peril. Justice Harlan concluded:

> The white race deems itself to be the dominant race in this country. And so it is, in prestige, in achievements, in education, in wealth, and in power. * * * But in view of the Constitution, in the eye of the law, there is in this country no superior, dominant, ruling class of citizens. There is no caste here. Our Constitution is color-blind, and neither knows nor tolerates classes among citizens. In respect of civil rights, all citizens are equal before the law. * * *

> * * * The present decision, it may well be apprehended, will not only stimulate aggressions, more or less brutal and irritating, upon the admitted rights of colored citizens, but will encourage the belief that it is possible, by means of state enactments, to defeat the beneficent purposes which the people of the United States had in view when they adopted the recent amendments of the constitution, * * * Sixty millions of whites are in no danger from the presence here of eight millions of blacks. The destinies of the two races, in this country are indissolubly linked together, and the interests of both require that the common government of all shall not permit the seeds of race hate to be planted under the sanction of law. What can more certainly arouse race hate * * * than state enactments which, in fact, proceed on the ground that colored citizens are so inferior and degraded that they cannot be allowed to sit in public coaches occupied by white citizens? *Id*. at 559–560.

Notwithstanding this dissent, Justice Harlan wrote the opinion for the Court in *Cumming v. Richmond County Board of Education*, 175 U.S. 528 (1899), extending the *Plessy* regime of "separate but equal" to school segregation.

Starting in the 1910s, however, the Supreme Court was more receptive to challenges against racial discrimination. Most of the cases involved violation of the separate but *equal* doctrine, *e.g.*, *Guinn v. United States*, 238 U.S. 347 (1915) (invalidating voting rule preventing blacks from voting, Fifteenth Amendment); *Missouri ex rel. Gaines v. Canada*, 305 U.S. 337 (1938) (invalidating law school segregation effectively denying blacks legal education, Fourteenth Amendment). The Court during and after World War II became immediately more aggressive in questioning race-based discrimination. The key cases were, ironically, two of the Court's most notorious decisions, the "Japanese Internment Cases."

Upholding the conviction of a citizen for disobeying a curfew imposed only upon Japanese Americans, the Court in *Kiyoshi Hirabayashi v. United States*, 320 U.S. 81, 100 (1943), stated: "Distinctions between citizens solely because of their ancestry are by their very nature odious to a free people whose institutions are founded upon the doctrine of equality. * * * [R]acial discriminations are in most circumstances irrelevant and therefore prohibited[.]" A bitterly divided Court in *Toyosaburo Korematsu v. United States*,

323 U.S. 214 (1944), upheld the detention of Japanese Americans in prison camps. Still, the majority announced a key precept of equal protection law:

> [A]ll legal restrictions which curtail the civil rights of a single group are immediately suspect. That is not to say that all such restrictions are unconstitutional. It is to say that courts must subject them to the most rigid scrutiny. Pressing public necessity may sometimes justify the existence of such restrictions; racial antagonism never can. *Id.* at 216.

Korematsu is the first case to announce that racial classifications must be subjected to "strict scrutiny": courts will invalidate laws classifying on the basis of race unless the state shows it has a "compelling" goal and that the racial classification is necessary to achieve that goal (i.e., nonracial alternatives are not available). *Korematsu* also stands for the propositions that "military necessity" is the sort of state interest that can satisfy strict scrutiny and that the Court is typically deferential to the national government when it makes claims based upon national security, especially in wartime. Note, finally, that Japanese Americans, like African Americans, served in segregated military units during World War II.

After World War II, the Court decided several very important race cases. Although the reasoning in each case was narrowly drawn, the pattern of decisions was friendly to claims against racial apartheid. In *Shelley v. Kraemer*, 334 U.S. 1 (1948), the Court held that racially restrictive covenants prohibiting the resale of property to people of color were constitutionally unenforceable in U.S. courts. But the decision focused only on the issue of state action (the Fourteenth Amendment's guarantees are only applicable to actions by the state). In *Morgan v. Virginia*, 328 U.S. 373 (1946), the Court held that states could not require segregation of buses traveling interstate, but that decision rested on Article I, § 8 (Congress' authority to regulate interstate commerce), which the Court has interpreted to forbid state regulations that unduly interfere with interstate commerce. Notwithstanding these decisions, and *Sipuel v. Board of Regents*, 332 U.S. 631 (1948) (Oklahoma's creation of a roped-off area as a "law school" violated the equality requirement of *Plessy*), the Court as of 1948 had made no overt move to overrule *Plessy* and its associated cases.

PROBLEM 4–1

LEGAL CONSIDERATIONS RE DESEGREGATING THE ARMED FORCES, 1948

You are a legal adviser to President Truman in 1948. The President is in a tough situation, caught between blacks demanding desegregation of the military and officers refusing to desegregate. Having read the previous notes, you should not be surprised to know that, according to President Truman's recollection (see Merle Miller, *Plain Speaking: An Oral Biography of Harry S. Truman* 79 note [1974]), every top military official he consulted was opposed to desegregation of the armed forces. On the other hand, strong political pressures pushed the President in that direction.

Many African Americans who fought in World War I resented serving in segregated units and, usually, in menial jobs. As the next great war loomed on the horizon, some black leaders opposed a repetition of that experience. A. Philip Randolph in 1941 called for a March on Washington, to pressure the Roosevelt Administration to end military segregation before the United States entered either the Pacific or European wars [Dalfiume 115–17]. The March on Washington Movement (MOWM) generated dozens of mass demonstrations against segregation, the formation of several committees working to end segregation, and was associated with the President's creation of the Committee on Fair Employment Practices. Although many African Americans were disappointed that the latter was all that was obtained from the MOWM, it was important as the first mass movement by blacks for their rights [Dalfiume 122]. It also lit a fire under the leaders of the more established black groups (the NAACP and the Urban League) to be more insistent on issues of African-American equality.

After World War II, Randolph formed the Committee Against Jim Crow in Military Service and Training, which pressed both the President and Congress on the segregation issue [Dalfiume 155–56, 163–65]. Randolph and others met with the President, testified before Congress, and engaged in a robust political campaign against military segregation. Randolph told a Senate Committee that he favored civil disobedience (refusal of African Americans to serve) if segregation were not ended [Dalfiume 164]. That pressure only increased with the report of the President's Committee on Civil Rights, which flatly condemned racial segregation in the military. The Committee found that "separate but equal" was a myth and condemned segregation generally. "Prejudice in any area is an ugly, undemocratic phenomenon," but "in the armed services where all men run the risk of death, it is particularly repugnant." [President's Committee on Civil Rights, *To Secure These Rights* 41 (1947).] The Committee rejected the view that the armed services could not be used for social experimentation, because it found that attitudes were inevitably formed or reformed in the caldron of battle, and that the military was the perfect place to "prove that the majority and minorities in our population can train and work and fight side by side in cooperation and harmony" [*id.* at 47].

Most of the major steps in reforming the military from the top down came in presidential election years—1940, 1944, and 1948—when the African–American vote was wooed by both the Republicans and Democrats. Since the latter were the party in power, they were under pressure to do something tangible for blacks in the military, as FDR had done in 1940 and 1944. Unlike his popular predecessor, Truman was in an impossible electoral situation in 1948: his popularity was dragging well below 50%, the Republicans were optimistic and united behind their crime-busting Governor Thomas Dewey, and the Democrats split into three factions—the regular Democratic Party, which nominated Truman; the Dixiecrats, who nominated Strom Thurmond; and the Progressives, who nominated Truman's predecessor as Vice President, Henry Wallace. Dewey courted the black vote, possibly key in the big cities, and the Republican platform promised that they would desegregate the armed forces (the Democrats' platform was typically silent). Black leaders asked Truman: Why should we support you, if Dewey will end segregation by the nation's largest employer?

The President asks you for an opinion on the constitutionality of the armed services' segregation. Is there a good argument against armed services segregation that can be constructed from the text of the Constitution, the Supreme Court's precedents, or constitutional theory? (There are also arguments from original intent, generally cutting in favor of permitting segregation, however.) Should the legal arguments play any significant role in the President's decision, or is the answer too indeterminate?

The President, for various reasons, decides to end the policy of segregation and again turns to you for advice. Given the overwhelming opposition within the armed forces, how should the Administration go about desegregation? In other words, Truman is unwilling to issue an order requiring immediate desegregation. What procedural or institutional approach would you recommend?

EXECUTIVE ORDER 9981

Establishing the President's Committee on Equality of Treatment and Opportunity in the Armed Services.

WHEREAS it is essential that there be maintained in the armed services of the United States the highest standards of democracy, with equality of treatment and opportunity for all those who serve in our country's defense:

NOW, THEREFORE, by virtue of the authority vested in me as President of the United States, by the Constitution and the statutes of the United States, and as Commander in Chief of the armed services, it is hereby ordered as follows:

1. It is hereby declared to be the policy of the President that there shall be equality of treatment and opportunity for all persons in the armed services without regard to race, color, religion or national origin. This policy shall be put into effect as rapidly as possible, having due regard to the time required to effectuate any necessary changes without impairing efficiency or morale.

2. There shall be created in the National Military Establishment an advisory committee to be known as the President's Committee on Equality of Treatment and Opportunity in the Armed Services, which shall be composed of seven members to be designated by the President.

3. The Committee is authorized on behalf of the President to examine into the rules, procedures and practices of the armed services in order to determine in what respect such rules, procedures and practices may be altered or improved with a view to carrying out the policy of this order. The Committee shall confer and advise with the Secretary of Defense, the Secretary of the Army, the Secretary of the Navy, and the Secretary of the

Air Force, and shall make such recommendations to the President and to said Secretaries as in the judgment of the Committee will effectuate the policy hereof. * * *

HARRY S. TRUMAN

THE WHITE HOUSE

July 26, 1948

NOTE ON THE TRUMAN ORDER AND THE PROCESS OF DESEGREGATING THE ARMED FORCES

Note the ambiguity of the Executive Order. Does it require complete integration? When? With all deliberate speed? Chaired by Charles Fahy, the Committee appointed under ¶ 2 of the Executive Order believed the order required integration and carried on negotiations with each branch to that effect.

The negotiations proceeded in different ways for different branches, given recent developments within each branch. The Air Force had developed its own plan for integration earlier in 1948, and that plan was immediately acceptable to the Fahy Committee; substantial integration was achieved in 1949. The Navy was at the same time committed to a policy of gradual integration, and the Fahy Committee was able to work out problems it had with the Navy's plans, yielding tangible policy commitments to integration in the Navy by mid–1949. The Army was committed to a separate but equal vision of equality established in its 1946 Gillem Report, and the Fahy Committee struggled with the Army through 1949 and into 1950. The Fahy Committee and the Army reached agreement on a new gradual integration policy on 16 January 1950. The Korean War speeded up the process of integration, and on 30 October 1954 the Secretary of Defense announced that the last racially segregated unit in the armed forces had been abolished.

A few words about the negotiation process are in order. Most obviously, the President's Executive Order did not produce integration by its own force, and each of the different branches had to be dealt with through some combination of direction (the President is the Commander in Chief) and persuasion. The process of persuasion was the more interesting. The experience of the armed forces with segregated units during World War II was not satisfactory [Lee ch. 11; Nalty ch. 11]. Especially when African–American units were commanded by white officers (the typical scenario), the units tended to have very low morale, and there were complaints during both World War I and World War II that all-black units fighting under white officers performed unevenly. Segregation created difficulties and extra expenses for sending black soldiers to the front. For example, it was often quite expensive to maintain separate but nominally equal facilities for blacks in combat as well as domestic settings.

As a result of these difficulties, and the Army's commitment to take African American recruits, some integration occurred during World War II [MacGregor ch. 2], and this experience proved to be a potent argument in 1949–50, when the Fahy Committee was pressuring the Army to follow President Truman's integration directive. Even the Gillem Board, which in 1946 laid out the Army's program for segregation-without-discrimination, predicted that in the event of a war the Army would have no choice but to deploy personnel "without regard to antecedents or race" [MacGregor 459]. This in fact occurred in the Korean conflict.

In short, segregation as a policy was already collapsing in 1948—in large part for a practical reason: it was very expensive, disruptive of morale, and counterproductive for the armed forces to accept African American recruits and volunteers, and then to segregate them. The Fahy Committee realized this in 1949. E.W. Kenworthy, the capable and committed anti-segregationist reporter for the Committee, urged Fahy in 1949 to confront the foot-dragging Army on its own terms and to force the Army to justify the "efficiency" of segregation [Letter from Kenworthy to Fahy (10 March 1949), described and excerpted in MacGregor 351–52]. Later in 1949, after the Army had given Fahy a jargon-filled report on what it proposed to do about Executive Order 9881, Kenworthy arranged for Fahy to meet Roy Davenport, who cited chapter and verse to the astounded (and annoyed) Fahy that the Army's report was worthless, that segregation was gravely inefficient, and that more forceful measures would have to be taken [meeting described in MacGregor 353]. At Committee hearings in April 1949, Davenport and Major James Fowler guided the Committee step by step through the Army's "career guidance" program, showing the Committee how the program squandered talent and personnel because of its commitment to the social policy of segregation [MacGregor 354–55]. Based upon this insight, the Fahy Committee basically nagged the Army (which had no responses to the detailed case made by Davenport and Fowler) into agreeing to integration in 1950, just in time for the Korean War, when integration actually occurred.

Given officer opposition to integration as destructive of troop morale and unit cohesion, the Army conducted studies of the adjustment by troops to integration. The Army's G–1 study reported that integration of black soldiers into white combat units in Korea had been accomplished generally "without undue friction and with better utilization of manpower." Combat commanders "almost unanimously favor integration" [DA Personnel Research Team, "A Preliminary Report on Personnel Research Data" (28 July 1951), quoted in MacGregor 441], a striking contrast to their pre-integration beliefs. Outside consultants also reviewed the situation, under the code name Project CLEAR. They reported that integration had not lowered white morale but greatly increased black morale; virtually all black soldiers supported integration, while white soldiers were not overtly hostile or were supportive; and in most instances white attitudes toward integration became more favorable with firsthand experience ["A Preliminary Report on the Utilization of Negro Manpower" (30 June 1951), described in MacGregor 442].[e] These findings were pretty much the same as those of secret Army surveys conducted during World War II, when the Army had desegregated a few units, found few if any problems, and then suppressed the findings.

The experience in the other services was the same. The Air Force found that integration progressed "rapidly, smoothly and virtually without incident" by the middle of 1950 [Memo from General Nugent to Ass't Sec'y Zuckert (14 July 1950), quoted in MacGregor 405]. Integration all but eliminated the stream of complaints about discrimination and racial incidents that had plagued the Air Force previously [MacGregor 409–10]. E.W. Kenworthy of the Fahy Committee reported in 1950: "The men apparently were more ready for equality of treatment and opportunity than the officer corps had realized." [Kenworthy Report, quoted in MacGregor 408.]

Reporter Lee Nichols interviewed members of all services in 1953 and wrote a book from what they told him.[f] He found that blacks and whites were amazed at how smoothly integration actually proceeded once the armed services decided to do it, but that blacks and whites continued to have different attitudes about military policy and practice. Whites tended to expect blacks to "prove themselves" in their assignments, while blacks were often skeptical that equal opportunities were really available to them. Tensions between blacks and whites were later to be even more problematic during the Vietnam War, but on the whole observers of all stripes believe that racial integration of the armed forces has been relatively successful from the perspectives of whites, African Americans, and other people of color.

e. This was the preliminary report. A seven-volume final report was prepared in November 1951. For years this report was classified. It was published under the title *Social Research and the Desegregation of the U.S. Army* (Leo Bogart ed. 1969).

f. Lee Nichols, *Breakthrough on the Color Front* (1954).

SECTION 2

THE EXCLUSION OF WOMEN FROM COMBAT

PART A. A HISTORY OF WOMEN IN THE MILITARY, 1861–1971[a]

Officially, women, like African Americans, have been excluded from the armed services for most of our history and then have been segregated once the formal exclusion ended. Unofficially, a surprising number of passing women served in the American military (and in combat roles!) during the nineteenth century. During the Civil War, Private Frank Fuller (née Frances Hook) of the Nineteenth Illinois Regiment served with distinction until she was wounded and captured in the Battle of Chattanooga. Mary Livermore, a nurse, estimated that more than 400 women "passed" as men and served in the Union Army. Most of these women were never detected. Sarah Emma Edmonds Seelye, alias Franklin Thomson, fled from home at age fifteen to escape an unwanted marriage. She donned male garb and supported herself selling Bibles; she enlisted in the Union Army and served for two years, retiring because of illness. Like hundreds, maybe thousands, of other women, her biological sex was never revealed during her service. We only "know" about it today because Seelye published her memoirs, *Nurse and Spy*, in 1864.[b]

Women were officially welcomed as nurses during the Civil War, an experience replicated in the Spanish–American War, but in both cases the women were viewed as civilian auxiliaries rather than as military personnel. The Nurse Corps were recognized as official auxiliaries by the Army in 1901 (by an act of Congress) and the Navy in 1908. World War I saw 34,000

---

a. See Major General Jeanne Holm, USAF, *Women in the Military: An Unfinished Revolution* (1982); Judith Hicks Stiehm, *Arms and the Enlisted Woman* (1989); Vern Bullough & Bonnie Bullough, *Cross Dressing, Sex, and Gender* ch. 7 (1993); Jill Laurie Goodman, "Women, War, and Equality: An Examination of Sex Discrimination in the Military," 5 *Women's Rights L. Rptr.* 243 (1979); Lori Kornblum, "Women Warriors in a Men's World: The Combat Exclusion," 2 *L. & Inequality* 351 (1984), for the account that follows.

b. A remarkable insight of her experience is how readily women could pass as men

simply by wearing male clothing. This was the testimony of Loreta Janet Velazquez, who served several years as a soldier in the Confederate Army: "So many men have weak and feminine voices that, provided the clothing is properly constructed and put on right, and the disguise is in other respects well arranged, a woman with even a very high-pitched voice need have little to fear" of being discovered. *The Woman in Battle* (1876). Unlike Seelye, Velazquez was found out, but she was sentenced to only ten days in jail for her "crime."

women serve in the Nurse Corps of the various branches of service. More important, on the eve of war, Secretary of the Navy Josephus Daniels directed that women be enrolled in the naval reserves as "yeomen" who could perform clerical and other duties that would free up men for combat. The Navy started taking female yeomen in March 1917, and they played a positive role in the war effort; the Marines followed suit immediately, but the Army was going to be damned if it were to accept women, and it didn't. Moreover, Congress in 1925 prohibited the Navy from enlisting women in the future.

The issue of women in the armed services went no further until General George C. Marshall became Army Chief of Staff in 1939. Believing that the U.S. would be hard put to staff a war machine, Marshall insisted that women be considered for service. The War Department dragged its feet, notwithstanding pressure from Marshall and a bill introduced in May 1941 by Representative Edith Rogers to create a women's auxiliary with the Army. Pearl Harbor ended the foot dragging. Congress adopted the Rogers bill to create the Women's Army Auxiliary Corps (WAAC, later WAC when the Auxiliary dropped out) in May 1942, Public Law No. 77–554, and a similar bill for the Navy and Marines was enacted in July, Public Law No. 77–689 (creating the Navy Women's Reserve, later called WAVES, and the Marine Corps Women's Reserve). The Air Force also acquired a female auxiliary, called SPAR (for "Semper Paratus [sic]— Always Ready").

World War II created unprecedented personnel needs which transformed the women's auxiliaries. They were originally viewed as staff for a few clerical jobs that could free up men for combat, but by 1944 women were performing a wide range of other military functions as well, including control tower operators, radio repair people and operators, air navigators, parachute riggers, gunner instructors, engine mechanics, aerophotographers. Highly classified projects included women. Still, most women served in clerical jobs that did not adequately exploit their skills, intelligence, and training. By 1943, women were also serving overseas. General Eisenhower opposed women in the armed forces until he saw how valuable they were in defending Britain, and after that he enthusiastically welcomed their support in the North African and then European Theatres. Of course, the nurse corps traveled wherever combat troops traveled. In all theatres, previously skeptical male officers rated women successful soldiers—not just supportive typists, but *soldiers*. By the end of the War, there were nearly 100,000 WACs, 86,000 WAVES, 18,000 Women Marines, and 11,000 SPARs, as well as over 18,000 nurses serving in the U.S. armed forces. Although most women as well as men were discharged after the war, General Eisenhower insisted that the WACs continue as a permanent part of the Army.

The post-war period was one of some consolidation and much retrenchment. On the one hand, the federal government established a permanent role for women when it enacted the Women's Armed Services Act of 1948, Public Law No. 80–625, the ironically dubbed "Integration Act." Fueled by hysterical fears that women would end up "commanding" men, the House initially rejected the bill, but Representatives Rogers and Margaret Chase Smith (R–Me.) were supported by General Eisenhower and thousands of telegrams in turning the House around on the matter. On the other hand, the Integration Act required segregation and marginalization of women in significant ways. Although the Act bestowed permanent military status on the women's corps and their members, the Act also imposed a 2% cap on the number of women who could serve in each branch, restricted the number of female officers and established a separate promotion list for women, set higher minimum ages for women wanting to enlist than were required for men, and allowed women to claim husbands or children as dependent only upon a showing of actual dependency (it was automatically assumed for the dependents of military men). Most important, the Act authorized the service Secretaries to assign women duties as they saw fit, provided that women could not be assigned flight or ship duties when the craft are "engaged in combat missions." This was a strange "Integration": separate but deliberately unequal.

The situation evolved in more conservative directions after 1948, which turned out to be the high point for almost a generation. During the Korean War, women played less of a role than they did in World War II; indeed, women volunteered at such low levels that they were no more than 1% of our troops in Korea (demand for women by commanders greatly exceeded supply). One reason for the decline was the increasingly marginal role of women in the armed forces; women were once again consigned to clerical and nursing jobs and became "typewriter soldiers." Relatedly, the training of military women grew increasingly obsessed with maintaining their "ladylike" image. The top brass grew obsessed with apparel, for example. "Hair styles had to be fashionable but 'conservative' and 'appropriate' to the uniform. Elaborate beehives and large boufants were frowned upon but were preferable to very short 'mannish' styles (there must be no appearance of lesbianism). According to Navy regulation, 'Hair shall be arranged and shaped to present a conservative, feminine appearance.'" (Holm 181–82.) The military's fetishism about appearance led to elaborate debates and regulations about skirt length (below the knee), pumps (in) versus boots (out), and hats and gloves (mandatory for most occasions).

The foregoing suggest that women were, basically, on the way out of the military in the 1950s and 1960s. This state of affairs was transformed by the war in Vietnam, which created a substantial demand for women in a full range of military jobs, and by the women's liberation movement, which problematized women's severely unequal treatment. The first tangible legal ramification of these circumstances was the enactment of Public Law No. 90–130, which was passed in 1967 and removed the formal restrictions on promotion of women. This was the first significant legal change since the 1948 Integration Act and solved a practical problem: women who had entered the armed services during and after World War II had run into a glass ceiling because of the promotion restrictions of the Integration Act; in the Navy, such women were being discharged after their thirteenth year and were thereby losing pension benefits that would vest after year twenty.

The 1967 law allowed these successful officers to be promoted and, without anyone much noticing removed the 2% ceiling on women in the armed services (a ceiling that had never been reached). The law did not, however, endorse equality of women's role in the armed services.[c] In 1970, the Army promoted two women to the rank of brigadier general, the first in Army history.

Women did not serve in the Vietnamese combat theatre until 1967, and then only after much bureaucratic maneuvering by female officers against the objections to having women anywhere near combat. The Tet Offensive launched in the early morning hours of 31 January 1968 was a stern test of female as well as male forces in Vietnam. Some believe that the female nurses performed more tirelessly and skillfully than any other service personnel, male or female, in this disastrous campaign (Holm 232–34). Women's performance under fire was all that staved off new efforts to exclude them from combat areas. An Air Force Master Sergeant wrote:

> One would expect the male members of the military to remain as calm as could be expected and that they would exert that little extra during a crisis such as was occurring here during the Tet Offensive—and they did just that. I guess what impressed me most was the relative calm that the female service members went about their duties (WAF, WAC, WAVES and Marine). That belief that the frail (or fair) sex will tremble at the first sign of trouble is not true. During February the MACV building would shake from US/RVN bombings in the nearby area, quite frequently and there is little difference in this noise and that made on the impact of a Viet Cong mortar round striking nearby. Yet I observed the female military members, in various offices of MACV, performing their duties no different than anyone else. If they had fears, which I am sure were no different than any male members, then they did a terrific job of concealing them. [Quoted in Holm 237.]

The women stayed, and about 7500 served in Vietnam. All received combat pay, many were decorated, and at least thirteen nurses died. [Holm 241–42.]

The role of women in the armed services changed in the 1970s, partly as a result of the Vietnam experience, but more importantly because of the end of the peacetime draft and the success of the Equal Rights Amendment (ERA), which was passed by large margins in Congress and ratified by almost three-quarters of the states. Reports from a House subcommittee and the Brookings Institution exposed the wastefulness and lost opportunities of the military's tokenist attitude toward women. The Army conducted a series of experiments to determine which level (0–35%) of women in combat and noncombat units would lower unit performance [note the

---

c. The Committee on the Armed Services wrote in its report that "there cannot be complete equality between men and women in the matter of military careers. The stern demands of combat, sea duty, and other types of assignments directly related to combat are not placed upon women in our society. The Defense Department assures the Committee that there would be no attempt to remove restrictions on the kind of military duties women will be expected to perform."

assumptions of the experiment]; all of the units performed well. Consistent with women's performance in every situation after 1942, the Army found that women's participation had no adverse consequences at any level tested (Holm 258).

The military's determined policy of separate but unequal imploded after 1972, and a series of interconnected policies were terminated: segregation in procurement and training, gender quotas for promotions (stealthily continued after 1967), unequal family policies, and some of the paternalism. Some of these changes were made in anticipation of adoption of the ERA, which supporters and opponents agreed would require the armed services to end their formal discrimination against women in the draft and even in combat duty. This was the congressional testimony of Assistant Attorney General William Rehnquist, for example. Other changes were in response to aggressive congressional pressure. Yet other changes were made, apparently, in response to lawsuits and Supreme Court doctrine, which in the early 1970s was evolving rather rapidly.

PART B. JUDICIAL REVIEW OF THE DIFFERENT TREATMENT OF WOMEN IN THE ARMED FORCES, 1971–81

Before 1971, the U.S. Supreme Court had never invalidated a statute because it discriminated against women or relied on a sex-based classification. The first decision to do so, *Reed v. Reed*, 404 U.S. 71 (1971), invalidated an Idaho statute preferring men over women as executors of estates. The next major case involved one of the policies established in the Integration Act of 1948. (See Chapter 1, Section 3[A] for an introduction to the Supreme Court's evolving scrutiny of sex-based classifications and the arguments for and against the heightened scrutiny given such classifications since the mid–1970s.)

Sharon A. Frontiero and Joseph Frontiero v. Elliot L. Richardson

United States Supreme Court, 1973.
411 U.S. 677, 93 S.Ct. 1764, 36 L.Ed.2d 583.

[Excerpted in Chapter 1, Section 3(A)]

PROBLEM 4–2

CONSTITUTIONAL ISSUES FOR WOMEN IN THE MILITARY, LATE 1970s

(A) All–Male Service Academies. West Point, the Naval Academy, and the Air Force Academy had always been exclusively male. In 1972, Senator Jacob Javits nominated a woman for the Naval Academy, which refused to consider her. At 1972 congressional hearings, Captain Robin Quigley explained: "The Academy exists for one viable reason, to train seagoing naval

officers * * * There is no room, no need, for a woman to be trained in this mode, since by law and by sociological practicalities, we would not have women in these seagoing or warfare specialties." Deputy Secretary of Defense William P. Clements, Jr. categorically rejected the Javits proposition: "Training cadets at the Academies is expensive, and it is imperative that these opportunities be reserved for those with potential for combat roles." At 1974 hearings, Navy Secretary J. William Middendorf II said: "Simply stated, unless the American people reverse their position on women in combat roles, it would be economically unwise and not in the national interest to utilize the expensive education and facilities of the Naval Academy to develop women officers." A woman sues the Naval Academy after *Frontiero* was decided. The Academy makes the arguments above. What arguments should she make? How would a court rule after *Frontiero*? See *Waldie v. Schlesinger*, 509 F.2d 508 (D.C.Cir.1974).[d]

(B) The Combat Exclusions. In 1977, 10 U.S.C. § 6015 (subsequently amended), provided that "women may not be assigned to duty in aircraft that are engaged in combat missions nor may they be assigned to vessels of the Navy other than hospital ships and transports." This was a statutory exclusion applicable to the Navy and Air Force; the Army by its own regulations excluded women from combat in 1972. See 10 U.S.C. § 3012(e) (authorizing the Army to determine assignment policies).

In 1976, a Supreme Court majority held that sex-based classifications are subjected to an intermediate version of heightened scrutiny. See *Craig v. Boren*, 429 U.S. 190 (1976) (invalidating state law allowing 18 year old females but not 18 year old males to buy alcoholic beer). Under *Craig*, a sex-based classification is invalid unless it is substantially related to the achievement of an important government objective. The "administrative convenience" argument in *Frontiero* would have failed this test, for example. Moreover, Justice Brennan's opinion for a six-Justice Court held that the state's reliance on traditional gender stereotypes (girls are responsible, boys are wild) not only failed to justify the statutory classification, but confirmed its invalidity under a regime where sex equality is the goal.

You are a litigator for a public interest law firm interested in challenging the combat exclusion in one of the branches. Several women from each branch have contacted your office about some kind of challenge. You want to file a lawsuit that wins, and then build on that win to get broader reform from Congress, the President, or the courts. (By the way, is that a smart strategy for this issue?) What would your ideal lawsuit look like? Which branch do you want to sue? See *Owens v. Brown*, 455 F. Supp. 291 (D.D.C.1978) (a successful lawsuit).

d. Public Law No. 94–106 (Oct. 1975), statutorily integrated the academies, with the first women admitted for the 1976–77 school year. For two divergent factual as well as normative accounts of gender integration at the Air Force Academy, compare Judith Hicks Stiehm, *Bring Me Men and Women: Mandated Change at the United States Air Force Academy* (1981), with Brian Mitchell, *Weak Link: The Feminization of the American Military* (1989).

(C) Registration for the Draft. Congressional hearings in 1979 pressured President Jimmy Carter to reinstitute draft registration, which the President resisted. As a response to Soviet aggression in Afganistan, the President in January acted on his own authority to reinstitute draft registration for men. With 150,000 women serving in the military, President Carter decided in February 1980 to request congressional authority to register women as well as men for the draft.[e] Congress was thrown into turmoil on the issue, with military hard-liners strongly supporting the President on registration and opposing him on registering women. Their stated reasons were (1) the limited number of noncombat jobs available to women, (2) the strain on training resources if equal numbers of women were introduced, and (3) the many ancillary issues that needed to be addressed (*e.g.*, the draft status of mothers). Most of the women in Congress—from liberal Representatives Patricia Schroeder (D–Colo.) and Barbara Mikulski (D–Md.) to conservative Senator Nancy Kassebaum (R–Kan.)—favored registration of women even if they were ambivalent about the draft. After extensive hearings, both House and Senate rejected the proposal by large margins, however.

Reviving a preexisting lawsuit, the District Court for the Eastern District of Pennsylvania rules that the new policy is unconstitutional. The Supreme Court stays the lower court injunction and accepts the case for immediate appeal. How will it rule? How should it rule? Read on.

Bernard Rostker v. Robert L. Goldberg et al.

United States Supreme Court, 1981.
453 U.S. 57, 101 S.Ct. 2646, 69 L.Ed.2d 478.

■ JUSTICE REHNQUIST delivered the opinion of the Court.

The question presented is whether the Military Selective Service Act, 50 U.S.C. App. § 451 *et seq.* (1976 ed. and Supp. III), violates the Fifth Amendment to the United States Constitution in authorizing the President to require the registration of males and not females.

Congress is given the power under the Constitution "To raise and support Armies," "To provide and maintain a Navy," and "To make Rules for the Government and Regulation of the land and naval Forces." Art. I, § 8, cls. 12–14. Pursuant to this grant of authority Congress has enacted the Military Selective Service Act, 50 U.S.C. App. § 451 *et seq.* (1976 ed. and Supp. III) (the MSSA or the Act). Section 3 of the Act, 62 Stat. 605, as amended, 50 U.S.C. App. § 453, empowers the President, by proclamation, to require the registration of "every male citizen" and male resident aliens between the ages of 18 and 26. The purpose of this registration is to facilitate any eventual conscription: pursuant to § 4(a) of the Act, 62 Stat.

---

e. "My decision to register women is a recognition of the reality that both women and men are working members of our society. It confirms what is already obvious through- out our society—that women are now providing all types of skills in every profession. The military should be no exception." (Quoted in Holm 347.)

605, as amended, 50 U.S.C. App. § 454 (a), those persons required to register under § 3 are liable for training and service in the Armed Forces. The MSSA registration provision serves no other purpose beyond providing a pool for subsequent induction. * * *

Whenever called upon to judge the constitutionality of an Act of Congress * * * the Court accords "great weight to the decisions of Congress." *Columbia Broadcasting System, Inc. v. Democratic National Committee*, 412 U.S. 94, 102 (1973). The Congress is a coequal branch of government whose Members take the same oath we do to uphold the Constitution of the United States. * * *

This is not, however, merely a case involving the customary deference accorded congressional decisions. The case arises in the context of Congress' authority over national defense and military affairs, and perhaps in no other area has the Court accorded Congress greater deference. * * * This Court has consistently recognized Congress' "broad constitutional power" to raise and regulate armies and navies, *Schlesinger v. Ballard*, 419 U.S. 498, 510 (1975). As the Court noted in considering a challenge to the selective service laws: "The constitutional power of Congress to raise and support armies and to make all laws necessary and proper to that end is broad and sweeping." *United States v. O'Brien*, 391 U.S. 367, 377 (1968). * * *

The Solicitor General argues, largely on the basis of the foregoing cases emphasizing the deference due Congress in the area of military affairs and national security, that this Court should scrutinize the MSSA only to determine if the distinction drawn between men and women bears a rational relation to some legitimate government purpose, and should not examine the Act under the heightened scrutiny with which we have approached gender-based discrimination [citing *Craig v. Boren* and *Reed*]. We do not think that the substantive guarantee of due process or certainty in the law will be advanced by any further "refinement" in the applicable tests as suggested by the Government. Announced degrees of "deference" to legislative judgments, just as levels of "scrutiny" which this Court announces that it applies to particular classifications made by a legislative body, may all too readily become facile abstractions used to justify a result. In this case the courts are called upon to decide whether Congress, acting under an explicit constitutional grant of authority, has by that action transgressed an explicit guarantee of individual rights which limits the authority so conferred. Simply labeling the legislative decision "military" on the one hand or "gender-based" on the other does not automatically guide a court to the correct constitutional result.

No one could deny that under the test of *Craig* v. *Boren*, the Government's interest in raising and supporting armies is an "important governmental interest." Congress and its Committees carefully considered and debated two alternative means of furthering that interest: the first was to register only males for potential conscription, and the other was to register both sexes. Congress chose the former alternative. When that decision is challenged on equal protection grounds, the question a court must decide is not which alternative it would have chosen, had it been the primary decision-maker, but whether that chosen by Congress denies equal protection of the laws.

Nor can it be denied * * * that judicial deference to such congressional exercise of authority is at its apogee when legislative action under the congressional authority to raise and support armies and make rules and regulations for their governance is challenged. As previously noted, deference does not mean abdication. The reconciliation between the deference due Congress and our own constitutional responsibility is perhaps best instanced in *Schlesinger* v. *Ballard*, 419 U.S., at 510, where we stated:

> "This Court has recognized that 'it is the primary business of armies and navies to fight or be ready to fight wars should the occasion arise.' [U.S. *ex rel.*] *Toth* v. *Quarles*, 350 U.S. 11, 17. The responsibility for determining how best our Armed Forces shall attend to that business rests with Congress, see U.S. Const., Art. I, § 8, cls. 12–14, and with the President. See U.S. Const., Art. II, § 2, cl. 1. We cannot say that, in exercising its broad constitutional power here, Congress has violated the Due Process Clause of the Fifth Amendment." * * *

The MSSA established a plan for maintaining "adequate armed strength ... to insure the security of [the] Nation." 50 U.S.C. App. § 451(b). Registration is the first step "in a united and continuous process designed to raise an army speedily and efficiently," *Falbo* v. *United States*, 320 U.S. 549, 553 (1944), and Congress provided for the reactivation of registration in order to "provid[e] the means for the early delivery of inductees in an emergency." S. Rep. No. 96–826, at 156. * * * Congress rather clearly linked the need for renewed registration with its views on the character of a subsequent draft. * * * As Senator Warner put it, "I equate registration with the draft." *Hearings on S. 2294*, at 1197. * * *

Congress determined that any future draft, which would be facilitated by the registration scheme, would be characterized by a need for combat troops. The Senate Report explained, in a specific finding later adopted by both Houses, that "[i]f mobilization were to be ordered in a wartime scenario the primary manpower need would be for combat replacements." S. Rep. No. 96–826, p. 160 (1980); see *id.*, at 158. * * *

Women as a group, however, unlike men as a group, are not eligible for combat. The restrictions on the participation of women in combat in the Navy and Air Force are statutory. Under 10 U.S.C. § 6015 (1976 ed., Supp. III), "women may not be assigned to duty on vessels or in aircraft that are engaged in combat missions," and under 10 U.S.C. § 8549 female members of the Air Force "may not be assigned to duty in aircraft engaged in combat missions." The Army and Marine Corps preclude the use of women in combat as a matter of established policy. Congress specifically recognized and endorsed the exclusion of women from combat in exempting women from registration. In the words of the Senate Report:

> "The principle that women should not intentionally and routinely engage in combat is fundamental, and enjoys wide support among our

people. It is universally supported by military leaders who have testified before the Committee.... Current law and policy exclude women
from being assigned to combat in our military forces, and the Committee reaffirms this policy." S. Rep. No. 96–826, *supra,* at 157.

The Senate Report specifically found that "[w]omen should not be intentionally or routinely placed in combat positions in our military services."
Id., at 160. See S. Rep. No. 96–226, *supra,* at 9. The President expressed his
intent to continue the current military policy precluding women from
combat, and appellees present their argument concerning registration
against the background of such restrictions on the use of women in combat.
* * *

The existence of the combat restrictions clearly indicates the basis for
Congress' decision to exempt women from registration. The purpose of
registration was to prepare for a draft of combat troops. Since women are
excluded from combat, Congress concluded that they would not be needed
in the event of a draft, and therefore decided not to register them. Again
turning to the Senate Report:

> "In the Committee's view, the starting point for any discussion of
> the appropriateness of registering women for the draft is the question
> of the proper role of women in combat.... The policy precluding the
> use of women in combat is, in the Committee's view, the most
> important reason for not including women in a registration system." S.
> Rep. No. 96–826, *supra,* at 157.

The District Court stressed that the military need for women was
irrelevant to the issue of their registration. As that court put it: "Congress
could not constitutionally require registration under the MSSA of only
black citizens or only white citizens, or single out any political or religious
group simply because those groups contain sufficient persons to fill the
needs of the Selective Service System." 509 F. Supp., at 596. This reasoning is beside the point. The reason women are exempt from registration is
not because military needs can be met by drafting men. This is not a case
of Congress arbitrarily choosing to burden one of two similarly situated
groups, such as would be the case with an all-black or all-white, or an all-
Catholic or all-Lutheran, or an all-Republican or all-Democratic registration. Men and women, because of the combat restrictions on women, are
simply not similarly situated for purposes of a draft or registration for a
draft.

Congress' decision to authorize the registration of only men, therefore,
does not violate the [Equal Protection component of the Fifth Amendment's] Due Process Clause. The exemption of women from registration is
not only sufficiently but also closely related to Congress' purpose in
authorizing registration. The fact that Congress and the Executive have
decided that women should not serve in combat fully justifies Congress in
not authorizing their registration, since the purpose of registration is to
develop a pool of potential combat troops. * * *

■ [The dissenting opinion of JUSTICE WHITE (joined by JUSTICE BRENNAN) is omitted.]

■ JUSTICE MARSHALL, with whom JUSTICE BRENNAN joins, dissenting. * * *

The Government does not defend the exclusion of women from registration on the ground that preventing women from serving in the military is substantially related to the effectiveness of the Armed Forces. Indeed, the successful experience of women serving in all branches of the Armed Services would belie any such claim. Some 150,000 women volunteers are presently on active service in the military, and their number is expected to increase to over 250,000 by 1985. See *Department of Defense Authorization for Appropriations for Fiscal Year 1981: Hearings on S. 2294 before the Senate Committee on Armed Services*, 96th Cong., 2d Sess., 1657, 1703 (1980) (*1980 Senate Hearings*); *Women in the Military Hearings before the Military Personnel Subcommittee of the House Committee on Armed Services*, 96th Cong., 1st and 2d Sess., 13–23 (1979 and 1980) (*Women in the Military Hearings*). At the congressional hearings, representatives of both the Department of Defense and the Armed Services testified that the participation of women in the All–Volunteer Armed Forces has contributed substantially to military effectiveness. Congress has never disagreed with the judgment of the military experts that women have made significant contributions to the effectiveness of the military. On the contrary, Congress has repeatedly praised the performance of female members of the Armed Forces, and has approved efforts by the Armed Services to expand their role. * * * Congress' decision to exclude women from registration—and therefore from a draft drawing on the pool of registrants—cannot rest on a supposed need to prevent women from serving in the Armed Forces. The justification for the MSSA's gender-based discrimination must therefore be found in considerations that are peculiar to the objectives of registration. * * *

* * * [The majority] states that "Congress determined that any future draft, which would be facilitated by the registration scheme, would be characterized by a need for combat troops." The Court then reasons that since women are not eligible for assignment to combat, Congress' decision to exclude them from registration is not unconstitutional discrimination inasmuch as "[m]en and women, because of the combat restrictions on women, are simply not similarly situated for purposes of a draft or registration for a draft." There is a certain logic to this reasoning, but the Court's approach is fundamentally flawed.

In the first place, although the Court purports to apply the *Craig v. Boren* test, the "similarly situated" analysis the Court employs is in fact significantly different from the *Craig v. Boren* approach. The Court essentially reasons that the gender classification employed by the MSSA is constitutionally permissible because nondiscrimination is not necessary to achieve the purpose of registration because they will not be needed in the event of a draft.

This analysis, however, focuses on the wrong question. The relevant inquiry under the *Craig v. Boren* test is not whether a *gender-neutral* classification would substantially advance important governmental interests. Rather, the question is whether the gender-based classification is itself substantially related to the achievement of the asserted governmental interest. Thus, the Government's task in this case is to demonstrate that excluding women from registration substantially furthers the goal of preparing for a draft of combat troops. Or to put it another way, the Government must show that registering women would substantially impede its efforts to prepare for such a draft. Under our precedents, the Government cannot meet this burden without showing that a gender-neutral statute would be a less effective means of attaining this end. As the court explained in *Orr v. Orr*, 440 U.S. [268, 283 (1979)] (emphasis added):

> "Legislative classifications which distribute benefits and burdens on the basis of gender *carry the inherent risk of reinforcing sexual stereotypes about the 'proper place' of women and their need for special protection....* Where, as here, the [Government's] ... purposes are as well served by a gender-neutral classification as one that gender classifies and therefore carries with it the baggage of sexual stereotypes, the [Government] cannot be permitted to classify on the basis of sex."

In this case, the Government makes no claim that preparing for a draft of combat troops cannot be accomplished just as effectively by *registering* both men and women but *drafting* only men if only men turn out to be needed. Nor can the Government argue that this alternative entails the additional cost and administrative inconvenience of registering women. This Court has repeatedly stated that the administrative convenience of employing a gender classification is not an adequate constitutional justification under the *Craig v. Boren* test.

The fact that registering women in no way obstructs the governmental interest in preparing for a draft of combat troops points up a second flaw in the Court's analysis. The Court essentially reduces the question of the constitutionality of male-only *registration* to the validity of a hypothetical program for *conscripting* only men. The Court posits a draft in which *all* conscripts are either assigned to those specific combat posts presently closed to women or must be available for rotation into such positions. By so doing, the Court is able to conclude that registering women would be no more than a "gestur[e] of superficial equality," since women are necessarily ineligible for every position to be filled in its hypothetical draft. If it could indeed be guaranteed in advance that conscription would be reimposed by Congress only in circumstances where, and in a form under which, all conscripts would have to be trained for and assigned to combat or combat rotation positions from which women are categorically excluded, then it could be argued that registration of women would be pointless.

But of course, no such guarantee is possible. Certainly, nothing about the MSSA limits Congress to reinstituting the draft only in such circumstances. For example, Congress may decide that the All–Volunteer Armed Forces are inadequate to meet the Nation's defense needs even in times of peace and reinstitute peacetime conscription. In that event, the hypothetical draft the Court relied on to sustain the MSSA's gender-based classification would presumably be of little relevance, and the Court could then be forced to declare the male-only registration program unconstitutional. This difficulty comes about because both Congress[12] and the Court have lost sight of the important distinction between *registration* and *conscription*. Registration provides "an inventory of what the available strength is within the military qualified pool in this country." *Reinstitution of Procedures for Registration Under the Military Selective Service Act: Hearing before the Subcommittee on Manpower and Personnel of the Senate Armed Services Committee*, 96th Cong., 1st Sess., 10 (1979) (*Selective Service Hearings*) (statement of Gen. Rogers). Conscription supplies the military with the personnel needed to respond to a particular exigency. The fact that registration is a first step in the conscription process does not mean that a registration law expressly discriminating between men and women may be justified by a valid conscription program which would, in retrospect, make the current discrimination appear functionally related to the program that emerged.

But even addressing the Court's reasoning on its own terms, its analysis is flawed because the entire argument rests on a premise that is demonstrably false. As noted, the majority simply assumes that registration prepares for a draft in which *every* draftee must be available for assignment to combat. But the majority's draft scenario finds no support in either the testimony before Congress, or more importantly, in the findings of the Senate Report. Indeed, the scenario appears to exist only in the Court's imagination, for even the Government represents only that "in the event of mobilization, *approximately two-thirds* of the demand on the induction system would be for *combat skills.*" Brief for Appellant 29 (emphasis added). For my part, rather than join the court in imagining hypothetical drafts, I prefer to examine the findings in the Senate Report and the testimony presented to Congress.

Nothing in the Senate Report supports the Court's intimation that women must be excluded from registration because combat eligibility is a prerequisite for *all* the positions that would need to be filled in the event of a draft. The Senate Report concluded only that "[i]f mobilization were to be ordered in a wartime scenario, the *primary* manpower need would be for combat replacements." S. Rep. No. 96–826, p. 160 (1980) (emphasis added). This conclusion was in keeping with the testimony presented at the congressional hearings. The Department of Defense indicated that in the event of a mobilization requiring reinstitution of the draft, the primary manpower requirement would be for combat troops and support personnel who can readily be deployed into combat. See *1980 Senate Hearings*, at

---

12. The Court quotes Senator Warner's comment: "'I equate registration with the draft.'" The whole of Senator Warner's statement merits quotation because it explains why Congress refused to acknowledge the distinction between registration and the draft. Senator Warner stated: "Frankly I equate registration with the draft because there is no way you can establish a registration law on a coequal basis and then turn right around and establish a draft law on a nonequal basis. I think the court would knock that down right away." *1980 Senate Hearings*, at 1197.

1395 (Principal Deputy Assistant Secretary of the Army Clark), 1390 (Lt. Gen. Yerks). But the Department indicated that conscripts would also be needed to staff a variety of support positions having no prerequisite of combat eligibility, and which therefore could be filled by women. Assistant Secretary of Defense (Manpower, Reserve Affairs, and Logistics) Pirie explained:

> "Not only will we need to expand combat arms, and as I said, that is the most pressing need, but we also will need to expand the support establishment at the same time to allow the combat arms to carry out their functions successfully. The support establishment now uses women very effectively, and in wartime I think the same would be true." *Registration of Women: Hearing on H.R. 6569 before the Subcommittee on Military Personnel of the House Committee on Armed Services* 96th Cong., 2d Sess., 17 (1980) (*1980 House Hearings*).

In testifying about the Defense Department's reasons for concluding that women should be included in registration plans, Pirie stated:

> "It is in the interest of national security that, in an emergency requiring the conscription for military service of the Nation's youth, the best qualified people for a wide variety of tasks in our Armed Forces be available. The performance of women in our Armed Forces today strongly supports the conclusion that many of the best qualified people for some military jobs in the 18–26 age category will be women." *Id.,* at 7.

* * * All four Service chiefs agreed that there are no military reasons for refusing to register women, and uniformly advocated requiring registration of women. The military's position on the issue was summarized by then Army Chief of Staff General Rogers: "[W]omen should be required to register for the reason that [Marine Corps Commandant] General Wilson mentioned, which is in order for us to have an inventory of what the available strength is within the military qualified pool in this country." *Selective Service Hearings,* at 10; see *id.,* at 10–11 (Adm. Hayward, Chief of Naval Operations; Gen. Allen, Air Force Chief of Staff; Gen. Wilson, Commandant, Marine Corps). * * *

This review of the findings contained in the Senate Report and the testimony presented at the congressional hearings demonstrates that there is no basis for the Court's representation that women are ineligible for *all* the positions that would need to be filled in the event of a draft. Testimony about personnel requirements in the event of a draft established that women could fill at least 80,000 of the 650,000 positions for which conscripts would be inducted. Thus, with respect to these 80,000 or more positions, the statutes and policies barring women from combat do not provide a reason for distinguishing between male and female potential conscripts; the two groups are, in the majority's parlance, "similarly situated." As such, the combat restrictions cannot be themselves supply the constitutionally required justification for the MSSA's gender-based classification. Since the classification precludes women from being drafted to fill positions for which they would be qualified and useful, the Government must demonstrate that excluding women from those positions is substantially related to the achievement of an important governmental objective. * * *

NOTE ON *ROSTKER*

By 1981, the Court was committed to applying an "intermediate" level of equal protection scrutiny to classifications based upon sex or gender (*Craig*, where the Court struck down a law allowing young women to obtain alcoholic beer at a younger age than young men). The classification in *Rostker* is one of the few that survived this level of scrutiny during the Burger Court, and the obvious reason is that the Court applies a more lenient level of scrutiny when it is a military classification that is at issue.

It is not clear why the Court defers so much to the military.[f] But as a matter of doctrine it has long done so, and continues to do so. *E.g., Weiss v. United States*, 510 U.S. 163, 181 (1994) (Scalia, J., concurring) (odd ad-hoc military judges arrangement would be patently unconstitutional in any setting but military); but cf. *id.* at 194 (Ginsburg, J., concurring) (military personnel do not abandon their constitutional rights when they join up). For a striking example, the Court in *Goldman v. Weinberger*, 475 U.S. 503 (1986), held that a general military regulation prohibiting the wearing of nonregulation headgear could be applied to prevent an orthodox rabbi (and officer) from wearing a yarmulke. It is probable that such a rule would not be tolerated in other public settings, but a divided Court did uphold it in the military setting.

Academic commentators have been critical of *Rostker*, generally agreeing with Justice Marshall's dissent.[g] An issue the Court did not resolve (because plaintiffs did not raise it) in *Rostker* was whether the exclusion of women from combat positions in the armed services was valid or whether such exclusion violated notions of equal protection. Judge John Sirica had struck down 10 U.S.C. § 6015, as applied to prevent Navy women from serving at sea. *Owens v. Brown*, 455 F.Supp. 291 (D.D.C.1978) (see Problem 4–2). Should groups critical of the military's policies have first attacked the

---

f. Possibilities include: (1) Judges don't know very much about military issues or feel incompetent to interfere with an organization that is set off from the rest of the government. (2) The military is a "total" environment, like a prison, and judges feel they have to give such institutions greater leeway to regulate and order their internal affairs. (3) The military is vested with protecting our national security, which is maybe more important than other government functions (if the trash is not picked up on Fridays the world will not end; if the military is not strong the world may very well end, for us!), and therefore justifies less interference from the judiciary.

g. *E.g.*, Lori Kornblum, "Women Warriors in Men's World: The Combat Exclusion," 2 *L. & Inequality* 351 (1984); Wendy Webster Williams, "The Equality Crisis: Some Reflections on Culture, Courts, and Feminism," 7 *Women's Rights L. Rep.* 175, 182–85 (1982). See also Note, "Women and the Draft: The Constitutionality of All–Male Registration," 94 *Harv. L. Rev.* 406 (1980).

exclusion from combat, and then the registration requirements? Does *Rostker* overrule *Owens*?

PART C. WOMEN'S EXCLUSION FROM COMBAT

A recurring theme of the history of women in uniform that we presented at the beginning of this section was the prevailing belief that women should not serve in combat positions. Note that women have in fact served in combat, albeit marginally. Military experts of all stripes agree that there can be no sharp demarcation between "combat" and "noncombat" positions; the latter are often subject to attack and are trained to defend themselves. Female nurses and doctors have served in combat zones since World War II, and women passing as men have served in combat in the Revolution, the Civil War, and the Spanish–American War. Women were also part of the World War II anti-aircraft artillery unit that was poised to defend Washington, D.C. against enemy attack. Most interestingly, women were integrated into the Office of Strategic Services (OSS), which performed dangerous and useful espionage activities during World War II.[h]

Nonetheless, public policy has long excluded women from combat roles, and it was not until the 1970s that defenders of this policy were called upon to explain themselves publicly. Their initial efforts have not held up well.[i] Originally, Defense Department defenders of the exclusion emphasized "real differences" between women and men in terms of strength (especially lifting and throwing ability) and speed. In hand-to-hand combat, units having women would be at a disadvantage. These arguments seem like red herrings. If strength is the key factor, then make combat roles turn on strength tests that women as well as men can take to qualify for combat duties. (No one disputes that many women are stronger than many men.) Moreover, in the technologically sophisticated armed services, hand-to-hand combat is no longer the norm. Many women possess the physical skills for

---

h. See George H. Quester, "The Problem," in *Female Soldiers—Combatants or Noncombatants? Historical and Contemporary Perspectives* 217, 226–28 (Nancy Loring Goldman ed., 1982). Other essays in *Female Soldiers* document the deployment of women in combat positions by other countries, from the Soviet Union, which deployed almost a million women in resisting Hitler, to Israel, whose widely esteemed army includes women in combat roles. For other historical accounts of women in combat, see Martin Binkin & Shirley J. Bach, *Women and the Military* (1977); John Lafflin, *Women in Battle* (1967).

i. Exemplary of the early efforts at justification are the statements in *Priorities and Economy in Government, the Role of Women*

in the Military: Hearings Before the Joint Economic Comm., 95th Congress, 1st Session (July 22 and Sept. 1, 1977); *Hearings Before Subcomm. No. 2 of the House Comm. on Armed Services*, 93d Congress, 2d Session, part 5 (May 29, 1974) (hearings on gender integration of the service academies). The military's arguments in the next two paragraphs in text are drawn from these hearings. See also the useful historical and analytical account by Jill Laurie Goodman, "Women, War, and Equality: An Examination of Sex Discrimination in the Military," 5 *Women's Rts. L. Rptr.* 243 (1979). For an author still making these arguments, see Brian Mitchell, *Weak Link: The Feminization of the American Military* (1989).

flying airplanes and deploying equipment that men do, and women may have a comparative advantage in some physical skills (possibly stamina) that are more relevant than the ability to bench press 500 pounds.[j] For practical reasons such as these, the armed forces have been moving toward more gender-neutral classifications which are based upon actual strength needs rather than stereotypes.

Relatedly, early defenders of the exclusion maintained that women are not as "aggressive" as men and could not take the "stress" of combat. This objection was even less well-considered than the physical differences objection, for military bureaucrats produced no data to support any such claim. In fact the experience of World War II, Korea, and Vietnam suggested that women can handle stress as well or better than men. While women in our culture may be less "aggressive" (whatever that actually means) than men, no one has made out a cogent case for why raw aggression is necessary or even useful in the modern armed forces. Do we want a pilot who runs on testosterone, or one who is capable, well organized, skillful at flying airplanes, follows orders, and is smart about taking only calculated risks? Critics of the foregoing arguments also reminded the military officials that eerily similar arguments have been advanced against opening any profession to women, from law to the presidency: women are "naturally" less aggressive or able to handle stress and the real world than men. So, too, eerily similar arguments had been advanced against racial integration in the 1940s: African Americans were "naturally" less aggressive or intelligent (or both) than white soldiers. All of these earlier arguments have been discredited by historical experience, and their repeated invocation ought to have diminished credibility.

It soon became clear that these arguments (especially the aggressiveness objection) were surrogates for deeper concerns. The Superintendent of the Air Force Academy explained that opening combat or even leadership roles to women "offends the dignity of womanhood and ignores the harsh realities of war. * * * Fighting is a man's job and should remain so."[k] General Robert H. Barrow, former Commandant of the Marine Corps, had this to say:

> War is man's work. Biological convergence on the battlefield would not only be dissatisfying in terms of what women could do, but it would be an enormous psychological distraction for the male who wants to think that he's fighting for that woman somewhere behind, not up there in the same foxhole with him. It tramples the male ego. When you get right down to it, you have to protect the manliness of war.

j. Discreet reservations have also been posed on the basis of women's menstrual cycles and possible pregnancies: these are said to be added diversions impairing combat readiness. It is pointed out, however, that men also have biological cycles. Although women's menstruation is more visible, it does not seem any more medically disruptive than men's cycles. Pregnancies would seem an administrative problem and are handled as such for noncombat positions.

k. *1974 Hearings* 135 (testimony of Lt. Gen. A.P. Clark, Superintendent, Air Force Academy).

We got this quote from the Karst article that opened this chapter.[1] Consistent with his overall thesis, Karst argues that the exclusion of women from combat subserves the symbolism of Victorian masculinity: men protect women and the family from the outside enemy, a trope that would be disrupted by women fighting for their own protection; war is the greatest test as well as crucible of manhood, a bit of male bonding that would be undermined by women in the foxhole; men are by nature aggressive fighters, in contrast to nurturing passive women. These images are increasingly recognized as stereotypes, and after *Frontiero* it is perilous to ground military policy on such obvious stereotypes. The manliness-of-war argument is losing its appeal and is legally dangerous besides.

Is there any refuge for the military's reluctance to allow women to serve in combat roles? The following excerpt is a particularly useful statement of the male-bonding/unit cohesion objection that may be the most thoughtful one.

Mady Wechsler Segal, The Argument for Female Combatants

In *Female Soldiers: Combatants or Noncombatants?* 267, 278–81.
Nancy Loring Goldman, Editor, 1982.*

The results of [the Army's] * * * studies showed that the proportion of women in combat support and combat service support units had no effect on measurable unit performance in field training exercises. These results surprised many people who assumed that raising the proportion of women beyond some minimal level would be detrimental to performance. Some remain unconvinced even by this evidence and insist that these trials were not adequate tests because they did not involve actual combat. * * *

The willingness to engage in actual combat, to kill and to risk being killed, depends upon a very strong devotion to the group. This commitment to the group is seen as depending, among other motivations, on male bonding. The presence of women would interfere with the process of devotion of men to each other, as women are outsiders who are not privy to the male subculture. There may also be competition among the men for the sexual favors of the women. No real evidence exists to support or refute these arguments. One point is clear: if men believe that women are not part of their group and that they cannot function with women around, this belief will disrupt such functioning and may hinder actual ability to cope with the stress of combat, thereby serving as a self-fulfilling prophecy.

Let me offer an additional explanation for men's resistance to allowing women in combat units. I conjecture that there is a psychological differenti-

---

1. Karst, "The Pursuit of Manhood," 38 *UCLA L. Rev.* at 534, quoting from Wright "The Marine Corps faces the Future," *N.Y. Times*, June 20, 1982, magazine section, at 16, 74.

ation between the "real world" and combat that enables some men to survive the enormous psychological stress of combat. One survives by preserving a mental picture of the normal world back home to which one will return from the horror world of combat. One is engaged in an elaborate game * * * and when the game is over, one can go home to an intact world. One of the major components of the world back home is women, "our women," who are warm, nurturant, ultra-feminine, and objects of sexual fantasy. Women (at least "our women") are not a part of war. Indeed, one of the reasons for fighting is to protect our women and the rest of what is in that image of the world back home. If we allow these women into combat with us, then this psychological differentiation cannot be maintained, and we lose this psychological defense. * * *

If these speculations are accurate, I do not know precisely what effect women in combat would have on combat unit cohesion. I suspect that the effects have already been felt in military units that used to be all male but now have women, including the academies. Various processes of social change resulting from gender integration have probably already begun and will continue to proceed in creating new styles of interaction in face-to-face working units. It is certainly hoped that women's presence in groups will not automatically result in low cohesion. New images of the "real world back home" may supplant the old ones. The new images may then serve the same psychological functions.

The concern that women in combat units will reduce unit cohesion is reminiscent of arguments that have been used in the past to justify excluding women from other occupations. It was not so long ago that women were excluded from law, medicine, police work, and fire fighting (to name a few). This exclusion was based partly on women's supposed inability as individuals to perform the jobs adequately and partly on the potential disruption of men's interpersonal relations if women were included. While such arguments were accepted in the past, they have now been shown to be fallacious. * * *

Even outside of combat situations, there are certain interpersonal problems already existing in the military that deserve attention. The lack of acceptance of women by many military men creates problems for the women. As in other predominantly male settings, military women often face prejudice from male superiors, peers, and subordinates and face certain male behavior that creates stress for the women. Such behavior includes differential treatment of women that interferes with their job performance and sexual harassment of varying degrees.** These problems also exist in institutional settings other than the military, but they must be addressed in the military before women can function most effectively.

** [Eds.] This is an understatement, as subsequent events and studies have revealed, most notably the Tailhook scandal. See Military Personnel and Compensation Subcomm. and Defense Policy Panel of the House Comm. on Armed Services, 102d Congress, 2d Session, Report, *Women in the Military: The Tailhook Affair and the Problem of Sexual Harassment* (Sept. 14, 1992).

The interpersonal problems associated with gender integration of previously all-male settings * * * are similar to problems that were experienced in the process of racial integration of the U.S. armed forces. * * * In the first half of this century, black men were underrepresented in the military and were largely excluded from combat jobs. * * *

* * * Many of the arguments being advanced to justify exclusion of women from combat are reminiscent of those used in the past to bar black men from combat. * * *

The cohesion of military units in general and combat units in particular, need not be based on the exclusion of women. The bonds that tie soldiers to their groups often derive from respect for their fellow group members, based on performance that contributes to the goals of the group (including survival). Such mutual interdependence and affective regard can develop in mixed gender groups. DeFleur's study of the Air Force Academy shows that over the course of the first four years of gender integration, there has been some increase in male acceptance or and interaction with the women. Women are far from being fully accepted and integrated [as of 1982], however, a situation at least partially attributable to the lack of interdependence among cadets.

Intragroup cohesion also depends on having a definition of those who are considered outsiders by the group. Such exclusions need not include all women, just as they need not include all members of other categories, for example, college men or blacks. Rather, women who are seen as poor soldiers (or as not being soldiers) are excluded, while women who are seen as good combat soldiers can be fully integrated into the group. * * *

NOTE ON CONGRESSIONAL RESPONSE TO THE DEMAND FOR A COMBAT ROLE FOR WOMEN

In 1988, hearings held by the Subcommittee on Military Personnel and Compensation of the House Committee on Armed Services led to the establishment by the Department of Defense, the Navy, and the Marine Corps of a task force on women. The result was that additional noncombat positions were opened to women and procedures to deal with sexual harassment were strengthened. In 1990, the Subcommittee held a follow up hearing[m] in which Representative Patricia Schroeder argued for a bill that would authorize a four-year study of women in all slots in the Army, including combat positions. Referring to women's role in operating "noncombat" communication vans, Schroeder said, "[W]omen can be the first killed, but they are not allowed at the front line and supposedly in the battle."

The military response was to praise the contributions that women make and to expound the numerous opportunities already open to women.

m. *Women in the Military: Hearing Before the Subcomm. on Military Personnel and Compensation of the House Comm. on the*   *Armed Services*, 101st Congress, 2d Session (Mar. 20, 1990).

According to Vice Admiral J.M. Boorda, Deputy Chief of Naval Operations, "Whether you approach the issue of women in the Navy from an equal opportunity viewpoint or simply from a readiness and best use of the Nation's resources viewpoint, I think we have a lot to be proud of." He listed the increase of women in various positions and concluded: "Getting women into non-traditional careers is the key to expanded opportunities for women in the Navy." (*1990 Hearings* 29.) Note that he did not say getting women into combat roles. Female officers backed up Admiral Boorda's testimony by describing their positive experience with a career in the military (*id.* at 83).

In 1991, the statutory limitation on assignment of women to combat aircraft (part of § 6015) was repealed, Public Law No. 102–190, § 531, 105 Stat. 1365, and a commission was established to assess the laws and policies restricting women from combat in general. *Id.* § 541. In 1992, the subcommittee held follow-up hearings on the implementation of the 1991 law.[n] While Subcommittee Chair Beverly Bryon did not "advocate the wholesale placement of women in combat roles," she was "disappointed with the well-publicized account that Secretary Cheney has decided to delay placing women in combat aircraft." (*1992 Hearings* 2.) In response, Christopher Jehn, Assistant Secretary of Defense for Force Management and Personnel, stated that the military had two priorities, military capability and fairness to other service members, that required a go-slow approach. He concluded that the military would wait for further study and analysis before implementing female aviators. (*Id.* at 26.)

The commission appointed pursuant to the 1991 law recommended against participation of women in ground combat, but favored a more flexible policy in other contexts. Following this latter idea, Secretary of Defense Les Aspin opened combat aircraft assignments to women. In his words,

> First, I directed all of the Services to permit women to compete for assignments in aircraft, including those engaged in combat missions. Second, I directed the Navy to open as many additional positions aboard ships as practicable * * * and to develop a legislative proposal to repeal remaining restrictions within Title 10, to permit the assignment of women to ships that are engaged in combat missions. Finally, the Army and Marine Corps will study opportunities for women to serve in additional ground positions, including those in field artillery and air defense artillery.

> Within this policy guidance, there will be exceptions that result in some positions being kept closed to women if the Services fully justify these exceptions. For example, I will allow exceptions for units engaged in direct combat on the ground and for assignments where physical requirements or the cost of berthing and privacy are restrictive. * * *

---

n. *Implementation of the Repeal of the Combat Exclusion of Female Aviators: Hearing Before the Subcomm. on Military Personnel and Compensation of the House Comm. on the Armed Services*, 102d Congress, 2d Session (Jan. 29, 1992).

After further hearings,[o] Congress repealed § 6015, the statutory restriction on the assignment of women in the Navy and Marine Corps. Public Law No. 103–160, § 541, 107 Stat. 1659 (Nov. 30, 1993). The Act also authorized the Secretary of Defense to change military personnel policies in order to make available to female members of the armed forces assignment to any type of combat unit, class of combat vessel, or type of combat platform that is not open to such assignments, but the Secretary must, not less than 30 days before such change is implemented, transmit to the Committees on Armed Services of the Senate and House of Representatives notice of the proposed change in personnel policy. (*Id.* § 542, 107 Stat. 1659–60.) In addition, § 543(a) of the statute requires gender-neutral occupational standards:

GENDER NEUTRALITY REQUIREMENT.—In the case of any military occupational career field that is open to both male and female members of the Armed Forces, the Secretary of Defense—

(1) shall ensure that qualification of members of the Armed Forces for, and continuance of members of the Armed Forces in, that occupational career field is evaluated on the basis of common, relevant performance standards, without differential standards or evaluation on the basis of gender;

(2) may not use any gender quota, goal, or ceiling except as specifically authorized by law; and

(3) may not change an occupational performance standard for the purpose of increasing or decreasing the number of women in that occupational career field. (107 Stat. 1661.)

Apparently there was some discontent about the possibility that women could be involved in ground combat if the Secretary notified Congress 90 days in advance. In 1994 a subcommittee of the House Armed Services Committee held a hearing to alleviate these fears.[p] Subcommittee Chair Ike Skelton stated, "Congress as a whole has consistently maintained the position that women should not serve in direct ground combat. I will repeat that: women should not serve in direct combat on the ground." (*Oct. 1994 Hearing* 1.)

In 1994, the subcommittee held hearings which explored people's attitudes about women in combat.[q] A Youth Tracking Study on opinions of women in combat had some interesting findings. In 1988, 1989, and 1991 respondents aged 16 to 21 were asked: "Currently, women are restricted by law from military duties involving combat. What is your opinion about

o. Particularly *Women in Combat: Hearing Before the Subcomm. on Military Personnel and Compensation of the House Comm. on the Armed Services*, 103d Congress, 1st Session (May 12, 1993).

p. *Assignment of Army and Marine Corps Women under the New Definition of Ground Combat: Hearing Before the Subcomm. on Military Forces and Personnel of the House Comm. on Armed Services*, 103d Congress, 2d Session (Oct. 6, 1994).

q. *Recruiting and Expanded Role for Women in the Military: Hearings Before the Subcomm. on Military Forces and Personnel of the House Comm. on Armed Services*, 103 Congress, 2d Session (Apr., July, 1994).

changing the law so that women could volunteer for any combat assignment?" In 1992 the question was modified to reflect policy restrictions, rather than statutory restrictions. It read: "Currently, Defense Department policy restricts women from military duties involving combat. What is your opinion about changing the policy so that women would be allowed to volunteer for combat assignments?" In 1993, the question was modified to state that women were excluded from "some" military duties and to ask whether women should be allowed to volunteer for "any" combat position. The results (*Apr. 1994 Hearings* 82):

	Favor	Neither Favor nor Oppose	Oppose
Males			
1988	47	25	27
1989	51	24	25
1991	53	27	19
1992	59	24	18
1993	60	21	18
Females			
1988	42	31	26
1989	49	27	23
1991	60	26	13
1992	64	23	13
1993	69	19	11

In 1992, another interesting question was added: "If you knew women in the military would serve under the same conditions as men, how would this effect your attitude toward enlistment?" The results (*id.* at 81):

	More likely	Neither	Less likely
Male 16–21	10	71	18
Male 22–24	8	75	17
Female 16–21	11	62	27
Female 22–24	7	63	30

PROBLEM 4–3

THE LEGALITY OF CURRENT POLICY EXCLUDING WOMEN FROM COMBAT

You are the same attorney as in Problem 4–2(B). Jane Able is a Navy officer who wants to serve on combat mission ships, which current Navy policy forbids. Pursuant to the Aspin directive of April 1993 and the now-governing statutes, Navy women can serve on combat aircraft but not combat ships. She wants to sue the Navy, and you take her case. What arguments do you make? How do you get around *Rostker*? What is the impact of *United States v. Virginia* (Chapter 1, Section 3[A])? Consider the following new evidence that you acquire from the government.

The General Accounting Office (GAO) in 1993 issued a report of women's combat or near-combat roles during the Persian Gulf War of

1991.[r] Based upon its on-site interviews and observations, the team of GAO experts made the following findings of fact: (1) Women were an integral part of military service operations, including combat operations, during that war. "Perceptions of favoritism, the tendency of men to want to protect women, and comparable award recognition generally were not considered impediments to the effective operation of mixed-gender units." *GAO Report* 15. (2) Women and men operated effectively under the same deployment conditions, including conditions of stress and little privacy. Neither men nor women appreciated the lack of privacy, but both groups handled the inconveniences well. Also, "women's health and hygiene issues were inconsequential." *Id.* at 29. (3) Gender homogeneity was not a prerequisite to unit cohesion. "Discipline problems during the deployment were considered to be infrequent, and women were more likely to be seen as having a positive or neutral effect on interpersonal friction than a negative one." *Id.* at 38. "The theory that only men can bond is misleading. Individuals who experience a crisis bond because of the crisis—not because they are women or men." *Id.* at 40. On the other hand, a few units did report negative effects on bonding, and there were reports of sexual harassment.

Does the GAO report change the arguments you want to emphasize? The calculus of prevailing? The relevance of *Rostker* or the VMI case?

---

r. U.S. General Accounting Office, Report to the Secretary of Defense, *Women in* *the Military: Deployment in the Persian Gulf War* (July 1993).

THE MILITARY'S EXCLUSION OF LESBIANS, GAY MEN, AND BISEXUALS

PART A. ORIGINS OF THE GAY EXCLUSION[a]

In 1778, the Continental Army was fortunate to receive Baron Frederich Wilhelm Ludolf Gerhard Augustin von Steuben of Prussia, the drillmaster who retrained General Washington's Army at Valley Forge and literally rewrote the Americans' manual on discipline and order. The men worshipped the Prussian, because he was organized, authoritative, and drilled them relentlessly in person (American and British officers delegated such duties to juniors). Historians consider his contribution to the Continental cause—and to eventual American independence—incalculable. Ironically, von Steuben was available for American service only because he had in late 1777 been accused of "having taken familiarities with young boys which the law forbids and punishes severely" in Prussia, and was in danger of being prosecuted by either the clergy or the state (Shilts 8–9).

The further irony is that at the very moment von Steuben rescued the flailing American cause, the Continental Army had set a precedent for excluding such men from service. Lieutenant General Gotthold Frederick Enslin was discovered in bed with Private John Monhart. On March 10, 1778, Lieutenant Colonel Aaron Burr (an American scoundrel) presided at Enslin's court martial trial for sodomy and perjury and found him guilty of the same. Enslin was, literally, drummed out of the Continental Army, immediately. He was, so far as we know, the first casualty of the U.S. military's efforts to police the same-sex intimacy of its soldiers. Subsequent prosecutions were highly episodic, however, until World War I.[b]

a. Our discussion draws from Allan Bérubé, *Coming Out Under Fire: The History of Gay Men and Women in World War Two* (1990); William N. Eskridge, Jr., *Gaylaw: Challenging the Apartheid of the Closet* chs. 1–2 (1998); Lawrence R. Murphy, *Perverts by Official Order: The Campaign Against Homosexuals by the United States Navy* (1988); Randy Shilts, *Conduct Unbecoming: Lesbians and Gays in the U.S. Military—Vietnam to the Persian Gulf* (1993); George Chauncey, Jr., "Christian Brotherhood or Sexual Perversion? Homosexual Identities and the Construction of Sexual Boundaries in the World War I Era," in *Hidden from History* 294 (Chauncey et al. eds., 1989); Major Jeffrey S. Davis, "Military Policy Toward Homosexuals: Scientific, Historical, and Legal Perspectives," 131 *Mil. L. Rev.* 55 (1991).

b. As you surely have discerned by now, the evolution of the U.S. military speeds up a good deal during wartime, and all sorts of unpredictable things happen which influence the course of law. Thus World War I

The Articles of War of 1916 were the first complete revision of military law since 1806. Article 93 ("miscellaneous crimes and offenses") prohibited assault to commit a felony, apparently including assault to commit sodomy.[c] The Articles of War adopted by Congress in 1920 enumerated sodomy as a separate offense under Article 93. Act of June 4, 1920, 41 Stat. 787. Various other wartime statutes prohibited lewd practices in or near U.S. military bases. Note that these newly specified regulations coincided with popular and medical perceptions that a new species of human—"sex perverts" or "degenerates"—could be defined by their desire to engage in sodomy with people of their own sex (usually men).

The first celebrated "event" in this new era of military regulation was the Newport Naval Training Station scandals of 1919–20 (Murphy; Chauncey). In February–March 1919, Lieutenant Erastus Hudson authorized Chief Machinists Mate Ervin Arnold (a former vice cop in Connecticut) to organize undercover operatives to ferret out "sex perverts" among the hospital and other military personnel at Newport, as well as among the townsfolk. Arnold was a highly organized zealot, and before long he and his operators had piles of evidence detailing oral sex, anal sex, cross-dressing, effeminate behavior, kissing, and mutual masturbation among naval personnel and townspeople. A board of inquiry in March 1919 assembled the evidence against a couple of dozen defendants, most of whom were arrested and court-martialed on charges of sodomy (before the 1920 Articles made sodomy an offense). Arnold was the first military investigator to integrate military vice with the surrounding community, to focus on gangs of "perverts" and assemble evidence by infiltrating the gangs with his undercover operatives, and to use the testimony of each "pervert" to implicate other "perverts" if possible. Newport was the first homosexual witch hunt in the U.S. armed forces.

Equally fascinating was the backlash against Arnold and his operatives. After starting the process by which the naval "degenerates" would be court-martialed, the military went after civilians as well, under a 1917 statute prohibiting lewd conduct with military personnel. Arnold had compiled a huge file on the Reverend Samuel Kent, an Episcopal chaplain associated with the training center and a member of the YMCA crowd. Operative after operative slept over with Kent and wrote up their experiences in reports of kissing, hugging, and oral sex. Kent's trial in U.S. District Court was a major public event. Kent denied the charges of half a dozen sworn operatives and introduced one prominent witness after another testifying to his character and probity. The jury acquitted, perhaps based

brought women into the military, stimulated African–American demands for integration, and created an exclusion that increasingly targeted "sex perverts."

c. The Manual for Courts–Martial, United States, 1917, ¶ 443 defined sodomy as "sexual connection with any brute animal, or in sexual connection, per annum, by a man with any man or woman." This was similar to the sodomy or crime against nature laws in most states, but some states also prohibited oral sex as sodomy or the "infamous crime against nature." Congress followed the newer state practice in 1920.

upon his lawyers' outrage that military operatives would seek to entrap a man of the cloth.

The Kent acquittal initiated yet a third inquisition, in which the investigators themselves came under fire. Kent's Bishop and other ministers in Newport pestered the Navy Department into convening a new court of inquiry in January 1920. The main charge of the new court was that the investigators themselves had violated the law by committing lewd and sodomitic practices with their targets. The poor operatives perjured themselves right and left as they tried to explain what it was they were instructed to do (were they supposed to go all the way?) and what they thought they were doing when they went along repeatedly with the targets' desire to have oral sex (wasn't that against the sodomy law?). What is most remarkable about the whole affair is the operatives' nonchallance about oral sex. For the most part they would not consent to anal sex, didn't like kissing the targets, would tolerate some hugging and fondling, but repeatedly erected themselves at the hint of oral sex and allowed themselves to be fellated.

Although the court of inquiry ended rather inconclusively, it did condemn the investigative practices and gave homosexual witch hunts a bad name for a while. There were broader lessons as well (Eskridge ch. 1). On the one hand, the whole process of court-martialing for consensual sodomy was problematic: evidence was hard to come by because the activity was usually in private and there was no complaining witness, and undercover tactics carried their own risks of embarrassment. After 1920, the typical way to deal with "perverted" practices was through administrative separation, with a threat of court-martial. After 1922, Section VIII of the separation regulations ("inaptness or undesirable habits or traits of character") was the mechanism by which homosexuals were quietly drummed out of the service, albeit in very small numbers. On the other hand, the experience of Newport and World War I generally revealed the importance of pre-induction screening. If it was so hard to kick "perverts" out, why not prevent their getting in? This was an idea that came of age during the next great war.

The creation of homosexuality as a legal and medical rather than just moral phenomenon came to have great significance during World War II. With the war came the draft, the need to enlist large numbers of men, and arguments from the psychiatric community that homosexuality should be treated as an illness rather than as a crime. Harry Stack Sullivan (himself homosexual) and Winfred Overholser—both schooled in the modern Freudian approach to psychoanalysis—were the psychiatrists who led this crusade (Bérubé ch. 1). Shortly after Congress enacted the conscription act in anticipation of war in 1940, Sullivan and Overholser met with FDR's Selective Service Director and persuaded him to screen inductees for psychiatric as well as physical problems; such screening would save millions of dollars in treatment costs.

Sullivan drafted the initial screening plan with no reference to homosexuality, but the bureaucratic process and scrutiny by other psychiatrists added glosses drawn from the dominant psychiatric view of homosexuality as a mental illness. Medical Circular No. 1 was issued by the Selective Service on November 7, 1940, explaining psychiatry to the 30,000 volunteer physicians at local draft boards; homosexuality was not mentioned. The Service revised the Circular in 1941 and included "homosexual proclivities" in the list of disqualifying "deviations." The Army listed "homosexual persons" among those to be rejected because of "psychopathic personality disorders" (recall Chapter 2, Section 2[C]). The Navy sought to screen out people "whose sexual behavior is such that it would endanger or disturb the morale of the military unit."

In 1941, Sullivan and Overholser initiated the second phase of their plan—to train doctors and psychiatrists to apply the new guidelines for mental screening of inductees (Bérubé 14–15). The discourse of the lecturers was distinctly "modern" (as of 1941, anyway): "homosexuals" were described exclusively through the argot of "mental illness" and pseudo–Freudian determinism ("latency," "tendencies," "personality types"). Homosexuals were considered "psychopaths" who were unable to control their sexual desires and hence would be troublemakers. They were "paranoid" personalities too introverted or repressed to adjust to the give-and-take of military life and the stress of combat situations. They were too effete or "sissy" to become good soldiers or to be accepted by their comrades. Lecturers questioned the popular faith that the armed forces could "make a man" out of such "sissies." The lecturers were less certain about how doctors could "diagnose" such "homosexuals" upon a physical examination (Bérubé 16–18). Some clues were imparted, however: an inductee's discomfort with displaying his nude body, his curiosity or embarrassment about masturbation, or possible admissions of awkwardness around women. Such men, the lecturers insisted, were subject to "homosexual panic" and could be excluded.

Sullivan never completed this second phase, in part because the Service feared that local draft boards would consider the psychiatric talk too weird, and then because the new Director, Major General Lewis Hershey, thoroughly distrusted this "science." Sullivan resigned in protest in November 1941, when Hershey eliminated separate psychiatric examinations at the local boards. Overholser, however, continued to advise the Service and worked a paragraph on "Sexual Perversions" into the 1942 revisions of the Army's mobilization regulations (Bérubé 19). These regulations, published in final form in 1943, were in place for the remainder of the war. The regulations were not as "sophisticated" as the work Sullivan had attempted and reflected nineteenth as well as twentieth century attitudes. "Persons habitually or occasionally engaged in homosexual or other perverse sexual practices" were "unsuitable for military service" as was anyone having "a record as a pervert." "Homosexuals" could be recognized by "feminine body characteristics" or "effeminacy in dress and manner" or "patulous [expanded] rectum." The regulations rejected physically "normal" but personally "effeminate" men because they "would become subject to ridicule and 'joshing' which will harm the general morale and will incapacitate the individuals."

This decision to medicalize homosexuality combined with the draft to bring millions of men under scrutiny. Draftees were certified as either heterosexual or homosexual, and processed accordingly. At the same time that this "more humanitarian" approach was being taken toward homosexuality, efforts to prevent "malingering" meant that discovered homosexuals were treated with revulsion. Thus, while physicians had hoped to ameliorate the military's policy on gays by using a psychiatric framework, other social forces, in particular the need to enlist large numbers of men, combined with the psychiatric effort to produce an opposite effect. The military labeled every potential inductee and imposed severe informal sanctions on discovered homosexuals, who were later discharged. During the course of the war, 18 million Americans were inducted; fewer than 5,000 were rejected for homosexuality. Clearly, little effort was made to open every closet door.

The military's decision to define homosexuality as a medical problem both failed to rid the service of homosexuals and contributed to the stigmatization of homosexuality. On the one hand, the military tried to conceive of homosexuality as a form of mental illness to increase efficiency. On the other hand, it did not want declarations of homosexuality to become a way of avoiding service. The military put research teams to work to uncover a screening device for weeding out homosexuals while also figuring out a way to determine if and how some homosexuals might be "salvaged." These research efforts did not meet with notable success. Indeed, researchers had difficulty even creating a useful classification system for homosexuality. Thus, while military policy continued to evolve, most homosexuals managed to remain in service the conventional way—by remaining in the closet.[d]

The detection of lesbians was even more lax. Because women did not serve in the military in large numbers before World War II, there were not in place preexisting alarms about sexual deviation; lesbian relations were not prosecuted, and Overholser's inquiries about effeminacy and patulous rectums had little meaning for examinations for lesbianism. Hence, overworked examiners let the matter slide, and lesbians were almost always able to enter the armed forces undetected. A good many women joined up *because* they "wanted to be with all those women," as Phillis Abry recalls (Bérubé 28). Although WAC and WAVE top brass pressed for better screening to keep their forces from becoming "dominated" by lesbians, the need for personnel and the lack of direction rendered the screening a

---

d. The primary explanation for the military's apparently laissez-faire policy toward homosexuality was the need for able-bodied men. Such pressure makes any military less selective. Thus, by 1942 the Army agreed to accept men previously rejected for venereal disease. By 1943 it inducted fathers. By 1942 it also stopped "section eighting" homosexuals who were doing their job well; a year later it discharged them only if "rehabilitation" was "impossible." By the time the war ended in 1945, discharged homosexuals were actually being re-inducted as long as they had committed no "in-service" acts. The main liberalizing practices in the Army were codified in AR 615–368 (issued March 7, 1945 and amended April 10, 1945).

porous sieve indeed. Only in 1944, near the end of the war, were regulations issued to detect lesbians.

According to Bérubé, a boatload of homosexual activity was unleashed by the war. People of the same sex serving under extreme stress in a deeply felt common cause are bound to grow physically as well as emotionally closer. Sex among military personnel was widely tolerated by the command structure for these practical reasons. The only big scandal we know about was the famous investigation of lesbian activity at the WAC training center at Fort Oglethorpe, Georgia (Eskridge ch. 1). The investigation was initiated by a May 1944 letter from a shocked mother, who had discovered love letters between her WAC trainee daughter and an older WAC. The mother charged that her "little girl [age 20] who I know was clean of heart and mind" was corrupted by this predatory older woman, and the mother demanded an investigation. The Inspector General took this letter seriously and dispatched a team immediately, Lieutenant Colonel Birge Holt and Captain Ruby Herman. The team conducted a professional but not inquisitorial investigation and uncovered mountains of letters and testimony involving explicit same-sex intimacy at Fort Oglethorpe. Still, only a couple of women were discharged, and the investigators invoked a series of War Department medical circulars to justify retention of most involved.

The medical leniency shown by the military during World War II ended soon after the war did. The period 1947–53 saw thousands of lesbian and gay soldiers hounded from their units, and thousands of others terrorized by the prospect of being discovered in the McCarthy-era witch hunts. Medical compassion was out the door, and anti-deviant hysteria was the order of the day. President Eisenhower's 1953 executive order denying federal employment to a range of political nonconformists lumped "sex perverts" with Communists as enemies of the state. The Army's post-war policy had some flexibility to retain people with "homosexual tendencies," but generally operated under a simple principle: "True, confirmed, or habitual homosexual personnel, irrespective of sex, will not be permitted to serve in the Army in any capacity and prompt separation of known homosexuals from the Army is mandatory." AR 600–443, § I, ¶ 2 (April 10, 1953). From 1953 into the 1970s more than a thousand people were discharged from the armed forces each year on grounds of homosexuality. Many more were negotiated out quietly and do not appear on the record books.

The main concern voiced about homosexuals by the military in the 1950s was their disloyalty. Although the discourse of sick homosexuals remained robust and shed most of its rehabilitative medical gloss, the focus was on potential disloyalty of homosexuals to their country. A standard script was that homosexuals would be particularly susceptible to blackmail: their status was so repugnant that Communists would be able to extract secret information out of them by threat of exposure. A 600-page internal Navy report compiled by Admiral Crittenden debunked the security and blackmail argument in 1957, but the Navy only suppressed the Crittenden

Report and maintained its public stance. So things remained until Stonewall.

PART B.   THE GAY EXCLUSION UNDER LEGAL SIEGE, 1976–94

Before the Stonewall riots (1969), expulsions of homosexuals from the armed forces were the result of military investigations and dragnets, where people were hunted down, interrogated, and expelled. The witch hunts continued after 1969, but a new breed of soldier came to the fore—the person who openly conceded her or his homosexuality and sued the armed forces to stay in. Several of the lawsuits were successful. The most notable successes were those of Copy Berg and Leonard Matlovich, whose cases set an important precedent. *Matlovich v. Secretary of the Air Force*, 591 F.2d 852 (D.C.Cir.1978); *Berg v. Claytor*, 591 F.2d 849 (D.C.Cir.1978). The court declined to hold the military's gay exclusions unconstitutional but held instead that the military vested illegal discretion with officials enforcing the exclusionary policy. Specifically, the services allowed for retention of homosexuals where appropriate but did not define when retention would be appropriate. Because Matlovich and Berg had exemplary service records and no evidence of misconduct, it was not clear why they should not have fallen under the exception.

These successful lawsuits ironically led to a hardening of the military's policy. The Department of Defense in the waning days of the Carter Administration decided not to compromise the gay exclusion and instead issued a new series of directives that were carried over by the new Reagan Administration. Directive 1332.14.1.H dealt with separations of enlisted personnel, 1332.30.1.H with separations of officers. The new directives stimulated a new series of lawsuits and court decisions, most of which upheld the directives.

Department of Defense Directive 1332.14

January 28, 1982.

Homosexuality (Part 1, Section H).

1. *Basis*

a.   Homosexuality is incompatible with military service. The presence in the military environment of persons who engage in homosexual conduct or who, by their statements, demonstrate a propensity to engage in homosexual conduct, seriously impairs the accomplishment of the military mission. The presence of such members adversely affects the ability of the Military Services to maintain discipline, good order, and morale; to foster mutual trust and confidence among servicemembers; to ensure the integrity of the system of rank and command; to facilitate assignment and worldwide deployment of servicemembers who frequently must live and work under close conditions affording minimal privacy; to recruit and retain members of the Military Services; to maintain the public acceptability of military service; and to prevent breaches of security.

b.   As used in this section:

(1) Homosexual means a person, regardless of sex, who engages in, desires to engage in, or intends to engage in homosexual acts;

(2) Bisexual means a person who engages in, desires to engage in, or intends to engage in homosexual and heterosexual acts;

(3) A homosexual act means bodily contact, actively undertaken or passively permitted, between members of the same sex for the purpose of satisfying sexual desires.

c.   The basis for separation may include preservice, prior service, or current service conduct or statements. A member shall be separated under this section if one or more of the following approved findings is made:

(1) The member has engaged in, attempted to engage in, or solicited another to engage in a homosexual act or acts unless there are approved further findings that:

(a) Such conduct is a departure from the member's usual and customary behavior;

(b) Such conduct under all the circumstances is unlikely to recur;

(c) Such conduct was not accomplished by use of force, coercion, or intimidation by the member during a period of military service;

(d) Under the particular circumstances of the case, the member's continued presence in the Service is consistent with the interest of the Service in proper discipline, good order, and morale; and

(e) The member does not desire to engage in or intend to engage in homosexual acts.

(2) The member has stated that he or she is a homosexual or bisexual unless there is a further finding that the member is not a homosexual or bisexual.

(3) The member has married or attempted to marry a person known to be of the same biological sex (as evidenced by the external anatomy of the persons involved) unless there are further findings that the member is not a homosexual or bisexual and that the purpose of the marriage or attempt was the avoidance or termination of military service.

PROBLEM 4–4

ISSUES UNDER DIRECTIVE 1332.14.1.H

(A) Transsexual Marriage? A male servicemember marries a post-operative male-to-female transsexual. (Post-operative means that the per-

son now has female rather than male external genitals; the person still has a male genetic make-up, however.) Is that grounds for separation? Would it make a difference if the partner identified as a male "homosexual" before the sex change?

(B) Military Volte-Face. An openly gay man was drafted in 1968, at the height of the Vietnam War. At the induction center he truthfully answered that he had "homosexual tendencies," and in a follow-up interview with a doctor truthfully said he enjoyed anal and oral sex with other men. The induction center accepted him for service, and the gay man did a tour in Vietnam. He also engaged in consensual oral and anal sex with other military men, both gay and straight. When the man reenlisted, he openly said he was homosexual, and no quarrel was made. Later in the 1970s, the servicemember became celebrated as a drag performer for military shows and was much in demand by commanding officers wanting to entertain the troops. In 1982 and operating under the new directive, the Army initiated proceedings to separate the gay man, who sued to retain his position. The man admits to homosexual activity with other servicemen. Will a court uphold this separation? See *Watkins*, below, as well as Mary Ann Humphrey, *My Country, My Right to Serve*, 248–57 (1990) (interview with Perry Watkins).

(C) Just a Statement? A serviceperson confesses homosexuality to the chaplain and commanding officer, but there is no evidence of homosexual activity. Will the armed forces separate the member for this statement? See *Steffan*, below.

Perry J. Watkins v. United States Army

United States Court of Appeals for the Ninth Circuit, 1988.
847 F.2d 1329, vacated, 875 F.2d 699 (1989).

[Excerpted in Chapter 1, Section 3(B)]

Joseph Steffan v. William J. Perry

United States Court of Appeals for the District of Columbia Circuit, en banc, 1994.
41 F.3d 677.

■ SILBERMAN, J., [delivered the opinion for the en banc Court.] * * *

[Joseph Steffan] enrolled in the Naval Academy in 1983. He successfully completed three of his four years of training, and consistently ranked near the top of his class. During his senior year, Steffan admitted privately that he was gay. At a performance board, Steffan was asked, "I'd like your word, are you a homosexual?" He replied, "Yes, sir." Based on this hearing the Performance Board recommended to the Commandant of the Academy that "Steffan be separated from the Naval Academy due to insufficient aptitude for commissioned service." Steffan was separated and subsequently sued for reinstatement. He maintained that the Naval Academy regulations requiring separation for simply being "homosexual" were unconstitutional, as were the underlying Department of Defense regulations. DOD Directive 1332.14.H.1.a, 32 C.F.R. Pt. 41, App. A (1991) (superseded).[1]

[A panel of the D.C. Circuit found the separation and the DOD Directive unconstitutional, *Steffan v. Aspin*, 8 F.3d 57 (1993), but the en banc court upheld the separation. Judge Silberman's opinion commanded an en banc majority for the following discussion of the constitutionality of the Naval Academy regulations, which were very similar to the DOD Directive. We have omitted his discussion of Steffan's procedural obstacles in challenging the Department of Defense Directive.]

* * * [W]e are required to ask two questions of the [Naval Academy] regulations. First, are they directed at the achievement of a legitimate governmental purpose? Second, do they rationally further that purpose? The first of these questions is not even in dispute in this case. * * * Steffan concedes that the military may constitutionally terminate service of all those who engage in homosexual conduct—wherever it occurs and at whatever time the conduct takes place. Counsel at oral argument further admitted, in connection with a discussion focused on the DOD Directives, that the military could ban even those who reveal an "intention" to engage in such conduct. It is common ground, then, that the regulations would be serving a legitimate purpose by excluding those who engage in homosexual conduct or who intend to do so.

The dispute between the parties is thus limited to the question whether the regulations (focusing now on the Academy regulations), by requiring the discharge of those midshipmen who describe themselves as homosexual—whether or not the Academy has information establishing that an individual has engaged in homosexual conduct or intends to do so— are rational. Steffan first argues that there is no necessary factual connection between such self-description and such conduct. But Steffan relies primarily on a more subtle and novel argument. Even if the government could rationally, as a factual matter, draw a connection between the statement and the conduct, other legal considerations prevent the government from so doing. The military may not, according to Steffan, "punish" homosexuals solely on the basis of their "status." Nor may the military presume that self-declared homosexuals will actually engage in homosexual conduct, for such conduct is illegal under the Code of Military Justice. (Sodomy is prohibited under 10 U.S.C. § 925 (1988).) Such a presumption—that someone will actually break the law—is inconsistent, he argues, with our legal traditions.

We consider first whether the Academy regulation has a rational factual basis. The appropriate question, it seems to us, is whether banning those who admit to being homosexual rationally furthers the end of

---

1. The Directives mandated that a "member shall be separated ... if one or more of the following approved findings is made." 1332.14.H.1.c. One such finding was that "[t]he member has stated that he or she is a homosexual ... unless there is a further finding that the member is not a homosexual." 1332.14.H.1.c.(2). And the term "homosexual" is defined as "a person, regardless of sex, who engages in, desires to engage in, or intends to engage in homosexual acts." 1332.14.H.1.b.(1).

banning those who are engaging in homosexual conduct or are likely to do so. The Academy can treat someone who intends to pursue homosexual conduct in the same manner as someone who engages in that conduct, because such an intent is a precursor to the proscribed conduct and makes subsequent homosexual conduct more likely than not. And the military may reasonably assume that when a member states that he is a homosexual, that member means that he either engages or is likely to engage in homosexual conduct. The inference seems particularly valid in this case because Steffan made no attempt to clarify what he meant by the term. He did not specify (nor was he asked by the Board) whether he had engaged in homosexual conduct in the past, whether he was presently engaged in homosexual conduct, whether he intended to engage in homosexual conduct in the future, or whether all three were true. * * *

Admittedly, it is conceivable that someone would describe himself as a homosexual based on his orientation or tendencies (and, perhaps, past conduct), notwithstanding the absence of any ongoing conduct or the probability of engaging in such conduct. That there may be exceptions to the assumption on which the regulation is premised is irrelevant, however, so long as the classification (the regulation) in the run of cases furthers its purpose, and we readily conclude that it does. As then-Judge Kennedy pointed out in *Beller v. Middendorf*, 632 F.2d 788 (9th Cir.1980), cert. denied, 454 U.S. 855 (1981) [excerpted in Chapter 3, Section 3(A)]:

> Nearly any statute which classifies people may be irrational as applied in particular cases. Discharge of the particular plaintiffs before us would be rational, under minimal scrutiny, not because their particular cases present the dangers which justify Navy policy, but instead because the general policy of discharging all homosexuals is rational. *Id*. at 808 n.20 (citation omitted).

The rule of law presupposes the creation of categories.

The military thus may rely on presumptions that avoid the administratively costly need to adduce proof of conduct or intent, so long as there is a rational basis for believing that the presumption furthers that end. And the military certainly furthers its policy of discharging those members who either engage in, or are likely to engage in, homosexual conduct when it discharges those who state that they are homosexual. The special deference we owe the military's judgment necessarily affects the scope of the court's inquiry into the rationality of the military's policy. Whether a certain course of conduct is rational does not depend solely upon the degree of correlation that exists between a surface characteristic and a corresponding hidden trait. For the question whether the degree of correlation justifies the action taken—i.e., whether it is rational—necessarily depends on one's assessment of the magnitude of the problem the action seeks to avoid. The military is entitled to deference with respect to its estimation of the effect of homosexual conduct on military discipline and therefore to the degree of correlation that is tolerable. Particularly in light of this deference, we think the class of self-described homosexuals is sufficiently close to the class of those who engage or intend to engage in homosexual conduct for the military's policy to survive rational basis review.

Because removing from the military all those who admit to being homosexual furthers the military's concededly legitimate purpose of excluding from service those who engage in homosexual conduct, Steffan's argument at bottom must be based on the notion that the classification drawn by the military is impermissibly over-inclusive—that the military may not presume that all admitted homosexuals will engage in homosexual conduct because some homosexuals would not. However, courts are compelled under rational-basis review to accept a legislature's generalizations even when there is an imperfect fit between means and ends. A classification does not fail rational-basis review because it " 'is not made with mathematical nicety or because in practice it results in some inequality.' The problems of government are practical ones and may justify, if they do not require, rough accommodations—illogical, it may be, and unscientific.' [*Heller v. Doe*, 113 S.Ct. 2637, 2643 (1993)] (quoting *Dandridge v. Williams*, 397 U.S. 471, 485 (1970) and *Metropolis Theatre Co. v. Chicago*, 228 U.S. 61, 69–70 (1913)).[7]

Steffan seeks to end-run this analysis by arguing that a prohibition triggered simply by an admission of homosexuality is one based on "status" rather than conduct, and therefore is legally impermissible regardless of its rational relationship, as a factual matter, to the military's objective. As the panel that initially decided this case put the point, "America's hallmark has been to judge people by what they do, and not by who they are." *Steffan v. Aspin*, 8 F.3d 57, 70 (D.C.Cir.1993), vacated and rehearing en banc granted (D.C.Cir. Jan. 7, 1994). In our view, however, Steffan's attempt to invoke a rule against "punishment" based on "status" is unavailing, because it derives from a misunderstanding of constitutional law.

It is true that the Constitution forbids criminal punishments based on a person's qualities—we assume that this is what is meant by "status"—rather than on his or her conduct. See *Robinson v. California*, 370 U.S. 660 (1962). Yet, this proposition has never meant that employment decisions—which is what this case is about—cannot be made on such a basis. One

---

7. In *Meinhold v. United States Dept. of Defense*, 34 F.3d 1469 (9th Cir.1994), the court addressed the "desires" portion of the DOD Directive in a case involving a serviceman who said on national television, "Yes, I am in fact gay." A discharge panel was convened to consider Meinhold's statement and as far as we can determine Meinhold did not appear before the Board. The Ninth Circuit construed the "desires" language to mean something akin to intent, and therefore concluded that separation could be based on a statement identifying oneself as a homosexual only when it was accompanied by evidence of conduct or intent. Finding that Meinhold's televised announcement failed to provide any such evidence, the court determined that Meinhold's discharge was illegal under the Navy's own regulations. The Ninth Circuit accepted Meinhold's characterization that the class of persons at issue was those "who say they are gay but have not acted in accordance with their propensity in the past." In our view, however, the proper characterization of the class is persons who say they are gay, but as to whom the military has no additional evidence as to their conduct. The *Meinhold* court also did not consider the rationality of treating all persons who identify themselves as homosexuals as likely violators of the prohibition on homosexual conduct.

cannot be put in jail for having been born blind (although a blind person who drives a truck and kills someone could be jailed for his act). But it obviously would be constitutional for the military to prohibit blind people from serving in the armed forces, even though congenital blindness is certainly a sort of "status." The logic of Steffan's argument and of the original panel's decision—that "America's hallmark" prohibits "punishment" (which term is meant to encompass discharge decisions) based on a person's "status"—would mean that the military acts unconstitutionally if it refuses to enlist blind individuals.

It is asserted that one does not choose to be homosexual and that therefore it is unfair for the military to make distinctions on that basis. But whether or not one's homosexuality is genetically predetermined, one's height certainly is. Steffan conceded at oral argument that the Navy's maximum height restrictions are constitutional because they rationally further a legitimate naval purpose. That concession amounts to an admission that employment decisions based on a person's characteristics are subject to the same analysis as decisions based on a person's conduct. Both are tested to see whether they rationally further a legitimate purpose.

The controversy before us is quite analogous to *Massachusetts Bd. of Retirement v. Murgia*, 427 U.S. 307 (1976) (per curiam), in which the Supreme Court upheld a mandatory retirement age of 50 for police officers on the grounds that the classification rationally furthered the government's purpose of excluding those who lacked the physical conditioning to be officers. In other words, the Court upheld a classification based on "status"—after all, a classification based on age turns on how old someone is, not on what he can do—that was aimed prophylactically at preventing the risk of unsatisfactory conduct. The connection between homosexuality and homosexual conduct is at least as strong (indeed, it seems much stronger) as the relationship upheld in *Murgia* between age—a paradigmatic "status"—and unsatisfactory job performance. * * *

■ [The separate opinions of JUDGE BUCKLEY, JUDGE RANDOLPH, and JUDGE GINSBURG are omitted.]

■ CIRCUIT JUDGE WALD [joined by CHIEF JUDGE EDWARDS and CIRCUIT JUDGE ROGERS], dissenting.

From the beginning, the central issue presented by Steffan's case has always been whether the military may constitutionally exclude from membership in the services individuals who admit to homosexual orientation, without any evidence of homosexual conduct or intent to engage in such conduct. Today's majority reformulates Steffan's appeal to avoid this critical issue. Through ingenious but totally unjustified uses of presumptions and inferences, the court seeks to transform Steffan's case into one concerning homosexual conduct—when in fact the Navy has never even alleged that Steffan engaged or intended to engage in such conduct.

The linchpin of the court's transformation strategy is its assertion that "a statement that one is a homosexual" may be "used by the Navy as a proxy for homosexual conduct—past, present, or future." We disagree in the most fundamental way with that claim, and believe that in the military context, where homosexual conduct results in automatic discharge or imposition of criminal sanctions, it is inherently unreasonable to equate an admission of homosexual identity with commission of or intent to engage in homosexual conduct. The en banc court's attempt to recast the case to avoid the issue that the parties, the trial court, and the original panel opinion have identified as at the core of this litigation must ultimately fail. The critical issue posed in the starkest fashion by Steffan's case is whether a member of the armed forces may be discharged on the sole basis of an admission of his homosexual orientation. We believe that he may not and we therefore dissent. * * *

* * * The nub of the majority's argument appears to be that when Steffan admitted his "homosexuality," he was actually "saying" any one of three things: (1) "I have already engaged in homosexual conduct"; (2) "I intend to engage in homosexual conduct"; or (3) "I desire to engage in homosexual conduct, but I do not engage or intend to engage in such conduct—I am simply homosexual by orientation." Given this trinity of possible meanings to Steffan's declaration of homosexuality, the argument continues, the military was entitled to infer that Steffan meant the first or second, but not the third. * * *

* * * Inferring future homosexual conduct from an admission of homosexuality presents the now-familiar "propensity" issue—whether the admission itself indicates that an individual will "one day" actually engage in proscribed homosexual conduct. [Judge Wald argues from the DOD Directive and the Department's interpretation of the Directive that the government as well as Steffan recognize the difference between homosexual "orientation" and homosexual "conduct." See also the Problem following this case, which describes the new "don't ask, don't tell" law.]

Given, then, that homosexual orientation and conduct are analytically distinct concepts, the "propensity" question reduces to whether an admission of homosexuality alone, without elaboration of any kind, may rationally give rise to an inference that a particular individual will "one day" engage in homosexual conduct, regardless of the inhibitions of his or her environment. Neither the majority nor the government offers any indication that such a presumption is rooted in reality. The government's brief baldly claims that there is a "sound factual connection between the proved and inferred facts," but offers no further support for this proposition. At oral argument, the government repeatedly relied on the incantation that the "nature of human sexuality" supported the inference. * * *

* * * The government's contention in this case smacks of precisely the sort of stereotypical assessment forbidden by *Stanton* and *Reed*; at bottom, the government and the majority seem to be saying that gay servicemembers—unlike heterosexuals—must be presumed incapable of controlling their sexual "desires" in conformity with the law.[18] While the government

---

18. The majority's attempt to explain this irrational difference in treatment on the ground that "heterosexuals have a permissible outlet for their particular sexual desires

is not obliged to offer evidence to support the rationality of an inference, neither are courts obliged to accept the naked assertion of an untenable position.

The irrationality of the government's inference is particularly patent in the military, where homosexual conduct is grounds for automatic discharge and, in the case of homosexual sodomy, punishable by incarceration. Indeed, it is much more reasonable to infer that a servicemember who admits to "homosexuality" will thereafter assiduously forego homosexual conduct. After all, servicemembers are surely aware that statements of homosexual orientation or desire will trigger close scrutiny of their subsequent behavior for evidence of homosexual "conduct" or "intent," as indeed occurred in Steffan's case. It would be foolhardy for servicemembers to freely admit "homosexuality," unless they were quite confident that no additional evidence of conduct or intent existed.

The Ninth Circuit is in agreement with this view, and has interpreted the regulation at issue here as not reaching simple, unadorned admissions of homosexuality. In so doing, it cited numerous inconsistencies in the military's position that raised, in the court's view there, serious doubts about the "rationality" of the same inference urged upon us here. In *Meinhold*, 34 F.3d at 1478 n.11, Judge Rymer noted that when an individual admits or has been found to engage in past homosexual acts, the military does not necessarily infer future homosexual conduct. Rather, so long as certain "approved findings" are made—including that the individual no longer "desires" to engage in homosexual acts—the DOD Directive permits such servicemembers to remain in the military. DOD Directives 1332.14 and 1332.30. Judge Rymer correctly concludes that it is not "wholly rational" to infer future homosexual conduct from a mere statement of "homosexuality" at the same time a similar inference is not necessarily made from past homosexual conduct by professed heterosexuals.

The *Meinhold* court also observed that the military's "propensity" inference treated homosexuals and heterosexuals differently for no reason. Judge Rymer wrote:

> Although courts defer to the military's judgment about homosexual conduct, and classifications having to do with homosexuality may survive challenge if there is any rational basis for them [citations omitted], at least a serious question is raised whether it can ever be

whereas homosexuals in the military do not," is undercut by the military's own definition of "homosexual," which includes individuals who admit to being "bisexual." DOD Directive 1332.14(H)(1)(b)(2). Bisexuals obviously have a "permissible outlet for their sexual desires." Moreover, recent events belie the notion that because heterosexuals have a "permissible outlet for their particular sexual desires," their "desires" are less likely than those of homosexuals to translate into forbidden conduct. Five West Point football players are currently facing charges of "groping" female cadets during a pep rally; seventy-six percent of the 1993 class of women cadets there report experiencing some form of harassment. Eleanor Randolph, "Army Players are Accused of 'Groping,'" *Washington Post*, Nov. 2, 1994, at A1 & A16. Under Academy disciplinary rules, the most severe punishment the accused athletes face for their alleged misconduct is suspension for ninety days.

rational to presume that one class of persons (identified by their sexual preference alone) will violate regulations whereas another class (identified by their preference) will not. *Id.* at 1478. * * *

The Supreme Court has repeatedly emphasized that even prior conduct does not demonstrate a "propensity" to engage in the same actions after they later become illegal. See, e.g., *Jacobson v. United States*, 503 U.S. 540 (1992) [excerpted in Chapter 11, Section 2(C)] ("Evidence of predisposition to do what once was lawful is not, by itself, sufficient to show predisposition to do what is now illegal, for there is a common understanding that most people obey the law even when they disapprove of it."). And if prior conduct does not permit an inference regarding future conduct, such a conclusion is still less justifiable when based on mere orientation or "desire." "[A] person's inclinations and 'fantasies ... are his own and beyond the reach of government'.... " *Id.* (quoting *Paris Adult Theatre I v. Slaton*, 413 U.S. 49, 67 (1973)). Indeed, as Justice Marshall wrote in *Stanley v. Georgia*, 394 U.S. 557, 565 (1969) [excerpted in Chapter 1, Section 1(B)], "Our whole constitutional heritage rebels at the thought of giving government the power to control men's minds." Clearly the Navy may not exercise this power over the minds of servicemembers by discharging them on the basis of inquiries about "homosexuality."

The "constitutional heritage" to which Justice Marshall referred in *Stanley* is evident in the evolution of the law of treason. Under a statute of Edward III, it was a crime to "compass or imagine the Death of ... the King." Statute of Treasons 25 Edw. III. This became the crime of "constructive treason," which was enforced against supposed "compassers" and "imaginers" even when no overt act (other than mere words) or agreement corroborated an intent to carry out the regicide.

Our Constitution expressly repudiates constructive treason. Article III, section 3 declares: "treason against the United States Shall consist only in levying War against them, or in adhering to their Enemies, giving them Aid and Comfort. No person shall be convicted of Treason unless on the Testimony of two Witnesses to the same overt Act, or on Confession in open Court." U.S. CONST. art. III, § 3 (emphasis added). The restrictions imposed by our Constitution, limiting the definition of treason to particular conduct and requiring an "overt act" for conviction, express the fundamental constitutional principle that a person's thoughts are his own—however distasteful they may be to the state or to the populace.

This same principle was accepted even in the cases that upheld the Smith Act's broad proscriptions of subversive activities. Despite the nation's widespread fears of Communist threats to overthrow the state, the Supreme Court never allowed prosecutions merely for private Communist sympathies. For example, in *Scales v. United States*, 367 U.S. 203, 221–24 (1961), the Supreme Court construed the Smith Act's "membership clause" to allow conviction only upon proof of both "active membership" in a Communist-affiliated organization and a "specific intent" to overthrow the Government of the United States. Only if intent accompanied membership, the Court held, would the statute be brought "within established, and therefore presumably constitutional standards of criminal imputability." *Scales*, 367 U.S. at 228. Any broader construction would render the statute constitutionally doubtful. *Id*. at 222, 224. * * *

Thus, even Cold War fears of internal subversion could not induce the Supreme Court to countenance the kind of presumption that the government argues and the majority adopts here—an inference of future misconduct on the basis of an admission of inchoate "desire," unaccompanied by any specific intent to engage in misconduct. Such an inference is repugnant to time-honored legal principles that guard the sanctity of a person's "thoughts and desires" against governmental control. * * *

The majority's attempt to analogize this case to *Massachusetts Bd. of Retirement v. Murgia*, 427 U.S. 307 (1976), upholding a mandatory retirement age of 50 for police officers on the ground that it rationally furthered a legitimate purpose of excluding officers lacking necessary physical fitness, misses the mark, as do its other examples of height and blindness disqualifications from government service. Of course the Navy can exclude individuals based on disqualifying physical or mental characteristics beyond their control. It is, however, an altogether different proposition to predicate exclusion on the assumption that certain individuals will not exert their will to prevent mere "desires" from translating into illegal actions.

To put the argument plainly, there is nothing a blind or tall person can do to negate those characteristics that disqualify him from military service. There is no will power that will spare an aging person the eventual loss of physical ability. And certainly there is no way that these people merely by conforming to the law can qualify for military service. But a servicemember who has homosexual desires can; he need only refrain from engaging in prohibited homosexual conduct, and by the Navy's own admission he will be as "fit" as the next person. Since a decision not to act is within the control of the individual servicemember—unlike the "decision" whether to age or be blind—it is not rational to assume that he will choose to engage in conduct that would subject him to discharge or even incarceration. * * *

NOTES ON *WATKINS* AND *STEFFAN* AND THE "OLD" EXCLUSION OF GAYS FROM THE ARMED FORCES

1. *Statutory and Common Law versus Constitutional Interpretation.* Note that all the judges in *Steffan* assume that the Naval Academy was correctly applying its regulations or the Department of Defense Directive. The Ninth Circuit in *Meinhold* interpreted the Department of Defense Directive as not clearly requiring separation of Navy officer Keith Meinhold, who like Steffan said he was a "homosexual" but never admitted to "homosexual conduct." Because separation based only on "status" would raise constitutional problems, the Ninth Circuit interpreted the Directive to preclude separation only for this reason. No judge in *Steffan* followed this approach to the case, perhaps because Naval Academy regulations were clearer or perhaps because the judges felt the Directive (quoted in our note 1 in Judge

Silberman's opinion) was sufficiently clear. Is there an advantage to the Ninth Circuit's approach?

In *Watkins*, the Ninth Circuit, sitting en banc, vacated Judge Norris' opinion. On reconsideration, the en banc Ninth Circuit upheld Perry Watkins' claim on the federal common law ground that the United States was "estopped" from kicking him out because of his homosexuality, after Watkins had enlisted and reenlisted and had made a military career, all with full disclosure on his part. 875 F.2d 699 (9th Cir. 1989) (en banc). Judges Norris and Canby (the original panel) concurred in the result, based upon their earlier analysis. Judge Reinhardt, a dissenter in the earlier panel, joined the opinion of the en banc Ninth Circuit. What are the arguments for this approach, as against Judge Norris' more direct approach?

2. *Level of Scrutiny.* Judge Norris' opinion in *Watkins* is the only federal appellate panel opinion to have applied "strict scrutiny" to a classification based on sexual orientation. Since *Watkins*, no federal appellate panel has applied strict equal protection scrutiny in a gay rights case (as of 1997). Is strict scrutiny defensible? If so, why have more judges not adopted it? Would intermediate scrutiny, similar to some of the gender cases (*Craig v. Boren*, for example), be more appropriate? How about an argument that the exclusion is sex discrimination or, in the case of lesbians, discriminates against women in practice? Recall the Law–Koppelman thesis (Chapter 1, Section 3[B][3]), and consider the Dodge and Benecke excerpt following these notes.

Instead of strict scrutiny, appellate judges have applied rational basis scrutiny. As *Cleburne* and *Romer* (Chapter 1, Section 3[B][1]) illustrate, rational basis scrutiny sometimes has bite, and *Meinhold* reflects concerns that the military exclusion might flunk even the rational basis test. If the exclusion in a particular case reflects nothing but "prejudice," it flunks *Romer*. By the way, both *Watkins* and *Steffan* were decided before *Romer*. Does the Supreme Court's analysis striking down the Colorado initiative have implications for the gays-in-the-military cases? How are the latter different?

3. *The Status–Conduct Distinction.* Judge Wald and the *Meinhold* Court made much of the Navy's penalizing people for simply declaring their sexual orientation but seemed open to penalty for homosexual "conduct." Indeed, Steffan's attorneys conceded this point for purposes of argument. Why is penalty for status so much more irrational than penalty for conduct? Steffan could have kept his mouth shut about his homosexuality (he confessed to two classmates and a chaplain before he was confronted by the military investigators), as could Meinhold. Why isn't the expression of identity conduct? Isn't the core objection that the government is trying to suppress people's identity? If that is so, isn't the government's regulation of private sexuality also suspect? Compare *Bowers v. Hardwick* (Chapter 1, Section 2), and *Romer v. Evans* (Chapter 1, Section 3[B][1]).

Note this status/conduct irony: a statement that "I am a heterosexual" is almost as probative evidence that one has and will commit illegal sodomy, as the statement "I am a homosexual." Studies have repeatedly shown that three-quarters of the American heterosexual population have engaged in active oral sex, three quarters receptive oral sex, and more than a fifth anal sex. *E.g.*, Edward O. Laumann et al., *The Social Organization of Sexuality: Sexual Practices in the United States* 98–99 (1994). Does this mean that open heterosexuals—the large majority of them sodomites by the government's inference—should be kicked out? If not, isn't the *Romer* equal protection problem exacerbated? Judge Wald makes the further point that the statement "I am a heterosexual man" is actually stronger evidence that the person will violate the Code of Military Justice than the statement "I am a homosexual man," because military regulations prohibit rape, sexual harassment, and other kinds of sexual assault which heterosexual men are much more likely to commit than any lesbian, gay, or bisexual group.

Michelle M. Benecke and Kristin S. Dodge, Military Women in Nontraditional Fields: Casualties of the Armed Forces' War on Homosexuals

13 *Harvard Women's Law Journal* 215, 219, 220–24, 226–28, 238–41 (1990).*

The belief that military women were particularly prone to lesbianism is apparent in the investigation and training procedures advocated by the services for ferreting out lesbians. A 1952 speech given to Navy Auxiliary (WAVE) recruits combined the topics of maintenance of femininity and avoidance of homosexuality, suggesting the degree to which suspicions of lesbianism were tied to popular stereotypes that lesbians were unfeminine in appearance and actions. Officers reminded recruits that they were "supplementing and complementing" the men, not competing with them and urged them to "be sure that we retain as much of our basic femininity as possible." * * *

* * * [A] combination of [various] factors resulted in women and lesbians becoming special targets for discharge. The 1980's were characterized by a wave of investigations and discharges for alleged lesbian activities, including the following: the investigation of women on the USS Norton Sound in 1980, which resulted in the discharge of eight women sailors; investigations on the hospital ship Sanctuary and on the USS Dixon; the Army's ouster of eight female military police officers from the United States Military Academy at West Point in 1986; the 1988 investigation of thirty women, including every African–American woman, on board the destroyer-tender USS Yellowstone, which resulted in the discharge of eight women; the 1988 investigation of five of the thirteen female crewmembers on board the USS Grapple; and the now infamous Parris Island investigation.

The Marine Corps' investigation of women drill instructors from 1986 to 1988 at the Marine Corps Recruit Training Depot at Parris Island, South

Carolina, is one of the most extensive investigations to come to public knowledge. Almost half of the post's 246 women were questioned about alleged lesbian activities, and sixty-five women eventually left the Marine Corps as a direct result of the investigation. At least twenty-seven of these women were administratively discharged. Three women Marines stationed at Parris Island were jailed as the result of criminal convictions for homosexual activity. Many women have chosen to resign or accept voluntary discharges rather than face extensive investigations and the possibility of criminal charges.

While the DOD policy on homosexuality does not distinguish between male and female servicemembers, recent reports indicate that women are discharged from the military services at a rate ten times that of men. The different investigative methods used to target women and men may account for this disparity. Men are typically investigated on a case-by-case basis, and allegations of male homosexuality tend to be handled quietly with efforts made to usher servicemen out of the service as quickly as possible. In sharp contrast, women are often targeted and discharged as the result of mass investigations, aptly referred to as "witchhunts."

Witchhunts are often initiated by military authorities on the basis of rumors started by male servicemembers about women who refuse the servicemen's sexual advances. The most frequent targets of witchhunts are competent, assertive, and athletic women. Witchhunts flourish when women under investigation are coerced by agents into naming other military women who are rumored to be lesbians. The 1988 investigation of women sailors on the USS Grapple is one example.

The USS Grapple investigation began when a male crew member started rumors about the close friendship between a woman who rebuffed his sexual advances and another sailor, Petty Officer Mary Beth Harrison. The rumors were followed by an incident in which this male sailor, in front of the ship's crew and at least one of its officers, shouted profanities and accusations that the women were lesbians. On a subsequent deployment, flyers bearing the sign "no dykes" appeared around the ship.

A woman who files complaints about such harassment often finds that her chain-of-command either is unresponsive or responds by initiating an investigation against the woman herself, presuming incorrectly that only lesbians are lesbian-baited. The experience of the women on the USS Grapple was no exception. Harrison's superiors actually advised her not to file a complaint and appeared to have dropped the matter until, in November 1988, she and three other women were questioned by the Naval Investigative Service (NIS) about alleged homosexual activities. Like many women targeted in witchhunts, the accused sailors were outstanding performers in nontraditional job assignments. According to Harrison, the fairness of these proceedings was dubious. "We were not asked if we were Gay—we were automatically presumed guilty."

Many women who have been investigated in witchhunts have reported that they were subjected to lengthy and harsh interrogations. Investigative techniques used during the USS Grapple witchhunt fit this pattern. Harrison's requests for an attorney were denied until after she had endured two and a half hours of "good guy, bad guy" questioning during her initial interrogation, and another woman was interrogated for six hours without a break.

One of the most common tactics used by investigators is to pressure women to name others who might be gay in order to save themselves. During the USS Grapple investigation, NIS agents told the sailors they would be "protected" if they turned the other women in, that the others had already confessed to being lesbians, and that the NIS had obtained "conclusive evidence" of their guilt. NIS agents have also threatened women with jail sentences and the loss of custody of their children if the women did not name others rumored to be lesbians or admit to participating in homosexual activities themselves. * * *

In July 1988, twenty-three-year-old Corporal Barbara Baum, a military policewoman, was convicted by a general court-martial of sodomy, seven counts of indecency, and conspiracy to obstruct justice. The charges against Baum arose from information provided to investigators by Baum's former lover, Lance Corporal Diana Maldonado, in exchange for a grant of testimonial immunity. Baum was sentenced to one year in jail, demotion to private, and a dishonorable discharge.

The brief affair between Baum and Maldonado was discovered by Maldonado's spurned boyfriend in October 1986 when he kicked in the door of their motel room and found them naked in bed together. An investigation of the women was not immediately initiated, however, because of the boyfriend's perceived lack of credibility.

Over a year later, Baum, en route to an assignment in Hawaii, was recalled for questioning. Military officials believed that she could provide information to agents conducting an investigation of alleged lesbian activities among female drill instructors at Parris Island. Baum's refusal to cooperate with investigators contributed to the military prosecutor's decision to try her case by general court-martial even though it involved no allegation of assault. This decision sent a strong message to other Marines to cooperate in the investigation.

Maldonado's account of oral sex with Baum on the night of the motel incident led to the charge of sodomy against Baum. Explicit questioning of Maldonado at Baum's trial provided sufficient evidence to prove the necessary elements of the sodomy offense. Maldonado also admitted to "passionate kissing and fondling of genitalia" between her and Baum at Baum's residence and gave uncorroborated testimony that Baum had told her of Baum's other physical contact with women during a game of "truth or dare" at a party in May 1986. This testimony was found sufficient to convict Baum under the ambiguous wording of UCMJ Article 134, Indecent Acts with Another.

In June 1988, three weeks after her imprisonment, Baum succumbed to agents' promises of clemency and an upgraded discharge if she cooperated in the ongoing investigation of women Marines. During fourteen hours of questioning, she gave investigators the names of over seventy-seven women she knew to be or suspected to be homosexual. Baum served 226 days of her one-year sentence before being released from the military prison at Quantico Marine Corps Base in Quantico, Virginia.

On February 15, 1990, a military appeals court overturned Baum's conviction, ruling that two jury members in Baum's trial had extrajudicial knowledge of the evidence and an interest in the outcome of the case and that the military trial judge had allowed uncorroborated testimony. * * *

A disturbing constant in the picture of harassment is the frequency with which lesbian-baiting is triggered by a servicewoman's refusal of sexual advances. For example, one officer interviewed by the authors told of sexual advances made by a male peer toward her and two colleagues. All three made it clear that they were not interested in pursuing a sexual relationship. Soon after, they learned that the spurned officer was suggesting to other men in the unit that the three were lesbians and were engaging in sexual acts together. In some respects, this follows the typical pattern of sexual harassment. The difference in the military is the degree of pressure which can be brought to bear against a woman not only by her superiors, but by her peers, and in the case of a woman officer or noncommissioned officer, by her subordinates. The legitimization of lesbian-baiting arms all men with a tool for sexual harassment because any time a woman is called a "dyke," her reputation, her career, and even her liberty are on the line. * * *

Recourse for women faced with lesbian-baiting or sexual harassment is limited. A woman who reports abuse is likely to be "labeled as ... not being a team player," an extremely degrading pronouncement in the military. As Harrison of the USS Grapple protested, "[t]hose times when I did move to make official reports I met hostility and reluctance to believe that incidents like these could happen aboard such a fine vessel." In addition, because of the military's anti-homosexual policy, a woman who reports lesbian-baiting harassment risks focusing increased scrutiny upon herself, which may lead to full-blown investigation. As a result, many women are reluctant to report incidents, and many accede to sexual demands.

Andrea Dworkin argues that sexual intercourse is a crucial means by which men prove their masculinity to themselves and to other men. Considered from the perspective of the gender identity theory explored above, it appears that sexual access to women servicemembers may help compensate men for the breakdown of gender boundaries in nontraditional job fields by providing an alternative means of proving masculinity. * * *

This sexual accessibility analysis appears to apply to the Parris Island investigation and may help to explain why investigations of drill instructors have taken place repeatedly at the installation. At Parris Island, Marine Corps policy segregates women recruits into their own units with women drill instructors and strictly separates male and female recruits during basic training. Servicemen on Parris Island find a host of psychological and social messages in this arrangement: they see a group of women sexually inaccessible to themselves or other men, grouped together under the instruction of assertive, competent female drill instructors who have sole access to the female recruits. The mixture is a potential powder keg of sexism, homophobia, and gender identity conflict to men who may be insecure in their masculinity.

PART C.   DON'T ASK, DON'T TELL, 1993–?

President Clinton in January 1993 announced his intention to end the exclusion of bisexuals, lesbians, and gay men by executive order. Facing a firestorm of protest from various quarters, the President immediately agreed with Senator Sam Nunn, the Chair of the Senate Armed Services Committee, and General Colin Powell, the Chair of the Joint Chiefs of Staff, to postpone any executive order until after Congress had studied the matter in a series of House and Senate hearings.

Policy Concerning Homosexuality in the Armed Forces: Hearings Before the Senate Committee on Armed Services

103d Congress, 2d Session.
595–97, 599–602, 606–09, 618–19 (May 11, 1993).

[Retired General H. Norman] SCHWARZKOPF: * * * Let me first state that my position on this matter is not based on any kind of moral outrage over what many consider immoral conduct. Also, I would like to state I am a very strong advocate of our Constitution's provisions for individual rights, and therefore my position is not a condemnation of anyone's right to choose their sexual orientation.

That said, I must say that I am opposed to an executive order lifting the ban on homosexuals in the military service, and my opposition grows out of honest concern for the impact that such a measure would have on the men and women of our Armed Forces and the resultant reduction in our Nation's ability to protect our vital interest.

The Armed Forces' principal mission is not to be instruments of social experimentation. The first, foremost, and all eclipsing mission of our military is to be ready to fight our Nation's wars and when called upon to do so to win those wars.

We send our troops into battle for God, country, and mom's homemade apple pie, but study after study of many different wars on many different battlefields time and time again come to the same conclusion.

What keeps soldiers in their foxholes rather than running away in the face of mass waves of attacking enemy, what keeps the marines attacking up the hills under withering machine gun fire, what keeps the pilots flying through heavy surface-to-air missile fire to deliver the bombs on targets, is the simple fact that they do not want to let down their buddies on the left or the right.

They do not want to betray their unit and their comrades with whom they have established a special bond through shared hardship and sacrifice not only in the war but also in the training and the preparation for the war.

It is called unit cohesion, and in my 40 years of army service in three different wars I have become convinced that it is the single most important factor in a unit's ability to succeed on the battlefield. Anyone who disputes this fact may have been to war, but certainly never led troops into battle.

Whether we like it or not, in my years of military service I have experienced the fact that the introduction of an open homosexual into a small unit immediately polarizes that unit and destroys the very bonding that is so important for the unit's survival in time of war.

For whatever reason, the organization is divided into a majority who oppose, a small minority who approve, and other groups who either do not care or just wish the problem would go away, and I do not find this surprising, given the divisiveness that I have encountered in our Nation in the past year. The attitudes of our servicemen and women simply reflect, in my opinion, the attitudes that I have encountered in the American people.

Do not get me wrong, please. I am not saying that homosexuals have not served honorably in our Armed Forces in the past. Of course they have, and I am quite sure that they will in the future, although I candidly must say that I completely reject the grossly overinflated numbers quoted by some organizations.

However, in every case that I am familiar with, and there are many, whenever it became known in a unit that someone was openly homosexual, polarization occurred, violence sometimes followed, morale broke down and unit effectiveness suffered. Plain and simply, that has been my experience.

I am also concerned from another standpoint. Today in our country we have the finest military units I have seen in my lifetime around the army. One of the reasons, of course, is the outstanding equipment provided to us by this committee and our Government, but far and above the biggest reason why our Armed Forces are as good as they are is the magnificent young men and women who serve our country in these Armed Forces.

This committee knows better than any that this did not happen by accident. It happened because as a result of the all-volunteer Armed Forces initiatives and legislation we have been able to dramatically improve the quality of the young men and women entering our military.

For the first time in anyone's memory, the pool of high quality men and women wanting the join the military greatly exceeded the number of people we needed to recruit. The result was top quality recruits capable of handling our modern high tech equipment who were four times more likely to complete their initial enlistment and far more likely to reenlist for military service.

It was these young men and women, far more than our equipment, who made it possible for us to accomplish such dramatic results in the Gulf War.

Lt. Gen. Barry McCaffrey, then the commander of the 24th Mechanized Infantry Division, summed it all up when he said, if the Iraqis had had our equipment and we had had theirs, we still would have won.

Will this same pool of high quality young men and women be available to us if the ban on homosexuals in the military is lifted? If what I am told by young men and women who talked to me is indicative, the answer is no. If what I am told by countless parents is indicative, the answer is clearly no.

What about those men and women already serving? Are they going to stick with us like they have in the past? There is little doubt that we will lose quite a few of them. The result of this decrease in quality of enlistees and reenlistees can only result in a decrease in the quality of our armed forces.

Often, various precepts of our Constitution clash. This has clearly been the case in the military. We have excluded people from serving due to height, weight, sex, mental capacity, and physical disability. We even retire brilliant, handsome, erudite general officers after 35 years of service. [Laughter.]

I mean, this is clearly a case of age discrimination. [Laughter.]

These exclusions have been contested over and over in the courts, and the decisions have been universally the same. The interest of the defense of our Nation has prevailed.

One last point. Our Armed Forces are already under severe pressure from ongoing deep budget cuts, resultant force drawdowns, inactivations and base closures, and what some all draconian personnel reductions in force, viewed by many as a breach of an implicit social contract.

Yet many who advocate lifting the ban on homosexuals in the military blithely say we can overcome all of the problems I have raised by ordering already overburdened military leaders at all levels to "institute training for all personnel on the acceptance of homosexual or bisexual orientation or conduct," even when a large majority of the leaders and the troops have clearly stated, "they oppose allowing homosexuals in the military" and "believe gays serving openly in the military would be very disruptive to discipline."

The military establishment is not fragile, but in my mind such actions would be seriously overloading their plate. They will faithfully try and execute the orders of their civilian leaders, but their hearts simply will not be in it. To me, they will be just like many of the Iraqi troops who sat in the deserts of Kuwait forced to execute orders they did not believe in.

And what about our troops' rights? Are we really ready to do this to the men and women of our Armed Forces and to risk a possible decrease in our Nation's ability to defend itself simply to force our servicemen and women to accept a lifestyle of a very well-organized, well-financed, and very vocal, but what turns out to be a very small minority of our society? I personally sincerely hope not. * * *

[Marine Colonel Frederick C.] PECK: * * * I have returned last Wednesday from Somalia. I spent 5 months in Somalia, and then a month before that in Kenya, working on the airlift in Operation Provide Relief, and then Restore Hope. * * *

* * * I will share with you very quickly that when we landed and I came ashore with the Marines at 4:30 a.m. in the morning on the 9th of December, in an AMTRAK across a now-infamous beach, past CNN and other enemy installations that were there, took the airfield and the port, it was an exciting experience.

And the grunts lived like grunts always do. We found wherever we could to throw down a bedroll, in abandoned buildings, or in worst cases, out in places like Badar and Baidoa, just digging a hole in the ground and putting a poncho over it. And when it rained out there, it got pretty miserable. Not to bore you with details, but the facilities were primitive; I am talking about toilet facilities. At first they were holes in the ground, and then they were improved to plywood 2–holers. You know, real fancy accommodations. And they never got much better than that.

We eventually moved out of crowded buildings and into tents, and we had cots, and put up some permanent structures, and living conditions got a little bit nicer. * * *

I have to tell you that among the troops out there, Topic A was this topic that we are discussing right here. And I also have to say that I served alongside, directly alongside, the Canadians and the Australians, who have had recent experience of their Legislatures dropping the ban. * * * [L]et me tell you that, amongst the Australians and the Canadians, how they handled it, how the troops handled it: And that is by intimidation.

They said no gays would dare assert themselves, where they were; and it would be barracks justice, and a very inhospitable environment for anyone who stepped forward. So they did not have a problem, because no one came out of the closet; no one was stepping forward, and it was very easy for them to deal with. I do not advocate that as necessarily as the right way to deal with things, I just want to tell you how it is, and how I saw it. * * *

[The witness describes his tour of duty with the Marines' "Hollywood Liaison Office."] I worked with a lot of people in Hollywood whose sexual orientations and a lot of other things about their personal lifestyles were much, much different than my own. I think I was successful there. * * * And I am saying this to tell you that I am not a homophobe, I am not the kind of person who has led some cloistered, sheltered military life, who has never had to deal with the homosexuals before. I have worked with them all the time. I can work with homosexuals, shoulder to shoulder.

But I do not think I can live with them and coexist with them in a military environment. It is one thing to share an office with someone, it is quite another thing to share a lifestyle; and that is what the military is: It is a way of life.

When you go to someplace like Somalia, there is not any off-duty time. It is not like working inside the beltway at the Pentagon where at the end of the day you go home. Your workplace is your living space, it is your home. And when you want to take someone of a different sexual orientation into that, let me tell you, think about what it would be in your personal, in your personal life. If you took someone of a different sexual orientation in, to live in your home, and how it would effect the way you carried out your daily life.

I am reminded of the President's saying that he had put up behind his desk there, that says, "It's the economy, stupid." And I keep wanting to say, "It's sexual orientation that we are talking about here." It is not the worth of the individual. We are not saying that, because people are too short or too tall, or mentally deficient or physically deficient somehow or another, that their personal worth is something less, we are just saying they do not fit in. And if you want to start breaking down those barriers, and trying to make people fit in where I do not think they belong, you are going to hurt the United States military.

I have three sons, I wrote to Senator Nunn and in my letter, and if the ban on gays and lesbians serving in the military were to be dropped, I would counsel all three of my sons to stay out of the military. Absolutely.

My oldest son, Scott, is a student at the University of Maryland, he is just about to graduate. If he were to walk into a recruiter's office, it would be the recruiter's dream come true[!] He is 6 foot 1, blue-eyed, blonde hair, great student.

I have not been the greatest father to him, I will confess that. His mother and I divorced when he was 6 years old. She later died of cancer, lymphoma, when he was 16. He has had a rough life, but he has come through it. And he has persevered, he switched colleges, switched majors, had the problems that most teenagers have growing up. But if he were to go and seriously consider joining the military, I would have to, number 1, personally counsel against it, and number 2, actively fight it.

Because my son, Scott, is a homosexual; and I do not think there is any place for him in the military. I love him; I love him as much as I do any of my sons. I respect him, I think he is a fine person; but he should not serve in the military. And that is the strongest testimonial I think I can give. I am the father of a homosexual boy, a young man, and I do not think he should serve in the military.

I spent 27 years of my life in the military, and I know what it would be like for him if he went in. And it would be hell. And if we went into combat, which as the General said is the whole purpose for us being here, he would be at grave risk if he were to follow in my footsteps as a infantry platoon leader or a company commander. I would be very fearful that his life would be in jeopardy from his own troops.

And I am not saying that that is right, or wrong, or whatever. I am telling you that is the way it is. You get into war, the first casualty is truth; the second is the value of human life. And fraggings, let me tell you, did not begin or end in Vietnam. Fratricide is something that exists out there, and there are people who would put my son's life at risk in our own Armed Forces. That is just one reason. That is a very important reason, for me, speaking personally about my own son, to counsel him not to go in the military.

I think I will end it right there. I hope we can talk later about unit cohesion, and issues like that. But I will leave my testimony at that point. * * *

Chairman [Samuel] NUNN: * * * [L]et me ask each of you this question. There are some who see this as a civil rights issue, or as an issue that is comparable to the debate about women and their role in the military, and certainly we hear over and over again that the same arguments are used against admitting openly gays and lesbians in the military as were used back in the 1940s and 1950s about the admission of blacks into integrated units in the military.

How would each of you respond to the general question as to whether you see an analogy between this debate and the debate that occurred in the civil rights era back in the forties and fifties, and also the question of women? * * *

Colonel PECK. * * * I think if someone declares their homosexuality that that is a statement that defines a behavior. It certainly connotes a behavior. If I say I am black or I am white or Jewish or Protestant or Catholic, it does not necessarily indicate how I am going to behave. But it does indicate a behavior if I say I am homosexual.

When I think of the analogy of race, I find that somewhat offensive. If I could use another analogy, it would be much akin to someone in the military saying I am a racist. Making that statement and then following up with, but I will not let my racial attitudes interfere with my behavior. You certainly would not expect the troops that had to follow that person to respect them or trust them. If the person says they are a racist, anyone of color or of the wrong ethnicity or religion working for him or her would be immediately suspect.

And it is the same analogy that I would have about someone who comes out and declares openly that they are gay or lesbian in the military. Once they do that, I think they compromise their position and it certainly has limited their effectiveness. * * *

General SCHWARZKOPF: There is certainly an analogy, but I do not agree that it is applicable here.

First of all, I do not think it is any secret that Colin Powell and my deputy, Cal Waller, have both said that there is no analogy, and they are certainly capable of speaking, since they entered the Armed Forces during that time and lived through a great deal of it. And I value their judgment greatly in this matter.

Second, we have a distinction between something that a person is born with and a chosen conduct. I know of no medical study anywhere that has validly proved that people are born homosexual. It is a question of choice of conduct in their case. An African–American is born black and they are black, and they are going to continue to be black. And they are going to continue to be African–Americans, and they have no choice in the matter whatsoever.

I think there is a very important point that we ought to remember, though. In 1953, I believe the statistic was that at the time the orders were issued to integrate our armed services, 30 percent of the people within the military were against the integration. Today, we have 78 or 80 percent of the people in the military against bringing homosexuals in. There is a rather considerable difference in the opinions of the people within our Armed Forces with regard to that issue.

I would also say that at that time I think there was a majority of the American people that were very much in favor of integration of African–Americans into our Armed Forces and, indeed, into our society. And my experience has been that it is just the opposite today. The majority of the American people are not in favor of the integration of homosexuals—a lifting of the ban on open homosexuality.

So there is a rather considerable difference on that point also that I do not think we can ignore. * * *

Major [Kathleen] BERGERON: * * * I do not see an analogy to either the race issue or the women's issue. I think color and gender are benign physical characteristics, as the General [Colin Powell] has said, that some-one is born with. They do not have a behavior that has the potential to affect other people and the people around them. And I personally resent the analogy to the females or to gender because the issue, and the issue that we are currently still struggling with in the military, I think, is a question of capabilities, and where women are going to be deployed * * *.

So, I do not see analogy with either one.

Chairman NUNN: And we also separate women and men in living quarters and give them at least as much privacy as possible, wherever they are, do we not?

Major BERGERON: Yes, sir. In my 17, almost 18, years, I have never been required or expected to cohabitate with males wherever I have gone, even in the field. We go to extraordinary measures to ensure that there is privacy. I think Colonel Peck stated it as either establishing different shower hours or different head hours, and even in sleeping arrangements, if you have to do it in shifts. But we go to extraordinary measures to ensure that that privacy is maintained.

General SCHWARZKOPF: Mr. Chairman, may I comment on the female issue also? * * *

We discriminate against women in the Armed Forces today, period. It is simply because we have come to a judgment that there are certain organizations where the defense of the nation will suffer if you made it $^{50}\!/_{50}$. And because of that we have adopted combat exclusion rules.

Now, some of them have been lifted, but a lot of them continue to be in effect for the very reason that we are interested in the defense of our Nation. So, yes, we have brought women in, and they do an outstanding job serving in our Armed Forces. But they are discriminated against. They are allowed to only serve in certain positions under certain circumstances, because we worry about the defense of our Nation, which is the foremost precept.

That just happens to be a matter of fact. And so, to say that this is an analogous issue to black Americans or to females, I think it completely misses the point that always, in every case, we have been looking at what's best for the defense of the Nation. * * *

Senator THURMOND: * * * General Schwarzkopf, last week we listened to experts, including Gen. Cal Waller, testify about the homosexual policies of foreign militaries. Some witnesses point to the Netherlands and Finland as examples of successful integration of homosexuals into the military.

Since you have a great deal of experience working with foreign militaries, can you tell us if it is better to compare the United States military to other nations for the purpose of determining homosexual policy?

If we were to permit openly homosexual soldiers to serve, would it change how our allies and coalition partners might view the United States military?

General SCHWARZKOPF: Senator, to be honest with you, most of the Armed Forces that have supposedly integrated homosexuals into them, practice a blatant form of hypocrisy. And for anyone to say that these homosexuals have been integrated in these organizations with no problems at all and no restrictions just obviously has not studied the subject.

Take Israel for example. Israel has a policy that the gays are allowed in their military. The gay soldiers do not sleep in the barracks. They are deliberately put in units where they go home at night. It is a clear fact that no gay commands any elite units. They are not even allowed in elite units in Israel. And no gay commands any unit in Israel. And there is also a very, very small number that even admit that they are gay in the Israeli military.

So to use that as an example is hypocrisy. * * *

Senator LEVIN: * * * Now let me get to the question that is the heart of the matter. Whether or not if someone is in the military, * * * and they say I am a homosexual, that that person should be removed. They do not say that they have engaged in homosexual activity. They simply say I am a homosexual. That would be enough, for you, to remove that person from the military.

General SCHWARZKOPF: Right, because that would polarize the organization. * * *

Senator LEVIN: * * * You said that the statement I am a homosexual, that is conduct in your book.

General SCHWARZKOPF: Of course. It also happens to be the DOD test today.

NOTE ON THE AFTERMATH OF THE GAYS IN THE MILITARY HEARINGS DON'T ASK, DON'T TELL

By most accounts, General Schwarzkopf[b] and Colonel Peck were effective witnesses, and Peck's was the most dramatic testimony of the hearings (you could hear a collective gasp from the packed hearing room audience when he announced that one of his sons was gay). Is there any response to the heartfelt confession of a father who felt so strongly about the issue that he would not only steer his son away from a career he loved, but was willing to "out" that son on national television? What are the implications of his uncontradicted assertion that straight soldiers might kill an openly gay soldier? Do you agree with what this might say about straight men? The military?

The Senate hearings yielded tons of testimony about unit cohesion, troop morale, shower facilities, close quarters on a ship, and popular views inside and outside the military. It all boiled down to: straight soldiers would not stand for gay soldiers to serve openly. The House hearings, chaired by Representative Ronald Dellums, were evenly balanced between witnesses supporting and those opposing the ban; the supporters of the ban made the same points they did in the Senate. When another witness made the Peck point (i.e., if openly gay people showed up in the Navy they would be chucked out the porthole), Chair Dellums expressed outrage that this would be tolerated in an organization that prides itself on discipline.

Quaere: Does this testimony establish a sufficient factual record to justify deference to the military on this issue?

On July 17, President Clinton announced his endorsement of Senator Nunn's "don't ask, don't tell" approach, and in the next week both House and Senate held hearings on the new policy. Senator Nunn's Committee

b. There is some irony in Stormin' Norman's testimony. When Michael Asen took the General's deposition in 1982, Schwarzkopf testified that homosexuality (status, not conduct) is incompatible with military service. Randy Shilts, *Conduct Unbecoming* 426 (1993) then reports:

> After the deposition, Asen and the general went to lunch. Asen recalls that they talked more about the case, off the record. * * * Over lunch, Schwarzkopf confided that although he would deny ever saying it if asked in court he really did not care whether or not gays ended up serving in the Army. He had known homosexuals who were fine soldiers. The policy was something he had inherited,

and it was a policy he had to enforce and defend. That was his job, but if the policy were thrown out tomorrow, he said, it would be fine with him.

Schwarzkopf called this account a "blatant lie" and maintained that all he meant to convey to the attorneys was his ambivalence about discriminating against gays on behalf of national security. (*May 1993 Senate Hearings* 625.)

Shilts also suggests (or hints) that some of the high-ranking military officials testifying in defense of the policy were themselves gay or lesbian, a suggestion also pressed in Michalangelo Signorile, *Queer in America: Sex, the Media, and the Closets of Power*, 97–122 (1993).

immediately assembled Secretary of Defense Leslie Aspin and the entire Joint Chiefs of Staff for a hearing on the new policy. The most dramatic point was when Senator Dan Coats (R–Ind.) polled the Joint Chiefs with the inquiry, "Is homosexuality incompatible with military service?" The actual response of the Joint Chiefs was split: General Colin Powell (the Chair of the Joint Chiefs), Admiral David Jeremiah (Navy), and General Merrill McPeak (Air Force) responded, *Open homosexuality* in a unit setting is incompatible with military service. Three other Joint Chiefs— General Carl Mundy (Marines), General Gordon Sullivan (Army), and Admiral Frank Kelso II (Naval Operations)—responded, *Homosexuality* is incompatible.

Representative Ike Skelton's Military Forces and Personnel Subcommittee of the House Committee on Armed Services held hearings on "Assessment of the Plan to Lift the Ban on Homosexuals in the Military" also in July 1993. Unable to attract the Joint Chiefs, Representative Skelton settled for Defense Department General Counsel Jamie Gorelick and several academics. Skelton explored the constitutionality of the don't ask, don't tell policy. Professor William Woodruff opined that the new policy raised more serious constitutional problems, especially under the First Amendment, than the old policy did and ran a somewhat greater risk of being declared unconstitutional as applied in some situations. Professor Cass Sunstein, who had earlier called the free speech issue a "red herring," disagreed: "[Y]ou won't get a court of appeals, and you will certainly not get five [J]ustices on the Supreme Court" to strike down the policy under any circumstances. "So if the worry is are the [J]ustices going to strike this one down, I think the answer is don't worry."[c] Do you agree with Professor Sunstein's confident assessment? Are there any circumstances where you could imagine five Justices invalidating the policy as applied?

With the new-found support of the President, Congress in Public Law No. 103–160, § 571(a)(1), 107 Stat. 1670, added the following new provision, codified at 10 U.S.C. § 654:

(a) Findings.—Congress makes the following findings: * * *

(4) The primary purpose of the armed forces is to prepare for and to prevail in combat should the need arise.

(5) The conduct of military operations requires members of the armed forces to make extraordinary sacrifices, including the ultimate sacrifice, in order to provide for the common defense.

(6) Success in combat requires military units that are characterized by high morale, good order and discipline, and unit cohesion.

(7) One of the most critical elements in combat capability is unit cohesion, that is, the bonds of trust among individual service members

c. *Assessment of the Plan to Lift the Ban on Homosexuals in the Military: Hearings Before the Military Forces and Personnel* Subcomm. of the House Comm. on Armed Services, 103d Congress, 1st Session 322 (July 22, 1993).

that make the combat effectiveness of a military unit greater than the sum of the combat effectiveness of the individual unit members.

(8) Military life is fundamentally different from civilian life in that—

(A) the extraordinary responsibilities of the armed forces, the unique conditions of military service, and the critical role of unit cohesion, require that the military community, while subject to civilian control, exist as a specialized society; and

(B) the military society is characterized by its own laws, rules, customs, and traditions, including numerous restrictions on personal behavior, that would not be acceptable in civilian society.

(9) The standards of conduct for members of the armed forces regulate a member's life for 24 hours each day beginning at the moment the member enters military status and not ending until that person is discharged or otherwise separated from the armed forces.

(10) Those standards of conduct, including the Uniform Code of Military Justice, apply to a member of the armed forces at all times that the member has a military status, whether the member is on base or off base, and whether the member is on duty or off duty.

(11) The pervasive application of the standards of conduct is necessary because members of the armed forces must be ready at all times for worldwide deployment to a combat environment.

(12) The worldwide deployment of United States military forces, the international responsibilities of the United States, and the potential for involvement of the armed forces in actual combat routinely make it necessary for members of the armed forces involuntarily to accept living conditions and working conditions that are often spartan, primitive, and characterized by forced intimacy with little or no privacy.

(13) The prohibition against homosexual conduct is a long-standing element of military law that continues to be necessary in the unique circumstances of military service.

(14) The armed forces must maintain personnel policies that exclude persons whose presence in the armed forces would create an unacceptable risk to the armed forces' high standards of morale, good order and discipline, and unit cohesion that are the essence of military capability.

(15) The presence in the armed forces of persons who demonstrate a propensity or intent to engage in homosexual acts would create an unacceptable risk to the high standards of morale, good order and discipline, and unit cohesion that are the essence of military capability.

(b) Policy.—A member of the armed forces shall be separated from the armed forces under regulations prescribed by the Secretary of Defense if one or more of the following findings is made and approved in accordance with procedures set forth in such regulations:

(1) That the member has engaged in, attempted to engage in, or solicited another to engage in a homosexual act or acts unless there are further findings, made and approved in accordance with procedures set forth in such regulations, that the member has demonstrated that—

(A) such conduct is a departure from the member's usual and customary behavior;

(B) such conduct, under all the circumstances, is unlikely to recur;

(C) such conduct was not accomplished by use of force, coercion, or intimidation;

(D) under the particular circumstances of the case, the member's continued presence in the armed forces is consistent with the interests of the armed forces in proper discipline, good order, and morale; and

(E) the member does not have a propensity or intent to engage in homosexual acts.

(2) That the member has stated that he or she is a homosexual or bisexual, or words to that effect, unless there is a further finding, made and approved in accordance with procedures set forth in the regulations, that the member has demonstrated that he or she is not a person who engages in, attempts to engage in, has a propensity to engage in, or intends to engage in homosexual acts.

(3) That the member has married or attempted to marry a person known to be of the same biological sex. * * *

(e) Rule of Construction.—Nothing in subsection (b) shall be construed to require that a member of the armed forces be processed for separation from the armed forces when a determination is made in accordance with regulations prescribed by the Secretary of Defense that—

(1) the member engaged in conduct or made statements for the purpose of avoiding or terminating military service; and

(2) separation of the member would not be in the best interest of the armed forces.

(f) Definitions.—In this section:

(1) The term "homosexual" means a person, regardless of sex, who engages in, attempts to engage in, has a propensity to engage in, or intends to engage in homosexual acts, and includes the terms "gay" and "lesbian".

(2) The term "bisexual" means a person who engages in, attempts to engage in, has a propensity to engage in, or intends to engage in homosexual and heterosexual acts.

(3) The term "homosexual act" means—

(A) any bodily contact, actively undertaken or passively permitted, between members of the same sex for the purpose of satisfying sexual desires; and

(B) any bodily contact which a reasonable person would understand to demonstrate a propensity or intent to engage in an act described in subparagraph (A).

On December 21, 1993, Secretary Aspin issued a memorandum and Directives concerning the implementation of the new policy. Memorandum from Secretary Aspin to the Secretaries of the Military Departments et al. (Dec. 21, 1993). They provided that an applicant to become a member will not be asked about his or her sexual orientation, that "homosexual orientation is not a bar" to "service entry or continued service," but that "homosexual conduct" is. Such "conduct" includes not only homosexual "acts" but also a statement by a member or applicant that "demonstrates a propensity or intent to engage" in such acts. A statement that demonstrates the "propensity" will thus require separation unless the member rebuts a presumption that he or she engages or intends to engage in "homosexual acts" or has a "propensity" to do so. Directives 1332.14 (separations [i.e., discharge] of enlisted personnel), 1332.30 (separations of officers), and 1304.26 (enlistment).

Department of Defense Directive Number 1332.14 Enlisted Administrative Separations

December 1993.

H. *Homosexual Conduct.*

 1. *Basis.*

 a.   Homosexual conduct is grounds for separation from the Military Services. Homosexual conduct includes homosexual acts, a statement by a member that demonstrates a propensity or intent to engage in homosexual acts, or a homosexual marriage or attempted marriage. A statement by a member that demonstrates a propensity or intent to engage in homosexual acts is grounds for separation not because it reflects the member's sexual orientation, but because the statement indicates a likelihood that the member engages in or will engage in homosexual acts. Sexual orientation is considered a personal and private matter, and homosexual orientation is not a bar to continued service unless manifested by homosexual conduct.

 b.   A member shall be separated under this section if one or more of the following approved findings is made:

 (1) The member has engaged in, attempted to engage in, or solicited another to engage in a homosexual act or acts, unless there are approved further findings that:

 (a) Such acts are a departure from the member's usual and customary behavior;

 (b) Such acts under all circumstances are unlikely to recur;

(c) Such acts were not accomplished by use of force, coercion, or intimidation;

(d) Under the particular circumstances of the case, the member's continued presence in the Armed Forces is consistent with the interest of the Armed Forces in proper discipline, good order, and morale; and

(e) The member does not have a propensity or intent to engage in homosexual acts.

(2) The member has made a statement that he or she is a homosexual or bisexual, or words to that effect, unless there is a further approved finding that the member has demonstrated that he or she is not a person who engages in, attempts to engage in, has a propensity to engage in, or intends to engage in homosexual acts. A statement by a Service member that he or she is a homosexual or bisexual, or words to that effect, creates a rebuttable presumption that the Service member engages in homosexual acts or has a propensity or intent to do so. The Service member shall be advised of this presumption and given the opportunity to rebut the presumption by presenting evidence that he or she does not engage in homosexual acts and does not have a propensity or intent to do so. Propensity to engage in homosexual acts means more than an abstract preference or desire to engage in homosexual acts; it indicates a likelihood that a person engages in or will engage in homosexual acts. In determining whether a member has successfully rebutted the presumption that he or she engages in or has a propensity or intent to engage in homosexual acts, some or all of the following may be considered:

(a) whether the member has engaged in homosexual acts;

(b) the member's credibility;

(c) testimony from others about the member's past conduct, character, and credibility;

(d) the Nature and circumstances of the member's statement;

(e) any other evidence relevant to whether the member is likely to engage in homosexual acts.

This list is not exhaustive; any other relevant evidence may also be considered.

(3) The member has married or attempted to marry a person known to be of the same biological sex (as evidence by the external anatomy of the persons involved).

2. *Burden of Proof.* * * * [Refers to H.4.e. and f., which provide as follows:

e.   The member shall bear the burden of proving, by a preponderance of the evidence, that retention is warranted under the limited circumstances described in paragraph H.1.b. except in cases where the member's conduct was solely the result of a desire to avoid or terminate military service.

f. Findings regarding whether or not retention is warranted under the limited circumstances of paragraph H.1.b. are required if the member clearly and specifically raises such limited circumstances.] * * *

HYPOTHETICAL TEACHING SCENARIOS * * *

The following hypothetical scenarios are for training purposes only. They are not meant to prescribe "correct" outcomes, but to illustrate how relevant personnel should approach issues that may arise under the DoD policy on homosexual conduct in the Armed Forces. * * *

2. *Situation*: An officer observes two male junior enlisted Service members walking and holding hands while off-duty and on liberty. The Service members are wearing civilian clothes and are in an isolated wooded park and, except for the officer, they are alone. He reports the incident to the commanding officer (CO) and adds that he is surprised to find out they appear to be homosexuals. He asks the CO what he proposes to do about the incident. The CO decides he will call the two Service members into his office, separately, and ask them about the officer's observations.

Issue: Was the CO's action appropriate? If not, what action should he have taken?

Discussion: The officer's observation of the two enlisted Service members walking and holding hands in the park constitutes credible information of homosexual conduct if the officer is someone the CO otherwise trusts and believes. The two Service members' hand-holding in these circumstances indicates a homosexual act and therefore the commanding officer may follow-up and inquire further. Probably, the extent of the inquiry will be two confidential one-on-one conferences between the CO and the two Service members to inquire into the incident.

Before the Service members are asked to discuss or explain the incident, the CO should advise them of the military's policy on homosexual conduct. Should they decline to discuss the matter, the questioning should stop. At that point, the CO may consider other relevant information and decide whether to initiate administrative separation actions based on the information he possesses. * * *

12. *Situation*: An enlisted Service member states to his commanding officer that he is a homosexual. He also tells this to several other enlisted members. An Administrative Discharge Board is convened. At the Board hearing, the member does not dispute that he stated on several occasions that he is a homosexual. He promises, however, that he will not engage in any homosexual acts during the remainder of his term of enlistment. The member presents no other evidence.

Issue: How should the Board consider whether the Service member has successfully rebutted the presumption?

Discussion: A statement by a Service member that he or she is a homosexual creates a rebuttable presumption that the member engages in or has a propensity or intent to engage in homosexual acts. This means that the statement itself is evidence that the member engages in or is likely to engage in homosexual acts. If the member fails to demonstrate that he or she in fact does not engage in homosexual acts and is not likely to do so, he or she may be discharged. * * *

If the only evidence that the member presented was his promise that he would not engage in any homosexual acts during the remainder of his term of enlistment, the Board would determine whether that promise, in light of the Board's assessment of the member's credibility and the nature and circumstances of his statements that he was a homosexual, was sufficient to demonstrate that he does not engage in homosexual acts and is not likely to do so. * * *

PROBLEM 4–5

APPLICATIONS OF DON'T ASK, DON'T TELL

(A) Hand–Holding. Assume that the Board in Hypothetical Situation No. 2 separates the two men based on the evidence of hand-holding. Both men deny they are homosexuals, and there is no evidence of other conduct. The men sue to remain in the Army. You are a federal district judge. How do you rule, and why?

(B) Hanging Out at a Lesbian Bar. A servicewoman has been observed on three occasions leaving a bar known to cater to a lesbian clientele. On one occasion she left with another woman, but there was no evidence of intimacy between the two; they were talking animatedly. Are these sightings the basis for separation? Should the commanding officer commence an investigation? See Hypothetical Situation No. 3 (omitted in our excerpt).

(C) Confessions of Status. Assume that the Board in Hypothetical No. 12 separates the man based only upon his verbal statement and without any evidence of homosexual activities. Would a judge sustain this action? Read the next cases.

Lt. Paul Thomasson, USN v. William J. Perry, 80 F.3d 915 (4th Cir., en banc, 1996). A fractured Fourth Circuit held § 654(b) was constitutionally applied to expel Lt. Paul Thomasson after he declared his homosexuality and then refused to offer evidence to rebut the presumption he had engaged in homosexual acts. Nine judges joined the majority opinion of Chief Judge J. Harvie Wilkinson, which followed *Steffan*: courts should defer to the political branches on military issues, statements of homosexuality are plausible evidence of illegal sodomy, and courts should defer to military judgments about that and about the effect of sodomy on unit cohesion. Four judges joined Judge K.K. Hall's opinion dissenting from this holding, for reasons similar to Judge Wald's dissent in *Steffan*.

Five judges joined a concurring opinion by Judge Michael Luttig, who adopted an argument advanced by the Family Research Council, that the

Department of Defense regulations are invalid. "The requirement that, in order to be discharged, one must at least demonstrate a likelihood to engage in homosexual acts exists only in a regulation promulgated by the Administration, ostensibly in implementation of the statute. That regulation redefines the statutory term 'propensity' so that only those homosexual service members who are *likely* to engage in homosexual acts will be discharged. Through this regulation the Administration has effectively secured the very policy regarding military service by homosexuals that it was denied by the Congress." In short, the gays in the military flap of 1993 ended up recodifying the prior policy, and the Clinton Administration's contrary "spin" is contrary to the statute.

As evidence for this position, Judge Luttig relied on the structure of § 654(b)(2), which flatly says personnel shall be separated if they state they are homosexual; the proviso ("unless") only allows personnel to stay in if they can persuade the armed forces that they are really *not* homosexual. Hence, Judge Luttig interpreted § 654(b)(2)'s exception for a soldier who can show that he or she is *not* a person with "propensity to engage in, or intends to engage in homosexual acts," to apply only to the *heterosexual who misspoke*, and not to the *celibate homosexual*. Judge Luttig argued that this reading is reinforced by § 654(b)(1), which allows a *heterosexual who slipped* and engaged in one homosexual act ("I was drunk and didn't know what I was doing and will never do it again") to stay in the armed forces, so long as he can persuade the military that he really is a heterosexual.

Judge Luttig also relied on statements during the July 1993 hearings on don't ask, don't tell, where slippery Administration witnesses were repeatedly pinned down by conservative Senators to confess that policy was not changing. For example, Secretary of Defense Aspin admitted, under cross-examination, to Senator Phil Gramm that military personnel "would at least be assured that no one would be self-professed homosexual and be allowed to continue to serve." Judge Luttig cited to other similar references and accused the Administration of deceiving the court and the public by its recharacterization of the statute and its policy in an effort to allow the *celibate homosexual* to serve. Hence, Judge Luttig would have invalidated the regulation, in part, but would still have expelled Thomasson based upon the statute itself.

Although only five of the twelve participating judges joined Judge Luttig, none of the Fourth Circuit judges responded to his arguments. Is there a response? Assume the regulation is invalid, and that homosexuals are excluded from service merely because of their status. Is Judge Luttig right that this is a constitutional policy? In light of *Romer v. Evans* (Chapter 1, Section 3[B][1])?

Lt. Col. Jane Able et al. v. United States, 88 F.3d 1280 (2d Cir.1996). Six plaintiffs serving the U.S. armed forces brought suit to enjoin enforcement of § 654. They stated in their complaint that they are "homosexuals." Judge Nickerson's trial court opinion held that the plaintiffs only had standing to challenge § 654(b)(2) (discharging personnel for statements of homosexuality) and that this provision violated the First

Amendment. Important First Amendment interests were implicated, both because they were conveying important information and because they were expressing their personal identity. "Regulation of the content of speech that involves First Amendment concerns is presumed invalid. The government may regulate its content only upon a showing that such regulation promotes a 'compelling interest' and that the government has chosen 'the least restrictive means' to further the interest."

Judge Nickerson found the unit cohesion rationale dubious and pointed out that the empirical studies by RAND for the Department of Defense and by the General Accounting Office found no factual basis for the disruption feared by military officials (see Problem 4–6). Moreover, the experience in other countries where gay people can serve openly (*e.g.*, Canada, Israel, Netherlands, Norway) has been devoid of disruption. Fears in the 1940s that service by African Americans would disrupt unit cohesion had no foundation and were disproved by experience in the Korean War. The district judge found that the goal (unit cohesion) was not carefully linked to the regulatory means (§ 654[b]). In any event, the regulatory means violated the First Amendment because it is content-based censorship.

On appeal, the Second Circuit held that plaintiffs had standing to attack the entire statutory policy—§ 654(b)(1)'s exclusion of those who engage in "homosexual conduct" as well as § 654(b)(2)'s exclusion of those who make statements of homosexuality. The panel then addressed and reversed the lower court's First Amendment critique of § 654(b)(2). Judge John Walker's panel opinion accepted part of the government's standard First Amendment argument: the statement "I am a homosexual" cannot be punished per se, but it can be used as evidence of a "propensity" to engage in illegal acts. See *Wisconsin v. Mitchell*, 508 U.S. 476 (1993), where the Supreme Court held that racist statements can be entered as evidence that an assault was motivated by racial hate and thereby eligible for an enhanced sentence.

Judge Walker agreed with Judge Nickerson that the government's regulation of speech did implicate First Amendment values, but reasoned that § 654(b)(2) was narrowly tailored to meet a compelling state objective, namely, the effective functioning of the nation's armed forces. As the Supreme Court did in *Goldman v. Weinberger*, the yarmulke case, the Second Circuit held that courts should defer to military judgments, even even when those judgments create regulations limiting First Amendment freedoms.

As this casebook goes to press, the case is back before Judge Nickerson, to evaluate the constitutionality of § 654(b)(1). The Second Circuit remanded the case to the trial court for further proceedings to determine whether these acts could still be criminalized. After the Supreme Court's opinion in *Romer v. Evans* (Chapter 1, Section 3[B][1]), it is no longer clear that the United States may constitutionally criminalize private, consensual sodomy, as the Code of Military Justice does.

PROBLEM 4–6

DEFERENCE TO CONGRESSIONAL JUDGMENTS EXCLUDING OR SEGREGATING CITIZENS IN THE ARMED FORCES

Like majorities of the D.C. and Fourth Circuits, sitting en banc, the Second Circuit in *Able* embraced a policy of deference to congressional and military judgments about unit cohesion as a basis for excluding citizens from military service. Query: Wouldn't such an approach have sustained the policy followed in 1946, where African Americans were segregated based upon "expert" military judgments that proved in retrospect to have been nothing but a heckler's veto compounded by the "experts" own bigotry? Note, too, that the Supreme Court in *Toyosaburo Korematsu* deferred to expert military judgment that Japanese Americans were prone to disloyalty during World War II and needed to be put in detention centers (nice language for concentration camps). That judgment was not only wrong but was perjured. As to matters of prejudice and equality, is the track record of the armed forces an inspiring one?

Perhaps deference is most appropriate as to issues of fact, such as the Administration's idea that statements of homosexuality are evidence of sodomy, which is illegal under the Uniform Code of Military Justice. This is actually quite true, but recall that the statement "I am a heterosexual" is just as probative evidence that one has and will commit sodomy in violation of the Code. *E.g.*, Edward O. Laumann et al., *The Social Organization of Sexuality: Sexual Practices in the United States* 98–99 (1994). The issue of deference, therefore, does not relate to a matter of fact (homosexuals are prone to commit illegal sodomy), but relates to a matter of discrimination law (why does the military treat presumptive heterosexual sodomites differently?).

As to military judgments that gay people would disrupt unit cohesion, the military used that to justify racial segregation and exclusion of women from a broad range of military positions. The available evidence, recounted in this chapter, suggests that the military was crying "wolf" both times. Is the gaylesbian exclusion the third "wolf"? A number of expert studies have been made of this argument by executive branch consultants. The most detailed study was that of the RAND Institute for the Department of Defense in 1993. Consistent with prior findings by the Government Accounting Office and the Defense Personnel Security Research and Education Center, RAND concluded: "concerns about the potential effect of permitting [open] homosexuals to serve in the military are not groundless, but the problems do not appear insurmountable, and there is ample reason to believe that heterosexual and homosexual personnel can work together effectively."[e] Do the views of people like retired General Schwarzkopf

---

e. RAND, National Defense Research Institute, Report to the Office of the Secretary of Defense, *Sexual Orientation and U.S. Military Personnel Policy: Options and Assessment* 329–30 (1993). See also U.S. General Accounting Office, Report to Congressional Requestors, *Defense Force Management: DOD's Policy on Homosexuality* (June 1992);

Theodore R. Sarbin & Kenneth E. Karois, Defense Personnel Security Research and Education Center, *Nonconforming Sexual Orientations and Military Suitability* (Dec. 1988), reprinted in *Gays in Uniform: The Pentagon's Secret Reports* (Kate Dyer ed. 1990).

suffice to justify the policy in light of objective expert evidence to the contrary?

*

CHAPTER 5

IDENTITY SPEECH IN THE BODY POLITIC

SECTION 1   Political Speech, Publication, and Association

SECTION 2   Privacy and Sexual "Outing"

SECTION 3   Hate Speech

Identity is a social as well as individual process. One develops as well as expresses one's identity through talking and associating with other people, expressing oneself orally and in the print or electronic media, and forming groups and organizations. Indeed, the factors that are considered important enough to frame one's identity are socially constructed factors. Those of us who are left-handed do not consider that feature critical to our identities, in large part because society attaches no real significance to that characteristic. Being a man or a woman, an African American or an Asian American, or a Jew or an Italian are all identity characteristics in ways that left-handedness is not.

Sexual orientation is likewise a consequential factor because of the significance society attaches to it. It is sometimes visible, sometimes not. Because heterosexuality is considered the norm, its existence is assumed and often not noticed (at least officially) or remarked upon until one acts in some way to signal that it should not be assumed. Once that signal is communicated, however, sexual orientation becomes highly visible in a particular situation, often dominating the perception of what is occurring.

If we think of gender as biological sex, it is generally assumed to be a visible categorization (despite what we studied in Chapter 2). If we think of gender as performative of cultural roles, however, it too becomes sometimes visible, sometimes not, with its impact determined by whether a person's gender presentation correlates with our expectations for his or her biological sex. And it is gender performativity that, correctly or not, often signals sexual orientation. All in all, gender and sexuality seem to depend a great deal on expression.

Can majority attitudes invoke the power of the state to prevent unpopular identity groups from associating with one another, to penalize individuals who openly espouse an unpopular identity, or to condition state benefits on foregoing such speech? The First Amendment provides that "Congress shall make no law * * * abridging the freedom of speech, or of the press; or the right of the people peaceably to assemble, and to petition the Government for a redress of grievances." The Supreme Court has held that the due process clause of the Fourteenth Amendment incorporates these protections against state as well as congressional laws. The First Amendment has been interpreted as a broad protection against state censorship, and stands as a barrier to state intervention along these lines (Section 1 of this Chapter). Does the First Amendment also empower private groups, including the press and "outing" activists, to invade people's privacy by exposing their sexual identities (Section 2)? Does the First Amendment prevent the invocation of state power to protect unpopular groups against private violence and hate speech (Section 3)? This Chapter challenges you to devise a theory of the First Amendment and its appropriate role in mediating public and private discourses of sexuality.

POLITICAL SPEECH, PUBLICATION, AND ASSOCIATION

The core First Amendment protection is for "political" speech and publication. Under the now discarded tendency-to-corrupt-morals test that defined obscenity until 1958, speech about sexuality outside of marriage was generally excluded from protection under the First Amendment. (On obscene sexual speech, see Chapter 6, Section 1.) Starting with the New York Supreme Court's ultimate decision in *Friede v. People* to overturn censorship of the *Well of Loneliness* (Chapter 2, Section 2[A][3]) through the 1970s, the courts gradually broadened the scope of sexually related speech that was not considered obscene. Throughout this period, however, sexual speech and political speech were still considered to be distinct and even mutually exclusive categories. Consider the following case, which challenges that approach. Read this case in light of which constitutional goals the First Amendment does or should embody. In other words, *why* does the Constitution restrict state regulation of speech and publication? Are these goals implicated when people *identified* by their gender or sexual orientation speak or publish about their commonalities? If so, does the divide between political and sexual speech collapse?

One, Inc. v. Otto K. Olesen

U.S. Court of Appeals for the Ninth Circuit, 1957.
241 F.2d 772, *reversed per curiam,* 355 U.S. 371 (1958).

■ ROSS, DISTRICT JUDGE.

[Responding to pressure from the Senate and the FBI, the U.S. Post Office confiscated copies of *One, Inc.*, the earliest continuously published homophile magazine in American history. The Post Office maintained that the magazine was nonmailable under 18 U.S.C. § 1461, which prohibits the Post Office from conveying or delivering "[e]very obscene, lewd, lascivious, or filthy book, pamphlet, picture, paper, letter, writing, print or other publication of an indecent character." *One* challenged the decision on the ground that it violated the First Amendment's right of a free press. The district court rejected the challenge, and the circuit court affirmed.]

* * * Our ultimate conclusion as to whether the magazine is mailable or not must be based upon the effect, or impact, that the wording of the various articles in the magazine have upon the reader. There is no precise pattern for reader reaction, so in determining whether the thought pat-

terns created by the words employed in the magazine articles are obscene, lewd, lascivious, filthy or indecent, we must ascertain how other courts met the problem. * * *

[The first] Justice Harlan in delivering the opinion of the court in *Rosen v. United States*, 161 U.S. 29, 43, * * * approved the following test of obscenity given in an instruction of the trial court: "The test of obscenity is whether the tendency of the matter is to deprave and corrupt the morals of those whose minds are open to such influence and into whose hands a publication of this sort may fall." "Would it * * * suggest or convey lewd thoughts and lascivious thoughts to the young and inexperienced?"

[The court quoted from many other opinions to the same effect. Slightly different was the test in *Burstein v. United States*, 178 F.2d 665, 666 (9th Cir.): matter is obscene "if it is offensive to the common sense of decency and modesty of the community, and tends to suggest or arouse sexual desires or thoughts in the minds of those who by means thereof may be depraved or corrupted in that regard."]

Plaintiff, as publisher, states on the second page of the magazine that it is published for the purpose of dealing primarily with homosexuality from the scientific, historical and critical point of view—to sponsor educational programs, lectures and concerts for the aid and benefit of social variants and to promote among the general public an interest, knowledge and understanding of the problems of [sexual] variation. The story "Sappho Remembered", appearing on pages 12 to 15 of the magazine, the poem "Lord Samuel and Lord Montagu" on pages 18 and 19, and the information given on page 29 as to where to obtain "The Circle," a magazine "with beautiful photos," do not comport with the lofty ideals expressed on page 2 by the publishers.

The article "Sappho Remembered" is the story of a lesbian's influence on a young girl only twenty years of age but "actually nearer sixteen in many essential ways of maturity", in her struggle to choose between a life with the lesbian, or a normal married life with her childhood sweetheart. The lesbian's affair with her room-mate while in college, resulting in the lesbian's expulsion from college, is recounted to bring in the jealousy angle. The climax is reached when the young girl gives up her chance for a normal married life to live with the lesbian. This article is nothing more than cheap pornography calculated to promote lesbianism. It falls far short of dealing with homosexuality from the scientific, historical and critical point of view.

The poem "Lord Samuel and Lord Montagu" is about the alleged homosexual activities of Lord Montagu and other British Peers and contains a warning to all males to avoid the public toilets while Lord Samuel is "sniffing round the drains" of Piccadilly (London). The poem pertains to sexual matters of such a vulgar and indecent nature that it tends to arouse a feeling of disgust and revulsion. It is dirty, vulgar and offensive to the moral senses.

An article may be vulgar, offensive and indecent even though not regarded as such by a particular group of individuals constituting a small segment of the population because their own social or moral standards are far below those of the general community. Social standards are fixed by and for the great majority and not by or for a hardened or weakened minority.
* * *

It is difficult to determine if the article contained on page 29 under the caption "Foreign Books and Magazines That Will Interest You", is an advertisement for the magazine "The Circle" or is merely information given by the publisher of "One" to its readers as to where to obtain other books and magazines that may be of interest. Regardless, the situation is the same, if information is given as to where, or how, or from whom, or by what means, obscene or filthy material may be obtained. Although on its face the information in this article appears harmless, it cannot be said that the purpose is harmless. It is for the information of those who read the magazine and particularly the homosexuals. It conveys information to the homosexual or any other reader as to where to get more of the material contained in "One."

An examination of "The Circle" clearly reveals that it contains obscene and filthy matter which is offensive to the moral senses, morally depraving and debasing, and that it is designed for persons having lecherous and salacious proclivities.

[The court described stories in "The Circle" and found them similar to "Sappho Remembered," except that they related to the actions of "homosexuals" rather than "lesbians." The court held that "The Circle," like the other matter, was obscene, thereby rendering "One, Inc." nonmailable.]

NOTE ON *ONE, INC.* AND POSSIBLE GOALS OF THE FIRST AMENDMENT

The Ninth Circuit's decision seems at first glance like a literal violation of the First Amendment, for it applies a congressional "law * * * abridging freedom of speech, or of the press." The Ninth Circuit's dodge around the literal text was to characterize *One* as "obscenity," a legal category of work not considered "speech" or, apparently, "press" either. Ironically, at the very point the Ninth Circuit promulgated its decision, the Supreme Court was beginning to rethink the breadth of the obscenity exception to the First Amendment.

The Supreme Court's per curiam decision in *One, Inc. v. Olesen*, 355 U.S. 371 (1958), reversed the Ninth Circuit's decision. The Court's one-sentence opinion indicated that the lower court's decision was inconsistent with *Roth v. United States*, 354 U.S. 476 (1957) [Chapter 6, Section 1], the First Amendment obscenity decision handed down six months earlier. Consider the constitutional policy basis, or bases, for this result. That is, what constitutional goals does the First Amendment potentially, or optimally, serve?[a] Are those goals implicated in the Post Office's suppression of *One*? The following are some candidates nominated by various scholars and judges; consider these theories critically.

1. *The Marketplace of Ideas.* According to John Stuart Mill, *On Liberty* (1857), truth or the best answer emerges from a competition in the marketplace of ideas. If some ideas are arbitrarily suppressed by the government, there will be a less robust public ventilation of ideas, and we shall be less likely to come to right answers and good policies. The Ninth Circuit's decision in *One* seems antithetical to a free marketplace of ideas, for Judge Ross is saying that there is *one* correct viewpoint about homosexuality (it is sick and abnormal), and any other viewpoint is simply wrong. Most educated people today would consider Judge Ross' position naive and ill-informed—and an example where the First Amendment should have been invoked to head off premature closure in an important debate about the nature of homosexuality and same-sex intimacy. On the other hand, a marketplace of ideas metaphor may not support a strong First Amendment. Consider our willingness in other settings to regulate dysfunctioning markets.[b] The state can prohibit false commercial advertising, for example. Why can't the state prohibit homosexuals from "falsely advertising" their condition?

2. *Democracy Values.* Alexander Meiklejohn, *Free Speech and Its Relation to Self–Government* (1948), argues that channels of communication about political and social issues need to be kept open for democratic self-government to work well. He invokes the American tradition of the town meeting to valorize the First Amendment. While the Ninth Circuit's position in *One* might be criticized as cutting off the flow of relevant information to the body politic, it might be defended on the ground that it expunges information that most townspeople find disgusting (that being the point of obscenity regulations). Does "gross" speech contribute to democracy in action?

Lee Bollinger, *The Tolerant Society: Freedom of Speech and Extremist Speech in America* (1986), extends Meiklejohn's argument to maintain that the First Amendment is a check against people's tendency to be intolerant of those different from themselves or who espouse unfamiliar ideas. Insisting that the polity think twice before suppressing a community of different people, the First Amendment instantiates a norm of tolerance that contributes to a particularly robust and diverse polity. The Ninth Circuit's opinion is intolerant and therefore inconsistent with this vision, but is tolerance a value we want to press at any price? Should society "tolerate" a community

a. Excellent philosophical introductions to this issue include Thomas Emerson, *The System of Freedom of Expression* (1970); Kent Greenawalt, *Speech, Crime, and the Uses of Language* (1989); Frederick Schauer, *Free Speech: A Philosophical Enquiry* (1982); Ronald Collins & David Skover, "The First Amendment in an Age of Paratroopers," 68 *Tex. L. Rev.* 1087 (1990).

b. Critics of the marketplace of ideas metaphor include Ronald Coase, "The Market for Goods and the Market for Ideas," 64 *Am. Econ. Rev.* 384 (1974); Owen Fiss, "Why the State?", 100 *Harv. L. Rev.* 781 (1987); Stanley Ingber, "The Marketplace of Ideas: A Legitimating Myth," 1984 *Duke L.J.* 1.

of vandals on the grounds that they simply reflect another "perspective"?[c] Would the tolerance idea require deregulation of prostitution [see Chapter 11, Section 3]?

3. *Autonomy Values.* Speech and publication are primary methods by which people express, and oftentimes discover, their individuality and personhood. A libertarian would argue that the state must leave the individual alone when she is expressing or exploring personhood, unless there is evidence she is harming others. See Mill, *On Liberty* ch. 4.[d] A communitarian could argue that the state should be encouraging individual flourishing. See Steven Shiffrin, *The First Amendment, Democracy, and Romance* (1990). The ethic of conformity reflected in the Ninth Circuit's opinion threatens to crush individual flourishing, yes?

But consider this. Some progressives maintain that words can and do wound other people, and in such cases the rights of some can justify suppressing or penalizing the speech of others. (See Section 3 of this Chapter, as well as Chapter 6, Section 3.) Can the Ninth Circuit's opinion not be read as a more traditionalist version of the same approach: the articles in *One* can be suppressed because of their tendency to wound others, either by disgusting them or by misleading them (especially "impressionable" young people)? Consistent with an autonomy theory of the First Amendment, can the state regulate public solicitation of sex? If not, the First Amendment has a broader reach than any American court has ever held. If so, how can you meaningfully distinguish *One*?

PART A.   RIGHTS OF ASSOCIATION

Although the First Amendment protects the right to assemble, it does not explicitly protect rights of association. Nonetheless, the Supreme Court held such rights protected by implication in *NAACP v. Alabama*, 357 U.S. 449 (1958). Justice Harlan's opinion reasoned that associational rights are prerequisites for rights to speak and publish that are explicitly protected. The Court disallowed a state's effort to obtain NAACP membership lists, because the disclosure of membership by an unpopular group would surely chill entry into the group. That sort of reasoning was just as applicable to homophile groups that had formed in the 1950s, particularly the Daughters of Billitis and the Mattachine Society. Not only did the homophile groups promise to keep their membership hidden from the authorities, but many and perhaps most members of the group were disinclined to reveal their real names and identities to the group itself! Hence, even though *NAACP v. Alabama* did not involve lesbian and gay plaintiffs, its holding was just as

---

c. Critics of the Meiklejohn and Bollinger tolerance theory include Robert Bork, "Neutral Principles and Some First Amendment Problems," 47 *Ind. L.J.* 1 (1971); David Strauss, "Why Be Tolerant?", 53 *U. Chi. L. Rev.* 1485 (1986); Pierre Schlag, Book Review, 34 *UCLA L. Rev.* 265 (1986).

d. Expressions of this argument include Edwin Baker, "Scope of the First Amendment Freedom of Speech," 25 *UCLA L. Rev.* 964 (1978); Martin Redish, "The Value of Free Speech," 130 *U. Pa. L. Rev.* 591 (1982).

important for homophile groups as it was for equally unpopular African–American civil rights groups.

More recent cases have confirmed and broadened the associational feature of the First Amendment recognized in *NAACP*. "[T]he Court has recognized a right to associate for the purpose of engaging in those activities protected by the First Amendment—speech, assembly, petition for the redress of grievances, and the exercise of religion. The Constitution guarantees freedom of association of this kind as an indispensable means of preserving other individual liberties." *Roberts v. United States Jaycees*, 468 U.S. 609, 618 (1984). Under what circumstances, if any, can the state limit people's rights of association? Consider the following cases.

Sol M. Stoumen v. George R. Reilly et al.

Supreme Court of California, 1951.
37 Cal.2d 713, 234 P.2d 969.

■ GIBSON, CHIEF JUSTICE.

[The State Board of Equalization suspended plaintiff's license to sell alcoholic beverages at the Black Cat Restaurant. The Board alleged violations of sections 58 and 61(a) of the Alcoholic Beverage Control Act. Section 58 provided:

> Every licensee or agent or employee of any licensee who keeps or permits to be used or suffers to be used, in conjunction with a licensed premises, any disorderly house or place in which people abide or to which people resort, to the disturbance of the neighborhood, or in which people abide or to which people resort for purposes which are injurious to the public morals, health, convenience or safety shall be guilty of a misdemeanor.

Section 61(a) provided:

> Every person who sells, furnishes, gives, or causes to be sold, furnished or given away any alcoholic beverage to any person under the age of twenty-one years shall be guilty of a misdemeanor.]

The hearing officer of the board, who received the evidence, found that plaintiff "kept and permitted his licensed premises to be used as a disorderly house in that * * * persons of known homosexual tendencies patronized said premises and used said premises as a meeting place," and that beer was sold to a minor as alleged. He concluded that plaintiff had violated sections 58 and 61(a) and recommended "indefinite suspension" of the license. The findings and recommendation were adopted by the board as its decision. Thereafter the superior court denied a writ of mandate after reviewing the matter on the record before the board.

The principal question with respect to count one [section 58] is whether the evidence is sufficient to warrant suspension of plaintiff's license. Several police officers testified that many of the patrons of the Black Cat were homosexuals and that it was reputed to be a "hangout" for such persons. A number of people were arrested there, some for vagrancy and some because they "demonstrated homosexual actions", but there was no showing that any of those arrested were convicted. There was no evidence of any illegal or immoral conduct on the premises or that the patrons resorted to the restaurant for purposes injurious to public morals.

Section 58 of the act makes it a misdemeanor for a licensee to permit his restaurant and bar to be used as a disorderly house or place "to which people resort for purposes which are injurious to the public morals." The terms of the section refer to conduct on the premises or resort thereto for improper purposes, and it is clear that it would be necessary to read something into that section before it could be construed as an attempt to regulate mere patronage by any particular class of persons without regard to their conduct on the premises. Members of the public of lawful age have a right to patronize a public restaurant and bar so long as they are acting properly and are not committing illegal or immoral acts; the proprietor has no right to exclude or eject a patron "except for good cause," and if he does so without good cause he is liable in damages. See Civ.Code, §§ 51, 52. In analogous cases it has been held that a liquor license could not be revoked on the ground that prostitutes had dined in the licensee's restaurant, *In re Farley*, 111 N.E. 479 (N.Y.1916), and that a conviction of maintaining a bawdy house was not supported by evidence that women of loose or immoral character had obtained lodging in defendant's hotel. *Patterson v. State*, 132 P. 693, 695 (Okla.Crim.App.1913). In the *Patterson* case the court pointed out that such women are human beings entitled to shelter and that it is not a crime to give them lodging unless it is done for immoral purposes. The same reasoning applies to the patronage of a public restaurant and bar by homosexuals, and mere proof of patronage, without proof of the commission of illegal or immoral acts on the premises, or resort thereto for such purposes, is not sufficient to show a violation of section 58.

The fact that the Black Cat was reputed to be a "hangout" for homosexuals indicates merely that it was a meeting place for such persons. Unlike evidence that an establishment is reputed to be a house of prostitution, which means a place where prostitution is practiced and thus necessarily implies the doing of illegal or immoral acts on the premises, testimony that a restaurant and bar is reputed to be a meeting place for a certain class of persons contains no such implication. Even habitual or regular meetings may be for purely social and harmless purposes, such as the consumption of food and drink, and it is to be presumed that a person is innocent of crime or wrong and that the law has been obeyed.

[The court reversed as to count one, discussed above, and remanded for further fact finding as to count two, which alleged the sale of liquor to a minor.]

NOTES ON THE BLACK CAT CASE: GAY BARS, NARROWING INTERPRETATIONS, AND UNCONSTITUTIONAL CONDITIONS

1. *Gay Bars as a Situs for "Political" Association?* Although there was state harassment of early homophile groups such as the Mattachine Society and its publishing arm, *One, Inc.*, the most common situs for state harassment of lesbians and gay men was bars and clubs. Such harassment was a byproduct of Prohibition's repeal in 1933. Once public consumption of alcohol was legal again, bars catering to lesbian and gay clientele grew like weeds in a vacant lot. Excluded from respectable establishments like churches, civic clubs, and the like, lesbians and gays formed their own institutions. Gay bars proliferated not just in major cities like San Francisco (the home of the Black Cat) and New York (the home of the Stonewall), but also smaller cities like Buffalo. See Elizabeth L. Kennedy & Madeline M. Davis, *Boots of Leather, Slippers of Gold* (1993). At the very same time lesbians and gay men were flocking to these new institutions, however, a new and more forceful regime of state regulation was being established.

One cost accompanying the end of Prohibition was the creation of a state apparatus to regulate nightclubs, bars, and other establishments that sold liquor. The regime was driven by the requirement of a license to sell alcohol. To get a license the applicant had to meet whatever requirements the state set; to keep the license, the licensee had to satisfy the state that it was following state rules on an ongoing basis. Some states, like California and New York, had fairly detailed rules the licensee had to satisfy, including rules against allowing "immoral" or "disorderly" (a synonym for "immoral") behavior on the premises. A pattern of immoral conduct, especially prostitution and homosexuality, justified license revocation and a police shutdown.

2. *First Amendment Considerations.* The lower court had sustained the order shutting down The Black Cat, finding:

> An occasional fortuitous meeting of such persons at restaurants for the innocent purpose mentioned is one thing. But for a proprietor of a restaurant knowingly to permit his premises to be regularly used 'as a meeting place' by persons of the type mentioned with all of the potentialities for evil and immorality drawing out of such meetings is, in my opinion, conduct of an entirely different nature which justifies action on the part of the Board of Equalization.

Quoted in Arthur S. Leonard, *Sexuality and the Law: An Encyclopedia of Major Legal Cases* 191 (1993). The California Supreme Court rejected that line of analysis, ostensibly as a matter of statutory interpretation, but perhaps informed by First Amendment considerations. What First Amendment value, if any, is served by the state supreme court's decision? *NAACP v. Alabama* can be distinguished as a pure "political association" case. Are bars and other instances of "social association" entitled to First Amendment protection?

Responding to *Stoumen*, the California legislature in 1955 amended the ABC law to require license revocation "[w]here the portion of the premises of the licensee upon which the activities permitted by the license are conducted are a resort for illegal possessors or users of narcotics, prostitutes, pimps, panderers, or sexual perverts. In addition to any other legally competent evidence, the character of the premises may be proved by the general reputation of the premises in a community as a resort for illegal possessors or users of narcotics, prostitutes, pimps, panderers, or sexual perverts." California Statutes 1955, chapter 1217, page 2230, codified at California Business and Professions Code § 242000(e). Within months of the new law, the ABC bureau sought to close down the Black Cat again.

Deciding a test case, the California Supreme Court struck down the 1955 law as a violation of the First Amendment in *Vallerga v. Department of Alcoholic Beverage Control*, 347 P.2d 909 (Cal. 1959). The court carefully distinguished cases where licenses were revoked for obscene, lewd, or other unlawful conduct. Later cases followed *Vallerga* in holding that the state could not punish bars simply for serving homosexual customers. See *One Eleven Wines & Liquors, Inc. v. Division of Alcoholic Beverage Control*, 235 A.2d 12 (N.J.1967); *Becker v. New York State Liquor Authority*, 234 N.E.2d 443 (N.Y.1967).

3. *Unconstitutional Conditions*. The constitutional issue underlying *Stoumen* and *Vallerga* is slightly different than the usual First Amendment case. In the typical case, the state is seeking a penalty (an injunction, a fine, jail) for an "illegal" speech or publication. In *Stoumen*, the state is merely imposing a speech-restrictive "condition" (no homosexuals) upon the state-conferred benefit (the liquor license). The U.S. Supreme Court has held that the state has greater freedom to impose conditions upon state-conferred benefits than to penalize similar conduct directly. For example, in *Rust v. Sullivan*, 500 U.S. 173 (1991), the Court upheld a federal regulation forbidding doctors funded by federal Title X programs (family planning services) from discussing or counseling their patients about abortion as a mode of family planning. Under either *Roe v. Wade* [Chapter 1, Section 1(C)] or the First Amendment (or both), the state could not directly prohibit private doctors or families from exploring this option, but the Supreme Court upheld the state's ability to impose a "gag order" as a condition of receiving the benefits of Title X. Is this a defensible posture in the modern regulatory state, where most entitlements flow from the state in some manner?

What "conditions" on state benefits would be unconstitutional? For speculation, see our materials on state funding of the arts in Chapter 6, Section 3(B). Consider also *Rosenberger v. University of Virginia*, excerpted in Part C of this Section.

POSTSCRIPT ON THE NINE LIVES OF THE BLACK CAT

After *Vallerga*, the Black Cat was again investigated by the ABC gendarmerie. This time the board sent undercover officers who reported in detail the conduct they observed at the establishment: dancing, kissing, and fondling between people of the same sex. One undercover officer reported that a male patron solicited him for sex in the Black Cat. Once again, the ABC department revoked the Black Cat's license. Would the California courts uphold the revocation? See *Stoumen v. Munro*, 33 Cal.Rptr. 305 (Cal.App.1963).

Gay Students Organization of the University of New Hampshire v. Thomas N. Bonner

U.S. Court of Appeals for the First Circuit, 1974.
509 F.2d 652.

■ COFFIN, CHIEF JUDGE.

The Gay Students Organization (GSO) was officially recognized as a student organization at the University of New Hampshire in May, 1973, and on November 9, 1973 the group sponsored a dance on campus. The dance itself was held without incident, but media coverage of the event and criticism by Governor Meldrim Thomson, Jr., led the University's Board of Trustees to reconsider its treatment of the organization. The next day, November 10, 1973, the Board issued a "Position Statement" which indicated that the University would attempt to have determined the "legality and appropriateness of scheduling social functions by the Gay Students Organization" and which "directed that in the interim the University administration would schedule no further social functions by the Gay Students Organization until the matter is legally resolved." The University subsequently filed a declaratory judgment action in Strafford County Superior Court on November 21, 1973.

When the GSO requested permission to sponsor a play on December 7 and have a social function afterward, the University permitted the play but denied permission for the social function. The play was given as scheduled, and the GSO held a meeting following it. Sometime during the evening copies of two "extremist" homosexual publications were distributed by individuals over whom the GSO claims it had no control. Governor Thomson wrote an open letter to the trustees after the play, warning that if they did not "take firm, fair and positive action to rid your campuses of socially abhorrent activities" he would "stand solidly against the expenditure of one more cent of taxpayers' money for your institutions." Dr. Thomas N. Bonner, President of the University, then issued a public statement condemning the distribution of the homosexual literature and announcing that a repetition of the behavior would cause him to seek suspension of the GSO as a student organization. Bonner also revealed that he had "ordered that the current Trustee ban on GSO social functions be interpreted more strictly by administrative authorities than had been the case before December 7, 1973." * * *

* * * [W]e are conscious of the tension between deeply felt, conflicting values or moral judgments, and the traditional legal method of extracting and applying principles from decided cases. First, this case deals with a university attempting to regulate student activity—in the *in loco parentis* tradition which most judges, being over thirty, acknowledged without much question during their years of matriculation. Second, the campus group sought to be regulated stands for sexual values in direct conflict with the deeply imbued moral standards of much of the community whose taxes support the university.

The underlying question, usually not articulated, is whether, whatever may be Supreme Court precedent in the First Amendment area, group activity promoting values so far beyond the pale of the wider community's values is also beyond the boundaries of the First Amendment, at least to the extent that university facilities may not be used by the group to flaunt its credo. If visceral reactions suggest an affirmative answer, the next task for judges is to devise a standard which, while damping down the First Amendment on a university campus, is generally applicable and free from the dangers of arbitrariness. At this point troubles arise. How are the deeply felt values of the community to be identified? On an issue such as permissive abortion, the wider community may well be divided among those believing in "the right to life", those believing in "the right to control over one's body", and those who do not feel deeply either way. Assuming that "community-wide values" could be confidently identified, and that a university could limit the associational activity of groups challenging those values, such an approach would apply also to socialists, conscientious objectors, vivisectionists, those favoring more oil refineries. As to each group, there are sectors of the community to whom its values are anathema. Or, if values be limited to morals, the barrier would reach those attracted to pre-marital sex, atheism, the consumption of alcoholic beverages, esoteric heterosexual activity, violence on television, or dirty books. This is not to suggest that a university is powerless to proscribe either harmful activity or incitement of illegal activity, but it is to say that we are unable to devise a tolerable standard exempting this case at the threshold from general First Amendment precedents. * * *

Given this standard by which a university regulation should be judged, we now must ask whether, even though GSO was recognized as a campus organization, its members' right of association was abridged. * * * *Healy v. James* [408 U.S. 169 (1972)] is controlling. It is true that there the university had refused to recognize the campus organization [Students for a Democratic Society (SDS)] altogether rather than denying it the use of campus facilities for certain activities. But the Court's analysis in *Healy* focused not on the technical point of recognition or nonrecognition, but on the practicalities of human interaction. While the Court concluded that the SDS members' right to further their personal beliefs had been impermissibly burdened by nonrecognition, this conclusion stemmed from a finding that the "primary impediment to free association flowing from nonrecognition is the denial of use of campus facilities for meetings and other appropriate purposes." The ultimate issue at which inquiry must be directed is the effect which a regulation has on organizational and associational activity, not the isolated and for the most part irrelevant issue of recognition *per se*.

Despite the language of *Healy* cited above, appellants argue that "social events" are not among the class of protected associational activities. One aspect of this argument is the suggestion that the ban on social events is permissible because other GSO activities such as discussions are allowed. A very similar contention was rejected in *Healy*. The university had pointed out that nonrecognition affected only on-campus activities, and that therefore the individuals wishing to form an SDS group could meet and distribute literature off campus, and even meet on campus if they did so informally. The Court was thus invited to find that the individuals were free to associate even though their on-campus activities were restricted. It held, however, that the other associational opportunities available to the individuals did not ameliorate significantly the disabilities imposed by the university. Once again, its standard was expressed in the clearest of terms—"[T]he Constitution's protection is not limited to direct interference with fundamental rights." Although the Supreme Court refused in *Healy* to characterize as insubstantial the impediments to association resulting from denial of access to campus bulletin boards and the school newspaper, that case could conceivably be read to shelter only those group efforts at self-promotion which utilize such conventional approaches.

There are, however, many other ways in which an organization might wish to go about attracting members and promoting its point of view. *Healy* has been interpreted to extend to the use of campus facilities for social events in the one case of which we are aware which has considered the issue. We are also led to this conclusion by the realization that efforts by a state to restrict groups other than the GSO to gatherings that were in no sense "social events" would be rejected out of hand. Even a lecture or discussion, which appear to be the only types of meetings which the appellants would allow the GSO to hold, becomes a social event if beer is served beforehand or coffee afterward. Teas, coffees and dinners form the backbone of many a political candidate's campaign, and yet these activities would seemingly be subject to prohibition. While a university may have some latitude in regulating organizations such as fraternities or sororities which can be purely social, its efforts to restrict the activities of a cause-oriented group like the GSO stand on a different footing. Considering the important role that social events can play in individuals' efforts to associate to further their common beliefs, the prohibition of all social events must be taken to be a substantial abridgment of associational rights, even if assumed to be an indirect one.

What we have been considering is appellants' contention that, so long as an association is allowed to meet, restrictions on some of its activities are permissible—i.e., that it is enough that the glass is half full. We now address appellants' contention that when we examine the other half of the glass, the activities barred by the campus regulation, we must conclude that the First Amendment offers no protection because the activities barred are not speech related. Putting aside for a moment the question of whether GSO social events constitute "speech" in their own right, we note the district court's conclusion, not disputed by appellants, that the GSO is a political action organization. The GSO's efforts to organize the homosexual minority, "educate" the public as to its plight, and obtain for it better treatment from individuals and from the government thus represent but another example of the associational activity unequivocally singled out for protection in the very "core" of association cases decided by the Supreme Court. Moreover, the activity engaged in by the GSO would be protected even if it were not so intimately bound up with the political process, for "it is immaterial whether the beliefs sought to be advanced by association pertain to political, economic, religious or cultural matters." *NAACP v. Alabama*, 357 U.S. at 460.

While we accept the district court's conclusion that the associational rights of GSO members have been impermissibly regulated, we cannot agree that their "more traditional First Amendment rights" have not been abridged as well. * * * Communicative conduct is subject to regulation as to "time, place and manner" in the furtherance of a substantial governmental interest, so long as the restrictions imposed are only so broad as required in order to further the interest and are unrelated to the content and subject matter of the message communicated. *Police Department v. Mosley*, 408 U.S. 92 (1972).

There can be no doubt that expression, assembly and petition constitute significant aspects of the GSO's conduct in holding social events. The GSO was created, as its Statement of Purpose attests, to promote the free exchange of ideas among homosexuals and between homosexuals and heterosexuals, and to educate the public about bisexuality and homosexuality. GSO claims that social events in which discussion and exchange of ideas can take place in an informal atmosphere can play an important part in this communication. It would seem that these communicative opportunities are even more important for it than political teas, coffees, and dinners are for political candidates and parties, who have much wider access to the media, being more highly organized and socially accepted. And beyond the specific communications at such events is the basic "message" GSO seeks to convey—that homosexuals exist, that they feel repressed by existing laws and attitudes, that they wish to emerge from their isolation, and that public understanding of their attitudes and problems is desirable for society.

Perhaps these claims, being self serving, fall short of establishing the speech-relatedness of GSO social events. But they receive the strongest corroboration from the interpretation placed on these events by the outside community, as related by appellants. Appellants have relied heavily on their obligation and right to prevent activities which the people of New Hampshire find shocking and offensive. In the brief for President Bonner and the University administrators we are told that the "activity of the GSO was variously labelled a spectacle, an abomination and similar terms of disapprobation" after the GSO dance on November 8, 1973; that the University has an obligation to prevent activity which affronts the citizens of the University and the town and which violates breach of the peace statutes; that the GSO dance constituted "grandstanding"; that recognition of the GSO inflamed a large segment of the people of the state; that the organization cannot be permitted to use its unpopularity without restriction to undermine the University within the state; and that "the ban on social functions reflects the distaste with which homosexual organizations are regarded in the State".

We do not see how these statements can be interpreted to avoid the conclusion that the regulation imposed was based in large measure, if not exclusively, on the content of the GSO's expression. It is well established that "above all else the First Amendment means that government has no power to restrict expression because of its message, its ideas, its subject matter, or its content." *Mosley*, 408 U.S. at 95. * * *

Another interest asserted by appellants is that in preventing illegal activity, which may include "deviate" sex acts, "lascivious carriage", and breach of the peace. But there has been no allegation that any such illegal acts took place at the GSO social events held on November 8 and December 7, 1973. Indeed, we emphasize the finding of the district court that "There were no official complaints about the dance, and no evidence was adduced to show that improper or illegal activities had taken place" at the dance. The only activity of even questionable legality discussed in the record involved the distribution of printed materials alleged to be obscene, and the district court found that no University of New Hampshire students were responsible for the distribution. Mere "undifferentiated fear or apprehension" of illegal conduct is not enough to overcome First Amendment rights, and speculation that individuals might at some time engage in illegal activity is insufficient to justify regulation by the state.

The University is by no means bereft of power to regulate conduct on campus. Not only may it act to prevent criminal conduct by policies focused on real and established dangers, but it can proscribe advocacy of illegal activities falling short of conduct, or conduct in itself noncriminal, if such advocacy or conduct is directed at producing or is likely to incite imminent lawless action. *Brandenburg v. Ohio*, 395 U.S. 444, 447 (1969).

Finally there is a residual power going beyond the prevention of criminal conduct and the kind of advocacy of such conduct we have described. In *Healy v. James*, the Supreme Court said that in a school environment, the power to prohibit lawless action is not limited to acts of a criminal nature: "Also prohibitable are actions which 'materially and substantially disrupt the work and the discipline of the school'." [*Healy*, 408 U.S. at 189, quoting *Tinker v. Des Moines Indep. Community Sch. Dist.*, 393 U.S. 503, 513 (1969).] We would assume that a university, so minded, would not be powerless to regulate public petting (heterosexual or otherwise), drinking in university buildings, or many other noncriminal activities which those responsible for running the institution rightly or wrongly think necessary "to assure that the traditional academic atmosphere is safeguarded." 408 U.S. at 194 n.24. Thus, if a university chose to do so, it might well be able to regulate overt sexual behavior, short of criminal activity, which may offend the community's sense of propriety, so long as it acts in a fair and equitable manner. The point in this case is that the district court has found no improper conduct, and it does not appear that the university ever concerned itself with defining or regulating such behavior. Defendants sought to cut back GSO's social activities simply because sponsored by that group. The ban was not justified by any evidence of misconduct attributable to GSO, and it was altogether too sweeping. * * *

NOTES ON *BONNER* AND CURRENT FIRST AMENDMENT
DOCTRINE

1. *First Amendment Formalism: If Protected Speech or Association, the State Cannot Engage in Content Discrimination.* Judge Coffin's thoughtful and scholarly decision in *Bonner* reflects First Amendment doctrine as it evolved during the Warren Court, and as it exists today (compare *R.A.V.* [Section 3]). The initial inquiry is whether the state is regulating protected "speech," which includes association. The next inquiry is what kind of regulation the state is engaged in. If the state regulation is just procedural (time, place, or manner), the state has substantial freedom but cannot impose unreasonable restrictions. If the state regulation is substantive (content-based), it can only do so if its regulation is narrowly tailored to meet a compelling state interest. This is an exceedingly hard test to pass.

Notice that Judge Coffin does not wonder why GSO is not proscribable as a group whose speech is per se "obscene," as the Ninth Circuit had done in *One, Inc.* By 1974 it was virtually impossible for judges to assume that pro-homosexual speech was obscene. Why was this so?

2. *Speech/Conduct Distinction.* In dicta, Judge Coffin says he would allow the university to regulate not only sodomy (then a crime), but also "public petting," and other activities that might undermine "the traditional academic atmosphere." Is his opinion a forerunner of the status-conduct distinction? So long as homosexuals don't "practice what they preach," they will be tolerated on state university campuses? Indeed, Judge Coffin's opinion might recreate the conundrum of *Stoumen* and the other gay bar cases. The state cannot adopt per se rules against homosocial associations, but it is virtually unlimited in regulating what can be done through those associations: no sodomy, no petting. No handholding?

The speech-conduct distinction blurs when the organization's speech is shown to create an "imminent danger" of "inciting" people to illegal conduct. *Brandenburg*, cited in Judge Coffin's opinion, remains the leading case for incitement. The Supreme Court overturned a conviction of the Ku Klux Klan for violating Ohio's Criminal Syndicalism Statute. The Court's per curiam opinion announced "the principle that the constitutional guarantees of free speech and free press do not permit a State to forbid or proscribe advocacy of the use of force or of law violation except where such advocacy is directed to inciting or producing imminent lawless action and is likely to incite or produce such action." Under *Brandenburg*, the university could not proscribe GSO for advocating the repeal of sodomy laws, or perhaps even for advocating the practice of sodomy by people of all orientations. Only if GSO were inciting "imminent lawless action" could it be censured in its advocacy. Does *Bonner*'s steep divide between speech and conduct subserve First Amendment goals?

3. *The First Amendment in the Classroom.* Note the school setting, in this case a university. Would Judge Coffin have been willing to protect GSO's social as well as educational activities if the setting had been a public high school? See Chapter 7, Section 1.

PART B.   STATE INSISTENCE UPON THE CLOSET

In Chapter 3, we introduced you to several cases where courts upheld state rules enforcing a sexual closetry; you might review those cases, especially *Rowland* (Chapter 3, Section 2[C]). The next two cases, like *Rowland*, arise in school settings where state rules seek to enforce an "apartheid of the closet." The third case in this part reflects a newer kind of state law, one that is interpreted to protect against sexual orientation discrimination because of its politically expressive character. The California Supreme Court decision is remarkable and deserves most careful study.

National Gay Task Force v. Board of Education of the City of Oklahoma City

U.S. Court of Appeals for the Tenth Circuit, 1984.
729 F.2d 1270, affirmed by an equally divided Court, 470 U.S. 903 (1985).

■ LOGAN, CIRCUIT JUDGE.

The National Gay Task Force (NGTF), whose membership includes teachers in the Oklahoma public school system, filed this action in the district court challenging the facial constitutional validity of Okla. Stat. tit. 70, § 6–103.15. The district court held that the statute was constitutionally valid. On appeal NGTF contends that the statute violates plaintiff's members' rights to privacy and equal protection, that it is void for vagueness, that it violates the Establishment Clause, and, finally, that it is overbroad.

The challenged statute, Okla. Stat. tit. 70, § 6–103.15, provides:

"A.   As used in this section:

1.   'Public homosexual activity' means the commission of an act defined in Section 886 of Title 21 of the Oklahoma Statutes [prohibiting sodomy], if such act is:

    a.   committed with a person of the same sex, and

    b.   indiscreet and not practiced in private;

2.   'Public homosexual conduct' means advocating, soliciting, imposing, encouraging or promoting public or private homosexual activity in a manner that creates a substantial risk that such conduct will come to the attention of school children or school employees; and

3.   'Teacher' means a person as defined in Section 1–116 of Title 70 of the Oklahoma Statutes.

B.   In addition to any ground set forth in Section 6–103 of Title 70 of the Oklahoma Statutes, a teacher, student teacher or a teachers' aide may be refused employment, or reemployment, dismissed, or suspended after a finding that the teacher or teachers' aide has:

1.   Engaged in public homosexual conduct or activity; and

2. Has been rendered unfit, because of such conduct or activity, to hold a position as a teacher, student teacher or teachers' aide.

C. The following factors shall be considered in making the determination whether the teacher, student teacher or teachers' aide has been rendered unfit for his position:

1. The likelihood that the activity or conduct may adversely affect students or school employees;

2. The proximity in time or place the activity or conduct to the teacher's, student teacher's or teachers' aide's official duties;

3. Any extenuating or aggravating circumstances; and

4. Whether the conduct or activity is of a repeated or continuing nature which tends to encourage or dispose school children toward similar conduct or activity."

The trial court held that the statute reaches protected speech but upheld the constitutionality of the statute by reading a "material and substantial disruption" test into it. We disagree. The statute proscribes protected speech and is thus facially overbroad, and we cannot read into the statute a "material and substantial disruption" test. Therefore, we reverse the judgment of the trial court.

We see no constitutional problem in the statute's permitting a teacher to be fired for engaging in "public homosexual activity." Section 6–103.15 defines "public homosexual activity" as the commission of an act defined in Okla. Stat. tit. 21, § 886, that is committed with a person of the same sex and is indiscreet and not practiced in private. * * *

The part of § 6–103.15 that allows punishment of teachers for "public homosexual conduct" does present constitutional problems. To be sure, this is a facial challenge, and facial challenges based on First Amendment overbreadth are "strong medicine" and should be used "sparingly and only as a last resort." *Broadrick v. Oklahoma*, 413 U.S. 601, 613 (1973). Nonetheless, invalidation is an appropriate remedy in the instant case because this portion of § 6–103.15 is overbroad, is "not readily subject to a narrowing construction by the state courts," and "its deterrent effect on legitimate expression is both real and substantial." *Erznoznik v. City of Jacksonville*, 422 U.S. 205, 216 (1975). Also, we must be especially willing to invalidate a statute for facial overbreadth when, as here, the statute regulates "pure speech."

Section 6–103.15 allows punishment of teachers for "public homosexual conduct," which is defined as "advocating, soliciting, imposing, encouraging or promoting public or private homosexual activity in a manner that creates a substantial risk that such conduct will come to the attention of school children or school employees." Okla. Stat. tit. 70, § 6–103.15(A)(2). The First Amendment protects "advocacy" even of illegal conduct except when "advocacy" is "directed to inciting or producing imminent lawless action and is likely to incite or produce such action." *Brandenburg v. Ohio*,

395 U.S. 444, 447 (1969). The First Amendment does not permit someone to be punished for advocating illegal conduct at some indefinite future time.

"Encouraging" and "promoting," like "advocating," do not necessarily imply incitement to imminent action. A teacher who went before the Oklahoma legislature or appeared on television to urge the repeal of the Oklahoma anti-sodomy statute would be "advocating," "promoting," and "encouraging" homosexual sodomy and creating a substantial risk that his or her speech would come to the attention of school children or school employees if he or she said, "I think it is psychologically damaging for people with homosexual desires to suppress those desires. They should act on those desires and should be legally free to do so." Such statements, which are aimed at legal and social change, are at the core of First Amendment protections. As in *Erznoznik*, the statute by its plain terms is not easily susceptible of a narrowing construction. The Oklahoma legislature chose the word "advocacy" despite the Supreme Court's interpretation of that word in *Brandenburg*. Finally, the deterrent effect of § 6–103.15 is both real and substantial. It applies to all teachers, substitute teachers, and teachers aides in Oklahoma. To protect their jobs they must restrict their expression. Thus, the § 6–103.15 proscription of advocating, encouraging, or promoting homosexual activity is unconstitutionally overbroad. * * *

■ BARRETT, CIRCUIT JUDGE, dissenting. * * *

The majority, unlike the district court, holds that portion of the statute which allows "punishment" for teachers for advocating "public homosexual conduct" to be overbroad because it is "not readily subject to a narrowing construction by the state courts" and "its deterrent effect on legitimate expression is both real and substantial." I disagree. Sodomy is *malum in se*, i.e., immoral and corruptible in its nature without regard to the fact of its being noticed or punished by the law of the state. It is not *malum prohibitum*, i.e., wrong *only* because it is forbidden by law and not involving moral turpitude. It is on this principle that I must part with the majority's holding that the "public homosexual conduct" portion of the Oklahoma statute is overbroad.

Any teacher who advocates, solicits, encourages or promotes the practice of *sodomy* "in a manner that creates a substantial risk that such conduct will come to the attention of school children or school employees" is in fact and in truth *inciting* school children to participate in the abominable and detestable crime against nature. Such advocacy by school teachers, regardless of the situs where made, creates a substantial risk of being conveyed to school children. In my view, it does not merit any constitutional protection. There is no need to demonstrate that such conduct would bring about a material or substantial interference or disruption in the normal activities of the school. A teacher advocating the practice of sodomy to school children is without First Amendment protection. This statute furthers an important and substantial government interest, as determined by the Oklahoma legislature, unrelated to the suppression of free speech. The incidental restriction on alleged First Amendment freedom is no greater than is essential to the furtherance of that interest. * * *

The Oklahoma legislature has declared that the advocacy by teachers of homosexual acts to school children is a matter of statewide concern. The Oklahoma statute does not condemn or in any wise affect teachers, homosexual or otherwise, except to the extent of the non-advocacy restraint aimed at the protection of school children. It does not deny them any rights as human beings. To * * * require proof that advocacy of the act of sodomy will substantially interfere or disrupt normal school activities is a bow to permissiveness. To the same extent, the advocacy of violence, sabotage and terrorism as a means of effecting political reform held in *Brandenburg* to be protected speech unless demonstrated as directed to and likely to incite or produce such action *did not* involve advocacy of a crime *malum in se* to school children by a school teacher. * * *

NOTES ON *GAY TASK FORCE* AND THE FADING BOUNDARY BETWEEN SEXUAL SPEECH AND POLITICAL SPEECH

On review before the Supreme Court, the Justices split four to four; in that event, the court of appeals decision is affirmed. Justice Powell took no part in the case because of illness. Leonard, *Sexuality and the Law* 616. The Tenth Circuit's decision remains the law of that circuit, but its affirmance by an equally divided Supreme Court means that it has no national precedential value. Would the *Romer v. Evans* Court [Chapter 1, Section 3(B)(1)] reach the same result? Consider some of the historical and analytical issues raised by the case.

1. *The Briggs Initiative and Identity Speech.* The Oklahoma statute challenged in *NGTF* was identical in substance to a proposal popularly known as the Briggs Initiative for its sponsor, state senator John Briggs, that was rejected by California voters. The campaign for and against the Briggs Initiative created the first large-scale consideration of a gay rights issue in electoral politics:

> The Briggs Initiative appeared on the November 1978 California state ballot as a referendum question. * * * It was widely understood to be a vote on whether the state should fire gay teachers and thus purge that group from the schools and from contact with children. * * *

> But the Briggs Initiative was configured to play a double role. It was framed in terms of banning a viewpoint, the "advocating" or "promoting" of homosexuality, rather than the exclusion of a group of persons. Lesbians and gay men easily fell within this proscription because to come out is to implicitly, or often explicitly, affirm the value of homosexuality. For that reason, a Briggs-style law could be used to target all lesbian and gay school employees who had expressed their sexual orientation, except in the most furtive contexts.

> The viewpoint target made the initiative more complicated, however. It threatened anyone, gay or straight, who voiced the forbidden ideas. Thus it simultaneously discriminated against gay people while extending its aim to everyone not gay who supported them.

The proposed law did not merely include the two distinct elements of viewpoint bias and group classification. It merged them into one new concept. This merger—what I would describe as the formation of a legal construct of identity that incorporates both viewpoint and status—would come to dominate both the right-wing strategy against gay rights and the claims of the lesbian and gay community for equality.

* * * The Briggs Initiative referendum campaign marked the moment when American politics began to treat homosexuality as something more than deviance, conduct, or lifestyle; it marked the emergence of homosexuality as an openly political claim and as a viewpoint. That, in turn, laid the foundation for the emergence of a new analysis of speech about homosexuality. Instead of treating such speech as the advocacy of conduct, courts shifted to a consideration of gay speech as the advocacy of ideas. The once-bright boundary between sexual speech and political speech began to fade.

Nan D. Hunter, "Identity Speech and Equality," 79 *Va. L. Rev.* 1695, 1703–05 (1993).

2. *Category Contest.* Drafters of the Oklahoma statute at issue in *NGTF* labeled "encouraging," "promoting," and "advocating" of certain illegal conduct (sodomy) as "public homosexual conduct." What is the rhetorical strategy behind that phrase? Analyze its three components: What must be "public" for the behavior to be prohibited? Which Oklahoma statutes are and are not limited to "homosexual" activity? What is the "conduct" at issue?

By contrast, plaintiffs framed the statute as endangering "pure" political speech and relied on its potential scope extending to out-of-classroom speech. What if the statute had been limited to in-classroom speech or speech advocating illegal sexual acts? (See Chapter 7.)

3. *Off Duty Political Speech by Government Employees.* In *Van Ooteghem v. Gray*, 654 F.2d 304 (5th Cir.1981), the court held that an assistant county treasurer could not be fired for addressing county commissioners as a citizen in favor of civil rights for lesbians and gay men. Compare *Singer v. U.S. Civil Service Commission*, 530 F.2d 247 (9th Cir.1976), vacated, 429 U.S. 1034 (1977) (gay man fired for "flaunting" his homosexuality by attempting to legalize gay marriage). See Chapter 10 for a series of cases, including *Singer*, involving speech and employment discrimination.

Joseph Acanfora, III v. Board of Education of Montgomery County

U.S. Court of Appeals for the Fourth Circuit, 1974.
491 F.2d 498.

[Excerpted in Chapter 7, Section 2(A)]

Marjorie Rowland v. Mad River Local School District

U.S. Court of Appeals for the Sixth Circuit, 1984.
730 F.2d 444, *cert. denied,* 470 U.S. 1009, 105 S.Ct. 1373, 84 L.Ed.2d 392 (1985).

[Excerpted in Chapter 3, Section 2(C)]

Gay Law Students Association et al. v. Pacific Telephone and Telegraph Co.

California Supreme Court, 1979.
24 Cal.3d 458, 156 Cal.Rptr. 14, 595 P.2d 592.

■ TOBRINER, JUSTICE.

[Plaintiffs, four individuals and two associations organized to promote equal rights for homosexual persons, sued Pacific Telephone and Telegraph Company (PT & T), alleging that PT & T practiced discrimination against homosexuals in the hiring, firing and promotion of employees, and seeking both injunctive and monetary relief under the California Labor Code. The trial court sustained defendant's demurrer and held that California statutory law did not give plaintiffs a claim for relief. The California Supreme Court reversed.]

Over 60 years ago the California Legislature, recognizing that employers could misuse their economic power to interfere with the political activities of their employees, enacted Labor Code sections 1101 and 1102 to protect the employees' rights. Labor Code section 1101 provides that "No employer shall make, adopt, or enforce any rule, regulation, or policy: (a) Forbidding or preventing employees from engaging or participating in politics.... (b) Controlling or directing, or tending to control or direct the political activities of affiliations of employees." Similarly, section 1102 states that "No employer shall coerce or influence or attempt to coerce or influence his employees through or by means of threat of discharge or loss of employment to adopt or follow or refrain from adopting or following any particular course or line of political action or political activity." These sections serve to protect "the fundamental right of employees in general to engage in political activity without interference by employers."

These statutes cannot be narrowly confined to partisan activity. As explained in *Mallard v. Boring* (1960) 182 Cal.App.2d 390, 395: "The term 'political activity' connotes the espousal of a candidate *or a cause,* and some degree of action to promote the acceptance thereof by other persons." (Emphasis added.) The Supreme Court has recognized the political character of activities such as participation in litigation (*N.A.A.C.P. v. Button* (1963) 371 U.S. 415, 429), the wearing of symbolic armbands (*Tinker v. Des Moines School Dist.* (1969) 393 U.S. 503), and the association with others for the advancement of beliefs and ideas (*N.A.A.C.P. v. Alabama* (1958) 357 U.S. 449).

Measured by these standards, the struggle of the homosexual community for equal rights, particularly in the field of employment, must be recognized as a political activity. Indeed the subject of the rights of homosexuals incites heated political debate today, and the "gay liberation movement" encourages its homosexual members to attempt to convince other members of society that homosexuals should be accorded the same fundamental rights as heterosexuals. The aims of the struggle for homosexual rights, and the tactics employed, bear a close analogy to the continuing struggle for civil rights waged by blacks, women, and other minorities.

A principal barrier to homosexual equality is the common feeling that homosexuality is an affliction which the homosexual worker must conceal from his employer and his fellow workers. Consequently one important aspect of the struggle for equal rights is to induce homosexual individuals to "come out of the closet," acknowledge their sexual preferences, and to associate with others in working for equal rights.

In light of this factor in the movement for homosexual rights, the allegations of plaintiffs' complaint assume a special significance. Plaintiffs allege that PT & T discriminates against "manifest" homosexuals and against persons who make "an issue of their homosexuality." The complaint asserts also that PT & T will not hire anyone referred to them by plaintiff Society for Individual Rights, an organization active in promoting the rights of homosexuals to equal employment opportunities. These allegations can reasonably be construed as charging that PT & T discriminates in particular against persons who identify themselves as homosexual, who defend homosexuality, or who are identified with activist homosexual organizations. So construed, the allegations charge that PT & T has adopted a "policy . . . tending to control or direct the political activities or affiliations of employees" in violation of section 1101, and has "attempt[ed] to coerce or influence . . . employees . . . to . . . refrain from adopting [a] particular course or line of political . . . activity" in violation of section 1102. * * *

■ RICHARDSON, JUSTICE, dissenting. * * *

* * * [T]he complaint herein fails to allege *any* attempted control or coercion by PT & T of any employee or applicant with respect to any "*political*" activity whatever. Significantly, plaintiffs' appellate briefs do not even raise the point. They cite neither section 1101 nor 1102 in support of their complaint. The "political" argument has never been advanced nor apparently even thought of by either lawyers or litigants.

The gist of plaintiff's allegations in the complaint herein is that plaintiffs have been damaged by reason of PT & T's alleged refusal to hire or promote "manifest homosexuals." As the "introduction" to the first amended complaint alleges, "PT & T has, since at least 1971, had an articulated policy of excluding homosexuals from employment opportunities with its organization." Again, in the "fact allegations" of the complaint, it is alleged that " ... PT & T has maintained and enforced a policy of employment discrimination against homosexuals.... PT & T refuses to hire any 'manifest homosexual' which [*sic*] may apply to it for employment at any occupational level or category." Nowhere in the complaint, from beginning to end, do plaintiffs allege that PT & T's asserted policy of discrimination is directed toward any of plaintiffs' *political* activity or affiliations. Rather, plaintiffs contend, and the gravamen of their complaint is, that employment discrimination is based solely on the overt and manifest nature of their sexual orientation itself. * * *

NOTE ON *PT & T* AND "COMING OUT" AS "POLITICAL" ACTIVITY

1. *California Law.* Note the timing of the decision in *PT & T*, namely, the year after California voters rejected the Briggs Amendment, which would have banned advocates of gay rights from teaching in the public schools. The *Pacific Telephone* case was eventually settled with a $5 million payment to the plaintiff class and the adoption by defendant of an antidiscrimination policy. Leonard, *Sexuality and the Law* 417. In 1992, the legislature amended the Labor Code to add an explicit protection against discrimination based on sexual orientation. Cal. Lab. Code § 1102.1 (West 1993). Was the amendment necessary, in light of the *PT & T* precedent?

2. *The Personal As Political?* Under *PT & T*, would it be political speech to put a photograph of one's same-sex lover on one's desk at work? What about a photo of one's opposite-sex partner? How could the first act be political speech if the second is not also?

Justice Tobriner's analysis links an individual's coming out to "the struggle of the homosexual community for equal rights." The phrase "coming out" has now become common parlance and is applied to numerous examples of self-identification. Recall from Eve Kosofsky Sedgwick, *Epistemology of the Closet* [Chapter 3, Section 2(C)] how one can "come out" as a fat person. Are all such statements political speech? If not, how would you draw the appropriate lines?

3. *Coming Out and the Military Exclusion.* In the military cases, as you have seen in Chapter 4, the government defends its policy of using "coming out" speech as the basis for expulsion by arguing that such speech is penalized, either because it is reasonably predictive of forbidden homosexual conduct, or because the homosexual identity offends other service personnel and therefore lowers morale. The latter argument would appear offensive to traditional First Amendment doctrine: the state cannot censor speech simply because of what it conveys to others.

The first argument would appear safe from First Amendment attack, but think again. If the "conduct" of displaying a photograph could be treated as political speech, what about sexual conduct itself? Consider the next excerpt.

David Cole and William N. Eskridge, Jr., From Hand–Holding to Sodomy: First Amendment Protection of Homosexual (Expressive) Conduct

29 *Harvard Civil Rights–Civil Liberties Law Review* 319, 321–22, 325, 326–29, 333–35 (1994).*

* * * [T]he government's restrictions on gays in the military directly implicate First Amendment values, and should be subject to strict scrutiny under current First Amendment case law. * * * Where [the government] argues that [identity] speech can be used as evidence of proscribable conduct, we contend that the underlying prohibition on homosexual conduct is in fact a restriction of expression. Homosexual conduct is expressive. While an act's expressiveness does not in itself entitle the conduct to stringent First Amendment protection, such protection is required where the government's reason for regulating the conduct is predicated on its communicative character, or where the government has selectively targeted some forms of conduct and not others based on their message. The only reasons the government offers for the military's regulation of homosexual conduct are based on what that conduct communicates to other service members who may be offended by knowledge that some of their fellow soldiers are gay or lesbian. Moreover, the military policy treats the very same conduct—hand-holding, kissing, marriage, and sexual contact—differently depending on whether it sends a heterosexual or homosexual message. Therefore, under established First Amendment doctrine, the military's policy is "related to the suppression of expression," and must be justified under the traditional strict scrutiny accorded to regulation of speech.

* * * The military's criminal prohibition of sodomy itself, and indeed all state sodomy statutes, also regulate expressive conduct based on what that conduct communicates to others, and, therefore, should also be subject to traditional strict First Amendment scrutiny. In *Bowers v. Hardwick*, the Supreme Court upheld a statute criminalizing sodomy against a due process challenge, finding that it was rationally related to the state's interest in upholding morality. No First Amendment argument was raised, and the Court subjected the statute to only relaxed rational basis scrutiny. But the rationale for regulating sodomy—upholding community morals—is inextricably related to what sodomy expresses to the community, and therefore sodomy statutes should have to satisfy strict scrutiny, not rational basis review. They cannot meet that more stringent standard. Thus, the argument advanced here offers a doctrinal method for rethinking, and ultimately overruling, *Bowers*.

If conduct is not expressive, the First Amendment is not implicated. If one engages in conduct without any intent to communicate, or if nobody would understand one's action as communicating anything, there is nothing for the First Amendment to protect. Thus, the threshold inquiry in any expressive conduct case is whether the plaintiff's conduct was intended to communicate a message, and would be understood by others as communicative. * * *

As the Supreme Court has recognized, sexual expression possesses deep communicative significance. Eight Justices of the Court agreed that nude dancing in public is "expressive conduct" in *Barnes v. Glen Theatre, Inc.* [Chapter 6, Section 1]. The ninth Justice, Scalia, defined "inherently expressive conduct" as activity "that is normally engaged in for the purpose of communicating an idea, or perhaps an emotion, to someone else." Sexual conduct—from hand-holding to kissing to intercourse—is expressive in precisely this way. While also engaged in for carnal pleasure and (in increasingly rare instances) procreative purposes, sex is intrinsically communicative and may express a wide range of emotions—love, desire, power, dependency, even rage or hatred. Indeed, the communicative power of sex is often unmatched by other forms of communication. To say "I love you" is one thing; to hold a lover's hand in public to express one's love can express something quite different; and "to make love" is often a still more profound expression of what one feels and thinks. * * * [A]ll of these acts are, to use Justice Scalia's terms, "normally engaged in for the purpose of communicating . . . an emotion to someone else."

Sexual conduct is also important to the developmental feature of the liberty value. The First Amendment protects the individual's freedom to explore, develop, and expand upon her identity. It assures that the state may not seek to control a person's thoughts or beliefs, those intellectual characteristics that are central to our identities. Sexual expression is equally important to individual development. Indeed, some philosophers consider expression of the passionate, sexual side of ourselves to be more identity-generative than expression of the verbal, intellectual side. [The authors invoke *Stanley v. Georgia* (Chapter 1, Section 1[B]) as an example of this libertarian value of sexual expression.]

The First Amendment also has a strong social or political component. Its protection of individual autonomy and liberty engenders collective benefits in the body politic, by fostering a diverse citizenry and assuring that "debate on public issues should be uninhibited, robust, and wide-open," as the Court said in *New York Times v. Sullivan.* Homosexual conduct, from public hand-holding and kissing by same-sex couples to private sexual conduct, fosters the diverse robust polity that the First Amendment envisions. Public expression of same-sex intimacy is as important a critique of gender assumptions and gender roles in American society as any published treatise. It is therefore not only individually expressive, but also socially valuable under the robust pluralism endorsed in *Sullivan.* The fact that gestures like kissing and hand-holding are symbolic of ideas and attitudes rather than literal statements of position in a debate does not diminish their importance. The public debate has never been limited to books, articles, letters to the editor, speeches, and signs; it has always included symbolic gestures such as dancing, visual art, advertising imagery, public demonstrations, clothing, and physical conduct. * * *

* * * The military's "bargain"—gays and lesbians may serve so long as they remain "in the closet" or so long as they publicly repudiate any desire to consummate their sexual desires—demonstrates that the military seeks to regulate not homosexuality itself, but its public acknowledgment and expression, that is, its communicative content.

The military's stated rationales for its policy also reflect a concern for what homosexual conduct communicates to others. The military has advanced two principal arguments for its regulation, each of which underscores its interest in regulating the expression of homosexuality rather than homosexuality itself. First, it argues that "morale" and "unit cohesion" will be threatened by the presence of openly gay, lesbian, and bisexual personnel. But the "don't ask" half of its policy concedes that "morale" and "unit cohesion" are not threatened by the presence of *closeted* gay, lesbian, and bisexual personnel. Thus, the problem has less to do with identity or conduct itself than with the expression of that identity or conduct to others. The military's interests are threatened only by the communication of gay members' sexual identities to other (presumably homophobic) members of a military unit.

Second, the government has contended that the presence of gay and lesbian soldiers in the military will invade the privacy of heterosexual soldiers, given the close quarters that military life frequently requires. But once again, the fact that the military allows closeted gay, lesbian, and bisexual personnel to serve suggests that the privacy concern is triggered not by the mere presence of such personnel, but by the public acknowledgement of their presence. * * *

How does consensual homosexual conduct (on or off base) harm the military community, except by virtue of what it expresses to that community? A consensual act of homosexual sodomy has no physical effect whatsoever on anyone other than the participants. It can affect the broader community only if the fact that it occurred is somehow communicated to the community, thereby offending or demoralizing its homophobic members. Because society's (or the military's) interests can be undermined only if the fact of the proscribed conduct is in some way communicated, the government's interest in regulating sodomy is necessarily related to sodomy's expressive character. * * *

PROBLEM 5–1

MISCONDUCT OR VIEWPOINT?

You are a lawyer for the American Civil Liberties Union. One morning, you receive two calls. The first is from a person employed as an equal opportunity specialist by an agency of your state government. She recently attended an annual departmental conference on EEO issues. One session at the conference featured a panel of lesbian, gay, and bisexual employees discussing discrimination based on sexual orientation. Asked to comment on it afterward by a local reporter, this individual replied, "Well, this is just my own personal opinion, of course, but I think this is a question of morality, not equality. We don't need to recreate Sodom and Gomorrah." She has just been reassigned to another job and seeks your assistance in challenging this action by the state.

The second call you receive is from the local gay rights group. They want the ACLU to file an *amicus* brief on their behalf in support of the forced re-assignment.

Which position should the ACLU take? What other information will you need to decide? For a real life analog, see Max Boot, "A Different Kind of Whistle–Blower," *Wall St. Journal*, Apr. 27, 1994; *Congressional Record*, S 9226–9231 (July 19, 1994) and S 9289–9302 (July 20, 1994).

PART C.   IDENTITY AND VIEWPOINT: THE CLASH OF NONDISCRIMINATION AND FIRST AMENDMENT NORMS

Identity can be constituted as much by what one is *not* as by what one *is*. The duality of identity formation often finds its way into the public arena, as when one group wants to self-identify in a context which threatens the self-identity of another group. Efforts by women to join all-male social clubs, colleges, and fraternities have generated clashing forms of identity expression. The all-male groups assert free association rights under the First Amendment, against women's equal protection rights under the Fifth or Fourteenth Amendments or under state or local laws prohibiting sex discrimination. Laws prohibiting discrimination on the basis of sexual orientation have been adopted in several states, the District of Columbia, and many cities. Such laws invariably generate fundamental legal clashes. How should such clashes be analyzed?

Kathryn Roberts v. United States Jaycees, 468 U.S. 609, 104 S.Ct. 3244, 82 L.Ed.2d 462 (1984). The Minnesota Human Rights Act, as amended in 1973, made it illegal for a "public accommodation" to "deny any person the full and equal enjoyment of the goods, services, facilities, privileges, advantages, and accommodations * * * because of race, color, creed, religion, disability, national origin or sex." The national Jaycees, a network of all-male civic clubs, disciplined its Minnesota chapters for admitting women pursuant to the state law, and the state courts held the national chapter in violation of the law. The Jaycees challenged the statute, as construed, on the ground that it violated the right of association in the First Amendment. The Supreme Court affirmed.

Justice Brennan's opinion for the Court recognized that "certain kinds of personal bonds have played a critical role in the culture and traditions of the Nation by cultivating and transmitting shared ideals and beliefs; they thereby foster diversity and act as critical buffers between the individual and the power of the State. * * * Protecting these relationships from unwarranted state interference therefore safeguards the ability independently to define one's identity that is critical to any concept of liberty." The core protection of this feature of the right of association is the family, "distinguished by such attributes as relative smallness, a high degree of selectivity in decisions to begin and maintain the affiliation, and seclusion from others in critical aspects of the relationship. * * * Conversely, an association lacking these qualities—such as a large business enterprise—seems remote from the concerns giving rise to the constitutional protection."

Under such a core-penumbra reasoning, the Jaycees were entitled to little special First Amendment protection, reasoned Justice Brennan. According to lower tribunals' findings of fact, the Jaycees were large and sprawling, relatively unselective in choosing members (essentially accepting everyone except women and a few other minorities), and unbonded in the interaction of members who remain strangers to one another. It was not clear that the Jaycees' interests triggered First Amendment protection.

In any event, infringements on even core associational rights can be justified by "regulations adopted to serve compelling state interests, unrelated to the suppression of ideas, that cannot be achieved through means significantly less restrictive of associational freedoms." Justice Brennan found the public accommodation law's "compelling interest in eradicating discrimination against its female citizens justifies the impact that application of the statute to the Jaycees may have on the male members' associational freedoms." He found it important that the statute did not discriminate "on the basis of viewpoint" and was not administered arbitrarily. Justice Brennan also emphasized the constitutional underpinnings of the state law.

John J. ["Wacko"] Hurley v. Irish–American Gay, Lesbian and Bisexual Group of Boston

Supreme Court of the United States, 1995.
___ U.S. ___ , 115 S.Ct. 2338, 132 L.Ed.2d 487.

■ JUSTICE SOUTER delivered the opinion of the Court.

[The South Boston Allied War Veterans Council, a private group, has since 1947 been granted authority by the City of Boston to organize the annual St. Patrick's Day Parade, an event of special significance to people of Irish ancestry. Every year the Council has applied for and been granted a permit for the parade. In 1992, a court ordered the Council to include the Irish–American Gay, Lesbian, and Bisexual Group of Boston (GLIB), the respondents. In 1993, GLIB sued the Council for violating the state law which prohibits discrimination on account of sexual orientation (inter alia) in the admission to a place of public accommodation. Relying on *Roberts*, the state courts interpreted the public accommodations law to require that GLIB be included and overruled the Council's claim that such an interpretation violated the First Amendment. The Supreme Court reversed.]

If there were no reason for a group of people to march from here to there except to reach a destination, they could make the trip without expressing any message beyond the fact of the march itself. Some people might call such a procession a parade, but it would not be much of one. Real "[p]arades are public dramas of social relations, and in them performers define who can be a social actor and what subjects and ideas are available for communication and consideration." S. Davis, *Parades and Power: Street Theatre in Nineteenth–Century Philadelphia* 6 (1986). Hence, we use the word "parade" to indicate marchers who are making some sort of collective point, not just to each other but to bystanders along the way. Indeed a parade's dependence on watchers is so extreme that nowadays, as with Bishop Berkeley's celebrated tree, "if a parade or demonstration receives no media coverage, it may as well not have happened." *Id.*, at 171. Parades are thus a form of expression, not just motion, and the inherent expressiveness of marching to make a point explains our cases involving protest marches. In *Gregory v. Chicago*, 394 U.S. 111, 112 (1969), for example, petitioners had taken part in a procession to express their grievances to the city government, and we held that such a "march, if peaceful and orderly, falls well within the sphere of conduct protected by the First Amendment." Similarly, in *Edwards v. South Carolina*, 372 U.S. 229 (1963), where petitioners had joined in a march of protest and pride, carrying placards and singing The Star Spangled Banner, we held that the activities "reflect an exercise of these basic constitutional rights in their most pristine and classic form."

The protected expression that inheres in a parade is not limited to its banners and songs, however, for the Constitution looks beyond written or spoken words as mediums of expression. Noting that "symbolism is a primitive but effective way of communicating ideas," *West Virginia Bd. of Ed. v. Barnette*, 319 U.S. 624, 632 (1943), our cases have recognized that the First Amendment shields such acts as saluting a flag (and refusing to do so), *id.*, at 632, 642, wearing an arm band to protest a war, *Tinker v. Des Moines Independent Community School Dist.*, 393 U.S. 503, 505–506 (1969), displaying a red flag, *Stromberg v. California*, 283 U.S. 359, 369 (1931), and even "[m]arching, walking or parading" in uniforms displaying the swastika, *National Socialist Party of America v. Skokie*, 432 U.S. 43 (1977). As some of these examples show, a narrow, succinctly articulable message is not a condition of constitutional protection, which if confined to expressions conveying a "particularized message," would never reach the unquestionably shielded painting of Jackson Pollock, music of Arnold Schönberg, or Jabberwocky verse of Lewis Carroll.

Not many marches, then, are beyond the realm of expressive parades, and the South Boston celebration is not one of them. Spectators line the streets; people march in costumes and uniforms, carrying flags and banners with all sorts of messages (e.g., "England get out of Ireland," "Say no to drugs"); marching bands and pipers play, floats are pulled along, and the whole show is broadcast over Boston television. To be sure, we agree with the state courts that in spite of excluding some applicants, the Council is rather lenient in admitting participants. But a private speaker does not forfeit constitutional protection simply by combining multifarious voices, or by failing to edit their themes to isolate an exact message as the exclusive subject matter of the speech. Nor, under our precedent, does First Amendment protection require a speaker to generate, as an original matter, each item featured in the communication. * * *

Respondents' participation as a unit in the parade was equally expressive. GLIB was formed for the very purpose of marching in it, as the trial court found, in order to celebrate its members' identity as openly gay, lesbian, and bisexual descendants of the Irish immigrants, to show that there are such individuals in the community, and to support the like men and women who sought to march in the New York parade. The organization distributed a fact sheet describing the members' intentions, and the record otherwise corroborates the expressive nature of GLIB's participation. In 1993, members of GLIB marched behind a shamrock-strewn banner with the simple inscription "Irish American Gay, Lesbian and Bisexual Group of Boston." GLIB understandably seeks to communicate its ideas as part of the existing parade, rather than staging one of its own. * * *

* * * The petitioners disclaim any intent to exclude homosexuals as such, and no individual member of GLIB claims to have been excluded from parading as a member of any group that the Council has approved to march. Instead, the disagreement goes to the admission of GLIB as its own parade unit carrying its own banner. Since every participating unit affects the message conveyed by the private organizers, the state courts' application of the statute produced an order essentially requiring petitioners to alter the expressive content of their parade. Although the state courts spoke of the parade as a place of public accommodation, once the expressive character of both the parade and the marching GLIB contingent is understood, it becomes apparent that the state courts' application of the statute had the effect of declaring the sponsors' speech itself to be the public accommodation. Under this approach any contingent of protected individuals with a message would have the right to participate in petitioners' speech, so that the communication produced by the private organizers would be shaped by all those protected by the law who wished to join in with some expressive demonstration of their own. But this use of the State's power violates the fundamental rule of protection under the First Amendment, that a speaker has the autonomy to choose the content of his own message. * * *

Petitioners' claim to the benefit of this principle of autonomy to control one's own speech is as sound as the South Boston parade is expressive. Rather like a composer, the Council selects the expressive units of the parade from potential participants, and though the score may not produce a particularized message, each contingent's expression in the Council's eyes comports with what merits celebration on that day. Even if this view gives the Council credit for a more considered judgment than it actively made, the Council clearly decided to exclude a message it did not like from the communication it chose to make, and that is enough to invoke its right as a private speaker to shape its expression by speaking on one subject while remaining silent on another. The message it disfavored is not difficult to identify. Although GLIB's point (like the Council's) is not wholly articulate, a contingent marching behind the organization's banner would at least bear witness to the fact that some Irish are gay, lesbian, or bisexual, and the presence of the organized marchers would suggest their view that people of their sexual orientations have as much claim to unqualified social acceptance as heterosexuals and indeed as members of parade units organized around other identifying characteristics. The parade's organizers may not believe these facts about Irish sexuality to be so, or they may object to unqualified social acceptance of gays and lesbians or have some other reason for wishing to keep GLIB's message out of the parade. But whatever the reason, it boils down to the choice of a speaker not to propound a particular point of view, and that choice is presumed to lie beyond the government's power to control. * * *

It might, of course, have been argued that a broader objective is apparent: that the ultimate point of forbidding acts of discrimination toward certain classes is to produce a society free of the corresponding biases. Requiring access to a speaker's message would thus be not an end in itself, but a means to produce speakers free of the biases, whose expressive conduct would be at least neutral toward the particular classes, obviating any future need for correction. But if this indeed is the point of applying the state law to expressive conduct, it is a decidedly fatal objective. Having availed itself of the public thoroughfares "for purposes of assembly [and] communicating thoughts between citizens," the Council is engaged in a use of the streets that has "from ancient times, been a part of the privileges, immunities, rights, and liberties of citizens." *Hague v. Committee for Industrial Organization*, 307 U.S. 496, 515 (1939) (opinion of Roberts, J.). Our tradition of free speech commands that a speaker who takes to the street corner to express his views in this way should be free from interference by the State based on the content of what he says. See, e.g., *Police Department of Chicago v. Mosley*, 408 U.S. 92, 95 (1972); cf. H. Kalven, Jr., *A Worthy Tradition* 6–19 (1988); O. Fiss, "Free Speech and Social Structure," 71 *Iowa L. Rev.* 1405, 1408–1409 (1986). The very idea that a noncommercial speech restriction be used to produce thoughts and statements acceptable to some groups or, indeed, all people, grates on the First Amendment, for it amounts to nothing less than a proposal to limit speech in the service of orthodox expression. The Speech Clause has no more certain antithesis. While the law is free to promote all sorts of conduct in place of harmful behavior, it is not free to interfere with speech for no better reason than promoting an approved message or discouraging a disfavored one, however enlightened either purpose may strike the government. * * *

NOTE ON *HURLEY*, STATE ACTION, AND THE SPEECH–IDENTITY DIVIDE

1. *State Action.* GLIB had challenged the exclusions of gays on the basis of the First Amendment as well as the state public accommodations law. They lost their initial claim on the ground that the First Amendment (like the other individual rights protections of the Constitution) only applies to "state action" and there was no "state actor" in this case (the Veterans Council being a private group). GLIB did not appeal this issue, and it was not before the Supreme Court.

There are several ways around this quandary. On the one hand, many state courts have interpreted free speech provisions in state constitutions to be applicable to large-scale private as well as public actors, on the ground that institutions such as shopping centers, *e.g., Robins v. Pruneyard Shopping Center*, 153 Cal.Rptr. 854, 592 P.2d 341 (Cal.1979), *aff'd*, 447 U.S. 74 (1980), universities, *e.g., State v. Schmid*, 423 A.2d 615 (N.J.1980), appeal dismissed, 455 U.S. 100 (1982), and train stations, *e.g., In re Hoffman*, 64 Cal.Rptr. 97, 434 P.2d 353 (Cal. 1967), exercise the functional equivalent of public power. Compare *Amalgamated Food Employees Local 590 v. Logan Valley Plaza, Inc.*, 391 U.S. 308 (1968) (similar analysis under the First Amendment), overruled by *Lloyd Corp. v. Tanner*, 407 U.S. 551 (1972). GLIB could have made a similar pitch under the Massachusetts Constitution.

On the other hand, even under federal constitutional law, a private actor may be deemed a state actor when "conspiring" with a state official, *e.g., Lugar v. Edmondson Oil Co.*, 457 U.S. 922 (1982), or when delegated to perform state functions, *e.g., Flagg Brothers, Inc. v. Brooks*, 436 U.S. 149 (1978) (dictum), or when closely intermingled with the state, e.g., *Burton v. Wilmington Parking Auth.*, 365 U.S. 715 (1961). The Court in *Edmonson v. Leesville Concrete Co.*, 500 U.S. 614 (1991), said that "in determining whether a particular action or course of conduct is governmental in character, it is relevant to examine * * * the extent to which the actor relies on government assistance and benefits; whether the actor is performing a traditional governmental function; and whether the injury caused is aggravated in a unique way by the incidents of governmental authority." What arguments did GLIB have for the proposition that the Veterans Council was so intermingled with the City of Boston that its parade could be treated as a "public" event?

Note how the dynamics of the litigation changes if GLIB is able to tag the Veterans Council as a state actor. The Council would then be in a dilemma: if it claims the parade is an expressive event it violates the First Amendment by excluding lesbian, gay, and bisexual speakers, but if it denies the expressiveness of a parade it has no defense to the public accommodations law.

2. *The Reach of Public Accommodations Laws.* The Massachusetts anti-discrimination law defines "public accommodation" as "any place * * * which is open to and accepts or solicits the patronage of the general public and, without limiting the generality of this definition, whether or not it be * * * (6) a boardwalk or other public highway [or] (8) a place of public amusement, recreation, sport, exercise or entertainment." Is a parade a "public accommodation under this law"? Should it be? (This was an issue of state law, and Justice Souter's opinion accepted as settled the Massachusetts Supreme Court's decision that a parade did fall within this statute.)

3. *The Identity–Speech Dichotomy.* Viewed sympathetically, the Council contended that it excluded GLIB because of its expression. GLIB contended that it was excluded because of its members' sexual orientation. The state trial court found that GLIB was "excluded because of its values and its message, i.e., its members' sexual orientation." Appendix to Petition for Cert., at B4 n.5. It is not so easy to choose between these two, because for gay people the two are interconnected. Unlike race and sex, sexual orientation is ordinarily an invisible characteristic. If women march in this parade, they are conveying a message (women are Irish and proud of it!) by their very presence. Lesbians and gay men can only be known by more explicit signals. For them to participate in a parade in the same way that women participate, they need some device to uncloset themselves.

Consider these complexities. The Council maintained that it was happy to have gay people participate, just not as a group. (Don't ask, don't tell!) Say the Council said the same thing to women: we shall let you march only in groups of men, and not as your own group. Could the state constitutionally prohibit this under *Roberts*? (By the way, *Roberts* is the governing authority. Why does Justice Souter ignore its analytical framework?) At oral argument, GLIB's attorney noted that GLIB was not asking to carry pro-homosexual signs (therefore nothing like "Gay Is Good"); it was only asking to be included as a self-identified group, and the only signs it was asking to carry were signs identifying the group. GLIB was even willing to abandon its signs if the Council adopted a general ban on signs. Doesn't this further undermine Justice Souter's effort to create a big gulf between expression and identity?

In the final question at oral argument, Justice Breyer asked the Council's attorney whether he thought GLIB's goal was identity or speech. Chester Darling, the attorney for the Council, exclaimed that it was "self-proclamation," expression, self-identity. Justice Breyer sighed wearily.

PROBLEM 5–2

PARADES AND EXCLUSIONS

The circus comes to Boston and applies for a permit for a "let's go to the circus and have fun" parade. Citizens object because the circus refuses to allow women to participate. "We support male supremacy," say the circus owners, "and our parade is intended to reflect that ideology." The state antidiscrimination law applies to parades, the holding of the state courts in *Hurley*. But after *Hurley*, can Boston constitutionally deny the permit? Would your answer be different if the parade organizers said: of course women are welcome in our parade, but they must dress in male clothing?

Gay Rights Coalition of Georgetown University Law Center et al. v. Georgetown University

District of Columbia Court of Appeals, en banc, 1987.
536 A.2d 1.

■ MACK, ASSOCIATE JUDGE.

In the District of Columbia, the Human Rights Act [Appendix 2 to this casebook] prohibits an educational institution from discriminating against any individual on the basis of his or her sexual orientation. Two student gay rights groups contend that Georgetown University violated this statutory command by refusing to grant them "University Recognition" together with equal access to the additional facilities and services that status entails. The University, relying on the trial court's factual finding that Georgetown's grant of "University Recognition" includes a religiously guided "endorsement" of the recipient student group, responds that the Free Exercise Clause of the First Amendment protects it from official compulsion to "endorse" an organization which challenges its religious tenets. Upholding the asserted constitutional defense, the trial court entered judgment in favor of Georgetown. The student groups appeal.

Our analysis of the issues differs from that of the trial court. At the outset, we sever the artificial connection between the "endorsement" and the tangible benefits contained in Georgetown's scheme of "University Recognition." With respect to the University's refusal to grant the status of "University Recognition," we do not reach Georgetown's constitutional defense. Contrary to the trial court's understanding, the Human Rights Act does not require one private actor to "endorse" another. Thus, Georgetown's denial of "University Recognition"—in this case a status carrying an intangible "endorsement"—does not violate the statute. Although affirming the trial court's entry of judgment for the University on that point, we do so on statutory rather than constitutional grounds.

We reach a contrary conclusion with respect to the tangible benefits that accompany "University Recognition." While the Human Rights Act does not seek to compel uniformity in philosophical *attitudes* by force of law, it does require equal *treatment.* Equality of treatment in educational institutions is concretely measured by nondiscriminatory provision of access to "facilities and services." D.C. Code § 1–2520 (1987). Unlike the "endorsement," the various additional tangible benefits that accompany a grant of "University Recognition" are "facilities and services." As such, they must be made equally available, without regard to sexual orientation or to any other characteristic unrelated to individual merit. Georgetown's refusal to provide tangible benefits without regard to sexual orientation violated the Human Rights Act. To that extent only, we consider the merits of Georgetown's free exercise defense. On that issue we hold that the District of Columbia's compelling interest in the eradication of sexual orientation discrimination outweighs any burden imposed upon Georgetown's exercise of religion by the forced equal provision of tangible benefits.
* * *

There are two reasons why, as a matter of statutory construction, the Human Rights Act cannot be read to compel a regulated party to express religious approval or neutrality towards any group or individual. First, the statute prohibits only a discriminatory denial of access to "facilities and services" provided by an educational institution. D.C. Code § 1–2520 (1987). An "endorsement" is neither. The Human Rights Act provides legal

[handwritten margin note: services must be equally available]

mechanisms to ensure equality of *treatment*, not equality of *attitudes*. Although we fervently hope that nondiscriminatory attitudes result from equal access to "facilities and services," the Human Rights Act contains nothing to suggest that the legislature intended to make a discriminatory state of mind unlawful in itself. Still less does the statute reveal any desire to force a private actor to express an idea that is not truly held. The Human Rights Act demands action, not words. It was not intended to be an instrument of mind control. * * *

Second, as we have already pointed out, unless the language of the statute is plainly to the contrary, we must construe it so as to uphold its constitutionality. To read into the Human Rights Act a requirement that one private actor must "endorse" another would be to render the statute unconstitutional. The First Amendment protects both free speech and the free exercise of religion. Its essence is that government is without power to intrude into the domain of the intellect or the spirit and that only conduct may be regulated. Interpreting the Human Rights Act so as to require Georgetown to "endorse" the student groups would be to thrust the statute across the constitutional boundaries set by the Free Speech Clause and also, where sincere religious objections are raised, the Free Exercise Clause. Nothing in the statute suggests, let alone requires, such a result. * * *

Freedom of expression is a right to which we all lay equal claim, irrespective of the content of our message. This is easily illustrated. Suppose that the Gay University of America (GUA) is established as a private educational institution. Part of its mission is to win understanding and acceptance of gay and bisexual persons in an intolerant society. Although open to everyone, regardless of sexual orientation, GUA does expect its faculty, staff and students to maintain a sympathetic attitude towards gay practices and the philosophies that support them. GUA has, as the trial court finds, a system of "University Recognition" through which it expresses its approval or tolerance of various student groups desiring that status. But the GUA administration refuses to grant "University Recognition" to the Roman Catholic Sexual Ethics Association (RCSEA). In that situation, the Human Rights Act's ban on discrimination based on religion could not avail the Catholic student group, for the simple reason that the statute does not require GUA to give expressions of approval or tolerance. Insincere statements of opinion are not what the Human Rights Act requires. On the other hand, the statute would require equal distribution of any attendant tangible benefits if GUA's denial of these was based on the religion of RCSEA members. Georgetown's protection against compelled expression is no more and no less.

The trial court's construction of the Human Rights Act would transform the statute into a violation of the First Amendment. It would compel Georgetown to "endorse" the student groups despite the Supreme Court's warning that a religious actor may not be forced to "say . . . anything in conflict with [its] religious tenets." This construction of the Human Rights Act is required neither by its language nor by its purpose of ensuring equal *treatment*—treatment concretely measured by access to "facilities and services," not by the educational institution's expressed approval of the "purposes and activities" of recipient student groups. * * *

Although the student groups were not entitled to summary judgment on the ground that Georgetown's denial of "University Recognition"—including an "endorsement"—violated the Human Rights Act, the statute does require Georgetown to equally distribute, without regard to sexual orientation, the tangible benefits contained in the same package. If discrimination appears from the record, this court may sustain the statutory ruling "on a ground different from that adopted by the trial court." Our review of the record reveals no genuine dispute that the tangible benefits were denied on the basis of sexual orientation. The Human Rights Act was violated to that extent.

The Human Rights Act cannot depend for its enforcement on a regulated actor's purely subjective, albeit sincere, evaluation of its own motivations. * * * It is particularly difficult to recognize one's own acts as discriminatory. Apart from organizations that failed to meet purely technical requirements such as a minimum membership, the record shows that Georgetown never denied "University Recognition" to a student group that was not mainly composed of persons with a homosexual orientation. Where, as here, those possessing characteristics identified by the legislature as irrelevant to individual merit are treated less favorably than others, the Human Rights Act imposes a burden upon the regulated actor to demonstrate that the irrelevant characteristic played no part in its decision. Georgetown failed to present facts that could show it was uninfluenced by sexual orientation in denying the tangible benefits.

One nondiscriminatory reason asserted by Georgetown for its denial of the tangible benefits contained in "University Recognition" was that it could not give its accompanying "endorsement" to the student groups without violating its religious principles. But as the Human Rights Act, properly construed, requires no direct, intangible "endorsement," Georgetown cannot avoid a finding of discrimination on that ground. The remaining nondiscriminatory reasons asserted by Georgetown may be summarized as follows: the "purposes and activities" of the student groups fell outside the boundaries set by "Recognition Criteria," rendering them ineligible for the tangible benefits they sought and not "otherwise qualified" within the meaning of the statute, D.C. Code § 1–2520 (1987); and, in any event, the denial of tangible benefits was based on the "purposes and activities" of the student groups, not on the homosexual status of their members, so that the sexual orientation of the students involved played no part in the decisionmaking process, *id.*

In this case, the nondiscriminatory reasons asserted by Georgetown have the effect of fusing together what would normally be two separate inquiries—are the student groups "otherwise qualified" for the tangible benefits they seek, and, if so, did Georgetown deny those tangible benefits due to the sexual orientation of their members? Here, because the answer to both of those distinct questions is determined by objective reference to the "purposes and activities" of the student groups, what are normally two separate inquiries collapse into one: did the homosexual orientation of the group members cause them to be treated differently from other applicants?

We are not bound by Georgetown's subjective perception of the "purposes and activities" to which it objected. Georgetown must view the "purposes and activities" of a student group in a way which is free from impermissible reliance upon factors unrelated to individual merit. Accordingly, if the homosexual status of group members entered into Georgetown's assessment of the "purposes and activities" of the student groups, albeit unconsciously, the denial of tangible benefits was itself based on sexual orientation. Put differently, it would be irrelevant that Georgetown saw itself as doing nothing more than applying neutral guidelines established by "Recognition Criteria" if sexual orientation had in fact influenced how those standards were applied.

In denying GPGU's application for "University Recognition" Georgetown adverted to that group's expressed purpose (one of four) to "provide a forum for the development of responsible sexual ethics consonant with one's personal beliefs." That purpose is at odds with Roman Catholic teachings. But GRC's constitution contained no comparable statement; Georgetown's stated objection was to GRC's much broader intention to "[p]rovide lesbians and gay men entering the Law Center with information about Washington's gay community, including educational, cultural, religious, social and medical services." Because GRC's purposes include an asexual commitment to serving the broad range of needs experienced by homosexual students, but no statement as to the propriety of homosexual conduct, Georgetown's objection to that organization must to some extent have been prompted by the sexual orientation of its members.

That Georgetown's treatment of the gay student groups was not exclusively influenced by a specific objection to "purposes and activities" inconsistent with Roman Catholic dogma was further evidenced by Debbie Gottfried, the University's Director of Student Activities. In clarifying GPGU's status after it had obtained "Student Body Endorsement," but had failed to obtain "University Recognition," Gottfried wrote that the University would not change its position "on what it feels would be interpreted as endorsement and official support of *the full range of issues associated with this cause.*" At no time has Georgetown defined what it meant by "the full range of issues" associated with the gay student groups, despite its insistence that Roman Catholic doctrine favors the provision of equal civil and political rights to homosexually oriented persons and that its religious objection was directed only to the promotion of homosexual conduct. Gottfried's statement was later repeated by Dean Schuerman, who wrote that the University would not lend its endorsement, support or approval to "the positions taken by the gay movement *on a full range of issues*" or "the major activities and issues which, *by definition*, are associated with a *gay organization.*" Similarly, when Dean McCarthy turned down GRC's application at the Law Center, he wrote that the University would not lend its official subsidy and support to a gay law student organization because that "would be interpreted by many as endorsement of the positions taken by the gay movement on *a full range of issues.*" George-town thus ascribed to the student groups not only "purposes and activities" which they may have had, but also a host of others automatically assumed to be a necessary attribute of their homosexual orientation. * * *

It is apparent from this correspondence, all of which was before Judge Braman when he granted summary judgment on the discrimination issue, that Georgetown's denial of tangible benefits was not closely tied to specific "purposes and activities" of the student groups promoting the homosexual conduct condemned by Roman Catholic doctrine. The conclusion is inescapable that the predominantly gay composition of the student groups played at least some role in their treatment by Georgetown. By objecting to the student groups' assumed connection, "by definition," to a "full range of issues" associated with the "gay movement," rather than to specific "purposes and activities" inconsistent with its Roman Catholic tradition, Georgetown engaged in the kind of stereotyping unrelated to individual merit that is forbidden by the Human Rights Act. In short, the record reveals no genuine doubt that Georgetown's asserted nondiscriminatory basis for its action was in fact tainted by preconceptions about gay persons. Georgetown did not apply "Recognition Criteria" on an equal basis to all groups without regard to the sexual orientation of their members. * * *

■ [CHIEF JUDGE PRYOR concurred in the result reached by JUDGE MACK. JUDGE NEWMAN wrote a concurring opinion one section of which commanded a majority of the Court. He observed that the Human Rights Act protected against race, sex, and sexual orientation discrimination (etc.) with no differentiation as to the importance of eradicating each kind of discrimination. All three goals were of equal importance.]

■ BELSON, ASSOCIATE JUDGE, with whom NEBEKER, ASSOCIATE JUDGE, RETIRED, joins, concurring in part and dissenting in part. * * *

The Human Rights Act, by its plain language, does not prohibit discrimination against persons or groups based upon their advocacy. Rather, it prohibits discrimination against persons based upon their "sexual orientation" which, in the words of the statute, "means male or female homosexuality, heterosexuality and bisexuality, by preference or practice." D.C.Code § 1–2502(28) (1987). It follows that Judge Braman erred if he granted summary judgment against Georgetown on the theory that it violated the Act by denying recognition because of the groups' advocacy of homosexual life-styles.

* * * [A] construction of the Act that would prohibit a private actor from differentiating among persons based on their advocacy of ideas would not only be untrue to the Act, it would also abridge the first amendment's guarantees of free speech and, in this case, the free exercise of religion. Judge Mack interprets the Act to prohibit the public and private educational institutions covered by it from engaging in certain types of conduct but, in an attempt to avoid conflict with the first amendment, she construes the Act not to reach the speech activities of a private institution. Judge Mack concludes that the Act therefore does not require one private actor to "endorse" another.

I would use a different analysis to determine whether Georgetown's denial of recognition to the student groups falls outside the scope of the Human Rights Act. I interpret the Act to prohibit adverse action taken against persons on the basis of their status as members of a protected class. The Act does not purport to prohibit actions taken against persons because of their promotion of ideas or activities (here, for example, promotion of ideas and conduct antithetical to Catholic teachings). Thus, in my view, if an entity covered by the Act fails to grant facilities and services to an individual because of his or her status as a member of a protected group, the Act is violated. In contrast, if an entity covered by the Act fails to provide facilities and services to an individual because of his or her promotion of ideas or activities, that conduct does not violate the Act. Furthermore, as developed below, a construction of the Act that would prevent a private actor from differentiating among others on the basis of the content of their speech would be unconstitutional, at least in the absence of a compelling state interest. Thus, a statutorily imposed requirement of neutrality toward the promotion of an idea, *viz.*, the morality of homosexual life-styles, would abridge first amendment rights. Similarly, an imposed duty either to endorse or to subsidize a position on that issue would also abridge those rights.

An analogy is illustrative. It could not seriously be suggested that the Human Rights Act could force a private, church-affiliated school to lend its endorsement or subsidy to a group that advocated or purposely facilitated fornication or adultery. Such a group, however, could argue that those activities reflect the group members' heterosexual orientation, an orientation that triggers the Act's protection to the same extent as does homosexual orientation. There can be no doubt that university authorities in such a case could recognize that the purposes and activities of an organization of this type would foster or promote acts that the Church deems immoral. While Catholic doctrine deems all homosexual acts immoral and only some heterosexual acts immoral, the principle is the same. Both this hypothetical group and the groups before us can properly be denied endorsement and subsidy by a religious institution because of their sponsorship and promotion of acts that the institution considers immoral, rather than on the basis of their members' status as homosexuals, heterosexuals, or bisexuals. See Tr. 541 (Georgetown would not subsidize activities of student "playboy" club); Tr. 628–30 (Georgetown would not support group that distributes information about abortion clinics to students). * * *

Even if there were a valid finding that Georgetown had violated the Human Rights Act, Georgetown should prevail in this litigation on the basis of its constitutional rights under the free speech and free exercise clauses of the first amendment. I discuss the constitutional issues here on the premise that Georgetown denied recognition to the student groups at least in large part because of the groups' sponsorship and promotion of ideas and activities. Although it has not yet been determined by a factfinder whether sexual orientation entered at all into Georgetown's motivation, it is clear from the record and from Judge Bacon's findings that Georgetown's concern over the groups' advocacy and speech activities permeated its consideration of the question of whether to grant them recognition. Therefore, Georgetown's right of free speech comes strongly into play. With respect to free exercise, Judge Bacon's findings firmly established that Georgetown denied recognition "because recognition would be inconsistent with its duties as a Catholic institution." * * *

■ FERREN, ASSOCIATE JUDGE, with whom TERRY, ASSOCIATE JUDGE, joins, concurring in part and dissenting in part.

I continue to subscribe to the views expressed in the opinion of the division vacated by the en banc court, *Gay Rights Coalition of Georgetown University v. Georgetown University*, 496 A.2d 567, 587 (D.C.1985). Thus, I continue to believe that Georgetown University may not lawfully refuse to accord the plaintiff gay rights groups "University recognition," which means (1) *status* equal to that of the other student groups formally recognized by the university, including permission to use the university name, and (2) the *tangible benefits* uniformly available to other recognized groups such as office space, supplies and equipment, a telephone, computer label and mailing services, student advertising privileges, financial counseling, and the opportunity to apply for lecture fund privileges and for other funding. I therefore concur, as far as it goes, in the result proposed by Judge Mack, joined by Chief Judge Pryor and Judge Newman, requiring the university to make the second category of (tangible) benefits available to the gay rights groups. But I respectfully dissent from the views of those three colleagues, as well as Judges Belson and Nebeker, who would deny the first category of (intangible) relief plaintiffs have requested. * * *

In contrast with Judge Mack, Judge Belson reads the Human Rights Act in a way that may not proscribe any of Georgetown's discriminatory conduct. He argues that the Act's reference to "sexual orientation" only forbids discrimination based on sexual "preference or practice," not discrimination based on "advocacy," meaning "promotion of ideas or activities." If Georgetown engaged only in the latter sort of discrimination, he says, it did not violate the Act. But for his disposition of the appeal on constitutional grounds, on the assumption that Georgetown has violated the Act, Judge Belson would remand for further proceedings to clarify the university's motives.

There are two problems with Judge Belson's analysis. First, given the trial court findings on which he relies—and which are supported by the record—no remand is necessary to determine the university's motives for purposes of evaluating whether Georgetown has violated the Human Rights Act. Indeed, on the basis of the findings by both trial judges in the statutory and constitutional phases of the proceedings—which Judge Belson himself suggests we can rely on for purposes of analyzing all issues in this case—the student groups are entitled to prevail on the statutory issue. Second, Judge Belson incorrectly argues that the Act can never, consistent with the Constitution, interdict discrimination directed at "speech" or "advocacy."

[The initial problem with Judge Belson's analysis is that it falls athwart findings of fact by both trial judges, Bacon and Braman, that

Georgetown denied recognition and services in part because of the sexual orientation of the students. At worst, from Judge Ferren's perspective, the trial judges both found issues of fact precluding Georgetown from receiving summary judgment. At best, the trial judges firmly established summary judgment against Georgetown because part of its motivation was the prohibited one.]

There is a more general, though fundamental weakness of Judge Belson's analysis—of his unqualified proposition that the Act cannot be construed to forbid the suppression of "speech" or "advocacy." The distinction between discrimination based on advocacy and on status will not work. Part of who a person is, is what he or she says; to deny the right to speak is to deny an essential aspect of one's person. In this sense, therefore, an asserted right to discriminate against someone's advocacy of homosexuality is clearly a claimed right to discriminate against the person on the basis of one's sexual "preference" and thus "sexual orientation." D.C.Code §§ 1–2502(28), –2520(1) (1987).

Assume, however, it is true, as Judge Belson contends, that the Act does not forbid discrimination motivated solely by a desire to prevent the speech activities of a group. Two caveats are in order. First, the means chosen to discriminate against advocacy (here, non-recognition of the plaintiff groups) does not necessarily prove that the underlying motive is merely to prevent the propagation of a repugnant doctrine on campus. The university's action may be directed solely at speech activities (let us assume it is), but that action may still be illegal under the Act if motivated, even in part, by dislike for those who prefer or practice homosexuality. I believe Judge Belson agrees.

Second, even if the university were motivated solely by a desire to shut down offensive speech activities, the means chosen to counter repugnant speech might nonetheless violate the Act. Even if the Act were construed not to forbid discrimination against homosexual ideas, it unquestionably does forbid discrimination against homosexuals because of their ideas. Discrimination that goes beyond the ideas to the person violates the Act no matter what the motive. *See* D.C. Code § 1–2532 (1987) (any practice having "effect or consequence" of violating Act is unlawful). Accordingly, even if censorship in this context, when properly motivated, were lawful, an act excluding or degrading a group to accomplish censorship would not be lawful.

As indicated, I believe any effort to distinguish under the Act between legal discrimination against ideas and illegal discrimination against persons fails to take into account that ideas—and advocacy—are an essential part of the person. But even if the distinction could be made, it is not easy to draw, in part because means capable of achieving the former may amount to the latter. I believe Judge Belson has overlooked, both in his analysis and in its application, the possibility that Georgetown's refusal to recognize the plaintiff groups, if only because of an aversion to their advocacy, is likely to be—indeed, inevitably is in the context of a university—an overly broad response that effectively discriminates against persons in violation of the Act. * * *

The fundamental [constitutional] question is: whether plaintiffs' request for "University recognition"—meaning full citizenship as student groups at Georgetown University—may be denied, even though in violation of the Human Rights Act, because of Georgetown's first amendment rights. * * * I want to emphasize again that, on this record, "University recognition" or "endorsement" of the plaintiff student groups does not mean, explicitly or implicitly, a statement of approval—or even of neutrality—toward homosexuality, gay rights, or related matters. Because of the nature of the university, the Human Rights Act in no way compels Georgetown to take a position in violation of its right to free exercise of religious beliefs.

In context—and context is critically important—the Act only requires Georgetown not to discriminate against student groups that wish to express their own views in what I believe we may call, without fear of contradiction, a typical private university marketplace of ideas, which inherently stands for freedom of expression. That marketplace is analogous, for constitutional purposes, to the shopping center in *PruneYard [Shopping Center v. Robins*, 447 U.S. 74 (1980)]. There, the Supreme Court held that the first amendment rights of the shopping center owner did not justify barring pamphleteers from exercising their own free speech rights in the common areas open to the public. A legal requirement that Georgetown make its university-wide forum available on a nondiscriminatory basis to all student citizens of the university does not, in my view, imply in any way that the university corporation/administration itself can be reasonably identified with the views of any particular student organization or that the university, as such, has a position—pro, con, or neutral—on any particular message a student group happens to spread. The Human Rights Act, therefore, does not require Georgetown to espouse any view or to intimate even a neutral opinion. * * *

There is a recognized constitutional distinction between a requirement that others be permitted to express what are clearly their own ideas in your forum, when you manifestly provide a public forum (*PruneYard*), and a requirement that you must express the ideas of others (*Barnette*) or must spread, and thus implicitly affirm, those ideas in your own private forum, absent a dissociative statement. * * * I believe the *PruneYard* analysis is controlling here. While there obviously are differences between a private university and a private shopping center, the fact that each, for entirely different reasons, has become a traditional forum for the expression of diverse, often conflicting ideas provides a context compelling a conclusion that, *by definition*, even a private university proprietor cannot *reasonably* be associated with any idea it does not affirmatively embrace. At most, therefore, "University recognition" of a gay rights group implies no more than the university's "official tolerance," of still another student organization in a pluralistic environment—a tolerance to be expected, indeed taken for granted, in any university that purports to be open to free expression of ideas, and thus a tolerance that implies no university position whatsoever about the ideas any group stands for. To tolerate another's values or speech is not to approve of them; nor is it to express indifference or neutrality. It is simply an expressed willingness to let someone else have a say without indicating what you think about it. This distinction between toleration and endorsement (or, more generally, between toleration and taking a position of some sort) lies at the heart of the first amendment's demand that government tolerate dissident beliefs and speech; it is equally essential to our civil rights statutes. Conceptually, perhaps, one could quibble about whether government-compelled toleration amounts to forced conduct or forced speech; but, for constitutional purposes, the salient point is that, in context, such "University recognition" does not suggest the university is taking a position on the group that it tolerates/recognizes. Thus, required "recognition" does not run afoul of the absolute protection against compelled utterances * * *. As I see it, therefore, only in refusing to recognize a student group expressly for ideological or theological reasons is the university making a statement about the group's ideas and thus making its own position known. * * *

NOTES ON THE GEORGETOWN CASE

1. *The Relevance of* Hurley? Does the Supreme Court's opinion in *Hurley* require a different result in this case? Doesn't it support Judge Belson's point of view? Or is *Georgetown* distinguishable?

2. *Viewpoint As Constituting Identity.* "Notions of identity increasingly form the basis for gay and lesbian equality claims. Those claims merge not only status and conduct, but also viewpoint, into one whole. To be openly gay, when the closet is an option, is to function as an advocate as well as a symbol. The centrality of viewpoint to gay identity explains the logic behind what has become the primary strategy of anti-gay forces: the attempted penalization of those who 'profess' homosexuality, in a series of 'no promo homo' campaigns." Nan D. Hunter, "Identity, Speech and Equality," 79 *Va. L. Rev.* 1695, 1696 (1993). Imagine that a group of lesbian, gay and bisexual students had formed to seek and provide support for becoming heterosexual. Would Georgetown have been likely to charter the group? If so, wouldn't viewpoint—not identity—be the only explanation for its different treatment of the plaintiffs in this case? Conversely, imagine that heterosexual students seek to form a chapter of "Straight But Not Narrow." What result?

3. *Must One Choose Between Viewpoint and Identity?* Judge Ferren's opinion tackles this dilemma in greater depth than any other judicial text. His central point is that "[e]ven if the Act were construed not to forbid discrimination against homosexual ideas, it unquestionably does forbid discrimination against homosexuals because of their ideas." Is that true? Is it illegal to discriminate against Latinos "because of their ideas"? Because of their ideas only about race or ethnicity? What *are* "homosexual ideas"?

4. *Litigation Binds.* In fact, gay plaintiffs have argued that discrimination against them is based on viewpoint (*Bonner*); based on anti-group bias and not on viewpoint (*Georgetown, Hurley*); and based on both (the military cases). Private sector defendants have argued that differential, adverse treatment of gay people is because of a clash of viewpoint. The military and other public sector defendants have argued that it is based on anything but viewpoint.

One can imagine a chart of the pros and cons of proceeding under either a viewpoint/dissent model or an equality model. A claim of viewpoint discrimination under the First Amendment carries the most powerful doctrinal punch. State actions that penalize speech based on viewpoint are subjected to exacting review and, if the viewpoint bias can be shown, are presumptively unconstitutional. Protecting disfavored points of view is part of the tradition associated with the doctrine. Appellate courts will re-examine *de novo* a trial court's findings of fact (normally entitled to deferential review), as well as any conclusions of law. However, First Amendment claims can be made *only* against the state.

A constitutional equality claim based on sexual orientation discrimination leads to a much more lenient standard of review for the defendant's actions: whether the classification is rationally related to a legitimate governmental interest. Efforts to obtain a more stringent standard of review send gay plaintiffs into the mire of arguing about immutability and relative powerlessness.

A statutory equality claim brings a standard of review equal to or perhaps higher than that under a First Amendment claim. To justify disparate treatment, a defendant may in some circumstances assert a bona fide occupational qualification (BFOQ), a very tough test to satisfy. To justify a facially neutral policy with disparate effects, a defendant must prove a business necessity for the policy. Most private entities are covered. Caveat: the First Amendment remains available to defendants as a shield.

To summarize, if one alleges that anti-gay discrimination is based on viewpoint, plaintiffs invoke a powerful claim against the state, but forfeit all claims against private actors. If one alleges an equality claim, plaintiffs in a few states get a powerful statutory claim against most public and private actors, except the federal government. (Federal government actions are governed only by federal, never by state, law. Thus state and local civil rights laws which include sexual orientation do not apply to the federal government.) Plaintiffs everywhere else get a weaker constitutional claim, and only against government.

5. *Race Analogies.* In a portion we have left out, Judge Ferren charged the plurality of consigning Georgetown's gay students to a "separate but equal" regime similar to that allowed for African Americans in *Plessy v. Ferguson.* His argument: the gay groups got access to equal facilities and resources but were left with the stigma as the only student group not "recognized" by the university. (In the subsequent settlement, the students agreed to put a statement on their correspondence and stationery saying that their group was not recognized by the university.) Hence, Georgetown was allowed to keep the homosexuals "separate" so long as they were given "equal" facilities. Is this a fair analogy?

If Georgetown were a state university, would Judge Mack's result be allowable? See *Bonner*. If not, why should large, non-government private centers of power be given "special immunities" from the First Amendment? Recall that in California, New Jersey, and other states free speech requirements have been extended to private institutions, including Princeton University.

6. *The Subsequent History of the Georgetown Case.* In 1988, Congress adopted the Armstrong Amendment requiring the D.C. Council to amend the Human Rights Act to exempt religious institutions from the prohibition against discrimination on the basis of sexual preference. A member of the D.C. Council successfully challenged the provision as violating his First Amendment speech rights, by requiring him to vote in a certain way. *Clarke v. United States*, 886 F.2d 404 (D.C.Cir.1989), vacated as moot, 915 F.2d 699 (1990). After this ruling, Congress adopted a second Armstrong Amendment directly rewriting the Human Rights Act. Public Law No. 101–168, § 141, 103 Stat. 1267 (1989).

Meanwhile, Georgetown University ultimately declined to seek Supreme Court review of the decision you read. The University settled the lawsuit with the students, and lent no support to efforts to overturn the ruling in Congress. Even after the Armstrong Amendments, the University adhered to its agreement with the students, and gay student groups have continuously existed and flourished at both the main campus and at the Law Center.

Ronald W. Rosenberger v. Rector and Visitors of the University of Virginia

Supreme Court of the United States, 1995.
___ U.S. ___ , 115 S.Ct. 2510, 132 L.Ed.2d 700.

■ JUSTICE KENNEDY delivered the opinion of the Court.

[Almost any student group at the University of Virginia can apply to be a "Contracted Independent Organization" (CIO). CIOs enjoy access to University facilities, including meeting rooms and computer terminals. Some CIOS are also entitled to apply for funds from the Student Activities Fund (SAF). Established and governed by University Guidelines, the purpose of the SAF is to support a broad range of extracurricular student activities that "are related to the educational purpose of the University." The SAF is based on the University's "recogni[tion] that the availability of a wide range of opportunities" for its students "tends to enhance the University environment." The Student Council has the initial authority to disburse the funds, but its actions are subject to review by a faculty body.]

[University] Guidelines recognize 11 categories of student groups that may seek payment to third-party contractors because they "are related to the educational purpose of the University of Virginia." One of these is "student news, information, opinion, entertainment, or academic communications media groups." The Guidelines also specify, however, that the costs of certain activities of CIOs that are otherwise eligible for funding will not be reimbursed by the SAF. The student activities which are excluded from SAF support are religious activities, philanthropic contributions and activities, political activities, activities that would jeopardize the University's tax exempt status, those which involve payment of honoraria or similar fees, or social entertainment or related expenses. The prohibition on "political activities" is defined so that it is limited to electioneering and lobbying. The Guidelines provide that "[t]hese restrictions on funding political activities are not intended to preclude funding of any otherwise eligible student organization which . . . espouses particular positions or ideological viewpoints, including those that may be unpopular or are not generally accepted." A "religious activity," by contrast, is defined as any activity that "primarily promotes or manifests a particular belie[f] in or about a deity or an ultimate reality." * * *

Petitioners' organization, Wide Awake Productions (WAP), qualified as a CIO. Formed by petitioner Ronald Rosenberger and other undergraduates in 1990, WAP was established "[t]o publish a magazine of philosophical and religious expression," "[t]o facilitate discussion which fosters an atmosphere of sensitivity to and tolerance of Christian viewpoints," and "[t]o provide a unifying focus for Christians of multicultural backgrounds." WAP publishes Wide Awake: A Christian Perspective at the University of Virginia. The paper's Christian viewpoint was evident from the first issue, in which its editors wrote that the journal "offers a Christian perspective on both personal and community issues, especially those relevant to college students at the University of Virginia." The editors committed the paper to a two-fold mission: "to challenge Christians to live, in word and deed, according to the faith they proclaim and to encourage students to consider what a personal relationship with Jesus Christ means." The first issue had articles about racism, crisis pregnancy, stress, prayer, C.S. Lewis' ideas about evil and free will, and reviews of religious music. In the next two issues, Wide Awake featured stories about homosexuality, Christian missionary work, and eating disorders, as well as music reviews and interviews with University professors. Each page of Wide Awake, and the end of each article or review, is marked by a cross. The advertisements carried in Wide Awake also reveal the Christian perspective of the journal. For the most part, the advertisers are churches, centers for Christian study, or Christian bookstores. By June 1992, WAP had distributed about 5,000 copies of Wide Awake to University students, free of charge.

WAP had acquired CIO status soon after it was organized. This is an important consideration in this case, for had it been a "religious organization," WAP would not have been accorded CIO status. As defined by the Guidelines, a "religious organization" is "an organization whose purpose is to practice a devotion to an acknowledged ultimate reality or deity." At no stage in this controversy has the University contended that WAP is such an organization.

A few months after being given CIO status, WAP requested the SAF to pay its printer $5,862 for the costs of printing its newspaper. The Appropriations Committee of the Student Council denied WAP's request on the ground that Wide Awake was a "religious activity" within the meaning of the Guidelines, *i.e.*, that the newspaper "promote[d] or manifest[ed] a particular belie[f] in or about a deity or an ultimate reality." It made its determination after examining the first issue. WAP appealed the denial to the full Student Council, contending that WAP met all the applicable Guidelines and that denial of SAF support on the basis of the magazine's religious perspective violated the Constitution. The appeal was denied without further comment, and WAP appealed to the next level, the Student Activities Committee. In a letter signed by the Dean of Students, the committee sustained the denial of funding. * * *

It is axiomatic that the government may not regulate speech based on its substantive content or the message it conveys. Other principles follow from this precept. In the realm of private speech or expression, government regulation may not favor one speaker over another. * * * The government must abstain from regulating speech when the specific motivating ideology or the opinion or perspective of the speaker is the rationale for the restriction. See *Perry Ed. Assn. v. Perry Local Educators' Assn.*, 460 U.S. 37, 46 (1983).

These principles provide the framework forbidding the State from exercising viewpoint discrimination, even when the limited public forum is one of its own creation. In a case involving a school district's provision of school facilities for private uses, we declared that "[t]here is no question that the District, like the private owner of property, may legally preserve the property under its control for the use to which it is dedicated." *Lamb's Chapel v. Center Moriches Union Free School Dist.*, 113 S.Ct. 2141, 2146 (1993). The necessities of confining a forum to the limited and legitimate purposes for which it was created may justify the State in reserving it for certain groups or for the discussion of certain topics. See, *e.g., Cornelius v. NAACP Legal Defense & Ed. Fund, Inc.*, 473 U.S. 788, 806 (1985); *Perry Ed. Assn.*, [460 U.S.] at 49. Once it has opened a limited forum, however, the State must respect the lawful boundaries it has itself set. The State may not exclude speech where its distinction is not "reasonable in light of the purpose served by the forum," *Cornelius*, [473 U.S.] at 804–806, nor may it discriminate against speech on the basis of its viewpoint, *Lamb's Chapel*, 113 S.Ct., at 2147. Thus, in determining whether the State is acting to preserve the limits of the forum it has created so that the exclusion of a class of speech is legitimate, we have observed a distinction between, on the one hand, content discrimination, which may be permissible if it preserves the purposes of that limited forum, and, on the other hand, viewpoint discrimination, which is presumed impermissible when directed against speech otherwise within the forum's limitations. See *Perry Ed. Assn.*, [460 U.S.] at 46.

The SAF is a forum more in a metaphysical than in a spatial or geographic sense, but the same principles are applicable. The most recent and most apposite case is our decision in *Lamb's Chapel*. There, a school district had opened school facilities for use after school hours by community groups for a wide variety of social, civic, and recreational purposes. The district, however, had enacted a formal policy against opening facilities to groups for religious purposes. Invoking its policy, the district rejected a request from a group desiring to show a film series addressing various child-rearing questions from a "Christian perspective." There was no indication in the record in *Lamb's Chapel* that the request to use the school facilities was "denied for any reason other than the fact that the presentation would have been from a religious perspective." 113 S.Ct., at 2145. Our conclusion was unanimous: "[I]t discriminates on the basis of viewpoint to permit school property to be used for the presentation of all views about family issues and child-rearing except those dealing with the subject matter from a religious standpoint." *Ibid.*

The University does acknowledge (as it must in light of our precedents) that "ideologically driven attempts to suppress a particular point of view are presumptively unconstitutional in funding, as in other contexts," but insists that this case does not present that issue because the Guidelines draw lines based on content, not viewpoint. Brief for Respondents 17, n.10. As we have noted, discrimination against one set of views or ideas is but a subset or particular instance of the more general phenomenon of content discrimination. And, it must be acknowledged, the distinction is not a precise one. It is, in a sense, something of an understatement to speak of religious thought and discussion as just a viewpoint, as distinct from a comprehensive body of thought. The nature of our origins and destiny and their dependence upon the existence of a divine being have been subjects of philosophic inquiry throughout human history. We conclude, nonetheless, that here, as in *Lamb's Chapel*, viewpoint discrimination is the proper way to interpret the University's objections to Wide Awake. By the very terms of the SAF prohibition, the University does not exclude religion as a subject matter but selects for disfavored treatment those student journalistic efforts with religious editorial viewpoints. Religion may be a vast area of inquiry, but it also provides, as it did here, a specific premise, a perspective, a standpoint from which a variety of subjects may be discussed and considered. The prohibited perspective, not the general subject matter, resulted in the refusal to make third-party payments, for the subjects discussed were otherwise within the approved category of publications.

The dissent's assertion that no viewpoint discrimination occurs because the Guidelines discriminate against an entire class of viewpoints reflects an insupportable assumption that all debate is bipolar and that anti-religious speech is the only response to religious speech. Our understanding of the complex and multifaceted nature of public discourse has not embraced such a contrived description of the marketplace of ideas. If the topic of debate is, for example, racism, then exclusion of several views on that problem is just as offensive to the First Amendment as exclusion of only one. It is as objectionable to exclude both a theistic and an atheistic perspective on the debate as it is to exclude one, the other, or yet another political, economic, or social viewpoint. The dissent's declaration that debate is not skewed so long as multiple voices are silenced is simply wrong; the debate is skewed in multiple ways.

The University's denial of WAP's request for third-party payments in the present case is based upon viewpoint discrimination not unlike the discrimination the school district relied upon in *Lamb's Chapel* and that we found invalid. The church group in *Lamb's Chapel* would have been qualified as a social or civic organization, save for its religious purposes. Furthermore, just as the school district in *Lamb's Chapel* pointed to nothing but the religious views of the group as the rationale for excluding its message, so in this case the University justifies its denial of SAF participation to WAP on the ground that the contents of Wide Awake reveal an avowed religious perspective. It bears only passing mention that the dissent's attempt to distinguish *Lamb's Chapel* is entirely without support in the law. Relying on the transcript of oral argument, the dissent seems to argue that we found viewpoint discrimination in that case because the government excluded Christian, but not atheistic, viewpoints from being expressed in the forum there. The Court relied on no such distinction in holding that discriminating against religious speech was discriminating on the basis of viewpoint. There is no indication in the opinion of the Court (which, unlike an advocate's statements at oral argument, is the law) that exclusion or inclusion of other religious or antireligious voices from that forum had any bearing on its decision. * * *

Vital First Amendment speech principles are at stake here. The first danger to liberty lies in granting the State the power to examine publications to determine whether or not they are based on some ultimate idea and if so for the State to classify them. The second, and corollary, danger is to speech from the chilling of individual thought and expression. That danger is especially real in the University setting, where the State acts against a background and tradition of thought and experiment that is at the center of our intellectual and philosophic tradition. See *Healy v. James*, 408 U.S. 169, 180–181 (1972); *Keyishian v. Board of Regents, State Univ. of N.Y.*, 385 U.S. 589, 603 (1967); *Sweezy v. New Hampshire*, 354 U.S. 234, 250 (1957). In ancient Athens, and, as Europe entered into a new period of intellectual awakening, in places like Bologna, Oxford, and Paris, universities began as voluntary and spontaneous assemblages or concourses for students to speak and to write and to learn. See generally R. Palmer & J. Colton, *A History of the Modern World* 39 (7th ed. 1992). The quality and creative power of student intellectual life to this day remains a vital measure of a school's influence and attainment. For the University, by regulation, to cast disapproval on particular viewpoints of its students risks the suppression of free speech and creative inquiry in one of the vital centers for the nation's intellectual life, its college and university campuses.

The Guideline invoked by the University to deny third-party contractor payments on behalf of WAP effects a sweeping restriction on student thought and student inquiry in the context of University sponsored publications. The prohibition on funding on behalf of publications that "primarily promot[e] or manifes[t] a particular belie[f] in or about a deity or an ultimate reality," in its ordinary and commonsense meaning, has a vast potential reach. The term "promotes" as used here would comprehend any writing advocating a philosophic position that rests upon a belief in a deity or ultimate reality. See *Webster's Third New International Dictionary* 1815 (1961) (defining "promote" as "to contribute to the growth, enlargement, or prosperity of: further, encourage"). And the term "manifests" would bring within the scope of the prohibition any writing that is explicable as resting upon a premise which presupposes the existence of a deity or ultimate reality. See *id.*, at 1375 (defining "manifest" as "to show plainly: make palpably evident or certain by showing or displaying"). Were the prohibition applied with much vigor at all, it would bar funding of essays by hypothetical student contributors named Plato, Spinoza, and Descartes. And if the regulation covers, as the University says it does, those student journalistic efforts which primarily manifest or promote a belief that there is no deity and no ultimate reality, then under-graduates named Karl Marx, Bertrand Russell, and Jean–Paul Sartre would likewise have some of their major essays excluded from student publications. If any manifestation of beliefs in first principles disqualifies the writing, as seems to be the case, it is indeed difficult to name renowned thinkers whose writings would be accepted, save perhaps for articles disclaiming all connection to their ultimate philosophy. Plato could contrive perhaps to submit an acceptable essay on making pasta or peanut butter cookies, provided he did not point out their (necessary) imperfections.

Based on the principles we have discussed, we hold that the regulation invoked to deny SAF support, both in its terms and in its application to these petitioners, is a denial of their right of free speech guaranteed by the First Amendment. It remains to be considered whether the violation following from the University's action is excused by the necessity of complying with the Constitution's prohibition against state establishment of religion. [The Court determined that the establishment clause was not violated.]

■ [We omit JUSTICE O'CONNOR's concurring opinion.]

■ JUSTICE SOUTER, joined by JUSTICES STEVENS, GINSBURG, and BREYER, dissenting. * * *

The Court acknowledges the necessity for a university to make judgments based on the content of what may be said or taught when it decides, in the absence of unlimited amounts of money or other resources, how to honor its educational responsibilities. Nor does the Court question that in allocating public funds a state university enjoys spacious discretion. Cf. *Rust v. Sullivan*, 500 U.S. 173, 194 (1991) ("[W]hen the government appropriates public funds to establish a program it is entitled to define the limits of that program"). Accordingly, the Court recognizes that the relevant enquiry in this case is not merely whether the University bases its funding decisions on the subject matter of student speech; if there is an infirmity in the basis for the University's funding decision, it must be that the University is impermissibly distinguishing among competing viewpoints * * *.

The issue whether a distinction is based on viewpoint does not turn simply on whether a government regulation happens to be applied to a speaker who seeks to advance a particular viewpoint; the issue, of course, turns on whether the burden on speech is explained by reference to viewpoint. As when deciding whether a speech restriction is content-based or content-neutral, "[t]he government's purpose is the controlling consideration." *Ward v. Rock Against Racism*, 491 U.S. 781, 791 (1989). So, for example, a city that enforces its excessive noise ordinance by pulling the plug on a rock band using a forbidden amplification system is not guilty of viewpoint discrimination simply because the band wishes to use that equipment to espouse antiracist views. Accord, *Rock Against Racism*, *supra*. * * *

Accordingly, the prohibition on viewpoint discrimination serves that important purpose of the Free Speech Clause, which is to bar the government from skewing public debate. Other things being equal, viewpoint discrimination occurs when government allows one message while prohibiting the messages of those who can reasonably be expected to respond. It is precisely this element of taking sides in a public debate that identifies viewpoint discrimination and makes it the most pernicious of all distinctions based on content. Thus, if government assists those espousing one point of view, neutrality requires it to assist those espousing opposing points of view, as well.

There is no viewpoint discrimination in the University's application of its Guidelines to deny funding to Wide Awake. Under those Guidelines, a "religious activit[y]," which is not eligible for funding is "an activity which primarily promotes or manifests a particular belief(s) in or about a deity or an ultimate reality." It is clear that this is the basis on which Wide Awake Productions was denied funding. The discussion of Wide Awake's content shows beyond any question that it "primarily promotes or manifests a particular belief(s) in or about a deity . . .," in the very specific sense that its manifest function is to call students to repentance, to commitment to Jesus Christ, and to particular moral action because of its Christian character.

If the Guidelines were written or applied so as to limit only such Christian advocacy and no other evangelical efforts that might compete with it, the discrimination would be based on viewpoint. But that is not what the regulation authorizes; it applies to Muslim and Jewish and Buddhist advocacy as well as to Christian. And since it limits funding to activities promoting or manifesting a particular belief not only "in" but "about" a deity or ultimate reality, it applies to agnostics and atheists as well as it does to deists and theists (as the University maintained at oral argument, and as the Court recognizes). The Guidelines, and their application to Wide Awake, thus do not skew debate by funding one position but not its competitors. As understood by their application to Wide Awake, they simply deny funding for hortatory speech that "primarily promotes or manifests" any view on the merits of religion; they deny funding for the entire subject matter of religious apologetics. * * *

The Guidelines are thus substantially different from the access restriction considered in *Lamb's Chapel*, the case upon which the Court heavily relies in finding a viewpoint distinction here. *Lamb's Chapel* addressed a school board's regulation prohibiting the after-hours use of school premises "by any group for religious purposes," even though the forum otherwise was open for a variety of social, civic, and recreational purposes. 113 S.Ct., at 2144 (citation and internal quotation marks omitted). "Religious" was understood to refer to the viewpoint of a believer, and the regulation did not purport to deny access to any speaker wishing to express a nonreligious or expressly antireligious point of view on any subject.

With this understanding, it was unremarkable that in *Lamb's Chapel* we unanimously determined that the access restriction, as applied to a speaker wishing to discuss family values from a Christian perspective, impermissibly distinguished between speakers on the basis of viewpoint. Equally obvious is the distinction between that case and this one, where the regulation is being applied, not to deny funding for those who discuss issues in general from a religious viewpoint, but to those engaged in promoting or opposing religious conversion and religious observances as such. If this amounts to viewpoint discrimination, the Court has all but eviscerated the line between viewpoint and content.

To put the point another way, the Court's decision equating a categorical exclusion of both sides of the religious debate with viewpoint discrimination suggests the Court has concluded that primarily religious and antireligious speech, grouped together, always provides an opposing (and not merely a related) viewpoint to any speech about any secular topic. Thus, the Court's reasoning requires a university that funds private publications about any primarily nonreligious topic also to fund publications primarily espousing adherence to or rejection of religion. But a university's decision to fund a magazine about racism, and not to fund publications aimed at urging repentance before God does not skew the debate either about racism or the desirability of religious conversion. The Court's contrary holding amounts to a significant reformulation of our viewpoint discrimination precedents and will significantly expand access to limited-access forums. * * *

NOTE ON *ROSENBERGER* AND RELIGIOUS–BASED IDENTITY SPEECH

As in *Bonner*, a student group was seeking access to university funds and services under the First Amendment's speech clause. As in *Georgetown*, the defendant University relied on one of the religion clauses as a defense. In all three cases, the courts required the universities to provide goods and services to controversial student groups. Does *Rosenberger* validate the approaches taken in *Bonner* and *Georgetown*?

In a secular world, are fundamentalist Christians an "identity group" similar to gays and lesbians (who are at odds with fundamentalists on many issues)? See Chapter 8, Section 1, where we treat the free exercise and establishment clause issues raised in *Georgetown* and *Rosenberger*, respectively.

SECTION 2

PRIVACY AND SEXUAL "OUTING"

The previous section explored the clash between free expression and nondiscrimination in cases involving sexuality and gender. This section explores the clash between free expression and privacy. The privacy to which we refer is informational privacy, specifically the authority to control information about one's own sexuality, as distinct from the autonomy branch of privacy in Chapter 1. We take up some of the very issues first broached by Samuel Warren and Louis Brandeis in their foundational article on the right to privacy: a press filled with gossip and "mechanical devices [that] threaten to make good the prediction that 'what is whispered in the closet shall be proclaimed from the house-tops.' " Samuel D. Warren & Louis D. Brandeis, "The Right to Privacy," 4 *Harv. L. Rev.* 193, 195 (1890).

We begin with the First Amendment and examine the constitutional limits placed on governmental authority to regulate the control of any information, even information about oneself. Other speakers and listeners, most notably the press, claim rights to a free flow of information despite the fact that it may be embarrassing, shocking, or intimate. Once outside those constitutional limits, however, how does the law regulate such disclosures? Tort law recognizes claims for both invasion of privacy and defamation. How has this branch of law developed in relationship to the realm of sexuality, and how have those two structures—tort law and the social understanding of sexuality—shaped each other? In that regard, we pay special attention to the arguments related to "outing," a practice used by some journalists and activists to publicize the sexual orientation of closeted gays and lesbians.

PART A.   FIRST AMENDMENT PARAMETERS

The Florida Star v. B.J.F.

Supreme Court of the United States, 1989.
491 U.S. 524, 109 S.Ct. 2603, 105 L.Ed.2d 443.

■ JUSTICE MARSHALL delivered the opinion of the Court.

Florida Stat. § 794.03 (1987) makes it unlawful to "print, publish, or broadcast . . . in any instrument of mass communication" the name of the victim of a sexual offense.[1] Pursuant to this statute, appellant *The Florida Star* was found civilly liable for publishing the name of a rape victim which it had obtained from a publicly released police report. The issue presented here is whether this result comports with the First Amendment. We hold that it does not.

[*The Florida Star* is a weekly newspaper which serves the community of Jacksonville, Florida, and which has an average circulation of approximately 18,000 copies. Its "Police Reports" section contains brief articles describing local criminal incidents under police investigation. On October 29, 1983, the section reported the details of a robbery and sexual assault on B.J.F. The newspaper obtained her name and the details of the assault from a public report on file in the pressroom of the Duval County Sheriff's Department. In printing B.J.F.'s full name, *The Florida Star* violated its internal policy of not publishing the names of sexual offense victims. B.J.F. successfully sued the newspaper for negligently violating § 794.03 and obtained $75,000 in compensatory and $25,000 in punitive damages. The Florida courts rejected the newspaper's defense that such liability violates the First Amendment.]

The tension between the right which the First Amendment accords to a free press, on the one hand, and the protections which various statutes and common-law doctrines accord to personal privacy against the publication of truthful information, on the other, is a subject we have addressed several times in recent years. Our decisions in cases involving government attempts to sanction the accurate dissemination of information as invasive of privacy, have not, however, exhaustively considered this conflict. On the contrary, although our decisions have without exception upheld the press' right to publish, we have emphasized each time that we were resolving this conflict only as it arose in a discrete factual context.

The parties to this case frame their contentions in light of a trilogy of cases which have presented, in different contexts, the conflict between truthful reporting and state-protected privacy interests. In *Cox Broadcasting Corp. v. Cohn*, 420 U.S. 469 (1975), we found unconstitutional a civil damages award entered against a television station for broadcasting the name of a rape-murder victim which the station had obtained from courthouse records. In *Oklahoma Publishing Co. v. Oklahoma County District Court*, 430 U.S. 308 (1977), we found unconstitutional a state court's pretrial order enjoining the media from publishing the name or photograph of an 11–year-old boy in connection with a juvenile proceeding involving that child which reporters had attended. Finally, in *Smith v. Daily Mail Publishing Co.*, 443 U.S. 97 (1979), we found unconstitutional the indict-

---

1. The statute provides in its entirety:

"Unlawful to publish or broadcast information identifying sexual offense victim.—No person shall print, publish, or broadcast, or cause or allow to be printed, published, or broadcast, in any instrument of mass communication the name, address, or other identify-ing fact or information of the victim of any sexual offense within this chapter. An offense under this section shall constitute a misdemeanor of the second degree, punishable as provided in § 775.082, § 775.083, or § 775.084." Fla.Stat. § 794.03 (1987).

ment of two newspapers for violating a state statute forbidding newspapers to publish, without written approval of the juvenile court, the name of any youth charged as a juvenile offender. The papers had learned about a shooting by monitoring a police band radio frequency and had obtained the name of the alleged juvenile assailant from witnesses, the police, and a local prosecutor. * * *

We conclude that imposing damages on appellant for publishing B.J.F.'s name violates the First Amendment, although not for either of the reasons appellant urges. Despite the strong resemblance this case bears to *Cox Broadcasting*, that case cannot fairly be read as controlling here. The name of the rape victim in that case was obtained from courthouse records that were open to public inspection, a fact which Justice White's opinion for the Court repeatedly noted. Significantly, one of the reasons we gave in *Cox Broadcasting* for invalidating the challenged damages award was the important role the press plays in subjecting trials to public scrutiny and thereby helping guarantee their fairness. That role is not directly compromised where, as here, the information in question comes from a police report prepared and disseminated at a time at which not only had no adversarial criminal proceedings begun, but no suspect had been identified.

Nor need we accept appellant's invitation to hold broadly that truthful publication may never be punished consistent with the First Amendment. Our cases have carefully eschewed reaching this ultimate question, mindful that the future may bring scenarios which prudence counsels our not resolving anticipatorily. Indeed, in *Cox Broadcasting*, we pointedly refused to answer even the less sweeping question "whether truthful publications may ever be subjected to civil or criminal liability" for invading "an area of privacy" defined by the State. Respecting the fact that press freedom and privacy rights are both "plainly rooted in the traditions and significant concerns of our society," we instead focused on the less sweeping issue "whether the State may impose sanctions on the accurate publication of the name of a rape victim obtained from public records—more specifically, from judicial records which are maintained in connection with a public prosecution and which themselves are open to public inspection." We continue to believe that the sensitivity and significance of the interests presented in clashes between First Amendment and privacy rights counsel relying on limited principles that sweep no more broadly than the appropriate context of the instant case.

In our view, this case is appropriately analyzed with reference to such a limited First Amendment principle. It is the one, in fact, which we articulated in *Daily Mail* in our synthesis of prior cases involving attempts to punish truthful publication: "[I]f a newspaper lawfully obtains truthful information about a matter of public significance then state officials may not constitutionally punish publication of the information, absent a need to further a state interest of the highest order." According the press the ample protection provided by that principle is supported by at least three separate considerations, in addition to, of course, the overarching " 'public interest, secured by the Constitution, in the dissemination of truth.' "   The cases on which the *Daily Mail* synthesis relied demonstrate these considerations.

First, because the *Daily Mail* formulation only protects the publication of information which a newspaper has "lawfully obtain[ed]," the government retains ample means of safeguarding significant interests upon which publication may impinge, including protecting a rape victim's anonymity. To the extent sensitive information rests in private hands, the government may under some circumstances forbid its nonconsensual acquisition, thereby bringing outside of the *Daily Mail* principle the publication of any information so acquired. To the extent sensitive information is in the government's custody, it has even greater power to forestall or mitigate the injury caused by its release. The government may classify certain information, establish and enforce procedures ensuring its redacted release, and extend a damages remedy against the government or its officials where the government's mishandling of sensitive information leads to its dissemination. Where information is entrusted to the government, a less drastic means than punishing truthful publication almost always exists for guarding against the dissemination of private facts.

A second consideration undergirding the *Daily Mail* principle is the fact that punishing the press for its dissemination of information which is already publicly available is relatively unlikely to advance the interests in the service of which the State seeks to act. It is not, of course, always the case that information lawfully acquired by the press is known, or accessible, to others. But where the government has made certain information publicly available, it is highly anomalous to sanction persons other than the source of its release. We noted this anomaly in *Cox Broadcasting*: "By placing the information in the public domain on official court records, the State must be presumed to have concluded that the public interest was thereby being served." * * *

A third and final consideration is the "timidity and self-censorship" which may result from allowing the media to be punished for publishing certain truthful information. *Cox Broadcasting* noted this concern with overdeterrence in the context of information made public through official court records, but the fear of excessive media self-suppression is applicable as well to other information released, without qualification, by the government. A contrary rule, depriving protection to those who rely on the government's implied representations of the lawfulness of dissemination, would force upon the media the onerous obligation of sifting through government press releases, reports, and pronouncements to prune out material arguably unlawful for publication. This situation could inhere even where the newspaper's sole object was to reproduce, with no substantial change, the government's rendition of the event in question.

Applied to the instant case, the *Daily Mail* principle clearly commands reversal. The first inquiry is whether the newspaper "lawfully obtain[ed] truthful information about a matter of public significance." It is undisputed that the news article describing the assault on B.J.F. was accurate. In addition, appellant lawfully obtained B.J.F.'s name. * * *

The second inquiry is whether imposing liability on appellant pursuant to § 794.03 serves "a need to further a state interest of the highest order." Appellee argues that a rule punishing publication furthers three closely related interests: the privacy of victims of sexual offenses; the physical safety of such victims, who may be targeted for retaliation if their names become known to their assailants; and the goal of encouraging victims of such crimes to report these offenses without fear of exposure.

At a time in which we are daily reminded of the tragic reality of rape, it is undeniable that these are highly significant interests, a fact underscored by the Florida Legislature's explicit attempt to protect these interests by enacting a criminal statute prohibiting much dissemination of victim identities. We accordingly do not rule out the possibility that, in a proper case, imposing civil sanctions for publication of the name of a rape victim might be so overwhelmingly necessary to advance these interests as to satisfy the *Daily Mail* standard. For three independent reasons, however, imposing liability for publication under the circumstances of this case is too precipitous a means of advancing these interests to convince us that there is a "need" within the meaning of the *Daily Mail* formulation for Florida to take this extreme step.

First is the manner in which appellant obtained the identifying information in question. As we have noted, where the government itself provides information to the media, it is most appropriate to assume that the government had, but failed to utilize, far more limited means of guarding against dissemination than the extreme step of punishing truthful speech. That assumption is richly borne out in this case. B.J.F.'s identity would never have come to light were it not for the erroneous, if inadvertent, inclusion by the Department of her full name in an incident report made available in a pressroom open to the public. Florida's policy against disclosure of rape victims' identities, reflected in § 794.03, was undercut by the Department's failure to abide by this policy. Where, as here, the government has failed to police itself in disseminating information, it is clear under *Cox Broadcasting* [*et al.*] that the imposition of damages against the press for its subsequent publication can hardly be said to be a narrowly tailored means of safeguarding anonymity. Once the government has placed such information in the public domain, "reliance must rest upon the judgment of those who decide what to publish or broadcast," and hopes for restitution must rest upon the willingness of the government to compensate victims for their loss of privacy and to protect them from the other consequences of its mishandling of the information which these victims provided in confidence. * * *

A second problem with Florida's imposition of liability for publication is the broad sweep of the negligence *per se* standard applied under the civil cause of action implied from § 794.03. Unlike claims based on the common law tort of invasion of privacy, see Restatement (Second) of Torts § 652D (1977), civil actions based on § 794.03 require no case-by-case findings that the disclosure of a fact about a person's private life was one that a reasonable person would find highly offensive. On the contrary, under the *per se* theory of negligence adopted by the courts below, liability follows automatically from publication. This is so regardless of whether the identity of the victim is already known throughout the community; whether the victim has voluntarily called public attention to the offense; or whether the identity of the victim has otherwise become a reasonable subject of public concern—because, perhaps, questions have arisen whether the victim fabricated an assault by a particular person. Nor is there a scienter requirement of any kind under § 794.03, engendering the perverse result that truthful publications challenged pursuant to this cause of action are less protected by the First Amendment than even the least protected defamatory falsehoods: those involving purely private figures, where liability is evaluated under a standard, usually applied by a jury, of ordinary negligence. We have previously noted the impermissibility of categorical prohibitions upon media access where important First Amendment interests are at stake. More individualized adjudication is no less indispensable where the State, seeking to safeguard the anonymity of crime victims, sets its face against publication of their names.

Third, and finally, the facial underinclusiveness of § 794.03 raises serious doubts about whether Florida is, in fact, serving, with this statute, the significant interests which appellee invokes in support of affirmance. Section 794.03 prohibits the publication of identifying information only if this information appears in an "instrument of mass communication," a term the statute does not define. Section 794.03 does not prohibit the spread by other means of the identities of victims of sexual offenses. An individual who maliciously spreads word of the identity of a rape victim is thus not covered, despite the fact that the communication of such information to persons who live near, or work with, the victim may have consequences as devastating as the exposure of her name to large numbers of strangers. (Appellee acknowledges that § 794.03 would not apply to "the backyard gossip who tells 50 people that don't have to know.")

When a State attempts the extraordinary measure of punishing truthful publication in the name of privacy, it must demonstrate its commitment to advancing this interest by applying its prohibition evenhandedly, to the smalltime disseminator as well as the media giant. Where important First Amendment interests are at stake, the mass scope of disclosure is not an acceptable surrogate for injury. A ban on disclosures effected by "instrument[s] of mass communication" simply cannot be defended on the ground that partial prohibitions may effect partial relief. See *Daily Mail* (statute is insufficiently tailored to interest in protecting anonymity where it restricted only newspapers, not the electronic media or other forms of publication, from identifying juvenile defendants). Without more careful and inclusive precautions against alternative forms of dissemination, we cannot conclude that Florida's selective ban on publication by the mass media satisfactorily accomplishes its stated purpose.

Our holding today is limited. We do not hold that truthful publication is automatically constitutionally protected, or that there is no zone of personal privacy within which the State may protect the individual from intrusion by the press, or even that a State may never punish publication of the name of a victim of a sexual offense. We hold only that where a newspaper publishes truthful information which it has lawfully obtained, punishment may lawfully be imposed, if at all, only when narrowly tailored to a state interest of the highest order, and that no such interest is satisfactorily served by imposing liability under § 794.03 to appellant under the facts of this case. * * *

■ [We omit the opinion of JUSTICE SCALIA, concurring in part and concurring in the judgment.]

■ JUSTICE WHITE, with whom THE CHIEF JUSTICE [REHNQUIST] and JUSTICE O'CONNOR join, dissenting.

"Short of homicide, [rape] is the 'ultimate violation of self.' " *Coker v. Georgia*, 433 U.S. 584, 597 (1977) (opinion of White, J.). For B.J.F., however, the violation she suffered at a rapist's knifepoint marked only the beginning of her ordeal. A week later, while her assailant was still at large, an account of this assault—identifying by name B.J.F. as the victim—was published by *The Florida Star*. As a result, B.J.F. received harassing phone calls, required mental health counseling, was forced to move from her home, and was even threatened with being raped again. Yet today, the Court holds that a jury award of $75,000 to compensate B.J.F. for the harm she suffered due to the Star's negligence is at odds with the First Amendment. I do not accept this result. * * *

Cox Broadcasting stands for the proposition that the State cannot make the press its first line of defense in withholding private information from the public—it cannot ask the press to secrete private facts that the State makes no effort to safeguard in the first place. In this case, however, the State has undertaken "means which avoid [but obviously, not altogether prevent] public documentation or other exposure of private information." No doubt this is why the Court frankly admits that *"Cox Broadcasting . . .* cannot fairly be read as controlling here."

Finding *Cox Broadcasting* inadequate to support its result, the Court relies on *Smith v. Daily Mail* Publishing Co. as its principal authority. But the flat rule from *Daily Mail* on which the Court places so much reliance— "[I]f a newspaper lawfully obtains truthful information . . . then state officials may not constitutionally punish publication of the information, absent a need to further a state interest of the highest order"—was introduced in *Daily Mail* with the cautious qualifier that such a rule was "suggest[ed]" by our prior cases, "[n]one of [which] . . . directly control[led]" in *Daily Mail*. * * *

More importantly, at issue in *Daily Mail* was the disclosure of the name of the perpetrator of an infamous murder of a 15–year-old student. Surely the rights of those accused of crimes and those who are their victims must differ with respect to privacy concerns. That is, whatever rights alleged criminals have to maintain their anonymity pending an adjudication of guilt—and after *Daily Mail*, those rights would seem to be minimal—the rights of crime victims to stay shielded from public view must be infinitely more substantial. *Daily Mail* was careful to state that the "holding in this case is narrow. . . . there is no issue here of privacy." But in this case, there is an issue of privacy—indeed, that is the principal issue—and therefore, this case falls outside of *Daily Mail*'s "rule" (which, as I suggest above, was perhaps not even meant as a rule in the first place).

[Justice White then examined the three "independent reasons" given by Justice Marshall for expanding *Cox Broadcasting* to B.J.F.'s case. Although the newspaper obtained B.J.F.'s name from the sheriff's department pressroom, including her name had been inadvertent and signs in the pressroom explicitly stated that the names of rape victims were not matters of public record.] Florida has done precisely what we suggested, in *Cox Broadcasting*, that States wishing to protect the privacy rights of rape victims might do: "respond [to the challenge] by means which avoid public documentation or other exposure of private information." By amending its public records statute to exempt rape victims names from disclosure, Fla.Stat. § 119.07(3)(h) (1983), and forbidding its officials to release such information, Fla.Stat. § 794.03 (1983), the State has taken virtually every step imaginable to prevent what happened here. This case presents a far cry, then, from *Cox Broadcasting* * * * : here, the State is not asking the media to do the State's job in the first instance. Unfortunately, as this case illustrates, mistakes happen: even when States take measures to "avoid" disclosure, sometimes rape victims' names are found out. As I see it, it is not too much to ask the press, in instances such as this, to respect simple standards of decency and refrain from publishing a victims' name, address, and/or phone number. * * *

NOTE ON THE IMPACT OF *FLORIDA STAR*

What is the status of the Florida statute after the Court's ruling? Why do you think the Court framed its holding so narrowly, rather than extending the principle of *Cox*? In a subsequent case, the Florida Supreme Court struck down another Florida statute that prohibited the identification of a victim of a sex crime in mass communications media. *State v. Globe Communications Corp.*, 648 So.2d 110 (Fl.1994). After this decision, can truthful speech ever invade privacy?

PROBLEM 5–3

BALANCING INTERESTS IN THE REPORTING OF RAPES

How would you draft a statute that accommodates both rape victims' privacy interests and the rights of the press, but that does not perpetuate the stigma of rape? What elements of proof would be required? What would be the permissible defenses? What would constitute a waiver of the cause of action? Would the claim be unique to rape? Consider the following as you draft.

Ellen Willis, Naming Names

Newsday, April 23, 1991.

Over 20 years ago, I was raped. Though I often write about my own experience, it has taken me this long to mention that particular experience in print. Despite my feminist convictions and the passage of time, I still find it hard to do. So it's not lack of empathy with the woman in Palm Beach who has accused a member of the Kennedy family of rape that makes me see the furor over publication of her name as somewhat beside the point. The real issue, it seems to me, is our cultural mythology about rape and the way the press perpetuates it, whether naming the victims or not.

I oppose the media's traditional policy of never identifying rape victims or complainants. To put sex crimes in a special category requiring protective silence is to pander to the belief that a woman who is raped should be ashamed of it, that it is somehow her fault, that she is damaged goods. To keep all rape victims anonymous is to strip them of their individual humanity and make them generic females, in an unnerving parody of what the rapist has done.

This isn't to say, however, that the press should automatically reveal a woman's name. After all, it's hardly unusual for reporters to honor a request for anonymity from a subject who isn't a public figure, whose identity is not crucial to the story and who might be harmed materially or emotionally by disclosure. I just think journalists should approach a rape case as they would any other story that involves a potential conflict between newsworthy information and personal privacy—they should be guided by ethical sensitivity, not by taboos.

Obviously, publishing a rape victim's name with her consent is an ethical and, I would argue, a socially constructive act. When The *Des Moines Register* published the story of Nancy Ziegenmeyer's rape, with her full cooperation, it was a powerful political statement that women should fight the sigma of rape by going public.

But at this historical moment rape victims are more likely to share the feelings of the Palm Beach woman. According to one account in the *New York Post*, which hasn't published her name, the publicity left her "reeling" and "humiliated." (*New York Newsday* has also decreed her anonymity, sparing me a choice.) It's not only that the stigma, like it or not, is real; public exposure of an assault on a woman's sexual being can't help but re-evoke the most odious aspect of rape—its forced intimacy. If the exposure is also forced, it must feel like a terrifying confirmation that her will means nothing.

Like the recent trend toward "outing" closeted gays, the thought of overriding rape victims' feelings to make a feminist political point appalls me. Yet I don't think it works simply to substitute "no identification without consent" for the old blanket taboo.

This solution still implies that rape is uniquely awful and degrading. In fact, there are other equally wrenching situations where the subject of a story—someone who has AIDS for instance—may fear disclosure. In such situations, ethical journalists weigh the subject's feelings heavily. Still, there are always the exceptions, the hard cases.

Ironically, Palm Beach is arguably such a hard case. The coverage of this event has been creepy in more ways than one. Somehow the media have managed the difficult feat of simultaneously portraying William Kennedy Smith, who has not yet been arrested or charged, as a presumptive criminal; his accuser as a bad girl, therefore a presumptive liar; and Ted Kennedy as guilty by association simply for going out drinking with them.

Smith, a public figure only because of his family, has had his name in the headlines, and his picture, with those suspicious-looking eyes, plastered all over the place. In this poisoned atmosphere, the woman's anonymity didn't feel right: It not only contributed to the presumption of Smith's guilt, but reinforced her own image as a designing woman out to victimize the Kennedys.

Still, I'm not giving NBC, *The New York Times*, or the supermarket tabloids that showed them the way any kudos for openness. This outing was politically motivated all right—by sexist and class hostility.

Surrounded by mixed messages, this one came across loud and clear: The Central Park jogger, who was attacked by black and Hispanic kids and had her skull bashed in while in the virtuous act of exercising, deserved to be protected; the Palm Beach woman, a single mother who gets speeding tickets, goes out drinking with her social betters, and can't prove her victimhood with disabling injuries, does not. Rather than demolishing a sexist taboo, the outers merely declared a certain woman unworthy of it. So what else is new?

PART B.   INVASION OF PRIVACY

Oliver W. Sipple v. The Chronicle Publishing Co.
California Court of Appeals, 1984.
154 Cal.App.3d 1040, 201 Cal.Rptr. 665.

■ CALDECOTT, PRESIDING JUDGE.

On September 22, 1975, Sara Jane Moore attempted to assassinate President Gerald R. Ford while the latter was visiting San Francisco, California. Plaintiff Oliver W. Sipple (hereafter appellant or Sipple) who was in the crowd at Union Square, San Francisco, grabbed or struck Moore's arm as the latter was about to fire the gun and shoot at the President. Although no one can be certain whether or not Sipple actually saved the President's life, the assassination attempt did not succeed and Sipple was considered a hero for his selfless action and was subject to significant publicity throughout the nation following the assassination attempt.

Among the many articles concerning the event was a column, written by Herb Caen and published by the *San Francisco Chronicle* on September 24, 1975. The article read in part as follows: "One of the heroes of the day, Oliver 'Bill' Sipple, the ex-Marine who grabbed Sara Jane Moore's arm just as her gun was fired and thereby may have saved the President's life, was the center of midnight attention at the Red Lantern, a Golden Gate Ave. bar he favors. The Rev. Ray Broshears, head of Helping Hands, and Gay Politico, Harvey Milk, who claim to be among Sipple's close friends, describe themselves as 'proud—maybe this will help break the stereotype'. Sipple is among the workers in Milk's campaign for Supervisor."

[Other newspapers picked up the story and, essentially, "outed" Sipple to his family, who were not aware that he was gay. On September 30, 1975, Sipple filed an action against the newspaper, Caen, and others, alleging that the publication constituted the tort of invasion of privacy. The trial judge granted summary judgment to the defendants, and Sipple appealed.]

* * * It is well settled that there are three elements of a cause of action predicated on tortious invasion of privacy. First, the disclosure of the *private facts* must be a *public disclosure*. Second, the facts disclosed must be *private facts*, and not public ones. Third, the matter made public must be one which would be *offensive* and objectionable to a reasonable person of ordinary sensibilities. It is likewise recognized, however, that due to the supreme mandate of the constitutional protection of freedom of the press even a tortious invasion of one's privacy is exempt from liability if the publication of private facts is truthful and newsworthy. The latter proposition finds support primarily in Restatement Second of Torts section 652D which provides that "One who gives publicity to a matter concerning the private life of another is subject to liability to the other for invasion of his privacy, if the matter publicized is of a kind that (a) would be highly offensive to a reasonable person, and (b) is not of legitimate concern to the public."

In interpreting the cited section, the cases and authorities emphasize that the privilege to publicize newsworthy matters incorporated in section 652D is not only immunity accorded by the common law, but also one of constitutional dimension based upon the First Amendment of the United States Constitution. As tersely stated in comment d to section 652D: "When the subject-matter of the publicity is of legitimate public concern, there is no invasion of privacy. [¶] This has now become a rule not just of common law of torts, but of the Federal Constitution as well." * * *

When viewed in light of the aforegoing principles, the summary judgment in this case must be upheld on two grounds. First, as appears from the record properly considered for the purposes of summary judgment, the facts disclosed by the articles were not private facts within the meaning of the law. Second, the record likewise reveals on its face that the publications in dispute were newsworthy and thus constituted a protective shield from liability based upon invasion of privacy.

(A) *The facts published were not private.*

As pointed out earlier, a crucial ingredient of the tort premised upon invasion of one's privacy is a public disclosure of *private facts*, that is the unwarranted publication of intimate details of one's private life which are outside the realm of legitimate public interest. In elaborating on the notion, the cases explain that there can be no privacy with respect to a matter which is already public or which has previously become part of the "public domain." Moreover, it is equally underlined that there is no liability when the defendant merely gives further publicity to information about the plaintiff which is already public or when the further publicity relates to matters which the plaintiff leaves open to the public eye.

The case at bench falls within the aforestated rules. The undisputed facts reveal that prior to the publication of the newspaper articles in question appellant's homosexual orientation and participation in gay community activities had been known by hundreds of people in a variety of cities, including New York, Dallas, Houston, San Diego, Los Angeles and San Francisco. Thus, appellant's deposition shows that prior to the assassination attempt appellant spent a lot of time in "Tenderloin" and "Castro," the well-known gay sections of San Francisco; that he frequented gay bars and other homosexual gatherings in both San Francisco and other cities; that he marched in gay parades on several occasions; that he supported the campaign of Mike Caringi for the election of "Emperor"; that he participated in the coronation of the "Emperor" and sat at Caringi's table on that occasion; that his friendship with Harvey Milk, another prominent gay, was well-known and publicized in gay newspapers; and that his homosexual association and name had been reported in gay magazines (such as *Data Boy, Pacific Coast Times, Male Express*, etc.) several times before the publications in question. In fact, appellant quite candidly conceded that he did not make a secret of his being a homosexual and that if anyone would ask, he would frankly admit that he was gay. In short, since appellant's sexual orientation was already in public domain and since the articles in question did no more than to give further publicity to matters which appellant left open to the eye of the public, a vital element of the tort was missing rendering it vulnerable to summary disposal. * * *

(B) *The publication was newsworthy.*

But even aside from the aforegoing considerations, the summary judgment dismissing the action against respondents was justified on the additional, independent basis that the publication contained in the articles in dispute was newsworthy.

As referred to above, our courts have recognized a broad privilege cloaking the truthful publication of all newsworthy matters. Thus, in *Briscoe v. Reader's Digest Assn., Inc.,* [483 P.2d 34 (Cal.1971)] our Supreme Court stated that a truthful publication is protected if (1) it is newsworthy and (2) it does not reveal facts so offensive as to shock the community notions of decency. While it has been said that the general criteria for determining newsworthiness are (a) the social value of the facts published; (b) the depth of the article's intrusion into ostensibly private affairs; and

(c) the extent to which the individual voluntarily acceded to a position of public notoriety, the cases and authorities further explain that the paramount test of newsworthiness is whether the matter is of legitimate public interest which in turn must be determined according to the community mores. As pointed out in *Virgil v. Time, Inc.* [527 F.2d 1122, 1129 (9th Cir.1975)]: " 'In determining what is a matter of legitimate public interest, account must be taken of the customs and conventions of the community; and in the last analysis what is proper becomes a matter of the community mores. *The line is to be drawn when the publicity ceases to be the giving of information to which the public is entitled, and becomes a morbid and sensational prying into private lives for its own sake*, with which a reasonable member of the public, with decent standards, would say that he had no concern.' " (Emphasis added.) (Accord, Rest., 2d Torts, § 652D, com. h.)

In the case at bench the publication of appellant's homosexual orientation which had already been widely known by many people in a number of communities was not so offensive even at the time of the publication as to shock the community notions of decency. Moreover, and perhaps even more to the point, the record shows that the publications were not motivated by a morbid and sensational prying into appellant's private life but rather were prompted by legitimate political considerations, i.e., to dispel the false public opinion that gays were timid, weak and unheroic figures and to raise the equally important political question whether the President of the United States entertained a discriminatory attitude or bias against a minority group such as homosexuals.[2] Thus appellant's case squarely falls within the language of [*Kapellas v. Kofman*, 459 P.2d 912 (Cal.1969)] in which the California Supreme Court emphasized that "when, [as here] the legitimate public interest in the published information is substantial, a much greater intrusion into an individual's private life will be sanctioned, especially if the individual willingly entered into the public sphere."

Appellant's contention that by saving the President's life he did not intend to enter into the limelight and become a public figure, can be easily answered. In elaborating on involuntary public figures, Restatement Second of Torts section 625D, comment f, sets out in part as follows: "There are other individuals who have not sought publicity or consented to it, but through their own conduct or otherwise have become a legitimate subject of public interest. They have, in other words, become 'news.' ... These persons are regarded as properly subject to the public interest, and publish-

---

2. For example, the *Los Angeles Times* reporters explained the newsworthiness of the publication in the following language: "First, since Sipple publicly performed a heroic act of national and international significance, reporting his connections to the gay community presented information contrary to the stereotype of homosexuals as lacking vigor—a concept apparently much desired to be reported by activist members of the San Francisco gay community.

"Second, the intimation that the President of the United States had refrained from expressing normal gratitude to an individual who perhaps had saved his life raised significant political and social issues as to whether the President entertained discriminatory attitudes toward a minority group, namely, homosexuals."

ers are permitted to satisfy the curiosity of the public as to its heroes, leaders, villains and victims, and those who are closely associated with them. As in the case of the voluntary public figure, the authorized publicity is not limited to the event that itself arouses the public interest, and to some reasonable extent includes publicity given to facts about the individual that would otherwise be purely private."

In summary, appellant's assertion notwithstanding, the trial court could determine as a matter of law that the facts contained in the articles were not private facts within the purview of the law and also that the publications relative to the appellant were newsworthy. Since the record thus fails to present any triable issue of fact, the trial court was justified (if not mandated) in granting summary judgment and dismiss the case against respondents by way of summary procedure. * * *

NOTES ON *SIPPLE* AND THE CONTINUUM OF THE CLOSET

1. *Private Facts and the Continuum of the Closet.* Is an individual's sexual orientation a private fact? Is the occurrence of sexual conduct a private fact? Is there a difference? What criteria could a court use to determine this? Consider Eve Kosofsky Sedgwick's idea of a "continuum of the closet": one may be "out" to one's parents but not one's employer, or to one's friends but not parents, and so forth. Where on the continuum does the "public disclosure" defense to the tort of invasion of privacy start: being out to friends? one's employer? the lesbian and gay subculture? the local community?

Should selective disclosure constitute a forfeiture of privacy? In her discussion of this case, Professor Ruthann Robson wrote:

> Sipple's choice not to come out to his family is legally over-ridden by his activity within his community and his exceptionality to discriminatory stereotypes. Both of these rationales are disturbing. There is no recognition that our communities are in any way unique: the Castro is like suburban Cincinnati, the *Male Express* like the *L.A. Times*. From the standpoint of the rule of law, our communities are simply assimilable. The dominant culture is the only culture; biases of the dominant culture control. Any nonconformance to those biases is noteworthy, newsworthy and part of the public domain. These rationales would limit privacy only to the most closeted and stereotypical lesbian.

Ruthann Robson, *Lesbian (Out)Law: Survival Under the Rule of Law* 74 (1992). Is Robson's implicit claim for uniqueness persuasive?

2. *Sexuality as Newsworthy.* In *Sipple*, the newsworthiness defense swallowed the claim. Will this always be true? If the personal is truly political, is the inclusion in the mass media of personal facts such as those related to sexuality inevitable, perhaps even positive? Is there any measure of the social value of such facts that would place them off-limits, as against a First Amendment-based defense? In a society, such as ours, that is both sex negative and sex obsessed, will sexuality issues always be newsworthy?

What about the identity of a rape victim? In *Ross v. Midwest Communications, Inc.*, 870 F.2d 271 (5th Cir.), *cert. denied*, 493 U.S. 935 (1989), a rape victim sued film makers who had used her first name and shown her former residence in a documentary that contended that a man convicted of another rape was innocent because plaintiff had stated that he was not the man who had raped her, and the details of the two rapes were strikingly similar. The court ruled that the inclusion of her name and the picture of her residence were newsworthy details because they "provide[d] a 'personalized frame of reference that fosters perception and understanding,' and avoid[ed] the loss of credibility that comes with anonymity." *Id.* at 274. When would a rape victim's name not be newsworthy?

3. *Role Reversal?* If one argues that sexual orientation is seldom or never newsworthy, as Sipple did, how does that square with a claim that coming out should be protected as political speech?

NOTE ON OUTING

The unstated assumption behind claims for invasion of privacy and defamation is that the revelation of homosexuality leads to ruin. In 1989, a group of gay activist journalists in New York challenged that assumption and began what came to be called the "outing" of closeted gay men and lesbians. Proponents of outing justify it as a means to promote positive images of gay people by "claiming" accomplished individuals as gay and by shattering stereotypes by revealing that a popular figure is homosexual; and as a means to expose the hypocrisy of secretly gay public officials who oppose equal rights for gay people. All these rationales seemingly apply only to public figures. Consider, however, whether a school teacher or a prominent businessperson in a small town would qualify as public figure. Would such a rationale itself, *ipso facto*, establish a newsworthiness defense if a victim of outing sued for invasion of privacy? How do these concerns apply to the outing of a heterosexual person's sexual relationships outside of marriage? For vigorous defenses of outing, see Michelangelo Signorile, *Queer in America* (1993), Richard D. Mohr, *Gay Ideas: Outing and Other Controversies* (1992), and Larry Gross, *Contested Closets: The Politics and Ethics of Outing* (1993).

One commentator has argued that a politically-motivated outing should be immunized under the law because of its relevance to self-governance interests, but that "role model outing" should be actionable. John P. Elwood, "Outing, Privacy and the First Amendment," 102 *Yale L.J.* 747 (1992). What are the strengths and weaknesses of that approach? Into which category does the *Sipple* case fall? Elwood believes that a public figure's homosexuality should have to be proven relevant to a matter of legitimate public concern other than the general issue of the role of gays in society. *Id.* at 776. Do you agree? Without such a limiting principle, is there anything left of the invasion of privacy tort, especially for public figures? Should there be?

Consider the following example of an outing.

Richard Rouilard, Comment.

The Advocate, August 27, 1991.*

Outing is a weapon of last resort. * * * Previously, we [*The Advocate*] never outed those who acquiesced to anti-gay activities, understanding that all of us have to make some accommodations in a principally heterosexual world and that some progress could, albeit slowly, be made by closeted homosexuals in high places. * * *

But what of those in very high positions, who are able to affect policy changes, and who do nothing? Can we afford to suffer these Uncle Toms in this increasingly violent time?

In almost all cases, yes. They are our people, whether we like it or not, whether they like it or not. But no longer can we abide *every* omission to act. We cannot support the acquiescence of Pete Williams, the assistant secretary of defense for public affairs, to the policies of the most homophobic department of the U.S. government. Too many gays and lesbians have been harmed too egregiously. We commit ourselves to this singular instance of outing in the name of the 12,966 lesbian and gay soldiers who have been outed by the military since 1982. * * *

Deciding to out Pete Williams did not require us to search our souls very long. * * * Pete Williams is not the innocent victim of rabid gay activists. We're talking about a man who knowingly assists in the promotion of policies designed to thoroughly undermine the community in which, part-time, he lives. All reports confirm that Williams has never once interceded on behalf of gay and lesbian soldiers. He remains silent. We choose not to be, and we have that right. We censure. * * *

There is a national distaste for gay and lesbian rights. In newsrooms around the country, most editors will not equate the gay and lesbian struggle with that of blacks, Hispanics or other minorities. The reason most editors will not participate in outing on any basis, we understand, is that labeling someone as homosexual is just too disgraceful a thing to do to someone. * * *

Pete Williams knows that the military's blanket exclusion of gays and lesbians is wrong. And that his silent complicity encourages the continuation of this vile and despotic activity. The U.S. military is awash in lies and hypocrisy. Williams is the proof that we are not perverts, liable to be blackmailed at every turn, incapable of containing our sexual urges when necessary—all that stereotypical bullshit that is used to justify this purge of good soldiers. For much less than the very same activities Williams has been involved in, many of these soldiers have had their lives ruined.

We do not want to ruin Pete Williams's life. We are asking Pete Williams to confirm what is true: that he has security clearance on the highest level; that he is an excellent and effective spokesman; that he has the confidence of the President, the secretary of defense, and his coworkers; and that his sexuality has not interfered with his position.

Except when he hides it.

PART C.   DEFAMATION

Kathleen Hayes v. Roger W. Smith, Jr. and Samantha Smith

Colorado Court of Appeals, 1991.
832 P.2d 1022.

■ Opinion by JUDGE DUBOFSKY.*

[Plaintiff, Kathleen Hayes, and defendants, Roger and Samantha Smith, were active participants in a conservative Christian community. Plaintiff and Samantha Smith jointly created a corporation to further business ideas related to their common religious outlook but the partnership degenerated into personal bitterness. Defendants made the following allegations against Hayes to her employer, the superintendent of schools: (1) plaintiff had tried to establish a homosexual relationship with Samantha Smith; (2) plaintiff had "proposed marriage" to Samantha Smith; and (3) plaintiff had in the past been discharged from a teaching position. Hayes sued for defamation and won $26,000 in damages.]

Defendants argue that the trial court erred in determining that the statements accusing plaintiff of homosexual conduct were slanderous *per se* and in, therefore, instructing the jury on that basis. We agree.

Cases in various jurisdictions have reached different conclusions in deciding whether statements which falsely accuse a person of being a homosexual or engaging in homosexual activity constitute slander *per se*. *Compare Moricoli v. Schwartz*, 361 N.E.2d 74 (Ill.App.1977) (statements referring to a singer as a "fag" held to be slander *per quod*, and not slander *per se*) and *Boehm v. American Bankers Insurance Group*, 557 So.2d 91 (Fla.Dist.Ct.App.1990) ("The modern view considering the issue, has not found statements regarding sexual preference to constitute slander *per se* let alone intrinsic evidence of express malice.") with *Manale v. New Orleans*, 673 F.2d 122 (5th Cir.1982) (police roll call statement referring to plaintiff as "ya little fruit" held to be slanderous *per se*) and *Mazart v. State*, 441 N.Y.S.2d 600 (N.Y.Sup.Ct.1981) (inasmuch as certain homosexual activity was still a crime in New York, reference to plaintiffs as being "members of a gay community" was slanderous *per se*). Our analysis of the present state of the law leads us to conclude that the *per se* classification is inappropriate for the statements at issue here.

Historically, defamation was actionable *per se* only if the defamatory remark imputed a criminal offense; a venereal or loathsome and communicable disease; improper conduct of a lawful business; or unchastity by a

---

* [Eds.] The author of this opinion, Judge Frank Dubofsky, is the spouse of Jean Dubofsky, who was lead counsel for plaintiffs in *Romer v. Evans* (Chapter 1, Section 3[B]).

woman. Restatement (First) of Torts § 569 (1983), and *Gertz v. Robert Welch, Inc.*, 418 U.S. 323 (1974).

However, the Restatement (Second) of Torts [§§ 571–574] reflects a trend toward limiting the *per se* category of slander to those instances in which the defamatory remark is apparent from the publication itself without reference to extrinsic facts. As to the specific matter at issue here, the Restatement (Second) of Torts expressly left open the issue whether an accusation of homosexuality fell into the *per se* category.

The primary advantage to a plaintiff claiming slander *per se* is that certain damages are presumed if the statement is so categorized, *e.g.*, loss of reputation, and therefore, need not be proved. This presumption has been considered desirable because injuries such as loss of reputation can be difficult to prove since the recipients of the information may be reluctant to testify that the publication affected their relationship with the plaintiff and because the words may affect the recipients' view of the relationship in subtle ways of which the recipient is not necessarily aware.

Another advantage to a *per se* classification is that the plaintiff need not prove the statements were defamatory within the context in which they were made. In *Gertz* the court was also concerned that *per se* classifications inhibit and punish freedom of speech by making it too easy to prove defamation and damages.

In *Gertz*, the majority indicated that *per se* classifications and presumed damages, even where constitutional, are not favored. Indeed, the *Gertz* court held that, as to a public official or public figure, a presumed damage award without proof of reckless or malicious conduct violates the First Amendment rights of the publisher of the false statement. [The trial court determined plaintiff to be a public figure.]

In *Gertz*, however, the court emphasized that, even though presumed damages may be unavailable, plaintiff can recover for any actual injuries caused by the defamation. The *Gertz* court stated:

> Suffice it to say that actual injury is not limited to out-of-pocket loss. Indeed the more customary types of actual harm inflicted by defamatory falsehood include impairment of reputation and standing in the community, personal humiliation, and mental anguish and suffering.

These non-economic and non-reputation damages can be awarded without an initial or predicate determination awarding damages because of either harm to reputation or economic loss. * * *

There are also several other factors which bear on our decision to conclude that accusations of homosexuality are not slanderous *per se*.

First, the fact that sexual activities between consenting adults of the same sex are no longer illegal in Colorado tends to indicate that an accusation of being a homosexual is not of such a character as to be slanderous *per se*.

Second, if a person is falsely accused of belonging in a category of persons considered deserving of social approbation, *i.e.*, thief, murderer, prostitute, etc., it is generally the court's determination as to whether such accusation is considered slander *per se* so that damages are presumed. A court should not classify homosexuals with those miscreants who have engaged in actions that deserve the reprobation and scorn which is implicitly a part of the slander/libel *per se* classifications.

For a characterization of a person to warrant a *per se* classification, it should, without equivocation, expose the plaintiff to public hatred or contempt. However, there is no empirical evidence in this record demonstrating that homosexuals are held by society in such poor esteem. Indeed, it appears that the community view toward homosexuals is mixed. *See* Denver Revised Municipal Code 28–91, et seq. (1990); Boulder Revised Code 12–1–2, et seq. (1981); Colorado Executive Order In Regard to Human Rights (Colo. Dec. 10, 1990). * * *

Although we agree that, in light of plaintiff's showing of malicious or reckless conduct by defendants, there is no constitutional prohibition against these false accusations of homosexuality being treated as slander *per se*, we, nevertheless, are unwilling to do so. We reach this conclusion because of the *Gertz* hostility to expanding the scope of defamation *per se* and because there are serious doubts whether homosexuality meets the criteria for such a classification. We, therefore, reverse the trial court on this issue. * * *

Janet Nazeri v. Missouri Valley College

Supreme Court of Missouri, 1993.
860 S.W.2d 303.

■ PRICE, JUDGE.

[Janet Nazeri was employed as Director of Teacher Education in the Missouri Department of Elementary and Secondary Education. Her duties included chairing the Department's teacher evaluation teams and visiting college campuses to conduct such evaluations. Responding in a newspaper interview to Nazeri's negative evaluation of the college's teacher education program, Dennis Spellmann, Vice–President of Missouri Valley College, described Nazeri as incompetent, out to get the college, prejudiced against the college, and opposed to church schools having education programs. He also asserted that "Janet Nazeri lives with S____ A____ , who is a well known homosexual and has lived with her for years", and that "You know Ms. Nazeri left her husband and children to live with S____ A____ ." Although these and other statements were not published, Nazeri alleged they became public knowledge.

[Nazeri sued Spellman and the college for defamation, alleging that the statements were untrue and damaged her personal and professional reputation and employment. After these events transpired, she was relieved of she responsibilities as chair of the evaluation teams and was prevented from completing the evaluation of Missouri Valley College and from performing the preliminary work for an evaluation of Lindenwood College. Count II of the complaint pleaded slander *per se*, based upon the allegation that the remarks imputed unchastity, adultery, homosexuality, and criminal conduct. Count I pleaded slander *per quod*, further alleging injury to appellant's reputation, employment, professional standing, and emotional harm.]

At common law, slander *per se* encompassed false statements that the plaintiff was guilty of a crime, afflicted with a loathsome disease, or unchaste, as well as false statements that concerned the plaintiff's ability to engage in his or her occupation or business. In such cases the plaintiff was not required to plead damages, as damages were presumed from the nature of the defamation. Where the words were not actionable as slander *per se*, the tort was referred to as slander *per quod* and the plaintiff was required to plead and prove, in addition, "special damages." Special damages in this sense meant a loss of money or of some advantage capable of being assessed in monetary value, such as the loss of a marriage, employment, income, profits, or even gratuitous hospitality.

These classifications do not correspond exactly to those found in libel law. There, *per se* referred to a statement whose defamatory nature was apparent upon the face of the publication, whereas *per quod* indicated a statement that required resort to extrinsic facts in order to become defamatory. Libel *per se* was actionable without proof of damages. Libel *per quod*, by analogy to slander *per quod*, required proof of special damages. Adding to the confusion was the fact that many courts permitted libel *per quod* to be actionable without proof of special damages if it imputed a matter that would constitute slander *per se* if the statement had been spoken.

The distinction between *per se* and *per quod* causes of action derived from the ancient conflict of jurisdiction between the royal and ecclesiastical courts of England. Initially, slander was the province of the ecclesiastical courts. The royal courts had jurisdiction only over those claims that could be shown to have resulted in "temporal," as opposed to "spiritual," injury. This is the origin of the requirement to prove "special damages" in the form of an actual out-of-pocket loss in all cases where such damages cannot be conclusively presumed. With the demise of the ecclesiastical courts, the rationale for this distinction evaporated—and so did the venue for defamation claims that did not result in direct economic losses. Nonetheless, by this time the presumed damages/special damages duality was entrenched in the very definition of the tort. As a result, even though libel and slander have evolved to the point where modern law combines them as the generic tort of defamation, the causes of action themselves have retained both the *per se/per quod* designation and many of the characteristics of the old common law torts.

The consequences of this anachronism were of more than academic interest. The presumed damages/special damages distinction controlled the right of plaintiffs to bring a defamation claim, even though it bore little relationship to either the magnitude of a plaintiff's injury or the wrongfulness of a defendant's conduct. It also exposed some defendants to liability that might be far in excess of the actual injury caused. * * *

* * * Missouri revised its MAI [jury] instructions for libel and slander in 1980. * * * The instructions result in shifting the historic slander *per se/per quod* duality to a duality that distinguishes between comments regarding public matters that are constitutionally protected and comments regarding private matters. * * *

Counts I and II rest upon the same alleged defamatory remarks. Paragraph 41 of Count II maintains that the statements portray plaintiff:

> ... as an unchaste woman, a woman engaged in illegal and immoral acts, and a person who abandoned her home, spouse and family, as well as portraying plaintiff as one engaged in adulterous and criminal conduct. All such statements being slander *per se.* * * *

The alleged defamatory remarks can be fairly divided into two categories. Appellant has alleged statements attacking her professional competence and integrity and statements attacking her sexual activities. [Going to professional competence included the statements that Nazeri was incompetent and "out to get" Missouri Valley College in particular and private colleges in general and that Nazeri was involved in a conspiracy with S____ A____ to use plaintiff's professional position to effect a bad educational program evaluation.]

Respondent's alleged remarks accuse appellant outright of a lack of skill and fitness to perform her official duties. They portray her as incompetent and prejudiced. Moreover, the accusation that appellant was involved in a conspiracy to "effect a bad education program evaluation" of the College questions her integrity and imputes misconduct in the line of her calling, by suggesting that she is willing to abuse her official position in order to advance her own personal agenda. Under traditional defamation law such statements are slanderous *per se.*

As to the remarks attacking plaintiff's sexual activities, it is alleged that Spellmann stated that "Janet Nazeri lives with S____ A____ , who is a well known homosexual and has lived with her for years", and that "You know Ms. Nazeri left her husband and children to live with S____ A____ ", and that he "would not tolerate fags on campus."

Respondents contend that the remarks pleaded in the petition do not insinuate that appellant is a homosexual, an adulteress, or an unchaste person; that she left her husband and family; or that she was involved in criminal activities, as the petition alleges. They also assert any references to homosexuality allude only to appellant's roommate, and therefore they are not defamatory of appellant personally. * * *

Although respondents' argument has technical merit, an objective reading simply does not allow these words an innocent sense. Respondent's comments clearly insinuate that appellant is a homosexual and an adulteress. In our vernacular, "living with" somebody is a common euphemism for a sexual relationship. The allegation that appellant "left" her husband and children to live with a "well known homosexual" would most obviously and naturally be interpreted to mean that appellant abandoned her family for the purpose of engaging in an adulterous and unchaste relationship with a lesbian woman. Moreover, the comments refer to appellant by name.

An allegation of unchastity is one of the four traditional categories of slander *per se*. In addition, we have a statute that makes it actionable "to publish falsely and maliciously, in any manner whatsoever, that any person has been guilty of fornication or adultery." Thus, the statements pleaded are actionable insofar as they impute adultery and unchastity.

The parties disagree as to whether a false imputation of homosexuality is slanderous *per se*. The few courts that have considered this issue are sharply divided. Some have held that an allegation of homosexuality is defamatory *per se*, in that it implies immorality, unchastity, or criminal conduct.

Other courts, citing the ongoing evolution of our social mores, have come to the contrary conclusion and require proof of damages as a condition of recovery. It is undisputed, however, that an imputation of homosexuality is "at least reasonably susceptible of a defamatory meaning."

The harm inflicted by defamation is particularly sensitive to the characteristics and situation of the injured party and of the society that surrounds him or her. Attitudes change slowly and unevenly among different groups. Despite the efforts of many homosexual groups to foster greater tolerance and acceptance, homosexuality is still viewed with disfavor, if not outright contempt, by a sizeable proportion of our population. Moreover, engaging in deviant sexual intercourse with another person of the same sex is still a class A misdemeanor in this state. Sec. 566.090, RSMo 1986. We hold that a false allegation of homosexuality is defamatory in Missouri.

Furthermore, the "unchastity" category of slander per se has been generalized by our court of appeals to make actionable any false allegation of "serious sexual misconduct." We agree with this approach. Matters of sexuality and sexual conduct are intensely private, intensely sensitive, and a false public statement concerning them is particularly harmful. In this society, an untruthful declaration concerning homosexual orientation must be considered as damaging to reputation as one concerning adulterous conduct. * * *

NOTES ON DEFAMATION LAW AND ISSUES OF SEXUALITY

1. *Per Se Rules and the Line Between Minority and Scandalous Sexuality.* The law's traditional recognition of slander or libel *per se* amounts to taking judicial notice of both the defendant's malice and the damage to the plaintiff by a particular kind of statement. What kinds of statements should fall within the scope of a *per se* rule? As the opinions you read indicate, state courts that have addressed the issue are split on whether assertions of homosexuality should be treated as defamatory *per se*. As a judge in Colorado, for example, how and by what criteria would you resolve that question? How would a Colorado judge classify the assertion that a person has AIDS? Dates adolescents? Engages in sadomasochistic sex? Recall Gayle

Rubin's "Thinking Sex" [Chapter 3, Section 2(B)], which sets forth a hierarchy of social approval for an array of sexual practices.

2. *Truth, Reputation, and Identity.* Truth is an affirmative defense to a defamation claim. If you were counsel for the defendants in either *Hayes* or *Nazeri*, how would you go about trying to prove that the plaintiff is lesbian? What would your strategy be if you were counsel for plaintiff? If you were a juror, what evidence would be necessary to persuade you?

What are the similarities and differences between the concepts of reputation and identity? In treating assertions of homosexuality as defamation *per se*, for example, isn't the law protecting heterosexual identity? If identity is a prized and central component of one's personhood, that must be as true for heterosexual as homosexual identity. Are there dangers with such protection for identity? Compare Cheryl I. Harris, "Whiteness as Property," 106 *Harv. L.Rev.* 1707 (1993). For an argument that the goal of cultural pluralism as applied to the power to create and re-create social meanings should weaken the claim of individuals to control even the commercial appropriations of their names and images, see Michael Madow, "Private Ownership of Public Image: Popular Culture and Publicity Rights," 81 *Calif. L. Rev.* 125 (1993).

3. *Distinguishing the Cases—The Relevance of Sodomy Laws?* Can *Hayes* and *Nazeri* be distinguished simply on the basis of each state's criminal law? Colorado repealed its sodomy law, while Missouri has not. See *State v. Walsh*, 713 S.W.2d 508 (Mo.1986) (en banc) (upholding Missouri's sodomy law against constitutional attack but reserving issue of whether consensual sodomy can be criminalized). On the other hand, the North Carolina Court of Appeals held that "referring to a person as 'gay' or 'bisexual' is not tantamount to charging that individual with commission of a crime" violative of that state's sodomy law. *Hunter v. Fiumara*, 442 S.E.2d 572, 576 (N.C.App.1994). Citing a later-reversed panel decision in one of the gay military cases, the court reasoned that "the label of 'gay' or 'bisexual' does not carry with it an automatic reference to any particular sexual activity; indeed, it does not necessarily connote sexual activity at all, but rather inclination or preference." *Id.* How would you analyze the relationship between sodomy laws and defamation?

Robert McCune v. Rose Neitzel

Nebraska Supreme Court, 1990.
235 Neb. 754, 457 N.W.2d 803.

■ FAHRNBRUCH, JUSTICE.

[Plaintiff, Robert L. McCune, appealed a district judge's order denying him the benefit of a $25,350 verdict rendered by a jury in his favor because he had been slandered. Finding plaintiff's appeal meritorious and defendant's cross-appeal not, the Supreme Court reinstated the verdict.]

McCune, a single, 27–year-old man, was raised in Springfield, Nebraska, which has a population of 800 inhabitants. Since the age of 15, the plaintiff at various times had been employed in the sprinkler business on a part-time and full-time basis. In March 1986, McCune began employment with a Gretna business owned by his brother. McCune's primary duties consisted of selling residential lawn sprinkler systems and managing the installation crews. The company operated within a 100–mile radius of Gretna.

During July 1987, the defendant's sister, Lois Keyes, was bedridden due to paralysis on her left side caused by a stroke. Patricia J. Dieleman was employed as a certified nurse's aide assigned by her employer to assist Keyes in her home. The plaintiff's mother, Betty Holz, with whom Dieleman shared a common employer, was [also] a home health aide.

On the evening of July 8, 1987, * * * Keyes' daughter, informed Keyes and Neitzel that she knew a friend of McCune's who was dying of AIDS. While Neitzel was visiting Keyes at her home the following afternoon, Keyes told Neitzel that she did not want Holz to take care of her because she was told that Holz' son had AIDS. Shortly thereafter, when Dieleman entered the room to attend to Keyes, Keyes, Dieleman, and Neitzel discussed Dieleman's coworkers with whom she was familiar. During the course of the conversation, Neitzel asked Dieleman if she knew the plaintiff's mother. After Dieleman indicated that she knew McCune's mother, Keyes became upset and stated that she did not want Holz in her home. When Dieleman asked why, Neitzel responded, "Didn't you know her son, Bobbie, has AIDS?" Dieleman thereupon asked, "Bobbie McCune has AIDS?" and Neitzel said, "Yes." Neitzel testified that she stated, "Lois said Bobbie McCune was in the hospital with AIDS." McCune was not afflicted with AIDS.

Dieleman testified that she was shocked when Neitzel made the statement to her. After Dieleman stated that she would have to warn somebody, Neitzel replied that she would warn her children if they were associating with a person that had AIDS. Later that same day, Dieleman reported Neitzel's remarks to a friend of hers and to McCune's mother. Neitzel testified that she spoke of the July 9 events with Keyes' seven daughters, her own husband, her sister, her brother, and her four sons.

The plaintiff testified that after he became aware of Neitzel's statement, he believed that people would regard him differently. McCune avoided Springfield, where he had previously visited his mother and friends at least two times per week. Furthermore, McCune, due to embarrassment, avoided some family gatherings. He testified that one Springfield resident confronted him regarding AIDS.

There was evidence that McCune was a very good employee of his brother's until approximately the third week of July 1987, when his productivity declined dramatically. McCune testified that he was having problems with the workers he supervised because of the rumor that he was suffering from AIDS. McCune's brother informed him near the end of July that the installation crews which the plaintiff managed had lost respect for him due to rumors in the community and that he had to resign or be fired. At that time, McCune resigned his job. The plaintiff eventually left the

Springfield area. He was able to find new employment in Ames, Iowa, commencing on April 1, 1988. The job in Ames entailed the same type of work in which the plaintiff was formerly engaged with his brother's company.

For about a month beginning the middle of July 1987, the plaintiff drank continuously. McCune had received alcohol abuse treatment in January 1987 and had remained sober until July 13 or 14. The plaintiff sought professional counseling and attended Alcoholics Anonymous meetings, after which he ceased drinking alcohol. McCune testified that it was a combination of factors in his life, including the AIDS rumors, which caused him to start drinking again. He also suffered from headaches and sleeplessness, was lethargic, and gained weight.

McCune filed a petition on September 24, 1987, alleging that Neitzel had falsely accused him of having AIDS. In her answer, Neitzel denied making any such statements. After trial, the jury returned a verdict in favor of McCune. * * *

Neitzel's first assignment of error claims the trial court erred in failing to properly instruct the jury on the law of slander per se. Defendant contends the trial court should have included her proposed instruction that read:

> Under Nebraska Law, language is actionable, i.e., slanderous per se, if by its nature and obvious meaning, it falsely imputes to another an existing venereal disease or other loathsome and communicable disease.

> In determining whether particular language is defamatory, words complained of cannot be isolated and must be considered in the context of the entire recital or verbal exchange.

> Language alleged to be defamatory, must be interpreted in its ordinary and popular sense, rather than in a technical manner. * * *

Without passing on the precision of the instructions given by the court, we hold that it would have been improper for the court to have included the defendant's slander per se instruction with those given to the jury. Whether a statement is actionable per se is a matter of law for the court. In a slander per se action where the statement is clear and unambiguous, the issue the jury is to determine is not whether a statement is defamatory but whether the statement was made by the defendant. Given the narrow issue Neitzel raises with regard to the trial court's instructions, the defendant's first assignment of error is meritless.

[The court also rejected Neitzel's second assertion of error, that the trial judge had not allowed her to impeach McCune for testifying that a friend of his had died of pneumonia and not AIDS. Neitzel's offer of proof was that McCune admitted to a coworker that his best friend died of AIDS. The appeals court held that the accuracy of this assertion had nothing to do with the slander and defamation issues on appeal. For similar procedural reasons, the appeals court rejected Neitzel's assertion that the trial court erroneously prohibited her from inquiring about, or making reference to, the sexual orientation of plaintiff or any other witness. Neitzel's final assignment of error maintained that the trial court erred in failing to sustain her motions for directed verdict at the close of plaintiff's case and again at the close of defendant's case.]

Defendant first contends that plaintiff was required to prove that her statements were made with malicious intent or ill will. Neitzel is correct that malice in the common-law sense of the term means hate, spite, or ill will toward the person about whom a statement has been published. However, proof of common-law malice is at issue only when truth or a conditional privilege has been asserted by the declarant. In the defendant's answer, she did not allege truth or conditional privilege as a defense. Instead, she relied upon denials of McCune's allegations. In this defamation action, truth or conditional privilege must be pled as an affirmative defense. Since Neitzel did not so plead, malice was not at issue in this case.

Neitzel also argues that since McCune failed to present any evidence that other individuals thought any less of him or had a lower opinion of him because of the remarks she made, she was entitled to have her motions for directed verdict granted. In a suit for slander per se, no proof of any actual harm to reputation or any other damage is required for the recovery of either nominal or substantial damages. "By definition, statements constituting slander per se are unambiguous in their defamatory meaning and do not require proof of extraneous facts." *Hennis v. O'Connor* [388 N.W.2d 470, 476 (Neb.1986)].

The defendant further contends that the trial court should have directed a verdict in her favor because the conversation she had with Keyes was private and she did not expect it to be repeated outside the family home. However, one who puts a libel or slander in circulation is liable for any subsequent publications that are the natural consequence of his or her act. Similarly, in proving a publication, a plaintiff is not required to show that the slander was made known to the public generally. It is enough that the plaintiff show that it was orally communicated to a single person other than the plaintiff. Neitzel also argues that plaintiff presented no evidence showing the rumors originated with or were disseminated by her. The record reflects, however, that Neitzel admittedly told at least one other person that McCune had AIDS. In addition, one who repeats or otherwise republishes defamatory matter is subject to liability as if he or she originally published it.

Viewing all evidence in favor of McCune as true and drawing all reasonable inferences therefrom, the trial court did not err in denying Neitzel's motions for a directed verdict. Neitzel's assignment of error is meritless.

As indicated, the trial court in part granted Neitzel's motion for a new trial. Finding that the $25,350 verdict in favor of McCune was awarded under the influence of passion and prejudice and in disregard of the evidence, the trial court granted a new trial on the issue of damages alone. McCune appeals from that order, claiming that there was sufficient competent evidence to support the jury verdict. In support of this, the plaintiff refers to his lost wages and benefits, physical and mental suffering, and impairment of reputation. * * *

In an action for defamation, the damages which may be recovered are (1) general damages for harm to reputation; (2) special damages; (3) damages for mental suffering; and (4) if none of these are proven, nominal damages. * * *

McCune testified that after the slander was perpetrated by Neitzel, he noticed that people in Springfield were less friendly and that he "felt like people would look at [him] like [he] was an outcast. . . . " There was evidence that the installation crews which McCune managed lost respect for him due to the rumors circulating in Springfield concerning his affliction with AIDS. A resident of Springfield confronted McCune regarding the statement concerning AIDS. McCune testified that due to the AIDS rumor, he avoided Springfield, where he had previously made visits to his mother and friends on at least two occasions per week. There was evidence that McCune did not attend some family gatherings because of the situation. The plaintiff testified that he was forced to leave the Springfield area in order to pursue his career.

As indicated, the record further reflects the plaintiff's mental suffering. After McCune became aware of Neitzel's statement, he dwelt on it for weeks, cognizant that Neitzel was very active in the community. Consequently, McCune isolated himself. He suffered from stress, sleeplessness, headaches, lethargy, and weight gain. McCune's therapist testified that the plaintiff felt ostracized by the community, was concerned about the rumors concerning him, and was having a difficult time in facing these problems. Significantly, the Omaha–Springfield area was an area McCune liked very much and was where he was raised, had always lived except when away at college, worked, and wished to remain.

In regard to special damages, there was evidence from which the jury could have concluded that the slander was the proximate cause of McCune's employment being terminated. McCune testified that after he left his brother's employment he actively sought permanent employment and was not able to secure such employment until April 1, 1988, with a firm in Ames, Iowa. * * *

After reviewing the record, we conclude that the verdict of $25,350 does not shock the judicial conscience and that the verdict was not the result of passion, prejudice, mistake, or some other means not apparent in the record. Thus, the trial court abused its discretion in sustaining the defendant's motion for a new trial on the issue of damages. * * *

NOTE ON SEXUALITY–BASED SPEECH AND INTENTIONAL INFLICTION OF EMOTIONAL DISTRESS

Even if it had been true, the sort of malicious gossip in *McCune* might have supported a cause of action for intentional infliction of emotional distress, a tort in most jurisdictions. Although the tort requires proof of either reckless or intentional statements causing severe emotional distress to the plaintiff, this tort does avoid the need to prove either falsity of the statement or invasion of privacy. Should Pete Williams have a cause of action against *The Advocate* for outing him?

Should outing speech ever be subject to tort claims on such a theory? In *Hustler Magazine v. Falwell*, 485 U.S. 46 (1988), the Supreme Court ruled that the Reverend Jerry Falwell, founder of the Moral Majority, could not recover against *Hustler Magazine* for intentional infliction of emotional distress for publication of a parody in which Falwell "states that his 'first time' was during a drunken incestuous rendezvous with his mother in an outhouse." The Court concluded that there was no principled standard for distinguishing between the portrayal of Falwell and traditional political satire, and that the state's interest in protecting public figures from intentional emotional distress was not sufficient to outweigh a First Amendment right to publish non-defamatory (because inherently incredible) ridicule.

The Alabama Supreme Court denied recovery to a non-public figure who was called, over the telephone, "as queer as a three-dollar bill." *Logan v. Sears, Roebuck & Co.*, 466 So.2d 121 (Ala.1985). The court reasoned:

> We are unwilling to say that the use of the word "queer" to describe a homosexual is atrocious and intolerable in civilized society. We recognize that there are other words favored by the homosexual community in describing themselves, but the word "queer" has been used for a long time by those outside that community. It has been in use longer than the term "gay," which has recently become the most frequently used term to describe homosexuals.

> Since Logan is admittedly a homosexual, can it be said realistically that being described as "queer" should cause him shame or humiliation? We think not. In order to create a cause of action, the conduct must be such that would cause mental suffering, shame, or humiliation to a person of ordinary sensibilities, not conduct which would be considered unacceptable merely by homosexuals.

Id. at 123–24. Would it be constitutional under the First Amendment for Alabama to enact a statute making it a tort or a hate crime to call someone a "queer" with the intent of wounding their feelings? Consider the next section.

SECTION 3

HATE SPEECH

Women, gay people, transvestites, transsexuals, and other sex or gender minorities are frequently victims of "hate speech." Hate speech might include catcalls, slurs, and demeaning comments, any speech that is viciously inspired and hurtful to the recipient as a woman, gay person, and so forth. Hate speech might be more narrowly defined to include only vicious speech that is likely to "incite" a breach of the peace. The Supreme Court in *Chaplinsky v. New Hampshire*, 315 U.S. 568 (1942), held that the state could regulate "fighting words" whose utterance threatened a breach of the peace.

Should the state try to regulate hate speech, either narrowly or broadly defined? If it should, what kinds of regulations would be constitutional, if any? Consider the issue, first, from the arguments for regulating racist speech, where most of the debate and litigation have focused. Then consider whether sexist or anti-homosexual speech represents a better or worse scenario for state regulation.

Mari J. Matsuda, Public Response to Racist Speech: Considering the Victim's Story

In *Words That Wound: Critical Race Theory, Assaultive Speech, and the First Amendment* 17, 25–26, 34–36, 37–38 (1993).*

Research in the psychology of racism suggests a related effect of racist hate propaganda: At some level, no matter how much both victims and well-meaning dominant-group members resist it, racial inferiority is planted in our minds as an idea that may hold some truth. The idea is improbable and abhorrent, but because it is presented repeatedly, it is there before us. "Those people" are lazy, dirty, sexualized, money-grubbing, dishonest, inscrutable, we are told. We reject the idea, but the next time we sit next to one of "those people" the dirt message, the sex message, is triggered. We stifle it, reject it as wrong, but it is there, interfering with our perception and interaction with the person next to us. In conducting research for this Article, I read an unhealthy number of racist statements. A few weeks after reading about a "dotbusters" campaign against immigrants from India, I passed by an Indian woman on my campus. Instead of thinking, "What a beautiful sari," the first thought that came into my mind was "dotbusters." Only after setting aside the hate message could I move on to my own thoughts. The propaganda I read had taken me one step back from casually treating a fellow brown-skinned human being as that, rather than as someone distanced from myself. For the victim, similarly, the angry rejection of the message of inferiority is coupled with absorption of the message. When a dominant-group member responds favorably, there is a moment of relief—the victims of hate messages do not always believe in their insides that they deserve decent treatment. This obsequious moment is degrading and dispiriting when the self-aware victim acknowledges it.

Psychologists and sociologists have done much to document the effects of racist messages on both victims and dominant-group members. Writers of color have given us graphic portrayals of what life is like for victims of racist propaganda. From the victim's perspective racist hate messages cause real damage.

If the harm of racist hate messages is significant, and the truth value marginal, the doctrinal space for regulation of such speech is a possibility. An emerging international standard seizes this possibility. * * *

In the area of commerce and industrial relations, expression is frequently limited. False statements about products, suggestions that prices be fixed, opinions about the value of stock, and pro-employer propaganda during union elections, are all examples of expressions of ideas that are limited by the law. An instrumental analysis might be that smooth operation of the entities of commerce and the need for a stable setting for the growth of capital have overcome the commitment to civil liberties in these instances. A doctrinal first amendment explanation is that those are examples of hard cases, representing more than the expression of an idea. Some statements are noncommunicative acts, subject to legal restraint. * * *

The override occurs again in the area of privacy and defamation. Expressing intimate and private facts about a private individual is subject to civil damages, as is the spread of untruths damaging to both public and private figures. First amendment protections are worked into the law of defamation and privacy, but they are not allowed to supersede completely the reputational interest and personal integrity of the victims of certain forms of expression. When courts are called into private disputes about defamatory speech, they are really mediating between competing interests of constitutional dimension: the right of expression, and the implicit right to a measure of personal integrity, peace of mind, and personhood.

Speech infringing on public order is another classic unprotected area. Bomb threats, incitements to riot, "fighting words," and obscene phone calls are a few of the speech-crimes that slip through the first amendment's web of protection. These categories edge close to the category of racist speech. Under existing law, insults of such dimension that they bring men—this is a male-centered standard—to blows are subject to a first amendment exception. The problem is that racist speech is so common that it is seen as part of the ordinary jostling and conflict people are expected to tolerate, rather than as fighting words. Another problem is that the effect of dehumanizing racist language is often flight rather than fight. Targets choose to avoid racist encounters whenever possible, internalizing the harm rather than escalating the conflict. Lack of a fight and admirable self-restraint then defines the words as nonactionable. When racist leaflets threatening Representative Tyrone Brooks urged whites to band together to keep civil rights activists out of Rome, Georgia, state officials felt that the first amendment prevented arrest because the leaflet "didn't threaten to kill anyone." * * *

A definition of actionable racist speech must be narrow in order to respect first amendment values. I believe racist speech is best treated as a sui generis category, presenting an idea so historically untenable, so dangerous, and so tied to perpetuation of violence and degradation of the very classes of human beings who are least equipped to respond that it is properly treated as outside the realm of protected discourse. * * *

In order to distinguish the worst, paradigm example of racist hate messages from other forms of racist and nonracist speech, I offer three identifying characteristics:

1. The message is of racial inferiority;

2. The message is directed against a historically oppressed group; and

3. The message is persecutory, hateful, and degrading.

Making each element a prerequisite to prosecution prevents opening of the floodgates of censorship. * * *

What is argued here, then, is that we accept certain principles as the shared historical legacy of the world community. Racial supremacy is one of the ideas we have collectively and internationally considered and rejected. As an idea connected to continuing racism and degradation of minority groups, it causes real harm to its victims. We are not safe when these violent words are among us.

Treating racist speech as sui generis and universally condemned on the basis of its content and the harmful effect of its content is precisely the censorship that civil libertarians fear. I would argue, however, that explicit content-based rejection of narrowly defined racist speech is more protective of civil liberties than the competing-interests tests or the likely-to-incite-violence tests that can spill over to censor forms of political speech. * * *

NOTES ON WHETHER THE FIRST AMENDMENT PROTECTS SEXIST AND HOMOPHOBIC SPEECH

Professor Matsuda's article has spawned a tremendous academic debate.[a]

a. See Peter Byrne, "Racist Insults and Free Speech Within the University," 79 *Geo. L.J.* 399 (1991); Richard Delgado, "Campus Antiracist Rules: Constitutional Narratives in Collision," 85 *Nw. L. Rev.* 343 (1991); Gerald Gunther, "Freedom for the Thought We Hate," *Academe*, Nov.-Dec. 1990, at 10; Charles R. Lawrence, III, "Acknowledging the Victim's Cry," *Academe*, Nov.-Dec. 1990, at 10, and "If He Hollers Let Him Go: Regulating Racist Speech on Campus," 1990 *Duke L.J.* 431; Robert Post, "Racist Speech, De-

1. *Does Hate Speech Serve Any First Amendment Goals?* Recall the constitutional policies theoretically subserved by the First Amendment (notes after *One, Inc.*). Is any First Amendment policy served by hate speech, as by calling a person a racist or homophobic name? Richard Delgado argues:

> * * * Uttering racial slurs may afford the racially troubled speaker some immediate relief, but hardly seems essential to self-fulfillment in any ideal sense. Indeed, social science writers hold that making racist remarks impairs, rather than promotes, the growth of the person who makes them, by encouraging rigid, dichotomous thinking and impeding moral development. * * *
>
> Additionally, slurs contribute little to the discovery of truth. Classroom discussion of racial matters and even the speech of a bigot aimed at proving the superiority of the white race might move us closer to the truth. But one-on-one insults do not. They neither state nor attack a proposition; they are like a slap in the face. * * *

Richard Delgado, "Campus Antirace Rules: Constitutional Narratives in Collision," 85 *Nw. L.Rev.* 343, 379 (1991).

Are there other First Amendment goals that hate speech might contribute to? Can a public slur be penalized but a public argument not? What if the argument contains slurs? What if the slur is uttered in private? Note, by the way, some similarities between Professor Delgado's arguments for suppressing racist speech and the Ninth Circuit's justification for suppressing *One, Inc.* Does that raise concerns?

2. *Should Protection Against Hate Speech Operate Just One Way?* Professor Matsuda would regulate only hate speech directed against historically persecuted minorities. Hence, a racist statement by an African American against whites would not be regulable under her theory, as we understand it. This position responds to Professor Nadine Strossen's criticism that hate speech laws would tend to be used against minorities, but it creates other difficulties for Professor Matsuda's theory. Not only does her theory have to answer First Amendment concerns because it suppresses speech and classifies speech according to content, but it then has to answer Fourteenth Amendment (equal protection) concerns because it classifies people according to race. See *Loving v. Virginia* [Chapter 9, Section 2], which seems to hold that any racial classification triggers heightened judicial scrutiny.

Another difficulty is presented by laws that target hate speech against women or gay people as well as against racial minorities. Would slurs by black men against women be actionable? Homophobic slurs made by black women? Racist remarks by lesbian Latinas? The concern is that once one creates a regime for regulating hate speech one becomes immediately enmeshed in controversial, and hurtful and extremely divisive, value choices.

mocracy, and the First Amendment," 32 *Wm. & Mary L. Rev.* 267 (1991); Nadine Strossen, "Regulating Racist Speech on Campus: A Modest Proposal," 1990 *Duke L.J.* 484.

3. *Does Hate Speech Regulation Serve a Compelling State Interest?* Recall *Roberts*, which stands for the proposition that state regulation of constitutionally protected activity can be justified by a compelling state interest such as the eradication of discriminatory practices. Is *Roberts* distinguishable from a hate speech regulation seeking to remove barriers to the advancement of racial minorities? Professor Charles Lawrence argues that *Brown* itself provides a justification, by its emphasis on the bad effects of school segregation on the "hearts and minds" of African–American children (Lawrence, "Victim's Cry").

NOTE ON UNIVERSITY HATE SPEECH CODES

In 1988 the University of Michigan adopted regulations prohibiting students in classrooms and other school facilities from engaging in "[a]ny behavior, verbal or physical, that stigmatizes or victimizes an individual on the basis of race, ethnicity, religion, sex, sexual orientation, creed, national origin, ancestry, age, marital status, handicap or Vietnam-era veteran status" *and* that threatens or interferes with an individual's academic efforts, employment, participation in university activities *or* "[c]reates an intimidating, hostile, or demeaning environment for educational pursuits, employment, or participation in University sponsored educational activities." Violation of these regulations can result in reprimands through expulsions from school.

Several cases that were targeted by or arose under these regulations included the following statements:

- Student *A* says in class: "Women just aren't as good in this field as men."

- Student *B* says in class: "Homosexuality is a treatable disease."

- Students *A* and *B* make their statements in a lunchroom conversation that is overheard by other students.

See Peter Byrne, "Racial Insults and Free Speech Within the University," 79 *Geo. L.J.* 399 (1991). Can these statements be penalized, consistent with the First Amendment, by a public university? Can these statements be penalized, consistent with the District of Columbia's Human Rights Act [Appendix 2], by Georgetown University?

R.A.V. v. City of St. Paul

Supreme Court of the United States, 1992.
505 U.S. 377, 112 S.Ct. 2538, 120 L.Ed.2d 305.

■ JUSTICE SCALIA delivered the opinion of the Court.

In the predawn hours of June 21, 1990, petitioner and several other teenagers allegedly assembled a crudely-made cross by taping together broken chair legs. They then allegedly burned the cross inside the fenced yard of a black family that lived across the street from the house where petitioner was staying. Although this conduct could have been punished under any of a number of laws,[1] one of the two provisions under which respondent city of St. Paul chose to charge petitioner (then a juvenile) was the St. Paul Bias–Motivated Crime Ordinance, St. Paul, Minn. Legis. Code § 292.02 (1990), which provides:

> "Whoever places on public or private property a symbol, object, appellation, characterization or graffiti, including, but not limited to, a burning cross or Nazi swastika, which one knows or has reasonable grounds to know arouses anger, alarm or resentment in others on the basis of race, color, creed, religion or gender commits disorderly conduct and shall be guilty of a misdemeanor." * * *

In construing the St. Paul ordinance, we are bound by the construction given to it by the Minnesota court. Accordingly, we accept the Minnesota Supreme Court's authoritative statement that the ordinance reaches only those expressions that constitute "fighting words" within the meaning of *Chaplinsky*. Petitioner and his *amici* urge us to modify the scope of the *Chaplinsky* formulation, thereby invalidating the ordinance as "substantially overbroad." We find it unnecessary to consider this issue. Assuming, *arguendo*, that all of the expression reached by the ordinance is proscribable under the "fighting words" doctrine, we nonetheless conclude that the ordinance is facially unconstitutional in that it prohibits otherwise permitted speech solely on the basis of the subjects the speech addresses.

The First Amendment generally prevents government from proscribing speech, or even expressive conduct, because of disapproval of the ideas expressed. Content-based regulations are presumptively invalid. From 1791 to the present, however, our society, like other free but civilized societies, has permitted restrictions upon the content of speech in a few limited areas, which are "of such slight social value as a step to truth that any benefit that may be derived from them is clearly outweighed by the social interest in order and morality." *Chaplinsky*, 315 U.S. at 572. We have recognized that "the freedom of speech" referred to by the First Amendment does not include a freedom to disregard these traditional limitations. See, *e.g.*, *Roth v. United States*, 354 U.S. 476 (1957) (obscenity); *Beauharnais v. Illinois*, 343 U.S. 250 (1952) ([group] defamation); *Chaplinsky v. New Hampshire* ("fighting" words). Our decisions since the 1960's have narrowed the scope of the traditional categorical exceptions for defamation and for obscenity, but a limited categorical approach has remained an important part of our First Amendment jurisprudence.

We have sometimes said that these categories of expression are "not within the area of constitutionally protected speech," or that the "protection of the First Amendment does not extend" to them. Such statements must be taken in context, however, and are no more literally true than is

---

1. The conduct might have violated Minnesota statutes carrying significant penalties. See, *e.g.*, Minn. Stat. § 609.713(1) (1987) (providing for up to five years in prison for terroristic threats); § 609.563 (arson) (providing for up to five years and a $10,000 fine, depending on the value of the property intended to be damaged); § 609.595 (supp. 1992) (criminal damage to property) (providing for up to one year and a $3,000 fine, depending upon the extent of the damage to the property).

the occasionally repeated shorthand characterizing obscenity "as not being speech at all." What they mean is that these areas of speech can, consistently with the First Amendment, be regulated *because of their constitutionally proscribable content* (obscenity, defamation, etc.)—not that they are categories of speech entirely invisible to the Constitution, so that they may be made the vehicles for content discrimination unrelated to their distinctively proscribable content. Thus, the government may proscribe libel; but it may not make the further content discrimination of proscribing *only* libel critical of the government. * * *

Our cases surely do not establish the proposition that the First Amendment imposes no obstacle whatsoever to regulation of particular instances of such proscribable expression, so that the government "may regulate [them] freely" (White, J., concurring in judgment). That would mean that a city council could enact an ordinance prohibiting only those legally obscene works that contain criticism of the city government or, indeed, that do not include endorsement of the city government. Such a simplistic, all-or-nothing-at-all approach to First Amendment protection is at odds with common sense and with our jurisprudence as well. It is not true that "fighting words" have at most a *"de minimis"* expressive content, or that their content is *in all respects* "worthless and undeserving of constitutional protection"; sometimes they are quite expressive indeed. We have not said that they constitute *"no* part of the expression of ideas," but only that they constitute "no *essential* part of any exposition of ideas." *Chaplinsky*, 315 U.S., at 572 (emphasis added). * * *

Applying these principles to the St. Paul ordinance, we conclude that, even as narrowly construed by the Minnesota Supreme Court, the ordinance is facially unconstitutional. Although the phrase in the ordinance, "arouses anger, alarm or resentment in others," has been limited by the Minnesota Supreme Court's construction to reach only those symbols or displays that amount to "fighting words," the remaining, unmodified terms make clear that the ordinance applies only to "fighting words" that insult, or provoke violence, "on the basis of race, color, creed, religion or gender." Displays containing abusive invective, no matter how vicious or severe, are permissible unless they are addressed to one of the specified disfavored topics. Those who wish to use "fighting words" in connection with other ideas—to express hostility, for example, on the basis of political affiliation, union membership, or homosexuality—are not covered. The First Amendment does not permit St. Paul to impose special prohibitions on those speakers who express views on disfavored subjects.

In its practical operation, moreover, the ordinance goes even beyond mere content discrimination, to actual viewpoint discrimination. Displays containing some words—odious racial epithets, for example—would be prohibited to proponents of all views. But "fighting words" that do not themselves invoke race, color, creed, religion, or gender—aspersions upon a person's mother, for example—would seemingly be usable *ad libitum* in the placards of those arguing *in favor* of racial, color, etc. tolerance and equality, but could not be used by that speaker's opponents. One could hold up a sign saying, for example, that all "anti-Catholic bigots" are misbegotten; but not that all "papists" are, for that would insult and provoke violence "on the basis of religion." St. Paul has no such authority to license one side of a debate to fight freestyle, while requiring the other to follow Marquis of Queensbury Rules.

What we have here, it must be emphasized, is not a prohibition of fighting words that are directed at certain persons or groups (which would be *facially* valid if it met the requirements of the Equal Protection Clause); but rather, a prohibition of fighting words that contain (as the Minnesota Supreme Court repeatedly emphasized) messages of "bias-motivated" hatred and in particular, as applied to this case, messages "based on virulent notions of racial supremacy." One must wholeheartedly agree with the Minnesota Supreme Court that "[i]t is the responsibility, even the obligation, of diverse communities to confront such notions in whatever form they appear," but the manner of that confrontation cannot consist of selective limitations upon speech. St. Paul's brief asserts that a general "fighting words" law would not meet the city's needs because only a content-specific measure can communicate to minority groups that the "group hatred" aspect of such speech "is not condoned by the majority." The point of the First Amendment is that majority preferences must be expressed in some fashion other than silencing speech on the basis of its content.

Despite the fact that the Minnesota Supreme Court and St. Paul acknowledge that the ordinance is directed at expression of group hatred, Justice Stevens suggests that this "fundamentally misreads" the ordinance. It is directed, he claims, not to speech of a particular content, but to particular "injur[ies]" that are "qualitatively different" from other injuries. This is wordplay. What makes the anger, fear, sense of dishonor, etc. produced by violation of this ordinance distinct from the anger, fear, sense of dishonor, etc. produced by other fighting words is nothing other than the fact that it is caused by a distinctive idea, conveyed by a distinctive message. The First Amendment cannot be evaded that easily. It is obvious that the symbols which will arouse "anger, alarm or resentment in others on the basis of race, color, creed, religion or gender" are those symbols that communicate a message of hostility based on one of these characteristics. St. Paul concedes in its brief that the ordinance applies only to "racial, religious, or gender-specific symbols" such as "a burning cross, Nazi swastika or other instrumentality of like import." Indeed, St. Paul argued in the Juvenile Court that "[t]he burning of a cross does express a message and it is, in fact, the content of that message which the St. Paul Ordinance attempts to legislate."

The content-based discrimination reflected in the St. Paul ordinance comes within neither any of the specific exceptions to the First Amendment prohibition we discussed earlier, nor within a more general exception for content discrimination that does not threaten censorship of ideas. It assuredly does not fall within the exception for content discrimination based on the very reasons why the particular class of speech at issue (here, fighting words) is proscribable. As explained earlier, the reason why fighting words are categorically excluded from the protection of the First Amendment is not that their content communicates any particular idea, but that their content embodies a particularly intolerable (and socially unnecessary) *mode* of expressing *whatever* idea the speaker wishes to convey. St. Paul has not singled out an especially offensive mode of expression—it has not, for example, selected for prohibition only those fighting words that communicate ideas in a threatening (as opposed to a merely obnoxious) manner. Rather, it has proscribed fighting words of whatever manner that communicate messages of racial, gender, or religious intolerance. Selectivity of this sort creates the possibility that the city is seeking to handicap the expression of particular ideas. That possibility would alone be enough to render the ordinance presumptively invalid, but St. Paul's comments and concessions in this case elevate the possibility to a certainty. * * *

Finally, St. Paul and its *amici* defend the conclusion of the Minnesota Supreme Court that, even if the ordinance regulates expression based on hostility towards its protected ideological content, this discrimination is nonetheless justified because it is narrowly tailored to serve compelling state interests. Specifically, they assert that the ordinance helps to ensure the basic human rights of members of groups that have historically been subjected to discrimination, including the right of such group members to live in peace where they wish. We do not doubt that these interests are compelling, and that the ordinance can be said to promote them. But the "danger of censorship" presented by a facially content-based statute, *Leathers v. Medlock*, 499 U.S. 439, 448 (1991), requires that that weapon be employed only where it is "*necessary* to serve the asserted [compelling] interest." *Burson v. Freeman*, 504 U.S. 191, 199 (1992) (plurality) (emphasis added). The existence of adequate content-neutral alternatives thus "undercut[s] significantly" any defense of such a statute, casting considerable doubt on the government's protestations that "the asserted justification is in fact an accurate description of the purpose and effect of the law." *Burson*, 504 U.S. at 213 (Kennedy, J., concurring). The dispositive question in this case, therefore, is whether content discrimination is reasonably necessary to achieve St. Paul's compelling interests; it plainly is not. An ordinance not limited to the favored topics, for example, would have precisely the same beneficial effect. In fact the only interest distinctively served by the content limitation is that of displaying the city council's special hostility towards the particular biases thus singled out. That is precisely what the First Amendment forbids. The politicians of St. Paul are entitled to express that hostility—but not through the means of imposing unique limitations upon speakers who (however benightedly) disagree.

Let there be no mistake about our belief that burning a cross in someone's front yard is reprehensible. But St. Paul has sufficient means at its disposal to prevent such behavior without adding the First Amendment to the fire. * * *

■ JUSTICE WHITE, with whom JUSTICES BLACKMUN, O'CONNOR, and STEVENS join, concurring in the judgment, and with whom JUSTICE STEVENS joins except as to Part I–A.

[I–A] * * * It is inconsistent to hold that the government may proscribe an entire category of speech because the content of that speech is evil, but that the government may not treat a subset of that category differently without violating the First Amendment; the content of the subset is by definition worthless and undeserving of constitutional protection.

The majority's observation that fighting words are "quite expressive indeed" is no answer. Fighting words are not a means of exchanging views, rallying supporters, or registering a protest; they are directed against individuals to provoke violence or to inflict injury. *Chaplinsky.* Therefore, a ban on all fighting words or on a subset of the fighting words category would restrict only the social evil of hate speech, without creating the danger of driving viewpoints from the marketplace.

Therefore, the Court's insistence on inventing its brand of First Amendment underinclusiveness puzzles me. The overbreadth doctrine has the redeeming virtue of attempting to avoid the chilling of protected expression, but the Court's new "underbreadth" creation serves no desirable function. Instead, it permits, indeed invites, the continuation of expressive conduct that in this case is evil and worthless in First Amendment terms, until the city of St. Paul cures the underbreadth by adding to its ordinance a catchall phrase such as "and all other fighting words that may constitutionally be subject to this ordinance."

Any contribution of this holding to First Amendment jurisprudence is surely a negative one, since it necessarily signals that expressions of violence, such as the message of intimidation and racial hatred conveyed by burning a cross on someone's lawn, are of sufficient value to outweigh the social interest in order and morality that has traditionally placed such fighting words outside the First Amendment.[4] Indeed, by characterizing fighting words as a form of "debate," the majority legitimates hate speech as a form of public discussion.

Furthermore, the Court obscures the line between speech that could be regulated freely on the basis of content (*i.e.*, the narrow categories of expression falling outside the First Amendment) and that which could be regulated on the basis of content only upon a showing of a compelling state interest (*i.e.*, all remaining expression). By placing fighting words, which the Court has long held to be valueless, on at least equal constitutional footing with political discourse and other forms of speech that we have

---

4. This does not suggest, of course, that cross burning is always unprotected. Burning a cross at a political rally would almost certainly be protected expression. Cf. *Brandenburg v. Ohio*, 395 U.S. 444, 445 (1969). But in such a context, the cross burning could not be characterized as a "direct personal insult or an invitation to exchange fisticuffs," *Texas v. Johnson*, 491 U.S. 397, 409 (1989), to which the fighting words doctrine * * * applies.

deemed to have the greatest social value, the majority devalues the latter category. * * *

[B.] Although the First Amendment does not apply to categories of unprotected speech, such as fighting words, the Equal Protection Clause requires that the regulation of unprotected speech be rationally related to a legitimate government interest. A defamation statute that drew distinctions on the basis of political affiliation or "an ordinance prohibiting only those legally obscene works that contain criticism of the city government," would unquestionably fail rational basis review.

Turning to the St. Paul ordinance and assuming arguendo, as the majority does, that the ordinance is not constitutionally overbroad * * * there is no question that it would pass equal protection review. The ordinance proscribes a subset of "fighting words," those that injure "on the basis of race, color, creed, religion or gender." This selective regulation reflects the City's judgment that harms based on race, color, creed, religion, or gender are more pressing public concerns than the harms caused by other fighting words. In light of our Nation's long and painful experience with discrimination, this determination is plainly reasonable. Indeed, as the majority concedes, the interest is compelling.

[Justice White concurred in the judgment, however, because the ordinance was overbroad in reaching beyond proscribable "fighting words." As interpreted by the Minnesota Supreme Court, the ordinance prohibited hate speech which by its very utterance inflicts injury. Citing the flag-burning cases, Justice White reasoned from the fact that the "mere fact that expressive activity causes hurt does not render the expression unprotected," to the conclusion that the ordinance was "substantially overbroad," regulating protected as well as unprotected expression. Under *Broadrick v. Oklahoma*, 413 U.S. 601 (1973), defendants engaged in unprotected expression have standing to challenge a law that is substantially overbroad.]

■ [We omit the separate concurring opinion of JUSTICE BLACKMUN.]

■ STEVENS, J., * * * concurring in the judgment. * * *

Looking to the context of the regulated activity, it is again significant that the statute (by hypothesis) regulates *only* fighting words. Whether words are fighting words is determined in part by their context. Fighting words are not words that merely cause offense; fighting words must be directed at individuals so as to "by their very utterance inflict injury." By hypothesis, then, the St. Paul ordinance restricts speech in confrontational and potentially violent situations. The case at hand is illustrative. The cross-burning in this case—directed as it was to a single African–American family trapped in their home—was nothing more than a crude form of physical intimidation. That this cross-burning sends a message of racial hostility does not automatically endow it with complete constitutional protection.[8]

---

8. The Court makes much of St. Paul's description of the ordinance as regulating "a message". As always, however, St. Paul's argument must be read in context:

Significantly, the St. Paul ordinance regulates speech not on the basis of its subject matter or the viewpoint expressed, but rather on the basis of the *harm* the speech causes. In this regard, the Court fundamentally misreads the St. Paul ordinance. The Court describes the St. Paul ordinance as regulating expression "addressed to one of [several] specified disfavored *topics*," as policing "disfavored *subjects*," and as "prohibit[ing] ... speech solely on the basis of the *subjects* the speech addresses." Contrary to the Court's suggestion, the ordinance regulates only a subcategory of expression that causes *injuries based on* "race, color, creed, religion or gender," not a subcategory that involves *discussions* that concern those characteristics. The ordinance, as construed by the Court, criminalizes expression that "one knows ... [by its very utterance inflicts injury on] others on the basis of race, color, creed, religion or gender." In this regard, the ordinance resembles the child pornography law at issue in [*New York v. Ferber*, 458 U.S. 747 (1982) (excerpted in Chapter 6, Section 1)], which in effect singled out child pornography because those publications caused far greater harms than pornography involving adults.

Moreover, even if the St. Paul ordinance did regulate fighting words based on its subject matter, such a regulation would, in my opinion, be constitutional. As noted above, subject-matter based regulations on commercial speech are widespread and largely unproblematic. As we have long recognized, subject-matter regulations generally do not raise the same concerns of government censorship and the distortion of public discourse presented by viewpoint regulations. Thus, in upholding subject-matter regulations we have carefully noted that viewpoint-based discrimination was not implicated. See *Young v. American Mini Theatres, Inc.* [427 U.S. 50, 67 (1976) (plurality opinion)] (emphasizing "the need for absolute neutrality by the government," and observing that the contested statute was not animated by "hostility for the point of view" of the theatres); *FCC v. Pacifica Foundation* [438 U.S. 726, 745–46 (1978) (plurality opinion)] (stressing that "government must remain neutral in the marketplace of ideas"). Indeed, some subject matter restrictions are a functional necessity in contemporary governance: "The First Amendment does not require States to regulate for problems that do not exist." *Burson v. Freeman*.

Contrary to the suggestion of the majority, the St. Paul ordinance does *not* regulate expression based on viewpoint. The Court contends that the ordinance requires proponents of racial intolerance to "follow the Marquis of Queensbury Rules" while allowing advocates of racial tolerance to "fight freestyle." The law does no such thing.

"Finally we ask the Court to reflect on the 'content' of the 'expressive conduct' represented by a 'burning cross'. It is no less than the first step in an act of racial violence. It was and unfortunately still is the equivalent of [the] waving of a knife before the thrust, the pointing of a gun before it is fired, the lighting of a match before the arson, the hanging of a noose before the lynching. It is not a political statement, or even a cowardly statement of hatred. It is the first step in an act of assault. It can be no more protected than holding a gun to a victim['s] head. It is perhaps the ultimate expression of 'fighting words'." App. to Brief for Petitioner C–6.

The Court writes:

> "One could hold up a sign saying, for example, that all 'anti-Catholic bigots' are misbegotten; but not that all 'papists' are, for that would insult and provoke violence 'on the basis of religion.'"

This may be true, but it hardly proves the Court's point. The Court's reasoning is asymmetrical. The response to a sign saying that "all [religious] bigots are misbegotten" is a sign saying that "all advocates of religious tolerance are misbegotten." Assuming such signs could be fighting words (which seems to me extremely unlikely), neither sign would be banned by the ordinance for the attacks were not "based on . . . religion" but rather on one's beliefs about tolerance. Conversely (and again assuming such signs are fighting words), just as the ordinance would prohibit a Muslim from hoisting a sign claiming that all Catholics were misbegotten, so the ordinance would bar a Catholic from hoisting a similar sign attacking Muslims.

The St. Paul ordinance is evenhanded. In a battle between advocates of tolerance and advocates of intolerance, the ordinance does not prevent either side from hurling fighting words at the other on the basis of their conflicting ideas, but it does bar *both* sides from hurling such words on the basis of the target's "race, color, creed, religion or gender." To extend the Court's pugilistic metaphor, the St. Paul ordinance simply bans punches "below the belt"—*by either party*. It does not, therefore, favor one side of any debate.

Finally, it is noteworthy that the St. Paul ordinance is, as construed by the Court today, quite narrow. The St. Paul ordinance does not ban all "hate speech," nor does it ban, say, all cross-burnings or all swastika displays. Rather it only bans a subcategory of the already narrow category of fighting words. Such a limited ordinance leaves open and protected a vast range of expression on the subjects of racial, religious, and gender equality. As construed by the Court today, the ordinance certainly does not " 'rais[e] the specter that the Government may effectively drive certain ideas or viewpoints from the marketplace.'" Petitioner is free to burn a cross to announce a rally or to express his views about racial supremacy, he may do so on private property or public land, at day or at night, so long as the burning is not so threatening and so directed at an individual as to "by its very [execution] inflict injury." Such a limited proscription scarcely offends the First Amendment.

In sum, the St. Paul ordinance (as construed by the Court) regulates expressive activity that is wholly proscribable and does so not on the basis of viewpoint, but rather in recognition of the different harms caused by such activity. Taken together, these several considerations persuade me that the St. Paul ordinance is not an unconstitutional content-based regulation of speech. Thus, were the ordinance not overbroad, I would vote to uphold it.

NOTES ON *R.A.V.* AND FIRST AMENDMENT LIMITS ON HATE SPEECH REGULATION

1. *The New Problem of Constitutional "Underbreadth" and the Aspiration of Neutrality.* If taken seriously, *R.A.V.* creates a new First Amendment "underbreadth" doctrine: a law proscribing expressive conduct ordinarily not protected by the First Amendment is invalid if it makes content-based distinctions, as for example, by prohibiting only hate speech directed against government officials. (Contrast *Rosenberger*, where the Court would allow content-based, but not viewpoint-based, distinctions when the state is creating a "public forum.") The concurring Justices vigorously objected that "underbreadth" not only went beyond, but went against precedent and was riddled with too many exceptions to be a useful doctrine. Consider, for example, the argument made in Cole & Eskridge, "From Handholding to Sodomy" (Section 1), that state laws criminalizing only same-sex, and not different-sex, sodomy violate *R.A.V.*, as does the military's policy of excluding people for saying they are gay but not for saying that they are straight. This is a logical application of *R.A.V.*, but is there any doubt that Justice Scalia himself would dismiss this argument out of hand? If you harbor doubts, reread his *Romer* dissent (Chapter 1, Section 3[B][1]).

What good is doctrine unless it meaningfully binds the Court in subsequent cases? The "state needs to be neutral" debate you saw in *Rosenberger* is anticipated in *R.A.V.* The alignment of Justices suggests a split along lines of "anti-political correctness" (the Scalia group) versus "give the state leeway to deal with bias" (the White group). Critical feminist and race theory maintains that the latitude allowed by the White group is necessary to allow the state to foster an environment where women, people of color, and gay people can feel free enough to assert their citizenship on equal terms with previously empowered citizens. The Scalia group might be considered reflective of "counter critical theory," where state neutrality means staying out of speech regulation.

2. *Is Sex or Sexual Orientation Different?* Most of the debate over hate speech has arisen in the context of racist speech or sexist speech. See Professor Matsuda's article and the references in note "a" to this Section. Should feminists and gay rights advocates favor hate speech codes? Consider this:

> [T]he Fourteenth Amendment [equal protection clause] has provided very little, if any, equality for lesbians and gay men, while, by contrast, the First Amendment has been the only consistent friend of lesbian and gay rights litigators since Stonewall. But more importantly, I do not find that "equality" belongs only to the Fourteenth Amendment and "speech" only to the First. The pureness of these legal categories collapses under the experience of lesbians and gay men: First Amendment cases are about equality and equal protection cases are about speech.

First Amendment cases are about equality. In the First Amendment cases in which gay litigants prevail, the narrative that can be weaved about these cases goes much farther than the vindication of free speech. When a state university, for instance, denies gay student group the right to meet on campus, it is not just striking a blow at free association, although it is indeed doing that. Rather, the university is sending out a message that lesbians and gay men are less equal than other persons. * * * Thus, I cherish the First Amendment not only because it protects free speech, but also because it is the most direct and powerful instrument of *equality* for lesbian and gay persons.

William B. Rubenstein, "Since When Is the Fourteenth Amendment Our Only Route to Equality? Some Reflections on the Construction of the 'Hate–Speech' Debate from a Lesbian/Gay Perspective," in Henry Louis Gates, Jr., et al., *Speaking of Race, Speaking of Sex: Hate Speech, Civil Rights and Civil Liberties* 290–91 (1994).

There is a paradox in the hate speech debate. Both racist speech and pro-gay speech express views that are disfavored (or at least disowned) in the larger culture. Their very unpopularity is one justification for the shelter accorded them under the First Amendment. And the argument that toleration implies endorsement applies as much to one as to the other. If one's goal is the advancement of both racial and sexual equality, it is impossible to avoid the conflict. How would you resolve it?

3. *Hate Crimes.* In 1990, Congress enacted the Hate Crime Statistics Act, which authorized the Department of Justice to collect data on crimes motivated by the victim's "race, religion, disability, sexual orientation or ethnicity." 28 U.S.C. § 534(b)(1) (West Supp. 1995). Its passage marked the first use of the term "sexual orientation" in a federal statute. A number of state and local laws create separate criminal offenses for crimes of violence motivated by bigotry, or provide for enhancement of the sentence for persons convicted of such crimes, some of which include sexual orientation as a protected category. See, *e.g.*, Fla. Stat. ch. 877.19; Ill. Rev. Stat. ch. 38–110–5.

Are these statutes constitutional after *R.A.V.*? Doesn't a statute that enlarges a sentence for physical assault because it expresses hate based on the victim's sex, sexual orientation, or race violate *R.A.V.*'s statement that the First Amendment has been violated when "the only interest distinctively served by the content limitation is that of displaying the city council's special hostility towards the particular biases thus singled out." Consider the next case.

Wisconsin v. Todd Mitchell, 508 U.S. 476, 113 S.Ct. 2194, 124 L.Ed.2d 436 (1993). Todd Mitchell, a black youth, was convicted of beating a white victim. His conviction of aggravated battery normally carried a two-year maximum sentence. Because the jury found that Mitchell had intentionally selected the victim because of his race, the maximum sentence was increased to seven years by Wisconsin Stat. § 939.645 (also applicable if the actor selects a victim because of "religion, color, disability, sexual orientation, national origin or ancestry"). The court sentenced

Mitchell to four years' imprisonment. The Wisconsin Supreme Court invalidated the sentence-enhancement scheme because it posed the same overbroad threat to speech as the *R.A.V.* ordinance did.

A unanimous Supreme Court reversed. Chief Justice Rehnquist's opinion emphasized that the criminal law has long considered defendants' motives when determining the severity of a crime and its appropriate punishment. Premeditated murder is a more serious crime than unpremeditated murder, and assault or murder for pecuniary gain has been considered an appropriate aggravating factor in setting criminal punishment. Moreover, race- and sex-based motives relevant to the imposition of liability under Title VII have been upheld or accepted by the Court's employment discrimination precedents.

While a defendant's abstract beliefs cannot be considered, *e.g.*, *Dawson v. Delaware*, 503 U.S. 159 (1992) (sentencing court cannot consider defendant's membership in a white supremacist prison gang), the Court held that defendant's motivations can be an aggravating factor. The Court distinguished *R.A.V.* as involving an ordinance "explicitly directed at expression," while the enhancement law was aimed only at violent "conduct unprotected by the First Amendment. Moreover, the Wisconsin statute singles out for enhancement bias-inspired conduct because this conduct is thought to inflict greater individual and societal harm. For example, according to the State and its amici, bias-motivated crimes are more likely to provoke retaliatory crimes, inflict distinct emotional harms on their victims, and incite community unrest."

Quaere: Isn't this argument precisely the one the Court rejected in *R.A.V.*? Is *Mitchell* a retreat from the earlier case? If so, how can you explain Justice Scalia's joining *Mitchell*, without so much as a separate statement? If not, how can the quoted language be reconciled with *R.A.V.*?

One common analogy for hate speech is that of an assault, executed by verbal rather than physical means. Think of the ways in which sexualized or sexually explicit speech is used to express hostility. Should such speech be presumptively categorized as hate speech? Does or should that conceptualization differ, depending on whether the object/victim of the speech is male or female, straight or gay, white or nonwhite? What are the legal problems with adopting that kind of approach? The theoretical problems? See Chapter 6.

CHAPTER 6

Sexual Speech

SECTION 1   Sexual Speech and the First Amendment: A Dysfunctional
            Dyad

SECTION 2   Feminist Theories of Sexual Speech and Its Regulation

SECTION 3   Cutting Edge Issues of Sexual Speech Law

SEXUAL SPEECH AND THE FIRST AMENDMENT: A DYSFUNCTIONAL DYAD

The endlessly recurring question in the law's treatment of sexually explicit speech has been whether sexual speech merits the protection accorded to nonsexual speech. Perhaps the starting point should be: Why not? That perspective, however, has never gained a majority within the Supreme Court. For many years, the Court avoided this issue. The general tenor of the Court's early jurisprudence can be found in *Chaplinsky v. New Hampshire*, 315 U.S. 568 (1942), the "fighting words" case, where the Court simply stated that "lewd and obscene" speech is unprotected by the First Amendment. Courts not only refused to protect obscene speech, but defined the category broadly. Recall *One, Inc.* (Chapter 5, Section 1), where the court of appeals held that a sympathetic story about two lesbians was obscene.

This section invites you to evaluate the issue historically and critically. Start with first principles: What are the goals of the First Amendment? (Consult Chapter 5's introductory section.) Does protecting sexual speech contribute to those goals? What sense can be made of the precedents? Consider the Court's first effort in this area.

Samuel Roth v. United States
David S. Alberts v. California

United States Supreme Court, 1957.
354 U.S. 476, 77 S.Ct. 1304, 1 L.Ed.2d 1498.

■ MR. JUSTICE BRENNAN delivered the opinion of the Court.

[The appeal involved the constitutionality of two statutes, one federal and one state. The federal law, 18 U.S.C. § 1461, prohibited the mailing of "[e]very obscene, lewd, lascivious, or filthy book, pamphlet, picture, paper, letter, writing, print, or other publication of an indecent character." New York businessman Samuel Roth was convicted of violating the federal statute because the materials and circulars mailed by his bookstore were held to be obscene. California Penal Code § 311, made guilty of a misdemeanor "[e]very person who wilfully and lewdly * * * 3. Writes, composes, stereotypes, prints, publishes, sells, distributes, keeps for sale, or exhibits any obscene or indecent writing, paper, or book; or designs, copies, draws, engraves, paints, or otherwise prepares any obscene or indecent picture or print; or molds, cuts, casts, or otherwise makes any obscene or indecent figure; or, 4. Writes, composes, or publishes any notice or advertisement of any such writing, paper, book, picture, print or figure; * * *." David Alberts ran a mail-order business that California prosecuted for selling lewd and obscene materials. Justice Brennan conceded that the issue whether "obscene" utterances were "speech" protected by the First Amendment was one of first impression with the Court.]

The guaranties of freedom of expression in effect in 10 of the 14 States which by 1792 had ratified the Constitution, gave no absolute protection for every utterance. Thirteen of the 14 States provided for the prosecution of libel, and all of those States made either blasphemy or profanity, or both, statutory crimes. As early as 1712, Massachusetts made it criminal to publish "any filthy, obscene, or profane song, pamphlet, libel or mock sermon" in imitation or mimicking of religious services. Acts and Laws of the Province of Mass. Bay, c. CV, § 8 (1712), Mass. Bay Colony Charters & Laws 399 (1814). Thus, profanity and obscenity were related offenses.

In light of this history, it is apparent that the unconditional phrasing of the First Amendment was not intended to protect every utterance. This phrasing did not prevent this Court from concluding that libelous utterances are not within the area of constitutionally protected speech. *Beauharnais v. Illinois*, 343 U.S. 250, 266. At the time of the adoption of the First Amendment, obscenity law was not as fully developed as libel law, but there is sufficiently contemporaneous evidence to show that obscenity, too, was outside the protection intended for speech and press.

The protection given speech and press was fashioned to assure unfettered interchange of ideas for the bringing about of political and social changes desired by the people. This objective was made explicit as early as 1774 in a letter of the Continental Congress to the inhabitants of Quebec:

> "The last right we shall mention, regards the freedom of the press. The importance of this consists, besides the advancement of truth, science, morality, and arts in general, in its diffusion of liberal sentiments on the administration of Government, its ready communication of thoughts between subjects, and its consequential promotion of union among them, whereby oppressive officers are shamed or intimidated, into more honourable and just modes of conducting affairs." 1 *Journals of the Continental Congress* 108 (1774).

All ideas having even the slightest redeeming social importance—unorthodox ideas, controversial ideas, even ideas hateful to the prevailing climate of opinion—have the full protection of the guaranties, unless excludable because they encroach upon the limited area of more important interests. But implicit in the history of the First Amendment is the rejection of obscenity as utterly without redeeming social importance. This rejection for that reason is mirrored in the universal judgment that obscenity should be restrained, reflected in the international agreement of over 50 nations, in the obscenity laws of all of the 48 States, and in the 20 obscenity laws enacted by the Congress from 1842 to 1956. This is the same judgment expressed by this Court in *Chaplinsky*:

> "* * * There are certain well-defined and narrowly limited classes of speech, the prevention and punishment of which have never been thought to raise any Constitutional problem. *These include the lewd and obscene * * *. It has been well observed that such utterances are no essential part of any exposition of ideas, and are of such slight social value as a step to truth that any benefit that may be derived from them is clearly outweighed by the social interest in order and morality* * * *." (Emphasis added.)

We hold that obscenity is not within the area of constitutionally protected speech or press. [This holding of the Court dispatched defendants' arguments that the state was penalizing "impure sexual *thoughts*, not shown to be related to any overt antisocial conduct which is or may be incited in the persons stimulated to such *thoughts*." Because "obscenity" was not speech of any cognizable sort, the state was fully free to regulate it, for the same reasons *Beauharnais* held that the state can regulate libel.]

However, sex and obscenity are not synonymous. Obscene material is material which deals with sex in a manner appealing to prurient interest.[20] The portrayal of sex, *e.g.*, in art, literature and scientific works, is not itself sufficient reason to deny material the constitutional protection of freedom of speech and press. Sex, a great and mysterious motive force in human life, has indisputably been a subject of absorbing interest to mankind through the ages; it is one of the vital problems of human interest and public concern. * * *

We perceive no significant difference between the meaning of obscenity developed in the case law and the definition of the A.L.I., Model Penal Code, § 207.10(2) (Tent. Draft No. 6, 1957), *viz.*:

> "... A thing is obscene if, considered as a whole, its predominant appeal is to prurient interest, *i.e.*, a shameful or morbid interest in nudity, sex, or excretion, and if it goes substantially beyond customary limits of candor in description or representation of such matters...."
> See comment, *id.*, at 10, and the discussion at page 29 *et seq*. * * *

The early leading standard of obscenity allowed material to be judged merely by the effect of an isolated excerpt upon particularly susceptible persons. *Regina v. Hicklin*, [1868] L.R. 3 Q.B. 360. Some American courts adopted this standard but later decisions have rejected it and substituted this test: whether to the average person, applying contemporary community standards, the dominant theme of the material taken as a whole appeals to prurient interest. The *Hicklin* test, judging obscenity by the effect of

---

20. *I.e.*, material having a tendency to excite lustful thoughts. *Webster's New International Dictionary* (Unabridged, 2d. ed., 1949) defines *prurient*, in pertinent part, as follows:

"... Itching; longing; uneasy with desire or longing; of persons, having itching, morbid, or lascivious longings; of desire, curiosity or propensity, lewd ..." * * *

isolated passages upon the most susceptible persons, might well encompass material legitimately treating with sex, and so it must be rejected as unconstitutionally restrictive of the freedoms of speech and press. On the other hand, the substituted standard provides safeguards adequate to withstand the charge of constitutional infirmity.

Both trial courts below sufficiently followed the proper standard. Both courts used the proper definition of obscenity. In addition, in the *Alberts* case, in ruling on a motion to dismiss, the trial judge indicated that, as the trier of facts, he was judging each item as a whole as it would affect the normal person, and in *Roth*, the trial judge instructed the jury as follows:

"... The test is not whether it would arouse sexual desires or sexual impure thoughts in those comprising a particular segment of the community, the young, the immature or the highly prudish or would leave another segment, the scientific or highly educated or the so-called worldly-wise and sophisticated indifferent and unmoved....

"The test in each case is the effect of the book, picture or publication considered as a whole, not upon any particular class, but upon all those whom it is likely to reach. In other words, you determine its impact upon the average person in the community. The books, pictures and circulars must be judged as a whole, in their entire context, and you are not to consider detached or separate portions in reaching a conclusion. You judge the circulars, pictures and publications which have been put in evidence by present-day standards of the community. You may ask yourselves does it offend the common conscience of the community by present-day standards.

. . .

"In this case, ladies and gentlemen of the jury, you and you alone are the exclusive judges of what the common conscience of the community is, and in determining that conscience you are to consider the community as a whole, young and old, educated and uneducated, the religious and the irreligious—men, women and children."

■ [On this note, Justice Brennan's opinion affirmed the lower courts' dispositions in both cases. We omit the opinion of MR. CHIEF JUSTICE WARREN, concurring in the Court's judgment.]

■ [MR. JUSTICE HARLAN concurred in the judgment affirming the state court conviction of *Alberts* but dissented from the judgment in *Roth*. Justice Harlan believed that principles of federalism justified a higher standard of review for the congressional enactment. Morals-based regulation should be located mainly at the local level. Justice Harlan also expressed doubts about Justice Brennan's community-norms focus for judicial review.]

■ MR. JUSTICE DOUGLAS, with whom MR. JUSTICE BLACK concurs, dissenting.

When we sustain these convictions, we make the legality of a publication turn on the purity of thought which a book or tract instills in the mind of the reader. I do not think we can approve that standard and be faithful to the command of the First Amendment, which by its terms is a restraint on Congress and which by the Fourteenth is a restraint on the States.

In the *Roth* case the trial judge charged the jury that the statutory words "obscene, lewd and lascivious" describe "that form of immorality which has relation to sexual impurity and has a tendency to excite lustful thoughts." He stated that the term "filthy" in the statute pertains "to that sort of treatment of sexual matters in such a vulgar and indecent way, so that it tends to arouse a feeling of disgust and revulsion." He went on to say that the material "must be calculated to corrupt and debauch the minds and morals" of "the average person in the community" not those of any particular class. "You judge the circulars, pictures and publications which have been put in evidence by present-day standards of the community. You may ask yourselves does it offend the common conscience of the community by present day standards."

The trial judge who, sitting without a jury, heard the *Alberts* case and the appellate court that sustained the judgment of conviction, took California's definition of "obscenity" from *People v. Wepplo*, 178 P.2d 853, 855 (Cal.App.1947). That case held that a book is obscene "if it has a substantial tendency to deprave or corrupt its readers by inciting lascivious thoughts or arousing lustful desire."

By these standards punishment is inflicted for thoughts provoked, not for overt acts nor antisocial conduct. This test cannot be squared with our decisions under the First Amendment. Even the ill-starred *Dennis* [*v. United States*, 341 U.S. 494, 502–11 (1951)] case conceded that speech to be punishable must have some relation to action which could be penalized by government. [In *Dennis*, the Court adopted the clear and present danger of imminent harm test for seditious speech.] This issue cannot be avoided by saying that obscenity is not protected by the First Amendment. The question remains, what is the constitutional test of obscenity?

The tests by which these convictions were obtained require only the arousing of sexual thoughts. Yet the arousing of sexual thoughts and desires happens every day in normal life in dozens of ways. Nearly 30 years ago a questionnaire sent to college and normal school women graduates asked what things were most stimulating sexually. Of 409 replies, 9 said "music"; 18 said "pictures"; 29 said "dancing"; 40 said "drama"; 95 said "books"; and 218 said "man." Alpert, "Judicial Censorship of Obscene Literature," 52 *Harv. L. Rev.* 40, 73.

The test of obscenity the Court endorses today gives the censor free range over a vast domain. To allow the State to step in and punish mere speech or publication that the judge or the jury thinks has an *undesirable* impact on thoughts but that is not shown to be a part of unlawful action is drastically to curtail the First Amendment. As recently stated by two of our outstanding authorities on obscenity, "The danger of influencing a change in the current moral standards of the community, or of shocking or offending readers, or of stimulating sex thoughts or desires apart from objective conduct, can never justify the losses to society that result from interference with literary freedom." Lockhart & McClure, Literature, "The Law of Obscenity and the Constitution," 38 *Minn. L. Rev.* 295, 387.

If we were certain that impurity of sexual thoughts impelled to action, we would be on less dangerous ground in punishing the distributors of this sex literature. But it is by no means clear that obscene literature, as so defined, is a significant factor in influencing substantial deviations from the community standards.

"There are a number of reasons for real and substantial doubts as to the soundness of that hypothesis. (1) Scientific studies of juvenile delinquency demonstrate that those who get into trouble, and are the greatest concern of the advocates of censorship, are far less inclined to read than those who do not become delinquent. The delinquents are generally the adventurous type, who have little use for reading and other non-active entertainment. Thus, even assuming that reading sometimes has an adverse effect upon moral conduct, the effect is not likely to be substantial, for those who are susceptible seldom read. (2) Sheldon and Eleanor Glueck, who are among the country's leading authorities on the treatment and causes of juvenile delinquency, have recently published the results of a ten year study of its causes. They exhaustively studied approximately 90 factors and influences that might lead to or explain juvenile delinquency, but the Gluecks gave no consideration to the type of reading material, if any, read by the delinquents. This is, of course, consistent with their finding that delinquents read very little. When those who know so much about the problem of delinquency among youth—the very group about whom the advocates of censorship are most concerned—conclude that what delinquents read has so little effect upon their conduct that it is not worth investigating in an exhaustive study of causes, there is good reason for serious doubt concerning the basic hypothesis on which obscenity censorship is defended. (3) The many other influences in society that stimulate sexual desire are so much more frequent in their influence, and so much more potent in their effect, that the influence of reading is likely, at most, to be relatively insignificant in the composite of forces that lead an individual into conduct deviating from the community sex standards. The Kinsey studies show the minor degree to which literature serves as a potent sexual stimulant. And the studies demonstrating that sex knowledge seldom results from reading indicates [sic] the relative unimportance of literature in sex thoughts as compared with other factors in society." Lockhart & McClure, *op. cit. supra*, pp. 385–386.

The absence of dependable information on the effect of obscene literature on human conduct should make us wary. It should put us on the side of protecting society's interest in literature, except and unless it can be said that the particular publication has an impact on action that the government can control.

As noted, the trial judge in the *Roth* case charged the jury in the alternative that the federal obscenity statute outlaws literature dealing with sex which offends "the common conscience of the community." That standard is, in my view, more inimical still to freedom of expression.

The standard of what offends "the common conscience of the community" conflicts, in my judgment, with the command of the First Amendment that "Congress shall make no law ... abridging the freedom of speech, or of the press." Certainly that standard would not be an acceptable one if religion, economics, politics or philosophy were involved. How does it become a constitutional standard when literature treating with sex is concerned?

Any test that turns on what is offensive to the community's standards is too loose, too capricious, too destructive of freedom of expression to be squared with the First Amendment. Under that test, juries can censor, suppress, and punish what they don't like, provided the matter relates to "sexual impurity" or has a tendency "to excite lustful thoughts." This is community censorship in one of its worst forms. It creates a regime where in the battle between the literati and the Philistines, the Philistines are certain to win. If experience in this field teaches anything, it is that "censorship of obscenity has almost always been both irrational and indiscriminate." Lockhart & McClure, *op. cit. supra*, at 371. The test adopted here accentuates that trend.

I assume there is nothing in the Constitution which forbids Congress from using its power over the mails to proscribe *conduct* on the grounds of good morals. No one would suggest that the First Amendment permits nudity in public places, adultery, and other phases of sexual misconduct.

I can understand (and at times even sympathize) with programs of civic groups and church groups to protect and defend the existing moral standards of the community. I can understand the motives of the Anthony Comstocks who would impose Victorian standards on the community. When speech alone is involved, I do not think that government, consistently with the First Amendment, can become the sponsor of any of these movements. I do not think that government, consistently with the First Amendment, can throw its weight behind one school or another. Government should be concerned with antisocial conduct, not with utterances. Thus, if the First Amendment guarantee of freedom of speech and press is to mean anything in this field, it must allow protests even against the moral code that the standard of the day sets for the community. In other words, literature should not be suppressed merely because it offends the moral code of the censor.

The legality of a publication in this country should never be allowed to turn either on the purity of thought which it instills in the mind of the reader or on the degree to which it offends the community conscience. By either test the role of the censor is exalted, and society's values in literary freedom are sacrificed. * * *

NOTES ON *ROTH* AND THE STATE'S POWER TO SUPPRESS "OBSCENITY"

1. *The Pre–History of* Roth. Early American laws often coupled obscenity with blasphemy. The first obscenity law in the colonies, enacted by Massachusetts in 1712, prohibited "the composing, writing, printing, or publishing of any filthy, obscene, or profane story, pamphlets, libel or mock sermon, in imitation of preaching or any other part of divine worship." (Quoted in *State v. Henry*, 732 P.2d 9, 12 (Or.1987)). The colonies routinely criminalized blasphemy, but did not single out sexual speech for proscription unless it was also anti-religious. *Id.*; see also Laurence H. Tribe, *American Constitutional Law* 904–05 (1988) (summarizing the early history). This approach derived from earlier English tradition, summarized by Justice Douglas in one of his repeated dissents in the obscenity cases:

> The advent of the printing press spurred censorship in England, but the ribald and the obscene were not, at first, within the scope of that which was officially banned. The censorship of the Star Chamber and the licensing of books under the Tudors and Stuarts was aimed at the blasphemous or heretical, the seditious or treasonous. At that date, the government made no effort to prohibit disseminations of obscenity. Rather, obscene literature was considered to raise a moral question properly cognizable only by ecclesiastical, and not the common-law, courts.

United States v. 12 200–Ft. Reels of Super 8mm. Film et. al. (Paladini, Claimant), 413 U.S. 123, 134–35 (1973) (Douglas, J., dissenting).

Obscenity as we understand it—graphic sexually explicit speech—emerged as an issue for the law in the nineteenth century, both in England and the United States.[a] A British court articulated what also became the American test for obscenity until it was replaced in *Roth*: "whether the tendency of the matter charged * * * is to deprave and corrupt those whose minds are open to such immoral influences, and into whose hands a publication of this sort may fall." *Regina v. Hicklin*, L.R. 3 Q.B. 360, 368 (1868). The *Hicklin* test produced nearly a century of judicial assessments of whether particular works tended to corrupt the morals of the audience. A New York court banned the classic lesbian novel *The Well of Loneliness* on the ground that "it seeks to justify the right of a pervert to prey upon normal members of a community and to uphold such relationship as noble and lofty." *People v. Friede* 233 N.Y.S. 565, 567 (Mag.Ct.1929) [Chapter 2, Section 2(A)(3)]. Other victims of the *Hicklin* test were *An American Tragedy*,[b] *Lady Chatterly's Lover*,[c] *God's Little Acre*,[d] and *Memoirs of Hecate County*.[e] It was also under the *Hicklin* regime that obscenity laws

---

a. The first federal statute, aimed at the "French post card trade," prohibited the importation of obscene pictorial matter. 5 Stat. 566 (1842). The first of the Comstock laws, named for the tireless anti-obscenity crusader Anthony Comstock, was enacted in 1868. 7 N.Y. Stats. 309 (1868) In Britain, Lord Campbell's Act criminalized the publication of obscene matter. 20 & 21 Vict., c. 83 (1857). The need for interpretation of Lord Campbell's Act prompted the judicial opinion in *Hicklin*.

b. *Commonwealth v. Friede*, 171 N.E. 472 (Mass.1930).

c. *Commonwealth v. Delacey*, 171 N.E. 455 (Mass.1930).

d. *Attorney General v. Book Named "God's Little Acre,"* 93 N.E.2d 819 (Mass. 1950).

e. *Doubleday & Co. v. New York*, 335 U.S. 848 (1948), affirming, *People v. Doubleday & Co.*, 77 N.E.2d 6 (N.Y.1947).

were used to suppress birth control materials. (See Chapter 1, Section 1.) The turning point in the acceptance of explicit sexuality in serious literature came with Judge Augustus Hand's decision allowing the importation of James Joyce's *Ulysses*. *United States v. One Book Entitled "Ulysses"*, 72 F.2d 705 (2d Cir. 1934.)

The meaning of the term "obscenity" has thus shifted to encompass very different kinds of disfavored expression in different time periods— from the blasphemous to the profane to the medical to the sexual. As always when considering historical evidence in the process of legal reasoning, the question is what to make of that. The Oregon Supreme Court determined that the historical record supported only the shielding of children from sexually explicit speech, and declared that state's obscenity statute invalid on state constitutional grounds. *State v. Henry*, 732 P.2d 9 (Or.1987). *Quaere* whether history reinforces the categorical approach, i.e., whatever "obscenity" has meant, it has signified an unprotected category of expression; or whether obscenity's longstanding kinship with blasphemy, which now would enjoy unquestioned First Amendment protection, renders the very category of obscenity rule highly suspect. Indeed, one might question whether a First Amendment inquiry should ever consider historical disfavor as a justification for limiting protection.

2. *Why Is Obscene Speech Treated Differently?* As *Roth* indicates, the Court has asserted a qualitative difference between sexual and political speech. In *Young v. American Mini Theatres, Inc.*, 427 U.S. 50, 70 (1976), for example, Justice Stevens' plurality opinion maintained that content-based regulation of sexual expression is permissible because "society's interest in protecting this type of expression is of a wholly different, and lesser, magnitude than the interest in untrammeled political debate." He continued, provocatively:

> Whether political oratory or philosophical discussion moves us to applaud or to despise what is said, every schoolchild can understand why our duty to defend the right to speak remains the same. But few of us would march our sons and daughters off to war to preserve the citizens' right to see "Specified Sexual Activities" exhibited in the theaters of our choice.

Based on deeming it less valuable, courts have assigned sexual speech a lower rung on the hierarchy of First Amendment values.

Although a majority of the Supreme Court rejected Justice Stevens' view in *American Mini Theatres*,[f] the Court's First Amendment doctrine

---

f. Justice Stevens wrote the opinion of the Court upholding a zoning ordinance imposed only on adult movie theaters. However, four Justices dissented, *American Mini Theatres*, 427 U.S. at 84 (Stewart, Brennan, Marshall, Blackmun, JJ., dissenting), and Justice Powell wrote separately to note that he disagreed with Justice Stevens' view "that non-obscene, erotic materials may be treated dif- ferently under First Amendment principles from other forms of protected expression." *Id.* at 73 n.1 (Powell, J., concurring). See also *FCC v. Pacifica Foundation*, 438 U.S. 726 (1978), where Justice Stevens again wrote a plurality opinion following the *American Mini Theatres* reasoning, four Justices again dissented, and Justice Powell again con-

nonetheless appears to depend upon the premise that sexual expression is less worthy than political expression. The Court allows government to regulate sexual expression in ways that it flatly forbids for political speech. Sexual expression can be zoned to remote parts of town, *City of Renton v. Playtime Theatres*, 475 U.S. 41 (1986), as well as *American Mini Theatres*; denied access to the airwaves until late at night, *FCC v. Pacifica Foundation*, 438 U.S. 726 (1978) (see Section 3, *infra*), and even criminally suppressed if the community finds it simultaneously arousing, offensive, and valueless. By contrast, the state is generally barred from regulating political expression, even if a majority of the public finds it offensive, immoral, and without redeeming value. In *Cohen v. California*, 403 U.S. 15 (1971), for example, the Court protected a young man's expression of opposition to the Vietnam War through the phrase, "Fuck the Draft" on his jacket.

3.   *Sex As Politics.* Can the sexual-versus-political speech distinction hold up? Consider the following:

- In a case involving, ironically, the film version of *Lady Chatterly's Lover*, the Court invalidated a New York statute that required the denial of a license to exhibit motion pictures "which are immoral in that they *portray* 'acts of sexual immorality . . . as desirable, acceptable or proper patterns of behavior.'" *Kingsley International Pictures Corp. v. Regents of the University of the State of New York*, 360 U.S. 684, 687 (1959) (quoting the lower court, 151 N.E.2d 197, 197 (N.Y.1958)). The New York Court of Appeals had found that the film was not obscene, but that, taken as a whole, it "alluringly portrays adultery as proper behavior." The Supreme Court found that the propriety of adultery was an idea, the advocacy of which was protected. There is no discussion in the opinion, however, of the impact of the presentation of an idea in eroticized form. The Court has seldom relied on *Kingsley* since, although it was cited in *Stanley v. Georgia* (See Chapter 1, Section 1[B]).

- In *Hustler Magazine v. Falwell*, 485 U.S. 46, 50 (1988), the Court held that *Hustler* magazine was protected against a libel suit for an illustrated satire depicting religious leader Reverend Jerry Falwell's first sexual experience as being with his mother in an outhouse. This case raises issues of personal privacy as well as sexual speech, yet the Supreme Court applied the First Amendment strenuously.

- Is the use of highly eroticized imagery to promote safer sex practices political? Medical? Or is a photograph of two persons about to engage in intercourse using a condom indistinguishable, for legal purposes, from the same image absent a condom? See Section 3, infra.

4.   *What Is Obscene Speech?* For 15 years after *Roth*, the Court's definition of obscenity evolved, but there was no majority on the Court in support of any single standard. In *Miller v. California*, 413 U.S. 15 (1973), Chief

curred in the Court's judgment but rejected
the Stevens reasoning.

Justice Burger obtained a majority of five Justices for the following limits on state regulation:

> [W]e now confine the permissible scope of such regulation to works which depict or describe sexual conduct. That conduct must be specifically defined by the applicable state law, as written or authoritatively construed. A state offense must also be limited to works which, taken as a whole, appeal to the prurient interest in sex, which portray sexual conduct in a patently offensive way, and which, taken as a whole, do not have serious literary, artistic, political, or scientific value.

Id. at 24. The opinion gave as "plain examples of what a state statute could define for regulation * * * [p]atently offensive representations or descriptions of ultimate sexual acts, normal or perverted, actual or simulated" and "[p]atently offensive representations or descriptions of masturbation, excretory functions, and lewd exhibition of the genitals." Chief Justice Burger made clear that the state could only regulate representations of "patently offensive 'hard core' sexual conduct." What is hard core or patently offensive is to be ascertained by "applying contemporary community standards" of the state or area in which the representations are purveyed.

Note that under *Miller* the state can regulate depictions or representations of some sexual activity more rigorously than it can regulate the activity itself under the *Griswold-Loving* line of cases. This is an inversion of the First Amendment, which usually protects representation more than conduct.

How helpful is the *Miller* definition? Specifically, what exactly is "the prurient interest"? A Washington statute that defined prurient interest as "that which incites lasciviousness or lust" came before the Court in *Brockett v. Spokane Arcades, Inc.*, 472 U.S. 491 (1985). The appeals court had invalidated the statute on the ground that "it reached material that incited normal as well as unhealthy interest in sex." The Supreme Court reversed, ruling that any overbreadth was curable, in that the scope of the term "lust" could be construed to cover only "that which appeals to a shameful or morbid interest in sex." *Id.* at 504–05. Most remarkable is what is missing from the opinion—any attempt at defining "normal," "unhealthy," "shameful," or "morbid."

5. *What Are the State's Interests?* One result of *Roth*'s categorical approach to sexual speech is that the government never has to justify its rationale for suppression. If expression is obscene, the state can elect to ban it on categorical grounds. If it is sexually explicit but stops short of obscenity, the case law establishes that zoning may be used to restrict its accessibility; there, the question usually becomes whether the geographic restrictions are too harsh. Thus, proof of the negative consequences of obscenity has been notoriously absent from lawmaking. Consider the impact of this when you read Section 2. How would feminist theories, such as those in Chapter 3, address this issue?

6. *Speech or Conduct? Public or Private?* Frederick Schauer, "Speech and 'Speech'—Obscenity and 'Obscenity': An Exercise in the Interpretation of

Constitutional Language," 67 *Geo. L.J.* 899 (1979), argues that "the prototypical pornographic item on closer analysis shares more of the characteristics of sexual activity than of the communicative process. The pornographic item is in a real sense a sexual surrogate." Hence, he maintains that obscene representations are not "speech" at all, but rather "conduct" unprotected by the First Amendment. Schauer served on President Reagan's Pornography Commission, which issued a report reflecting these views. Consider how the feminist anti-pornography ordinance described in Section 2 draws on that approach.

The Court held in *Stanley v. Georgia*, 394 U.S. 557 (1969) [Chapter 1, Section 1(B)], that the possession of obscene materials in one's home cannot be criminalized. The contrast between that holding and those discussed in this chapter starkly illustrates the fundamental role played by notions of a sharp break between public and private realms in the legal doctrine on sexual speech. A challenge to an Indiana law prohibiting public nudity triggered an attempt by the Court to map more precisely the bounds of those two realms and to justify the extremely anomalous result that, for obscene speech alone, expression that is private is entitled to greater protection than that which is public.

Barnes v. Glen Theatre, Inc., 501 U.S. 560, 111 S.Ct. 2456, 115 L.Ed.2d 504 (1991). Section 35–45–4–1 of the Indiana Code prohibited nudity in a public place and defined "nudity" to include wearing less than a G-string, not covering female breast nipples with "pasties," or showing male genitals "in a discernibly turgid state." This statute was the basis for prosecution of the Kitty Kat Lounge, where female go-go dancers took off all their clothes, and Glen Theatre, an adult bookstore offering booths where patrons could watch female strippers through glass windows. These defendants claimed that erotic dance, including nudity, involved "expressive conduct" protected by the first amendment. For this reason, the public nudity statute should not have been applied to their establishments. The Seventh Circuit, sitting en banc, agreed. Judge Posner wrote a concurring opinion containing a learned discussion of erotic art and dancing, as well as the First Amendment's protection of "expressive conduct." A fragmented Supreme Court rejected defendants' claim and reversed the Seventh Circuit.

Writing for himself and Justices O'Connor and Kennedy, Chief Justice Rehnquist's plurality opinion started with the premise that nude dancing can be "expressive conduct within the outer limits of the First Amendment, though we view it as only marginally so." He evaluated the public nudity regulation under the framework of *United States v. O'Brien*, 391 U.S. 367 (1968) (upholding rules against burning draft cards). The statute easily satisfied the *O'Brien* requirement that the law further a "substantial" governmental interest, namely, "protecting societal order and morality." The Chief Justice pointed to the laws of 47 states that regulated public indecency and, as authority, cited *Bowers v. Hardwick* [Chapter 1, Section 2]. The Indiana law also met *O'Brien*'s requirement that the government interest be "unrelated to the suppression of free expression." According to the Chief Justice, the requirement that dancers utilize G-strings and pasties did not detract from whatever erotic message they were conveying. *Quaere*: Is this a realistic view of erotic dancing? Judge Posner's concurring opinion suggests the Chief Justice's point is not factually supportable.

Justice Scalia concurred only in the Court's judgment. He believed that no First Amendment interest was involved and that the polity can broadly prohibit any conduct just because its citizens consider it immoral. "In American society, such prohibitions have included, for example, sadism, cockfights, bestiality, suicide, drug use, prostitution, and sodomy. While there may be great diversity of view on whether various of these prohibitions should exist (though I have found few ready to abandon, in principle, all of them), there is no doubt that * * * the Constitution does not prohibit them simply because they regulate 'morality.' " [Following the Chief Justice, Justice Scalia cited *Bowers* as his main authority.] Only where the government prohibits conduct "precisely because of its communicative attributes" does the Court rigorously scrutinize state regulation. *Quaere*: Isn't the communication of erotic possibilities exactly the reason why Indiana prohibits nudity in general and nude dancing even more so? Wouldn't it be unconstitutional under *Stanley* to arrest someone for nude, lewd dancing in his or her own home—and indeed would anyone even care? What people care about is expression of eroticism to others. Doesn't that then bring nude dancing under the First Amendment? Isn't the case for First Amendment protection for nude dancing stronger than its protection for racist cross-burning, to which Justice Scalia gave innovative First Amendment protection in *R.A.V.* [Chapter 5, Section 3]?

Justice Souter also concurred only in the Court's judgment, providing the critical fifth vote for sustaining the law and the prosecution. He agreed with the Chief Justice that nude dancing is expressive conduct governed by the *O'Brien* standard but was unwilling to find morality alone a sufficiently "substantial" state interest. Following suggestions in *Renton v. Playtime Theatres, Inc.*, 475 U.S. 41 (1986) (upholding restrictive zoning for establishments of adult entertainment), Justice Souter required harmful third-party effects to justify restrictions on expression. He found "secondary effects of adult entertainment establishments" to include sexual assault and prostitution. *Quaere*: There was no evidence that the Indiana statute was adopted for any reason but morality-based ones, as the Chief Justice found. Did Justice Souter simply make up his own justifications? Does nude dancing stimulate sexual assault, in fact? If the prevention of sexual assault can be a substantial state interest justifying the restriction of fundamental constitutional rights, does that mean that the state can segregate the sexes, or the races or gays from straights, on the ground that segregation is needed to prevent assaults? (Recall military justifications for segregating African Americans, excluding women from combat, and expelling gay men and lesbians, Chapter 4.)

Justice White, joined by Justices Marshall, Blackmun, and Stevens, dissented. They argued that the statute was aimed at the "communicative aspect of the erotic dance" and therefore was not content-neutral, as required by *O'Brien*.

David Cole, Playing by Pornography's Rules: The Regulation of Sexual Expression

143 *University of Pennsylvania Law Review* 111, 143–50, 176–77 (1994).*

The most recent example of the Court's sanctioning of public/private policing is *Barnes v. Glen Theatre, Inc.*, in which the Court upheld an Indiana "public nudity" statute that required nude dancers to wear pasties and a G-string. This case is about nothing but the public/private line; as Justice Scalia noted, "Indiana bans nudity in public places, but not within the privacy of the home." The Court's judgment in *Barnes* rested tenuously on three separate opinions * * *. Virtually the only point of agreement [among] the five Justices who made up the majority was that Indiana's law was unrelated to the suppression of expression. Reaching this conclusion was necessary to uphold the statute because the Court had previously recognized nude dancing as expressive conduct, and had recently reaffirmed that where regulation of expressive conduct is related to its communicative aspects, it violates the First Amendment absent a compelling state interest. But the conclusion is highly dubious.

Rehnquist and Scalia reasoned that the state's interest in regulating public nudity was unrelated to expression because the state sought to protect "societal order and morality." Neither Justice explained, however, *how* public nudity harms public morality other than by virtue of what it expresses. Scalia insisted that the ban was unrelated to expression because it "generally" prohibited public nudity, irrespective of its message. But Scalia's use of "generally" is question-begging. The Indiana law does not "generally" prohibit all nudity, but singles out *public* nudity, that is, nudity communicated to others in public.

Ordinarily, where government selectively regulates public but not private conduct or expression, there is reason to suspect that the government is attempting to suppress the message communicated to the public, and strict scrutiny is triggered. In *Texas v. Johnson*, for example, the fact that the Texas statute prohibited only those flag burnings that would "seriously offend one or more persons likely to observe or discover" the conduct led the Court to conclude that the government's regulatory interest was related to the message that the conduct expressed, and therefore to apply stringent First Amendment scrutiny. By contrast, in *United States v. O'Brien*, the Court justified application of relaxed scrutiny to a statute prohibiting destruction of draft cards by noting that the law "does not distinguish between public and private destruction, and it does not punish only destruction engaged in for the purpose of expressing views." Like the flag burning statute in *Johnson* and unlike the draft card law in *O'Brien*,

Indiana banned only *public* nudity, and did not attempt a *general* regulation of nudity.

Chief Justice Rehnquist justified his conclusion that the suppression of expression was not intended by claiming that "[p]ublic nudity is the evil the state seeks to prevent, whether or not it is combined with expressive activity." But public nudity has no effect on public morals except by virtue of what it expresses to those who see it: offensiveness, immodesty, sensuality, disrespect for social mores, etc. If public nudity expressed nothing, society would have no interest in suppressing it. It is only because public nudity is expressive that it is regulated.

Justice Souter's rationale for finding the Indiana law "unrelated to the suppression of expression" is no less strained. He reasoned that because Indiana might have determined that forbidding nude barroom dancing would further its "interest in preventing prostitution, sexual assault, and associated crimes," the public nudity law should be viewed as directed at those secondary effects, and not at nude dancing's expressive elements. In order to reach this result, Souter had to clear several hurdles.

First, there was no indication that Indiana actually sought to further these interests. Second, there was no basis for believing that the secondary effects Justice Souter identified as flowing from nude dancers would be mitigated by pasties and a G-string. If bars featuring nude dancing attract "prostitution, sexual assault, and associated crime," it is difficult to see why bars featuring nude dancing under a pasties-and-G-string regime would not. Third, the public nudity law on its face extended beyond nude barroom dancing, reaching instances of public nudity—such as skinny-dipping, nude sunbathing, and "streaking"—with no connection to the secondary effects Souter posited as the law's justification. Although Scalia and Rehnquist relied on what they viewed as the law's "general" scope to support their determination that the statute was not targeted at suppressing the erotic messages of nude dancers, Souter relied on the law's specific application to nude barroom dancers to uphold it as a regulation directed at the secondary effects of nude dancing. In essence, the Justices upheld different laws. The nude dancing law Souter upheld would fail under Rehnquist and Scalia's analysis, which was predicated on the law generally banning all public nudity. And the law that Rehnquist and Scalia upheld would have failed Justice Souter's test, because Indiana could not possibly demonstrate secondary effects with respect to *all* public nudity.

Finally, and most problematically, even if nude barroom dancing has the effects Souter identified, those effects are not "secondary," but are directly linked to its communicative content. Where government regulates speech because its content is said to cause harmful effects, the government must satisfy the *Brandenburg v. Ohio* test; here, Indiana would have had to show that nude dancing was directed to causing unlawful conduct, and was likely to produce that effect imminently. In response to this concern, Souter opined that the effects might not have been caused by, but only correlated with, the nude dancing, thereby obviating the need to apply *Brandenburg*.
* * *

Putting aside the wisdom of grounding First Amendment protection on an evanescent distinction between effects caused by or correlated with speech, each of the possibilities Souter identified is inextricably tied to nude dancing's expressive character. If "the simple viewing of nude bodies" has any effect, it must be by virtue of what the nude bodies communicate visually. Similarly, if nude dancing attracts a crowd of predisposed men, it must be because they are drawn to what nude dancing communicates to them, unless one believes that nude dancers have some magnetic force of attraction irrespective of what they communicate. What is going on may not be "persuasive" in the strictly rational sense, but the First Amendment is not restricted to protecting rational persuasion.

Thus, all of the Justices in the *Barnes* majority strained mightily to reach the conclusion that the regulation at issue was unrelated to the suppression of expression. In an exchange with the *Barnes* dissenters, Justice Scalia provides a clue as to why the Justices were driven to such great lengths. The dissent had argued that the Indiana law was unconstitutional, at least as applied to nude barroom dancing, because such an application had nothing to do with avoiding offense to nonconsenting parties, and therefore "the only remaining purpose must relate to the communicative elements of the performance." Scalia responded:

> Perhaps the dissenters believe that "offense to others" *ought* to be the only reason for restricting nudity in public places generally, but there is no basis for thinking that our society has ever shared that Thoreauvian "you-may-do-what-you-like-so-long-as-it-does-not-injure-someone-else" beau ideal—much less for thinking that it was written into the Constitution.

Invoking the remarkable image of "60,000 fully consenting adults crowded into the Hoosier Dome to display their genitals to one another," Scalia maintained that such an event could be prohibited "even if there were not an offended innocent in the crowd." He argued that "[o]ur society prohibits, and all human societies have prohibited, certain activities not because they harm others but because they are considered, in the traditional phrase, '*contra bonos mores*,' *i.e.*, immoral," and one of those activities is public exposure of one's private parts.

Thus, Scalia not only accepts the public/private line, he makes it a moral imperative. But one might as easily say flag burning, criticizing one's elected leaders, and blasphemy are "immoral." The First Amendment usually demands more than a Latin phrase to justify the regulation of expression and specifically bars regulation based solely on a judgment that the expression is immoral. Thus, the majority was driven to find the Indiana statute "unrelated to expression" because it otherwise could not have upheld the law as a regulation of morals.

Left unstated is *how* requiring otherwise nude dancers to don pasties and G-strings will uphold the morals of the community. The moral difference between an entirely nude dancer and a dancer wearing pasties and a G-string is not immediately apparent. But the pasties and G-string do serve an important symbolic function: they insist that the law is present in this public space, very literally enforcing a line, albeit a very fine one. The thinness of the line is ultimately less important than the fact that the line exists. The statute regulates the public sphere precisely by demanding that dancers keep their "private parts" private, but only in the most minimal sense. Thus, the pasties and G-string are an apt metaphor for the regulation of sexual expression: they symbolically police the public sphere by barring certain "private" topics from surfacing, even as they permit (and possibly even increase the desirability of) *regulated* sexual expression in the public sphere. They reflect society's compromise on sexual expression: such expression may remain relatively free in the private sphere, but its public expression, although far from forbidden altogether, must be subject to legal regulation. The Court has in turn sanctioned that compromise, but in order to do so it has had to invert the First Amendment. * * *

[Cole then argues that what drives the society to regulate public expressions of sexuality is the need to impose limits on sexuality, "that which risks being beyond control * * * for the sake ultimately of the limit itself." Because pornography is dependent upon its taboo status for its appeal as well as its threat, this action by the state also helps to define what is sexy, with serious consequences for how all of us experience our sexuality. In developing this line of argument, Cole draws upon Michel Foucault's theory of sexuality as a discourse, and one that is the product of ostensibly repressive laws as well as normalizing social categories. See Chapter 3, Section 2(A).]

Although the public/private line is conventionally seen as essential to maintain the values of civilization, it plays an equally central role in the construction of sexuality. In large part, what makes sexual expression sexy in our culture is the potential for transgression, for abandonment of inhibitions, and for the play of fantasy. Social prohibitions ironically contribute to this conception of sexuality by constructing lines to transgress, inhibitions to abandon, and a "normal" reality against which fantasies may be played out. Pornographers play along with the lines society draws and even go further by drawing their own lines. Society regulates sexual expression because of its perceived dangers, yet without such regulation sexual expression might well lose some of its "dangerous" appeal.

Thus, while conventional accounts of sexual regulation portray the sex drive as an otherwise unrestrained libidinal instinct that must be contained, sublimated, and regulated to serve the interests of civilization, I have suggested that the sex drive is itself shaped by the regulatory lines we draw and precisely by the excitement that transgressing those taboos promises. The regulation of sexual expression reveals at bottom, not a struggle between social order and sexual anarchy, but a dynamic in which both law and sex are inextricably dependent on the drawing of lines. Paradoxically, then, sexual expression to some extent will always elude society's desperate attempts to regulate it, because sexual expression transforms whatever taboo is imposed into a fetish.

By our regulatory obsession we have constructed a very particular type of sexuality, one in which transgressing lines and violating taboos is central to sexual excitement. We should not (and most of us do not) assume that such a construction of sexuality is necessary or inevitable. But this construction of sexuality is so strongly determined in our culture—by the very regulations we impose—that it is difficult to conceive of sexuality in other than transgressive terms. This construction of sexuality limits the possibilities for alternative visions of sexuality, visions that are not delimited by the transgression of taboos. Both the traditional critics of pornography, who envision a sexuality characterized by love and devotion, and the feminist critics, who seek a sexuality predicated on equality between women and men, undermine their own causes by focusing on suppression as the means for achieving those ideals. They would do better *not* to seek to control sexual expression, but instead to participate in affirmative private and public exploration of alternative visions. In the end, not only the First Amendment, but sexuality itself, demand more speech, not less. More regulation and less speech will only ensure that we remain bound to a pornographic conception of sexuality.

PROBLEM 6–1

REGULATION OF CHILD PORNOGRAPHY

In 1977, the New York Legislature enacted Article 263 of its Penal Law. N.Y. Penal Law art. 263 (McKinney 1989). Section 263.05 criminalized as a class C felony the use of a child in a sexual performance:

> "A person is guilty of the use of a child in a sexual performance if knowing the character and content thereof he employs, authorizes or induces a child less than sixteen years of age to engage in a sexual performance or being a parent, legal guardian or custodian of such child, he consents to the participation by such child in a sexual performance."

A "[s]exual performance" was defined as "any performance or part thereof which includes sexual conduct by a child less than sixteen years of age." § 263.00(1). "Sexual conduct" was in turn defined in § 263.00(3):

> " 'Sexual conduct' means actual or simulated sexual intercourse, deviate sexual intercourse, sexual bestiality, masturbation, sado-masochistic abuse, or lewd exhibition of the genitals."

"Performance" was defined as "any play, motion picture, photograph or dance" or "any other visual representation exhibited before an audience." § 263.00(4). Section 263.15 made the following a Class D felony: "A person is guilty of promoting a sexual performance by a child when, knowing the character and content thereof, he produces, directs or promotes any performance which includes sexual conduct by a child less than sixteen years of age." Section 263.00(5) defined "promote" to mean "to procure, manufacture, issue, sell, give, provide, lend, mail, deliver, transfer, transmute, publish, distribute, circulate, disseminate, present, exhibit or advertise, or to offer or agree to do the same." Section 263.10 banned the knowing distribution of "obscene" material of this nature.

A bookseller is charged with knowingly selling photographs of naked children; the children's faces are covered, but their genitals are bared for the camera. Consider the following queries:

(A) Will or ought the New York courts interpret Article 263 to impose criminal penalties upon the bookseller? Would such criminal penalties be constitutional under *Roth*? *Miller*?

(B) Does it make a statutory or constitutional difference that the books are medical textbooks and that the bookseller only handles medical texts? How about if the books are collections of artistic photographs and the bookseller is the Whitney Museum? What if the children are simply posed, and the bookseller is an adult entertainment shop in Times Square?

(C) Is the statute a regulation of sexual content, or of child labor? If the latter is the intent, how would you draft a statute to address the particular situation of children being used for sexually explicit modeling?

After you have analyzed these doctrinal issues, think about how David Cole or Michel Foucault would analyze the issues.

New York v. Paul Ira Ferber

United States Supreme Court, 1982.
458 U.S. 747, 102 S.Ct. 3348, 73 L.Ed.2d 1113.

■ JUSTICE WHITE delivered the opinion of the Court.

In recent years, the exploitive use of children in the production of pornography has become a serious national problem. The Federal Government and 47 States have sought to combat the problem with statutes specifically directed at the production of child pornography. At least half of such statutes do not require that the materials produced be legally obscene. Thirty-five States and the United States Congress have also passed legislation prohibiting the distribution of such materials; 20 States prohibit the distribution of material depicting children engaged in sexual conduct without requiring that the material be legally obscene.[2]

[Paul Ferber, the proprietor of a Manhattan bookstore specializing in sexually oriented products, sold two films to an undercover police officer. The films are devoted almost exclusively to depicting young boys mastur-

---

2. In addition to New York, 19 States have prohibited the dissemination of material depicting children engaged in sexual conduct regardless of whether the material is obscene. [Citations to laws in Arizona, Colorado, Delaware. Florida, Hawaii, Kentucky, Louisiana, Massachusetts, Michigan, Mississippi, Montana, New Jersey, Oklahoma, Pennsylvania, Rhode Island, Texas, Utah, West Virginia, and Wisconsin.] Fifteen states prohibit dissemination of such material only if it is obscene. [Citation to statutes in Alabama, Arkansas, California, Illinois, Indiana, Maine, Minnesota, Nebraska, New Hampshire, North Dakota, Ohio, Oregon, South Dakota, Tennessee, and Washington.] The federal statute also prohibits dissemination only if the material is obscene as to minors. 18 U.S.C. § 2252(a). Two states prohibit dissemination only if the material is obscene as to minors. [Connecticut and Virginia.] Twelve States prohibit only the use of minors in the production of the material. [Alaska, Georgia, Idaho, Iowa, Kansas, Maryland, Missouri, Nevada, New Mexico, North Carolina, South Carolina, Wyoming.]

bating. Ferber was indicted on two counts of violating section 263.10 and two counts of violating section 263.15, the two New York laws controlling dissemination of child pornography [quoted in Problem 6–1]. After a jury trial, Ferber was found guilty of the two counts under section 263.15, which did not require proof that the films were obscene. The New York Court of Appeals overturned Ferber's conviction as inconsistent with the First Amendment as interpreted in *Miller*. The Supreme Court reversed.]

The Court of Appeals' assumption [that the *Miller* obscenity standard governed] was not unreasonable in light of our decisions. This case, however, constitutes our first examination of a statute directed at and limited to depictions of sexual activity involving children. We believe our inquiry should begin with the question of whether a State has somewhat more freedom in proscribing works which portray sexual acts or lewd exhibitions of genitalia by children. * * *

The *Miller* standard, like its predecessors, was an accommodation between the State's interests in protecting the "sensibilities of unwilling recipients" from exposure to pornographic material and the dangers of censorship inherent in unabashedly content-based laws. Like obscenity statutes, laws directed at the dissemination of child pornography run the risk of suppressing protected expression by allowing the hand of the censor to become unduly heavy. For the following reasons, however, we are persuaded that the States are entitled to greater leeway in the regulation of pornographic depictions of children.

First. It is evident beyond the need for elaboration that a State's interest in "safeguarding the physical and psychological well-being of a minor" is "compelling." *Globe Newspaper Co. v. Superior Court*, 457 U.S. 596, 607 (1982). "A democratic society rests, for its continuance, upon the healthy, well-rounded growth of young people into full maturity as citizens." *Prince v. Massachusetts*, 321 U.S. 158, 168 (1944). Accordingly, we have sustained legislation aimed at protecting the physical and emotional well-being of youth even when the laws have operated in the sensitive area of constitutionally protected rights. In *Prince v. Massachusetts*, the Court held that a statute prohibiting use of a child to distribute literature on the street was valid notwithstanding the statute's effect on a First Amendment activity. In *Ginsberg v. New York*, [390 U.S. 629 (1968)], we sustained a New York law protecting children from exposure to nonobscene literature. Most recently, we held that the Government's interest in the "well-being of its youth" justified special treatment of indecent broadcasting received by adults as well as children. *FCC v. Pacifica Foundation*, 438 U.S. 726 (1978).

The prevention of sexual exploitation and abuse of children constitutes a government objective of surpassing importance. The legislative findings accompanying passage of the New York laws reflect this concern:

"[T]here has been a proliferation of exploitation of children as subjects in sexual performances. The care of children is a sacred trust and should not be abused by those who seek to profit through a commercial network based upon the exploitation of children. The public policy of the state demands the protection of children from exploitation through sexual performances." 1977 N.Y.Laws, ch. 910, § 1.

We shall not second-guess this legislative judgment. Respondent has not intimated that we do so. Suffice it to say that virtually all of the States and the United States have passed legislation proscribing the production of or otherwise combating "child pornography." The legislative judgment, as well as the judgment found in the relevant literature, is that the use of children as subjects of pornographic materials is harmful to the physiological, emotional, and mental health of the child. That judgment, we think, easily passes muster under the First Amendment.

Second. The distribution of photographs and films depicting sexual activity by juveniles is intrinsically related to the sexual abuse of children in at least two ways. First, the materials produced are a permanent record of the children's participation and the harm to the child is exacerbated by their circulation.[10] Second, the distribution network for child pornography must be closed if the production of material which requires the sexual exploitation of children is to be effectively controlled. Indeed, there is no serious contention that the legislature was unjustified in believing that it is difficult, if not impossible, to halt the exploitation of children by pursuing only those who produce the photographs and movies. While the production of pornographic materials is a low-profile, clandestine industry, the need to market the resulting products requires a visible apparatus of distribution. The most expeditious if not the only practical method of law enforcement may be to dry up the market for this material by imposing severe criminal penalties on persons selling, advertising, or otherwise promoting the product. Thirty-five States and Congress have concluded that restraints on the distribution of pornographic materials are required in order to effectively combat the problem, and there is a body of literature and testimony to support these legislative conclusions.

[These demonstrated third-party effects persuaded Justice White that the *Miller* standard of looking at community values was too permissive of child pornography.]

Third. The advertising and selling of child pornography provide an economic motive for and are thus an integral part of the production of such materials, an activity illegal throughout the Nation. "It rarely has been suggested that the constitutional freedom for speech and press extends its immunity to speech or writing used as an integral part of conduct in violation of a valid criminal statute." *Giboney v. Empire Storage & Ice Co.*, 336 U.S. 490, 498 (1949). We note that were the statutes outlawing the

---

10. As one authority has explained:

"[P]ornography poses an even greater threat to the child victim than does sexual abuse or prostitution. Because the child's actions are reduced to a recording, the pornography may haunt him in future years, long after the original misdeed took place. A child who has posed for a camera must go through life knowing that the recording is circulating within the mass distribution system for child pornography." Shouvlin, "Preventing the Sexual Exploitation of Children: A Model Act," 17 *Wake Forest L. Rev.* 535, 545 (1981). * * *

employment of children in these films and photographs fully effective, and the constitutionality of these laws has not been questioned, the First Amendment implications would be no greater than that presented by laws against distribution: enforceable production laws would leave no child pornography to be marketed.

Fourth. The value of permitting live performances and photographic reproductions of children engaged in lewd sexual conduct is exceedingly modest, if not *de minimis*. We consider it unlikely that visual depictions of children performing sexual acts or lewdly exhibiting their genitals would often constitute an important and necessary part of a literary performance or scientific or educational work. As a state judge in this case observed, if it were necessary for literary or artistic value, a person over the statutory age who perhaps looked younger could be utilized. Simulation outside of the prohibition of the statute could provide another alternative. Nor is there any question here of censoring a particular literary theme or portrayal of sexual activity. The First Amendment interest is limited to that of rendering the portrayal somewhat more "realistic" by utilizing or photographing children.

Fifth. Recognizing and classifying child pornography as a category of material outside the protection of the First Amendment is not incompatible with our earlier decisions. "The question whether speech is, or is not, protected by the First Amendment often depends on the content of the speech." *Young v. American Mini Theatres* (opinion of Stevens, J.). "[I]t is the content of [an] utterance that determines whether it is a protected epithet or an unprotected 'fighting comment.'" *Id*. Leaving aside the special considerations when public officials are the target, a libelous publication is not protected by the Constitution. Thus, it is not rare that a content-based classification of speech has been accepted because it may be appropriately generalized that within the confines of the given classification, the evil to be restricted so overwhelmingly outweighs the expressive interests, if any, at stake, that no process of case-by-case adjudication is required. When a definable class of material, such as that covered by § 263.15, bears so heavily and pervasively on the welfare of children engaged in its production, we think the balance of competing interests is clearly struck and that it is permissible to consider these materials as without the protection of the First Amendment.

There are, of course, limits on the category of child pornography which, like obscenity, is unprotected by the First Amendment. As with all legislation in this sensitive area, the conduct to be prohibited must be adequately defined by the applicable state law, as written or authoritatively construed. Here the nature of the harm to be combated requires that the state offense be limited to works that *visually* depict sexual conduct by children below a specified age. The category of "sexual conduct" proscribed must also be suitably limited and described.

The test for child pornography is separate from the obscenity standard enunciated in *Miller*, but may be compared to it for the purpose of clarity. The *Miller* formulation is adjusted in the following respects: A trier of fact need not find that the material appeals to the prurient interest of the average person; it is not required that sexual conduct portrayed be done so in a patently offensive manner; and the material at issue need not be considered as a whole. We note that the distribution of descriptions or other depictions of sexual conduct, not otherwise obscene, which do not involve live performance or photographic or other visual reproduction of live performances, retains First Amendment protection. As with obscenity laws, criminal responsibility may not be imposed without some element of scienter on the part of the defendant.

Section 263.15's prohibition incorporates a definition of sexual conduct that comports with the above-stated principles. The forbidden acts to be depicted are listed with sufficient precision and represent the kind of conduct that, if it were the theme of a work, could render it legally obscene: "actual or simulated sexual intercourse, deviate sexual intercourse, sexual bestiality, masturbation, sado-masochistic abuse, or lewd exhibition of the genitals." § 263.00(3). The term "lewd exhibition of the genitals" is not unknown in this area and, indeed, was given in *Miller* as an example of a permissible regulation. A performance is defined only to include live or visual depictions: "any play, motion picture, photograph or dance ... [or] other visual representation exhibited before an audience." § 263.00(4). Section 263.15 expressly includes a scienter requirement.

[Justice White held that the statute was constitutionally applied to Ferber's case. As to Ferber's further claim that the statute was overbroad in its regulation, perhaps in other cases, Justice White reasoned that the Court's First Amendment overbreadth jurisprudence did not reach this far. Compare *R.A.V.*, Chapter 5, Section 3.]

■ JUSTICE O'CONNOR, concurring.

Although I join the Court's opinion, I write separately to stress that the Court does not hold that New York must except "material with serious literary, scientific, or educational value," from its statute. The Court merely holds that, even if the First Amendment shelters such material, New York's current statute is not sufficiently overbroad to support respondent's facial attack. The compelling interests identified in today's opinion suggest that the Constitution might in fact permit New York to ban knowing distribution of works depicting minors engaged in explicit sexual conduct, regardless of the social value of the depictions. For example, a 12–year-old child photographed while masturbating surely suffers the same psychological harm whether the community labels the photograph "edifying" or "tasteless." The audience's appreciation of the depiction is simply irrelevant to New York's asserted interest in protecting children from psychological, emotional, and mental harm.

An exception for depictions of serious social value, moreover, would actually increase opportunities for the content-based censorship disfavored by the First Amendment. As drafted, New York's statute does not attempt to suppress the communication of particular ideas. The statute permits discussion of child sexuality, forbidding only attempts to render the "portrayal[s] somewhat more 'realistic' by utilizing or photographing children."

Thus, the statute attempts to protect minors from abuse without attempting to restrict the expression of ideas by those who might use children as live models.

On the other hand, it is quite possible that New York's statute is overbroad because it bans depictions that do not actually threaten the harms identified by the Court. For example, clinical pictures of adolescent sexuality, such as those that might appear in medical textbooks, might not involve the type of sexual exploitation and abuse targeted by New York's statute. Nor might such depictions feed the poisonous "kiddie porn" market that New York and other States have attempted to regulate. Similarly, pictures of children engaged in rites widely approved by their cultures, such as those that might appear in issues of the *National Geographic,* might not trigger the compelling interests identified by the Court. It is not necessary to address these possibilities further today, however, because this potential overbreadth is not sufficiently substantial to warrant facial invalidation of New York's statute.

■ [JUSTICE BLACKMUN concurred in the result, without opinion. JUSTICE STEVENS concurred in the judgment only. The following excerpt is from the opinion concurring in the judgment written by JUSTICE BRENNAN, joined by JUSTICE MARSHALL:]

* * * [I]n my view application of § 263.15 or any similar statute to depictions of children that in themselves do have serious literary, artistic, scientific, or medical value, would violate the First Amendment. As the Court recognizes, the limited classes of speech, the suppression of which does not raise serious First Amendment concerns, have two attributes. They are of exceedingly "slight social value," and the State has a compelling interest in their regulation. The First Amendment value of depictions of children that are in themselves serious contributions to art, literature, or science, is, by definition, simply not *"de minimis."* At the same time, the State's interest in suppression of such materials is likely to be far less compelling. For the Court's assumption of harm to the child resulting from the "permanent record" and "circulation" of the child's "participation," lacks much of its force where the depiction is a serious contribution to art or science. The production of materials of serious value is not the "low-profile, clandestine industry" that according to the Court produces purely pornographic materials. In short, it is inconceivable how a depiction of a child that is itself a serious contribution to the world of art or literature or science can be deemed "material outside the protection of the First Amendment." * * *

NOTE ON APPLICATION OF *FERBER* TO CUSTOMERS

After *Ferber,* New York prosecutes a man who purchased magazines and videotapes portraying children simulating sexual activity. The defendant purchased the pornography from an undercover police officer who sent the material through the mail to defendant's home. The state charged the defendant with violating § 263.15 by "procuring" the pornography and thereby contributing to the exploitation of children. *Quaere:* Can the defendant constitutionally be sent to prison for purchasing these materials? Consider the following defenses:

- Defendant argues that his conduct does not fall within the statute. See *People v. Keyes*, 75 N.Y.2d 343 (1990).

- Defendant argues that the statute cannot constitutionally be applied to him. Even if the application passes muster under *Ferber*, he is protected by *Stanley v. Georgia* (Chapter 1, Section 1[B]).

- Defendant maintains that he believed in good faith that the performers in the video were not minors and, therefore, that he did not have the *mens rea* needed for conviction under the statute. Assume that he did believe that in good faith. Is that a defense? See *United States v. X–Citement Video, Inc.*, 115 S. Ct. 464 (1994).

PROBLEM 6–2

CHILD PORN WITHOUT LIVE MODELS

Consider the lawfulness of drawings, cartoons, computer graphics, or other visuals that depict sex by a minor without actually involving a minor. The Child Pornography Prevention Act of 1996, Pub.Law 104–208, defines child pornography to include "any visual depiction * * * of sexually explicit conduct, where

(A) the production of such visual depiction involves the use of a minor engaging in sexually explicit conduct;

(B) such visual depiction is, or appears to be, of a minor engaging in sexually explicit conduct;

(C) such visual depiction has been created, adapted, or modified to appear that an identifiable minor is engaging in sexually explicit conduct; or

(D) such visual depiction is advertised, promoted, presented, described or distributed in such a manner that conveys the impression that the material is or contains a visual depiction of a minor engaging in sexually explicit conduct * * *."

A person can be prosecuted who knowingly mails, transports, receives or distributes such material. Constitutional? Can the film *Lolita* be prosecuted?

FEMINIST THEORIES OF SEXUAL SPEECH AND ITS REGULATION

PROBLEM 6–3

THE DWORKIN–MACKINNON PORNOGRAPHY ORDINANCES

In 1983, Andrea Dworkin and Catharine MacKinnon drafted and the Minneapolis City Council passed the first feminist anti-pornography ordinance, with the following stated purpose:

> The council finds that pornography is central in creating and maintaining the civil inequality of the sexes. Pornography is a systematic practice of exploitation and subordination based on sex which differentially harms women. * * *

Minneapolis Ordinance (Dec. 30, 1983; July 13, 1984), amending Minneapolis Code of Ordinances tit. 7, chs. 139 & 141.

The ordinance defined pornography as "the sexually explicit subordination of women, graphically depicted, whether in pictures or in words, that also includes one or more of the following:

(i) women are presented as dehumanized sexual objects, things, or commodities; or

(ii) women are presented as sexual objects who enjoy pain or humiliation; or

(iii) women are presented as sexual objects who experience sexual pleasure in being raped; or

(iv) women are presented as sexual objects tied up or cut up or mutilated or bruised or physically hurt; or

(v) women are presented in postures of sexual submission; or

(vi) women's body's parts—including but not limited to vaginas, breasts, and buttocks—are exhibited, such that women are reduced to those parts; or

(vii) women are presented as whores by nature; or

(viii) women are presented being penetrated by objects or animals; or

(ix) women are presented in scenarios of degradation, injury, abasement, torture, shown as filthy or inferior, bleeding, bruised, or hurt in a context that makes these conditions sexual."

533

The mayor of Minneapolis twice vetoed the ordinance, but a similar one was later adopted by the city of Indianapolis. Both created civil law causes of action for monetary and injunctive relief against anyone who produced, sold, exhibited, or distributed "pornography."

Is this ordinance constitutional under *Miller*? *Ferber*? Should there be a new exception to First Amendment protection for sexual speech? Consider the following materials.

Catharine A. MacKinnon, Pornography, Civil Rights, and Speech

20 *Harvard Civil Rights–Civil Liberties Law Review* 1, 16–20, 22–24, 32–33, 26–27, 43–59 (1985).*

* * * In pornography, there it is, in one place, all of the abuses that women had to struggle so long even to begin to articulate, all the *unspeakable* abuse: the rape, the battery, the sexual harassment, the prostitution, and the sexual abuse of children.[a] Only in the pornography it is called something else: sex, sex, sex, sex, and sex, respectively. Pornography sexualizes rape, battery, sexual harassment, prostitution, and child sexual abuse; it thereby celebrates, promotes, authorizes, and legitimizes them. More generally, it eroticizes the dominance and submission that is the dynamic common to them all. It makes hierarchy sexy and calls that "the truth about sex" or just a mirror of reality. Through this process, pornography constructs what a woman is as what men want from sex. This is what the pornography means. * * *

Pornography constructs what a woman is in terms of its view of what men want sexually, such that acts of rape, battery, sexual harassment, prostitution, and sexual abuse of children become acts of sexual equality. Pornography's world of equality is a harmonious and balanced place. Men and women are perfectly complementary and perfectly bipolar. Women's desire to be fucked by men is equal to men's desire to fuck women. All the ways men love to take and violate women, women love to be taken and violated. The women who most love this are most men's equals, the most liberated; the most participatory child is the most grown-up, the most equal to an adult. Their consent merely expresses or ratifies these preexisting facts.

The content of pornography is one thing. There, women substantively desire dispossession and cruelty. We desperately want to be bound, battered, tortured, humiliated, and killed. Or, to be fair to the soft core, merely taken and used. This is erotic to the male point of view. Subjection itself with self-determination ecstatically relinquished is the content of women's

* Copyright © President and Fellows of Harvard College. Reprinted by permission.

a. These abuses are based in part on the author's findings from *Public Hearings on Ordinances to Add Pornography as Discrimination Against Women*, Committee on Government Operations, City Council, Minneapolis, Minn., (Dec. 12–13, 1983) [hereinafter Hearings].

sexual desire and desirability. Women are there to be violated and possessed, men to violate and possess us either on screen or by camera or pen on behalf of the consumer. On a simple descriptive level, the inequality of hierarchy, of which gender is the primary one, seems necessary for the sexual arousal to work. Other added inequalities identify various pornographic genres or sub-themes, although they are always added through gender: age, disability, homosexuality, animals, objects, race (including anti-semitism), and so on. Gender is never irrelevant.

What pornography *does* goes beyond its content: It eroticizes hierarchy, it sexualizes inequality. It makes dominance and submission sex. Inequality is its central dynamic; the illusion of freedom coming together with the reality of force is central to its working. Perhaps because this is a bourgeois culture, the victim must look free, appear to be freely acting. Choice is how she got there. Willing is what she is when she is being equal. It seems equally important that then and there she actually be forced and that forcing be communicated on some level, even if only through still photos of her in postures of receptivity and access, available for penetration. Pornography in this view is a form of forced sex, a practice of sexual politics, an institution of gender inequality.

From this perspective, pornography is neither harmless fantasy nor a corrupt and confused misrepresentation of an otherwise natural and healthy sexual situation. It institutionalizes the sexuality of male supremacy, fusing the erotization of dominance and submission with the social construction of male and female. To the extent that gender is sexual, pornography is part of constituting the meaning of that sexuality. Men treat women as who they see women as being. Pornography constructs who that is. Men's power over women means that the way men see women defines who women can be. Pornography is that way. Pornography is not imagery in some relation to a reality elsewhere constructed. It is not a distortion, reflection, projection, expression, fantasy, representation, or symbol either. It is a sexual reality.

In Andrea Dworkin's definitive work on pornography, sexuality itself is a social construct gendered to the ground. Male dominance here is not an artificial overlay upon an underlying inalterable substratum of uncorrupted essential sexual being. Dworkin's *Pornography: Men Possessing Women* presents a sexual theory of gender inequality of which pornography is a constitutive practice. The way in which pornography produces its meaning constructs and defines men and women as such. Gender has no basis in anything other than the social reality its hegemony constructs. Gender is what gender means. The process that gives sexuality its male supremacist meaning is the same process through which gender inequality becomes socially real. * * *

At the request of the city of Minneapolis, Andrea Dworkin and I conceived and designed a local human rights ordinance in accordance with our approach to the pornography issue. We define pornography as a practice of sex discrimination, a violation of women's civil rights, the opposite of sexual equality. Its point is to hold accountable, to those who are injured, those who profit from and benefit from that injury. It means that women's injury—our damage, our pain, our enforced inferiority—should outweigh their pleasure and their profits, or sex equality is meaningless.

We define pornography as the graphic sexually explicit subordination of women through pictures or words that also includes women dehumanized as sexual objects, things, or commodities, enjoying pain or humiliation or rape, being tied up, cut up, mutilated, bruised, or physically hurt, in postures of sexual submission or servility or display, reduced to body parts, penetrated by objects or animals, or presented in scenarios of degradation, injury, torture, shown as filthy or inferior, bleeding, bruised, or hurt in a context that makes these conditions sexual. Erotica, defined by distinction as not this, might be sexually explicit materials premised on equality. We also provide that the use of men, children or transsexuals in the place of women is pornography. The definition is substantive in that it is sex-specific, but it covers everyone in a sex-specific way, so is gender neutral in overall design.

There is a buried issue within sex discrimination law about what sex, meaning gender, is. If sex is a *difference*, social or biological, one looks to see if a challenged practice occurs along the same lines; if it does, or if it is done to both sexes, the practice is not discrimination, not inequality. If, by contrast, sex inequality is a matter of *dominance*, the issue is not the gender difference but the difference gender makes. In this more substantive, less abstract approach, the concern is whether a practice *subordinates* on the basis of sex. The first approach implies that marginal correction is needed; the second suggests social change. Equality to the first centers on abstract symmetry between equivalent categories; the asymmetry that occurs when categories are not equivalent is not inequality, it is treating unlikes differently. To the second approach, inequality centers on the substantive, cumulative disadvantagement of social hierarchy. Equality to the first is nondifferentiation; to the second, equality is nonsubordination. Although it is consonant with both approaches, our anti-pornography statute emerges largely from an analysis of the problem under the second approach.

To define pornography as a practice of sex discrimination combines a mode of portrayal that has a legal history—the sexually explicit—with an active term central to the inequality of the sexes—subordination. Among other things, subordination means to be placed in a position of inferiority or loss of power, or to be demeaned or denigrated. To be someone's subordinate is the opposite of being their equal. The definition does not include all sexually explicit depictions *of* the subordination of women. That is not what it says. It says, this which *does* that: the sexually explicit which subordinates women. To these active terms to capture what the pornography *does*, the definition adds a list of what it must also contain. This list, from our analysis, is an exhaustive description of what must be in the pornography for it to do what it does behaviorally. Each item in the definition is supported by experimental, testimonial, social, and clinical evidence. We made a legislative choice to be exhaustive and specific and concrete rather than conceptual and general, to minimize problems of chilling effect, making it hard to guess wrong, thus making self-censorship less likely, but encouraging (to use a phrase from discrimination law) voluntary compliance, knowing that if something turns up that is not on the list, the law will not be expansively interpreted. * * *

The first victims of pornography are the ones in it. To date, it has only been with children, and male children at that, that the Supreme Court has understood that before the pornography became the pornographer's speech, it was somebody's life. This is particularly true in visual media, where it takes a real person doing each act to make what you see. This is the double meaning in a statement one ex-prostitute made at our hearing: "[E]very single thing you see in pornography is happening to a real woman right now." Linda Marchiano, in her book *Ordeal*, recounts being coerced as "Linda Lovelace" into performing for "Deep Throat," a fabulously profitable film, by abduction, systematic beating, being kept prisoner, watched every minute, threatened with her life and the lives of her family if she left, tortured, and kept under constant psychological intimidation and duress. Not all pornography models are, to our knowledge, coerced so expressly; but the fact that some are not does not mean that those who are, aren't. It only means that coercion into pornography cannot be said to be biologically female. The further fact that prostitution and modeling are structurally women's best economic options should give pause to those who would consider women's presence there a true act of free choice. In the case of other inequalities, it is sometimes understood that people do degrading work out of a lack of options caused by, say, poverty. The work is not seen as *not* degrading "for them" because they do it. With women, it just proves that this is what we are really for, this is our true nature. I will leave you wondering, with me, why it is that when a woman spreads her legs for a camera, what she is assumed to be exercising is free will. Women's freedom is rather substantively defined here. And as you think about the assumption of consent that follows women into pornography, look closely some time for the skinned knees, the bruises, the welts from the whippings, the scratches, the gashes. Many of them are not simulated. One relatively soft core pornography model said, "I knew the pose was right when it hurt." It certainly seems important to the audiences that the events in the pornography be real. For this reason, pornography becomes a motive for murder, as in "snuff" films in which someone is tortured to death to make a sex film. They exist. * * *

* * * It is therefore vicious to suggest, as many have, that women like Linda Marchiano should remedy their situations through the exercise of more speech. Pornography makes their speech impossible and where possible, worthless. Pornography makes women into objects. Objects do not speak. When they do, they are by then regarded as objects, not as humans, which is what it means to have no credibility. Besides, how Ms. Marchiano's speech is supposed to redress her injury, except by producing this legal remedy, is unclear since no amount of saying anything remedies what is being *done* to her in theatres and on home videos all over the world,

where she is repeatedly raped for public entertainment and private profit.
* * *

Specific pornography directly causes some assaults. Some rapes are performed by men with paperback books in their pockets. One young woman testified in our hearings about walking through a forest at thirteen and coming across a group of armed hunters reading pornography. As they looked up and saw her, one said, "There is a live one." They gang-raped her at gunpoint for several hours. One native American woman told us about being gang-raped in a reenactment of a videogame on her.

> [T]hat's what they screamed in my face as they threw me to the ground, "This is more fun than Custer's Last Stand." They held me down and as one was running the tip of his knife across my face and throat he said, "Do you want to play Custer's Last Stand? It's great, you lose but you don't care, do you? You like a little pain, don't you, squaw? . . . Maybe we will tie you to a tree and start a fire around you."

Received wisdom seems to be that because there is so little difference between convicted rapists and the rest of the male population in levels and patterns of exposure, response to, and consumption of pornography, pornography's role in rape is insignificant. A more parsimonious explanation of this data is that knowing exposure to, response to, or consumption of pornography will not tell you who will be reported, apprehended, and convicted for rape. But the commonalities such data reveal between convicted rapists and other men are certainly consistent with the fact that only a tiny fraction of rapes ever come to the attention of authorities. It does not make sense to assume that pornography has no role in rape simply because little about its use or effects distinguishes convicted rapists from other men, when we know that a lot of those other men *do* rape women; they just never get caught. In other words, the significance of pornography in acts of forced sex is one thing if sex offenders are considered deviants and another if they are considered relatively nonexceptional except for the fact of their apprehension and incarceration. Professionals who work with that tiny percentage of men who get reported and convicted for such offenses, a group made special only by our ability to assume they once had sex by force in a way that someone (in addition to their victim) eventually regarded as serious, made the following observations about the population they work with. "Pornography is the permission and direction and rehearsal for sexual violence." "[P]ornography is often used by sex offenders as a stimulus to their sexually acting out." It is the "tools of sexual assault," "a way in which they practice" their crimes, "like a loaded gun," "like drinking salt water," "the chemical of sexual addiction." They hypothesize that pornography leads some men to abusiveness out of fear of loss of control that has come to mean masculinity when real women won't accept sex on the one-sided terms that pornography gives and from which they have learned what sex is. "[Because pornography] is reinforcing, [and leads to sexual release, it] leads men to want the experience which they have in photographic fantasy to happen in 'real' life." "They live vicariously through the pictures. Eventually, that is not satisfying enough and they end up acting out sexually." "[S]exual fantasy represents the hope for reality." These professionals are referring to what others are fond of terming "just an idea."

Although police have known it for years, reported cases are increasingly noting the causal role of pornography in some sexual abuse. In a recent Minnesota case, a fourteen-year-old girl on a bicycle was stopped with a knife and forced into a car. Her hands were tied with a belt, she was pushed to the floor and covered with a blanket. The knife was then used to cut off her clothes, and fingers and a knife were inserted into her vagina. Then the man had her dress, drove her to a gravel pit, ordered her to stick a safety pin into the nipple of her left breast, and forced her to ask him to hit her. After hitting her, he forced her to commit fellatio and to submit to anal penetration, and made her use a cigarette to burn herself on her breast and near her pubic area. Then he defecated and urinated on her face, forced her to ingest some of the excrement and urine and made her urinate into a cup and drink it. He took a string from her blouse and choked her to the point of unconsciousness, leaving burn marks on her neck, and after cutting her with his knife in a couple of places, drove her back to where he had gotten her and let her go. The books that were found with this man were: *Violent Stories of Kinky Humiliation, Violent Stories of Dominance and Submission*—you think feminists made up these words?—*Bizarre Sex Crimes, Shamed Victims,* and *Water Sports Fetish, Enemas and Golden Showers.* The Minnesota Supreme Court said "It appears that in committing these various acts, the defendant was giving life to some stories he had read in various pornographic books."

To reach the magnitude of this problem on the scale it exists, our law makes trafficking in pornography—production, sale, exhibition, or distribution—actionable. Under the obscenity rubric, much legal and psychological scholarship has centered on a search for the elusive link between pornography defined as obscenity and harm. They have looked high and low—in the mind of the male consumer, in society or in its "moral fabric," in correlations between variations in levels of anti-social acts and liberalization of obscenity laws. The only harm they have found has been one they have attributed to "the social interest in order and morality." Until recently, no one looked very persistently for harm to women, particularly harm to women through men. The rather obvious fact that the sexes *relate* has been overlooked in the inquiry into the male consumer and his mind. The pornography doesn't just drop out of the sky, go into his head and stop there. Specifically, men rape, batter, prostitute, molest, and sexually harass women. Under conditions of inequality, they also hire, fire, promote, and grade women, decide how much or whether or not we are worth paying and for what, define and approve and disapprove of women in ways that count, that determine our lives.

If women are not just born to be sexually used, the fact that we are seen and treated as though that is what we are born for becomes something in need of explanation. If we see that men relate to women in a pattern of who they see women as being, and that forms a pattern of inequality, it becomes important to ask where that view came from or, minimally, how it is perpetuated or escalated. Asking this requires asking different questions about pornography than the ones obscenity law made salient.

Now I'm going to talk about causality in its narrowest sense. Recent experimental research on pornography shows that the materials covered by our definition cause measurable harm to women through increasing men's attitudes and behaviors of discrimination in both violent and nonviolent forms. Exposure to some of the pornography in our definition increases normal men's immediately subsequent willingness to aggress against women under laboratory conditions. It makes normal men more closely resemble convicted rapists attitudinally, although as a group they don't look all that different from them to start with. It also significantly increases attitudinal measures known to correlate with rape and self-reports of aggressive acts, measures such as hostility toward women, propensity to rape, condoning rape, and predicting that one would rape or force sex on a woman if one knew one would not get caught. This latter measure, by the way, begins with rape at about a third of all men and moves to half with "forced sex."

As to that pornography covered by our definition in which normal research subjects seldom perceive violence, long-term exposure still makes them see women as more worthless, trivial, non-human, and object-like, i.e., the way those who are discriminated against are seen by those who discriminate against them. Crucially, all pornography by our definition acts dynamically over time to diminish one's ability to distinguish sex from violence. The materials work behaviorally to diminish the capacity of both men and women to perceive that an account of a rape is an account of a rape. X-only materials, in which subjects perceive no force, also increase perceptions that a rape victim is worthless and decrease the perception she was harmed. The overall direction of current research suggests that the more expressly violent materials accomplish on less exposure what the less overtly violent—that is, the so-called "sex only materials"—accomplish over the longer term. Women are rendered fit for use and targeted for abuse. The only thing that the research cannot document is which individual women will be next on the list. (This cannot be documented experimentally because of ethics constraints on the researchers—constraints which do not operate in life.) Although the targeting is systematic on the basis of sex, it targets individuals at random. They are selected on the basis of roulette. Pornography can no longer be said to be just a mirror. It does not just reflect the world or some people's perceptions. It *moves* them. It increases attitudes that are lived out, circumscribing the status of half the population. * * *

In our hearings, women spoke, to my knowledge for the first time in history in public, about the damage pornography does to them. * * * Asked if anyone ever tried to inflict sex acts on them they did not want that they knew came from pornography, ten percent of women in a recent random study said yes. Twenty-four percent of married women said yes. That is a lot of women. A lot more don't know. Some of those who do testified in Minneapolis. One wife said of her ex-husband: "He would read from the pornography like a text book, like a journal. In fact when he asked me to be bound, when he finally convinced me to do it, he read in the magazine how to tie the knots...." Another woman said of her boyfriend: "[H]e went to this party, saw pornography, got an erection, got me ... to inflict his erection on.... There is a direct causal relationship there." One woman who said her husband had rape and bondage magazines all over the house, discovered two suitcases full of Barbie dolls with rope tied on their arms and legs and with tape across their mouths. Now think about the silence of women. She said, "He used to tie me up and he tried those things on me." A therapist in private practice reported:

> Presently or recently I have worked with clients who have been sodomized by broom handles, forced to have sex with over 20 dogs in the back seat of their car, tied up and then electrocuted on their genitals. These are children, [all] in the ages of 14 to 18, all of whom [have been directly affected by pornography,] [e]ither where the perpetrator has read the manuals and manuscripts at night and used these as recipe books by day or had the pornography present at the time of the sexual violence.

One woman, testifying that all the women in a group of ex-prostitutes were brought into prostitution as children through pornography, characterized their collective experience: "[I]n my experience there was not one situation where a client was not using pornography while he was using me or that he had not just watched pornography or that it was verbally referred to and directed me to pornography." "Men," she continued, "witness the abuse of women in pornography constantly and if they can't engage in that behavior with their wives, girl friends or children, they force a whore to do it."

Men also testified about how pornography hurts them. One young gay man who had seen *Playboy* and *Penthouse* as a child said of heterosexual pornography:

> It was one of the places I learned about sex and it showed me that sex was violence. What I saw there was a specific relationship between men and women.... [T]he woman was to be used, objectified, humiliated and hurt; the man was in a superior position, a position to be violent. In pornography I learned that what it meant to be sexual with a man or to be loved by a man was to accept his violence.

For this reason, when he was battered by his first lover, which he described as "one of the most profoundly destructive experiences of my life," he accepted it.

Pornography also hurts men's capacity to relate to women. One young man spoke about this in a way that connects pornography—not the prohibition on pornography—with fascism. He spoke of his struggle to repudiate the thrill of dominance, of his difficulty finding connection with a woman to whom he is close. He said:

My point is that if women in a society filled by pornography must be wary for their physical selves, a man, even a man of good intentions, must be wary for his mind.... I do not want to be a mechanical, goose stepping follower of the Playboy bunny, because that is what I think it is.... [T]hese are the experiments a master race perpetuates on those slated for extinction.

The woman he lives with is Jewish. There was a very brutal rape near their house. She was afraid; she tried to joke. It didn't work. "She was still afraid. And just as a well-meaning German was afraid in 1933, I am also very much afraid."

Pornography stimulates and reinforces, it does not cathect or mirror, the connection between one-sided freely available sexual access to women and masculine sexual excitement and sexual satisfaction. The catharsis hypothesis is fantasy. The fantasy theory is fantasy. Reality is: Pornography conditions male orgasm to female subordination. It tells men what sex means, what a real woman is, and codes them together in a way that is behaviorally reinforcing. This is a real five-dollar sentence but I'm going to say it anyway: Pornography is a set of hermeneutical equivalences that work on the epistemological level. Substantively, pornography defines the meaning of what a woman is by connecting access to her sexuality with masculinity through orgasm. The behavior data show that what pornography means *is* what it does. * * *

Lisa Duggan, Nan D. Hunter, and Carole S. Vance, False Promises: Feminist Anti–Pornography Legislation

38 *New York Law School Law Review* 133 (1993).*

* * * Although proponents claim that the Minneapolis and Indianapolis ordinances represent a new way to regulate pornography, the strategy is still laden with our culture's old, repressive approach to sexuality. The implementation of such laws hinges on the definition of pornography as interpreted by the judiciary. The definition provided in the Minneapolis legislation is vague, leaving critical phrases such as "the sexually explicit subordination of women," "postures of sexual submission," and "whores by nature" to the interpretation of the citizen who files a complaint and to the judge who hears the case. The legislation does not prohibit just the images of rape and abusive sexual violence that most supporters claim to be its target, but instead drifts toward covering an increasingly wide range of sexually explicit material.

The most problematic feature of this approach is a conceptual flaw embedded in the law itself. Supporters of this type of legislation say that the target of their efforts is misogynous, sexually explicit, and violent representation, whether in pictures or words. Indeed, the feminist anti-

* First published in *Women Against Censorship* (Varda Burstyn, ed. 1985). Reprinted by permission of the authors.

pornography movement is fueled by women's anger at the most repugnant examples of pornography. But a close examination of the wording of the model legislative text, and examples of purportedly actionable material offered by proponents of the legislation in briefs defending the Indianapolis ordinance in a court challenge, suggests that the law is actually aimed at a range of material considerably broader than what the proponents claim is their target. The discrepancies between the law's explicit and implicit aims have been almost invisible to us because these distortions are very similar to distortions about sexuality in the culture as a whole. The legislation and supporting texts deserve close reading. Hidden beneath illogical transformations, non sequiturs, and highly permeable definitions are familiar sexual scripts drawn from mainstream, sexist culture that potentially could have very negative consequences for women.

[A] Venn diagram illustrates the three areas targeted by the law, and represents a scheme that classifies words or images that have any of three characteristics: violence, sexual explicitness, or sexism.

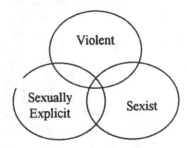

Clearly, a text or an image might have only one characteristic. Material can be violent but not sexually explicit or sexist: for example, a war movie in which both men and women suffer injury or death without regard to or because of their gender. Material can be sexist but not sexually explicit or violent. A vast number of materials from mainstream media—television, popular novels, magazines, newspapers—come to mind, depicting, for example, either distraught housewives or the "happy sexism" of the idealized family, with mom self-sacrificing, other-directed, and content. Finally, material can be sexually explicit but not violent or sexist: for example, the freely chosen sexual behavior depicted in sex education films or women's own explicit writing about sexuality.

As the diagram illustrates, areas can also intersect, reflecting a range of combinations of the three characteristics. Images can be violent and sexually explicit without being sexist—for example, a narrative about a rape in a men's prison, or a documentary about the effect of a rape on a woman. The latter example illustrates the importance of context in evaluating whether material that is sexually explicit and violent is also sexist. The intent of the maker, the context of the film, and the perception of the viewer together render a depiction of a rape sympathetic, harrowing, even educational, rather than sensational, victim-blaming, and laudatory.

Another possible overlap is between material that is violent and sexist but not sexually explicit. Films or books that describe violence directed against women by men in a way that clearly shows gender antagonism and inequality, and sometimes strong sexual tension, but no sexual explicitness, fall into this category—for example, the popular genre of slasher films in which women are stalked, terrified, and killed by men, or accounts of mass murder of women, fueled by male rage. Finally, a third point of overlap arises when material is sexually explicit and sexist without being violent—that is, when sex is consensual but still reflects themes of male superiority and female abjectness. Some sex education materials could be included in this category, as well as a great deal of regular pornography.

The remaining domain, the inner core, is one in which the material is simultaneously violent, sexually explicit, and sexist—for example, an image of naked woman being slashed by a knife-wielding rapist. The Minneapolis ordinance, however, does not by any means confine itself to this material.

To be actionable as pornography under the law, material must be judged by the courts to be "the sexually explicit subordination of women, graphically depicted whether in pictures or in words that also includes at least one or more" of nine criteria. Of these, only four involve the intersection of violence, sexual explicitness, and sexism, and then only arguably. Even in these cases, many questions remain about whether images with all three characteristics do in fact cause violence against women. And the task of evaluating material that is ostensibly the target of these criteria becomes complicated—indeed, hopeless—because most of the clauses that contain these criteria mix actions or qualities of violence with those that are not particularly associated with violence.

The section that comes closest to the stated purpose of the legislation is clause (iii): "women are presented as sexual objects who experience sexual pleasure in being raped." This clause is intended to cover depictions of rape that are sexually explicit and sexist; the act of rape itself signifies the violence. But other clauses are not so clear cut because the list of characteristics often mixes signs or by-products of violence with phenomena that are unrelated or irrelevant to judging violence.

Such a problem occurs with clause (iv): "women are presented as sexual objects tied up or cut up or mutilated or bruised or physically hurt." All these except the first, "tied up," generally occur as a result of violence. "Tied up," if part of consensual sex, is not violent and, for some practitioners, not particularly sexist. Women who are tied up may be participants in nonviolent sex play involving bondage, a theme in both heterosexual and lesbian pornography. Clause (ix) contains another mixed list, in which "injury," "torture," "bleeding," "bruised," and "hurt" are combined with phrases such as "degradation" and "shown as filthy or inferior," neither of which is violent. Depending on the presentation, "filthy" and "inferior" may constitute sexually explicit sexism, although not violence. "Degradation" is a sufficiently inclusive term to cover most acts of which a viewer disapproves.

Several other clauses have little to do with violence at all; they refer to material that is sexually explicit and sexist, thus falling outside the triad of characteristics at which the legislation is supposedly aimed. For example, movies in which "women are presented as dehumanized sexual objects, things, or commodities" may be infuriating and offensive to feminists, but they are not violent.

Finally, some clauses describe material that is neither violent nor necessarily sexist. Clause (v)—"women ... in postures of sexual submission [or sexual servility, including by inviting penetration]"—and clause (viii)—"women ... being penetrated by objects or animals"—are sexually explicit, but not violent and not obviously sexist unless one believes that penetration—whether heterosexual, lesbian, or autoerotic—is indicative of gender inequality and female oppression. Similarly problematic are clauses that invoke representations of "women ... as whores by nature" and "women's body parts ... such that women are reduced to those parts."

Texts cited in support of the Indianapolis law show how broadly it could be applied. In the amicus brief filed on behalf of Linda Marchiano in Indianapolis, Catharine MacKinnon offered the film *Deep Throat* as an example of the kind of pornography covered by the law. *Deep Throat* served a complicated function in this brief because the movie, supporters of the ordinance argue, would be actionable on two counts: coercion into pornographic performance because Marchiano alleges that she was coerced into making the movie; and trafficking in pornography because the content of the film falls within one of the categories in the Indianapolis ordinance's definition—that which prohibits presenting women as sexual objects "through postures or positions of servility or submission or display." Proponents of the law have counted on women's repugnance at allegations of coerced sexual acts to spill over and discredit the sexual acts themselves in this movie.

The aspects of *Deep Throat* that MacKinnon considered to be indicative of "sexual ... subordination" are of particular interest because any movie that depicted similar acts presumably could be banned under the law. MacKinnon explained in her brief that the film "subordinates women by using women ... sexually, specifically as eager servicing receptacles for male genitalia and ejaculate. The majority of the film presents 'Linda Lovelace' in, minimally, postures of submission and/or servility." In its brief, the City of Indianapolis concurred: "In the film *Deep Throat*, a woman is being shown as being ever eager for oral penetration by a series of men's penises, often on her hands and knees. There are repeated scenes in which her genitalia are graphically displayed and she is shown as enjoying men ejaculating on her face."

These descriptions are very revealing since they suggest that multiple partners, group sex, and oral sex subordinate women and hence are sexist. The notion that the female character is "used" by men suggests that it is improbable that a woman would engage in fellatio of her own accord. *Deep Throat* does draw on several sexist conventions common in advertising and the entire visual culture of woman as object of the male gaze, and the assumption of heterosexuality, for example. But it is hardly an unending paean to male dominance, since the movie contains many contrary themes. In it, the main female character is shown as both actively seeking her own pleasure and as trying to please men; a secondary female character is shown directing encounters with multiple male partners. Both briefs describe a movie quite different from the one viewers see.

At its heart, this analysis implies that heterosexual sex itself is sexist, that women do not engage in it of their own volition, and that behavior pleasurable to men is intrinsically repugnant to women. In some contexts, for example, the representation of fellatio and multiple partners can be sexist, but are we willing to concede that they always are? If not, then what is proposed as actionable under the Indianapolis law includes merely sexually explicit representation (the traditional target of obscenity laws), which proponents of the legislation vociferously insist they are not interested in attacking. * * *

Certain troubling questions arise here, for if one claims, as some anti-pornography activists do, that there is a direct relationship between images and behavior, why should images of violence against women or scenarios of sexism in general not be similarly proscribed? Why is sexual explicitness singled out as the cause of women's oppression? For proponents to exempt violent and sexist images, or even sexist images, from regulation is inconsistent, especially since they are so pervasive. * * *

* * * [W]hat underlies this legislation, and the success of its analysis in blurring and exceeding boundaries, is an appeal to a very traditional view of sex: Sex is degrading to women. By this logic, any illustrations or descriptions of explicit sexual acts that involve women are in themselves affronts to women's dignity. In its brief, the City of Indianapolis was quite specific about this point: "The harms caused by pornography are by no means limited to acts of physical aggression. The mere existence of pornography in society degrades and demeans all women." Embedded in this view are several other familiar themes: that sex is degrading to women, but not to men; that men are raving beasts; that sex is dangerous for women; that sexuality is male, not female; that women are victims, not sexual actors; that men inflict "it" on women; that penetration is submission; that heterosexual sexuality, rather than the institution of heterosexuality, is sexist.

These assumptions, in part intended, in part unintended, lead us back to the traditional target of obscenity law: sexually explicit material. What initially appeared novel, then, is really the reappearance of a traditional theme. It is ironic that a feminist position on pornography incorporates most of the myths about sexuality that feminism has struggled to displace.
* * *

Not only does pornography not cause the kind and degree of harm that can justify the restraint of speech, but its existence serves some social functions which benefit women. Pornographic speech has many, often anomalous, characteristics. Certainly one is that it magnifies the misogyny present in the culture and exaggerates the fantasy of male power. Another, however, is that the existence of pornography has served to flout conventional sexual mores, to ridicule sexual hypocrisy, and to underscore the importance of sexual needs. Pornography carries many messages other than woman-hating; it advocates sexual adventure, sex outside of marriage, sex for no reason other than pleasure, casual sex, anonymous sex, group sex, voyeuristic sex, illegal sex, public sex. Some of these ideas appeal to women reading or seeing pornography, who may interpret some images as legitimating their own sense of sexual urgency or desire to be sexually aggressive. Women's experience of pornography is not as universally victimizing as the ordinance would have it. * * *

Supporters of the anti-pornography ordinances both endorse the concept that pornographic speech contains no ideas or expressive interest, and at the same time attribute to pornography the capacity to trigger violent acts by the power of its misogyny. The City's brief in defense of the Indianapolis ordinance expanded this point by arguing that all sexually explicit speech is entitled to less constitutional protection than other speech. The anti-pornography groups have cleverly capitalized on this approach—a product of a totally nonfeminist legal system—to attempt, through the mechanism of the ordinances, to legitimate a new crusade for protectionism and sexual conservatism.

The consequences of enforcing such a law, however, are much more likely to obstruct than advance feminist political goals. On the level of ideas, further narrowing of the public realm of sexual speech coincides all too well with the privatization of sexual, reproductive and family issues sought by the far right. Practically speaking, the ordinances could result in attempts to eliminate the images associated with homosexuality. Doubtless there are heterosexual women who believe that lesbianism is a "degrading" form of "subordination." Since the ordinances allow for suits against materials in which men appear "in place of women," far-right anti-pornography crusaders could use these laws to suppress gay male pornography. Imagine a Jerry Falwell-style conservative filing a complaint against a gay bookstore for selling sexually explicit materials showing men with other men in "degrading" or "submissive" or "objectified" postures—all in the name of protecting women. * * *

NOTES ON THE FEMINIST DEBATE OVER PORNOGRAPHY

1. *Unpacking the Arguments: Feminism and the Construction of Sexuality.* Both the "pro-censorship" and the "pro-sex" sides agree that sexuality is in fundamental ways socially constructed. Both agree that most commercial pornography at best ignores women's sexuality and at worst glorifies misogyny. Why such a bitter debate?

One historical analogy is the debate among women in the early twentieth century over whether to seek prohibition of alcohol. Although now often thought of as a silly, puritanical campaign to extinguish drinking, the temperance movement was led by committed feminists who documented the association of drunkenness with domestic violence. In both debates, women argued about what the real chain of causation was. (Does drinking/pornography lead to abuse? Would elimination of drinking/pornography substantially alleviate the problem?) More fundamentally, they also argued about using strategies designed to constrain male freedom versus strategies to expand the social space for women to act without conforming to traditional expectations.

Another way to analyze the pornography debate is to position the two feminist viewpoints in the context of existing legal doctrine on sexual speech. Both sides would de-privatize sexual speech. Rather than treating it as immoral under the obscenity approach, both see it as politically charged. The Dworkin–MacKinnon approach would continue to treat it as unique, however, albeit under a new rationale. The anti-censorship approach would abolish the separate, undervalued category of sexually explicit speech.

How do essentialist notions of male and female sexuality function in these arguments about pornography? Carlin Meyer argues in "Sex, Sin, and Women's Liberation: Against Porn–Suppression," 72 *Tex. L. Rev.* 1097, 1130–3, 1172–8 (1994), that the glorification of romantic love and its near saturation of popular culture have a more powerful and more insidious effect than does pornography on the construction of women's sexuality.

2. *What Are the Behavioral Effects of Viewing Pornography?* A key issue in the legal debate is whether exposure to certain materials induces criminal behavior.[b] In a comprehensive review of the literature, three of the leading social scientists in the field concluded that "for the most part * * * sexually explicit images, per se, do not in the short run facilitate aggressive behavior against women, change attitudes about rape, or influence other forms of antiscoial behavior. Instead, the research indicates that it is the violent images fused with sexual images in some forms of pornography, or even the violent images alone, that account for many of the antisocial effects reported by social science researchers." Edward Donnerstein, Daniel Linz and Steven Penrod, *The Question of Pornography: Research Findings and Policy Implications* 2 (1987). What the researchers call violent or aggressive pornography has been shown to influence aggression toward women, at least in a laboratory situation, and to have negative effects on attitudes about women. *Id.* ch. 5. "It is important to note that materials that were merely sexual in nature had no effect on aggressive behavior." *Id.* at 98.

Is this the same material that the Indianapolis ordinance defined as pornography? Donnerstein, et al. define it as "depict[ions of] sexual coercion in a sexually explicit way," combined with a depiction of the female victim as initially resisting, then enjoying the rape. "[I]t is this unique feature of violent pornography—the presentation of the idea that women

---

b. Surveys of the empirical literature on the relationship between reading pornography and violence against women include Catharine A. MacKinnon, *Feminism Unmodified* 163 ff. (1987); Richard A. Posner, *Sex and Reason* 366–73 (1992); Frederick Schauer, "Causation Theory and the Causes of Sexual Violence," 1987 *Am. Bar Found. Res. J.* 737, analyzing the conclusions about causation in the Report of the Attorney General's Commission on Pornography, on which Professor Schauer served.

find sexual violence arousing—that plays an important role in producing violent pornography's harmful effects." *Id.* at 89.

Many of the materials that produce the most troubling effects are eroticized but not sexually explicit and thus would not fall within the ordinance's definition of pornography (nor within the category of obscenity). Research has found that exposure to "slasher films" (*e.g.*, *The Texas Chain Saw Massacre*), in which graphic depictions of violence against women are mixed with erotic scenes, negatively affects men's responses to victims of sexual violence, at least in laboratory situations. *Id.* ch. 6.

3. *Is Sadomasochistic Imagery "Violent"?* Note the repeated emphasis in much of the advocates' discussion of pornography on images of bondage and sadomasochism (SM). (See discussion in Chapter 11, Section 1[C].) Does SM imagery that depicts mutually desired bondage, for example, fall within the ordinance definition of pornography? Within the social scientists' definition of violent pornography? Obscenity law is also grappling with how to treat SM imagery, particularly when it does not depict genital, anal or breast contact. Obscenity statutes have been revised to attempt to cover such images. Consider the North Carolina statute, which defines "sexual conduct" in the *Miller* test to include: "an act or condition that depicts torture, physical restraint by being fettered or bound, or flagellation of or by a nude person or a person clad in undergarments or in revealing or bizarre costume." N.C. Gen. Stat. § 14–190.1(c)(3) (1995). Valid?

Next we see the law's response to the Indianapolis ordinance. Consider as you read whether the court "heard" the feminist arguments being presented on both sides of the case. The case following *American Booksellers* shows how our neighbor Canada reached a different resolution.

American Booksellers Association, Inc. v. William H. Hudnut, III

U.S. Court of Appeals for the Seventh Circuit, 1985.
771 F.2d 323, *aff'd mem.*, 475 U.S. 1001 (1986).

■ EASTERBROOK, CIRCUIT JUDGE.

Indianapolis enacted an ordinance defining "pornography" as a practice that discriminates against women. "Pornography" is to be redressed through the administrative and judicial methods used for other discrimination. The City's definition of "pornography" is considerably different from "obscenity," which the Supreme Court has held is not protected by the First Amendment. * * *

"Pornography" under the ordinance is "the graphic sexually explicit subordination of women, whether in pictures or in words, that also includes one or more of the following:

(1) Women are presented as sexual objects who enjoy pain or humiliation; or

(2) Women are presented as sexual objects who experience sexual pleasure in being raped; or

(3) Women are presented as sexual objects tied up or cut up or mutilated or bruised or physically hurt, or as dismembered or truncated or fragmented or severed into body parts; or

(4) Women are presented as being penetrated by objects or animals; or

(5) Women are presented in scenarios of degradation, injury, abasement, torture, shown as filthy or inferior, bleeding, bruised, or hurt in a context that makes these conditions sexual; or

(6) Women are presented as sexual objects for domination, conquest, violation, exploitation, possession, or use, or through postures or positions of servility or submission or display."

Indianapolis Code § 16–3(q). The statute provides that the "use of men, children, or transsexuals in the place of women in paragraphs (1) through (6) above shall also constitute pornography under this section." The ordinance as passed in April 1984 defined "sexually explicit" to mean actual or simulated intercourse or the uncovered exhibition of the genitals, buttocks or anus. An amendment in June 1984 deleted this provision, leaving the term undefined.

The Indianapolis ordinance does not refer to the prurient interest, to offensiveness, or to the standards of the community. It demands attention to particular depictions, not to the work judged as a whole. It is irrelevant under the ordinance whether the work has literary, artistic, political, or scientific value. The City and many *amici* point to these omissions as virtues. They maintain that pornography influences attitudes, and the statute is a way to alter the socialization of men and women rather than to vindicate community standards of offensiveness. * * *

[Judge Easterbrook quoted from Catherine A. MacKinnon, "Pornography, Civil Rights and Speech," 20 *Harvard Civ.Rts.-Civ.L.Rev.* 1 (1985); see excerpts in this section.]

Civil rights groups and feminists have entered this case as *amici* on both sides. Those supporting the ordinance say that it will play an important role in reducing the tendency of men to view women as sexual objects, a tendency that leads to both unacceptable attitudes and discrimination in the workplace and violence away from it. Those opposing the ordinance point out that much radical feminist literature is explicit and depicts women in ways forbidden by the ordinance and that the ordinance would reopen old battles. It is unclear how Indianapolis would treat works from James Joyce's *Ulysses* to Homer's *Iliad*; both depict women as submissive objects for conquest and domination.

We do not try to balance the arguments for and against an ordinance such as this. The ordinance discriminates on the ground of the content of the speech. Speech treating women in the approved way—in sexual encounters "premised on equality" (MacKinnon, *supra*, at 22)—is lawful no matter how sexually explicit. Speech treating women in the disapproved way—as submissive in matters sexual or as enjoying humiliation—is unlawful no matter how significant the literary, artistic, or political qualities of the work taken as a whole. The state may not ordain preferred viewpoints in this way. The Constitution forbids the state to declare one perspective right and silence opponents.

The ordinance contains four prohibitions. People may not "traffic" in pornography, "coerce" others into performing in pornographic works, or "force" pornography on anyone. Anyone injured by someone who has seen or read pornography has a right of action against the maker or seller.

Trafficking is defined in § 16–3(g)(4) as the "production, sale, exhibition, or distribution of pornography." The offense excludes exhibition in a public or educational library, but a "special display" in a library may be sex discrimination. Section 16–3(g)(4)(C) provides that the trafficking paragraph "shall not be construed to make isolated passages or isolated parts actionable."

"Coercion into pornographic performance" is defined in § 16–3(g)(5) as "[c]oercing, intimidating or fraudulently inducing any person ... into performing for pornography...." The ordinance specifies that proof of any of the following "shall not constitute a defense: I. That the person is a woman; ... VI. That the person has previously posed for sexually explicit pictures ... with anyone ...; ... VIII. That the person actually consented to a use of the performance that is changed into pornography; ... IX. That the person knew that the purpose of the acts or events in question was to make pornography; ... XI. That the person signed a contract, or made statements affirming a willingness to cooperate in the production of pornography; XII. That no physical force, threats, or weapons were used in the making of the pornography; or XIII. That the person was paid or otherwise compensated."

"Forcing pornography on a person," according to § 16–3(g)(5), is the "forcing of pornography on any woman, man, child, or transsexual in any place of employment, in education, in a home, or in any public place." The statute does not define forcing, but one of its authors states that the definition reaches pornography shown to medical students as part of their education or given to language students for translation. MacKinnon, *supra*, at 40–41.

Section 16–3(g)(7) defines as a prohibited practice the "assault, physical attack, or injury of any woman, man, child, or transsexual in a way that is directly caused by specific pornography."

For purposes of all four offenses, it is generally "not ... a defense that the respondent did not know or intend that the materials were pornography...." Section 16–3(g)(8). But the ordinance provides that damages are unavailable in trafficking cases unless the complainant proves "that the respondent knew or had reason to know that the materials were pornography." It is a complete defense to a trafficking case that all of the materials in question were pornography only by virtue of category (6) of the definition of pornography. In cases of assault caused by pornography, those who seek damages from "a seller, exhibitor or distributor" must show that the defendant knew or had reason to know of the material's status as pornography. By implication, those who seek damages from an author need not show this.

A woman aggrieved by trafficking in pornography may file a complaint "as a woman acting against the subordination of women" with the office of equal opportunity. Section 16–17(b). A man, child, or transsexual also may protest trafficking "but must prove injury in the same way that a woman is injured...." *Ibid.* Subsection (a) also provides, however, that "any person claiming to be aggrieved" by trafficking, coercion, forcing, or assault may complain against the "perpetrators." We need not decide whether § 16–17(b) qualifies the right of action in § 16–17(a).

The office investigates and within 30 days makes a recommendation to a panel of the equal opportunity advisory board. The panel then decides whether there is reasonable cause to proceed (§ 16–24(2)) and may refer the dispute to a conciliation conference or to a complaint adjudication committee for a hearing (§§ 16–24(3), 16–26(a)). The committee uses the same procedures ordinarily associated with civil rights litigation. It may make findings and enter orders, including both orders to cease and desist and orders "to take further affirmative action ... including but not limited to the power to restore complainant's losses...." Section 16–26(d). Either party may appeal the committee's decision to the board, which reviews the record before the committee and may modify its decision.

Under Indiana law an administrative decision takes effect when rendered, unless a court issues a stay. Ind. Stat. § 4–22–1–13. The board's decisions are subject to review in the ordinary course. Ind. Stat. § 4–22–1–14. Judicial review in pornography cases is to be de novo, Indianapolis Code § 16–27(e), which provides a second complete hearing. When the board finds that a person has engaged in trafficking or that a seller, exhibitor, or distributor is responsible for an assault, it must initiate judicial review of its own decision, *ibid.*, and the statute prohibits injunctive relief in these cases in advance of the court's final decision. (This is unlike the usual procedure under state law, which permits summary enforcement. Ind.Stat. §§ 4–22–1–18 and 4–22–1–27.) * * *

"If there is any fixed star in our constitutional constellation, it is that no official, high or petty, can prescribe what shall be orthodox in politics, nationalism, religion, or other matters of opinion or force citizens to confess by word or act their faith therein." *West Virginia State Board of Education v. Barnette*, 319 U.S. 624, 642 (1943). Under the First Amendment the government must leave to the people the evaluation of ideas. Bald or subtle, an idea is as powerful as the audience allows it to be. A belief may be pernicious—the beliefs of Nazis led to the death of millions, those of the Klan to the repression of millions. A pernicious belief may prevail. Totalitarian governments today rule much of the planet, practicing suppression of billions and spreading dogma that may enslave others. One of the things that separates our society from theirs is our absolute right to propagate opinions that the government finds wrong or even hateful. * * *

Under the ordinance graphic sexually explicit speech is "pornography" or not depending on the perspective the author adopts. Speech that "subordinates" women and also, for example, presents women as enjoying pain, humiliation, or rape, or even simply presents women in "positions of servility or submission or display" is forbidden, no matter how great the literary or political value of the work taken as a whole. Speech that portrays women in positions of equality is lawful, no matter how graphic the sexual content. This is thought control. It establishes an "approved" view of women, of how they may react to sexual encounters, of how the sexes may relate to each other. Those who espouse the approved view may use sexual images; those who do not, may not.

Indianapolis justifies the ordinance on the ground that pornography affects thoughts. Men who see women depicted as subordinate are more likely to treat them so. Pornography is an aspect of dominance. It does not persuade people so much as change them. It works by socializing, by establishing the expected and the permissible. In this view pornography is not an idea; pornography is the injury.

There is much to this perspective. Beliefs are also facts. People often act in accordance with the images and patterns they find around them. People raised in a religion tend to accept the tenets of that religion, often without independent examination. People taught from birth that black people are fit only for slavery rarely rebelled against that creed; beliefs coupled with the self-interest of the masters established a social structure that inflicted great harm while enduring for centuries. Words and images act at the level of the subconscious before they persuade at the level of the conscious. Even the truth has little chance unless a statement fits within the framework of beliefs that may never have been subjected to rational study.

Therefore we accept the premises of this legislation. Depictions of subordination tend to perpetuate subordination. The subordinate status of women in turn leads to affront and lower pay at work, insult and injury at home, battery and rape on the streets. In the language of the legislature, "[p]ornography is central in creating and maintaining sex as a basis of discrimination. Pornography is a systematic practice of exploitation and subordination based on sex which differentially harms women. The bigotry and contempt it produces, with the acts of aggression it fosters, harm women's opportunities for equality and rights [of all kinds]." Indianapolis Code § 16–1(a)(2).

Yet this simply demonstrates the power of pornography as speech. All of these unhappy effects depend on mental intermediation. Pornography affects how people see the world, their fellows, and social relations. If pornography is what pornography does, so is other speech. Hitler's orations affected how some Germans saw Jews. Communism is a world view, not simply a *Manifesto* by Marx and Engels or a set of speeches. Efforts to suppress communist speech in the United States were based on the belief that the public acceptability of such ideas would increase the likelihood of totalitarian government. Religions affect socialization in the most pervasive way. The opinion in *Wisconsin v. Yoder*, 406 U.S. 205 (1972), shows how a religion can dominate an entire approach to life, governing much more than the relation between the sexes. Many people believe that the existence of television, apart from the content of specific programs, leads to intellectual laziness, to a penchant for violence, to many other ills. The Alien and Sedition Acts passed during the administration of John Adams rested on a sincerely held belief that disrespect for the government leads to social collapse and revolution—a belief with support in the history of many nations. Most governments of the world act on this empirical regularity, suppressing critical speech. In the United States, however, the strength of the support for this belief is irrelevant. Seditious libel is protected speech unless the danger is not only grave but also imminent. See *New York Times Co. v. Sullivan*, 376 U.S. 254 (1964); cf. *Brandenburg v. Ohio*, [395 U.S. 444 (1969)]; *New York Times Co. v. United States*, 403 U.S. 713 (1971) [the Pentagon Papers Case].

Racial bigotry, anti-semitism, violence on television, reporters' biases—these and many more influence the culture and shape our socialization. None is directly answerable by more speech, unless that speech too finds its place in the popular culture. Yet all is protected as speech, however insidious. Any other answer leaves the government in control of all of the institutions of culture, the great censor and director of which thoughts are good for us.

Sexual responses often are unthinking responses, and the association of sexual arousal with the subordination of women therefore may have a substantial effect. But almost all cultural stimuli provoke unconscious responses. Religious ceremonies condition their participants. Teachers convey messages by selecting what not to cover; the implicit message about what is off limits or unthinkable may be more powerful than the messages for which they present rational argument. Television scripts contain unarticulated assumptions. People may be conditioned in subtle ways. If the fact that speech plays a role in a process of conditioning were enough to permit governmental regulation, that would be the end of freedom of speech. * * *

Much of Indianapolis's argument rests on the belief that when speech is "unanswerable," and the metaphor that there is a "marketplace of ideas" does not apply, the First Amendment does not apply either. The metaphor is honored; Milton's *Aeropagitica* and John Stewart Mill's *On Liberty* defend freedom of speech on the ground that the truth will prevail, and many of the most important cases under the First Amendment recite this position. The Framers undoubtedly believed it. As a general matter it is true. But the Constitution does not make the dominance of truth a necessary condition of freedom of speech. To say that it does would be to confuse an outcome of free speech with a necessary condition for the application of the amendment.

A power to limit speech on the ground that truth has not yet prevailed and is not likely to prevail implies the power to declare truth. At some point the government must be able to say (as Indianapolis has said): "We know what the truth is, yet a free exchange of speech has not driven out falsity, so that we must now prohibit falsity." If the government may declare the truth, why wait for the failure of speech? Under the First Amendment, however, there is no such thing as a false idea, so the government may not restrict speech on the ground that in a free exchange truth is not yet dominant. * * *

We come, finally, to the argument that pornography is "low value" speech, that it is enough like obscenity that Indianapolis may prohibit it. Some cases hold that speech far removed from politics and other subjects at the core of the Framers' concerns may be subjected to special regulation. [Citing *Pacifica; Mini Theatres; Chaplinsky*.] These cases do not sustain statutes that select among viewpoints, however. In *Pacifica* the FCC sought to keep vile language off the air during certain times. The Court held that it may; but the Court would not have sustained a regulation prohibiting scatological descriptions of Republicans but not scatological descriptions of Democrats, or any other form of selection among viewpoints. See *Planned Parenthood Ass'n v. Chicago Transit Authority*, 767 F.2d 1225, 1232–33 (7th Cir.1985).

At all events, "pornography" is not low value speech within the meaning of these cases. Indianapolis seeks to prohibit certain speech because it believes this speech influences social relations and politics on a grand scale, that it controls attitudes at home and in the legislature. This precludes a characterization of the speech as low value. True, pornography and obscenity have sex in common. But Indianapolis left out of its definition any reference to literary, artistic, political, or scientific value. The ordinance applies to graphic sexually explicit subordination in works great and small. The Court sometimes balances the value of speech against the costs of its restriction, but it does this by category of speech and not by the content of particular works. Indianapolis has created an approved point of view and so loses the support of these cases.

Any rationale we could imagine in support of this ordinance could not be limited to sex discrimination. Free speech has been on balance an ally of those seeking change. Governments that want stasis start by restricting speech. Culture is a powerful force of continuity; Indianapolis paints pornography as part of the culture of power. Change in any complex system ultimately depends on the ability of outsiders to challenge accepted views and the reigning institutions. Without a strong guarantee of freedom of speech, there is no effective right to challenge what is. * * *

Regina v. Donald Victor Butler

Supreme Court of Canada, 1992.
[1992] 1 S.C.R. 452, 89 D.L.R.4th 449.

■ SOPINKA, J.

[Section 163 of Canada's obscenity law includes as prohibited obscenity "any publication a dominant characteristic of which is the undue exploitation of sex, or of sex and any one or more of the following subjects, namely, crime, horror, cruelty and violence." Criminal Code, R.S.C. 1985, c. C–46, s. 163(8). Justice Sopinka's opinion held that this rule violates article 2(b) of the Canadian Charter, which prohibits restrictions on freedom of expression. The opinion then held that s. 163 is nonetheless "saved" by article 1 of the Charter, which permits restrictions on other Charter rights (including expression) so long as the restrictions are narrowly tailored to serve a "pressing and substantial" public purpose.

[Justice Sopinka then considered s. 163(8)'s public purpose. In 1959, when the statute was enacted, the overriding purpose was apparently to reinforce traditional moral standards. Justice Sopinka held, however, that a law's purpose is not static. As evidence of the law's current, rather than historical, purpose, the opinion reasoned as follows.]

The harm was described in the following way in the *Report on Pornography* by the Standing Committee on Justice and Legal Affairs (MacGuigan Report) (1978), at p.18:4:

> The clear and unquestionable danger of this type of material is that it reinforces some unhealthy tendencies in Canadian society. The effect of this type of material is to reinforce male-female stereotypes to the detriment of both sexes. It attempts to make degradation, humiliation, victimization, and violence in human relationships appear normal and acceptable. A society which holds that egalitarianism, non-violence, consensualism, and mutuality are basic to any human interaction, whether sexual or other, is clearly justified in controlling and prohibiting any medium of depiction, description or advocacy which violates these principles. * * *

[Reconciling this statement with the original discussions, the Court had this to say:] First, the notions of moral corruption and harm to society are not distinct, as the appellant suggests, but are inextricably linked. It is moral corruption of a certain kind which leads to the detrimental effect on society. Secondly, and more importantly, I am of the view that with the enactment of s. 163, Parliament explicitly sought to address the harms which are linked to certain types of obscene materials. The prohibition of such materials was based on a belief that they had a detrimental impact on individuals exposed to them and consequently on society as a whole. Our understanding of the harms caused by these materials has developed considerably since that time; however, this does not detract from the fact that the purpose of this legislation remains, as it was in 1959, the protection of society from harms caused by the exposure to obscene materials. * * *

> In 1959, the harm to society caused by the undue exploitation of sex or of sex and other named matters may well have been defined more strictly in terms of public morality, *i.e.*, that such expression offended society's sense of right and wrong. It may well be that if such was the only identifiable harm today that the legislation could not be

said to pertain to pressing and substantial concerns thereby warranting an infringement of the right of expression. But that is not so. The harm goes beyond public morality in this narrow sense.

[quoting the analysis of Charron Dist. Ct. J. in *R. v. Fringe Product Inc.*, (1990) 53 C.C.C. (3d) 422, 443.]

A permissible shift in emphasis was built into the legislation when, as interpreted by the courts, it adopted the community standards test. Community standards as to what is harmful have changed since 1959.

This being the objective, is it pressing and substantial? Does the prevention of the harm associated with the dissemination of certain obscene materials constitute a sufficiently pressing and substantial concern to warrant a restriction on the freedom of expression? In this regard, it should be recalled that in [*Regina v. Keegstra*, (1990), 61 C.C.C. (3d) 1, [1990] 3 S.C.R. 697], this court unanimously accepted that the prevention of the influence of hate propaganda on society at large was a legitimate objective. Dickson C.J.C. wrote with respect to the changes in attitudes which exposure to hate propaganda can bring about (at pp. 747–48):

> ... the alteration of views held by the recipients of hate propaganda may occur subtly, and is not always attendant upon conscious acceptance of the communicated ideas. Even if the message of hate propaganda is outwardly rejected, there is evidence that its premise of racial or religious inferiority may persist in a recipient's mind as an idea that holds some truth, an incipient effect not to be entirely discounted....
>
> The threat to the self-dignity of target group members is thus matched by the possibility that prejudiced messages will gain some credence, with the attendant result of discrimination, and perhaps even violence, against minority groups in Canadian society.

This court has thus recognized that the harm caused by the proliferation of materials which seriously offend the values fundamental to our society is a substantial concern which justifies restricting the otherwise full exercise of the freedom of expression. In my view, the harm sought to be avoided in the case of the dissemination of obscene materials is similar. In the words of Nemetz C.J.B.C. in *R. v. Red Hot Video Ltd.* (1985), 18 C.C.C. (3d) 1 at p. 8, 45 C.R. (3d) 36, 15 C.R.R. 206 (B.C.C.A.), there is a growing concern that the exploitation of women and children, depicted in publications and films can, in certain circumstances, lead to "abject and servile victimization". As Anderson J.A. also noted in that same case, if true equality between male and female persons is to be achieved, we cannot ignore the threat to equality resulting from exposure to audiences of certain types of violent and degrading material. Materials portraying women as a class as objects for sexual exploitation and abuse have a negative impact on "the individual's sense of self-worth and acceptance".

In reaching the conclusion that legislation proscribing obscenity is a valid objective which justifies some encroachment of the right to freedom of expression, I am persuaded in part that such legislation may be found in most free and democratic societies. As Nemetz C.J.B.C. aptly pointed out in

R. v. Red Hot Video, *supra*, for centuries democratic societies have set certain limits to freedom of expression. He cited (at p. 40) the following passage of Dickson J.A. (as he then was) in *R. v. Great West News Ltd.*, *supra*, at p. 309:

> ... all organized societies have sought in one manner or another to suppress obscenity. The right of the state to legislate to protect its moral fibre and well-being has long been recognized, with roots deep in history. It is within this frame that the Courts and Judges must work.

The advent of the *Charter* did not have the effect of dramatically depriving Parliament of a power which it has historically enjoyed. * * *

The enactment of the impugned provision is also consistent with Canada's international obligations (*Agreement for the Suppression of the Circulation of Obscene Publications and the Convention for the Suppression of the Circulation of and Traffic in Obscene Publications*).

Finally, it should be noted that the burgeoning pornography industry renders the concern even more pressing and substantial than when the impugned provisions were first enacted. I would therefore conclude that the objective of avoiding the harm associated with the dissemination of pornography in this case is sufficiently pressing and substantial to warrant some restriction on full exercise of the right to freedom of expression. The analysis of whether the measure is proportional to the objective must, in my view, be undertaken in light of the conclusion that the objective of the impugned section is valid only in so far as it relates to the harm to society associated with obscene materials. Indeed, the section as interpreted in previous decisions and in these reasons is fully consistent with that objective. The objective of maintaining conventional standards of propriety, independently of any harm to society, is no longer justified in light of the values of individual liberty which underlie the *Charter*. This, then, being the objective of s. 163, which I have found to be pressing and substantial, I must now determine whether the section is rationally connected and proportional to this objective. As outlined above, s. 163(8) criminalizes the exploitation of sex and sex and violence, when, on the basis of the community test, it is undue. The determination of when such exploitation is undue is directly related to the immediacy of a risk of harm to society which is reasonably perceived as arising from its dissemination.

The proportionality requirement [for a regulation of free expression to be "saved" under the Canadian Charter] has three aspects:

(1) the existence of a rational connection between the impugned measures and the objective;

(2) minimal impairment of the right or freedom, and

(3) a proper balance between the effects of the limiting measures and the legislative objective. * * *

The values which underlie the protection of freedom of expression relate to the search for truth, participation in the political process, and individual self-fulfillment. The Attorney–General for Ontario argues that of these, only "individual self-fulfillment", and only in its most base aspect, that of physical arousal, is engaged by pornography. On the other hand, the civil liberties groups argue that pornography forces us to question conventional notions of sexuality and thereby launches us into an inherently political discourse. In their factum [brief], the British Columbia Civil Liberties Association adopts a passage from R. West, "The Feminist–Conservative Anti–Pornography Alliance and the 1986 Attorney General's Commission on Pornography Report", (1987) 4 *Am. Bar Found. Res. Jo.* 681, at p. 696:

> Good pornography has value because it validates women's will to pleasure. It celebrates female nature. It validates a range of female sexuality that is wider and truer than that legitimated by the non-pornographic culture. Pornography when it is good celebrates both female pleasure and male rationality.

A proper application of the test should not suppress what West refers to as "good pornography". The objective of the impugned provision is not to inhibit the celebration of human sexuality. However, it cannot be ignored that the realities of the pornography industry are far from the picture which the British Columbia Civil Liberties Association would have us paint. Shannon J., in *R. v. Wagner, supra,* described the materials more accurately when he observed, at p. 331:

> Women, particularly, are deprived of unique human character or identity and are depicted as sexual playthings, hysterically and instantly responsive to male sexual demands. They worship male genitals and their own value depends upon the quality of their genitals and breasts.

In my view, the kind of expression which is sought to be advanced does not stand on equal footing with other kinds of expression which directly engage the "core" of the freedom of expression values.

This conclusion is further buttressed by the fact that the targeted material is expression which is motivated, in the overwhelming majority of cases, by economic profit. This court held in *Rocket v. Royal College of Dental Surgeons of Ontario* [1990] 2 S.C.R. 232, 47 C.R.R. 193, that an economic motive for expression means that restrictions on the expression might "be easier to justify than other infringements".

I will now turn to an examination of the three basic aspects of the proportionality test.

The message of obscenity which degrades and dehumanizes is analogous to that of hate propaganda. As the Attorney General of Ontario has argued in its factum, obscenity wields the power to wreak social damage in that a significant portion of the population is humiliated by its gross misrepresentations.

Accordingly, the rational link between s. 163 and the objective of Parliament relates to the actual causal relationship between obscenity and the risk of harm to society at large. On this point, it is clear that the literature of the social sciences remains subject to controversy. In *Fringe Product Inc.,* supra, Charron D.C.J. considered numerous written reports and works and heard six days of testimony from experts who endeavored to describe the status of the social sciences with respect to the study of the effects of pornography. Charron D.C.J. reached the conclusion that the relationship between pornography and harm was sufficient to justify Parliament's intervention. This conclusion is not supported unanimously.

The recent conclusions of the Fraser Report could not postulate any causal relationship between pornography and the commission of violent crimes, the sexual abuse of children, or the disintegration of communities and society. This is in contrast to the findings of the MacGuigan Report.

While a direct link between obscenity and harm to society may be difficult, if not impossible, to establish, it is reasonable to presume that exposure to images bears a causal relationship to changes in attitudes and beliefs. The Meese Commission Report concluded in respect of sexually violent material (vol. 1, at p. 326):

> ... the available evidence strongly supports the hypothesis that substantial exposure to sexually violent materials as described here bears a causal relationship to antisocial acts of sexual violence and, for some subgroups, possibly to unlawful acts of sexual violence.

> Although we rely for this conclusion on significant scientific empirical evidence, we feel it worthwhile to note the underlying logic of the conclusion. The evidence says simply that the images that people are exposed to bear a causal relationship to their behavior. This is hardly surprising. What would be surprising would be to find otherwise, and we have not so found. We have not, of course, found that the images people are exposed to are a greater cause of sexual violence than all or even many other possible causes the investigation of which has been beyond our mandate. Nevertheless, it would be strange indeed if graphic representations of a form of behavior, especially in a form that almost exclusively portrays such behavior as desirable, did not have at least some effect on patterns of behavior. * * *

I am in agreement with Twaddle J.A. who expressed the view that Parliament was entitled to have a "reasoned apprehension of harm" resulting from the desensitization of individuals exposed to materials which depict violence, cruelty, and dehumanization in sexual relations.

Accordingly, I am of the view that there is a sufficiently rational link between the criminal sanction, which demonstrates our community's disapproval of the dissemination of materials which potentially victimize women and which restricts the negative influence which such materials have on changes in attitudes and behavior, and the objective.

[Justice Sopinka concluded by determining that there is no less intrusive alternative that would meet the objectives of the government, in part because "materials which have scientific, artistic, or literary merit" are exempt from the definition of obscenity. We omit the separate opinion, concurring in the disposition, by Justice Gonthier.]

NOTES ON *BUTLER* VERSUS *HUDNUT*

1. *Conflating Sexual Speech and Hate Speech.* Note that the primary authority in *Butler* for this new interpretation of obscenity is *Keegstra,* a decision in which the court upheld restrictions on hate speech. Recall our analysis of that issue in Chapter 5, Section 3. This analysis in some ways seems to get to the heart of what the Dworkin–MacKinnon approach is about: banning speech that promotes sexism. Yet it does so only by assuming that all sufficiently graphic sexually explicit speech—the fundamental and enduring definition of obscenity—is sexist, or hate speech. Valid?

2. *Similarities Between Canadian and American Free Expression Law, and a Key Difference Reflected in the Hate Speech and Pornography Cases.* Notwithstanding the distinct constitutional regimes, note how similarly Canada and the United States protect freedom of expression. Both countries allow its regulation only when the state can show that it is narrowly tailored to subserve a compelling or important social purpose. The same goals—free market of ideas, participation in the political process, personal autonomy—animate the judicial constructions in both countries. The Canadian Supreme Court is more willing to allow regulation of "assaultive" expression, specifically hate speech (*Keegstra*) and obscenity (*Butler*). Contrast the U.S. Supreme Court's decisions in *R.A.V.* (Chapter 5, Section 3) and *Hudnut* (affirming Judge Easterbrook).

Apart from your views about whether such speech should be regulated, which legal regime is overall the better? Is a risk of the Canadian approach that constitutional protection will be too shallow when more oppressive censorship comes? Is a risk of the American approach that a First Amendment absolutism will disable the government from needed regulations?

3. *Irony in the Canadian Approach: Say Feminism, Do Homophobia.* The first prosecution for obscenity initiated by Canadian police after the *Butler* ruling was against the owners of a gay bookstore for its sale of *Bad Attitude*, a lesbian sex magazine published in Boston. They were found guilty, with the court ruling that the combination in one short story of "bondage in various forms, the pulling of hair, a hard slap and explicit sex" met the *Butler* test. *R. v. Scythes*, Ontario Court (Provincial Division) (Feb. 16, 1993) (unreported).

Lesbian and gay bookstores in Canada have been engaged in a long running battle with Canadian customs over the repeated confiscation of shipments of erotic or explicit books. The bookstores won a major victory in 1996 when a Provincial Court in Vancouver ruled that the customs agency had been systematically infringing their rights by targeting shipments to gay bookstores for sequestration. *Little Sisters Book and Art Emporium v. The Minister of Justice and Attorney General of Canada*, No. A901450, (Sup.Ct.Brit. Colum., Jan. 19, 1996). For an in-depth description of the Canadian situation and a blow-by-blow account of the Little Sister's trial, see Janine Fuller & Stuart Blackley, *Restricted Entry: Censorship On Trial* (1995).

NOTE ON LESBIAN AND GAY PORNOGRAPHY

The Dworkin–MacKinnon ordinance includes pornography where men are subordinated in the same ways that women are, and so the ordinance was intended to regulate gay porn as well as straight porn. See Andrea Dworkin, *Pornography: Men Possessing Women* 44–45 (1989). As to gay male porn, we are aware of no empirical, or even anecdotal, evidence to support a link between degradation of men and violence against women. Carl Stychin argues that gay male pornography is liberating rather than oppressive from a feminist perspective, because it "has the unique ability to destabilize the coherence of the male *subject* * * * [and] thus subverts phallocracy." Carl F. Stychin, "Exploring the Limits: Feminism and the Legal Regulation of Gay Male Pornography," 16 *Vt. L. Rev.* 859 (1992) (emphasis in the original).

Jeffrey G. Sherman, "Love Speech: The Social Utility of Pornography," 47 *Stan. L. Rev.* 661 (1995), maintains that pornography serves unusually strong First Amendment purposes for gay male adolescents in particular: it provides useful practical information (i.e., can be a how-to-do-it handbook), and even shows gay teenagers that they are not unique in their desires. See also Scott Tucker, *Radical Feminism and Gay Male Porn* (1983) (making Sherman's arguments in greater detail). Of course, Sherman's argument may prove too much: straight male porn could be considered a how-to handbook for misogyny. For a critique of gay male pornography as degrading, see John Stoltenberg, *Refusing To Be A Man: Essays on Sexual Justice* (1989). Stoltenberg argues that pornography, both gay and straight, "eroticizes domination and subordination of the female and [of] effeminacy." *Id.* at 132.

As to lesbian pornography, many of the considerations are similar. Should the Dworkin–MacKinnon approach apply to sexually explicit imagery created by and/or for lesbians? How could one identify those materials, given that much commercial pornography depicts only women, and most of that is directed to a male audience? Even if they could be identified, how would such an approach square with equality theory?

SECTION 3

CUTTING EDGE ISSUES OF SEXUAL SPEECH LAW

The following developments reflect some cutting edges in American obscenity law: the criminal prosecution of Cincinnati's Contemporary Art Center and its director, Dennis Barrie, for displaying Robert Mapplethorpe's racy photographs of interracial sex, sadomasochistic images, and male nudes[a] and criminal prosecutions of rap groups, notably 2 Live Crew, for their sexually explicit lyrics (see Part A of this section);[b] denial of public funding by the National Endowment for the Arts (NEA) to artists whose themes are feminist, lesbian, and gay, including performance artists Karen Finley, John Fleck, Holly Hughes and Tim Miller (Part B);[c] censorship by the Center for Disease Control of AIDS-education materials that the CDC thought Americans would find "offensive" and efforts by parents seeking to limit information about homosexuality, abortion, and AIDS (see Chapter 7); and regulation of sexuality on cable television and the internet, the latter through the Communications Decency Act of 1996 (Part C of this section).

Read the following materials with one eye on recurring themes in this chapter and this book. Consider, for example, how censorship itself is society's way of setting limits that demarcate public and private spheres (Chapter 1), but often has the greater effect of creating discourses of perverse sexualities (Chapter 3). Consider also how profoundly First Amendment values of a marketplace of ideas, individual autonomy, and political participation are implicated in conditioning state funding on sexual conformity, in contrast to the traditional First Amendment case, where the state is trying to put someone in jail or to confiscate obscene materials. Finally, consider the ways in which the state's deployment of sexual repression is a means for controlling and monitoring people of color, women, and gay people in particular (cf. Chapter 4).

a. See Elizabeth Hess, "Art on Trial: Cincinnati's Dangerous Theatre of the Ridiculous," in *Culture Wars: Documents from the Recent Controversies in the Arts* 269 (Richard Bolton ed. 1992).

b. Alabama prosecuted a record store owner for selling 2 Live Crew records, and Florida prosecuted 2 Live Crew themselves. See Marjorie Heins, *Sex, Sin, and Blasphemy: A Guide to America's Censorship Wars* (1993).

c. See John Frohnmayer [NEA Chair during the controversy], *Leaving Town Alive: Confessions of an Arts Warrior* (1993), as well as C. Carr, *On Edge: Performance at the End of the Twentieth Century* (1993).

PART A. INTERSECTIONS OF RACE AND SEX

Luke Records, Inc. et al. v. Nick Navarro

U.S. Court of Appeals for the Eleventh Circuit, 1992.
960 F.2d 134.

■ PER CURIAM.

In this appeal, appellants Luke Records, Inc., Luther Campbell, Mark Ross, David Hobbs, and Charles Wongwon seek reversal of the district court's declaratory judgment that the musical recording "As Nasty As They Wanna Be" is obscene under Fla. Stat. § 847.011 and the United States Constitution, contending that the district court misapplied the test for determining obscenity. We reverse.

Appellants Luther Campbell, David Hobbs, Mark Ross, and Charles Wongwon comprise the musical group "2 Live Crew," which recorded "As Nasty As They Wanna Be." In response to actions taken by the Broward County, Florida Sheriff's Office to discourage record stores from selling "As Nasty As They Wanna Be," appellants filed this action in federal district court to enjoin the Sheriff from interfering further with the sale of the recording. The district court granted the injunction, finding that the actions of the Sheriff's office were an unconstitutional prior restraint on free speech. The Sheriff does not appeal this determination.

In addition to injunctive relief, however, appellants sought a declaratory judgment pursuant to 28 U.S.C.A. § 2201 that the recording was not obscene. The district court found that "As Nasty As They Wanna Be" is obscene under *Miller v. California*.

This case is apparently the first time that a court of appeals has been asked to apply the *Miller* test to a musical composition, which contains both instrumental music and lyrics. Although we tend to agree with appellants' contention that because music possesses inherent artistic value, no work of music alone may be declared obscene, that issue is not presented in this case. The Sheriff's contention that the work is not protected by the First Amendment is based on the lyrics, not the music. The Sheriff's brief denies any intention to put rap music to the test, but states "it is abundantly obvious that it is only the 'lyrical' content which makes 'As Nasty As They Wanna Be' obscene." Assuming that music is not simply a sham attempt to protect obscene material, the *Miller* test should be applied to the lyrics and the music of "As Nasty As They Wanna Be" as a whole. * * *

[The court states that there are several problems in reviewing the record.]

First, the Sheriff put in no evidence other than the cassette tape. He called no expert witnesses concerning contemporary community standards, prurient interest, or serious artistic value. His evidence was the tape recording itself.

The appellants called psychologist Mary Haber, music critics Gregory Baker, John Leland and Rhodes Scholar Carlton Long. Dr. Haber testified that the tape did not appeal to the average person's prurient interest.

Gregory Baker is a staff writer for *New Times Newspaper*, a weekly arts and news publication supported by advertising revenue and distributed free of charge throughout South Florida. Baker testified that he authored "hundreds" of articles about popular music over the previous six or seven years. After reviewing the origins of hip hop and rap music, Baker discussed the process through which rap music is created. He then outlined the ways in which 2 Live Crew had innovated past musical conventions within the genre and concluded that the music in "As Nasty As They Wanna Be" possesses serious musical value.

John Leland is a pop music critic for *Newsday* magazine, which has a daily circulation in New York, New York of approximately six hundred thousand copies, one of the top ten daily newspaper circulations in the country. Leland discussed in detail the evolution of hip hop and rap music, including the development of sampling technique by street disc jockeys over the previous fifteen years and the origins of rap in more established genres of music such as jazz, blues, and reggae. He emphasized that a Grammy Award for rap music was recently introduced, indicating that the recording industry recognizes rap as valid artistic achievement, and ultimately gave his expert opinion that 2 Live Crew's music in "As Nasty As They Wanna Be" does possess serious artistic value.

Of appellants' expert witnesses, Carlton Long testified most about the lyrics. Long is a Rhodes scholar with a Ph.D. in Political Science and was to begin an assistant professorship in that field at Columbia University in New York City shortly after the trial. Long testified that "As Nasty As They Wanna Be" contains three oral traditions, or musical conventions, known as call and response, doing the dozens, and boasting. Long testified that these oral traditions derive their roots from certain segments of Afro–American culture. Long described each of these conventions and cited examples of each one from "As Nasty As They Wanna Be." He concluded that the album reflects many aspects of the cultural heritage of poor, inner city blacks as well as the cultural experiences of 2 Live Crew. Long suggested that certain excerpts from "As Nasty As They Wanna Be" contained statements of political significance or exemplified numerous literary conventions, such as alliteration, allusion, metaphor, rhyme, and personification.

The Sheriff introduced no evidence to the contrary, except the tape.

Second, the case was tried by a judge without a jury, and he relied on his own expertise as to the community standard and artistic prongs of the *Miller* test.

The district court found that the relevant community was Broward, Dade, and Palm Beach Counties. He further stated:

This court finds that the relevant community standard reflects a *more* tolerant view of obscene speech than would other communities within the state. This finding of fact is based upon this court's personal knowledge of the community. The undersigned judge has resided in Broward County since 1958. As a practicing attorney, state prosecutor, state circuit judge, and currently, a federal district judge, the under-signed has traveled and worked in Dade, Broward, and Palm Beach. As a member of the community, he has personal knowledge of this area's demographics, culture, economics, and politics. He has attended public functions and events in all three counties and is aware of the commu-nity's concerns as reported in the media and by word of mouth.

In almost fourteen years as a state circuit judge, the undersigned gained personal knowledge of the nature of obscenity in the community while viewing dozens, if not hundreds of allegedly obscene films and other publications seized by law enforcement.

. . . .

The plaintiffs' claim that this court cannot decide this case with-out expert testimony and the introduction of specific evidence on community standards is also without merit. The law does not require expert testimony in an obscenity case. The defendant introduced the *Nasty* recording into evidence. As noted by the Supreme Court in *Paris Adult Theatre I*, when the material in question is not directed to a "bizarre, deviant group" not within the experience of the average person, the best evidence is the material, which "can and does speak for itself." *Paris Adult Theatre I [v. Slaton*, 413 U.S. 49], 56 & n. 6. [(1973)]. * * *

* * * In this case, it can be conceded without deciding that the judge's familiarity with contemporary community standards is sufficient to carry the case as to the first two prongs of the *Miller* test: prurient interest applying community standards and patent offensiveness as defined by Florida law. The record is insufficient, however, for this Court to assume the fact finder's artistic or literary knowledge or skills to satisfy the last prong of the *Miller* analysis, which requires determination of whether a work "lacks serious artistic, scientific, literary or political value."

In *Pope v. Illinois*, the Court clarified that whether a work possesses serious value was not a question to be decided by contemporary community standards. The Court reasoned that the fundamental principles of the First Amendment prevent the value of a work from being judged solely by the amount of acceptance it has won within a given community * * *

The Sheriff concedes that he has the burden of proof to show that the recording *is* obscene. Yet, he submitted no evidence to contradict the testimony that the work had artistic value. A work cannot be held obscene unless each element of the *Miller* test has been met. We reject the argument that simply by listening to this musical work, the judge could determine that it had no serious artistic value.

Kimberlé Williams Crenshaw, Mapping the Margins: Intersectionality, Identity Politics, and Violence Against Women of Color

43 *Stanford Law Review* 1241, 1285–95 (1991).*

An initial problem with the obscenity prosecution of 2 Live Crew was its apparent selectivity. Even the most superficial comparison between 2 Live Crew and other mass-marketed sexual representations suggests the likelihood that race played some role in distinguishing 2 Live Crew as the first group ever to be prosecuted for obscenity in connection with a musical recording, and one of a handful of recording artists to be prosecuted for a live performance. Recent controversies about sexism, racism, and violence in popular culture point to a vast range of expression that might have provided targets for censorship, but was left untouched. Madonna has acted out masturbation, portrayed the seduction of a priest, and insinuated group sex on stage, but she has never been prosecuted for obscenity. While 2 Live Crew was performing in Hollywood, Florida, Andrew Dice Clay's recordings were being sold in stores and he was performing nationwide on HBO. Well-known for his racist "humor," Clay is also comparable to 2 Live Crew in sexual explicitness and misogyny. In his show, for example, Clay offers, "Eenie, meenie, minee, mo/Suck my [expletive] and swallow slow," and "Lose the bra, bitch." Moreover, graphic sexual images—many of them violent—were widely available in Broward County where the performance and trial took place. According to the testimony of a Broward County vice detective, "nude dance shows and adult bookstores are scattered throughout the county where 2 Live Crew performed." Given the availability of other forms of sexually explicit "entertainment" in Broward County, Florida, one might wonder how 2 Live Crew could have been seen as uniquely obscene by the lights of the "community standards" of the county. After all, patrons of certain Broward County clubs "can see women dancing with at least their breasts exposed," and bookstore patrons can "view and purchase films and magazines that depict vaginal, oral and anal sex, homosexual sex and group sex." In arriving at its finding of obscenity, the court placed little weight on the available range of films, magazines, and live shows as evidence of the community's sensibilities. Instead, the court apparently accepted the sheriff's testimony that the decision to single out *Nasty* was based on the number of complaints against 2 Live Crew "communicated by telephone calls, anonymous messages, or letters to the police."

Evidence of this popular outcry was never substantiated. But even if it were, the case for selectivity would remain. The history of social repression of Black male sexuality is long, often violent, and all too familiar. Negative reactions to the sexual conduct of Black men have traditionally had racist overtones, especially where that conduct threatens to "cross over" into the mainstream community. So even if the decision to prosecute did reflect a widespread community perception of the purely prurient character of 2

Live Crew's music, that perception itself might reflect an established pattern of vigilante attitudes directed toward the sexual expression of Black men. In short, the appeal to community standards does not undercut a concern about racism; rather, it underscores that concern.

A second troubling dimension of the case brought against 2 Live Crew was the [trial] court's apparent disregard for the culturally rooted aspects of 2 Live Crew's music. Such disregard was essential to a finding of obscenity given the third prong of the *Miller* test requiring that material judged obscene must, taken as a whole, lack literary, artistic, or political value. 2 Live Crew argued that this criterion of the *Miller* test was not met in the case of *Nasty* since the recording exemplified such African–American cultural modes as "playing the dozens," "call and response," and "signifying." The court denied each of the group's claims of cultural specificity, recharacterizing in more generic terms what 2 Live Crew contended was distinctly African American. According to the court, "playing the dozens" is "commonly seen in adolescents, especially boys, of all ages"; "boasting" appears to be "part of the universal human condition"; and the cultural origins of "call and response"—featured in a song on Nasty about fellatio in which competing groups chanted "less filling" and "tastes great"—were to be found in a Miller beer commercial, not in African–American cultural tradition. The possibility that the Miller beer commercial may have itself evolved from an African–American cultural tradition was apparently lost on the court.

In disregarding the arguments made on behalf of 2 Live Crew, the court denied that the form and style of *Nasty* and, by implication, rap music in general had any artistic merit. This disturbing dismissal of the cultural attributes of rap and the effort to universalize African-American modes of expression are a form of colorblindness that presumes to level all significant racial and ethnic differences in order to pass judgment on intergroup conflicts. The court's analysis here also manifests a frequently encountered strategy of cultural appropriation. African-American contributions that have been accepted by the mainstream culture are eventually absorbed as simply "American" or found to be "universal." Other modes associated with African–American culture that resist absorption remain distinctive and are either neglected or dismissed as "deviant."

The court apparently rejected as well the possibility that even the most misogynistic rap may have political value as a discourse of resistance. The element of resistance found in some rap is in making people uncomfortable, thereby challenging received habits of thought and action. Such challenges are potentially political, as are more subversive attempts to contest traditional rules by becoming what is most feared. Against a historical backdrop in which the Black male as social outlaw is a prominent theme, "gangsta' rap" might be taken as a rejection of a conciliatory stance aimed at undermining fear through reassurance, in favor of a more subversive form of opposition that attempts to challenge the rules precisely by becoming the very social outlaw that society fears and attempts to proscribe. Rap representations celebrating an aggressive Black male sexuality can be easily construed as discomforting and oppositional. Not only does reading rap in this way preclude a finding that *Nasty* lacks political value, it also defeats the court's assumption that the group's intent was to appeal solely to prurient interests. To be sure, these considerations carry greater force in the case of other rap artists, such as N.W.A., Too Short, Ice Cube, and The Geto Boys, all of whose standard fare includes depictions of violent assault, rape, rape-murder, and mutilation. In fact, had these other groups been targeted rather than the comparatively less offensive 2 Live Crew, they might have successfully defeated prosecution. The graphic violence in their representations militate against a finding of obscenity by suggesting an intent not to appeal to prurient interests but instead to more expressly political ones. So long as violence is seen as distinct from sexuality, the prurient interest requirement may provide a shield for the more violent rap artists. However, even this somewhat formalistic dichotomy may provide little solace to such rap artists given the historical linkages that have been made between Black male sexuality and violence. Indeed, it has been the specter of violence that surrounds images of Black male sexuality that presented 2 Live Crew as an acceptable target of an obscenity prosecution in a field that included Andrew Dice Clay and countless others.

The point here is not that the distinction between sex and violence should be rigorously maintained in determining what is obscene or, more specifically, that rap artists whose standard fare is more violent ought to be protected. To the contrary, these more violent groups should be much more troubling than 2 Live Crew. My point instead is to suggest that obscenity prosecutions of rap artists do nothing to protect the interests of those most directly implicated in rap—Black women. On the one hand, prevailing notions of obscenity separate out sexuality from violence, which has the effect of shielding the more violently misogynistic groups from prosecution; on the other, historical linkages between images of Black male sexuality and violence permit the singling out of "lightweight" rappers for prosecution among all other purveyors of explicit sexual imagery.

Although Black women's interests were quite obviously irrelevant in the 2 Live Crew obscenity judgment, their images figured prominently in the public case supporting the prosecution. George Will's *Newsweek* essay provides a striking example of how Black women's bodies were appropriated and deployed in the broader attack against 2 Live Crew. Commenting on "America's Slide into the Sewers," Will laments that

> America today is capable of terrific intolerance about smoking, or toxic waste that threatens trout. But only a deeply confused society is more concerned about protecting lungs than minds, trout than black women. We legislate against smoking in restaurants; singing "Me So Horny" is a constitutional right. Secondary smoke is carcinogenic; celebration of torn vaginas is "mere words."

Lest one be misled into thinking that Will has become an ally of Black women, Will's real concern is suggested by his repeated references to the Central Park jogger assault. Will writes, "Her face was so disfigured a friend took 15 minutes to identify her. 'I recognized her ring.' Do you recognize the relevance of 2 Live Crew?" While the connection between the threat of 2 Live Crew and the image of the Black male rapist was suggested subtly in the public debate, it is blatant throughout Will's discussion. Indeed, it bids to be the central theme of the essay. "Fact: Some members of a particular age and societal cohort—the one making 2 Live Crew rich— stomped and raped the jogger to the razor edge of death, for the fun of it." Will directly indicts 2 Live Crew in the Central Park jogger rape through a fictional dialogue between himself and the defendants. Responding to one defendant's alleged confession that the rape was fun, Will asks, "Where can you get the idea that sexual violence against women is fun? From a music store, through Walkman earphones, from boom boxes blaring forth the rap lyrics of 2 Live Crew." Since the rapists were young Black males and *Nasty* presents Black men celebrating sexual violence, 2 Live Crew was in Central Park that night, providing the underlying accompaniment to a vicious assault. Ironically, Will rejected precisely this kind of argument in the context of racist speech on the ground that efforts to link racist speech to racist violence presume that those who hear racist speech will mindlessly act on what they hear. Apparently, the certain "social cohort" that produces and consumes racist speech is fundamentally different from the one that produces and consumes rap music.

Will invokes Black women—twice—as victims of this music. But if he were really concerned with the threat of 2 Live Crew to Black women, why does the Central Park jogger figure so prominently in his argument? Why not the Black woman in Brooklyn who was gang-raped and then thrown down an airshaft? In fact, Will fails even to mention Black victims of sexual violence, which suggests that Black women simply function for Will as stand-ins for white women. Will's use of the Black female body to press the case against 2 Live Crew recalls the strategy of the prosecutor in Richard Wright's novel *Native Son*. Bigger Thomas, Wright's Black male protagonist, is on trial for killing Mary Dalton, a white woman. Because Bigger burned her body, it cannot be established whether Bigger had sexually assaulted her, so the prosecutor brings in the body of Bessie, a Black woman raped by Bigger and left to die, in order to establish that Bigger had raped Mary Dalton.

These considerations about selectivity, about the denial of cultural specificity, and about the manipulation of Black women's bodies convince me that race played a significant, if not determining, role in the shaping of the case against 2 Live Crew. While using antisexist rhetoric to suggest a concern for women, the attack on 2 Live Crew simultaneously endorses traditional readings of Black male sexuality. The fact that the objects of these violent sexual images are Black women becomes irrelevant in the representation of the threat in terms of the Black rapist/ white victim dyad. The Black male becomes the agent of sexual violence and the white community becomes his potential victim. The subtext of the 2 Live Crew prosecution thus becomes a re-reading of the sexualized racial politics of the past.

While concerns about racism fuel my opposition to the obscenity prosecution of 2 Live Crew, the uncritical support for, and indeed celebration of, 2 Live Crew by other opponents of the prosecution is extremely troubling as well. If the rhetoric of antisexism provided an occasion for racism, so, too, the rhetoric of antiracism provided an occasion for defending the misogyny of 2 Live Crew. That defense took two forms, one political, the other cultural, both advanced prominently by Henry Louis Gates. Gates's political defense argues that 2 Live Crew advances the antiracist agenda by exaggerating stereotypes of Black male sexuality "to show how ridiculous [they] are." The defense contends that by highlighting to the extreme the sexism, misogyny, and violence stereotypically associated with Black male sexuality, 2 Live Crew represents a postmodern effort to "liberate" us from the racism that perpetuates these stereotypes.

Gates is right to contend that the reactions of Will and others confirm that the racial stereotypes still exist, but even if 2 Live Crew intended to explode these stereotypes, their strategy was misguided. Certainly, the group wholly miscalculated the reaction of their white audience, as Will's polemic amply illustrates. Rather than exploding stereotypes, as Gates suggests, 2 Live Crew, it seems most reasonable to argue, was simply (and unsuccessfully) trying to be funny. After all, trading in sexual stereotypes has long been a means to a cheap laugh, and Gates's cultural defense of 2 Live Crew recognizes as much in arguing the identification of the group with a distinctly African–American cultural tradition of the "dozens" and other forms of verbal boasting, raunchy jokes, and insinuations of sexual prowess, all of which were meant to be laughed at and to gain for the speaker respect for his word wizardry, and not to disrupt conventional myths of Black sexuality. Gates's cultural defense of 2 Live Crew, however, recalls similar efforts on behalf of racist humor, which has sometimes been defended as antiracist—an effort to poke fun at or to show the ridiculousness of racism. More simply, racist humor has often been excused as "just joking"—even racially motivated assaults have been defended as simple pranks. Thus the racism of an Andrew Dice Clay could be defended in either mode as an attempt to explode racist stereotypes or as simple humor not meant to be taken seriously. Implicit in these defenses is the assumption that racist representations are injurious only if they are intended to injure, or to be taken literally, or are devoid of some other nonracist objective. It is highly unlikely that this rationale would be accepted by Blacks as a persuasive defense of Andrew Dice Clay. Indeed, the Black community's historical and ongoing criticism of such humor suggests widespread rejection of these arguments.

The claim that a representation is meant simply as a joke may be true, but the joke functions as humor within a specific social context in which it frequently reinforces patterns of social power. Though racial humor may sometimes be intended to ridicule racism, the close relationship between the stereotypes and the prevailing images of marginalized people complicates this strategy. And certainly, the humorist's positioning vis-à-vis a targeted group colors how the group interprets a potentially derisive stereotype or gesture. Although one could argue that Black comedians have broader license to market stereotypically racist images, that argument has no force here. 2 Live Crew cannot claim an in-group privilege to perpetuate misogynist humor against Black women: the members of 2 Live Crew are not Black women, and more importantly, they enjoy a power relationship over them.

Humor in which women are objectified as packages of bodily parts to serve whatever male-bonding/male-competition needs men please subordinates women in much the same way that racist humor subordinates African Americans. Claims that incidences of such humor are just jokes and are not meant to injure or to be taken literally do little to blunt their demeaning quality—nor, for that matter, does the fact that the jokes are told within an intragroup cultural tradition.

The notion that sexism can serve antiracist ends has proponents ranging from Eldridge Cleaver to Shahrazad Ali, all of whom seem to expect Black women to serve as vehicles for the achievement of a "liberation" that functions to perpetuate their own subordination. Claims of cultural specificity similarly fail to justify toleration of misogyny. While the cultural defense of 2 Live Crew has the virtue of recognizing merit in a form of music common to the Black community, something George Will and the court that convicted 2 Live Crew were all too glib in dismissing, it does not eliminate the need to question both the sexism within the tradition it defends and the objectives to which the tradition has been pressed. The fact that playing the dozens, say, is rooted in the Black cultural tradition, or that themes represented by mythic folk heroes such as "Stackolee" are African–American does not settle the question of whether such practices oppress Black women. Whether these practices are a distinctive part of the African-American cultural tradition is decidedly beside the point. The real question is how subordinating aspects of these practices play out in the lives of people in the community, people who share the benefits as well as the burdens of a common culture. With regard to 2 Live Crew, while it may be true that the Black community has accepted the cultural forms that have evolved into rap, that acceptance should not preclude discussion of whether the misogyny within rap is itself acceptable.

With respect to Gates's political and cultural defenses of 2 Live Crew, then, little turns on whether the "word play" performed by the Crew is a postmodern challenge to racist sexual mythology or simply an internal group practice that crossed over into mainstream America. Both defenses are problematic because they require Black women to accept misogyny and its attendant disrespect and exploitation in the service of some broader group objective, whether it be pursuing an antiracist political agenda or maintaining the cultural integrity of the Black community. Neither objective obligates Black women to tolerate such misogyny.

Likewise, the superficial efforts of the anti–2 Live Crew movement to link the prosecution of the Crew to the victimization of Black women had little to do with Black women's lives. Those who deployed Black women in the service of condemning 2 Live Crew's misogynist representations did not do so in the interest of empowering Black women; rather, they had other interests in mind, the pursuit of which was racially subordinating. The implication here is not that Black feminists should stand in solidarity with the supporters of 2 Live Crew. The spirited defense of 2 Live Crew was no more about defending the entire Black community than the prosecution was about defending Black women. After all, Black women whose very assault is the subject of the representation can hardly regard the right to be represented as bitches and whores as essential to their interest. Instead, the defense primarily functions to protect 2 Live Crew's prerogative to be as misogynistic as they want to be. * * *

PART B.   CENSORSHIP OF STATE-SUBSIDIZED SPEECH

Karen Finley, John Fleck, Holly Hughes, Tim Miller, and the National Association of Artists' Organizations v. National Endowment for the Arts

U. S. Court of Appeals for the Ninth Circuit, 1996.
100 F.3d 671.

■ CIRCUIT JUDGE BROWNING.

Plaintiffs Karen Finley, John Fleck, Holly Hughes, and Tim Miller were refused fellowships under the defendant National Endowment for the Arts' ("NEA") solo performance artists program. They filed suit, alleging, among other things, that a provision of the NEA's governing statute identifying the standard for approval of funding applications violated the Fifth and First Amendments because it was impermissibly vague and imposed content-based restrictions on protected speech. * * *

Congress gave the NEA authority "to establish and carry out a program of ... grants-in-aid ... to ... individuals of exceptional talent engaged in or concerned with the arts." 20 U.S.C. § 954(c). The Chairperson of the NEA has ultimate authority to approve or disapprove grants. 20 U.S.C. §§ 954(c), 955(f). Before making a decision on a particular grant application, however, the Chairperson must consult and receive the advice of the 26–member National Council on the Arts. 20 U.S.C. § 955(f). The Chairperson may not approve any application disapproved by the National Council. The Chairperson must also utilize advisory panels to review applications and make recommendations to the National Council. 20 U.S.C. § 959(c).

An advisory panel recommended approval of plaintiffs' applications; a majority of the Council recommended disapproval; the Chairperson denied the applications. The district court concluded the statutory standard under which the applications were judged, which requires the NEA to "take into consideration general standards of decency and respect for the diverse beliefs and values of the American public," 20 U.S.C. § 954(d)(1), violated plaintiffs' due process and free speech rights. * * *

NEA and the dissent argue the "decency and respect" provision is not subject to a vagueness challenge because it does not regulate conduct directly but merely subsidizes speech. Although the need for fair warning may be less when a statute does not directly regulate conduct, the need for specific standards to prevent arbitrary and discriminatory application of provisions that touch upon speech may be even greater when a statute subsidizes speech and the risk that the provision on its face will inhibit speech remains. *Big Mama Rag, Inc. v. United States*, 631 F.2d 1030, 1039 (D.C.Cir.1980) (holding void for vagueness a tax exemption for educational and charitable organizations).

The "decency and respect" provision was enacted to prevent the funding of particular types of art. To that end, it places a mandatory duty on the Chairperson to ensure that grant applications are judged according to "general standards of decency and respect for the diverse beliefs and values of the American public." The Chairperson has no discretion to ignore this obligation, enforce only part of it, or give it a cramped construction. Rather, the Chairperson, Council, and advisory panels must examine each grant application to determine if it comports with "general standards of decency" and shows "respect for diverse beliefs and values" as they subjectively understand these terms. The record indicates this is exactly how the Chairperson and Council interpreted the provision prior to this litigation.

So construed, the "decency and respect" provision violates due process because "no standard of conduct is specified at all," *Coates v. City of Cincinnati*, 402 U.S. 611, 614 (1971), and the statute thus provides no "ascertainable standard for inclusion and exclusion." *Smith v. Goguen*, 415 U.S. 566, 578 (1974). Without doubt, persons "of common intelligence must necessarily guess at [the] meaning and differ as to [the] application" of the terms "decency" and "respect." See *Connally v. General Constr. Co.*, 269 U.S. 385, 391 (1926). These terms are inherently ambiguous, varying in meaning from individual to individual. See *Smith*, 415 U.S. at 573 ("What is contemptuous to one ... may be a work of art to another."); *Coates*, 402 U.S. at 614 ("Conduct that annoys some people does not annoy others."); *Cohen v. California*, 403 U.S. 15, 25 (1971) ("One['s] vulgarity is another's lyric."). The content of the term "diverse beliefs and values of the American public" is also impossible to define. The individual members of a pluralistic society, and particularly our own, have a great variety of beliefs and values, largely unascertainable.

Since it is not susceptible to objective definition, the "decency and respect" standard gives rise to the danger of arbitrary and discriminatory application. It grants government officials power to deny an application for funding if the application offends the officials' subjective beliefs and values. Inevitably, NEA's decision not to fund a particular artist or project as indecent or disrespectful will depend in part on who is judging the application and whether that official agrees with the artist's point of view. Under such a grant of authority, funding may be refused because of the artist's political or social message or because the art or the artist is too controversial. This danger is especially pronounced because a vague statute effectively shields decisions from review. Where First Amendment liberties are at stake, such a grant of authority violates fundamental principles of due process. * * *

Our holding that § 954(d)(1) is unconstitutionally vague effectively disposes of this case. However, in view of the dissent's argument that the government may restrict the content of speech it funds, we briefly explain why the First Amendment's prohibition on content- and viewpoint-based restrictions provides an alternate ground for our decision.

"It is axiomatic" that under the First Amendment, "the government may not regulate speech based on its substantive content or the message it conveys." *Rosenberger v. Rector & Visitors of the Univ. of Virginia*, 115 S. Ct. 2510, 2519–20 (1995) [excerpted in Chapter 5, Section 1(C)]. A content-based restriction on speech is therefore presumed unconstitutional, and must be subjected to "'the most exacting scrutiny.'" *Texas v. Johnson*, 491 U.S. 397, 412 (1989) (quoting *Boos v. Barry*, 485 U.S. 312, 321 (1988)). To survive this scrutiny, the government must advance a compelling interest served by its regulation of the content of protected speech, and the regulation must be narrowly tailored to serve that interest. *Sable Communications v. F.C.C.*, 492 U.S. 115, 126 (1989); *Denver Area Educ. Telecommunications Consortium, Inc. v. F.C.C.*, 116 S. Ct. 2374, 2385 (1996) [excerpted in Part C below] (government may directly regulate speech "to address extraordinary problems, where its regulations are appropriately tailored to resolve those problems without imposing an unnecessarily great restriction on speech"); *Action for Children's Television*, 58 F.3d at 659.

The presence of government funding alters this framework somewhat. The government may make content-based choices "when it is the speaker or when it enlists private entities to convey its own message." *Rosenberger*, 115 S. Ct. at 2518. Thus, the Supreme Court has upheld regulations that granted tax deductions for veterans' groups but not for other charitable groups engaged in lobbying, see *Regan v. Taxation With Representation*, 461 U.S. 540, 545–48 (1983), and barred recipients of federal family planning funds from providing information on abortion. *Rust v. Sullivan*, 500 U.S. 173, 200 (1991) [excerpted in this Part]. As the Court explained in *Rust*, "when the government appropriates public funds to establish a program it is entitled to define the limits of that program." *Id.* at 194.

Government funding does not invariably justify government control of the content of speech, however. In *Rust*, the Court cautioned that its holding would not apply to public fora or to universities, which occupied "a traditional sphere of free expression so fundamental to the functioning of our society that the Government's ability to control speech within that sphere by means of conditions attached to the expenditure of Government funds is restricted." *Rust*, 500 U.S. at 200.

In addition, *Rust* and *Rosenberger* identify two related contexts in which the government may subsidize speech only if it does so in a way that is viewpoint-neutral. Neutrality may be required because the area is a "traditional sphere of free expression," *Rust*, 500 U.S. at 200, or because the government has declared its intention to "encourage a diversity of views from private speakers." *Rosenberger*, 115 S. Ct. at 2519. Both approaches support the district court's conclusion that government funding of the arts, in the circumstances of this case, must be viewpoint-neutral.

As the district court explained, the arts, no less than the university, are "at the core of a democratic society's cultural and political vitality." * * * Similarly, Congress has clearly indicated the NEA's purpose is to support a diverse array of artistic expression. Even the most cursory review of the NEA's enabling statute reveals this intent. In its findings, Congress emphasized that a democracy must "honor and preserve its multicultural artistic heritage as well as support new ideas" and declared its intent "to help create and sustain ... a climate encouraging freedom of thought, imagination, and inquiry." 20 U.S.C. § 951(10), (7). * * * The NEA and its programs were created to encourage diverse private speech and not, as the dissent suggests, to engage in "speech for hire."

We cannot agree with NEA's assertion that the "decency and respect" provision does not reflect viewpoint discrimination. In *Rosenberger*, the Supreme Court found viewpoint discrimination in a university regulation that "selected for disfavored treatment those student journalistic efforts with religious editorial viewpoints." 115 S. Ct. at 2517. Central to the court's decision was the fact that under the regulation, any topic treated from a religious perspective would be denied funding. See *id*. ("Religion ... provides ... a specific premise, a perspective, a standpoint from which a variety of subjects may be discussed and considered. The prohibited perspective, not the general subject matter, resulted in the refusal to make third-party payments."). Here too, it is the treatment of a subject, not the subject itself, that is disfavored. Two depictions of the same subject matter—an American flag, for example—could be treated differently if NEA believed one depiction symbolized an "indecent" perspective or demonstrated disrespect for "the diverse beliefs and values of the American public," and the other did not.

The dissent argues we have erred in applying the body of law for regulation of speech and generally available entitlements to prizes. According to the dissent, since the NEA grants are a prize given to a select few, rather than a generally available benefit, the government can choose to support only a certain viewpoint. The Supreme Court explicitly rejected a similar argument by the University in *Rosenberger*. As the Court explained, "the government cannot justify viewpoint discrimination among private speakers on the economic fact of scarcity." 115 S. Ct. at 2519. Although NEA awarded only 88 grants from an applicant pool of 5,168, it cannot provide those scarce grants to favor a particular viewpoint. See *id*. at 2519–20 (rejecting the University's argument that "scarcity would give the State the right to exercise viewpoint discrimination that is otherwise impermissible"). * * *

The "decency and respect" provision authorizes viewpoint discrimination, an "egregious form of content discrimination." *Rosenberger*, 115 S. Ct. at 2516. Because the government has made no attempt to articulate a compelling interest served by the provision, § 954(d)(1) cannot survive strict scrutiny.* * *

■ KLEINFELD, CIRCUIT JUDGE, dissenting.

* * * First Amendment law has taken some odd turns lately. We now live in a legal context prohibiting display of a cross or menorah on government property. *American Jewish Congress v. City of Beverly Hills*, 1996 WL 409164 (9th Cir.1996), *Separation of Church and State Committee v. City of Eugene*, 93 F.3d 617 (9th Cir.1996). But if a cross is immersed in urine, a government grant cannot be withheld on the ground that the art would offend general standards of decency and respect for the religious beliefs of most Americans. The government, under today's decision, cannot even consider "general standards of decency and respect for the diverse beliefs and values of the American public" when it gives artists grants. Yet we penalize private employers for slowness in firing employees who do not show decency and respect for other employees. See *Steiner v. Showboat Operating Company*, 25 F.3d 1459 (9th Cir.1994). This self-contradictory silliness is not built into the Bill of Rights. The First Amendment does not prohibit the free exercise of common sense.

Artists, and for that matter, non-artists, are constitutionally entitled to express themselves indecently and disrespectfully toward the beliefs and values of as much of the American public as they like. Indecency sometimes helps to communicate an idea effectively, and it is constitutionally protected. See *Cohen v. California*, 403 U.S. 15 (1971). Lenny Bruce's monologues needed offensive indecency to accomplish their legitimate artistic objective. The same language that gave rise to liability in *Steiner* was essential to Allen Ginsberg's artistic expression in *Howl* and *Kaddish*. The great Modigliani nudes are frankly erotic and focus on the models' pubic hair; our Constitution unquestionably protects them from censorship. Less artistically distinguished attempts to communicate by means of offensiveness and indecency are also entitled to First Amendment protection. Molly Bloom's soliloquy, Aristophanes' jokes about passing gas, Shakespeare's double entendres, the indecent kiss in Chaucer's *Miller's Tale*, and countless works by lesser artists, such as Samuel Clemens' *1601* and Vladimir Nabakov's *Lolita*, are all part of the ancient artistic tradition of using the impolite or indecent in art. Every general art history textbook reproduces and discusses Edouard Manet's *Luncheon On the Grass*, a painting of a nude woman looking at the artist while two fully clothed men sit next to her and talk to each other. The content and viewpoint doubtless offend, but the art history books are constitutionally protected regardless. There can be no constitutional excuse for allowing the government to censor art on grounds of indecency or offensiveness. I hope that it is still as clear as it was when *Cohen* came down that anyone in America, artist or not, has a constitutional right to express himself indecently and offensively.

That offensive or indecent expression cannot be censored does not mean that the government has to pay for it. By drawing the line between private expression and government conduct, we preserve liberty for individual expression, while preserving democracy for governmental decisions.

Any time government enters a previously private sphere of conduct, the line becomes blurred, and the issues difficult. Government subsidy of art was an easy issue when the Medicis hired artists—the Medicis could freely impose their preferences. But when a democratic government pays artists to stick their thumbs in the public's eye, the public naturally becomes annoyed, and attempts to exercise its ordinary authority in a democracy to control through Congress how tax monies are spent.

Whether government can consider content and viewpoint depends on whether the money it gives out is generally available to all who meet some basic standard, or whether it is a prize given to a select few. Only 88 out of 5168 applicants for Visual Artists Fellowships won grants in fiscal year 1994. 1994 Annual Report, National Endowment for the Arts 10. Applying for an NEA arts grant is not like applying for welfare, social security, a tax exemption, or a student activity grant. NEA grants are prizes for the fortunate few, not entitlements.

The case at bar does not involve government censorship. If Congress had prohibited artists from expressing themselves indecently or disrespect-fully, the Constitution would make such a law null and void. The NEA statute before us is not such a law. It does not restrict what artists do. It restricts what the NEA can do. This case is about whether the American people can require a government agency to consider, in giving grants to very few of the many artists in the country, "general standards of decency and respect for the diverse beliefs and values of the American public."
* * *

The majority * * * misreads *Rosenberger*. The university which lost *Rosenberger* paid expenses for virtually all student organizations, but denied the money to plaintiffs because they expressed a Christian view-point. In its zeal to steer clear of the establishment clause, the university * * * overlooked the free speech clause. * * * The context was a program in which grants went to virtually all speakers but those with a Christian viewpoint, not to everyone except for a few prizewinners. * * * The majority uses principles for entitlement and regulation cases in a prize case. The principles are by and large right, the application wrong. * * *

When the government gives a prize rather than an entitlement, it necessarily discriminates by content and viewpoint. * * *

The artists who brought this lawsuit may have difficulty (the record does not say) attracting enough patrons to support their art. Finley alleges in her complaint that she is a "performance artist whose performances address such issues as the sexual stereotyping and objectification of women, rape and other forms of violence against women, and the powerlessness and victimization of women and others in our society." Fleck alleges that his performances "openly challenge traditional notions of gender and sexuali-ty" and "address AIDS, birth, death, religion, consumption in a capitalist society, and the environment." Hughes alleges that her work "addresses issues of women's power in society and women's sexuality, including lesbian relationships." Miller alleges that his "often autobiographical work addresses the relation between the individual and society, and particularly concerns social activism on issues affecting gay people, including AIDS." These works may lack the mass market of art appealing to more broadly shared sentiments.

There is no constitutional principle, however, which requires the government to replace the market and pump up the incomes of less popular artists. Government support of the arts is a policy choice, and perhaps a good one, but it is not constitutionally compelled. Lack of market appeal is an obstacle "not of [the government's] own creation." *Regan v. Taxation with Representation Wash.*, 461 U.S. 540, 549–50 (1983). So long as the artists are free to perform, people are free to patronize their performances, and the artists are not deprived of government money to which artists generally are entitled, the artists' freedom of expression is not abridged by content or viewpoint discrimination in the grant process.

The only practical guarantee of artistic freedom is private money.* * *

Irving Rust v. Louis W. Sullivan, 500 U.S. 173, 111 S.Ct. 1759, 114 L.Ed.2d 233 (1991). Doctors and grantees challenged regulations issued by the Department of Health and Human Services that prohibited family planning clinics receiving federal funds from engaging in activities that "encourage, promote or advocate abortion as a method of family planning." Plaintiffs asserted that the regulations violated the First Amendment rights of clinic staff and burdened the privacy rights of patients. The Court upheld the regulations as a permissible implementation of Title X of the Public Health Service Act, which in part prohibits use of those funds for "programs where abortion is a method of family planning."

Chief Justice Rehnquist's opinion for a five-Justice majority described the matter this way: "The challenged regulations implement the statutory prohibition by prohibiting counseling, referral, and the provision of information regarding abortion as a method of family planning. They are designed to ensure that the limits of the federal program are observed. The Title X program is designed not for prenatal care, but to encourage family planning. A doctor who wished to offer prenatal care to a project patient who became pregnant could properly be prohibited from doing so because such service is outside the scope of the federally funded program. The regulations prohibiting abortion counseling and referral are of the same ilk; 'no funds appropriated for the project may be used in programs where abortion is a method of family planning,' and a doctor employed by the project may be prohibited in the course of his project duties from counseling abortion or referring for abortion. This is not a case of the Government 'suppressing a dangerous idea,' but of a prohibition on a project grantee or its employees from engaging in activities outside of its scope.

"To hold that the Government unconstitutionally discriminates on the basis of viewpoint when it chooses to fund a program dedicated to advance certain permissible goals, because the program in advancing those goals necessarily discourages alternate goals, would render numerous government programs constitutionally suspect. When Congress established a National Endowment for Democracy to encourage other countries to adopt democratic principles, 22 U.S.C. § 4411(b), it was not constitutionally required to fund a program to encourage competing lines of political philosophy such as Communism and Fascism. Petitioners' assertions ultimately boil down to the position that if the government chooses to subsidize one protected right, it must subsidize analogous counterpart rights. But the Court has soundly rejected that proposition. Within far broader limits than petitioners are willing to concede, when the government appropriates public funds to establish a program it is entitled to define the limits of that program."

The Court next distinguished the "unconstitutional conditions" line of cases. It held that the underlying statutory provision that prohibited funding for programs offering abortion as a means of family planning did not improperly condition a benefit, but rather simply delimited the scope of the service being funded. Title X grantees can obtain funds from other sources to support abortion-related advocacy, as long as such activities are "physically and financially separate" from family planning services, a requirement the Court also upheld. Likewise, the Court said, clinic staff could engage in abortion-related activities "when they are not acting under the auspices of the Title X project."

"This is not to suggest that funding by the Government, even when coupled with the freedom of the fund recipients to speak outside the scope of the Government-funded project, is invariably sufficient to justify government control over the content of expression. For example, this Court has recognized that the existence of a Government 'subsidy,' in the form of Government-owned property, does not justify the restriction of speech in areas that have 'been traditionally open to the public for expressive activity,' or have been 'expressly dedicated to speech activity.' Similarly, we have recognized that the university is a traditional sphere of free expression so fundamental to the functioning of our society that the Government's ability to control speech within that sphere by means of conditions attached to the expenditure of Government funds is restricted by the vagueness and overbreadth doctrines of the First Amendment, *Keyishian v. Board of Regents* [385 U.S. 589 (1967)]. It could be argued by analogy that traditional relationships such as that between doctor and patient should enjoy protection under the First Amendment from government regulation, even when subsidized by the Government. We need not resolve that question here, however, because the Title X program regulations do not significantly impinge upon the doctor-patient relationship."

In dissent, Justice Blackmun objected: "Until today, the Court never has upheld viewpoint based suppression of speech simply because that suppression was a condition upon the acceptance of public funds. Whatever may be the Government's power to condition the receipt of its largess upon the relinquishment of constitutional rights, it surely does not extend to a condition that suppresses the recipient's cherished freedom of speech based solely upon the content or viewpoint of that speech.

"It cannot seriously be disputed that the counseling and referral provisions at issue in the present cases constitute content-based regulation of speech. Title X grantees may provide counseling and referral regarding any of a wide range of family planning and other topics, save abortion.

"The Regulations are also clearly viewpoint based. While suppressing speech favorable to abortion with one hand, the Secretary compels anti-abortion speech with the other. * * *

"Remarkably, the majority concludes that 'the Government has not discriminated on the basis of viewpoint; it has merely chosen to fund one activity to the exclusion of another.' But the majority's claim that the Regulations merely limit a Title X project's speech to preventive or preconceptional services rings hollow in light of the broad range of nonpreventive services that the Regulations authorize Title X projects to provide. By refusing to fund those family-planning projects that advocate abortion *because* they advocate abortion, the Government plainly has targeted a particular viewpoint. The majority's reliance on the fact that the Regulations pertain solely to funding decisions simply begs the question. Clearly, there are some bases upon which government may not rest its decision to fund or not to fund. For example, the Members of the majority surely would agree that government may not base its decision to support an activity upon considerations of race. As demonstrated above, our cases make clear that ideological viewpoint is a similarly repugnant ground upon which to base funding decisions."

Hilton Kramer, Is Art Above the Laws of Decency?

New York Times, July 2, 1989, Section 2, page 1.

* * * [The] homoerotic idealizations of male sexuality are not the most extreme of Mapplethorpe's pictures. That dubious honor belongs to the pictures that celebrate in graphic and grisly detail what Richard Marshall, the curator who organized a Mapplethorpe retrospective at the Whitney Museum last summer, * * * identified as the "sadomasochistic theme." In this case, it is a theme enacted by male homosexual partners whom we may presume to be consenting adults—consenting not only to the sexual practices depicted but to Mapplethorpe's role in photographing them.

I cannot bring myself to describe these pictures in all their gruesome particularities, and it is doubtful that this newspaper would agree to publish such a description even if I could bring myself to write one. (There can be no question either, of course, of illustrating such pictures on this page, which raises an interesting and not irrelevant question: Should public funds be used to exhibit pictures which the press even in our liberated era still finds too explicit or repulsive to publish?) * * *

Even in a social environment as emancipated from conventional sexual attitudes as ours is today, to exhibit photographic images of this sort, which are designed to aggrandize and abet erotic rituals involving coercion, degradation, bloodshed and the infliction of pain, cannot be regarded as anything but a violation of public decency. Such pictures have long circulated in private, of course. They belonged, and were seen to belong, to the realm of specialized erotica. In that realm, it was clearly understood that the primary function of such images was to promote sexual practices commonly regarded as unruly and perverse, or to aid in fantasizing about such practices. The appeal of such images for those who were drawn to them lay precisely in the fact that they were forbidden. They belonged, in other words, to the world of pornography.

* * * How we, as adult citizens, wish to deal in our own lives with this antisocial element in the arts should not, I think, be a matter for the Government to determine, for systematic programs of censorship are likely to have consequences that are detrimental to our liberties. (The question of protecting children is another matter entirely.) It is when our Government intervenes in this process by supporting the kind of art that is seen to be antisocial that we as citizens have a right to be heard—not, I hasten to add, in order to deny the artist his freedom of expression, but to have a voice in determining what our representatives in the Government are going to support and thus validate in our name. * * *

NOTES ON FUNDING FOR SEXUALLY EXPLICIT ART

1. *The Public Forum Issue.* The analytical difference between the majority and the dissent in *Finley* is that the former sees the NEA as a kind of public forum and so follows *Rosenberger*, while the latter sees the NEA as a prize-giving fund and so follows *Rust*. Which is the closer analogy?

2. *The Public–Private Boundary.* Few areas of law illustrate as dramatically the tension over how law treats efforts to influence discourse as the current debate over whether the First Amendment applies with equal force to programs in which the state subsidizes expression. We think it is not coincidental that so many of the key cases have arisen over speech associated with sexuality, such as *Finley* and *Rust*. Sexual speech has for so long seemed the quintessential example of private speech, as we have seen. Now traditionalists assert that advocates are not just making a claim that sexual speech ranks with core political speech in value, but that it merits government support as well! But that isn't the point, if one is assessing the power dynamics involved. Owen Fiss has written:

> The constitutional wrong of an obscenity prosecution arises from the effect such an exercise of state power upon public discourse, and although there is an analytic difference in the subsidy situation, arising from the scarcity factor, the focus should remain on the effect of the government action. * * * A court [should] ascertain whether the allocative decision would contribute to a debate on national issues that is "uninhibited, robust, and wide-open," or whether its effect would be just the opposite.

Owen Fiss, "State Activism and State Censorship," 100 *Yale L. J.* 2087, 2102 (1991). For a very different perspective, see Richard Epstein, "Foreword: Unconstitutional Conditions, State Power, and the Limits of Consent," 102 *Harv. L. Rev.* 4 (1988).

3. *The Claim for Viewpoint Discrimination.* Much of the argument in these cases turns on whether explicit or "indecent" speech can be said to have a viewpoint. The lawyers for the NEA Four (including one of us) asserted that "decency" was being used as a code word for anti-feminist and anti-gay rights expression. Persuasive? Or is "decency" too incoherent a word, too vague as we also argued, to fulfill that function? Should one assess whether a viewpoint is being suppressed from the perspective of the agency seeking to suppress or from that of the speaker? Does Hilton Kramer's interpretation of the art in question inadvertently make Justice Blackmun's point in his *Rust* dissent?

PART C.   "INDECENCY" AND ELECTRONIC MEDIA

Should different rules for the regulation of sexual speech govern when broadcast or other electronic media are involved? The Supreme Court has traditionally allowed more state regulation of the electronic media than of the print media or of face-to-face speech, originally because radio and television were considered "scarce" resources. *Red Lion Broadcasting v. FCC*, 395 U.S. 367 (1969) (upholding the FCC's "fairness doctrine," requiring television to provide equal time for competing political viewpoints). Although the scarcity rationale has dissipated over time, the Court has never overruled *Red Lion* and continues to treat the electronic media as a special forum. *E.g., Turner Broadcasting System, Inc. v. FCC*, 512 U.S. 622 (1994). Consider this doctrine in light of the following problem and Supreme Court precedents.

NOTE ON THE SUPREME COURT'S RULINGS ON INDECENT SPEECH IN THE ELECTRONIC MEDIA

In *FCC v. Pacifica Foundation*, 438 U.S. 726 (1978), the Court upheld the FCC's action prohibiting Pacifica from airing George Carlin's "Seven Dirty Words" monologue, against both statutory and constitutional attack. Writing for five Members of the Court, Justice Stevens analogized the rationale for suppression in this instance to nuisance law, holding that speech which might be permissible in other contexts could be suppressed when presented in a medium that has a "uniquely pervasive presence" and is "uniquely accessible to children."

Writing only for himself and two other Justices, Stevens argued that non-obscene but indecent speech is of such low value that it merits less than full protection under the First Amendment. "[W]e may assume, *arguendo*, that this monologue would be protected in other contexts. Nonetheless the constitutional protection accorded to a communication containing such patently offensive sexual and excretory language need not be the same in every context. It is a characteristic of speech such as this that both its capacity to offend and its 'social value' * * * vary with the circumstances.''

Writing for himself and Justice Blackmun, Justice Powell refused to accept a sliding scale of First Amendment protection for speech dependent upon its social value. These concurring Justices believed that *indecent* as well as *obscene* speech could be regulated in this context because it is broadcast directly into the home, where children are likely to hear it.

Four Justices dissented, arguing that the case was not materially different from *Cohen v. California*, 403 U.S. 15 (1971), where the Court had disallowed state regulation of a young man whose jacket displayed the words "Fuck the Draft" in public places. Commentators have tended to be more shocked by the Court's opinion than by the seven dirty words.[a]

In *Sable Communications v. FCC*, 492 U.S. 115 (1989), the Court struck down a ban on indecent interstate telephone messages (i.e., dial-a-porn) on the grounds that it did not intrude upon a captive audience or unwilling listeners, in the way that radio and television could, and that the statute at issue there was a total ban, rather than the FCC order in *Pacifica*, which was a specific sanction geared to a particular broadcast. Three years later the Court let stand the invalidation of a 24–hour ban on broadcasting indecent speech on the ground that some preservation for such material was required. *Action for Children's Television v. FCC*, 932 F.2d 1504 (D.C.Cir.1991), *cert. denied sub. nom. Children's Legal Fdn., Inc. v. Action for Children's Television*, 503 U.S. 913 (1992).

Thus, the cases have established that both for broadcast media and for telephone services, Congress cannot enact a total ban on speech that is indecent but not obscene. Moreover, regulation of indecent speech must be narrowly tailored so that it is effectuated by mechanisms that achieve the goal of shielding children but do not unduly restrict access by adults. On this point, a statute was upheld that required that phone company customers affirmatively subscribe to dial-a-porn access, or otherwise opt-in, rather allow access to all except those who had opted out by requesting central blocking of such calls. *Dial Information Services Corp. v. Thornburgh*, 938 F.2d 1535 (2d Cir.1991), *cert. denied sub nom. Dial Information Services Corp. v. Barr*, 502 U.S. 1072 (1992).

What exactly *is* indecent speech? Beginning with *Pacifica*, the Court has upheld the following definition:

> language that describes, in terms patently offensive as measured by contemporary community standards for the broadcast medium, sexual or excretory activities and organs * * *.

Pacifica, 438 U.S. at 731–32. Statutes using essentially the same definition have been found constitutional in application to dial-a-porn, *Dial Informa-*

a. *E.g.,* Steven Shiffrin, *The First Amendment, Democracy, and Romance* 80 (1990).

tion Services Corp. v. Thornburgh, 938 F.2d 1535 (2d Cir.1991), *cert. denied sub nom., Dial Information Services Corp. v. Barr*, 502 U.S. 1072 (1992).

Important questions remain unanswered, however. How are community standards ascertained when one is broadcasting to the entire United States? In *Sable*, the Court held that this was a problem of the dial-a-porn business, not a constitutional issue. "If Sable's audience is comprised of different communities with different local standards, Sable ultimately bears the burden of complying with the prohibition on obscene messages." *Sable Communications v. FCC*, 492 U.S. at 126. Should the same approach apply to indecent speech?

Under the definition as it has evolved, speech may be declared to be indecent even though it does not appeal to prurient interest, as required in the definition of obscenity. Nor is there an exception for speech which has serious artistic, scientific, educational or other value. Are AIDS education materials indecent?

Denver Area Educational Telecommunications Consortium v. Federal Communications Commission

United States Supreme Court, 1996.
___ U.S. ___, 116 S.Ct. 2374, 135 L.Ed.2d 888.

■ JUSTICE BREYER announced the judgment of the Court and delivered the opinion of the Court with respect to Part III, an opinion with respect to Parts I, II, and V, in which JUSTICE STEVENS, JUSTICE O'CONNOR, JUSTICE SOUTER join, and an opinion with respect to Parts IV and VI, in which JUSTICE STEVENS and JUSTICE SOUTER join.

These cases present First Amendment challenges to three statutory provisions that seek to regulate the broadcasting of "patently offensive" sex-related material on cable television. Cable Television Consumer Protection and Competition Act of 1992 (1992 Act or Act), 106 Stat. 1486, §§ 10(a), 10(b), and 10(c), 47 U.S.C. §§ 532(h), 532(j), and note following § 531. * * *

We conclude that the first-provision—that *permits* the operator to decide whether or not to broadcast such programs on *leased* access channels—is consistent with the First Amendment. The second provision, that *requires* leased channel operators to segregate and to block that programming, and the third provision, applicable to public, educational, and governmental channels, violate the First Amendment, for they are not appropriately tailored to achieve the basic, legitimate objective of protecting children from exposure to "patently offensive" material.

Cable operators typically own a physical cable network used to convey programming over several dozen cable channels into subscribers' houses. Program sources vary from channel to channel. Most channels carry programming produced by independent firms, including "many national and regional cable programming networks that have emerged in recent years," *Turner Broadcasting System, Inc. v. FCC*, 114 S.Ct. 2445, 2452

(1994), as well as some programming that the system operator itself (or an operator affiliate) may provide. Other channels may simply retransmit through cable the signals of over-the-air broadcast stations. Certain special channels here at issue, called "leased channels" and "public, educational, or governmental channels," carry programs provided by those to whom the law gives special cable system access rights.

A "leased channel" is a channel that federal law requires a cable system operator to reserve for commercial lease by unaffiliated third parties. About 10 to 15 percent of a cable system's channels would typically fall into this category. See 47 U.S.C. § 532(b). "[P]ublic, educational, or governmental channels" (which we shall call "public access" channels) are channels that, over the years, local governments have required cable system operators to set aside for public, educational, or governmental purposes as part of the consideration an operator gives in return for permission to install cables under city streets and to use public rights-of-way. Between 1984 and 1992 federal law (as had much pre–1984 state law, in respect to public access channels) prohibited cable system operators from exercising *any* editorial control over the content of any program broadcast over either leased or public access channels. See 47 U.S.C. §§ 531(e) (public access), 47 U.S.C. §§ 532(c)(2) (leased access).

In 1992, in an effort to control sexually explicit programming conveyed over access channels, Congress enacted the three provisions before us. The first two provisions relate to leased channels. The first says:

> "This subsection shall permit a cable operator to enforce prospectively a written and published policy of prohibiting programming that the cable operator reasonably believes describes or depicts sexual or excretory activities or organs in a patently offensive manner as measured by contemporary community standards." 1992 Act, § 10(a)(2), 106 Stat. 1486.

The second provision applicable only to leased channels requires cable operators to segregate and to block similar programming if they decide to permit, rather than to prohibit, its broadcast. The provision tells the Federal Communications Commission (FCC or Commission) to promulgate regulations that will (a) require "programmers to inform cable operators if the program[ming] would be indecent as defined by Commission regulations"; (b) require "cable operators to place" such material "on a single channel"; and (c) require "cable operators to block such single channel unless the subscriber requests access to such channel in writing." 1992 Act, § 10(b)(1). The Commission issued regulations defining the material at issue in terms virtually identical to those we have already set forth, namely as descriptions or depictions of "sexual or excretory activities or organs in a patently offensive manner" as measured by the cable viewing community. First Report and Order, ¶¶ 33–38, 8 FCC Rcd, at 1003–1004. The regulations require the cable operators to place this material on a single channel and to block it (say, by scrambling). They also require the system operator to provide access to the blocked channel "within 30 days" of a subscriber's written request for access and to re-block it within 30 days of a subscriber's request to do so. 47 CFR § 76.701(c) (1995).

The third provision is similar to the first provision, but applies only to public access channels. The relevant statutory section instructs the FCC to promulgate regulations that will

> "enable a cable operator of a cable system to prohibit the use, on such system, of any channel capacity of any public, educational, or governmental access facility for any programming which contains obscene material, sexually explicit conduct, or material soliciting or promoting unlawful conduct." 1992 Act, § 10(c).

The FCC, carrying out this statutory instruction, promulgated regulations defining "sexually explicit" in language almost identical to that in the statute's leased channel provision, namely as descriptions or depictions of "sexual or excretory activities or organs in a patently offensive manner" as measured by the cable viewing community. See 47 CFR § 76.702(1995) (incorporating definition from 47 CFR § 76.701(g)).

The upshot is, as we said at the beginning, that the federal law before us (the statute as implemented through regulations) now *permits* cable operators either to allow or to forbid the transmission of "patently offensive" sex-related materials over both leased and public access channels, and *requires* those operators, at a minimum, to segregate and to block transmission of that same material on leased channels. * * *

[Part II] We turn initially to the provision that *permits* cable system operators to prohibit "patently offensive" (or "indecent") programming transmitted over leased access channels. 1992 Act, § 10(a). * * *

We recognize that the First Amendment, the terms of which apply to governmental action, *ordinarily* does not itself throw into constitutional doubt the decisions of private citizens to permit, or to restrict, speech—and this is so ordinarily even where those decisions take place within the framework of a regulatory regime such as broadcasting. Were that not so, courts might have to face the difficult, and potentially restrictive, practical task of deciding which, among any number of private parties involved in providing a program (for example, networks, station owners, program editors, and program producers), is the "speaker" whose rights may not be abridged, and who is the speech-restricting "censor." Furthermore, as this Court has held, the editorial function itself is an aspect of "speech," see *Turner*, 114 S.Ct., at 2456, and a court's decision that a private party, say, the station owner, is a "censor," could itself interfere with that private "censor's" freedom to speak as an editor. Thus, not surprisingly, this Court's First Amendment broadcasting cases have dealt with governmental efforts to restrict, not governmental efforts to provide or to maintain, a broadcaster's freedom to pick and to choose programming. * * *

Nonetheless, petitioners, while conceding that this is ordinarily so, point to circumstances that, in their view, make that analogy with private broadcasters inapposite and make this case a special one, warranting a different constitutional result. As a practical matter, they say, cable system operators have considerably more power to "censor" program viewing than do broadcasters, for individual communities typically have only one cable system, linking broadcasters and other program providers with each community's many subscribers. Moreover, concern about system operators' exercise of this considerable power originally led government—local and federal—to insist that operators provide leased and public access channels free of operator editorial control. H.R.Rep. No. 98–934, at 30–31. To permit system operators to supervise programming on leased access channels will create the very private-censorship risk that this anticensorship effort sought to avoid. At the same time, petitioners add, cable systems have two relevant special characteristics. They are unusually involved with government, for they depend upon government permission and government facilities (streets, rights-of-way) to string the cable necessary for their services. And in respect to leased channels, their speech interests are relatively weak because they act less like editors, such as newspapers or television broadcasters, than like common carriers, such as telephone companies.

Under these circumstances, petitioners conclude, Congress' "permissive" law, in actuality, will "abridge" their free speech. And this Court should treat that law as a congressionally imposed, content-based, restriction unredeemed as a properly tailored effort to serve a "compelling interest." They further analogize the provisions to constitutionally forbidden content-based restrictions upon speech taking place in "public forums" such as public streets, parks, or buildings dedicated to open speech and communication. And, finally, petitioners say that the legal standard the law contains (the "patently offensive" standard) is unconstitutionally vague.
* * *

[T]he First Amendment embodies an overarching commitment to protect speech from Government regulation through close judicial scrutiny, thereby enforcing the Constitution's constraints, but without imposing judicial formulae so rigid that they become a straightjacket that disables Government from responding to serious problems. This Court, in different contexts, has consistently held that the Government may directly regulate speech to address extraordinary problems, where its regulations are appropriately tailored to resolve those problems without imposing an unnecessarily great restriction on speech. Justices Kennedy and Thomas would have us further declare which, among the many applications of the general approach that this Court has developed over the years, we are applying here. But no definitive choice among competing analogies (broadcast, common carrier, bookstore) allows us to declare a rigid single standard, good for now and for all future media and purposes. That is not to say that we reject all the more specific formulations of the standard—they appropriately cover the vast majority of cases involving Government regulation of speech. Rather, aware as we are of the changes taking place in the law, the technology, and the industrial structure, related to telecommunications, see, *e.g.*, Telecommunications Act of 1996, 110 Stat. 56; S.Rep. No. 104–23 (1995); H.R.Rep. No. 104–204 (1995), we believe it unwise and unnecessary definitively to pick one analogy or one specific set of words now. We therefore think it premature to answer the broad questions that Justices

Kennedy and Thomas raise in their efforts to find a definitive analogy, deciding, for example, the extent to which private property can be designated a public forum; whether public access channels are a public forum; * * * whether the Government's viewpoint neutral decision to limit a public forum is subject to the same scrutiny as a selective exclusion from a pre-existing public forum; whether exclusion from common carriage must for all purposes be treated like exclusion from a public forum; and whether the interests of the owners of communications media always subordinate the interests of all other users of a medium.

Rather than decide these issues, we can decide this case more narrowly, by closely scrutinizing § 10(a) to assure that it properly addresses an extremely important problem, without imposing, in light of the relevant interests, an unnecessarily great restriction on speech. The importance of the interest at stake here—protecting children from exposure to patently offensive depictions of sex; the accommodation of the interests of programmers in maintaining access channels and of cable operators in editing the contents of their channels; the similarity of the problem and its solution to those at issue in *Pacifica*; and the flexibility inherent in an approach that permits private cable operators to make editorial decisions, lead us to conclude that § 10(a) is a sufficiently tailored response to an extraordinarily important problem.

[Justice Breyer concluded that the factors which justified in FCC order in *Pacifica* are also true of the provision allowing operators of leased cable channels to bar "indecent" programming: the easy accessibility of cable TV to children; the "uniquely pervasive presence" of broadcast media in the home; and the ability of adults to secure "indecent" programming by alternative means, such as in theaters or on tapes.]

[Part III] The statute's second provision significantly differs from the first, for it does not simply permit, but rather requires, cable system operators to restrict speech—by segregating and blocking "patently offensive" sex-related material appearing on leased channels (but not on other channels). 1992 Act, § 10(b). In particular, as previously mentioned, this provision and its implementing regulations require cable system operators to place "patently offensive" leased channel programming on a separate channel; to block that channel; to unblock the channel within 30 days of a subscriber's written request for access; and to reblock the channel within 30 days of a subscriber's request for reblocking. 1992 Act, § 10(b); 47 CFR §§ 76.701(b), (c), (g) (1995). Also, leased channel programmers must notify cable operators of an intended "patently offensive" broadcast up to 30 days before its scheduled broadcast date. §§ 76.701(d), (g).

These requirements have obvious restrictive effects. The several up-to–30–day delays, along with single channel segregation, mean that a subscriber cannot decide to watch a single program without considerable advance planning and without letting the "patently offensive" channel in its entirety invade his household for days, perhaps weeks, at a time. These restrictions will prevent programmers from broadcasting to viewers who select programs day by day (or, through "surfing," minute by minute); to viewers who would like occasionally to watch a few, but not many, of the programs on the "patently offensive" channel; and to viewers who simply tend to judge a program's value through channel reputation, *i.e.*, by the company it keeps. Moreover, the "written notice" requirement will further restrict viewing by subscribers who fear for their reputations should the operator, advertently or inadvertently, disclose the list of those who wish to watch the "patently offensive" channel. Cf. *Lamont v. Postmaster General*, 381 U.S. 301, 307 (1965) (finding unconstitutional a requirement that recipients of Communist literature notify the Post Office that they wish to receive it). Further, the added costs and burdens that these requirements impose upon a cable system operator may encourage that operator to ban programming that the operator would otherwise permit to run, even if only late at night.

The Government argues that, despite these adverse consequences, the "segregate and block" requirements are lawful because they are ."the least restrictive means of realizing" a "compelling interest," namely "protecting the physical and psychological well-being of minors." It adds that, in any event, the First Amendment, as applied in *Pacifica*, "does not require that regulations of indecency on television be subject to the strictest" First Amendment "standard of review."

We agree with the Government that protection of children is a "compelling interest." But we do not agree that the "segregate and block" requirements properly accommodate the speech restrictions they impose and the legitimate objective they seek to attain. Nor need we here determine whether, or the extent to which, *Pacifica* does, or does not, impose some lesser standard of review where indecent speech is at issue, compare 438 U.S., at 745–748 (opinion of Stevens, J.) (indecent materials enjoy lesser First Amendment protection), with id., at 761–762 (Powell, J., concurring in part and concurring in judgment) (refusing to accept a lesser standard for nonobscene, indecent material). That is because once one examines this governmental restriction, it becomes apparent that, not only is it not a "least restrictive alternative," and is not "narrowly tailored" to meet its legitimate objective, it also seems considerably "more extensive than necessary." * * *

Several circumstances lead us to this conclusion. For one thing, the law, as recently amended, uses other means to protect children from similar "patently offensive" material broadcast on *un*leased cable channels, *i.e.*, broadcast over any of a system's numerous ordinary, or public access, channels. The law, as recently amended, requires cable operators to "scramble or ... block" such programming on any (unleased) channel *"primarily dedicated* to sexually-oriented programming." Telecommunications Act of 1996, § 505, 110 Stat. 136 (emphasis added). In addition, cable operators must honor a subscriber's request to block any, or all, programs on any channel to which he or she does not wish to subscribe. § 504, *ibid.* And manufacturers, in the future, will have to make television sets with a so-called "V-chip"—a device that will be able automatically to identify and block sexually explicit or violent programs. § 551, *id.*, at 139–142.

Although we cannot, and do not, decide whether the new provisions are themselves lawful (a matter not before us), we note that they are significantly less restrictive than the provision here at issue. They do not force the viewer to receive (for days or weeks at a time) all "patently offensive" programming or none; they will not lead the viewer automatically to judge the few by the reputation of the many; and they will not automatically place the occasional viewer's name on a special list. They therefore inevitably lead us to ask why, if they adequately protect children from "patently offensive" material broadcast on ordinary channels, they would not offer adequate protection from similar leased channel broadcasts as well? Alternatively, if these provisions do not adequately protect children from "patently offensive" material broadcast on ordinary channels, how could one justify more severe leased channel restrictions when (given ordinary channel programming) they would yield so little additional protection for children? * * *

[Part IV] The statute's third provision, as implemented by FCC regulation, is similar to its first provision, in that it too *permits* a cable operator to prevent transmission of "patently offensive" programming, in this case on public access channels. 1992 Act, § 10(c); 47 CFR § 76.702 (1995). But there are * * * important differences.

The first is the historical background. * * * [C]able operators have traditionally agreed to reserve channel capacity for public, governmental, and educational channels as part of the consideration they give municipalities that award them cable franchises. In the terms preferred by Justice Thomas, the requirement to reserve capacity for public access channels is similar to the reservation of a public easement, or a dedication of land for streets and parks, as part of a municipality's approval of a subdivision of land. Significantly, these are channels over which cable operators have not historically exercised editorial control. H.R.Rep. No. 98–934, *supra*, at 30. Unlike § 10(a) therefore, § 10(c) does not restore to cable operators editorial rights that they once had, and the countervailing First Amendment interest is nonexistent, or at least much diminished.

The second difference is the institutional background that has developed as a result of the historical difference. When a "leased channel" is made available by the operator to a private lessee, the lessee has total control of programming during the leased time slot. See 47 U.S.C. § 532(c)(2). Public access channels, on the other hand, are normally subject to complex supervisory systems of various sorts, often with both public and private elements. See § 531(b) (franchising authorities "may require rules and procedures for the use of the [public access] channel capacity"). Municipalities generally provide in their cable franchising agreements for an access channel manager, who is most commonly a nonprofit organization, but may also be the municipality, or, in some instances, the cable system owner. See * * * P. Aufderheide, *Public Access Cable Programming, Controversial Speech, and Free Expression* (1992) reprinted in App. 61, 63 (surveying 61 communities; the access manager was: a nonprofit organization in 41, a local government official in 12, the cable operator in 5, and an unidentified entity in 3). * * * Access channel activity and management are partly financed with public funds—through franchise fees or other payments pursuant to the franchise agreement, or from general municipal funds.

This system of public, private, and mixed nonprofit elements, through its supervising boards and nonprofit or governmental access managers, can set programming policy and approve or disapprove particular programming services. And this system can police that policy by, for example, requiring indemnification by programmers, certification of compliance with local standards, time segregation, adult content advisories, or even by prescreening individual programs. Whether these locally accountable bodies prescreen programming, promulgate rules for the use of public access channels, or are merely available to respond when problems arise, the upshot is the same: there is a locally accountable body capable of addressing the problem, should it arise, of patently offensive programming broadcast to children, making it unlikely that many children will in fact be exposed to programming considered patently offensive in that community.

Third, the existence of a system aimed at encouraging and securing programming that the community considers valuable strongly suggests that a "cable operator's veto" is less likely necessary to achieve the statute's basic objective, protecting children, than a similar veto in the context of leased channels. Of course, the system of access managers and supervising boards can make mistakes, which the operator might in some cases correct with its veto power. Balanced against this potential benefit, however, is the risk that the veto itself may be mistaken; and its use, or threatened use, could prevent the presentation of programming, that, though borderline, is not "patently offensive" to its targeted audience. See Aufderheide, App. 64–66 (describing the programs that were considered borderline by access managers, including sex education, health education, broadcasts of politically marginal groups, and various artistic experiments). And this latter threat must bulk large within a system that already has publicly accountable systems for maintaining responsible programs. * * *

The upshot, in respect to the public access channels, is a law that could radically change present programming-related relationships among local community and nonprofit supervising boards and access managers, which relationships are established through municipal law, regulation, and contract. In doing so, it would not significantly restore editorial rights of cable operators, but would greatly increase the risk that certain categories of programming (say, borderline offensive programs) will not appear. At the same time, given present supervisory mechanisms, the need for this particular provision, aimed directly at public access channels, is not obvious. Having carefully reviewed the legislative history of the Act, the proceedings before the FCC, the record below, and the submissions of the parties and *amici* here, we conclude that the Government cannot sustain its burden of showing that § 10(c) is necessary to protect children or that it is appropriately tailored to secure that end. Consequently, we find that this third provision violates the First Amendment. * * *

■ [We omit the concurring opinions of JUSTICES STEVENS and SOUTER and the opinion concurring in part and dissenting in part by JUSTICE O'CONNOR.]

■ [JUSTICE KENNEDY, joined by JUSTICE GINSBURG, concurred in striking down § 10(b), (c) and dissented from upholding § 10(a). Because a public access channel is a public forum, Justice Kennedy maintained that *Sable* requires § 10(a) to be struck down. Justice Kennedy was most troubled, however, by the plurality's avoidance of standards. "Indeed, the creation of standards and adherence to them, even when it means affording protection to speech unpopular or distasteful, is the central achievement of our First Amendment jurisprudence. Standards are the means by which we state in advance how to test a law's validity, rather than letting the height of the bar be determined by the apparent exigencies of the day. They also provide notice and fair warning to those who must predict how the courts will respond to attempts to suppress their speech."]

■ [JUSTICE THOMAS, joined by CHIEF JUSTICE REHNQUIST and JUSTICE SCALIA, concurred in upholding § 10(a) and dissented from striking down § 10(b), (c). As to the latter, Justice Thomas maintained that the government had shown those provisions narrowly tailored to a compelling state interest in shielding minors from indecent as well as obscene speech. Recall *Ferber* as well as *Pacifica*.]

NOTES ON "INDECENCY" AND NEW MEDIA

1. *The Impact of Evolving Technologies.* Justice Breyer's opinion conveys a reluctance to commit the Court to a specific approach to regulation of non-obscene, sexual speech in light of the possibility of technological solutions. Most proposals for such solutions center on versions of a blocking system often known as the "V-chip." V-chips depend on a process in which each program is rated prior to broadcast. A consumer can use the chip to block all incoming programs with certain ratings. Someone other than the consumer, however, decides what those ratings will be, and applies them to specific programs. The film industry has for many years engaged in voluntary, industry-administered ratings of movies. Should such an approach be used for cable television? Could the FCC rate programs without running afoul of the First Amendment?

2. *How Should Violence Be Judged?* There is no tier of lesser protection for portrayals of violence on television that is equivalent to the category of "indecency." Efforts to restrict dissemination of violent programming would be likely to engender more debate over the meaning of social science findings. The effects of television violence on children has been extensively studied, but with inconclusive results. An early and still influential study found that TV violence may lead to some aggression in children, but it tends to affect only children predisposed to aggression and even then only under certain environmental conditions. Albert Bandura, Dorothea Ross & Sheila A. Ross, "Limitation of Film–Mediated Aggressive Models," 66 *J. Abnormal & Soc. Psychol.* 3 (1963). Could stronger social science evidence justify a lower tier of protection based on violence?

3. *Is the Internet More Like TV or the Press?* Should ratings and blocking chips be required for material on the internet? Opponents argue that consumers of interactive media need not rely on a single rating system, but that market demand will produce many different screening systems, giving parents and other users the opportunity to purchase a system which closely tracks their own individualized criteria for desirable content.

With the widespread popular access to the internet, battles are underway to regulate or insulate explicit speech in that medium. In *American Civil Liberties Union v. Reno*, 929 F.Supp. 824 (E.D.Pa.1996), a three judge court invalidated portions of the Communications Decency Act of 1996 [the C.D.A.],[b] and ruled that internet communications were entitled to the highest degree of protection under the First Amendment, comparable to that afforded the press, rather than the lesser standard used to regulate indecent speech in other electronic media.

> [T]he Internet may fairly be regarded as a never-ending world-wide conversation. The Government may not, through the C.D.A., interrupt that conversation. As the most participatory form of mass speech yet developed, the Internet deserves the highest protection from governmental intrusion.

Id. at 883. An appeal is pending before the Supreme Court. *Reno v. ACLU*, 117 S.Ct. 554 (1996) (noting probable jurisdiction).

b. Part of the Communications Decency Act (CDA), Title V of the Telecommunications Act of 1996, Pub. L. No. 104–104, 110 Stat. 56, 133–34 (1996), amends 47 U.S.C. § 223(a)(1)(B) to make it a criminal offense when any person in interstate or foreign commerce by means of a telecommunications device "knowingly * * * makes, creates, or solicits" and "imitates the transmission" of "any comment, request, suggestion, proposal, image or other communication which is obscene or indecent, knowing that the recipient of the communication is under 18 years of age." The CDA also amends § 223(d)(1) to make it a crime to use "an interactive computer service," such as the internet, to send or display to a person under age 18, "any comment, request, suggestion, proposal, image or other communication that, in context, depicts or describes, in terms patently offensive as measured by contemporary community standards, sexual or excretory activities or organs, regardless of whether the user of such service placed the call or initiated the communication." Section 223(a)(2), (d)(2) makes it a crime for anyone to "knowingly permit[] any telecommunications facility under [her or his] control to be used for any activity prohibited" by § 223(a)(1), (d)(1).

New § 223(e) provides safe harbor defenses to prosecutions under § 223 where (1) the person merely provided access or connection to a "facility, system or network" not under that person's control, or where (4) an employer is charged with an employee's violation unless the employee knows about and ratifies the illegal conduct, or where (5) the person (A) "has taken, in good faith, reasonable, effective and appropriate actions under the circumstances to restrict or prevent access by minors" or (B) has restricted access to the communication by requiring use of a credit card, access code, or adult identification number.

The ACLU challenged the constitutionality of these new provisions insofar as they apply to indecent material on the internet. They did not challenge pre-existing provisions making it criminal to communicate obscenity or child pornography on the internet, as these items were already prohibited by 18 U.S.C. §§ 1464–1465 and 2251–2252.

CHAPTER 7

SEXUALITY AND GENDER IN EDUCATION

SECTION 1   Regulating Student Exploration and Expression of Sexuality

SECTION 2   Academic Freedom and Issues of Gender and Sexuality

SECTION 3   Legal Issues Arising Out of Public Sex Education

Three distinct issues are embodied in public school disputes involving sexuality and gender. One is the debate between the view (widely held by parents and often practiced by school personnel) that public schools should primarily seek to *inculcate* good ideas and useful facts into the students, and the view (widely held by educational theorists and often practiced by school personnel) that education seeks to foster *critical thinking* by students. An inculcation approach is more prone to prescribe, or censor, student comments and pedagogic materials than is a critical thinking approach.

If a school's goal is at least in part inculcative, what views about gender and sexuality should it be inculcating? The debate is more intense here. A traditionalist perspective might urge that sexuality is best not discussed in schools at all; it should be left to parents. This has been the prevailing approach in America for most of this century. After the Kinsey Institute reports on men's (1948) and women's (1953) sexuality and sexual experiences galvanized national public discourse about sexuality, the openness of sexual activity among adolescents has galvanized local and state public discourses about sexuality. Pregnancy and AIDS are now recognized as critical issues for adolescents in this country, and the school system has become the most important forum for addressing those issues. Accordingly, traditionalist discourse has shifted from avoidance of public sex education to its acceptance, but only to the extent that it inculcates "natural law" gender norms (boys aggressive and girls passive, for example), sexual abstinence until marriage or at least maturity, and heterosexuality as compulsory.

Just as traditionalist discourse has changed, so has liberal discourse. A liberal perspective usually insists that sexuality be discussed in schools and that it be discussed without emphasis on traditional gender roles, heterosexual norms, or abstinence. Liberals emphasize tolerance of sexual diversity and deemphasize gender stereotypes. In the wake of increased teenage pregnancies and AIDS, however, liberals are more likely to problematize sex or at least emphasize its risks; feminist-inspired liberals warn of the disparity of risk, with women and girls taking on the bulk of the risks, now as before.

A third issue focuses on who decides what to teach and what to suppress. Should a court defer to the school board? To a high school principal? Should the school board and principal defer to the front-line teachers? Librarians? To what extent are students' views worth considering? How much deference must a court pay to legislative judgments about what factual and ethical materials must be conveyed to students?

REGULATING STUDENT EXPLORATION AND EXPRESSION OF SEXUALITY

John F. Tinker et al. v. Des Moines Independent Community School District, 393 U.S. 503, 89 S.Ct. 733, 21 L.Ed.2d 731 (1969). To protest the war in Vietnam, Des Moines public school students wore black armbands to classes in December 1965. Principals at several Des Moines junior high and high schools suspended students for wearing these armbands. The Supreme Court, in an opinion by Justice Fortas, held that the suspensions unconstitutionally penalized students for expression protected by the First Amendment. The critical issue in the case was whether the First Amendment's protection of core political expression should be attenuated in the school setting. The Court had this to say:

"First Amendment rights, applied in light of the special characteristics of the school environment, are available to teachers and students. It can hardly be argued that either students or teachers shed their constitutional rights to freedom of speech or expression at the schoolhouse gate. [On] the other hand, the Court has repeatedly emphasized the need for affirming the comprehensive authority [of] school officials, consistent with fundamental constitutional safeguards, [to] control conduct in the schools. * * *

"The school officials [sought] to punish [the students] for a silent, passive expression of opinion, unaccompanied by any disorder or disturbance on the part of [the students]. There is no evidence whatever of [the students'] interference, actual or nascent, with the schools' work or of collision with the rights of other students to be secure and to be let alone. [There] is no indication that the work of the schools or any class was disrupted. Outside the classrooms, a few students made hostile remarks to the children wearing armbands, but there were no threats or acts of violence on school premises.

"The [trial judge] concluded that the action of the school authorities was reasonable because it was based upon their fear of a disturbance from the wearing of the armbands. But, in our system, undifferentiated fear or apprehension of disturbance is not enough to overcome the right to freedom of expression. * * * [In] order for the State in the person of school officials to justify prohibition [of] expression of [a single] opinion, it must be able to show that its action was caused by something more than a mere desire to avoid the discomfort and unpleasantness that always accompany an unpopular viewpoint.''

Dissenting, Justice Hugo Black referred to events in the record where other students made fun of the armbands, and one armband student threatened the hecklers. Also, a math teacher complained that his lesson plan was wrecked by the protest. According to Black, the ''armbands'' did exactly what the [officials] foresaw they would, that is, took the students' minds off their classwork and diverted them to thoughts about the highly emotional subject of the Vietnam war.

Aaron Fricke v. Richard B. Lynch

U.S. District Court for the District of Rhode Island, 1980.
491 F.Supp. 381.

■ PETTINE, CHIEF JUDGE. * * *

[Aaron Fricke, a senior at Cumberland High School in Cumberland, Rhode Island, proposed to bring another man, Paul Guilbert, as his date to the high school prom. The high school principal, Richard Lynch, denied Fricke's request for the following reasons:

1. The real and present threat of physical harm to you, your male escort and to others; 2. The adverse effect among your classmates, other students, the School and the Town of Cumberland, which is certain to follow approval of such a request for overt homosexual interaction (male or female) at a class function; 3. Since the dance is being held out of state and this is a function of the students of Cumberland High School, the School Department is powerless to insure protection in Sutton, Massachusetts. That protection would be required of property as well as persons and would expose all concerned to liability for harm which might occur * * *.

Fricke sought an injunction requiring Lynch to allow him to bring a male date. At the preliminary injunction hearing, Lynch testified about student hostility expressed the year before when Guilbert had made a similar request, and about Fricke's being shoved and punched by other students after his request.]

The starting point in my analysis of Aaron's First Amendment free speech claim must be, of course, to determine whether the action he proposes to take has a ''communicative content sufficient to bring it within the ambit of the First Amendment.'' *Gay Students Organization v. Bonner*, 509 F.2d 652 (1st Cir.1974) [Chapter 5, Section 1]. * * * Aaron testified that he wants to go because he feels he has a right to attend and participate just like all the other students and that it would be dishonest to his own sexual identity to take a girl to the dance. He went on to acknowledge that he feels his attendance would have a certain political element and would be a statement for equal rights and human rights. * * * I believe Aaron's testimony that he is sincerely—although perhaps not irrevocably—committed to a homosexual orientation and that attending the dance with another young man would be a political statement. While mere communicative intent may not always transform conduct into speech, * * * this exact type of conduct as a vehicle for transmitting this very message can be considered protected speech.[4]

Accordingly, the school's action must be judged by the standards articulated in *United States v. O'Brien*, 391 U.S. 367 (1968), and applied in *Bonner*: (1) was the regulation within the constitutional power of the government; (2) did it further an important or substantial governmental interest; (3) was the governmental interest unrelated to the suppression of free expression; and (4) was the incidental restriction on alleged First Amendment freedoms no greater than essential to the furtherance of that interest?

* * * [T]he school's action fails to meet the last criterion set out in *O'Brien*, the requirement that the government employ the "least restrictive alternative" before curtailing speech. The plaintiff argues, and I agree, that the school can take appropriate security measures to control the risk of harm. Lynch testified that he did not know if adequate security could be provided, and that he would still need to sit down and make the necessary arrangements. In fact he has not made any effort to determine the need for and logistics of additional security. Although Lynch did not say that any additional security measures would be adequate, from the testimony I find that significant measures could be taken and would in all probability critically reduce the likelihood of any disturbance. As Lynch's own testimony indicates, police officers and teachers will be present at the dance, and have been quite successful in the past in controlling whatever problems arise, including unauthorized drinking. Despite the ever-present possibility of violence at sports events, adequate discipline has been maintained. * * *

The analysis so far has been along traditional First Amendment lines, making no real allowance for the fact that this case arises in a high school setting. The most difficult problem this controversy presents is how this setting should affect the result. *Tinker* makes clear that high school students do not "shed their constitutional rights to freedom of speech or expression at the schoolhouse gate." As the *Tinker* Court stated:

> But, in our system, undifferentiated fear or apprehension of disturbance is not enough to overcome the right to freedom of expression. Any departure from absolute regimentation may cause trouble. Any variation from the majority's opinion may inspire fear. Any word spoken, in class, in the lunchroom, or on the campus, that deviates from the views of another person may start an argument or cause a

---

4. The defendant argues that Aaron has selected an inappropriate time and place for his speech activity. Admittedly, Aaron seeks to express a political message in a social setting. His message, however, will take a form uniquely consonant with the setting he wishes to attend and participate like everyone else. Thus, while a purer form of speech such as leafleting or speechmaking might legitimately be barred at a dance, prohibiting Aaron's attendance does not fall within the rubric of a time, place, and manner restriction. This is especially so because the school's action is not entirely content-neutral.

disturbance. But our Constitution says we must take this risk; and our history says that it is this sort of hazardous freedom, this kind of openness that is the basis of our national strength and of the independence and vigor of Americans who grow up and live in this relatively permissive, often disputatious, society. In order for the State in the person of school officials to justify prohibition of a particular expression of opinion, it must be able to show that its action was caused by something more than a mere desire to avoid the discomfort and unpleasantness that always accompany an unpopular viewpoint. Certainly where there is no finding and no showing that engaging in the forbidden conduct would "materially and substantially interfere with the requirements of appropriate discipline in the operation of the school," the prohibition cannot be sustained. * * *

Tinker did, however, indicate that there are limits on First Amendment rights within the school:

> A student's rights, therefore, do not embrace merely the classroom hours. When he is in the cafeteria, or on the playing field, or on the campus during the authorized hours, he may express his opinions, even on controversial subjects like the conflict in Vietnam, if he does so without "materially and substantially interfer(ing) with the requirements of appropriate discipline in the operation of the school" and without colliding with the rights of others. *But conduct by the student, in class or out of it, which for any reason whether it stems from time, place or type of behavior materially disrupts classwork or involves substantial disorder or invasion of the rights of others is, of course, not immunized by the constitutional guarantee of freedom of speech.*

It seems to me that here, not unlike in *Tinker*, the school administrators were acting on "an undifferentiated fear or apprehension of disturbance." True, Aaron was punched and then security measures were taken, but since that incident he has not been threatened with violence nor has he been attacked. There has been no disruption at the school; classes have not been cancelled, suspended, or interrupted. In short, while the defendants have perhaps shown more of a basis for fear of harm than in *Tinker*, they have failed to make a "showing" that Aaron's conduct would "materially and substantially interfere" with school discipline. However, even if the Court assumes that there is justifiable fear and that Aaron's peaceful speech leads, or may lead, to a violent reaction from others, the question remains: may the school prohibit the speech, or must it protect the speaker?

It is certainly clear that outside of the classroom the fear—however justified—of a violent reaction is not sufficient reason to restrain such speech in advance, and an actual hostile reaction is rarely an adequate basis for curtailing free speech. *Gregory v. City of Chicago*, 394 U.S. 111 (1969); *Terminiello v. Chicago*, 337 U.S. 1 (1949). Thus, the question here is whether the interest in school discipline and order, recognized in *Tinker*, requires a different approach.

After considerable thought and research, I have concluded that even a legitimate interest in school discipline does not outweigh a student's right to peacefully express his views in an appropriate time, place, and manner. To rule otherwise would completely subvert free speech in the schools by granting other students a "heckler's veto," allowing them to decide—through prohibited and violent methods—what speech will be heard. The First Amendment does not tolerate mob rule by unruly school children. This conclusion is bolstered by the fact that any disturbance here, however great, would not interfere with the main business of school education. No classes or school work would be affected; at the very worst an optional social event, conducted by the students for their own enjoyment, would be marred. In such a context, the school does have an obligation to take reasonable measures to protect and foster free speech, not to stand helpless before unauthorized student violence. * * *

As to the other concern raised by *Tinker*, some people might say that Aaron Fricke's conduct would infringe the rights of the other students, and is thus unprotected by *Tinker*. This view is misguided, however. Aaron's conduct is quiet and peaceful; it demands no response from others and—in a crowd of some five hundred people—can be easily ignored. Any disturbance that might interfere with the rights of others would be caused by those students who resort to violence, not by Aaron and his companion, who do not want a fight. * * *

As a final note, I would add that the social problems presented by homosexuality are emotionally charged; community norms are in flux, and the psychiatric profession itself is divided in its attitude towards homosexuality. This Court's role, of course, is not to mandate social norms or impose its own view of acceptable behavior. It is instead, to interpret and apply the Constitution as best it can. The Constitution is not self-explanatory, and answers to knotty problems are inevitably inexact. All that an individual judge can do is to apply the legal precedents as accurately and as honestly as he can, uninfluenced by personal predilections or the fear of community reaction, hoping each time to disprove the legal maxim that "hard cases make bad law."

ROCK LOBSTER POSTSCRIPT

The world did not end after Judge Pettine's decision, and the prom went ahead as scheduled on May 30, 1980. Principal Lynch isolated Aaron and Paul at a side table, and the evening started off miserably. Finally, Aaron and Paul came together on the dance floor to slow-dance to Bob Seger's *We've Got the Night*. As Aaron Fricke tells the story in his book, *Reflections of a Rock Lobster* (1981),

"The crowd receded. As I laid my head on Paul's shoulder, I saw a few students start to stare at us. I closed my eyes and listened to the music, my thoughts wandering over the events of that evening. When the song ended, I opened my eyes. A large crowd of students had formed a ring around us. Probably most of them had never before seen two happy men embracing in a slow dance. For a moment I was uncomfortable. Then I heard the sound that I knew so well as a B–52's fan. One of my favorite songs was coming up: 'Rock Lobster.'

"Paul and I began dancing free-style. Everyone else was still staring at us, but by the end of the first stanza, several couples had also begun dancing. The song has a contagious enthusiasm to it, and with each bar, more dancers came onto the floor. * * *

"A quarter of the way into the song, thirty people were on the dance floor. 'Down, Down, Down,' commanded the lyrics. Everyone on the dance floor sank to their knees and crouched on the ground. * * *

"As Paul and I danced, we had gradually drifted from our original space on the floor. 'Down, Down, Down,' cried the B–52s again, and we all went down. * * * There were at least a hundred people on the dance floor. The tempo became more frenetic and everyone danced faster.

" 'Let's Rock!!!' bellowed the speakers, and to my surprise, when I looked up, I saw that Paul had disappeared. I looked around; several other guys were dancing with each other, and girls were dancing with girls. Everybody was rockin'. Everybody was fruggin'. Who cared why? * * * I danced with girls, I danced with guys, I danced with the entire group."

Bethel School District No. 403 v. Matthew N. Fraser, a Minor, and E.L. Fraser, Guardian Ad Litem

United States Supreme Court, 1986.
478 U.S. 675, 106 S.Ct. 3159, 92 L.Ed.2d 549.

■ CHIEF JUSTICE BURGER delivered the opinion of the Court. * * *

On April 26, 1983, respondent Matthew N. Fraser, a student at Bethel High School in Pierce County, Washington, delivered a speech nominating a fellow student for student elective office. Approximately 600 high school students, many of whom were 14–year-olds, attended the assembly. Students were required to attend the assembly or to report to the study hall. The assembly was part of a school-sponsored educational program in self-government. * * * During the entire speech, Fraser referred to his candidate in terms of an elaborate, graphic, and explicit sexual metaphor.

Two of Fraser's teachers, with whom he discussed the contents of his speech in advance, informed him that the speech was "inappropriate and that he probably should not deliver it," and that his delivery of the speech might have "severe consequences."

During Fraser's delivery of the speech, a school counselor observed the reaction of students to the speech. Some students hooted and yelled; some by gestures graphically simulated the sexual activities pointedly alluded to in respondent's speech. Other students appeared to be bewildered and embarrassed by the speech. One teacher reported that on the day following the speech, she found it necessary to forgo a portion of the scheduled class lesson in order to discuss the speech with the class.

A Bethel High School disciplinary rule prohibiting the use of obscene language in the school provides:

"Conduct which materially and substantially interferes with the educational process is prohibited, including the use of obscene, profane language or gestures."

The morning after the assembly, the Assistant Principal called Fraser into her office and notified him that the school considered his speech to have been a violation of this rule. Fraser was presented with copies of five letters submitted by teachers, describing his conduct at the assembly; he was given a chance to explain his conduct, and he admitted to having given the speech described and that he deliberately used sexual innuendo in the speech. Fraser was then informed that he would be suspended for three days, and that his name would be removed from the list of candidates for graduation speaker at the school's commencement exercises. * * *

[The lower court found the school's actions unconstitutional under *Tinker*, and the Supreme Court reversed.]

The role and purpose of the American public school system were well described by two historians, who stated: "[P]ublic education must prepare pupils for citizenship in the Republic.... It must inculcate the habits and manners of civility as values in themselves conducive to happiness and as indispensable to the practice of self-government in the community and the nation." C. Beard & M. Beard, *New Basic History of the United States* 228 (1968). In *Ambach v. Norwick*, 441 U.S. 68, 76–77 (1979), we echoed the essence of this statement of the objectives of public education as the "inculcat[ion of] fundamental values necessary to the maintenance of a democratic political system."

These fundamental values of "habits and manners of civility" essential to a democratic society must, of course, include tolerance of divergent political and religious views, even when the views expressed may be unpopular. But these "fundamental values" must also take into account consideration of the sensibilities of others, and, in the case of a school, the sensibilities of fellow students. The undoubted freedom to advocate unpopular and controversial views in schools and classrooms must be balanced against the society's countervailing interest in teaching students the boundaries of socially appropriate behavior. Even the most heated political discourse in a democratic society requires consideration for the personal sensibilities of the other participants and audiences.

In our Nation's legislative halls, where some of the most vigorous political debates in our society are carried on, there are rules prohibiting the use of expressions offensive to other participants in the debate. The Manual of Parliamentary Practice, drafted by Thomas Jefferson and adopted by the House of Representatives to govern the proceedings in that body, prohibits the use of "impertinent" speech during debate and likewise provides that "[n]o person is to use indecent language against the proceedings of the House." *Jefferson's Manual of Parliamentary Practice* § 359, reprinted in *Manual and Rules of House of Representatives*, H.R.Doc. No.

97–271, pp. 158–159 (1982); see id., at 111, n. *a* (*Jefferson's Manual* governs the House in all cases to which it applies). The Rules of Debate applicable in the Senate likewise provide that a Senator may be called to order for imputing improper motives to another Senator or for referring offensively to any state. See Senate Procedure, S.Doc. No. 97–2, Rule XIX, pp. 568–569, 588–591 (1981). Senators have been censured for abusive language directed at other Senators. Can it be that what is proscribed in the halls of Congress is beyond the reach of school officials to regulate?

The First Amendment guarantees wide freedom in matters of adult public discourse. A sharply divided Court upheld the right to express an antidraft viewpoint in a public place, albeit in terms highly offensive to most citizens. See *Cohen v. California*, 403 U.S. 15 (1971). It does not follow, however, that simply because the use of an offensive form of expression may not be prohibited to adults making what the speaker considers a political point, the same latitude must be permitted to children in a public school. * * * As cogently expressed by Judge Newman, "the First Amendment gives a high school student the classroom right to wear Tinker's armband, but not Cohen's jacket." *Thomas v. Board of Education, Granville Central School Dist.*, 607 F.2d 1043, 1057 (C.A.2 1979) (opinion concurring in result).

Surely it is a highly appropriate function of public school education to prohibit the use of vulgar and offensive terms in public discourse. Indeed, the "fundamental values necessary to the maintenance of a democratic political system" disfavor the use of terms of debate highly offensive or highly threatening to others. Nothing in the Constitution prohibits the states from insisting that certain modes of expression are inappropriate and subject to sanctions. The inculcation of these values is truly the "work of the schools." *Tinker*. The determination of what manner of speech in the classroom or in school assembly is inappropriate properly rests with the school board.

The process of educating our youth for citizenship in public schools is not confined to books, the curriculum, and the civics class; schools must teach by example the shared values of a civilized social order. Consciously or otherwise, teachers—and indeed the older students—demonstrate the appropriate form of civil discourse and political expression by their conduct and deportment in and out of class. Inescapably, like parents, they are role models. The schools, as instruments of the state, may determine that the essential lessons of civil, mature conduct cannot be conveyed in a school that tolerates lewd, indecent, or offensive speech and conduct such as that indulged in by this confused boy.

The pervasive sexual innuendo in Fraser's speech was plainly offensive to both teachers and students—indeed to any mature person. By glorifying male sexuality, and in its verbal content, the speech was acutely insulting to teenage girl students. The speech could well be seriously damaging to its less mature audience, many of whom were only 14 years old and on the threshold of awareness of human sexuality. Some students were reported as bewildered by the speech and the reaction of mimicry it provoked.

This Court's First Amendment jurisprudence has acknowledged limitations on the otherwise absolute interest of the speaker in reaching an unlimited audience where the speech is sexually explicit and the audience may include children. In *Ginsberg v. New York*, 390 U.S. 629 (1968), this Court upheld a New York statute banning the sale of sexually oriented material to minors, even though the material in question was entitled to First Amendment protection with respect to adults. And in addressing the question whether the First Amendment places any limit on the authority of public schools to remove books from a public school library, all Members of the Court, otherwise sharply divided, acknowledged that the school board has the authority to remove books that are vulgar. *Board of Education v. Pico*, 457 U.S. 853 (1982) [excerpted below]. These cases recognize the obvious concern on the part of parents, and school authorities acting *in loco parentis*, to protect children—especially in a captive audience—from exposure to sexually explicit, indecent, or lewd speech.

We have also recognized an interest in protecting minors from exposure to vulgar and offensive spoken language. In *FCC v. Pacifica Foundation*, 438 U.S. 726 (1978), we dealt with the power of the Federal Communications Commission to regulate a radio broadcast described as "indecent but not obscene." There the Court reviewed an administrative condemnation of the radio broadcast of a self-styled "humorist" who described his own performance as being in "the words you couldn't say on the public, ah, airwaves, um, the ones you definitely wouldn't say ever." The Commission concluded that "certain words depicted sexual and excretory activities in a patently offensive manner, [and] noted that they 'were broadcast at a time when children were undoubtedly in the audience.'" [The Supreme Court upheld this order.]

We hold that petitioner School District acted entirely within its permissible authority in imposing sanctions upon Fraser in response to his offensively lewd and indecent speech. Unlike the sanctions imposed on the students wearing armbands in *Tinker*, the penalties imposed in this case were unrelated to any political viewpoint. The First Amendment does not prevent the school officials from determining that to permit a vulgar and lewd speech such as respondent's would undermine the school's basic educational mission. A high school assembly or classroom is no place for a sexually explicit monologue directed towards an unsuspecting audience of teenage students. Accordingly, it was perfectly appropriate for the school to disassociate itself to make the point to the pupils that vulgar speech and lewd conduct is wholly inconsistent with the "fundamental values" of public school education. * * *

■ JUSTICE BLACKMUN concurs in the result.

■ JUSTICE BRENNAN concurring in the judgment.

Respondent gave the following speech at a high school assembly in support of a candidate for student government office:

" 'I know a man who is firm—he's firm in his pants, he's firm in his shirt, his character is firm—but most . . . of all, his belief in you, the students of Bethel, is firm.

" 'Jeff Kuhlman is a man who takes his point and pounds it in. If necessary, he'll take an issue and nail it to the wall. He doesn't attack things in spurts—he drives hard, pushing and pushing until finally—he succeeds.

" 'Jeff is a man who will go to the very end—even the climax, for each and every one of you.

" 'So vote for Jeff for A.S.B. vice-president—he'll never come between you and the best our high school can be.' "

The Court, referring to these remarks as "obscene," "vulgar," "lewd," and "offensively lewd," concludes that school officials properly punished respondent for uttering the speech. Having read the full text of respondent's remarks, I find it difficult to believe that it is the same speech the Court describes. To my mind, the most that can be said about respondent's speech—and all that need be said—is that in light of the discretion school officials have to teach high school students how to conduct civil and effective public discourse, and to prevent disruption of school educational activities, it was not unconstitutional for school officials to conclude, under the circumstances of this case, that respondent's remarks exceeded permissible limits. * * *

■ [JUSTICE MARSHALL dissented on the ground that the official reaction was too extreme in light of the trivial nature of the student's action. JUSTICE STEVENS dissented on the ground that the school's regulation gave Fraser insufficient notice that use of sexual metaphors in a speech would trigger such an extreme official reaction.]

NOTES ON *FRASER* AND THE ROCK LOBSTER CASE

1. *Theories of Education: Inculcation versus Independent Thinking. Tinker* was criticized for applying standard First Amendment doctrine (the "free marketplace of ideas") in an inappropriate setting, secondary schools.[a] To the extent that a public school's mission is to convey to students at least some standard social and political norms (e.g., that democracy is good) and some standard factual material (e.g., the United States is a representative rather than direct democracy), allowing and indeed encouraging students to protest or resist would seem oxymoronic. But, to the extent that the school system wants to avoid conveyor-belt approaches to learning and wants to stimulate independent individual thought by students, allowing school officials to censor students at will

a. *E.g.*, David A. Diamond, "The First Amendment and Public Schools," 59 *Tex. L. Rev.* 477 (1981); Jack Garvey, "Children and the First Amendment," 57 *Tex. L. Rev.* 321 (1979); Stephen R. Goldstein, "Reflections on Developing Trends in the Law of Student Rights," 118 *U. Pa. L. Rev.* 612 (1970); R. George Wright, "Free Speech Values, Public Schools, and the Role of Judicial Deference," 22 *New Eng. L. Rev.* 59 (1987).

would seem equally counterproductive. This is the "First Amendment paradox of public education." Stanley Ingber, "Socialization, Indoctrination, or the 'Pall of Orthodoxy': Value Training in the Public Schools," 1987 *U. Ill. L. Rev.* 15, 15–20.

Tinker seems to value the independent thinking model at the expense of the inculcation model (espoused in Justice Black's dissent), while *Fraser* seems to value the inculcation model at the expense of the independent thinking model (espoused in Justice Brennan's concurring opinion and Justice Marshall's dissent). In *Hazelwood School District v. Kuhlmeier*, 484 U.S. 260 (1988), the Court upheld a high school's censorship of school newspaper articles describing students' experiences with pregnancy and the effect of divorce on students. Writing for a six-Justice majority, Justice Byron White said:

> A school must be able to set high standards for the student speech that is disseminated under its auspices—standards that may be higher than those demanded by some newspaper publishers or theatrical producers in the "real" world—and may refuse to disseminate student speech that does not meet those standards. *Id.* at 271–72.

The Court held that "educators do not offend the First Amendment by exercising editorial control over the style and content of student speech in school-sponsored expressive activities so long as their actions are reasonably related to legitimate pedagogical activities."

Justice White reconciled *Kuhlmeier* with *Tinker*:

> The question whether the First Amendment requires a school to tolerate particular student speech—the question that we addressed in *Tinker*—is different from the question whether the First Amendment requires a school affirmatively to promote particular student speech [the question addressed in *Fraser* and *Kuhlmeier*]. The former question addresses educators' ability to silence a student's personal expression that happens to occur on the school's premises. The latter question concerns educators' authority over school-sponsored publications, theatrical productions, and other expressive activities that students, parents, and members of the public might reasonably perceive to bear the imprimatur of the school. * * * Educators are entitled to exercise greater control over this second form of student expression to assure that participants learn whatever lessons the activity is designed to teach, that readers or listeners are not exposed to material that may be inappropriate for their level of maturity, and that the views of the individual speaker are not erroneously attributed to the school. *Id.* at 270–71.

Is this a satisfactory reconciliation? How should *Fricke* be resolved under this standard?

2. *The Relevance of Sex. Has* Fricke *Been Nullified?* Another way to understand, and perhaps reconcile, the cases focuses on the content of the expression. *Tinker* was a classic "political" speech case, *Fraser* and *Kuhlmeier* somewhere in between "political" speech and "sexual" speech. Note Chief Justice Burger's skittishness about Matthew Fraser's speech, which

Burger refused to quote (Justice Brennan playfully provides the text for the reader who labors through the Chief's opinion with only a vague idea as to what the opinion is talking about). Is the Court embarrassed talking about sexuality? See Richard A. Posner, *Sex and Reason* (1991) (yep).

Justice White's opinion in *Kuhlmeier* suggests other reasons why a school might have greater latitude regulating sexual speech:

> [A] school must be able to take into account the emotional maturity of the intended audience in determining whether to disseminate student speech on potentially sensitive topics, which might range from the existence of Santa Claus in an elementary school setting to the particulars of teenage sexual activity in a high school setting. A school must also retain the authority to refuse to sponsor student speech that might reasonably be perceived to advocate drug or alcohol use, irresponsible sex, or conduct otherwise inconsistent with "the shared values of a civilized social order," *Fraser*, or to associate the school with any position other than neutrality on matters of political controversy. Otherwise, the schools would be unduly constrained from fulfilling their role as "a principal instrument in awakening the child to cultural values, in preparing him for later professional training, and in helping him to adjust normally to his environment." *Brown v. Board of Education*.

Consider also Chief Justice Burger's suggestion in *Fraser* that female students might be particularly chilled by raunchy sexual speech. Public employers have a legal obligation to suppress employee expression which creates a "hostile work environment" for women. Public schools may have an obligation to suppress student expression which creates a hostile environment for female students (see Section 3[B]). In your opinion, was this a substantial risk in *Fraser*? *Kuhlmeier*?

If the Justices were skittish about Matthew Fraser's phallic allusions, would they respond even more strongly to Aaron Fricke's same-sex date to the prom? Do *Fraser* and *Kuhlmeier* nullify *Fricke*? Or is there a persuasive way to defend Judge Pettine's decision under current doctrine?

3. *Problems with the Court's Tilt Toward Deference and Inculcation.* Certainly, the later Supreme Court cases are more deferential to school authorities and receptive to inculcation as the primary goal of public schools. Richard L. Roe, "Valuing Speech: The Work of the Schools as Conceptual Development," 79 *Calif. L. Rev.* 1269 (1991), questions the Court's recent tilt. Roe argues that allowing schools to suppress student speech in cases like *Fraser* and *Kuhlmeier* undermines the more important goal of education at the high school level, namely, cognitive development. More important, Roe demonstrates that American public schools themselves declare that their goal is conceptual development, rather than just inculcation. See Benjamin Bloom, editor, *Taxonomy of Educational Objectives* (1956) (leading statement of American educational theory). The curricular guides for states as dissimilar as New York, Missouri, and Washington (surveyed by Roe) reject inculcation as the goal of education and insist upon conceptual development.

The problem, Roe maintains, is that educators are constantly tempted to fall back on an inculcative approach (*e.g.*, as a better way of keeping order in the classroom). Also, parents tend to see public education in these terms, and so PTAs and elected school boards can be expected to press strongly in this direction. The issue of deference then becomes difficult. Should courts defer to educational theory, or to parent-driven political decisions? Or is it not so simple?

Under a conceptual development model, there needs to be more room for student expression and dissent, even if expressed crudely (as in *Fraser*). William Buss, "School Newspapers, Public Forum, and the First Amendment," 74 *Iowa L. Rev.* 505, 516–22 (1989), argues that *Tinker* establishes that schools cannot easily regulate student expression that "contradicts" the official curriculum or ideology, while *Fraser* and *Kuhlmeier* establish that schools can regulate student expression that "interferes" with or "intercepts" the official curriculum.

PROBLEM 7–1

EXCLUDING GAY CLUBS IN PUBLIC HIGH SCHOOLS

The Smallville High School allows students to form clubs for any "valid educational purpose." Such clubs can use school property for their meetings, advertise free-of-charge in the school newspaper, and post announcements in school areas devoted to such purposes. Clubs that have been approved include those devoted to science, chess, prayer, wrestling, debate, drama, leadership, farming, ethnicity, and antismoking/antidrugs. Clark Kent and Lana Lang, two students at Smallville High, submit an application on behalf of themselves and five other interested students to form a "gay and lesbian student club," whose purpose would be to "help students understand different sexual orientations" by bringing in speakers, providing informative pamphlets, and sponsoring sessions where students exchange views and feelings they have. The school principal refuses to approve the club and refuses to allow it to meet on school property. Lang and Kent sue the school to require it to recognize their club on an equal basis with other clubs. Does the First Amendment require the high school to recognize the club? Does *Bonner* (Chapter 5, Section 1) govern gay clubs in high schools?

Consider also the Equal Access Act, 98 Stat. 1302, 20 U.S.C. §§ 4071–4074, which applies to public secondary schools which receive federal financial assistance. Such a school creates a "limited public forum" when it "grants an offering to or opportunity for one or more noncurriculum related student groups to meet on school premises during noninstructional time." *Id.* § 4071(b); see *Board of Education v. Mergens*, 496 U.S. 226 (1990) ("limited public forum" triggered by school's recognition of scuba, chess, and service clubs as "noncurriculum related"). If a covered school creates a "limited public forum," it is unlawful for it "to deny equal access or a fair opportunity to, or discriminate against, any students who wish to conduct a meeting within the limited open forum on the basis of the religious, philosophical, or other content of the speech at such meetings." 20 U.S.C. § 4071(a). Smallville High concedes that it has created a "limited public forum" because it has recognized chess and religious clubs. Does the Equal Access Act require it to recognize the gay club? Consider the relevance of *Fraser* and *Kuhlmeier* to the proper construction of the statute.

Board of Education, Island Trees Union Free School District No. 26 et al. v. Steven A. Pico

United States Supreme Court, 1982.
457 U.S. 853, 102 S.Ct. 2799, 73 L.Ed.2d 435.

■ JUSTICE BRENNAN announced the judgment of the Court and delivered an opinion, in which JUSTICE MARSHALL and JUSTICE STEVENS joined, and in which JUSTICE BLACKMUN joined except for Part II–A–1. * * *

In September 1975, petitioners Ahrens, Martin, and Hughes attended a conference sponsored by Parents of New York United (PONYU), a politically conservative organization of parents concerned about education legislation in the State of New York. At the conference these petitioners obtained lists of books described by Ahrens as "objectionable," and by Martin as "improper fare for school students." It was later determined that the High School library contained nine of the listed books, and that another listed book was in the Junior High School library.[3] In February 1976, at a meeting with the Superintendent of Schools and the Principals of the High School and Junior High School, the Board gave an "unofficial direction" that the listed books be removed from the library shelves and delivered to the Board's offices, so that Board members could read them. When this directive was carried out, it became publicized, and the Board issued a press release justifying its action. It characterized the removed books as "anti-American, anti-Christian, anti-Sem[i]tic, and just plain filthy," and concluded that "[i]t is our duty, our moral obligation, to protect the children in our schools from this moral danger as surely as from physical and medical dangers."

A short time later, the Board appointed a "Book Review Committee," consisting of four Island Trees parents and four members of the Island Trees schools staff, to read the listed books and to recommend to the Board whether the books should be retained, taking into account the books' "educational suitability," "good taste," "relevance," and "appropriateness to age and grade level." In July, the Committee made its final report to the

3. The nine books in the High School library were: *Slaughter House Five*, by Kurt Vonnegut, Jr.; *The Naked Ape*, by Desmond Morris; *Down These Mean Streets*, by Piri Thomas; *Best Short Stories of Negro Writers*, edited by Langston Hughes; *Go Ask Alice*, of anonymous authorship; *Laughing Boy*, by Oliver LaFarge; *Black Boy*, by Richard Wright; *A Hero Ain't Nothin' But A Sandwich*, by Alice Childress; and *Soul On Ice*, by Eldridge Cleaver. The book in the Junior High School library was *A Reader for Writers*, edited by Jerome Archer. Still another listed book, *The Fixer*, by Bernard Malamud, was found to be included in the curriculum of a twelfth-grade literature course.

Board, recommending that five of the listed books be retained and that two others be removed from the school libraries. As for the remaining four books, the Committee could not agree on two, took no position on one, and recommended that the last book be made available to students only with parental approval. The Board substantially rejected the Committee's report later that month, deciding that only one book should be returned to the High School library without restriction, that another should be made available subject to parental approval, but that the remaining nine books should "be removed from elementary and secondary libraries and [from] use in the curriculum." The Board gave no reasons for rejecting the recommendations of the Committee that it had appointed. * * *

[Petitioners, students at the high school and junior high school, brought suit challenging this censorship on the grounds that it deprived them of useful materials. The district judge granted summary judgment for the school board. The court of appeals reversed that judgment; the Supreme Court affirmed the court of appeals.]

[II–A–1] The Court has long recognized that local school boards have broad discretion in the management of school affairs. *Epperson v. Arkansas*, 393 U.S. [97, 104 (1968)] reaffirmed that, by and large, "public education in our Nation is committed to the control of state and local authorities," and that federal courts should not ordinarily "intervene in the resolution of conflicts which arise in the daily operation of school systems." * * * We are therefore in full agreement with petitioners that local school boards must be permitted "to establish and apply their curriculum in such a way as to transmit community values," and that "there is a legitimate and substantial community interest in promoting respect for authority and traditional values be they social, moral, or political." Brief for Petitioners 10.

At the same time, however, we have necessarily recognized that the discretion of the States and local school boards in matters of education must be exercised in a manner that comports with the transcendent imperatives of the First Amendment. In *West Virginia Board of Education v. Barnette*, 319 U.S. 624 (1943), we held that under the First Amendment a student in a public school could not be compelled to salute the flag. We reasoned:

> "Boards of Education ... have, of course, important, delicate, and highly discretionary functions, but none that they may not perform within the limits of the Bill of Rights. That they are educating the young for citizenship is reason for scrupulous protection of Constitutional freedoms of the individual, if we are not to strangle the free mind at its source and teach youth to discount important principles of our government as mere platitudes." *Id.* at 637.

Later cases have consistently followed this rationale. Thus *Epperson* invalidated a State's anti-evolution statute as violative of the Establishment Clause, and reaffirmed the duty of federal courts "to apply the First Amendment's mandate in our educational system where essential to safeguard the fundamental values of freedom of speech and inquiry." 393 U.S.

at 104. *Tinker* held that * * * students do not "shed their constitutional rights to freedom of speech or expression at the schoolhouse gate," [393 U.S.] at 506, and therefore local school boards must discharge their "important, delicate, and highly discretionary functions" within the limits and constraints of the First Amendment. * * *

* * * [T]he First Amendment rights of students may be directly and sharply implicated by the removal of books from the shelves of a school library. Our precedents have focused "not only on the role of the First Amendment in fostering individual self-expression but also on its role in affording the public access to discussion, debate, and the dissemination of information and ideas." *First National Bank of Boston v. Bellotti*, 435 U.S. 765, 783 (1978). And we have recognized that "the State may not, consistently with the spirit of the First Amendment, contract the spectrum of available knowledge." *Griswold v. Connecticut*, 381 U.S. 479, 482 (1965) [excerpted in Chapter 1, Section 1(A)]. In keeping with this principle, we have held that in a variety of contexts "the Constitution protects the right to receive information and ideas." *Stanley v. Georgia*, 394 U.S. 557, 564 (1969) [excerpted in Chapter 1, Section 1(B)]; see *Kleindienst v. Mandel*, 408 U.S. 753, 762–763 (1972) (citing cases). This right is an inherent corollary of the rights of free speech and press that are explicitly guaranteed by the Constitution, in two senses. First, the right to receive ideas follows ineluctably from the *sender's* First Amendment right to send them: "The right of freedom of speech and press ... embraces the right to distribute literature, and necessarily protects the right to receive it." *Martin v. Struthers*, 319 U.S. 141, 143 (1943) (citation omitted). "The dissemination of ideas can accomplish nothing if otherwise willing addressees are not free to receive and consider them. It would be a barren marketplace of ideas that had only sellers and no buyers." *Lamont v. Postmaster General*, 381 U.S. 301, 308 (1965) (Brennan, J., concurring).

More importantly, the right to receive ideas is a necessary predicate to the recipient's meaningful exercise of his own rights of speech, press, and political freedom. Madison admonished us:

> "A popular Government, without popular information, or the means of acquiring it, is but a Prologue to a Farce or a Tragedy; or, perhaps both. Knowledge will forever govern ignorance: And a people who mean to be their own Governors, must arm themselves with the power which knowledge gives." 9 *Writings of James Madison* 103 (G. Hunt ed. 1910).

As we recognized in *Tinker*, students too are beneficiaries of this principle:

> "In our system, students may not be regarded as closed-circuit recipients of only that which the State chooses to communicate.... [S]chool officials cannot suppress 'expressions of feeling with which they do not wish to contend.'" 393 U.S. at 511 (quoting *Burnside v. Byars*, 363 F.2d 744, 749 [5th Cir. 1966]).

In sum, just as access to ideas makes it possible for citizens generally to exercise their rights of free speech and press in a meaningful manner, such access prepares students for active and effective participation in the pluralistic, often contentious society in which they will soon be adult members. Of course all First Amendment rights accorded to students must be construed "in light of the special characteristics of the school environment." *Tinker*, 393 U.S. at 506. But the special characteristics of the school *library* make that environment especially appropriate for the recognition of the First Amendment rights of students.

A school library, no less than any other public library, is "a place dedicated to quiet, to knowledge, and to beauty." *Brown v. Louisiana*, 383 U.S. 131, 142 (1966) (opinion of Fortas, J.). *Keyishian v. Board of Regents*, 385 U.S. 589 (1967), observed that " 'students must always remain free to inquire, to study and to evaluate, to gain new maturity and understanding.' " [*Id.* at 603, quoting *Sweezy v. New Hampshire*, 354 U.S. 234, 250 (1957).] The school library is the principal locus of such freedom. * * * Petitioners emphasize the inculcative function of secondary education, and argue that they must be allowed *unfettered* discretion to "transmit community values" through the Island Trees schools. But that sweeping claim overlooks the unique role of the school library. It appears from the record that use of the Island Trees school libraries is completely voluntary on the part of students. Their selection of books from these libraries is entirely a matter of free choice; the libraries afford them an opportunity at self-education and individual enrichment that is wholly optional. Petitioners might well defend their claim of absolute discretion in matters of curriculum by reliance upon their duty to inculcate community values. But we think that petitioners' reliance upon that duty is misplaced where, as here, they attempt to extend their claim of absolute discretion beyond the compulsory environment of the classroom, into the school library and the regime of voluntary inquiry that there holds sway. * * *

[II–A–2] With respect to the present case, the message of these precedents is clear. Petitioners rightly possess significant discretion to determine the content of their school libraries. But that discretion may not be exercised in a narrowly partisan or political manner. If a Democratic school board, motivated by party affiliation, ordered the removal of all books written by or in favor of Republicans, few would doubt that the order violated the constitutional rights of the students denied access to those books. The same conclusion would surely apply if an all-white school board, motivated by racial animus, decided to remove all books authored by blacks or advocating racial equality and integration. Our Constitution does not permit the official suppression of *ideas*. Thus whether petitioners' removal of books from their school libraries denied respondents their First Amendment rights depends upon the motivation behind petitioners' actions. If petitioners *intended* by their removal decision to deny respondents access to ideas with which petitioners disagreed, and if this intent was the decisive factor in petitioners' decision, then petitioners have exercised their discretion in violation of the Constitution. To permit such intentions to control official actions would be to encourage the precise sort of officially prescribed orthodoxy unequivocally condemned in *Barnette*. On the other hand, respondents implicitly concede that an unconstitutional motivation would *not* be demonstrated if it were shown that petitioners had decided to remove the books at issue because those books were pervasively vulgar. And again, respondents concede that if it were demonstrated that the removal decision was based solely upon the "educational suitability" of the books in question, then their removal would be "perfectly permissible." In other words, in respondents' view such motivations, if decisive of petitioners' actions, would not carry the danger of an official suppression of ideas, and thus would not violate respondents' First Amendment rights.* * *

[Justice Brennan quoted an example of impermissible motivation (note 25 of his opinion): "When asked to give an example of 'anti-Americanism' in the removed books, petitioners Ahrens and Martin both adverted to [Alice Childress'] *A Hero Ain't Nothin' But A Sandwich*, which notes at one point that George Washington was a slaveholder. Petitioner Martin stated: 'I believe it is anti-American to present one of the nation's heroes, the first President, . . . in such a negative and obviously one-sided life [sic]. That is one example of what I would consider anti-American.' Deposition of Petitioner Martin 22."]

■ JUSTICE BLACKMUN, concurring in part and concurring in the judgment. [Justice Blackmun did not concur in the plurality opinion's discussion of the right to receive information (II–A–1) but did find the following principle in those cases: "the State may not suppress exposure to ideas—for the sole *purpose* of suppressing exposure to those ideas—absent sufficiently compelling reasons." He also agreed with the plurality that "state action calculated to suppress novel ideas or concepts is fundamentally antithetical to the values of the First Amendment."]

■ JUSTICE WHITE concurring in the judgment. [Justice White avoided the constitutional issue altogether and voted to affirm the court of appeals because there were legitimate factual issues going to the school board's motivation; those issues precluded the summary judgment granted by the district court.]

■ CHIEF JUSTICE BURGER, with whom JUSTICE POWELL, JUSTICE REHNQUIST, and JUSTICE O'CONNOR join, dissenting.

* * * In an attempt to deal with a problem in an area traditionally left to the states, a plurality of the Court, in a lavish expansion going beyond any prior holding under the First Amendment, expresses its view that a school board's decision concerning what books are to be in the school library is subject to federal-court review. Were this to become the law, this Court would come perilously close to becoming a "super censor" of school board library decisions. * * *

It is true that where there is a willing distributor of materials, the government may not impose unreasonable obstacles to dissemination by the third party. And where the speaker desires to express certain ideas, the government may not impose unreasonable restraints. *Tinker*. It does not follow, however, that a school board must affirmatively aid the speaker in his communication with the recipient. In short the plurality suggests today that if a writer has something to say, the government through its schools must be the courier. None of the cases cited by the plurality establish this broad-based proposition.

First, the plurality argues that the right to receive ideas is derived in part from the sender's First Amendment rights to send them. * * * Never before today has the Court indicated that the government has an obligation to aid a speaker or author in reaching an audience.

Second, the plurality concludes that "the right to receive ideas is a necessary predicate to the recipient's meaningful exercise of his own rights of speech, press, and political freedom." However, the "right to receive information and ideas," *Stanley*, 394 U.S. at 564, does not carry with it the concomitant right to have those ideas affirmatively provided at a particular place by the government. The plurality cites James Madison to emphasize the importance of having an informed citizenry. We all agree with Madison, of course, that knowledge is necessary for effective government. Madison's view, however, does not establish a right to have particular books retained on the school library shelves if the school board decides that they are inappropriate or irrelevant to the school's mission. Indeed, if the need to have an informed citizenry creates a "right," why is the government not also required to provide ready access to a variety of information? This same need would support a constitutional "right" of the people to have public libraries as part of a new constitutional "right" to continuing adult education. * * *

* * * If, as we have held, schools may legitimately be used as vehicles for "inculcating fundamental values necessary to the maintenance of a democratic political system," *Ambach v. Norwick*, 441 U.S. 68, 77 (1979), school authorities must have broad discretion to fulfill that obligation. Presumably all activity within a primary or secondary school involves the conveyance of information and at least an implied approval of the worth of that information. How are "fundamental values" to be inculcated except by having school boards make content-based decisions about the appropriateness of retaining materials in the school library and curriculum. * * *

We can all agree that as a matter of *educational policy* students should have wide access to information and ideas. But the people elect school boards, who in turn select administrators, who select the teachers, and these are the individuals best able to determine the substance of that policy. The plurality fails to recognize the fact that local control of education involves democracy in a microcosm. In most public schools in the United States the *parents* have a large voice in running the school. Through participation in the election of school board members, the parents influence, if not control, the direction of their children's education. A school board is not a giant bureaucracy far removed from accountability for its actions; it is truly "of the people and by the people." A school board reflects its constituency in a very real sense and thus could not long exercise unchecked discretion in its choice to acquire or remove books. If the parents disagree with the educational decisions of the school board, they can take steps to remove the board members from office. Finally, even if parents and students cannot convince the school board that book removal is inappropriate, they have alternative sources to the same end. Books may be acquired from bookstores, public libraries, or other alternative sources unconnected with the unique environment of the local public schools.* * *

[Chief Justice Burger criticized the plurality opinion for inviting judges to usurp or second-guess the educational decisions of school boards. The standards of review announced by the plurality—courts can overturn "partisan" censorship but should allow censorship of materials that are "pervasively vulgar"—are too vague to be constraining on trial judges. They will, therefore, be free to impose their own standards and to displace those adopted by the local boards.]

■ [The separate dissenting opinions of JUSTICE POWELL and JUSTICE REHN-QUIST are omitted. Our Notes to this case excerpt portions of the Appendix to Justice Powell's dissent.]

NOTES ON *PICO* AND STUDENTS' RIGHT TO KNOW

1. *More About the Censored Books.* Justice Powell's dissent contained excerpts from the censored books. Consider a few:

- From Eldridge Cleaver's *Soul on Ice*, pages 157–58: "There are white men who will pay you to fuck their wives. They approach you and say, 'How would you like to fuck a white woman?' 'What is this?' you ask. 'On the up-and-up,' he assures you. 'It's all right. She's my wife. She needs black rod, is all. She has to have it. It's like a medicine or drug to her. She has to have it. I'll pay you. It's all on the level, no trick involved. Interested?' You go with him and he drives you to their home. The three of you go into the bedroom. There is a certain type who will leave you and his wife alone and tell you to pile her real good. After it is all over, he will pay you and drive you to wherever you want to go. Then there are some who like to peep at you through a keyhole and watch you have his woman, or peep at you through a window, or lie under the bed and listen to the creaking of the bed as you work out. There is another type who likes to masturbate while he stands beside the bed and watches you pile her. There is the type who likes to eat his woman up after you get through piling her. And there is the type who only wants you to pile her for a little while, just long enough to thaw her out and kick her motor over and arouse her to heat, then he wants you to jump off real quick and he will jump onto her and together they can make it from there by themselves."

- Langston Hughes, editor, *The Best Short Stories by Negro Writers*, page 228: "that no-count bitch of a daughter of yours is up there up North making a whore of herself." *Id.* at 237: "they made her get out and stand in front of the headlights of the car and pull down her pants and raise her dress—they said that was the only way they could be sure. And you can imagine what they said and what they did—." *Id.* at 303: "You need some pussy. Come on, let's go up to the whore house on the hill." "Oh, these bastards, these bastards, this God damned Army and the bastards in it. The sons of bitches!'' *Id.* at 436: "he produced a brown rag doll, looked at her again, then grabbed the doll by its legs and tore it part way up the middle. Then he jammed his finger into the rip between the doll's legs. The other men laughed...." etc.

- Richard Wright, *Black Boy*, pages 70–71: "We black children—seven or eight or nine years of age—used to run to the Jew's store and shout:

  ... Bloody Christ Killers

  Never trust a Jew

  Bloody Christ Killers

  What won't a Jew do ...

  Red, white and blue

  Your pa was a Jew

  Your ma a dirty dago

  What the hell is you?"

  Id. at 265: " 'Crush that nigger's nuts, nigger!' 'Hit that nigger!' 'Aw, fight, you goddam niggers!' 'Sock 'im, in his f-k-g-piece!' 'Make 'im bleed!' ''

If you were the trial judge, would you be inclined to allow the school board to remove any of these books? Should Justice Powell have included these excerpts in a Supreme Court opinion that is readily accessible to children, and indeed more readily accessible to very young children than the books in a high school library (the Powell excerpts can be found on the internet, for example)? If Justice Powell was trying both to titillate as well as scandalize his audience, should we include such material in our casebook? All three of these books, and most of the nine censored books, were written or edited by African–American authors. What light, if any, does that shed on the controversy?

2. *Do High School Students Have a General Right to Know? To Sex Education?* Three Justices in *Pico* agreed that high school students have a constitutional right to know, which entails access to important intellectual materials; one Justice (Blackmun) agreed with a negative right, not to withhold ideas from students. Four Justices rejected a right to know and, perhaps, even Justice Blackmun's negative right. Justice White took no firm position. On the one hand, he believed the school board does not have unfettered discretion in removing books and saw a point to a trial determining if the board removed the books simply because of their "vulgarity." His opinion in *Kuhlmeier* bespoke a deferential, inculcative view of public education, however.

Should high school students have some kind of right to know? If so, should it extend beyond the library setting? That is, does a school have an obligation to expose students to "useful" information? How can judges decide what information is "useful" and what is not? Consider the following quandaries that may be of life and death significance: Does a teenage girl have the right to know about the risks of pregnancy and how to prevent it? Does a teenage boy have a similar need? Does he need to know how to use a condom? Does a gay teenager have a right to know that homosexuality is not a mental or physical disease? Do teenagers of all genders and sexualities have a right to know about how HIV, the virus that is associated with AIDS, is transmitted?

3. *Removal of Lesbian Novels from High School Libraries?* A federal district court, in *Case v. Unified School District No. 233*, 908 F.Supp. 864 (D.Kan.1995), applied the First Amendment to a school board's removal of *Annie on My Mind*, an award-winning book about a romantic relationship between two teenage girls. Accompanied by substantial publicity, Project 21 (since renamed the P.E.R.S.O.N. project) donated several copies of the book, along with copies of *All American Boys*, a similar story involving teenage boys, to the Kansas City-area school district for placement in the district's high school libraries. Ironically, the libraries already had a number of copies of *Annie*. All of the district's high school librarians agreed that *Annie* had literary merit, but that *Boys* did not. A school official then wrote Project 21, accepting *Annie* but declining *Boys*. The school district's superintendent then unilaterally determined that all of the district's copies of *Annie*, including those previously present, would be removed.

The district court followed the plurality opinion in *Pico*, as this was the only Supreme Court opinion specifically addressing the removal of books from a public school library. The court found the board's action invalid under the *Pico* (plurality) rule, as the four board members voting to support the removal of *Annie* stated that they had done so because the book "glorified and promoted" homosexuality. In making this assessment, the court looked behind the board members' invocation of "educational unsuitability," which the court found to represent nothing more than viewpoint discrimination. The court also deemed it important that the board disregarded its own established procedures for reviewing the suitability of library books, and that the board failed to consider less restrictive alternatives to the complete removal of the book. Rejecting the board's claims in defense, the court held that the board did not have unfettered discretion to "transmit community values," while the book's availability in other libraries in the area did not cure the constitutional violation. What arguments could the school board make on appeal? Should the board prevail?

PROBLEM 7–2

AVAILABILITY OF GAY PUBLICATIONS IN PUBLIC LIBRARIES

The Washington Blade is a free weekly gay publication published in the Washington, D.C. metropolitan area. It carries news stories, with a progay point of view, and also contains advertisements of all sorts: commercial businesses, upcoming events of interest to the lesbian and gay community, and personal ads. The newspaper is distributed at local centers, usually bookstores, where people can simply take a copy from a stack located in a public area. The public libraries of Fairfax County, Virginia are among the hundreds of distribution centers in the D.C. area.

Concerned parents object to *The Blade*'s being so readily available to adolescents and petition the Fairfax County Council to instruct the newspaper's publishers not to leave copies at the county's public libraries; the parents do not ask for the county to limit circulation at privately owned properties. The parents believe that the newspaper is too provocative and point to personal ads in *The Blade* that solicit same-sex dates ("GWM gym rat, 26, ISO similar versatile GWM, blond a definite +"), as well as ads for social events that display nearly naked male bodies, ads for gay sexual "chat" lines (900 numbers), and ads by male escorts and massage therapists who will perform sensual services for a fee.

The County Council considers this an important issue, and the County Attorney schedules a public hearing on the matter. You are a lawyer advising *The Blade*. What do you advise? What action can you and your client take to head off this proposal? What arguments can you make to the County Attorney before the hearing?

ACADEMIC FREEDOM AND ISSUES OF GENDER AND SEXUALITY

Academic freedom involves the insulation of scholarship and liberal education from "extracurricular" political interference.[a] Academic freedom subserves both substantive and procedural values, according to its adherents. Substantively, defenders of academic freedom maintain that teachers need to be left alone, so that the "marketplace of ideas" can work freely. Procedurally, the polity should defer to educational choices made by educators. When the educational institution is run by the state, academic freedom of educators is protected by the First Amendment.[b]

There are profound ambiguities at the core of academic freedom, however. How can one balance the values of academic freedom against educational responsibilities to create an environment in which all students can learn? Does academic freedom protect teachers from employer interference? Or does it protect institutional employers from outside interference? Including interference from judges (*Fraser* and *Pico*)? Which is more important: the teacher's autonomy in running the classroom, or the institution's autonomy in running the curriculum? Also, does the educational level make a difference: Should college (or law school!) teachers enjoy greater autonomy than high school or grade school teachers?

PART A.   ACADEMIC FREEDOM AND SILENCING CLASSROOM DISCUSSION OF SEXUALITY

What limits does the Constitution impose upon school boards that discipline teachers who open up discourse on controversial topics such as sexuality? The leading case for First Amendment limits on disciplining secondary school teachers is *Pickering v. Board of Education*, 391 U.S. 563 (1968). In that case, the teacher criticized the Board of Education (his

---

a. For useful discussions of academic freedom, from which our account draws, see Peter Byrne, "Academic Freedom: A 'Special Concern of the First Amendment,'" 99 *Yale L.J.* 251, 255 (1989); E. Edmund Reutter, Jr., "Academic Freedom Advisory: Be Wary of the Long Arm of *Kuhlmeier*," 89 *Ed. L. Rep.* 347. Jordan Young, Georgetown University Law Center Class of 1998, authored the first

draft of the introductions to Section 2, Parts A, B, and C.

b. Academic freedom was first officially recognized as protected by the First Amendment in *Sweezy v. New Hampshire*, 354 U.S. 234, 250 (1957), see Byrne, "Academic Freedom," 256, and received its most eloquent enunciation in *Keyishian v. Board of Regents*, 385 U.S. 589 (1967).

employer) in a public letter for the manner in which the district allocated funds between academic and athletic activities, and the teacher was fired for so doing. The Supreme Court upheld a teacher's right to speak out on matters of public interest without fear of reprisal by his employer, as long as the teacher's speech didn't affect his performance in the classroom, or "interfere with the regular operation of the schools."

Left unanswered in *Pickering* was the question of what happened when a teacher's speech was part of classroom or school-based activities. In those cases, arguably, academic freedom cuts both ways: failure of courts to intervene undermines the academic freedom of the teacher, but intervention undermines the academic freedom of the institution. *Epperson v. Arkansas*, 393 U.S. 97 (1968) states that "public education . . . is committed to the control of state and local authorities [school boards]," and that federal courts should be loathe to "intervene in the resolution of conflicts which arise in the daily operation of school systems." The Supreme Court has said that teachers and administrators in secondary schools may regulate and censor the "style and content of student speech in school-sponsored expressive activities so long as their actions are reasonably related to legitimate pedagogical concerns" (*Kuhlmeier*). The question then becomes whether teachers are also bound by those same "legitimate pedagogical concerns." Are educators allowed to teach and espouse views, in the classroom, which are contrary to those advanced by the school board and stated in established curricula? If the views focus on issues of sexuality, does that make a difference? Does an educator's own sexuality justify institutional remediation? Consider the following cases.

David O. Solmitz et al. v. Maine School Administration District No. 59

Supreme Judicial Court of Maine, 1985.
495 A.2d 812.

■ McKUSICK, CHIEF JUSTICE. * * *

In the fall of 1984, David Solmitz, a teacher at Madison High School, began planning an all-day "Symposium on Tolerance" in reaction to the tragic drowning of a Bangor homosexual by three Bangor high school students. Tolerance Day, as the program became known, was designed to bring to the school representatives of some dozen different groups who have experienced prejudice in society. The program, to begin with a school-wide assembly, would replace scheduled classes throughout the school day on Friday, January 25, 1985.

On January 14, Solmitz met with the school's principal, Anthony Krapf, to discuss the proposed symposium. At that meeting, Krapf instructed Solmitz that he should not invite a homosexual to speak at Tolerance Day. The next day the two men met with Robert Woodbury, superintendent of S.A.D. 59, who also advised Solmitz that he should not include a homosexual in the program. On Friday, January 18, Solmitz and Woodbury reached a compromise whereby Dale McCormick, a lesbian who had agreed to speak at Tolerance Day, would participate in the symposium. As modified, the program would begin with a mandatory assembly of all students at which a speaker would discuss the issue of tolerance in general and the representatives of the various groups would be introduced. Those representatives would then disperse to different classrooms, and each would speak separately for two class periods. The students would have the option of attending such sessions as they might choose or of attending a study hall.

* * * News of the proposed symposium appeared in the local papers on Saturday morning, January 19, and during the weekend school administrators and school board members received fifty or more telephone calls and visits from people critical of McCormick's scheduled appearance. Some callers suggested that picketing might occur on the day of the program, and some parents threatened to keep their children out of school, or to attend school themselves to monitor the symposium. A few of the phone calls warned the Board to expect bomb threats against the school and sabotaging of the school furnace if the program were held.* * *

[As a result of these events, the Board ordered that Tolerance Day not proceed. On the next day, Solmitz, McCormick, and Sonja Roach, a freshman student in Solmitz's history class, sued the Board and some members for violating their First Amendment rights. The trial court denied relief, and the state supreme court affirmed.]

It is beyond question that "local school boards have broad discretion in the management of school affairs." *Pico*, 457 U.S. at 863. In Maine local control over education is established by article VIII, § 1 of our constitution, providing that "the legislature are authorized, and it shall be their duty to require, the several towns to make suitable provision, at their own expense, for the support and maintenance of public schools...." Moreover, 20–A [Maine Revised Statutes Annotated, M.R.S.A.] § 2(2) (1983) provides:

> It is the intent of the Legislature that the control and management of the public schools shall be vested in the legislative and governing bodies of local school administrative units, as long as those units are in compliance with appropriate state statutes.

Additionally, 20–A M.R.S.A. § 1001(6) (1983) requires that the school board "shall direct the general course of instruction." In the case at bar, plaintiffs could make no realistic claim that the Tolerance Day program was anything other than a proposed addition to the course of instruction at Madison High School. Even the compromise Tolerance Day program would have required all students to attend a morning assembly and would have displaced the school's regular classes for part of the day. * * *

Plaintiff Solmitz argues that the Board's rejection of his plans for a school-wide Tolerance Day program violated his rights to academic freedom under the First Amendment. See *Keyishian*, 385 U.S. at 603 ("[academic] freedom is ... a special concern of the First Amendment"). Solmitz, however, does not, nor could he, contend that the Board's veto infringed in any way upon his right to teach his assigned courses as he deemed appropriate, or to express himself freely on tolerance, prejudice against homosexuals, or any other subject. However broad the protections of academic freedom may be, they do not permit a teacher to insist upon a given curriculum for the whole school where he teaches. The facts as found by the Superior Court demonstrate beyond any doubt that Tolerance Day was designed by Solmitz to add to the school-wide curriculum of Madison High School. No right of Solmitz to speak freely was violated by the Board's decision to veto his curriculum proposal, and in cancelling the symposium the Board acted well within the permissible range of its discretion to direct the general course of instruction in S.A.D. 59.

We stress that in this case there is no indication that the Board was attempting to "cast a pall of orthodoxy over the classroom," *Keyishian*, 385 U.S. at 603, or restrict impermissibly the marketplace of ideas within the high school. The Superior Court justice found as a fact that "concerns about disruptions [by those opposed to having a homosexual speak] and the fact that such disruptions might make Tolerance Day 'a lost day educationally' . . . were the *decisive factors* in the decision to vote to cancel." (Emphasis added) The justice further found that "concerns about disruption of educational activities, *not desire to suppress ideas*," motivated the Board to cancel the proposed Tolerance Day program; "concerns directed at potential disruption . . . were the *actual* factors leading to the cancellation." (Emphasis added) There is no reason to disturb those findings. * * *

In announcing our decision in the case at bar, we stress what this case does not involve. The Board did not attempt to discipline Solmitz for proposing and organizing the Tolerance Day symposium. It did not tell Solmitz how he was to teach his history course. It did not restrict Solmitz in any way in freely expressing his views on any subject within or without the school. Similarly, the Board did not prohibit any other discussions of tolerance or of prejudice against homosexuals, whether in Solmitz's classes or otherwise within Madison High School. When the Board cancelled a proposed forum disruptive to the education of its students, it exercised its responsibility for directing the course of instruction of the school. That action did not infringe on the rights of teacher Solmitz and did not impermissibly restrict the free marketplace of ideas at Madison High School.

The free speech rights of Sonja Roach, a student of Solmitz, similarly were not violated by the action of the Board. Students have no right to demand a curriculum of their own choice. In the *Pico* case, the various opinions of the justices demonstrate that at least five members of the United States Supreme Court believe that the right to receive information as a component of the First Amendment does not allow students to insist upon a given curriculum.[8] We follow their analysis in interpreting article I, § 4 of the Maine Constitution.

---

8. In *Pico* only three justices in the plurality explicitly found that "the right to receive ideas follows ineluctably from the *sender's* First Amendment rights to send them.... [And that] the right to receive ideas is a necessary predicate to the *recipient's* meaningful exercise of his own rights of speech...." 457 U.S. at 867 (emphasis in original). The four-judge dissent wrote that a student should not be able to force a school

Again, we stress that the findings of the Superior Court that we have ruled to be beyond reversal on appeal demonstrate that Tolerance Day was cancelled for safety, order, and security reasons, and not in an attempt to cast a "pall of orthodoxy" over the school. Sonja Roach has no right to impose upon the Board her ideas for the curriculum at Madison High School, and none of her freedoms under article I, § 4 of the Maine Constitution or the First Amendment was in any way infringed by the action of the Board.

Plaintiff Dale McCormick has no right to speak at Madison High School arising from the invitation she received from Solmitz, and she could demand successfully to address the student body only if the school had become a public forum. See *Perry Education Association v. Perry Local Educators' Association*, 460 U.S. 37 (1983). We hold that Madison High School is not a public forum, and deny this plaintiff's appeal.

[Although the school generally aspired to present "controversial ideas" to its students, it had a more specific policy that "no individual or group may claim the right to present arguments directly to students." The court found this sufficient to refute the possibility that the school was a limited public forum which is prohibited from discriminating based on viewpoint. (Recall *Rosenberger*, Chapter 5, Section 1.)]

NOTE ON *SOLMITZ* AND INSTITUTIONAL CONTROL OF SEXUALITY DISCOURSE IN THE CLASSROOM

In *Miles v. Denver Public Schools*, 944 F.2d 773, 777 (10th Cir.1991), a teacher commenting on the decline in values among the student body referred to "two students making out on the tennis courts," naming one of the students. As a result, the teacher was placed on paid administrative leave, and a letter of reprimand stating that he had shown poor judgment was placed in his file. The Tenth Circuit rejected his claim that the reprimand violated his First Amendment right to academic freedom. In light of *Fraser* and *Pico*, would the U.S. Supreme Court agree?

As in *Miles*, the cases where schools are most successful in defending the disciplining of a teacher, are those in which the teacher's speech touches on sexual issues. Courts seem very willing to support administration claims that censure was based on the "vulgar" content of the "speech" involved, and the need to protect students from such "offensive" material. For example, *O'Connor v. Sobol*, 577 N.Y.S.2d 716 (N.Y.App.Div.1991)

"to be the conduit for [any] particular information." *Id.* at 889 (Burger, C.J., dissenting). And Justice Blackmun, while concurring with the plurality, wrote: "I do not suggest that the State has any affirmative obligation to provide students with information or ideas, something that may well be associated with a 'right to receive.' " *Id.* at 878 (Blackmun, J., concurring). Justice White also concurred separately in the judgment affirming the court of appeals' reversal of the grant of summary judgment by the district court, but he did not discuss the first amendment question. *Id.* at 883 (White, J., concurring). *Pico* was limited to the removal of library books from the school, and even the plurality opinion recognized the broad power of school boards in controlling curriculum. *See id.* at 862, 869.

upheld, against First Amendment attack, the reprimand of a New York teacher for distributing a sexually explicit article to high school seniors. Similarly, an Illinois federal district court held that a school board's decision not to renew the contract of a teacher because he showed a high school class the R-rated film "About Last Night" as a modern version of Thornton Wilder's *Our Town* was justifiable under *Kuhlmeier*. See *Krizek v. Board of Education of Cicero–Stickney Township High School District No. 201*, 713 F.Supp. 1131 (N.D.Ill.1989).

While school boards are given considerable leeway in determining what is appropriate classroom behavior, the constitutional decisions are not thoroughly one-sided. In *Ward v. Hickey*, 996 F.2d 448 (1st Cir.1993), the First Circuit followed *Keyishian* to overturn the denial of tenure to a teacher alleging that the reviewing panel was biased against her for discussing abortions of Downs Syndrome fetuses; the court found that the teacher had insufficient notice to apprise her of the standards that would be applied. The court invoked *Keyishian* to qualify the *Kuhlmeier* standard. "[W]hether a regulation is reasonably related to legitimate pedagogical concerns will depend on, among other things, the age, sophistication of the students, the relationship between teaching method and valid educational objective, and the context and manner of presentation."

Joseph Acanfora III v. Board of Education of Montgomery County

U.S. Court of Appeals for the Fourth Circuit, 1974.
491 F.2d 498.

■ BUTZNER, CIRCUIT JUDGE.

Joseph Acanfora III appeals from an order of the district court denying him reinstatement to a teaching position in Montgomery County, Maryland. The district court held that the school officials wrongfully transferred Acanfora to a nonteaching position when they discovered that he was a homosexual, but it denied relief because of Acanfora's subsequent press and television interviews. We hold that Acanfora's public statements were protected by the first amendment. We conclude, however, that he is not entitled to relief because of material omissions in his application for a teaching position. Consequently, without reaching Acanfora's claim that his denial of a teaching position is unconstitutional, we affirm the district court, but on different grounds.* * *

[While Acanfora was a junior at Penn State University he joined an organization known as the Homophiles of Penn State, which had as its purpose the development of public understanding about homosexuality. When Acanfora applied for teacher certification, Penn State officials differed as to his qualifications and forwarded his application to the Pennsylvania Secretary of Education without recommendation. In the meantime, he was hired by Montgomery County as a junior high school science teacher. They didn't learn of his homosexuality until several weeks after school opened in the fall, and only then as a result of a widely publicized press conference at which the Pennsylvania Secretary of Education announced favorable action on Acanfora's application for teacher certification in that state. Shortly after this disclosure, the Montgomery County deputy superintendent of schools transferred Acanfora, without reduction in pay, from teaching to administrative work in which he had no contact with pupils. When the school officials did not accede to Acanfora's demands that he be returned to his classroom assignment, he commenced this action.]

Following his transfer to an administrative position, Acanfora granted several press and television interviews. The district court characterized the television programs as tending to spark controversy, and noted an element of sensationalism in Acanfora's remarks. It held that Acanfora's appearances were not reasonably necessary for self-defense, but instead exhibited an indifference to the bounds of propriety governing the behavior of teachers. Consequently, the court, ruling that the refusal to reinstate Acanfora or renew his contract was neither arbitrary nor capricious, dismissed his suit.

The Supreme Court has explained the general principles that govern the intricate balance between the rights of a teacher to speak as a citizen on public issues related to the schools and the importance the state properly attaches to the uninterrupted education of its youth. Balancing these interests, the court has ruled that a teacher's comments on public issues concerning schools that are neither knowingly false nor made in reckless disregard of the truth afford no ground for dismissal when they do not impair the teacher's performance of his duties or interfere with the operation of the schools. *Pickering v. Board of Education*, 391 U.S. 563 (1968). Acanfora's public statements must be judged by these constitutional principles, and not, as the district court suggested, by the common law doctrine of self-defense to defamation.

At the invitation of the Public Broadcasting System, Acanfora appeared with his parents on a program designed to help parents and homosexual children cope with the problems that confront them. Acanfora also consented to other television, radio, and press interviews. The transcripts of the television programs, which the district court found to be typical of all the interviews, disclose that he spoke about the difficulties homosexuals encounter, and, while he did not advocate homosexuality, he sought community acceptance. He also stressed that he had not, and would not, discuss his sexuality with the students.

In short, the record discloses that press, radio, and television commentators considered homosexuality in general, and Acanfora's plight in particular, to be a matter of public interest about which reasonable people could differ, and Acanfora responded to their inquiries in a rational manner. There is no evidence that the interviews disrupted the school, substantially impaired his capacity as a teacher, or gave the school officials reasonable grounds to forecast that these results would flow from what he said. We hold, therefore, that Acanfora's public statements were protected by the first amendment and that they do not justify either the action taken by the school system or the dismissal of his suit.

On his application for a teaching position in the Montgomery County Schools, Acanfora responded to a request for information about his professional, service and fraternal organizations by mentioning only his student membership in the Pennsylvania State Education Association. In response to a request for information about his extracurricular activities, he listed swimming, bowling, student council, magazine and newspaper staffs, honor society, and Naval Reserve Officers Training Corps. He made no mention of his membership and official position in the organization known as the Homophiles of Penn State. Nevertheless, he verified that the information he submitted was accurate to the best of his knowledge. His omission of the Homophiles was not inadvertent. To the contrary, he realized that this information would be significant, but he believed disclosure would foreclose his opportunity to be considered for employment on an equal basis with other applicants.

Acanfora protests that refusal to employ or retain him as a teacher violates the first and fourteenth amendments. He contends that the school system cannot defend on any deficiency in his application because it was his homosexuality, not omissions from the application, that led to the unconstitutional discrimination against him. The school officials admit that if Acanfora had revealed his affiliation with the Homophiles they would not have employed him. They assert, however, that Acanfora's intentional omission of his connection with the Homophiles bars his attack on the constitutionality of the school system's employment policy. * * *

Not every omission of information in an employment application will preclude an employee from attacking the constitutionality of action taken by the governing body that employs him. But here Acanfora wrongfully certified that his application was accurate to the best of his knowledge when he knew that it contained a significant omission. His intentional withholding of facts about his affiliation with the Homophiles is inextricably linked to his attack on the constitutionality of the school system's refusal to employ homosexuals as teachers. Acanfora purposely misled the school officials so he could circumvent, not challenge, what he considers to be their unconstitutional employment practices. He cannot now invoke the process of the court to obtain a ruling on an issue that he practiced deception to avoid. * * *

NOTES ON *ACANFORA* AND THE DOUBLE BIND FACED BY SEXUAL MINORITIES IN TEACHING

1. *"Immoral Conduct" Exclusions for Teachers: The "Sexual Psychopath" Anxiety.* Most states require teachers to be certified by the state, and state certification laws have traditionally allowed state boards of education to revoke certificates for teachers who engage in "immoral conduct" or "gross immorality" or "crimes of moral turpitude." These statutes were originally aimed at keeping adulterers out of the classroom, but in the 1950s they were applied mostly against "homosexuals." In California, teachers could be decertified for violating the state's "lewd vagrancy" statute, a misdemeanor offense for making a lewd proposition. Florida in the late 1950s and early 1960s used investigators to ferret out closeted gay teachers and professors and got those apprehended to name others who would then be investigated and suspended. See William N. Eskridge, Jr., *Gaylaw: Challenging the Apartheid of the Closet* ch. 2 (forthcoming 1998).

These and other states explicitly relied on the fear that sexually "deviant" people were "sexual psychopaths" who could not control their sexual feelings (recall Chapter 2, Section 2[B]). Accordingly, they were potential or even presumptive "child molesters"; homosexuals were the worst, according to Florida's report on them in 1965, because they needed to "recruit" young people in order to perpetuate themselves. This reasoning made it imperative that such people not be permitted as teachers of impressionable young people. (The same hysteria is depicted in Lillian Hellman's play *The Children's Hour*, where the awakening lesbian attraction between two teachers culminates in their disgrace and in the suicide of one.) Scientific studies since the 1950s have overwhelmingly rejected this understanding of gay people; although men are greatly overrepresented in the child molester population, gay men are no more, nor any less, likely to be molesters than straight men.

2. *Shifting Discourse for Excluding Gay Teachers: From the Predatory Homosexual to the Untruthful Homosexual.* The law in the 1960s was moving in the same direction as the science. After *Griswold*, it was no longer clear that "private" sexual activity could be the basis for teacher discharges. The California Supreme Court in *Morrison v. State Board of Education*, 82 Cal.Rptr. 175, 461 P.2d 375 (Cal. 1969), held that the state could not decertify a teacher because of a private homosexual encounter with another teacher. "No person can be denied government employment because of factors unconnected with the responsibilities of that employment," said Justice Tobriner for a divided court. "The power of the state to regulate the professions and conditions of government employment must not arbitrarily impair the right of the individual to live his private life, apart from his job, as he deems fit."

This decision was arguably inconsistent with *Acanfora*, which assumes that homosexuality (not even homosexual conduct) is materially relevant to the decision to hire a teacher. Recall *National Gay Task Force v. Board of Education of Oklahoma City* [Chapter 5, Section 1(B)], where the Tenth Circuit held that a teacher could not constitutionally be disciplined for "speech" concerning homosexuality, even though the teacher could be disciplined for homosexual "conduct." On the other hand, no one was trying to take away Acanfora's teaching certificate, or even his job; recall that Montgomery County was only trying to transfer him away from students.

Acanfora reflects the new privacy discourse: the trial court faulted Acanfora for being "public" about his homosexuality, and hence beyond *Griswold*'s protection; and the appeals court faulted him for being "dishonest" about his homosexuality, and hence also beyond *Griswold*'s protection. Recall *Rowland* [Chapter 3, Section 2(C)], where the Sixth Circuit allowed the firing of a teacher who revealed her bisexuality. This is similar to what Eve Kosofsky Sedgwick calls the "double bind," the Catch–22 of gay litigation—the way in which society's ambiguous thinking about homosexuality (as both a weird minority and a frightening thing in all of us) penalizes the gay person whichever way she or he argues (Chapter 2, Section 2[C]).

In light of the U.S. Supreme Court's precedents—especially *Bowers* and *Romer* [Chapter 1], *Hurley* and *National Gay Task Force* [Chapter 5], and *Fraser* and *Pico* [this Chapter]—did the Fourth Circuit reach the right result in *Acanfora*?

3. *Don't Ask, Don't Tell.* An anecdote from *Acanfora* suggests the underlying policy. Michael Gottesman, counsel for Acanfora and now a law professor at Georgetown, remembers that his client testified in his deposition that gay teachers were everywhere in Montgomery County's schools. The counsel for Montgomery County idly asked Acanfora to name some of these teachers who were "everywhere." Realizing that Montgomery County viewed itself as "tolerant" and not like the witch-hunting fifties folks, Gottesman suggested that opposing counsel consult with his client to be sure that the defendants *really* wanted that question answered (Gottesman would have instructed Acanfora not to answer in any event). The next day, counsel indicated that his client had no interest in the names of other gay teachers.

Note the parallel between General Colin Powell's justification for the military's "don't ask, don't tell" policy: so long as "homosexuals" are in the closet, they can and do serve honorably in the nation's armed forces; only the openly gay person disrupts morale and unit cohesion [Chapter 4, Section 3(C)]. Is "don't ask, don't tell" less justifiable in the teaching setting than in the military setting? Or does parental concern about gay teachers serve the "heckler's veto" function that soldiers' concern about gay bunkmates serves in the military setting?

PROBLEM 7–3

OTHER SEXUALITY–BASED LIMITS ON TEACHING PERSONNEL

Assume that *Acanfora* is wrongly decided. Figure out a principle justifying the opposite decision and then apply that principle to the following variations:

(A) Adultery. Acanfora is a married man who is having an extramarital affair with a woman not his wife; that affair becomes public knowledge. Can the school system transfer Acanfora out of a classroom teaching job?

(B) Pregnancy. Acanfora is a single woman who is pregnant. Can the school transfer her? Think of reasons the school might give. (This issue is taken up in the employment context generally by Chapter 10, Section 2[A].)

(C) Hebephilia. Acanfora writes a journal article criticizing laws criminalizing sexual relations between adults and adolescents between the ages of 14 and 18. Although there is no evidence he has ever molested a student

or broken state laws against hebephilia (sex with adolescents), the school board gets heavy pressure from parents to transfer Acanfora. Can it constitutionally do so? Would it make a difference in your answer if Acanfora confesses to the school board that he harbors sexual feelings for adolescents but has never acted upon them?

PART B. TITLE IX AND RESPONSIBILITIES OF EDUCATIONAL INSTITUTIONS TO PREVENT SEXUAL HARASSMENT

Title IX of the Education Amendments of 1972 provides in relevant part: "No person in the United States shall, on the basis of sex, be excluded from participation in, be denied the benefits of, or be subjected to discrimination under any education program or activity receiving Federal financial assistance * * *." 20 U.S.C. § 1681(a).[c] Virtually all public schools and most private schools receive federal financial assistance as defined by the statute, and the Supreme Court in *Cannon v. University of Chicago*, 441 U.S. 677 (1979), held that Title IX's intended beneficiaries have a private cause of action against institutions violating this directive. Thus if a school told girls they could not take advanced calculus, a course open to boys, female students could obtain an injunction requiring the school to offer the course without sex-based limits.

Does Title IX provide a remedy for sexual harassment in educational settings? Studies have found great incidence of sexual harassment of female students at all levels of education. As many as a third of female college students report some form of sex-based harassment from their professors, a figure that would be higher if peer-group harassment is included.[d] The numbers may be even higher for secondary schools, as an American Association of University Women (AAUW) survey found that four out of five students in grades 8 through 11 had experienced some form of sexual harassment, most often from their peers.[e] The AAUW survey included boys as well as girls, but girls were greatly more likely to have been traumatized by the harassment. In short, the evidence indicates that sexual harassment

---

c. The language in text is the general rule of § 1681(a), which is then followed by nine exceptions, § 1681(a)(1)-(9). Exceptions include (1) primary and secondary school admissions policies, (3) educational institutions controlled by religious organizations and discriminating for religious reasons, (4) educational institutions training individuals for U.S. military service, (5) public colleges which from their establishment have only admitted students of one sex, and (6) social fraternities and sororities.

d. See Billie Wright Dziech & Linda Weiner, *The Lecherous Professor: Sexual Harassment on Campus* (2d ed. 1990); Jean O'Gorman Hughes & Bernice R. Sandler,

Peer Harassment: Hassles for Women on Campus (1988); Nan Stein et al., *Secrets in Public: Sexual Harassment in Our Schools* (1992).

e. Educational Foundation of the American Association of University Women, *Hostile Hallways: The AAUW Survey on Sexual Harassment in America's Schools* 8–10 (1993); see Carrie M.H. Herbert, *Talking of Silence: The Sexual Harassment of Schoolgirls* (1989); Karen Bogart et al., "Breaking the Silence: Sexual and Gender–Based Harassment in Elementary, Secondary, and Postsecondary Education," in *Sex Equity and Sexuality in Education* 191 (Susan Shurberg Klein ed. 1992).

in educational settings is a major phenomenon, and one that disproportionately disadvantages female students. Does Title IX provide a legal remedy for this conduct?

The Supreme Court in *Franklin v. Gwinnett County Public Schools*, 503 U.S. 60 (1992), held that Christine Franklin (a tenth grader) had a cause of action for damages against her high school because she was sexually harassed by Andrew Hill, a teacher-coach at the school. Among the allegations were that Hill quizzed Franklin about her personal sex life, pressed her about having sex with an older man, kissed her on the mouth, and called her at home with social invitations. The school discouraged Franklin from pressing charges and never disciplined Hill (he later resigned, though), and she sued. The Supreme Court held that

> Title IX placed on the Gwinnett County Schools the duty not to discriminate on the basis of sex, and "when a supervisor sexually harasses a subordinate because of the subordinate's sex that supervisor 'discriminate[s]' on the basis of sex." *Meritor Savings Bank, FSB v. Vinson* [a Title VII sexual harassment case]. We believe the same rule should apply when a teacher sexually harasses and abuses a student. Congress did not intend for federal monies to be expended to support the intentional actions it sought by statute to proscribe. * * *

Id. at 1037. The Office for Civil Rights of the Department of Education, which is charged with implementing Title IX, takes the position that sexual harassment is prohibited under *Franklin*.[f]

To the extent the Supreme Court was importing Title VII's sexual harassment jurisprudence into Title IX by its reliance on *Meritor* [see our treatment in Chapter 10, Section 2(C)], it might be found that Title IX is violated *either* when an educational officer demands sex in return for some educational benefit or the avoidance of a detriment (quid pro quo sexual harassment, the kind in *Franklin*) *or* "[w]hen the [educational environment] is permeated with 'discriminatory intimidation, ridicule, and insult' that is 'sufficiently severe or pervasive to alter the conditions of the victim's employment and create an abusive ... environment'" (hostile environment sexual harassment). *Harris v. Forklift Sys., Inc.*, 510 U.S. 17 (1993) (Title VII case quoting and elaborating on *Meritor*). Under a *Harris-Meritor* standard, if the conduct is not so severe or pervasive that a reasonable person would find it hostile or abusive, it is beyond Title IX's purview. Similarly, if the plaintiff does not subjectively perceive the environment to be abusive, the conduct has not actually altered the conditions of her employment, and there is no Title IX violation. Thus, the court must consider not only the actual effect of the harassment on the plaintiff, but also the effect such conduct would have on a reasonable person in the plaintiff's position. Cf. *Bougher v. University of Pittsburgh*, 882 F.2d 74 (3d Cir. 1989) (professor's staring at female student on campus, after they had dissolved their sexual relationship, did not violate Title IX).

---

f. See Carrie N. Baker, "Proposed Title IX Guidelines on Sex–Based Harassment of Students," 43 *Emory L.J.* 271, 272 (1994) (student comment).

Franklin hardly settles all the important issues surrounding sexual harassment under Title IX. Can a teacher's mode of instruction constitute sexual harassment actionable under Title IX? Is gay-bashing sexual harassment under Title IX? Does Title IX establish a duty for educational institutions to protect against sexual harassment by other students? These questions are addressed in the cases and notes that follow.

Dean Cohen v. San Bernardino Valley College

U.S. District Court for the Central District of California, 1995.
883 F.Supp. 1407, *rev'd,* 92 F.3d 968 (9th Cir.1996).

■ LEW, DISTRICT JUDGE.* * *

[Dean Cohen was a tenured professor of English and Film Studies at San Bernardino Valley College (SBVC). In spring term 1992, he taught a remedial English course, English 015.]

By his own admission, Cohen uses a confrontational teaching style designed to shock his students and make them think and write about controversial subjects. He assigns provocative essays such as Jonathan Swift's "A Modest Proposal" and discusses subjects such as obscenity, cannibalism, and consensual sex with children. At times, Cohen uses vulgarities and profanity in the classroom.

One of the students in the spring semester English 015 class, Anita Murillo, became offended by Cohen's repeated focus on topics of a sexual nature, his use of profanity and vulgarities, and by his comments which she believed were directed intentionally at her and some other female students in a humiliating and harassing manner. In February of 1992, Cohen began a class discussion in his English 015 class on the issue of pornography and played the "devil's advocate" by asserting controversial viewpoints. During classroom discussion on this subject, Cohen stated in class that he wrote for Hustler and Playboy, and he read some articles out loud in class. Cohen concluded the class discussion by requiring his students to write essays defining pornography. When Cohen assigned the "Define Pornography" paper, Murillo asked for an alternative assignment but Cohen refused to give her one.

According to Murillo, Professor Cohen then told her that if she met him in a bar he would help her get a better grade. She also claimed that Cohen would look down her shirt, as well as the shirts of other female students, and that he told her she was overreacting because she was a woman.

Murillo stopped attending Cohen's class and received a failing grade for the semester. She subsequently complained about Cohen's statements and conduct to the chair of the English Department, asserting that Cohen had sexually harassed her. Murillo then filed a formal written student grievance against Cohen on May 12, 1993.

On May 26, 1993, the SBVC Faculty Grievance Committee held a hearing to determine whether Murillo's complaint was well-founded. Both

Cohen and Murillo testified, submitted documents, and called witnesses on their own behalf. At the conclusion of the hearing, the Grievance Committee found that Professor Cohen had violated the Community College District's policy against sexual harassment by creating a hostile learning environment. * * *

[Based on its policy prohibiting conduct which "has the purpose or effect of unreasonably interfering with an individual's academic performance or creating an intimidating, hostile, or offensive learning environment," the Grievance Committee recommended disciplinary action. The President and the Board of Trustees agreed. The latter required Cohen to attend a sexual harassment seminar, undergo a formal evaluation procedure, and modify his teaching strategy "when it becomes apparent that his techniques create a climate which impedes the students' ability to learn."

[Cohen sued under 42 U.S.C. § 1983, seeking an injunction against this disciplinary action. He maintained that the discipline violated his free speech rights under either the First Amendment to the U.S. Constitution or article I, § 2(a) of the California Constitution: "Every person may freely speak, write and publish his or her sentiments on all subjects, being responsible for the abuse of this right. A law may not restrain or abridge liberty of speech or press."]

Cohen argues that his right to "academic freedom" prevents the College from punishing him for his classroom speech. In support of his argument, Cohen cites numerous cases. The concept of academic freedom, however, is more clearly established in academic literature than it is in the courts. As one commentator has written,

> * * * The cases, shorn of panegyrics, are inconclusive, the promise of their rhetoric reproached by the ambiguous realities of academic life.
>
> The problems are fundamental: There has been no adequate analysis of what academic freedom the Constitution protects or of why it protects it. Lacking definition or guiding principle, the doctrine floats in the law, picking up decisions as a hull does barnacles.

J. Peter Byrne, "Academic Freedom: A 'Special Concern of the First Amendment,'" 99 *Yale L.J.* 251, 252–53 (1989). * * *

While Supreme Court cases contain strongly worded defenses of "academic freedom," their rhetoric is broader than their holdings. Namely, many cases restrict the government from regulating teachers' *non-classroom* conduct. For example, teachers like other government employees cannot be punished or excluded under unconstitutional statutes requiring them to take "loyalty oaths" or otherwise disclose their allegiance to "subversive" groups. *Sweezy v. New Hampshire*, 354 U.S. 234 (1957). Nor may teachers be punished under unconstitutionally vague statutes forbidding "treasonable" or "seditious" words or actions. *Keyishian v. Board of Regents*, 385 U.S. 589 (1967). The state is also precluded from punishing a teacher for publicly expressing his views on matters of public concern in regards to education. *Pickering v. Board of Educ.*, 391 U.S. 563 (1968) (holding unconstitutional a school board's firing of a high school teacher for writing a letter to a local newspaper criticizing the school board).

[None of the appellate cases cited by Cohen was on point. Most of the cases, like *Pickering*, involved teacher comments outside the classroom. The only cases dealing with instructional comments were establishment clause cases disallowing statutes requiring that creation science be taught. *Edwards v. Aguillard*, 482 U.S. 578 (1987); *Epperson v. Arkansas*, 393 U.S. 97 (1968). Other cases involved only student, rather than teacher, expression. E.g., *Tinker* and *Healy*. Compare *Fraser* and *Kuhlmeier*, which have expanded the discretion of educational institutions at the expense of students, Judge Lew observed. He also relied on lower court decisions which vested broad discretion in colleges' treatment of nonconforming professors. E.g., *Hetrick v. Martin*, 480 F.2d 705, 708–09 (6th Cir.) (upholding university's decision to decline to renew a nontenured teacher because of her pedagogical methods; the pedagogical methods at issue included stating, in the classroom, "I am an unwed mother"), *cert. denied*, 414 U.S. 1075 (1973).]* * *

Other courts, however, have placed limits on the state's control of classroom discussion. *Keefe v. Geanakos*, 418 F.2d 359, 362 (1st Cir.1969) (finding that a high school teacher's classroom use of an obscenity for demonstrated educational purpose was protected); *Dube v. State Univ.*, 900 F.2d 587, 598 (2d Cir.1990) (denying qualified immunity to defendants on the grounds that a professor's classroom discussion of controversial topics was protected by the First Amendment), cert. denied, 501 U.S. 1211 (1991); *Parducci v. Rutland*, 316 F.Supp. 352, 356 (M.D.Ala.1970) (holding that a high school English teacher could not be penalized for assigning a Kurt Vonnegut short story which was not inappropriate or disruptive). * * *

Because the doctrine of academic freedom does not clearly protect Cohen's classroom, curriculum-based speech, the Court now turns to the line of cases dealing with the government's ability to regulate its employees' speech. The Supreme Court has acknowledged the conflict inherent in public employers' restriction of employee speech. In *Connick v. Myers*, the Supreme Court confirmed the government's right as an employer to restrict employee speech, unless that speech pertains to matters of "public concern." 461 U.S. 138, 142 (1983) (citing *Pickering*, as the root of this doctrine). *Connick* discussed the discharge of a Louisiana assistant district attorney. The assistant district attorney was terminated for her workplace distribution of a "questionnaire" on office policies and morale which essentially asked for a "vote of no-confidence" in office supervisors. She argued that, inasmuch as the questionnaire dealt with the workings of a governmental agency, it was speech on a matter of public concern and therefore protected. The *Connick* Court disagreed, finding that the survey was designed to support the assistant district attorney's own personal battle with her superiors over a proposed transfer, not to objectively evaluate or comment on the workings of the district attorneys' office.

Under *Connick*, this Court must first determine whether Cohen's speech can be characterized as "constituting speech on a matter of public concern." If it can be so characterized, then the Defendants must show that the speech "substantially interfered" with government duties. If it is not speech on a matter of public concern, then the government is entitled to "wide latitude in managing [its employees], without intrusive oversight by the judiciary in the name of the First Amendment," and this Court may not interfere in such managerial decisionmaking. [See also *Waters v. Churchill*, 114 S. Ct. 1878 (1994), for a more recent explication of the government's wide discretion as an employer to cashier disruptive employees who disrupt office cohesion.]

[Judge Lew found that Professor Cohen's use of obscenity was not speech about a matter of public concern, and therefore that SBVC had the widest latitude to discipline him for it. Accord, *Martin v. Parrish*, 805 F.2d 583, 585 (5th Cir.1986); see *Dambrot v. Central Michigan Univ.*, 839 F.Supp. 477, 488 (E.D.Mich.1993) (finding that university basketball coach's use of a racial epithet during team pep-talk was not speech on a matter of public concern). The speech about pornography, on the other hand, was a "matter of public concern," the judge held.]

Because Cohen's speech in assigning sexually focused topics and his commentary on those topics relates to a matter of public concern, the burden shifts to Defendants to show that their legitimate interests outweigh Cohen's First Amendment interests. [See *Rankin v. McPherson*, 483 U.S. 378, 388 (1987), applying and elaborating upon *Pickering*.] In applying this balancing test, the Court must consider the manner, time, place, and context of the employee's expression. The state's burden in justifying the regulation varies according to the nature of the employee's expression. Other pertinent considerations include "whether the statement impairs discipline by superiors or harmony among co-workers, has a detrimental impact on close working relationships for which personal loyalty and confidence are necessary, or impedes the performance of the speaker's duties or interferes with the regular operation of the enterprise." *Rankin*, 483 U.S. at 388 (citing *Pickering*). Essentially, the state's interest is based on "the effective functioning of the public employer's enterprise."

The Court must consider the employer's interest in effectively functioning, and whether that effective function is disrupted. In so determining the government's interest, the Court should consider whether the statement at issue impairs discipline, co-worker relations, or impedes the performance of the speaker's duties or the operation of the enterprise. If the speech at issue directly deals with issues of public concern, a stronger showing of disruption is required. The context of the situation determines how strong a showing must be made. A showing of real, not imagined disruption, is required. * * *

The College brings forth substantial, uncontroverted evidence showing that the educational process was disrupted by Cohen's focus on sexual topics and teaching style. There is testimony from the complaining student and from other students in the class that Cohen's sexually suggestive remarks, use of vulgarities and obscenities, and the topics for discussion prevented them from learning.

Furthermore, written evaluations of Cohen by his colleagues done in November of 1992, before Murillo filed her grievance against Cohen, show that while his colleagues respected Cohen as a teacher, several of them entertained doubts as to the efficacy of his confrontational teaching methods. [Two colleagues found Cohen's discussion of consensual sex with children reductionist and insensitive. On the other hand, Cohen's teaching evaluations from students were generally quite positive. Other colleagues describe Cohen as a gifted teacher, and the chair of the department (and defendant here) found Cohen's pedagogy within the realm of "acceptable academic practice."]

In applying a "hostile environment" prohibition, there is the danger that the most sensitive and the most easily offended students will be given veto power over class content and methodology. Good teaching should challenge students and at times may intimidate students or make them uncomfortable. In a different context, the Supreme Court has previously refused to ban all material which offends the sensibilities of society's most sensitive and vulnerable members. *Butler v. Michigan*, 352 U.S. 380, 383–84 (1957) (holding that a state statute prohibiting all distribution of written material harmful to minors was "burn[ing] the house to roast the pig" because it "reduce[d] the adult population of Michigan to reading only what is fit for children"). Colleges and universities, as well as the courts, must avoid a tyranny of mediocrity, in which all discourse is made bland enough to suit the tastes of all students.

However, colleges and universities must have the power to require professors to effectively educate all segments of the student population, including those students unused to the rough and tumble of intellectual discussion. * * *

The restrictions imposed by Defendants are not onerous. The College has required Cohen to issue a syllabus at the beginning of each semester for each of his classes. Cohen must attend a sexual harassment seminar. Cohen must be formally evaluated, and he is directed to "be sensitive" to students. These restrictions are tailored and reasonable, in light of the issues involved. The College is not directly censoring Cohen's choice of topics or teaching style. In essence, the College is requiring Cohen to warn students of his teaching style and topics so that those students for whom this approach is ineffective may make an informed choice as to their educations. * * *

As an alternative basis for its ruling, the Court recognizes the constitutional implications of the College's substantial interest in preventing the creation of a hostile, sexually discriminatory environment which would disrupt the educational process. The Supreme Court has found that creating a "hostile environment" based on gender is a form of sexual harassment which violates Title VII. *Harris v. Forklift Sys., Inc.*, 114 S. Ct. 367, 370–71 (1993); *Meritor Savs. Bank v. Vinson*, 477 U.S. 57, 64 (1986) [examined in Chapter 10]. Several circuits, including the Ninth Circuit, have held that sexual harassment is a type of sexual discrimination which violates the Equal Protection Clause of the Fourteenth Amendment. *Bator* *v. Hawaii*, 39 F.3d 1021, 1027 (9th Cir.1994) (holding that a claim of sexual harassment "can be impermissible sex discrimination in violation of the Equal Protection Clause"); *Bohen v. City of East Chicago*, 799 F.2d 1180, 1185 (7th Cir.1986) ("Sexual harassment of female employees by a state employer constitutes sex discrimination for purposes of the equal protection clause of the fourteenth amendment."); *Starrett v. Wadley*, 876 F.2d 808, 814–15 (10th Cir.1989) (holding that terminated state employee plaintiff had a 42 U.S.C. § 1983 cause of action for supervisor's propositions, physical contact, and quid pro quo threats). * * *

NOTES ON THE BALANCE BETWEEN ACADEMIC FREEDOM AND AVOIDING A HOSTILE EDUCATIONAL ENVIRONMENT

1. *Doctrinal Complexities of the Speech-in-the-Classroom Cases.* One reason we chose Judge Lew's decision for inclusion is that he nicely weaves together the various lines of cases relevant to Professor Cohen's discipline. Let us be explicit about the different doctrinal issues relevant to this case: Does Cohen have an independent First Amendment academic freedom right? (No said Judge Lew.) Cohen does have First Amendment rights as a public employee. Has his *Pickering-Connick* right to speak out on matters of "public concern" been violated by SBCV's discipline against him? (No: the use of obscenity in class is not protected at all; the pornography exercises are protected, but the school's interests outweigh Cohen's.) Relevant to the school's interest in regulating classroom speech on matters of public concern, is Judge Lew's conclusion that Cohen's speech created a hostile environment in violation of Title IX and the equal protection clause; both have been interpreted to incorporate Title VII's guidelines against workplace sexual harassment. Indeed, Alice Murillo would seem to have a claim against SBVC for damages, and future students would have claims for an injunction against SBVC if its (rather tame) disciplinary measures do not alleviate the sexually hostile environment Professor Cohen created.

As the caption to the case indicates, Judge Lew was reversed on appeal. What argument persuaded the Ninth Circuit? Should Judge Lew have been reversed?

We have edited out other doctrinal issues (not relevant to the Ninth Circuit's reversal) that should at least be noted: (a) Section 1983 usually requires that the violation of federal rights be by state actors, such as SBVC and its agents. If the college were private, § 1983 would not have been a viable cause of action. The California Constitution, however, has not been interpreted to require state action to assert violations of individual rights, and a lawsuit under the state equal protection guarantee might have been possible. (b) Some of the defendants in these cases are or may be "immune" from § 1983 lawsuits. The Supreme Court has held that the state government and its subdivisions are immune from suit under that statute, and it is less than perfectly clear that Congress could subject the states to direct damages suits. See *Seminole Tribe of Florida v. Florida,* 116 S.Ct. 1114 (1996) (interpreting Eleventh Amendment). (c) As to the Title

IX issues, note that the judge relied on Title VII principles and case law by analogy, as the Supreme Court briefly did in *Franklin*. The next case will follow a different approach to the relationship between Title VII and Title IX.

2. *Variations on* Cohen. Assume that Judge Lew was correct in holding that Professor Cohen's conduct violated Title IX and the equal protection clause. Consider variations: Under what circumstances, if any, would discussion of rape constitute sexual harassment? When if ever would discussion of a particular student's sexual orientation be appropriate? What obligations does a professor have when students make upsetting comments, such as "Everybody knows that 'no' means 'yes,' coming from a woman." What is required by Title IX? What is allowed by the First Amendment, if the professor teaches at a public university?

It might be argued that Professor Cohen's conduct reflects the attitudes that penalize female professors as well as female students. Dale Spender, *Women of Ideas (and What Men Have Done to Them)* 30–31 (1983), illustrates how women scholars have systematically been belittled as thinkers via attacks on their sexuality:

> * * * [I]n relation to women's intellectual work, * * * we witness the technique of bringing a woman's character into disrepute by means of her sexuality, so that her ideas need not be addressed at all * * * for if a woman can be classified as 'promiscuous' then her ideas can be classified as unreliable and not worthy of serious consideration, and if she can be classified as embittered and twisted * * * then the same rule applies. * * * Such abuse has served to discourage other women from expressing their ideas * * * This also * * * promotes their disappearance.

The extensive litigation that has been required by women to receive tenure in institutions of higher education supports Spender's argument.

3. *The Hate Speech Analogy.* Professor Cohen relied on cases striking down university hate speech codes as overbroad under the First Amendment. See *Doe v. University of Michigan*, 721 F.Supp. 852 (E.D.Mich.1989) (invalidating a code restricting speech which, among other things "stigmatizes or victimizes an individual on the basis of race, ethnicity, religion, sex ... and that ... [c]reates an intimidating, hostile, or demeaning environment for educational pursuits"), and *UWM Post, Inc. v. Board of Regents*, 774 F.Supp. 1163 (E.D.Wis.1991) (invalidating University of Wisconsin regulations prohibiting "racist or discriminatory comments, epithets or other express behavior directed at an individual ... if such comments ... intentionally * * * [c]reate an intimidating, hostile, or demeaning environment for education"). Judge Lew distinguished those decisions on the ground that they protected student speech (*Tinker*) rather than teacher speech, which is subject to more regulation (*Pickering-Connick*). Is this a persuasive distinction?

James S. Nabozny v. Mary Podlesny et al., 92 F.3d 446 (7th Cir.1996). The Seventh Circuit ruled that a gay student's constitutional rights were violated when his school did not protect him from anti-gay harassment and violence. For example, when several boys attacked eighth grader James Nabozny in the school bathroom, Mary Podlesney (who was responsible for school discipline) told James and his parents that such acts should be expected because James was openly gay. Although they promised to take action, school officials did nothing to prevent the harassment against James. Towards the end of the school year a district attorney purportedly suggested that James take time off from school. When James returned after one and a half weeks off, the harassment continued and James attempted suicide. The harassment of James continued in further high school years.

The Seventh Circuit found that Nabozny had made out a claim for unconstitutional discrimination on the basis of both sex and sexual orientation. "We find it impossible to believe that a female lodging a similar complaint would have received the same response. * * * More important, the defendants do not deny that they aggressively punished male-on-female battery and harassment." The court concluded its sex discrimination discussion: "The question is not whether they are required to treat every harassment complaint the same way; as we have noted, they are not. The question is whether they are required to give male and female students equivalent levels of protection; they are, absent an important governmental objective, and the law clearly said so prior to Nabozny's years in middle school."

"Nabozny introduced sufficient evidence to show that the discriminatory treatment was motivated by the defendants' disapproval of Nabozny's sexual orientation, including statements by the defendants that Nabozny should expect to be harassed because he is gay." As to whether such discrimination is constitutionally actionable, the court said yes: "Our discussion of equal protection analysis thus far has revealed a well established principle: the Constitution prohibits intentional invidious discrimination between otherwise similarly situated persons based on one's membership in a definable minority, absent a least a rational basis for the discrimination. There can be little doubt that homosexuals are an identifiable minority subjected to discrimination in our society. * * * We are unable to garner any rational basis for permitting one student to assault another based on the victim's sexual orientation, and the defendants do not offer us one."

Would this fact situation justify a claim for relief under Title IX? Would it have justified such a claim if Nabozny had been female? Consider the following decision.

Debra Rowinsky, for Herself and as Next Friend of * * * Her Minor Children, et al. v. Bryan Independent School District

U.S. Court of Appeals for the Fifth Circuit, 1996.
80 F.3d 1006, *cert. denied*, 117 S.Ct. 165 (1996).

■ JERRY E. SMITH, CIRCUIT JUDGE * * *

During the 1992–93 school year, students proceeding in this litigation under the pseudonyms of Jane and Janet Doe were eighth graders at Sam

Rayburn Middle School in the Bryan Independent School District ("BISD") who rode a BISD school bus to and from school. Boys and girls were required to sit on different sides of the bus, and the bus driver, Bob Owens, enforced the restriction, even, on occasion, telling Jane and Janet not to sit on the boys' side of the bus.

Beginning in September 1992, a male student, whom we identify only by his initials, "G.S.," physically and verbally abused Janet on the bus. G.S. regularly swatted Janet's bottom whenever she walked down the aisle and made comments such as, "When are you going to let me fuck you?", "What bra size are you wearing?", and "What size panties are you wearing?" He also called Janet a "whore." At one point, G.S. groped Janet's genital area.

Janet complained to Owens no fewer than eight times that G.S. had swatted her and Jane on their bottoms and used foul language. Owens took down names on a pad of paper. Janet eventually stopped reporting the incidents.

On September 24, G.S. grabbed Jane in her genital area, and, a few minutes later, grabbed her breasts. Jane, Janet, and their parents visited Assistant Principal Randy Caperton the next day to complain about the incident. Caperton told the Rowinsky family that he had already heard about the sexual assault from another student and that he believed the nature of the assault merited expelling G.S. Caperton suspended G.S. from riding the bus for three days and required him to sit in the second row behind the driver.

On September 29, Mrs. Rowinsky visited Caperton again to discuss the incident, complaining that other girls were being harassed on the bus. Caperton showed her a bus report that documented the incident with Jane. The report, however, contained numerous inaccuracies, including the fact that it did not name G.S. and listed the wrong date and length of punishment. Caperton corrected the assailant's name in a new report.

The three-day suspension did not deter G.S. He violated the seating requirement, and, as a result, Owens restricted Jane and Janet to the front of the bus. Mrs. Rowinsky called Jay Anding, assistant director of the transportation office, and demanded that he restrict G.S. to the second row seat because of the continuing remarks and misbehavior. Anding told Mrs. Rowinsky that he would speak with Owens. * * *

[Notwithstanding such assurances, incidents continued to occur on the schoolbus, with another male student, "L.H.," then groping and harassing Janet. Mrs. Rowinsky continued to complain and continued to get assurances from Anding; the bus driver was replaced, but G.S. remained on the bus. Another male student, "F.F.," groped Janet during class; he was suspended for the rest of the day. Mrs. Rowinsky continued to ask school officials to take harsher action against G.S. and L.H. The school authorities responded that L.H. was no longer a student and that they did not consider the actions of G.S. and F.F. to be sexual in nature. Rowinsky finally brought a lawsuit against the school for tolerating a hostile environment of sexual harassment against female students, including her daughters, in violation of title IX.

[Disagreeing with *Davis v. Monroe County Bd. of Educ.*, 74 F.3d 1186 (11th Cir.1996), which had found a claim for relief in similar circumstances, Judge Smith affirmed the trial court's dismissal of Rowinsky's lawsuit.]

The linchpin of Rowinsky's theory is the assumption that a grant recipient [the school] need not engage in prohibited conduct to violate title IX. The specific statutory phrase at issue [20 U.S.C. § 1681(a)] is the prohibition that "[n]o person be subjected to discrimination under any educational program or activities." Rowinsky focuses solely upon that phrase and argues that "under" means "in" and not "by." By making this substitution, she reasons that the statute cannot be limited to acts of discrimination by grant recipients.[11]

* * * The Supreme Court has repeatedly stated that the purpose of title IX is to prevent discrimination by grant recipients. In *Cannon*, the Court reviewed the legislative history of title IX and concluded that

> title IX, like its model title VI, sought to accomplish two related, but nevertheless somewhat different, objectives. First Congress wanted to avoid the use of federal resources to support *discriminatory practices*; second, it wanted to provide individual citizens effective protection against those practices. Both of these purposes were repeatedly identified in the debates on the two statutes.

441 U.S. at 704 (emphasis added).

Throughout the legislative history, both supporters and opponents of the amendment focused exclusively on acts by the grant recipients. Senator Bayh introduced the amendment and listed the types of sex discrimination, *all by grant recipients*, that prompted the legislation. 118 Cong.Rec. at 5803 (1972) ("It is clear to me that sex discrimination reaches into all facets of education—admissions, scholarship programs, faculty hiring and promotion, professional staffing, and pay scales."). The senator described the "heart" of the amendment as "a provision banning sex discrimination in educational programs receiving Federal funds. The amendment would cover

---

11. * * * At a theoretical level, the problem with sexual harassment is "the unwanted imposition of sexual requirements in the context of unequal power." Catherine MacKinnon, *Sexual Harassment of Working Women* 1 (1979). In an employment context, the actions of a co-worker sometimes may be imputed to an employer through a theory of respondeat superior.

In an educational setting, the power relationship is the one between the educational institution and the student. In the context of two students, however, there is no power relationship, and a theory of respondeat superior has no precedential or logical support. Unwanted sexual advances of fellow students do not carry the same coercive effect or abuse of power as those made by a teacher, employer or co-worker. This is not to say that the behavior does not harm the victim, but only that the analogy is missing a key ingredient—a power relationship between the harasser and the victim. * * *

such crucial aspects as admissions procedures, scholarships, and faculty employment, with limited exceptions." *Id.* * * *

The OCR's interpretation of title IX is consistent with refusing to impose liability for the acts of third parties. The primary interpretation of title IX is found in its implementing regulations. See 34 C.F.R. § 106.31. The entire section is devoted to acts by the recipients themselves.

The most definitive statement by the OCR on sexual harassment focuses on conduct by employees or agents of the recipient. The OCR's Policy Memorandum contains the following definition:

> Sexual harassment consists of verbal or physical conduct of a sexual nature, imposed on the basis of sex, *by an employee or agent of the recipient*, that denies, limits, provides different, or conditions the provision of aid, benefits, services or treatment protected under title IX.

OCR Policy Memorandum from Antonio J. Califa, Director of Litigation, Enforcement, and Policy Service, to Regional Civil Rights Directors (Aug. 31, 1981) (emphasis added). In particular, the agency left unresolved the issue of peer sexual harassment. *Id.* at 10 ("The other unresolved issue relates to a recipient's responsibility for the sexual harassment acts of students against fellow students in the context of the situation in which neither student is in a position of authority, derived from the institution, over the other students.").

The only OCR documents to apply title IX to peer sexual harassment, i.e., recent Letters of Finding, should be accorded little weight. Any weight the letters do have are outweighed by both the implementing regulations and the Policy Memorandum promulgated by the OCR. As a legislative regulation, the implementing regulations found at 34 C.F.R. § 106 are accorded far greater deference than are interpretive regulations such as Letters of Finding. The Policy Memorandum deserves more deference because it represents a deliberate policy statement by the agency and is consistent with past agency interpretations. * * *

The mere existence of sexual harassment does not necessarily constitute sexual discrimination. Both men and women can be the victims or perpetrators of sexual harassment. For example, this circuit has recognized that same-sex sexual harassment is not always sex discrimination under title VII. In the same vein, sexual overtures directed at both sexes, or behavior equally offensive to both males and females, is not sex discrimination.

In the case of peer sexual harassment, a plaintiff must demonstrate that the school district responded to sexual harassment claims differently based on sex. Thus, a school district might violate title IX if it treated sexual harassment of boys more seriously than sexual harassment of girls, or even if it turned a blind eye toward sexual harassment of girls while addressing assaults that harmed boys. As the district court correctly pointed out, however, Rowinsky failed to allege facts to support such a claim. * * *

■ DENNIS, CIRCUIT JUDGE, dissenting.* * *

* * * [T]he *Franklin* Court interpreted Title IX as placing on the school board a duty not to discriminate on the basis of sex, by knowingly failing to take appropriate corrective action when a male teacher has sexually harassed and abused a female high school student and thereby created for her a hostile educational environment. [By explicitly relying on *Meritor*, the leading Title VII case on sexual harassment, *Franklin* imported the Title VII jurisprudence into Title IX, Judge Dennis argued.]

As explained in *Meritor*, as well as antecedent cases and EEOC Guidelines discussed therein, an employer's liability for "hostile environment" sex discrimination generally is based on the employer's failure to take reasonable corrective measures after receiving knowledge that an employee is being subjected to sexual harassment or abuse in the work environment by co-workers (or non-employees over whom the employer has a degree of control or legal responsibility). In other words, employer liability for hostile environment harassment by coworkers and non-employees under Title VII is predicated on the *employer's failure* to act in accordance with its statutory duty not to discriminate in the workplace on the basis of "race, color, religion, sex or national origin" with respect to its "terms, conditions, or privileges of employment," 42 U.S.C. § 2000e–2(a)(1), by requiring an employee to work in an environment permeated with "discriminatory intimidation, ridicule, and insult ... sufficiently severe or pervasive to alter the conditions of the victim's employment and create an abusive working environment.... " *Harris*, 114 S. Ct. at 370 (quoting *Meritor*, 477 U.S. at 65, 67). Consequently, the *Franklin* Court's recognition of this type of claim under Title IX necessarily indicates that a student subjected to severe sexual harassment by other students in the school environment may recover for damages sustained thereby from a federally funded educational institution if its board had knowledge of the harassment and failed to take appropriate corrective action.

[Judge Dennis argued that *Meritor* assumed the responsibility of employers for dealing with sexual harassment by other employees as well as by supervisors, a position explicitly taken by the EEOC's Guidelines which were relied upon by the Supreme Court in *Meritor*. Section 1604.11(d), (e) of the EEOC Guidelines make the employer responsible for sexual harassment by other employees or nonemployees "where the employer knows or should have known of the conduct, unless it can show that it took immediate and appropriate corrective action."] The rule expressed by the Guidelines pertaining to sexual harassment by non-supervisory co-workers has been uniformly applied by the courts. It is not a controversial area; results in each case simply depend on an interpretation of the facts: whether the employer had sufficient notice, investigated properly, disciplined offenders, and so forth. * * *

Apparently underlying the majority's conclusion that summary judgment is appropriate here is the incorrect assumption that, in general, school boards have no duty with respect to students' safety and no power of discipline to control educationally pernicious student conduct. Even if the school board had not accepted federal funds, however, it owes a much higher duty to its students and has far greater powers of control over them than that described in the majority opinion. * * *

NOTE ON TITLE IX AND ATHLETIC PROGRAMS

1. *Participation on Boys' Teams? (No.)* Before 1980 several courts held that qualified girls had the right to try out for boys' teams. Denying a procedural application, Justice Stevens (as circuit Justice), cast doubt on that proposition in *O'Connor v. Board of Educ.*, 449 U.S. 1301 (1980). He worried that "[w]ithout a gender-based classification in competitive contact sports, there would be a substantial risk that boys would dominate the girls' programs." Since *O'Connor*, lower courts have upheld sex segregation in athletics. See Virginia P. Croudace & Steven A. Desmarais, "Where the Boys Are: Can Separate Be Equal in School Sports?," 58 *S. Cal. L. Rev.* 1425 (1985). The Title IX regulations allow separate teams. 45 C.F.R. § 86.41(b). Should this issue be revisited after the VMI decision (Chapter 1, Section 3[A])?

2. *Separate But Equal? (Not Exactly.)* The Title IX regulations not only allow sex segregation, but fail to require sex equity: "Unequal aggregate expenditures for members of each sex or unequal expenditures for male and female teams if a recipient [school] operates or sponsors separate teams will not constitute noncompliance" with Title IX, but can be considered as one of several factors suggesting noncompliance. 45 C.F.R. § 86.41(c). According to Susan K. Cahn, *Coming on Strong: Gender and Sexuality in Twentieth–Century Women's Sport* (1994), female participation in both high school and college athletics has boomed in the last 25 years, *but* programs allocate much more money to male teams, both absolutely and relatively; the ratio of female to male coaches for women's teams has actually fallen from 90% to 50% in recent years; and only 17% of women's programs are headed by women. Would such a regime come close to meeting the requirements for "separate but equal" in the VMI case?

3. *Sexuality and Athletics.* A number of authors have remarked on sports and the articulation of manhood (similar perhaps to Karst's thesis about the military, Chapter 4). Mariah Burton Nelson, *The Stronger Women Get, The More Men Love Football: Sexism and the American Culture of Sports* (1994), argues that sports is not just a major situs of sexism, but the last refuge of sexism and male prerogative. Brian Pronger, *The Arena of Masculinity: Sports, Homosexuality, and the Meaning of Sex* (1990), argues that the locker room is the situs for male homoeroticism and, at the same time, homophobia, the latter being necessary to displace attention from the former. What implications do these theories have for Title IX and high school or college athletics?

PART C. GENDER EQUITY AND THE ISSUE OF SAME-SEX SCHOOLS

There is ample evidence that American education treats female students differently than male students, and to the disadvantage of females.

Whether intentionally, or not, teachers discriminate against girls in the manner in which they encourage students to participate in the learning experience. According to the leading systematic study of the issue, teachers have a tendency to convey curricula in a manner "that will appeal to boys' interests and to select presentation formats in which boys excel or are encouraged more than girls." American Association of University Women, *How Schools Shortchange Girls* 71 (1992) (AAUW Report); see *Achieving Gender Equity in the Classroom and on the Campus: The Next Steps* (AAUW Symposium 1995). For example, boys are asked academically related questions 80% more often than girls in lecture classes.

Curricula tend to focus on the achievements of men—or, at least, they don't focus on the accomplishments of women. According to an AAUW survey of book-length works taught in high school English courses, only one of the ten books most frequently assigned by teachers was authored by a woman, and none were authored by minorities (AAUW Report 62). Such lack of emphasis on women's achievements in school curricula slowly and subtly conveys a message to girls that women's accomplishments in society are not as important as those of men. It is not surprising that girls' self-esteem tends to drop as they go through adolescence, when they are constantly taught, in essence, that they are not as valuable to society as their male peers. In schools that provide vocational education for students who plan not to attend college, women have been "routed into sex-stereotyped course work that leads to dead-end, low-paying jobs" generally focused on "home economics" (*id.* at 42, 43). Although girls tend to get better grades and score higher on standardized tests in high school and in college, scholarships awarded on the basis of grades and standardized test scores are twice as likely to be awarded to boys.

Some academics argue that these problems can be solved by single-sex education.[e] In an all-girls environment, female students cannot be passed over for attention by the teacher, and there is no class of people to whom girls can be made to feel inferior. In such an environment, girls receive all of the attention and encouragement that the teachers can give. There are, however, some serious legal problems with single-sex education which must be addressed.

Title IX only protects against discrimination in admissions policies of "institutions of vocational education, professional education, and graduate higher education, and to public institutions of undergraduate higher education." 20 U.S.C. § 1681(a)(1). Thus public school districts seem free to

---

e. See Deborah Rhode, "Association and Assimilation," 81 *Nw. U.L. Rev.* 106 (1986); Kristin S. Caplice, "The Case for Public Single–Sex Education," 18 *Harv. J.L. & Pub. Pol'y* 227 (1994), as well as older studies discussed in the dissenting opinions by Chief Justice Burger and Justice Powell in *Mississippi Univ. for Women v. Hogan*, 458 U.S. 718 (1982). Cornelius Riordan analyzed data from the Nat'l Center for Educational Stats. and found that girls in single-sex schools score a half-grade above their coeducational counterparts on four academic ability tests, and a full grade higher on science tests. Riordan's and other findings are discussed in Comment, "Inner–City Single–Sex Schools: Educational Reform or Invidious Discrimination?," 105 *Harv. L. Rev.* 1741, 1757 (1992).

establish single-sex schools under Title IX, and the legislative history indicates that Congress excepted elementary and secondary schools from Title IX because of the potential benefits of single-sex education. Of greater concern to proponents of single-sex education may be the Equal Educational Opportunity Act (EEOA) of 1974. While the goal of the act was to limit the use of busing to achieve racially diverse school systems, it includes a congressional finding that "dual school systems" where students assignation is based solely upon "race, color, *sex*, or national origin denies to those students equal protection of the laws guaranteed by the fourteenth amendment." 20 U.S.C. § 1701(a)(2) (emphasis added). But there is no specific proscription against segregation of schools based on sex in the EEOA, even though there are specific prohibitions based on race, color or national origin in the body of the EEOA. 20 U.S.C. § 1703(a).

The leading case is *Vorchheimer v. School Dist.*, 532 F.2d 880, 884–85 (3d. Cir. 1976), *aff'd by an equally divided Court*, 430 U.S. 703 (1977). Philadelphia's school system included single-sex schools for academically advanced students. Susan Vorchheimer applied to Central High School, the all-boys "academic" school, and was denied entry because of her sex. She then filed suit, alleging that her exclusion, based solely on her sex, was a violation of her right to equal protection under the EEOA and the Fourteenth Amendment. The Third Circuit rejected her constitutional argument on the grounds that a school board can maintain single-sex schools provided they are "voluntary and the educational opportunities offered to girls and boys are essentially equal." As to her statutory argument, the court held that the EEOA must be read in light of the busing controversy that led to the law's enactment; hence, the policy statement was meant only to apply to sex segregation for the purpose of preventing interracial mixing (and, one can infer, different-race dating).

Other courts have read the EEOA more broadly. The Fifth Circuit, distinguishing *Vorchheimer*, ruled that the EEOA bans single-sex schools. *United States v. Hinds County School Board* 560 F.2d 619 (5th Cir.1977). The Fifth Circuit distinguished its case, in which an entire district was sex-segregated, from *Vorchheimer*, which involved only two single-sex schools in a predominantly coeducational district. Furthermore, the court's ruling was possibly motivated by evidence that the district was using sex discrimination as a means to an end—racial segregation—in direct conflict with the policy goals of the EEOA, even as noted by the Third Circuit in *Vorchheimer*. Viewed together, *Hinds* and *Vorchheimer* may tolerate the establishment of single-sex schools, provided both single-sex and coeducational alternatives are provided to both girls and boys, so long as single-sex schools are not a smokescreen for racial segregation.

A final problem with single-sex education, if accomplished in public schools, is that it might violate the equal protection clause of the Fourteenth Amendment. Recall that sex-based classifications are subject to heightened scrutiny (Chapter 1, Section 3[A]). Two of the leading sex discrimination precedents involve same-sex colleges. One was *Mississippi University for Women v. Hogan*, 458 U.S. 718 (1982), where the Court struck down a women-only nursing school. Justice O'Connor's opinion for the Court held that the state had made no sufficient showing that a single-sex school was necessary in the field of nursing, where women's opportunities have long been substantial. If anything, limiting a nursing school to women smacked of gender stereotyping (men = doctors, women = nurses), precisely the sort of historical pattern the equal protection clause jurisprudence was supposed to overturn. Chief Justice Burger's dissenting opinion worried that *Hogan* problematized single-sex education that would be truly useful to women in particular. Consider the Court's next word on the subject.

United States v. Virginia

United States Supreme Court, 1996.
___ U.S. ___, 116 S.Ct. 2264, 135 L.Ed.2d 735..

[In an opinion by Justice Ruth Bader Ginsburg, the Supreme Court held that Virginia's maintenance of Virginia Military Institute (VMI) as a same-sex school excluding women was sex discrimination that was not justified by the state's post-hoc rationalization that it contributed to educational diversity. Reread Justice Ginsburg's opinion for the Court, which is excerpted in Chapter 1, Section 3(A). We reproduce here a portion of the dissenting opinion that we edited out of the excerpt in Chapter 1.]

■ JUSTICE SCALIA, dissenting. * * *

Under the constitutional principles announced and applied today, single-sex public education is unconstitutional. By going through the motions of applying a balancing test—asking whether the State has adduced an "exceedingly persuasive justification" for its sex-based classification—the Court creates the illusion that government officials in some future case will have a clear shot at justifying some sort of single-sex public education. Indeed, the Court seeks to create even a greater illusion than that: It purports to have said nothing of relevance to other public schools at all. "We address specifically and only an educational opportunity recognized ... as 'unique'...."

The Supreme Court of the United States does not sit to announce "unique" dispositions. Its principal function is to establish precedent—that is, to set forth principles of law that every court in America must follow. As we said only this Term, we expect both ourselves and lower courts to adhere to the *"rationale* upon which the Court based the results of its earlier decisions." *Seminole Tribe of Fla. v. Florida*, 517 U.S. ___, ___ (1996) (emphasis added). That is the principal reason we publish our opinions.

And the rationale of today's decision is sweeping: for sex-based classifications, a redefinition of intermediate scrutiny that makes it indistinguishable from strict scrutiny. Indeed, the Court indicates that if any program restricted to one sex is "uniqu[e]," it must be opened to members of the opposite sex "who have the will and capacity" to participate in it. I suggest that the single-sex program that will not be capable of being characterized as "unique" is not only unique but nonexistent.

In any event, regardless of whether the Court's rationale leaves some small amount of room for lawyers to argue, it ensures that single-sex public education is functionally dead. The costs of litigating the constitutionality of a single-sex education program, and the risks of ultimately losing that litigation, are simply too high to be embraced by public officials. Any person with standing to challenge any sex-based classification can haul the State into federal court and compel it to establish by evidence (presumably in the form of expert testimony) that there is an "exceedingly persuasive justification" for the classification. Should the courts happen to interpret that vacuous phrase as establishing a standard that is not utterly impossible of achievement, there is considerable risk that whether the standard has been met will not be determined on the basis of the record evidence—indeed, that will necessarily be the approach of any court that seeks to walk the path the Court has trod today. No state official in his right mind will buy such a high-cost, high-risk lawsuit by commencing a single-sex program. The enemies of single-sex education have won; by persuading only seven Justices (five would have been enough) that their view of the world is enshrined in the Constitution, they have effectively imposed that view on all 50 States.

This is especially regrettable because, as the District Court here determined, educational experts in recent years have increasingly come to "suppor[t] [the] view that substantial educational benefits flow from a single-gender environment, be it male or female, *that cannot be replicated in a coeducational setting*." 766 F. Supp., at 1415 (emphasis added). "The evidence in th[is] case," for example, "is virtually uncontradicted" to that effect. *Ibid.* Until quite recently, some public officials have attempted to institute new single-sex programs, at least as experiments. In 1991, for example, the Detroit Board of Education announced a program to establish three boys-only schools for inner-city youth; it was met with a lawsuit, a preliminary injunction was swiftly entered by a District Court that purported to rely on *Hogan*, see *Garrett v. Board of Education of School Dist. of Detroit*, 775 F. Supp. 1004, 1006 (E.D.Mich.1991), and the Detroit Board of Education voted to abandon the litigation and thus abandon the plan. Today's opinion assures that no such experiment will be tried again.

There are few extant single-sex public educational programs. The potential of today's decision for widespread disruption of existing institutions lies in its application to private single-sex education. Government support is immensely important to private educational institutions. Mary Baldwin College—which designed and runs VWIL—notes that private institutions of higher education in the 1990–1991 school year derived approximately 19 percent of their budgets from federal, state, and local government funds, not including financial aid to students. Charitable status under the tax laws is also highly significant for private educational institutions, and it is certainly not beyond the Court that rendered today's decision to hold that a donation to a single-sex college should be deemed contrary to public policy and therefore not deductible if the college discriminates on the basis of sex. See also *Bob Jones Univ. v. United States*, 461 U.S. 574 (1983). * * *

NOTE ON THE IMPACT ON THE VMI CASE ON THE LEGALITY OF SAME–SEX EDUCATIONAL INSTITUTIONS

1. *Are Public All–Male Educational Institutions Unconstitutional?* The only public college restricted to men, apart from VMI, was The Citadel, in South Carolina. Ironically, The Citadel litigated the sex discrimination issue throughout the 1990s and was ordered to admit Shannon Faulkner in 1995; after the exacting regimen of the first week, and the pressure caused by intense publicity, Faulkner withdrew and another plaintiff came forth. Days after the VMI decision, The Citadel announced that it would follow the "law of the land" and open its admissions to women; women enrolled during the fall of 1996. (VMI fell into line several months later.) Two women dropped out after the first semester, however; they alleged severe sexual harassment by male students, including setting their clothing on fire, and timid regulatory efforts by The Citadel to control this unusually violent "hazing."

Both VMI and The Citadel were freighted with nineteenth century origins for their men-only admissions policies, and the six Justices who joined Justice Ginsburg's opinion relied heavily on that background in traditional sex stereotypes. Is Justice Scalia right that the state is precluded now from establishing new colleges that are limited to the same sex? What if Virginia set up two new colleges—one for women and one for men—and gave them equal endowments and other state support? Are you as confident as Justice Scalia that such a set-up would be unconstitutional?

Consider also the Michigan decision striking down public secondary schools for inner-city boys. In 1991 the Board of Education of the City of Detroit planned to open three male "academies" to address the problems facing male inner-city youths—specifically high unemployment, drop-out, and homicide rates among urban males. These "academies" were to have, among other things, a specialized curriculum including a class called "Rites of Passage," an Afrocentric (pluralistic) curriculum, an emphasis on male responsibility, mentor programs, Saturday classes, individualized counseling, and extended classroom hours. Shawn Garrett, the father of a four year old daughter, Crystal, sued on her behalf on the grounds that the all-male schools violated Title IX, the EEOA, and the equal protection clause. In *Garrett v. Board of Education*, 775 F.Supp. 1004, 1006 (E.D.Mich.1991), the court granted a preliminary injunction against the opening of the academies. Although the state's objective of helping to improve chances for economic and literal survival of inner-city males was a valid state interest, the court found that the district failed to prove, or demonstrate in any way at all, that the problems faced by young inner-city males was at all related to the coeducational environment, or how women's absence form the classroom would improve their lot. Furthermore, the Court found that "the gender specific data presented * * * ignores the fact that all children in the Detroit public schools face significant obstacles to success." Even the school board acknowledged an "equally urgent and unique crisis facing" girls.

2. *Are Public All–Female Educational Institutions Unconstitutional?* Recall the gender equity discussion above. If the state shows that girls are disadvantaged by required coeducation and can learn more productively in single-sex schools, with equal schools for boys, can the state justify girls-only schools? In other words, is addressing gender equity the sort of "extremely persuasive" justification Justice Ginsburg would accept under the VMI decision? Would it matter that such schools were not compulsory (i.e., parents would have to apply to send their daughters to them)? For an early (pre-*Hogan*) decision, see *Williams v. McNair*, 316 F.Supp. 134 (D.S.C.1970). After the VMI decision, New York City announced that it was opening a girls-only school. The school did open in the fall of 1996. Was Justice Scalia right that Justice Ginsburg's opinion "assure[d] that no such experiment [in public same-sex education] will be tried again"? Is the New York experiment likely to be upheld? What would the city have to show to meet the VMI standard?

3. *Are Private Single–Sex Educational Institutions Doomed?* Assume that Justice Scalia is right that public same-sex educational institutions are unconstitutional. If so, would he also be right in saying that private same-sex schools are also doomed, because such colleges ought to lose various federal entitlements, including their income tax exemption as charitable or educational institutions (Internal Revenue Code § 501[c]). The Court ignored this charge, and the United States denied that this would happen, but the Court in *Bob Jones* held that private schools discriminating on the basis of race could not claim § 501(c) tax exemptions because they were not "charitable." If elimination of sex discrimination now has an importance similar to the elimination of race discrimination, isn't Justice Scalia right? Cf. *Norwood v. Harrison*, 413 U.S. 455 (1973), where the Court held it "axiomatic that a state may not induce, encourage or promote private persons to accomplish what it is constitutionally forbidden to accomplish," namely, discrimination on the basis of race in education.

Even if sex discrimination now assumes the same rank as race discrimination, an issue the VMI case neither addresses nor resolves, *Bob Jones* might still be distinguished in the following way. As Justice Scalia himself would be quick to realize, § 501(c) gives tax exemptions, without caveat, to "educational" as well as "charitable" institutions. Hence its plain language did not lend itself to the Court's interpretation that an "uncharitable" but clearly "educational" institution could not take advantage of the benefit. Chief Justice Burger's labored opinion for a near-unanimous Court emphasized the strong public policies against racial discrimination, but the laws and constitutional provisions he pointed to did not clearly render illegal the race discrimination of a private college like Bob Jones. More persuasive is the fact, neglected in the opinion, that 42 U.S.C. § 1981 (as interpreted) makes it illegal for a private college to discriminate on the basis of race; enacted during Reconstruction to address problems faced by the freed slaves, § 1981 does not apply to discrimination on the basis of sex. If one believed (as the Court has) that the federal tax code should not be interpreted to subsidize illegal conduct, one might deny race-discriminating schools tax benefits because their conduct is flatly illegal, even while allowing sex-discriminating schools tax benefits, so long as they do not violate a specific statutory or constitutional requirement.

Perhaps a better argument for Justice Scalia's charge would rest upon Title IX. A private college accepting federal financial assistance in any of its programs is covered by Title IX for all its programs. See The Civil Rights Restoration Act of 1987, 42 U.S.C. § 1687(2)(A), overriding *Grove City College v. Bell*, 465 U.S. 555 (1984). Because it is exceedingly hard to operate a college without federal funds, Title IX would be a more certain incentive for private colleges to abandon single-sex status (assuming Justice Scalia is right that the policy is not otherwise justifiable under the criteria of the VMI case). Recall that Title IX does not apply to admissions policies of primary and secondary schools, 20 U.S.C. § 1681(a)(1).

LEGAL ISSUES ARISING OUT OF PUBLIC SEX EDUCATION

A generation ago, the big debate (and often a ferocious one) was whether it was appropriate for public schools to teach sex education. An ancillary issue was whether disapproving parents could get their children excused from a sex education program. Although cases held that the state could require sex education for children over their parents' objections, school districts tended to allow parents to opt out, *e.g., Citizens for Parental Rights v. San Mateo County Bd. of Educ.*, 124 Cal.Rptr. 68 (Cal.App.1975), *appeal dismissed*, 425 U.S. 908 (1976), and sex education courses tended to be euphemistic "health and anatomy" courses, with little explicit instruction about sex.

The situation has changed dramatically, in large part because most teenagers are now sexually active and because the dangers of sexual experimentation are higher than before due to AIDS. According to the National Abortion Rights Action League (NARAL), *Sexuality Education in America: A State-by-State Review* v (Sept. 1995), 22 states[a] and the District of Columbia require schools to provide both sex and AIDS education. An additional 15 states[b] require schools to provide AIDS education. Although 13 states do not require any kind of sex education,[c] those states do not forbid it either; some of them (such as Louisiana, explored below) regulate the sex education chosen by local school boards. These 1995 figures will surely change, as sex education remains an area of strong legislative interest.

In short, some kind of sex education is now part of the American agenda. The key issue now is: What are the schools teaching? This has been a focus of state law, and the NARAL Review gives this overview, as of 1995:

- Twenty-six states require the schools to emphasize the importance of abstinence as the best method of birth control and avoidance of sexually transmitted diseases (especially AIDS). Only 14 of those 26

---

a. Alabama, Arkansas, Delaware, Florida, Georgia, Illinois, Iowa, Kansas, Maryland, Minnesota, Nevada, New Jersey, New Mexico, North Carolina, Rhode Island, South Carolina, Tennessee, Texas, Utah, Vermont, Virginia, West Virginia.

b. Arizona, California, Connecticut, Idaho, Indiana, Mississippi, Missouri, New Hampshire, New York, Ohio, Oklahoma, Oregon, Pennsylvania, Washington, Wisconsin.

c. Alaska, Colorado, Hawaii, Kentucky, Louisiana, Maine, Maryland, Massachusetts, Montana, Nebraska, North Dakota, South Dakota, Wyoming.

states[d] also require schools to provide useful information about contraception and pregnancy.

- Five states[e] prohibit discussion of abortion. One state (Vermont) and the District of Columbia require schools to instruct on abortion.

- At least 19 states[f] prohibit or discourage school health programs from making contraceptives available to students.

- Eight states[g] require or recommend schools to teach that homosexuality is not an acceptable "lifestyle" or that homosexual conduct is an offense under state law. One state (Rhode Island) requires schools to teach respect for others, regardless of sexual orientation.

- Twenty-six states[h] and the District of Columbia require that schools provide family life instruction as a component of sexuality education.

As these figures suggest, the contest is now over what sex education courses will teach students. Roughly speaking, the polar approaches are an approach that anchors the student on sexual abstinence until heterosexual marriage, on the one hand, and an approach that provides the student with neutral or sympathetic information about contraception, abortion, and homosexuality, on the other.

Is constitutional or statutory law relevant to these essentially political choices? Surprisingly, the law is mighty relevant. Consider these issues: students' right not to be exposed to inaccurate material (Part A); parental rights to control over materials, especially condoms, made available to their children (Part B); and state and local policies against "promoting" or even "normalizing" homosexuality in educational materials and instruction (Part C).

PART A.   STUDENTS' RIGHTS TO SEXUALITY INSTRUCTION THAT IS FACTUALLY ACCURATE

Recall the debate in *Pico*. If the Brennan plurality opinion is right, students might have a constitutional "right to know" accurate information about sexuality. Even if the Burger dissenting opinion correctly states the law, schools might have a constitutional obligation to present accurate information about sexuality if they undertake sex education at all. This is

d. Arizona, California, Delaware, Georgia, Illinois, North Carolina, Oklahoma, Oregon, Rhode Island, South Carolina, Tennessee, Vermont, Virginia, Washington.

e. Connecticut, Illinois, Louisiana, Michigan, South Carolina.

f. Arizona, Delaware, Georgia, Hawaii, Iowa, Kentucky, Louisiana, Maryland, Michigan, Minnesota, Mississippi, Missouri, North Carolina, North Dakota, Rhode Island, South Carolina, Texas, Utah, Wisconsin.

g. Alabama, Arizona, Georgia, Louisiana, North Carolina, South Carolina, Texas, Virginia.

h. Alabama, Arizona, California, Connecticut, Delaware, Florida, Georgia, Illinois, Indiana, Iowa, Louisiana, Maryland, Minnesota, Nevada, New Jersey, New Mexico, North Carolina, Oregon, Rhode Island, South Carolina, Tennessee, Texas, Utah, Vermont, Virginia, West Virginia.

the approach taken by many state laws. Some allow local school boards wide latitude as to teaching sex education but impose minimum requirements if localities do offer courses. Consider the Alabama statute.

Alabama Statutes § 16–40A–2, Minimum Contents to Be Included in Sex Education Program or Curriculum

(Added 1992).

(a) Any program or curriculum in the public schools in Alabama that includes sex education or the human reproductive process shall, as a minimum, include and emphasize the following:

(1) Abstinence from sexual intercourse is the only completely effective protection against unwanted pregnancy, sexually transmitted diseases, and acquired immune deficiency syndrome (AIDS) when transmitted sexually.

(2) Abstinence from sexual intercourse outside of lawful marriage is the expected social standard for unmarried school-age persons.

(b) Course materials and instruction that relate to sexual education or sexually transmitted diseases should be age-appropriate.

(c) Course materials and instruction that relate to sexual education or sexually transmitted diseases should include all of the following elements:

(1) An emphasis on sexual abstinence as the only completely reliable method of avoiding unwanted teenage pregnancy and sexually transmitted diseases.

(2) An emphasis on the importance of self-control and ethical conduct pertaining to sexual behavior.

(3) Statistics based on the latest medical information that indicate the degree of reliability and unreliability of various forms of contraception, while also emphasizing the increase in protection against pregnancy and protection against sexually transmitted diseases, including HIV and AIDS infection, which is afforded by the use of various contraceptive measures.

(4) Information concerning the laws relating to the financial responsibilities associated with pregnancy, childbirth, and child rearing.

(5) Information concerning the laws prohibiting sexual abuse, the need to report such abuse, and the legal options available to victims of sexual abuse.

(6) Information on how to cope with and rebuff unwanted physical and verbal sexual exploitation by other persons.

(7) Psychologically sound methods of resisting unwanted peer pressure.

(8) An emphasis, in a factual manner and from a public health perspective, that homosexuality is not a lifestyle acceptable to the

general public and that homosexual conduct is a criminal offense under the laws of the state.

(9) Comprehensive instruction in parenting skills and responsibilities, including the responsibility to pay child support by non-custodial parents, the penalties for non-payment of child support, and the legal and ethical responsibilities of child care and child rearing.

PROBLEM 7–4

RECONCILING ALABAMA'S EDUCATION DIRECTIVES AND STUDENTS' NEED TO KNOW ABOUT SEXUALITY

The Alabama Department of Education is charged with implementing the foregoing law. Its Health Education Bulletin No. 25 (1988) provides a grade-by-grade review of what schools have to do under the statute. In sixth and seventh grades, for example, schools must teach basic facts about physical and psychological changes in adolescents as they pass through puberty, the ways AIDS and other sexually transmitted diseases are spread and modes of prevention, and the need for family planning and the usefulness of resisting peer pressure to have sex too early. High school health instruction is supposed to provide detailed information about sexually transmitted diseases, individual responsibility for setting limits during dates, and the superiority of family and love to pornography and promiscuity in the development of an individual's sexuality. (See NARAL Review 2–3.) Consider the following hypothetical applications of the Alabama statute and the Board's guidelines. You are the state lawyer advising the Board as to its legal obligation.

(A) Abortion. The Board is asked to develop guidelines for teachers to respond to student questions about abortion. The Board is inclined to forbid teachers from talking about abortion altogether. Is that legal? Cf. *Rust v. Sullivan* (excerpted in Chapter 6, Section 3[B]).

(B) Contraceptives. Some legislators have learned that contraceptives are being distributed by school health officials in some high schools; those legislators want the Board to adopt a rule prohibiting school personnel from distributing contraceptives and to require mandatory dismissal of personnel who violate such a rule. The Board asks you whether it has authority to adopt such a rule.

(C) The Immorality of Premarital Sex. At one high school, the sex education class had a one-hour session in which the teacher brought in a woman who told the class that she had sex and an abortion before she was married and that these experiences "almost ruined my life." The woman witnessed before the students about the spiritual value of sex within marriage and the "sinfulness" of sex outside of marriage. The teacher assigned *Sex Respect* as the text for the class; those materials emphasize the "guilt" and psychological as well as physical harm that come from having premarital sex. The school district is uncertain whether this teacher's conduct of the sex education class is consistent with Alabama law and asks the Board for its opinion. How would you advise? Consider this query

under Louisiana law, which is summarized and applied to *Sex Respect* in the next case.

Bettye Coleman et al. v. Caddo Parish School Board et al.

Court of Appeal of Louisiana, Second Circuit, 1994.
635 So.2d 1238.

■ MARVIN, CHIEF JUDGE. * * *

[Bettye Coleman and other concerned parents sued the Caddo Parish School Board for adopting *Sex Respect: The Option of True Sexual Freedom*, for use in the 7th and 8th grades, and *Facing Reality: A New Approach to the Real World of Today's Teen*, for use in the 10th grade. The parents claimed that the curricula violated Louisiana Revised Code § 17:281, which provides that public elementary and secondary schools may, but are not required to, offer sex education instruction in grades seven and higher, provided the instruction is offered as part of an existing course such as biology, science, physical hygiene or physical education. The statute further provides:

> A(2). It is the intent of the legislature that, for the purposes of this Section, "sex education" shall mean the dissemination of factual biological or pathological information that is related to the human reproduction system and may include the study of sexually transmitted disease, pregnancy, childbirth, puberty, menstruation, and menopause, as well as the dissemination of factual information about parental responsibilities under the child support laws of the state. However, the dissemination of factual information about parental responsibilities under the child support laws of the state may be offered only in grade nine or above. It is the intent of the legislature that "sex education" shall not include religious beliefs, practices in human sexuality, nor the subjective moral and ethical judgments of the instructor or other persons. Students shall not be tested, quizzed, or surveyed about their personal or family beliefs or practices in sex, morality, or religion.

> A(3). * * * The major emphasis of any sex education instruction offered in the public schools of the state shall be to encourage sexual abstinence between unmarried persons. * * *

> F.   No program offering sex education instruction shall in any way counsel or advocate abortion.

The parents claimed that *Sex Respect* (a curriculum promulgated by traditionalist groups) contained factually inaccurate information and pressed a sectarian viewpoint onto the students, in violation of the statute. The Board responded that the curriculum's emphasis on abstinence saved it from the alleged improprieties. The Board relied on a recent amendment to the statute, Acts 1993, No. 921, which moved the statement about emphasizing abstinence before marriage from subsection A(3) to subsection A(4), and lengthened the statement to read:

A(4). The major emphasis of any sex education instruction offered in the public schools of this state shall be to encourage sexual abstinence between unmarried persons and any such instruction shall:

(a) Emphasize abstinence from sexual activity outside of marriage as the expected standard for all school-age children.

(b) Emphasize that abstinence from sexual activity is a way to avoid unwanted pregnancy, sexually transmitted diseases, including acquired immune deficiency syndrome, and other associated health problems.

(c) Emphasize that each student has the power to control personal behavior and to [sic] encourage students to base action on reasoning, self-esteem, and respect for others.]

Several of the passages that plaintiffs challenged as including religious beliefs or subjective moral and ethical judgments were found not to violate the statute. Examples are:

* * * Natural law is the basis of good health, as has been discovered in many other areas of modern medicine. *Sex Respect* uses the natural law of respect for one another and the power of our human sexuality to address the health problems we face today, without teaching absolute morals.

For many American families, the most abiding reasons in the struggle to practice self-mastery are religious ones. It is very important that you, as a parent, pass on your religious beliefs to your teen. They may choose to reject some of them. They may choose to embrace them. As part of their heritage, though, it could be said they have a right to be familiar with them. Remember, others will not be shy about proselytizing your teen.

The trial court found that the first passage "does not clearly include religious beliefs or subjective moral judgment. To conclude otherwise would be to read more into the passage than is present." About the second passage, the court said, "Because of the generality of these [statements], it cannot be said that they include religious beliefs or subjective moral judgments."

The trial court's analysis thus allows statements encouraging individual behavior choices based on reasoning, self-esteem and respect for others to remain in the curricula, provided the statements do not include religious beliefs or subjective moral and ethical judgments. The trial court's analysis is correct, under either the pre- or post–1993 wording of the statute. * * *

Religious Beliefs or Subjective Moral and Ethical Judgments

[The first set of challenged statements were alleged by plaintiffs to be animated by "religious beliefs," contrary to A(2) of the statute. The trial court upheld the use of general statements such as "As human beings, we gain confidence by doing what is right according to the laws of nature." These findings were sustained on appeal. The trial court found other statements in the teaching materials to violate the statute's prohibition, such as: "Sexual intercourse is designed ... to renew marriage vows and bind a couple that is united for life."]

The parent/teacher guide to *Facing Reality* candidly states, "Some of the main questions raised by this book are moral ones," and asks, "Is it moral for your sons and daughters to engage in sexual activity before marriage?" These passages clearly show the intent of the curriculum to present its message in moral terms. The Board does not deny that this is the intent of both curricula, but broadly urges that the moral judgments expressed are objective, rather than subjective, and are therefore not prohibited by the statute. Even though we may agree with the moral standard that is stated, neither our agreement nor the record allows us or the trial court to declare a "generally accepted objective moral standard about teenage sex." The Board's Dr. Carney said there is none. Plaintiffs' experts effectively agreed. The trial court's findings that the challenged passages stating and soliciting the moral aspects of premarital sex, explicitly or implicitly, violate the statute, are not clearly wrong. * * *

The trial court's findings that the passages [in *Sex Respect*] which define sexual intercourse as an action designed to be performed only by married persons include religious beliefs or subjective moral and ethical judgments are also not clearly wrong. While many of us in the current population may believe this to be true, whether on religious, moral or ethical grounds, we must recognize the expert testimony accepted below that some people do not. * * *

Many of the passages challenged by plaintiffs, as indicated, refer to the "spiritual" aspects of sexuality. Plaintiffs' religious and theological expert, Rabbi Matuson, opined that these passages include religious beliefs, while the Board's expert in religious and secular ethics, Dr. Carney, opined that most passages use the terms "spiritual" or "spiritually" in a secular context and that a few use the terms with a religious meaning but in a way appropriate for a secular text. Before discussing the trial court's assessment of the expert testimony, we review the definitions of the terms "spiritual" and "spiritually" that appear in *Sex Respect*.

Sex Respect asks students, "What does it mean to be mature? Emotionally, Mentally, Socially, Spiritually." The suggested answer in the teacher's guide, with respect to *spiritual maturity*, is:

> Accepting things you can't change but willing to work hard to change what you can, putting others first, taking time to consider the deeper meaning of life, setting goals that put faith in a greater power or principle than oneself.

The student text then asks, "What can you do to help yourself mature in each way? Emotionally, Mentally, Socially, Spiritually." The suggested answer for achieving spiritual maturity is:

> Attend worship services regularly, seek out friends who have strong moral values, develop a love for other people and a hunger for truth.

Rabbi Matuson opined that these passages, by including references to "faith in a greater power or principle than oneself" and regularly attending "worship services," clearly include religious beliefs and practices as an integral part of "spiritual maturity." Rabbi Matuson opined that a similar meaning of the word "spiritual" was intended in other parts of *Sex Respect*, such as those referring to *spiritual values* as an important part of sexuality and to the "spiritual parts of our sexuality." Rabbi Matuson attributed the same meaning to the term "spiritual" in *Facing Reality*, which refers to the "spiritual consequences" of promiscuity, although that curriculum does not expressly define spiritual consequences.

Dr. Carney conceded that the passage in *Sex Respect* that refers to attending worship services regularly "has a religious function," but opined that the passage was appropriate for a secular text because the conduct is merely suggested for, but not required of, students, and is one of many examples of conduct that will foster maturity of the four types listed. * * *

The experts also gave conflicting testimony about this passage in *Sex Respect*:

> Well, no one can deny that nature is making some kind of a comment on sexual behavior through the AIDS and herpes epidemics.

Rabbi Matuson opined that the word "nature" was used as a substitute for the word "God," explaining that, in his view, "Nature makes no comment besides what God commands it to do." Dr. Carney opined that the statement is a metaphorical rather than a literal description of nature sending a message and said, "It can do that with regard to sexual disease without ... requiring the belief that this is a surrogate for God."* * *

[The trial court credited Rabbi Matuson's explanation and found that the quoted passages violated the statute's stricture against religious imposition. The trial court also ruled that the following comments in the parent-teacher guide to *Facing Reality* violated the statute:

> The teacher should not be afraid to address the subject of homosexuality when it arises. Students should be directed to the choice that best serves the individual and the community. This is clearly the choice to abstain from homosexual activity, just as they should abstain from heterosexual activity.

> Discussions of the compassion and respect due to all persons should certainly include those who identify themselves as homosexual. To subjectively judge any individual is certainly not within the purview of any teacher. To objectively discuss the wisdom of certain choices is. A promiscuous lifestyle is an unhealthy lifestyle, regardless of the sex of one's partners.]

The court concluded that any discussion about whether a student's choice regarding sexual orientation "best serves the individual and the community" or is "wise" would necessarily include religious beliefs or subjective moral and ethical judgments.

The Board contends the passages simply direct teachers to instruct students that they should abstain from homosexual activity, just as they should abstain from heterosexual activity, if the subject of homosexuality arises. The Board claims the passages do not purport to allow or encourage religious, moral or ethical judgments about a student's sexual orientation.

We agree that a fair reading of the passages supports the Board's interpretation rather than the trial court's. The passages state, implicitly or explicitly, that the "choice" to be discussed with students is abstinence, *not* sexual orientation. The promotion of abstinence in the second passage is based solely on health considerations. Neither passage purports to make religious, moral or ethical statements or judgments about homosexuality or, for that matter, about abstinence. * * *

Counseling Abortion * * *

The litigants agree that the curricula do not recommend abortion. Plaintiffs cite, as violative of the statute, passages in *Sex Respect* which list numerous health risks of abortion, tout the advantages of adoption with only passing reference to disadvantages, and direct teachers to "[h]ave a speaker from Birthright or some other pro-life organization come and talk about the risks of abortion and the benefits of adoption."

Plaintiffs' expert psychiatrist, Dr. Seiden, defined the term "counsel" [in § 281(F)'s requirement that curricula cannot "counsel" abortion] as "therapeutic advice giving," either for or against something, and opined that these passages violate the statute by giving advice on the subject of abortion.

Dr. Coulson, the Board's clinical psychologist, agreed that the term "counsel" is sometimes used to mean "therapeutic advice giving," as when a doctor counsels someone about a particular problem, but opined that that meaning has no application in a classroom setting. Dr. Coulson testified that the term "counsel," when used in the context of counseling something rather than someone, means to favorably recommend the thing. Dr. Coulson distinguished "counseling" a subject, which, in his view, means only to speak in favor of it, from "counseling on" a subject, which may including speaking either for or against it. He opined that the challenged passages do not "counsel abortion" because they speak against it rather than in favor of it. * * *

[The trial court accepted the parents' understanding of counseling and declared the quoted passages contrary to the statute's prohibition of counseling abortion. The court of appeal disagreed and reinstated those passages. The court of appeal agreed with the trial court that other passages from *Sex Respect* were inappropriate for injecting religious beliefs into instruction: one asking "Does she get an abortion to kill the baby?" and another referring to abortion as "the killing of a grandchild."]

Factually Inaccurate Information * * *

* * * Examples of passages deemed facially inaccurate by the experts and the trial court are:

Teens with a low opinion of themselves are more likely than other teens to get involved in pre-marital sex.

Saving sex until marriage, by contributing to our emotional growth, will help us become better parents when we are married.

There's no way to have pre-marital sex without hurting someone.

A male can experience complete sexual release with a woman he doesn't even like, whereas a woman usually can't do so unless she loves her partner. * * *

The court also found effectively inaccurate and excluded a passage in *Sex Respect* which states that anyone who has an abortion "will feel guilt, depression, and anxiety . . . in the long run" and lists numerous physical risks of abortion, such as "damage to . . . reproductive organs, [h]eavy loss of blood, infection, . . . increased risk of miscarriage or birth complications with future pregnancies . . . [and possibly] infertility." Drs. Bocchini and Seiden opined that the statement of the psychological risks of abortion is inaccurate for describing these risks as inevitable, when in fact many women who have abortions do not experience guilt, depression or anxiety. These experts agreed that some women may experience one or more of the physical risks listed, but noted that the curriculum emphasizes the negative aspects of abortion without discussing the physical risks of carrying a child to term. Dr. Otterson described the passage as "blatantly incorrect."

Two passages that were stricken for including religious beliefs or subjective moral and ethical judgments were also found to be factually inaccurate. They state:

As the AIDS plague and herpes are proving, faithful marital relations are good not only for society's moral tone, but for the individual's health too.

Well, no one can deny that nature is making some kind of a comment on sexual behavior through the AIDS and herpes epidemics.

The trial court accepted the testimony of Drs. Bocchini and Seiden that AIDS and herpes are diseases resulting from contact with viruses, which may be transmitted through means other than sexual contact, and that, from a medical standpoint, the development of a disease is not considered to be a "comment" on individual behavior or on society's moral tone. The trial court found these passages to be factually inaccurate, concluding they have "no redeeming value in educating students about human reproduction or the transmission of sexually communicable diseases." * * * [The Board maintained that some of the passages were not inaccurate, while others were only partially inaccurate; the Board objected that the courts should defer to its judgment as to what is accurate. The court of appeals found the trial court's findings, based upon an examination of the expert testimony, acceptable.]

[The court of appeals reversed the trial court's holding the Board and certain individuals in contempt for assertedly disrespecting the court after it had issued its opinion.]

■ [JUDGE HIGHTOWER concurred in the court's reversal of the trial court in all respects and dissented from the court's affirming the trial court in other respects.]

PART B.   AIDS EDUCATION[i]

1.   THE CASE FOR AIDS EDUCATION

AIDS, a breakdown of the body's immune system, is associated with the HIV virus. Unlike the cold or flu virus, deadly HIV is not easily spread from one human to another; so far as we know in 1997, it is only spread through the exchange of an infected person's bodily fluid into another person, usually directly into the bloodstream. The two main means of HIV transmission are fluid exchange into a porous part of the body (usually rectum or vagina, apparently also the mouth) during sexual intercourse, and sharing needles by intravenous drug users. Because it is so deadly and because it is essentially preventable, HIV transmission is a classic subject for public education to tackle.

Evidence from the mid–1980s suggests that adolescents in large cities knew that HIV could be transmitted through sexual intercourse, but large numbers of teenagers (including sexually active ones) were unaware that HIV could also be transmitted through needle-sharing, that condoms could lower the risk of transmission, and that AIDS could not be cured. By 1990–91, adolescents in big cities were much more knowledgeable, in part because of government programs to reach out to adolescents.[j] Some adolescent subgroups remain ill-informed of basic facts about AIDS. Adolescents in the African–American and Latino communities are often less well informed than their counterparts in other communities, in part because of fewer educational opportunities and in part because these adolescents consider AIDS a "white gay male plague" that has little relevance to them.[k]

One problem, therefore, is simply imparting "facts" about HIV and AIDS to students. Another but related problem is to address the way teenagers, in particular, process information. Human decisionmaking generally is subject to several documented, and irrational, biases. Typical errors are that people give too much weight to vivid information which is presented dramatically to them or otherwise triggers an emotional re-

---

i. This Note is adapted from William N. Eskridge, Jr. & Brian D. Weimer, "The Economics Epidemic in an AIDS Perspective," 61 *U. Chi. L. Rev.* 733 (1994) (review essay).

j. After 1986 the Surgeon General insisted upon a media campaign to educate adolescents, and more than 30 states passed statutes requiring HIV education in their school systems; this effort at education paid off with greater teenager knowledge about the means of HIV transmission and its consequences. See Ralph Hingson & Lee Strunin, "Monitoring Adolescents' Response to the AIDS Epidemic: Changes in Knowledge, Attitudes, Beliefs and Behaviors," in *Adolescents and AIDS* 17, 18–21.

k. See Ralph DiClemente et al., "Minorities and AIDS: Knowledge, Attitudes and Misconceptions Among Black and Latino Adolescents," 78 *Am. J. Pub. Health* 55 (1988).

sponse, and that people overgeneralize from unrepresentative samples.[1] These biases affect people's views about HIV infection. Some people are overcautious, because they have been scared by AIDS stories. Other people have been undercautious. Adolescents in particular are prone to biases of undercaution.[m] Because of the long incubation period for HIV infection to develop into AIDS, adolescents tend not to know other adolescents who have symptoms associated with AIDS, and that contributes to their erroneous belief that their uncondomed sex and drug use with one another do not place them at risk. Overgeneralizing that AIDS is an older persons' disease is a frequent rationale for unsafe sex by the young.[n]

A third problem that education might address is cultural: the scripts that people follow in their sexual and other interactions. Although many experts believe that the incidence of new HIV infections has declined in recent years, virtually everyone agrees that new infections continue at an unacceptable rate, especially among young people, and perhaps especially young women. Some experts believe that in 1992 heterosexual transmission of HIV became the leading cause of the disease in women, overtaking first place from needle-sharing during intravenous drug use.[o] Additionally, there is substantial evidence of "relapses" into unsafe sex by young gay and bisexual men, as well as by adolescent heterosexuals.[p] These alarming statistics suggest that even with knowledge about the disease and a properly functioning brain, many adolescents are engaging in risky conduct.

2. EDUCATIONAL THEORY

Most of the AIDS literature starts with or focuses on the health belief model of decisionmaking.[q] The health belief model postulates that per-

l. See *Judgment Under Uncertainty: Heuristics and Biases* (Daniel Kahneman et al. eds. 1982); Richard E. Nisbett & Leon Ross, *Human Inferences: Strategies and Shortcomings of Social Judgment* (1980).

m. See Susan D. Cochran et al., "Sexually Transmitted Diseases and Acquired Immunodeficiency Syndrome (AIDS)," 17 *Sexually Transmitted Diseases* 80 (1990); see also Marshall H. Becker, "AIDS and Behavioral Change to Reduce Risk: A Review," 78 *Am. J. Pub. Health* 394 (1988).

n. See Robert B. Hays et al., "High HIV Risk–Taking Among Young Gay Men," 4 *AIDS* 901 (1990).

o. Carole A. Campbell, "Women and AIDS," 30 *Soc. Sci. Med.* 407 (1990); Olga A. Grinstead et al., "Sexual Risk for HIV Infection Among Women in High–Risk Cities," 25 *Family Planning Perspectives* 252 (1993); Lisa Krieger, "HIV Rates for Blacks, Women, and Young Rising," *San Francisco Examiner*, Dec. 13, 1993.

p. See David E. Kanouse et al., *AIDS-Related Knowledge, Attitudes, Beliefs, and Behaviors in Los Angeles County* 18–31 (Rand 1991); S.M. Adib et al., "Relapse in Sexual Behaviour Among Homosexual Men: A 2–Year Follow–Up from the Chicago MACS/CCS," 5 *AIDS* 757 (1992); Jane McCusker et al., "Maintenance of Behavioral Change in a Cohort of Homosexually Active Men," 6 *AIDS* 861 (1992); Michael C. Samuel et al., "Changes in Sexual Practices over 5 Years of Follow–Up among Heterosexual Men in San Francisco," 4 *J. AIDS* 896 (1991); Robert Stall et al., "Relapse from Safer Sex: The Next Challenge for AIDS Prevention Efforts," 3 *AIDS* 1181 (1990).

q. Set forth in Marshall H. Becker, ed., *The Health Belief Model and Personal Health Behavior*, in 2 *Health Educ. Monographs* 455 (1974) (special issue), and reviewed in Nancy K. Janz & Marshall H. Becker, "The Health Belief Model: A Decade Later," 11 *Health*

ceived high susceptibility to a disease, with severe consequences if infected and a belief in the efficacy of proposed preventive behavior, will induce people to change their behavior. The health belief model posits self-interested individuals performing cost-benefit analyses and altering their conduct in response to an infectious disease. This would seem to make sense: just as a rational human being will jump to the side to avoid an oncoming car, so one would expect such a human to cease behavior exposing her or him to a painful and early death. The implications for AIDS education are easy: teach students the facts and consequences, and let them internalize the data to mold or change their conduct.

The model has been empirically tested in connection with decisions to engage in HIV-risky activities, mainly condomless sex. A large majority of the empirical studies have found that knowledge about HIV risk and its consequences has a surprisingly low effect on condom use[r] or has an explanatory power for condom use that is less robust than the power of two other theories of decisionmaking.[s] One is a conflict model of decisionmaking, which posits that people's decisions are influenced by the level or type of stress created by a new situation.[t] New health threats create stress for individuals, who seek to reduce the stress through ameliorative strategies. This is consistent with the health belief model, but unlike that model the conflict model further posits that a high degree of stress (like the threat of AIDS) can trigger defense mechanisms such as denial of the risk, shifting responsibility for decision to someone else, and/or hypervigilance, in which the individual makes the most convenient choice.

Educ. Q. 1 (1984). The AIDS Risk Reduction Model developed in Joseph A. Catania et al., "The AIDS Risk Reduction Model (ARRM): A Model for Predicting High Risk Sexual Behavior," 17 *Health Educ.* 27 (1990) is analytically drawn from the health belief model. For further applications of this or related models to HIV infective choices, see also Tomas J. Philipson & Richard A. Posner, *Public Choices and Public Health: The AIDS Epidemic in an Economic Perspective* (1993); Susan M. Kegeles & Joseph A. Catania, "Understanding Bisexual Men's AIDS Risk Behavior: The AIDS Risk–Reduction Model," in *Bisexuality and HIV/AIDS: A Global Perspective* 139 (Rob Tielman et al., eds., 1991).

r. The main study finding some effect reported only a low one, see Ralph W. Hingson et al., "AIDS Transmission: Changes in Knowledge and Behaviors among Adolescents—Massachusetts Statewide Surveys 1986–1988," 85 *Pediatrics* 25 (1990). For studies finding no effect, or even a negative effect, see Anthony Biglan et al., "Social and Behavioral Factors Associated with High–Risk Behavior Among Adolescents," 13 *J. Behav. Med.* 245 (1990); John Vincke et al., "Factors Affecting AIDS–Related Sexual Be-

havior Change Among Flemish Gay Men," 52 *Hum. Org.* 260 (1993); Heather J. Walter et al., "Factors Associated with AIDS Risk Behaviors Among High School Students in an AIDS Epicenter," 82 *Am. J. Pub. Health* 528 (1992).

s. Daniel E. Klein et al., "Changes in AIDS Risk Behaviors Among Homosexual Male Physicians and University Students," 144 *Am J Psychiatry* 742 (1987); Madeline M. Gladis, "High School Students' Perceptions of AIDS Risk: Realistic Appraisal or Motivated Denial?," 11 *Health Psychol.* 307 (1992); Mary–Ann Shafer & Cherrie B. Bayer, "Psychosocial and Behavioral Factors Associated with Risk of Sexually Transmitted Diseases, Including Human Immunodeficiency Virus Infection, Among Urban High School Students," 119 *J. Pediatrics* 826 (1991); Vincke et al., "Flemish Gay Men."

t. See Janis & Mann, *Decision Making*; Kenneth H. Beck & Arthur Frankel, "A Conceptualization of Threat Communications and Protective Health Behavior," 14 *Social Psychol. Q.* 28 (1981).

These reactions to anxiety-provoking health threats do not involve a simple cost-benefit analysis, as the health benefit model does, but rather involve more intuitive responses. Thus, even if one partner knows of the other's high-risk behavior she still might have risky sex with him, because the anxiety aroused by AIDS-fear could be so high that she denies its applicability for her life or simply shifts responsibility for dealing with the risk to the risk-taking partner. This is not an uncommon strategy for people engaging in risky activities, including gay men, young people generally, and women in poverty.

Another model that helps explain responses to AIDS is the social norm model. Under this model, an individual's response to a health risk is strongly conditioned by social norms and attitudes. Under the health benefit model, one would expect a sixteen year-old person not to have risky sex with older men, but the social norm model suggests that the former might go along with risky sex if the adolescent culture stigmatizes condoms ("they're for squares"), thereby making adolescents embarrassed to bring up the subject. This, in turn, plays into the dynamics suggested by the conflict model. A sixteen year old's anxiety about AIDS might impel her or him to defer to the older person, an irrational but not uncommon strategy. Also, if the adolescent feels incapable of successfully negotiating with the adult to use condoms or of using the condoms correctly, she or he will be deterred from insisting upon safer sex.

Health education theorists believe that a successful AIDS education program for adolescents, especially for those most likely to engage in risky behaviors, must borrow from all three models: provide information to young people, teach them how successfully to negotiate risk-prone situations through role-playing and the like, and set in motion ideas and practices that affect youth culture generally. Thus researchers have found that programs inspired by the health belief model (and hence just supplying information to adolescents), are not very effective in reducing risk-taking adolescent behavior.[u] Consistent with the view that anxiety and social factors decisively influence decisionmaking, especially among adolescents, the medical literature has shown the greater success of programs that go well beyond providing information. Such (modestly) successful interventions tie behavior to consequences in concrete ways, engage the students in exercises designed to improve their perceived self-efficacy (namely, their ability to engage in safer behaviors skillfully), and change the peer culture regulating what is socially acceptable and what is not.

---

u. See Ralph Di Clemente, "Preventing HIV/AIDS Among Adolescents: Schools as Agents of Behavior Change," 270 *J. Am. Med. Ass'n* 760 (1993) (editorial); Ralph J. DiClemente & Amanda Houston–Hamilton, "Health Promotion Strategies for Prevention of Human Immunodeficiency Virus Infection Among Minority Adolescents," 20 *Health Educ.* 39 (1989); Douglas Kirby et al., "Reducing the Risk: Impact of a New Curriculum on Sexual Risk–Taking," 23 *Family Planning Perspectives* 253 (1991); Heather J. Walter & Roger D. Vaughan, "AIDS Risk Reduction Among A Multiethnic Sample of Urban High School Students," 270 *J. Am. Med. Ass'n* 725 (1993). See generally *Preventing AIDS: Theories and Methods of Behavioral Interventions* (Ralph J. DiClemente & J.L. Peterson eds. 1994).

Thus, a typical teenager will not stop having risky sex simply because he or she learns in the abstract that AIDS can be transmitted in this way. The sixteen year old is more likely to change his or her behavior if his attention is also engaged by simulated negotiations, which suggest how easy and normal it can be to have a condom ready and use it correctly. He or she is much more likely to demand safer sex if his peer group decides that condoms are "in" and that "only dopes take risks for unsafe sex."

3. LEGAL ISSUES RAISED BY AIDS EDUCATION

There is substantial political resistance to any kind of sex education in many communities, and such education that deals with homosexual feelings, shows adolescents how condoms and vaginal dams work, and engages in simulated negotiations regarding safe sex practices is beyond the imagination of most school boards. Does a school district have a legal or constitutional obligation to teach young people fundamental "facts" about human sexuality and reproduction? There is little if any support for the proposition that school systems have a constitutional obligation to teach students about sex, however.

Three other issues have generated legal controversy. One is whether parents have a fundamental right to control what information about sexuality is imparted to their children in the public schools, and a second is under what circumstances sex education can amount to a legally cognizable "hostile environment" for some students. These issues are explored in the cases that follow. A third set of issues, discussed in Part C of this section, involve discrimination, in which state sex education must be presented in a way that disapproves of homosexuality or that is admonished not to present homosexuality in an attractive light.

Ignacia Alfonso et al. v. Joseph A. Fernandez et al.

N.Y. Supreme Court, Appellate Division, Second Department, 1993.
195 A.D.2d 46, 606 N.Y.S.2d 259.

■ PIZZUTO, JUSTICE. * * *

In September 1987 the New York State Commission of Education directed all elementary and secondary schools to include, as part of health education programs, instruction concerning the Human Immunodeficiency Virus (HIV) which causes Acquired Immune Deficiency Syndrome (AIDS) (see, 8 NYCRR 135.3[b][2]; [c][2]). In late 1990, Joseph Fernandez, then Chancellor of the New York City Board of Education, suggested enlarging the existing HIV/AIDS curriculum to impart additional education about the transmission and prevention of HIV/AIDS. The former Chancellor also suggested that condoms be made available to high school students upon request. On February 27, 1991, the New York City Board of Education voted to establish an expanded HIV/AIDS Education Program in New York City's public high schools, consisting of two components. * * *

[The first component calls for classroom instructions on various aspects of HIV/AIDS; although mandatory for the students, this component allows a parent to opt his or her minor unemancipated child out of the classroom instruction upon the assurance that the child will receive such instruction at home. The second component of the program calls for the high schools to make condoms available to students who request them; this component is not mandatory for students but also does not have a parental opt-out provision. The School Board considered an opt-out provision but rejected it because they believed it would deny condoms to students most in need of them. The parent-plaintiffs challenged this second component for its lack of parental opt out.]

At common law it was for parents to consent or withhold their consent to the rendition of health services to their children. The general incapacity of minors to consent to health services derives from this common-law rule that treated a minor's "normal condition [as] that of incompetency". As legal incompetents, minors could no more consent to medical treatment than they could enter into binding contracts and they continued to be incompetent in many circumstances to give effective consent to health care. The courts identified exceptions to the common-law rule regarding the incapacity of minors. For example, children were regarded as emancipated and competent to consent when they were married; or supported themselves; or were inducted into military service; or when their parents abandoned them or failed to support them. In addition, a physician could render health services to a minor in an emergency without first consulting his or her parents.

Public Health Law § 2504, which was enacted in 1972 * * * reads as follows:

"1. Any person who is eighteen years of age or older, or is the parent of a child or has married, may give effective consent for medical, dental, *health* and hospital *services* for himself or herself, and the consent of no other person shall be necessary.

"2. Any person who has been married or who has borne a child may give effective consent for medical, dental, *health* and hospital *services* for his or her child.

"3. Any person who is pregnant may give effective consent for medical, dental, *health* and hospital *services* relating to prenatal care.

"4. Medical, dental, *health* and hospital *services* may be rendered to persons of any age without the consent of a parent or legal guardian when, in the physician's judgment an emergency exists and the person is in immediate need of medical attention and an attempt to secure consent would result in delay of treatment which would increase the risk to the person's life or health.

"5. Anyone who acts in good faith based on the representation by a person that he is eligible to consent pursuant to the terms of this section shall be deemed to have received effective consent" (emphasis supplied). * * *

[The court first determined that condom distribution is a "health service," as the parents argued, and not an "educational" service, as the school maintained.]* * * The distribution of condoms is not * * * an aspect of education in disease prevention, but rather is a means of disease prevention. Supplying condoms to students upon request has absolutely nothing to do with education, but rather is a health service occurring after the educational phase has ceased. Although the program is not intended to promote promiscuity, it is intended to encourage and enable students to use condoms if and when they engage in sexual activity. This is clearly a health service for the prevention of disease which requires parental consent. * * *

Requiring parental consent or opt-out for the condom availability component of the respondents' program would not violate State and Federal statutory and constitutional law as urged by the *amici*, nor would it stymie every health care provider, compelling parental consent whenever an unemancipated minor seeks contraceptive services.

Under the sections of the Social Security Act governing Aid to Families with Dependent Children and Medicaid, family planning services and supplies must be provided to all eligible recipients, including sexually active minors (*see*, 42 U.S.C. §§ 602[a][15]; 1396d[a][4][C]). The State laws governing these programs also require that contraception be made available to "eligible persons of childbearing age, including children who can be considered sexually active" (Social Services Law § 350[1][e]; *see*, Social Services Law § 365–a[3][c]; *see also*, 18 NYCRR 431.7, 463.2[b][1]; [b][2]; 463.6 [requiring provision of family planning services to minors eligible for public assistance, Medicaid, or supplemental security income, and to foster children]). These laws entitle eligible minors to confidential services from any provider who treats them under the auspices of one of the public assistance programs previously mentioned.

In addition, title X of the Public Health Service Act, the largest source of Federal funding for family planning programs throughout the nation, mandates that minors receive confidential services (*see*, 42 U.S.C. § 300[a]; 42 CFR 59.5[a][4], 59.15). Interpreting these statutes as requiring that adolescents be treated confidentially, on the basis of their own consent, the Federal courts have invalidated both state laws and Federal and state regulations that imposed parental consent or notification requirements on teenagers entitled to family planning services under these programs (*see*, *Jones v. T.H.*, 425 U.S. 986 [invalidating state regulations that mandated parental consent for family planning services to otherwise eligible minors]).

These statutes are merely legislatively-enacted exceptions to requirements of parental consent (*see also*, Public Health Law § 2781[1] [providing that HIV-related tests may be administered upon the written, informed consent of anyone, including a minor if the person has an ability to understand and the capacity to consent]; Public Health Law § 2305[2] [which dispenses with consent or knowledge of a parent in the diagnosis or treatment of a sexually transmissible disease]). It is for the Congress or the Legislature, not the courts—and certainly not the State Commissioner of Education or a Board of Education—to provide the exceptions to parental consent requirements. Neither Congress nor the New York State Legislature has enacted an exception for the health service at issue here. The distribution of condoms in our public high schools, where attendance is compulsory, even though condoms are nonmedicinal and require no prescription, is quite different from making them available at clinics, where attendance is wholly voluntary, or as part of public assistance programs. There is no specific authority for the condom availability component of the respondents' program, no matter how commendable its purpose may be. * * *

The petitioner parents are being compelled by State authority to send their children into an environment where they will be permitted, even encouraged, to obtain a contraceptive device, which the parents disfavor as a matter of private belief. Because the Constitution gives parents the right to regulate their children's sexual behavior as best they can, not only must a compelling State interest be found supporting the need for the policy at issue, but that policy must be essential to serving that interest as well. We do not find that the policy is essential. No matter how laudable its purpose, by excluding parental involvement, the condom availability component of the program impermissibly trespasses on the petitioners' parental rights by substituting the respondents in loco parentis, without a compelling necessity therefore. * * *

This is not a case in which parents are complaining solely about having their children exposed to ideas or a point of view with which they disagree or find offensive. We would agree that, standing alone, such opposition would falter in the face of the public school's role in preparing students for participation in a world replete with complex and controversial issues. However, the condom availability component of the respondents' distribution program creates an entirely different situation. Students are not just exposed to talk or literature on the subject of sexual behavior; the school offers the means for students to engage in sexual activity at a lower risk of pregnancy and contracting sexually transmitted diseases. The extent to which individual minors would be affected by the availability of contraceptives in the public school system if the distribution of condoms on the scale envisioned by the respondents were to become commonplace, cannot presently be ascertained. * * *

■ EIBER, JUSTICE (dissenting).* * *

[Justice Eiber disagreed with the majority's holding that the health law required parental consent for condom distribution as a "health service." In a footnote, Justice Eiber noted, "While the majority seems to suggest that the dictates of the common-law rule could be satisfied by allowing parents to opt their children out of the voluntary program, this position is inconsistent. If the condom distribution program is indeed a health service as contemplated by Public Health Law § 2504 and the common law, students under the age of 18 may participate in the program only with parental consent. A parent or guardian's failure to 'opt-out' is not the equivalent of consent." Additionally, the 1972 health law on which the majority relied was a contraction of the common-law rights of parents and in no way addressed the novel threats posed by AIDS.]

Moreover, * * * to engraft a parental consent requirement onto the condom distribution program would run counter to the United States Supreme Court's holding in *Carey v. Population Services Intl.*, 431 U.S. 678. At issue in *Carey* was the constitutionality of a New York statute which made it a crime for any person to sell or distribute a contraceptive device to a minor under the age of 16. In concluding that the statute was invalid, the plurality opinion noted that minors, as well as adults, are protected by the Constitution and possess constitutional rights, including the right to privacy in connection with decisions affecting procreation. The plurality opinion further reasoned that:

> "Since the State may not impose a blanket prohibition, or even a blanket requirement of parental consent, on the choice of a minor to terminate her pregnancy, the constitutionality of a blanket prohibition of the distribution of contraceptives is a fortiori foreclosed. The State's interests in protection of the mental and physical health of the pregnant minor, and in protection of potential life are clearly more implicated by the abortion decision than by the decision to use a nonhazardous contraceptive"

Furthermore, the majority's conclusion that the distribution of condoms is encompassed by the common-law prohibition against providing medical treatment without consent, is at odds with the fact that minors in this State are permitted to obtain abortions and treatment for sexually transmitted diseases without parental consent or notification (see, Public Health Law § 2305). Surely, if minors are permitted to obtain treatment for the consequences of unprotected sexual intercourse without parental consent or notification, it is inconsistent to restrict their access to the means by which they can prevent an unwanted pregnancy or protect themselves from sexually transmitted diseases, including the deadly HIV virus.

In addition, while the majority turns a blind eye to the potential ramifications of its interpretation of the common-law rule, the fact remains that if the distribution of condoms is a "health service" which cannot be undertaken without parental consent, then the many family planning clinics throughout this State which distribute condoms and other contraceptive devices to minors must also be deemed in violation of the common law and statute. Similarly, if condoms cannot be provided to minors in the absence of parental consent, then it logically follows that the commercial sale of condoms to minors violates the Public Health Law and is illegal. Thus, a broad interpretation of the term "health services" to preclude distribution of condoms to minors without parental consent would have a significant impact upon the ability of minors to obtain condoms, and thus violate their constitutionally-recognized right to make such decisions privately.

* * * If an opt-out feature is adopted * * * students will no longer be able to request condoms anonymously. The respondents have reasonably

concluded that this loss of confidentiality would deter student participation in the condom distribution program, thus reducing its effectiveness. In the years following the Supreme Court's decision in *Carey*, the spread of AIDS has reached alarming proportions giving rise to a compelling state interest to halt the growth of the epidemic. Clearly, many parents, such as the petitioners, are seeking to provide guidance to their children and to protect their health and morality. The majority overlooks the unfortunate reality that many children lack such interested parents. Many children have no parents to provide guidance and discipline or who are even available to consent to the child's participation in the program should an "opt-out" be mandated. Since the consequence of contracting AIDS is death, providing practical protection against the spread of the virus which causes it, to a high-risk population, in my view, outweighs the minimal intrusion into the parent/child relationship of the more protected, more fortunate portion of the adolescent population of New York City.* * *

■ [JUSTICE MILLER's separate dissenting opinion, agreeing with that of JUSTICE EIBER, is omitted.]

NOTES ON THE LEGALITY OF CONDOM DISTRIBUTION PROGRAMS AND PARENTS' CONSTITUTIONAL RIGHTS IN THEIR CHILDREN'S UPBRINGING

In *Doe v. Irwin*, 615 F.2d 1162 (6th Cir.), *cert. denied*, 449 U.S. 829 (1980), the Sixth Circuit rejected parents' substantive due process challenge to the practice of a publicly operated family planning center distributing contraceptives (including condoms) upon request to minors without notice to or consent by parents. Is *Irwin* distinguishable from *Alfonso*? If so, how? If not, which is correctly decided? Consider analytical issues common to the cases:

1. *Parental Rights.* The majority in *Alfonso* relied on both the common law and constitutional rights of parents. Does the majority have any answer to the dissent's charge that, if parents have a common law or constitutional right to control their children's health materials or education, an actual waiver and not just a failure to opt out is required to provide condoms or other useful information to minors? If the majority is right that parents have a constitutional right to determine what sex education their children are receiving, is the dissent right that this right cannot be taken away by an opt-out procedure?

The constitutional rights of parents are founded on two elderly substantive due process precedents. In *Meyer v. Nebraska*, 262 U.S. 390 (1923), the Court struck down a state law prohibiting parents from permitting their children to study a foreign language until after completion of the eighth grade. The Court held that the liberty guaranteed by the due process clause includes "not merely freedom from bodily restraint but also the right of the individual to contract, to engage in any of the common occupations of life, to acquire useful knowledge, to marry, to establish a home and bring up children, to worship God according to the dictates of his own conscience, and generally to enjoy those privileges long recognized at common law as essential to the orderly pursuit of happiness by free men." Two years later the Court in *Pierce v. Society of Sisters*, 268 U.S. 510 (1925), struck down a state statute requiring public school attendance—and thus precluding attendance at parochial schools—because it "unreasonably interfere[d] with the liberty of parents or guardians to direct the upbringing and education of children under their control." The *Meyer* and *Pierce* decisions have since been interpreted by the Court as recognizing that, under our constitutional scheme, "the custody, care and nurture of the child reside first in the parents." *Prince v. Massachusetts*, 321 U.S. 158, 166 (1944).

The *Alfonso* dissent distinguished these cases on the ground that the condom distribution program was not mandatory and therefore did not invade parents' rights to direct their children's upbringing. Persuasive?

2. *The Rights of Minors.* Like the *Alfonso* dissent, *Irwin* relied on the Supreme Court's decision in *Carey*, which recognized the rights of minors to obtain contraceptives without the knowledge or consent of their parents. In both contexts the underlying tension is between parents' desire to know and perhaps control their adolescent children's sexual behavior, and the adolescents' desire that their parents not know. While *Carey* seems to decide the tension in favor of the rights of minors, the case may be distinguishable from *Alfonso*, which combined compulsory public schooling with condom distribution. Also, *Carey* may be weakened by the Supreme Court's decision in *Hodgson v. Minnesota* [Chapter 2, Section 2(C)], which held that states can require parental notification of a female minor's attempt to obtain an abortion. The minor's rights to obtain an abortion and to obtain contraceptives both derive from the right of privacy now ensconced in the due process clause, and requiring parental consent in both cases serves parents' interests in knowing that their children are sexually active, at the expense of the children's sexual freedom. Is there a persuasive argument that *Carey* survives *Hodgson*?

3. *The Public Interest.* The *Alfonso* dissent relies on the strong public interest in fighting AIDS to tip the balance in favor of condom distribution. The school board believed that adolescents were going to be sexually active, whether they had condoms or not, and that making condoms available would prevent some kids from being infected by the HIV virus. For every person whose life is saved in this way there is a multiplier effect, because also saved would the people he might infect in turn. Public health professionals are in overwhelming agreement with this logic, and the school board agreed—but the New York Appellate Division was underwhelmed. Should the judges have been cautious about sacrificing what it considered common law or constitutional rights in the face of a public health emergency? If the AIDS emergency justifies sacrificing parental rights, might it not also be held to override other privacy rights, to justify mandatory HIV testing or even quarantines of people who test positive for this virus?

PROBLEM 7–5

AIDS INSTRUCTION AS SEXUAL HARASSMENT?

On April 8, 1992, Jason Mesiti and Shannon Silva attended a mandatory, school-wide assembly at Chelmsford High School. Both students were fifteen years old at the time. The assembly consisted of a ninety-minute presentation characterized by the school as an AIDS awareness program. The Program was staged by Suzi Landolphi and her corporation, Hot, Sexy, and Safer, Inc. Landolphi gave sexually explicit monologues and participated in sexually suggestive skits with several minors chosen from the audience.

Specifically, she allegedly (a) told the students that they were going to have a "group sexual experience, with audience participation"; (b) used profane, lewd, and lascivious language to describe body parts and excretory functions; (c) advocated and approved oral sex, masturbation, homosexual sexual activity, and condom use during promiscuous premarital sex; (d) simulated masturbation; (e) referred to being in "deep sh—" after anal sex; (f) had a male minor lick an oversized condom with her, after which she had a female minor pull it over the male minor's entire head and blow it up; (g) encouraged a male minor to display his "orgasm face" with her for the camera; (h) closely inspected a minor and told him he had a "nice butt"; and (i) made eighteen references to orgasms, six references to male genitals, and eight references to female genitals.

Mesiti and Silva were raised in very traditional homes and adhere to conservative views about human sexuality; both feel that people's sexuality is one of the most intimate things about them and should not be publicly displayed or made sport of. They were embarrassed by Landolphi's speech and its fallout among students. Many students copied Landolphi's routines and generally displayed overtly sexual behavior in the weeks following the program. They expressed their feelings to the school administration, complaining that they could not concentrate on their schoolwork because of the embarrassment they felt and the "unsettled" atmosphere created by the program.

The administration ignored the complaints, and Mesiti's and Silva's parents complained to the Office of Civil Rights of the Department of Education that such mandatory programs constituted sexual harassment under Title IX. Should the OCR intervene? Cf. *Brown v. Hot, Sexy and Safer Productions, Inc.*, 68 F.3d 525 (1st Cir.1995), *cert. denied*, 116 S.Ct. 1044 (1996).

PART C. NO PROMO HOMO POLICIES

Since 1987, when Senator Jesse Helms started introducing "no promotion of homosexuality" language into federal spending bills, a big issue of education policy has been what schools can or should say about homosexuality. States like Alabama, Arizona, Texas, and Utah have adopted statewide policies, but most of the battles have been fought at the school board level. Three different approaches have been floated and tried.

One approach would provide students with information from all sides of the issue but would positively encourage toleration and understanding of gay and lesbian youth. This approach responds to the traumas lesbian and gay adolescents suffer in high school, typically at the hands of their peers, but often exacerbated by insensitive teacher and administrative attitudes. HHS estimates that gay youth are two or three times more likely to commit suicide because of these pressures.[v] "An education system that openly and accurately addresses homosexuality benefits all students, not only those who may be gay. * * * [P]roviding accurate information helps students to understand and respect people who may seem 'different,' an essential lesson for ensuring stability in our diverse society."[w]

A second approach would send only negative messages about homosexuality. An extreme example of this approach was the requirement in Oregon's 1992 Ballot Measure 9 that would have required public schools to "recognize[] homosexuality, pedophilia, sadism and masochism as abnormal, wrong, unnatural and perverse and * * * to be discouraged and avoided." More typical is the Alabama statute quoted above, and the Arizona statute quoted just below. The rationale of these moderately antihomosexual policies is to inculcate a respect for heterosexuality among adolescents, so as to influence their sexual development in ways the society deems productive.

A third approach would avoid the issue altogether. In 1991, New York City School District 24 mandated that "any reference to * * * homosexuality * * * be eliminated from the curriculum."[x] This approach has the supposed advantage of neutrality: the state neither condemns nor endorses this controversial sexual orientation. Also, it is a policy many parents are most comfortable with. Consider the following state statute and the accompanying problem.

Arizona Revised Statutes § 15–716, Instruction on Acquired Immune Deficiency Syndrome

(Added 1991, amended 1995).

A. Each common, high and unified school district may provide instruction to kindergarten programs through the twelfth grade on acquired immune deficiency syndrome and the human immunodeficiency virus.

---

v. Paul Gibson, "Gay Male and Lesbian Youth Suicide," in Report of the [HHS] Secretary's Task Force on Youth Suicide 3–110 (1989).

w. Nancy Tenney, "The Constitutional Imperative of Reality in Public School Curricula: Untruths About Homosexuality as a Violation of the First Amendment," 60 *Brooklyn L. Rev.* 1599, 1614 (1995) (student note).

x. Letter from the Superintendent to Parents et al., for 1991–92 school year (quoted in Tenney, supra note w, at 1603 n.16).

B.   Each district is free to develop its own course of study for each grade. At a minimum, instruction shall:

1.   Be appropriate to the grade level in which it is offered.

2.   Be medically accurate.

3.   Promote abstinence.

4.   Discourage drug abuse.

5.   Dispel myths regarding transmission of the human immunodeficiency virus.

C.   No district shall include in its course of study instruction which:

1.   Promotes a homosexual life-style.

2.   Portrays homosexuality as a positive alternative life-style.

3.   Suggests that some methods of sex are safe methods of homosexual sex.

D.   At the request of a school district, the department of health services or the department of education shall review instruction materials to determine their medical accuracy.

E.   At the request of a school district, the department of education shall provide the following assistance:

1.   A suggested course of study.

2.   Teacher training.

3.   A list of available films and other teaching aids.

F.   At the request of a parent, a pupil shall be excused from instruction on the acquired immune deficiency syndrome and the human immunodeficiency virus as provided in subsection A of this section. The school district shall notify all parents of their ability to withdraw their child from the instruction.

PROBLEM 7–6

STATE AIDS EDUCATION AND THE POLICY AGAINST PROMOTING HOMOSEXUALITY

You are the general counsel to Arizona's department of education. School districts describe their proposed AIDS awareness programs to you, and you counsel them on whether their proposals violate the statute. Consider the following three programs:

(A) Hot, Sexy and Safer. Recall the program described in Problem 7–5, and assume that it does not constitute illegal sexual harassment. What modifications would have to be made in the program to make it minimally acceptable under the Arizona statute?

(B) Safe Lesbian Sex. One high school wants to teach a class on "Sexuality and Disease" (including AIDS). The school submits materials, which include a detailed description of safer sex techniques, including

explicit statements that oral sex with a condom or dental dam is 99.99% safe. Also the materials note that the rate of HIV infection is lower for lesbians than it is for straight women, straight or bisexual men, and gay men. You notify the school that these portions of the instruction seem to violate § 15–716(C)(3), as they suggest that homosexual oral sex and sex between women are relatively safe. The school rejoins that § 15–716(C)(3) is unconstitutional on its face or as applied. What do you have to say to that?

(C) The Homosexual Life Style. Another high school submits a program which contains an entire segment on gay youth. According to the compiled materials, the segment teaches that adolescents generally do not choose their sexual orientation, that this is a neutral feature of someone's person-hood, and that straight as well as gay youth should consult with a health professional to learn about safer sex before they become sexually active. The segment includes stories by gay, bisexual, and straight adolescents who have been infected with HIV by their different-sex and same-sex partners; the stories warn of the ease with which inexperienced youth can lapse into unsafe sex. Throughout the materials, homosexual attraction is treated as normal but is not singled out for special attention. Do these materials pass muster under the statute?

Gay Men's Health Crisis et al. v. Dr. Louis Sullivan

U.S. District Court for the Southern District of New York, 1992.
792 F.Supp. 278.

■ KRAM, DISTRICT JUDGE. * * *

Subsequent to [*GMHC v. Sullivan*, 733 F.Supp. 619 (S.D.N.Y.1989) ("*GMHC I*")], the CDC [Center for Disease Control] published a notice of revised grant terms and requested public comment on the proposed changes. See 55 Fed.Reg. 10667 (March 22, 1990). Parts (a) and (b) of the proposed revised Basic Principles read as follows:

> a. Language used in written materials ..., audiovisual materials ..., and pictorials ... to describe dangerous behaviors and explain less risky practices concerning HIV transmission should use terms, descriptors, or displays necessary for the intended audience to understand the messages.

> b. Written materials, audiovisual materials, and pictorials should not include terms, descriptors, or displays which will be offensive to a majority of the intended audience or to a majority of persons outside the intended audience.

The CDC received 133 comments on the proposed revised grant terms. 55 Fed.Reg. 23414 (June 7, 1990). [Although none objected to the require-ment that materials not be offensive to a majority of the intended audience, 86 objected to the requirement that materials not be offensive "to a majority of persons outside the intended audience" (5 concurred with this requirement). The CDC's Revised Grant Terms revised Part (b) as follows:

b. Written materials, audiovisual materials, and pictorials should not include terms, descriptors, or displays which will be offensive to a majority of the intended audience or to a majority of adults outside the intended audience unless, in the judgment of the Program Review Panel [PRP], the potential offensiveness of such materials is outweighed by the potential effectiveness in communicating an important HIV prevention message. 55 Fed.Reg. 23414 (June 7, 1990).

[The CDC's Revision of Requirements for Content of HIV/AIDS–Related Written materials, Pictorials, Audiovisuals, Questionnaires, Survey Instruments, and Educational Sessions in Centers for Disease Control Assistance Programs eliminated the requirements of the Kennedy–Cranston Amendment from its grant terms. The Kennedy/Cranston Amendment, first incorporated into the fiscal year 1989 appropriations act, P.L. 100–436 (1988), provided that AIDS education programs funded by CDC "shall not be designed to promote or encourage, directly, intravenous drug abuse or sexual activity, homosexual or heterosexual." This language was incorporated into funding statutes for fiscal years 1989–91. But the CDC opined that the underlying standards remain unchanged, as "any material which would have failed to meet the Kennedy–Cranston standard ... would also fail to meet the 'offensiveness' standard that continues as part of the Basic Principles to be applied by Program Review Panels."]

Plaintiffs argue that * * * the CDC acted beyond its statutory authority in promulgating the Revised Grant Terms. According to plaintiffs, by adopting the "offensiveness" criterion, the CDC contravened its statutory authority, which bars funding only of "obscene," not "offensive," material. See 42 U.S.C. § 300ee. Further, plaintiffs claim that the Revised Grant Terms must be invalidated because they were not the product of detailed and reasoned decisionmaking. * * *

The Court * * * finds that in using the "offensiveness" criterion, the CDC has contravened its statutory authority which bars funding only of obscene, not offensive material. 42 U.S.C. § 300ee(d). Defendants' argument that Congress intended only to set a floor in enacting subsection (d) is untenable in light of the legislative history of the statute. In fact, the legislative history makes clear that Congress intended the language of 42 U.S.C. § 300ee(d) to be a ceiling on the conditions that can be placed on AIDS education materials. The legislative history makes reference to the "necessity of reaching the highest risk groups *by whatever means will catch their attention*." S.Rep. No. 100–133 at 6–7, 1988 U.S.Code Cong. & Admin.News at 4181 (emphasis added). Moreover, Senator Cranston explained that the language that became 42 U.S.C. § 300ee was added to the legislation to allow "an aggressive education and prevention campaign." Further, a letter by Senator Cranston, which was incorporated into his remarks, noted that through repeated votes, Congress "has made clear its intent: The federal government *must not interfere with or hamstring public health efforts to educate* all Americans, including gay and bisexual men, about AIDS.... " 134 Cong.Rec. S15693 (Oct. 13, 1988) (emphasis added). * * *

[The court found that the CDC's offensiveness standard was contrary to the statute. In the next part of its opinion, the court found the standards unconstitutional in any event, because they provided vague and standard-less criteria for decisionmakers and therefore opened the door for censorship of information about AIDS.]

[T]he "offensiveness" standard remains essentially undefined. To date, the CDC has made no affirmative statement as to what constitutes "offensive" materials, nor has it set forth a method by which to determine what materials will be deemed "offensive" under the Revised Grant Terms. As such, plaintiffs are correct when they assert that the Revised Grant Terms provide no way of answering questions such as: Can educational material be offensive simply because it mentions homosexuality? Because it depicts an interracial couple? Can a proposed AIDS education project be offensive because it traps a captive audience, such as subway riders, and forces them to look at a condom? Does offensive apply to all descriptions of sexual behavior, graphic depictions of sexual behavior, or descriptions of unusual sexual behavior? * * *

This lack of guidance is especially troubling given that the Revised Grant Terms require PRP members to gauge the reactions of members of the public, see *Big Mama Rag, Inc. v. United States*, 631 F.2d 1030, 1037 (D.C.Cir.1980) (the regulation's vagueness is especially apparent in that portion of the test expressly based on an individualistic—and therefore necessarily varying and unascertainable—standard: the reactions of members of the public), as well as engage in two levels of subjective analysis, i.e., PRP members have to form their own subjective opinions about the subjective opinions of a majority of other adults. Specifically, PRP members have to make a subjective determination as to what a majority of other adults will think offensive. * * *

Defendants contend that the core meaning of the "offensiveness" standard has been defined not only by examples contained in the Revised Grant Terms themselves, but by reference to the obscenity standard. According to the defendants, since the "offensiveness" standard clearly encompasses legally "obscene" materials, the Revised Grant Terms contain a core meaning. The Court disagrees.

As the plaintiffs assert, a restriction that prohibited the funding of all "rude," "unpopular," "erotic," "annoying," "controversial," or "upsetting" materials would also likely encompass legally obscene materials. However, the fact that a broad, undefined, and vague term overlaps with a more specific, well-defined and constitutional prohibition, does not make the broader language constitutional. Because the obscenity standard is inherently narrower than the offensiveness criterion, there is a vast amount of material that could be developed that would be deemed offensive, but not obscene. As such, the Court finds that reference to the obscenity standard offers no real guidance or clarification to either AIDS educators or PRP members.

Moreover, the Court will not permit the defendants to rely on the judicially defined obscenity standard to provide the grant terms with core meaning, when they have chosen instead to impose a nebulous and unde-fined "offensiveness" standard. If defendants seek to rely on the constitu-tional obscenity standard, they should adopt it, as the plaintiffs have urged. Such adoption would be consistent with the National Endowment for the Art's (NEA) decision to tailor its restrictions to the legal standard for obscenity. Under the terms of a recent settlement, the NEA will demand return of its funds from a grantee only if the grantee is convicted in a judicial proceeding of violating a criminal obscenity or child pornography statute. See *New School for Social Research v. Frohmayer*, No. 90 Civ. 3510 (LLS) (S.D.N.Y. Feb. 19, 1991) (settled by stipulation). * * *

* * * [T]he results of various PRP decisions indicate the arbitrariness of the Revised Grant Terms. In one instance, the National Association of Black and White Men Together ("BWMT") received a $1 million, five-year grant from the CDC to educate minority men who have sex with men. As part of its application, the organization included information about and a sample advertising poster for "Hot, Horny, and Healthy Playshops." The CDC approved the application without comment. The San Francisco PRP also approved the advertising poster as well as a second poster that depicted a white man and black man sitting on the floor together. In the District of Columbia and in Los Angeles, however, local affiliates of BWMT suffered disapprovals of proposals to hold such workshops with locally-distributed CDC money because the workshops were perceived as offensive and contrary to the grant terms. They also suffered disapprovals of the two advertising posters. * * *

Second, documents regarding the panels' deliberations as to the Origi-nal Grant Terms provide additional evidence of the unpredictable applica-tion of the grant terms. A review of the documents indicates that PRP members were unable to recognize any core meaning in the "offensiveness" criterion. For example, all of the following were given by PRP members as reasons for disapproving materials as "offensive":

(a) "I don't think cartoon figures are necessary to get the facts of AIDS across."

(b) "The patriotic connection with protection in the case of AIDS demeans Uncle Sam and all of us."

(c) "Tacky use of a respected symbol [Uncle Sam]"

(d) "Poor Taste"

(e) "Information on detailed safe sex practices should not be included in a general informational brochure on AIDS."

(f) "I have major concerns about using the image of a noted, deceased public figure, especially a Black leader [Dr. Martin Luther King]. While a poster for alcohol and drug abuse may be acceptable, there are certain implications regarding AIDS." Declaration of David Cole, executed on March 16, 1989 ("Cole Dec."), at ¶ 7 (filed with plaintiffs' first motion for summary judgment) and Exhibits "A"-"J", attached to Cole Declaration.

Since there has been no effective clarification of the "offensiveness" criterion, there is no reason to believe that the Revised Grant Terms are being applied in a less arbitrary fashion. In fact, those that have attended PRP meetings under the Revised Grant Terms "cannot say for sure the precise test that [the panel] is applying."

Evidence of self-censorship by AIDS education groups also provides evidence of the vagueness of the Revised Grant Terms. Because the grant terms are subjective and imprecise, AIDS educators cannot predict with any certainty what materials will be approved. Thus, they are forced to censor themselves and concentrate on proposals that will pass the "offensiveness" test with room to spare.* * *

As evidence of this chilling effect, plaintiff Horizons, as well as the American Red Cross, the Reimer Foundation, and the Tucson AIDS Project, have provided the Court with specific examples of projects that have been abandoned or toned down because of anticipated problems with PRP approval. See Trowbridge Dec., at ¶ 8 ("The offensiveness criterion . . . and the unpredictability of how that criterion would be administered led me to drop a plan to develop explicit, attention-grabbing brochures for a gay male audience"); id. at ¶ 9 ("We determined that to avoid PRP rejection we would have to use . . ." "semen," "feces," and "urine" [instead of "cum," "shit," and "piss"]); Comment letter from the American Red Cross, included in Exhibit B to Harlow Dec. I ("In developing brochures jointly with the CDC intended for adult women and men, we had to remove the colloquialism 'cum.' "); Felshman Dec., at ¶¶ 12, 14 (The Reimer Foundation, using private resources, produced and circulated explicit, clear palm cards that discussed safer sex for distribution in gay bars. The language on the cards was toned down before submitting them to the PRP); DeGroff Dec., at ¶ 9 (had to make compromises in creating the campaign so as to have a good chance of approval).

Moreover, all of the declarations from AIDS educators submitted in support of plaintiffs' motion describe the need to speculate ahead of time about what might happen under the indiscernible standard of the grant terms.

Further, for some organizations the deterrent effect of the grant terms is so strong, they avoid seeking CDC funding. Plaintiff Hetrick Martin Institute, for example, focuses its services on the gay and lesbian youth population. To reach this population, the Institute has determined that comic books, other materials that use vernacular language, and a gay-positive approach are essential. Under the Revised Grant Terms, however, Hetrick Martin believes that "we probably would be unable to secure approval of our educational materials by a Program Review Panel. Thus, it does not make practical sense for us to apply for CDC funding, although we could put additional funding for HIV prevention to good use in serving lesbian and gay youth." * * *

NOTE ON CONSTITUTIONAL CHALLENGES TO "NO PROMO HOMO" POLICIES

Gay Men's Health Crisis suggests three different kinds of legal problems with "no promo homo" policies. Because the decision is that of a federal district court, its precepts must be tested against those announced by the Supreme Court, of course. (The Department of Justice did not appeal Judge Kram's decision.)

1. *Consistency with Statutory Scheme.* The first problem is always whether a policy is consistent with the governing statute. Recall *Coleman*, where the Louisiana court struck down local sex education policies because they conflicted with the commands of the statute. Note, however, that the courts in *GMHC* and *Coleman* may have read the statutes narrowly because of the underlying constitutional issues. Statutory and constitutional interpretation frequently intermingle in this way. See William N. Eskridge, Jr. & Philip P. Frickey, "Quasi–Constitutional Law: Clear Statement Rules as Constitutional Lawmaking," 45 *Vand. L. Rev.* 593 (1992).

2. *Suppression of Expression.* A policy that prohibits officials from speaking about homosexuality, or that directs their speech in one direction, might violate the core command of the First Amendment: speech about an important public topic can almost never be censored. Recall *National Gay Task Force v. Oklahoma City* (Chapter 5, Section 1[B]), where the appeals court invalidated a state statute prohibiting school teachers from talking about homosexuality. That decision might be distinguished from cases where the school system is censoring what teachers can say in the classroom. Compare *Solmitz* (Section 2 of this chapter). Would the Arizona statute in Problem 7–6 pass muster under the precedents?

3. *Vagueness.* When the state or the school system establishes directives abridging speech, especially speech about important public topics, the courts require that the directives provide precise guidelines for those administering the directives, lest the administrators be left to act as censors at large. This was Judge Kram's big problem with the CDC's offensiveness regulation, which would probably have been constitutional in any arena but the free speech one. It was also the basis for the Ninth Circuit's decision overturning the district court's decision in *Cohen v. San Bernardino Valley College* (Section 2[B] of this chapter); the appeals court held that a general policy against creating a "hostile" school environment did not put Professor Cohen on notice that his classroom methods were inappropriate. Does the Arizona statute in Problem 7–6 satisfy this kind of stringent vagueness test? Recall, again, that none of these decisions was delivered by the Supreme Court.

*

CHAPTER 8

CITIZENSHIP AND COMMUNITY IN A SEXUALIZED WORLD

SECTION 1   Accommodating Religion in a Sexualized World

SECTION 2   Citizens in Conflict: Anti-Civil Rights and Anti-Gay Initiatives

SECTION 3   Sexuality and Citizenship in an International Setting

Political citizenship has long been gendered, in that feminized groups (women, mainly) have been devalued in the political process. (As a formal matter, political citizenship is less severely gendered than it was in the nineteenth century, when women were generally not given the right to vote or hold office.) Starting in the late nineteenth century, citizenship has also become sexualized, in that groups deviating from traditional sexual norms—prostitutes, polygamists, lesbians and gay men, bisexuals, cross dressers, and transsexuals—have been specified and devalued in the political process. In response, and ironically, the political process has recently had occasion to respond to claims of sex, gender, and sexual orientation minorities by enacting antidiscrimination laws that are offensive to religious minorities. This, in turn, has inspired a religious or traditionalist response that has often bypassed the legislative process, by appealing to judges to enforce the free exercise clause of the First Amendment (Section

1 of this chapter) or to the voters to override antidiscrimination laws through initiatives and referenda (Section 2).

This process is what some call "culture clash" (or, incorrectly, *Kulturkampf*). When groups come into conflict, they tend to deploy legal coercion where they can. What role should law play in culture clash? What role should courts play, in their capacity as enforcers of constitutional norms? Reread Justice Scalia's dissent in *Romer v. Evans* (Chapter 1, Section 3), for it suggests a passive, neoholmesian role for the rule of law in a culture clash: neither legislative nor constitutional law should stand in the way of the victory of one group over another. Viewing hostility to women and gay people as nothing more than a culture clash, however, denies the existence of "community" or its possibility. That point of view can also be applied to deny America's responsibilities under international law to respect and even embrace women and gay people persecuted here and in other parts of the world (Section 3 of this chapter).

In the context of the free exercise of religion (where Justice Scalia has consistently followed his neoholmesian perspective to allow the great majority of state burdens on religion), Section 1 provides another way of thinking about "community" and "citizenship" and of law's responsibility to intergroup hostility. One way of thinking about these issues is through Robert Cover's concept of "nomic" (value-laden) communities within the larger political community. Religious groups can readily be understood as nomic communities, and so can at least some sexualized minorities. What obligations does the larger political community owe to these nomic communities? When a nomic community is a religious one, the free exercise clause of the First Amendment or the Religious Freedom Restoration Act, provides formal protection against state burdens. What protections are available to sexualized minorities? Most important: What is a constructive role for law when these protections come into direct conflict?

ACCOMMODATING RELIGION IN A SEXUALIZED WORLD

Sexuality and religion are an odd couple. Many organized religions in this country are nervous about issues of sexuality, and the main political forces favoring sodomy laws, restricting abortions, censoring information about sexuality in schools, curtailing condom distribution, and regulating sexual speech are expressly or implicitly aligned with some organized religions, especially the Southern Baptist Convention and the Roman Catholic Church. Conversely, many and perhaps most women who have abortions, lesbians and gay men, and consumers of pornography are themselves religious—and not a few are Baptists and Roman Catholics. Many lesbians, bisexuals, transgendered people, and gay men are members of the Metropolitan Community Church, a denomination founded by the Reverend Troy Perry in 1968 to be a spiritual home for gays. In turn, some religions consider the MCC the devil's workplace, an antithesis of religion, and some feminists and gender benders consider organized religion to be reactionary or a thin cover for expressing bigoted views.

This clash might be viewed as culture war. Under such a win-lose understanding, the role of the courts might be conceptualized as simply letting the secular state burden or benefit religious communities in any way it sees fit so long as the regulation is not targeted to destroy a religion or elevate it to official status (this is Justice Scalia's view). Contrariwise, the role of the courts might be to invoke the free exercise clause against such burdens and the establishment clause against undue favoritism (this was Justice Brennan's point of view). Consider the following introduction to these issues.

John Ware et al. v. Valley Stream High School District

New York Court of Appeals, 1989.
75 N.Y.2d 114, 551 N.Y.S.2d 167, 550 N.E.2d 420.

■ KAYE, JUDGE. * * *

[The individual plaintiffs were members of the Plymouth Brethren, a religious organization of approximately 35,000 adherents worldwide, 2,000 of whom live in the United States. The Brethren are a devoutly religious group established in the 1820's by biblically literalist Irish Christians who had become disenchanted with the established churches of the period. Fundamental to the Brethren creed is a precept of spiritual separatism by which members seek to distance themselves from all things they consider evil. Accordingly, the Brethren spend much of their time in group prayer, and they shun many modern technological innovations they consider evil.]

Plaintiffs complain that they are faced with evil in the form of the mandate that each school district promulgate an AIDS curriculum for its elementary and secondary school students. Specifically, the regulations required that elementary schools provide such instruction as part of the health education program for all pupils beginning in kindergarten (8 NYCRR 135.3[b][2]); secondary schools similarly must incorporate AIDS instruction into the required health instruction courses (8 NYCRR 135.3[c][2]).

[Each curriculum must include instruction concerning the nature of the disease, methods of transmission and methods of prevention (8 NYCRR 135.3[b][2]). Recognizing the delicacy of some of the subject matter, the regulations further provide that: "No pupil shall be required to receive instruction concerning the methods of prevention of AIDS if the parent or legal guardian of such pupil has filed with the principal of the school which the pupil attends a written request that the pupil not participate in such instruction, with an assurance that the pupil will receive such instruction at home." (8 NYCRR 135[b][2]; [c][2].)

[Thirty-five Brethren children attended public school in the Valley Stream High School District, which planned 22 lessons of AIDS instruction for the 1988–89 school year. Plaintiffs asked for exemption of their children from the entire AIDS curriculum; the school board granted exemption from five lessons on "prevention," which was all the statute allowed it to exempt (8 NYCRR 135[b][2]; [c][2]). The Commissioner of Education was empowered to grant a broader exemption under state law (Education Law 3204[5]) but declined to do so because of the compelling health goals of AIDS education. The Brethren brought suit in state court to require their exemption. At trial they submitted evidence along the following lines.]

First, the Plymouth Brethren are an identifiable religious group with a long history of maintaining a cohesive community separated and insulated from society. Members—who have been accorded "conscientious objector" status by the Selective Service System—are strongly moral and principled individuals practicing and reinforcing personal purity and other exemplary moral behavior. Apart from the practical necessity for this very small group to attend public school and earn a livelihood in the community, members' associations are limited to other Brethren.

Second, plaintiffs' children are not permitted to socialize with non-member children after school, or even to eat with them at school. The Brethren do not allow television or radio, and they do not see movies or read magazines. Their lives are spent in worship, or in social activities limited to association with other members under the constant moral guidance and supervision of parents and other community adults in an "extended family."

Third, insistence upon rigorous morality is interwoven with the movement's strong sense of separateness. The central principle of the Brethren's religion is the obligation to "separate from evil." Even to know the details of evil is regarded as subversive. This injunction forms the basis of their teaching and practice.

Fourth, in that the Brethren condemn all sexual relations outside of marriage as evil and the details of that evil as subversive, "[t]he religious tenets of its members flatly * * * forbid exposure to instruction concerning sexual relations and moral teachings other than those imparted by members of the community to members of the community." Consequently, plaintiffs believe that their children's exposure to the contents of the AIDS curriculum is inimical to their religious, moral, ethical and personal well-being. In plaintiffs' own words: "to expose our children to the detail of evil amplified in the entire sex, drug and AIDS curriculum would undermine the foundations of our faith and scar the moral values which have been instilled into our children from their very earliest days and could even jeopardize their place in the holy fellowship of God's Son, our Lord Jesus Christ, if they were diverted from a path of righteousness."

Fifth, exposure to the AIDS curriculum would undermine the Brethren's ability to guide their children's moral lives in accordance with their faith. In short, as plaintiffs affirmed, such exposure "carries with it the very real threat of undermining [plaintiff's] religious community and religious practice."

Sixth, by reason of the extent to which the Brethren involve themselves in instilling exemplary behavior in their children—including the teaching of the moral and health dangers of AIDS, the abstinence from all sexual relations outside of marriage, and the avoidance of illegal drugs in order to remain physically and spiritually "pure"—no public health risk will result from the exemption. Whatever the failings of society at large in educating children to avoid the dangerous and unhealthy practices by which AIDS is transmitted, in Brethren society such instruction is successful.

[Notwithstanding these factual proofs, the trial court dismissed the complaint, and the appellate division affirmed. Recognizing the burden that AIDS instruction placed on the Brehren's religious beliefs, the lower courts held that such burden was outweighed by the state's compelling interest in public health instruction; the lower courts also deferred to the expert judgment of the public school authorities.]

Reflecting the rich religious pluralism that characterizes and distinguishes this Nation, the First Amendment to the Federal Constitution enjoins the State from enacting any laws "prohibiting the free exercise" of religion. Under this clause a claimant may seek a religious exemption from a government requirement linked to a benefit program such as public education (*Wisconsin v. Yoder*, 406 U.S. 205 [1972]).

In deciding whether a claimant is entitled to such an exemption, the Supreme Court has formulated a two-step analysis, both steps obviously fact-sensitive. First, a claimant must show a sincerely held religious belief that is burdened by a State requirement. Second, the State must demonstrate that the requirement nonetheless serves a compelling governmental purpose, and that an exemption would substantially impede fulfillment of that goal. With respect to both prongs of the test, this case presents material issues of fact that preclude summary judgment. * * *

It is generally acknowledged that mere exposure to ideas that contradict religious beliefs does not impermissibly burden the free exercise of religion. The First Amendment does not stand as a guarantee that a school curriculum will offend no religious group. Moreover, parents have no constitutional right to tailor public school programs to individual preferences, including religious preferences (see, *Epperson v. Arkansas*, 393 U.S. 97, 106 [1968]).

Plaintiffs accept that the Constitution offers no protection against exposure to ideas that offend their religion. They maintain, however, that the Supreme Court recognized an exception to the "mere exposure" rule in *Yoder*, and that they fall squarely within that exception.

Yoder involved members of two Amish groups who refused, on the basis of religious belief, to send their children to school beyond the eighth grade. The parents were convicted of violating Wisconsin's compulsory school-attendance law, which required parents to send their children until age 16. At trial the Amish asserted that the law required what their religion forbade and thus violated the Free Exercise Clause. In addition, the Amish adduced testimony from expert witnesses, scholars on religion and education, who explained the relationship between the Amish belief concerning school attendance and the more general tenets of their religion, and described the devastating impact that compulsory high school attendance could have on the continued survival of the religious community.

The Supreme Court in *Yoder* held Wisconsin could not require the Amish to send their children to public school after the eighth grade. In finding an impermissible burden on free exercise, the Supreme Court examined Amish life and culture in some detail, ultimately concluding that what was in issue were long-standing beliefs shared by an organized group, that the beliefs related to religious principles and pervaded and regulated Amish daily life, and that the State law threatened the continuing existence of the Old Order Amish church community.

The reach of *Yoder* is plainly limited. The Supreme Court itself made that clear in cautioning that its holding would apply to "probably few other religious groups or sects" and that "courts must move with great circumspection in performing the sensitive and delicate task of weighing a State's legitimate social concern when faced with religious claims for exemption from generally applicable educational requirements." * * *

Nevertheless, the present case bears some striking similarities to *Yoder*. As in *Yoder*, plaintiffs seek a religious exemption from exposure to ideas that are not merely offensive but allegedly abhorrent to their central religious beliefs. And like *Yoder*, governmental action purportedly compels them to participate in instruction that is at odds with a fundamental tenet of their religious belief—remaining simple from evil. The Brethren assert, like the Amish in *Yoder*, that these are entrenched religious beliefs, not the product of "a way of life and mode of education by a group claiming to have recently discovered some 'progressive' or more enlightened process for rearing children for modern life." Their adherence to "the Principle of Separation," they say, also stems from "a sustained faith pervading and regulating [their] entire mode of life."

Thus, on this record we cannot agree with the sweeping conclusions reached by the Trial Judge in granting summary judgment that the mandated AIDS curriculum is neither contrary to the Brethren's religious beliefs nor destructive of the community as a whole. Rather, the record better supports the conclusion reached by the Appellate Division that "compulsory education which exposes [plaintiffs'] children to the 'details of evil' which their religion instructs them to avoid may place a limited burden upon the free exercise of their religion."

But it is as much plaintiffs' alleged differences from the Amish in *Yoder* as their similarities that give pause and persuade us that further factual development is required before a conclusion can be reached—either way—on the question whether the free exercise of sincerely held religious beliefs is burdened by compulsory AIDS education, how great such a burden might be, and what if any further accommodation should be made. With such significant public and private interests in the balance, on this record it is at the least prudent to withhold judgment until there is a firmer basis for the necessary findings of fact than the brief, contentious, often conclusory affidavits both sides have submitted. The trial record in *Yoder* is replete with fact, scholarly and expert testimony that has no parallel in the present record. [Among the issues to be developed were (1) exactly how integrated the Brethren were in the overall community (the Amish were established as almost wholly segregated from the larger community in *Yoder*); (2) whether instruction in sexuality would threaten the Brethren's ability to maintain their religion; and (3) whether instruction of these Brethren children is really necessary to effectuate the state's compelling interest in public health instruction, the next issue examined by Judge Kaye.]

* * * Both the trial court and the Appellate Division were satisfied that the State's interests in AIDS education on its face was so compelling that it necessarily would override plaintiffs' free exercise rights. While that conclusion may ultimately prove correct, it was error to reach it on the present record.

As a blanket proposition, the State has a compelling interest in controlling AIDS, which presents a public health concern of the highest order. Nor can there be any doubt as to the blanket proposition that the State has a compelling interest in educating its youth about AIDS. Education regarding the means by which AIDS is communicated is a powerful weapon against the spread of the disease and clearly an essential component of our nationwide struggle to combat it.

But the Education Law and regulations themselves provide for exemptions from the prescribed curriculum. Moreover, history teaches that constitutional protections do not readily yield to blanket assertions of exigency. As with other grave risks we have faced during the past two centuries, the threat of AIDS cannot summarily obliterate this Nation's fundamental values (see, Orland and Wise, "The AIDS Epidemic: A Constitutional Conundrum," 14 *Hofstra L. Rev.* 137, 150 [discussing *Korematsu v. United States*, 323 U.S. 214 (1944)]). That compelling public interests underlie the mandate for AIDS education thus does not, in and of itself, end all inquiry as to whether 35 Brethren children must be denied an exemption. * * *

In supporting the compelling need to educate Brethren children about AIDS, defendants point both to plaintiffs' extensive life within the community and to the possibility that some of them may go astray, or leave the fellowship, or be cast out, thus consigned to living among the general population ignorant of AIDS. Plaintiffs rejoin that their lives are indeed separate, and that the State's allegations regarding defections are pure speculation; there is no evidence either way as to defections among the New York State Brethren. Even assuming that a defection could be said to pose a public health threat, plaintiffs strenuously dispute that the education they provide their children leaves them ill equipped to cope with the dangers of AIDS. These contentions cannot be determined by the existing record.

Again somewhat relatedly, given the particular means by which AIDS is transmitted a real question is raised about the education Brethren children do receive, and whether the State can achieve its goal of AIDS control by means that would not unduly burden plaintiffs' religious practice. If plaintiffs showed that the education they offered their children was the functional equivalent of the AIDS curriculum—giving due regard to the physical as well as moral concerns—the State might well be required to accommodate their beliefs.

On this point the parties are at loggerheads. Defendants allege that Brethren parents do not offer a suitable alternative form of education, in that they provide their children only with moral instruction which is not an adequate substitute for clinical information. The Appellate Division characterized Brethren teaching as "uncontradicted religious indoctrination which denies the existence of undeniable health crises". But plaintiffs strenuously contest those assertions. Although Brethren children are provided with moral instruction regarding sex and drug use, plaintiffs have never stated that this is all they teach their children and they represent that, if granted an exemption, they would "instruct [their] children at home or in their assembly concerning the AIDS virus and epidemic." They further submit that, as a practical matter, by teaching their children to avoid all sexual activity outside of marriage and to avoid all illegal drugs in order to remain physically and spiritually "pure," they have developed "a strong AIDS-prevention program" that has been singularly successful in preventing its members from either contracting the disease themselves or transmitting it to others. This factual dispute also requires a fuller record.

[Speaking for the Court, Judge Kaye remanded the case for trial on these disputed factual issues.]

■ TITONE, JUDGE (dissenting).

[Judge Titone believed that plaintiffs were entitled to summary judgment and, therefore, disagreed with the remand for further evidence-taking. The key legal issues—the sincerity of plaintiffs' religious beliefs and their relation to sexuality instruction and plaintiffs' assurances of effective home education—were not, in Judge Titone's view placed in material dispute by defendants' submissions.]

In my view, neither this case, nor *Yoder*, is simply an example of a religious sect's effort to obtain First Amendment protection from the "mere exposure" to inimical ideas. Instead this case, like *Yoder*, is an attempt by plaintiffs to secure a judicial dispensation from having to perform an affirmative act that their religion forbids. Although the gist of what plaintiffs seek to avoid is, indeed, "exposure" to a certain category of information, plaintiffs are motivated not merely by a desire to steer clear of offensive or contradictory ideas, but rather by a religious precept that requires them, and their children, to remain innocent of "the details of evil." In a sense, plaintiffs are forbidden by their religious beliefs to eat of the tree of secular knowledge on the subject of AIDS in the same way that some observant Jewish and Muslim individuals are forbidden to eat pork— and in the same way that the Amish individuals in Yoder were forbidden to send their teen-age children to public high school, thereby removing them from the traditional farm community at a time that was critical to their spiritual development. Accordingly, plaintiffs are entitled to the same protection, without regard to whether the continuing vitality of their religious community has been threatened. * * *

Finally, as a matter of common sense and experience, I have difficulty crediting any claim by the State that its interests would be seriously impaired by granting an exemption to these plaintiffs. As the majority suggests, the statutory and regulatory provisions for granting exemptions on a case-by-case basis belie any potential contention by the State that strict universal AIDS education, without exception, is necessary to satisfy its interests. Moreover, although education is, unfortunately, the most effective weapon we now have against this contemporary plague, we should not lose sight of the fact that knowledge is not the equivalent of a serum that would ensure immunity. To the contrary, the efficacy of education in this context might well be questioned, since the individuals who are most at risk, such as intravenous drug users, are also among those who are least susceptible to the influence of educators. Furthermore, given the nature of this disease and the manner in which it is spread, it seems clear that prevention depends upon a combination of personal factors, only one of which involves clinical knowledge. Equally critical are such factors as an individual's choice of life-style and sense of self-esteem—precisely the areas which the Brethren's moral and spiritual training addresses.

In the final analysis, the continued existence of our pluralistic society depends not only upon our commitment to tolerating minority viewpoints, but also upon our willingness to accommodate them. Further, I believe that we jeopardize an important element of our social structure when we too readily displace the moral and spiritual guidance that may be derived from family and church with the secular and purportedly value-neutral instruction that our public schools are equipped to provide. While I share the abhorrence of ignorance that characterizes much of modern western culture, I cannot overlook the fact that our contemporary faith in the power of secular education has not immunized us from such social ills as rampant drug abuse, an inordinately high drop-out rate, family dissolution and spiritual demoralization, as well as socially transmitted diseases such as AIDS. Accordingly, like the *Yoder* court I am most reluctant to assume that today's prevailing culture, which places its faith in objective knowledge, is "right" while plaintiffs and others like them, who place their faith in moral and spiritual guidance, are "wrong." * * *

■ BELLACOSA, JUDGE (dissenting). * * *

The simple landscape on which this controversy is viewed includes the conceded compelling State interest of educational instruction in the transmission and prevention of a public health menace—the AIDS epidemic—and the pervasive, voluntary integration of the Brethren believers in work, education and dwelling within their chosen general community. Indisputably then, this is not a *Yoder* case. It is not at all like that case, and even is distinguishable in a constitutionally crucial respect—here, plaintiffs' children were granted a substantial exemption pursuant to the challenged regulation itself, which also authorizes that flexible outlet.

The majority recognizes, as the United States Supreme Court has taught, that *Yoder* is an extraordinarily exceptional dispensation from the primacy of a universal public educational curriculum—in this case, a primacy enhanced by the urgency of a rampant public health problem, thus far apparently controllable only by educational means. Fragmentation of the curriculum, especially in this area, and segmentation of the student population are not warranted and plaintiffs have not advanced sufficient proof, within the summary judgment rubric, to withstand the defendant Commissioner's record presentations of a dominant, compelling State interest.

The essential "factual dispute," forming the primary premise for this court's rationale upsetting the lower courts' grant of summary judgment to the Commissioner of Education, springs from an assertion by plaintiffs that they have "minimal" contacts in the community and from a claimed sufficient relatedness to *Yoder*. Denominating their claims as fact issues, however, cannot so facilely justify this inconclusive procedural remedy not even sought by plaintiffs, because the claims are facially and evidentially, in the summary judgment sense, belied by the realities and the record. The Brethren's conceded participation in the community, especially in the core relevant category of the students' otherwise full involvement in their public school education, is substantial, not "minimal." Moreover, these primary attributes of community, i.e., work, school and dwelling, cannot be diminished or denied just because the Brethren find it "not feasible * * * to do otherwise." (Majority opn.) The facts are the facts for whatever reason—and if undeniable, they are not triable. Indeed, some categories of cases are, for transcendent jurisprudential and policy reasons, particularly suitable to summary judgment resolution. This is such a case and such a category, and the record supports only that relief in my view.

[Like Judge Titone, Judge Bellacosa rejected the majority's insistence upon a new hearing. Unlike Judge Titone, who thought the Brethren were entitled to summary judgment under *Yoder*, Judge Bellacosa thought the state was entitled to summary judgment because *Yoder* was so different from this case.]

PROBLEM 8–1

RETHINKING AIDS EDUCATION IN LIGHT OF LATER FREE EXERCISE DECISIONS AND THE RELIGIOUS FREEDOM RESTORATION ACT

Although a recent decision, *Ware* came before recent upheavals in the meaning of "free exercise of religion." Consider subsequent developments and the light they cast upon the positions taken by Judges Kaye, Titone, and Bellacosa, especially their different readings of *Wisconsin v. Yoder*, 406 U.S. 205 (1972).

(A) The Demise of Yoder? Notwithstanding *Yoder*, the Supreme Court rarely struck down a state policy because it impermissibly burdened religious free exercise, and many of its decisions belied a commitment to *Yoder*'s compelling interest test.[a] The Court rejected that test altogether in *Employment Division, Department of Human Resources v. Smith*, 494 U.S. 872 (1990), where Oregon had applied its antidrug laws to prosecute a Native American using peyote for ceremonial religious purposes. Justice Scalia's opinion for a five Justice Court held that the free exercise clause afforded people no right to exemption from laws of general application that incidentally and as applied burdened their free exercise of religion. Three Justices dissented from the Court's rejection of *Yoder* and *Sherbert v. Verner*, 374 U.S. 398 (1963). Justice O'Connor concurred in the Court's judgment but did not agree that *Sherbert*'s compelling interest approach should have been overruled or rejected. Under *Smith*, the Court was willing to strike down a municipal law apparently targeted at an unpopular religious group, *Church of the Lukumi Babalu Aye, Inc. v. City of Hialeah*,

---

a. *E.g., Lyng v. Northwest Indian Cemetery Protective Ass'n*, 485 U.S. 439 (1988) (allowing state to build a road on public lands sacred to Native Americans because no direct "coercion" of religious belief); *Goldman v. Weinberger*, 475 U.S. 503 (1986) (refusing strict scrutiny when military dress code burdens free exercise by preventing rabbi from wearing yarmulke); *Bowen v. Roy*, 476 U.S. 693 (1986) (declining to require compelling state justification when alleged burden, use of social security numbers to identify welfare recipients, was merely a procedural, housekeeping rule); *United States v. Lee*, 455 U.S. 252 (1982) (administratively sound tax system is a state interest sufficient to justify ancillary burdens on religious belief). See generally Ira Lupu, "Of Time and the RFRA: A Lawyer's Guide to the Religious Freedom Restoration Act," 56 *Mont. L. Rev.* 171 (1994).

508 U.S. 520 (1993), but otherwise the free exercise clause was apparently deprived of its prior constitutional bite (or overbite, as Justice Scalia might put it).

After *Smith*, is there any defense for the approach taken by either Judge Titone or Kaye in *Ware*? Does Judge Bellacosa now carry the day?[b]

(B) The Religious Freedom Restoration Act (RFRA): Yoder Redivivus? *Smith* was greeted with the proverbial firestorm of protest, as it offended what seemed like just about everybody: organized and unorganized religions alike, Native Americans and a broad range of civil liberties groups, and lawyers who felt that courts should adhere to stare decisis, or original intent, or plain meaning, in constitutional interpretation. Congress overrode *Smith* by near-unanimous margins in November 1993 with the Religious Freedom Restoration Act of 1993 (RFRA), Pub. L. No. 103–141, 107 Stat. 1488–89, codified at 42 U.S.C. §§ 2000bb through 2000bb–4.

RFRA rejected *Smith* as firmly as Congress has ever overridden the Supreme Court. Section 1 of the Act, 42 U.S.C. § 2000bb(b)(1), stated that the purpose of RFRA was "to restore the compelling interest test as set forth in *Sherbert v. Verner* and *Wisconsin v. Yoder*," and RFRA's statutory findings criticized *Smith* by name. *Id.* § 2000bb(a)(4). Section 3(b) directs that "Government may substantially burden a person's exercise of religion only if it demonstrates that application of the burden to the person—

(1) is in furtherance of a compelling governmental interest; and

(2) is the least restrictive means of furthering that compelling governmental interest."

Id. § 2000bb–1(b). "Government" is defined in RFRA § 5 to include all branches, departments, and instrumentalities of the federal and state governments (including the District of Columbia). Section 6(a) of RFRA provides that the law should have retroactive effect, applying to state and federal statutes adopted before 1993. *Id.* § 2000bb–3(a). The reason was that Congress viewed RFRA as "restorative" legislation, restoring the "true" free exercise law expressed in *Yoder* and *Sherbert* and temporarily displaced in *Smith*.

After RFRA, is there any defense for the approach taken by Judge Bellacosa or Kaye? Does Judge Titone's approach now carry the day?

(C) RFRA in Action: Muddy Waters? The enactment of RFRA has not entirely cleared up free exercise jurisprudence. Commentators Christopher Eisgruber and Lawrence Sager, argue that RFRA is unconstitutional in "Why the Religious Freedom Restoration Act Is Unconstitutional," 69 *N.Y.U. L. Rev.* 437 (1994). See also the debate in *Hamilton v. Schiro*, 74 F.3d 1545 (8th Cir.1996). Their argument, in brief, is that Congress cannot reset constitutional rights under its authority to implement the Fourteenth Amendment and that RFRA not only overrides *Smith* (which Eisgruber and Sager believe to have been rightly decided) but confuses prior free exercise

b. Consider Angela C. Carmella, "State Constitutional Protection of Religious Exercise: An Emerging Post-*Smith* Jurispru- dence," 1993 *B.Y.U. L. Rev.* 275; *State v. Hershberger*, 462 N.W.2d 393 (Minn.1990).

jurisprudence as well. Other commentators believe RFRA constitutional, either because they think *Smith* was wrong or they believe Congress has the power to create a statutory right in situations where the Court has refused to create a constitutional right. See generally "Symposium on RFRA," 55 *Mont. L. Rev.* 303 (1994).

For all the *sturm und drang*, it appears that RFRA is being applied with only a little more bite than *Yoder* had been, but the evidence is still provisional. On the one hand, *Cheffer v. Reno*, 55 F.3d 1517 (11th Cir. 1995), held that the Federal Access to Clinics Entrances Act does not violate RFRA, even accepting plaintiffs' assertion that it chills their expression of religious prolife views. Accord, *American Life League v. Reno*, 47 F.3d 642 (4th Cir.1995). On the other hand, courts have applied RFRA to overturn state orders preventing a Roman Catholic school from discharging a nonCatholic teacher, *Porth v. Roman Catholic Diocese*, 532 N.W.2d 195 (Mich.App.1995); requiring the Amish to mark their vehicles with orange triangles rather than the silver tape they prefer, *State v. Hershberger*, 538 N.W.2d 573 (Wis.App.1995); and imprisoning Rastafarians for using marijuana, *United States v. Bauer*, 75 F.3d 1366 (9th Cir.1996).

Is RFRA constitutional? (As this book goes to press in 1997, this issue is pending before the Supreme Court.) If so, how *should* it affect cases like *Ware*? Consider the following cases, the first one post-RFRA and the next one pre-RFRA. Both involve conflict between secular nondiscrimination duties involving sexuality, versus religious beliefs held by mainstream rather than marginal religious groups.

Evelyn Smith v. Fair Employment and Housing Commission, 12 Cal.4th 1143, 51 Cal.Rptr.2d 700, 913 P.2d 909 (1996). Evelyn Smith owned four apartment units which she rented out. She refused to consider renting a unit to Gail Phillips and Gary Randall because they were an unmarried couple; a devout Presbyterian, Smith considered their status sinful and did not want her units used for sinful relations. Phillips and Randall complained to the state Fair Employment and Housing Commission (FEHC), which found that Smith violated California's fair housing law, which makes it illegal to discriminate on the basis of "marital status" in housing rentals. Smith's main defense was that the FEHC position burdened her religious beliefs, in violation of the free exercise clause of the First Amendment, RFRA, and the California Constitution. A fragmented California Supreme Court held that she violated the law and that her religious beliefs were no defense.

The plurality opinion of Justice Werdegar, joined by two other Justices, ruled that the fair housing law was a law of general application which burdened Smith's religious beliefs only incidentally. Under *Employment Division v. Smith,* no free exercise violation was established. This part of the opinion commanded a majority of the court. The plurality opinion then ruled that Smith's religious beliefs were not "substantially burdened" and therefore did not trigger RFRA. Justice Werdegar recognized that RFRA meant to override *Smith* in favor of the *Sherbert/Yoder* approach, which requires compelling state justification, but only when action "substantially burden[s] a person's free exercise of religion."

Justice Werdegar distinguished *Sherbert*, where the person risked losing her job if she did not compromise her religious principles, and *Yoder*, where the state instruction was thought to violate core Amish principles regarding their children's education. In contrast, "Smith's religion does not require her to rent apartments, nor is investment in rental units the only available income-producing use of her capital. Thus, she can avoid the burden on her religious exercise without violating her beliefs or threatening her livelihood. The asserted burden is the result not of a law directed against religious exercise, but of a religion-neutral law that happens to operate in a way that makes Smith's religious exercise more expensive. Finally, to grant the requested accommodation would not affect Smith alone, but would necessarily impair the rights and interests of third parties." Accord, *Swanner v. Anchorage Equal Rights Comm'n*, 874 P.2d 274 (Alaska 1994), *cert. denied*, 115 S. Ct. 460 (1994).

Justice Mosk concurred on the ground that RFRA is unconstitutional. Because RFRA adjusts constitutional rights in both directions—depriving some of their rights while empowering others—it is not authorized by section 5 of the Fourteenth Amendment, he maintained.

Three Justices dissented from the RFRA holding of the court majority. Justice Kennard argued that FEHC's action substantially burdened Smith's religious beliefs and that such burden was not justified by the state interest in preventing discrimination on the basis of marital status. Unmarried people can easily find apartments in California, and any discrimination—if it exists—is mighty slender. Justice Kennard distinguished sexual orientation discrimination, which he believed to be substantially more invidious. Justice Baxter, joined by Justice Lucas, believed that RFRA applied because Smith's religion was substantially burdened by the FEHC order. They supported a remand to the FEHC for factual hearings on the significance of the state interest criticized by Justice Kennard.

Gay Rights Coalition of Georgetown University Law Center v. Georgetown University

District of Columbia Court of Appeals, *en banc*, 1987.
536 A.2d 1.

[Additional Excerpts in Chapter 5, Section 1(c)]

■ MACK, ASSOCIATE JUDGE [delivered the judgment of the Court].

[The Gay People of Georgetown University (GPGU) was established on the university's main campus in late 1977. Its constitution listed as goals to "provide an atmosphere in which gay people can develop a sense of pride, self-worth, awareness and community," to "provide information and encourage understanding and dialogue between gay and non-gay people," and to "provide a forum for the development of responsible sexual ethics consonant with one's personal beliefs." A similar group, Gay Rights Coalition (GRC), was formed at the Law Center. In 1979, the Dean of Student Affairs refused to afford university "recognition" of GPGU. and its attendant benefits (office space, telephone service, supplies at the university) because of Georgetown's tradition as a Roman Catholic institution. His letter concluded:

> This situation involves a controversial matter of faith and the moral teachings of the Catholic Church. "Official" subsidy and support of a gay student organization would be interpreted by many as endorsement of the positions taken by the gay movement on a full range of issues. While the University supports and cherishes the individual lives and rights of its students it will not subsidize this cause. Such an endorsement would be inappropriate for a Catholic University.

[The student groups unsuccessfully appealed this action within the university and then brought suit under the District's Human Rights Act (Appendix 2). Superior Court Judge Leonard Braman granted the students summary judgment to the effect that Georgetown had violated § 1–2520, which prohibits discrimination by an educational institution in the provision of "facilities and services" on the basis of sexual orientation and other illegitimate criteria (including sex and race). Superior Court Judge Sylvia Bacon tried the case and found that Georgetown's refusal to recognize was based upon its sincere religious beliefs and, therefore, that the District could not, consistent with the free exercise clause of the First Amendment, require the school to recognize student groups which the school found religiously objectionable.]

Through two centuries of growth, Georgetown University has been guided by the religious hope of its founder, John Carroll. All of its forty-six presidents have been Roman Catholic clergymen. On four occasions, the University has been headed by a bishop. In particular, Georgetown has continued a close relationship with the Jesuits. Since about 1825, without exception, members of that order have filled the presidential office. * * *

[Georgetown President Timothy S. Healy, S.J.] testified that throughout its existence Georgetown has invariably defined itself as a Roman Catholic institution. This perception is illustrated by some of the opening words in its undergraduate bulletin: "Georgetown is committed to a view of reality which reflects Catholic and Jesuit influences.... As an institution that is Catholic, Georgetown believes that all men are sons of God, called to a life of oneness with Him now and in eternity." Georgetown University, University Bulletin—Undergraduate Schools 1 (1980–81) (hereinafter "Undergraduate Bulletin"). * * * The Faculty Handbook describes "Georgetown University as an American, Catholic, Jesuit institution of higher learning," seeking to "uphold, defend, propagate, and elucidate the integral Christian and American cultural heritage" through "certain established principles, specific ideals, and definite traditions." Georgetown University, Faculty Handbook vi (1971) (hereinafter "Faculty Handbook"). The "established principles" are "the demonstrated philosophical truths about the nature of man, the universe and God; the truths of Christian revelation and their crystallization through the centuries.... " *Id.* Among the "specific ideals" are "the perfectability of society through the acquisition and practice by its members of the theological, intellectual, moral virtues and their derivatives [and] the value of service to the community as an expression of Christian democratic ideals." *Id.* And the "definite traditions" include "the Christian culture and conduct having their source and inspiration in the teachings and example of Christ. . . ." *Id.*

Georgetown University is a member of several associations of Roman Catholic educational institutions. As a Pontifical University, it is one of only two American universities entered in the Annuario Pontificio, an annual listing by the Holy See of all such institutions throughout the world. Chapels are scattered throughout its properties and Masses offered several times each day. Almost all of its directors are Catholic, although there is no formal requirement that they be so. During a five-year period just prior to trial, Jesuits made up between one third and one half of the board. Faculty members must "maintain a sympathetic attitude towards Catholic beliefs and practices. . . ." Georgetown has the largest number of ministers in residence among the Jesuit colleges and universities in the United States.

Roman Catholic doctrine influences some of Georgetown's policy decisions. Abortions and other proscribed procedures are not performed in the University hospital. Student newspapers may not carry advertisements for abortion clinics. Birth control devices may not be sold in the student stores. Cohabitation is forbidden between single students in the dormitories. In 1981, Georgetown returned a gift of $750,000 to the Libyan government due to the conflict between Roman Catholic teachings and that nation's perceived links with terrorist activity. Religious considerations, the trial court found, influenced Georgetown's denial of "University Recognition" and accompanying tangible benefits to the student groups. * * *

* * * [T]he student groups urge us to disregard as clearly erroneous Judge Bacon's factual finding that "University Recognition" at Georgetown includes an "endorsement." They point out that other groups with "University Recognition" occupy a broad range of the political, social and philosophical spectrum, and argue that Georgetown cannot claim that all of these organizations are strictly Roman Catholic in outlook. In particular, the student groups refer us to the recognized existence of such diverse bodies as the Jewish Students Association, the Organization of Arab Students, the Young Americans for Freedom, and the Democratic Socialist Organizing Committee. * * *

The student groups also sought to undermine Georgetown's claim of "endorsement" by pointing to views on artificial birth control, abortion, divorce and lesbianism associated with members of the Women's Rights Collective (WRC) and the Women's Political Caucus (WPC). However, one of their witnesses, Sister Mary K. Liston, stated that WPC, another campus group of which she was a member, had not and could not take a pro-abortion position "[b]ecause of the stand of the Catholic Church on the issue of abortion." Sona Jean Vandall, a representative of WRC, acknowledged that the only formally stated purpose of that organization is the eradication of policies and practices which alienate and discriminate against women. She further testified that views contrary to Roman Catholic teachings were carried in none of WRC's published information and that no such positions had been voted on by its membership. * * *

With regard to the plaintiff student groups, President Healy saw the matter differently. He testified that the University does not distinguish between students on the basis of their sexual orientation and said that group activity merely promoting the legal rights of gay people would present no religious conflict. But, according to President Healy and other Georgetown representatives, including its theological expert, the purposes set forth in the GPGU Constitution described an organization for which "University Recognition" would be inappropriate for a Catholic institution.

"The statement that stopped me most," said President Healy, was GPGU's stated commitment to "the development of responsible sexual ethics consonant with one's personal beliefs." See GPGU Constitution [quoted above]. Under Roman Catholic doctrine, as expert testimony established, responsible sexual ethics are not a question of personal belief. "The University cannot make that statement about any area of front line morality without insisting upon the objectivity of moral fact and that it is not left strictly to individual determination within any context which can reasonably be read as Catholic." Under Roman Catholic doctrine, contrary to GPGU's suggestion, sexual ethics are the subject of an absolute and unyielding moral law, one laid down by God.

President Healy also testified that GPGU's expressed intention to "establish a program of activities which reflect the above purposes," *id.*, was "open-ended enough to involve the University in a host of positions and activities which together or singly it would find inappropriate." He had similar reservations about GRC's stated commitment to the provision of information to gay and lesbian law students concerning "Washington's gay community, including educational, cultural, religious, social and medical services." See GRC Constitution. According to President Healy, GRC's association with the range of activities engaged in by the Washington gay community would "involve Georgetown University in positions it would not wish publicly to adopt."

Roman Catholic teachings establish "moral norms" which prevent believers from recognizing homosexual conduct, as distinguished from homosexual orientation, as anything other than sinful. * * *

Reverend Richard J. McCormick, S.J., Georgetown's theological expert, testified * * * that a Roman Catholic university "has a duty to act in a way consistent with those teachings and not to undermine them in its public policies." Thus, "in its public policies and public acts," the University "ought not to adopt a public policy of explicit endorsement or implicit endorsement" of, for example, abortion, premarital intercourse, or homosexual conduct. Georgetown should not "in its public actions, policies, decisions, take a position that would equivalently establish another normative lifestyle equally valid with the one that is in a normative position." According to President Healy, a grant of "University Recognition" to

GPGU and GRC would conflict with Georgetown's duty not to undermine the Roman Catholic teaching that "human sexuality can be exercised only within marriage...." * * *

* * * To read into the Human Rights Act a requirement that one private actor must "endorse" another would be to render the statute unconstitutional. The First Amendment protects both free speech and the free exercise of religion. Its essence is that government is without power to intrude into the domain of the intellect or the spirit and that only conduct may be regulated. Interpreting the Human Rights Act so as to require Georgetown to "endorse" the student groups would be to thrust the statute across the constitutional boundaries set by the Free Speech Clause and also, where sincere religious objections are raised, the Free Exercise Clause. Nothing in the statute suggests, let alone requires, such a result.

Because similar interests are often implicated, the Supreme Court has relied on both the Free Speech Clause and the Free Exercise Clause to protect against government intrusion into the inner domain. The Court has made clear that the state is without power to regulate the intellect or the spirit; its rule is over actions and behavior only. In its initial decision interpreting the Free Exercise Clause, the Court described the division between opinion and action as "the true distinction between what properly belongs to the Church and what to the State." *Reynolds v. United States*, 98 U.S. (8 Otto) 145, 163 (1878). With the adoption of the Free Exercise Clause, "Congress was deprived of all legislative power over mere opinion, but was left free to reach actions which were in violation of social duties or subversive of good order." *Id.* at 164. The Court quoted with approval a statute drafted by Thomas Jefferson to protect religious freedom in Virginia: "[i]t is time enough for the rightful purposes of civil government for its officers to interfere when principles break out into overt acts against peace and good order." *Id.* (quoting 12 Hening's Stat. 84 (1784)). "[T]o suffer the civil magistrate to intrude his [or her] powers into the field of opinion, and to restrain the profession or propagation of principles on supposition of their ill tendency, is a dangerous fallacy which at once destroys all religious liberty." *Id.* The Court concluded, as a matter of constitutional principle, that "[l]aws are made for the government of actions, and while they cannot interfere with mere religious belief and opinions, they may with practices." *Id.* at 166.

That principle has been emphatically reaffirmed in a later free exercise case: "the Amendment embraces two concepts—freedom to believe and freedom to act. The first is absolute but, in the nature of things, the second cannot be. Conduct remains subject to regulation for the protection of society." *Cantwell v. Connecticut*, 310 U.S. [296,] 303–04 [1940] (citations omitted). The principles embraced within the "absolute" core of the clause, freedom of conscience, thought and expression of religious belief, as "sacred private interests, basic in a democracy," *Prince v. Massachusetts*, 321 U.S. 158, 165 (1944), cannot be forced to jostle for position with other values regarded by the state as more deserving. * * *

Although the student groups were not entitled to summary judgment on the ground that Georgetown's denial of "University Recognition"—including an "endorsement"—violated the Human Rights Act, the statute does require Georgetown to equally distribute, without regard to sexual orientation, the tangible benefits contained in the same package. * * * Our review of the record reveals no genuine dispute that the tangible benefits were denied on the basis of sexual orientation. The Human Rights Act was violated to that extent. * * *

[Judge Mack considered whether this application of the Human Rights Act was consistent with the Free Exercise Clause. Unlike a required endorsement, required benefits—or burdens—entailed a balancing analysis.] One who invokes the Free Exercise Clause in order to gain exemption from a governmentally imposed obligation must initially establish that forced compliance with the regulation will impose a burden on his or her religious exercise. Although not all burdens on religious exercise are unconstitutional, an exemption accommodating the religious practice must be granted unless the government can demonstrate that it has a compelling or an overriding interest in enforcing the challenged regulation. If so, the court must assure itself that the promotion of the compelling governmental objective outweighs the burden imposed upon the practice of religion and, moreover, that the challenged regulation is the least restrictive means by which the government can attain its compelling end. *See, e.g., Bob Jones University v. United States*, 461 U.S. 574, 602–04 (1983); *United States v. Lee*, 455 U.S. 252, 257–60 (1982); *Thomas v. Review Board*, 450 U.S. 707, 718–19 (1981); *Wisconsin v. Yoder*, 406 U.S. [205, 219–21 (1972)]; *Sherbert v. Verner*, 374 U.S. [398, 402–09 (1963)].

[Judge Mack found that Georgetown's sincere religious objections extended beyond official recognition, to include provision of equal facilities and benefits to the gay student groups. After a lengthy factual analysis, Judge Mack also found that the District had a compelling interest in eradicating sexual orientation discrimination, based upon the factual findings that sexual orientation has no relation to an individual's ability to contribute to society and that prejudice against lesbians and gay men is irrational. In a remarkable survey, Judge Mack concluded that old notions of homosexuality as a mental disorder "have been widely abandoned" and that experts agree that sexual orientation is irrelevant to citizenship. Moreover, gay people are subjected to "ongoing prejudice in all walks of life, ranging from employment to education," a situation that the District properly sought to remedy in its Human Rights Act. "Although by no means a prerequisite to our conclusion of a compelling governmental interest, we note parenthetically that sexual orientation appears to possess most or all of the characteristics that have persuaded the Supreme Court to apply strict or heightened scrutiny to legislative classifications under the Equal Protection Clause."]

The compelling interests, therefore, that any state has in eradicating discrimination against the homosexually or bisexually oriented include the fostering of individual dignity, the creation of a climate and environment in which each individual can utilize his or her potential to contribute to and benefit from society, and equal protection of the life, liberty and property that the Founding Fathers guaranteed to us all. [Judge Mack then resolved the clash between the burden on Georgetown's religious free exercise and this compelling state interest.]

In this case, compelling equal access to the tangible benefits, without requiring the intangible "endorsement" contained in "University Recognition," imposes a relatively slight burden on Georgetown's religious practice. As Georgetown itself concedes, "[t]he only tangible benefits plaintiffs could receive by the grant of official recognition are relatively insignificant—such as mailing and computer labeling services." Supplemental Brief at 2. It then argues that "[s]uch minor perquisites cannot outweigh the substantial burden on the University's religious liberty that would flow from compelled recognition of the student groups." *Id.* But its argument fails because the "substantial burden" to which it refers—compulsion to grant the intangible "endorsement" contained in "University Recognition"—is not required by the Human Rights Act. By Georgetown's own admission, what the Human Rights Act actually does require—equal distribution of the tangible benefits—is considerably less burdensome.

Our conclusion that the burden on religious liberty does not outweigh the District's compelling interest receives additional support from the facts that Georgetown voluntarily gives the student groups the fewer tangible benefits that come with "Student Body Endorsement" and that it has never objected to the student groups meeting on campus. Without interference from the Georgetown administration, the student groups are an active force in the university community. GPGU, for example, has held campus meetings almost weekly, hosting discussions, speakers, and educational and social events. Finally, the burden imposed upon Georgetown's religious exercise is further diminished by the parties' representations that GPGU has already been given a mailbox, one of the tangible benefits theoretically in dispute.

[Judge Mack found that the equal benefits requirement was the "least restrictive means" to achieve the statutory goal of nondiscrimination.] To tailor the Human Rights Act to require less of the University than equal access to its "facilities and services," without regard to sexual orientation, would be to defeat its compelling purpose. The District of Columbia's overriding interest in eradicating sexual orientation discrimination, if it is ever to be converted from aspiration to reality, requires that Georgetown equally distribute tangible benefits to the student groups. Other than compelling the equal provision of tangible benefits, there are no available means of eradicating sexual orientation discrimination in educational institutions that would be less restrictive of Georgetown's religious exercise.

■ [We omit the separate opinion of CHIEF JUDGE PRYOR, who concurred with Judge Mack's result, allowing the students equal access to tangible benefits but not requiring Georgetown to provide "intangible" recognition. JUDGE NEWMAN also concurred in Judge Mack's judgment, adding the following discussion of the free exercise issue.]

The Supreme Court has held a variety of governmental interests sufficient to sustain facially neutral laws or regulations challenged by religious objectors under the free exercise clause. In *Goldman*, the Court held that the military's interest in "uniformity" permitted it to enforce its dress regulations to prohibit an Orthodox Jewish serviceman from wearing a yarmulke while on duty. In *Lee* the "broad public interest in maintaining a sound tax system" prevented exemption from the Social Security tax for an Amish employer employing other Amish. In *Braunfeld v. Brown*, 366 U.S. 599, 603 (1961), the state's interest in "improving the health, safety, morals and general well-being of ... citizens" permitted enforcement of Sunday closing laws against merchants who observed a Saturday Sabbath. In *Prince v. Massachusetts*, 321 U.S. 158, 165 (1944), the "interests of society to protect the welfare of children" permitted the state to apply its child labor law to bar a Jehovah's Witness from distributing religious literature on the streets.

By contrast, in those cases in which the Court has upheld a free exercise challenge and required the government to make exception to its general scheme in order to accommodate a religious objector, it has made clear that the government presented only the weakest of interests to support its refusal to make such an accommodation. In *Thomas* and *Sherbert*, the Court found that the states' asserted interests were without support in the record or had not been raised below. These cases involved the denial of unemployment compensation to employees who had left their employment rather than comply with a job task, *Thomas*, or work schedule, *Sherbert*, that conflicted with religious beliefs. The states argued that granting compensation would lead to fraudulent claims and dilution of the fund.

In *Yoder*, the Court determined to uphold the free exercise claim because to reject it "would do little to serve those interests" that the state had advanced in favor of enforcement of its law. 406 U.S. at 222. Taking into consideration the Amish way of life and the fact that the Amish were willing to comply with the state's requirements up through the eighth grade, the Court concluded that "Wisconsin's interest in compelling the school attendance of Amish children to age 16 emerges as somewhat less substantial than requiring such attendance for children generally." [*Id.*] at 228–29. * * *

While government cannot compel religious or other belief, it can require persons and institutions to comport their behavior to secular moral norms. *Reynolds* (refusing to exempt Mormons from application of anti-polygamy statute). Nondiscrimination is such a secular norm. In a series of recent decisions, the Supreme Court has extinguished any doubt that the enforcement of antidiscrimination laws is a compelling governmental interest when poised against a first amendment objection. In *Bob Jones University v. United States*, 461 U.S. 574, 604 (1983), the Court recognized that the government's "fundamental, overriding interest in eradicating racial discrimination in education" outweighed the free exercise claim of a private religious school that challenged the denial of tax-exempt status. In *Roberts v. United States Jaycees*, 468 U.S. 609, 626 (1984), the Court held that Minnesota's law "[a]ssuring women equal access to ... goods, privileges, and advantages clearly furthers compelling state interests." *Roberts* permitted the state to enforce its public accommodations law to require a private organization to admit women members in the face of a freedom of association claim. Most recently, in *Board of Directors of Rotary International v. Rotary Club of Duarte*, 107 S.Ct. 1940, 1948 (1987), confronted by a similar challenge to the application of a California statute, the Court reaffirmed that "public accommodations laws 'plainly serv[e] compelling state interests of the highest order,' " quoting *Roberts*, 468 U.S. at 624.

Finally, the Supreme Court has indicated that the compass of the right to free exercise of religion is measured not only by the importance of the governmental interest but by the nature of the burden imposed on the religious objector. See, e.g., *Braunfeld* (cautioning against "strik[ing] down, without the most critical scrutiny, legislation which imposes only an indirect burden on the exercise of religion, i.e., legislation which does not make unlawful the religious practice itself"). I do not understand Georgetown to argue that discrimination against any persons or groups is a tenet of its faith. * * *

■ FERREN, ASSOCIATE JUDGE, with whom TERRY, ASSOCIATE JUDGE, joins, concurring in the result in part and dissenting in part. * * *

* * * As I see it (and to this extent I agree with Judges Belson and Nebeker), compelled "University recognition" either is constitutional in both its aspects or is altogether unconstitutional; there is no middle ground.

If Judge Mack and her colleagues are correct—if gay rights groups must have access to tangible benefits equal to that of other groups but may lawfully be excluded from the list of officially "recognized" student groups having access to the same benefits—then the Act permits a "separate but equal" access to university facilities and services reminiscent of the justification that once permitted blacks on public buses, but only in the back. The Act's protections are not so narrow. * * *

An analogy to a similar form of discrimination helps underscore the point. Suppose, hypothetically, that a local private college religiously wedded to the views of the clergy who once offered a Biblical defense of slavery, or to the more recently expressed views of Bob Jones University, sought to limit black student groups to the tangible benefits of student activities by stressing that, because of their racial inferiority and/or their advocacy of racial intermarriage, they could not be officially "recognized" by the college on a par equal with other groups, such as a student chapter of the local Masonic lodge. Or, suppose that the same local college admitted self-acknowledged homosexuals to all degree-granting programs but carried them on all official college rosters, including the commencement program, under the exclusive heading of "evil" students. I cannot imagine anyone seriously would contend that the Human Rights Act does not prohibit such second-class, restricted access to college facilities and services—that the Act tolerates such a "hostile environment." *Meritor Savings Bank v. Vinson*, 477 U.S. 57 (1986). * * *

Just as Judge Mack's distinction between tangible and intangible benefits is not helpful in defining the reach of the Human Rights Act, it provides little enlightenment for resolving the constitutional question that is at the heart of Judge Mack's statutory analysis. Judge Mack distinguishes tangible from intangible benefits because she believes that compelling the university to give equal access to the intangible benefit of "recognition" would force it to speak in conflict with its religious tenets, whereas government-ordered access to tangible benefits would compel only conduct, not speech. The difference is critical, Judge Mack contends, because the first amendment absolutely forbids the government to compel speech but does not necessarily bar compelled conduct burdening religious practice. Consequently, she says, only the demand to provide the status of "University recognition" automatically violates the free exercise clause; requiring the mere "conduct" of giving equal access to tangible benefits, while burdening Georgetown's free exercise rights, is nonetheless constitutionally permitted if justified by a compelling state interest.

* * * I do not believe that either the intangible or the tangible benefits of "University recognition," if required, would violate Georgetown's free exercise rights. But, if Judge Mack were correct that compelled verbal "recognition" of the student groups would be a compelled religious stand in violation of the first amendment, I do not comprehend how enforcement of student access to visible, tangible benefits such as an office, a telephone, mailing services, and advertising privileges financed by the university would be any less evidently an unconstitutional requirement. Forced financial support for particular ideas is, in general, no less a required endorsement than compelled verbal support: depending on the circumstances, compelled financial support may well constitute an infringement of first amendment protections. Judge Mack's analysis virtually ignores this constitutional reality. * * *

■ BELSON, ASSOCIATE JUDGE, with whom NEBEKER, ASSOCIATE JUDGE, Retired, joins, concurring in part and dissenting in part. * * *

Georgetown's free exercise rights would * * * be infringed if it were required to subsidize ideas or activities that are contrary to Catholic doctrine. This defense applies with full force not only to the speech-related activity of the groups, but also to all other activities of the groups that are antithetical to Catholic doctrine. * * *

It has long been part of this country's first amendment jurisprudence that an individual cannot be compelled to fund the dissemination of religious views of others. James Madison, a drafter of the first amendment, wrote: "Who does not see ... [t]hat the same authority which can force a citizen to contribute three pence only of his property for the support of any one establishment, may force him to conform to any other establishment in all cases whatsoever?" J. Madison, *Memorial and Remonstrance Against Religious Assessments*, reprinted in *Everson v. Board of Education*, 330 U.S. 1 app. at 65–66 (1947). Thomas Jefferson expressed his agreement when he drafted the Virginia Bill for Religious Liberty, which stated in its preamble that "to compel a man to furnish contributions of money for the propagation of opinions which he disbelieves, is sinful and tyrannical." 12 *Hening, Statutes of Virginia* 84 (1823), quoted in *Everson.*

Since Georgetown is a private, Catholic-affiliated institution and since the promotion of homosexuality is incompatible with Catholic doctrine, it would infringe Georgetown's right to the free exercise of religion if it were required to subsidize student groups that foster and promote a homosexual life-style. Georgetown's interest in not being compelled to subsidize activities antithetical to Catholicism must be given great weight under our Constitution. * * *

* * * The Human Rights Act forbids an educational institution from discriminating

> based upon the race, color, religion, national origin, sex, age, marital status, personal appearance, sexual orientation, family responsibilities, political affiliation, source of income or physical handicap of any individual....

D.C.Code § 1–2520 (1987). While neither the statutory language nor its legislative history indicates whether the Council intended to assign any hierarchy to the several proscribed bases for discrimination, it is reasonable to postulate that it did not intend them to be equal. One must doubt, for example, that the eradication of discrimination based upon source of income or personal appearance was meant to be as compelling an interest as the eradication of discrimination based upon race.

In any event, it cannot be said that the goal of eliminating discrimination on the basis of sexual orientation, as undesirable as such discrimination may be, has attained the same high priority as public policy, in the District of Columbia or nationally, as has the goal of eliminating racial discrimination. This difference of emphasis is manifested in many ways. One is the equal protection clause jurisprudence of the United States Supreme Court. Under it, for example, a racial classification leading to different treatment has been identified as one that demands strict scrutiny—but no such scrutiny has been demanded of sexual orientation discrimination. * * *

Weighing the District of Columbia's interest in eradicating sexual orientation discrimination, I observe too that not every application of that interest is equally compelling. Indeed, in deciding what weight to assign to that interest, the most pertinent question is not simply whether the District's interest in proscribing sexual orientation discrimination is, in the abstract, compelling. Rather, it is how important this application of the Human Rights Act is to the accomplishment of that interest. Therefore, in weighing the competing interests involved, one can consider that in addition to endorsement petitioners are seeking only the tangible benefits of a mailbox, mailing services, and computer labeling services, and also the right to apply for university funds. This case does not involve denial of fundamental aspects of higher education such as admission to the university, course selection, or use by a student of the physical facilities of the university. Nor does it involve such deprivations as discriminatory discharge from employment or exclusion from a place of public accommodation based on sexual orientation, the elimination of which may well be compelling. Indeed, Georgetown permits these student organizations to conduct their activities without hindrance, merely requiring that they do so without university subsidization or endorsement. On this point, Judge Bacon found that "the interests of Georgetown students in gay issues and their needs can be served without 'university recognition' of the plaintiff organizations." She noted specifically that "[w]ithout 'university recognition,' clubs may be formed, meetings may be held on campus and application may be made for lecture funds."

On the other side of the balance, Georgetown is claiming constitutional rather than statutory rights, and they are the fundamental rights of freedom of speech and the free exercise of religion. Moreover, the burden on Georgetown would be direct compulsion, i.e., an injunction ordering the university to violate its religious beliefs.[19] Therefore, upon considering the constitutional issues and balancing the opposing interests, I would find the District's interest in preventing the asserted sexual orientation discrimination regarding endorsement and limited tangible benefits is outweighed by Georgetown's interest in not endorsing and subsidizing activities and an ideological message repugnant to its religious creed. This is the conclusion Judge Bacon reached upon weighing Georgetown's free exercise rights against the statutory right of petitioners to receive the benefits in question. That decision is supported by the record and by the applicable case law.

* * *

■ [Part VI of ASSOCIATE JUDGE NEWMAN's concurring opinion responded to Judge Belson's belief that some discriminations in the Human Rights Act are more important than others. The statutory language and legislative history evidence no such hierarchy of favored and less favored categories of discrimination. "The District of Columbia Council, determining to pioneer where the federal government, and indeed many state governments, have not, has chosen to include sexual orientation discrimination within the

---

19. Although the record bears out Judge Newman's observation that discrimination against homosexuals is not a tenet of the Catholic faith, I disagree with his conclusion that providing facilities and services to the student groups is, therefore, only an indirect burden on Georgetown's free exercise of religion. Forcing Georgetown to subsidize the dissemination of a doctrine of sexual ethics deemed immoral by the Catholic Church is a direct burden on its free exercise rights. In this respect, this case differs from *Bob Jones*. There, the burden on that university's free exercise of religion from the denial of its tax-exempt status was much lighter than the burden that would be imposed here. The Su-

preme Court said in Bob Jones that although "[d]enial of tax benefits will inevitably have a substantial impact on the operation of private religious schools, [it] will not prevent those schools from observing their religious tenets." In contrast, the burden on Georgetown would constitute direct compulsion to violate its religious tenets by subsidizing a group whose purposes are antithetical to Catholicism. Furthermore, Bob Jones University ran afoul of the public policy against racial discrimination, which has constitutional underpinnings, while the "state" interest at issue here is the enforcement of a statutory provision.

ambit of those forms of discrimination which it deems anathema in this jurisdiction. This provision, no less than the Act's more traditional provisions, deserves the deference of this court." This part of Judge Newman's opinion was joined by ASSOCIATE JUDGES MACK, FERREN, and TERRY. It was the only analysis that commanded a majority of the seven-judge court of appeals.]

NOTES ON THE GEORGETOWN CASE AND THE ACCOMMODATION OF FREE EXERCISE AND NONDISCRIMINATION NORMS

1. *Doctrinal Update.* You can perform the same exercise for this case that Problem 8–1 poses for *Ware*, the AIDS education case. After *Employment Division v. Smith*, would Judge Ferren carry the day? After RFRA, would Judge Belson have the better arguments? Or does RFRA just return doctrine to where Judge Newman said it was all along? Or do you think RFRA, whose constitutionality will be evaluated and which will be interpreted by the same Justices who handed down *Smith*, will not have as much bite as Congress expected?

2. *The Analogies to Race and Marital Status.* Judges Belson and Nebeker were alone in believing there is a hierarchy in the Human Rights Act nondiscrimination categories: race and perhaps sex discrimination are the most important, with sexual orientation discrimination being of less consequence to the Council. A majority of the court disagreed. Were those judges right as a normative matter? Should it make a difference that in 1987 consensual sodomy was a felony in the District?

Given this understanding of the Act, is there any way to distinguish *Bob Jones*, where the Court allowed a fundamentalist college to lose its tax exemption because it discriminated on the basis of race? Has Judge Ferren trapped Judges Mack and Newman with his hypothetical? Was *Bob Jones* rightly decided under RFRA? Bob Jones University lost its tax exemption—which is a major big deal for educational institutions—because it did not allow interracial dating on campus. Before 1975, Bob Jones had discriminated against African–American applicants in some ways, but it claimed that its only discrimination after 1975 was against interracial dating. Is that race discrimination that would violate the equal protection clause or the Human Rights Act? Is that discrimination enough to satisfy RFRA?

Given Judge Newman's view that the Council did not create a hierarchy of discriminations, does Georgetown violate the Human Rights Act's "marital status" protections by refusing to rent apartments to cohabiting students? Recall Evelyn Smith's case, and the California Supreme Court's analysis of the free exercise issues.

3. *Accommodating Colliding Norms.* The quandary in the Georgetown case was how to accommodate two attractive norms, free exercise and nondiscrimination. Judges Ferren and Belson insisted that the rights of one side trump the rights of the other; the former believed nondiscrimination trumps free exercise, the latter believed the opposite. Both attack Judge Mack, who sought to accommodate colliding norms rather than simply choose one. One of us teaches at Georgetown, and the other is an alumna. We think Judge Mack's accommodation has been workable, and that both students and the university have profited from her moderation. Do you agree that moderation works here? Is there a theoretically attractive way of defending it? (Don't stop with Solomon and his baby-cutting hypothetical.) Consider the following and see what you think.

Robert M. Cover, The Supreme Court, 1982 Term—Foreword: *Nomos* and Narrative

97 *Harvard Law Review* 4, 14–16, 30, 32–33, 40, 60–62 (1983).*

[Cover identifies two patterns for forming a *nomos*, a normative world. One is "world-creating," or *paideic*. "Discourse is initiatory, celebratory, expressive, and performative, rather than critical and analytic. Interpersonal commitments are characterized by reciprocal acknowledgment, the recognition that individuals have particular needs and strong obligations to render person-specific responses." A second model is "world-maintaining," or *imperial*. "In this model, norms are universal and enforced by institutions. They need not be taught at all, as long as they are effective. Discourse is premised on objectivity—upon that which is external to the discourse itself. Interpersonal commitments are weak, premised only upon a minimalist obligation to refrain from the coercion and violence that would make impossible the objective mode of discourse and the impartial and neutral application of norms."]

Of course, no normative world has ever been created or maintained wholly in either the *paideic* or the imperial mode. I am not writing of types of societies, but rather isolating in discourse the coexisting bases for the distinct attributes of all normative worlds. Any *nomos* must be *paideic* to the extent that it contains within it the commonalities of meaning that make continued normative activity possible. Law must be meaningful in the sense that it permits those who live together to express themselves with it and with respect to it. It must both ground predictable behavior and provide meaning for behavior that departs from the ordinary.

* * * [T]he very act of constituting tight communities about common ritual and law is jurisgenerative by a process of juridical mitosis. New law is constantly created through the sectarian separation of communities. The 'Torah' becomes two, three, many Toroth as surely as there are teachers to teach or students to study. The radical instability of the *paideic nomos* forces intentional communities—communities whose members believe themselves to have common meanings for the normative dimensions of their common lives—to maintain their coherence as *paideic* entities by expulsion and exile of the potent flowers of normative meaning.

It is the problem of the multiplicity of meaning—the fact that never only one but always many worlds are created by the too fertile forces of jurisgenesis—that leads at once to the imperial virtues and the imperial mode of world maintenance. Maintaining the world is no small matter and requires no less energy than creating it. Let loose, unfettered, the worlds created would be unstable and sectarian in their social organization, dissociative and incoherent in their discourse, wary and violent in their interactions. The sober imperial mode of world maintenance holds the mirror of critical objectivity to meaning, imposes the discipline of institutional justice upon norms, and places the constraint of peace on the void at which strong bonds cease. * * *

In the world of the modern nation-state—at least in the United States—the social organization of legal precept has approximated the imperial ideal type that I have sketched above, while the social organization of the narratives that imbue those precepts with rich significance has approximated the *paideic*. We exercise rigid social control over our precepts in one fashion or another on a national level. There is a systematic hierarchy—only partially enforced in practice, but fully operative in theory—that conforms all precept articulation and enforcement to a pattern of nested consistency. The precepts we call law are marked off by social control over their provenance, their mode of articulation, and their effects. But the narratives that create and reveal the patterns of commitment, resistance, and understanding—patterns that constitute the dynamic between precept and material universe—are radically uncontrolled. They are subject to no formal hierarchical ordering, no centralized, authoritative provenance, no necessary pattern of acquiescence. Such is the radical message of the first amendment: an interdependent system of obligation may be enforced, but the very patterns of meaning that give rise to effective or ineffective social control are to be left to the domain of Babel.

* * * [T]here is a radical dichotomy between the social organization of law as power and the organization of law as meaning. This dichotomy, manifest in folk and underground cultures in even the most authoritarian societies, is particularly open to view in a liberal society that disclaims control over narrative. The uncontrolled character of meaning exercises a destabilizing influence upon power. Precepts must 'have meaning,' but they necessarily borrow it from materials created by social activity that is not subject to the strictures of provenance that characterize what we call formal lawmaking. Even when authoritative institutions try to create meaning for the precepts they articulate, they act, in that respect, in an unprivileged fashion. * * *

The free exercise clause is only one of many principles that may be employed to create boundaries for communities and their quasiautonomous law. Professor Carol Weisbrod's excellent study of nineteenth century utopian communities [*Boundaries of Utopia* (1980)] demonstrates the power of freedom of contract to create nomic insularity. It is not surprising that she finds that the voluntaristic character of the ideology of these communities—especially the Shaker community—dominated their constitutional thought, just as the vision of free exercise dominates Amish and Mennonite constitutional theory. * * *

Freedom of association is the most general of the Constitution's doctrinal categories that speak to the creation and maintenance of a common life, the social precondition for a *nomos*. From the point of view of state doctrine, the simplest way to generalize the points that I have made concerning the ways in which various groups have built their own normative worlds is to recognize that the norm-generating aspects of corporation law, contract, and free exercise of religion are all instances of associational liberty protected by the Constitution. Freedom of association implies a degree of norm-generating autonomy on the part of the association. It is not a liberty to be but a liberty and capacity to create and interpret law—minimally, to interpret the terms of the association's own being. * * *

Liberty of association is not exhausted by a model of insular autonomy. People associate not only to transform themselves, but also to change the social world in which they live. Associations, then, are a sword as well as a shield. They include collective attempts to increase revenue from market transactions, to transform society through violent revolution, to make converts for Jesus, and to change the law or the understanding of the law. Despite the interactive quality that characterizes transformational associations, however, such groups necessarily have an inner life and some social boundary; otherwise, it would make no sense to think of them as distinct entities. It is this social organization, not the datum of identity of interest, that requires the idea of liberty of association. Commonality of interests and objectives may lead to regularities in social, political, or economic behavior among numbers of individuals. Such regularities, however, can be accommodated within a framework of individual rights. When groups generate their own articulate normative orders concerning the world as they would transform it, as well as the mode of transformation and their own place within the world, the situation is different—a new *nomos*, with its attendant claims to autonomy and respect, is created. Insofar as the vision and objectives of such a group are integrative, however, the structure of its *nomos* differs from that of the insular sectarian model.

[Distinguishing the vision of these groups from the *insular constitutionalism* of the Amish and Mennonites, Cover uses the term *redemptive constitutionalism* to describe "the positions of associations whose sharply different visions of the social order require a transformational politics that cannot be contained within the autonomous insularity of the association itself." Examples of redemptive constitutionalism are the antislavery jurisprudence of the mid-nineteenth century (William Lloyd Garrison) and the civil rights jurisprudence of the mid-twentieth century (Martin Luther King, Jr.). Redemptive constitutional thinking also characterizes the women's liberation as well as right-to-life movements of the late twentieth century.]

[T]he jurisgenerative principle by which legal meaning proliferates in all communities never exists in isolation from violence. Interpretation always takes place in the shadow of coercion. And from this fact we may come to recognize a special role for courts. Courts, at least the courts of the state, are characteristically 'jurispathic.'

It is remarkable that in myth and history the origin of and justification for a court is rarely understood to be the need for law. Rather, it is understood to be the need to suppress law, to choose between two or more laws, to impose upon laws a hierarchy. It is the multiplicity of laws, the fecundity of the jurisgenerative principle, that creates the problem to which the court and the state are the solution.

* * * To state, as I have done, that the problem is one of too much law is to acknowledge the nomic integrity of each of the communities that have generated principles and precepts. It is to posit that each 'community of interpretation' that has achieved 'law' has its own *nomos*—narratives, experiences, and visions to which the norm articulated is the right response. And it is to recognize that different interpretive communities will almost certainly exist and will generate distinctive responses to any normative problem of substantial complexity. * * *

* * * Just as living in the economic world entails an understanding of price, so living in the normative world entails an understanding of the measures of commitment to norms in the face of contrary commitments of others. Such a view of the normative import of coercion avoids privileging the violence or the interpretations of the state. If there is a state and if it backs the interpretations of its courts with violence, those of us who participate in extrastate jurisgenesis must consider the question of resistance and must count the state's violence as part of our reality. * * *

* * * Keeping the peace is no simple or neutral task. For in the normative worlds created around us, not all interpretive trajectories are insular. The worlds of law we create are all, in part, redemptive. With respect to a world of redemptive constitutionalism, the Court must either deny the redemptionists the power of the state (and thereby either truncate the growth of their law or force them into resistance) or share their interpretation. * * * The courts may well rely upon the jurisdictional screen and rules of toleration to avoid killing the law of the insular communities that dot our normative landscape. But they cannot avoid responsibility for applying or refusing to apply power to fulfill a redemptionist vision.

The problem is exemplified in the Supreme Court's treatment of competing claims concerning the education of children and youth. The claims of both insular and redemptionist visions have particular force: the bond between group and individual is by definition *paideic*, and disputes over educational issues raise the question of the character of the *paideia* that will constitute the child's world. The American constitutional treatment of schooling has responded by assuming a twofold form. Certain decisions have acknowledged the dangerous tendencies of a statist *paideia* and marked its boundaries through formal specification of the limits of public meaning. * * * Although these decisions suggest that the state's specification of meaning is most dangerous when religion and politics are concerned, the issues in these cases are presented by every public curriculum. No sharp line between the problems of *Epperson* [prohibiting the state from teaching religious theories of creation] and those of a typical history curriculum can be drawn. Similarly, the confessional or sacramental character of the utterances in *Barnette* [prohibiting the state from requiring schoolchildren to pledge allegiance to the flag] and the School Prayer Cases distinguish them only in degree from the confessional character of all claims of truth and meaning.

* * * The public curriculum is an embarrassment, for it stands the state at the heart of the *paideic* enterprise and creates a statist basis for the meaning as well as for the stipulations of law. The recognition of this dilemma has led to the second dimension of constitutional precedent regarding schooling—a breathtaking acknowledgment of the privilege of insular autonomy for all sorts of groups and associations. The principle of *Pierce v. Society of Sisters* [prohibiting the state from requiring public school attendance] was always grounded on a substantive due process that protected not only religious education, but also private education in general, and it has proved the single, solid survivor from the era of substantive due process. *Wisconsin v. Yoder* recognized an even broader autonomy for religious community. The state's extended recognition of associational autonomy in education is the natural result of the understanding of the problematic character of the state's *paideic* role. There must, in sum, be limits to the state's prerogative to provide interpretive meaning when it exercises its educative function. But the exercise is itself troublesome; thus, the private, insular alternative is specially protected. Any alternative to these limits would invite a total crushing of the jurisgenerative character. The state might become committed to its own meaning and destroy the personal and educative bond that is the germ of meanings alternative to those of the power wielders. * * *

NOTE ON THE ESTABLISHMENT CLAUSE AS A LIMITATION ON STATE ENDORSEMENT OF RELIGIOUS MESSAGES

The First Amendment guarantees not only the free exercise of religion but also prohibits the "establishment" of a state religion. According to *Everson v. Board of Education*, 330 U.S. 1 (1947), the establishment clause prohibits not only the formal establishment of an official state religion, but also state encouragement or even subsidization. (*Everson* pointed to Madison's opposition to a religious assessment in Virginia. In his *Remonstrance Against Religious Assessments*, Madison insisted that "religious liberty could be achieved best under a government which was stripped of all power to tax, to support, or otherwise to assist any or all religions, or to interfere with the beliefs of any religious individual or group.") Notwithstanding this general precept, *Everson* allowed New Jersey to compensate parents for transportation of their children to parochial schools when this was part of a general program of compensating all parents for such costs, including those who sent their children to public schools or nonreligious private schools.

The wall of separation between church and state, Justice Black's ideal in *Everson*, has been harder and harder to apply in the modern regulatory era, where so many benefits flow directly from the state. While the Court has been firm in denying the state any power to impose compulsory prayers on a captive audience, *e.g.*, *Lee v. Weisman*, 505 U.S. 577 (1992), it has wandered a bit in figuring out whether various forms of state aid to religious schools are permissible. Compare *Lemon v. Kurtzman*, 403 U.S. 602 (1971) (salary supplement for teachers at private religious schools yields too much "entanglement" of state and religion), with *Mueller v. Allen*, 463 U.S. 388 (1983) (tax deduction for expenses of private religious schools is fine).

Recall *Rosenberger v. Rector and Visitors of the University of Virginia*, 115 S.Ct. 2510 (1995) (Chapter 5, Section 1[C]), where a split Court required the University of Virginia to subsidize a sectarian newspaper, *Wide Awake: A Christian Perspective at the University of Virginia*. Holding that the university was required by the free speech clause to give the newspaper funding on an equal basis as other student newspapers and groups, the Court necessarily confronted the establishment clause problem its decision created. All the Justices agreed that the establishment clause required state "neutrality" toward religion but differed as to what neutrality meant in the particular case. Justice Kennedy's opinion for the Court reasoned from *Everson* that neutrality is respected "when the government, following neutral criteria and evenhanded policies, extends benefits to recipients whose ideologies and viewpoints, including religious ones, are broad and diverse." *Id.* at 2521. Because the university was providing a public forum open to all student opinions and groups, the establishment clause allowed—and the free speech clause required—the university to assure the forum to religious viewpoints on a nondiscriminatory basis.

Writing for four dissenting Justices, Justice Souter reasoned from Madison's *Remonstrance* that "direct subsidization of preaching the word is categorically forbidden under the Establishment Clause." *Id.* at 2535. He argued that state neutrality requires avoidance of any entanglement of the state with explicitly religious messages, and certainly cannot countenance a state subsidy for "proselytizing." The state should, on the whole, stay away from religion. (Justice Thomas, in a concurring opinion, disputed Justice Souter's history. The Souter–Thomas debate is an interesting historical one.)

How would Cover analyze this debate? The university saw itself as a nomic community dedicated to secular knowledge and education. The student group saw itself as part of a nomic community of born-again Christians. Was it jurispathic for the Court to reject the university's understanding of its mission? Was that preferable to rejecting the students' ability to engage in their form of redemptive constitutionalism?

CITIZENS IN CONFLICT: ANTI-CIVIL RIGHTS AND ANTI-GAY INITIATIVES

The tension between religious groups and sexualized groups (cohabiting couples, lesbians and gay men) explored in Section 1 has a flip side in this section. Where the earlier disputes arose out of the application of the nondiscrimination norm to religious institutions or persons, the disputes in this section arise out of popular efforts—often spearheaded by fundamentalist churches—to repeal nondiscrimination norms adopted by legislatures. Some of the same religious groups, mainly fundamentalist Protestant ones, had earlier spearheaded campaigns to repeal civil rights laws protecting African Americans, and this section uses the earlier anti-civil rights initiatives (and their case law) to illuminate the more recent anti-gay initiatives and the recent Supreme Court decision striking down Colorado's effort.

PART A. INTRODUCTION TO DIRECT DEMOCRACY

The initiative is a method whereby a certain percentage of the electorate may petition to have a proposed statute or amendment to the state constitution put on the ballot for a vote of the electorate at large. The direct initiative refers to the method in which the issue goes on the ballot automatically after the requisite signatures of voters are collected. In contrast, under the format of the indirect initiative, upon the collection of the requisite signatures the proposed statute is submitted to the legislature, which is given a period of time in which to approve or disapprove the measure. If the legislature fails to pass the proposed statute, or if it adopts an amended version, the proposed statute in its original form is placed on the ballot, often along with any legislatively approved variation.

The referendum is a method whereby the electorate may approve or disapprove of a law proposed by or already enacted by the legislature. The voter referendum is a method under which, upon the collection of the requisite signatures, a law already passed by the legislature may be approved or rejected by the electorate. The legislative referendum is a format in which the legislature may place before the electorate a proposed law either for the voters' approval or disapproval (a "binding legislative referendum") or for their advice (an "advisory legislative referendum").

Almost one-half of the states have one form or another of statewide initiative, and about three-fourths have some form of statewide referendum. *The Book of the States 1986–87*, at 214–16 (1986). In many states, the

715

initiative and referendum are available at the local level as well, even if one or both are not available statewide. In addition, state constitutions generally require proposed constitutional amendments to be submitted to the electorate for approval or disapproval. For more information and theory about direct democracy, see William N. Eskridge, Jr. & Philip P. Frickey, *Legislation: Statutes and the Creation of Public Policy* ch. 5 (2d ed. 1994), a book which opens its discussion of direct democracy with the following case involving an early anti-gay initiative.

St. Paul Citizens for Human Rights v. City Council of the City of St. Paul

Supreme Court of Minnesota, 1979.
289 N.W.2d 402.

[The St. Paul City Charter provides:

Sec. 8.01.   *Initiative, referendum and recall.* The people shall have the right to propose ordinances, to require ordinances to be submitted to a vote, and to recall officials by processes known as initiative, referendum, and recall.

Sec. 8.02.   *Petition.* Initiative, referendum, or recall shall be initiated by a petition signed by registered voters of the city equal to eight per cent of those who voted for the office of mayor in the last preceding city election in the case of initiative or referendum, and twenty per cent in the case of recall. * * *

Sec. 8.04.   *Initiative.* Any ordinance may be proposed by a petition which shall state at the head of each page or attached thereto the exact text of the ordinance sought to be proposed. If the council fails to enact the ordinance without change within sixty days after the filing of the petition with the city clerk, it shall be placed on the ballot at the next election occurring in the city. * * * If a majority of those voting on the ordinance vote in its favor, it shall become effective immediately.

Sec. 8.05.   *Referendum.* Any ordinance * * * may be subjected to referendum by a petition filed within forty-five days after its publication. The petition shall state, at the head of each page or in an attached paper, a description of the ordinance * * * involved. Any ordinance * * * upon which a petition is filed, other than an emergency ordinance, shall be suspended in its operation as soon as the petition is found sufficient. If the ordinance * * * is not thereafter entirely repealed, it shall be placed on the ballot at the next election, or at a special election called for that purpose, as the council shall determine. The ordinance * * * shall not become operative until a majority of those voting on the ordinance * * * vote in its favor.

Sec. 8.06.   *Repeal of ordinances * * * submitted to voters.* No ordinance adopted by the voters on initiative or ordinance * * * approved by referendum shall be repealed within one year after its approval.

[In April 1978 a majority of those voting in St. Paul voted "yes" on the following initiative question:

Should Chapter 74 of the St. Paul Legislative Code which prohibits discrimination in employment, education, housing, public accommodations and public services based on race, creed, religion, sex, color, national origin or ancestry, affectional or sexual preference, age or disability be amended by removing "affectional or sexual preference" from the ordinance and should Section 74.04 which provides as follows:

"No person shall discriminate, on grounds of race, creed, religion, color, sex, national origin or ancestry, affectional or sexual preference, age or disability, with respect to access to, use of, or benefit from any institution of education or services and facilities rendered in connection therewith, except that a school operated by a religious denomination may require membership in such denomination as a condition of enrollment, provided such requirement is placed upon all applicants."

be further amended by removing "provided such requirement is placed upon all applicants"?]

■ TODD, JUSTICE.

* * * Plaintiffs contend that voters in St. Paul cannot use the initiative process to repeal an ordinance; they claim that council action or a referendum are the only means by which an ordinance can be repealed. Defendants argue that the power to legislate includes the power to repeal, that there are no restrictions on the power of initiative, and, thus, that an initiative can be used to repeal an existing ordinance. Whether or not voters have the power to repeal an existing ordinance by initiative is a question of first impression in Minnesota.

Municipal ordinances are enacted either by action of the city council or by the initiative process. The power to enact ordinances generally implies the power to repeal them. The city council repeals existing ordinances by enacting new ordinances. The voters of St. Paul are, therefore, also able to repeal existing ordinances by enacting new ordinances through the initiative process unless the grant of authority provides otherwise.

The St. Paul City Charter grants the people "the right to propose ordinances, to require ordinances to be submitted to a vote, and to recall elective officials by processes known respectively as initiative, referendum, and recall." St. Paul City Charter, § 8.01. It also provides that "[a]ny ordinance may be proposed by [initiative] petition * * *." St. Paul City Charter, § 8.04. These two provisions indicate that the city charter commission intended the voters to be able to repeal or amend existing ordinances by initiative. * * *

Plaintiffs also claim that the ballot question repealing the St. Paul Gay Rights Ordinance was improperly drawn because it actually contained two questions. The first question dealt with deleting all reference to "affectional or sexual preference" from the St. Paul Human Rights Ordinance, and the second question dealt with deleting the clause "provided such requirement is placed upon all applicants" from the provision which permits a religious institution to require membership in its denomination as a condition of enrollment.

A municipal ordinance must contain only a single subject. See, St. Paul City Charter, § 6.04. An ordinance violates this proscription only when it contains subjects which are so dissimilar as to have no legitimate connection. See, *City of Duluth v. Cerveny*, 16 N.W.2d 779 (Minn.1944), where we held that an ordinance providing for the forfeiture of intoxicating liquor did not violate the Duluth Charter provision that no law shall embrace more than one subject because the question of forfeiture had a logical and material connection to the subject of regulating the sale of intoxicating liquor. The purpose of such a charter provision is to avoid the possibility of logrolling, deceit, or voter confusion. See, *Bogen v. Sheedy*, 229 N.W.2d 19 (Minn.1975), where we held that a referendum petition concerning two ordinances was valid despite the fact that it contained two questions, because the ordinances had been debated together, considered together, were passed at the same council meeting, and dealt with the same subject matter.

In the instant case, both questions concerned the same subject matter—the St. Paul Human Rights Ordinance. Given the public debate on the initiative, there was little possibility of deceit, voter confusion, or logrolling. Because the St. Paul City Council could have deleted all reference to "affectional or sexual preference" and the clause relating to religious institutions by enacting one ordinance, there is no reason that the voters could not do the same through the initiative process. * * *

■ ROGOSHESKE, J., took no part in the consideration or decision of this case.

■ WAHL, JUSTICE [joined by JUSTICES OTIS and SCOTT], dissenting.

I respectfully dissent from the majority holding that the voters of St. Paul can repeal an existing ordinance by the initiative process. Few courts have addressed this issue, and the case is one of the first impression in Minnesota. We must consider this decision in terms of its long-range implications and not on the basis of any one issue brought before the voters by the initiative process. Whether an existing ordinance can be repealed through the initiative process depends on the constitutional and/or statutory grant of authority.

Initiative and referendum provisions were introduced in this country early in this century by reformers who hoped that these processes would (1) increase voter involvement in the legislative process, (2) provide a check on the domination of legislatures by special interest groups, and (3) permit voters to act more objectively by considering issues rather than personalities so that there would be greater accuracy in expressing the public will.

The experience with initiative and referendum provisions has indicated that these hopes have been frustrated. First, ordinances enacted through the initiative process may be poorly drafted because only one person or a small group drafts the ordinance to be placed on the initiative petition. There is no review to ensure that the ordinance is internally consistent, not in conflict with existing laws or policies, or based on inaccurate factual premises. Further, there is no critical evaluation, input, or feedback from those in society who may be affected by the legislation; nor is there the refining process that occurs in the legislature. Second, the fact that the issues may be very complex necessitates long, detailed explanations and perhaps specialized knowledge in order that voters may make an informed choice. An election campaign does not lend itself to such explanations but to simple fact statements or slogans. As a result voters may be confused and make decisions, not on a factual or philosophical basis, but for emotional or political reasons. Third, the initiative process does not necessarily avoid domination of the legislature or council by special interest groups, because small groups, e.g., only eight percent of the voters of the City of St. Paul, can place an initiative question on the ballot. Because of the small voter turnout, a well-organized minority can secure or block passage of an ordinance. Thus, the initiative process is not always the voice of the people.

Because of these grave problems, I believe that statutory and charter provisions providing for initiative and referendum must be narrowly construed. I am confirmed in this belief by the fact that neither the framers of the state constitution nor the legislature has seen fit to provide for initiative and referendum on a statewide level. In Minnesota, the powers of initiative and referendum are confined by statute to the municipal level of government. The statute provides that municipalities "may also provide for submitting ordinances to the council by petition of the electors of such city and for the repeal of ordinances in like manner." Minn.St. 410.20. Instead of using the statutory language, however, the St. Paul City Charter grants the people "the right to propose ordinances, to require ordinances to be submitted to a vote, and to recall elective officials by processes known respectively as initiative, referendum, and recall." St. Paul City Charter, § 8.01. The St. Paul City Charter permits voters to vote on emergency ordinances by referendum, and all ordinances submitted to the voters by initiative or referendum can be repealed in one year.

Although the repeal of an ordinance may be considered an act of proposing legislation in a broad sense, there is a recognized distinction between an initiative, which is designed to propose new legislation, and a referendum, which is designed to review existing legislation. See, *Landt v. City of Wisconsin Dells*, 141 N.W.2d 245 (Wis.1966). Under Chapter 8 of the St. Paul City Charter, the only distinction between the initiative and the referendum is the time limit in which a petition must be filed. To hold that the St. Paul voters can repeal an existing ordinance by initiative would be to render the referendum provision meaningless, because it would eliminate the need to file the referendum petition within 45 days. It is not reasonable to suppose that the St. Paul City Charter Commission intended such a result. On this ground I would reverse the decision of the trial court.

NOTES ON *ST. PAUL CITIZENS* AND THE LIMITATIONS OF DIRECT DEMOCRACY

1. *Is Direct Democracy Reliable?* Justice Wahl, dissenting in the *St. Paul* case, makes this argument: given the exceptional nature of direct democracy, courts ought to be exacting in their scrutiny of the results. Thus courts should stand ready to prevent flawed initiatives or referendums from even getting on the ballot, to invalidate them more freely than they invalidate products of the legislature, and to construe such laws narrowly. The majority of the Minnesota Supreme Court might respond that judges should be no more activist when direct democracy produces law than when the legislature does so; the people, after all, are the ultimate sovereigns in our society.

James Madison in *Federalist* No. 10 cautioned against direct democracy, and firmly advocated representative democracy such as that instantiated in the Constitution, on the ground that pure democracy was too easily swayed by temporary passions and factional laws not in the longterm public interest. Madison would be attracted to Justice Wahl's position. Progressive reformers in the early twentieth century believed that Madison's views were outdated and that popular democracy would enhance citizen participation and be a breath of fresh air into the lawmaking process. Who is right?

Derrick Bell, Jr., in "The Referendum: Democracy's Barrier to Racial Equality," 54 *Wash.L.Rev.* 1, 20 (1978), says: "Appeals to prejudice, over-simplification of the issues, and exploitation of legitimate concerns by promising simplistic solutions to complex problems often characterize referendum and initiative campaigns." Based upon an empirical analysis of direct democracy in action, David Magleby, *Direct Legislation* (1984), points to several problems:

- Because of threshold signature-gathering requirements and the difficulty of educating the electorate, most successful initiatives are sponsored by organized interest groups that lost in the legislative process. In this way direct democracy might be wasteful and could contribute to legislative enervation (if the legislature is cowed by the possibility of popular override).

- Since voters get no chance to express views on alternative approaches to the ballot issue, their simple "yes" or "no" vote is not a good measure of their true beliefs. Moreover, ballot measures are often too lengthy and complex for the average voter to digest, and many voters simply respond by abstaining. Thus, while those particularly concerned with the measure will vote, the average voter, and particularly the less sophisticated voter, is likely to forego voting. Thus, the citizens who vote on a ballot proposition are often less representative of the electorate than those who vote for candidates.

- Because direct democracy often deals with sensitive issues, and because it cannot work a compromise or accommodation, by its nature it "appeal[s] to passions and prejudices, spotlight[s] tensions, and result[s] only in greater conflict and disagreement." Recall Madison's argument in *Federalist* No. 10, that representative government is to be preferred over direct democracy, lest temporary "factions" obtain hasty legislation.

Other commentators have viewed direct democracy more favorably than Bell and Magleby. For example, Professors Butler and Ranney state that their "preliminary verdict would be that the referendum is a politically neutral device that generally produces outcomes favored by the current state of public opinion." *Referendums: A Comparative Study of Practice and Theory* 224 (David Butler & Austin Ranney eds. 1978). They acknowledge that the all-or-nothing choice given the electorate, in discouraging deliberation and compromise, is a "great deficiency." *Id.* at 226. Yet they suggest that

> in every polity there are times and circumstances when some decision is better than no decision, when continuing delay is itself disruptive of consensus and good temper, when the likelihood of working out a just compromise that will please anyone is slim or nonexistent. In such a situation the referendum has at least one great virtue: not only will it produce a decision, but the decision it produces is, in this democratic age, more likely to be regarded as legitimate and therefore acceptable than is a decision produced indirectly by elected officials. The people are always likely to think better of themselves than of their leaders, and thus any decision they make directly is likely to strike them as more legitimate than a decision made for them by others.

Id. Butler & Ranney take a moderate position, concluding that "[r]eferendums have often proved to be useful devices for solving or setting aside problems too hot for representative bodies to handle." *Id.*

2. *Procedural Judicial Review as a Corrective for Problems with Direct Democracy.* Perhaps surprisingly in light of his many criticisms, David Magleby concludes that "[d]irect legislation has been neither as positive in its effect as proponents have frequently asserted nor as dire in its consequences as opponents have predicted." *Direct Legislation* 196. Magleby's equivocal conclusion is based in part on his perception that courts "have been active in protecting individual rights, minimizing the harmful effects of short-term majorities on minority and individual rights." *Id.* The courts did strike down, in whole or in part, six of the ten initiatives adopted in California from 1960 to 1980. *Id.* at 53.

Most decisions invalidating initiatives and referenda are by state courts applying procedural norms derived from state and local sources of law; note that the debate in *St. Paul* focuses only upon the St. Paul Charter, with reference to state statutory and constitutional sources. Three kinds of state and local procedural limitations are often litigated:

(A) Jurisdictional. Because initiatives and referenda are exceptional methods of lawmaking in our political culture, they must be explicitly authorized. In *St. Paul*, that meant that the Minnesota Constitution (or statutes) had to allow St. Paul to make or unmake law by initiatives and referenda *and* the St. Paul Charter (or ordinance) had to authorize and establish procedures for such direct lawmaking. These requirements were not in dispute in the *St. Paul* case, but a related issue was: Was the measure a "referendum" subject to the requirement that the measure be submitted within 45 days of the ordinance it proposed to repeal, or was it

an "initiative" not subject to the 45–day rule? Justice Wahl seems to have a good argument that the measure was functionally a referendum and therefore failed the 45–day requirement. Is there any answer to this argument?

(B) The Single–Subject Rule. Most state constitutions and city charters that allow initiatives and referenda require that they only cover a "single subject," so that they offer clear-cut and unconfusing choices to voters. The challengers in *St. Paul* argued that the initiative covered more than a single subject, but even the dissenting justices did not adopt that argument. Why not?

(C) Technical Requirements. Although not at issue in *St. Paul*, technical requirements imposed by the authorizing provision of state or municipal law are the most frequently litigated, and challengers often win with such arguments as: The petitioners did not collect enough signatures to get their measure on the ballot. Some of the signatures are invalid (*e.g.*, because signatories are not registered voters). The measure was not perfected in the required time. And so on. How strictly judges hold the petitioners to these and other technicalities may depend, in part, on the judicial attitude toward direct democracy in general, or the particular measure.

3. *Substantive Judicial Review as a Corrective for Problems with Direct Democracy.* Like laws adopted in the legislature, laws adopted by popular election are invalid if they abridge individual rights protected by state or federal constitutions. Consider John Hart Ely, *Democracy and Distrust* (1980), who argues that courts ought to be perfecters of the democratic process and that judicial review is most legitimate under the Constitution when judges are correcting for dysfunctions in the political process. Developing the theory of judicial review suggested in *United States v. Carolene Products Co.*, 304 U.S. 144, 152–53 n. 4 (1938), Ely maintains that courts should be particularly scrutinizing of legislation that enables political insiders to squelch dissent from outsiders or that burdens "discrete and insular minorities" who are effectively excluded from the democratic process. Neither Ely nor Justice Harlan Stone (the author of *Carolene*) addresses the direct-versus-representative- democracy issue, but the implications of their approach might be something like the following.

The insiders-choking-off-channels-of-political-change argument for judicial review ought to be more relevant to representative than direct democracy. Elected representatives are more prone to protect insiders (themselves!) and stifle dissent; while direct democracy might be prone to some of these pressures, its proponents are likely to be people or groups the representative process has not accommodated. On the other hand, the discrete-and-insular-minorities-subject-to-prejudice argument for judicial review ought to be more relevant to direct than representative democracy. Especially where the legislature is bicameral and the chief executive has a veto, there are more points for the minority to be protected against precipitous action than there is in the simple one-shot initiative or referendum process. To the extent that the discrete and insular minority is subject to popular "prejudice" (the *Carolene* assumption or prerequisite), the prejudice can be more directly mobilized and expressed in the simpler initiative than in the more complex legislative process. This *Carolene*-based theory is normally enforced under the equal protection clause of the Fourteenth Amendment or of state constitutions. The remainder of this section explores two lines of cases.

PART B.   EQUAL PROTECTION LIMITS TO ANTI-CIVIL RIGHTS INITIATIVES

State, local, and federal legislatures enacted a variety of civil rights laws in the 1960s and 1970s. The laws prohibited discrimination on the basis of race, ethnicity, and sometimes sex in a variety of locations: the workplace, public accommodations, housing, and so forth. California's fair housing law, the source of dispute in *Smith v. Fair Employment and Housing Commission* (Section 1 above) is an example of such a law, although the category of "marital status" was a more recent add-on. Civil rights laws protecting against race discrimination sometimes stirred a "white backlash," which was often expressed in popular initiatives and referenda, whose constitutionality was litigated in celebrated court cases. The first big case was *Reitman v. Mulkey*, 387 U.S. 369 (1967). The Supreme Court held that it was a violation of the equal protection clause for California voters to amend their state constitution in order to encourage racial discrimination. That was an easy case, because there was substantial evidence of racial animus driving the initiative. Subsequent cases were more indirect. The following ones are the leading authorities.

Nellie Hunter v. Erickson et al., 393 U.S. 385, 89 S.Ct. 557, 21 L.Ed.2d 616 (1969). The Citizens of Akron, Ohio voted to amend the city charter to require that any ordinance regulating real estate on the basis of race, color, religion, or national origin could not take effect without approval by a majority of those voting in a city election. The amendment also suspended the operation of the existing city ordinance assuring "equal opportunity to all persons to live in decent housing facilities regardless of race, color, religion, ancestry or national origin." Ordinances prohibiting other types of housing discrimination or otherwise regulating real estate did not require referendum approval.

The Supreme Court concluded that the amendment created an explicitly racial classification, treating anti-race-discrimination housing laws differently from other racial and housing matters. Hence, the case fell under the *Reitman* rule. "Because the core of the Fourteenth Amendment is the prevention of meaningful and unjustified official distinctions based on race, racial classifications are 'constitutionally suspect' * * * and subject to the 'most rigid scrutiny.' * * * They 'bear a far heavier burden of justification than other classifications.' " The amendment flunked strict scrutiny.

James et al. v. Anna Valtierra et al., 402 U.S. 137, 91 S.Ct. 1331, 28 L.Ed.2d 678 (1971). The voters of California adopted a New Article XXXIV for the California Constitution to bring public housing decisions under California's referendum provisions. Article XXXIV provided that a state public body could not develop, construct, or acquire in any manner a low-rent housing project until a majority of the voters at a community election approved the project. Citizens of San Jose and San Matteo, where the defeat of low-cost housing referenda meant that housing authorities could not apply for federal funds, sued to overturn Article XXXIV as inconsistent with the equal protection clause as interpreted in *Erickson* and *Reitman*.

The Supreme Court rejected the challenge. Justice Black's opinion for the Court distinguished the California amendment from the Akron amendment on the ground that the latter rested on "distinctions based on race," while the former did not. The Court declined to extend *Erickson* beyond its explicit race-based classification. "The people of California have also decided by their own vote to require referendum approval of low-rent public housing projects. This procedure ensures that all the people of a community will have a voice in a decision which may lead to large expenditures of local governmental funds for increased public services and to lower tax revenues. It gives them a voice in decisions that will affect the future development of their own community. This procedure for democratic decisionmaking does not violate the constitutional command that no State shall deny to any person 'the equal protection of the laws.' "

Justice Marshall, joined by Justices Brennan and Blackmun, dissented. He argued that the amendment's imposition of substantial burdens upon the poor required more justification than the state could provide.

Washington v. Seattle School District No.1, 458 U.S. 457, 102 S.Ct. 3187, 73 L.Ed.2d 896 (1982). Voters in the state of Washington adopted initiative 350, designed to terminate the use of mandatory busing for purposes of racial integration in the public schools in Washington. The Supreme Court decided that the initiative used the racial nature of an issue to define the governmental decisionmaking structure and therefore imposed substantial and unique burdens on racial minorities. The district court found that by carefully tailoring the initiative, the initiative permitted almost all of the busing previously taking place in Washington, except for desegregative busing. Although Initiative 350 was facially neutral because the initiative did not mention "race" or "integration," the Court did not doubt that the initiative organizers effectively drew the initiative for racial purposes.

Next, the Court concluded that from a practical standpoint, the initiative reallocated "the authority to address a racial problem—and only a racial problem—from the existing decisionmaking body, in such a way as to burden minority interests." Since local school boards previously had the discretion to determine what program would most appropriately fill a school district's educational needs, the Court concluded that "Initiative 350 worked a major reordering of the State's educational decisionmaking process."

Although "the simple repeal or modification of desegregation or anti-discrimination laws, without more, never has been viewed as embodying a presumptively invalid racial classification." As Justice Harlan noted in his *Erickson* concurring opinion, the voters of the polity may express their displeasure through an established legislative or referendum procedure when particular legislation "arouses passionate opposition." Had Akron's fair housing ordinance been defeated at a referendum, for example, "Negroes would undoubtedly [have lost] an important political battle but they would not thereby [have been] denied equal protection." Since Initiative 350 "burden[ed] all future attempts to integrate Washington schools in districts throughout the State, by lodging decisionmaking authority over the question at a new and remote level of government," the initiative "work[ed] something more than the 'mere repeal' of a desegregation law by the political entity that created it."

PROBLEM 8–2

INITIATIVES HAVING INDIRECT RACE–BASED EFFECTS

Toledo, Ohio's city council adopted ordinances authorizing its public housing authority to construct sewer extensions to two proposed public housing sites outside the inner city. This was in response to federal threats to cut off funds to the city, because it had dragged its feet in establishing public housing outside the (mostly African–American) inner city and inside the (mostly Caucasian–American) outer rim of the city. Toledo's voters repealed both ordinances by referendum, and a class of African Americans with low incomes sues to overturn the referendum. You represent the plaintiffs and want to avoid a motion to dismiss. What allegations do you need to find support for? See *Arthur v. City of Toledo*, 782 F.2d 565 (6th Cir.1986).

PART C.   THE CONSTITUTIONALITY OF ANTI–GAY INITIATIVES

The extension of civil rights protection to gay men and lesbians in the 1970s and (especially) 1980s has proven just as controversial, as evidenced by the introduction of anti-gay ballot measures. This controversy boiled over into popular initiatives and referenda repealing pro-gay measures. Between 1972 and 1996, approximately 75 anti-gay ballot proposals were put before voters in jurisdictions across the United States.   The first referendum to receive national publicity was Anita Bryant's "Save the Children" campaign in 1977, which was able to revoke Dade County, Florida's anti-discrimination measure. The campaign was characterized by general vilification of gays and lesbians as "human garbage" and predators threatening children.

The first statewide anti-gay initiative appeared on the California ballot in 1978. Inspired by Bryant's campaign, the "Briggs Amendment" targeted gay and lesbian teachers. It would have empowered school boards to fire or refuse to hire teachers and school superintendents for "soliciting, imposing, encouraging, or promoting homosexual conduct." Although the measure initially enjoyed strong popular support, it was opposed by figures as diverse as Jerry Brown and Ronald Reagan and was defeated.

Anti-gay ballot initiatives picked up steam in the late 1980s, in large part as a reaction to affirmative legal protections that were at last being afforded gay men and lesbians. In 1988, for example, Oregon voters approved Measure 8, which overturned a gubernatorial executive order protecting state employees from discrimination on the basis of sexual orientation. There was a similar attempt in 1990 to repeal the Massachusetts 1989 gay civil rights law, but the Massachusetts Supreme Judicial Court blocked the measure from reaching the voters based on a state constitutional provision barring questions involving religion from appearing on the ballot. *Collins v. Secretary of the Commonwealth*, 556 N.E.2d 348 (Mass.1990).

The next wave of initiatives sought to nullify increasingly common municipal and county gay rights ordinances. In 1992, Oregon and Colorado voted on initiatives that sought not only to repeal local gay rights ordinances, but also to prevent the enactment of any future state or local gay civil rights laws. These measures sought to impose a unique political disability on gay men and lesbians, who alone among citizen groups would be barred by state constitutional amendment from seeking civil rights legislation. Oregon's Measure 9 would have repealed local gay rights measures, barred the future legislative enactment of such laws, and affirmatively obligated government to teach that homosexuality is "wrong, unnatural, and perverse."[a] In contrast, Colorado's Amendment 2 neither explicitly condemned homosexuality nor conscripted government into teaching that homosexuality is wrong. While the Oregon measure was defeated in 1992, Colorado's Amendment 2 was approved by the voters:

> No Protected Status Based on Homosexual, Lesbian, or Bisexual Orientation. Neither the State of Colorado, through any of its branches or departments, nor any of its agencies, political subdivisions, municipalities or school districts, shall enact, adopt or enforce any statute, regulation, ordinance or policy whereby homosexual, lesbian or bisexual orientation, conduct, practices or relationships shall constitute or otherwise be the basis of or entitle any person or class of persons to have or claim any minority status quota preferences, protected status

---

a. Measure 9 provided as follows:

(1) This state shall not recognize any categorical provision such as "sexual orientation," "sexual preference," and similar phrases that includes homosexuality. Quotas, minority status, affirmative action, or any similar concepts, shall not apply to these forms of conduct, nor shall government promote these behaviors.

(2) State, regional and local governments and their properties and monies shall not be used to promote, encourage, or facilitate homosexuality, pedophilia, sadism or masochism.

(3) State, regional and local governments and their departments, agencies and other entities, including specifically the State Department of Higher Education and the public schools, shall assist in setting a standard for Oregon's youth that recognizes homosexuality, pedophilia, sadism and masochism as abnormal, wrong, unnatural, and perverse and that these behaviors are to be discouraged and avoided.

or claim of discrimination. This Section of the Constitution shall be in all respects self-executing.

Amendment 2 was invalidated under the equal protection clause, but pursuant to two different theories, one advanced by the Colorado Supreme Court (below) and the other by the U.S. Supreme Court (excerpted in Chapter 1, Section 3[B][1]). Please read both decisions.

Richard G. Evans et al. v. Roy Romer et al.

Supreme Court of Colorado, *en banc*, 1993.
854 P.2d 1270, *cert. denied*, 510 U.S. 959 (1993).

■ CHIEF JUSTICE ROVIRA delivered the opinion of the Court. * * *

The right of citizens to participate in the process of government is a core democratic value which has been recognized from the very inception of our Republic up to the present time. See John Hart Ely, *Democracy and Distrust* 87 (1980) (the Constitution "is overwhelmingly concerned, on the one hand, with procedural fairness in the resolution of individual disputes (process writ small), and on the other, with ... process writ large—with ensuring broad participation in the processes and distributions of government") * * *.

The value placed on the ability of individuals to participate in the political process has manifested itself in numerous equal protection cases decided by the Supreme Court over the last thirty years. These include the reapportionment cases, cases concerning minority party rights, cases involving direct restrictions on the exercise of the franchise, and cases involving attempts to limit the ability of certain groups to have desired legislation implemented through the normal political processes. When considered together, these cases demonstrate that the Equal Protection Clause guarantees the fundamental right to participate equally in the political process and that any attempt to infringe on an independently identifiable group's ability to exercise that right is subject to strict judicial scrutiny.[9]

The Supreme Court has consistently struck down legislation which establishes preconditions on the exercise of the franchise. These cases,

---

9. Strict judicial scrutiny is warranted when participatory rights are infringed not only because a fundamental right is at stake, but also because

> [t]he presumption of constitutionality and the approval given "rational" classifications in other types of enactments[ ] are based on an assumption that the institutions of state government are structured so as to represent fairly all the people. However, when the challenge to the statute is in effect a challenge of this basic assumption, the assumption

can no longer serve as the basis for presuming constitutionality.

[*Kramer v. Union Free Sch. Dist. No. 15*, 395 U.S. 628 (1969).] That is, the ordinary assumption which informs judicial review of legislation that "even improvident decisions will eventually be rectified by the democratic process[ ] and that judicial intervention is generally unwarranted no matter how unwisely we may think a political branch has acted," *Vance v. Bradley*, 440 U.S. 93, 97 (1979), is rendered inapplicable when participatory rights are at issue.

generally speaking, are the types which most clearly violate the guarantee of equal protection because the legislation under review has the effect of directly "[f]encing out," *Carrington v. Rash*, 380 U.S. 89, 94 (1965), certain classes of voters. Thus, the Court has held that the requirement that voters pay a poll tax, *Harper v. Virginia Bd. of Elections*, 383 U.S. 663 (1966), be civilians, *Carrington*, or have property or children, *Kramer v. Union Free Sch. Dist. No. 15*, 395 U.S. 621 (1969), before they can exercise the right to vote runs afoul of the Equal Protection Clause. * * *

This same emphasis on the value of equal participation emerges from a second group of cases which addresses the issue of reapportionment. In *Reynolds v. Sims*, 377 U.S. 533 (1964), for example, the Court acknowledged the importance of political participation and the need for the most searching standard of judicial scrutiny when any effort is made to limit participation, in recognition of the fact that "since the right to exercise the franchise in a free and unimpaired manner is preservative of other basic civil and political rights, any alleged infringement of the right of citizens to vote must be carefully and meticulously scrutinized."

Unlike the situations presented in *Carrington, Kramer*, and *Harper*, however, the *Reynolds* Court was not confronted with legislation which set a precondition on the right to vote—no individual or group was precluded, or even impeded, from voting. Rather, the question presented in *Reynolds* concerned the Equal Protection Clause's bearing on participatory effectiveness, i.e., the right to have one's vote be as meaningful as the votes of others. Consequently, the Court's opinion in *Reynolds*, as well as in the other reapportionment cases, reflects the judgment that dilution in the effectiveness of certain voters' exercise of the franchise violates the guarantee of equal protection of the laws not simply because citizens are guaranteed the right to vote, but because that right must be preserved in a meaningful, effective manner. In short, equal protection requires that voters are able to exercise the right of franchise on an even footing with others.

This principle has also been consistently relied on to strike down legislation in a third category of political participation cases—the "candidate eligibility" cases. For example, the Supreme Court in *Williams v. Rhodes*, 393 U.S. 23 (1968), reviewed a series of Ohio statutes which "made it virtually impossible," for new political parties with widespread support, or an old party which enjoyed very little support, to be placed on the state ballot to choose electors pledged to particular candidates for the Presidency and Vice Presidency of the United States. The Court observed that the state statutes placed significant burdens on "the right of qualified voters, regardless of their political persuasion, to cast their votes effectively," because a "vote may be cast only for one of two parties at a time when other parties are clamoring for a place on the ballot." * * *

The "precondition," reapportionment, and "candidate eligibility" cases are not dispositive of, or directly controlling on, our decision here, as Amendment 2 falls within none of those three categories of cases. Admittedly, those decisions addressed entirely distinct questions and constitutional problems from those presented here. Nevertheless, it would be erroneous to conclude that those decisions are entirely inapposite. In the course of invalidating the laws at issue in those cases, the Court consistently recognized the paramount importance of political participation in our system of government, and articulated the fundamental principle which guided its decision in those cases: The Equal Protection Clause guarantees the fundamental right to participate equally in the political process, and thus any attempt to infringe on that right must be subject to strict scrutiny and can be held constitutionally valid only if supported by a compelling state interest. This principle is what unifies the cases, in spite of the different factual and legal circumstances presented in each of them. Thus, while all three categories of cases are distinguishable from the present controversy, the common thread which unites them with one another, and with the case before us, is the principle that laws may not create unequal burdens on identifiable groups with respect to the right to participate in the political process absent a compelling state interest.

This principle has received its most explicit, and nuanced, articulation in yet another category of cases where the legislation at issue bore a much closer resemblance to the question presented by Amendment 2. This category of cases involves legislation which prevented the normal political institutions and processes from enacting particular legislation desired by an identifiable group of voters. In each case, the legislation was held to be violative of equal protection. [The court then discussed *Hunter v. Erickson*, *Washington v. Seattle School District No. 1*, and *James v. Valtierra*, all digested in Part B.]

We conclude that the Equal Protection Clause of the United States Constitution protects the fundamental right to participate equally in the political process, and that any legislation or state constitutional amendment which infringes on this right by "fencing out" an independently identifiable class of persons must be subject to strict judicial scrutiny. * * *

■ [The dissenting opinion of Justice Erickson is omitted, but its main points are discussed in the following notes.]

Roy Romer et al. v. Richard G. Evans et al.

United States Supreme Court, 1996.
___ U.S. ___, 116 S.Ct. 1620, 134 L.Ed.2d 855.

[Excerpted in Chapter 1, Section 3(B)(1)]

NOTES ON THE COLORADO INITIATIVE DECISIONS AND EQUAL PROTECTION LIMITS ON DIRECT DEMOCRACY

1. *The Colorado Supreme Court's Theory: Fundamental Right of Political Participation?* Justice Erickson's dissent argued that all the court's authorities are either race cases (*Hunter*) or right-to-vote (*Reynolds* and *Harper*) and ballot-access (*Rhodes*) cases—and therefore distinguishable from the present case. The race cases implement the core values of the Reconstruction Amendments, namely, to eradicate slavery and its vestiges. Those core values may not be applicable to eradicating the public signs of homophobia, the dissent argued. The right-to-vote and ballot-access cases struck down state efforts to dilute the franchise of voting groups. Dissenting Justice Erickson maintained that these cases only stand for the proposition that formal barriers to *electoral* participation are suspect, and cannot be expanded to cover rules that merely make it harder for certain groups to have their way in the *political* process. Moreover, the ballot-access cases do not support strict scrutiny, because the Supreme Court has in recent cases applied a pure balancing approach. See *Burdick v. Takushi*, 504 U.S. 428 (1992); *Anderson v. Celebrezze*, 460 U.S. 780 (1983).

The court's response was that these cases are all illustrations of a common constitutional principle: identifiable "groups" of people cannot be excluded from the political process. See Laurence Tribe, *American Constitutional Law* 1482–88 (2d ed. 1988). Justice Rovira maintained that the judiciary ought to serve as a brake on the desire of popular majorities to exclude unpopular groups from the political process. One problem with the court's response is that gays and lesbians do have available to them the "normal" political process—appeal to Congress in Washington, D.C., to exercise its authority under the Fourteenth Amendment to override Amendment 2 to the Colorado Constitution, or to legislate the antidiscrimination protections directly. Are gays and lesbians being deprived of their rights of political participation?

Another problem is that groups are routinely denied access to the "normal" political process. The main effect of Amendment 2 would be to override local antidiscrimination laws, but states routinely prohibit their municipalities from legislating in certain areas, and the federal government routinely prohibits the states from legislating in certain areas. If Congress exercises its power to preempt state laws protecting toxic polluters from liability, for example, toxic polluters as a group are disabled from going to the state legislature to protect themselves—yet no one would contend that this is unconstitutional, yes?

The Colorado court, therefore, has to have a theory as to why federal preemption disabling toxic polluters from obtaining protective legislation from state legislatures is different from state constitutional preemption disabling bisexuals, gay men, and lesbians from obtaining anti-discrimination legislation from county and municipal legislatures. Consider the argument of Note, "Constitutional Limits on Anti–Gay Rights Initiatives," 106 *Harv. L. Rev.* 1905, 1918 (1993): "Toxic polluters are defined solely by * * * the ability to engage in toxic polluting. By contrast, lesbians and gay men are defined by *more* that just what the anti-gay initiatives outlaw (the ability to enact gay rights laws); gay people are defined by the broader criterion of sexual orientation. The distinction is important because it shows that, unlike the hypothetical [case], anti-gay-rights initiatives are aimed at diluting the political power of a particular group and not the regulation of an activity."

2. *The Supreme Court's Decision: Irrational Prejudice.* The Supreme Court decision affirmed the Colorado Supreme Court's second opinion in *Evans* (which in turn affirmed the trial court's decision, on remand from *Evans I*, to invalidate Amendment 2). Nowhere did the Court majority take a position on the state supreme court's right of political participation, and Justice Scalia's dissenting opinion lampooned it.

The U.S. Supreme Court made two important, but cross-cutting, criticisms of Amendment 2. The first criticism is that it was unusual to the point of being unprecedented: the initiative not only repealed job discrimination protections for lesbians and gay men, but was phrased so broadly that it could be read to deny judicial enforcement of laws of general applicability. This extraordinary impact was exacerbated by the fact that Amendment 2 only denied protection to "homosexuals"; heterosexuals remained protected by those laws. This criticism suggests that *Evans* might be narrowly read, to invalidate only anti-gay initiatives that operate so partially.

The other criticism suggests that *Evans* should be read more broadly: imposing legal penalties against gay people is not a "rational," much less "compelling," state interest; an initiative that seeks to penalize gays as a group is illegitimate under the rational basis test (usually an easy test to pass). This criticism draws the most fire from Justice Scalia's dissenting opinion, however. He challenged the majority to distinguish Amendment 2 from other laws that allow the state to create a "criminal class" (drug users! polygamists!! sodomites!!!) and then treat them differently, as by preempting local laws that are more favorable than state policy thinks those people should be treated.

The majority's rationale is hard to reconcile with the constitutional and statutory provisions of twenty-one states denying individuals convicted of certain crimes, even if the individual is no longer incarcerated, from being elected to, or from holding public office. See Steven Snyder, "Let My People Run: The Rights of Voters and Candidates Under State Laws Barring Felons from Holding Elective Office," 4 *J.L. & Pol.* 453 app. A (1988) (listing jurisdictions that specifically disqualify ex-felons from holding public office). It is hard to imagine any greater form of participation in the political process than serving as an elected or appointed public official, and surely the majority's analysis would have struck down a state law or constitutional provision saying that bisexual, gay, and lesbian citizens are ineligible to hold state office in Colorado. And one would think that its analysis would be hostile to laws excluding ex-felons, yes? But, as Colorado Justice Erickson noted in his state court dissent, not one of these provisions has been struck down based on an equal protection challenge for infringing on a fundamental right to participate equally in the political process. How should the U.S. Supreme Court respond to this kind of argument? Would an initiative cancelling local civil rights for polygamists be unconstitutional if it were based upon the population's moral disapproval of polygamy?

3. *Issues of Community and Citizenship.* Set aside the issues of judicial activism and direct versus representative democracy, and consider another political theory perspective, one suggested by Justice Harlan's dissenting opinion in *Plessy v. Ferguson* (invoked at the beginning of Justice Kennedy's opinion in *Evans* and originally suggested as the basis for striking down Colorado's Amendment 2 in William N. Eskridge, Jr. & Philip P. Frickey, "The Supreme Court, 1993 Term—Foreword: Law as Equilibrium," 108 *Harv. L. Rev.* 26, 92–95 [1994]).

Justice Harlan warned against law's becoming part of a "caste" system, and his warning was stunningly prescient as to racial castes; the Supreme Court has repeatedly disgraced itself (*e.g., Plessy* and *Toyosaburo Korematsu*) when it has upheld race classifications and has seen some of its finest moments (*e.g., Brown* and *Loving*) when it has struck down efforts to use the state to maintain race-based caste. Justice Scalia challenged this parallel with his own: polygamy. The Supreme Court's deference to popular disapproval of polygamy has never gotten it in trouble and seems uncontroversial today.

Which parallel is the best one for *Evans*? One argument for the Court's position is that the state's track record for sexual orientation classifications is about as bad as for race classifications: such laws have been hurtful and have produced vicious and predatory conduct. See William N. Eskridge, Jr., *Gaylaw: Challenging the Apartheid of the Closet* chs. 1–2 (forthcoming 1998) (history of sexual orientation classifications, especially 1920s through 1950s, almost all of which have been abandoned even by social conservatives). *Evans* is an effort by the Court to discourage use of the state as an instrument for bashing gay people. The Court is sending this message not because it thinks gay people are "good" or even nondisgusting, but because the Court recognizes that gay people pose no threat to straight people and that anti-gay bigotry is unproductive. The Supreme Court tolerated much more vicious state-sponsored gay-bashing in cases like *Bowers* (Chapter 1) and *Boutilier* (Chapter 2), so long as it believed that gays were basically invisible and could be exterminated without harm to the body politic. Once it has become apparent to the Court that gay people are here to stay, and state-sponsored violence against gay people is bound to create anger and resentment, it makes sense for the Court to insist that the state be relatively neutral.

Justice Scalia would respond that the state is not "neutral" after *Evans*, for the anti-discrimination ordinances of Boulder, Aspen, and Denver now create "special rights" for "homosexuals." How might one respond to this kind of argument?

PROBLEM 8–3

ANTI-GAY INITIATIVES AFTER *ROMER*

Citizens of the city of Riverside, California present a petition containing the requisite number of signatures to place on the ballot an initiative prohibiting the city council from adopting any law that "promotes, encourages, endorses, legitimizes or justifies homosexual conduct" without the approval of city voters. You are a judge who must certify this initiative in order for it to be on the ballot in November, and you believe that you should not certify it if you think it violates either the California or United States Constitution. What constitutional arguments should you consider? What role would the U.S. Supreme Court's *Evans* opinion (Chapter 1) play in your consideration? The Colorado Supreme Court's opinion (above)? Would you refuse to certify this initiative? See *Citizens for Responsible Behavior v. Superior Court*, 2 Cal.Rptr.2d 648 (Cal.App.1991).

Jane S. Schacter, The Gay Civil Rights Debate in the States: Decoding the Discourse of Equivalents

29 *Harvard Civil Rights–Civil Liberties Law Review* 283, 285, 291–96, 298, 300–02, 306–09 (1994).*

As anti-gay ballot measures have proliferated [since 1977] opponents of gay civil rights have opened a significant new line of attack. These opponents have increasingly stressed what I call a "discourse of equivalents." The structure of the new discourse is comparative, focusing on whether gay men and lesbians are sufficiently "like" other protected groups, and whether sexual orientation is sufficiently "like" race, gender, disability, religion, or national origin, to merit the legal protection of civil rights laws. Current civil rights laws are held out as the normative baseline against which the gay civil rights claim is tested to determine whether the fit between established and aspiring law is sufficiently close to confer legitimacy. * * *

The discourse of equivalents claims that the legitimacy of gay civil rights laws can be determined only by express comparison with existing anti-discrimination law. The discourse invokes two related themes in rejecting the gay civil rights claim: first, that the experience of gay men and lesbians is insufficiently "like" the experience of other already-protected groups; and second, that sexual orientation is insufficiently "like" other protected aspects of identity, such as race, gender, disability, religion, and national origin.

These themes sustain two contradictory lines of argument that gay rights opponents frequently offer. The first *denies* that gay men and lesbians are victims of discrimination at all. It depicts homosexuals as privileged and powerful actors who covet new and unwarranted "special rights." The underlying theme is that the *experience* of gay men and lesbians does not reflect the same kinds of disadvantage as that suffered by groups protected by existing civil rights law. The second argument concedes that gay men and lesbians are the objects of discrimination, but *defends* such discrimination as fully appropriate, based on the claim that homosexuality is an objectionable "chosen behavior." Sexual orientation is depicted as different from other protected aspects of identity in ways that disqualify gay men and lesbians from the protection of civil rights laws. * * *

[O]pponents of gay rights frequently invoke explicit comparisons with the experience of African Americans. Because the African American experience in many ways represents the paradigm for thinking about American civil rights law, the discourse of equivalents aggressively uses it to discredit and undermine the gay civil rights claim. Some arguments thus focus on the forms of discrimination that African Americans have experienced as a group, but gay men and lesbians as a group have not. A gay rights opponent in Florida, for example, notes that African Americans were "lynched, beaten by police, not allowed to vote, not allowed to eat in restaurants, not allowed to drink at public fountains, not allowed to hold jobs." Along similar lines, a video entitled "Gay Rights/Special Rights," produced by a conservative group called the Traditional Values Coalition and aimed at minority audiences, features a screen with the heading "Ever denied the right to vote?" and the answers "Homosexuals: No"; "African Americans: Yes." The history of racism in this country is thus offered as a provocative contrast to what opponents allege is the gay and lesbian experience.

The claim that gay men and lesbians have suffered no real social disadvantage sustains the related notion that gay men and lesbians illegitimately seek "special rights." The "special rights" claim has become increasingly prominent in denying that anti-gay discrimination exists. Opponents of gay civil rights claim that the drive for civil rights masks a "blatant power grab" by a powerful "special interest group" bent on accruing unfair advantage. The discourse of equivalents uses the rhetoric of "special rights" and a "power grab" to appeal to fears of quotas and reverse discrimination. * * *

Unlike arguments denying that gay men and lesbians suffer from discrimination, the alternative approach employed by the discourse of equivalents concedes that there is anti-gay discrimination, but argues that there are good reasons to permit it. The core claim made in defense of anti-gay discrimination is that homosexuality is different from other protected aspects of identity because it is both *chosen* and *behavioral* and is therefore categorically beyond the pale of civil rights protection. * * *

The discourse of equivalents misconceives and undermines civil rights law in three principal ways. First, it is grounded in a misguided search for sameness. Second, even as it purports to support existing civil rights law, its rhetoric about "special rights" works to undermine the foundation of all civil rights law. Finally, its exclusion of "chosen behavior" is incoherent and incompatible with a strong conception of civil rights law.

The discourse of equivalents' comparative dynamic is built on a conceptual foundation of sameness. Its premise is that the entry barrier for civil rights protection can be overcome only if the forms and phenomenology of discrimination against gay men and lesbians are the same as for other protected groups. This search for sameness severely limits the meaning and reach of civil rights law both by treating civil rights as a closed category and by erasing complexity and difference.

The discourse of equivalents treats the category "civil rights law" as constant in meaning, impervious to change, and reducible to an irrefutable essence. This representation, however, ignores the history of civil rights laws as open-textured and ever-evolving products of changing legal and social norms. Characterizing anti-discrimination law as fixed and static, moreover, enables the discourse of equivalents to transform civil rights laws from instruments of social change into instruments for *resisting* social change. * * *

Because these experiences are so diverse, a particular group's claim to civil rights protection should not establish a simple, universal definition of the *kind* of disadvantage that qualifies a group for the protection of anti-discrimination law. To resist a singular definition of discrimination, however, is hardly to concede the factual premise of opponents of gay civil rights—namely, that gay men and lesbians as a class, in contrast to other groups, suffer no disadvantage requiring legal redress. It is only to insist that the ways in which that disadvantage is different from the experience of other subordinated groups in our society does not disqualify gay men and lesbians from civil rights protection. What gay men and lesbians share with other groups already protected under civil rights laws is not the reductive social similarity demanded by the discourse of equivalents. The common ground can be found at a higher level of generality: social subordination and stigmatization subject gay men and lesbians—like other subordinated groups—to systematic exclusion and disadvantage at the hands of dominant groups. * * *

* * * [T]he suggestion that gay men and lesbians can opt out of discrimination by staying hidden from public view fails to recognize the tyranny of the closet and the way the closet can itself be an instrument of stigma and social exclusion. Far from the innocuous safe haven pictured by opponents of gay rights, the closet exacts a high price in self-esteem, emotional health, and access to the community.[82] It is not only the constant stress of maintaining a wall of secrecy around life's most intimate associations that makes the closet so onerous, but also the way in which it can powerfully sustain the kind of "internalized homophobia" that makes difficult "the emergence of positive identity in a context of external oppression." The isolation from the support of a larger community that secrecy imposes on gay men and lesbians only compounds these problems. * * *

---

82. For explorations of the high personal cost of the closet, see, for example, John C. Gonsiorek & James R. Rudolph, "Homosexual Identity: Coming Out and Other Developmental Events," in *Homosexuality: Research Implications for Public Policy* 161, 164–76 (John C. Gonsioek & James D. Weinrich eds., 1991); Gregory M. Herek, "Sigma ...," in [*id.*] at 60, 73–75; Marc Fajer, "Can Two Real Men Eat Quiche Together? Storytelling, Gender–Role Stereotypes, and Legal Protection for Lesbians and Gay Men," 46 *U. Miami L. Rev.* 511, 592–602 (1992).

The rhetoric of "special rights" that pervades the discourse of equivalents is laden with corrosive double messages that are hostile to civil rights law in general. On the surface, the claim that gay men and lesbians seek "special rights" targets the legitimacy of gay civil rights. Anti-gay activists juxtapose a greedy gay "power grab" against the meritorious protection sought by groups protected under existing law. Notwithstanding this posture of support for civil rights law, however, the very rhetoric of special rights is heavily coded with the most powerful symbols and ideas of backlash against all civil rights law.

The rhetoric of "special rights" used by the anti-gay movement is a powerful example of the "symbolic uses of politics." Theories of symbolic politics challenge the conventional assumption that political events and choices reflect stable, pre-existing public values. These theories argue, instead, that political language and symbols heavily influence how the public understands and views contested policy questions * * *.

Public opinion surveys demonstrate the power of political rhetoric in shaping public attitudes about gay and lesbian civil rights. In a typical recent poll, for example, a lopsided majority agreed that "homosexuals should ... have equal rights in terms of job opportunities," yet only a minority favored "extending [existing] civil rights laws to include homosexuals." Many people are unwilling to equate civil rights laws with what they say they support—equal job rights. Similarly, polls about civil rights more generally reflect that opinion is strongly influenced by the words and concepts used, with support for civil rights laws and remedies decreasing as the words "quota" and "preference" are used in the question.

The concept of "special rights" is potent precisely because it appeals to the deepest public fears about civil rights law and remedies. Like the closely related, but more ubiquitous phrase "special interest group," "special rights" is an ambiguous term, subject to varying interpretations. In political culture, however, these terms have become heavily freighted with negative messages. They both reflect a deep reservoir of antagonism toward civil rights laws and, in turn, reify and intensify that antagonism. Invocation of these terms taps into "strong affective commitments to certain symbols, which remain constant for many years due to long histories of reinforcement."

[Schacter identifies three recurring rhetorical themes in opposition to the Civil Rights Act of 1964 and other laws outlawing race and sex discrimination: (1) such laws are partial and reflect the political power of beneficiary groups, envisioned as just another "special interest"; (2) such laws constitute "reverse discrimination," denying rights to other Americans; (3) these laws will "balkanize" Americans, dividing the country into "warring" groups. These rhetorical tropes constitute an "inversion" of anti-discrimination legislation. Precisely the same themes are the basis for rhetoric opposing laws against sexual orientation discrimination, such as Colorado's Amendment 2.] Opponents lament, for example, the "resentment it will cause among co-workers who are not in any protected classification." The underlying idea is that rather than promoting tolerance, gay civil rights laws will produce rancor and strife.

The consistency and continuity of the rhetoric and arguments used against civil rights laws supply the larger context in which the symbolic power of the "special rights" rhetoric can be understood. The discourse of equivalents attacks gay civil rights by exploiting the public's greatest hostility and fear about civil rights laws. By invoking the familiar strategies of inversion through the abstract symbol of "special rights," opponents of gay rights not only tap into an existing reservoir of anxiety and antagonism, but they strengthen the association of civil rights laws with quotas, reverse discrimination, minority domination, and balkanization. The discourse of equivalents thus sabotages the very civil rights law that it claims to support.

The discourse of equivalents also works against a strong conception of civil rights, even as it is cast as a defense of "real" civil rights, by claiming that "chosen behavior" is outside the legitimate domain of antidiscrimination law. This claim is offered as a boundary doctrine for civil rights, and thus as a way to defend the legal prerogative to discriminate against gay men and lesbians. * * *

The use of "choice" and "behavior" as boundaries for civil rights protection assumes a controversial normative proposition: that civil rights laws protect only those who "cannot help it," whose distinguishing characteristics are not of their own making. Thus, if one *can* conform one's behavior to prevailing cultural norms, one *should* do so. Conformity is socially expected, and deviation from prevailing norms is tolerated only if unavoidable.

Providing legal protection only to attributes perceived as involuntary reduces civil rights laws to codes of conformity and implicitly stigmatizes difference. If applied to current civil rights protections, this penalty on "choice" would produce perverse results. Must a Buddhist or Muslim relinquish statutory civil rights protection because each could "choose" to follow the dictates of Christianity? Does someone who declines the opportunity to marry waive protection from discrimination based on marital status? If a Latino can "pass" as white, must he do so? Must a deaf woman accept a cochlear implant if it can give her partial hearing, even if doing so would require her to forsake valued cultural ties to the deaf community?

These questions test whether a theory of civil rights is driven by a norm of assimilation or diversity, stasis or social change. By assigning central meaning to the idea of "choice," and protecting only that which is not "chosen," the discourse of equivalents once again reconstitutes civil rights law as a force for resisting social change—this time by adopting a conformity-based theory that works systematically to narrow the range of diversity protected by law.

Just as excluding "choice" from the legitimate ambit of civil rights law is problematic, so is excluding "behavior." Indeed, what might be called "behavior" can be seen as the very core of civil rights protection. For example, statutes prohibiting religious discrimination would be hollow if they offered no protection for the choice to "behave" in particular ways, such as wearing religious garb. Similarly, exempting "behavior" might well leave legally unprotected an African American man fired because he was perceived to be "acting 'too black' "; an African American woman fired for wearing a braided hairstyle; or a Filipino American denied a job based on a Filipino "accent." Employing the same reasoning in the context of gender discrimination, such an approach would permit a woman to be fired for having a personality regarded as too "masculine." Only the bare fact of race, national origin, or gender, and not any "behaviors" associated with identity, would be protected. * * *

The chosen behavior concept is also misguided because it relies on two distinctions that are deeply problematic: the distinction between "doing" and "being," and the distinction between sexual orientation as "chosen" versus that which is "given." Two contemporary debates about lesbian and gay identity reveal that these distinctions are fraught with uncertainty: the debate about the relationship of sexuality to identity and the debate about the origins of same-sex desire. Ultimately, the discourse of equivalents exploits the instability of these distinctions, even as it treats them as self-evident and coherent. * * *

The discourse of equivalents [categorically equates] sexual orientation and sexual behavior. Having drawn a strong distinction between "doing" and "being," the discourse then collapses that distinction by suggesting that gay men and lesbians can never "be" more, or other, than what they "do" sexually. Those resisting gay rights regularly resort to the caricatured idea that gay men and lesbians are essentially *sexual* beings, thus reconstructing "homosexual" as "omnisexual" and erasing the complexity of the human personality. In opposing gay civil rights, for example, one Florida minister argued that gay men want the protection of civil rights laws in order to "walk down the streets j____ing off." A caricature of predatory sexuality similarly structured the recent debate over the ban on gays in the military, where talk of showers, submarines, and the loss of military "privacy" and "morale" predominated. The construction of sexual desire as the totalizing aspect of gay and lesbian identity represents a strategic manipulation of the uncertainty about the relationship of sexuality to identity. * * *

NOTE ON THE "DISCOURSE OF EQUIVALENTS"

Reread the majority and dissenting opinions in *Evans* (Chapter 1, Section 3[B][1]). What light does Professor Schacter's thesis shed on the rhetorical strategies deployed by the majority and dissenting opinions? Does her analysis undermine the cogency of either opinion?

SEXUALITY AND CITIZENSHIP IN AN INTERNATIONAL SETTING

Sections 1 and 2 have been concerned with fractures in our political community on account of tensions between traditionalists, often people of faith, and the sexualized society we are becoming. This section treats issues of citizenship and America's treatment of sexuality in the context of other countries' policies and experiences. Chapter 2, Section 2(B) was an historical introduction to American immigration exclusions of prostitutes and "sexual deviants." Compare those materials to the evolution of U.S. policy toward naturalization and citizenship once the immigrant is in this country (Part A of this section). Part B introduces you to some of this country's international obligations as regards issues of gender, privacy, and sexual orientation. Part C treats issues of asylum, particularly for women subjected to sexual violence elsewhere in the world.

PART A. SEXUALITY AND CITIZENSHIP

Naturalization of people from other countries as U.S. citizens is governed by the Immigration and Nationality Act of 1940. Note that a different statute governs immigration, namely, the McCarran–Walter Act of 1952, as amended (see Chapter 2, Section 2[B]). Section 316(a) of the 1940 Act requires that a person seeking naturalization as a U.S. citizen be of "good moral character" for the statutory period of five years preceding her or his application for citizenship. 8 U.S.C. § 1427(a). Section 101(f) of the statute provides that a person is not of "good moral character" if he or she was a "habitual drunkard," a gambler, a state prisoner for a period of 180 days or more, or a person convicted of murder or any other "aggravated felony." 8 U.S.C. § 1101(f). Section 101(f)(3) stipulates that a person is not of "good moral character"

- if she or he is engaged in prostitution or commercialized vice, smuggling, or polygamy, or

- if he or she has been convicted of or admits to acts constituting the essential elements of "a crime involving moral turpitude" or two or more "offenses" of any sort, or

- if the U.S. official knows or has reason to believe that the noncitizen is an "illicit trafficker" in a "controlled substance," except 30 grams or less of marihuana.

Section 101(f) concludes: "The fact that a person is not within any of the foregoing classes shall not preclude a finding that for other reasons such person is or was not of good moral character." Do §§ 101 and 316 operate as citizenship bars against people who have not followed traditional sexual practices?

Marie Posusta v. United States

U.S. Court of Appeals for the Second Circuit, 1961.
285 F.2d 533.

■ Before CLARK, FRIENDLY, and [LEARNED] HAND, CIRCUIT JUDGES.

■ HAND, CIRCUIT JUDGE.

This is an appeal from an order of the District Court for the southern District of New York denying a petition of Marie Posusta to be naturalized. The petitioner is a Czechoslovakian by birth and was admitted into the United States for permanent residence in 1952. She married Posusta in this country on January 24, 1959, and filed her petition on April 20 of that year. The question is whether she had proved that she was a person of "good moral character" from April 20, 1954 to April 20, 1959. The facts are as follows.

She had become Posusta's paramour in Czechoslovakia some time in 1936 when she was about nineteen, and she bore him one child in August, 1940, and another in January, 1947. Posusta had himself married a woman, named Krausova, on December 30, 1939, by whom he had previously had a child. It is to be assumed that the petitioner's relations with Posusta, remained the same from 1937 or 1938, until he took his wife and her child with him to France in 1948. The petitioner followed them with her two children, and later took them to this country in 1952. After a visit back to France in January, 1953, she returned to the United States in July, 1954, Posusta having preceded her in May of that year. His marriage with Krausova ended in a divorce in March, 1954, so that there was not, and indeed could not have been, any adultery between them after April 20, 1954—five years before the petition was filed. On October 27, 1954, he and the petitioner took out a marriage license, and, although they did not marry until January 24, 1959, they continued their former relation with occasional interruptions.

Their explanation for the delay in marrying after Posusta had been divorced, was that he "wanted to take charge of" the education of Krausova's son which he thought he "could do better than" Krausova, and that, if he married again, "she would not give me the child at all." This child was apparently still a minor which to some extent confirms the avowed reason for their failure to marry for more than five years after they had the license. Moreover, the judge appears to have accepted this explanation of the delay. * * *

Section 1101 of Title 8 of the U.S.C.A. states eight specific conditions which an alien must satisfy in order to be naturalized, and then concludes that, although he may not be within any of the prohibited classes, he may nevertheless be denied naturalization if he "is or was not of good moral character." Much has been written as to the scope of that phrase, and, as was inevitable, there has been disagreement as to its meaning. However, it is settled that the test is not the personal moral principles of the individual judge or court before whom the applicant may come; the decision is to be based upon what he or it believes to be the ethical standards current at the time.

Moreover, a person may have a "good moral character" though he has been delinquent upon occasion in the past; it is enough if he shows that he does not transgress the accepted canons more often than is usual. In this respect this differs from the eight previously specified disqualifications which are unconditional. Obviously it is a test incapable of exact definition; the best we can do is to improvise the response that the "ordinary" man or woman would make, if the question were put whether the conduct was consistent with a "good moral character." Values are incommensurables; and the law is full of standards that admit of no quantitative measure; the most frequent instances are those that require "reasonable" appraisals between conflicting values or desires.

In the case at bar we think it enough that during the five years before she filed her petition the petitioner on the whole did what, as things stood, was consonant with "good moral character." We do not indeed mean that her relations with Posusta are to be condoned, or indeed that persistent incontinence may never preclude having "a good moral character"; but during the probationary period there were greatly extenuating circumstances. So far as appears, Posusta was her only lover and she had been true to him for over twenty years. Her relations with him were not concealed; indeed when they were both in this country they lived under the same roof. People will of course differ in their degree of condemnation of such breaches of the moral code; we can say no more than that even a continued illicit relation is not inevitably an index of a bad "moral character." If she married Posusta, he would lose all power over his son to the son's great disadvantage. True, she would legitimatize her own children, but she could do that anyway after the boy grew up, as she did in fact. It seems at least a reasonable solution to let things stand as they were until the boy became old enough to be independent of his mother. We do not forget that she was not obliged to continue her relations with Posusta; but these had been in all respects connubial for many years except for the absence of a legal marriage. We cannot think that good "morals" compelled her to separate from him and leave her children fatherless in substance as they already were in law. Any decision was complicated, but situated as she was, the better course in 1954 was to accept the situation until Krausova lost her power over Krausova's son. * * *

The statute is not penal; it does not mean to punish for past conduct, but to admit as citizens those who are likely to prove law-abiding and useful. Their past is of course some index of what is permanent in their make-up, but the test is what they will be, if they become citizens. We hold that the petitioner was a person of as "good moral character" as is necessary in order to become a citizen. * * *

NOTES ON *POSUSTA* AND THE EVOLUTION OF NATURALIZATION POLICY IN THE ERA OF *GRISWOLD*

1. *Sexual Fidelity as a Requirement for Citizenship?* Section 1101(f)(2) provided in 1963, "No person shall be regarded as, or found to be, a person of good moral character who, during the period for which good moral character is required to be established, is, or was * * * one who during such period has committed adultery * * *." How can the statute be squared with Judge Hand's learned opinion? Does the statute make sexual fidelity a requirement of citizenship? (Public Law No. 97–116, § 2[c][1], 95 Stat. 1611 [1981], repealed § 1101[f][2], but that law was adopted 18 years after *Posusta*.)

2. *The Relevance of* Griswold? *Posusta* overturned the INS' policy of excluding from citizenship people who were found to have engaged in sexual fornication. The INS did not immediately abandon that policy. Must it do so after *Griswold* in 1965? Does the right to privacy mean that adultery cannot be used to deny citizenship?

3. *Heterosexuality as a Requirement for Citizenship?* Horst Nemetz was a 41-year-old citizen of West Germany who was admitted into the U.S. as a permanent resident. Since his admission, he lived in Virginia (a state with laws criminalizing fornication, adultery, and consensual sodomy) with a male roommate. He petitioned for naturalization as a citizen and met all the statutory requirements, with the following possible problem. The INS' inquiry board suspected he was a homosexual and compiled the following record:

Q. Mr. Nemetz, are you now or have you ever been a homosexual?

A. I'm now.

Q. Do you have sexual relations with your roommate?

A. Well, we have a relationship. I like him.

Q. Have you ever had sexual relationships with him?

A. Yes.

Q. Mr. Nemetz, have you ever committed a homosexual act in public?

A. No.

Q. Have you ever recruited for any type of sexual activities in public?

A. No.

Q. Have you ever been arrested or been questioned by the police for any of these activities?

A. No.

Q. So what you're saying is that your relationship in the United States has been with one individual. Is that correct?

A. Yes.

Transcript (with deletions) from *Nemetz v. INS*, 647 F.2d 432 (4th Cir. 1981).

The INS denied Nemetz citizenship because this colloquy revealed that he lacked "good moral character." (The Fourth Circuit reversed.) By the 1970s, the INS did not consider either fornication or adultery to be disqualifying, but it still considered private homosexual conduct disqualifying. Would Judge Hand agree? If you were a judge in the Second Circuit in the 1970s, when Nemetz was excluded, how would you decide his case? What is the relevance of the Supreme Court's decision in *Boutilier v. INS* (Chapter 2, Section 2[B][3]), which interpreted the 1952 immigration statute to bar anyone who was a "known" homosexual or bisexual? (The INS administers both the immigration statute and the citizenship statute.)

In re Petition of Naturalization of Manuel Labady

U.S. District Court for the Southern District of New York, 1971.
326 F.Supp. 924.

■ MANSFIELD, DISTRICT JUDGE.

Petitioner, a 24–year old native and citizen of Cuba, was lawfully admitted into the United States as a permanent resident on December 3, 1960. On May 6, 1969, he filed his Petition for Naturalization pursuant to 8 U.S.C. § 1427. The Immigration and Naturalization Service ("the Service") opposes his petition on the ground that since he has been a homosexual he has not sustained his burden of establishing that within the five years immediately preceding the date of filing his petition he "has been and still is a person of good moral character * * *" within the meaning of 8 U.S.C. § 1427(a).

Petitioner was a homosexual in Cuba and made this fact known to the Service authorities when he entered this country at the age of 14. The Medical Director and Chief of the Psychiatry Department of the United States Public Health Service Hospital in Staten Island, however, did not certify him as a "sexual deviate" or "psychopathic personality" under 8 U.S.C. § 1182(a)(4).

Since petitioner validly entered the country without deceit, the Service concedes that he is not now deportable. After entering the United States in 1960 petitioner engaged in homosexual activities with several consenting adults. On the average he has been the active or passive partner in such activities about once a month, but the last occasion was about six months before his preliminary examinations by the Service upon his Petition for Naturalization. He has never engaged in homosexual activities with minors; all of his sexual acts have taken place in privacy, behind locked doors in hotel rooms. He has never engaged in such activity in any park, theatre, subway station, or any other public or semi-public place. He is unmarried and lives with his mother. There is no suggestion that his homosexual activities could harm a marriage relationship.

Petitioner has never been arrested. Though he has not applied for psychiatric treatment in the United States, he did unsuccessfully undergo therapy in Cuba. He does not drink; he does not frequent bars; he does not use narcotics. The Service stipulates that he has never been in trouble and, as his employer testified, he is highly regarded at his place of employment.

"Good moral character" is partially defined in 8 U.S.C. § 1101(f), which lists eight classes of conduct that preclude a finding of good moral character if engaged in during the five-year period immediately preceding the Naturalization Petition. These categories—e.g., habitual drunkard; adulterer; perjurer; convicted murderer (even if the conviction occurred before the five-year period); a person who within the five-year period was confined in a penal institution for 180 days or more; etc.—do not include petitioner's admitted conduct, but § 1101(f) is not definitive and so provides by its own terms:

> "The fact that any person is not within any of the foregoing classes shall not preclude a finding that for other reasons such person is or was not (within the five-year statutory period) of good moral character."

In determining good moral character, "the test is not the personal moral principles of the individual judge or court before whom the applicant may come; the decision is to be based upon what he or it believes to be the ethical standards current at the time." *Posusta*. If the criterion were our own personal moral principles, we would deny the petition, subscribing as we personally do to the general "revulsion" or "moral conviction or instinctive feeling" against homosexuality. E.g., Report of the Committee on Homosexual Offenses and Prostitution Presented to Parliament by the Secretary of State for the Home Department and the Secretary of State for Scotland by Command of her Majesty (Sept. 1957 Cmmd. 247) (The Wolfenden Report) § B(54).

The test of "good moral character" prescribed by Judge Hand in *Posusta* was recognized by him as one that is "incapable of exact definition," and in an earlier opinion he had confirmed that "good moral character" does not necessarily turn upon a popular vote. * * *

We believe that the most important factor to be considered is whether the challenged conduct is public or private in nature. If it is public or if it involves a large number of other persons, it may pose a threat to the community. If, on the other hand, it is entirely private, the likelihood of harm to others is minimal and any effort to regulate or penalize the conduct may lead to an unjustified invasion of the individual's constitutional rights. For instance, it is now established that official inquiry into a person's private sexual habits does violence to his constitutionally protected zone of privacy. Just as the state may not search "the sacred precincts of marital bedrooms for telltale signs of the use of contraceptives," *Griswold*, the state may not prohibit a person from possessing obscene matter in his home, because of the "right to be free * * * from unwarranted governmental intrusion into one's privacy." *Stanley*.

In short, private conduct which is not harmful to others, even though it may violate the personal moral code of most of us, does not violate public morality which is the only proper concern of § 1427. To hold otherwise would be to encourage governmental inquisition into an applicant's purely personal private temperament and habits (e.g., whether he harbors hate, malice or impure thoughts; whether he has ever engaged in masturbation, autoeroticism, fornication, or the like, etc.) even though such attitudes or conduct would not harm others.

Without condoning the purely private conduct here involved, we accept the principle that the naturalization laws are concerned with public, not private, morality. As Judge Hand stated in *Posusta*, § 1427 "is not penal; it does not mean to punish for past conduct, but to admit as citizens those who are likely to prove law-abiding and useful." The distinction between public and private morality is further recognized in the American Law Institute's Model Penal Code pp. 277–78, Tent. Draft No. 4 (1955), which provides:

> "No harm to the secular community is involved in atypical sex practice in private between consenting adult partners. This area in private morals is the distinctive concern of spiritual authorities. It has been so recognized in a recent report by a group of Anglican clergy, with medical and legal advisers, calling upon the British Government to reexamine its harsh sodomy laws." (Footnote omitted)

There is nothing to indicate that private conduct of the type here involved would affect petitioner's ability to be "lawabiding and useful" to society.

We reject the Service's contention that petitioner's conduct has violated New York Penal Law § 130.38 which provides that

> "A person is guilty of consensual sodomy when he engages in deviate sexual intercourse with another person."

The statute does not specifically extend to consensual sodomy performed in private. At common law a lewd, obscene, or indecent act included only open or public behavior. We have found no prosecution of private homosexual acts under § 130.38. One New York court has stated in dictum that the private conduct of an admitted homosexual was not violative of any criminal statute. *In re Petition of Olga Schmidt*, 289 N.Y.S.2d 89, 92 (Sup.Ct.1968). Many state statutes prohibiting homosexual conduct explicitly require "openness" or publicity. Under these circumstances, and bearing in mind that criminal laws should be strictly construed, it is highly unlikely that petitioner's private conduct has violated any state law.

[Section] 130.38, which is a Class B misdemeanor carrying a maximum punishment of three months imprisonment, would not necessarily preclude a finding of good moral character within the meaning of § 1427(a). *In re Van Dessel*, 243 F.Supp. 328 (E.D.Pa.1965), the court approved citizenship for a woman who had engaged in sexual relations with an unmarried man over a period of years. They had not married because of religious differences. The court concluded that although petitioner's acts of fornication were illegal in the state in which she was residing, crimes involving fornication were common in the law, and that the crime by itself—with consent of the other adult, also unmarried, and with the act done in private, not done for money, and with no begetting of an illegitimate child—was far less serious than the crimes listed in 8 U.S.C. § 1101(f) (e.g., adultery, murder, perjury, trafficking in narcotic drugs, aiding in the illegal entry into the United States, or conviction for any offense resulting in confinement in a penal institution for a period of 180 days or more). Petitioner's conduct similarly does not reach the seriousness of such crimes. [Judge Mansfield also pointed to the substantial nonenforcement of sodomy laws against consensual adult same-sex intimacy.]

The extent to which homosexuals are offered employment is also relevant in determining public attitudes toward private homosexual conduct, since one purpose of the "good moral character" clause is to insure that prospective citizens will be useful to society and lawabiding. Turning to local government, we find that the New York City Civil Service Commission has adopted a policy of accepting homosexuals as workers, except in some positions such as penitentiary guards and playground attendants. On the federal level, the Civil Service Commission no longer excludes all homosexuals from government service. The Commission as a matter of practice now "avoids expelling (homosexual) employees with many years service. It does not consider minor criminal conduct occurring two or more years before application for employment. It excludes only those whose homosexuality is a matter of public knowledge or record. Results have apparently been satisfactory." Note, "Government–Created Employment Disabilities of the Homosexual," 82 *Harv. L. Rev.* 1738, 1745–46 (1969). The Civil Service's power to fire homosexual employees has also been narrowed by the courts. * * *

Upon the record before us we conclude that petitioner has sustained his burden of compliance with Title 8 U.S.C. § 1427. He has led a quiet, peaceful, law-abiding life as an immigrant in the United States. Although he has engaged on occasion in purely private homosexual relations with consenting adults, he has not corrupted the morals of others, such as minors, or engaged in any publicly offensive activities, such as solicitation or public display. He is gainfully employed, highly regarded by his employer and associates, and he has submitted to therapy that was unsuccessful. Under all of the circumstances, setting aside our personal moral views, we cannot say that his conduct has violated public morality or indicated that he will be anything other than a law-abiding and useful citizen.

PROBLEM 8–4

FORMULATING A COHERENT APPROACH TO "GOOD MORAL CHARACTER"

The courts generally followed *Posusta* (private adultery and fornication) and *Labady* (private homosexual conduct), and the INS had no choice in the 1970s but to retreat from its earlier views about "good moral character." You are the INS General Counsel today. As a matter of law, how should the INS apply the "good character" requirement to the following cases:

(a) a female to male transsexual who has come to the United States for a sex change operation in order to cure his disjuncture between gender and sex.

(b) a male noncitizen who was convicted of carnal knowledge of a fifteen year old girl. See *Castle v. INS*, 541 F.2d 1064 (4th Cir. 1976).

(c) a female noncitizen who was convicted for having sexual relations with a fifteen year old boy.

(d) a male noncitizen who admits to having had sexual relations with a seventeen year old boy when the noncitizen was twenty years old.

(e) a female noncitizen who was convicted of adultery with a married man; the INS hearing examiner finds that the noncitizen took the initiative to break up the previously happy marriage.

(f) a female noncitizen who is an exotic dancer and has been convicted five times of indecent exposure under state law banning public nudity.

Which of these folks should be eligible for citizenship?

PART B. INTERNATIONAL OBLIGATIONS AND UNITED STATES' REGULATION OF SEXUALITY

The Universal Declaration of Human Rights, G.A. Res. 217 A(III), Dec. 10, 1948, U.N. Doc. A/810 (1948), is a resolution adopted by the U.N. General Assembly. The Declaration seeks to implement the general principles of the U.N. Charter; it has no formally binding character, although it is a source of customary international law. Various bodies, including the U.N. High Commissioner for Human Rights and the U.N. Sub–Commission on Prevention of Discrimination and Protection of Minorities, charged with investigating human rights violations, look to the Declaration as a statement of fundamental principles. Among other rights, the Declaration assures all people the right not to be discriminated against on the basis of "race, colour, sex, language, religion, political or other opinion, national or social origin, property, birth or other status" (art. 2). On the other hand, article 29(2) subjects the nondiscrimination and other rights to "such limitations as are determined by law solely for the purpose of securing due recognition and respect for the rights and freedoms of others and of meeting the just requirements of morality, public order and the general welfare in a democratic society."

The International Covenant on Civil and Political Rights (ICCPR), G.A. Res. 2200 A(XXI), Dec. 16, 1966, 21 U.N. GAOR Supp. (No. 16), 999 U.N.T.S. 171, U.N. Doc. A/6316 (1966), is a treaty entered into by the United States and other countries under the auspices of the United

Nations. It provides most of the same general guarantees as the Universal Declaration, but with greater specificity and without the general reservation found in article 29(2) of the Declaration. Also, as a treaty, the ICCPR has greater binding force against signatories. The U.N. Human Rights Committee adjudicates complaints brought against signatory parties which have signed onto the ICCPR's "Optional Protocol" and which are alleged to be in violation of the ICCPR's assurances.

Consider the following excerpts from the ICCPR and the problem that follows. Excellent introductions to the ICCPR and other agreements are James D. Wilets, "International Human Rights Law and Sexual Orientation," 18 *Hastings Int'l & Comp. L. Rev.* 1 (1994), and Richard Lillich, *Invoking International Human Rights Law in Domestic Courts* (1985).

International Covenant on Civil and Political Rights

General Assembly Resolution 2200A(XXI), 1966.
21 U.N. GAOR Supp. (No. 16), 999 U.N.T.S. 171, U.N. Doc. A/6316.

Article 2

1.   Each State Party to the present Covenant undertakes to respect and to ensure to all individuals within its territory and subject to its jurisdiction the rights recognized in the present Covenant, without distinction of any kind, such as race, colour, sex, language, religion, political or other opinion, national or social origin, property, birth or other status.
* * *

Article 7

No one shall be subjected to torture or to cruel, inhuman, or degrading treatment or punishment. In particular, no one shall be subjected without his free consent to medical or scientific experimentation. * * *

Article 9

1.   Everyone has the right to liberty and security of person. No one shall be subjected to arbitrary arrest or detention. No one shall be deprived of his liberty except on such grounds and in accordance with such procedure as are established by law.

2.   Anyone who is arrested shall be informed, at the time of arrest, of the reasons for his arrest and shall be promptly informed of any charges against him.

3.   Anyone arrested or detained on a criminal charge shall be brought promptly before a judge or other officer authorized by law to exercise judicial power and shall be entitled to trial within a reasonable time or to release. It shall not be the general rule that persons awaiting trial shall be detained in custody, but release may be subject to guarantees to appear for trial, at any other stage of the judicial proceedings, and should occasion arise, for execution of the judgment. * * *

Article 10

1. All persons deprived of their liberty shall be treated with humanity and with respect for the inherent dignity of the human person. * * *

Article 17

1. No one shall be subjected to arbitrary or unlawful interference with his privacy, family, home or correspondence, nor to unlawful attacks on his honour and reputation.

2. Everyone has the right to the protection of the law against such interference or attacks. * * *

Article 19

1. Everyone shall have the right to hold opinions without interference.

2. Everyone shall have the right to freedom of expression; this right shall include freedom to seek, receive and impart information and ideas of all kinds, regardless of frontiers, either orally, in writing or in print, in the form of art, or through any other media of his choice. * * *

Article 20

1. The right of peaceful assembly shall be recognized. No restrictions may be placed on the exercise of this right other than those imposed in conformity with the law and which are necessary in a democratic society in the interests of national security or public safety, public order (*ordre public*), the protection of public health or morals or the protection of the rights and freedoms of others.

2. Any advocacy of national, racial or religious hatred that constitutes incitement to discrimination, hostility or violence shall be prohibited by law. * * *

Article 22

1. Everyone shall have the right to freedom of association with others, including the right to form and join trade unions for the protection of his interests.

2. No restriction may be placed on the exercise of this right other than those which are prescribed by law and which are necessary in a democratic society in the interests of national security or public safety, public order (*ordre public*), the protection of public health or morals or the protection of the rights and freedoms of others. This article shall not prevent the imposition of lawful restrictions on members of the armed forces and of the police in their exercise of this right. * * *

Article 23

1. The family is the natural and fundamental group unit of society and is entitled to promotion by society and the State.

2. The right of men and women of marriageable age to marry and to found a family shall be recognized.

3. No marriage shall be entered into without the free and full consent of the intending spouses.

4. States Parties to the present Covenant shall take appropriate steps to ensure equality of rights and responsibilities of spouses as to marriage, during marriage and at its dissolution. In the case of dissolution, provision shall be made for the necessary protection of any children. * * *

Article 26

All persons are equal before the law and are entitled without any discrimination to the equal protection of the law. In this respect, the law shall prohibit any discrimination and guarantee to all persons equal and effective protection against discrimination on any ground such as race, colour, sex, language, religion, political or other opinion, national or social origin, property, birth or other status. * * *

PROBLEM 8–5

APPLYING THE ICCPR TO AMERICAN SODOMY LAWS[a]

Reconsider the issue in *Bowers v. Hardwick* [Chapter 1, Section 2] from an international perspective. Georgia's sodomy law makes it a felony for two adults to have consensual oral intercourse, and the Supreme Court upheld the law's constitutionality only as to homosexual intercourse (leaving open the issue of heterosexual intercourse). Twenty other states have sodomy laws, although most such laws penalize consensual sodomy only as a misdemeanor, not as a felony; six states explicitly criminalize only same-sex and not different-sex sodomy.

The Supreme Court in *Bowers* did not consider the applicability of the ICCPR, which was not ratified by the United States until 1992. Consider the following points of international law and practice (see Wilets 40–45):

1. The ICCPR is not a "self-executing" treaty, because the Senate's ratification explicitly said so (Wilets 40). Therefore, the ICCPR cannot serve as an independent claim for relief under federal law, as a self-enforcing treaty would. See *The Head Money Cases*, 112 U.S. 580 (1884).

2. Having ratified the ICCPR, the United States has accepted international obligations under the covenant but has not agreed to amenability to international adjudication of grievances before the U.N. Human Rights Committee; at least half the parties to the ICCPR have agreed to amenabil-

---

a. This problem is informed by the discussion in James D. Wilets, "Using International Law to Vindicate the Civil Rights of Gays and Lesbians in United States Courts," 27 *Colum. Human Rights L. Rev.* 33 (1995), as well as Richard Lillich, "The Constitution and International Human Rights," 83 *Am. J.* *Int'l L.* 851 (1989), and David Catania, "The Universal Declaration of Human Rights and Sodomy Laws: A Federal Common Law Right to Privacy for Homosexuals Based on Customary International Law," *Am. Cr. L. Rev.* 289 (1994) (student note).

ity. On the other hand, the United States has complied with requests by the Committee for information as to American compliance with the ICCPR and has expressed a "readiness * * * to take such further measures as may be necessary to ensure that the States of the Union implement the rights guaranteed by the Covenant." *Consideration of Reports Submitted by States Parties Under Article 40 of the Covenant*, U.N. GAOR Hum. Rts. Comm., 53d Sess., U.N. Doc. CCPR/C/79/Add 50, ¶ 9 (1995).

3.   Even when a treaty is not self-executing, U.S. courts will often interpret ambiguous federal law to be consistent with America's international commitments or with international law generally. E.g., *Murray v. Schooner Charming Betsy*, 6 U.S. (2 Cranch) 64, 118 (1804) (Marshall, C.J.); *Restatement (Third) of the Foreign Relations Law of the United States* § 114 (1987). Moreover, non-self-executing treaties "may sometimes be held to be federal policy superseding State law or policy." *Id.* § 115, comment (e); see *Toll v. Moreno*, 458 U.S. 1 (1982).

With this legal background in mind, turn back to the ICCPR and construct an argument for invalidating Georgia's sodomy law in cases like Michael Hardwick's (oral sex between two consenting adults). Consider also the following decision by the Human Rights Committee.

Nicholas Toonen v. Australia

United Nations Human Rights Committee, 1994.
U.N. Doc. CCPR/c/50/D/488/1992.

2.1   [Nicholas Toonen] is an activist for the promotion of the rights of homosexuals in Tasmania, one of Australia's six constitutive states. He challenges two provisions of the Tasmanian Criminal Code, namely, sections 122 (a) and (c) and 123, which criminalize various forms of sexual contact between men, including all forms of sexual contact between consenting adult homosexual men in private.

2.2   The author observes that the above sections of the Tasmanian Criminal Code empower Tasmanian police officers to investigate intimate aspects of his private life and to detain him, if they have reason to believe that he is involved in sexual activities which contravene the above sections. * * *

2.3   Although in practice the Tasmanian police has not charged anyone either with "unnatural sexual intercourse" or "intercourse against nature" (section 122) nor with "indecent practice between male persons" (section 123) for several years, the author argues that because of his long-term relationship with another man, his active lobbying of Tasmanian politicians and the reports about his activities in the local media, and because of his activities as a gay rights activist and gay HIV/AIDS worker, his private life and his liberty are threatened by the continued existence of sections 122 (a) and (c) and 123 of the Criminal Code. * * *

3.1   The author affirms that sections 122 and 123 of the Tasmanian Criminal Code violate articles 2, paragraph 1; 17; and 26 of the Covenant because:

(a) They do not distinguish between sexual activity in private and sexual activity in public and bring private activity into the public domain. In their enforcement, these provisions result in a violation of the right to privacy, since they enable the police to enter a household on the mere suspicion that two consenting adult homosexual men may be committing a criminal offence. Given the stigma attached to homosexuality in Australian society (and especially in Tasmania), the violation of the right to privacy may lead to unlawful attacks on the honour and the reputation of the individuals concerned;

(b) They distinguish between individuals in the exercise of their right to privacy on the basis of sexual activity, sexual orientation and sexual identity;

(c) The Tasmanian Criminal Code does not outlaw any form of homosexual activity between consenting homosexual women in private and only some forms of consenting heterosexual activity between adult men and women in private. That the laws in question are not currently enforced by the judicial authorities of Tasmania should not be taken to mean that homosexual men in Tasmania enjoy effective equality under the law. * * *

[The Committee took jurisdiction over this communication in November 1992. Australia's response, filed in September 1993, admitted that Tasmania's sodomy law arbitrarily interfered with Toonen's privacy rights. Australia conveyed to the Committee Tasmania's defense of its law but pointedly disagreed with several of Tasmania's arguments, especially its argument that the sodomy law was needed as part of a health campaign to prevent transmission of the virus that leads to AIDS.]

6.2   With regard to article 17, the Federal Government notes that the Tasmanian government submits that article 17 does not create a "right to privacy" but only a right to freedom from arbitrary or unlawful interference with privacy, and that as the challenged laws were enacted by democratic process, they cannot be an unlawful interference with privacy. The Federal Government, after reviewing the *travaux préparatoires* of article 17, subscribes to the following definition of "private": "matters which are individual, personal, or confidential, or which are kept or removed from public observation". The State party acknowledges that based on this definition, consensual sexual activity in private is encompassed by the concept of "privacy" in article 17.

6.9   In respect of the alleged violation of article 26, the State party seeks the Committee's guidance as to whether sexual orientation may be subsumed under the term "... or other status" in article 26. In this context, the Tasmanian authorities concede that sexual orientation is an "other status" for the purposes of the Covenant. The State party itself, after review of the *travaux préparatoires,* the Committee's general comment on articles 2 and 26 and its jurisprudence under these provisions, contends that there "appears to be a strong argument that the words of the two articles should not be read restrictively." ... The formulation of the provisions "without distinction of any kind, such as" and "on any ground such as" support an inclusive rather than exhaustive interpretation. While the *travaux préparatoires* do not provide specific guidance on this question, they also appear to support this interpretation. * * *

6.11 The State party concedes that section 123 of the Tasmanian Criminal Code clearly draws a distinction on the basis of sex, as it prohibits sexual acts only between males. If the Committee were to find that sexual orientation is an "other status" within the meaning of article 26, the State party would concede that this section draws a distinction on the basis of sexual orientation. * * *

8.1 The Committee is called upon to determine whether Mr. Toonen has been the victim of an unlawful or arbitrary interference with his privacy, contrary to article 17, paragraph 1, and whether he has been discriminated against in his right to equal protection of the law, contrary to article 26.

8.2 In so far as article 17 is concerned, it is undisputed that adult consensual sexual activity in private is covered by the concept of "privacy", and that Mr. Toonen is actually and currently affected by the continued existence of the Tasmanian laws. The Committee considers that sections 122 (a) and (c) and 123 of the Tasmanian Criminal Code "interfere" with the author's privacy, even if these provisions have not been enforced for a decade. In this context, it notes that the policy of the Department of Public Prosecutions not to initiate criminal proceedings in respect of private homosexual conduct does not amount to a guarantee that no actions will be brought against homosexuals in the future, particularly in the light of undisputed statements of the Director of Public Prosecutions of Tasmania in 1988 and those of members of the Tasmanian Parliament. The continued existence of the challenged provisions therefore continuously and directly "interferes" with the author's privacy. * * *

8.5 As far as the public health argument of the Tasmanian authorities is concerned, the Committee notes that the criminalization of homosexual practices cannot be considered a reasonable means or proportionate measure to achieve the aim of preventing the spread of AIDS/HIV. The Government of Australia observes that statutes criminalizing homosexual activity tend to impede public health programmes "by driving underground many of the people at the risk of infection". Criminalization of homosexual activity thus would appear to run counter to the implementation of effective education programmes in respect of the HIV/AIDS prevention. Secondly, the Committee notes that no link has been shown between the continued criminalization of homosexual activity and the effective control of the spread of the HIV/AIDS virus.

8.6 The Committee cannot accept either that for the purposes of article 17 of the Covenant, moral issues are exclusively a matter of domestic concern, as this would open the door to withdrawing from the Committee's scrutiny a potentially large number of statutes interfering with privacy. It further notes that with the exception of Tasmania, all laws criminalizing homosexuality have been repealed throughout Australia and that, even in Tasmania, it is apparent that there is no consensus as to whether sections 122 and 123 should not also be repealed. Considering further that these provisions are not currently enforced, which implies that they are not deemed essential to the protection of morals in Tasmania, the Committee concludes that the provisions do not meet the "reasonableness" test in the circumstances of the case, and that they arbitrarily interfere with Mr. Toonen's right under article 17, paragraph 1.

8.7 The State party has sought the Committee's guidance as to whether sexual orientation may be considered an "other status" for the purposes of article 26. The same issue could arise under article 2, paragraph 1, of the Covenant. The Committee confines itself to noting, however, that in its view, the reference to "sex" in articles 2, paragraph 1, and 26 is to be taken as including sexual orientation.

9. The Human Rights Committee, acting under article 5, paragraph 4, of the Optional Protocol to the International Covenant on Civil and Political Rights, is of the view that the facts before it reveal a violation of articles 17, paragraph 1, and 2, paragraph 1, of the Covenant.

10. Under article 2, paragraph 3 (a), of the Covenant, the author, as a victim of a violation of articles 17, paragraph 1, and 2, paragraph 1, of the Covenant, is entitled to a remedy. In the opinion of the Committee, an effective remedy would be the repeal of sections 122 (a) and (c) and 123 of the Tasmanian Criminal Code.

11. Since the Committee has found a violation of Mr. Toonen's rights under articles 17, paragraph 1, and 2, paragraph 1, of the Covenant requiring the repeal of the offending law, the Committee does not consider it necessary to consider whether there has also been a violation of article 26 of the Covenant. * * *

NOTE ON TRANSNATIONAL DEREGULATION OF CONSENSUAL SAME–SEX INTIMACY[b]

International experience supports the proposition that laws criminalizing same-sex intimacy are anachronistic for modern urbanized societies. According to James Wilets' recent survey, virtually all the countries with laws against consensual sodomy are nonindustrialized societies in Africa and Asia. Japan, Hong Kong, China, Taiwan, South Korea, Canada, Mexico, Brazil, Argentina, Columbia, Venezuela, and most of the states in Europe have no consensual sodomy laws. The few straggler countries (such as Ireland and Cyprus) or provinces (such as Tasmania [Australia] and Northern Ireland [United Kingdom]) have been subjected to legal as well as political pressure to abandon such anachronistic laws.

b. See James Wilets, "International Human Rights Law and Sexual Orientation," 18 *Hastings Int'l & Comp. L. Rev.* 1 (1994). See *The Third Pink Book* (Aart Hendriks et al., eds., 1993), for a country-by-country review as of 1993.

Most member states of the European Community have repealed their sodomy laws, and the few that have not have been found in violation of the European Convention on Human Rights. Unlike the U.S. Constitution, the European Convention is not formally binding on EC states, but member states are expected nonetheless to respond cooperatively to inconsistencies. Also unlike the U.S. Constitution, the European Convention, in Article 8, explicitly protects citizens' right to personal privacy.

In *Dudgeon v. United Kingdom*, 4 Eur. Hum. Rts. Rep. 149 (Eur. Ct. Hum. Rts. 1981), the European Court of Human Rights ruled that Northern Ireland's consensual sodomy prohibition contravened the right to privacy set forth in Article 8 of the European Convention. The decision affected only Northern Ireland, as the remainder of the United Kingdom had already decriminalized same-sex intimacy. The Court in *Norris v. Ireland*, 13 Eur. Hum. Rts. Rep. 186 (Eur. Ct. Hum. Rts. 1991), applied *Dudgeon* to require an entire country, Ireland, either to decriminalize homosexuality or disavow the European Convention on Human Rights. In 1993, the Court held that Cyprus' anti-sodomy law was likewise in derogation of the Convention, thereby completing a clean sweep of such regulations in the EC. *Modinos v. Cyprus*, 16 Eur. Hum. Rts. Rep. 485 (Eur. Ct. Hum. Rts. 1993).

From this comparative law data, construct an argument that *Bowers v. Hardwick* ought to be overruled.

Part C.   Gender, Sexuality, and Asylum

The United Nations Convention Relating to the Status of Refugees, 19 U.S.T. 6259, 189 U.N.T.S. 150, and its Protocol Relating to the Status of Refugees, 19 U.S.T. 6223, 606 U.N.T.S. 267, guarantee "refugees" the right not to be deported to their country of origin. A "refugee" is defined in Article 1 of the Protocol as someone who, "owing to a well-founded fear of being persecuted for reasons of race, religion, nationality, membership of a particular social group or political opinion is outside the country of his nationality and is unable or, owing to such fear, is unwilling to avail himself of the protection of that country."

The United States has ratified the Convention and its Protocol and has implemented its guarantees in the nation's immigration laws. Section 243(h) of the Immigration and Naturalization Act, as amended, requires the INS to withhold deportation of an otherwise illegal immigrant whose life would be "threatened on account of race, religion, nationality, membership in a particular social group, or political opinion." Relief for such a refugee is mandatory, but the refugee bears the burden of proving, by a preponderance of the evidence, that there actually will be persecution if she or he returns to the home country. *INS v. Stevic*, 467 U.S. 407 (1984).

Section 208(a) gives the INS the authority to give asylum to refugees who have a "well-founded fear of persecution on account of race, religion, nationality, membership in a particular social group, or political opinion."

This is discretionary with the INS, but the Supreme Court has held that the INS cannot arbitrarily deport a refugee who has shown a mere fear of persecution, so long as it is "well-founded"—a standard much less demanding than § 243(h)'s preponderance of the evidence standard. *INS v. Cardoza-Fonseca*, 480 U.S. 421 (1987). In *Cardoza-Fonseca*, the Supreme Court's lenient standard was strongly influenced by the international materials underlying the Convention and the Protocol, which were extensively canvassed by the Court.

In *Matter of Acosta*, 19 I & N Dec. 211 (Bd.Imm.App.1985), the Board of Immigration Appeals interpreted the phrase "persecution on account of membership in a particular social group" to mean persecution directed toward an individual "who is a member of a group of persons all of whom share a common, immutable characteristic. The shared characteristic might be an innate one. * * * [W]hatever the common characteristic that defines the group, it must be one that the members of the group either cannot change, or should not be required to change because it is fundamental to their individual identities or consciences." *Id.* at 234. Consider the following recent decision.

In re Fauziya Kasinga

Dep't of Justice, Board of Immigration Appeals, *en banc*, 1996.
File A73 476 695.

■ SCHMIDT, CHAIRMAN: * * *

[Fauziya Kasinga] is a 19–year-old native and citizen of Togo. She attended 2 years of high school. She is a member of the Tchamba–Kusuntu Tribe of northern Togo. She testified that young women of her tribe normally undergo FGM [female genital mutilation] at age 15. However, she did not because she was protected from FGM by her influential, but now deceased, father.

The applicant stated that upon her father's death in 1993, under tribal custom her aunt, her father's sister, became the primary authority figure in the family. The applicant's mother was driven from the family home, left Togo, and went to live with her family in Benin. * * *

The applicant further testified that her aunt forced her into a polygamous marriage in October 1994, when she was 17. The husband selected by the aunt was 45 years old and had three other wives at the time of marriage. The applicant testified that, under tribal custom, her aunt and her husband planned to force her to submit to FGM before the marriage was consummated.

[With the help of her older sister and ultimately her mother, Kasinga fled Togo and ultimately ended up in the United States in December 1994. She did not attempt to enter the United States illegally and immediately requested asylum. She was detained by the INS from December 1994 through April 1996.]

The applicant testified that the Togolese police and the Government of Togo were aware of FGM and would take no steps to protect her from the practice. She further testified that her aunt had reported her to the Togolese police. Upon return, she would be taken back to her husband by the police and forced to undergo FGM. She testified at several points that there would be nobody to protect her from FGM in Togo. * * *

According to the applicant's testimony, the FGM practiced by her tribe, the Tchamba–Kunsuntu, is of an extreme type involving the cutting the genitalia with knives, extensive bleeding, and a 40–day recovery period. The background materials confirm that the FGM practiced in some African countries, such as Togo, is of an extreme nature causing permanent damage, and not just a minor form of genital ritual. See, e.g., Nahid Toubia, *Female Genital Mutilation: A Call for Global Action* 9, 24–25 (Gloria Jacobs ed., Women Ink. 1993).

The record material establishes that FGM in its extreme forms is a practice in which portions of the female genitalia are cut away. In some cases, the vagina is sutured partially closed. This practice clearly inflicts harm or suffering upon the girl or woman who undergoes it.

FGM is extremely painful and at least temporarily incapacitating. It permanently disfigures the female genitalia. FGM exposes the girl or woman to the risk of serious, potentially life-threatening complications. These include, among others, bleeding, infection, urine retention, stress, shock, psychological trauma, and damage to the uerthra and anus. It can result in permanent loss of genital sensation and can adversely affect sexual and erotic functions. * * *

The record also contains a May 26, 1995 memorandum from Phyllis Coven, Office of International Affairs, INS, which is addressed to all INS Asylum Officers and sets forth guidelines for adjudicating women's asylum claims. Coven, U.S. Dep't of Justice, *Considerations for Asylum Officers Adjudicating Claims From Women* (1995). Those guidelines state that "rape ..., sexual abuse and domestic violence, infanticide and genital mutilation are forms of mistreatment primarily directed at girls and women and they may serve as evidence of past persecution on account of one or more of the five grounds [for granting asylum]." Coven, *supra*, at 4.

[State Department reports confirmed that extreme FGM is practiced in Togo and that police were unwilling to intervene to protect women against this or other kinds of violence. Notwithstanding this evidence, the Immigration Judge found Kasinga's story not entirely credible and denied her asylum application. The Board's de novo review found Kasinga's account credible and held that she met the statutory criteria for asylum in 8 U.S.C. § 1101(a)(42)(A). The Board found that Kasinga suffered "persecution," namely, the infliction of harm or suffering by a government or persons a government is unwilling or unable to control, to overcome a characteristic of the victim. Also, the persecution related to one of the five categories, in this case "particular social group," namely, "[y]oung women of the Tchamba–Kunsuntu Tribe who have not had FGM, as practiced by that tribe, and who oppose the practice."]

In accordance with *Acosta*, the particular social group is defined by common characteristics that members of the group either cannot change, or should not be required to change because such characteristics are fundamental to their individual identities. The characteristics of being a "young woman" and a "member of the Tchamba–Kunsuntu Tribe" cannot be changed. The characteristic of having intact genitalia is one that is so fundamental to the individual identity of a young woman that she should not be required to change it. * * *

Record materials state that FGM "has been used to control women's sexuality," *FGM Alert* [an INS publication]. It also is characterized as a form of "sexual oppression" that is "based on the manipulation of women's sexuality in order to assure male dominance and exploitation." Toubia, *supra*, at 42 (quoting Raqiya Haji Dualeh Abdalla, Somali Women's Democratic Organizations). During oral argument before us, the INS General Counsel [David Martin] agreed with the latter formulation. He also stated that the practice is a "severe bodily invasion" that should be regarded as meeting the asylum standard even if done with "subjectively benign intent."

We agree with the parties that, as described and documented in this record, FGM is practiced, at least in some significant part, to overcome sexual characteristics of young women of the tribe who have not been, and do not wish to be, subjected to FGM. We therefore find that the persecution the applicant fears in Togo is "on account of" her status as a member of the defined social group. * * *

We have determined that the applicant is eligible for asylum because she has a well-founded fear of persecution on account of her membership in a particular group in Togo. A grant of asylum to an eligible applicant is discretionary. The final issue is whether the applicant merits a favorable exercise of discretion. The danger of persecution will outweigh all but the most egregious adverse factors. The type of persecution faced by the applicant is very severe.

To the extent that the Immigration Judge suggested that the applicant had a legal obligation to seek refuge in Ghana or Germany, the record does not support such a conclusion. The applicant offered credible reasons for not seeking refuge in either of those countries in her particular circumstances.

The applicant purchase someone else's passport and used it to come to the United States. However, upon arrival, she did not attempt to use the false passport to enter. She told the immigration inspector the truth.

We have weighed the favorable and adverse factors and are satisfied that discretion should be exercised in favor of the applicant. Therefore, we will grant asylum to the applicant. * * *

■ [The concurring opinions of FILIPPU, BOARD MEMBER, and of ROSENBERG, BOARD MEMBER, have been omitted. VACCA, BOARD MEMBER, dissented without opinion.]

NOTES ON *KASINGA* AND ASYLUM FOR GENDER OPPRESSION

1. *The Breadth of the Board's Ruling?* Note that the INS acquiesced in reversing the Immigration Judge's denial of asylum and argued only for a remand for further fact-gathering. More important, the INS agreed with Kasinga that female genital mutilation constituted "persecution for reasons of * * * membership in a particular social group" under the refugee law. The INS was concerned, however, with the breadth of the Board's ruling. The INS "estimated that over eighty million females have been subjected to FGM" (Brief 13)—a potentially huge refugee class. The General Counsel maintained that there was no indication that "Congress considered application of [the asylum laws] to broad cultural practices of the type involved here" (*id.* at 14) and, more pointedly, that "the underlying purposes of the asylum system * * * are unavoidably in tension" with broad federal control over entry of noncitizens into the United States (*id.* at 14–15).

Because the U.S. "cannot simply grant asylum to all who might be subjected to a practice deemed objectionable or a violation of a person's human rights," the INS urged the Board to limit its holding to women who are immediately threatened with genital mutilation as would "shock the conscience" (*id.* at 15). The Board took no position on the INS' approach, and the two concurring opinions we omitted said that the Board and the Immigration Judges should follow an ad hoc approach and see where that leads. Congress is the appropriate forum for legislating the general approach suggested by the INS.

In the spirit of the concurring Board Members, start with *Kasinga* and decide whether you would grant asylum to the following applicants:

   (a) a Togolese woman from another tribe that practices female genital mutilation, but not of the "extreme" sort practiced by the Tchamba–Kunsuntu, and who was not in immediate danger of being mutilated;

   (b) a Togolese woman from a tribe for which the State Department has no evidence of female genital mutilation, but the applicant testifies that it is practiced and that she was told it would be practiced on her when she married; and

   (c) a woman from another country where there are documented examples of female genital mutilation, and the applicant testifies that she feared being mutilated when she married.

Consider also: Would *Kasinga* permit a claim for asylum by a woman who had already been mutilated but who feared more severe mutilation?

2. *Other Forms of Gender–Based Oppression.* Given the reasoning and result in *Kasinga*, isn't there a valid asylum claim for women who are able to show that they are subjected to rape and other sexual violence and that their home states offer no protection? Consider Fauziya Kasinga's claim without the gential mutilation element: she alleged that she was forced to marry a man whom she did not love and who had three other wives; implicit in her allegations was the suggestion that sex with this man would have been unwelcome. Should a woman like Kasinga have a right of asylum if their culture forces them into polygamous marriages and acquiescence in marital rape?

The People's Republic of China forbids families to have more than one child and requires pregnant women to have abortions if they already have a child. Americans from a variety of perspectives find this policy repellent: pro-life people consider this policy state-required murder, and pro-choice people consider this policy an invasion of a woman's right to control her body. The applicant for asylum is a pregnant Chinese woman who has fled her society in order to save her (second) baby from abortion. Should the INS grant her asylum? See *Matter of Chang*, 20 I & N Dec. 38 (Bd. Imm.App.1989).

Are these examples excessively ambitious extensions of *Kasinga*?

3. *Female Genital Mutilation in the United States.* Layli Miller Bashir, Kasinga's attorney before the INS, reports that FGM is not uncommon in the United States itself. "Female Genital Mutilation in the United States: An Examination of Criminal and Asylum Law," 4 *Am. U.J. Gender & L.* 415 (1996). Federal legislation has been introduced to make FGM a felony, and many other western countries have such laws already. Bashir argues, however, that the British law criminalizing FGM (the model for the proposed federal regulation) has been extremely ineffective. Why do you think that has been the case?

PROBLEM 8–6

ASYLUM FOR GAY PEOPLE?

In 1990 Marcelo Tenorio left his native Brazil, where he had been the victim of a brutal gay-bashing incident in 1989. Having left a gay discotheque in Rio de Janeiro, Tenorio was waiting for a bus when a carload of youths taunted him. "A strong black man like you. What are you doing here in a place of faggots," they yelled. The youths then beat him, and one stabbed him in the side. Although the attack required Tenorio to be hospitalized and to miss work (as a chef) for two weeks, he did not report it to the Rio police. He testifies credibly that the police in Rio do not respond to gay-bashing complaints and that some police form gangs that actually engage in such violence. Other incidents of verbal abuse followed, and in 1980 Tenorio sought to come to the United States. He was repeatedly denied visas to the U.S., and at no point did he rely on the gay-bashing incidents in his applications. Instead, Tenorio entered the United States illegally through Mexico. He petitions the INS for asylum.

Should the INS grant asylum? The matter was adjudicated in *In re Tenorio*, Dep't of Justice, Off. Imm. Rev., File No. A72 093 558 (July 26, 1993).

Consider the following in framing your answer:

1. Dr. Luiz Mott, a professor at the Federal University of Bahia, with degrees in ethnology and anthropology, has published a book about the

history and repression of sexuality in Brazil. He is also the founder of *Grupo Gay de Bahia*. He testifies that a gay person is murdered every five days in Brazil, the victim of macho attitudes repelled by homosexuality and of official tolerance of (and sometimes complicity in) anti-gay violence. A recent newspaper article referred to homosexuals in Brazil as "deer" and opined that killing homosexuals was more like "hunting" than killing. Dr. Mott testifies that if Tenorio is sent back to Brazil, his physical safety will be imperilled.

2. The State Department's *Country Reports on Human Rights Practices for 1992* refers to claims that there are 12 paramilitary groups in Brazil dedicated to killing gay and transgendered people. Allegedly, there are groups whose members wear "Hunt the Gays" teeshirts.

3. The United Nations High Commissioner for Refugees' *Handbook on Procedures and Criteria for Determining Refugee Status* says nothing—pro or con—about including gay or transgendered people as a "particular social group." The only decision found under the Convention is that of Canada's Immigration and Refugee Board, which in 1992 determined that persecution on the basis of homosexuality was a basis for refugee status under Canada's Immigration Act (which implements the Convention); the Board determined that homosexuality is an immutable characteristic and is fundamental to a person's identity.

If the INS grants Tenorio asylum, should it also grant asylum to a gay person who has been engaged in nonsexual criminal activity, such as burglary or drugs? This matter was adjudicated in *Matter of Toboso–Alfonso*, Int. Dec. No. A23 220 644, Dep't of Justice, Off. Imm. Rev., File No. A72 093 558 (Mar. 12, 1990).

In 1994, Attorney General Janet Reno issued a directive stating that persecution based on sexual orientation could be the basis for granting political asylum. In addition to the United States, nine other countries recognize anti-gay persecution as a basis for asylum: Australia, Belgium, Canada, Finland, Germany, Ireland, the Netherlands, New Zealand, and the United Kingdom.

*

CHAPTER 9

FAMILIES WE CHOOSE

SECTION 1   The Privatization of Family Law

SECTION 2   The Expanding Right to Marry

SECTION 3   Children in Families of Choice

"Family" in western civilization has traditionally meant ties created by marriage and blood, and the typical family was a husband, wife, and as many children as possible. As we enter the next millennium, marriage and blood remain centrally important, but have made way for "families we choose," as anthropologist Kath Weston terms it.[a] The relative ascendancy of families we choose is the family law parallel of Sir Henry Maine's observation that modern law consists in the ongoing transition from status relations to contractual relations. Thus it is that families today are both easier to form and easier to exit. This is the phenomenon Jana Singer calls the "privatization of family law," explored in Section 1 of this chapter. Our focus will be on the questionable features of privatization—its contradictory effects upon women and children, its tendency toward commodification and baby selling—but the reader should also consider the ways privatization has changed the face of the American family. The mom/dad/two kids model of family in the 1950s now competes with mom/mom/two kids, mom/dad/two careers, and mom/kids/no money models of family.

Section 1 closes with a problem on domestic partnership, a new legal institution tailor-made for families of choice. Section 2 begins with the flip

---

a.   Kath Weston, *Families We Choose: Lesbians, Gays, Kinship* (1991).

side of privatization: the possible expansion of marriage to include new arrangements, especially same-sex couples. As barriers to marriage fall for different-sex couples and marriage is rendered an easy way to solidify a family of choice, why should lesbian and gay couples not have the same choices? You will not be surprised to learn that the law has found this proposition impossible to swallow. You might be more surprised to see how controversial this idea has been in the bisexual, lesbian, and gay community.

What about children's role in families of choice? The law recognizes the parent's fundamental right to raise her children, but the litmus test in key areas is the "best interests of the child" (Section 3). That test has, in our society, traditionally been loaded with racial and sexual fears. When lesbian and gay families with children are assaulted by the state, relatives, or former spouses, the child's "best interests" become beclouded with societal as well as family issues. For families we choose, the hardest case in the chapter is one pitting a lesbian couple against a gay man, quarreling over rights to a child begotten by the man and one of the women by artificial insemination. This chapter will do little more than skim the surface of the many legal issues raised by insemination, surrogacy, and children's welfare but hopes to identify some of the legal cutting edges.

THE PRIVATIZATION OF FAMILY LAW

Jana B. Singer, The Privatization of Family Law

1992 *Wisconsin Law Review* 1443, 1447–53, 1456–59, 1460–64, 1470–71, 1478–79, 1488.*

Over the past twenty-five years, family law has become increasingly privatized. In virtually all doctrinal areas, private norm creation and private decision making have supplanted state-imposed rules and structures for governing family-related behavior. * * *

Perhaps the most significant way the law traditionally regulated intimate behavior was by distinguishing sharply, in virtually all important contexts, between married persons and persons in nonmarital intimate relationships. Through laws criminalizing adultery, fornication and nonmarital cohabitation, the law carved out marriage as the only legitimate arena for sexual intercourse. Tort causes of action for enticement, alienation of affections and criminal conversation penalized third parties who intentionally interfered with the marriage relationship; loss of consortium claims protected husbands (and later wives) against those who negligently impaired marital relations. No similar doctrines protected nonmarital intimate relationships from deliberate or negligent third party impairment.

An elaborate network of statutes and common law doctrines also distinguished sharply between children born within marriage and those born outside of it. * * * Similarly, state and federal programs designed to compensate families for the death or disability of a wage-earner typically excluded out-of-wedlock children as eligible beneficiaries. A major justification for these sharp distinctions between marital and nonmarital children was to protect the exclusivity of the marital unit and to punish adults (particularly women) who engaged in sex outside of marriage.

A series of Supreme Court decisions between 1968 and 1983 eliminated as unconstitutional most of the categorical legal distinctions between marital and nonmarital children.[11] These decisions explicitly rejected the traditional notion that differential treatment of legitimate and illegitimate offspring was justified as a way of encouraging matrimony and of expressing society's "condemnation of irresponsible liaisons beyond the bonds of

---

* Copyright © 1991, Wisconsin Law Review. Reprinted by permission.

11. Between 1968 and 1983, the Supreme Court decided more than 20 cases involving statutory classifications based on illegitimacy. [Citing cases, starting with *Levy v. Louisiana*, 391 U.S. 68 (1968), and *Stanley v. Illinois*, 405 U.S. 645 (1972).]

marriage."[12] A related series of Supreme Court decisions established that unmarried fathers who develop a relationship with their children must be given the same rights with respect to adoption and custody decisions as are accorded to married fathers.[13] These judicial declarations were paralleled and reinforced by the Uniform Parentage Act, promulgated in 1973 and approved by the American Bar Association in 1974. The Act abandons the concept of legitimacy and declares that "[t]he parent and child relationship extends equally to every child and to every parent, regardless of the marital status of the parents."[14] * * *

Another way the law traditionally privileged marriage over nonmarital intimate relationships was by denying unmarried cohabitants access to the judicial system for resolving financial disputes arising out of their relationship. In particular, contracts between unmarried cohabitants that related in any way to their sexual relationship were considered unenforceable as contrary to public policy. The rationale for this traditional rule was that the law should not "lend its aid to either party to a contract founded upon an illegal or immoral consideration." * * *

[In the 20 years since *Marvin v. Marvin, infra* Section 1(B)], courts in many states applied both express and implied contract remedies to resolve disputes about property and financial arrangements arising out of cohabitation relationships. In doing so, courts largely abandoned public policy objections to enforcing the private agreements of parties engaged in sexual relationships outside of marriage. A few courts have reached beyond contract in resolving cohabitation disputes, and have applied principles of partnership law or have reasoned by analogy to state marital property division statutes. Consistent with the modern emphasis on private ordering, however, most courts have been unwilling to grant nonagreement-based support rights to unmarried cohabitants or to extend statutory divorce obligations, such as the payment of attorneys fees. * * *

The shift from public to private control over the definition and structure of family relationships extends as well to control over the consequences of marital status. Traditionally, the law underscored the public nature of marriage by defining for all participants the salient aspects of the marriage bond, particularly the legal and economic relationship between spouses. Although marriage has often been described as a civil contract, until recently it was the state, and not the parties, that set the terms of this contract. * * *

The state-imposed terms of the traditional marriage contract were both hierarchical and rigidly gender-based. The husband, as head of household,

---

12. *Weber v. Aetna Casualty & Sur. Co.,* 406 U.S. 164, 175 (1972).

13. See *Stanley v. Illinois,* 405 U.S. 645 (1972); *Caban v. Mohammed,* 441 U.S. 380 (1979). Unwed fathers who have not developed a parent-child relationship need not be accorded such similar treatment. *Lehr v. Robertson,* 463 U.S. 248 (1983); *Quilloin v. Walcott,* 434 U.S. 246 (1978). [See out Note on the Constitutional Rights of Biological Fathers in Section 3(B).]

14. Uniform Parentage Act § 2, 9B U.L.A. 296 (1987). Under the Act, marriage between the parents remains relevant as an important, but not exclusive, indicator of paternity. *Id.* § 4, 9B U.L.A. 298.

was responsible for the financial support of his wife and children. The wife, as the domestic partner, was responsible for providing household services, including housework, sex and childcare. This compulsory gender-based division of labor persisted well into the 1960s, as did the inability of spouses to alter in any binding way the legal and economic incidents of marriage. [Thus, courts refused to enforce agreements, including prenuptial ones, between husbands and wives.]

Over the past twenty-five years, the law has loosened its control over the legal and economic incidents of marriage in three related ways. First, the state-imposed marriage contract is a far less comprehensive or precise instrument than it was a generation or two ago. In particular, the reciprocal rights and obligations of spouses are both less well-defined and less extensive than they were in previous generations. Second, individual couples today have considerably more freedom than in the past to vary by private agreement what little remains of the state-imposed marriage contract. Third, the law increasingly treats marriage partners as individuals, rather than as a single merged unit, for purposes of doctrinal analysis.

The modern trend in favor of sex-based equality has eliminated many of the explicitly gender-based terms of the traditional marriage contract. A wife is no longer required to assume her husband's surname or to accede to his choice of domicile. Wives are not automatically entitled to their husbands' financial support, nor husbands to their wives' domestic services. In most community property states, laws that previously gave husbands the right to manage and control community property during marriage have been repealed or replaced by statutes providing for joint management by both spouses. * * *

Even where state-imposed marital obligations remain as the background legal regime, spouses today have considerable freedom to alter those background obligations by private contract, either before or during marriage. For example, the Uniform Premarital Agreement Act, which has been adopted by sixteen states since its promulgation in 1983, authorizes prospective spouses to contract with each other with respect to their property rights and support obligations, as well as "any other matter, including their personal rights and obligations, not in violation of public policy or a statute imposing a criminal penalty." The commentary explains that this provision is meant to cover such matters as the choice of abode, the freedom to pursue career opportunities and the upbringing of children. Similarly, while the Second Restatement of Contracts continues to disapprove of marital contracts that would change an essential incident of marriage "in a way detrimental to the public interest in the marriage relationship," the Restators' comments make clear that both the essential incidents of marriage and the public's interest in the marriage relationship are to be interpreted more narrowly than in the past. * * *

A third way in which the state has ceded control over the legal and economic incidents of marriage is by treating married persons as individuals, rather than as a merged unit, for purposes of legal analysis. Traditionally, the common law treated married persons not as individuals, but as a single legal entity. Marriage stripped a woman of her independent legal existence and merged it into that of her husband; she became a "femme couvert," literally "a woman under cover" of her husband. This notion of marital merger had far-reaching legal consequences in a wide variety of doctrinal areas. Because husbands and wives were considered one, they could neither contract with nor sue each other. Nor could spouses testify for or against each other in civil or criminal proceedings. As the legal representatives of their wives, husbands were considered responsible for any torts their wives committed. * * * More generally, the legal fiction that the husband and wife were a single entity was one of the rationales that supported the law's traditional refusal to recognize marital rape or to provide remedies for victims of spousal violence.

* * * [T]he trend in most areas of law today is to view married persons as two separate individuals, rather than as a single unit, for purposes of legal analysis. Since 1971, at least twenty-five states have abolished interspousal tort immunity, thus allowing spouses to sue each other for negligent and other tortious behavior. Judicial decisions abrogating the immunity have explicitly rejected the argument that the doctrine is justified as a means of preserving marital harmony. Even those jurisdictions that continue to recognize some aspects of interspousal immunity, disclaim reliance on the notion of marital unity. The increased ability of spouses to contract with each other is similarly grounded in the notion of married persons as separate individuals, with potentially disparate interests.

Changes in the laws of evidence and the doctrines governing criminal responsibility also reflect the legal individuation of the married couple. The common law rule that a husband and wife could not make up the two parties necessary to constitute a conspiracy has been abolished in virtually all jurisdictions. In 1980, the Supreme Court abolished a criminal defendant's privilege against adverse spousal testimony, noting that the ancient foundations for so sweeping a privilege—including the denial to women of a separate legal identity—had long since disappeared.[89] The marital rape exemption has been abolished or narrowed in many jurisdictions.[90] Virtually all states have enacted or strengthened civil and criminal statutes designed to protect victims of domestic violence.

[Singer observes that entry into marriage is still restricted by state age (parental consent usually required for people under age 18), consanguinity (cannot marry relatives), and bigamy (one spouse at a time) limitations.

---

89. *Trammel v. United States*, 445 U.S. 40, 52 (1980). Under *Trammel*, the privilege is vested in the witness spouse; a witness spouse may choose not to testify but a defendant can no longer prevent his spouse from voluntarily testifying against him. *Id.* at 53.

90. See, e.g., *People v. Liberta*, 474 N.E.2d 567, 573–76 (N.Y.1984); *Shunn v. State*, 742 P.2d 775, 778 (Wyo.1987); *State v. Smith*, 426 A.2d 38 (N.J.1981). For examples of legislative abolishment of the exemption, see Colo. Rev. Stat. ch. 18–3–409 (Supp. 1989); Me. Rev. Stat. Ann. tit. 17A, § 251 (1983 & Supp.1989); id. § 252 (1983) (repealed 1989); Neb. Rev. Stat. §§ 28–319 to 320 (1985); N.J. Stat. Ann. § 2C:14–5(b) (West 1982); N.D. Cent. Code § 12.1–20–01 to 03 (1985 & Supp.1989); Or. Rev. Stat. § 163.335 (1971) (repealed 1977); Vt. Stat. Ann. tit. 13, § 3252 (Supp.1989); Wis. Stat. Ann. § 940.225(6) (West Supp.1989).

Other restrictions have been repealed or even invalidated by the Supreme Court's right to marry cases (see Section 2). Gone are laws prohibiting marriages that involve people with mental or physical disabilities (in some states these marriages can still be annulled by the parties), interracial couples, people with a contagious disease, paupers. Couples "have substantially more freedom than did their counterparts a generation ago to determine whether and under what circumstances they will wed, and to effectuate their choice of marriage partner." There are also fewer and simpler formal prerequisites imposed by the state; states do not require a religious ceremony anymore, for example.]

The shift from public to private ordering of marriage has been accompanied by the privatization of divorce and its financial consequences. Until the late 1960s, American law recognized no such thing as a consensual or privately-ordered divorce. Rather, statutes in each state established specific grounds for terminating a marriage. Most of these grounds required the spouse seeking a divorce to prove to a court that her partner had committed a marital offense and that she was innocent of marital fault. Thus, divorce was not the recognition of a private decision to terminate a marriage; it was a privilege granted by the state to an innocent spouse against a guilty one. * * *

The model of divorce as a state-bestowed remedy for an innocent spouse began eroding long before the formal adoption of no-fault divorce statutes. The adoption of these statutes, however, signaled an important shift in the legal paradigm governing divorce. The state, in essence, abandoned its role as the moral arbiter of marital behavior. In particular, the state "washed its hands" of attempting to determine when the goal of providing relief to an innocent spouse outweighed the strong public interest in preserving marriage. With the adoption of no-fault divorce statutes, the state ceded to the spouses themselves—and often to one spouse acting unilaterally—the authority to make this judgment. Thus, under no-fault divorce, the decision to end a marriage generally rests on unreviewed private judgment; the state's role is diminished to one of solemnization and recording, akin to its role in marital licensing. * * *

[The advent of no-fault divorce also initiated a process by which state reduced its supervision of the terms on which the parties parted. Not only were separation agreements routinely enforced by the courts, but so were prenuptial agreements. See the Uniform Premarital Agreement Act (1983), which provided for enforcement of such agreements unless fraudulent or unconscionable. In order to invalidate a premarital agreement on grounds of unconscionability, an objecting party must show that he or she (i) was not provided a fair and reasonable disclosure of the other party's assets or obligations; (ii) did not waive disclosure; and (iii) did not have an adequate knowledge of the other party's assets or finances. Singer observes that in Western Europe, which has also seen significant liberation of the terms of divorce, judges are much more active in reviewing the terms of separation and divorce decrees, especially to prevent hardship to a vulnerable party or to the children.]

In the context of adoption, the shift from public to private ordering has been more subtle, but equally profound. Most significantly, there has been a change in the perceived purpose of American adoption law, from promoting the welfare of children in need of parents—traditionally and unproblematically a "public" function—to fulfilling the needs and desires of couples who want children.

This shift in purpose is most evident in the context of surrogate mothering, where the procreative desires of couples who are unable (or unwilling) to bear children drive the process and where there is no child in existence at the time the "adoption arrangement" is entered into. The shift is also evident in the increased popularity of so-called independent or private placement adoptions, in which prospective adoptive parents solicit available infants directly through newspaper ads and physician referrals. Finally, the transformation of adoption from a publicly-regulated child welfare institution to a privately ordered consumer system is reflected in the increased acceptance (at least within the legal academy) of calls for the legalization of a (modified) free market in babies, championed by United States Court of Appeals Judge Richard Posner. * * *

[Singer demonstrates how the privatization of family law coincides with other developments in public law. Most notable is the gender equality revolution (Chapter 1, Section 3(A); Chapter 4, Section 2 of this book), which has rendered problematic any formal requirements that discriminate on the basis of sex or (sometimes) that rest upon traditional gender stereotypes. See *Orr v. Orr*, 440 U.S. 268 (1979), which invalidated state laws which impose alimony payments only on husbands and not on wives. Also, the Supreme Court's right to privacy jurisprudence (Chapter 1, Section 1) has focused on individuals, rather than the marriage unit, as the possessors of legal entitlements. Singer also notes how economic analysis has seeped into family law; this reflects a change in perceptions, from the family as separate and alien from the market, to the family as a setting in which exchange-like behavior is common and expected.]

NOTES ON IMPLICATIONS OF PRIVATIZATION FOR SEXUALITY AND GENDER

Recall the Ross and Rapp thesis (Chapter 3, Section 3[A]) that law pervasively affects sexuality by creating incentives and affecting behavior of individuals. Consider possible ways the privatization of family law interacts with people's sex lives and their thinking about sexuality.

1. *Sex (and More Sex) as a Consumer Good.* The new privatized family law contributes to the delinking of sex and procreation, a phenomenon already found in a middle class urban society such as ours has become in the last 100 years. With surrogacy and artificial insemination, pregnancy is now possible without sex. With contraception (*Griswold*) and abortion (*Roe*), sex is now possible without procreation. These developments might contribute to an ever greater focus on the pleasurable or sociable qualities of sex. (This is a far cry from the eighteenth century, when public discourse about sex focused overwhelmingly on its procreative purpose.) Like other pleasurable things, sex might then be viewed as a luxury good, obtainable whenever and wherever the mood strikes. Is this good? For a critique of the law's tendency to "commodify" intangibles and thereby degrade social goods, see Margaret Jane Radin, "Market Inalienability," 100 *Harv. L. Rev.* 1847 (1986).

Once sex is delinked from procreation and viewed as a pleasurable good, the demand for it might go up. People would have more sex and would start earlier. The increase in the amount of sex might also increase the variety of sex. In a culture where everyone has twice as much sex as they have in another culture, one would expect to find greater sexual variety. A sexual connoiseurship might evolve in some quarters. The foregoing developments might undermine some gender differences. In our culture, men have traditionally been more interested in having lots of sex, early and often. Pressed by the developments above, women could become increasingly interested in sex. Especially as women become increasingly active in the professions and business, we might expect to see women treating sex as a commodity (the traditional male thing) rather than as a relationship (the traditional female thing). There is some evidence for this speculation in popular culture: *Playgirl*, the Chippendales revue, beefcake advertisements, *Melrose Place* (shirtless "himbos" toyed with by sexually aggressive females).

2. *Sexuality and Commitment.* Under the new family law, sex without commitment is a little easier, and commitment without sex a lot harder. As to the former point, the costs of sex outside of marriage are diminished primarily by the availability of contraception and abortion, but also by the law's liberality toward children born outside of wedlock (the idea of "bastards" has been legally quashed in family law). Thus we should expect women in particular to be somewhat more willing to engage in extramarital sex.

As to the latter point, the death of sex life will more often be fatal to interpersonal commitment. It is both logically and empirically apparent that no-fault divorce has contributed to the higher rate of marital dissolutions; marriage today may last not "till death do us part," but rather "till the sex gets boring." Once sex is valorized for reasons beyond procreation, it becomes an increasingly important part of marriage. If the sex is bad, the marriage will not work, and we would expect women as well as men to seek divorce for this reason. Any kind of more intense link between sex and marriage threatens the stability of marriage and commitment. Commitment under the new family law would thereby be less stable, and this would have profound ramifications for children of the marriage in particular.

3. *Sex and the Single Mother.* The phenomena speculated in Notes 1 and 2 contribute to the phenomenon of "broken" families: children raised by single parents, usually the mother.[b] With more sex outside of marriage and

---

b. We would expect this to change, though it appears that any change is very slow. Because gender roles are changing, partly in response to the new family law, we

the removal of stigmas for children born outside of wedlock, there ought to be more children born out of wedlock, and less social pressure for the man to marry the mother. These children are then raised by one parent, as are children of divorce (on the rise for the reasons above). To the extent the parent raising the children is the mother, the new family law often creates a new difficulty: the state will not insure her financial security. Under the new family law, the state is less likely to scrutinize a separation or divorce agreement to ensure its fairness to the mother or the children or to amend the divorce decree later on to account for changed circumstances such as the father's improved economic position. For the consequences of this development, see the next note.

For low-income mothers, the situation is especially threatening. They have no realistic opportunity to bargain privately for better arrangements, since most of the men with whom they would bargain also lack basic economic resources. Indeed, for poor women, there has been a much more contradictory process than the term "privatization" would imply. Aid to Families with Dependent Children (AFDC), the primary welfare program, was conditioned for many years for unmarried recipients on not being sexually active, on the theory that any male who was a sexual partner ought to be supporting the woman's children. See *King v. Smith*, 392 U.S. 309 (1968). Home visits, including night-time searches, were standard methods of enforcement. See *Wyman v. James*, 400 U.S. 309 (1971); *Parrish v. Civil Serv. Comm'n of Alameda County*, 425 P.2d 223 (Cal.1967). After "man-in-the-house" disqualifications were found to be inconsistent with the statute, states began the policy of decreasing the incremental AFDC support payment for additional children, born after the mother began receiving welfare. See *Dandridge v. Williams*, 397 U.S. 471 (1970) (upholding such a policy). The paradigm shifted completely with enactment of the Personal Responsibility and Work Opportunity Reconciliation Act of 1996 ("welfare reform"), which imposed strict work requirements and a lifetime maximum eligibility of five years. 104 Pub.Law 193, 110 Stat. 2105. Much of the debate surrounding welfare reform concerned the public's unwillingness to expend funds for the support of indigent women having babies. Curbing welfare was intended, in part, to police sexuality and reproduction. What effects would you expect welfare reform to have on American sexuality?

NOTE ON FEMINIST CRITIQUES OF PRIVATIZATION[c]

Although originally supported by many feminists, no-fault divorce has been criticized as bad for women's interests. Leonore Weitzman estimates

would expect more single fathers than in the past. An important cultural benchmark was *Kramer v. Kramer*, in which Meryl Streep walked out of her marriage with Dustin Hoffman and left him with their child. (An earlier benchmark was of course Ibsen's *Doll's House*.)

c. Portions of this note draw on Megan Ann Barnett, "What's Love Got to Do With It? Status Contract Marriage and Divorce" (Yale Law School SAW Paper, 1996–97).

that during the 1970s (when no-fault divorce was becoming the rule) the standard of living for divorced mothers fell 73%, while that of their divorced husbands increased 42%.[d] As many as 39% of divorced women with children live below the poverty line; 20% receive welfare.[e] The reasons for this are apparent. Unlike a real contract regime, no-fault divorce does not realistically compensate the nonbreaching party for her (or his) economic losses.[f] Women's and men's contributions to the joint marital enterprise tend to be asymmetric: women's tend to be backloaded, men's frontloaded, as when the wife sacrifices her career to support the husband while in school and to raise children. This is a common but not universal scenario, and so long as it persists no-fault divorce is unfair to the wife unless it realistically values her contribution to the husband's increased earning power (which often does not happen). Moreover, to the extent that wives tend to be less restless in marriage than husbands, no-fault divorce is bad because its allowance of unilateral termination empowers the husband to escape marriage without the wife's consent or, in a bargaining game, the necessity of paying her off to obtain consent.

These problems are not insuperable. Where the wife's contribution to the family has been homebound or front-loaded, alimony courts in some jurisdictions are willing to consider commercial "goodwill" in the husband's career, *Dugan v. Dugan*, 457 A.2d 1 (N.J.1983), or even (in one jurisdiction) the income stream flowing from the husband's professional degree or license. *O'Brien v. O'Brien*, 498 N.Y.S.2d 743, 489 N.E.2d 712 (N.Y. 1985). How would this approach apply to blue collar families? Other courts have revived permanent rather than temporary alimony as justified in cases where longterm marriages have broken up. *E.g., Casper v. Casper*, 510 S.W.2d 253 (Ky.1974). Generally, however, academics have been much more in favor of innovative alimony arrangements than judges have.[g]

There are theoretical reasons to think that women will fare badly under a regime of marriage privatization, even where there is free contracting and even where courts award alimony more realistically. The foregoing analysis shows how the parties who start off the bargaining process with fewer entitlements (women) will not do as well in the process. With less

d. Leonore J. Weitzman, *The Divorce Revolution: The Unexpected Social and Economic Consequences for Women and Children in America* (1985). We understand that cogent criticisms have been leveled against Weitzman's methodology that would yield lower figures, but do not believe her overall point has been refuted.

e. Demie Kurz, *For Richer, For Poorer* 3–4 (1995).

f. See Alan M. Parkman, *No-Fault Divorce: What Went Wrong?*; Jana B. Singer, "Alimony and Efficiency: The Gendered Costs and Benefits of the Economic Justification for Alimony," 82 *Geo. L.J.* 2423 (1994); Milton C. Regan, Jr., "Spouses and Strang-ers: Divorce Obligations and Property Rheto-ric," 82 *Geo. L.J.* 2303 (1994); Joan Williams, "Is Coverture Dead? Beyond a New Theory of Alimony," 82 *Geo. L.J.* 2227 (1994).

g. See June Carbone & Margaret Brinig, "Rethinking Marriage: Feminist Ideology, Economic Change, and Divorce Reform" 65 *Tul. L. Rev.* 953 (1991); Ira M. Ellman, "The Theory of Alimony," 77 *Calif. L. Rev.* 1 (1989); Milton C. Regan, Jr., "Spouses and Strangers: Divorce Obligations and Property Rhetoric," 82 *Geo. L.J.* 2303 (1994); Jana D. Singer, "Alimony and Efficiency: The Gendered Costs and Benefits of the Economic Justification for Alimony," 82 *Geo. L.J.* 2423 (1994).

skilled lawyers, they will not do as well in the courts, either. Carol Rose suggests that in a bargaining situation women will tend to fall further behind men if it is true or widely assumed that women are more "cooperative" than men.[h] In either event, men will exact higher prices for their initial and continuing cooperation—an explanation for why men usually get a better deal from prenuptials, why women working outside the home still do most of the work inside the home too, and why men shirk their responsibilities during and after marriage (they think they can get away with it, and they usually do). In the new no-fault regime, men can unilaterally get out of marriages when they get tired, and the ease of exit fatally undermines the wife's bargaining position during the marriage if it is the case that she is more "invested" in the marriage and any children than the husband is.

Carole Pateman maintains that marriage, even as it is being reconfigured, is still gendered. What is most distinct about marriage is that it is a "sexual contract," with "sexual" taking on the meaning men give it: "to possess and to have access to sexual property. * * * In modern patriarchy, masculinity provides the paradigm of sexuality; and masculinity means sexual mastery. The 'individual' [who enters into the 'marriage contract'] is a man who makes use of a woman's body (sexual property); the converse is much harder to imagine."[i] Pateman acknowledges that the decline of a pure status regime, where a wife was essentially the husband's property, was necessary for women's rights and, further, that feminists themselves fought for no-fault divorce and other reforms that treat marriage more like a contract. But the defects of a pure status regime do not make out a case for a regime of private contracting. "For marriage to become merely a contract of sexual use—or, more accurately, for sexual relations to take the form of universal prostitution—would mark the political defeat of women *as women*," and "the patriarchal construction of sexual difference as mastery and subjection remains intact but repressed." (Pateman 187.)

One of us has argued that two separate discourses on privatization of family law—feminist and gaylegal—have developed in unfortunate isolation from each other.[j] Gay rights advocates tend to celebrate contractual models such as domestic partnerships; many feminists seek to instantiate implied and unstated duties, even constructive marriage. Certainly if same-sex marriage comes to pass, the hidden collision course will surface quickly. Even without same-sex marriage, however, the question of which fundamental direction lies ahead for family law is a critical one.

PART A.   SURROGACY AND BABY SELLING

Most states explicitly prohibit the "selling" of babies, and many prohibit fee-generating agencies from brokering baby contracts. A newer

---

h. Carol Rose, *Property and Persuasion* (1994).

i. Carole Pateman, *The Sexual Contract* 184–85 (1988).

j. Nan D. Hunter, "Marriage, Law and Gender: A Feminist Inquiry," 1 *Law & Sexuality* 9 (1991).

issue is "surrogacy": whether a woman can contract with a man to bear his child and then give up parental rights in return for a fee. Consider the leading case and the normative issues raised in the notes afterwards.

In the Matter of Baby M

New Jersey Supreme Court, 1988.
109 N.J. 396, 537 A.2d 1227.

■ The opinion of the Court was delivered by WILENTZ, J.

In this matter the Court is asked to determine the validity of a contract that purports to provide a new way of bringing children into a family. For a fee of $10,000, a woman agrees to be artificially inseminated with the semen of another woman's husband; she is to conceive a child, carry it to term, and after its birth surrender it to the natural father and his wife. The intent of the contract is that the child's natural mother will thereafter be forever separated from her child. The wife is to adopt the child, and she and the natural father are to be regarded as its parents for all purposes. The contract providing for this is called a "surrogacy contract," the natural mother inappropriately called the "surrogate mother." We invalidate the surrogacy contract because it conflicts with the law and public policy of this State. While we recognize the depth of the yearning of infertile couples to have their own children, we find the payment of money to a "surrogate" mother illegal, perhaps criminal, and potentially degrading to women. Although in this case we grant custody to the natural father, the evidence having clearly proved such custody to be in the best interests of the infant, we void both the termination of the surrogate mother's parental rights and the adoption of the child by the wife/stepparent. We thus restore the "surrogate" as the mother of the child. We remand the issue of the natural mother's visitation rights to the trial court, since that issue was not reached below and the record before us is not sufficient to permit us to decide it de novo.

[Richard Stern and Mary Beth Whitehead entered into a contract for Whitehead to bear Stern's child and then to give the child up to Stern and his wife, Elizabeth Stern, in return for $10,000. Whitehead was successfully inseminated by Stern at a fertility center and bore the child, a girl the Sterns named Melissa. Whitehead, however, became connected with the child even during pregnancy and became disconsolate when she gave the child to the Sterns. Fearing suicide, the Sterns allowed Whitehead to have the child for five days. Whitehead and her husband fled with the child to Florida, where the Sterns found them and obtained the baby, through police intervention. The Sterns initiated a lawsuit to enforce the surrogacy contract, which the trial court granted. The trial court terminated Whitehead's parental rights.]

We have concluded that this surrogacy contract is invalid. Our conclusion has two bases: direct conflict with existing statutes and conflict with the public policies of this State, as expressed in its statutory and decisional law.

One of the surrogacy contract's basic purposes, to achieve the adoption of a child through private placement, though permitted in New Jersey "is very much disfavored." *Sees v. Baber*, 377 A.2d 628 (1977). Its use of money for this purpose—and we have no doubt whatsoever that the money is being paid to obtain an adoption and not, as the Sterns argue, for the personal services of Mary Beth Whitehead—is illegal and perhaps criminal. N.J.S.A. 9:3–54. In addition to the inducement of money, there is the coercion of contract: the natural mother's irrevocable agreement, prior to birth, even prior to conception, to surrender the child to the adoptive couple. Such an agreement is totally unenforceable in private placement adoption. *Sees*, 377 A.2d 628. Even where the adoption is through an approved agency, the formal agreement to surrender occurs only after birth (as we read N.J.S.A. 9:2–16 and–17, and similar statutes), and then, by regulation, only after the birth mother has been offered counseling. N.J.A.C. 10:121A–5.4(c). Integral to these invalid provisions of the surrogacy contract is the related agreement, equally invalid, on the part of the natural mother to cooperate with, and not to contest, proceedings to terminate her parental rights, as well as her contractual concession, in aid of the adoption, that the child's best interests would be served by awarding custody to the natural father and his wife—all of this before she has even conceived, and, in some cases, before she has the slightest idea of what the natural father and adoptive mother are like. * * *

The surrogacy contract's invalidity, resulting from its direct conflict with the above statutory provisions, is further underlined when its goals and means are measured against New Jersey's public policy. The contract's basic premise, that the natural parents can decide in advance of birth which one is to have custody of the child, bears no relationship to the settled law that the child's best interests shall determine custody. * * *

The surrogacy contract guarantees permanent separation of the child from one of its natural parents. Our policy, however, has long been that to the extent possible, children should remain with and be brought up by both of their natural parents. That was the first stated purpose of the previous adoption act. While not so stated in the present adoption law, this purpose remains part of the public policy of this State. This is not simply some theoretical ideal that in practice has no meaning. The impact of failure to follow that policy is nowhere better shown than in the results of this surrogacy contract. A child, instead of starting off its life with as much peace and security as possible, finds itself immediately in a tug-of-war between contending mother and father.

The surrogacy contract violates the policy of this State that the rights of natural parents are equal concerning their child, the father's right no greater than the mother's. "The parent and child relationship extends equally to every child and to every parent, regardless of the marital status of the parents." N.J.S.A. 9:17–40. As the Assembly Judiciary Committee noted in its statement to the bill, this section establishes "the principle that regardless of the marital status of the parents, all children *and all parents* have equal rights with respect to each other." Statement to Senate

No. 888, Assembly Judiciary, Law, Public Safety and Defense Committee (1983) (emphasis supplied). The whole purpose and effect of the surrogacy contract was to give the father the exclusive right to the child by destroying the rights of the mother. * * *

The point is made that Mrs. Whitehead agreed to the surrogacy arrangement, supposedly fully understanding the consequences. Putting aside the issue of how compelling her need for money may have been, and how significant her understanding of the consequences, we suggest that her consent is irrelevant. There are, in a civilized society, some things that money cannot buy. In America, we decided long ago that merely because conduct purchased by money was "voluntary" did not mean that it was good or beyond regulation and prohibition. Employers can no longer buy labor at the lowest price they can bargain for, even though that labor is "voluntary," 29 U.S.C. § 206 (1982), or buy women's labor for less money than paid to men for the same job, 29 U.S.C. § 206(d), or purchase the agreement of children to perform oppressive labor, 29 U.S.C. § 212, or purchase the agreement of workers to subject themselves to unsafe or unhealthful working conditions, 29 U.S.C. §§ 651 to 678 (Occupational Safety and Health Act of 1970). There are, in short, values that society deems more important than granting to wealth whatever it can buy, be it labor, love, or life. Whether this principle recommends prohibition of surrogacy, which presumably sometimes results in great satisfaction to all of the parties, is not for us to say. We note here only that, under existing law, the fact that Mrs. Whitehead "agreed" to the arrangement is not dispositive.

The long-term effects of surrogacy contracts are not known, but feared—the impact on the child who learns her life was bought, that she is the offspring of someone who gave birth to her only to obtain money; the impact on the natural mother as the full weight of her isolation is felt along with the full reality of the sale of her body and her child; the impact on the natural father and adoptive mother once they realize the consequences of their conduct. Literature in related areas suggests these are substantial considerations, although, given the newness of surrogacy, there is little information. See N. Baker, *Baby Selling: The Scandal of Black Market Adoption*; *Adoption and Foster Care, 1975: Hearings on Baby Selling Before the Subcomm. on Children and Youth of the Senate Comm. on Labor and Public Welfare*, 94th Cong. 1st Sess. (1975).

The surrogacy contract is based on principles that are directly contrary to the objectives of our laws. It guarantees the separation of a child from its mother; it looks to adoption regardless of suitability; it totally ignores the child; it takes the child from the mother regardless of her wishes and her maternal fitness; and it does all of this, it accomplishes all of its goals, through the use of money.

Beyond that is the potential degradation of some women that may result from this arrangement. In many cases, of course, surrogacy may bring satisfaction, not only to the infertile couple, but to the surrogate mother herself. The fact, however, that many women may not perceive surrogacy negatively but rather see it as an opportunity does not diminish its potential for devastation to other women.

* * * [T]he proper bases for termination are found in the statute relating to proceedings by approved agencies for a termination of parental rights, N.J.S.A. 9:2–18, the statute allowing for termination leading to a private placement adoption, N.J.S.A. 9:3–48c(1), and the statute authorizing a termination pursuant to an action by DYFS, N.J.S.A. 30:4C–20. The statutory descriptions of the conditions required to terminate parental rights differ; their interpretation in case law, however, tends to equate them.

Nothing in this record justifies a finding that would allow a court to terminate Mary Beth Whitehead's parental rights under the statutory standard. It is not simply that obviously there was no "intentional abandonment or very substantial neglect of parental duties without a reasonable expectation of reversal of that conduct in the future," N.J.S.A. 9:3–48c(1), quite the contrary, but furthermore that the trial court never found Mrs. Whitehead an unfit mother and indeed affirmatively stated that Mary Beth Whitehead had been a good mother to her other children.

[Unlike the termination of parental rights issue, the custody issue turned entirely on the best interests of the child. Considering all the evidence, including the stability of the parents and the family unit and the ability to provide for the child, Justice Wilentz found that custody with the Sterns would best serve baby Melissa's interests.]

NOTES ON FEMINIST AND GAYLEGAL DEFENSES AND CRITIQUES OF SURROGACY

New Jersey's *Baby M* decision has been broadly influential. As of 1995, surrogacy arrangements were explicitly prohibited by statute in at least nine states and the District of Columbia[k] and heavily regulated in other jurisdictions.[l] The California legislature passed a law explicitly allowing surrogacy arrangements, but Governor Pete Wilson vetoed it. Should surrogacy arrangements be allowed? Should "gestational surrogacy," where the woman who bears the child has no genetic link to the child, be allowed?[m]

k. See D.C. Code § 16–401 (1993); Ind. Code §§ 31–8–1–1 to–8–2–3 (1994); Ky. Rev. Stat. § 199.590 (1993); La. Rev. Stat. § 9:2713 (1991); Mich. Stat. §§ 25.248(153), (155), (159) (1994); Neb. Rev. Stat. § 25–21.200 (1993); N.Y. Dom. Rel. Law § 122; N.D. Cent. Code § 14–18–05 (1991); Utah Code § 76–7–204 (1994); Wash. Rev. Code § 26.26.210 (1994).

l. See, *e.g.*, Ark. Code § 9–10–201 (1993); Fla. Stat. ch. 742.15, .16 (1994); Nev.

Rev. Stat. § 126.045 (1993); N.H. Rev. Stat. §§ 168–B:1 to B:32 (1993); Va. Code §§ 20–159 to–165 (1994).

m. A gestational surrogacy contract was upheld in *Johnson v. Calvert*, 19 Cal. Rptr.2d 494, 851 P.2d 776 (Cal. 1993), upon the theory that the "mother" for purposes of the Uniform Parentage Act is the genetic and not the gestational mother.

1. *Defense: Leave the Market Alone.* Richard Posner, ''The Regulation of the Market in Adoption,'' 67 *B.U.L. Rev.* 59 (1987), maintains that policies regulating or prohibiting baby-selling and surrogacy are questionable, because they obstruct and drive underground a normally functioning market in babies.[n] While such a market involves a much more precious good, human beings themselves, the truths of market dynamics are just as applicable: people's needs and preferences will be satisfied better through the market than through state regulation. But this is true only if the market is a well-functioning one. Is the market for babies a well-functioning market? To take only one example, a woman agreeing to give up a baby she carries to term will usually undervalue the loss she will feel when she gives up the baby, especially if she has never borne a child. If this is true, the mother should have the option of changing her mind after delivery, an option that would destroy surrogacy for many.

2. *Critique: Market Inalienability.* A deeper response to the Posnerian economic argument is that the intrinsic nature of reproductive labor is so different from other labor that it should be ''market inalienable,'' to use Margaret Radin's term.[o] Reproductive labor is different along several dimensions, such as the genetic connection between the laborer and the ''product'' and the duration of the enterprise. Carole Pateman, *The Sexual Contract* 206–18 (1988) and Elizabeth Anderson, ''Is Women's Labor a Commodity?'' *Phil. & Pub. Affs.*, Winter 1990, at 71–92, maintain the key difference is that reproductive labor is more ''integral'' to a woman's identity than other labor; hence, selling this capacity invades a woman's dignity.[p] But how is selling the use of one's uterus more undignified than selling the temporary use of other intimate body parts, as women do when they pose for magazines such as *Playboy*? Are a woman's ideas not integral to her identity as well—yet we would not regulate her ability to market them, or even change them for monetary consideration, right? Anderson and Pateman treat sexuality as unique, to be guarded by the state if not by the woman. Is this too close to old-fashioned attitudes about women's sexuality to be considered feminist? Even more controversial is the idea that the body is sacred and to be regulated much more than the mind.

   Robin West, ''Jurisprudence and Gender,'' 55 *U. Chi. L. Rev.* 1 (1988), believes the feature that makes women most unlike men is the greater connectedness they feel to other people, a connectedness that derives from their bearing children, or even just their ability to bear children. The connection that a mother feels with the child inside her might be considered the most unique quality that human beings can have. This quality therefore might justify treating reproductive labor as a category by itself,

---

n. See also Richard A. Posner, *Sex and Reason* 409–29 (1992). This line of argument is criticized from a libertarian point of view in Martha A. Field, *Surrogate Motherhood* (1990).

o. Margaret Jane Radin, ''Market Inalienability,'' 100 *Harv. L. Rev.* 1849 (1987).

p. See also Judith Areen, ''Baby M Reconsidered,'' 76 *Geo. L.J.* 1741 (1988); Mary Warnock, *A Question of Life: The Warnock Report on Human Fertilisation and Embryology* (1985). This line of argument is criticized in Debra Satz, ''Markets in Women's Reproductive Labor,'' *Phil. & Pub. Affs.*, Spring 1992, at 107, 112–16.

different from any other. But recall that even this unique relationship is alienable: women can give up their children for adoption, and women can choose to abort a pregnancy. If adoptions generally and abortions often are permitted, how can the state justify banning the woman's relinquishment of rights for money? (This argument would better support a rule allowing the mother to change her mind after the child's birth.)

3. *Critique: The Interests of the Child.* Susan Okin, "A Critique of Pregnancy Contracts," 8 *Pol. & Life Sci.* 205–10 (1990), claims that surrogacy contracts do not adequately consider the interests of the child (a big theme in the *Baby M* decision). By weakening biological ties between parents and children and, more important, by inculcating a consumerist attitude toward children (much like the consumerist attitude we now have toward marriage), surrogacy can encourage parental exits and thereby undermine the security children need. The main problem with this argument is that there are not sufficient data to evaluate it one way or the other. Do surrogacy families (biological father and his wife) stick with the child as well as nonsurrogacy families (biological father and mother are married or partnered)? Do adoptive parents generally bond with children as well as biological parents? Even if the child of surrogacy is generally less secure, however, it is not clear how much that should count. Should a little bit of increased insecurity offset a great deal of happiness for a family that otherwise would not have children at all? Remember, by allowing no-fault divorce, our society has made a decision to sacrifice the interests of minor children for the satisfaction of parents and their intimate relationships.

4. *Defense: Economic Opportunities for Women.* In *Birthpower* (1989), Carmel Shalev makes a liberal feminist case for surrogacy contracts. See also Lori B. Andrews, *Between Strangers: Surrogate Mothers, Expectant Fathers, and Brave New Babies* (1989). Shalev rejects the idea that the state should "protect" women from using any of their natural endowments for economic gain. (One can recall that earlier "protective" legislation, such as special maximum hour laws for women, operated to deny women economic opportunities.) She argues that the market should be neutral as between competing conceptions of human relationships, as it should be for abortion, to take a primary example. Contract pregnancy is a potentially large source of wealth for women, and women who choose ought to be able to take advantage of it. Recall, however, Carol Rose's model of bargaining relations between men and women, in which women systematically fail to achieve equitable deals. One might be more pessimistic than Shalev about how much of an economic bonanza contract pregnancy would be for women. Shalev might respond that women's bargaining strategies—the key assumption in Rose's model—might themselves change over time.

5. *Critique: Reinforcing Women's Actual Inequality in the United States.* Debra Satz, "Markets in Women's Reproductive Labor," *Phil. & Pub. Affs.*, Spring 1992, at 107, criticizes both the market and the market-inalienability approaches to surrogacy. She maintains that the primary objection to surrogacy is that in our gender-unequal society contract pregnancy will turn women's labor into an activity used and controlled by others and will reinforce gender stereotypes, mainly the idea of women as breeders deployed to serve male fetishes about maintaining lineage.[q] Note, however, that a great many economic opportunities for women reinforce traditional gender stereotypes and are severely undervalued partly for that reason: secretary (who serves the "bossman"), hired caregiver for a family's children, domestic servant cleaning house, and so forth. If you do not accept the market-inalienability arguments, as Satz does not, how can you deny women opportunities to enter pregnancy contracts while allowing them to enter badly paid contracts to be wet nurses, babysitters, and domestic servants?

6. *Defense: Homosexual Choice and Surro-gaycy.* Marla J. Hollandsworth, "Gay Men Creating Families Through Surro–Gay Arrangements: A Paradigm for Reproductive Freedom," 3 *Am. U.J. Gender & Law* 183 (1995), reveals that gay men have quietly been echoing the "lesbian baby boom" of the 1980s with their own "gay-by boomlet" in the 1990s. Gay male couples can have biological children through "surro-gay" arrangements, as Hollandsworth calls them. Her article, excerpted in Section 3(B) of this chapter, shows how the law discriminates against these men, not only by prohibiting or regulating surro-gaycy (most state regulations insist that only married couples can have a child through surrogacy), but also by artificial insemination laws that refuse to recognize the biological father's rights. She argues that state regulation is blind to the possibility of men's being nurturing and interested in raising children, while appalled by the possibility that a mother would not. Is the parental interest of a gay couple sufficient to offset the feminist criticisms of surrogacy developed in prior notes? Should Hollandsworth accept some regulation as valid, such as an option for the surrogate mother to change her mind when the child is born?

PART B.   LEGAL RECOGNITION AND ENFORCEMENT OF NONMARITAL OBLIGATIONS AND BENEFITS

Michelle Marvin v. Lee Marvin

California Supreme Court, 1976.
18 Cal.3d 660, 134 Cal.Rptr. 815, 557 P.2d 106.

■ TOBRINER, JUSTICE. * * *

In the instant case plaintiff [Michelle Marvin] and defendant [actor Lee Marvin] lived together for seven years without marrying; all property acquired during this period was taken in defendant's name. When plaintiff sued to enforce a contract under which she was entitled to half the

---

q. Anita Allen, "Surrogacy, Slavery and the Ownership of Life," 13 *Harv. J.L. & Pub. Pol'y* 139–49 (1990), adds that surrogacy bears disturbing semblance to the appropriation of slave women by their masters. Some of the cases involve the use of African–American women as the "gestational" surrogate (she carries the fertilized egg of the biological mother and father).

property and to support payments, the trial court granted judgment on the pleadings for defendant, thus leaving him with all property accumulated by the couple during their relationship. Since the trial court denied plaintiff a trial on the merits of her claim, its decision * * * must be reversed. * * *

In *Trutalli v. Meraviglia* (1932) 12 P.2d 430 we established the principle that nonmarital partners may lawfully contract concerning the ownership of property acquired during the relationship. We reaffirmed this principle in *Vallera v. Vallera* (1943) 134 P.2d 761, 763, stating that "If a man and a woman [who are not married] live together as husband and wife under an agreement to pool their earnings and share equally in their joint accumulations, equity will protect the interests of each in such property." * * *

Defendant [responds] that the alleged contract is so closely related to the supposed "immoral" character of the relationship between plaintiff and himself that the enforcement of the contract would violate public policy.[4] He points to cases asserting that a contract between nonmarital partners is unenforceable if it is "involved in" an illicit relationship, or made in "contemplation" of such a relationship. A review of the numerous California decisions concerning contracts between nonmarital partners, however, reveals that the courts have not employed such broad and uncertain standards to strike down contracts. The decisions instead disclose a narrower and more precise standard: a contract between nonmarital partners is unenforceable only *to the extent* that it *explicitly* rests upon the immoral and illicit consideration of meretricious sexual services. * * *

* * * [A]dults who voluntarily live together and engage in sexual relations are nonetheless as competent as any other persons to contract respecting their earnings and property rights. Of course, they cannot lawfully contract to pay for the performance of sexual services, for such a contract is, in essence, an agreement for prostitution and unlawful for that reason. But they may agree to pool their earnings and to hold all property acquired during the relationship in accord with the law governing community property; conversely, they may agree that each partner's earnings and the property acquired from those earnings remains the separate property of the earning partner. So long as the agreement does not rest upon illicit meretricious consideration, the parties may order their economic affairs as they choose, and no policy precludes the courts from enforcing such agreements.

---

4. Defendant also contends that the contract was illegal because it contemplated a violation of former Penal Code section 269a, which prohibited living "in a state of cohabitation and adultery." (§ 269a was repealed by Stats.1975, ch. 71, eff. Jan. 1, 1976.) Defendant's standing to raise the issue is questionable because he alone was married and thus guilty of violating section 269a. Plaintiff, being unmarried could neither be convicted of adulterous cohabitation nor of aiding and abetting defendant's violation.

The numerous cases discussing the contractual rights of unmarried couples have drawn no distinction between illegal relationships and lawful nonmarital relationships. * * *

[Justice Tobriner held that Michelle Marvin had made out a proper claim of express contract, based on her allegations that she and Lee Marvin had entered into an oral agreement in 1964 to live together, hold themselves out as husband and wife, and pool their incomes. In return for her services as "companion, homemaker, housekeeper and cook," Michelle would be supported financially by Lee Marvin. In the next part of his decision for the court, Justice Tobriner held that Michelle Marvin could amend her complaint to add further causes of action founded upon theories of "implied contract" and "equitable relief."

[*Vallera* and other early decisions allowing actions founded upon express contracts refused to allow nonmarital partners to assert claims for relief based upon contracts implied from the conduct of the parties. The court of appeal decision *In re Marriage of Cary* (1973) 34 Cal. App. 3d 345, held that these earlier decisions were inconsistent with the Family Law Act of 1970, which eliminated fault as a basis for dividing marital property and which gave "putative spouses" (people who believed they were spouses but whose marriage was invalid) half the "quasi marital property." The California Supreme Court was not persuaded that the 1970 statute overrode *Vallera* and the earlier decisions but held that those decisions were no longer viable on the merits.]

We conclude that the judicial barriers that may stand in the way of a policy based upon the fulfillment of the reasonable expectations of the parties to a nonmarital relationship should be removed. As we have explained, the courts now hold that express agreements will be enforced unless they rest on an unlawful meretricious consideration. We add that in the absence of an express agreement, the couples may look to a variety of other remedies in order to protect the parties' lawful expectations.

The courts may inquire into the conduct of the parties to determine whether the conduct demonstrates an implied contract or implied agreement of partnership or joint venture, or some other tacit understanding between the parties. The courts may, when appropriate, employ principles of constructive trust or resulting trust. Finally, a nonmarital partner may recover in quantum meruit for the reasonable value of household services rendered less the reasonable value of support received if he can show he has rendered services with the expectation of monetary reward.[25] * * *

■ [The concurring and dissenting opinion of JUSTICE CLARK is omitted.]

NOTES ON *MARVIN* AND THE TREATMENT OF FAMILIES WE CHOOSE

The courts in most states have followed *Marvin* to provide contractual or quasi-contractual remedies for cohabiting partners. A minority of juris-

---

25. Our opinion does not preclude the evolution of additional equitable remedies to protect the expectations of the parties to a nonmarital relationship in cases where exist- ing remedies prove inadequate; the suitability of such remedies may be determined in later cases in light of the factual setting in which they arise.

dictions flatly rejected *Marvin*, e.g., *Hewitt v. Hewitt*, 394 N.E.2d 1204 (Ill. 1979), and several jurisdictions adopted a diluted version of *Marvin*. *Morone v. Morone*, 429 N.Y.S.2d 592, 413 N.E.2d 1154 (N.Y. 1980), for example, limited *Marvin* remedies to cases where there was an express oral or written agreement between the cohabiting parties. Minnesota courts followed *Marvin, Carlson v. Olson*, 256 N.W.2d 249 (Minn.1977), but the legislature overrode the decision with a rule requiring an express written contract. Minn. Stat. § 513.075.

1.   *Quasi–Contract or Contract as a Basis for Gender Equity?* The *Marvin* cause of action in quasi- or implied contract can operate in feminist ways, as illustrated by *Alderson v. Alderson*, 225 Cal.Rptr. 610 (Cal.App.1986). The courts there applied *Marvin* to create an implied contract for community property division of assets in favor of Jonne Alderson, based on these facts: she and Steve Alderson held themselves out as husband and wife for twelve years; Jonne and their three children took Steve's name; Jonne participated in Steve's business and property dealings, including both money and management. The Aldersons' arrangement bore traces of traditional bargaining where women get less than men: Jonne acquiesced in the decision to live together after the couple originally planned to marry; Steve depended on Jonne's support and expertise and then expected to walk away with most of the tangible assets; Jonne not only kept house and took care of the children, but also had a job outside the home and contributed to purchase of the properties, yet Steve believed she was not entitled to an equal division. Moreover, the courts invalidated a quitclaim deed signed by Jonne that renounced her interest in the acquired properties, on the ground that she signed under duress (physical assaults and threats by Steve). Are there disadvantages to *Marvinizing*, from a feminist perspective?[p]

2.   *Unequal Application of Contract Principles to Same–Sex Relationships.* Both *Marvin* and *Alderson* rejected arguments that implied or express contracts arising out of sexual relationships rest upon "meretricious" consideration, even though it was apparent that sexual companionship was part of the deal. This approach has not been characteristic of courts' treatment of gay relationships. In *Jones v. Daly*, 176 Cal.Rptr. 130 (Cal. App.1981), the court flatly refused to enforce an express "cohabitors' agreement" between two men. The gay couple agreed to pool earnings. As consideration, the plaintiff agreed to be "lover, companion, homemaker, traveling companion, housekeeper and cook," virtually the same agreement made by Michelle and Lee Marvin. Nonetheless, the courts found that the gay contract rested upon "meretricious" consideration. Although California courts say that same-sex relationships are protected by *Marvin*, courts in the 1980s are more likely to sexualize those relationships than different-sex

---

p.   For feminist critiques that *Marvin* is the law's imposition of bourgeois ideals on unconventional families and "repressive benevolence" on women like Jonne Alderson, see Michael D.A. Freeman & Christina M. Lyon, *Cohabitation Without Marriage* (1983); Ruth L. Deech, "The Case Against Legal Recognition of Cohabitation," 29 *Int'l & Comp. L.Q.* 480 (1980). Compare Grace Ganz Blumberg, "Cohabitation Without Marriage: A Different Perspective," 28 *UCLA L. Rev.* 1125 (1981).

ones. A case that resisted this temptation, somewhat, is *Whorton v. Dillingham*, 248 Cal.Rptr. 405 (Cal.App.1988).

As *Marvin* illustrates, many of the legal benefits of marriage can be created by private contracts, including wills, joint tenancies and banking accounts, powers of attorney, and so forth. See Barbara J. Cox, "Alternative Families: Obtaining Traditional Family Benefits Through Litigation, Legislation, and Collective Bargaining," 2 *Wis. Women's L.J.* 1 (1986), and Hayden Curry & Denis Clifford, *A Legal Guide for Lesbian and Gay Couples* (6th ed. 1991). As *Jones v. Daly* illustrates, however, courts have traditionally failed to enforce wills and other contracts sealing "homosexual" relationships. See Jeffrey Sherman, "Undue Influence and the Homosexual Testator," 42 *U.Pitt.L.Rev.* 225 (1981) (surveying the caselaw). *Whorton* may reflect a recent willingness of courts to give effect to contract-like expectations between same-sex couples. This new-found willingness is not limited to California. See *Crooke v. Gilden,* 414 S.E.2d 645 (Ga.1992).

3. *Limits of Marvinizing Even in California.* Should *Marvin* be extended to create marriage-like benefits when a nonmarital partner is injured? A California intermediate appeals court held in *Butcher v. Superior Court,* 188 Cal.Rptr. 503 (Cal.App.1983), that the surviving partner in a "stable and significant relationship" may assert a cause of action for loss of consortium in a lawsuit for the wrongful death of her or his partner. Like most other states, California allows a spouse to sue for lack of consortium, and the court held that *Marvin* augurs for an expansion of that right. "Evidence of the stability and significance of the relationship could be demonstrated by the duration of the relationship; whether the parties have a mutual contract; the degree of economic cooperation and entanglement; exclusivity of sexual relations; whether there is a 'family' relationship with children."

Other state courts have rejected such a cause of action, *e.g., Tremblay v. Carter*, 390 So.2d 816 (Fla.App.1980); *Sostock v. Reiss*, 415 N.E.2d 1094 (Ill.App.1980); *Laws v. Griep*, 332 N.W.2d 339 (Iowa 1983); *Haas v. Lewis*, 456 N.E.2d 512 (Ohio App.1982); *Sawyer v. Bailey*, 413 A.2d 165 (Me.1980); *Gillespie-Linton v. Miles*, 473 A.2d 947 (Md.App.1984), as have other intermediate appellate courts in California. The third district court of appeal held in *Lewis v. Hughes Helicopter, Inc.*, that nonmarital spouses have no consortium cause of action. After noting that there must be some limit on the consortium cause of action, the court mainly relied on the state's strong public policy favoring marriage, which had been mentioned in *Marvin* and emphasized in later cases. Also, the court found the "stable and significant relationship" test unworkable.

The court in *Coon v. Joseph*, 237 Cal.Rptr. 873 (Cal.App.1987), held that a stable and intimate gay relationship does not establish the "close relationship" required in California for a third party to sue for infliction of emotional distress after witnessing an intentional tort to his or her loved one. California courts have held that close relationships entitling one to sue include parent-child, husband-wife, and common-law husband-wife. Recovery has been denied to cousin-cousin and lover-lover relationships. The court emphasized the need for limits to the third-party cause of action for infliction of emotional distress and believed that social policy rendered marriage and parenthood the best place to draw the line. A concurring opinion by Justice Barry–Deal distinguished *Marvin* on the ground that it did not involve third-party responsibilities to the unmarried couple and asserted that the legislature alone can extend third-party obligations to same-sex couples. Judge White dissented from this reasoning, noting that some California courts had extended recovery to foster parents witnessing injuries to foster children and that it was unfair to deny lesbian and gay couples the same tort rights as straight couples.

A TRILOGY OF NEW YORK CASES WHERE FAMILIES WE CHOOSE TRY TO FIT INTO TRADITIONAL FAMILY LAW

In the Matter of the Adoption of Robert Paul P., 63 N.Y.2d 233, 481 N.Y.S.2d 652, 471 N.E.2d 424 (1984). A 57–year-old gay man petitioned to adopt his 50–year-old gay partner of more than 25 years. Section 110 of New York's Domestic Relations Law defines adoption as "the legal proceeding whereby a person takes another person into the relation of child and thereby acquires the rights and incurs the responsibilities of parent." Since 1915, New York's adoption law has allowed adults to be adopted and now explicitly allows one to adopt any other "person." Nonetheless, the Family Court denied the petition.

The New York Court of Appeals, in an opinion by Judge Jasen, held that the petition was properly denied. Adoption "is plainly not a quasi-matrimonial vehicle to provide nonmarried partners with a legal imprimatur for their sexual relationship, be it heterosexual or homosexual. Moreover, any such sexual intimacy is utterly repugnant to the relationship between child and parent in our society, and only a patently incongruous application of our adoption laws—wholly inconsistent with the underlying public policy of providing a parent-child relationship for the welfare of the child—would permit the employment of adoption as the legal formalization of an adult relationship between sexual partners under the guise of parent and child."

The purpose of the adoption was to assure that the younger man would enjoy, as a matter of law, inheritance and other family rights not available to unmarried people. Judge Jasen responded: "Adoption is not a means of obtaining a legal status for a nonmarital relationship—whether homosexual or heterosexual. Such would be a 'cynical distortion of the function of adoption.' (*Matter of Adult Anonymous II*, 88 A.D.2d 30, 38 [Sullivan, J., dissenting].) Nor is it a procedure to legitimize an emotional attachment, however sincere, but wholly devoid of the filial relationship that is fundamental to the concept of adoption."

Joined by Chief Judge Cooke, Judge Meyer dissented. The plain language of the adoption law was narrowed by the court without either legislative authorization or a good policy reason in the wake of *People v. Onofre*, where the New York Court of Appeals invalidated the state's consensual sodomy law (Chapter 1, Section 2). "[N]othing in the statute requires an inquiry into or evaluation of the sexual habits of the parties to an adult adoption or the nature of the current relationship between them. It is enough that they are two adults who freely desire the legal status of parent and child. The more particularly is this so in light of the absence from the statute of any requirement that the adopter be older than the adoptee, for that, if nothing else, belies the majority's concept that adoption under New York statute imitates nature, inexorably and in every last detail."

Postscript on Adoption as a Way to Legalize Families of Choice. Most states, like New York, allow adults to "adopt" other adults, thereby creating rights of inheritance and surrogate decisionmaking in the event of incapacity. See Jeffrey Sherman, "Undue Influence and the Homosexual Testator," 42 *U.Pitt.L.Rev.* 225 (1981). Although New York's Court of Appeals refused to allow the Robert Paul P. adoption, other same-sex adult adoptions have been approved, so long as the petition is discreet. *E.g., 333 East 53d Street Assocs. v. Mann,* 503 N.Y.S.2d 752 (N.Y.App.1986). Note that state incest laws, if gender neutral, might apply to same-sex "adoption" couples, however.

Miguel Braschi v. Stahl Associates Company, 74 N.Y.2d 201, 544 N.Y.S.2d 784, 543 N.E.2d 49 (1989). Miguel Braschi was the surviving partner of a man who lived in a New York City rent-controlled apartment until his death. Stahl Associates, the landlord, sued to remove Braschi from the apartment pursuant to York City rent and eviction regulations 9 NYCRR 2204.6(d), which provides that upon the death of a rent-control tenant, the landlord may repossess the apartment (and rent it for a higher rate), unless the apartment is inhabited by "the surviving spouse of the deceased tenant or some other member of the deceased tenant's family who has been living with the tenant." Braschi claimed that he was a member of the decedent's "family" due to their stable partnership, and Stahl responded that "family" should be limited to relatives by blood or marriage, such as those given inheritance rights under New York's intestate decedent rules.

In an opinion by Judge Titone, a plurality of the New York Court of Appeals held that "the term family, as used in 9 NYCRR 2204.6(d), should not be rigidly restricted to those people who have formalized their relationship by obtaining, for instance, a marriage certificate or an adoption order. The intended protection against sudden eviction should not rest on fictitious legal distinctions or genetic history, but instead should find its foundation in the reality of family life. In the context of eviction, a more realistic, and certainly equally valid, view of a family includes two adult lifetime partners whose relationship is long term and characterized by an emotional and financial commitment and interdependence. This view comports both with our society's traditional concept of 'family' and with the expectations of individuals who live in such nuclear units."

Judge Titone then considered what partners should be considered "family" for purposes of the statute: "The determination as to whether an individual is entitled to noneviction protection should be based upon an objective examination of the relationship of the parties. In making this assessment, the lower courts of this State have looked to a number of factors, including the exclusivity and longevity of the relationship, the level of emotional and financial commitment, the manner in which the parties have conducted their everyday lives and held themselves out to society, and the reliance placed upon one another for daily family services. These factors are most helpful, although it should be emphasized that the presence or absence of one or more of them is not dispositive since it is the totality of the relationship as evidenced by the dedication, caring and self-sacrifice of the parties which should, in the final analysis, control." Because Braschi and the decedent had lived together as "permanent life partners" for more than 10 years, held themselves out and socialized as a couple, pooled their assets, and established the rent-controlled apartment as their joint home, Judge Titone found Braschi to fit the idea of family.

Three judges joined this plurality opinion, and Judge Bellacosa agreed with its holding and with its general analysis. Judge Simons, joined by another judge, dissented. He believed that the objectives of the rent control law "require a weighing of the interests of certain individuals living with the tenant of record at his or her death and the interests of the landlord in regaining possession of its property and rerenting it under the less onerous rent-stabilization laws. The interests are properly balanced if the regulation's exception is applied by using objectively verifiable relationships based on blood, marriage and adoption, as the State has historically done in the estate succession laws, family court acts and similar legislation. The distinction is warranted because members of families, so defined, assume certain legal obligations to each other and to third persons, such as creditors, which are not imposed on unrelated individuals and this legal interdependency is worthy of consideration in determining which individuals are entitled to succeed to the interest of the statutory tenant in rent-controlled premises. Moreover, such an interpretation promotes certainty and consistency in the law and obviates the need for drawn out hearings and litigation focusing on such intangibles as the strength and duration of the relationship and the extent of the emotional and financial interdependency. So limited, the regulation may be viewed as a tempered response, balancing the rights of landlords with those of the tenant. To come within that protected class, individuals must comply with State laws relating to marriage or adoption. Plaintiff cannot avail himself of these institutions, of course, but that only points up the need for a legislative solution, not a judicial one."

Postscript on Same–Sex Families under Landlord–Tenant Law. New York's Division of Housing and Community Renewal codified *Braschi* in its regulations and extended it to rent-stabilized as well as rent-controlled apartments. N.Y. Compiled Codes, Rules & Regulations tit. 9, § 2204.6(d)(3)(i). On the other hand, New York courts have enforced lease provisions for unregulated apartments that limit occupancy to persons related by blood or marriage. E.g., *Hudson View Properties v. Weiss,* 463 N.Y.S.2d 428, 450 N.E.2d 234 (1983).

In the Matter of Alison D. v. Virginia M., 77 N.Y.2d 651, 569 N.Y.S.2d 586, 572 N.E.2d 27 (1991). Alison D. and Virginia M. were a lesbian couple who raised a child together. When the child was two years old, the parents split up. Virginia, the biological mother, retained custody of the child, but Alison continued to contribute to his support and well-being. The child called both parents "mommy." After 1987, Virginia terminated Alison's contact with the child, and Alison sued for visitation rights under Domestic Relations Law § 70, which authorizes "either parent" of a child to bring suit for a judicial determination of "guardianship, charge and custody" of a minor child. The Court of Appeals, in a perfunctory *per curiam* opinion, dismissed Alison's arguments. "We decline petitioner's invitation to read the term parent in section 70 to include categories of nonparents who have developed a relationship with a child or who have had prior relationships with a child's parents and who wish to continue visitation with the child."

Judge Kaye dissented from the court's adherence to a stiff biological definition of parent. Section 70 did not define or otherwise limit the term "parent," and set forth as its overriding goal the "best interests of the child." As for a limiting principle, she said this: "It should be required that the relationship with the child came into being with the consent of the biological or legal parent, and that the petitioner at least have had joint custody of the child for a significant period of time. Other factors likely should be added to constitute a test that protects all relevant interests— much as we did in *Braschi*."

Postscript on Child Visitation Rights When Same–Sex Couples Split Up. Some courts have followed *Alison D.*, e.g., *Nancy S. v. Michele G.*, 279 Cal.Rptr. 212 (Cal.App.1991); *Music v. Rachford*, 654 So.2d 1234 (Fla.App. 1995); *Kulla v. McNulty*, 472 N.W.2d 175 (Minn.App.1991), while other courts have exercised their equitable or legal power to entertain such petitions. E.g., *Holtzman v. Knott*, 533 N.W.2d 419 (Wis.1995); *A.C. v. C.B.*, 829 P.2d 660 (N.M.App.1992).

NOTE ON THE NEW YORK COURT OF APPEALS' APPROACH[ES] TO SAME–SEX FAMILIES

Can these three cases be reconciled? Note this similarity to the California cases described in the notes to *Marvin*. Both jurisdictions take a functional approach to heterosexual families we choose but revert to formalist line-drawing when lesbian and gay families are involved. The main exception, *Braschi*, came in the policy area easiest to limit (rent control). Contrast the commonsense reasoning of the next case. Given the foregoing trilogy, is it possible to predict how the New York Court of Appeals would have decided it? Or is it just an easier case?

In re Guardianship of Sharon Kowalski, 478 N.W.2d 790 (Minn. App.1991). Sharon Kowalski was mentally and physically disabled in an automobile accident in 1983. At the time of the accident, she had been living for four years with her partner, Karen Thompson. In 1984, both

Thompson and Sharon's father, Donald Kowalski, petitioned to be Sharon's guardian. The courts made Donald the guardian. *In re Guardianship of Kowalski*, 382 N.W.2d 861 (Minn.App.1986). Donald denied that his daughter was a lesbian and accused Thompson of "preying" on her; Thompson was denied any right to see Sharon until 1989. In 1988, Donald's own health problems required his relinquishing guardianship, and Thompson petitioned. Her petition was supported by 16 medical witnesses who had treated Sharon and was opposed by Sharon's sister and two friends. The trial court appointed a friend who had rarely seen Sharon after her accident.

Minnesota requires appointment of the guardian who would operate in the "best interests of the ward." Minn. Stat. § 525.551(5). The statute says that all "relevant factors" should be considered, including (1) the "reasonable preference of the ward" if she has the capacity to form a preference; (2) "the interaction between the proposed guardian * * * and the ward"; and the (3) "interest and commitment" of the guardian "in promoting the welfare of the ward" and her ability to do so sympathetically. "Kinship is not a conclusive factor in determining the best interests of the ward * * * but should be considered to the extent that it is relevant to the other factors." *Id.* § 525.539(7).

Writing for the Minnesota Court of Appeals, Judge Davies held that the trial court had erred and directed that Thompson be appointed guardian. The factors militating for the appointment were overwhelming: all the doctors and medical staff testified that Thompson was the only person Sharon wanted as guardian, that Sharon made rehabilitative progress only with her, and that only Thompson visited her regularly; only Thompson offered the possibility that Sharon could live outside an institution, as she had built a house equipped to accommodate Sharon's disabilities; Thompson displayed a detailed knowledge of Sharon's needs and possible therapies; only Thompson impressed the social worker as someone who could cope with Sharon's difficult needs.

The trial court's findings of fact were surely animated by two other concerns. One was the Kowalski family's threats that they would never visit Sharon again if Thompson were the guardian. The appeals court refused to be cowed by such threats, especially in light of Thompson's overtures and willingness to accommodate Sharon's blood family. "It is not the court's role to accommodate one side's threatened intransigence, where to do so would deprive the ward of an otherwise suitable and preferred guardian." The trial court also objected to Thompson's "outing" their lesbian relationship, which it viewed as tantamount to a breach of Sharon's privacy and an exploitation of her situation. Judge Davies rebuked the trial judge for ignoring Sharon's needs and held that the evidence overwhelmingly supported the proposition that Sharon was in no way "exploited" by her new status as a "celebrity victim" of judicial and familial gay-bashing. Explicit in the appeals court opinion was the view that it was important for both Sharon and her doctors that her sexual orientation to be uncloseted. Judge Davies ended his opinion with an extraordinary warning to the trial court that the appeals court would not countenance irrational "conditions" to be attached to Thompson's guardianship.

PART C.   NEW LEGAL FORMS FOR RECOGNIZING RELATIONSHIPS: DOMESTIC PARTNERSHIP LAWS

The developments above have impelled a broad range of scholars to call for the creation of new legal categories for family law purposes. Some scholars have favored revival and extension of "common law marriage" to longterm couples, including same-sex couples perhaps.[q] Others advocate new legal forms. William A. Reppy, "Property and Support Rights of Unmarried Cohabitants: A Proposal for Creating a New Legal Status," 44 *La. L. Rev.* 1677 (1984), for example, called for a new status of "lawful cohabitation" applicable to parties who expressly declare their partnership status *or* have attained its functional equivalent in terms of interdependence and sharing their lives, and bestowing on these parties some of the benefits and obligations of marriage. One problem with such proposals is that when they impose a new category on unwilling families, they may be undermining privacy concerns.   Professor Martha Fineman calls for abolishing marriage altogether, replacing it with a protected status for persons in caretaker-dependent relationships, unrelated to sexual bonds.   See Martha A. Fineman, *The Neutered Mother, the Sexual Family, and Other Twentieth Century Tragedies* (1995).[r]

A formal legal move falling somewhere between privatization and marriage is the enactment of laws and ordinances that recognize "domestic partnerships" of two individuals, including same-sex couples.[s] The first major domestic partnership bill was passed by the San Francisco Board of Supervisors in 1982, but Mayor Diane Feinstein vetoed it on the ground that anything that even faintly "mimics a marriage license" was unacceptable to straight society.[t] Two years later, the Berkeley City Council adopted the first operative municipal domestic partnership policy, which ultimately allowed city employees to obtain health benefits for their registered domestic partners. The West Hollywood ordinance (reproduced in Appendix 5 to this casebook) came the next year. Local coalitions of gay activists and allies obtained similar or slightly broader domestic partner-

---

q. See David Chambers, "The Legalization of the Family: Toward a Policy of Supportive Neutrality," 18 *J.L. Reform* 805 (1985); Ellen Kandolian, "Common Law Marriage, and the Possibility of a Shared Moral Life," 75 *Geo. L.J.* 1829 (1987).

r. See Note, "Looking for Family Resemblance: The Limits of the Functional Approach to the Legal Definition of Family," 104 *Harv. L. Rev.* 1640 (1991).

s. See generally Craig A. Bowman & Blake M. Cornish, "A More Perfect Union: A Legal and Social Analysis of Domestic Partnership Ordinances," 92 *Colum. L. Rev.* 1164 (1992) (student note); Robert L. Eblin, "Domestic Partnership Recognition in the Workplace: Equitable Employee Benefits for Gay Couples (and Others)," 51 *Ohio St. L.J.* 1067 (1990) (student note).

t. "San Francisco Mayor Says No to Gay Marriage," *The Blade*, Jan. 26, 1983, at 9.

ship ordinances, executive orders, or policies in Santa Cruz and Madison (1986), Los Angeles (1988), Seattle and New York City (1989), San Francisco (1991 after a referendum repealed the 1989 ordinance), Washington, D.C. (1991), Chicago and Baltimore (1993), New Orleans and San Diego (1994), and Denver (1995). The first countywide domestic partnership policy was adopted in 1990 by Santa Cruz County. Vermont was the first state to offer domestic partnership benefits to its employees (1994). In the same year, the California legislature passed a domestic partnership bill. Like Mayor Feinstein a dozen years earlier, Governor Pete Wilson vetoed the bill on the ground that it would be a "foot in the door" for same-sex marriage.[u]

Most domestic partnership ordinances, like West Hollywood's (Appendix 5), extend health insurance and other benefits to the registered partners of municipal employees. (Private employers often and increasingly extend fringe benefits to domestic partners as a matter of policy, but not of law.) Opponents have successfully challenged such ordinances as inconsistent with state "home rule" law's allowance of municipal legislation. See *City of Atlanta v. McKinney,* 454 S.E.2d 517 (Ga.1995); *Lilly v. City of Minneapolis,* 527 N.W.2d 107 (Minn.App.1995).

PROBLEM 9–1

LEGAL CONSEQUENCES OF DOMESTIC PARTNERSHIP?

You are a lawyer in West Hollywood, California, whose domestic partnership law is reproduced in Appendix 5 to this casebook. Joan Roe, the registered domestic West Hollywood partner of Jane Doe, becomes a client of yours. Over a period of several years, she comes to you with the following inquiries. What advice would you give? What further inquiries would you make, if any?

(A) Tort Suit. Doe was attacked by lesbian-bashers cruising around in West Hollywood. Doe and Roe want to sue the assailants. They know that they can get compensation for the injuries Doe suffered, but they want to know from you what the odds are that Roe can sue for emotional injury because she witnessed the attack and was powerless to stop it and loss of consortium because of Doe's hospitalization.

(B) Inheritance. Doe ultimately dies of her injuries. Like many other people her age, Doe left no will. Assume that under state law, the estate of an intestate decedent (one who dies without a will) passes to the "spouse" and, if there is no spouse, to the next of kin (Doe's parents in this case). Can Roe qualify as a "spouse" for inheritance purposes?

(C) Child Custody. During their partnership, Doe had borne a child, Sarah. After a year continuing to raise Sarah, Roe is sued by Doe's parents for custody of their blood grandchild. Assume that state law follows a "best interests of the child" approach to custody issues. What are the odds that Doe's parents will prevail?

---

u. Daniel Weintraub & Bettina Boxall, "Ballot Fallout Expected from Wilson's Veto," *Los Angeles Times,* Sept. 13, 1994, at 3.

NOTE ON THE BENEFITS AND OBLIGATIONS CONFERRED BY MARRIAGE AND EUROPEAN REGISTERED PARTNERSHIPS

If Doe and Roe in Problem 9–1 had been married rather than domestic partners, they would in most jurisdictions have the following rights and benefits:

- the right to receive, or the obligation to provide, spousal support and (in the event of separation or divorce) alimony and an equitable division of property;

- preference in being appointed the personal representative of an intestate decedent, that is, someone who dies without a will;

- priority in being appointed guardian of an incapacitated individual, or to act for an incapacitated person in making health care decisions;

- all manner of rights relating to the involuntary hospitalization of the spouse, including the right to petition, the right to be notified, and the right to initiate proceedings leading to release;

- the right to bring a lawsuit for the wrongful death of the spouse and for the intentional infliction of emotional distress through harm to one's spouse;

- the right to spousal benefits statutorily guaranteed to public employees, including health and life insurance and disability payments, plus similar contractual benefits for private-sector employees;

- the right to claim an evidentiary privilege for marital communications;

- the right to adopt children, or a preference in such adoptions;

- a presumption of joint ownership of real estate as a tenancy in common, and a right not to be held to a mortgage or assignment of rights to creditors without the spouse's written permission;

- a right to priority in claiming human remains, and to make anatomical donations on behalf of the deceased spouse;

- various inheritance rights, including priority in inheriting the property of an intestate decedent, the right to a family allowance, and the right to dower;

- the right for one's non-American spouse to qualify as an "immediate relative" given preferential immigration treatment, 8 U.S.C. § 1151(b)(2)(A)(i), and become an American citizen under federal law, *id*. § 1430(a), (b), (d);

- the right to receive additional Social Security benefits based upon the spouse's contribution, 42 U.S.C. §§ 401–403; and

- survivor's benefits upon the death of a veteran spouse. 38 U.S.C. §§ 1310–1318.

Which of these rights and benefits is afforded by domestic partnership laws like that of West Hollywood? Does our society "overreward" marriage? Are too many benefits and rights tied to marriage?

In 1987, Sweden adopted a nationwide law providing many legal benefits (fewer than marriage, more than American domestic partnership laws) for cohabiting couples. In 1989, Denmark enacted a Registered Partnership Act, Danish Act Number 372, June 7, 1989 (the Registered Partnership Act); Danish Act Number 373, June 7, 1989 (amending the Danish marriage, inheritance, penal, and tax laws to conform to the Registered Partnership Act).[v] The Act applies only to same-sex couples (section 1), and at least one partner must have his or her permanent residence in Denmark and be a Danish citizen (section 2[2]). To obtain the benefits of the Act, the partners must register according to rules laid down by the Minister of Justice (sections 1, 2[3]). Once registered, the partners have most of the rights, benefits, and obligations of married spouses (section 3). The main exception is that registered partners do not enjoy the same rights of adoption that married couples enjoy (section 4[1]). Danish divorce law generally governs the terms by which a registered partnership is dissolved (section 5). Norway adopted a similar statute in 1993, and Sweden expanded its cohabitation law to the same effect in 1994.

In the United States, there is no federal recognition of domestic partners. Perhaps the closest analog, other than the mostly local laws described above, has developed in the field of domestic violence. The Interstate Domestic Violence Act, enacted in 1994, provides federal criminal penalties for abusing a spouse or "intimate partner" and requires that full faith and credit be granted to orders of protection that meet its requirements. 18 U.S.C. §§ 2261–2266. "Spouse or intimate partner" includes:

> a spouse, a former spouse, a person who shares a child in common with the abuser, and a person who cohabits or has cohabited with the abuser as a spouse; and any other person similarly situated to a spouse who is protected by the domestic or family violence laws of the State in which the injury occurred or where the victim resides.

18 U.S.C. § 2266. One state appellate court has interpreted "cohabit" in a domestic violence statute to include a same-sex partner, *State v. Hadinger,* 573 N.E.2d 1191 (Ohio App.1991), and anecdotal reports indicate that many judges in family courts adjudicate complaints of abuse between same-sex partners.

Outside the realm of public law entirely, advocates have made stunning progress toward the recognition of non-marital relationships by lobbying private companies to provide health and other benefits for domestic partners. As of 1996, the National Gay and Lesbian Task Force listed more than 300 employers—half of them for-profit businesses, some with tens of thousands of employees—that had started to offer such benefits. Further proof of privatization?

v. See Linda Nielsen, "Family Rights and the 'Registered Partnership' in Denmark," 4 *Int'l J.L. & Family* 297 (1990), as well as Henning Bech, "Report From a Rotten State: 'Marriage' and 'Homosexuality' in 'Denmark,'" in *Modern Homosexualities* 134 (Ken Plummer ed., 1992).

THE EXPANDING RIGHT TO MARRY

One consequence of privatization has been the decline of marriage. This relative decline is evidenced by the increased number of people who never marry and the shorter duration of their marriages when they do wed. Marriages are not for everyone and no longer for life, although the recidivism rate is high. As its popularity has done a slow swoon, marriage as an institution has also encountered unprecedented criticism, mainly from feminists and Marxists. Feminists have criticized marriage as stacked against women. Although these critics acknowledge that formal constraints against women have largely vanished, they maintain that some remain (such as more restrictive rules for defining rape when it is within marriage) and that the institution itself carries with it sexist expectations (man works outside the home, woman keeps house and raises the children).[a] Marxist critics of marriage argue that it has been an institution that apes the oppressive market, with its assumptions of "ownership" and "exclusivity."

Just as marriage has fallen into decline, barriers to entering it have decreased. Just as old barriers have fallen, new groups long excluded from the institution want to join up, and society has rejected them, under the aegis of protecting the institution. The first group to win the right to marry are "miscegenosexuals" (Samuel Marcosson's term), people of different races who love one another. Then came lesbians and gay men, and then transsexuals. Who will be next? Polygamists? Incestophiles?

PART A. THE CONSTITUTIONAL RIGHT TO MARRY

Richard and Mildred Loving v. Virginia

United States Supreme Court, 1967.
388 U.S. 1, 87 S.Ct. 1817, 18 L.Ed.2d 1010.

■ CHIEF JUSTICE WARREN delivered the opinion of the Court.

[In 1958, two residents of Virginia, a black woman (Mildred Jeter) and a white man (Richard Loving), were married in the District of Columbia. Upon returning to Virginia and making their home there, they were prosecuted for violating the state anti-miscegenation statutes. After they

---

a. See, *e.g.*, Carole Pateman, *The Sexual Contract* ch. 6 (1988); Lenore J. Weitzman, *The Marriage Contract: Spouses, Lovers, and* the Law (1981); Margaret Shultz, "Contractual Ordering of Marriage: A New Model for State Policy," 70 *Calif. L. Rev.* 2 (1982).

795

pleaded guilty in 1959, the Virginia state trial judge imposed a one year jail sentence, but suspended the sentence for 25 years on condition that the Lovings leave Virginia and not return together for 25 years. In 1963, the Lovings requested that the state trial court vacate the conviction and sentence on the ground that the anti-miscegenation statutes violated the Fourteenth Amendment. The state trial and appellate courts denied the request, holding that the statutes were constitutional.]

Virginia is now one of 16 States which prohibit and punish marriages on the basis of racial classifications.[5] Penalties for miscegenation arose as an incident to slavery and have been common in Virginia since the colonial period. The present statutory scheme dates from the adoption of the Racial Integrity Act of 1924, passed during the period of extreme nativism which followed the end of the First World War. * * *

I.

In upholding the constitutionality of these provisions in the decision below, the Supreme Court of Appeals of Virginia referred to its 1955 decision in *Naim v. Naim*, 87 S.E.2d 749 * * *. In *Naim*, the state court concluded that the State's legitimate purposes were "to preserve the racial integrity of its citizens," and to prevent "the corruption of blood," "a mongrel breed of citizens," and "the obliteration of racial pride," obviously an endorsement of the doctrine of White Supremacy. *Id.* at 90. * * *

* * * [T]he State argues that the meaning of the Equal Protection Clause, as illuminated by the statements of the Framers, is only that state penal laws containing an interracial element as part of the definition of the offense must apply equally to whites and Negroes in the sense that members of each race are punished to the same degree. Thus, the State contends that, because its miscegenation statutes punish equally both the white and the Negro participants in an interracial marriage, these statutes, despite their reliance on racial classifications do not constitute an invidious discrimination based upon race. The second argument advanced by the State assumes the validity of its equal application theory. The argument is that, if the Equal Protection Clause does not outlaw miscegenation statutes because of their reliance on racial classifications, the question of constitutionality would thus become whether there was any rational basis for a State to treat interracial marriages differently from other marriages. On this question, the State argues, the scientific evidence is substantially in doubt and, consequently, this Court should defer to the wisdom of the state legislature in adopting its policy of discouraging interracial marriages.

Because we reject the notion that the mere "equal application" of a statute containing racial classifications is enough to remove the classifications from the Fourteenth Amendment's proscription of all invidious racial discriminations, we do not accept the State's contention that these statutes should be upheld if there is any possible basis for concluding that they

---

5. * * * Over the past 15 years, 14 states have repealed laws outlawing interra- cial marriages. * * *

serve a rational purpose. The mere fact of equal application does not mean that our analysis of these statutes should follow the approach we have taken in cases involving no racial discrimination where the Equal Protection Clause has been arrayed against a statute discriminating between the kinds of advertising which may be displayed on trucks in New York City, *Railway Express Agency, Inc. v. People of State of New York*, 336 U.S. 106 (1949), or an exemption in Ohio's ad valorem tax for merchandise owned by a non-resident in a storage warehouse, *Allied Stores of Ohio, Inc. v. Bowers*, 358 U.S. 522 (1959). In these cases, involving distinctions not drawn according to race, the Court has merely asked whether there is any rational foundation for the discriminations, and has deferred to the wisdom of the state legislatures. In the case at bar, however, we deal with statutes containing racial classifications, and the fact of equal application does not immunize the statute from the very heavy burden of justification which the Fourteenth Amendment has traditionally required of state statutes drawn according to race.

The State argues that statements in the Thirty-ninth Congress about the time of the passage of the Fourteenth Amendment indicate that the Framers did not intend the Amendment to make unconstitutional state miscegenation laws. Many of the statements alluded to by the State concern the debates over the Freedmen's Bureau Bill, which President Johnson vetoed, and the Civil Rights Act of 1866, 14 Stat. 27, enacted over his veto. While these statements have some relevance to the intention of Congress in submitting the Fourteenth Amendment, it must be understood that they pertained to the passage of specific statutes and not to the broader, organic purpose of a constitutional amendment. As for the various statements directly concerning the Fourteenth Amendment, we have said in connection with a related problem, that although these historical sources "cast some light" they are not sufficient to resolve the problem; "[a]t best, they are inconclusive. The most avid proponents of the post-War Amendments undoubtedly intended them to remove all legal distinctions among 'all persons born or naturalized in the United States.' Their opponents, just as certainly, were antagonistic to both the letter and the spirit of the Amendments and wished them to have the most limited effect." *Brown v. Board of Education*, 347 U.S. 483, 489 (1954). We have rejected the proposition that the debates in the Thirty-ninth Congress or in the state legislatures which ratified the Fourteenth Amendment supported the theory advanced by the State, that the requirement of equal protection of the laws is satisfied by penal laws defining offenses based on racial classifications so long as white and Negro participants in the offense were similarly punished. *McLaughlin v. Florida*, 379 U.S. 184 (1964).

The State finds support for its "equal application" theory in the decision of the Court in *Pace v. Alabama*, 106 U.S. 583 (1883). In that case, the Court upheld a conviction under an Alabama statute forbidding adultery or fornication between a white person and a Negro which imposed a greater penalty than that of a statute proscribing similar conduct by members of the same race. The Court reasoned that the statute could not be said to discriminate against Negroes because the punishment for each participant in the offense was the same. However, as recently as the 1964 Term, in rejecting the reasoning of that case, we stated *"Pace* represents a limited view of the Equal Protection Clause which has not withstood analysis in the subsequent decisions of this Court." *McLaughlin* [379 U.S.] at 188. As we there demonstrated, the Equal Protection Clause requires the consideration of whether the classifications drawn by any statute constitute an arbitrary and invidious discrimination. The clear and central purpose of the Fourteenth Amendment was to eliminate all official state sources of invidious racial discrimination in the States.

There can be no question but that Virginia's miscegenation statutes rest solely upon distinctions drawn according to race. The statutes proscribe generally accepted conduct if engaged in by members of different races. Over the years, this Court has consistently repudiated "[d]istinctions between citizens solely because of their ancestry" as being "odious to a free people whose institutions are founded upon the doctrine of equality." *Hirabayashi v. United States*, 320 U.S. 81, 100 (1943). At the very least, the Equal Protection Clause demands that racial classifications, especially suspect in criminal statutes, be subjected to the "most rigid scrutiny," *Korematsu v. United States*, 323 U.S. 214, 216 (1944), and, if they are ever to be upheld, they must be shown to be necessary to the accomplishment of some permissible state objective, independent of the racial discrimination which it was the object of the Fourteenth Amendment to eliminate. * * *

There is patently no legitimate overriding purpose independent of invidious racial discrimination which justifies this classification. The fact that Virginia prohibits only interracial marriages involving white persons demonstrates that the racial classifications must stand on their own justification, as measures designed to maintain White Supremacy.[11] We have consistently denied the constitutionality of measures which restrict the rights of citizens on account of race. There can be no doubt that restricting the freedom to marry solely because of racial classifications violates the central meaning of the Equal Protection Clause.

---

11. Appellants point out that the State's concern in these statutes, as expressed in the words of the 1924 Act's title, "An Act to Preserve Racial Integrity," extends only to the integrity of the white race. While Virginia prohibits whites from marrying any nonwhite (subject to the exception for the descendants of Pocahontas), Negroes, Orientals, and any other racial class may intermarry without statutory interference. Appellants contend that this distinction renders Virginia's miscegenation statutes arbitrary and unreasonable even assuming the constitutional validity of an official purpose to preserve "racial integrity." We need not reach this contention because we find the racial classifications in these statutes repug- nant to the Fourteenth Amendment, even assuming an even-handed state purpose to protect the "integrity" of all races. [*Editors' note*: The Virginia statutes stated that "the term 'white person' shall apply only to such person as has no trace whatever of any blood other than Caucasian; but persons who have one-sixteenth or less of the blood of the American Indian and have no other non-Caucasic blood shall be deemed to be white persons." In an earlier footnote, Chief Justice Warren explained this exception by quoting a 1925 publication by a state official, who wrote that it reflected " 'the desire of all to recognize as an integral and honored part of the white race the descendants of John Rolfe and Pocahontas.' "]

II.

These statutes also deprive the Lovings of liberty without due process of law in violation of the Due Process Clause of the Fourteenth Amendment. The freedom to marry has long been recognized as one of the vital personal rights essential to the orderly pursuit of happiness by free men.

Marriage is one of the "basic civil rights of man," fundamental to our very existence and survival. *Skinner v. State of Oklahoma*, 316 U.S. 535, 541 (1942). To deny this fundamental freedom on so unsupportable a basis as the racial classifications embodied in these statutes, classifications so directly subversive of the principle of equality at the heart of the Fourteenth Amendment, is surely to deprive all the State's citizens of liberty without due process of law. The Fourteenth Amendment requires that the freedom of choice to marry not be restricted by invidious racial discriminations. Under our Constitution, the freedom to marry or not marry, a person of another race resides with the individual and cannot be infringed by the State.

These convictions must be reversed.

John F. Singer and Paul C. Barwick v. Lloyd Hara

Washington Court of Appeals, 1974.
11 Wash. App. 247, 522 P.2d 1187, review denied, 84 Wash.2d 1008 (1974).

■ SWANSON, CHIEF JUDGE.

Appellants Singer and Barwick, both males, appeal from the trial court's order denying their motion to show cause by which they sought to compel King County Auditor Lloyd Hara to issue a marriage license to them. * * *

Appellants * * * argue that if, as we have held, our state marriage laws must be construed to prohibit same-sex marriages, such laws * * * violate[] the ERA which recently became part of our state constitution.[4] The question thus presented is a matter of first impression in this state and, to our knowledge, no court in the nation has ruled upon the legality of same-sex marriage in light of an equal rights amendment. The ERA provides, in relevant part:

> Equality of rights and responsibility under the law shall not be denied or abridged on account of sex.

In seeking the protection of the ERA, appellants argue that the language of the amendment itself leaves no question of interpretation and that the essential thrust of the ERA is to make sex an impermissible legal classification. Therefore, they argue, to construe state law to permit a man to marry a woman but at the same time to deny him the right to marry

---

4. HJR 61, commonly known as the 'equal rights amendment,' was approved by the voters November 7, 1972, and became effective December 7, 1972. Const. amend. 61, adding article 31. The language of the ERA is substantially similar to the federal ERA now before the states for ratification as the twenty-seventh amendment to the United States Constitution.

another man is to construct an unconstitutional classification "on account of sex."[5] In response to appellants' contention, the state points out that all same-sex marriages are deemed illegal by the state, and therefore argues that there is no violation of the ERA so long as marriage licenses are denied equally to both male and female pairs. In other words, the state suggests that appellants are not entitled to relief under the ERA because they have failed to make a showing that they are somehow being treated differently by the state than they would be if they were females. Appellants suggest, however, that the holdings in *Loving*; *Perez v. Lippold*, 32 Cal.2d 711, 198 P.2d 17 (1948); and *J.S.K. Enterprises, Inc. v. City of Lacey*, 492 P.2d 600 (1971), are contrary to the position taken by the state. We disagree.

In *Loving*, the state of Virginia argued that its anti-miscegenation statutes did not violate constitutional prohibitions against racial classifications because the statutes affected both racial groups equally. The Supreme Court, noting that the fact of equal application does not immunize the statute from the very heavy burden of justification which the Fourteenth Amendment has traditionally required of state statutes "drawn according to race," held that the Virginia laws were founded on an impermissible racial classification and therefore could not be used to deny interracial couples the "fundamental" right to marry. The California court made a similar ruling as to that state's anti-miscegenation law in *Perez*.

Although appellants suggest an analogy between the racial classification involved in *Loving* and *Perez* and the alleged sexual classification

---

5. Appellants also argue that prior to the November 7, 1972 election, the voters were advised that one effect of approval of the ERA (HJR 61) would be the legalization of same-sex marriages, but nevertheless voted in favor of the amendment. In this connection, appellants direct our attention to the following language in the "Statement against" HJR 61 contained in the 1972 Voters Pamphlet published by the Secretary of State:

> HJR 61 would establish rules in our society which were not intended and which the citizenry simply could not support. Examples are numerous: * * *
>
> (3) Homosexual and lesbian marriage would be legalized, with further complication regarding adopting children into such a "family." People will live as they choose, but the beauty and sanctity of marriage must be preserved from such needless desecration; * * *

We are not persuaded that voter approval of the ERA necessarily included an intention to permit same-sex marriages. On the contrary, the "Statement for" HJR 61 in the Voters Pamphlet indicated that the basic principle of the ERA

> is that both sexes be treated equally under the law. The States could not pass or enforce any law which places a legal obligation, or confers a special legal privilege on one sex but not the other.

Similarly, the Attorney General's explanation of the effect of HJR 61, also set forth in the Voters Pamphlet, focused on the idea that government "could not treat persons differently because they are of one sex or the other." In other words, as we discuss in the body of this opinion, to be entitled to relief under the ERA, appellants must make a showing that they are somehow being treated differently by the government than they would be if they were females.

[The court cited and quoted from newspaper accounts published at the time of the November 7, 1972 election, to show that proponents of the ERA consistently denied that it would require gender-neutral marriages and that voters as well as proponents saw the ERA only in terms of women's rights and not gay rights.]

involved in the case at bar, we do not find such an analogy. The operative distinction lies in the relationship which is described by the term "marriage" itself, and that relationship is the legal union of one man and one woman. Washington statutes, specifically those relating to marriage (RCW 26.04) and marital (community) property (RCW 26.16), are clearly founded upon the presumption that marriage, as a legal relationship, may exist only between one man and one woman who are otherwise qualified to enter that relationship. Similarly although it appears that the appellate courts of this state until now have not been required to define specifically what constitutes a marriage, it is apparent from a review of cases dealing with legal questions arising out of the marital relationship that the definition of marriage as the legal union of one man and one woman who are otherwise qualified to enter into the relationship not only is clearly implied from such cases, but also was deemed by the court in each case to be so obvious as not to require recitation. Finally, the courts known by us to have considered the question have all concluded that same-sex relationships are outside of the proper definition of marriage. *Jones v. Hallahan*, 501 S.W.2d 588 (Ky.1973); *Baker v. Nelson*, 291 Minn. 310, 191 N.W.2d 185 (1971); *Anonymous v. Anonymous*, 67 Misc.2d 982, 325 N.Y.S.2d 499 (1971). Appellants have cited no authority to the contrary.

Given the definition of marriage which we have enunciated, the distinction between the case presented by appellants and those presented in *Loving* and *Perez* is apparent. In *Loving* and *Perez*, the parties were barred from entering into the marriage relationship because of an impermissible racial classification. There is no analogous sexual classification involved in the instant case because appellants are not being denied entry into the marriage relationship because of their sex; rather, they are being denied entry into the marriage relationship because of the recognized definition of that relationship as one which may be entered into only by two persons who are members of the opposite sex. As the court observed in *Jones v. Hallahan*, 501 S.W.2d at 590: "In substance, the relationship proposed by the appellants does not authorize the issuance of a marriage license because what they propose is not a marriage." *Loving* and *Perez* are inapposite.

J.S.K. Enterprises, Inc. v. City of Lacey is also factually and legally dissimilar to the case at bar. In that case, this court held that a city ordinance which permitted massagists to administer massages only to customers of their own sex constituted discrimination on the basis of sex, prohibited by the equal protection clause of the fourteenth amendment to the United States Constitution, and also violated RCW 49.12.200, relating to the right of women to pursue any employment. We see no analogy between the right of women to administer massages to men and the question of whether the prohibition against same-sex marriages is unconstitutional. The right recognized in *J.S.K. Enterprises, Inc.* on the basis of principles applicable to employment discrimination has nothing to do with the question presented by appellants.

Appellants apparently argue, however, that notwithstanding the fact that the equal protection analysis applied in *Loving, Perez,* and *J.S.K. Enterprises, Inc.* may render those cases distinguishable from the case at bar, the absolute language of the ERA requires the conclusion that the prohibition against same- sex marriages is unconstitutional. In this context, appellants suggest that definition of marriage, as the legal union of one man and one woman, in and of itself, when applied to appellants, constitutes a violation of the ERA. Therefore, appellants contend, persons of the same sex must be presumed to have the constitutional right to marry one another in the absence of a countervailing interest or clear exception to the ERA.

* * * We do not believe that approval of the ERA by the people of this state reflects any intention upon their part to offer couples involved in same-sex relationships the protection of our marriage laws. A consideration of the basic purpose of the ERA makes it apparent why that amendment does not support appellants' claim of discrimination. The primary purpose of the ERA is to overcome discriminatory legal treatment as between men and women "on account of sex." The popular slogan, "Equal pay for equal work," particularly expresses the rejection of the notion that merely because a person is a woman, rather than a man, she is to be treated differently than a man with qualifications equal to her own.

Prior to adoption of the ERA, the proposition that women were to be accorded a position in the law inferior to that of men had a long history. Thus, in that context, the purpose of the ERA is to provide the legal protection, as between men and women, that apparently is missing from the state and federal Bills of Rights, and it is in light of that purpose that the language of the ERA must be construed. To accept the appellants' contention that the ERA must be interpreted to prohibit statutes which refuse to permit same-sex marriages would be to subvert the purpose for which the ERA was enacted by expanding its scope beyond that which was undoubtedly intended by the majority of the citizens of this state who voted for the amendment. * * *

In the instant case, it is apparent that the state's refusal to grant a license allowing the appellants to marry one another is not based upon appellants' status as males, but rather it is based upon the state's recognition that our society as a whole views marriage as the appropriate and desirable forum for procreation and the rearing of children. This is true even though married couples are not required to become parents and even though some couples are incapable of becoming parents and even though not all couples who produce children are married. These, however, are exceptional situations. The fact remains that marriage exists as a protected legal institution primarily because of societal values associated with the propagation of the human race. Further, it is apparent that no same-sex couple offers the possibility of the birth of children by their union. Thus the refusal of the state to authorize same-sex marriage results from such impossibility of reproduction rather than from an invidious discrimination "on account of sex." Therefore, the definition of marriage as the legal union of one man and one woman is permissible as applied to appellants, notwithstanding the prohibition contained in the ERA, because it is founded upon the unique physical characteristics of the sexes and appellants are not being discriminated against because of their status as males per se. In short, we hold the ERA does not require the state to authorize same-sex marriage.

[The court also rejected appellants' arguments under the federal due process and equal protection clauses. The court first determined that "rational basis" scrutiny is all that such a classification must meet and, then, that this law passed the rational basis test. The court concluded with this quotation from *Baker v. Nelson*, 191 N.W.2d at 186:]

> The institution of marriage as a union of man and woman, uniquely involving the procreation and rearing of children within a family, is as old as the book of Genesis.... This historic institution manifestly is more deeply founded than the asserted contemporary concept of marriage and societal interests for which petitioners contend. The due process clause of the Fourteenth Amendment is not a charter for restructuring it by judicial legislation. The equal protection clause of the Fourteenth Amendment, like the due process clause, is not offended by the state's classification of persons authorized to marry. * * *

NOTE ON CONSTITUTIONAL ARGUMENTS ALLOWING THE STATE TO DENY SAME–SEX MARRIAGE

1. *Definitional Arguments.* As of 1993, not a single judge or state attorney general had expressed an opinion that same-sex marriage is required by any principle of law.[f] Their main argument against same-sex marriage has

f. A chronological array of judicial decisions rejecting same-sex couples' petition for equal marriage rights is as follows: *Baker v. Nelson*, 191 N.W.2d 185 (Minn.1971), appeal dismissed, 409 U.S. 810 (1972); *Jones v. Hallahan*, 501 S.W.2d 588 (Ky.1973); *Singer v. Hara*, 522 P.2d 1187 (Wash.App.), review denied, 84 Wash. 2d 1008 (Wash. 1974); *Adams v. Howerton*, 486 F.Supp. 1119 (C.D.Cal. 1980), affirmed on other grounds, 673 F.2d 1036 (9th Cir.1982); *Jacobson v. Jacobson*, 314 N.W.2d 78 (N.D.1981); *Slayton v. State*, 633 S.W.2d 934 (Tex.App.1982); *De Santo v. Barnsley*, 476 A.2d 952 (Pa.Super.Ct.1984); *Cuevas v. Mills*, No. 86–3244 (D. Kan., October 27, 1986) (unpublished opinion); *In re Succession of Bacot*, 502 So.2d 1118 (La. App.), writ denied, 503 So.2d 466 (La.1987); *Gajovski v. Gajovski*, 610 N.E.2d 431 (Ohio App.1991); *VanDyck v. VanDyck*, 425 S.E.2d 853 (Ga.1993); *Callender v. Corbett*, No. 296666 (Ariz. Super. Ct., April 13, 1994) (un-

published opinion); *Dean v. District of Columbia*, 653 A.2d 307 (D.C.1995).

For negative responses from state attorneys general, see 190 Opinions of the Attorney General of Alabama 30 (1983); Opinions of the Attorney General of Arkansas (April 26, 1995); 1975 Opinions of the Attorney General of Colorado (1975); 1993 Opinions of the Attorney General of Idaho 11 (1993); 77 Opinions of the Attorney General of Kansas (Aug. 4, 1977); 1992 Opinions of the Attorney General of Louisiana 699(A) (1992); 1984 Opinions of the Attorney General of Maine 28 (1984); 1978 Opinions of the Attorney General of Mississippi 684 (July 10, 1978); 1977 Opinions of the Attorney General of Nebraska 170 (1977); 1976 Opinions of the Attorney General of South Carolina 423 (1976); 88 Opinions of the Attorney General of Tennessee 43 (1988); 1977–1978 Opinions of the Attorney General of Virginia 154 (1977).

been definitional: marriage is necessarily different-sex and therefore cannot include same-sex couples. Hence, any statute that talks of "marriage" can only contemplate different-sex couples, even if the statute is not gendered (i.e., does not use the specific terms "husband" and "wife"). Typical is the discussion in *Jones v. Hallahan*, 501 S.W.2d 588, 589 (Ky.1973):

> Marriage was a custom long before the state commenced to issue licenses for that purpose. For a time the records of marriage were kept by the church. * * * [M]arriage has always been considered as the union of a man and a woman and we have been presented with no authority to the contrary. * * * It appears that appellants are prevented from marrying, not by the statutes of Kentucky or the refusal of the County Clerk of Jefferson County to issue them a license, but rather by their own incapability of entering into a marriage as that term is defined.

This definitional approach naturally dispatches any statutory interpretation argument, since all the state marriage statutes (whether gendered or not) do use the term "marriage." Note that the Kentucky court relied on history and tradition to figure out what marriage is, definitionally. Other courts have also defined the essence of marriage more philosophically, as requiring procreation as one purpose. See *Baker v. Nelson*, 191 N.W.2d 185 (Minn.1971), appeal dismissed, 409 U.S. 810 (1972). Courts have also used the definitional argument as a way to reject constitutional challenges based upon the right to marriage recognized in *Loving*. By defining marriage as essentially different-sex, *Singer* was able to avoid the charge that the state was creating an invidious discrimination by denying licenses to same-sex couples.

What results when a post-operative male-to-female transsexual wants to marry a man? See the contradictory case law in Chapter 12, Section 2. How is that different from same-sex marriage? What about the case of a person with Klinefelter's syndrome (XXY chromosomes, rather than the male XY pattern or the female XX pattern)? See Chapter 2, Section 3(A) for a description of chromosomal variations and the determination of a person's sex.

2. *Functional Arguments.* The opponents of same-sex marriage have also developed functional justifications for this definitional barrier. Accordingly, the second type of oppositionist argument invokes community values, including the values of traditional morality. The federal court in *Adams v. Howerton*, 486 F.Supp. 1119, 1123 (C.D.Cal.1980), affirmed on other grounds, 673 F.2d 1036 (9th Cir.1982), made the definitional argument by linking it to traditions of Judeo–Christian morality:

> The definition of marriage, the rights and responsibilities implicit in that relationship, and the protections and preferences afforded to marriage, are now governed by the civil law. The English civil law took its attitudes and basic principles from canon law, which, in early times, was administered in the ecclesiastical courts. Canon law in both

> Judaism and Christianity could not possibly sanction any marriage between persons of the same sex because of the vehement condemnation in the scriptures of both religions of all homosexual relationships. Thus there has been for centuries a combination of scriptural and canonical teaching under which a "marriage" between persons of the same sex was unthinkable and, by definition, impossible.

Although this decision rested upon a suspiciously sectarian vision of morality, it could as easily have invoked general "family values," as some courts and commentators have done.[g]

3. *Pragmatic Arguments.* A milder argument against same-sex marriage appeals to pragmatism. The pragmatist unconstrained by formal definitions and uninterested in traditional morality might still be reluctant to allow same-sex marriages if such marriages would be impractical and disruptive. Judge Richard Posner's *Sex and Reason* (1991) presents a pragmatic case against same-sex marriage at this time. Recognizing same-sex relationships as marriage would be problematic, he suggests, because it would "be widely interpreted as placing a stamp of approval on homosexuality"; would carry an "information cost" in that the socially informative value of knowing someone is married would be somewhat reduced as the term is broadened; and would have "many collateral effects, simply because marriage is a status rich in entitlements, many of which were not designed with same-sex couples in mind." *Id.* at 311–13. The last point is the most important. If the state suddenly recognized same-sex marriage, employers would have to refigure fringe benefits for many of their newly married gay and lesbian employees; legislatures would become embroiled in a spate of controversies about which (if any) marriage entitlements they would deny to same-sex couples, and then litigation over the constitutionality of any new but more specific discriminations; and agencies would have to rethink their regulations and cost-benefit analyses in a number of areas. For a pragmatic response, see William N. Eskridge, Jr., "A Social Constructionist Critique of Posner's *Sex and Reason*," 102 *Yale L.J.* 333, 352–59 (1992).

Thomas E. Zablocki v. Roger C. Redhail, 434 U.S. 374, 98 S.Ct. 673, 54 L.Ed.2d 618 (1978). The Supreme Court invalidated Wisconsin's law precluding the issuance of marriage licenses to people with outstanding (owed but unpaid) support obligations to children from a previous marriage. Justice Thurgood Marshall's opinion for the Court started with the *Loving* proposition that the "right to marry" is a fundamental due process right. "It is not surprising that the decision to marry has been placed on the same level of importance as decisions relating to procreation, childbirth, child rearing, and familial relationships. As the facts of these cases illustrate, it would make little sense to recognize a right to privacy with respect

---

g. "The majority, therefore, may reasonably believe that legal recognition of same-sex marriage in the eyes of society and, by so doing, would impair the ability of opposite-sex marriage to advance the individual and community values that it has traditionally promoted." C. Sydney Buchanan, "Same-Sex Marriage: The Linchpin Issue," 10 *U. Dayton L. Rev.* 541, 567 (1985); see *id.* at 559–60 (state ought to be able to implement community moral standards by discouraging conduct inconsistent with those standards).

to other matters of family life and not with respect to the decision to enter into a relationship that is the foundation of the family in our society."

Justice Marshall then reasoned that any state discrimination in allocating the right to marry must be scrutinized strictly under the equal protection clause as well. "When a statutory classification significantly interferes with the exercise of a fundamental right, it cannot be upheld unless it is supported by sufficiently important state interests and is closely tailored to effectuate only those interests." The Wisconsin statute flunked this stringent test. Although ensuring collection of support obligations owed one's children is an important state interest, the state has other, less constitutionally intrusive, ways of effectuating that interest.

Concurring only in the judgment, Justice Powell objected to the broad sweep of the opinion of the Court. (Five Justices joined Justice Marshall's opinion; three Justices concurred on the judgment; only Justice Rehnquist dissented.) He believed that federal law should not intrude on traditional state regulation of the marital relationship. "State regulation has included bans on incest, bigamy, and homosexuality, as well as various preconditions to marriage, such as blood tests. Likewise, a showing of fault on the part of one of the partners traditionally has been a prerequisite to the dissolution of an unsuccessful union. A 'compelling state purpose' inquiry would cast doubt on the network of restrictions that the States have fashioned to govern marriage and divorce."

William R. Turner v. Leonard Safley, 482 U.S. 78, 107 S.Ct. 2254, 96 L.Ed.2d 64 (1987). A unanimous Court in an opinion by Justice Sandra Day O'Connor struck down a state regulation barring the ability of prisoners to marry. The Court held that the right to marry was implicated even in prison settings, where sex with outsiders is normally prohibited. "First, inmate marriages, like others, are expressions of emotional support and public commitment. These elements are an important and significant aspect of the marital relationship. In addition, many religions recognize marriage as having spiritual significance; for some inmates and their spouses, therefore, the commitment of marriage may be an exercise of religious faith as well as an expression of personal dedication. Third, most inmates eventually will be released by parole or commutation, and therefore most inmate marriages are formed in the expectation that they will be fully consummated. Finally, marital status often is a precondition to the receipt of government benefits (*e.g.*, Social Security benefits), property rights (*e.g.*, tenancy by the entirety, inheritance rights), and other, less tangible benefits (*e.g.*, legitimation of children born out of wedlock). These incidents of marriage, like the religious and personal aspects of the marriage commitment, are unaffected by the fact of confinement or the pursuit of legitimate corrections goals."

Because of the prison setting, Justice O'Connor applied the Court's precedents requiring a "reasonable relationship" between a prison regulation and legitimate penological objectives. Another part of her opinion (joined only by five Justices) upheld prison surveillance of inmate mail, usually protected under the First Amendment. Unlike opening inmate mail, preventing inmate marriages did not narrowly serve legitimate penological purposes, Justice O'Connor reasoned. The regulation was invalidated.

PROBLEM 9–2

SAME-SEX MARRIAGE IN THE DISTRICT OF COLUMBIA?

Joan Doe and Jane Roe are a lesbian couple residing in the District of Columbia. They desire to marry, but the District's Marriage License Bureau refuses to issue licenses to same-sex couples. In 1977, Doe and Roe come to you, a lawyer, to file a lawsuit seeking an injunction requiring the District to issue them a marriage license. Originally enacted by Congress in 1901, the District's Marriage Law is gender neutral, except for its consanguinity prohibitions: a man may not marry his sister etc.; a woman may not marry her brother etc.   Also, the District's Divorce Law repeatedly refers to "husband" and "wife."   What arguments would you make in light of the foregoing case law?

Consider the impact of two local statutes. The District's Human Rights Act, which is reprinted in Appendix 2, prohibits discrimination on the basis of sex and sexual orientation (as well as other categories). Is the denial of a marriage license to same-sex couples sex discrimination? Sexual orientation discrimination? Does the Human Rights Act's nondiscrimination duty apply to the District government? In 1982, the District of Columbia Council adopted the "Gender Rule of Construction Act," which provides: "Unless the Council of the District of Columbia specifically provides that this section shall be inapplicable to a particular act or section, all the words thereof importing 1 gender include and apply to the other gender as well." D.C. Code § 49–203.

For the real-life outcome, see *Dean v. District of Columbia*, 653 A.2d 307 (D.C.1995). For competing doctrinal analyses of *Loving/Zablocki/Turner*, compare William N. Eskridge, Jr., *The Case for Same–Sex Marriage* chs. 5–6 (1996), with Lynn D. Wardle, "A Critical Analysis of Constitutional Claims for Same–Sex Marriage," 1996 *Brigham Young L. Rev.* 1.

PART B.   THE SAME-SEX MARRIAGE DEBATE

Ninia Baehr and Genora Dancel et al. v. John C. Lewin

Hawaii Supreme Court, 1993.
74 Haw. 530, 852 P.2d 44.

■ LEVINSON, JUDGE, in which MOON, CHIEF JUDGE, joins.

The plaintiffs-appellants Ninia Baehr, Genora Dancel, Tammy Rodrigues, Antoinette Pregil, Pat Lagon, and Joseph Melilio appeal the circuit court's order * * * granting the motion of the defendant-appellee John C. Lewin, in his official capacity as Director of the Department of Health (DOH), State of Hawaii, for judgment on the pleadings, resulting in the dismissal of the plaintiffs' action with prejudice for failure to state a claim against Lewin upon which relief can be granted. * * *

[In 1991, the three plaintiff couples—Baehr/Dancel, Rodriguez/Pregil, and Lagon/Melilio—filed a lawsuit for declaratory judgment that Hawaii's Marriage Law, Hawaii Revised Statutes § 572–1, unconstitutionally denied same-sex couples the same marriage rights as different-sex couples. Plaintiffs further sought an injunction requiring the DOH to issue them marriage licenses. Plaintiffs' claims were based on the privacy and equal protection clauses of the Hawaii Constitution.]

* * * [A]rticle I, section 6 of the Hawaii Constitution expressly states that "[t]he right of the people to privacy is recognized and shall not be infringed without the showing of a compelling state interest." * * *

When article I, section 6 of the Hawaii Constitution was being adopted, the 1978 Hawaii Constitutional Convention, acting as a committee of the whole, clearly articulated the rationale for its adoption:

> By amending the Constitution to include a separate and distinct privacy right, it is the intent of your Committee to insure that privacy is treated as a fundamental right for purposes of constitutional analysis. . . . This right is similar to the privacy right discussed in cases such as *Griswold, Eisenstadt, Roe v. Wade*, etc. * * * By inserting clear and specific language regarding this right into the [Hawaii] Constitution, your Committee intends to alleviate any possible confusion over the source of the right and the existence of it.

Comm. Whole Rep. No. 15, 1 Proceedings, at 1024. * * * We ultimately concluded in [*State v. Mueller*, 671 P.2d 1351 (1983)] that the federal cases cited by the Convention's committee of the whole should guide our construction of the intended scope of article I, section 6.

Accordingly, there is no doubt that, at a minimum, article I, section 6 of the Hawaii Constitution encompasses all of the fundamental rights expressly recognized as being subsumed within the privacy protections of the United States Constitution. In this connection, the United States Supreme Court has declared that "the right to marry is part of the fundamental 'right of privacy' implicit in the Fourteenth Amendment's Due Process Clause." *Zablocki v. Redhail*, 434 U.S. 374, 384 (1978). The issue in this case is, therefore, whether the "right to marry" protected by article I, section 6 of the Hawaii Constitution extends to same-sex couples. Because article I, section 6 was expressly derived from the general right to privacy under the United States Constitution and because there are no Hawaii cases that have delineated the fundamental right to marry, this court, as we did in *Mueller*, looks to federal cases for guidance.

The United States Supreme Court first characterized the right of marriage as fundamental in *Skinner v. Oklahoma ex rel. Williamson*, 316 U.S. 535 (1942). In *Skinner*, the right to marry was inextricably linked to the right of procreation. The dispute before the Court arose out of an Oklahoma statute that allowed the state to sterilize "habitual criminals" without their consent. In striking down the statute, the *Skinner* court indicated that it was "dealing ... with legislation which involve[d] *one of the basic civil rights of man. Marriage and procreation are fundamental to the very existence and survival of the race." Id.* at 541 (emphasis added). Whether the Court viewed marriage and procreation as a single indivisible right, the least that can be said is that it was obviously contemplating unions between men and women when it ruled that the right to marry was fundamental. This is hardly surprising inasmuch as none of the United States sanctioned any other marriage configuration at the time.

The United States Supreme Court has set forth its most detailed discussion of the fundamental right to marry in *Zablocki*, which involved a Wisconsin statute that prohibited any resident of the state with minor children "not in his custody and which he is under an obligation to support" from obtaining a marriage license until the resident demonstrated to a court that he was in compliance with his child support obligations. The *Zablocki* court held that the statute burdened the fundamental right to marry; applying the "strict scrutiny" standard to the statute, the Court invalidated it as violative of the fourteenth amendment to the United States Constitution. In so doing, the *Zablocki* court delineated its view of the evolution of the federally recognized fundamental right of marriage as follows:

> Long ago, in *Maynard v. Hill*, 125 U.S. 190 (1888), the Court characterized marriage as "the most important relation in life," *id.* at 205, and as "the foundation of the family and of society, without which there would be neither civilization nor progress." *Id.* at 211. In *Meyer v. Nebraska*, 262 U.S. 390 (1923), the Court recognized that the right "to marry, establish a home and bring up children" is a central part of the liberty protected by the Due Process Clause, *id.* at 399, and in *Skinner* marriage was described as "fundamental to the very existence and survival of the race." 316 U.S., at 541.

> . . . .

> It is not surprising that the decision to marry has been placed on the same level of importance as decisions relating to procreation, childbirth, child rearing, and family relationships. As the facts of this case illustrate, it would make little sense to recognize a right of privacy with respect to other matters of family life and not with respect to the decision to enter into the relationship that is the foundation of the family in our society. The woman whom appellee desired to marry had a fundamental right to seek an abortion of their expected child, see *Roe v. Wade*, 410 U.S. 113 (1973), or to bring the child into life to suffer the myriad social, if not economic disabilities that the status of illegitimacy brings.... Surely, a decision to marry and raise the child in a traditional family setting must receive equivalent protection. And, if appellee's right to procreate means anything at all, it must imply some right to enter the only relationship in which the State of Wisconsin allows sexual relations legally to take place.

[*Zablocki*, 434 U.S.] at 384–86. Implicit in the *Zablocki* court's link between the right to marry, on the one hand, and the fundamental rights of procreation, childbirth, adoption, and child rearing, on the other, is the assumption that one is simply the logical predicate of the others.

The foregoing case law demonstrates that the federal construct of the fundamental right to marry—subsumed within the right to privacy implicitly protected by the United States Constitution—presently contemplates unions between men and women. (Once again, this is hardly surprising inasmuch as such unions are the only state-sanctioned marriages currently acknowledged in this country.)

Therefore, the precise question facing this court is whether we will extend the *present* boundaries of the fundamental right of marriage to include same-sex couples, or, put another way, whether we will hold that same-sex couples possess a fundamental right to marry. In effect, as the applicant couples frankly admit, we are being asked to recognize a new fundamental right. [Justice Levinson read his Court's prior privacy cases as expressing a reluctance to read Hawaii's privacy protection more expansively than the federal protection in *Zablocki*.]

* * * [W]e do not believe that a right to same-sex marriages is so rooted in the traditions and collective conscience of our people that failure to recognize it would violate the fundamental principles of liberty and justice that lie at the base of all our civil and political institutions. Neither do we believe that a right to same-sex marriage is implicit in the concept of ordered liberty, such that neither liberty nor justice would exist if it were sacrificed. Accordingly, we hold that the applicant couples do not have a fundamental constitutional right to same-sex marriage arising out of the right to privacy or otherwise. * * *

The applicant couples correctly contend that the DOH's refusal to allow them to marry on the basis that they are members of the same sex deprives them of access to a multiplicity of rights and benefits that are contingent upon that status. * * * [Those rights] include: (1) a variety of state income tax advantages, including deductions, credits, rates, exemptions, and estimates; (2) public assistance from and exemptions relating to the Department of Human Services; (3) control, division, acquisition, and disposition of community property; (4) rights relating to dower, curtesy, and inheritance; (5) rights to notice, protection, benefits, and inheritance under the Uniform Probate Code; (6) award of child custody and support payments in divorce proceedings; (7) the right to spousal support; (8) the right to enter into premarital agreements; (9) the right to change of name; (10) the right to file a nonsupport action; (11) post-divorce rights relating to support and property division; (12) the benefit of the spousal privilege and confidential marital communications; (13) the benefit of the exemption of real property from attachment or execution; and (14) the right to bring a wrongful death action. For present purposes, it is not disputed that the applicant would be entitled to all of these marital rights and benefits, but for the fact that they are denied access to the state-conferred legal status of marriage. * * *

* * * Article I, section 5 of the Hawaii Constitution provides in relevant part that "[n]o person shall ... be denied the equal protection of the laws, *nor be denied the enjoyment of the person's civil rights or be discriminated against in the exercise thereof because of* race, religion, *sex*, or ancestry." (Emphasis added.) Thus, by its plain language, the Hawaii Constitution prohibits state-sanctioned discrimination against any person in the exercise of his or her civil rights on the basis of sex.

"The freedom to marry has long been recognized as one of the vital personal rights essential to the orderly pursuit of happiness by free [people]." *Loving*, 388 U.S. at 12. So "fundamental" does the United States Supreme Court consider the institution of marriage that it has deemed marriage to be "one of the 'basic civil rights of [men and women].'" *Id.* (quoting *Skinner*, 316 U.S. at 541).

[Justice Levinson found that the Hawaii Marriage Law, and Lewin acting under it, discriminated against the plaintiff couples in the exercise of this important "civil right" because of their "sex." That is, a female/female couple would be denied a marriage license simply because of the sex of one of the partners—if she were a man, the license would be routinely granted.]

* * * Lewin contends that "the fact that homosexual [sic—actually, same-sex] partners cannot form a state-licensed marriage is not the product of impermissible discrimination" implicating equal protection considerations, but rather "a function of their biologic inability as a couple to satisfy the definition of the status to which they ascribe." Lewin's answering brief at 21. Put differently, Lewin proposes that "the right of persons of the same sex to marry one another does not exist because marriage, by definition and usage, means a special relationship between a man and a woman." *Id.* at 7. We believe Lewin's argument to be circular and unpersuasive. * * *

The facts in *Loving* and the respective reasoning of the Virginia courts, on the one hand, and the United States Supreme Court, on the other, * * * unmask the tautological and circular nature of Lewin's argument that HRS § 572–1 does not implicate article I, section 5 of the Hawaii Constitution because same-sex marriage is an innate impossibility. Analogously to Lewin's argument * * *, the Virginia courts declared that interracial marriage simply could not exist because the Deity had deemed such a union intrinsically unnatural, and, in effect, because it had theretofore never been the "custom" of the state to recognize mixed marriages, marriage "always" having been construed to presuppose a different configuration. With all due respect to the Virginia courts of a bygone era, we do not believe that trial judges are the ultimate authorities on the subject of Divine Will, and, as *Loving* amply demonstrates, constitutional law may mandate, like it or not, that customs change with an evolving social order. * * *

* * * Accordingly, we hold that sex is a "suspect category" for purposes of equal protection analysis under article I, section 5 of the Hawaii Constitution and that HRS § 572–1 is subject to the "strict scrutiny" test. It therefore follows, and we so hold, that (1) [the Hawaii Marriage Law] is presumed to be unconstitutional (2) unless Lewin ... can show that (a) the statute's sex-based classification is justified by compelling state interests and (b) the statute is narrowly drawn to avoid unnecessary abridgements of the applicant couples' constitutional rights.

[Justice Levinson then directed a remand to the circuit court for a hearing to determine whether Lewin and the State could overcome the presumption that the Marriage Law is unconstitutional, by showing that its sex discrimination furthers a compelling state interest and is narrowly drawn. He concluded his opinion with some responses to dissenting Judge Heen.]

We understand that Judge Heen disagrees with our view in this regard based on his belief that "HRS § 572–1 treats everyone alike and applies equally to both sexes[,]" with the result that "neither sex is being *granted* a right or benefit the other does not have, and neither sex is being *denied* a right or benefit that the other has." The rationale underlying Judge Heen's belief, however, was expressly considered and rejected in *Loving*:

> Thus, the State contends that, because its miscegenation statutes punish equally both the white and the Negro participants in an interracial marriage, these statutes, despite their reliance on racial classifications do not constitute an invidious discrimination based upon race.... [W]e reject the notion that the mere "equal application" of a statute containing racial classifications is enough to remove the classifications from the Fourteenth Amendment's proscriptions of all invidious discriminations.... In the case at bar, ... we deal with statutes containing racial classifications, and the fact of equal application does not immunize the statute from the very heavy burden of justification which the Fourteenth Amendment has traditionally required of state statutes drawn according to race.

388 U.S. at 8. Substitution of "sex" for "race" and article I, section 5 for the fourteenth amendment yields the precise case before us together with the conclusion we have reached. * * *

■ BURNS, INTERMEDIATE COURT OF APPEALS CHIEF JUDGE [specially appointed to hear this case], concurs in the result. * * *

* * * In my view, the Hawaii Constitution's reference to "sex" includes all aspects of each person's "sex" that are "biologically fated." The decision whether a person when born will be a male or female is "biologically fated." Thus, the word "sex" includes the male-female difference. Is there another aspect of a person's "sex" that is "biologically fated"?

[Judge Burns then quoted from three accounts in the popular press as to the basis for a person's sexual orientation. Two of the accounts suggest the hormonal and genetic basis for a homosexual orientation. A third account disputed that claim.]

If heterosexuality, homosexuality, bisexuality, and asexuality are "biologically fated[,]" then the word "sex" also includes these differences. Therefore, the questions whether heterosexuality, homosexuality, bisexuality, and asexuality are "biologically fated" are relevant questions of fact which must be determined before the issue presented in this case can be answered. If the answers are yes, then each person's "sex" includes both the "biologically fated" male-female difference and the "biologically fated" sexual orientation difference, and the Hawaii Constitution probably bars the State from discriminating against the sexual orientation difference by permitting opposite-sex Hawaii Civil Law Marriages and not permitting same-sex Hawaii Civil Law Marriages. If the answers are no, then each person's "sex" does not include the sexual orientation difference, and the Hawaii Constitution may permit the State to encourage heterosexuality and discourage homosexuality, bisexuality, and asexuality by permitting opposite-sex Hawaii Civil Law Marriages and not permitting same-sex Hawaii Civil Law Marriages.

■ HEEN, INTERMEDIATE COURT OF APPEALS JUDGE [also specially appointed to hear this case], dissenting.

[Judge Heen distinguished *Loving* and *Zablocki*, two right to marry cases on which the plurality opinion relied. Neither case involved a same-sex marriage. Instead, he urged the court to follow other state courts that had considered and rejected a right to same-sex marriage, particularly *Singer*.]

HRS § 572–1 treats everyone alike and applies equally to both sexes. The effect of the statute is to prohibit same sex marriages on the part of professed or non-professed heterosexuals, homosexuals, bisexuals, or asexuals, and does not effect an invidious discrimination. * * *

HRS § 572–1 does not establish a "suspect" classification based on gender because all males and females are treated alike. A male cannot obtain a license to marry another male, and a female cannot obtain a license to marry another female. Neither sex is being *granted* a right or benefit the other does not have, and neither sex is being *denied* a right or benefit that the other has. * * *

In my view, the statute's classification is clearly designed to promote the legislative purpose of fostering and protecting the propagation of the human race through heterosexual marriage and bears a reasonable relationship to that purpose. I find nothing unconstitutional in that.

■ [On motion for rehearing, the court by a vote of four to one denied the state's request to reconsider the foregoing decision. Judge Heen dissented and Judge Burns concurred, as they had earlier. Newly appointed Justice Paula Nakayama joined Chief Justice Moon and Justice Levinson in voting to deny the rehearing.]

NOTES ON THE HAWAII SAME–SEX MARRIAGE CASE AND INTERSTATE RECOGNITION OF SAME–SEX MARRIAGES

1. *The Miscegenation Analogy and the Court's Sex Discrimination Argument.* Note the three ways in which *Loving* is relevant to Justice Levinson's opinion in *Baehr*. Its due process fundamental right to marry holding, the basis for *Zablocki* and *Turner*, was found insufficient to establish a right for same-sex couples to marry. But *Loving*'s equal protection holding that race-based classifications in marriage statutes are suspect was extended by the Hawaii justices to form the analytical basis for a claim that sex-based classifications in marriage statutes are suspect under the state ERA. How can Justice Levinson reject the *Zablocki* privacy argument on tradition-based grounds, while accepting the *Loving* argument against tradition-based attack? Also, is there something of a "transvestic" quality to the sex discrimination argument? Judge Heen suggests that it dresses up gay rights in feminist garb.

Sylvia Law, "Homosexuality and the Social Meaning of Gender," 1988 *Wis. L. Rev.* 187, and Andrew Koppelman, "Why Discrimination Against Lesbians and Gay Men Is Sex Discrimination," 69 *NYU L. Rev.* 197 (1994) (excerpted in Chapter 1, Section 3[B][3]), have suggested a similar argument that could support *Baehr*: the prohibition against same-sex marriage is a gender *classification*, because the license is denied to a female-female couple simply because of their gender (a female-male couple would be treated differently), and it contributes to the subordination of a gender *class* (women). Hence, not only should heightened scrutiny be applicable (and lethal) to the discrimination, but the fit with *Loving* becomes quite snug. Should it be extended to the federal equal protection clause, as interpreted in the VMI case (Chapter 1, Section 3[A])? For a critical historical examination of the Law–Koppelman argument, see William N. Eskridge, Jr., *Gaylaw: Challenging the Apartheid of the Closet* ch. 5 (forthcoming 1998). For a constructionist analysis of the gendered structure of marriage, see Nan D. Hunter, "Marriage, Law and Gender: A Feminist Inquiry," 1 *Law & Sexuality* 9 (1991).

Note how Justice Levinson deployed *Loving* to rebut the *Singer* argument that same-sex couples are being discriminated against only because of the "nature" of marriage—this was exactly the kind of argument that had been the basis of statutes prohibiting different-race marriage.[h] For example, the Georgia Supreme Court upheld its statute in part because "amalgamation of the races is ... unnatural," yielding offspring who are "generally sickly, effeminate, and ... inferior in physical development and strength, to the full-blood of either race" and in part because

> equality [of the races] does not in fact exist and never can. The God of nature made it otherwise, and no human law can produce it, no human tribunal can enforce it. There are gradations and classes throughout the universe. From the tallest arch angel in Heaven, down to the meanest reptile on earth, moral and social inequalities exist, and must continue to exist through all eternity.

Scott v. Georgia, 39 Ga. 321, 324 (1869). The Tennessee Supreme Court emphasized the necessity of such laws "[t]o prevent violence and bloodshed which would arise from such cohabitation, distasteful to our people, and unfit to produce the human race in any of the types in which it was

---

h. See Eva Saks, "Representing Miscegenation Law," 8 *Raritan* (1988), and Paul Lombardo, "Miscegenation, Eugenics, and Racism: Historical Footnotes to *Loving v. Virginia*," 21 *U.C. Davis L. Rev.* 421 (1988).

created." *Lonas v. State*, 50 Tenn. 287, 299–300 (1871). What is the legal relevance of this rhetorical deployment of *Loving*?

2. *Is There a Rational or Substantial Justification for Denying Same–Sex Couples Marriage Licenses?* The effect of *Baehr* was to remand for trial to determine whether the state can justify its discrimination against same-sex couples. What justifications could Hawaii offer for this policy? Hawaii advanced various state interests, such as encouraging procreation and protecting state financial resources and the freedom of religious groups who are prejudiced against homosexuals,[i] but emphasized and presented evidence on only one interest when the case went to trial in September 1996: protecting children. The state argued that children raised by same-sex spouses would lose intimate contact with a parent of one gender and never observe at close hand the modeling of male-female relationships. It identified encouragement of children being raised by male-female couples as a compelling state interest. All of the evidence introduced at trial, by both sides, addressed the impact on children of lesbian and gay family settings. The trial judge found this evidence insufficient to justify the sex discrimination and in December 1996 invalidated the state's bar to same-sex marriages.   As this book goes to press, both the state's appeal and a state constitutional convention are pending.

3. *Recognition of Hawaii Marriages in Other States.* Assume that Hawaii does ultimately recognize same-sex marriages. Article IV, § 1 of the U.S. Constitution requires: "Full Faith and Credit shall be given in each State to the public Acts, Records, and judicial Proceedings of every other State." Does this full faith and credit clause require Kansas to recognize the same-sex marriage of a Hawaii couple that later moves to Kansas? Like a number of other states, Kansas has enacted a statute precluding its courts from recognizing Hawaii same-sex marriages in Kansas. Is the Kansas statute constitutional, or does it violate the full faith and credit clause?

The Supreme Court has held that divorces are judgments that must be recognized in all other states, unless the state of divorce lacked jurisdiction over the parties or subject matter. *Williams v. North Carolina*, 317 U.S. 287 (1942); *Williams v. North Carolina*, 325 U.S. 226 (1945). Marriage, on the other hand, has never been recognized as a "judgment," but is probably an "act" or "record" for full faith and credit purposes. Common law

---

i. Hawaii's tentative responses as of 1995 are noted and answered in Evan Wolfson, "Crossing the Threshold: Equal Marriage Rights for Lesbians and Gay Men, and the Intra–Community Critique," 21 *NYU J.L. & Soc. Change* 567 (1995). See also Jennifer Gerarda Brown, "Competitive Federalism and the Legislative Incentives to Recognize Same–Sex Marriages," 68 *S.Cal.L.Rev.* 745 (1995). Commentators have attacked state restrictions on same-sex couples' right to marry "because states cannot articulate legitimate interests that are rationally relat-ed to the restrictions they impose." "Developments in the Law: Sexual Orientation & the Law," 102 *Harv. Law Rev.* 1508, 1609 (1989); see Alissa Friedman, "The Necessity for State Recognition of Same–Sex Marriage: Constitutional Requirements and Evolving Notions of the Family," 3 *Berkeley Women's L.J.* 134, 157–160 (1988); Jed Rubenfield, "The Right to Privacy," 102 *Harv. Law Rev.* 737, 800 (1989); Claudia Lewis, "From This Day Forward: A Feminine Moral Discourse on Homosexual Marriage," 97 *Yale L.J.* 1783 (1988) (student note).

marriages valid under the law of the partners' domicile are recognized in other states. *E.g., Thomas v. Sullivan*, 922 F.2d 132, 134 (2d Cir.1990); *Parish v. Minvielle*, 217 So.2d 684, 688 (La.Ct.App.1969). Some states recognize "child marriages" if valid in the state of the partners' domicile (states have varying ages of consent). *E.g., Wilkins v. Zelichowski*, 129 A.2d 459 (N.J.Super.1957). It is not clear how much these decisions were inspired by full faith and credit considerations.

Eleven states and D.C. allow first cousins to marry, which is considered incest elsewhere. Some cases recognize "incestuous" first-cousin marriages if valid in the state of the partners' domicile. *E.g., In re Miller's Estate*, 214 N.W. 428 (Mich.1927). Other cases, however, refuse to recognize out-of-state first-cousin marriages, though the only cases we have found are ones where domiciliaries of one state go to another state in order to evade the no-first-cousin rule of their home state. *E.g., In re Mortenson's Estate*, 316 P.2d 1106 (Ariz.1957). Should there be a "public policy exception" to full faith and credit obligations? For commentary on this issue, see Joseph W. Hovermill, "A Conflict of Law and Morals: The Choice of Law Implications of Hawaii's Recognition of Same–Sex Marriages," 53 *Md.L.Rev.* 450 (1994); Thomas M. Keane, "Aloha, Marriage? Constitutional and Choice of Law Arguments for Recognition of Same–Sex Marriages," 47 *Stan.L.Rev.* 499 (1995) (student note).

PROBLEM 9–3

THE DEFENSE OF MARRIAGE ACT

Responding to the possibility of same-sex marriages in Hawaii, Congress passed and the President signed the "Defense of Marriage Act" (DOMA) in 1996. Section 1 of the bill forbids any federal recognition of same-sex marriages for purposes such as income tax or Social Security. Section 2 of the bill relieves other states from giving full faith and credit to "any public act, record, or judicial proceeding * * * respecting a relationship between persons of the same sex." Assume that Kansas, our example above, would be prohibited by the full faith and credit clause from refusing to recognize a same-sex marriage entered into by Hawaii domiciliaries (hence, ignore the issue of evasion). DOMA would be taking away constitutional rights under this assumption.

Can Congress derogate from rights created in the Constitution? Usually not, but the sponsors of the bill point to the second sentence of the full faith and credit clause: "And the Congress may by general Laws prescribe the Manner in which such Acts, Records and Proceedings shall be proved, *and the Effect thereof.*" (Our emphasis.) Does Congress' authority to "prescribe * * * the Effect" of state marriages mean that it can take away constitutional rights? Section 5 of the Fourteenth Amendment gives Congress "power to enforce, by appropriate legislation, the provisions" of the amendment. Does this section permit Congress to take away constitutional rights? Most Americans dislike different-race marriages, according to recent polls. Can Congress adopt a statute which deprives different-race couples of their Fourteenth Amendment right to marry, recognized in *Loving v. Virginia*? Assuming Congress cannot enact such a statute, could Congress adopt a statute similar to the DOMA which says that no state will have to recognize a different-race marriage entered into in another state? Would this be permissible under the "prescribe Effect" sentence of the full faith and credit clause?

In a one-page letter, the Department of Justice represented to a House subcommittee in May 1996 that DOMA is constitutional. The letter gave no reasons. Do you agree?

Paula L. Ettelbrick, Since When Is Marriage a Path to Liberation?

OUT/LOOK, Autumn 1989, Pages 8–12.*

* * * Marriage runs contrary to two of the primary goals of the lesbian and gay movement: the affirmation of gay identity and culture and the validation of many forms of relationships. * * *

The fight for justice has as its goal the realignment of power imbalances among individuals and classes of people in society. A pure "rights" analysis often fails to incorporate a broader understanding of the underlying inequities that operate to deny justice to a fuller range of people and groups. * * * At this point in time, making legal marriage for lesbian and gay couples a priority would set an agenda of gaining rights for a few, but would do nothing to correct power imbalances between those who are married (whether gay or straight) and those who are not. Thus, justice would not be gained.

Justice for gay men and lesbians will be achieved only when we are accepted and supported in this society *despite* our difference from the dominant culture and the choices we make regarding our relationships. * * * Being queer means pushing the parameters of sex, sexuality, and family, and in the process transforming the very fabric of society. Gay liberation is inexorably linked to women's liberation. Each is essential to the other.

The moment we argue, as some amongst us insist on doing, that we should be treated as equals because we are really just like married couples and hold the same values to be true, we undermine the very purpose of our movement and begin the dangerous process of silencing our different voices. As a lesbian, I am fundamentally different from nonlesbian women. That's the point. Marriage, as it exists today, is antithetical to my liberation as a lesbian and as a woman because it mainstreams my life and voice. I do not want to be known as "Mrs. Attached–To–Somebody–Else." Nor do I want to give the state the power to regulate my primary relationship. * * *

---

* Reprinted by permission of the author.

The thought of emphasizing our sameness to married heterosexuals in order to obtain this "right" terrifies me. It rips away the very heart and soul of what I believe it is to be a lesbian in this world. It robs me of the opportunity to make a difference. We end up mimicking all that is bad about the institution of marriage in our effort to appear to be the same as straight couples.

By looking to our sameness and de-emphasizing our differences, we do not even place ourselves in a position of power that would allow us to transform marriage from an institution that emphasizes property and state regulation of relationships to an institution that recognizes one of many types of valid and respected relationships. * * * We would be perpetuating the elevation of married relationships and of "couples" in general, and further eclipsing other relationships of choice.

Ironically, gay marriage, instead of liberating gay sex and sexuality, would further outlaw all gay and lesbian sex that is not performed in a marital context. Just as sexually active nonmarried women face stigma and double standards around sex and sexual activity, so too would nonmarried gay people. * * *

Undoubtedly, whether we admit it or not, we all need to be accepted by the broader society. * * * Those closer to the norm or to power in this country are more likely to see marriage as a principle of freedom and equality. Those who are more acceptable to the mainstream because of race, gender, and economic status are more likely to want the right to marry. It is the final acceptance, the ultimate affirmation of identity.

On the other hand, more marginal members of the lesbian and gay community (women, people of color, working class and poor) are less likely to see marriage as having relevance to our struggles for survival. After all, what good is the affirmation of our relationships (that is, marital relationships) if we are rejected as women, people of color, or working class? * * *

If the laws change tomorrow and lesbians and gay men were allowed to marry, where would we find the incentive to continue the progressive movement we have started that is pushing for societal and legal recognition of all kinds of family relationships? To create other options and alternatives? * * * To get the law to acknowledge that we may have more than one relationship worthy of legal protection? * * *

Thomas B. Stoddard, Why Gay People Should Seek the Right to Marry

OUT/LOOK, Autumn 1989, Pages 8–12.*

* * * [D]espite the oppressive nature of marriage historically, and in spite of the general absence of edifying examples of modern heterosexual marriage, I believe very strongly that every lesbian and gay man should have the right to marry the same-sex partner of his or her choice, and that

---

* Reprinted by permission of the author.

the gay rights movement should aggressively seek full legal recognition for same-sex marriages. To those who may not agree, I respectfully offer three explanations, one practical, one political, and one philosophical.

The legal status of marriage rewards the two individuals who travel to the altar (or its secular equivalent) with substantial economic and practical advantages. Married couples * * * are entitled to special government benefits, such as those given surviving spouses and dependents through the Social Security program. They can inherit from one another even when there is no will. They are immune from subpoenas requiring testimony against the other spouse. And marriage to an American citizen gives a foreigner a right to residency in the United States.

Other advantages have arisen not by law but by custom. Most employers offer health insurance to their employees, and many will include an employer's spouse in the benefits package, usually at the employer's expense. Virtually no employer will include a partner who is not married to an employee, whether of the same sex or not. * * *

In short, the law generally presumes in favor of every marital relationship, and acts to preserve and foster it, and to enhance the rights of the individuals who enter into it. It is usually possible, with enough money and the right advice, to replicate some of the benefits conferred by the legal status of marriage through the use of documents like wills and power-of-attorney forms, but that protection will inevitably, under current circumstances, be incomplete. [Stoddard notes the "suspicion" many judges cast upon documents protecting lesbian and gay families, the cost of obtaining such documents, and the inability of private contracting to affect the public advantages of marriage, such as spousal immunities.]

* * * Why devote resources to such a distant goal? Because marriage is, I believe, the political issue that most fully tests the dedication of people who are not gay to full equality for gay people, and it is also the issue most likely to lead ultimately to a world free from discrimination against lesbians and gay men.

Marriage is much more than a relationship sanctioned by law. It is the centerpiece of our entire social structure, the core of the traditional notion of "family." Even in its present tarnished state, the marital relationship inspires sentiments suggesting that it is something almost suprahuman. The Supreme Court, in striking down an anticontraception statute in 1965, called marriage "noble" and "intimate to the degree of being sacred." * * *

Lesbians and gay men are now denied entry to this "noble" and "sacred" institution. The implicit message is this: two men or two women are incapable of achieving such an exalted domestic state. Gay relationships are somehow less significant, less valuable. Such relationships may, from time to time and from couple to couple, give the appearance of a marriage, but they can never be of the same quality or importance.

I resent—indeed, I loathe—that conception of same-sex relationships. And I am convinced that ultimately the only way to overturn it is to remove the barrier to marriage that now limits the freedom of every gay man and lesbian. * * *

I confessed at the outset that I personally found marriage in its present state rather unattractive. Nonetheless, even from a philosophical perspective, I believe the right to marry should become a goal of the gay-rights movement.

First, and most basically, the issue is not the desirability of marriage, but rather the desirability of the *right* to marry. That I think two lesbians or two gay men should be entitled to a marriage license does not mean that I think all gay people should find appropriate partners and exercise the right, should it eventually exist. * * *

Furthermore, marriage may be unattractive and even oppressive as it is currently structured and practiced, but enlarging the concept to embrace same-sex couples would necessarily transform it into something new. If two women can marry, or two men, marriage—even for heterosexuals—need not be a union of a "husband" and a "wife." Extending the right to marry to gay people—that is, abolishing the traditional gender requirements of marriage—can be one of the means, perhaps the principal one, through which the institution divests itself of the sexist trappings of the past. * * *

NOTES ON THE ETTELBRICK–STODDARD DEBATE

The Ettelbrick–Stoddard exchange triggered a renewed debate within the lesbian and gay community over whether the right to marry should be a priority.[j] Consider some key points of disagreement:

1. *Would Same–Sex Marriage Change the Institution for the Better?* One of us has argued: "Marriage between men or between women could also destabilize the cultural meaning of marriage. It would create for the first time the possibility of marriage as a relationship between members of the same social status categories. However valiantly individuals try to build marriages grounded on genuine equality, no person can erase his or her status in the world as male or female, or create a home life apart from culture. Same-sex marriage could create the model in law for an egalitarian

j. See William N. Eskridge, Jr., *The Case for Same–Sex Marriage* (1996); Richard D. Mohr, *A More Perfect Union: Why Straight America Must Stand Up for Gay Rights* ch. 3 (1994); Andrew Sullivan, *Virtually Normal* (1995); "Noose or Knot? The Debate Over Lesbian Marriage," *OUT/WEEK*, Sept. 18, 1989, at 38–43 (articles by Sarah Petitt, Ashley McNeely, and Catherine Saalfield); Nitya Duclos, "Some Complicating Thoughts on Same–Sex Marriage," 1 Law & Sexuality 31 (1991); Marc A. Fajer, "Can Two Real Men Eat Quiche Together? Storytelling, Gender-Role Stereotypes, and Legal Protection for Lesbians and Gay Men," 46 *U. Miami L. Rev.* 511 (1992); Steven K. Homer, "Against Marriage," 29 *Harv. C.R.-C.L. L. Rev.* 505 (1994) (student note); Nan D. Hunter, "Marriage, Law, and Gender: A Feminist Inquiry," 1 *Law & Sexuality* 9 (1991); Christine Pierce, "Gay Marriage," *J. Soc. Phil.*, Fall 1995, at 5–16; Nancy D. Polikoff, "We Will Get What We Ask For: Why Legalizing Gay and Lesbian Marriage Will Not 'Dismantle the Structure of Gender in Every Marriage,'" 79 *Va. L. Rev.* 1535 (1993); Ruthann Robson and S.E. Valentine, "Lov(h)ers: Lesbians as Intimate Partners and Lesbian Legal Theory," 63 *Temple L. Rev.* 511 (1990).

kind of interpersonal relation, outside the gendered terms of power, for many marriages. At the least, it would radically strengthen and dramatically illuminate the claim that marriage partners are presumptively equal." (Hunter, "Marriage, Law, and Gender," 11.)

Nancy Polikoff responded, based upon evidence that the other of us collected(!): "[M]ost of the marriages Eskridge uncovered support rather than subvert hierarchy based upon gender. His historical and anthropological evidence contradicts any assumption that 'gender dissent' is inherent in marriage between two men or two women. Rather, most of the unions reported were in fact gendered. Although both partners were biologically of the same sex, one partner tended to assume the characteristics and responsibilities of the opposite gender, with both partners then acting out their traditional gender roles." (Polikoff, "We Will Get What We Ask For," 1538; see Eskridge, *Case for Same–Sex Marriage* ch. 2.)

2. *Transformation and Assimilation.* Ettelbrick and her allies make a pitch for radical transformation, while those on the other side discreetly favor a higher degree of assimilation into the American mainstream. What, exactly, is *wrong* with assimilation? Do most lesbians, gay men, and bisexuals want to transform America?

Polikoff says that once a movement turns to the courts the assimilationists get the upper hand: "Demands for social change often have begun with a movement at first articulating the rhetoric of radical transformation and then later discarding that rhetoric to make the demands more socially acceptable. The movement's rhetoric is modified or altered when those opposing reform explore the radical and transformative possibilities of that rhetoric, causing its advocates to issue reassurances promising that such transformation is not what the movement is about at all." Polikoff cites the abortion movement as an "example of a movement redefining its goals to make them more politically palatable. * * * In the face of conservative voices decrying abortion as a facilitator of unchecked sexual freedom, 'pro-choice' voices denied or downplayed the relationship between women's access to abortion and women's ability to enjoy guilt-free sexual pleasure." (Polikoff, "We Will Get What We Ask For," 1541–42.)

Why not a "menu" approach, in which couples of all varieties could choose among (1) do-it-yourself structures for their relationship, through informal agreements and formal contracts; (2) registered domestic partnership that would provide some off-the-rack rules and public legal benefits but that would be easy to terminate; and (3) marriage, with lots of off-the-rack benefits and obligations that are difficult to terminate. Critics of same-sex marriage believe that marriage will drain any support from the domestic partnership movement or for other institutional alternatives to marriage. Is that so?

3. *The Impact of AIDS.* What is the role of the AIDS epidemic? On the one hand, the specter of AIDS might increase the value of having a committed relationship. Because the HIV virus most easily spreads and mutates through unsafe sex with a variety of partners, collective strategies against it might focus on both safer sex and fewer and better monitored partners. If marriage is monogamous, the number of partners is reduced; even if it is a more open relationship, marriage contributes to better monitoring and responsibility so long as there is genuine mutual caring within the relationship. Marriage also has this social insurance feature: most people do not want to die alone and uncared for. The commitment entailed in marriage is a mutual pact to care for one another, and this additional layer of security ought to be comforting.

On the other hand, this response would be a retreat from the "sexual revolution" features of gay liberation. (Is that regrettable?) Also, the campaign against AIDS should focus most of all on safer sex. Marital sex that is unsafe might be riskier over time than safer sex with a variety of partners. This is certainly true is one of the marital partners is HIV-positive, and probably true if one of the partners is having sex outside of marriage as well (whether secretly or openly). Marriage is not a panacea for AIDS, one might worry.

PART C.   THE CONSTITUTIONALITY OF OTHER RESTRICTIONS ON MARRIAGE

After *Zablocki* and *Turner* there was much hand-wringing that the right to marry would open the door to same-sex marriages and child marriages. After *Baehr*, there has been much hand-wringing that polygamy would have to be recognized by the state. Note, of course, that the Hawaii Supreme Court structured its opinion in precisely the way to avoid this charge: the court did not recognize a right to marry, it only questioned a sex-based discrimination. Nonetheless, the polygamy debate persists. Consider the post-*Zablocki* constitutionality of other restrictions.

1.   AGE RESTRICTIONS

In all 50 states and the District of Columbia, eighteen year olds can marry. If the children's parents consent, all 50 states plus the District of Columbia allow seventeen year olds to marry as well. Forty-nine states (all but Oregon) allow sixteen year olds to marry under such circumstances. Forty states allow fourteen year olds to marry; usually a court order as well as the consent of the child's parents are required for these marriages. Nine states allow children under 18 years old to marry if the female is pregnant or has borne a child by the male; in these cases parental consent is usually not required.

John Doe, age 16, wants to marry Jane Roe, age 19. Doe's parents refuse permission, and the state refuses to issue a marriage license. Doe and Roe sue the state under *Zablocki* and *Turner*. What arguments does the state have in response? What are the odds the judge will require the state to issue a marriage license?

2. INCEST

All 50 states and the District of Columbia prohibit "incestuous" marriages, including parent-child, grandparent-grandchild, aunt-nephew, uncle-niece, brother-sister marriages. Thirty-eight states prohibit marriages by first cousins. Eleven states and the District of Columbia prohibit marriages by step-relatives, that is, persons related within the prohibited degree, but only by marriage and not by blood. Two states (Alaska and Louisiana) prohibit persons within four degrees of consanguinity from marrying. One state (Utah) prohibits persons within five degrees from marrying. Are all of these restrictions constitutional? Consider the following decision.

Martin Richard Israel and Tammy Lee Bannon Israel v. Allen, 577 P.2d 762 (1978). Plaintiffs were siblings by marriage and adoption: Martin's father married Tammy Lee's mother when the two were 18 and 13 years old, respectively, and father Israel adopted Tammy Lee as his child. Martin and Tammy Lee asked to be married, and the state refused a license because its statute prohibited marriages to people closely related by adoption. The Colorado Supreme Court held that this refusal violated their *Zablocki* right to marry. Indeed, the court said the prohibition of marriage by adoptive siblings fails even the rational basis test.

"Nonetheless, defendant argues that this marriage prohibition furthers a legitimate state interest in family harmony. We do not agree. As the instant case illustrates it is just as likely that prohibiting marriage between brother and sister related by adoption will result in family discord." The court pointed to the fact that father and mother Israel filed affidavits saying they had no objection to the marriage; the Roman Catholic Bishop of Denver filed a similar affidavit.

Quoting 1 *Vernier, American Family Laws* 183, the court analogized this marriage restriction to those based upon "affinity," or relationship by marriage (*e.g.*, the sister of my wife). " 'The objections that exist against consanguineous marriages are not present where the relationship is merely by affinity. The physical detriment to the offspring of persons related by blood is totally absent. The natural repugnance of people toward marriages of blood relatives, that has resulted in well-nigh universal moral condemnation of such marriages, is quite generally lacking in application to the union of those related only by affinity. It is difficult to construct any very logical case for the prohibition of marriage on grounds of affinity.' "

NOTES ON THE DIFFICULTY OF DEFENDING PROHIBITIONS AGAINST INCESTUOUS MARRIAGES

1. *The Slippery Slope.* Can a man marry a woman who is the widow of his blood uncle (i.e., his aunt by marriage)? Dicta in *Israel* suggest that in Colorado the state could not constitutionally deny the marriage license. Could a man marry his father's second wife? (Shades of Oedipus!) Would the Colorado courts really require the state to issue such a license? Would other courts be inclined to follow?

Israel views marriage between blood relatives differently than relatives by adoption or affinity. But what is the rationale for prohibiting those marriages? The court seems to think it is biological: "the physical detriment to the offspring of persons related by blood." The biologists say that there is virtually no eugenic reason to prohibit marriages among close relatives; even brother-sister marriages pose little risk of genetic defects. The evidence is assembled in Carolyn S. Bratt, "Incest Statutes and the Fundamental Right of Marriage: Is Oedipus Free to Marry?," 18 *Family L.Q.* 257 (1984). She thinks that Oedipus has a *Zablocki* right to marry. Does he? Could the *Israel* court accept that?

2. *The Incest Taboo.* Foucault thought the incest taboo is a product of the modern construction of childhood sexuality. The home has been sexualized at least since Freud, but the law exists to keep that sexuality within bounds. See Chapter 3, Section 2. Foucault opposed the taboo and maintained that the discourse of incest itself sexualizes the family and contributes to the impulse to commit incest. Is this a credible view?

You can press Foucault's insight in either direction. Like Foucault, you might use it to strike down all incest prohibitions and allow Oedipus to marry his mother, Jocasta (but he still may not kill his father to do so). Contra Foucault, you might justify all sorts of affinity-based incest rules and sustain Colorado's objections to the Israel marriage. If the state concern is an effort to control sexuality in the home, should it make a difference that Tammy Lee and Richard were adoptive rather than blood siblings? Note, also, the disparity in ages: Richard was a legal adult and Tammy Lee still a child when their parents married. Should that make a difference?

3. *Parental Consent as the Linchpin?* The parents agreed to the marriage in *Israel*. Should it be constitutional for Colorado to prohibit such marriages when the parents do not consent? This is similar to the rule for child marriages: they can usually proceed if the parents consent. Are the two situations different?

3. POLYGAMY

All 50 states and the District of Columbia prohibit bigamy, marriage to more than one person at the same time. Assume that John Doe, still married to another person, desires to marry Jane Roe as well. Informed of the existing wife, Roe still wants to marry Doe. Making both due process and equal protection arguments, they sue the state. Is there any chance they will prevail? Consider the leading case.

George Reynolds v. United States, 98 U.S. 145, 25 L.Ed. 244 (1878). George Reynolds, a member of the Church of Latter Day Saints, had several wives, a practice dictated by his Mormon religion. He was convicted of criminal bigamy and cohabitation and appealed that conviction as inconsistent with his free exercise of religion. Not questioning the sincerity of Reynolds' beliefs, Chief Justice Morris Waite's opinion for a unanimous court held that the First Amendment was not violated. He had this to say about polygamy:

"Polygamy has always been odious among the northern and western nations of Europe, and, until the establishment of the Mormon Church, was almost exclusively a feature of the life of Asiatic and African people. At common law, the second marriage was always void, and from the earliest history of England polygamy has been treated as an offence against society." In the seventeenth century the penalty for bigamy was death, in both England and (later) in the colonies.

"In the face of all this evidence, it is impossible to believe that the constitutional guaranty of religious freedom was intended to prohibit legislation in respect to this most important feature of social life. Marriage, while from its very nature a sacred obligation, is nevertheless in most civilized nations, a civil contract, and usually regulated by law. Upon it society may be said to be built, and out of its fruits spring social relations and social obligations and duties, with which government is necessarily required to deal. In fact, according as monogamous or polygamous marriages are allowed, do we find the principles on which the government of the people, to a greater or less extent, rests. Professor Lieber says, polygamy leads to the patriarchal principle, and which, when applied to large communities, fetters the people in stationary despotism, while that condition cannot long exist in connection with monogamy."

NOTES ON POLYGAMY

1. *Polygamy and Gay Marriage.* Opponents of gay marriage invoke polygamy: if society allows two women to marry, there is no principle to prevent it from allowing a man and two women to marry. On the one hand, note the eery similarity between *Reynolds'* reasons for disrespecting polygamy and the reasons drummed up against gay marriage: (a) Both institutions have been demonized by English common law and have flourished in "Asiatic and African" cultures.[k] (b) Both violate mainstream religious doctrines shared by the Roman Catholic and Protestant churches and by Judaism. (c) Both have been attacked as undermining the foundations of the state itself. Rousseau's idea that the "good husband" is the "good citizen" rests upon a model of marriage that is binary, heterosexual, and patriarchal. The man-woman marriage is considered the foundation of political life, and anything deviating from that model is considered politically as well as morally subversive. For an argument that same-sex marriage contributes to a healthy polity but polygamy does not, see Maura I. Strassberg, "Distinctions of Form or Substance: Monogamy, Polygamy, and Same–Sex Marriage," *N.C.L.Rev.* (1997).

---

k. Same-sex marriages have flourished in prewestern or nonwestern cultures, including Africa, Asia, and Native America. It has been suppressed in Western culture since the thirteenth century. See William N. Eskridge, Jr., *The Case for Same–Sex Marriage* ch. 2 (1996).

2. *Polygamy and Sex Discrimination.* Opponents tend not to read the Hawaii Supreme Court decision, which criticized the prohibition against same-sex marriage because it is sex discrimination; prohibiting polygamy is only discrimination on the basis of "numbers," not a suspicious category. As Nan Hunter and Andrew Koppelman have argued, barring same-sex marriage is not only formal discrimination on the basis of sex, but it perpetuates traditional gender roles that undermine women's place as equal citizens. Polygamy offers women a bad deal and reinforces traditional gender roles: the one man is the head of the household, and the "harem" of women are presumably secondary. Not so says Elizabeth Joseph, who argues that polygamy can foster a cooperative sisterhood that is extremely useful for women, like herself (a lawyer), who work outside the home. "My Husband's Nine Wives," *N.Y. Times*, May 23, 1991, at A31. Carol Rose, *Property and Persuasion* 233–34 (1994) (discussed in Chapter 3, Section 1[B]) sketches the following feminist argument for polygamy. If women on the whole are more cooperative than men, many cooperative women will end up accepting a marriage with "loutish" men, which is a recipe for heartbreak. Polygamy allows cooperative women to cluster around cooperative (nonloutish) men. This is good for cooperative men, good for cooperative women, and is what loutish men deserve. Indeed, if polygamy were allowed, men as a group might change their ways.

3. *Polygamy and Sexual Orientation Discrimination.* Recall Justice Scalia's dissenting opinion in *Romer v. Evans* (Chapter 1, Section 3[B][1]). He relied on a Supreme Court decision upholding discrimination against polygamists. How could the Court have responded to Justice Scalia's polygamy analogy?

SECTION 3

CHILDREN IN FAMILIES OF CHOICE

One concomitant of the privatization of family law has been a delinkage of sex within the adult relationship and the existence of children in the family. The law has played a major role in this phenomenon, through liberalization of adoption rules and the gradual deregulation of sexual behavior. Technology has contributed much as well: the availability of artificial insemination at prices many middle class people can afford has spawned gestational hetero-surrogacy (another woman carries the fertilized egg of the male-female couple), regular hetero-surrogacy (another woman is inseminated by the sperm of the man in a male-female couple), single parenting by women (the woman is inseminated by an anonymous or known donor with the understanding that she will raise the child), the lesbian baby boom (a woman is inseminated by an anonymous or known donor with the understanding that the woman and her female partner will be the custodial parents), and the "gay-by boom" (Marla Hollandsworth's term for gay male couples who have children through surrogacy arrangements).

We introduce the materials that follow in a chronological sequence: custody disputes when families break up (Part A), the increasingly complex law surrounding artificial insemination and surrogacy arrangements (Part B), and the phenomenon of second-parent adoptions (Part C). As you read these materials, consider several larger themes. One theme is how child-placement law has adapted to the decline of the Ozzie-and-Harriet model of the stable husband-wife family. Nowadays, marriages are no longer for life, many parents in couples do not marry their partners, and many single persons become parents by choice or accident. Another theme is that many lesbians and gay men are raising children in same-sex households.[a] How does a legal culture typified by *Bowers v. Hardwick*, where the Court opined that "[n]o connection between family * * * on the one hand and

---

a. See Laura Benkov, *Reinventing the Family: The Emerging Story of Lesbian and Gay Parents* (1994); *Homosexuality and the Family* (Frederick W. Bozett ed., 1989); Sharon Elizabeth Rush, "Breaking with Tradition: Surrogacy and Gay Fathers," in *Kindred Matters: Rethinking the Philosophy of the Family* 102 (1993); E. Donald Shapiro & Lisa Schultz, "Single–Sex Families: The Impact of Birth Innovations Upon Traditional Family Notions," 24 *J. Family L.* 271 (1985–1986); Randy Shilts, "Gay People Make Babies Too," *The Advocate*, October 22, 1975, 25. See also The Editors of the Harvard Law Review, *Sexual Orientation and the Law* 119 (1989) (as many as "three million gay men and lesbians in the United States are parents, and between eight and ten million children are raised in gay or lesbian households").

homosexual activity on the other has been demonstrated,"[b] deal with issues that arise from gay people's involvement in procreation, child rearing, and family formation? Yet another theme is the ways in which the law still reflects Victorian ideas about gender. The constitutional law against sex discrimination has purged law of much gender stereotyping, but not all. Is a complete purge possible? Desirable?

PART A.   STATE DECISIONS ABOUT THE PLACEMENT OF CHILDREN

In a variety of contexts the state is an arbiter of who raises children: family break-ups, where state judges ultimately approve or even craft the terms of separation and divorce; adoption and foster care, either run or supervised by state agencies; and social service intervention to protect abused or neglected children. In all of these contexts, the legal requirement is that the state must serve the "best interests of the child," but such a general inquiry surely involves many moral judgments (including a judgment whether to consider traditional moral judgments). The materials in this part will focus on custody and visitation disputes among parents (and in one case a grandparent) and then conclude with issues involving adoption.

1.   SEXUALITY, RACE, AND CHILD CUSTODY

The traditional rule in divorce cases was that custody of children was routinely awarded to the mother, with provision for alimony and child support by the father. The strong presumption of maternal custody was rebutted when the mother did not live up to "maternal" standards established by the courts—especially when she was "guilty" of sexual infidelity or, especially in the South, a romantic relationship with someone of another race. These norms reflected not only traditional gender stereotypes (the mother must be desexualized and nurturing), but also fears of interracial sex and of sexualizing the child's household environment.

Is either of these factors a legitimate consideration in child custody determinations? Would either tend to undermine the child's best interests? Is it constitutional for the state to consider these factors?

Virginia Whaley v. Robert Whaley

Ohio Court of Appeals, 1978.
61 Ohio App.2d 111, 399 N.E.2d 1270.

■ GREY, JUDGE.

[In 1977, the marriage of Robert and Virginia Whaley was dissolved, with Virginia being given custody of their four-year-old daughter. Later in

b. *Bowers v. Hardwick*, 478 U.S. 186, 191 (1986).

1977, the trial court amended the order to transfer custody to Robert, on the ground that Virginia was romantically involved with a married man, which was criminal adultery in Ohio. The rule in Ohio, as elsewhere, was that a custody decree could not be altered unless there is a showing of "changed circumstances" affecting the best interests of the child.

[Revised Code 3109.04(B) strongly presumed against modification of a prior custody decree and specified only three exceptions: (1) the custodian agrees to a change in custody; (2) the child, with the consent of the custodian, has been integrated into the family of the person seeking custody; or (3) "[t]he child's present environment endangers significantly his physical health or his mental, moral, or emotional development and the harm likely to be caused by a change of environment is outweighed by the advantages of such change to the child."]

Applying the clear language of the statute to this case, we find that the record is devoid of any showing of a change of circumstances in the child or the custodian, or that the child has been neglected, injured or harmed in any way. The sole basis for the motion to modify was that appellant was seeing a married man, who was separated from his wife and seeking a divorce, and that the two of them hoped to get married. * * *

* * * [The trial court] made the following finding:

"You see Ma'am, you and Mr. Bell apparently have violated the most sacred contract anyone ever enters into, and that's a marital relationship. The fact that you have this affection for him doesn't change your obligations. *It would be wrong for the Court to permit it to continue, and it would be especially wrong if you and Mr. Bell ultimately get married*, that two people who apparently have caused the problem and have forsaken your spouses *would be the beneficiaries of, of the child*." (Emphasis supplied.)

The judge's decision demonstrates that the change in custody was ordered to punish Mrs. Whaley for conduct the court considered morally wrong.

This is not the standard in the state of Ohio. R.C. 3109.04. The state is concerned with the child's welfare. A child must not be used to punish or reward conduct a particular judge might condemn or condone. * * *

If then the issue of immoral conduct by the custodial parent is relevant only to the extent that it affects the child, what standard is to be used by a trial court in deciding such a question? In a well written article by Lauerman, "Nonmarital Sexual Conduct and Child Custody," 46 *Cin.L.R.* 647 (1977), various standards are set forth. In the interest of brevity we shall attempt to summarize those standards.

Where a custodial parent engages in nonmarital sexual conduct, (1) it is conclusively presumed that the person is unfit to have custody or (2) it is rebuttably presumed that the person is unfit to have custody, or (3) it must be shown that such conduct has a direct adverse impact on the child, or (4) it is presumed that such conduct has a direct adverse impact on the child.

The author gives her opinion, at page 670, as to the standard to be followed.

"Of the four approaches to custody disputes involving parental non-marital sexual conduct, three—the conclusive disqualification rule, the presumptive unfitness position, and the presumptive direct adverse impact stance—are unsatisfactory. The direct adverse impact rule, however, is very satisfactory, assuming a certain mode of application is adopted. The assumption upon which the conclusive disqualification and presumptive unfitness rules are premised, namely, that a sexually active parent necessarily or probably lacks the ability to be a good parent, is invalid simply because it is untrue in many cases. Although these approaches may each have the advantage of producing relatively consistent results, both positions appear to aim more at punishing the parent than at furthering the best interests of the child. In cases in which the child is not likely to be affected by parental sexual conduct and might benefit from the offending parent's care (as, for instance, where the mother is the sexually active parent and the child is very young), use of either the conclusively disqualified rule or the presumptive unfitness test punishes the child as well as the parent. Since the best interests of the child and not the punishment of either parent or child should be the polestar in custody cases, summary espousal of the conclusively disqualified rule or of the presumptively unfit approach constitutes an unacceptable judicial attempt to enforce a particular moral code, a moral code which is by no means accepted by everyone. That some courts have carved out exceptions to the conclusive disqualification rule which emphasize consideration of the child's welfare rather than parental character may reflect at least limited recognition of this proposition."

[The trial court apparently adopted a legal presumption of adverse impact, which the appeals court rejected for the reasons in Professor Lauerman's article. The appeals court required proof of a nexus between nonmarital sexual conduct and adverse impact, for the reasons advanced by Professor Lauerman and because the court found the trial court's standard unworkable.]

* * * It is unworkable because it requires the court to determine what is moral and immoral, and requires the parties to speculate on what is and what may become "morally acceptable." In *In re Anonymous* (1962), 238 N.Y.S.2d 422, 423, we have this language:

"* * * It therefore has devolved upon the courts to establish the moral standards to be followed by persons to whom is entrusted the care and custody of children. And never has there been a greater need for the courts to maintain a high level of moral conduct than exists today. * * * Our courts will continue to insist upon a high level of moral conduct on the part of custodians of children, and will never succumb to the 'Hollywood' type of morality so popular today, which seems to condone and encourage the dropping of our moral guard."

A mere 13 years later, about the time it takes to raise a child to junior high school age, we have this:

"* * * Residence together of an unmarried male and female without the benefit of a sermonized marriage is not per se evil nor one of immorality. * * * The criterion to be applied to determinations of custody is not whether the court condones the mother's mode of living or considers it contrary to good morals, but whether the child is best located with the mother and there well behaved and cared for." *S. v. J.* (1975), 367 N.Y.S.2d 405, 410.

These two cases exemplify the problem for both the parents and the courts. If immoral conduct is presumed to be harmful, the party seeking a change of custody need not show a change of circumstances which is harmful to the child that is presumed. The burden of proof on that party is to show "immorality," and impliedly to prove a moral norm which the custodial party has violated. Disregarding the momentous constitutional implications of such a standard, and in light of the diversity of religious and moral practice in this country we find it simply an unworkable standard beyond the realm of legitimate judicial inquiry. * * *

Linda Sidoti Palmore v. Anthony J. Sidoti, 466 U.S. 429, 104 S.Ct. 1879, 80 L.Ed.2d 421 (1984). When Linda and Anthony Sidoti (both white) were divorced in 1980, Linda was awarded custody of their three-year-old daughter. In 1981, Anthony moved for an order changing custody, on the ground that Linda was living with a person of color, Clarence Palmore, Jr., whom she married two months later. The Florida judge agreed:

> The father's evident resentment of the mother's choice of a black partner is not sufficient to wrest custody from the mother. It is of some significance, however, that the mother did see fit to bring a man into her home and carry on a sexual relationship with him without being married to him. Such action tended to place gratification of her own desires ahead of her concern for the child's future welfare. This Court feels that despite the strides that have been made in bettering relations between the races in this country, it is inevitable that Melanie will * * * suffer from the social stigmatization that is sure to come.

A unanimous Supreme Court reversed, on the ground that such a race-based decision violates the equal protection clause. "The question * * * is whether the reality of private biases and the possible injury they might inflict are permissible considerations for removal of an infant child from the custody of its natural mother. We have little difficulty concluding that they are not. The Constitution cannot control prejudices but neither can it tolerate them. Private biases may be outside the reach of the law, but the law cannot, directly or indirectly, give them effect."

NOTE ON THE IMPLICATIONS OF *PALMORE v. SIDOTI*

1. *Race.* Does *Palmore* stand for the proposition that race can *never* be considered in child custody determinations? What if there were studies showing that children of color would be deprived of their intangible but psychologically important cultural or ethnic heritage if they were raised by white families? What if there were psychiatric evidence that, for a particular child, the trauma of living in a mixed-race household would be substantial?

2. *Sexuality.* Note that the *Whaley* approach allows more judicial discretion in considering sexual relations outside of marriage than *Palmore* seems to permit for interracial relationships. Would there be a constitutional problem if the Florida judge in *Palmore* had changed custody simply based on Linda Sidoti's extramarital relationship with Clarence Palmore, without mentioning the race element? When would it be unconstitutional for the state to deprive Linda Sidoti Palmore of custody of her child?

3. *Homosexuality.* Would it be constitutional for Ohio to follow the approach of *Whaley* when the extramarital affair is heterosexual, but follow a stricter approach when it is homosexual? Would that be sex discrimination similar to the race discrimination in *Palmore*? Would the sexual orientation discrimination be invalid under *Romer v. Evans* (Chapter 1, Section 3[B][1])?

2.   SEXUAL ORIENTATION AND CUSTODY

During the first wave of lesbian and gay custody disputes, courts strongly discriminated against the lesbian or gay parents. One discrimination was a *per se* rule that homosexuality disqualified a parent from custody. Early cases rested the *per se* rule on the "immorality" of the gay parent's "lifestyle," *e.g., Bennett v. Clemens*, 196 S.E.2d 842 (Ga.1973); *Immerman v. Immerman*, 1 Cal.Rptr. 298 (Cal.App.1959); *Commonwealth v. Bradley*, 91 A.2d 379 (Pa.Super.1952), a proposition that came under intense fire in the 1970s. A key case was *Schuster v. Schuster*, 585 P.2d 130 (Wash.1978), where a lesbian couple, Sandy Schuster and Madeliene Isaacson, presented expert psychiatric evidence that parental orientation is irrelevant to the child's development and that their children were healthy and normal. The courts left custody with the mothers, but with conditions. The trial court admonished the mothers not to "use" the children as a showcase for "homosexuality," and the appeals court refused to allow the mothers to live together. See Rhonda R. Rivera, "Our Straight-Laced Judges: The Legal Position Of Homosexual Persons In The United States," 30 *Hastings L.J.* 799, 898–900 (1979) (discussing *Schuster*, with excellent discussion of other pre–1979 cases, including several unreported cases).

During the 1970s, the anti-homosexual discourse shifted from the *per se* rule based upon the intrinsic immorality of the lesbian or gay parent, to a rule requiring judges to consider the overall best interests of the child, but slanting the inquiry by insisting that homophobic third-party reactions be considered. In *S. v. S.*, 608 S.W.2d 64 (Ky.App.1980), the Kentucky Court of Appeals reversed a trial court for failing to change child custody from mother to father when the mother came out as a lesbian. Based upon a journal article, the court accepted as a fact that "the lesbianism of the mother, because of the failure of the community to accept and support such a condition, forces on the child a need for secrecy and the isolation imposed by such a secret, thus separating the child from his or her peers." The leading case insisting upon a more neutral best interests of the child inquiry was *Bezio v. Patenaude*, 410 N.E.2d 1207 (Mass.1980), where the Massachusetts Supreme Court held that there had to be a specific showing of harm to the child, exclusive of general cultural prejudice, to justify depriving a lesbian or gay parent of custody. For an early explication of the nexus argument, see Nan D. Hunter & Nancy D. Polikoff, "Custody Rights of Lesbian Mothers: Legal Theory and Litigation Strategy," 25 *Buff.L.Rev.* 691 (1976).

Ohio has not decided this issue when the following case comes before its courts. Which approach would you predict Ohio to take, in light of *Whaley*?

Charles L. Conkel v. Kim D. Conkel

Ohio Court of Appeals, 1987.
31 Ohio App.3d 169, 509 N.E.2d 983.

■ GREY, JUDGE.

[Charles and Kim Conkel were married in 1972 and bore two children, both boys. The parents divorced in 1981; the separation agreement gave custody of the children to Kim and reasonable visitation rights to Charles, who also was required to pay child support. In 1985, Kim (now remarried and named Kim Brown) moved the court to cite Charles for contempt because he failed to pay child support, and Charles (now partnered with a male lover) moved to cite Kim for contempt for obstructing his visitation rights. The trial court granted Charles overnight visitation with his children but on the condition that he was not to exercise his visitation in the presence of any non-related male person.

[Kim appealed this disposition, citing the following:] (1) she is fearful for the physical and mental well-being of the children because visitation with their father may trigger homosexual tendencies in them; (2) during visitation with their father they may contract AIDS; (3) homosexuality is a basis to change custody; (4) an extended visitation would force the children to "confront the homosexual problem" and "suffer the slings and arrows of a disapproving society" * * *.

The purpose of visitation orders is to promote the children's continuing contact with the non-custodial parent. The need for visitation is recognized in Ohio. The Ohio Supreme Court made the importance of visitation clear in *Porter v. Porter* (1971), 267 N.E.2d 299, paragraph three of the syllabus:

"The need of a child for visitation with a separated parent is a natural right of the child, and is as worthy of protection as is the parent's rights of visitation with the child; thus, the failure, without just cause, of a divorced or separated parent having custody of a child to accord visitation rights to the other parent is not only an infringement of the other parent's right to visitation but is also an infringement of the child's right to receive the love, affection, training and companionship of the parent."

The bond between parent and child has been accorded constitutional protection. In 1972, the Supreme Court in *Stanley v. Illinois* (1972), 405 U.S. 645, 651, recognized that the interest of parents in their children "undeniably warrants deference and, absent a powerful countervailing interest, protection. * * *" In *Stanley*, the court set aside a presumption that a father was unfit based solely on his status as an unwed father. Recently, the Supreme Court limited the *Stanley* protection to fathers who had had a prior relationship to their children. *Lehr v. Robertson* (1983), 463 U.S. 248. However, at the same time, the court re-emphasized that the parental "interest in personal contact with * * * [the] child acquires substantial protection under the Due Process Clause." *Id.* at 261.

Brown's contentions constitute an unconstitutional "status" argument, i.e., that the appellee father's status as a homosexual man establishes conclusive proof of a judicial abuse of discretion. This court rejects such an argument. See *Robinson v. California* (1962), 370 U.S. 660. Secondly, Brown's contentions posit an irrebuttable presumption of unfitness based on sexual activity. This court has already rejected that argument in *Whaley*. Such an irrebuttable presumption offends the constitutional standards of *Stanley* and *Lehr*. In *Whaley*, this court held that the issue of immoral conduct is relevant only to the extent that it affects the child. Such conduct can be considered in the grant of custody or modification of a custody order only if the conduct of the parent has a direct adverse impact on the child.

Ohio courts have followed *Whaley*, but only in cases involving divorced heterosexual parents. Other jurisdictions have considered homosexual parents. In *A. v. A.* (1973), 514 P.2d 358, 360, the Oregon Court of Appeals held that the homosexuality of a parent should not result in a determination of unfitness per se. See, also, *Nadler v. Superior Court* (1967), 63 Cal.Rptr. 352. In a well-written article, Rivera, "The Legal Position of Homosexual Persons in the United States" (1979), 30 *Hastings L.J.* 799, the status of a homosexual or lesbian parent attempting to assert custody or visitation rights is discussed in depth. The article points out that courts are beginning to apply an objective standard of the best interests of the child rather than looking to the sexual habits of the parent. *Id.* at 903–904.
* * *

Too long have courts labored under the notion that divorced parents must somehow be perfect in every respect. The law should recognize that parents, married or not, are individual human beings each with his or her own particular virtues and vices. The children of married parents are expected to take their parents as they find them—as Oliver Cromwell said to his portraitist, "with warts and all." Whatever their faults, unless the married parent's conduct is harming the child, the courts will not intervene in the parent-child relationship.

In divorce cases, however, the court has no choice but to intervene to establish custody and visitation. Nonetheless, the same standard should be used. In domestic relations cases the courts should recognize that all parents have faults, and look not to the faults of the parents, but to the needs of the child. A child needs to know that both his parents, divorced or not, love him. Where the parent is removed from the child's environment, the child feels a sense of loss. If the courts are concerned with the best interests of the child, then visitation by the non-custodial parent must be recognized as necessary to the child's well-being. The denial of visitation should only be done when egregious conduct by the non-custodial parent results in harm to the child. * * *

Brown expresses "fear" that contact with their father will trigger homosexual tendencies in the two boys. No evidence was presented to support this contention. This court takes judicial notice that there is no consensus on what causes homosexuality, but there is substantial consensus among experts that being raised by a homosexual parent does not increase the likelihood that a child will become homosexual.

Dr. Richard Green, Professor of Psychiatry, State University of New York at Stony Brook, an expert on gender identity in children, has said that "* * * [n]o theory in the developmental psychology literature suggests that having homosexual parents leads to a homosexual outcome. Rather, heterosexual parents raise pre-homosexual children." [Green], "The Best Interests of the Child with a Lesbian Mother" (1982), 10 *Bulletin of the American Academy of Psychiatry and the Law* 7, at 9. * * *

[The court also rejected Kim's fears that the children might contract AIDS (there was evidence that Charles was not infected and that casual contact could not spread the HIV virus in any event) and might be subjected to social stigmas associated with homosexuality.] In a similar case in New Jersey, *M.P. v. S.P.* (1979), 404 A.2d 1256, a New Jersey appellate court noted that changing custody would not remove the source of stigma and potential embarrassment. The New Jersey court left the children with their homosexual parent and postulated a beneficial effect for the children, i.e., overcoming "the constraints of currently popular sentiment or prejudice." *Id.* at 1263.

This court cannot take into consideration the unpopularity of homosexuals in society when its duty is to facilitate and guard a fundamental parent-child relationship. The Supreme Court of the United States faced the question of popular disapproval in 1984 in the case of *Palmore v. Sidoti* (1984), 466 U.S. 429. In *Palmore*, the trial court removed a white child from her natural mother because the white mother was cohabiting with a black man, whom she later married. The white father relied on the issue of social stigma. The Supreme Court recognized that such a child might "be subject to a variety of pressures and stresses not present if the child were living with parents of the same racial or ethnic origin."

Nonetheless, Chief Justice Burger, in overruling the trial court, wrote, "* * * The Constitution cannot control such prejudices but neither can it tolerate them. Private biases may be outside the reach of the law, but the law cannot, directly or indirectly, give them effect. * * * "*Id.* The Supreme Court of Alaska in May 1985 applied the *Palmore* case to a lesbian mother custody case, *S.N.E. v. R.L.B.* (Alaska 1985), 699 P.2d 875. The court held: "[I]t is impermissible to rely on any real or imagined social stigma attaching to [the] Mother's status as a lesbian. * * * " *Id.* at 879.

■ [The Court affirmed the decree of the trial court. JUDGE ABELE dissented without opinion.]

NOTE ON CUSTODY AND VISITATION DISPUTES INVOLVING LESBIAN, BISEXUAL, AND GAY PARENTS

1. *The "Nexus" Approach to Lesbian and Gay Custody.* Courts in most jurisdictions have adopted the so-called "nexus" approach: sexual orientation of the parent is not *per se* disqualifying in custody determinations, but it may justify denying custody to a lesbian or gay parent if there is a nexus between the sexual orientation and harm to the child. Leading cases (and one statutory codification) are listed in the margin.[c]

The Ohio decisions excerpted above reflect a relatively neutral approach to the issues of visitation and custody: the sexuality of the parent is largely irrelevant to custody and visitation decisions; the only relevant evidence is the best interests of the child; and social attitudes about the parent's sexuality will not be relevant to determine that. An historical note may help explain this: the judge who had been assigned to write the decision in *Conkel* sought out the assistance of Professor Rhonda Rivera of Ohio State University School of Law, and author of some of the first legal scholarship in the area of gay rights. Professor Rivera helped draft the opinion.

The nexus requirement seems to be the prevailing approach also in Alaska, California, Indiana, Massachusetts, New Jersey, New Mexico, New York, Vermont, Washington, and other states. Other states utilizing the nexus approach, such as Kentucky, consider third-party attitudes (such as classmate jibes) such as those disapproved in different-race cases by *Palmore v. Sidoti*. Should *Palmore*'s reasoning be applied to prevent this skewed application of the nexus approach?

2. *Discrimination in Conditions on Parental Custody and Visitation.* Note that, by affirming the trial court, the appeals court left in place the restriction that Charles Conkel cannot have the children overnight if there is a nonrelated male present, such as his same-sex partner. Would such a

---

c. See *S.N.E. v. R.L.B.*, 699 P.2d 875 (Alaska 1985); *In re Marriage of Birdsall*, 243 Cal.Rptr. 287 (Cal.App.1988); *Charpentier v. Charpentier*, 536 A.2d 948 (Conn.1988); D.C. Code § 16–911(a)(5) (D.C.); *Davis v. Davis*, 335 So.2d 857 (Fla.App.1976); *In re Marriage of Williams*, 151 Ill.Dec. 89, 563 N.E.2d 1195 (Ill.App.1990); *D.H. v. J.H.*, 418 N.E.2d 286 (Ind.App.1981); *In re Marriage of Wiarda*, 505 N.W.2d 506 (Iowa App.1993); *S. v. S.*, 608 S.W.2d 64 (Ky.App.1980); *Bezio v. Patenaude*, 410 N.E.2d 1207 (Mass.1980); *People v. Brown*, 212 N.W.2d 55 (Mich.App.1973); *M.P. v. S.P.*, 404 A.2d 1256 (N.J. Super.1979); *A.C. v. C.B.*, 829 P.2d 660 (N.M.App.1992); *Anonymous v. Anonymous*, 503 N.Y.S.2d 466 (N.Y.App.Div.1986); *Jacobson v. Jacobson*, 314 N.W.2d 78 (N.D.1981); *Matter of Marriage of Ashling*, 599 P.2d 475 (Or.App.1979); *Blew v. Verta*, 617 A.2d 31 (Pa.Super.1992); *Stroman v. Williams*, 353 S.E.2d 704 (S.C.App.1987); *Nickerson v. Nickerson*, 605 A.2d 1331 (Vt.1992); *Schuster v. Schuster*, 585 P.2d 130 (Wash.1978).

condition have been constitutional in *Palmore* if Linda Sidoti had not married Clarence Palmore? Note that there was no such condition in *Whaley*. Under a truly neutral "nexus" approach, is there any defense for treating Charles Conkel differently from Virginia Whaley?

There is ample precedent for the *Conkel* conditions, however. New Jersey's Superior Court ruled in *In re J.S. & C.*, 324 A.2d 90 (N.J.Super.1974), *affirmed*, 362 A.2d 54 (N.J.Super.App.1976), that a gay father's constitutional interest in the companionship of his child militated against a per se rule prohibiting any visitation or contact with the children. Nonetheless, the court held that the welfare of the children justified severe restrictions on that visitation. The court relied on the father's advocacy of gay rights (he was a member of Gay Activists Alliance) and the "speculative" possibility that, according to the mother's expert, the children "would be subject to either overt or covert homosexual seduction which would detrimentally influence their sexual development." Accordingly, the court limited the gay father's visitation time and conditioned any visitation on the father's agreement that he "not involve the children in any homosexual related activities or publicity" or have his lover present at any time. Such discriminatory conditions on visitation by gay parents were commonly imposed and approved by state appellate courts. *E.g., J.L.P. v. D.J.P.*, 643 S.W.2d 865 (Mo.App.1982); *In re Jane B.*, 380 N.Y.S.2d 848 (N.Y.Sup.Ct. 1976).

On the other hand, more recent appellate decisions have been more skeptical of such conditions. The California Court of Appeal in *Birdsall v. Birdsall*, 243 Cal.Rptr. 287 (Cal.App.1988), vacated a prohibition of a gay father's overnight visitation in the presence of another homosexual, based upon the nexus test. "The unconventional life style of one parent, or the opposing moral positions of the parties, or the outright condemnation of one parent's beliefs by the other parent's religion, which may result in confusion for the child, do not provide an adequate basis for restricting visitation rights. Evidence of one parent's homosexuality, without a link to detriment to the child, is insufficient to constitute harm," the court held. To the same effect are *In re Marriage of Diehl*, 582 N.E.2d 281 (Ill.App. 1991); *North v. North*, 648 A.2d 1025 (Md.App.1994); *Blew v. Verta*, 617 A.2d 31 (Pa.Super.1992). In light of these decisions, should Ohio reconsider the *Conkel* conditions in future cases?

3. *States Following More Traditional Approaches to Lesbian and Gay Custody.* Other states follow a more traditional approach, presuming against gay or lesbian custody and imposing special conditions on gay and lesbian visitation. In Alabama and Florida, for example, the custody statutes require the court to consider the "moral fitness" of the parent. In most states, however, moral fitness requirements have been introduced by judges. Missouri and Virginia courts have created presumptions against custody with lesbian or gay parents when their straight former spouses desire custody. See *Roe v. Roe*, 324 S.E.2d 691 (Va.1985); *G.A. v. D.A.*, 745 S.W.2d 726 (Mo.App.1987). What if the grandparent wants to take away a child from her own lesbian daughter? Can she do so in such states?

Compare *Bottoms v. Bottoms*, 444 S.E.2d 276 (Va.App.1994), with the Virginia Supreme Court decision reversing the court of appeals, 457 S.E.2d 102 (Va.1995), which immediately follows.

Pamela Kay Bottoms v. Sharon Lynne Bottoms

Supreme Court of Virginia, 1995.
249 Va. 410, 457 S.E.2d 102.

■ COMPTON, JUSTICE. * * *

[The court summarized the facts as found by the trial court, which entered judgment transferring custody of Tyler Doustou from his mother, Sharon Bottoms, to his grandmother, Pamela Kay Bottoms. The trial court judgment had been reversed on appeal, but the supreme court reinstated it.]

During the two-year period before the trial court hearing, the child had spent 70 percent of the time with the grandmother and 30 percent with his mother. The grandmother has kept the child for "weeks at a time" and during "every weekend since he's been born." On at least three occasions during that period, the mother left the child with the grandmother without informing her of the mother's whereabouts or how she could be reached "in the event something happened to the child."

Following the mother's separation from Doustou, she continued a "relationship" with another man that had begun during her marriage. She contracted a venereal disease during this relationship that prevents her from having additional children. During the child's first year, the mother "slept with two or three different guys, maybe four, in the same room" with the child "where his crib was." At the time, the mother "lived two blocks away" from the grandmother, and the mother kept the child's "suitcase packed" for visits to the grandmother's home. The mother said that she has "had trouble" with her temper, and that when the child was about "a year" old, she "popped him on his leg too hard a couple of times," and left her fingerprints there. She has had "counseling" in an effort to control her temper. * * *

Except for brief employment as a grocery store cashier, the mother had been unemployed during most of the three-year period prior to the trial court hearing. She was receiving "welfare money" which often was spent to "do her fingernails before the baby would get any food."

During May 1992, ten months before the juvenile court hearing, 16 months before the trial court hearing, and when her son was ten months old, the mother met April Wade, a lesbian. Wade, born in April 1966, had been discharged from the U.S. Army in 1986. Wade is a "recovering alcoholic." The mother and Wade "moved in together" in September 1992. From that time, with the exception of a two-week period, the mother and Wade have lived in "a lesbian relationship." According to the mother, the relationship involves hugging and kissing, patting "on the bottom," sleeping in the same bed, "fondling," and "oral sex." The mother testified that she loves Wade and that they "have a lifetime commitment."

At the time of the juvenile court hearing, the mother, the child, and Wade were living in a two-bedroom apartment with "Evelyn," another lesbian. "At one time," the child's bed was in the room where the mother and Wade slept, having "sex in the same bed." At one point in her testimony, however, when asked "how many times did you do it when the child was sleeping in the same bedroom," the mother responded, "None." She said that she and Wade displayed other signs of affection "in front of" the child.

Wade, employed as a gift shop manager, supports the mother. The pair lives in an apartment complex in Western Henrico County. Wade has become "a parent figure" to the child, who calls Wade "Da Da."

Two months before the petition for custody was filed, the mother revealed her lesbian relationship to the grandmother. This disclosure alienated the two. During the period after the juvenile court hearing, when regimented visitation with the mother began, the child demonstrated certain traits. For example, when the child returned to the grandmother from being with the mother, he would "stomp" his foot, tell himself to "go to the corner," and then would stand in the corner of a room, facing the wall. He curses, saying "shit" and "damn," language never used in the grandmother's home. On one occasion, when the mother and Wade "came to pick him up," the child "held his breath, turned purple. He didn't want to go with her," according to the grandmother. During a period in mid–1993, each time the mother "would come pick him up," the child would scream and cry.

Wade has admitted she "hit" the child. Also, on one occasion, when an argument developed between the mother and Wade, on the one hand, and the grandmother, on the other, about the timing of the exchange of the child for visitation, Wade said during the quarrel, "I might end up killing somebody." According to the grandmother, the child is "always neglected." For example, when the child returns to the grandmother's home, she testified that he "can't even sit down in the bathtub. That's neglect from changing his diaper. He is so red." * * *

The trial judge, announcing his decision from the bench at the conclusion of the hearing, said the dispute "presents the question ... whether the child's best interest is served by a transfer of the custody of the child from [his] mother to [his] maternal grandmother." Stating that the mother's conduct is "illegal," and constitutes a felony under the Commonwealth's criminal laws, and that "her conduct is immoral," the court recognized the "presumption in the law in favor of the custody being with the natural parent."

Mentioning the evidence of lesbianism and specified "other evidence" in the case not involving homosexual conduct, the trial court concluded from "all the facts and circumstances ... of the case," that "the custody will be with the grandmother."

The Court of Appeals concluded that "the evidence fails to prove" that the mother "abused or neglected her son, that her lesbian relationship with April Wade has or will have a deleterious effect on her son, or that she is an unfit parent." "To the contrary," said the Court of Appeals, the evidence showed that the mother "is and has been a fit and nurturing parent who has adequately provided and cared for her son. No evidence tended to prove that the child will be harmed by remaining with his mother." The court held "that the trial court abused its discretion by invoking the state's authority to take the child from the custody of his natural mother ... and by transferring custody to a non-parent, ... the child's maternal grand-mother."

[The Virginia Supreme Court held that the court of appeals had not properly deferred to the trial court's findings of fact.]

We have held * * * that a lesbian mother is not per se an unfit parent. *Doe v. Doe*, 284 S.E.2d 799, 806 (1981). Conduct inherent in lesbianism is punishable as a Class 6 felony in the Commonwealth, Code § 18.2–361; thus, that conduct is another important consideration in determining custody.

And, while the legal rights of a parent should be respected in a custody proceeding, those technical rights may be disregarded if demanded by the interests of the child. In the present case, the record shows a mother who, although devoted to her son, refuses to subordinate her own desires and priorities to the child's welfare. For example, the mother disappears for days without informing the child's custodian of her whereabouts. She moves her residence from place to place, relying on others for support, and uses welfare funds to "do" her fingernails before buying food for the child. She has participated in illicit relationships with numerous men, acquiring a disease from one, and "sleeping" with men in the same room where the child's crib was located. To aid in her mobility, the mother keeps the child's suitcase packed so he can be quickly deposited at the grandmother's.

The mother has difficulty controlling her temper and, out of frustra-tion, has struck the child when it was merely one year old with such force as to leave her fingerprints on his person. While in her care, she neglects to change and cleanse the child so that, when he returns from visitation with her, he is "red" and "can't even sit down in the bathtub."

Unlike *Doe*, relied on by the mother, there is proof in this case that the child has been harmed, at this young age, by the conditions under which he lives when with the mother for any extended period. For example, he has already demonstrated some disturbing traits. He uses vile language. He screams, holds his breath until he turns purple, and becomes emotionally upset when he must go to visit the mother. He appears confused about efforts at discipline, standing himself in a corner facing the wall for no apparent reason.

And, we shall not overlook the mother's relationship with Wade, and the environment in which the child would be raised if custody is awarded the mother. We have previously said that living daily under conditions stemming from active lesbianism practiced in the home may impose a burden upon a child by reason of the "social condemnation" attached to such an arrangement, which will inevitably afflict the child's relationships with its "peers and with the community at large." *Roe v. Roe*, 324 S.E.2d 691, 694 (1985). We do not retreat from that statement; such a result is likely under these facts. Also, Wade has struck the child and, when there was a dispute over visitation, she has threatened violence when her views were not accepted. * * *

■ KEENAN, JUSTICE, dissents with whom WHITING and LACY, JUSTICES, join. [Justice Keenan faulted the trial court for violating the *Doe* rule in its finding that Sharon Bottoms was *per se* unfit because she was a lesbian. Because the trial court applied the wrong rule of law, its other findings cannot be rehabilitated, and the case should have been remanded for a new hearing.]

PROBLEM 9–4

THE CONSTITUTION, SHARON LYNNE BOTTOMS, AND THE VIRGINIA SUPREME COURT

You are the attorney for Sharon Lynne Bottoms; she wants to appeal this decision all the way to the United States Supreme Court. What chances do you think she has? What is her best argument? What *amicus* briefs do you want to line up if an appeal is taken and granted?

3.   SEXUAL ORIENTATION, RACE, AND ADOPTION

In re Adoption of Charles B.

Ohio Supreme Court, 1990.
50 Ohio St.3d 88, 552 N.E.2d 884.

■ PER CURIAM.

[Charles B. was a minor who had suffered from an abusive and neglectful childhood. His parents surrendered him to an adoption agency which made several unsuccessful attempts to place Charles in a family-oriented home where the parents also had the patience and desire to help Charles with his learning and emotional disabilities. In 1987, Mr. B. indicated a desire to adopt Charles, and in 1988 he filed a petition with probate court for adoption. The agency opposed the adoption on the ground that Mr. B. is a gay man. The trial judge rejected that position and granted Mr. B.'s petition, based on evidence that Mr. B. offered Charles a good home, that Mr. B. (unlike other candidates) was willing to invest time and resources in Charles' rehabilitation, and that Charles liked Mr. B. and wanted to make his home with this man. The court of appeals reversed, holding that a gay man should never be allowed to adopt a child.]

[Revised Code (R.C.)] 3107.02 sets forth who may be adopted. R.C. 3107.02(A) provides: "Any minor may be adopted." R.C. 3107.03 sets forth those persons who may adopt. R.C. 3107.03 provides in relevant part: "The following persons may adopt: * * * (B) An unmarried adult[.]"

Charles is included within R.C. 3107.02(A) and thus may be adopted. Mr. B. is included within R.C. 3107.03(B) and is, therefore, *statutorily* permitted to adopt. * * *

Having so stated, we hasten to add that the right to adopt is not absolute. Both R.C. 3107.02 and 3107.03 use the discretionary word "may." Accordingly, we also hold that while an unmarried adult in Ohio is eligible to adopt, the right is permissive and not absolute as both R.C. 3107.02 and R.C. 3107.03 use the verb "may." * * *

[We] further hold that pursuant to R.C. 3107.14, adoption matters must be decided on a case-by-case basis through the able exercise of discretion by the trial court giving due consideration to all known factors in determining what is in the best interest of the person to be adopted. * * *

The court in *In re Burrell* (1979), 388 N.E.2d 738, addressed whether two minor girls lacked proper parental care and supervision solely because their mother, with whom they lived, was also living with her boyfriend. We found that the evidence showed no conditions adverse to the normal development of the girls other than the fact that the mother lived with her boyfriend. We held:

> "* * * [S]uch conduct is only significant if it can be demonstrated to have an adverse impact upon the child sufficiently to warrant state intervention. That impact cannot be simply inferred in general, but must be specifically demonstrated in a clear and convincing manner. * * *" *Id.* at 739.

[The court invoked *Whaley* and *Conkel* as support for following a nexus approach to child placement decisions: "that immoral sexual conduct must be shown to have a direct or probable adverse impact on the welfare of the child" for it to be relevant.] [T]he test to be used in *any* adoption is the "best interest of the child" standard. If there is information available that shows or indicates that adoption of a particular child would not be in the child's best interest, then that evidence should be presented at the adoption hearing.

What evidence was offered at the hearing? [The department] offered one witness. The witness, who is the Administrator of Social Services for appellee, testified that, except for a few classes in those areas, she had no formal education in either social work, or psychology. She had met with Charles individually on only one occasion and for one hour. She had not observed Charles with Mr. B. * * *

In contrast, Mr. B. himself testified and presented six other witnesses. These other witnesses were: (1) Dr. Joseph Shannon, who holds a Ph.D. in psychology, (2) Dr. Victoria Blubaugh, who also holds a doctorate in psychology, (3) Mr. B.'s mother, (4) Mr. B.'s sister, (5) Carol Menge, vice-president of Lutheran Social Services and herself an adoptive parent, and (6) Mr. K. Finally, the guardian ad litem gave an oral report recommending that the adoption be approved.

* * * Dr. Blubaugh * * * testified that in her counseling role she had observed a bonding develop between Charles and Mr. B. She testified that it was in Charles's best interest to be adopted by Mr. B. especially given the specific needs of Charles. * * * Mr. B.'s mother and sister stated that Charles had become integrated into their family and that a relationship of grandmother-grandson and aunt-nephew had been developed with Charles. * * *

[Ohio law allows child placement over the objection of the adoption agency where in the best interest of the child. The Ohio Supreme Court held that the trial court had not abused its discretion in finding that adoption by Mr. B. would be in Charles's best interest. The court reinstated the judgment of the trial court.]

■ ALICE ROBIE RESNICK, JUSTICE, dissenting.

* * * Existing Ohio law is very clear that a homosexual is not as a matter of law barred from adopting a child under R.C. 3107.03(B). * * * The fact that the party seeking to become an adoptive parent is a homosexual should not, in and of itself, be determinative. However, neither can it be ignored. When a homosexual seeks to adopt a minor, a trial court must have before it sufficient evidence to show that the prospective parent's homosexuality will not have an adverse effect on the minor. * * *

* * * Charlie has leukemia which presently is in remission. The treatment which Charlie received for leukemia has altered his immune system. * * *

Mr. B. * * * was tested, proving to be HIV negative. However, we must remember that adoption is not just for today but forever. Mr. B. falls within a high-risk population for AIDS. Why place a child whose immune system has already been altered in such an environment? It was best stated by Kathleen Handley, Administrator of Social Services for the Licking County Department of Social Services, at the hearing that "[o]ur feeling is that professionally it would be an adoption risk * * * to place a child in a setting where there is no practiced precedent to give us support. We do not view this as a child that needs experimentation. He has too many other issues that he has to conquer in his life." * * *

NOTE ON SEXUAL ORIENTATION AND ADOPTION

Adoption proceedings do not yield as much appellate litigation as custody proceedings; most adoptions are quietly resolved at the agency or department of social services level. Most states seem to follow the Ohio approach, but even in those states there is strong resistance to adoption by lesbian and gay adults. Consider several themes:

1. *The Per Se Immoral Argument.* In a few states, adoption by gay people is substantially or wholly forbidden on the old "immorality" ground. Arizona has yielded the leading decision, in a case involving an unmarried, openly bisexual man. "It would be anomalous for the state on the one hand to declare homosexual conduct unlawful and on the other create a parent after that proscribed model, in effect approving that standard, inimical to the natural family, as head of a state-created family." *In re Appeal in Pima County Juvenile Action B–10489*, 727 P.2d 830, 835 (Ariz.App.1986). Can this kind of reasoning survive *Romer v. Evans* (Chapter 1, Section 3[B][1])? The Arizona case reflects a staple argument of anti-homosexual rhetoric, that gay equality is "special rights" and state "approval" of the "homosexual lifestyle." Recall Jane Schacter's article on "The Discourse of Equivalents" in Chapter 8, Section 2(C).

Florida's legislature in 1977 prohibited adoptions by "homosexuals." Fla.Stat. § 63.042(3). In response to an array of constitutional arguments, a Florida district court held that the prohibition has a defensible "rational basis" to protect children: because most children are expected to be heterosexual, they will not benefit as much from homosexual as heterosexual "role models." *State Dep't of Health v. Cox,* 627 So.2d 1210 (Fla.App. 1993). The Florida Supreme Court remanded the case to develop a more complete factual record on this issue, however. *Cox v. Florida Dep't of Health & Rehab. Servs.,* 656 So.2d 902 (Fla.1995) (*per curiam*). In light of *Romer v. Evans* (Chapter 1, Section 3[B][1]) and the materials following these notes, how should the court rule on remand?

2. *The AIDS Argument.* Justice Resnick's dissent in Charles's case relies on the possibility of the parent's passing on the HIV virus to the adoptive child. On its face, this argument is factually groundless: not only was Mr. B. not infected with the virus and was living in a monogamous relationship, but HIV is not passed on through casual household contact. Families operate normally with an HIV-infected member. Justice Resnick's dissent may be more than factually vacuous, however. Reading between the lines, do you think that she is alleging that there is a good chance that Mr. B.'s bonding with Charles is sexual in nature, and that presumptively "promiscuous" Mr. B. will "prey" on poor Charles? There is no scientific evidence to suggest that gay or lesbian parents, adoptive or otherwise, are more likely than heterosexual parents to "prey" on their children sexually.

3. *The Best–Scenario-for-Raising–Children Argument.* Most anti-homosexual discourse in the 1990s eschews openly prejudiced appeals to sodomy laws and AIDS. The "kinder, gentler" anti-homosexual discourse focuses on the best interests of the child. Lesbian and gay households are, under this approach, defective in their inability to conform to the husband-wife pattern and, therefore, inappropriate places for children. (Recall that this is how Hawaii is defending its marriage statute.) Consider the following problem as an example of this new strategy.

PROBLEM 9–5

PROHIBITING "HOMOSEXUAL" ADOPTION, FOSTER CARE, AND CHILD CARE

As of 1987, only Florida prohibited gay people from adopting children as a matter of statute. The New Hampshire House of Representatives considered the issue in 1987. In that state (and a few others), the legislature can obtain a preliminary judgment of constitutionality of proposed legislation from its Supreme Court. The House adopted a resolution asking for advice on the constitutionality of House Bill 70, an act prohibiting homosexuals from adopting, being foster parents, or running day care centers. The Supreme Court requested greater specificity, and the House adopted this resolution:

"That for the purposes of HB 70, a homosexual is defined as any person who performs or submits to any sexual act involving the sex organs of one person and the mouth or anus of another person of the same gender; and

"That the general court has chosen over the years to enact statutes relative to adopting children, providing foster care, and licensing day care centers in order to further the best interests of our state's children. These statutory enactments of the state do not involve intrusion into the private lives of consenting adults, but rather further the public and governmental interest in providing for the health, safety, and proper training for children who will be the subject of governmentally approved or licensed activities relating to such children. The general court finds that, as a matter of public policy, the provision of a healthy environment and a role model for our children should exclude homosexuals, as defined by this act, from participating in governmentally sanctioned programs of adoption, foster care, and day care. Additionally, the general court finds that being a child in such programs is difficult enough without the added social and psychological complexities that a homosexual lifestyle could produce. The general court makes this statement in a deliberative and balanced manner both recognizing the rights of consenting adults, as limited by the Supreme Court of the United States in *Bowers v. Hardwick*, 106 S.Ct. 2841 (1986), and the rights of the children of this state, who are intimately affected by the policies of this state in the above governmentally sanctioned programs, to positive nurturing and a healthy environment for their formative years * * *."

The bill if enacted would amend New Hampshire's Revised Statutes §§ 170–B:4 (homosexuals could not adopt), 170–F:6 (disqualifying as a foster family any family "in which one or more of the adults is a homosexual"), 161:2 (the department could not grant a license to be a foster home to a family which contains one or more adult homosexuals), and 170–E:4 (requiring denial of any application to operate a child care facility "if the department determines that the applicant is unfit for licensure by reason of being a homosexual"). Consider this bill from several different angles.

(A) Constitutional Interpretation. Does this bill infringe upon gay people's rights to privacy, equal protection, or freedom of expression under the U.S. Constitution? For this inquiry, remember, the New Hampshire Supreme Court is bound by decisions of the U.S. Supreme Court. What answer? See *Opinion of the Justices*, 530 A.2d 21 (N.H.1987). What about under the state constitution? Here the court is not bound by federal precedent. Should the court create broader rights for gay people?

(B) Statutory Interpretation. Consider the following queries about the breadth of the bill's application. Are the following people disqualified from adopting under the statute?

- a 40 year-old married woman who had a lesbian affair when she was 20 years old;

- a 40 year-old married man who "fooled around" with other boys when he was 12 years old and admits to having had oral sex then but not since;

- a 30 year-old married woman who admits that her feelings are predominantly lesbian and that she has kissed other women passionately, but denies that she has ever had oral or anal sex with another woman.

Does your answer to this inquiry affect how you answer the first portion of this Problem? See *Opinion of the Justices, supra.*

(C) Theoretical Interpretation. How would Eve Kosofsky Sedgwick approach this bill? Ellen Ross and Rayna Rapp? Michel Foucault? See Chapter 3 for excerpts from these authors.

Charlotte J. Patterson, Adoption of Minor Children by Lesbian and Gay Adults: A Social Science Perspective, 2 *Duke Journal of Gender Law and Policy* 191, 197, 199–200 (1995). Discussing the *Charles B.* adoption case and the *Bottoms* custody case, Professor Charlotte Patterson, a psychologist at the University of Virginia, reports social science research about how children fare in lesbian and gay households. "Not only have the studies failed to produce conclusive evidence that the children of lesbian mothers or gay fathers have significant difficulties in development relative to children of heterosexual parents, but they have produced no evidence at all in support of this proposition. In fact, in study after study, children of lesbian mothers have been found to develop normally." We cite in the margin the main studies reported in Patterson's article.[d]

Patterson ties the studies to specific concerns raised by courts in adoption as well as custody cases. One concern: "Would girls in lesbian or gay homes grow up thinking of themselves as boys? Would boys grow up acting effeminate, or girls grow up behaving in masculine ways? Might

---

d. Patricia Falk, "Lesbian Mothers: Psychosocial Assumptions in Family Law," 44 *Am. Psychol.* 941 (1989); Susan Golombok et al., "Children in Lesbian and Single Parent Households: Psychosexual and Psychiatric Appraisal," 24 *J. Child Psychol. & Psy.* 551 (1983); David J. Kleber et al. "The Impact of Parental Homosexuality in Child Custody Cases: A Review of the Literature," 14 *Bull. Am. Academy Psychol. & Law* 81 (1986); Mary E. Hotvedt & Jane Barclay Mandel, "Children of Lesbian Mothers," in William Paul et al., *Homosexuality: Social,* *Psychological, and Biological Issues* 275, 282 (1982). Reviews of the empirical literature are contained in Charlotte J. Patterson, "Children of Lesbians and Single–Parent Households: Psychosexual and Psychiatric Appraisals," 63 *Child Dev.* 1025 (199); Alisa Steckel, "Psychosexual Development of Children of Lesbian Mothers," in *Gay and Lesbian Parents* 75 (Frederick W. Bozett ed. 1987); Fiona L. Tasker & Susan Golombok, "Children Raised by Lesbian Mothers: The Empirical Evidence," 21 *Fam. L.* 184 (1991).

children of lesbian or gay parents themselves grow up to be lesbian or gay?'' Patterson reported 12 studies that addressed this issue and found no evidence of any of these traits.

"A second concern that courts have expressed about children in lesbian and gay families involves other difficulties in personal development, such as low self-esteem, problems of adjustment, and psychiatric disorders. Reviewing research on these questions, I found a number of studies, not one of which provides any reason to believe that children of lesbian or gay parents are at risk. Courts have also expressed the view that these children are more likely to be sexually abused by parents or by parents' friends. However, the existing research suggests that the great majority of child sexual abuse is committed by heterosexual men, not by lesbians or gay men. Again, no evidence validates the courts' concerns.''

Patterson found no empirical basis for a third concern, that children of lesbian and gay households would be teased or stigmatized in their peer group because of their parents' sexual orientation. There is anecdotal evidence cutting in a number of different directions, she reports. On the one hand, when adults are not hysterical about the matter, children can assimilate alternate households without any difficulty. On the other hand, so much of the social environment is anti-homosexual, that many children do experience stress because of the teasing. Perhaps typical of others is the experience of 12 year-old Carl Cade:

> Everybody keeps asking me things. When they see my moms, they say, "I thought that other one was your mother." ... I shrug the questions off. I told one kid that one was my aunt and I just call her my mom. My mom is not very happy about me saying that. But it's hard sometimes. I don't know what the kids would do if they knew. (Carl Cade, "Two Moms, No Hamburgers," in *Different Mothers: Sons and Daughters of Lesbians Talk About Their Lives* 50, 51 [Louise Rafkin ed. 1990].)

Patterson's own studies have found that children of lesbian households report a little more stress of this sort than children of different-sex households, but also report somewhat greater feelings of self-esteem.

Although not discussed in Patterson's article, there are a few studies have found that children raised in a two-parent lesbian household are better adjusted than children raised in single-parent households, whether the single parent is straight or lesbian.[e] There have been no major empirical studies of children raised by gay male couples (that we know of).

---

e. See Richard Green et al., "Lesbian Mothers and Their Children: A Comparison with Solo Parent Heterosexual Mothers and Their Children," 15 *Archives Sexual Behav.* 167 (1986); Golombok et al., "Children in Lesbian and Single Parent Households," 562–67. See also Rhonda R. Rivera, "Legal Issues in Gay and Lesbian Parenting," in *Gay and Lesbian Parents*, 199, 226 note 79 (reporting unpublished study comparing children in households having two lesbian parents, with those in households having a single female parent, whether straight or lesbian).

Would the foregoing studies support a state adoption preference for lesbian couples over single women, single men, or gay male couples to enhance the "best interests of the child"? What if the child were lesbian-identified? See Joseph Evall, "Sexual Orientation and Adoptive Matching," 25 *Fam.L.Q.* 347 (1991). Do these studies undermine the court decisions from Florida (*Cox*), New Hampshire (*Opinion of the Justices*), and Virginia (*Bottoms*)? Does an exclusion of lesbian couples and parents in these cases pass the rational basis test of *Cleburne* or *Romer v. Evans* (Chapter 1, Section 3[B][1])? Professor Patterson testified in the trial of the Hawaii marriage case, to rebut the state's assertedly compelling interest in limiting marriage to male-female couples.

NOTE ON RACE AND ADOPTION

Under *Palmore v. Sidoti*, can a state adoption agency prefer couples of the same race as the children they adopt? Can the agency prefer different-race couples when placing children born of different-race couples? There is a debate within critical scholarship as to whether or not it is good ever to place African–American babies in non-African–American households, as such babies would be deprived of their racial heritage.[f] Could a stringent policy of not placing such children outside their race survive *Palmore*?

The Multiethnic Placement Act of 1994, Pub. L. No. 103–382, 108 Stat. 3518 (1994), codified at 42 U.S.C. § 5115a, provides that an adoption agency or service that is run or subsidized by the state cannot "categorical-ly" discriminate on the basis of race in its child placement policies. The law also provides that such an agency "may consider the cultural, ethnic, or racial background of the child and the capacity of the prospective foster or adoptive parents to meet the needs of a child of this background as one of a number of factors used to determine the best interests of the child." 42 U.S.C. § 5115a(a)(2). Are there constitutional problems with this provision? See also the Indian Child Welfare Act of 1978, codified at 25 U.S.C. § 1901 *et seq.*

PART B.   ISSUES ARISING OUT OF SURROGACY AND ARTIFICIAL INSEMINATION

Many male-female couples have difficulty conceiving the children they desire, and they turn to doctors who can increase their odds of conception through artificial insemination and sperm-washing techniques. Beginning in the 1970s, couples where the wife was infertile sometimes turned to another woman, a "surrogate," to be artificially inseminated by the hus-

---

f. See generally Rita James Simon, *Transracial Adoption* (1977); Elizabeth Bar-   tholet, "Where Do Black Children Belong?

band. Such surrogacy arrangements were controversial.[g] Critics, including the New Jersey Supreme Court in the celebrated "Baby M" case, maintained that surrogacy arrangements were tantamount to baby-selling, put women to an unbearable choice of giving up their babies for money, and exploited poor women in favor of yuppie couples. Proponents maintained that surrogacy is empowering to women and fulfills human needs of families that otherwise might not be able to bear children. See the analysis in Section 1(A) of this chapter.

Whilst heterosexuals were involved in the messy battle over the surrogacy issue, lesbians and some single heterosexual women were quietly taking advantage of surrogacy's flip side: artificial insemination, usually through sperm banks using unknown donors or through do-it-yourself "turkey baster" insemination using known donors. The lesbian baby boom of the 1980s was the result, and thousands of children are now coming of age within lesbian families. Gay men completed the circle in the 1990s, when they turned to surrogacy to create a tiny "gay-by" boomlet.

Surrogacy and artificial insemination might be the ultimate in privatization of the family, for they delink baby creation from connubial sex, and in many cases from even having a partner. (Families we choose might just be one parent and one child.) To the contrary, this phenomenon is highly regulated. Consider the following.

Marla J. Hollandsworth, Gay Men Creating Families Through Surro–Gay Arrangements: A Paradigm for Reproductive Freedom

3 *American University Journal of Gender & the Law* 183, 202–03, 204–13 (1995).*

In 1988, the National Conference of Commissioners on Uniform State Laws approved the USCACA [the Uniform Status of Children of Assisted Conception Act]. "The Act was designed primarily to effect the security and well being of those children born and living in our midst as a result of assisted conception," specifically artificial insemination by donor, in vitro fertilization, and surrogacy agreements. The intent of the Act is to give such a child "the same rights in property and inheritance as though conceived through natural means." It purports to accomplish this in three parts. The first part, sections 1–4, defines the legal relationship of the child to the adults involved in the assisted conception. The second part, Alternative A, creates a court-supervised surrogacy arrangement that is enforceable 180 days after the surrogate's last artificial insemination, provided she

---

The Politics of Race Matching in Adoption," 139 *U. Pa. L. Rev.* 1163 (1991).

g. Critical literature includes Martha A. Field, *Surrogate Motherhood: The Legal and Human Issues* (2d ed. 1990); "Colloquy: *In re Baby M,*" 76 Geo.L.J. 1717–1844 (1988). Literature supporting surrogacy includes Lori B.

Andrews, *Between Strangers: Surrogate Mothers, Expectant Fathers, and Brave New Babies* (1989); Carmel Shalev, *Birth Power: The Case for Surrogacy* (1989).

has not exercised her right to terminate the agreement. Alternative B of the Act provides that surrogacy agreements are void. Any child born to a married surrogate, with the consent of her husband, is the child of both her and her husband. In cases where her husband is not a party to the agreement or she is not married, paternity of the child is governed by the Uniform Parentage Act.

Under the USCACA, the following definitions apply:

"[S]urrogate" means an adult woman who enters into an agreement to bear a child through assisted conception for intended parents. "Intended parents" means a man and a woman, married to each other, who enter into an agreement under this [Act] providing that they will be the parents of a child born to a surrogate through assisted conception using egg or sperm of one or both of the intended parents.

The surrogacy agreement is effectuated by placing the child with the father and his wife, who then adopts the child through a stepparent adoption. Under the USCACA definitions, therefore, an unmarried man would not be an *intended parent*. Moreover, gay men, because they cannot legally marry, cannot use the stepparent adoption statutes as a way to terminate the birth mother's parental rights. If the jurisdiction in which the gay father resides has adopted the language of the USCACA, he would have to rely on an independent legal basis for terminating the birth mother's parental rights.
* * *

Several states have adopted a version of the USCACA, Alternative A, to regulate surrogacy.[98] These regulatory schemes restrict the *intended parents* to married couples, precluding an unmarried person from entering into a surrogacy agreement. Washington state surrogacy statutes, on the other hand, do not restrict surrogacy to a married couple; and under the broad language of the statutes, an unmarried man could enter into a surrogacy agreement where the surrogate mother voluntarily relinquishes her parental rights to the child. Arkansas is the only state that specifically acknowledges that an unmarried man may contract with a woman to have a child whom he will parent.

Many states have adopted statutes that make surrogacy agreements void and unenforceable.[102] While these prohibitions preclude a party to the agreement from obtaining specific performance on the contract, in some states, the donor may still be held to be the father of the child pursuant to the states' artificial insemination statutes. In these states the court is left with little direction concerning the respective parental rights of the donor and birth mother, leaving open the option of proceeding with the agreement and placing the child with the biological father pursuant to the best interests of the child. However, in other states the statutory provisions

---

98. [The author describes the statutes in Florida, Nevada, New Hampshire, Virginia.]

102. [The author describes the statutory schemes in the District of Columbia, Indiana, Kentucky, Louisiana, Michigan, Nebraska, New York, North Dakota, and Oregon.]

making such agreements void and unenforceable as a matter of public policy are accompanied by criminal and/or civil sanctions in agreements that involve compensation. In these states the donor and birth mother's respective parental rights remain unclear. The practice commentaries that accompany the New York statute indicate that the donor is the legal father, and the birth mother may consent to the adoption by the father but would forfeit any payment exceeding those allowed in adoptions. Furthermore, Utah and Washington criminalize compensated surrogacy but recognize surrogacy contracts and resolve any resulting custody disputes pursuant to the best interests of the child standard.

Unless a state regulates surrogacy arrangements, the sperm donor's parental rights are uncertain. Because surrogacy arrangements are accomplished through donor insemination, artificial insemination statutes may govern the determination of the legal status of the donor with respect to the child born as a result of the insemination. This section addresses the various means courts use to make that determination. Many states have adopted statutory constructs that do not treat the donor as the father of the child as a matter of law.[108] However, a few possibilities exist that allow the donor to be recognized as the father.

The majority of states that address donor insemination follow the Uniform Parentage Act in providing that the donor of sperm used by a married couple is not the legal father of a child conceived through assisted conception performed under the supervision of a licensed physician.[110] In this statutory construct, the sperm donor may or may not be considered the father of the child if the insemination is performed by someone other than a licensed physician. Other states, which do not specifically follow the Uniform Parentage Act but that seem to have a similar scheme, also provide that an insemination performed through a physician abrogates all donor's rights as the father of the child.[111] In *Jhordan C. v. Mary K.*,[113] however, the California Court of Appeals held that the sperm donor was the legal father of the child because the parties had failed to avail themselves of the "physician inseminator" provision of the statute. The court reasoned that this statutory provision was created to protect the parties from undesired assertions of paternity. Had the parties desired to ensure that the donor could not assert parental rights, according to the

---

108. [The author cites statutes from Alabama, Alaska, Arizona, Arkansas, California, Colorado, Florida, Georgia, Illinois, Kansas, Maryland, Massachusetts, Michigan, Minnesota, Missouri, Montana, Nevada, New Jersey, New Mexico, New York, North Carolina, Tennessee, Washington, Wisconsin, Wyoming.]

110. Thirteen states have adopted identical language providing that if an insemination is performed with sperm not from the husband under the supervision of a licensed physician with written consent of the husband and wife, the husband is treated under the law as the natural father of a child thereby conceived. The donor of sperm provided to a physician for use in artificial insemination to a woman not his wife is treated as if he is not the father of the child. [Citing statutes from Alabama, California, Colorado, Illinois, Minnesota, Missouri, Montana, Nevada, New Jersey, New Mexico, Washington, Wisconsin, and Wyoming.]

111. [Describing statutes from Alaska, Connecticut, the District of Columbia, Idaho, New York, Ohio.]

113. 224 Cal.Rptr. 530 (Cal.App.1986).

court, they should have required a physician to perform the insemination. The implication derived from the case is that men who desire to use donor insemination to create a child should not use a physician to inseminate. That is, an insemination performed directly between the donor and the woman, with the donor anticipating the privileges of fatherhood, would more likely result in the donor being considered the legal father.

Many statutes provide that paternity is established, as a matter of law, to the husband of a woman who conceives through assisted conception, provided the woman obtains written consent from her husband. Similarly, other states simply provide that, as a matter of law, the sperm donor shall have no rights or obligations to a child born as a result of donor insemination.[114] In this situation the donor would have no standing to assert paternity, thus making it unlikely that the surro-gay arrangement could be effectuated. * * *

In states that do not define the donor's legal rights as a matter of law, paternity may be established pursuant to the legitimacy statutes as a question of fact. Courts consider the intent of the parties as substantiated or modified by subsequent behavior of the parties. Placement of the donor's name on the birth certificate creates a presumption that he is the father, as does his declaration of paternity. These two actions should give the donor standing to assert paternity, unless the birth mother's husband had consented to the insemination.

Another means by which the donor's rights can be defined is based on statutory schemes that allow the parties to determine the donor's rights to the child.[125] These statutes vary to the extent that they allow the intent of the parties to govern, from almost complete discretion to assign parental rights to an acknowledgment that the donor may be the legal father of the child. The most progressive of the intent statutes is the Arkansas statute, which acknowledges that children born through assisted conception may have a married couple as parents, or may have only one parent: an unmarried woman or an unmarried man. This statutory scheme allows the parties to define the intended parent or parents of the child.[127]

Although perhaps not as progressive as Arkansas, New Hampshire and Washington also have statutes that address intent. In New Hampshire a "sperm donor may be liable for support [of a child born through donor insemination] only if he signs an agreement with the other parties to that effect."[128] Thus, the child born to an unmarried woman through donor insemination would have no father as a matter of law. An unmarried donor of sperm, however, may be the legal father if he and an unmarried woman, who would be the mother of the child, agree in writing in advance of the

114. [Describing statutes from Connecticut, Idaho, North Dakota, Ohio, Oklahoma, Oregon, Texas, Virginia.]

125. [Describing, as examples, the statutes in Arkansas, New Hampshire, and Washington.]

127. Ark. Code Ann. §§ 9–10–201 to–202 (Michie 1993).

128. N.H. Rev. Stat. Ann. § 168–B:11 (1993). The statute does not specifically provide that the donor is not the legal father of the child; rather it relieves him of all legal responsibility for support of the child.

procedure that he will be the father of the child. Section 168–B:4 of the New Hampshire Revised Statutes Annotated provides for the parental rights of the birth mother to be terminated and transferred to the intended parents in a surrogacy arrangement. Because *intended parents* is defined as "persons who are married to each other," there is no statutory procedure for terminating the parental rights of the birth mother when the intended parent is an unmarried man. Although a child may be born with no legal father, no provisions are made for the birth mother to divest herself of the legal obligations of parenthood. The statute thus allows the parties to choose whether the donor will or will not be the father, but it does not allow the unmarried mother to terminate her parental rights.

Similar to New Hampshire, Washington has no provisions for terminating the mother's parental rights to the child, although the statute provides that the child can be born with no father as a matter of law.[132] This statutory scheme creates inherent inequities between men and women in the utilization of assisted conception. Thus, with the exception of the Arkansas statute, an implicit policy holds that the woman who gives birth must parent the child whereas the biological father, or donor in artificial insemination situations, is responsible for the child only if he agrees to be held as such.

NOTE ON THE CONSTITUTIONAL RIGHTS OF BIOLOGICAL FATHERS

Hollandsworth's helpful analysis makes it clear that USCACA discriminates in several ways. First, it discriminates against unmarried parents, who cannot be "intended parents" under the statute. Second, it discriminates against men who are donors. The USCACA makes sure that a child will always start off life with a mother (the biological mother) but often and increasingly leaves the child without a legal father, as when an unmarried woman becomes pregnant through insemination. Third, it discriminates against gay men who want to utilize the surrogacy option. Are any, or all, of these discriminations constitutional?[h] Hollandsworth thinks there are substantial constitutional problems, and she invokes a complicated line of cases that bear, perhaps equivocally, on the issue.

In *Stanley v. Illinois*, 405 U.S. 645 (1972), the state tried to take away a man's children after his lover, their mother, died. The Supreme Court held that an unwed father has a "liberty" in his biological child, and that the state cannot deprive the father of this liberty without "due process of law," per the Fourteenth Amendment. Yet in *Quilloin v. Walcott*, 434 U.S.

---

132. Wash. Rev. Code Ann. § 26.26.050(2) (West 1994). * * *

h. Jennifer L. Heeb, "Homosexual Marriage, the Changing American Family, and the Heterosexual Right to Privacy," 24 *Seton Hall L. Rev.* 347 (1993), argues that it would violate *Eisenstadt* (Chapter 1, Section 1[B])

for the state to limit insemination access to married women only. Contrast Ann McLean Massie, "Restricting Surrogacy to Married Couples: A Constitutional Problem? The Married–Parent Requirement in the Uniform Status of Children of Assisted Conception Act," 18 *Hastings Const'l L.Q.* 487 (1991).

246 (1978), the Court said a biological father has no right to intervene in an adoption proceeding when the father had not been active in the child's upbringing. *Quillon* allows the state to treat biological fathers differently, based upon the extent of their "commitment to the welfare of the child."

Michael H. v. Gerald D., 491 U.S. 110, 109 S.Ct. 2333, 105 L.Ed.2d 91 (1989). Carole, wife of Gerald, was having an affair with Michael and gave birth to a baby who was probably Michael's. Carole and the baby lived with Michael for several years, but when Carole reconciled with Gerald she and Gerald denied Michael visitation rights to his daughter. Michael's suit for visitation was dismissed by reason of California Evidence Code § 621, which establishes a conclusive presumption that a baby born in wedlock is the husband's child. A fractured Supreme Court upheld this result.

Justice Scalia's plurality opinion (joined in full by Chief Justice Rehnquist) found no liberty interest whatsoever, because there is no "traditional" state protection of children born in an adulterous relationship. Justice Scalia read *Stanley* as resting upon "the historic respect—indeed, sanctity would not be too strong a term—traditionally accorded to the relationships that develop within the unitary family." He found no evidence of common law respect for the Carole–Michael relationship and cited the common law's strong presumption of legitimacy as evidence that an "adulterous natural father" has no standing to assert fundamental rights. In footnote 6 of his plurality opinion, Justice Scalia invoked *Bowers* for the proposition that the Court ought not recognize as "fundamental" rights that do not have a deep and specific common law reference. Justice Scalia emphatically rejected the dissent's suggestion that "traditional" ideas of liberty be set at a higher level of generality, say "parenthood." Justice Scalia said:

> We refer to the most specific level at which a relevant tradition protecting, or denying protection to, the asserted right can be identified. If, for example, there was no societal tradition, either way, regarding the rights of the natural father of the child adulterously conceived, we would have to consult, and (if possible) reason from, the traditions regarding natural fathers in general. But there is a more specific tradition [in this case, the presumption of legitimacy], and it unqualifiedly denies protection to such a parent.

Justices O'Connor and Kennedy concurred in all of Justice Scalia's opinion except footnote 6. They feared footnote 6 to be inconsistent with *Griswold* and *Eisenstadt*, as well as *Loving*. "I would not foreclose the unanticipated by the prior imposition of a single mode of historical analysis," they said, citing Justice Harlan's opinion in *Poe*.

Justice Stevens, the fifth vote to uphold the statute, concurred only in the Court's judgment. He suggested that "a natural father might * * * have a constitutionally protected interest in his relationship with a child whose mother was married to and cohabiting with another man," in some cases at least.

Justice Brennan's dissenting opinion (joined by Justices Marshall and Blackmun) found it "ironic that an approach so utterly dependent on tradition is so indifferent to our precedents," from *Griswold* through *Stanley* through the abortion cases. Justice Brennan observed that the old common law presumption of legitimacy has lost much of its value in a world where blood tests can actually determine paternity with some precision, where women are not property of their husbands, and where marriage is not for life. New technological, cultural, and legal developments require the Court to set "tradition" at a higher level of abstraction—parenthood, child-rearing, family—than Justice Scalia would. Justice White dissented in a separate opinion.

Although Justice Scalia's footnote 6 only garnered two votes in the end, what would be the consequences of its adoption by the Court? Would *Griswold* have to be overruled? *Roe v. Wade*? *Loving v. Virginia*? Consider the consequences of *Michael H.* for the next case.

In re Thomas S. v. Robin Y.

N.Y. Supreme Court, Appellate Division, 1st Department, 1994.
209 A.D.2d 298, 618 N.Y.S.2d 356.

■ MEMORANDUM DECISION. * * *

The child, Ry R.-Y., now 12 years old, lives with her mother, respondent Robin Y., the mother's lifetime companion, Sandra R., and Sandra's child, Cade, now 14, who was also conceived through artificial insemination by a donor known to her mother. Petitioner, who is also gay, was sought out by Robin Y. as a known donor and, after several attempts in both New York and California, Robin Y. successfully inseminated herself with petitioner's semen in February 1981 at the home of a mutual friend.

Ry was born on November 16, 1981 in San Francisco, where the household temporarily relocated in connection with Sandra R.'s employment. Like Cade, Ry was given the last names of R. and Y. Petitioner is not listed on Ry's birth certificate, and R. and Y. paid all expenses associated with the pregnancy and delivery. Petitioner was, however, informed of the birth and brought congratulatory flowers to R. and Y.'s home. Later that year, the household moved back to New York where they currently occupy an apartment located in a building owned by Sandra R.

For the first three years of her life, petitioner saw Ry only once or twice while in New York on business. In accordance with an oral agreement with R. and Y., he did not call, support or give presents to her during this period. When Cade, at the age of approximately five years, started asking questions about her father, R. and Y., as they had agreed between themselves, made arrangements for Ry and Cade to meet their biological fathers.

Petitioner testified that there were approximately 26 visits with the R. and Y. family over the following six-year period, ranging in duration from a few days to two weeks. Robin Y. estimates that appellant spent a total of sixty days with the R.-Y. family over the course of those six years, and petitioner estimates 148 days. Whatever the figure, it appears that all parties concerned developed a comfortable relationship with one another. Photographs included in the exhibits depict a warm and amicable relationship between petitioner and Ry, and there are numerous cards and letters from Ry to petitioner in which she expressed her love for him.

In July 1990, petitioner asked Robin Y. for permission to take Ry and Cade to see his parents and stay at a beach house with some of his siblings and their children. It seems that petitioner felt awkward about introducing R. and Y. to his parents. R. and Y., however, were not willing to allow petitioner to take the girls unless the mothers accompanied them.

It was apparently during the course of these negotiations that petitioner revealed his desire to establish a paternal relationship with Ry. Y. and R. regarded this as a breach of their oral agreement, insisting that visitation continue on the same terms as over the past six years, viz., with their supervision. They also rejected petitioner's suggestion to consult a family counselor or mediator. Unable to resolve his differences with R. and Y. and unable to see his daughter for a period of several months, petitioner moved, by order to show cause, for an order of filiation and for visitation.

During the course of the proceedings, Family Court ordered blood tests and a psychiatric evaluation of Ry. Petitioner, Robin Y. and Ry all submitted to blood genetic marker tests pursuant to Family Court Act § 532. The tests indicated a 99.9% probability of petitioner's paternity. Psychiatric evaluation revealed a belief on Ry's part that any relationship with petitioner would necessarily disrupt her relationship with Robin Y. and Sandra R. and might therefore undermine the legitimacy of her perception of the family unit. It also revealed that, since these proceedings were instituted, Ry has expressed a desire to end all contact with petitioner.

Family Court found by clear and convincing evidence, based upon the blood tests, that petitioner is the biological father of Ry. Nevertheless, citing the doctrine of equitable estoppel, the court refused to enter an order of filiation and dismissed the proceeding. The court characterized petitioner as an "outsider attacking her [Ry's] family and refusing to give it respect," concluding that "a declaration of paternity would be a statement that her family is other than what she knows it to be and needs it to be" and, therefore, "would not be in her best interests." The court added, "Even were there an adjudication of paternity, I would deny [petitioner's] application for visitation."

It is appropriate to begin with the observation that the effect of Family Court's order is to cut off the parental rights of a man who is conceded by all concerned—the child, her mother and the court—to be the biological father. The legal question that confronts us is not, as Family Court framed it, whether an established family unit is to be broken up. Custody of the child is not now, and is unlikely ever to be, an issue between the parties. Rather the question is whether the rights of a biological parent are to be terminated. Absent strict adherence to statutory provisions, termination of those rights is in violation of well established standards of due process and cannot stand.

The asserted sanctity of the family unit is an uncompelling ground for the drastic step of depriving petitioner of procedural due process (*Lehr v. Robertson*, 463 U.S. 248). Whatever concerns and misgivings Family Court and the dissenters may entertain about visitation, custody and the child's best interests, it is clear that they are appropriately reserved for a later stage of the proceedings. * * *

The reasoning advanced by the dissent to obviate further proceedings involves the predetermination of the very issues that would normally be resolved by hearings on visitation and, if warranted, termination of parental rights. Without the order of filiation to which the law entitles him, petitioner lacks standing to seek visitation (Family Ct.Act § 549) or challenge respondent's (and the dissent's) concept of what may or may not be in the child's best interests (Social Services Law § 384–b). * * *

Even more disturbing is the suggestion that the judicial process will pose "severe traumatic consequences" to the child whose interests it is designed to protect. Petitioner is portrayed by the dissent as the villain of this case for having the temerity to request that Ry and her sister accompany him on an unsupervised visit to meet his parents, causing a "rift" and precipitating this litigation. The record, however, indicates that it was Robin Y. and Sandra S. who opposed this visit and does not reflect any initial resistance on the part of Ry. It was only some period of time after Robin Y. and Sandra S. refused petitioner any further visitation with his daughter that Ry developed overt animosity towards the man she had called "Dad" and regarded with great affection. As the Court of Appeals has noted, "The desires of young children, capable of distortive manipulation by a bitter, or perhaps even well-meaning, parent, do not always reflect the long-term best interest of the children" (*Matter of Nehra v. Uhlar*, 43 N.Y.2d 242, 249). * * *

* * * [T]he extent of petitioner's involvement in Ry's life is at once characterized by the dissent as both inadequate and overly intrusive. He is vilified for failing to sufficiently undertake his parental responsibility to provide ongoing support for the child and her education, without any consideration for whether support was necessary, solicited or even deemed desirable by her mother and Sandra R. He is criticized for having only a limited experience with the day-to-day events in his child's life, without regard for the three-thousand-mile distance between residences or the degree to which access to the child was limited by respondent and Sandra R. At the same time, petitioner's desire to communicate and visit with his daughter is portrayed as a threat to the stability and legitimacy of the family unit constituted by Ry, respondent and Sandra R. It is distressing that petitioner, who seems to have exhibited sensitivity and respect for the relationship between respondent and her domestic partner, is proposed to be compensated for his understanding by judicial extinguishment of his rights as a father. Such a result is offensive to the Court's sense of equity. Moreover, such an injustice hardly serves to promote tolerance and restraint among persons who may confront similar circumstances. It discourages resolution of disputes involving novel and complex familial relation-

ships without resort to litigation which, ideally, should only be pursued as a last resort. * * *

Family Court's disposition is no more compelled by the equities of this matter than by the law. The notion that a lesbian mother should enjoy a parental relationship with her daughter but a gay father should not is so innately discriminatory as to be unworthy of comment. Merely because petitioner does not have custody of his daughter does not compel the conclusion, embraced by the dissent, that he may not assert any right to maintain a parental relationship with her. While much is made by Family Court of the alleged oral understanding between the parties that petitioner would not assume a parental role towards Ry, any such agreement is unenforceable for failure to comply with explicit statutory requirements for surrender of parental rights (Social Services Law § 384; Family Ct. Act § 516), as the dissent concedes. * * *

Family Court presumed to apply the doctrine of equitable estoppel to foreclose any attempt by petitioner to obtain judicial consideration of his rights as a parent. However, the doctrine is more appropriately applied against the mother than against petitioner. If respondent now finds petitioner's involvement in his daughter's life to be inconvenient, she cannot deny that her predicament is the result of her own action. Not content with the knowledge of the identity of the biological father that her chosen method of conception afforded, Robin Y. initiated and fostered a relationship between petitioner and Ry. * * *

Having initiated and encouraged, over a substantial period of time, the relationship between petitioner and his daughter, respondent is estopped to deny his right to legal recognition of that relationship. The provisions of Family Ct. Act § 542(a) are clear and unambiguous and, therefore, there is no room for judicial interpretation. Having found that petitioner is the father of Ry R.-Y., Family Court was commanded by statutory direction to enter an order of filiation.

[The majority remanded the case to Family Court for further proceedings on the issue of visitation.]

■ ELLERIN, JUSTICE [joined by ROSENBERGER, PRESIDING JUSTICE] (dissenting).

* * * The complexity of the human relationships that permeate this case and the contemporary reality of millions of households that maintain alternative family life styles strongly militate against the rigid, abstract application of legal principles, not designed for situations such as this, in a way that will grievously impact upon an innocent child, now twelve years of age. This case also demonstrates, as do most emotionally charged situations, the inadequacy of current law and litigation as instruments capable of satisfactorily accommodating the competing desires and interests of each of the parties involved. Since, however, I believe that the overriding factor which must guide us is the best interests of this child, I dissent and would affirm the trial court's sensitive and well founded decision which denied a declaration of paternity to petitioner sperm donor on the basis of equitable estoppel. * * *

The record clearly establishes that for Ry's first 9 and half years of life the appellant at no time sought to establish a true parental relationship with her either by way of seeking to legally establish his paternity and assuming the responsibilities and obligations which that status entailed or by any involvement in her upbringing or schooling or by attempting to provide any support for her. He was not there when she cut her baby teeth, started to walk, was sick or in need of parental comfort or guidance, nor did he seek to involve himself in the every day decisions which are peculiarly the domain of parents—decisions as to what schools she should attend, what camps, what doctors should be consulted, the extent of her after school and social activities, the need for tutors and the like. Perhaps Ry herself best stated it when she said that to her a parent is a person who a child depends on to care for her needs. * * *

The trial court, sensitive to the issues involved, appointed a law guardian for the child and obtained the agreement of all parties to submit the child to a psychiatric evaluation. Both the law guardian and the psychiatrist strongly recommended against the declaration of paternity and further recommended that there be no court-ordered visitation. Their intensive examination of Ry's progress while raised with the family unit that she has known since birth showed that she, and Cade, in addition to having a very close and warm sisterly relationship and a warm and loving relationship with both their mothers have also functioned well in the private school which they attend and that they have strong peer relationships. Ry is a well adjusted child, who, despite experiencing some external incidents of intolerance and insensitivity to her family lifestyle, views that family as a warm, loving, supportive environment. Most significantly, Ry views this proceeding as a threat to her sense of family security. She is angry at petitioner and feels betrayed by him because she and her family had counted on him as a supporter of their unconventional family unit. The thought of visiting appellant, and her deep-seated fear that he might seek custody of her, have caused Ry anxiety and nightmares and the psychiatrist opined that forced visitation with appellant would exacerbate that anxiety and have untoward consequences. The law guardian in a lengthy and well-documented brief details the specifics of the relationships involved and the completely nonparental role occupied by appellant until the instant proceeding was commenced when Ry was almost 10 years old. Both the law guardian and the court appointed psychiatrist make clear that the best interests of Ry, now 12 years old, will be served by an affirmance of the denial of filiation, which will also eliminate Ry's custody concerns. * * *

The threshold issue that must first be determined is what rights, if any, arise from the fact that petitioner was the sperm donor and paternal biological progenitor of the child Ry. The Court of Appeals has made clear that absent "a full commitment to the responsibilities of parenthood" the mere existence of a biological link does not merit constitutional protection (*Matter of Robert O. v. Russell K.*, 604 N.E.2d 99, quoting *Lehr v. Robertson*, 463 U.S. at 261). Thus, an unwed biological father does not automatically have parental rights which must be recognized by the state independent of the child's best interests * * *.

While providing support for the child, and the child's education, would appear to be a minimal requirement for the manifestation of parenthood (see, Family Ct.Act § 513), the criteria which are particularly relevant in determining whether an unwed biological father has sufficiently undertaken his parental responsibilities to give him a protected parental interest may be garnered by reference to Domestic Relations Law § 111 which governs adoptions and delineates the various criteria which must be met before an unwed father has any protected right vis-à-vis the child. That statute provides that when the child is more than six months old, the father has a protected parental right to the extent of requiring his consent to the child's adoption, *only* if he has

maintained substantial and continuous or repeated contact with the child as manifested by: (i) the payment by the father toward the support of the child of a fair and reasonable sum, according to the father's means, and either (ii) the father's visiting the child at least monthly when physically and financially able to do so and not prevented from doing so by the person or authorized agency having lawful custody of the child, or (iii) the father's regular communication with the child or with the person or agency having the care or custody of the child, when physically and financially unable to visit the child or prevented from doing so by the person or authorized agency having lawful custody of the child. (Domestic Relations Law § 111[1][d].)

In this case there is no question that petitioner has never sought to contribute to the ongoing support of the child, or to see to her educational or other needs despite the fact that he is a professional of substantial means. On the contrary, all of the child's economic and educational needs have been provided for through her mothers and she has enjoyed a comfortable standard of living. Nor, after not seeing the child at all for the first 3 years of her life, has petitioner ever sought to visit the child on anything close to a monthly basis. His failure to do so cannot be attributed to respondent since, until very recently, the pattern of occasional visits was one with which he was in full agreement. Whether viewed within the framework of the statutory criteria or the common understanding of what parenthood entails vis-à-vis the multiple daily facets of a child's life, petitioner's conduct until the commencement of this proceeding fell far short of manifesting the willingness to take on the parental responsibilities necessary to invest him with any constitutionally recognized parental "rights" which could be terminated subject to the provisions of Social Services Law § 384–b.

[The dissenting Justices believed that the plain language of Family Law § 542, which would appear to require petitioner's parentage to be established, is subject to an implied exception based upon the principle of equitable estoppel. In the context of this case, equitable estoppel is grounded in the same considerations as the best interests of the child: the father's failure to contribute to the child's support, his infrequent contact with the child during her formative years, and the disruption threatened by his intervention in her life.]

Furthermore, and perhaps most important, a declaration of paternity in this case would be counter to this child's interests because it clearly would be only the first step in ongoing litigation which will inevitably cause severe traumatic consequences to the child and her family. Indeed, the majority's decision has already provided for further litigation in its remand for a decision on visitation. A declaration of paternity creates a platform for petitioner, as well as his parents and other members of his family, who will, by means of the order, become the child's legal relations, to seek changes in visitation and, of course, to seek custody. Indeed, even were visitation never to be granted and further litigation never to succeed, the constant, frightening potential for it is a burden that this child, who is already aware that her family is vulnerable to attack on a number of fronts, should not have to bear. It is clear that this specific fear has already taken its toll. According to the psychiatric testimony, the child believes that the order of filiation would mean that "anytime [petitioner] didn't like something he could sue." In particular, the psychiatric testimony emphasized Ry's haunting fear of the consequences should her birth mother die or become unable to care for her and the resulting ambiguous status of the woman whom she has consistently thought of as her second parent. * * *

NOTE ON ROBIN Y.'s ARGUMENTS ON APPEAL

Assume that Robin Y. wants to appeal the foregoing decision to the state's highest court, the New York Court of Appeals. What is her strongest argument? Is she likely to prevail?

As you evaluate her position, consider the following: (1) the court of appeals' precedents on issues of alternative families, especially *Alison D.* and *Braschi*; (2) issues of equity and jurisprudence, including feminist jurisprudence; and (3) legal developments or precepts from other states, such as California's *Marvin* line of cases or New Jersey's *Baby M* decision. (How would a California court handle this case?)

Finally, consider the issues in this case from a lesbian and gay perspective. Is this the defining case for differences between lesbian and gay perspectives? Or are these lesbian-feminist arguments for Thomas S.'s position and gaylegal arguments for Robin Y.'s position? See generally Katharine Arnup & Susan Boyd, "Familial Disputes? Sperm Donors, Lesbian Mothers, and Legal Parenthood," in *Legal Inversions: Lesbians, Gay Men, and the Politics of Law* 77 (Didi Herman & Carl Stychin eds., 1995).

PART C.   SECOND-PARENT ADOPTIONS

Consider the following conundrum. One partner in a same-sex couple is the legal parent of a child, whether through a custody decree, adoption, surrogacy, or artificial insemination. The three are a family of choice, but there are legal disabilities if only one of two parents has legal rights to the child. If the legal parent dies or is incapacitated, the "other" parent has few or no legal rights, and the stability of the child's family environment might be, and frequently has been, disrupted. (Recall the *Bottoms* case, where the lesbian-bashing was accomplished by the woman's own mother; there are many others involving in-laws.)

The "second" parent would like to adopt the child, but of course without terminating the parental rights of the "first" parent. State adoption statutes pose a problem, as they rest upon a heterosexual family model which assumes that adoptions will typically involve a husband-and-wife couple. Consider the statutory scheme in place for the District of Columbia. D.C.Code § 16–302 ("Persons who may adopt") provides:

> Any person may petition the court for a decree of adoption. A petition may not be considered by the court unless petitioner's spouse, if he [or she] has one, joins in the petition, except that if either the husband or wife is a natural parent of the prospective adoptee, the natural parent need not join in the petition with the adopting parent, but need only give his or her consent to the adoption. If the marital status of the petitioner changes after the time of filing the petition and before the time the decree of adoption is final, the petition must be amended accordingly.

Section 16–305 ("Petition for adoption") lists the categories of information a petitioner must supply and then concludes: "If more than one petitioner joins in a petition, the requirements of this section apply to each." Finally, § 16–312 ("Legal effects of adoption") provides in paragraph (a):

> (a) A final decree of adoption establishes the relationship of natural parent and natural child between adopter and adoptee for all purposes, including mutual rights of inheritance and succession as if adoptee were born to adopter. The adoptee takes from, through, and as a representative of his [or her] adoptive parent or parents in the same manner as a child by birth, and upon the death of an adoptee intestate, his [or her] property shall pass and be distributed in the same manner as if the adoptee had been born to the adopting parent or parents in lawful wedlock. All rights and duties including those of inheritance and succession between the adoptee, his [or her] natural parents, their issue, collateral relatives, and so forth, are cut off, except that when one of the natural parents is the spouse of the adopter, the rights and relations as between adoptee, that natural parent, and his [or her] parents and collateral relatives, including mutual rights of inheritance and succession, are in no wise altered.

What is the best statutory or constitutional argument around § 16–312(a)? Nancy Polikoff, the author of the leading article on "second-parent adoptions"—"This Child Does Have Two Mothers: Redefining Parenthood to Meet the Needs of Children in Lesbian–Mother and Other Nontraditional Families," 78 *Geo. L.J.* 459 (1990)—faced this problem when she litigated the legality of second-parent adoptions in the District. See also Suzanne Bryant, "Second Parent Adoptions: A Model Brief," 2 *Duke J. Gender L. & Pol'y* 233 (1995). The following is the result of Polikoff's efforts.

In re M.M.D. & B.H.M.

District of Columbia Court of Appeals, 1995.
662 A.2d 837.

■ FERREN, ASSOCIATE JUDGE. * * *

[Judge Ferren's statement of the facts of the case was taken from the trial court's opinion.]

Hillary is a healthy, happy, and delightful 2 ½ year-old Black/Hispanic child who was born on August 15, 1991 in the District of Columbia. Hillary's biological mother is a young, attractive Black woman who met Bruce and Mark after reading an advertisement that they had placed in a local newspaper. The ad identified the petitioners as a gay couple who were seeking to adopt a child. Bruce and Mark are adult, white, homosexual males who have shared an intimate relationship for almost five years.

At the time she read the newspaper advertisement, the birth mother was several months pregnant and was not on good terms with her mother with whom she then lived. The birth mother, therefore, not only answered the ad, but shortly after meeting the petitioners, she began living with them. Eventually, she delivered Hillary on August 15, 1991. All went as planned when Hillary's mother signed her consent to an adoption of Hillary on September 9, 1991. Bruce filed the first petition to adopt the child on the following day.

The baby's natural mother and Bruce reached an agreement that the mother would continue to have visitation privileges with Hillary, even after the adoption was finalized. These visitation arrangements, however, did not proceed smoothly. Rather, the mother accused Bruce of denying her access to Hillary, and eventually she filed a motion to vacate her consent to the adoption. This motion was submitted to this court and was scheduled for a hearing.

After much discussion and several preliminary hearings, the parties reached an accord which they reduced to writing. Essentially, Hillary's mother and Bruce agreed again to permit the mother to visit with Hillary even after a final decree of adoption was issued.

In their discussion with the court about this agreement, the parties expressly stated that they understood that under the District of Columbia law, the natural mother had no enforceable right to visit Hillary after a final decree of adoption was signed because the law in the District of Columbia, as the parties understood it, mandated that upon the signing of the final decree of adoption, all of the mother's rights as a parent would be terminated. No one suggested that this severance of Hillary's mother's rights was waivable. At the parties' request, this court reviewed the agreement and satisfied itself that the natural mother understood that she was in no way obligated to settle the case; that she could instead proceed with the hearing on her motion to vacate her consent; and that the agreement to allow continued visitation with Hillary could not be enforced under the law as it existed in the District of Columbia. This court was further satisfied that the mother's decision to reaffirm her consent to the adoption and to withdraw her motion to vacate her consent was voluntarily made. Therefore, since all of the evidence supported a finding that Bruce M. was a suitable person to adopt Hillary, and since Hillary was clearly suitable to be adopted, and because this court found that the adoption was in Hillary's best interest, this court signed the final decree of adoption in favor of Bruce M.

In March 1993, both Bruce M. and Mark D. petitioned to adopt Hillary. In addition, Bruce M. signed his consent to the petition to adopt in favor of himself and Mark D.

The petitioners, Bruce and Mark, are thirty and thirty-five respectively. They are both Catholics who are members of a gay and lesbian religious organization called Dignity. Bruce has a Bachelor's Degree in Electrical Engineering and a Master's Degree in Engineering Computer Science. He currently works as an engineer for a major corporation. Mark has a Bachelor's Degree in Political Science and a Master's Degree in Public Administration. He now works as a Court Administrator in the state of Pennsylvania.

The petitioners own a condominium that they bought jointly and have shared since 1990. They have committed themselves to each other as a family to the extent legally possible, and they seek to raise Hillary together, *whether or not* their joint petition to adopt her is approved. They have, for example, introduced Hillary to, and included her as, a part of both of their extended families. They shared in her baptism at their church. They have enrolled her in a monthly play group arranged by the Gay and Lesbian Parent Coalition of Washington. Hillary is a beneficiary in their wills, insurance policies and other funds.

Hillary appears to be bonded equally well to both Bruce and Mark. She calls Bruce "Daddy" and Mark "Poppy." Bruce cooks most of the meals, while Mark often reads the bedtime stories. They both take Hillary on outings. The Department of Human Services has recommended in favor of their joint petition.

[The lower court, however, held that the adoption law did not permit the joint petition, even though it satisfied the best interests of Hillary. Writing for the court majority (himself and Judge Mack), Judge Ferren reversed. The following is his summary of the grounds for interpreting the adoption statutes to permit this join adoption.]

1. D.C.Code § 16–302 (1989 Repl.) expressly authorizes adoptions by "[a]ny person," without limitation. It then imposes a restriction on adoption by a spouse of the natural parent (that parent must "consent"), as well as a restriction on adoption by every other married petitioner (the petitioner's spouse must "join[ ]in the petition"). There is no mention of adoptions by unmarried couples. A later provision, D.C.Code § 16–305, refers generally to adoptions by "more than one petitioner," and D.C.Code § 16–312(a) acknowledges the "adopting parent or parents." Finally, D.C.Code § 49–202 (1990 Repl.), which antedates the adoption statute, provides that "[w]ords importing the singular . . . shall be held to include

the plural" unless that "construction would be unreasonable." These provisions, taken together, neither assuredly authorize adoptions by unmarried couples nor conclusively preclude them. The court, therefore, must consider this ambiguous statutory language in light of other interpretive criteria.

2.   The legislative histories of the 1954 (present) adoption statute and of its 1937 predecessor add little to our understanding of legislative intent except for a significant, unexplained omission: beginning with the 1937 statute, Congress withheld language found in the first (1895) District of Columbia adoption statute limiting adoptions by couples to "husband and wife." After 1895, no committee report or comment from the House or Senate floor addressed "who may adopt." And nothing in the legislative history can be said to exclude adoptions by unmarried couples.

3.   Because the statutory language and legislative history of the 1954 statute do not indicate that Congress paid attention to unmarried couples, one way or another, the language in D.C.Code § 16–302 specifying restrictions that apply "if" a petitioner has a "spouse" does not provide a basis for inferring that Congress consciously decided to exclude unmarried couples from eligibility to adopt. According to applicable case law, the *expressio unius* canon of construction (expression of one thing excludes another) only applies when the legislature is aware of the matter excluded.

4.   In contrast, the doctrine of "strict construction" would limit adoptions to couples who are married, regardless of whether Congress thought about the matter, simply because the statute refers to married couples and no others. This court, however, has rejected strict construction of the adoption statute in favor of "liberal construction" in other adoption contexts. Moreover, courts in other states have employed liberal construction to allow adoptions by unmarried couples under statutes similar to the District of Columbia statute, in order to further the statute's beneficial purposes. The trial court's adherence to strict construction, therefore, is not easily justified.

5.   The traditional interpretive criteria cautioning against statutory construction that leads to "absurd results" or "obvious injustice," while marginally relevant (if relevant at all), cut in favor of a liberal construction that includes unmarried couples as eligible adopters.

6.   Under the circumstances, where the statutory language, legislative history, and other applicable criteria are not dispositive, the controlling interpretive criterion, according to applicable case law, is the court's obligation to effectuate the legislative purpose of the adoption statute. There is no proper way of discerning legislative intent based on how Congress in 1954 would have answered the question whether unmarried couples should be eligible to adopt. This court, therefore, must focus on the general purpose or policy that motivated Congress to pass the adoption statute. There is considerable case law emphasizing that the "paramount concern" of the adoption statute—its central beneficial purpose—is the "best interests of the prospective adoptee." We conclude that this purpose is better served by applying a liberal, inclusionary reading of the statute to

the facts presented here, for which there is persuasive decisional precedent; this case and others demonstrate that adoption by an unmarried couple can be in a child's best interests—especially when the alternative would be a child's living in a family with two unmarried parents, only one of whom would be allowed to establish a formal parental relationship.

7. As indicated earlier, the statutory rule of construction in D.C.Code § 49–202 would convert § 16–302 to say "any persons," not merely "any person," may petition for an adoption if that construction would not be "unreasonable." Because we have concluded that liberal construction of the statute is appropriate here, and because this case and others show that adoptions by unmarried couples can be in the best interests of children, there is no basis for concluding that adoptions by unmarried couples would, categorically, be "unreasonable." We therefore are satisfied that § 49–202 supports the analysis here and that § 16–302 should be construed accordingly.

8. We conclude, finally, that the so-called "stepparent exception" in D.C.Code § 16–312(a) would apply, under the circumstances, to prevent termination of the relationship between Hillary and her unmarried natural parent (Bruce by adoption) if his life partner (Mark) is allowed to adopt the child and live as a family with Bruce and Hillary.

9. The trial court's order is reversed and the case remanded for further proceedings to determine whether it will be in Hillary's best interest for Mark, as well as Bruce, to adopt her. * * *

■ [We omit the concurring opinion of ASSOCIATE JUDGE MACK and the dissenting opinion of ASSOCIATE JUDGE STEADMAN.]

Postscript. On remand, the trial court granted Bruce and Mark's adoption petition.

NOTE ON RACE, SEXUAL ORIENTATION, AND SECOND–PARENT ADOPTIONS

1. *Lesbian and Gay Families We Choose.* Second-parent adoptions are a way to assure that the child is not harmed by the same-sex parents' inability to marry. Thus, if the biological parent or, as in the D.C. case, the first adoptive parent were to die, the "second" parent would automatically retain custody over the child. In the absence of such legal relationship, other blood relatives sometimes take the child away from the second parent, usually to the detriment of the child. For a heart-rending example of a child who was torn from her surviving parent by the biological grandparents, see Laura Benkov, *Reinventing the Family: The Emerging Story of Lesbian and Gay Parents* (1994).

Second-parent adoptions are a relatively new legal issue, and so there are authoritative resolutions in only a few states. They are apparently routine in California, and some other state supreme courts have been as receptive as the District's Court of Appeals was. See *In re Adoption of B.L.V.B.*, 628 A.2d 1271 (Vt.1993) (allowing second-parent adoption under statute that included a "cut off" provision with a "stepparent" exception similar to D.C.Code § 16–312[a]); *Adoption of Tammy*, 619 N.E.2d 315, 320 (Mass.1993) (sustaining joint petition for adoption of child by biological mother and her same-sex, committed life partner, without termination of biological mother's parental relationship under termination provision similar to D.C.Code § 16–312[a]); *In re Adoption of Two Children by H.N.R.*, 666 A.2d 535 (N.J.Super.1995) (following Vermont and Massachusetts precedents); *In re Evan*, 583 N.Y.S.2d 997, 1000 (Sur.Ct.1992) (upholding adoption of child by biological mother's same-sex partner under statutory provision similar to D.C.Code § 16–312[a]). The leading decision rejecting second-parent adoptions is *In re Angel Lace M.*, 516 N.W.2d 678, 683 & nn. 8–9, 11 (Wis.1994) (unmarried mother's life partner could not adopt child without terminating mother's parental rights because statute literally required such termination unless birth parent is spouse of adoptive parent).

2.   *Adoption versus Marriage.* Judge Ferren's opinion was a highly dynamic interpretation of the District's adoption laws. Judge Steadman's dissent relied on the *expressio unius* canon to argue that adoption should be confined to the cases clearly contemplated by the legislature. Judge Ferren responded that (1) the adoption law should be liberally and not strictly interpreted; (2) the legislature was not thinking about unmarried couples generally; and (3) the D.C. Code states that singular words should also be read to be plural unless unreasonable. Are these persuasive responses? Is it plausible to think that the legislature would have acquiesced in a gay male couple's adopting a child?

Note how each of Judge Ferren's arguments supports an interpretation of the District's marriage laws to include same-sex marriage (Problem 9–2): (1) the marriage law should be liberally construed to be consistent with the District's Human Rights Act, which prohibits sex and sexual orientation discrimination by the District; (2) the legislature was not thinking about same-sex couples generally, and in 1977 when the issue did arise the legislature rejected the Catholic Church's proposal to make its gender-neutral language more specific; (3) the D.C. Code states that male terms shall include their female equivalents, and vice versa, unless the statute specifically says otherwise, which means that the marriage law's gendered consanguinity provisions and the divorce law's gendered provisions are constructively gender neutral. While it is doubtful that the legislature intended to allow gay and lesbian couples to marry, it is just as doubtful that the legislature intended such couples to adopt children as couples.

The irony is that all these arguments were rejected in the D.C. same-sex marriage case—and the opinion rejecting them was written by Judge Ferren! See *Dean v. District of Columbia*, 653 A.2d 307 (D.C.App.1995). How can you explain the different results?

3.   *The Submerged Race Issue.* Note the important race issue in the case: a white couple is adopting a Latino–African–American child. Black social workers in the 1970s maintained that such adoptions are wrong, because they displace the African–American child from her or his racial heritage. This view retains a vigorous constituency. See Twilo L. Perry, "The

Transracial Adoption Controversy: An Analysis of Discourse and Subordination," 21 *N.Y.U. Rev. L. & Soc. Change* 33 (1993–94). Harlon Dalton argues, in an excerpt reprinted in Chapter 12, Section 1, that the African–American community is also very ambivalent about homosexual relationships. Anita Allen, "Surrogacy, Slavery and the Ownership of Life," 13 *Harv. J.L. & Pub. Pol'y* 139–49 (1990), argues that surrogacy is especially problematic in this context, where a white couple is "buying" a black baby.

The department of social services in *M.M.D.* favored the adoption of Hillary by Mark and Bruce, but what if the department had opposed the adoption for reasons of racial heritage? How should that affect the court's exercise of its discretion? Would consideration of such factors be inconsistent with *Palmore v. Sidoti* in Part A of this section? The Multiethnic Placement Act of 1994 described in the notes to *Palmore*? For examples of adoptions by white lesbian couples of children of color, over the objections of blood kin, see *In re Adoption of Jessica N.*, 609 N.Y.S.2d 209 (N.Y.App. 1994); *In re Commitment of J.N.*, 601 N.Y.S.2d 215 (N.Y.Fam.Ct.1993).

PROBLEM 9–6

SECOND–PARENT ADOPTIONS IN NEW YORK

Two cases are before the New York Court of Appeals. Roseanne M.A. is the mother of Jacob and is no longer living with Jacob's biological father. Since Jacob was a year old, however, she has been living with Stephen T.K. Stephen files a petition to adopt Jacob. P.I. is the biological mother of Dana, whom she conceived through artificial insemination. Her lesbian partner of 19 years is G.M. G.M. files a petition to adopt Dana. In both cases the biological mothers would retain all their parental rights.

The relevant statutes are the following: Domestic Relations Law (DRL) § 110 provides that an "adult unmarried or an adult husband and his adult wife together may adopt another person." DRL § 114 says that when it is "satisfied that the best interests of the * * * child will be promoted thereby," a court "shall make an order approving the adoption." DRL § 117 says: "After the making of an order of adoption the natural parents of the adoptive child shall be relieved of all parental duties toward and of all responsibilities for and shall have no rights over such adoptive child or to his property by descent or succession."

Recall from Section 1(B) of this chapter that the Court of Appeals has interpreted the DRL in *Robert Paul P.* and *Alison D.*, two precedents binding on the court. What arguments can be made against the adoptions of Jacob and Dana? How do you think the Court of Appeals should rule? How will it rule? See *In re Jacob*, 636 N.Y.S.2d 716, 660 N.E.2d 397 (N.Y. 1995).

CHAPTER 10

SEXUALITY AND GENDER IN THE WORKPLACE

SECTION 1   Exclusions From Government Employment

SECTION 2   The Statutory Ban Against Sex Discrimination

SECTION 3   Current Issues in Workplace Discrimination

What does it mean to talk about "sexuality in the workplace"? Some possibilities include:

- sexualized persons (women, unmarried pregnant women, gay men, lesbians) assertedly not belonging in the workplace;

- the visible manifestation of sexuality, the traditional example being pregnancy and the more recent example being AIDS;

- the choreographed display of gendered ideals, such as a waitress' wearing tight, body-revealing clothing, or their confusion, such as a man's wearing such clothing;

- eroticized behavior, exhibiting one's sexuality in the workplace;

- the use of sexuality to gain advantages in the workplace (e.g., sleeping your way to the top);

- the use of sexuality as a mechanism of harassment, usually to dominate the space and dynamics of the workplace by those traditionally empowered.

All of these meanings emerge in the cases and other materials that you will read in this chapter. Much of the law in this field implicitly seeks the expurgation of sexuality from the workplace. Is this merely an appropriate, rational suppression of eroticization from an arena in which it does not belong? Consider the following analysis.

Rosemary Pringle, Sexuality at Work

From *Secretaries Talk* (1988).*

If the boss-secretary relation is organised around sexuality and family imagery this seems to place it outside the modern bureaucratic structures that are a feature of all large organisations. The relationship is often conceptualised either as archaic or as marginal to the workings of bureaucracy 'proper'. It is argued here that, on the contrary, the boss-secretary relationship is the most visible aspect of a pattern of domination based on desire and sexuality. Far from being an exception, it vividly illustrates the workings of modern bureaucracies. Gender and sexuality are central not only in the boss-secretary relation but in all workplace power relations.

Two bodies of theory are important to the development of this argument. A variety of feminist analyses, particularly of sexual harassment, indicate the ubiquity of coercive sexual encounters in the workplace; and theorists such as Marcuse and Foucault have indicated, in their different ways, the connections between sexual *pleasure* and the operations of *power*. By contrast, most organisation theory continues to treat sexuality and gender as marginal or incidental to the workplace. In doing so, however, it expresses a widely held view that while gender was central to 'traditional' social relations it has become outmoded in 'modern' society which is more concerned with 'personhood'. Since degendering is implicit in the modernist emphasis on rationality and in the development of liberal democratic institutions, it is important to start by considering the ways in which gender is suppressed in the main texts.

For [Max] Weber bureaucracy is progressive in that it breaks down the old patriarchal structures and removes the arbitrary power held by fathers and masters in traditional society. He distinguishes between traditionalism, which is patriarchal, and the rational-legal order of the modern world which promises the end of tyranny and despotism and the development of liberal democracy. All attempts to theorise bureaucracy have been carried out in the shadow of Weber's classical account. He still sets the terms of the dominant frameworks for studies of power and organisations. Although the limits of his theory have been clearly shown in more than half a century of organisation studies, Weber's version retains a powerful ideological hold. People's views of how organisations actually do work and how they 'ought' to work are still filtered through Weber and the theory becomes, in some sense, a self-fulfilling prophecy.

Weber has been given a favourable reading by liberal feminists because he does appear to provide a basis for understanding breakdown of patriarchal relations. Equal Employment Opportunity and Affirmative Action plans, for example, emphasize the importance of excluding 'private' considerations and insist on the impersonal application of rules. Secretaries, it is thought, should ignore or reject the sexual and familial images and focus on skills and career ladders. The implication here is that secretarial work should be 'rationalized', made to fit the bureaucratic pattern. In her broadly liberal feminist analysis, *Men and Women of the Corporation* [1977], Rosabeth Moss Kanter denies that gender or sexuality have much explanatory potential. She observes that 'what look like sex differences may really be power differences' and that 'power wipes out sex' [pp. 201–12]. In this framework the problem for secretaries is that they lack power; they are caught up in an old-fashioned patriarchal relationship that is out of kilter with 'modern' business practices. The question then becomes how can individual secretaries remove themselves from these backwaters and place themselves on the management ladder? Kanter's very lucid analysis of the power structure is designed to help individuals articulate their positions and thereby improve their own manoeuvering for power.

It is not surprising that Weber should have had such influence for he is one of the great spokespersons of 'modernity'. Thinkers of his stature are not easily 'overturned'. Even theorists who take a critical stance, or who self-consciously define themselves as 'post-modern', find themselves returning to at least some of the 'modernist' assumptions. Kanter herself was explicitly rejecting the Weberian emphasis on the rationality and goal-directedness of bureaucracies, yet by playing down gender and sexuality she eventually returned to that which she had criticized. Whatever modifications or even radical revisions are made to the theory it retains a core of 'truth' which makes it difficult to move outside it. This 'core' needs to be deconstructed if gender and sexuality are to be made central to the analysis of the workplace. While 'modernist' analyses and bureaucratic structures offer certain gains for women they are not, in fact, gender-neutral and may in fact represent a subtler and hence more stable version of male domination than the earlier models. Feminist and 'post-modern' critiques are therefore very important in informing political and workplace strategies.

According to Weber the overriding concerns of bureaucratic organisations are efficiency and consistency in the application of rules. Authority established by rules stands in contrast to the 'regulation of relationships through individual privilege and bestowals of favour' which characterizes patrimonialism. Traditional forms of domination are based on the household unit and are patriarchal in the direct sense that the father, as head of the family, possesses authority. In larger forms of traditional organisation authority is patrimonial, that is, it takes the form of personal allegiance to the master. In bureaucracy, by contrast, loyalty is to an office not to a particular person. Impersonality and the separation of the public and private spheres distinguish bureaucracy from traditionalism. As theorised by Weber, bureaucracy 'has a "rational" character: rules, means, ends, and matter-of-factness dominate its bearing ... The march of bureaucracy has destroyed structures of domination which had no rational character, in the special sense of the term'.

According to Weber's 'ideal type', bureaucracies are based on impersonality, functional specialisation, a hierarchy of authority and the impartial application of rules. There are well-defined duties for each specialised position and recruitment takes place on criteria of demonstrated knowledge and competence. Authority is held in the context of strict rules and regulations and graded hierarchically with the supervision of lower offices by higher ones. Authority established by rules stands in contrast to the 'regulation of relationships through individual privileges and bestowals of favor' which characterised traditional structures. Above all there is a separation of the public world of rationality and efficiency from the private sphere of emotional and personal life.

The boss-secretary relationship runs against every one of these criteria. By having direct access to the powerful, secretaries are outside the hierarchy of authority. Far from being specialised, they can be called upon to do just about anything, and their work may overlap with that of their bosses. The relationship is based on personal rapport, involves a degree of intimacy, day-to-day familiarity and shared secrets unusual for any but lovers or close friends, and is capable of generating intense feelings of loyalty, dependency and personal commitment. How are we to explain this least 'bureaucratic' of relationships? Is it merely an exception or does its existence suggest problems with the way bureaucracy itself has been theorised? * * *

It remains important to analyse the discourse of 'bureaucratic rationality' as it affects men and women. This involves not so much a rejection of Weber as a rereading designed to bring out the underlying assumptions. It can be argued that while the rational-legal or bureaucratic form presents itself as gender-neutral, it actually constitutes a new kind of patriarchal structure. The apparent neutrality of rules and goals disguises the class and gender interests served by them. Weber's account of 'rationality' can be interpreted as a commentary on the construction of a particular kind of masculinity based on the exclusion of the personal, the sexual and the feminine from any definition of 'rationality'. The values of instrumental rationality are strongly associated with the masculine individual, while the feminine is associated with that 'other' world of chaos and disorder. This does not mean that men are in fact 'rational' or that women are 'emotional' but rather that they learn to recognise themselves in these conceptions.

It may be argued that 'rationality' requires as a condition of its existence the simultaneous creation of a realm of the Other, be it personal, emotional, sexual or 'irrational'. Masculine rationality attempts to drive out the feminine but does not exist without it. 'Work' and 'sex' are implicitly treated as the domains of the 'conscious' and the 'unconscious'. But far from being separate spheres the two are thoroughly intertwined. Despite the illusion of ordered rationality, workplaces do not actually manage to exclude the personal or sexual. Rather than seeing the presence of sexuality and familial relations in the workplace as an aspect of traditional, patriarchal authority, it makes more sense to treat them as part of modern organisational forms. I am concerned here not with 'actual' families but with the family symbolism that structures work as well as personal relationships. The media, advertising and popular culture are saturated in such imagery, which provides a dominant set of social meanings in contemporary capitalist society. * * *

If we accept that a series of discourses on sexuality underpin bureaucratic control it is possible to see secretaries not as marginal but as paradigmatic of how that power operates. Thus the boss-secretary relation need not be seen as an anomalous piece of traditionalism or of an incursion of the private sphere, but rather as a site of strategies of power in which sexuality is an important though by no means the only dimension. Far from being marginal to the workplace, sexuality is everywhere. It is alluded to in dress and self-presentation, in jokes and gossip, looks and flirtations, secret affairs and dalliances, in fantasy, and in the range of coercive behaviours that we now call sexual harassment. Rather than being exceptional in its sexualisation, the boss-secretary relation is an important nodal point for the organisation of sexuality and pleasure. This is no less true when the boss happens to be a woman.

Sex at work is very much on display. It is undoubtedly true that for both men and women sexual fantasies and interactions are a way of killing time, of giving a sense of adventure, of livening up an otherwise boring day. As Michael Korda put it, 'the amount of sexual energy circulating in any office is awe-inspiring, and given the slightest sanction and opportunity it bursts out'.[a] Marcuse was one of the first to recognise the pervasiveness of sexuality in the workplace and to try to theorise it. He recognised that it was not just an instance of incomplete repression but was encouraged as a means of gratification in otherwise boring jobs. If open-plan offices are about surveillance they are also, he suggests, about controlled sex.

Marcuse introduced the concept of 'repressive desublimation' to explain how people were being integrated into a system which in its sweeping rationality, which propels efficiency and growth, is itself irrational.[b] He pointed to the ways in which,

> without ceasing to be an instrument of labour, the body is allowed to exhibit its sexual features in the everyday work world and in work relations ... The sexy office and sales girls, the handsome, virile junior executive and floor worker are highly marketable commodities, and the possession of suitable mistresses ... facilitates the career of even the less exalted ranks in the business community ... Sex is integrated into work and public relations and is thus made susceptible to (controlled) satisfaction ... But no matter how controlled ... it is also gratifying to the managed individuals ... Pleasure, thus adjusted, generates submission.[c]

a. [Eds.] Michael Korda, *Male Chauvinism! How It Works* 108 (1972).

b. [Eds.] Herbert Marcuse, *One Dimensional Man* 12 (1968).

c. [Eds.] *Id.* at 70–71.

In Foucault's account, sexuality in the workplace is not simply repressed or sublimated or subjected to controlled expression. It is actively produced in a multiplicity of discourses and interactions. Modern Western societies have accumulated a vast network of discourses on sex and pleasure. We expect to find pleasure in self-improvement in both our work and non-work activities. Purposive activity operates not through the denial of pleasure but its promise: we will become desirable. * * *

The difficulty with both Marcuse and Foucault is that they are gender-blind. While they establish the centrality of sexuality in the workplace they pay very little attention to gender. Marcuse presumes that men and women are equally and similarly oppressed, ignoring the ways that women are required to market sexual attractiveness to men. Foucault acknowledges gender struggles but does not afford them any priority or permanence. Central to his work is the idea that there is no constant human subject or any rational course to history. If there is no human subject then for Foucault there is no gendered subject. Feminist struggles are, like any others, merely immediate responses to local and specific situations. Foucault's account of power is counterposed to any binary opposition between rulers and ruled. Though he underplays the significance of gender he does provide the basis for developing a more dynamic and fluid conception of power relations between men and women. 'Male power' is not simply and unilaterally imposed on women—gender relations are a process involving strategies and counter-strategies of power.

Where organisation theorists have maintained a division between sex and work, women are left in little doubt that the two go together. Women are constantly aware of sexual power structures and the need to put up barriers against men. Though they might enjoy male company and male jokes they are careful to limit their participation and to make it clear to men 'how far they can go'. Many secretaries have chosen their current jobs on the basis of minimising any further experiences of sexual harassment. One head office, nicknamed the 'twenty five year club' because of the length of time most of the managers had been there, was regarded as something of a refuge. If there was no sexual excitement on the sixteenth floor, at least there was no danger.

The term 'sexual harassment' came into the language around 1976 and was quickly taken up as a dimension of gender inequality at work. MacKinnon argued that 'intimate violation of women by men is sufficiently pervasive ... as to be nearly invisible. Contained by internalized and structural forms of power, it has been nearly inaudible ... Tacitly, it has been both acceptable and taboo; acceptable for men to do, taboo for women to confront, even to themselves'.[d] In the 1980s it became possible in Australia to bring sexual harassment cases under anti-discrimination legislation.

Sexual harassment has often been dismissed either as trivial and isolated or as referring to universal 'natural' behaviours. Secretaries who

---

d. [Eds.] Catharine A. MacKinnon, *Sexual Harassment of Working Women* 1 (1979).

discussed it in the interviews tended to feel that they are responsible for controlling men's behaviour, that women should be able to deal with unwanted advances and preferably avoid getting into the situation in the first place. Yet a number of them had experienced sexual harassment and had even left jobs because of it. Feminists have insisted that sexual harassment is not only an individual problem but part of an organised expression of male power. Sexual harassment functions particularly to keep women out of non-traditional occupations and to reinforce their secondary status in the workplace. * * *

The sexual division of labour is mediated by gender constructions that in numerous aspects bear on sexuality. Rich's notion of 'compulsory hetero-sexuality' (1983) can be applied here,[e] for the sexual 'normality' of daily life in the office is relentlessly heterosexual. The norm is reproduced in concrete social practices ranging from managerial policies through to every-day informal conversations.[f] It involves the domination of men's heterosex-uality over women's heterosexuality and the subordination of all other forms of sexuality. It was striking how few homosexuals, either bosses or secretaries, we turned up via our workplace visits, though we attempted to give cues that it was 'safe' to talk about the subject. Those who identified as homosexual were nearly all volunteers who had been contacted via 'non-work' channels. Few of them were 'out' at work in any more than a limited way. Those who were tended to be in 'creative' areas where it was acceptable, or they were treated by the rest of the office as the tame pervert. The only secretary who was completely open about her lesbianism was a woman who had been married and had children and could thus claim to have paid her dues to 'normality'. She said, 'I think I'm good PR for lesbians . . . because I'm so bloody ordinary. You know, I've been married, I've had children, I own a house, I own a car. I'm Ms. Middle class Suburbia!' Another secretary told me that she deliberately chose temporary work so that she could move on before having to face the chit-chat over morning tea about private life. * * *

e. [Eds.] Adrienne Rich, "Compulsory Heterosexuality and Lesbian Existence," in *Blood, Bread, and Poetry: Selected Prose 1979–1985*, at 23 (1986), discussed in Chapter 3, Section 2(B).

f. [Eds.] J. Hearn and W. Parkin, *'Sex' At 'Work': The Power and Paradox of Organi-sation Sexuality* 94–5 (1987).

EXCLUSIONS FROM GOVERNMENT EMPLOYMENT

PART A. STATE DISCRIMINATION ON THE BASIS OF SEX

A dominant historical theme of Anglo–American law has been the state's willingness to exclude sexualized minorities from the workplace. The first, and longest lived, exclusion was of women. Women's exclusion from jobs and from the professions was invisible for most of American history, so "natural" did it seem that women's "place" was in the home. It was not until the mid-nineteenth century that women became a sufficiently serious employment threat that unstated, implicit exclusions of women from jobs came to be stated and explicit. At the same time, the New Women started pressing their claims in court. After the adoption of the Fourteenth Amendment in 1868, women had colorable claims that their exclusions by the state were unconstitutional.

Myra Bradwell's application for a license to practice law was denied by the Illinois Supreme Court solely because she was a (married) woman. The U.S. Supreme Court affirmed this judgment against attack in *Bradwell v. Illinois*, 83 U.S. (16 Wall.) 130 (1873). The Court held that Bradwell's exclusion did not violate the privileges and immunities clause. Justice Bradley, speaking for himself and Justices Swayne and Field, concurred in the judgment on broad grounds, reflecting a widely held theory of sex and gender:

> [T]he civil law, as well as nature herself, has always recognized a wide difference in the respective spheres and destinies of man and woman. Man is, or should be, woman's protector and defender. The natural and proper timidity and delicacy which belongs to the female sex evidently unfits it for many of the occupations of civil life. The constitution of the family organization, which is founded in the divine ordinance, as well as in the nature of things, indicates the domestic sphere as that which properly belongs to the domain and functions of womanhood. The harmony, not to say identity, of interests and views which belong, or should belong, to the family institution is repugnant to the idea of a woman adopting a distinct and independent career from that of her husband. So firmly fixed was this sentiment in the founders of the common law that it became a maxim of that system of jurisprudence that a woman had no legal existence separate from her husband. * * *

It is true that many women are unmarried and not affected by any of the duties, complications, and incapacities arising out of the married state, but these are exceptions to the general rule. The paramount destiny and mission of woman are to fulfil the noble and benign offices of wife and mother. This is the law of the Creator. And the rules of civil society must be adapted to the general constitution of things, and cannot be based upon exceptional cases.

The humane movements of modern society, which have for their object the multiplication of avenues for woman's advancement, and of occupations adapted to her condition and sex, have my heartiest concurrence. But I am not prepared to say that it is one of her fundamental rights and privileges to be admitted into every office and position, including those which require highly special qualifications and demanding special responsibilities. * * *

After *Bradwell*, the privileges and immunities clause was a dead end for challenges to state exclusions of women from the workplace, but constitutional litigation over sex discrimination issues continued under the due process and equal protection clauses of the Fourteenth Amendment. The structure of the litigation was quite different, but both lines of cases reflected the prevailing jurisprudence of difference accepted by the American legal establishment.

The due process cases involved industry attacks on legislation providing workplace protections for women. Early in the women's rights movement, Elizabeth Cady Stanton and Susan B. Anthony had advocated equal pay for equal work, eight hour days, and better workplace conditions for women. The mainstream unions after the turn of the century tended to fight for maximum hour laws mainly for women and children, arguably as a way to prevent women from competing on equal terms with men in the workplace. As a result of this and many other factors, women—who constituted about one-fifth of the workforce at the turn of the century— tended to be segregated into "women's work," jobs reflecting home-based values (teaching, helping, nurturing).[a]

Hence, "protective" legislation was often favored by male workers as a way to channel women into "women's work" and away from competition with men. Thus, when Oregon's law setting maximum hours for women was challenged, the main supporters of the law were the male-dominated state, the National Consumers' League, and its chief theoretician and advocate, Louis Brandeis. Notwithstanding its precedents protecting employer-employee "liberty of contract," the Supreme Court unanimously upheld the law, based upon the state's compelling interest in protecting women:

a. See Philip Foner, *Women and the American Labor Movement* (1979); Alice Kessler–Harris, *Out to Work: A History of Wage–Earning Women in the United States* 201–02 (1982); Julie Matthei, *An Economic History of Women in America* (1982); Elizabeth Brandeis, "Labor Legislation," in 3 *History of Labor in the United States* 462 (John Commons et al. eds. 1935).

That woman's physical structure and the performance of maternal functions place her at a disadvantage in the struggle for subsistence is obvious. * * * [B]y abundant testimony of the medical fraternity continuance for a long time on her feet at work, repeating this from day to day, tends to injurious effects upon the body, and as healthy mothers are essential to vigorous offspring, the physical well-being of woman becomes an object of public interest and care in order to preserve the strength and vigor of the race.

Still again, history discloses the fact that woman has always been dependent upon man. * * * As minors * * * she has been looked upon in the courts as needing especial care that her rights may be preserved. * * * Differentiated by these matters from the other sex, she is properly placed in a class by herself, and legislation designed for her protection may be sustained even when like legislation is not necessary for men and could not be sustained. It is impossible to close one's eyes to the fact that she still looks to her brother and depends upon him. * * *

Muller v. Oregon, 208 U.S. 412, 421 (1908). The Court followed a similar "paternalistic" approach in *Radice v. New York*, 264 U.S. 292 (1924) (upholding law forbidding nightwork for waitresses but exempting female entertainers and ladies' room attendants), and *Bosley v. McLaughlin*, 236 U.S. 385 (1915) (rejecting challenge by female pharmacist to 8–hour law preventing her employment with hospital). Most middle-class "progressive" groups applauded these decisions, and the NCL's "Brandeis brief" and its detailed empirical policy arguments became a new standard for influencing the Court.

Yet in the wake of *Muller*, many women came to oppose "protective" legislation, arguing that "unequal wages and bad factory conditions, and not special laws for adult women workers, are the things in which we should all interest ourselves. * * * When we limit women's opportunities to work, we simply create more poverty, and we postpone the day when equal pay for equal work will be universal." Views of Rheta Childe Dorr, *Good Housekeeping*, Sept. 1925, at 156 ff. The only case where the Supreme Court struck down a statute "protecting" women was its decision in *Adkins v. Children's Hospital*, 261 U.S. 525 (1923), which invalidated a federal statute fixing minimum wages for women and children in the District of Columbia.

Like the due process cases, the equal protection cases involved statutes that "protected" women in traditional "women's" occupations, while excluding or restricting them from traditional "men's" occupations. In *Quong Wing v. Kirkendall*, 223 U.S. 59 (1912), the Court upheld against equal protection attack a statute exempting from a ten dollar licensing charge for laundries, any laundry operation of two or fewer women. Justice Holmes wrote for the Court, finding the legislature's "ground of distinction in sex * * * not without precedent," citing *Muller*. "If Montana deems it advisable to put a lighter burden upon women than upon men with regard to an employment that our people commonly regard as more appropriate for the former, the Fourteenth Amendment does not interfere by creating a fictitious equality where there is a real difference."

In *Goesaert v. Cleary*, 335 U.S. 464 (1948), the Court upheld a statute allowing a woman to work as a bartender only if she were the wife or daughter of the bar owner. *Goesaert* approached the problem as simply a matter of rationality review: "The Constitution does not require legislatures to reflect sociological insight, or shifting social standards, any more than it requires them to keep abreast of the latest scientific standards." Before 1974, we are aware of no Supreme Court case invalidating a state sex-based employment discrimination.

Of course, that first case, *Frontiero* [Chapter 1, Section 3(A)], was the Court's introduction to "heightened" scrutiny for an employment statute discriminating on the basis of sex. Responding to the women's rights movement, the Court struck down many sex-based employment discriminations. Enforcement of the anti-discrimination provisions in Title VII accelerated. But consider the leading constitutional analysis of sex-based employment discrimination from the 1970s. Is its result defensible?

Personnel Administrator of Massachusetts v. Helen Feeney, 442 U.S. 256, 99 S.Ct. 2282, 60 L.Ed.2d 870 (1979). During her 12–year tenure as a public employee, Helen Feeney took and passed a number of open competitive civil service examinations. In 1971 she received the second highest score on an examination for a job with the Board of Dental Examiners, and in 1973 the third highest on a test for an Administrative Assistant position with a mental health center. Her high scores, however, did not win her a place on the certified eligible list. Because Massachusetts had an absolute statutory preference for war veterans, Feeney was ranked sixth behind five male veterans on the Dental Examiner list, one of whom was eventually appointed. On the 1973 examination, Feeney was placed in a position on the list behind 12 male veterans, 11 of whom had lower scores.

In the 1970s, more than 98% of the veterans in Massachusetts were male; only 1.8% were female. And more than one-quarter of the Massachusetts population were veterans. During the decade between 1963 and 1973 when Feeney was actively participating in the State's merit selection system, 47,005 new permanent appointments were made in the classified official service. Forty-three percent of those hired were women, and 57% were men. Of the women appointed, 1.8% were veterans, while 54% of the men had veteran status. A large unspecified percentage of the female appointees were serving in lower paying positions for which males traditionally had not applied. On each of 50 sample eligible lists that are part of the record in this case, one or more women who would have been certified as eligible for appointment on the basis of test results were displaced by veterans whose test scores were lower.

The Supreme Court, in an opinion by Justice Stewart, upheld the statutory discrimination against equal protection attack. The opinion relied on race precedents which had held that statutes that do not discriminate on their face, but only have discriminatory "effects," are not entitled to heightened scrutiny. See *Washington v. Davis*, 426 U.S. 229 (1976). The Court in *Davis* held that where the actual "purpose" of the law was discriminatory, heightened scrutiny would apply. Feeney argued that the State, by favoring veterans, "intentionally" discriminated against women. The Court rejected this argument, on the ground that the trial court had found as a matter of fact that Massachusetts' veterans' preferences were motivated by desires to "help" veterans, not "hurt" women.

PART B.   STATE DISCRIMINATION ON THE BASIS OF SEXUAL ORIENTATION

The primary, current as well as historical, example of state job discrimination on the basis of sexual orientation is the U.S. armed forces, a story told and examined in Chapter 4. Consider the parallel history of U.S. Civil Service and state civil service policies.

David K. Johnson, Homosexual Citizens: Washington's Gay Community Confronts the Civil Service

Washington History, Fall/Winter 1994–95, at 45–51, 53, 55–57, 59–61.*

It was 2:00 a.m. on a Tuesday night in the fall of 1963, and Washington's principal downtown gay bars, the Chicken Hut and the Derby Room, had just closed. On his way home, Clifford Norton, a budget analyst with the National Aeronautics and Space Administration, decided to drive by nearby Lafayette Park, a popular meeting and trysting site for gay men since the early part of the century. Seeing Madison Proctor standing on the corner, Norton stopped his car, rolled down the window and struck up a conversation. After inviting Proctor home for a drink, he drove him to his nearby parked car. Norton then drove home to his Southwest Washington apartment, and Proctor followed. When they arrived, however, they discovered they had been followed by two District of Columbia police officers assigned to the Morals Division. Outside the parking lot, the officers questioned Norton and Proctor about their interaction at the park and, because they had trailed them at speeds exceeding 45 miles per hour, brought the two in to police headquarters on a "traffic violation."

At headquarters, Roy Blick, chief of the Morals Division, interrogated Norton and Proctor for two hours concerning their activities that night and their sexual histories in general. "How long have you been a homosexual?" Blick repeatedly asked the NASA employee. Norton refused to answer. Blick eventually relented and issued Norton only a traffic summons. But since Norton had revealed his place of employment, Blick telephoned NASA's security director, who came to police headquarters and continued to interrogate Norton about his sexual history until 6:30 a.m. Several days later, despite a 15–year record of exemplary government service, NASA

---

discharged Norton for "immoral, indecent and disgraceful conduct." Although they acknowledged that issues of national security were not involved, NASA officials claimed that a recurrence of this type of activity might "embarrass" the agency. The Civil Service Commission concurred and determined that Norton's dismissal would promote "the efficiency of the service."

The attempt to ferret gay men and lesbians from the federal civil service is commonly associated with the anti-Communist witch hunts of the McCarthy era. But the "purge of the perverts" actually began before McCarthy made headlines with his attacks on the State Department and continued long after his death in 1957. Norton's detention and subsequent dismissal was only one of thousands of similar incidents that occurred in Washington from the later 1940s through the late 1960s. Washington's gay community reluctantly found itself on the front lines as the government attempted to eliminate sexual deviants from the ranks of the Civil Service reputedly to protect "national security."

Despite the heated rhetoric of the McCarthy era, the purge had little to do with national security. Instead, it reflected an underlying anxiety over the bureaucratization and urbanization of Washington, changes largely precipitated by the New Deal and World War II.

Norton's otherwise routine 1963 arrest marked a turning point in the hostile relationship between the city's gay community and the federal government. A closeted middle-aged gay man, Norton was no activist, but he had heard about a new organization of gays and lesbians called the Mattachine Society of Washington. Founded in 1961 by a handful of gay men, some of whom had been fired similarly from the federal government, Mattachine of Washington had received considerable publicity in the local press. The group helped Norton contest his dismissal * * *. Norton's case demonstrates how, by the early 1960s, Washington's gay community was beginning to fight back.

The issue of gays in government first came to public attention in 1950. In February, just days after Senator McCarthy made national headlines with his claim that 205 Communists (later reduced to 57) were working for the State Department, the under secretary of state for security revealed that 91 homosexuals had been fired. By that summer Washington had "gone crazy," according to Saturday Evening Post reporters Joseph and Stewart Alsop, with congressional leaders railing about Communists and sexual deviants infiltrating the government. Fear and suspicion gripped the city, as numerous "good men" quit the government, and many who stayed, even powerful U.S. senators, presumed that their telephone lines were tapped. * * *

* * * Under congressional pressure, the dismissals spread beyond the State Department. Throughout the executive branch, hundreds of civil servants were called in by their agency's personnel officer. Thousands lived in dread that they too would be summoned. The routine was always the same. Employees knew that it had nothing to do with loyalty or subversion; nonetheless they could expect to lose their jobs. "Information has come to

our attention indicating that you are a homosexual," the interrogator would begin. "What comment do you care to make?" Regardless of the response, the civil servant was usually granted "the opportunity" to resign quietly.

By November 1950, an additional 400 federal civil servants across the country had resigned or were fired following such interviews. By the end of the decade the number was in the thousands. Suspicion shrouded anyone who left the government. A *New Yorker* cartoon depicted a man explaining to a potential employer, "It's true, sir, that the State Department let me go, but that was solely because of incompetence." * * *

The question senators wanted answered that summer was, "Who put the 91 homosexuals in our State Department?" The question implied that "an unseen master hand" had placed them there in order to weaken America's foreign policy apparatus. Homosexuals were not assumed to be Communists—although some observers would come to equate the two—but they were thought to be vulnerable to blackmail and therefore to pose a "security risk." Homosexuals might not be intrinsically disloyal, but they could be used by those who were, so the thinking went. * * *

Although the rhetoric fueling much of the hysteria over gays in the government in the 1950s centered on the alleged threat to national security, this was never an issue in any actual dismissals. A combination of congressional actions and executive orders did increase the power of the Civil Service Commission and of the various agencies themselves to dismiss federal employees determined to be "security risks." The Eisenhower administration even issued an executive order banning the government from employing anyone guilty of "sexual perversion." Still, none of these measures were used against suspected homosexuals. If the alleged gay man or lesbian did not simply resign, he or she was generally dismissed for "immoral conduct," a disqualification that had been included in civil service regulations since the administration of Theodore Roosevelt. An even earlier Department of the Interior prohibition on immorality led to the termination of gay poet Walt Whitman's employment in 1865. The purges of the 1950s represented more a change in rhetoric and enforcement than in government policy.

Senator Joseph McCarthy is commonly associated with the height of both the red and lavender witch hunts, but he did not originate either campaign; in the case of gays and lesbians, he was not the principal accuser. Several State Department employees on McCarthy's famous list of subversives were accused of "sex perversion," but they were incidental to his main "Communist" targets. Even at the time, some speculated that the reason for McCarthy's comparative reticence on the gay issue, despite its appeal to his constituency, was "the danger of a boomerang," as the *New York Post* Max Lerner suggested in 1950. Not only was McCarthy's principal aide, Roy Cohn, a closeted gay man, but allegations had been made against McCarthy himself. According to Richard Rovere, the New Yorker's political reporter in Washington in the 1950s, "many people were firmly convinced that [McCarthy] was a homosexual," although the evidence was "wholly circumstantial." * * *

The two scares [fear of homosexuals and of Communists] were linked because both constituted attacks on Franklin D. Roosevelt's New Deal. FDR's policies had long been denounced as socialistic and communistic because they expanded the federal bureaucracy as "a national menace," and Congressman Martin Dies, Democrat of Texas and first chairman of the House Un–American Activities Committee, justified his attacks on New Deal agencies by referring to a "new philosophy" in the world, "which in one country is communism, in another fascism, in another country Nazism and in another country bureaucracy."

The 1940 revelation that Roosevelt was harboring at least one homosexual in a key administration position gave critics another angle of attack. Under–Secretary of State Sumner Welles was a friend of Roosevelt's and, like the president, came from a wealthy eastern family. Because of this close connection, Welles served as the de facto head of the department, with more influence over foreign policy than Secretary of State Cordell Hull. But then, in 1940, complaints that Welles had made "lewd homosexual advances" to several African–American railroad porters fell into the hands of his enemy, U.S. Ambassador to France William Bullitt. For two years, Roosevelt resisted firing Welles, but when Bullitt leaked the information to Republican Senator Ralph O. Brewster of Maine, who threatened to launch a Senate probe, the president was forced to seek his resignation. The press reported the resignation as the result of a power struggle with Secretary Hull, but Washington insiders knew that was only half the story.

Although foreign service officers had long been denounced as "cookie pushers in striped pants," no one did more to link the New Deal and the State Department with homosexuality than Welles. In 1950, when the issue of gays in the State Department came out in the press, several journalists pointed somewhat obliquely to Welles as the origin of the problem. * * * Many saw Sumner Welles, abetted by his friend President Roosevelt, as the center of a gay fifth column threatening the integrity of the government. * * *

* * * Critics of the New Deal believed that the large increase in the federal bureaucracy under the Roosevelt administration offered a haven for deviants. "The exceptional ones" may go to New York and Hollywood, [rightwing journalists] Lait and Mortimer argued, but the more mediocre queers were attracted by the security of the Civil Service. "If you're wondering where your wandering semi-boy is tonight, he's probably in Washington," they warned the nation.

In the "mediocrity and virtual anonymity of commonplace tasks" within the federal bureaucracy, they theorized, "the sexes—all four of them—are equal in the robot requirements and qualifications." Not only had the Civil Service erased gender distinctions, but "there is no color line, no social selectivity; not even citizenship is always a prerequisite." The rising scope and power of government bureaucracy was seen as somehow emasculating society, creating a world of gender-neutral bureaucrats. Like

Communism itself, bureaucracy raised the specter of a face-less, gender-less, family-less welfare state. Homosexual civil servants were seen as the natural conclusion of this frightening trend. * * *

The total number of gays and lesbians affected by the purge cannot be calculated. However, some published figures give a sense of its impact. In the two years between May 1953 and June 1955, more than 800 federal employees nationwide either resigned or were terminated with "files contain[ing] information indicating sex perversion," according to documents submitted to Senate investigators. Many more dismissals occurred on an informal undocumented basis, ostensibly to protect the reputation of the employee. Other gay and lesbian civil servants resigned before their sexual orientation was discovered. Ray Mann, for example, decided to leave the State Department in the summer of 1954 because "being unmarried, I just didn't think my future lay in working for the U.S. government in the McCarthy era." Large numbers of applicants were also rejected because of their sexual orientation, and thousands of men and women were discharged from the military, where the sexual witch hunt was even more severe.

The impact was not limited to federal employees. Millions of private-sector employees worked for government contractors who required security clearances. Other private industries adopted the policies of the federal government—the nation's largest single employer—even though they had no direct federal contracts. * * *

Only slowly did any effort at collective political resistance emerge. Even Frank Kameny, who in 1957 became one of the first to fight his dismissal from the Civil Service, initially distanced himself from the charge of homosexuality, asking that he be examined as an individual and not be judged like other homosexuals. But by 1960, when his case reached the U.S. Supreme Court, Kameny realized that it was not about him as an individual at all. In petitioning the court for a writ of certiorari—his attorney having abandoned the case—Kameny charged that he, along with 15 million other Americans, was being treated as a second-class citizen. He was not being persecuted for illegal conduct but for his sexual identity. This was "no less illegal," he argued, "than discrimination based on religious or racial grounds."

Kameny's brief showed the influence of Donald Webster Cory's 1950 book, *The Homosexual in America*, the first systematic argument published in the United States for categorizing gays and lesbians as an oppressed minority group. It also drew on new federal government policies aimed at protecting African Americans and other racial minorities. Kameny argued that gays and lesbians faced harsher discrimination because "instead of being mitigated and ameliorated by the government's attitudes and practices," anti-gay sentiment "has instead been intensified by them." While the governmental rhetoric and policy, however ineffective, was aimed at protecting the rights of religious and racial minorities, homosexuals were the only group "barred, in toto, from Federal employment." Kameny was asking for the court to examine "the propriety, the legality, and the constitutionality" of the government's policy toward homosexuals, an open examination that had never taken place, even during the intense publicity of the summer of 1950.

When the Supreme Court declined to hear his case in 1961, Kameny began casting about for others who might join his cause. Social contacts at gay bars and parties helped, but a mailing list of the Mattachine Society of New York provided the largest group of supporters. In August 1961, New York Mattachine set up an organizational meeting at the Hay–Adams Hotel for those interested in forming a group in Washington. Among the approximately 16 men in the room that night was Lieutenant Louis Fochet of the Metropolitan Police Department's Morals Division. Ron Balin, who recognized Fochet, alerted Kameny. During the discussion period after a formal presentation by Mattachine of New York, Kameny rose and said, "I understand that there is a member of the Metropolitan Police Department here. Could he please identify himself and tell us why he's here?" Fochet, visibly flustered, explained that he had been invited and quickly left. Kameny's conduct at this initial organizational meeting set the tone for the future activities of what became the Mattachine Society of Washington (MSW). * * *

In contrast to the secretive genesis of almost all previous gay organizations, MSW distributed press releases announcing its formation to every member of Congress, President Kennedy, and the Cabinet. But while coming out publicly, MSW simultaneously wrapped itself metaphorically in the American flag. In the organization's constitution, hammered out in the fall of 1961, the ground based its objectives on the two founding documents of American democracy, dedicating itself to "act by any lawful means . . . to secure for homosexuals the right to life, liberty, and the pursuit of happiness, as proclaimed for all men by the Declaration of Independence and . . . the basic rights and liberties established by the word and spirit of the Constitution of the United States." They were coming out not just as homosexuals but as "homosexual citizens."

Because they were fighting for their rights as American citizens, MSW members adopted the methods of traditional reform groups, particularly those of the civil rights movement. As an advocacy group, MSW modeled itself after the National Association for the Advancement of Colored People (NAACP) and the American Civil Liberties Union (ACLU). It sought meetings with the government officials, shepherded test discrimination cases through the courts, leafleted government buildings with pamphlets on how to handle an arrest or federal interrogation, and publicized its cause wherever possible. [Conservatively dressed MSW members picketed the headquarters of the Commission on June 26, 1965, the first such protest by a homophile organization.]

Perhaps even more intimidating to the Civil Service Commission than gay and lesbian protesters was a June 1965 court victory for Bruce Scott, MSW's secretary. Based on a 1947 arrest for loitering in Lafayette Park, Scott had been fired from the Department of Labor in 1956 after 17 years of service. When he reapplied to the department in 1962, he was again judged unsuitable, but with the help of MSW and the ACLU he filed suit.

As the *Washington Post* pointed out in an editorial supporting Scott's lawsuit, "no specific act of immoral conduct was charged against him." The U.S. Court of Appeals [for the District of Columbia Circuit] overturned his disqualification, charging that the commission "may not rely on a determination of 'immoral conduct' based only on such vague labels as 'homosexual' or 'homosexual conduct' as a ground for disqualifying [Scott]." The court demanded for the first time that the commission define its terms and explain the rationale behind its policy.

After publicity over the pickets and its defeat in the Scott case, the commission finally agreed to meet with Mattachine representatives in the fall of 1965. In September Lawrence Meloy, Civil Service Commission general counsel, and Kimbell Johnson, director, Bureau of Personnel Investigations, met with five MSW members at the commission's headquarters. At the conclusion of the hour-and-a-half long meeting, the commission representatives requested that MSW submit a formal statement of its position and promised a response.

As a result of this exchange, the commission made the first attempt to explain its position on homosexuality * * *. In his letter to MSW, Chairman Macy claimed that the commission did not discriminate against a class of people but simply excluded individuals based on illegal or immoral conduct when it became public, such as through an arrest record or general "notoriety." As long as one did not "publicly proclaim that he engages in homosexual conduct" or "that he prefers such relationships," Macy asserted that the commission would not pry into an individual's private life. However, the commission did have to consider how the public would react to transacting government business with "a known or admitted sexual deviate."

By requiring federal employees to keep their homosexual behavior hidden, the commission's letter was an admonition to gay and lesbian employees: stay in the closet. In a 1969 interview Kimbell Johnson stated that many people continued to view the presence of known homosexuals in government service as "repugnant" and that the commission therefore disqualified them "in order to retain public confidence." Lesbians were less likely to be investigated because the public finds them "less repugnant." The issue of vulnerability to blackmail was never mentioned. The commission was not concerned with security but with its own image. The Civil Service did not want to be seen as a haven for deviants as it had been portrayed in the 1950s by critics of the New Deal. * * *

Clifford L. Norton v. John Macy et al.

U.S. Court of Appeals for the District of Columbia Circuit, 1969.
417 F.2d 1161.

■ BAZELON, CHIEF JUDGE.

Appellant, a former GS–14 budget analyst in the National Aeronautics and Space Administration (NASA), seeks review of his discharge for "immoral conduct" and for possessing personality traits which render him "unsuitable for further Government employment." As a veterans preference eligible, he could be dismissed only for "such cause as will promote the efficiency of the service."[1] Since the record before us does not suggest any reasonable connection between the evidence against him and the efficiency of the service, we conclude that he was unlawfully discharged.

[Judge Bazelon recounted the facts of Norton's nocturnal escapade, his interrogation and arrest, and discharge from government service.]

Congress has provided that protected civil servants shall not be dismissed except "for such cause as will promote the efficiency of the service." The Civil Service Commission's regulations provide that an appointee may be removed, *inter alia,* for "infamous * * *, immoral, or notoriously disgraceful conduct" and for "any * * other disqualification which makes the individual unfit for the service."[4] We think—and appellant does not strenuously deny—that the evidence was sufficient to sustain the charge that, consciously or not, he made a homosexual advance to Procter. Accordingly, the question presented is whether such an advance, or appellant's personality traits as disclosed by the record, are "such cause" for removal as the statute requires.

* * * The Government's obligation to accord due process sets at least minimal substantive limits on its prerogative to dismiss its employees: it forbids all dismissals which are arbitrary and capricious. These constitutional limits may be greater where, as here, the dismissal imposes a "badge of infamy," disqualifying the victim from any further Federal employment, damaging his prospects for private employ, and fixing upon him the stigma of an official defamation of character. The Due Process Clause may also cut deeper into the Government's discretion where a dismissal involves an intrusion upon that ill-defined area of privacy which is increasingly if indistinctly recognized as a foundation of several specific constitutional protections.[10] Whatever their precise scope, these due process limitations apply even to those whose employment status is unprotected by statute. And statutes such as the Veterans' Preference Act were plainly designed to confer some additional job security not enjoyed by unprotected federal employees. * * *

Preliminarily, we must reject appellee's contention that once the label "immoral" is plausibly attached to an employee's off-duty conduct, our inquiry into the presence of adequate rational cause for removal is at an end. A pronouncement of "immorality" tends to discourage careful analysis because it unavoidably connotes a violation of divine, Olympian, or otherwise universal standards of rectitude. However, the Civil Service Commission has neither the expertise nor the requisite anointment to make or enforce absolute moral judgments, and we do not understand that it

1. 5 U.S.C. § 863 (1964), recodified in 5 U.S.C. § 7512(a) (Supp.1965–68).

4. 5 C.F.R. § 731.201(g) (1968).

10. See, e.g., *Stanley v. Georgia,* 394 U.S. 557 (1969) [Chapter 1, Section 1(B)];

Griswold v. Connecticut, 381 U.S. 479 (1965) [Chapter 1, Section 1(A)] * * *.

purports to do so. Its jurisdiction is at least confined to the things which are Caesar's, and its avowed standard of "immorality" is no more than "the prevailing mores of our society."[18]

So construed, "immorality" covers a multitude of sins. Indeed, it may be doubted whether there are in the entire Civil Service many persons so saintly as never to have done any act which is disapproved by the "prevailing mores of our society." Analytical philosophers would distinguish between acts conventionally regarded as morally wrong and acts which are disapproved merely as indecent, repulsive, or unesthetic; but if the Commission makes such a distinction, it is of no benefit to employees, who may assertedly be dismissed for "indecent and disgraceful" conduct as well as for "immorality."

We are not prepared to say that the Commission could not reasonably find appellant's homosexual advance to be "immoral," "indecent," or "notoriously disgraceful" under dominant conventional norms. But the notion that it could be an appropriate function of the federal bureaucracy to enforce the majority's conventional codes of conduct in the private lives of its employees is at war with elementary concepts of liberty, privacy, and diversity. And whatever we may think of the Government's qualifications to act *in loco parentis* in this way, the statute precludes it from discharging protected employees except for a reason related to the efficiency of the service. Accordingly, a finding that an employee has done something immoral or indecent could support a dismissal without further inquiry only if all immoral or indecent acts of an employee have some ascertainable deleterious effect on the efficiency of the service. The range of conduct which might be said to affront prevailing mores is so broad and varied that we can hardly arrive at any such conclusion without reference to specific conduct. Thus, we think the sufficiency of the charges against appellant must be evaluated in terms of the effects on the service of what in particular he has done or has been shown to be likely to do. * * *

The homosexual conduct of an employee might bear on the efficiency of the service in a number of ways. Because of the potential for blackmail, it might jeopardize the security of classified communications. * * * [I]t may in some circumstances be evidence of an unstable personality unsuited for certain kinds of work. If an employee makes offensive overtures while on the job, or if his conduct is notorious, the reactions of other employees and of the public with whom he comes in contact in the performance of his official functions may be taken into account. Whether or not such potential consequences would justify removal, they are at least broadly relevant to "the efficiency of the service."

The peculiar feature of appellant's dismissal, however, is that it rests on none of these possible effects on the service. The NASA official who fired him, Mr. Garbarini, testified that appellant was a "competent employee" doing "very good" work. In fact, Garbarini was "not worried" about any

---

18. Letter from John W. Macy, Jr., Chairman, United States Civil Service Commission, to The Mattachine Society of Washington, Feb. 25, 1966, p. 3. * * *

possible effect on appellant's performance, and went so far as to inquire of personnel officers "if there was any way around this kind of problem for the man. * * *" He "considered whether or not we had real security problems here to worry about" and concluded "there was not enough of that to influence me." Appellant's duties apparently did not bring him into contact with the public, and his fellow employees were unaware of his "immorality." Nonetheless, Garbarini's advisers told him that dismissal for any homosexual conduct was a *"custom* within the agency," and he decided to follow the custom because continued employment of appellant might "turn out to be embarrassing to the agency" in that "if an incident like this occurred again, it could become a public scandal on the agency."

Thus, appellee is now obliged to rely solely on this possibility of embarrassment to the agency to justify appellant's dismissal. The assertion of such a nebulous "cause" poses perplexing problems for a review proceeding which must accord broad discretion to the Commission. We do not doubt that NASA blushes whenever one of its own is caught *in flagrante delictu;* but if the possibility of such transitory institutional discomfiture must be uncritically accepted as a cause for discharge which will "promote the efficiency of the service," we might as well abandon all pretense that the statute provides any substantive security for its supposed beneficiaries. A claim of possible embarrassment might, of course, be a vague way of referring to some specific potential interference with an agency's performance; but it might also be a smokescreen hiding personal antipathies or moral judgments which are excluded by statute as grounds for dismissal. A reviewing court must at least be able to discern some reasonably foreseeable, specific connection between an employee's potentially embarrassing conduct and the efficiency of the service. Once the connection is established, then it is for the agency and the Commission to decide whether it outweighs the loss to the service of a particular competent employee.

In the instant case appellee has shown us no such specific connection. Indeed, on the record appellant is at most an extremely infrequent offender, who neither openly flaunts nor carelessly displays his unorthodox sexual conduct in public. Thus, even the potential for the embarrassment the agency fears is minimal. We think the unparticularized and unsubstantiated conclusion that such possible embarrassment threatens the quality of the agency's performance is an arbitrary ground for dismissal.[28]

28. We note that the Civil Service Commission of the City of New York has recently determined that homosexual conduct is not an automatic bar to employment by the City. Rather, the Commission says:

Policy dictates that with reference to a homosexual applicant the commission would be required to determine the personal qualities reasonably considered indispensable to the duties of the position, and then to reasonably determine whether the applicant's condition is inconsistent with the possession of these qualities to the extent of rendering him unfit to assume the duties of the position.

New York Times, May 9, 1969, pp. 1, 23.

The most widely accepted study of American sexual practices estimates that "at least 37 per cent" of the American male population have at least one homosexual experience during their lifetime. Kinsey, Pomeroy & Martin, *Sexual Behavior in the Human Male* 623 (1948). If this is so, a policy of excluding all persons who have engaged in homosexual

Lest there be any doubt, we emphasize that we do not hold that homosexual conduct may never be cause for dismissal of a protected federal employee. Nor do we even conclude that potential embarrassment from an employee's private conduct may in no circumstances affect the efficiency of the service. What we do say is that, if the statute is to have any force, an agency cannot support a dismissal as promoting the efficiency of the service merely by turning its head and crying "shame."

■ TAMM, CIRCUIT JUDGE dissenting:

* * * I would affirm. To do otherwise would implicate me in the setting of precedent for the proposition that offduty homosexual conduct, coupled with a capacity for "blacking out" while intoxicated, bears no real relationship to the functioning of an efficient service within a government agency. Homosexuals, sadly enough, do not leave their emotions at Lafayette Square and regardless of their spiritual destinies they still present targets for public reproach and private extortion. I believe this record supports the finding that this individual presents more than a potential risk in this regard and that his termination will serve the efficiency of the service. Despite the billows of puffery that continue to float out of recent opinions on this subject, I believe that the theory that homosexual conduct is not in any way related to the efficiency and effectiveness of governmental business is not an evil theory—just a very unrealistic one.

NOTES ON *NORTON* AND ITS INSISTENCE THAT THE STATE SHOW A "NEXUS" BETWEEN SEXUAL ORIENTATION AND JOB REQUIREMENTS

1. *Subsequent Civil Service Developments.* The principle in *Norton* (that a gay or lesbian person cannot be fired without a showing that there is a "nexus" between sexual orientation and job fitness) has been codified, first by administrative policy guidance and then by statute. A Civil Service Bulletin dated December 21, 1973, instructed supervisors:

> You may not find a person unsuitable for Federal employment merely because that person is a homosexual or has engaged in homosexual acts, nor may such exclusion be based on a conclusion that a homosexual person might bring the public service into contempt. You are, however, permitted to dismiss a person or find him or her unsuitable for Federal employment where the evidence establishes that such person's homosexual conduct affects job fitness—excluding from such consideration, however, unsubstantiated conclusions concerning possible embarrassment to the Federal service.

conduct from government employ would disqualify for public service over one-third of the male population. This result would be both inherently absurd and devastating to the public service. The public service is protected from the consequences of any such policy by its inability to identify most of the offending males. But we must assume that the Government carries many such potentially embarrassing employees on its roles without noticeable impact on the efficiency of the service.

In 1975, the Commission promulgated formal regulations to the same effect, 5 C.F.R. § 731.202(b). In 1978, the statute governing the Civil Service was amended to add the following:

> Any employee who has authority to take, direct others to take, recommend or approve any personnel action, shall not, with respect to such authority— * * * (10) discriminate for or against any employee or applicant for employment on the basis of conduct which does not adversely affect the performance of the employee or applicant or the performance of others * * *

5 U.S.C. § 2302(b)(10). Beginning with the Carter Administration, this language has been officially interpreted to preclude civil service discrimination on the basis of sexual orientation. See Letter from James B. King, Director, Office of Personnel Management, to Representative Barney Frank, Jan. 26, 1994, quoted *infra* page 895.

2. *Security Clearances.* The "security risk" rationale continued to be cited as the primary rationale for excluding lesbian, gay, and bisexual employees by some federal agencies exempted from the normal civil service rules, most prominently the Federal Bureau of Investigation and the Central Intelligence Agency. The FBI's exclusionary policy was upheld in *Padula v. Webster*, 822 F.2d 97, 104 (D.C.Cir.1987) (relying on *Bowers v. Hardwick* to justify anti-homosexual discrimination). In addition, it was used to justify separate and more stringent investigations of hundreds of thousands of federal and private sector workers who have needed security clearances in order to obtain jobs or promotions. See *High Tech Gays v. Defense Industrial Security Clearance Office*, 895 F.2d 563 (9th Cir.1990).

In 1995, President Clinton signed an Executive Order prohibiting discrimination based on sexual orientation in the granting of security clearances. Executive Order No. 12968, 60 Fed. Reg. 40245 (Aug. 7, 1995). The Order ended the practice by federal agencies of automatically subjecting lesbian and gay applicants for clearances to an extensive background investigation on that basis alone. Although the Order directed that sexual orientation may not be a basis for denying security clearance, previous executive orders, following from Executive Order 10450, 18 Fed.Reg. 2489 (Apr. 29, 1953), required investigation for "notoriously disgraceful conduct" and "sexual perversion." President Clinton's Order specifically preserved Order 10450. If someone convicted of sodomy seeks a security clearance, is the government supposed to investigate? Can it deny a clearance?

3. *State Cases.* State courts did not immediately follow *Norton*'s nexus approach or applied it conservatively. An exception was California, whose supreme court soon thereafter ruled that laws banning immoral and unprofessional conduct and conduct involving moral turpitude by teachers must be limited to conduct shown to indicate unfitness to teach. *Morrison v. State Board of Education*, 82 Cal.Rptr. 175, 461 P.2d 375 (Cal. 1969). In later cases, the definition of "unfitness" became the central issue.

PROBLEM 10–1

CIVIL SERVICE DISCRIMINATION AFTER *NORTON*

Consider these variations on the *Norton* facts. In which, if any, would the D.C. Circuit protect the employee against discharge? Under which, if any, would the 1978 statute protect against discharge?

(a) NASA employee Norton marries Procter in a publicized same-sex marriage ceremony and then sues the District of Columbia, in an equally publicized lawsuit, to obtain a marriage license.

(b) On several occasions, Norton shows up for work wearing a dress and announces his intention to have a sex change operation. Coworkers take this news in stride. Should the result be different if some employees are upset?

(c) Norton is a CIA analyst. See *Dobbs v. CIA*, 866 F.2d 1114 (9th Cir.1989). Or Norton is a special agent for the FBI. See *Padula v. Webster*, 822 F.2d 97 (D.C.Cir.1987); *Buttino v. FBI*, 801 F.Supp. 298 (N.D.Cal.1992).

John Singer v. U.S. Civil Service Commission

U.S. Court of Appeals for the Ninth Circuit, 1976.
530 F.2d 247, *vacated*, 429 U.S. 1034 (1977).

■ JAMESON, DISTRICT JUDGE. * * *

On August 2, 1971, Singer was hired by the Seattle Office of the Equal Employment Opportunity Commission (EEOC) as a clerk typist. Pursuant to 5 C.F.R. § 315.801 *et seq.*, he was employed for one year on probationary status, subject to termination if "his work performance or conduct during this period (failed) to demonstrate his fitness or his qualifications for continued employment" (§ 315.804). At the time he was hired Singer informed the Director of EEOC that he was a homosexual.

On May 12, 1972, an investigator for the Civil Service Commission sent a letter to Singer inviting him "to appear voluntarily for an interview to comment upon, explain or rebut adverse information which has come to the attention of the Commission" as a result of its investigation to determine Singer's "suitability for employment in the competitive Federal service." The interview was set for May 19. Singer appeared at the appointed time with his counsel. Singer was advised that the investigation by the Commission disclosed that "you are homosexual. You openly profess that you are homosexual and you have received wide-spread publicity in this respect in at least two states." Specific acts were noted, which may be summarized as follows:

(1) During Singer's previous employment with a San Francisco mortgage firm Singer had "flaunted" his homosexuality by kissing and embracing a male in front of the elevator in the building where he was employed and kissing a male in the company cafeteria;

(2) The *San Francisco Chronicle* wrote an article on Singer in November of 1970 in which he stated his name and occupation and views on "closet queens";

(3) At the Seattle EEOC office Singer openly admitted being "gay" and indicated by his dress and demeanor that he intended to continue homosexual activity as a "way of life";

(4) On September 20, 1971, Singer and another man applied to the King County Auditor for a marriage license, which was eventually refused by the King County Superior Court;[a]

(5) As a result of the attempt to obtain the marriage license Singer was the subject of extensive television, newspaper and magazine publicity;

(6) Articles published in the Seattle papers of September 21, 1971 included Singer's identification as a typist employed by EEOC and quoted Singer as saying, in part, that he and the man he sought to marry were "two human beings who happen to be in love and want to get married for various reasons"; * * *

[By letter dated June 26, 1972 the Chief of the Investigations Division of the Seattle office of the Civil Service Commission notified Singer that by reason of his "immoral and notoriously disgraceful conduct" he was disqualified under the Civil Service Regulations, 5 C.F.R. § 731.201(b). The letter stated: "The information developed by the investigation, taken with your reply, indicate that you have flaunted and broadcast your homosexual activities and have sought and obtained publicity in various media in pursuit of this goal. * * * Your activities in these matters are those of an advocate for a socially repugnant concept. * * * In determining that your employment will not promote the efficiency of the service, the Commission has considered such pertinent factors as the potential disruption of service efficiency because of the possible revulsion of other employees to homosexual conduct and/or their apprehension of homosexual advances and solicitations; the hazard that the prestige and authority of a Government position will be used to foster homosexual activity, particularly among youth; the possible use of Government funds and authority in furtherance of conduct offensive to the mores and law of our society; and the possible embarrassment to, and loss of public confidence in, your agency and the Federal civil service."

[The Hearing Officer rejected Singer's appeal. Although Singer's co-workers and supervisor had voiced no complaint about Singer's job performance, the overall "efficiency of the service" was compromised by "notoriously disgraceful conduct." The Civil Service Commission, Board of Appeals and Review affirmed, saying:

"There is evidence in the file which indicated that appellant's actions establish that he has engaged in immoral and notoriously disgraceful conduct, openly and publicly flaunting his homosexual way of life and indicating further continuance of such activities. Activities of the type

---

a. [Eds. Singer's marriage license application was denied, and the Washington courts rejected Singer's constitutional challenge to the marriage exclusion. See Chapter 9, Section 2.]

he has engaged in are such that general public knowledge thereof reflects discredit upon the Federal Government as his employer, impeding the efficiency of the service by lessening general public confidence in the fitness of the Government to conduct the public business with which it is entrusted."]

Appellant contends that he was discharged because of his status as a homosexual without the Commission showing any "rational nexus" between his homosexual activities and the efficiency of the service, in violation of the Due Process Clause of the Fifth Amendment; and that he has been denied freedom of expression and the right to petition the Government for redress of grievances, in violation of the First Amendment. [The court held that the scope of judicial review was very narrow, because Singer was a probationary employee; such employees generally have no right to continued employment, but only a right to be shielded from arbitrary and capricious action.]

With the foregoing principles and trends in mind, we turn to those cases which have considered homosexual activities as a basis for dismissal of Civil Service employees. The leading case is *Norton v. Macy* * * *. The court noted, however, that homosexual conduct cannot be ignored as a factor in determining fitness for federal employment since it might "bear on the efficiency of the service in a number of ways." More specifically the court said: "If an employee makes offensive overtures while on the job, or if his conduct is notorious, the reactions of other employees and of the public with whom he comes in contact in the performance of his official functions may be taken into account. Whether or not such potential consequences would justify removal, they are at least broadly relevant to 'the efficiency of the service.' " * * *

We conclude from a review of the record in its entirety that appellant's employment was not terminated because of his status as a homosexual or because of any private acts of sexual preference. The statements of the Commission's investigation division, hearing examiner, and Board of Appeals make it clear that the discharge was the result of appellant's "openly and publicly flaunting his homosexual way of life and indicating further continuance of such activities," while identifying himself as a member of a federal agency. The Commission found that these activities were such that "general public knowledge thereof reflects discredit upon the Federal Government as his employer, impeding the efficiency of the service by lessening public confidence in the fitness of the Government to conduct the public business with which it was entrusted."

[The court denied Singer's First Amendment claim on the ground that cases protecting speech about homosexuality had not "involved the open and public flaunting or advocacy of homosexual conduct."]

POSTSCRIPTS TO *SINGER* AND THE FALL OF THE CIVIL SERVICE EXCLUSION OF "IMMORAL" HOMOSEXUALS

1. *Postscript: Singer's Case.* The Ninth Circuit opinion was vacated by the Supreme Court, which remanded the case to the Civil Service Commission for reconsideration in light of new Civil Service regulations adopted during the pendency of the case. In 1978, the Federal Employee Appeals Authority (FEAA) cancelled the personnel action that caused Singer's dismissal. The FEAA found a "complete absence of any evidence which indicates that appellant's presence on the rolls of the agency impeded the agency's ability to carry out its missions" and concluded that the dismissal had been based on "unsubstantiated conclusions." Rhonda Rivera, "Sexual Preference Law," 30 *Drake L. Rev.* 317–18 (1980–81). However, that resolution is not part of the published legal record, and subsequent courts have probably not been aware of it.

2. *The Evolving Civil Service Regulations.* Singer was discharged and sued in 1972. The Civil Service Bulletin adopting a *Norton* (nexus) approach was issued at the end of 1973. The district court dismissed the case in 1974. Final Civil Service regulations were issued in 1975. The court of appeals affirmed in 1976. Why was the commission's new policy not dispositive?

In a May 12, 1980 memorandum, Alan K. Campbell, Director of the Office of Personnel Management, elaborated on the application of the statutory provision barring consideration of non-job-related conduct in federal employment matters. He stated, "Thus, applicants and employees are to be protected against inquiries into, or actions based upon, non-job-related conduct, such as religious, community or social affiliations, or sexual orientation." A February 17, 1994 memorandum from OPM Director James B. King stated, "The 1980 memorandum continues to reflect the Federal Government's longstanding policy on the matter of discrimination based on non-job-related conduct." Most agencies and departments of the federal government have, in the 1990s, adopted internal policies explicitly prohibiting job discrimination and harassment based on sexual orientation.

3. *Postscript: A New Double Bind—Don't Ask, Don't Tell.* A majority of the post-*Singer* cases have adopted the rationale that state and local governments cannot penalize public employees for being gay but can penalize them for public announcements of homosexuality. Illustrative is *Childers v. Dallas Police Department*, 513 F.Supp. 134 (N.D.Tex.1981), which upheld the Police Department's refusal to promote Childers because of his pro-gay activism. Relying on *Singer*, Judge Porter held that because "Childers was in no way inclined to be discreet about his homosexuality," his expressive activity would undermine the community respect needed for police work and the efficiency of the department (the latter because Childers' gay activism would "foment controversy and conflict within the department"). Judge Porter distinguished *Norton* upon the familiar ground that the plaintiff had been discharged "because of his homosexual preference and personality," not "substantial overt homosexual conduct." 513 F. Supp. at 147 n. 20. Compare *Childers* to *Shahar v. Bowers* [Chapter 1, Section 3(C)].

Courts adjudicating cases brought by teachers also adopted the reasoning of *Singer*. For example, in *Gaylord v. Tacoma School District No. 10*, 559 P.2d 1340 (Wash.), *cert. denied*, 434 U.S. 879 (1977), the court ruled that negative reactions to a gay teacher's homosexuality by students, teachers and parents justified his firing. See also *Rowland v. Mad River Local School Dist.* (Chapter 3, Section 2[C]). To what extent would such a decision be buttressed by *Bowers v. Hardwick* (Chapter 1, Section 2)? Or rendered suspect by *Romer v. Evans* (Chapter 1, Section 3[B][1])?

PART C. STATE DISCRIMINATION ON THE BASIS OF PREGNANCY

One of the persistent problems in equal protection jurisprudence has been how to analyze pregnancy—as inextricably intertwined with gender or as coincidental medical condition. The issue arose in a series of cases litigated in the late 1960s and early 1970s against school boards, which were not then covered by Title VII. School districts at that time commonly had mandatory leave policies, forcing pregnant teachers to resign their position at least four to five months before the expected birth. As was noted in the case which reached the Supreme Court, *Cleveland Board of Education v. LaFleur*, 414 U.S. 632, 653 (1974) (Powell, J., concurring), "The records before us abound with proof that a principal purpose behind the adoption of the regulations was to keep visibly pregnant teachers out of the sight of schoolchildren." Although this and several other pregnant teacher cases had been litigated and won by plaintiffs below on the ground that such policies constituted sex discrimination in violation of the equal protection clause, the Supreme Court in *LaFleur* grounded its ruling of invalidity on a due process basis, that the policies "employ irrebuttable presumptions that unduly penalize a female teacher for deciding to bear a child." *Id.* at 648. In the next case, the Supreme Court reached the equal protection argument.

Dwight Geduldig v. Carolyn Aiello, 417 U.S. 484, 94 S.Ct. 2485, 41 L.Ed.2d 256 (1974). California's disability insurance program paid benefits to persons in private employment temporarily unable to work because of a physical disability not covered by worker's compensation. The program excluded from coverage disabilities associated with pregnancy. The Court held that the exclusion was constitutional. Justice Stewart's opinion for the Court found the exclusion rationally related to the program's self-supporting goals (benefits are covered by premiums) and the need to draw lines of exclusion. Indeed, noted Justice Stewart, the annual claim rate and the annual claim cost were greater for women than for men under the existing program. *Id.* at 497 n.21.

Three dissenting Justices (Brennan, Douglas, Marshall) argued that a more exacting scrutiny was required to justify any such discrimination on the basis of sex or gender, under *Reed* and *Frontiero* (the latter just decided). Justice Stewart responded: "The lack of identity between the excluded disability and gender as such under this insurance program becomes clear upon the most cursory analysis. The program divides potential recipients into two groups—pregnant women and nonpregnant persons.

While the first group is exclusively female, the second includes members of both sexes. The fiscal and actuarial benefits of the program thus accrue to members of both sexes." *Id.* at 496 n.20. In the same footnote, Justice Stewart held out the possibility of stricter scrutiny if "distinctions involving pregnancy are mere pretexts designed to effect an invidious discrimination against the members of one sex or another."

The Court's decision in *Geduldig* apparently remains good law as an analysis of equal protection doctrine applicable to discrimination based on pregnancy. However, adoption of the Pregnancy Discrimination Act, *infra*, sapped *Geduldig* of its practical effect in the workplace. Because of the existence of that statutory protection, subsequent litigation has largely ignored the constitutional dimensions of pregnancy-based policies.

THE STATUTORY BAN AGAINST SEX DISCRIMINATION

Title VII of the Civil Rights Act of 1964, codified as amended [in 1972 and 1991] at 42 U.S.C. § 2000e et seq., is the primary federal protection against job discrimination in the private sector; since 1972, the statute has also applied to state and federal employment. The prime directive of Title VII is found in § 703(a), 42 U.S.C. § 2000e–2(a):

It shall be an unlawful employment practice for an employer—

(1) to fail or refuse to hire or to discharge any individual, or otherwise to discriminate against any individual with respect to his compensation, terms, conditions, or privileges of employment, because of such individual's race, color, religion, sex, or national origin; or

(2) to limit, segregate, or classify his employees or applicants for employment in any way which would deprive or tend to deprive any individual of employment opportunities or otherwise adversely affect his status as an employee, because of such individual's race, color, religion, sex, or national origin.

Section 703(b)–(c), *id.* § 2000e–2(b)–(c), sets forth similar prohibitions of "unlawful employment practices" by employment agencies and labor organizations (unions). Section 703(d), *id.* § 2000e–2(d), applies the anti-discrimination principle specifically to apprenticeship or training programs.

As proposed by the Kennedy Administration and its House and Senate sponsors, the early versions of what was to become Title VII originally targeted only discrimination because of race, color, religion, or national origin. The title's prohibition of sex discrimination was proposed by Representative Howard Worth Smith, a southern Democrat vehemently opposed to the civil rights bill. Having failed to kill the 1963 bill in his Rules Committee, as he had killed previous bills, Smith proposed to the House of Representatives the addition of the word "sex" to Title VII's list of impermissible bases for employment decisions. Smith hoped that by transforming the civil rights bill into a law guaranteeing women equal employment rights with men—thus drastically affecting virtually every employer, labor union, and governmental body in the country—the bill would become so controversial that it would fail, if not in the House, certainly in the Senate.[a]

a. See Charles Whalen & Barbara Whalen, *The Longest Debate: A Legislative* *History of the 1964 Civil Rights Act* 115–16 (1985); Katharine M. Franke, "The Central

The shocked, flustered (and perhaps chauvinistic) House sponsor of the bill, Representative Emmanuel Celler (D–N.Y.), immediately rose to speak in opposition to Smith's "killer" amendment. While the Republican supporters of the bill sat on the sidelines, many Democratic liberals joined Celler in speaking against the amendment. Then five Congresswomen— Frances Bolton (R–Ohio), Martha Griffiths (D–Mich.), Katherine St. George (R–N.Y.), Catherine May (R–Wash.), and Edna Kelly (D–N.Y.)—rose in support "of this little crumb of equality. The addition of the little, terrifying word 's-e-x' will not hurt this legislation in any way," argued St. George. With a coalition of southerners and women supporting it and the rest of the House divided on the apparent choice between equal rights for blacks and equal rights for women, the Smith amendment passed, 168–133. (Vaas 442.) " 'We've won, we've won!' cried a lady in the gallery jubilantly." (Whalens 117.) House attendants escorted her from the chamber.

As it turned out, the Smith amendment did nothing to hurt the bill's chances in either the House or the Senate. Although the sex discrimination prohibition was retained, it and the other prohibitions were diluted by various "exemptions" or "defenses" to the charge of unlawful employment practices under Title VII. The main defenses are those which qualify the meaning of "unlawful employment practice" in § 703. Section 703(e), *id.* § 2000e–2(e), presents a defense for practices based on bona fide occupational qualifications ("BFOQ"):

> Notwithstanding any other provision of this subchapter, (1) it shall not be an unlawful employment practice for an employer to hire and employ employees, for an employment agency to classify, or refer for employment any individual, for a labor organization to classify its membership or to classify or refer for employment any individual, or for an employer, labor organization, or joint labor-management committee controlling apprenticeship or other training or retraining programs to admit or employ any individual in any such program, on the basis of his religion, sex, or national origin in those certain instances where religion, sex, or national origin is a bona fide occupational qualification reasonably necessary to the normal operation of that particular business or enterprise * * *.

Section 703(h), *id.* § 2000e–2(h), protects employment decisions based upon bona fide seniority or merit systems. Section 713(b)(1), *id.* § 2000e–12(b)(1), provides a defense to a person charged with violating Title VII "if he pleads and proves that the act or omission complained of was in good faith, in conformity with, and in reliance on any written interpretation or opinion of the Commission," which is charged with enforcement of Title VII.[b]

Mistake of Sex Discrimination Law: The Disaggregation of Sex from Gender," 144 *U.Pa.L.Rev.* 1, 23–25 (1995); Francis Vaas, "Title VII: Legislative History," 7 *B.C. Indus. & Com. L. Rev.* 431, 441–42 (1966).

b. Under Title VII procedures, a person "claiming to be aggrieved" may not file suit herself, but should file a "charge" with the EEOC asserting violation of the substantive norms of Title VII, pursuant to § 706(a), 42 U.S.C. § 2000e–5(a). Once the aggrieved per-

After the enactment of Title VII, the EEOC interpreted the law to prohibit not just "disparate treatment" of employees because of their race or sex, but also the adoption or retention of employment policies that have an unjustified (not job-related) "disparate impact" on employees that is race- or sex-based. The Supreme Court ratified that EEOC view in *Griggs v. Duke Power Co.*, 401 U.S. 424 (1971). Although *Griggs*, and indeed § 703(a) generally, were not applied with full force to sex discrimination cases immediately, *e.g., Dothard v. Rawlinson*, 433 U.S. 321 (1977) (allowing sex discrimination in state prison system), it proved to have significant bite over time. In response to the Supreme Court's perceived retreat from *Griggs* in 1989, Congress codified its understanding of this cause of action in the Civil Rights Act of 1991, Pub. L. No. 102–166, 105 Stat. 1071, which added a new § 703(k)(1) to Title VII, 42 U.S.C. § 2000e–2(k). Section 703(k)(1) recognizes a claim for relief if the plaintiff can show that the employer uses an employment practice that causes a disparate impact on the basis of race, sex, etc., and the employer "fails to demonstrate that the challenged practice is job related for the position in question and consistent with business necessity."

For a comprehensive introduction to Title VII doctrine and evolution, see Barbara Allen Babcock, Ann E. Freedman, Susan Deller Ross, Wendy Webster Williams, Rhonda Copelon, Deborah L. Rhode, and Nadine Taub, *Sex Discrimination and the Law: History, Practice, and Theory* ch. 2 (1996).

PART A.   PREGNANCY DISCRIMINATION UNDER TITLE VII

One of the most important early questions of statutory interpretation involving the prohibition against sex discrimination was whether it covered discrimination based on pregnancy. The EEOC initially viewed pregnancy-based discrimination as outside the purview of the Act (see Opinion Letter from the EEOC General Counsel, Oct. 17, 1966), but adopted a regulation holding such discrimination to be sex discrimination in 1972.

Following the reasoning of *Geduldig*, the Supreme Court held in *General Electric v. Gilbert*, 429 U.S. 125 (1976), that pregnancy-based discrimination does not constitute sex-based discrimination, because although only women can become pregnant, the class of "non-pregnant persons" includes both women and men. In 1978, Congress responded to the Court's decision by amending Title VII to "prohibit sex discrimination

son has filed a timely charge, the EEOC determines whether there is "reasonable cause to believe that the charge is true," and if so it will try to eliminate the unlawful practice informally through "conference, conciliation, and persuasion" (§ 706(a), *id.* § 2000e–5(a)). If the EEOC is unable to obtain voluntary compliance with Title VII, it notifies the aggrieved person and informs her that she may bring a lawsuit in federal court within thirty days (§ 706(e), *id.* § 2000e–5(e)). To remedy an unlawful employment practice, a court may enjoin the practice and order "such affirmative action as may be appropriate, which may include reinstatement or hiring of employees, with or without back pay" (§ 706(g), *id.* § 2000e–5(g)).

on the basis of pregnancy." The new amendment, entitled the Pregnancy Discrimination Act ("PDA"), added a new § 701(k):

> The terms "because of sex" or "on the basis of sex" include, but are not limited to, because of or on the basis of pregnancy, childbirth, or related medical conditions; and women affected by pregnancy, childbirth, or related medical conditions shall be treated the same for all employment-related purposes, including receipt of benefits under fringe benefit programs, as other persons not so affected but similar in their ability or inability to work * * *

42 U.S.C. § 2000e(k). This provision "made clear that, for all Title VII purposes, discrimination based on a woman's pregnancy is, on its face, discrimination because of her sex." The Supreme Court in *Newport News Shipbuilding & Dry Dock Co. v. EEOC*, 462 U.S. 669 (1983), held that the 1978 amendment not only overrode the *Gilbert* result, but overruled *Gilbert*'s stingy approach to sex discrimination in the context of pregnancy.

NOTE ON THE EQUAL TREATMENT/SPECIAL TREATMENT DEBATE AND THE PDA'S APPLICATION TO PREGNANCY–BASED PROTECTIONS

Although the PDA "fixed" the problem created by the *Geduldig-Gilbert* line of cases, it also set the stage for one of the most contentious feminist debates of the 1980s. The intent behind the enactment of the PDA was to equalize "up," by forcing employers to include pregnancy in their comprehensive health insurance coverage and medical leave policies. At least theoretically, it is always possible to also equalize "down," which in this instance would have meant denying such coverage to everyone, for all conditions. As a practical matter, workers who already had health insurance and sick leave could be counted on to oppose such a proposal by employers; and, in a reasonably competitive market for labor, most companies would not want to be seen as such an unattractive employer. For small businesses, however, these assumptions did not necessarily hold true, especially for the issue of sick leave. Responding to business concerns opposing a mandate requiring medical leave for all workers but persuaded by women's rights advocates that California should amend its state law to counter the effect of *Gilbert,* the California legislature enacted the following statute while the PDA was still pending in Congress:

> It shall be an unlawful employment practice unless based upon a bona fide occupational qualification: * * * (b) For any employer to refuse to allow a female employee affected by pregnancy, childbirth, or related medical conditions * * * (2) To take a leave on account of pregnancy for a reasonable period of time; provided, such period shall not exceed four months * * *. Reasonable period of time means that period during which the female employee is disabled on account of pregnancy, childbirth, or related medical conditions. * * *

Cal. Gov't Code Ann. § 12945(b)(2) (West 1980).

When Lillian Garland sought to return from her pregnancy leave in 1982, her employer, California Federal Savings & Loan Association, informed her that it had not saved her position. She charged the bank with violating the California statute, and it sought a declaration that the California statute was invalid as inconsistent with and pre-empted by the PDA. The bank argued that it treated male and female workers identically and thus was in compliance with the PDA and that the pregnancy leave mandated by the state statute would force it to treat pregnant workers differently, which the PDA prohibited.

Feminists filed briefs on all sides of the case, and scholars engaged in lengthy debates in the pages of law reviews. The group that became known as the "special treatment" advocates argued in support of the California statute, reasoning that its effect was to produce an outcome that put women on equal footing with men, even if it violated formal strictures of equality in doing so. Pregnancy had been excluded from coverage and leave policies because the underlying norm was the male worker, they reasoned. The California approach guaranteed that women's life experiences, including pregnancy, had to be treated also as the norm. Without the promise that they could return to their jobs after childbirth, women could never achieve equality in the workforce.[c] Professor Christine Littleton and others authored a brief for the Coalition for Reproductive Equality in the Workplace which supported the California law.

The "equal treatment" feminists saw that approach as a trap. For decades, protectionist labor laws had been enacted with the purported goal of helping women, but had functioned only to help keep them in their place. A California-style system would reinforce the old notion that women were more expensive as workers and generated bothersome special rules, ultimately hurting women. Such laws would also reinforce and perpetuate the assumption that children were women's concern and responsibility; a father who sought to spend even one day caring for an infant could be fired for doing so.[d] Joan Bertin and others authored a brief for the ACLU opposing the California law and arguing that it was preempted. Professors Wendy Webster Williams and Susan Deller Ross, authors of the PDA, wrote a brief for the National Organization for Women and the Women's Legal Defense Fund, arguing that the benefits of the California law should be extended to men in order to meet the requirements of the PDA.

At a more theoretical level, feminists disagreed over how special pregnancy and childbirth were; do they amount to a "real" difference? The text of the PDA reflects the position that the experience of giving birth is analogous to any number of other temporarily disabling conditions. Some

---

c. See, *e.g.*, Sylvia A. Law, "Rethinking Sex and the Constitution," 132 *U. Penn. L. Rev.* 955 (1984); Christine Littleton, "Reconstructing Sexual Equality," 75 *Calif. L. Rev.* 1279 (1987); Linda J. Krieger & Patricia N. Cooney, "The Miller–Wohl Controversy: Equal Treatment, Positive Action and the Meaning of Women's Equality," 13 *Golden Gate L. Rev.* 513 (1983).

d. See, *e.g.*, Wendy Williams, "Equality's Riddle: Pregnancy and the Equal Treatment/Special Treatment Debate," 13 *N.Y.U. Rev. L. & Soc. Change* 325 (1985).

special treatment feminists characterized insistence on that analogy as assimilationism. At bottom, this was a debate about the extent to which the meaning of pregnancy was a social construct, and an intense battle over what was the best strategy to advance the interests of most women, in both the long term and the short term. It touched a nerve underlying many disputes in feminism. Recall the debate over protectionist laws in the early twentieth century from Part A of Section 1 of this chapter. As women's studies scholar Ann Snitow wrote in her analysis of whether women (or mothers) should claim a special insight for making anti-war arguments:

> Th[e] tension between needing to act as women and needing an identity not overdetermined by our gender is as old as Western feminism. It is at the core of what feminism is. The divide runs, twisting and turning, right through movement history. The problem of identity it poses was barely conceivable before the eighteenth century, when almost everyone saw women as a separate species. Since then absolute definitions of gender difference have fundamentally eroded, and the idea "woman" has become a question rather than a given.

Ann Snitow, "A Gender Diary," in *Feminism and History* 506 (Joan Wallach Scott ed., 1996).

California Federal Savings and Loan Association v. Mark Guerra

Supreme Court of the United States, 1987.
479 U.S. 272, 107 S.Ct. 683, 93 L.Ed.2d 613.

■ JUSTICE MARSHALL delivered the opinion of the Court. * * *

In order to decide whether the California statute requires or permits employers to violate Title VII, as amended by the PDA, or is inconsistent with the purposes of the statute, we must determine whether the PDA prohibits the States from requiring employers to provide reinstatement to pregnant workers, regardless of their policy for disabled workers generally.

Petitioners argue that the language of the federal statute itself unambiguously rejects California's "special treatment" approach to pregnancy discrimination, thus rendering any resort to the legislative history unnecessary. They contend that the second clause of the PDA forbids an employer to treat pregnant employees any differently than other disabled employees. Because " '[t]he purpose of Congress is the ultimate touchstone' " of the pre-emption inquiry, however, we must examine the PDA's language against the background of its legislative history and historical context. * * *

* * * By adding pregnancy to the definition of sex discrimination prohibited by Title VII, the first clause of the PDA reflects Congress' disapproval of the reasoning in *Gilbert*. Rather than imposing a limitation on the remedial purpose of the PDA, we believe that the second clause was intended to overrule the holding in *Gilbert* and to illustrate how discrimination against pregnancy is to be remedied. * * * [W]e agree with the Court

of Appeals' conclusion that Congress intended the PDA to be "a floor beneath which pregnancy disability benefits may not drop—not a ceiling above which they may not rise."

The context in which Congress considered the issue of pregnancy discrimination supports this view of the PDA. Congress had before it extensive evidence of discrimination *against* pregnancy, particularly in disability and health insurance programs like those challenged in *Gilbert* * * *. The Reports, debates, and hearings make abundantly clear that Congress intended the PDA to provide relief for working women and to end discrimination against pregnant workers. In contrast to the thorough account of discrimination against pregnant workers, the legislative history is devoid of any discussion of preferential treatment of pregnancy, beyond acknowledgments of the existence of state statutes providing for such preferential treatment. Opposition to the PDA came from those concerned with the cost of including pregnancy in health and disability-benefit plans and the application of the bill to abortion, not from those who favored special accommodation of pregnancy. * * *

Title VII, as amended by the PDA, and California's pregnancy disability leave statute share a common goal. The purpose of Title VII is "to achieve equality of employment opportunities and remove barriers that have operated in the past to favor an identifiable group of . . . employees over other employees." *Griggs v. Duke Power Co.*, 401 U.S. 424, 429–430 (1971). Rather than limiting existing Title VII principles and objectives, the PDA extends them to cover pregnancy. As Senator Williams, a sponsor of the Act, stated: "The entire thrust . . . behind this legislation is to guarantee women the basic right to participate fully and equally in the workforce, without denying them the fundamental right to full participation in family life." 123 Cong. Rec. 29658 (1977).

Section 12945(b)(2) also promotes equal employment opportunity. By requiring employers to reinstate women after a reasonable pregnancy disability leave, § 12945(b)(2) ensures that they will not lose their jobs on account of pregnancy disability. * * * By "taking pregnancy into account," California's pregnancy disability-leave statute allows women, as well as men, to have families without losing their jobs.

We emphasize the limited nature of the benefits § 12945(b)(2) provides. The statute is narrowly drawn to cover only the period of *actual physical disability* on account of pregnancy, childbirth, or related medical conditions. Accordingly, unlike the protective labor legislation prevalent earlier in this century, § 12945(b)(2) does not reflect archaic or stereotypical notions about pregnancy and the abilities of pregnant workers. A statute based on such stereotypical assumptions would, of course, be inconsistent with Title VII's goal of equal employment opportunity. * * *

■ [The concurring opinions of JUSTICES STEVENS and SCALIA are omitted.]

■ JUSTICE WHITE, with whom THE CHIEF JUSTICE [REHNQUIST] and JUSTICE POWELL join, dissenting. * * *

The second clause [of the PDA] could not be clearer: it mandates that pregnant employees "shall be treated the same for all employment-related purposes" as nonpregnant employees similarly situated with respect to their ability or inability to work. This language leaves no room for preferential treatment of pregnant workers. * * *

Contrary to the mandate of the PDA, California law requires every employer to have a disability leave policy for pregnancy even if it has none for any other disability. An employer complies with California law if it has a leave policy for pregnancy but denies it for every other disability. On its face, § 12945(b)(2) is in square conflict with the PDA and is therefore preempted. Because the California law permits employers to single out pregnancy for preferential treatment and therefore to violate Title VII, it is not saved by § 708 which limits pre-emption of state laws to those that require or permit an employer to commit an unfair employment practice.

The majority nevertheless would save the California law on two grounds. First, it holds that the PDA does not require disability from pregnancy to be treated the same as other disabilities; instead, it forbids less favorable, but permits more favorable, benefits for pregnancy disability. The express command of the PDA is unambiguously to the contrary, and the legislative history casts no doubt on that mandate.

The legislative materials reveal Congress' plain intent not to put pregnancy in a class by itself within Title VII, as the majority does with its "floor ... not a ceiling" approach. The Senate Report clearly stated:

> "By defining sex discrimination to include discrimination against pregnant women, the bill rejects the view that employers may treat pregnancy and its incidents as *sui generis*, without regard to its functional comparability to other conditions. Under this bill, the treatment of pregnant women in covered employment must focus not on their condition alone but on the actual effects of that condition on their ability to work. Pregnant women who are able to work must be permitted to work on the same conditions as other employees; and when they are not able to work for medical reasons, they must be accorded the same rights, leave privileges and other benefits, as other workers who are disabled from working."

[S.Rep. No. 95–331, p. 4 (1977).] * * *

The majority correctly reports that Congress focused on discrimination against, rather than preferential treatment of, pregnant workers. There is only one direct reference in the legislative history to preferential treatment. Senator Brooke stated during the Senate debate: "I would emphasize most strongly that S. 995 in no way provides special disability benefits for working women. They have not demanded, nor asked, for such benefits. They have asked only to be treated with fairness, to be accorded the same employment rights as men." [123 Cong.Rec. 29664 (1977).] Given the evidence before Congress of the wide-spread discrimination against pregnant workers, it is probable that most Members of Congress did not seriously consider the possibility that someone would want to afford preferential treatment to pregnant workers. The parties and their *amici* argued vigorously to this Court the policy implications of preferential treatment of pregnant workers. In favor of preferential treatment it was urged with conviction that preferential treatment merely enables women, like men, to have children without losing their jobs. In opposition to preferential treatment it was urged with equal conviction that preferential treatment represents a resurgence of the 19th-century protective legislation which perpetuated sex-role stereotypes and which impeded women in their efforts to take their rightful place in the workplace. See, *e.g., Muller; Bradwell* (Bradley, J., concurring). It is not the place of this Court, however, to resolve this policy dispute. Our task is to interpret Congress' intent in enacting the PDA. Congress' silence in its consideration of the PDA with respect to preferential treatment of pregnant workers cannot fairly be interpreted to abrogate the plain statements in the legislative history, not to mention the language of the statute, that equality of treatment was to be the guiding principle of the PDA. * * *

NOTE ON SUBSEQUENT PARENTAL LEAVE LEGISLATION

Throughout the 1980s and early 1990s, women's rights advocates sought a law guaranteeing leave for both parents. In 1993, the Family and Medical Leave Act became law. Under it, all employers of 50 or more workers have to offer employees up to 12 weeks of unpaid leave, with continuation of health benefits and a right to return to the same or similar job, in order for the worker to care for a newly-born or newly-adopted child, to deal with a serious health problem of his own, or to care for a spouse, child, or parent of the employee who has a serious health problem. 29 U.S.C. §§ 2601–2654 (1996). Anecdotal reports indicate that the overwhelming majority of workers who take leave upon the arrival of a child are women, even though men are equally entitled to do so. In other words, although many firms now have a "mommy track," there is in practice no "daddy track." Where does this leave the special treatment/equal treatment debate?

Crystal Chambers v. Omaha Girls Club, Inc.

U.S. Court of Appeals for the Eighth Circuit, 1987.
834 F.2d 697, *rehearing en banc denied,* 840 F.2d 583 (1988).

■ WOLLMAN, CIRCUIT JUDGE:

[The Omaha Girls Club is a private, non-profit corporation that offers programs designed to assist young girls between the ages of eight and eighteen to maximize their life opportunities, through creating trusting relationships among girls and with adult mentors. Among the Club's many activities are programs directed at pregnancy prevention. Most of the girls and staff members who participate in this and other programs in two Omaha locations are African American. One of the Club's "role model rules" is a ban of single-parent pregnancies among its staff members.

Crystal Chambers, a black single woman, was employed by the Club as an arts and crafts instructor at the Club's North Omaha facility. The Club terminated her when she became pregnant, in violation of the role model rule. Chambers challenged the rule against single-mother pregnancies as a "disparate treatment" in violation of Title VII, as amended by the PDA, and as having a "disparate impact" on African–American women, in violation of Title VII's ban on race discrimination. Her claims were dismissed by the trial court.]

A plaintiff seeking to prove discrimination under the disparate impact theory must show that a facially neutral employment practice has a significant adverse impact on members of a protected minority group. The burden then shifts to the employer to show that the practice has a manifest relationship to the employment in question and is justifiable on the ground of business necessity. Even if the employer shows that the discriminatory employment practice is justified by business necessity, the plaintiff may prevail by showing that other practices would accomplish the employer's objectives without the attendant discriminatory effects. The district court found that "because of the significantly higher fertility rate among black females, the rule banning single pregnancies would impact black women more harshly." Thus, Chambers established the disparate impact of the role model rule. The Club then sought to justify the rule as a business necessity.

Establishing a business necessity defense presents an employer with a "heavy burden." Business necessity exists only if the challenged employment practice has " ' "a manifest relationship to the employment in question." ' " The employer must demonstrate that there is a " 'compelling need * * * to maintain that practice,' " and the practice cannot be justified by " 'routine business considerations.' " Moreover, the employer may be required to show that the challenged employment practice is " 'necessary to safe and efficient job performance,' " or that the employer's goals are "significantly served by" the practice.

The district court found that the role model rule is justified by business necessity because there is a manifest relationship between the Club's fundamental purpose and the rule. Specifically, the court found:

> The Girls Club has established by the evidence that its only purpose is to serve young girls between the ages of eight and eighteen and to provide these women with exposure to the greatest number of available positive options in life. The Girls Club has established that teenage pregnancy is contrary to this purpose and philosophy. The Girls Club established that it honestly believed that to permit single pregnant staff members to work with the girls would convey the impression that the Girls Club condoned pregnancy for the girls in the age group it serves. The testimony of board members * * * made clear that the policy was not based upon a morality standard, but rather, on a belief that teenage pregnancies severely limit the available opportunities for teenage girls. The Girls Club also established that the policy was just one prong of a comprehensive attack on the problem of

teenage pregnancy. The Court is satisfied that a manifest relationship exists between the Girls Club's fundamental purpose and its single pregnancy policy.

The court also relied in part on expert testimony to the effect that the role model rule could be helpful in preventing teenage pregnancy. Chambers argues, however, that the district court erred in finding business necessity because the role model rule is based only on speculation by the Club and has not been validated by any studies showing that it prevents pregnancy among the Club's members. * * *

We believe that "the district court's account of the evidence is plausible in light of the record viewed in its entirety." Therefore, we cannot say that the district court's finding of business necessity is clearly erroneous. The district court's conclusion on the evidence is not an impermissible one. Although validation studies can be helpful in evaluating such questions, they are not required to maintain a successful business necessity defense. Indeed, we are uncertain whether the role model rule by its nature is suited to validation by an empirical study. * * *

Chambers argues further, however, that the district court erred in discounting alternative practices that the Club could have used to ameliorate the discriminatory effects of the role model rule. Chambers contends that the Club either could have granted her a leave of absence or transferred her to a position that did not involve contact with the Club's members. The Club responds that neither of these alternatives was available in this case. The Club has a history of granting leaves of up to six weeks, but the purposes of the role model rule would have required a five to six month leave for Chambers, given that the pregnancy would have become visually apparent probably within three or four months. Moreover, employing a temporary replacement to take Chamber's position would itself have required six months of on-the-job training before the replacement would have been able to interact with the girls on the level that the Club's approach requires. The use of temporary replacements would also disrupt the atmosphere of stability that the Club attempts to provide and would be inconsistent with the relationship-building and interpersonal interaction entailed in the Club's role model approach. Furthermore, transfer to a "noncontact position" apparently was impossible because there are no positions at the Club that do not involve contact with Club members. The district court found that the Club considered these alternatives and determined them to be unworkable. We are unable to conclude that the district court's finding that there were no satisfactory alternatives to the dismissal of Chambers pursuant to the role model rule is clearly erroneous. Accordingly, we hold that the district court's finding that the role model rule is justified by business necessity and thus does not violate Title VII under the disparate impact theory is not clearly erroneous.

Unlike the disparate impact theory, the disparate treatment theory requires a plaintiff seeking to prove employment discrimination to show discriminatory animus. The plaintiff must first establish a prima facie case of discrimination. The burden of production then shifts to the employer to show a legitimate, nondiscriminatory reason for the challenged employment practice. If the employer makes such a showing, then the plaintiff may show that the reasons given by the employer were pretextual. No violation of Title VII exists, however, if the employer can show that the challenged employment practice is a bona fide occupational qualification (BFOQ). * * *

The BFOQ exception is " 'an extremely narrow exception to the general prohibition of discrimination on the basis of sex.' " In *Dothard v. Rawlinson*, the Supreme Court found that a rule that prohibited employment of women in contact positions in all-male Alabama prisons was a BFOQ under the particular circumstances of that case, which involved a prison system rife with violence. The statutory language is, of course, the best guide to the content of the BFOQ exception; however, the courts, including the Supreme Court in *Dothard*, have noted the existence of several formulations for evaluating whether an employment practice is a BFOQ. The formulations include: whether " 'the essence of the business operation would be undermined' " without the challenged employment practice; whether safe and efficient performance of the job would be possible without the challenged employment practice; and whether the challenged employment practice has " 'a manifest relationship to the employment in question.' "

Although the district court did not clearly conclude that the role model rule qualified as a BFOQ, several of the court's other findings are persuasive on this issue. The court's findings of fact, many of which are relevant to the analysis of a potential BFOQ exception, are binding on this court unless clearly erroneous. The facts relevant to establishing a BFOQ are the same as those found by the district court in the course of its business necessity analysis. As already noted, the district court found that the role model rule has a manifest relationship to the Club's fundamental purpose and that there were no workable alternatives to the rule. Moreover, the district court's finding of business necessity itself is persuasive as to the existence of a BFOQ. This court has noted that the analysis of a BFOQ "is similar to and overlaps with the judicially created 'business necessity' test." The various standards for establishing business necessity are quite similar to those for determining a BFOQ. Indeed, this court has on different occasions applied the same standard—"manifest relationship"—to both business necessity and BFOQ. Inasmuch as we already have affirmed the district court's finding of business necessity as not clearly erroneous, we feel compelled to conclude that "[i]n the particular factual circumstances of this case," the role model rule is reasonably necessary to the Club's operations. Thus, we hold that the role model rule qualifies as a bona fide occupational qualification. * * *

■ McMILLAN, CIRCUIT JUDGE, dissenting. * * *

* * * I would reject the BFOQ or business necessity exceptions offered by OGC because there is no evidence to support a relationship between teenage pregnancies and the employment of an unwed pregnant instructor,

and therefore I am left with the definite and firm conclusion that the district court made a mistake.

The district court, and now this court, accepts without any proof OGC's assumption that the presence of an unwed pregnant instructor is related to teenage pregnancies. OGC failed to present surveys, school statistics or any other empirical data connecting the incidence of teenage pregnancy with the pregnancy of an adult instructor. OGC also failed to present evidence that other girls clubs or similar types of organizations employed such a rule. OGC instead relied on two or three highly questionable anecdotal incidents to support the rule.

* * * OGC had the burden of establishing a reasonable basis, that is a factual basis, for its belief, and in the absence of such proof, OGC may not implement the discriminatory rule.

Although there are no cases that have considered precisely the issue raised in this case, a few courts have considered the role model defense in school settings and all have rejected the schools' role model defenses. In *Andrews v. Drew Municipal Separate School District*, 507 F.2d 611 (5th Cir.1975), two unwed mothers challenged the school district's policy that prohibited the employment of teachers and teachers' aides who were unwed parents. Not unlike OGC, the school district defended the policy on the basis that such teachers would be poor role models for the children and that employing such teachers could lead to schoolgirl pregnancies. The Fifth Circuit struck down the rule.

> In the absence of overt, positive statements to which the children can relate, we are convinced that the likelihood of inferred learning that unwed parenthood is necessarily good or praiseworthy, is highly improbable, if not speculative. We are not at all persuaded by defendants' suggestions, quite implausible in our view, that students are apt to seek out knowledge of the personal and private life-styles of teachers or other adults within the school system (i.e. whether they are divorced, separated, happily married or single, etc.), and, when known, will approve and seek to emulate them.

[*Andrews v. Drew Municipal Separate Sch. Dist.*, 507 F.2d 611, 617 (5th Cir. 1975).

[Courts also rejected the role model defense in *Avery v. Homewood City Board of Education*, 674 F.2d 337 (5th Cir.1982) (school district justified the firing of an unwed pregnant teacher), and in *Ponton v. Newport News School Board*, 632 F.Supp. 1056 (E.D.Va.1986) (similar).]

The district court in the present case, although correctly articulating the BFOQ and business necessity tests, failed to actually apply the tests. Instead of requiring OGC to demonstrate a reasonable relationship between teenage pregnancy and the employment of single pregnant women, the district court accepted the beliefs and assumptions of OGC board members. * * *

Neither an employer's sincere belief, without more, (nor a district court's belief), that a discriminatory employment practice is related and necessary to the accomplishments of the employer's goals is sufficient to establish a BFOQ or business necessity defense. The fact that the goals are laudable and the beliefs sincerely held does not substitute for data which demonstrate a relationship between the discriminatory practice and the goals. The district court, recognizing that there was no data to support such a relationship, should have held that OGC failed to carry its burden of showing a BFOQ or business necessity.

Even if I were to accept for purposes of argument that OGC established a relationship between the single pregnancy policy and the work of the club, the BFOQ and the business necessity exceptions must still fail because OGC did not establish that there were no less discriminatory alternatives available. Unlike the district court and the panel majority, I am unimpressed by OGC's rejection of alternatives with less discriminatory impact. OGC's personnel policy provided leave of absences for up to six weeks for pregnancies and other sicknesses and longer leaves upon approval of the board. It is clear that OGC could have accommodated its stated mission and the pregnancy of Crystal Chambers by granting her a leave of absence or by placing her in a noncontact position. Administrative inconvenience is not a sufficient justification for not utilizing these less discriminatory alternatives. * * *

NOTES ON *CHAMBERS*, TITLE VII DISPARATE IMPACT LIABILITY, AND ROLE MODEL ARGUMENTS

In constitutional sex discrimination cases like *Feeney*, plaintiffs alleging that a state employment practice has a disparate impact upon them must also show that the disparate impact was "intended" by the state. In short, in the constitutional context, disparate impact cases are turned into disparate treatment cases. Title VII as the Supreme Court interpreted it in *Griggs* is more liberal, because a plaintiff like Crystal Chambers can recover if she is able to show *either* that the employer treated her differently because of her sex *or* that the employer's policy had a disparate impact upon a sex-based group (women) that is not justified. The court's opinion separates these two kinds of claims and reveals their analytical structure. How do the two kinds of claims operate in pregnancy cases?

1. *Race, Gender and Sexuality. Chambers* is an excellent example of a case in which issues pertaining to gender and sexuality are thoroughly "raced." The plaintiff uses race as part of her claim, asserting successfully that the role model policy has a disparate impact on African–American women, because they are more likely to be single mothers. But the fact that both she and her charges are African American seems to strengthen the defendant's argument about the extent to which the role model effect actually operates. Would such an effect be accepted if the adult and the teenagers were all white? If the adult were African American, but the girls were white?

Professor Regina Austin sees *Chambers* as a battle over racialized meanings of sexuality. Noting that most of the teenagers' own mothers were not married, Austin reads a deeper meaning into the case:

> Although Crystal Chambers' firing was publicly justified on the ground that she would have an adverse impact on the young Club members, it is likely that the Club in part sacked her because she resisted its effort to model her in conformity with white and middle-class morality. In its struggles against the culture of the girls' mothers, Crystal Chambers, employee and arts and crafts instructor, was supposed to be on the Club's side. But like a treasonous recruit, Crystal turned up unmarried and pregnant. As such, she embodied the enemy. If the Club could not succeed in shaping and restraining the workers whose economic welfare it controlled, how could it expect to win over the young members and supplant their mothers' cultural legacy. * * *
>
> The critique of the images of black women whites have historically promoted is relevant to the assessment of the treatment accorded contemporary role models. Role models are supposed to forgo the vices of Jezebel and exhibit the many virtues of Mammy. The case of Crystal Chambers illustrates this quite well. When Crystal Chambers refused to subordinate her interest in motherhood to the supposed welfare of the Club girls, she essentially rejected the Club's attempt to impose upon her the "positive" stereotype of the black female as a repressed, self-sacrificing, nurturing woman whose heart extends to other people's children because she cannot (or should not) have kids of her own. Instead, like a Jezebel, Crystal Chambers "flaunted" her sexuality and reproductive capacity, but, unlike her counterpart in slavery, she did so in furtherance of her own ends, in defiance of her white employers, and in disregard of a rule that forbade her from connecting with a man outside of the marriage relationship.

Regina Austin, "Sapphire Bound!," 1989 *Wis.L.Rev.* 539, 557, 571.

2. *Analytical Ramifications for Gay Rights Cases.* Should social science evidence have been necessary in this case, as the dissent charged? Is suppressing teenage pregnancy a legitimate goal? Is suppressing teenage homosexuality a legitimate goal? If suppressing teenage pregnancy or homosexuality is a legitimate goal, will a BFOQ such as was found in this case control decisions even under a law prohibiting discrimination on the basis of sexual orientation? (See the District of Columbia Human Rights Act [Appendix 2], Wisconsin's employment discrimination law [Appendix 3], and the proposed Employment Nondiscrimination Act [Appendix 4].) What will the role of validation studies be in such a case? Which side in a gay teacher case will seek to prove what? Could schools distinguish between open and closeted gay men or lesbians? In *Thompson v. Wisconsin Dept. of Public Instruction*, 541 N.W.2d 182 (Wis.App.1995) a gay teacher kept his job after having been convicted of two criminal offenses involving sexual fondling in a public park. The court ruled that there was no nexus between those offenses and his abilities as a teacher. Compare the policy on excluding gay scoutmasters upheld in *Curran v. Mt. Diablo Council of the Boy Scouts of America*, 29 Cal.Rptr.2d 580 (Cal.App.1994), appeal pending.

3. *Nondiscriminatory Reasons?* The Sixth Circuit upheld the firing of an unmarried pregnant teacher, finding that she had been fired because she had sex outside of marriage, and not because of her pregnancy *per se*. *Boyd v. Harding Academy of Memphis*, 88 F.3d 410 (6th Cir.1996). In *Harvey v. YWCA*, 533 F.Supp. 949 (W.D.N.C.1982), the court upheld the firing of an unmarried pregnant program director by the Young Women's Christian Association on the ground that her expressed intent to offer herself as an "alternative role model" constituted a legitimate nondiscriminatory reason for her termination. Do such grounds fall outside the scope of the PDA? How would your opinion be affected by evidence that the defendant had fired both males and females for this reason?

PROBLEM 10–2

PREGNANCY DISCRIMINATION TO PROTECT THE FETUS

Johnson Controls manufactures batteries. Because some of its process-es involve the use of lead, certain tasks risking exposure to lead could be harmful to a human fetus. In 1982 it adopted a policy of excluding pregnant women and women of childbearing age from jobs presenting significant risks of lead exposure. Female employees, including one woman who has been sterilized and one 50-year-old woman who was transferred out of a lead-exposure job, sue Johnson Controls for violation of Title VII as amended by the PDA. What defense does Johnson Controls have? Should it prevail? Would a more narrowly tailored policy pass PDA scrutiny? See *International Union, UAW v. Johnson Controls, Inc.*, 499 U.S. 187 (1991).

PART B.   GENDER AND SEXUAL ORIENTATION DISCRIMINATION UNDER TITLE VII

Given the language, history, and purposes of Title VII's prohibition of job discrimination on the basis of "sex," which if any of the following hypothetical associates has a claim for relief under Title VII?[e]

Alice, Bob, and Calvin are sixth-year associates at a law firm. All three are up for partnership, along with seven other candidates. A, B, and C are the top three associates in terms of billable hours and generation of business, and their work evaluations are also the tops. Yet the partnership decides to deny them promotion and to make the other seven partners.

A, B, and C all file Title VII complaints with the EEOC and then the courts, making the following allegations: Alice claims that she was rejected because her "tough macho behavior" and "unladylike lan-

---

e. This hypothetical is taken from I. Bennett Capers, "Sex(ual) Orientation and   Title VII," 91 *Colum. L. Rev.* 1158 (1991) (student note).

guage" ruffled the all-male partnership. Bob is told that the partners consider him "too soft" and wondered whether he "has lace in his jockey shorts." Calvin claims that he was rejected because he is openly gay.

Outline your answers, and then read the following decisions.

Robert DeSantis et al. v. Pacific Telephone & Telegraph Co.
Donald Strailey v. Happy Times Nursery School, Inc.
Judy Lundin and Barbara Buckley v. Pacific Telephone & Telegraph Co.

U.S. Court of Appeals for the Ninth Circuit, 1979.
608 F.2d 327.

■ Choy, Circuit Judge. * * *

Appellant Strailey, a male, was fired by the Happy Times Nursery School after two years' service as a teacher. He alleged that he was fired because he wore a small gold ear-loop to school prior to the commencement of the school year. * * *

DeSantis, Boyle, and Simard, all males, claimed that Pacific Telephone & Telegraph Co. (PT&T) impermissibly discriminated against them because of their homosexuality. DeSantis alleged that he was not hired when a PT&T supervisor concluded that he was a homosexual. According to appellants' brief, "BOYLE was continually harassed by his co-workers and had to quit to preserve his health after only three months because his supervisors did nothing to alleviate this condition." Finally, "SIMARD was forced to quit under similar conditions after almost four years of employment with PT&T, but he was harassed by his supervisors [as well].... In addition, his personnel file has been marked as not eligible for rehire, and his applications for employment were rejected by PT&T in 1974 and 1976." Appellants DeSantis, Boyle, and Simard also alleged that PT&T officials have publicly stated that they would not hire homosexuals. * * *

Lundin and Buckley, both females, were operators with PT&T. They filed suit in federal court alleging that PT&T discriminated against them because of their known lesbian relationship and eventually fired them. They also alleged that they endured numerous insults by PT&T employees because of their relationship. Finally, Lundin alleged that the union that represented her as a PT&T operator failed adequately to represent her interests and failed adequately to present her grievance regarding her treatment. * * *

[All the above plaintiffs brought suit under Title VII, charging sex discrimination. The district court in all three sets of cases dismissed plaintiffs' claims under Title VII. The Ninth Circuit consolidated the different cases for purpose of appeals and affirmed.]

Appellants argue first that the district courts erred in holding that Title VII does not prohibit discrimination on the basis of sexual preference. They claim that in prohibiting certain employment discrimination on the basis of "sex," Congress meant to include discrimination on the basis of sexual orientation. They add that in a trial they could establish that discrimination against homosexuals disproportionately effects men and that this disproportionate impact and correlation between discrimination on the basis of sexual preference and discrimination on the basis of "sex" requires that sexual preference be considered a subcategory of the "sex" category of Title VII. See 42 U.S.C. § 2000e–2.

In *Holloway v. Arthur Andersen & Co.*, 566 F.2d 659 (9th Cir.1977), plaintiff argued that her employer had discriminated against her because she was undergoing a sex transformation and that this discrimination violated Title VII's prohibition on sex discrimination. This court rejected that claim, writing:

> The cases interpreting Title VII sex discrimination provisions agree that they were intended to place women on an equal footing with men.
>
> Giving the statute its plain meaning, this court concludes that Congress had only the traditional notions of "sex" in mind. Later legislative activity makes this narrow definition even more evident. Several bills have been introduced to *amend* the Civil Rights Act to prohibit discrimination against "sexual preference." None have been enacted into law.
>
> Congress has not shown any intent other than to restrict the term "sex" to its traditional meaning. Therefore, this court will not expand Title VII's application in the absence of Congressional mandate. The manifest purpose of Title VII's prohibition against sex discrimination in employment is to ensure that men and women are treated equally, absent a bona fide relationship between the qualifications for the job and the person's sex.

Id. at 662–63 (footnotes omitted).

Following *Holloway*, we conclude that Title VII's prohibition of "sex" discrimination applies only to discrimination on the basis of gender and should not be judicially extended to include sexual preference such as homosexuality. See *Smith v. Liberty Mutual Insurance Co.*, 569 F.2d 325, 326–27 (5th Cir.1978); *Holloway*, 566 F.2d at 662–63; *Voyles v. Ralph K. Davies Medical Center*, 403 F. Supp. 456, 456–57 (N.D.Cal.1975), *aff'd without published opinion*, 570 F.2d 354 (9th Cir. 1978). * * *

Appellants argue that recent decisions dealing with disproportionate impact require that discrimination against homosexuals fall within the purview of Title VII. They contend that these recent decisions, like *Griggs v. Duke Power Co.*, 401 U.S. 424 (1971), establish that any employment criterion that affects one sex more than the other violates Title VII. They quote from *Griggs*:

> What is required by Congress [under Title VII] is the removal of artificial, arbitrary, and unnecessary barriers to employment when the barriers operate invidiously to discriminate on the basis of racial or other impermissible classifications.

401 U.S. at 431. They claim that in a trial they could prove that discrimination against homosexuals disproportionately affects men both because of the greater incidence of homosexuality in the male population and because of the greater likelihood of an employer's discovering male homosexuals compared to female homosexuals.

Assuming that appellants can otherwise satisfy the requirement of *Griggs*, we do not believe that *Griggs* can be applied to extend Title VII protection to homosexuals. In finding that the disproportionate impact of educational tests on blacks violated Title VII, the Supreme Court in *Griggs* sought to effectuate a major congressional purpose in enacting Title VII: protection of blacks from employment discrimination. * * *

The *Holloway* court noted that in passing Title VII Congress did not intend to protect sexual orientation and has repeatedly refused to extend such protection. Appellants now ask us to employ the disproportionate impact decisions as an artifice to "bootstrap" Title VII protection for homosexuals under the guise of protecting men generally.

This we are not free to do. Adoption of this bootstrap device would frustrate congressional objectives as explicated in *Holloway*, not effectuate congressional goals as in *Griggs*. It would achieve by judicial "construction" what Congress did not do and has consistently refused to do on many occasions. It would violate the rule that our duty in construing a statute is to "ascertain . . . and give effect to the legislative will." We conclude that the *Griggs* disproportionate impact theory may not be applied to extend Title VII protection to homosexuals. * * *

Appellant Strailey contends that he was terminated by the Happy Times Nursery School because that school felt that it was inappropriate for a male teacher to wear an earring to school. He claims that the school's reliance on a stereotype—that a male should have a virile rather than an effeminate appearance—violates Title VII.

In *Holloway* this court noted that Congress intended Title VII's ban on sex discrimination in employment to prevent discrimination because of gender, not because of sexual orientation or preference. Recently the Fifth Circuit similarly read the legislative history of Title VII and concluded that Title VII thus does not protect against discrimination because of effeminacy. *Liberty Mutual*, 569 F.2d at 326–27. We agree and hold that discrimination because of effeminacy, like discrimination because of homosexuality (*supra*) or transsexualism (*Holloway*), does not fall within the purview of Title VII. * * *

■ SNEED, CIRCUIT JUDGE.

I respectfully dissent from [that part of the disposition] which holds that male homosexuals have not stated a Title VII claim under the disproportionate impact theories of *Griggs*. My position is not foreclosed by our holding, with which I agree, that Title VII does not afford protection to homosexuals, male or female. The male appellants' complaint, as I understand it, is based on the contention that the use of homosexuality as a disqualification for employment, which for *Griggs'* purposes must be treated as a facially neutral criterion, impacts disproportionately on males because of the greater visibility of male homosexuals and a higher incidence of homosexuality among males than females.

To establish such a claim will be difficult because the male appellants must prove that as a result of the appellee's practices there exists discrimination against males *qua* males. That is, to establish a prima facie case under *Griggs* it will not be sufficient to show that appellees have employed a disproportionately large number of female *homosexuals* and a disproportionately small number of male *homosexuals*. Rather it will be necessary to establish that the use of homosexuality as a bar to employment disproportionately impacts on *males,* a class that enjoys Title VII protection. Such a showing perhaps could be made were male homosexuals a very large proportion of the total applicable male population.

My point of difference with the majority is merely that the male appellants in their *Griggs* claim are not using that case "as an artifice to 'bootstrap' Title VII protection for homosexuals under the guise of protecting men generally." Their claim, if established properly, would in fact protect males generally. I would permit them to try to make their case and not dismiss it on the pleadings. * * *

Price Waterhouse v. Ann B. Hopkins

United States Supreme Court, 1989.
490 U.S. 228, 109 S.Ct. 1775, 104 L.Ed.2d 268.

[Excerpted in Chapter 3, Section 2(B)]

NOTE ON HOPKINS AND TITLE VII'S APPLICATION TO GENDER–STEREOTYPE DISCRIMINATION

Before *Hopkins*, an employer that does not hire women discriminates on the basis of sex under Title VII, unless justified by a statutory defense (BFOQ). Ditto for an employer that does not hire men. After *Hopkins*, an employer can be sued for refusing to hire or promote women because they do not conform to traditional "feminine" characteristics. Is it not necessary under *Hopkins* to protect men who are penalized for not conforming to traditional "masculine" characteristics? In other words, *Hopkins* makes clear that Title VII protects against discrimination because of "wrong gender" as well as "wrong sex." Professor Mary Anne Case summarizes the state of the law in the following chart:

	SEX OF EMPLOYEE	GENDER OF EMPLOYEE	GENDER OF JOB	EMPLOYER DEMAND	ANALYSIS & RESULT UNDER TITLE VII
1	Female	Masculine	Masculine (e.g., accountant) or none	Act more femininely[1]	Disparate treatment: *Price Waterhouse v. Hopkins*
2	Male	Feminine	Feminine (e.g., nursery school teacher) or none	Act more masculinely[2]	Disparate treatment: result governed by *Hopkins*: impermissible sex stereotyping
3	Female	Feminine	Masculine (e.g., commission salesperson) or none	Act more masculinely[2]	Disparate impact: once employee shows that requiring masculine or disfavoring feminine qualities has disparate impact on females, who are disproportionately feminine and not masculine, employer must then show that requiring masculine or disfavoring feminine characteristics is job-related and consistent with business necessity
4	Male	Feminine	Masculine	Act more masculinely[2]	*Ius tertii* claim, raising argument made by feminine woman in row 3 above
5	Male	Masculine	Feminine (e.g., Jenny Craig counselor)	Act more femininely[1]	Disparate impact: analysis is mirror image of row 3 above
6	Female	Masculine	Feminine	Act more femininely[1]	Analysis is mirror image of row 4 above

Notes:

[1] "Act more femininely" is here a shorthand for, e.g., the advice given Ann Hopkins to "walk more femininely, talk more femininely, dress more femininely, wear make-up, have [your] hair styled, . . . wear jewelry" and go to "charm school." 490 U.S. at 235 (1989).

[2] Or act less femininely. Both phrases are shorthand for the reverse of the advice given Hopkins, e.g., take off your makeup and jewelry, cut your hair short and go to assertiveness training class.

TABLE 1. ANALYSIS OF GENDER DISCRIMINATION CLAIMS UNDER TITLE VII

Mary Anne C. Case, "Disaggregating Gender from Sex and Sexual Orientation: The Effeminate Man in the Law and Feminist Jurisprudence," 105 *Yale L.J.* 1, 5 (1995). If this summary is correct, should *DeSantis* be overruled, at least in part?

PART C.   SEXUAL HARASSMENT AND HOSTILE WORK ENVIRONMENT UNDER TITLE VII[f]

The language of Title VII broadly prohibits employment discrimination "because of * * * sex." Shortly following its enactment, plaintiffs brought cases alleging that as a condition of employment, they were subjected to *quid pro quo* sexual harassment because of their sex. In a typical *quid pro quo* case, a plaintiff alleges that her boss or supervisor required her to have sex with him (or continue a previous consensual relationship) as a condition for not being fired, receiving satisfactory job performance evaluations, gaining choice job assignments or earning promotions. The earliest courts rejected this claim on the grounds that the discrimination was not because of sex.[g] The harassment was a result of the plaintiff's behavior and actions, i.e., refusing to have sex. She was not discriminated against because she was a woman. (This line of reasoning was particularly popular in cases in which the plaintiff had had a previous sexual relationship with the defendant, where the defendant could claim that the discrimination only occurred after the plaintiff refused sexual advances.) However, later courts rejected those holdings, finding that in the archetype situations described above, if not for the fact that the plaintiff was a woman, she would never have been approached for sexual favors, and therefore she was subjected to sexual harassment because of her sex.[h] Moreover, feminist theorists were developing sophisticated analyses of the gendered dynamics of the workplace and the ways in which sexual harassment effectively denies women job opportunities as much as traditional "no women need apply" policies.[i]

As the agency responsible for enforcement of Title VII, the Equal Employment Opportunity Commission issued "Guidelines On Discrimina-

---

f. The introduction to this section was drafted by Mitsuka Herrera, Georgetown University Law Center, Class of 1998.

g. *Barnes v. Train*, 13 FEP Cases 123, 124 (D.D.C.1974), *reversed sub nom., Barnes v. Costle*, 561 F.2d 983 (D.C. Cir.1977) (discrimination was because plaintiff rejected "sexual affair with her supervisor" and thus had an "inharmonious personal relationship with him," not because she was a woman); *Corne v. Bausch & Lomb, Inc.*, 390 F.Supp. 161 (D.Ariz.1975), *vacated*, 562 F.2d 55 (9th Cir.1977); *Miller v. Bank of Am.*, 418 F.Supp. 233, 236 (N.D.Cal.1976), *reversed on other grounds*, 600 F.2d 211 (9th Cir.1979) (sexual demands are not prohibited by Title VII because, "the attraction of males to females and females to males is a natural sex phenomenon and it is probable that this attraction plays at least a subtle role in most personnel decisions").

h. *Barnes v. Costle*, 561 F.2d 983, 990 (D.C.Cir.1977) ("But for her womanhood, . . . [the plaintiff's] participation in sexual activity would never have been solicited. To say then that she was victimized in her employment simply because she declined the invitation is to ignore the asserted fact that she was invited only because she was a woman."); *Henson v. City of Dundee*, 682 F.2d 897, 904 (11th Cir.1982) ("In the typical case in which a male supervisor makes sexual overtures to a female worker, it is obvious that the supervisor did not treat male employees in the same fashion. It will therefore be a simple matter for the plaintiff to prove that, but for her sex, she would not have been subjected to sexual harassment.").

i. See Lin Farley, *Sexual Shakedown: The Sexual Harassment of Women on the Job* (1978); Catharine A. MacKinnon, *Sexual Harassment of Working Women* (1979).

tion Because Of Sex," codified at 29 CFR ch. XIV § 1604. 45 Fed. Reg. 25,024 (Apr. 11, 1980). Section 1604.11(a)(1) and (2) defined *quid pro quo* sexual harassment as prohibited conduct, while subsection (3) declared that sexual harassment conduct which creates an "intimidating, hostile, or offensive working environment" because of a employee's sex is also a form of prohibited sex discrimination.[j] In *Meritor Sav. Bank, FSB v. Vinson*, 477 U.S. 57 (1986), the Supreme Court unanimously adopted the EEOC position that sexual discrimination which creates a hostile or abusive work environment is a violation of Title VII. The Court then laid out the framework necessary to prove this type of sexual harassment claim:

> To prevail on a hostile environment claim, plaintiff must establish: (1) she belongs to a protected group, (2) she was subject to unwelcome sexual harassment, (3) the harassment was based on sex, (4) the harassment affected a "term, condition, or privilege" of employment, and (5) the employer knew or should have known of the harassment in question and failed to take proper remedial action. *Id.* at 57.

Although this decision is framed in terms of a male harasser and female harassee, both the EEOC and other courts have held that Title VII applies to cases where the harasser is female and the harassee is male. To meet (1), a plaintiff merely need show that she or he is a woman or a man. The key element of (2) is the "unwelcomeness."[k] It is not necessary for the plaintiff to have resisted all sexual advances[l] or to have formally complained about the harassment prior to bringing a Title VII claim.[m]

With respect to conditions (3), (4) and (5), in a *quid pro quo* claim, the plaintiff must show that the harassment was a sexual advance tied to a tangible job benefit by a supervisor. This is the essence of *quid pro quo*. In contrast, hostile environment claims may be brought in situations in which

---

j. **"Sexual Harassment.** (a) Harassment on the basis of sex is a violation of section 703 of title VII. Unwelcome sexual advances, requests for sexual favors, and other verbal or physical conduct of a sexual nature constitute sexual harassment when (1) submission to such conduct is made either explicitly or implicitly a term or condition of employment, (2) submission to or rejection of such conduct by an individual is used as the basis for employment decisions that affect such individual, or (3) such conduct has the purpose or effect of unreasonably interfering with an individual's work performance or creating an intimidating, hostile or offensive working environment." 29 CFR ch. XIV § 1604.11(a) (1995).

k. "[S]exual conduct becomes unlawful only when it is unwelcome." EEOC Compliance Manual, vol. III, N:4037, Bureau of Nat'l Affairs, D.C. (Dec. 1995). "[T]he challenged conduct must be unwelcome, 'in the sense that the employee did not solicit or incite it, and in the sense that the employee regarded the conduct as undesirable or offensive.' " *Id.* quoting *Henson v. City of Dundee*, 682 F.2d at 903.

l. "[T]he fact that sex-related conduct was 'voluntary', in the sense that the complainant was not forced to participate against her will, is not a defense to a sexual harassment suit brought under Title VII. * * * The correct inquiry is whether [the victim][sic] by her conduct indicated that the alleged sexual advances were unwelcome, not whether her actual participation in sexual intercourse was voluntary." *Id.* at N:4036, quoting *Meritor*.

m. "While a complaint or protest is helpful to charging party's case, it is not a necessary element of the claim. Indeed, the Commission recognizes that victims may fear repercussions from complaining about the harassment and that such fear may explain a delay in opposing the conduct." *Id.* at N:4038.

the complainant suffered no direct economic harm, but was expected to endure harassment by co-workers as a condition of her employment.

Finally, with regard to conditions (2) and (3) in hostile environment claims, the harassment must be because of the plaintiff's sex, but prohibited conduct is not limited to sexual advances. As § 1604.11(a)(3) states, and as courts have held, threats or acts of physical violence (including restraint, assault, rape), physical conduct (such as urinating in someone's gas tank, exposing oneself, ejaculating in a co-worker's work area, leaving pornographic photos or graffiti for co-workers), and verbal abuse (repeatedly calling someone "whore," "bitch," "cunt," etc.) can be considered harassment because of sex. Additionally, conduct of a nonsexual nature, such as refusing to fix the trucks driven by female employees, can be used to support other evidence of a generally hostile environment because of sex.[n]

Against this lengthy backdrop, two new forms of sexual harassment claims have emerged: sexual harassment in which both the harasser and harassee are of the same sex, and in which an employee is harassed because she or he violates gender or sexuality norms. How should such cases be analyzed under the EEOC's guidelines? Under *Hopkins*?

Lisa Ann Burns v. McGregor Electronic Industries, Inc.

U.S. Court of Appeals for the Eighth Circuit, 1992.
955 F.2d 559.

■ WOLLMAN, CIRCUIT JUDGE. * * *

On August 30, 1985, Burns filed a complaint alleging constructive discharge from her employment with McGregor, a stereo speaker manufacturer employing fifty to seventy-five workers. She sought back pay, reinstatement, and all other related relief. Burns had worked at McGregor during three separate periods: October 14, 1980 through August 10, 1981; September 15, 1981 through June 20, 1983; and September 26, 1983 through July 19, 1984.

McGregor, which is located in McGregor, Iowa, is owned by Paul Oslac, a resident of Chicago, Illinois. Burns testified that during her first period of employment with McGregor, manager-trainee Marla Ludvik often made sexual comments as Burns left the restroom, such as "have you been playing with yourself in there?" Ludvik also made almost daily comments to other workers that she did not think Burns took douches, that she saw Burns riding in Oslac's car, and that Burns was going out with Oslac. Ludvik tried to convince Burns to date male employees. Supervisors Cleo Martin and Eldon Rytilahti heard Ludvik's remarks. Burns complained to Martin and to Mary Jean Standford, then the plant manager, but nothing changed.

---

n. See generally Jane Dolkart, "Hostile Environment Harassment: Equality, Objectivity and the Shaping of Legal Standards," 43 *Emory L.J.* 151 (1994).

The plant consisted of assembly lines in the basement and on the main floor, an office, a laboratory, and a third floor apartment used by Oslac when he visited the plant. Burns testified that Oslac showed her advertisements for pornographic films in *Penthouse* magazine, talked about sex, asked her to watch pornographic movies with him, and made lewd gestures, such as ones imitating masturbation. A former worker, Kim Heisz, saw one of Oslac's gestures. Oslac asked Burns for dates at least once a week. She gave him excuses rather than direct refusals because, she testified, she feared the loss of her job. She stated that his behavior made her angry, upset, and "real nervous," and that sometimes she would cry at work or at home. Burns also testified that there was no one above Oslac to whom she could complain; and that although she received no complaints, her work slowed down and she started dropping assembly parts. She voluntarily left McGregor on August 10, 1981.

Burns returned on September 15, 1981, because, she maintained, she needed the work. The newly-hired plant manager, Virginia Kelley, placed her in a higher-paying quality control job. Burns testified that during this period Oslac visited the plant from 11:00 a.m. Monday until 9:00 a.m. Tuesday of each week and that he spent most of this time with her. He continued to ask for dates and wanted to engage in oral sex so she would "be able to perform [her] work better." When Burns refused a date, Oslac told her, "I'm tired of your fooling around and always turning me down. You must not need your job very bad." Believing that Oslac intended to fire her, she accepted an invitation to dinner at his apartment on the condition that her mother would join them. Burns testified that her mother refused to go, so her father, Daniel Burns, went with her. As the district court found, Oslac appeared shocked when Burns' father appeared at the dinner with Burns. After the meal, Daniel Burns told Oslac he knew what was going on and for Oslac "to leave the girls alone at work."

Burns further testified that during her second period of employment Ludvik, who was then a supervisor, circulated a petition to have Burns fired because nude photographs of her, taken by her father, appeared in two motorcycle magazines—*Easyrider* and *In the Wind*. One full frontal view of Burns revealed a pelvic tatoo; two photographs highlighted jewelry attached to her pierced nipples. Burns testified that she had willingly allowed her father to do the piercing and photography. She did not take copies of the magazines into the plant. Former employee Deborah Johnson testified that she saw Ludvik showing employees the magazine and the petition. Burns testified that after Oslac learned about the nude photos from Ludvik, he told her, "They're ganging up on you and trying to get rid of you. If you don't go out with me, I might just let them do it." Oslac then asked Burns to pose nude for him in the plant in return for overtime pay.

Burns further testified that she was humiliated by plant gossip that she was Oslac's girlfriend; that supervisor June Volske tried to get her to sit on Oslac's lap, to go out with him, or to go up to his apartment; and that coworker Eugene Ottaway called her vulgar names. She complained to Kelley, who appeared to try to "do something" for a period of time, and to

Kelley's successor. Burns testified that her second period of employment was "hostile" and "extremely worse" than the first. She quit again on June 20, 1983.

Burns returned to McGregor for the third time on September 26, 1983, because, she said, Kelley had returned to the plant and because she needed work to support herself, her father, and her brother. When Burns expressed concerns about Oslac's behavior, Kelley assured her that Oslac would no longer enter the plant. Oslac continued to visit Burns, although he did not spend as much time with her as he had previously. According to Burns, he repeatedly asked her to go out, pose nude, and watch pornographic movies. On one occasion when other employees were present, Oslac threw his arm around her, cupped his hand as if to grab her breast, and said, "Well, I see I got you back, lover." He also gave her an *Easyrider* calendar.

Oslac had not visited the plant within the four to six weeks preceding Burns' last day, July 19, 1984. On that day, Burns asked Ottaway to move stacks of speakers, and he refused. Burns reported this to a supervisor, who instructed Ottaway to move the speakers. Ottaway then pushed and shoved the stacks, all the while calling Burns a series of vulgar names similar to those he admitted to having called her on other occasions, and placed the speakers so high she could not reach them. When Burns asked him to make the stacks lower, Ottaway threw the speakers across the room. Burns began crying and tried to get a supervisor to stop Ottaway, but the supervisor did nothing. Burns left work and did not return.

Burns testified that the overall work environment was "hostile and offensive." She testified that during the last six weeks of her third period of employment at McGregor she overheard Ottaway tell a fellow worker that "he should throw [Burns] over the [conveyor] belts" and commit an act of sodomitic intercourse upon her. Called as a witness for McGregor, Ottaway denied making the statement attributed to him by Burns about "throwing her over the belts." He admitted on direct examination, however, that he had called Burns names—"anything nasty." He testified that Burns had responded by calling him similar names. He further testified that during the speaker-throwing incident on July 19, 1984, he was angry at Burns and had "called her every name in the book." [Other witnesses confirmed that Ottaway called Burns abusive names and that Oslac routinely touched women in improper ways and make lewd gestures while in the plant.]

Testifying by way of deposition, Oslac denied Burns' allegations. He testified that he had invited Burns and her father to dinner at his apartment because Burns was planning to quit and that he convinced her father to talk her into staying. He claimed that he never talked to Burns at all during her last period of employment. He admitted spending quite a bit of time in her testing booth during her second period of employment, but said that Burns needed a lot of encouragement. He admitted showing several workers a bruise, but said that he pulled his pant leg up to do so and did not drop his pants to his knees. He claimed that the *Easyrider* calendar was given to him by Burns, not the other way around.

On the basis of this and other testimony, the district court indicated that it had some difficulty in determining what actually went on at McGregor because "rumor and gossip ran rampant." The court found that several forces contributed to Burns' decision to quit her job: the general working conditions; gossip about the nude photos (and the resulting treatment by co-employees); unwanted sexual advances by Oslac; and the sexually-charged name-calling during the running dispute with other employees about moving and stacking speakers. The district court found "the primary reason [Burns quit] was the incident on the last day during which she and Eugene Ottaway got into a violent name-calling argument and speakers were knocked about."

The district court found that the sexual harassment that Burns received from her co-workers peaked during the second period of employment and resulted from the publication of the nude photos. The court found that there was little or no sexual harassment directed toward Burns by her co-workers during her third period of employment at McGregor. The court found that "[i]n view of [Burns'] willingness to display her nude body to the public in Easy Riders publications, crude magazines at best, her testimony that she was offended by sexually directed comments and Penthouse or Playboy pictures is not credible." The court stated that it had no doubt that Oslac had made unwelcome sexual advances to Burns during her first two employment periods, but that Burns had exaggerated the severity and pervasiveness of the harassment and its effect upon her. The district court concluded that, in light of the whole record and the totality of the circumstances, Burns had failed to prove "by a preponderance of credible evidence" that the sexual harassment was sufficiently severe or pervasive to alter the conditions of her employment and create an abusive work environment, citing *Meritor Savings Bank v. Vinson*, 477 U.S. 57, 66 (1986). * * *

To prevail in her sexual harassment claim based on "hostile [work] environment," Burns must show that 1) she belongs to a protected group; 2) she was subject to unwelcome sexual harassment; 3) the harassment was based on sex; 4) the harassment affected a term, condition, or privilege of employment; and 5) McGregor knew or should have known of the harassment and failed to take proper remedial action.

The district court found that Burns had satisfied the first, third, and fifth elements, findings that are clearly supported by the record. First, Title VII forbids discrimination on the basis of sex and Burns, as a woman, is a member of a protected group. Second, sexual behavior directed at a woman raises the inference that the harassment is based on her sex. The record is replete with instances of sexual behavior directed at Burns, such as Oslac's cretinous sexual advances, Ludvik's sexual comments, and Ottaway's obscene name-calling. Thus, the harassment, because of its sexual nature, was based on Burns' sex. Third, the employer clearly knew of the harassment. Oslac is the owner of the plant. Additionally, Burns complained to Martin and Ludvik, both supervisors in the plant, about the harassment from her coworkers; she complained to Kelley about the harassment from Oslac.

There is evidence that Oslac knew about the harassment of the coworkers and that he used that harassment to further his own harassment of Burns, telling her that he might just let them get her fired.

The second element requires the plaintiff to show that she was subject to unwelcome sexual harassment. The district court had "no doubt" that Oslac made unwelcome sexual advances toward Burns during the first two periods she was employed, but found that there were few opportunities for Oslac to see her during the third period. The court also found that Burns lacked credibility when she testified that she was offended by the pornographic pictures and by the sexual comments.

The threshold for determining that conduct is unwelcome is "that the employee did not solicit or incite it, and the employee regarded the conduct as undesirable or offensive." The district court's finding that Oslac's advances were unwelcome necessarily required the district court to believe Burns' testimony that Oslac's behavior was offensive to her. Thus, the district court's finding that Oslac made unwelcome advances toward Burns and its finding that Burns was not credible when she stated that Oslac's behavior was offensive appear on their face to be internally inconsistent.

There is no evidence in the record that Burns solicited any of the conduct that occurred. However, the gossip, lewd talk, and the petition all occurred after the nude photographs of Burns appeared. These incidents were incited by the nude photographs and must be considered separately from Oslac's conduct. His conduct occurred both before and after Burns appeared in the magazines and did not change in kind or intensity after the appearance of the photos, though his advances tapered off during Burns' third period of employment. Eugene Ottaway's conduct and that of Burns' supervisors must also be analyzed separately from the conduct that occurred after Burns appeared nude. Ludvik, a plant supervisor, made inappropriate sexual and personal remarks and encouraged Burns to go out with Oslac, both before and after the nude pictures appeared. When Burns complained to supervisors about Oslac's behavior, she received either no response or promises that were not kept. Ottaway, according to the record, knew of the nude pictures and harassed Burns about them, but he also called Burns and other employees names of a sexual nature. Burns' complaints to her supervisor about Ottaway's conduct bore no results. The district court should, on remand, take all of this conduct into account as part of the "totality of the circumstances" in determining whether Burns found the conduct unwelcome. "The correct inquiry is whether [the plaintiff] by her conduct indicated that the alleged sexual advances were unwelcome[.]" *Meritor*, 477 U.S. at 68.

Evidence regarding a plaintiff's sexually provocative speech or dress is relevant "in determining whether he or she found particular sexual advances unwelcome." *Id.* at 69. Thus, in making the determination as to whether the conduct directed at Burns was unwelcome, the nude photo evidence, though relating to an activity engaged in by Burns outside of the work place, may be relevant to explain the context of some of the comments and actions directed by Oslac and coworkers to Burns.

Last, the district court found that the harassment Burns underwent was not so severe or pervasive that it affected a term, condition or privilege of employment. To affect a "term, condition, or privilege" of employment within the meaning of Title VII, the harassment "must be sufficiently severe or pervasive 'to alter the conditions of [the victim's] employment and create an abusive working environment.'" *Id.* at 67. The E.E.O.C. guidelines state that conduct is prohibited by Title VII where it "has the purpose or effect of unreasonably interfering with an individual's work performance *or* creating an intimidating, hostile, or offensive working environment." 29 C.F.R. § 1604.11(a)(3) (emphasis added). In approving this language, the Supreme Court cited cases involving racial discrimination and stated that "[o]ne can readily envision working environments so heavily polluted with discrimination as to destroy completely the emotional and psychological stability of [the] workers." *Meritor*, 477 U.S at 66. The court went on to state that "[n]othing in Title VII suggests that a hostile environment based on discriminatory *sexual* harassment should not be likewise prohibited." *Id.* (emphasis in original).

The district court reasoned that a person who would appear nude in a national magazine could not be offended by the behavior which took place at the McGregor plant. It also believed that Burns had exaggerated the severity and pervasiveness of the harassment and its effect on her. Again, these findings are at odds with the district court's finding that Oslac's advances were unwelcome.

We believe that a reasonable person would consider the conduct of Oslac and Burns' supervisors to be sufficiently severe or pervasive to alter the conditions of employment and create an abusive work environment. Burns testified that she was offended by the pictures in the pornographic magazines because they depicted couples engaged in various acts of sexual intercourse. She testified that she found Oslac's sexual advances and Ludvik's and Ottaway's comments humiliating and degrading. Burns continually complained to different supervisors, and she quit three separate times when she could no longer tolerate the conduct. The question is whether Burns has shown she is an "affected individual," that is, whether she was at least as affected as the reasonable person under like circumstances. On remand, the district court must determine whether Burns was as affected as that hypothetical "reasonable person." * * *

Ernest Dillon v. Frank

U.S. Court of Appeals for the Sixth Circuit, 1992.
952 F.2d 403.*

■ BOGGS, CIRCUIT JUDGE.

[Ernest Dillon worked as a mail handler at the Postal Service's Bulk Mail Center at Allen Park, Michigan. He started work in 1980. Beginning

---

* The original opinion, excerpted here, was withdrawn from publication but is available on electronic sources. The citation in text is to the memorandum notation of a summary disposition.

in 1984, he was subjected to a stream of coworker abuse based upon the belief that he was homosexual, including homophobic epithets ("fag") shouted in his face, a vicious physical assault, antihomosexual graffiti informing all that "Dillon sucks dicks" and "Dillon gives head." Management was aware of these incidents yet did nothing to curtail them. Dillon endured these circumstances for three years before he finally resigned in 1988 upon advice from his psychiatrist. He brought suit for sex discrimination under Title VII. The trial court dismissed Dillon's complaint primarily for procedural reasons, mainly a failure to exhaust his administrative remedies with the EEOC and the Post Office. The appellate court leapfrogged those issues in order to reach the merits.]

* * * Title VII makes it illegal "to discriminate against any individual with respect to ... compensation, terms, conditions, or privileges of employment, because of such individual's race, color, religion, sex, or national origin." 42 U.S.C. § 2000e–2(a). The Supreme Court has held that an employer who creates a hostile working environment for members of a class protected by Title VII, such as blacks or women, is discriminating "with respect to ... terms [and] conditions" of employment. *Meritor*. The question Dillon poses for us is whether such a hostile working environment involving sexual epithets and directed at a person because of perceived sexual behavior (homosexuality) is also proscribed by Title VII. In effect, Dillon asks us to define "because of sex" to mean "because of anything relating to being male or female, sexual roles, or to sexual behavior." Because we believe that only discrimination based on being male or female is prohibited by Title VII, and that the cases proscribing hostile environment sexual harassment are not to the contrary, we affirm the district court.

This would be an easy case if Dillon alleged that he was discriminated against because he was believed to be a homosexual. The circuits are unanimous in holding that Title VII does not proscribe discrimination based on sexual activities or orientation. * * * This is not an easy case, because Dillon does not allege that he is entitled to Title VII protection simply because he is alleged to be a homosexual. Rather, Dillon alleges that he was the victim of sexual harassment that was so pervasive that it rises to the level of a hostile work environment. He analogizes his circumstances to those under which it is clear plaintiffs can recover under Title VII. He directs us to cases where women who were subjected to demeaning and cruel verbal abuse (unaccompanied by demands for sexual favors) were able to secure a remedy through Title VII. [E.g., *Wall v. AT & T Technologies, Inc.*, 754 F.Supp. 1084 (M.D.N.C.1990).] He further points to cases where plaintiffs subjected to demands by a boss for homosexual intercourse have been permitted to bring an action under Title VII. [E.g., *Joyner v. AAA Cooper Transp.*, 597 F. Supp. 537 (M.D.Ala.1983), *aff'd*, 749 F.2d 732 (11th Cir.1984).] These cases, he contends, hold that all extremely unpleasant working environments that arise because of verbal and other abuse regarding sex are proscribed, and that therefore the fact that the harassment in his case was predicated upon a belief that he is a homosexual, rather than specifically on his being male, is irrelevant. He contends that he was subjected to this abuse relating to homosexuality solely because he was a man, and therefore has stated a claim under Title VII.

Dillon also advanced a separate contention at oral argument. He pointed to the Supreme Court's decision in *Price Waterhouse v. Hopkins*, which considered a claim that a female plaintiff had been denied partnership at a prestigious accounting firm in part because she was not considered feminine enough. Dillon notes that the Court stated that evidence of such sex stereotyping is admissible to prove sex discrimination. He contended that he was subjected to such stereotyping in that he was not deemed "macho" enough by his co-workers for a man, and that the verbal abuse resulted from this stereotyping. It is clear that claims that the work environment was made hostile by animus against a person because that person was a man or a woman, even if the person was not subjected to demands for sexual favors, are cognizable under Title VII. The reason is simple: requiring a person to submit to abuse based on the fact that the person is male or female introduces sex as a factor in the workplace. It does so by forcing some persons, solely because they are male or female, to endure hostile working conditions, while permitting the other group to enjoy their workplace. Thus, a "condition" of employment includes whether the workplace is free from ridicule and other devices that stigmatize the recipient as inferior, and the refusal to provide that workplace because a person is male or female violates Title VII. * * *

Dillon's analogy is appealing because of the cruel treatment he was subjected to, and its similarity to the facts of many cases involving heterosexual hostile environment claims. The harassment that he was subjected to was clearly sexual in nature. It seriously affected Dillon's psychological well-being, to the point that Dillon felt compelled to resign. The Postal Service knew about the harassment, and yet it continued unabated, raising the strong possibility that there would be employer liability for the actions of Dillon's co-workers. It appears undeniable that Dillon was denied the "condition" of employment at issue in hostile environment cases, a workplace where each employee is treated with appropriate dignity and respect.

* * * Although the cases recognizing claims for hostile environment sexual harassment hold that employees have a right to a work environment free from denigrating comments, verbal abuse, and other tactics of marginalization, that body of law does not hold that right to be absolute. Rather, Title VII only punishes those employers who withhold such environments from employees based on certain proscribed criteria: race, color, sex, religion, or national origin.

* * * In none of [the leading] cases is the content of the harassment the deciding factor in determining if Title VII provides a remedy; it is whether the harassment was directed at the plaintiff for a statutorily impermissible reason.

Thus, Dillon cannot escape our holding, and those of the other circuits, that homosexuality is not an impermissible criteria on which to discriminate with regard to terms and conditions of employment. Dillon's co-workers deprived him of a proper work environment because they believed him to be homosexual. Their comments, graffiti, and assaults were all directed at demeaning him solely because they disapproved vehemently of his alleged homosexuality. These actions, although cruel, are not made illegal by Title VII.

In a perfect world, the "right" to dignified treatment by one's employer and co-workers would be absolute: all workers of the world would unite in being "nice" toward one another. In our less than perfect world, both criminal and tort law may provide workers with protection against cruel harassment by their co-workers. Indeed, some of the actions Dillon complains of seem capable of remedy under both tort and criminal law, such as Barrett's beating (battery) and his co-workers taunting and graffiti-writing (intentional infliction of emotional distress). If Dillon can prove that the harassment ever caused him to be immediately apprehensive of another physical assault—and given the increase of the harassment after his recovery from Barrett's beating, this is not at all implausible—he can also sue for assault. In fact, to the extent that his co-workers and employer wanted to see Dillon quit, he could even sue for tortious interference with contract or employment relationship. The base result, however, is undisturbed; our decision today does not leave those in Dillon's situation without legal remedy.

We interpret Title VII to prescribe only specified discriminatory actions. What Title VII proscribes, although vitally important, is easily exceeded by what it does not. Employers or co-workers can still make the workplace unpleasant based on political belief ("damned Republican"); a co-worker's discussing sexual topics at work; family antagonism ("damned Rockefeller"); college attended ("I'm a Harvardian, you Yalie"); eating practices ("how can you eat something that used to be alive"); or rooting for particular sports teams ("the Dodgers are bums").

Work environments can be made extremely unpleasant based upon disagreement over beliefs closely related to factors protected by Title VII. Persons who hold beliefs or support practices repugnant to most in our society, such as the Indian practice of widow-burning known as "suttee," or a belief in "racial purity" based on Norse mythology, do not receive Title VII protection. * * *

Dillon attempts to avoid this problem by alleging that he was discriminated against because he was male. His argument is that but for his being male, he would not have been abused. We find this argument unpersuasive, primarily because he has not shown that his co-workers would have treated a similarly situated woman any differently. Dillon's argument must presume that the abuse was either directed at his supposed homosexuality or at specific sexual practices (such as anal sex or fellation). In two of its cases, the District of Columbia Circuit has raised the figure of the bisexual sexual harasser, preying equally on men and women, as a way to demonstrate that Title VII proscribes certain motives behind discrimination, not the practices used to implement those motives. Dillon has not shown such unisexual oppression: he has not argued that a lesbian would have been accepted at the Center, nor has he argued that a woman known to engage in the disfavored sexual practices would have escaped abuse. See *Porta v. Rollins Envtl. Serv. (NJ), Inc.*, 654 F.Supp. 1275, 1279 (D.N.J.1987) (graffiti alleging "Judy sucks Bernie's dick" part of sexual harassment claim). Without such a showing, his claim to have been discriminated against because he is male cannot succeed.

Price Waterhouse v. Hopkins does not direct a different result. *Price Waterhouse* was not a hostile environment case. It involved a specific management decision and the plaintiff's allegation "that gender played a part in a particular employment decision." Because of this difference, we do not read the Court to mean that any treatment that could be based on sexual stereotypes would violate Title VII.

First, there is no specific evidence of "sex stereotyped remarks" in our case. In *Price Waterhouse*, the plaintiff's superiors had criticized her aggressiveness, advised her to use makeup, and suggested she go to "charm school." The Court emphasized that in showing "that the employer actually relied on her gender in certainly be evidence that gender played a part." In our case there is no evidence provided that Dillon's co-workers justified their outrageous behavior based on, or accompanied it with remarks indicating, a belief that his practices would be acceptable in a female but unacceptable in a male.

Further, the Court emphasized the "intolerable and impermissible Catch–22" in the stereotyping in that case. A desirable trait (aggressiveness) was believed to be peculiar to males. If Hopkins lacked it, she would not be promoted; if she displayed it, it would not be acceptable. In our case, Dillon's supposed activities or characteristics simply had no relevance to the workplace, and did not place him in a "Catch–22." * * *

Mark McWilliams v. Fairfax County Board of Supervisors

United States Court of Appeals, Fourth Circuit, 1996.
72 F.3d 1191, *cert. denied*, 117 S.Ct. 72 (1996).

■ PHILLIPS, SENIOR CIRCUIT JUDGE.

[Mark McWilliams, a man with a learning disability, was an auto mechanic working for the Newington Facility of the Fairfax County Equipment Management Transportation Agency (EMTA). Beginning sometime in 1989, McWilliams' coworkers, collectively known as the "lube boys," beset McWilliams with a variety of offensive conduct. They teased him, asked him about his sexual activities, and exposed themselves to him. They taunted him with remarks such as, "The only woman you could get is one who is deaf, dumb, and blind." On one occasion, a coworker placed a condom in McWilliams' food. On at least three occasions, coworkers tied

McWilliams' hands together, blindfolded him, and forced him to his knees. On one of these occasions, a coworker, Doug Witsman, placed his finger in McWilliams' mouth to simulate an oral sexual act. During another of these incidents, a coworker and another person placed a broomstick to McWilliams' anus while a third exposed his genitals to McWilliams. On yet another occasion, the coworker entered the bus on which McWilliams was working and fondled him.

[McWilliams complained about most of these abusive episodes to the EMTA management. Receiving no relief, he brought suit under Title VII for sexual harassment and under § 1983 for unconstitutional sex discrimination. The trial court granted summary judgment for the County.]

The County raises serious questions as to whether McWilliams has proffered sufficient admissible evidence to support the necessary finding that any of his supervisors, hence the County, were on actual or constructive notice of coworker conduct sufficient to have created a hostile workplace environment. We need not address those problems, however, for we hold that McWilliams' hostile-environment claim fails for the more fundamental reason that such a claim does not lie where both the alleged harassers and the victim are heterosexuals of the same sex. Here, both McWilliams and all his alleged harassers were indisputably males, and no claim is made that any was homosexual.[5]

We believe this result compelled by a commonsense reading of the critical causation language of the statute: "because of the [claimant's] sex". As a purely semantic matter, we do not believe that in common understanding the kind of shameful heterosexual-male-on-heterosexual-male conduct alleged here (nor comparable female-on-female conduct) is considered to be "because of the [target's] *sex*.'" Perhaps "because of" the victim's known or believed prudery, or shyness, or other form of vulnerability to sexually-focussed speech or conduct. Perhaps "because of" the perpetrators' own sexual perversion, or obsession, or insecurity. Certainly, "because of" their vulgarity and insensitivity and meanness of spirit. But not specifically "because of" the victim's *sex*.

5. Though there is no allegation or proffered proof that either McWilliams or any of the "lube boys" was in fact homosexual, our dissenting brother apparently would either find that fact properly inferable from the nature of some of the harassing conduct, or consider it unnecessary to prove homosexuality-in-fact, homosexual innuendo being sufficient. And, on this basis he would reach the homosexuality issue and hold that same-sex "harassment" claims may lie under Title VII where homosexuality (either in-fact or as merely suggested by conduct) is involved. With respect, we believe that were Title VII to be so interpreted, the fact of homosexuality (to include bisexuality) should be considered an essential element of the claim, to be alleged and proved. The dissent expresses concern, because of proof (and privacy?) problems, about requiring such allegation and proof, but we believe it critical and eminently fair to require it if homosexuality is to be the critical fact making same-sex harassment claims cognizable under Title VII. The (ordinarily different) sexes of the relevant actors always has been an essential element of either form of Title VII sexual harassment claims. If such claims were to reach past different-sex to same-sex situations where homosexuality of one or the other or both of the actors is involved, that added fact would seem equally essential to the statement and proof of such a claim. * * *

The difficulty of construing this causation language to reach such same-sex claims and the commonsense of not doing so are emphasized when the practical implications are considered. That this sort of conduct is utterly despicable by whomever experienced; that it may well rise to levels that adversely affect the victim's work performance; and that no employer knowingly should tolerate it are all undeniable propositions. But to interpret Title VII to reach that conduct when only heterosexual males are involved as harasser and victim would be to extend this vital statute's protections beyond intentional discrimination "because of" the offended worker's "sex" to unmanageably broad protection of the sensibilities of workers simply "in matters of sex." We cannot believe that Congress in adopting this critical causation language and the Supreme Court in interpreting it to reach discrimination by the creation of hostile workplace environments could have intended it to reach such situations. There perhaps "ought to be a law against" such puerile and repulsive workplace behavior even when it involves only heterosexual workers of the same sex, in order to protect the victims against its indignities and debilitations, but we conclude that Title VII is not that law. * * *

■ MICHAEL, CIRCUIT JUDGE, dissenting.

It is too early to write this case off to meanness and horseplay. * * *

I believe the majority makes a mistake to affirm summary judgment on the ground that there is no allegation that McWilliams and his male harassers are of different sexual orientations. That puts too fine a point on the "discriminat[ion] ... *because of [his] ... sex* " issue. I would simply hold that Title VII is implicated whenever a person physically abuses a co-worker for sexual satisfaction or propositions or pressures a co-worker out of sexual interest or desire. This can be established by an account of what the harasser did or said to the victim, and proof of the harasser's sexual orientation should not be required. The harassment must, of course, be sufficiently pervasive to create a hostile working environment.

I recognize that in a same-sex harassment claim, evidence of sexual orientation could be relevant to either side's case. However, it should not be elevated to a required element of the plaintiff's proof. See *Mogilefsky v. Superior Court*, 26 Cal.Rptr.2d 116 (1993). That would burden the statute too much because the focus would shift from an examination of what happened to the plaintiff to a pursuit (surely to be complicated, far-ranging and elusive) of the "true" sexual orientation of the harasser.

Here, McWilliams alleges that his co-workers (i) "approach[ed] him in a sexual manner, touch[ed] him," Amend.Compl. ¶ 6, (ii) "asked him to perform sexual acts on them," id. ¶ 7 and (iii) "restrained him and touched him in a sexual manner," id. ¶ 8. The details are amply provided in the summary judgment record. On several occasions defendant Witsman told McWilliams that he wanted to have sex with him. At least once Witsman offered McWilliams money for sex. Witsman would do things such as flick his tongue at McWilliams, say "I love you, I love you," and ask for sex. Witsman would also follow McWilliams into the restroom where Witsman, with one hand in his unzipped fly, would put his arm around McWilliams or invite him into a stall. On several occasions Witsman asked McWilliams if he (Witsman) could masturbate McWilliams. Once when McWilliams was working under the dashboard of a bus, Witsman came up and rubbed McWilliams' penis until it became erect. At least three times defendants Pinnock, Riddle and Witsman tied McWilliams' hands together, blindfolded him and pushed him to his knees. During one of these incidents Witsman put his finger in McWilliams' mouth and simulated a sex act. In a separate incident, Riddle and Witsman held McWilliams down while Pinnock exposed himself and defendant Shelton put a broom handle between McWilliams' buttocks. These assaults and propositions were against the backdrop of constant obsessive talk about sex—and not just male-female sex. One defendant even talked about having sex with little boys.

I would not require McWilliams to allege on top of these facts that his harassers were homosexual. The acts of assault and harassment are sufficiently direct and suggestive by themselves to raise the question whether they were done "because of [McWilliams'] ... sex." * * *

NOTES ON *BURNS*, *DILLON*, AND *MCWILLIAMS*

1. *"Because of Sex."* Recall that the EEOC and the Supreme Court have interpreted Title VII's rule against discrimination "because of sex" very liberally to include the various kinds of sexual harassment and the discrimination in *Hopkins* (which was gender-based). *Burns* falls within the EEOC's Guidelines, but *Dillon* and *McWilliams* do not. Why not? In all three cases, employees were assaulted and abused because they were sexualized by other employees and management did nothing about the abuse. Why should the lube boys be free to simulate sodomy with McWilliams but not Burns? If Ann Hopkins had been abused because she was considered too "macho," wouldn't she have had a claim for relief? Why doesn't Ernest Dillon then have a claim? Or Mark McWilliams? In your analysis, is the sexual orientation of Hopkins, Dillon, or McWilliams relevant? Why or why not?

Rejecting the reasoning of *McWilliams*, the Eighth Circuit ruled that "evidence that members of one sex were the primary targets of the harassment is sufficient to show that the conduct was gender based." *Quick v. Donaldson Co.*, 90 F.3d 1372, 1378 (8th Cir.1996). The facts there involved a heterosexual man who filed an harassment complaint after being the object of repeated "bagging," a practice in which male employees grabbed or feigned grabbing another man's testicles. Relying heavily on *Burns*, the Eighth Circuit reversed the district court's grant of summary judgment for defendants, and remanded the case for a trial on whether the totality of the circumstances demonstrated sexual harassment.

2. *The Contrast with Quid Pro Quo Cases.* The one area in which same-sex harassment consistently has been found to be a valid cause of action under Title VII has been cases in which acquiescence to sexual contact was expected as a condition of a job-related benefit. *See, e.g., EEOC v. Walden Book Co.*, 885 F.Supp. 1100 (M.D.Tenn.1995); *Roe v. K-Mart*, 1995 WL

316783 (D.S.C.1995); *Wright v. Methodist Youth Services*, 511 F.Supp. 307 (N.D.Ill.1981). Why the difference between the *quid pro quo* and hostile environment doctrines? In the former, there is pressure to engage in sexual activity. In the latter, sexual activity as such is usually not an issue. How does this difference affect whether discrimination is "based on sex"?

3. *Gendered Meanings?* A series of cases have held that men failed to establish a hostile environment claim when same-sex harassment was alleged. In most, as in *McWilliams*, the courts have found that the gay-baiting constituted a form of teasing, unrelated not only to sex but also to sexual orientation. Consider:

> Mr. Feltner's male co-worker called the plaintiff a "dick sucker." This was a common epithet, not a sexual advance. The "harasser" taunted Mr. Feltner by calling him a homosexual, but there was no evidence or even allegation that either man was homosexual or believed the other to be. While the epithet used and the taunting had a "sexual" component, as do most expletives, the crucial point is that the "harasser" was not aiming expletives at the victim because of the victim's male-ness. He was taunting the victim because he did not like him; Mr. Feltner's gender was irrelevant. There was no evidence that the abuse was based on the "harasser's" disdain for the victim's gender. Thus, it was not actionable under Title VII.

Vandeventer v. Wabash National Corp., 887 F.Supp. 1178, 1181 n.2 (N.D.Ind.1995). If anti-gay sexual orientation harassment is not covered by Title VII, and anti-straight male harassment of a sexual nature (but not because of sex) is not covered, does any cause of action remain for men harassed by men? What beliefs about gender and sexuality does such a position reflect? What structures of gender and sexuality do such holdings help to construct?

4. *The Purpose of the Statute.* The difference between *Burns* and the other two cases might be that *Burns* directly subserves the purpose of Title VII to help women in the workplace, while the others do not. Recalling the argument that sexual orientation discrimination is a kind of sex discrimination (Chapter 1, Section 3[B][3]), EEOC lawyer Samuel Marcosson responded:

> [T]he dominance of male attitudes in the workplace as a barrier to women's equal participation in economic life, and the woman-directed nature of the sexual conduct that takes place provide a powerful basis for the conclusion that offensive, hostile work environments that are sexual in nature are sex discrimination. * * * Because [the harassment in *Dillon*] was sexual in nature, the harassment reinforced male-created and male-dominated norms regarding the appropriateness of sexual conversation and conduct in the workplace. In this sense, it was directed at women, even if the immediate target was a man. More fundamentally, antigay harassment * * * is "targeted" at women because it reinforces stereotypes about appropriate gender roles.

Samuel A. Marcosson, "Harassment on the Basis of Sexual Orientation: A Claim of Sex Discrimination Under Title VII," 81 *Geo. L. J.* 1, 23–4 (1992). How does this theory square with the facts in *Vandeventer*?

5. *When the Employee Is Held Responsible for Sexualizing the Workplace.* Note the role that Burns' private life conduct, in posing for nude photographs, plays in the court's analysis. The trial court may have denied her claim in part because it held her responsible for sexualizing the workplace. Recall Rosemary Pringle's thesis at the beginning of this chapter. Given a "totality of the circumstances" standard, is this evidence relevant? For a trenchant comparison of the legal doctrines underlying sexual harassment law and rape law, see Susan Estrich, "Sex At Work," 43 *Stan. L. Rev.* 813 (1991).

6. *Other Remedies.* Claims of a hostile work environment caused by same-sex harassment have been accepted as the basis for disability caused by mental stress, *Rendon v. United Airlines*, 881 P.2d 482 (Colo.App.1994), and unemployment compensation benefits based on a good cause to quit, *Hanke v. Safari Hair Adventure*, 512 N.W.2d 614 (Minn.App.1994).

7. *Variations under Title VII.* Would a Title VII claim based on each of the following fact patterns withstand a motion to dismiss:

(a) Heterosexual men create a hostile work environment for a heterosexual woman by calling her a "lesbian" and "cunt licker" because of her refusal to have sex with them;

(b) Same as (a), except that the woman *is* a lesbian;

(c) Heterosexual woman refers to a male co-worker during weekly staff meetings as a "fairy" and "the in-house cocksucker";

(d) Same as (c), except the harasser is a heterosexual male.

(e) Same as (c), except the harasser is a gay male.

(f) Same as (c), and it is clear that the victim is straight.

8. *Variations under ENDA.* Appendix 4 to this casebook reproduces the proposed Employment NonDiscrimination Act (ENDA), which came within one vote of passing the Senate in 1996. If ENDA became law, would Dillon have a claim for relief? McWilliams? How about each of the claimants in Note 7?

9. *Variations under State Law.* Appendices 2 and 3 to this casebook reproduce employment discrimination laws for the District of Columbia and Wisconsin, respectively. Would Dillon and McWilliams have claims under either of these laws, if they had been applicable to their cases?

PROBLEM 10–3

THE FIRST AMENDMENT AND HOSTILE WORKPLACE RULES

Assume that Congress enacts ENDA (Appendix 4) and that ENDA is interpreted to prohibit workplace harassment based on the sexual orientation of employees like Ernest Dillon. Dillon's supervisor, A, tells him, "I don't like working with fags, and I only put up with you because the courts are making me." She repeatedly denigrates male homosexuals as "carriers of AIDS" and "asshole buddies" but does not otherwise sanction or penalize Dillon on the job. B is a fellow Post Office employee who daily criticizes the new workplace rules protecting gay people. B uses offensive language and points at Dillon as an example of the sort of people who are an "embarrassment" to the government because they "flaunt" their homosexuality and "perversions." A, who supervises both Dillon and B, does nothing to stop this torrent of "verbal abuse," as Dillon calls it.

The Post Office fires both A and B for harassment. Both sue for reinstatement on the ground that their firing violated their First Amendment rights [see Chapter 5]. Assuming such action is consistent with ENDA's statutory override, is it likely that either will succeed?

Recall *R.A.V. v. City of St. Paul*, 505 U.S. 377 (1992) (Chapter 5, Section 3), which struck down St. Paul's hate speech law on the ground that it regulated only certain disfavored types of hate speech (racist, sexist, etc.). Justice White's opinion concurring in the judgment feared that the broadly written majority opinion cast the EEOC's workplace harassment regulation into constitutional doubt:

> The regulation does not prohibit workplace harassment generally; it focuses on what the majority would characterize as the "disfavored topi[c]" of sexual harassment. In this way, Title VII is similar to the St. Paul ordinance that the majority condemns because it "impose[s] special prohibitions on those speakers who express views on disfavored subjects." Under the broad principle the Court uses to decide the present case, hostile work environment claims based on sexual harassment should fail First Amendment review; because a general ban on harassment in the workplace would cover the problem of sexual harassment, any attempt to proscribe the subcategory of sexually harassing expression would violate the First Amendment.

> Hence, the majority's second exception, which the Court indicates would insulate a Title VII hostile work environment claim from an underinclusiveness challenge because "sexually derogatory 'fighting words' . . . may produce a violation of Title VII's general prohibition against sexual discrimination in employment practices." But application of this exception to a hostile work environment claim does not hold up under close examination.

> First, the hostile work environment regulation is not keyed to the presence or absence of an economic *quid pro quo*, but to the impact of the speech on the victimized worker. Consequently, the regulation would no more fall within a secondary effects exception than does the St. Paul ordinance. Second, the majority's focus on the statute's general prohibition on discrimination glosses over the language of the specific regulation governing hostile working environment, which reaches beyond any "incidental" effect on speech. If the relationship between the broader statute and specific regulation is sufficient to bring the Title VII regulation within [*United States v. O'Brien*, 391

U.S. 367 (1968)], then all St. Paul need do to bring its ordinance within this exception is to add some prefatory language concerning discrimination generally.

Id. at 409 (White, J., concurring in the judgment). Is the EEOC's regulation generally unconstitutional after *R.A.V.*? Even if constitutional generally, would the regulation be unconstitutionally applied to the firing of A? The firing of B?

CURRENT ISSUES IN WORKPLACE DISCRIMINATION

PART A. THE PERSISTENCE OF GENDER: SEX–SEGREGATED JOBS

Equal Employment Opportunity Commission v. Sears, Roebuck & Co.

U.S. District Court for the Northern District of Illinois, 1986.
628 F.Supp. 1264, *affirmed*, 839 F.2d 302 (7th Cir.1988).

■ NORDBERG, DISTRICT JUDGE.

This opinion marks the culmination of a lengthy dispute between the Equal Employment Opportunity Commission ("EEOC") and Sears, Roebuck & Co. ("Sears"), the world's largest retail seller of general merchandise. In 1973, an EEOC commissioner's charge was filed. After an extensive investigation and extensive conciliation discussions, EEOC filed this suit in 1979, alleging nationwide discrimination by Sears against women in virtually all aspects of its business, in violation of Title VII of the Civil Rights Act of 1964, as amended, 42 U.S.C. § 2000e et seq. ("Title VII"), and the Equal Pay Act, 29 U.S.C. § 206(d).

This is a case of claimed statistical disparities. * * * The two allegations EEOC sought to prove at trial were that Sears engaged in a nationwide pattern or practice of sex discrimination: (1) by failing to hire female applicants for commission selling on the same basis as male applicants, and by failing to promote female non-commission salespersons into commission sales on the same basis as it promoted male non-commission salespersons into commission sales (commission sales claim); and (2) by paying female checklist management employees in certain job categories lower compensation than similarly situated male checklist management employees (checklist compensation claim). [After a ten-month trial, the court ruled that the EEOC had failed to prove either claim.]

* * * EEOC's statistical analyses are based on two essential assumptions for which there is no credible support in the record. In designing all of his statistical analyses relating to commission sales, [EEOC expert witness] Dr. Siskin made the important assumptions that (1) all male and female sales applicants are equally likely to accept a job offer for all commission sales positions at Sears, and (2) all male and female sales applicants are equally qualified for all commission sales positions at Sears. The court finds

that both of these assumptions were proven untrue.[a] Without these assumptions, EEOC's statistical analyses are virtually meaningless.

EEOC has offered no credible evidence to support its assumption of equal interest by male and female applicants in all commission sales positions at Sears. Sears, on the other hand, has offered much credible evidence that employees' and applicants' interests, preferences and aspirations are extremely important in determining who applies for and accepts commission sales jobs at Sears. Sears has proven, with many forms of evidence, that men and women tend to have different interests and aspirations regarding work, and that these differences explain in large part the lower percentage of women in commission sales jobs in general at Sears, especially in the particular divisions with the lowest proportion of women selling on commission.

The most credible and convincing evidence offered at trial regarding women's interest in commission sales at Sears was the detailed, uncontradicted testimony of numerous men and women who were Sears store managers, personnel managers and other officials, regarding their efforts to recruit women into commission sales. As discussed above, attracting women to commission sales has been an important priority in Sears' affirmative action programs since the first affirmative action questionnaire was circulated in 1968. Sears managers and other witnesses with extensive store experience over the entire relevant time period testified that far more men than women were interested in commission selling at Sears. Numerous managers described the difficulties they encountered in convincing women to sell on commission. Sears managers continually attempted to persuade women to accept commission selling or other non-traditional jobs. Women who expressed an interest in commission selling were given priority over men when an opening occurred. Managers attempted to persuade even marginally qualified women to accept commission selling positions. They would sometimes guarantee a woman her former position if she would try commission selling for a certain period. Store managers reported that they had interviewed every woman in the store and none were willing to sell on commission. Managers often had to "sell" the job to reluctant women, even though enthusiasm and interest in the positions were qualities management valued highly in commission salespeople. Despite these unusual efforts, managers had only limited success in attracting women to commission sales.

Female applicants who indicated an interest in sales most often were interested in selling soft lines of merchandise, such as clothing, jewelry, and cosmetics, items generally not sold on commission at Sears. Male applicants were more likely to be interested in hard lines, such as hardware, automotive, sporting goods and the more technical goods, which are more likely to be sold on commission at Sears. These interests generally paralleled the

---

a. [Eds.] The court found in a later portion of the opinion that women applicants in the sales pool were younger, less educated, less likely to have commission sales experience and less likely to have prior work experience with the products that Sears sold on commission than were male applicants.

interest of customers in these product lines. Men, for example, were usually not interested in fashions, cosmetics, linens, women's or children's clothing, and other household small ticket items. Women usually lacked interest in selling automotives and building supplies, men's clothing, furnaces, fencing and roofing. Women also were not as interested as men in outside sales in general [*i.e.*, the fencing, floorcoverings, plumbing and heating, building materials, kitchens and dishwashers divisions], and did not wish to invest the time and effort necessary to learn to sell in the home improvements divisions [*i.e.*, the fencing and garden tractor, plumbing etc., building materials, and kitchen etc. divisions]. Women often disliked Division 45 (men's clothing) because it sometimes involved taking personal measurements of men.

Custom draperies, however, was one division in which women were willing to sell on a commission basis, even though it could require some outside selling. More women were willing to sell custom draperies on commission because they enjoyed the fashion and creative aspect of the job, most had past experience in the field, and it was a relatively low pressure commission division. Applicants expressing an interest in the division were almost all women. Very few men were willing to sell draperies.

The percentage of women hired in the various categories generally paralleled their interests and background in the product line involved. This illustrates how much an applicant's interest in the product sold can influence his willingness to accept a particular commission sales position. As is evident from the above discussion, interests of men and women often diverged along patterns of traditional male and female interest. * * *

Women at Sears who were not interested in commission sales expressed a variety of reasons for their lack of interest. Some feared or disliked the perceived "dog-eat-dog" competition. Others were uncomfortable or unfamiliar with the products sold on commission. There was fear of being unable to compete, being unsuccessful, and of losing their jobs. Many expressed a preference for noncommission selling because it was more enjoyable and friendly. They believed that the increased earnings potential of commission sales was not worth the increased pressure, tension, and risk.

These reasons for women not taking commission sales jobs were confirmed in a study performed by Juliet Brudney on behalf of Sears. Ms. Brudney conducted structured interviews of women in nontraditional jobs at Sears, including women in automotive and service technician jobs, and their supervisors. She also interviewed women who were seeking jobs or changing jobs, and found that they perceived commission sales as requiring cut-throat competitiveness that prevents friendships at work. They were also reluctant to sell products with which they were unfamiliar and preferred the security of a steady salary to the risks of making less in commission sales.

The results of Ms. Brudney's study were supported by the testimony of Sears' expert, Dr. Rosalind Rosenberg, who testified that women generally prefer to sell soft-line products, such as apparel, housewares or accessories sold on a non-commission basis, and are less interested in selling products such as fencing, refrigeration equipment and tires. Women tend to be more interested than men in the social and cooperative aspects of the workplace. Women tend to see themselves as less competitive. They often view non-commission sales as more attractive than commission sales, because they can enter and leave the job more easily, and because there is more social contact and friendship, and less stress in noncommission selling. This testimony is consistent with the uncontradicted testimony of Sears' witnesses regarding the relative lack of interest of women in commission selling at Sears, and with the testimony of Ms. Brudney, and is further evidence that men and women were not equally interested in commission sales at Sears.

[Sears also introduced survey evidence.] Sears presented extensive evidence of differences in the general interests and attitudes of men and women in American society over the past 50 years. This evidence was developed by Dr. Irving Crespi from an exhaustive study of national surveys and polls taken from the mid–1930's through 1983 which related to the changing status of women in American society. Although the evidence presented by Dr. Crespi demonstrated many changes in attitudes over the past 50 years, he made a number of conclusions directly relevant to women's interest in commission sales. Dr. Crespi found that: (1) men were more likely than women to be interested in working at night or on weekends, (2) women were more likely than men to be interested in regular daytime work; (3) men were more likely than women to be interested in sales jobs involving a high degree of competition among salespersons; (4) men were more likely to be interested in jobs where there was a chance of making more money, even though it involved a risk of losing the job if they did not sell enough; and (5) men were more likely than women to be motivated by the pay of a job than by the nature of the job and whether they like it. All of these conclusions support Sears' contention that women were less likely than men to be interested in commission selling in general.
* * *

The morale surveys [of Sears employees] demonstrated that most non-commission salespeople were happy with their work, and that more non-commission saleswomen preferred to stay in their present jobs than non-commission salesmen. In 1974–1976, noncommission saleswomen were much less interested than noncommission salesmen in promotion to division management or a higher level. They were far more likely than noncommission salesmen to want to remain in the job they had or one like it. In 1978–1980, only 14% of full time noncommission salesmen and 8.4% of noncommission saleswomen were interested in a different position. Thus, although only a small percentage were interested in other jobs, almost twice as many men as women were interested in new jobs. In addition, almost twice the percentage of female (56.4%) as male (30.3%) full time noncommission salespeople expressed a preference to remain in their present jobs.

The morale of noncommission salespersons was higher than that of all other timecard nonsupervisory employees. Noncommission salespersons were satisfied with their work, and noncommission saleswomen were more satisfied than noncommission salesmen. Most noncommission salespersons, and especially females, enjoyed their work and took pride in their jobs.

Noncommission saleswomen were more likely than noncommission salesmen to believe that their pay levels favorably influenced their attitudes toward their jobs, and were less likely to feel underpaid and to report that their pay at Sears was inadequate to meet their needs. Noncommission saleswomen were also more likely than noncommission salesmen to feel good about their futures at Sears. * * *

NOTE ON GENDERED JOB PREFERENCES AND FEMINIST "DIFFERENCE" THEORY

A study of moral development asked children to resolve the following moral dilemma (the Heinz dilemma): Heinz works for a drug store; his wife is sick, and he cannot afford needed drugs. Should he steal the drug from the store? Researchers found that boys had clearer moral visions about what to do (generally, steal the drug, because life is more important than property) than girls did. Carol Gilligan, *In a Different Voice: Psychological Theory and Women's Development* (1982) argued that the studies showed nothing about relative moral development and, instead, revealed "different voices" of boys and girls. Gilligan argued that women tend to define themselves and be defined by others in a context of human relationships. The "goodness" of women has traditionally been defined in terms of their cooperativeness and their care for and their sensitivity towards others. On the other hand, the "goodness" of men has been defined by their independence, their motivation to succeed, and their ability to provide for others. These cultural differences, Gilligan argued, show up in different modes of reasoning for her archetypical children, "Jake" and "Amy." Judge Nordberg's opinion can be read as an application of feminist "difference" analysis: when Jake and Amy go work for Sears Roebuck, Jake is much more likely to end up making more money because he prefers commission work, while Amy is happier with the more cooperative noncommission work. Should this be the end of the legal analysis?

Feminists have sharply attacked Gilligan's work. Most, including Gilligan, agree that the very basis of neutrality is itself defined from a masculine perspective. But where Gilligan emphasizes the differences between men and women and calls for the valuation of the feminine, Catharine MacKinnon responds:

> Difference is the velvet glove of the iron fist of domination. The problem then is not that differences are not valued; the problem is that they are defined by power. This is as true when difference is affirmed as when it is denied, when its substance is applauded or disparaged.

Catharine MacKinnon, *Toward a Feminist Theory of the State* 219 (1989). MacKinnon refuses to celebrate the feminine, for such a celebration is simply the flip side of male domination. Deborah Rhode critiques Gilligan's work for overstating the extent of difference and warns that its popularizers have reframed its message as a a ground for believing in the biological, rather than social, basis for gender differences. She counsels against an either-or approach:

> In many contexts, rights impose responsibilities, and responsibilities imply rights. Often the concepts serve identical ends. * * * [W]e need a jurisprudence that can transcend such dichotomies. Conventional rights-oriented frameworks have often served more to restate than resolve fundamental social conflict. Yet women have also made substantial gains through a rhetoric of rights. Further progress is possible only through an approach that insists on integrating ethics of both autonomy and connection. Our problem is less a poverty of moral vocabulary than an absence of concrete strategies * * *

Deborah L. Rhode, *Justice and Gender: Sex Discrimination and the Law* 312 (1989). Construct an argument from feminist theory for reversing Judge Nordberg, and then read the following analysis.

Vicki Schultz, Telling Stories About Women and Work: Judicial Interpretations of Sex Segregation in the Workplace in Title VII Cases Raising the Lack of Interest Argument

103 *Harvard Law Review* 1749, 1769, 1787–8, 1800, 1805–08, 1815–16 (1990).*

An analysis of lower court decisions shows that the courts have relied on two mutually exclusive explanations for sex segregation in the workplace. The conservative explanation accepts the lack of interest argument and attributes sex segregation to women workers' own "choice," while the more liberal explanation rejects the lack of interest argument and attributes segregation to employer "coercion." Even though these interpretations lead to different results, the fact that they are conceptualized as mutually exclusive reveals that they share a common assumption that women form their choices about work, independently of employer action or coercion, in private pre-work realms. * * *

There is a distinction in the historical sensibilities of conservative and liberal courts, but it is a distinction without a difference. In the conservative approach, women have always had a timeless set of "feminine" attributes that include a preference for traditionally female work. This conservative vision is ultimately ahistorical, for history reveals only the expression of an unchanging "truth" that gender and gendered work aspirations are so deeply ingrained that they may be considered part of human nature. The liberal approach is more complex. Even apparently sympathetic liberal judges who reject the idea that contemporary women "choose" female-dominated work have been unwilling to abandon the notion that women of the past did "choose'" such work. The liberal approach thus rests on a story of historical progress that imagines a "modern" woman who has emerged only since the passage of Title VII and whose aspirations for nontraditional work represent a sharp break from those of most women in the past. Unlike the conservative vision, the liberal one is not completely ahistorical, for it acknowledges implicitly that human consciousness is subject to historical influences and change. But it attributes the historical change in women's work aspirations not to changed labor market conditions, but rather to other, unspecified "societal" influences.

The liberal approach ultimately converges with the conservative one for Title VII purposes. Neither clearly acknowledges the influence of historical labor market discrimination on the formation of working women's job aspirations. Conservatives and liberals alike have found implausible the proposition that sex segregation exists because employers have historically reserved higher-paying jobs for men and restricted women to lower- paying, less desirable jobs. It is unclear why judges have adopted this view, for it denies the primary reason women needed Title VII's protection. The history of employer discrimination relegating women to female-dominated jobs is well documented. * * *

The conservative story of choice is the familiar one told by the *Sears* court: women are "feminine," nontraditional work is "masculine," and therefore women do not want to do it. The story rests on an appeal to masculinity and femininity as oppositional categories. Women are "feminine" because that is the definition of what makes them women. Work itself is endowed with the imagined human characteristics of masculinity or femininity based on the sex of the workers who do it. "Femininity" refers to a complex of womanly traits and aspirations that by definition precludes any interest in the work of men. Even though the story always follows this same logic, the story changes along class lines in the way it is told. Cases involving blue-collar work emphasize the "masculinity" of the work, drawing on images of physical strength and dirtiness. Cases involving white-collar work focus on the "femininity" of women, appealing to traits and values associated with domesticity. * * *

In the end, the logic of the story of choice converges in both blue-collar and white-collar cases. It makes no difference that in blue-collar cases gender is described in physical imagery, while in white-collar cases gender is described in social and psychological terms. In both contexts, the story portrays gender as so complete and natural as to render invisible the processes through which gender is socially constructed by employers. The story is powerful because it appeals to the widely held perception that the sexes are different. It extends this perception into an account of gendered job aspirations: if women have different physical characteristics or have had different life experiences from men, then they must have different work interests, too. There is no room for the possibility that women are different from men in certain respects, yet still aspire to the same types of work. If gender is all-encompassing, it is also so natural as to be unalterable. Women's preferences for "feminine" work are so central to the definition of womanhood itself that they remain unchanged (and unchangeable), regardless of what women experience at work. Because there is no room for change, employers do not and cannot contribute to shaping women's job preferences.

The flip side of the coin is that work itself is somehow inherently "masculine" or "feminine," apart from anything employers do to make it that way. With the world neatly compartmentalized into gendered people and jobs, sex segregation becomes easy to explain. Women bring to the workplace their preexisting preferences for traditionally female work, and employers merely honor those preferences. In the story of choice, workplace segregation implies no oppression or even disadvantage for women. Courts telling this story often describe women's jobs as "more desirable" than men's jobs, even where women's jobs pay lower wages, afford less prestige, and offer fewer opportunities for advancement than men's. The implicit point of reference for evaluating the desirability of the work, is, of course, the courts' own construction of women's point of view: no court would describe women's work as more desirable to men. The moral of the conservative story is that working women choose their own economic disempowerment.

Like their conservative counterparts, liberal courts assume that women form their job preferences before they begin working. This shared assumption, however, drives liberal courts to a rhetoric that is the opposite of conservative rhetoric. Whereas the conservative story has a strong account of gender that implies a preference for "feminine" work, the liberal story has no coherent account of gender. To the contrary, liberal courts suppress gender difference, because the assumption of stable, preexisting preferences means that they can hold employers responsible for sex segregation only by portraying women as ungendered subjects who emerge from early life realms with the same experiences and values, and therefore the same work aspirations, as men.

The liberal story centers around the prohibition against stereotyping. * * * This anti-stereotyping reasoning is the classic rhetoric of gender neutrality: it invokes the familiar principle that likes are to be treated alike. The problem lies in determining the extent to which women are "like" men. On its face, the anti-stereotyping reasoning seems to deny the existence of group-based gender differences and asserts that, contrary to the employer's contention, the women in the proposed labor pool are no less interested than the men in nontraditional work. Below the surface, however, this reasoning reflects a basic ambiguity (and ambivalence) about the extent of gender differences. For the anti-stereotyping rule may be interpreted to admit that women are as a group less interested than men in nontraditional work, and to assert only that some individual women may nonetheless be exceptions who do not share the preferences of most women. Under such an individualized approach, the employer is forbidden merely from presuming that all women are so "different" from men that they do not aspire to nontraditional work.

This individualized approach finds support in a number of cases, which emphasize the exceptional woman who does not "share the characteristics generally attributed to [her] group." Some courts condemn employers who raise the lack of interest argument for "stereotyping" all women as being uninterested in nontraditional work. Other courts reject the interest argument by observing that although some women do not desire nontraditional jobs, others do. These courts reason that "Title VII rights are peculiar to the individual, and are not lost or forfeited because some members of the protected classes are unable or unwilling to undertake certain jobs." Logically, however, this reasoning does not suffice to refute the lack of interest argument. The employer is not asserting that no individual woman is interested in nontraditional work, but rather that, within the pool of eligible workers, the women are as a group sufficiently less interested than men to explain their underrepresentation. * * *

* * * [W]hen employers present testimony from other women, who say that they are happier doing traditionally female jobs and that they would not take more highly rewarded nontraditional jobs even if offered, the liberal story confronts a dilemma. Often, liberal courts have simply characterized these women as unrepresentative of the larger group of women in the labor pool. But they have no way of explaining why these women should be considered less representative of most women than the victims, or how they came to have more gendered job aspirations than other women. Because liberal courts have no coherent explanation for gender difference, more conservative courts can easily portray the victims, rather than those satisfied with traditionally female work, as the anomalous unrepresentative group. * * *

There is a need for a new story to make sense of sex segregation in the workplace. Gender conditioning in pre-work realms is too slender a reed to sustain the weight of sex segregation. To explain sex segregation, the law needs an account of how employers actively construct gendered job aspirations—and jobs—in the workplace itself. * * *

The new account suggests a more transformative role for the law in dismantling sex segregation at work. Once we realize that women's work aspirations are shaped not solely by amorphous "social" forces operating in early pre-work realms, but primarily by the structures of incentives and social relations within work organizations, it becomes clear that Title VII can play a major role in producing the needed changes. Title VII cases challenging segregation seek to alter (at least indirectly) the very structural conditions that prevent women from developing and realizing aspirations for higher-paid, more challenging nontraditional jobs. By attributing women's aspirations to forces external and prior to the workworld, courts deny their own ability to (re)construct workplace arrangements and the work aspirations that arise out of those arrangements. In a very real sense, the legal system has perpetuated the status quo of sex segregation by refusing to acknowledge its own power to dismantle it. * * *

NOTE ON GENDER GHETTOES AND THE LAW: AFFIRMATIVE ACTION FOR WOMEN IN THE WORKPLACE?

1. *The Persistence of Gender Ghettoes in the Workplace.* As economic opportunities for women continued to open up, occupational segregation by sex declined in the 1970s (especially in managerial and professional positions), but women continued, on the whole, to be channeled into traditionally "female" jobs.[o] Many firms remained entirely sex segregated into the 1980s, and many women remained effectively closed off from traditionally "male" jobs. Experts fear that even less progress has been made since the 1980s and that there might even be a resegregation ahead. For example, bank tellers were once a "male" job, but women entered it in great numbers during the 1970s—so much so that after a certain "tipping point" was reached, the job became freshly identified with women and is now predominantly "female." Structural concerns also do not bode well. Women greatly outnumber men as part-time workers. With greater employer demand for contingent workers (receiving lesser benefits), women may be increasingly trapped in a double (gendered, part-time) ghetto.

2. *Affirmative Action as a Remedy?* Schultz tries to chart a path between an oversimplified rationale of choice and a paternalistic one of coercion. Does she succeed? By what means would the law most effectively address the concerns she raises: new litigation approaches? legislation? contractual models such as collective bargaining?

The primary response to date has been for the employer to affirmatively recruit women for jobs they have not traditionally held. Workplace historian Alice Kessler–Harris testified at the *Sears* trial that women's choices are strongly influenced by employer signals, sometimes subtle ones: when employers steer women toward traditional "female" jobs or reinforce such choices, women will "choose" those jobs, whereas when employers show positive interest in having women in "male" jobs, women will respond favorably. See also Sylvia A. Law, "'Girls Can't Be Plumbers'— Affirmative Action for Women in Construction: Beyond Goals and Quotas," 24 *Harv. C.R.-C.L. L. Rev.* 45 (1989). Note that Judge Nordberg found that Sears engaged in affirmative action to recruit women for commissioned positions. Wendy Webster Williams, "From Exclusion to Inclusion: Protective Legislation and Affirmative Action" (draft 1993) (excerpted in Babcock et al., *Sex Discrimination and the the Law* 782–87), tells a different story: Sears initiated its affirmative action plan in response to the EEOC's investigation, and the hiring of women in commission sales went up more than threefold.

Assuming affirmative action plans have the strong possibilities Williams and Schultz ascribe to them, the issue of their legality remains. Do such plans violate Title VII's general requirement that employment decisions not be made "because of * * * sex"? The Supreme Court upheld voluntary affirmative action to place women in nontraditional jobs (road

o. See generally *Women's Work, Men's Work: Sex Segregation on the Job* (Barbara F. Reskin & Heidi Hartmann eds. 1986).

dispatcher for a county transportation agency) in *Johnson v. Transportation Agency, Santa Clara County*, 480 U.S. 616 (1987). Justice Brennan's opinion for the Court broadly allowed affirmative action plans for women whenever there is a "manifest imbalance" between men and women in a particular job category, a requirement easily met because no woman had ever been a road dispatcher in Santa Clara County. Concurring in the judgment, Justice O'Connor (who is now the swing vote within the Court on this issue) maintained that a public or private employer can prefer women for a position when there is a "firm basis" for believing the preference necessary to remedy past job discrimination. Would that test allow affirmative action whose purpose is, as Schultz urges, to open the door to changing preferences? A more recent affirmative action decision (authored by Justice O'Connor) disallowed federal race-based set-asides as unconstitutional. *Adarand v. Pena*, 115 S.Ct. 2097 (1995), might signal a more restrictive approach to affirmative action in Title VII cases.

3. *In Defense of* Sears. The *Sears* decision is not without its defenders. Professor Richard Epstein describes it as "an island of good sense in a sea of judicial adventurism." Richard A. Epstein, "Gender Is For Nouns," 41 *DePaul L. Rev.* 981, 998 (1992). Epstein argues that the gender differences illustrated in the facts presented in *Sears* are "real." In direct contradiction to Schultz, he sees nature and the state as mutually exclusive realms:

> The question is whether the state should seek to interfere with the pattern of job sorting by sex that is likely to take place in employment markets. In this regard, it is sometimes said that the protection is strictly necessary to avoid the sense of "caste" that is created by the differences in occupational patterns. But caste itself is a system of formal classification that creates legal barriers to entry for certain classes of people. Whatever the problems in job markets today, formal limitations on contractual capacity of the sort that were common in the nineteenth century are no part of the problem. The issue is not whether women have full contractual capacity, but the way in which they choose to turn that capacity to their own self-advantage. If anything, the insistence that women are a protected class under the statute introduces the same kinds of formal caste distinctions that the supporters of the employment discrimination laws claim they seek to abolish.

Id. at 999. Epstein argues that markets adjust as social realities change, and that legal interventions to eliminate discrimination, especially disparate outcomes rather than intentional discrimination, backfire in terms of social costs for all concerned. How would Schultz respond?

PART B.   LEGAL BANS AGAINST SEXUAL ORIENTATION DISCRIMINATION

Nine states and the District of Columbia have adopted statutes prohibiting employment discrimination because of the employee's sexual orientation.[p] (The District's and Wisconsin's statutes are reproduced as Appendices 2 and 3 to this casebook.) All of these statutes provide legal or equitable remedies or both for employees against private as well as government employers. At least 13 states have executive orders prohibiting sexual orientation discrimination against state employees.[q] Several of these orders are enforceable only administratively and provide neither legal or equitable rights enforceable in court. More than 150 cities and counties have ordinances prohibiting job discrimination because of sexual orientation, either generally or just for municipal employment. There is no federal statute that prohibits discrimination based on sexual orientation, however. Legislation to create such a cause of action as to employment, the Employment Non–Discrimination Act (ENDA, Appendix 4 to this casebook),[r] fell one vote short of Senate passage in September 1996.

A principal objection to ENDA is that lesbians, gay men, and bisexuals are affluent and therefore in no need of anti-discrimination protections. (This was a minor theme of Justice Scalia's dissent in *Romer v. Evans* [Chapter 1, Section 3(B)(1)].) Economist Lee Badgett of the University of Maryland's School of Public Affairs analyzed pooled 1989–91 data from a national random sample, the General Social Survey.[s] The annual average earnings of employees by sex and sexual orientation were as follows:

Heterosexual Men	$28,312
Homosexual/Bisexual Men	$26,321
Heterosexual Women	$18,341
Homosexual/Bisexual Women	$15,056

Professor Badgett's data reflect the previously documented wage gap between women and men and demonstrate that a similar wage gap exists between gay/bisexual and straight employees for each sex. Professor Badgett also subjected the data to "regression" analysis which considers whether other factors such as education explain the income differences, or whether sexual orientation alone explains the difference. She found that no other factor could explain gay/bisexual men's income differential, which was 11% to 27% less than straight male incomes after accounting for other variables. Professor Badgett found persistent lower income for gay/bisexual women, ranging from 12% to 30% lower income than straight female

p. See Cal. Labor Code § 1102.1 (adopted 1992); Conn. Gen. Stat. §§ 46a–81c (adopted 1991); D.C. Code § 1–2501 *et seq.* (adopted 1977); Haw. Rev. Stat. § 378–2 (adopted 1991); Mass. Gen. Laws ch. 151B, § 4 (adopted 1989); Minn. Stat. § 363.03 (adopted 1991); N.J. Stat. §§ 10:5–4,–12 (adopted 1991); R.I. Stat. (adopted 1995); Vt. Stat. tit. 3, § 961(6) and tit. 21 §§ 495(a), 1726(a)(7) (adopted 1991); Wis. Stat. § 101.22 (adopted 1982).

q. Pennsylvania (1975); California (1979); New York (1983); Ohio (1983); New Mexico (1985); Oregon (1987); Colorado (1990); Washington (1991); Louisiana (1992); Maryland (1993); Rhode Island (1993); Minnesota (1994); Illinois (1996).

r. The Senate Committee on Labor and Human Resources held hearings on the bill in 1994. *Employment Discrimination on the Basis of Sexual Orientation: Hearings on S. 2238 Before the Senate Comm. on Labor and Human Resources*, 103d Cong., 2d Sess. (1994).

s. M.V. Lee Badgett, "The Wage Effects of Sexual Orientation Discrimination," *Indus. & Labor Rels. Rev.* 726 (1995).

incomes. The differential for lesbians was not measured at a statistically significant level, however. This may have been a consequence of the smaller sample for lesbians or, more likely, may indicate that lesbian employees are mainly penalized for their sex, and only secondarily for their sexual orientation.

PROBLEM 10–4

DRAFTING A SEXUAL ORIENTATION NONDISCRIMINATION LAW

You are a lawyer with a lesbian and gay rights group and have been asked to draft a provision prohibiting discrimination based on sexual orientation for your local jurisdiction, which already has a general civil rights law. Consider the legal, political, and theoretical issues raised by these questions:

- Will you draft a freestanding provision, or add "sexual orientation" to the existing law?
- Should your bill allow disparate impact discrimination claims? (Recall the distinction between disparate impact and disparate treatment in *Chambers, supra.*) How should the issue of affirmative action be handled?
- Will your legislation compel employers to furnish health and other benefits for employees' domestic partners (recall Chapter 9, Section 1[C])? If so, will it cover only gay, lesbian, and bisexual workers, or will it extend to straight workers as well?
- Should religious institutions be covered? Excluded? Accorded an affirmative defense?
- What about the Boy Scouts? Are there other arguably expressive associations that would have a valid, or least plausible, claim for exemption?
- What about discrimination against transgendered persons? See Chapter 12, Section 2. Transvestites? See Chapter 12, Section 3.

How did the drafters of ENDA and the various other legislative provisions deal with these issues?

Chad Leibert v. Transworld Systems, Inc.

California Court of Appeal, First Appellate District, 1995.
32 Cal.App.4th 1693, 39 Cal.Rptr.2d 65.

■ JUDGE HAERLE.

Appellant brought a civil action against respondent, his former employer, in which he based various causes of action on the allegation that respondent harassed and terminated him on the basis of his sexual orientation. In response to numerous pretrial motions, the trial court dismissed all of appellant's causes of action. On appeal, appellant seeks reinstatement of four claims: (1) violation of Labor Code sections 1101, 1102, and 1102.1

[which prohibit discrimination on the basis of sexual orientation]; (2) violation of the state constitutional right to privacy; (3) wrongful termination in violation of public policy; and (4) intentional infliction of emotional distress. We affirm the trial court rulings with respect to claims 1 and 2 and reverse with respect to claims 3 and 4. * * *

Although the complaint in this matter was amended several times, the pertinent factual allegations remained consistent throughout. On or about April 4, 1991, appellant was hired by respondent to be a collection specialist in its Rohnert Park office. During the course of appellant's employment, respondent learned that appellant was a homosexual. Subsequently, co-workers and managerial employees referred to appellant as a "fag." His supervisor portrayed him in an "effeminate manner." On or about May 7, 1991, a vice-president of respondent met with another employee and instructed him to "keep a close watch on [appellant] and that any mistake by [appellant] would result in [appellant's] immediate termination because 'I do not need a fag working for me in this office.' "Appellant was, he contends, terminated without good cause on or about August 15, 1991. Appellant alleges that his sexual orientation was the reason for his discharge.

Appellant's first amended complaint alleged a cause of action for violations of sections 1101, 1102, 1102.1 which, together, prohibit discrimination on the basis of sexual orientation. Appellant alleged neither exhaustion of, unavailability of, nor futility of administrative remedies. Respondent demurred to this claim on the ground that appellant was required to allege exhaustion of administrative remedies. The trial court agreed and sustained the demurrer with leave to amend. [The court upheld the demurrer on the ground that plaintiff failed to satisfy the pleading requirement and did not produce admissible evidence that pursuit of his administrative remedies would have been futile.]

Appellant next contends that the trial court erred in sustaining without leave to amend respondent's third demurrer to his cause of action for invasion of privacy. The gravamen of appellant's cause of action was that his state constitutional right to privacy was violated when respondent used information about his sexual orientation as grounds to terminate his employment. Appellant specifically alleged that the information misused by respondent "was not improperly obtained and not confidential."

* * * [California law recognizes two categories of privacy protected under its constitution: informational privacy and autonomy privacy. The latter is the interest "in making intimate personal decisions or conduct personal activities without observation, intrusion or interference." The court ruled plaintiff's claim under this cause of action was also properly dismissed. As to the first category of privacy,] appellant specifically alleged that his sexual orientation was not confidential. Therefore, appellant, as a matter of law, cannot state a claim for infringement of a legally protected *informational* privacy interest. * * *

[As to the second category,] he alleged that respondent harassed and discharged him because of his sexual orientation or, in other words, his status as a homosexual. Although deplorable if true, we do not believe that respondent's alleged conduct amounts to an "intrusion," "observation" or "interference" with the making of "intimate personal decisions" or the conduct of "personal activities" of the type protected by the state constitutional right to privacy. * * *

Appellant further contends that the trial court erred in granting respondent judgment on the pleadings on his claim for wrongful termination in violation of public policy [under *Tameny v. Atlantic Richfield Co.*, 610 P.2d 1330 (Cal.1980)]. Appellant's *Tameny* claim alleged that respondent's conduct violated the public policies expressed in sections 1101, 1102, 1102.1 and the state constitutional right to privacy contained in article I, section 1 of the California Constitution. In its motion for judgment on the pleadings, respondent argued that appellant could not state a *Tameny* claim when the trial court had previously removed from the case direct causes of action brought pursuant to the statutory and constitutional provisions relied upon by appellant to support that claim.

* * * We begin our review here by considering the adequacy of appellant's first theory supporting his *Tameny* claim: violation of the enumerated Labor Code sections. We conclude that appellant's claim remains viable notwithstanding the dismissal of his direct action premised on those statutes. Because we uphold appellant's cause of action on this first theory, we do not reach the question of whether the cause of action can be upheld on plaintiff's alternative, constitutional, theory also.

Initially, we observe that respondent did not challenge this cause of action in the trial court on the ground that Labor Code sections 1101, 1102, and 1102.1 fail to state a fundamental public policy of this state against employment discrimination and harassment based upon sexual orientation sufficient to sustain a *Tameny* claim. (See *Gantt v. Sentry Insurance* (1992) [824 P.2d 680] [hereafter *Gantt*] [clarifying sources of public policy to support *Tameny* claim].) In fact, respondent's counsel expressly conceded this point at oral argument. Such a concession is both warranted and appropriate: discrimination on the basis of sexual orientation is outlawed under the prohibitions on discrimination on the basis of political activities or affiliations found in sections 1101 and 1102. (*Gay Law Students Assn. v. Pacific Tel. & Tel. Co.* (1979) [595 P.2d 592] [statutes protect manifest homosexuals]; 69 Ops. Cal. Atty. Gen. 80 (1986) [statutes protect employees from discrimination on the basis of undisclosed or suspected homosexual orientation]; *Delaney v. Superior Fast Freight* [(1993) 18 Cal.Rptr.2d 33] [tracing history of prohibition against discrimination on basis of sexual orientation]; Dickey, "Reorienting the Workplace: Examining California's New Labor Code Section 1102.1 and Other Legal Protections Against Employment Discrimination Based on Sexual Orientation" (1993) 66 *So. Cal. L. Rev.* 2297, 2299–2306 [same].)

Section 1102.1, effective January 1, 1993, provides in relevant part: "(a) Sections 1101 and 1102 prohibit discrimination or different treatment in any aspect of employment or opportunity for employment based on actual or perceived sexual orientation." The Legislature specifically declared that the law "codifies existing law and practice.... " (Historical Note, 44 West's Ann. Lab. Code (1995 pocket supp.) § 1102.1, p. 68, quoting § 1 of Stats. 1992, ch. 915 (Assem. Bill No. 2601).) Given this history, we conclude that the fundamental public policy against discrimination on the basis of sexual orientation was adequately expressed in the statutes of this state to meet the requirements set forth in *Gantt* at the time relevant to this suit. * * *

Finally, appellant argues that the trial court erred in sustaining without leave to amend the demurrer to his cause of action for intentional infliction of emotional distress on the ground that the workers' compensation laws provide the exclusive remedy. We agree.

Appellant's emotional distress claim is premised upon the same alleged actions of his employer that support his *Tameny* claim. As explained above, these alleged actions constitute discrimination in violation of a fundamental public policy of this state. Such misconduct lies outside of the exclusive remedy provisions of the Labor Code. * * *

Employment discrimination, whether based upon sex, race, religion or sexual orientation, is invidious and violates a fundamental public policy of this state. * * *

NOTES ON SEXUAL ORIENTATION DISCRIMINATION CLAIMS

At common law and unless abrogated by a statute such as a civil rights law or by a specific contract, a private sector employer may fire an employee for any reason. The common saying is that an employee can be fired for any reason, or for no reason, but not for a prohibited reason. However, the "at will" doctrine embodies an exception, that an employer cannot terminate an employee for a reason that runs counter to public policy. Numerous plaintiffs have asserted that a firing based on sexual orientation violates public policy, but Leibert is the first to succeed, at least at the appellate level. One Catch–22 in the at will analysis is that, without an anti-discrimination law in place in that jurisdiction, the courts find that there is no evidence that public policy frowns on such firings. Of course, if there is such a law covering the case, few plaintiffs will base their case on an exception to the at will doctrine when their chances of success are usually greater under a statute. Here, Liebert asserted multiple claims: statutory, contract, and tort. A defect in pleadings sank his statutory claim, but two others survived. How will his potential remedies be affected by this result?

Another strategy for employees not covered by anti-discrimination statutes is a contract claim seeking enforcement of company policies against discrimination based on sexual orientation. Such policies are difficult to enforce, because they run headlong into the at will doctrine. *See, e.g., Joachim v. AT & T Information Systems,* 793 F.2d 113 (5th Cir.1986) (holding that statement in personnel handbook that sexual orientation would not be a basis for job discrimination did not create a contractual obligation to the employee). Nonetheless, a plaintiff who can demonstrate a sufficiently clear promise, amounting to an agreement understood by both parties as a contract, that the employee relied on, may succeed in enforcing such a claim. *Compare Torosyan v. Boehringer Ingelheim Pharmaceuticals, Inc.*, 662 A.2d 89 (Conn.1995) (court found contract binding employer to dismiss only for cause based on company manual and recruiter's promise).

Mary K. Ross v. Denver Department of Health and Hospitals

Colorado Court of Appeals, 1994.
883 P.2d 516.

■ JUDGE KAPELKE.

This is an appeal from a judgment of the district court reversing the determination of the Denver Career Service Board (Board) that plaintiff, Mary K. Ross, was not entitled to receive family sick leave benefits to care for her same-sex domestic partner. We reverse and remand with directions.

Ross was formerly employed as a social worker by the Department of Health and Hospitals (Department). In December 1991, she requested family sick leave benefits for the three days she took off work to care for her domestic partner. * * *

The eligibility for sick leave benefits to take care of other persons is prescribed in C.S.A. Rule 11–32, which provides, in pertinent part, that "sick leave may be used . . . for necessary care and attendance during sickness . . . of a member of the employee's immediate family."

The term "immediate family" is defined in C.S.A. Rule 1 as follows:

Husband, wife, son, daughter, mother, father, grandmother, grandfather, brother, sister, son-in-law, daughter-in-law, mother-in-law, father-in law, brother-in-law, sister in law.

As Ross acknowledges, a same-sex partner does not fall within the agency's definition of "immediate family." Nevertheless, before both the hearings officer and the district court, Ross successfully argued that the family definition in C.S.A. Rule 1 has been superseded and, in effect, invalidated by the agency's promulgation of C.S.A. Rule 19–10(c), which provides as follows:

The following administrative actions relating to personnel matters shall be subject to appeal: . . . . c) Discriminatory actions: any action of any officer or employee resulting in alleged discrimination because of race, color, creed, national origin, sex, age, political affiliation, or sexual orientation.

Thus, the dispositive issues are whether C.S.A. Rule 19–10(c) superseded the definition of "immediate family," and whether the denial of sick leave benefits to Ross was an action resulting in discrimination because of her sexual orientation. * * *

There is no evidence that Ross' employer singled her out and treated her differently than it would have treated a similarly situated heterosexual employee. Nor is there any evidence that the Department's decision to deny Ross' request for sick leave was motivated by discriminatory animus. Accordingly, the Board properly based its decision on an interpretation of the rule itself.

We conclude that the Board's interpretation of its rules was reasonable and that the regulatory definition of "immediate family" does not impermissibly discriminate against Ross by reason of her sexual orientation. The definition in the rule applies equally to heterosexual and homosexual employees and thus does not discriminate on the basis of sexual orientation.

A homosexual employee is not precluded from enjoying family sick leave benefits. He or she may take family sick leave to care for a son, daughter, mother, father, grandmother, grandfather, brother, sister, son-in-law, daughter-in-law, mother-in-law, father-in-law, brother-in-law, or sister-in-law.

The only portion of the definition of "immediate family" that arguably affects homosexuals differently is the language allowing an employee to take family sick leave to care for a husband or wife. This portion of the rule does not differentiate between heterosexual and homosexual employees but rather between married and unmarried employees.

Ross was not denied family sick leave benefits to care for her same-sex partner because she is homosexual. An unmarried heterosexual employee also would not be permitted to take family sick leave benefits to care for his or her unmarried opposite-sex partner. Thus, the rule does not treat homosexual employees and similarly situated heterosexual employees differently. *See Hinman v. Department of Personnel Administration*, 213 Cal. Rptr. 410 (Cal.Ct.App.1985); *Phillips v. Wisconsin Personnel Commission*, 482 N.W.2d 121 (Wis.App.1992).

In Hinman v. Department of Personnel Administration, the plaintiff was a homosexual employee who challenged an administrative denial of dental benefits to his same-sex partner. His contention, like Ross' here, was that the state's definition of "family member" for determining eligibility for dental benefits improperly failed to include same-sex partners and that the denial of benefits ran athwart of the California Constitution and an executive order prohibiting employment discrimination based on sexual orientation in state government. We find the court's analysis both persuasive and apposite to the situation here:

> Rather than discriminating on the basis of sexual orientation, therefore, the dental plans distinguish eligibility on the basis of marriage. There is no difference in the effect of the eligibility requirement on unmarried homosexual and unmarried heterosexual employees.

> Thus, plaintiffs are not similarly situated to heterosexual state employees with spouses. They are similarly situated to other unmarried state employees. Unmarried employees are all given the same benefits; plaintiffs have not shown that unmarried homosexual employees are treated differently than unmarried heterosexual employees.

Hinman v. Department of Personnel Administration, supra, 213 Cal. Rptr. at 416.

The court in *Phillips v. Wisconsin Personnel Commission*, undertook a similar analysis. There, a state employee contended that the agency's denial of health insurance coverage for her lesbian companion violated the Wisconsin Fair Employment Act which prohibits discrimination based on, among other things, sexual orientation.

The *Phillips* court construed the rule defining "dependents," which did not include same-sex partners, to be compatible with the anti-discrimination order based upon a finding that the differentiation turned on marital status rather than sexual orientation. "[T]he challenged ... rule distinguishes between married and unmarried employees, not between homosexual and heterosexual employees." *Phillips v. Wisconsin Personnel Commission, supra*, 482 N.W.2d at 127.

In both *Hinman* and *Phillips*, the courts emphasized that, absent a finding of statutory or constitutional violation, the decision to extend various employee benefits to same-sex partners or, for that matter, to unmarried opposite-sex partners, was one properly within the province of the legislature rather than the courts. We concur in that conclusion.

We recognize that under current Colorado law, a homosexual's same-sex partner cannot be a "spouse" and therefore cannot be considered part of the partner's "immediate family" under the present definition in C.S.A. Rule 1. Ross urges that her inability to marry her same-sex partner thus distinguishes her situation from that of an unmarried heterosexual employee. That distinction, however, does not alter our conclusion that the Career Service Rules do not discriminate on the basis of sexual orientation. In this regard, Ross' concern is with a perceived unfairness of the state's marital laws. The decision to change the marriage laws to permit same-sex marriages, however, is a matter for the legislature, not the courts.

Similarly, the definition of "family" is a policy question entrusted to the political branches of government, and we have no judicial authority to substitute our political judgments for those of the other branches.

The Career Service Authority rule contains an exhaustive listing of the categories of persons for whose care a Denver employee may obtain sick leave time. That rule could, of course, be amended to include nonmarital domestic partners.

Other cities have adopted sick leave rules which expressly cover care for unmarried domestic partners. See Note, "A More Perfect Union: A Legal and Social Analysis of Domestic Partnership Ordinances," 92 *Colum. L. Rev.* 1164, 1190 (fns. 125, 128, 129) (1992).

Ross relies on *Braschi v. Stahl Associates Co.*, 543 N.E.2d 49 (N.Y. 1989) [Chapter 9, Section 1(B)], in urging us to adopt a more expansive, sociologically based definition of "family." However, the critical distinction here is that the Career Service Authority has already formulated a definition, while in *Braschi* there were no statutory or regulatory guidelines. The

New York Court of Appeals therefore had to supply its own judicial meaning of that term.

Unlike the New York court, we are not free to design our own definition based upon what might be our perception of a contemporary family. Nor are we bound, as Ross contends, to adhere to the definition set forth in the testimony of the expert witness on families who testified before the hearings officer. If the agency definition is rational and valid, as we determine it is here, we must apply its plainly worded provisions. * * *

NOTES ON EXTENDING EMPLOYMENT BENEFITS TO DOMESTIC PARTNERS

1. *Legislative Action.* Two years after this decision, Denver adopted an ordinance that extended health insurance benefits to the partners of lesbian and gay city employees. James Brooke, "Denver Extends Health Coverage to Partners of Gay Employees," *New York Times*, Sept. 18, 1996, at A17. The *Times* reported that similar policies had been adopted by 313 businesses, 36 cities, 12 counties and four states (Delaware, Massachusetts, New York and Vermont). At least some municipal laws, however, have run afoul of state statutes that do not make such provisions, and have been held pre-empted by inconsistent state law. See, *e.g.*, *Lilly v. City of Minneapolis*, 527 N.W.2d 107 (Minn.App.1995).

The city of San Francisco took this trend a step further in 1996 by amending its administrative code to require all city contractors to grant the same benefits to their employees' domestic partners as to employees' spouses. The new provision had two exceptions: if the actual cost of the same benefit was greater for a domestic partner than for a spouse, the employer could require the affected employee to pay the difference; and if the employer could not provide the benefit, after attempting to do so, it could pay the affected employee the cash equivalent. Catholic Charities of San Francisco, which had $5.5 million worth of city contracts, threatened to sue, seeking a religious exemption. Do you think the new law is valid?

2. *Discrimination Based on Marital Status.* Lesbian and gay employees have also argued that denial of partner benefits to them constituted discrimination based on marital status. No federal employment law prohibits marital status discrimination, but a number of state and local laws do include it as a prohibited basis. Wisconsin's employment discrimination law (Appendix 3) prohibits marital status as well as sexual orientation discrimination, but its courts have held that lesbian and gay employees are not similarly situated to married employees, and thus there is no discrimination:

> Here, the legislature has declared that eligibility for family health insurance coverage is determined by marriage or the presence of dependent children. We have no doubt that Phillips and Tommerup have a committed relationship that partakes of many of the attributes of marriage in the traditional sense. Despite this, however, the fact that Phillips regards Tommerup as her "spouse equivalent" does not

make her "similarly situated" to a married employee in the context of a discrimination analysis. For good or ill, the fact is that under current Wisconsin law Phillips, unlike a spouse, has no legal relationship to Tommerup. The law imposes no mutual duty of general support, and no responsibility for provision of medical care, on unmarried couples of any gender, as it does on married persons. See, for example, § 49.90(1)(m), Stats., which declares that "[e]ach spouse has an equal obligation to support the other spouse," an obligation that may be compelled by the state and enforced in the courts. Thus, Phillips's legal status is not similar to that of a married employee, and, for the reasons discussed, we conclude that the trial court and the commission properly rejected her claim of marital status discrimination under the Fair Employment Act.

Phillips v. Wisconsin Personnel Commission, 482 N.W.2d 121, 125 (Wis. App.1992).

3. *Would ENDA Make a Difference?* Consider the impact of ENDA (Appendix 4) if enacted. Would federal courts reach a different result than the state courts in California, Colorado, or Wisconsin? Would this issue be analyzed differently under the District of Columbia's Human Rights Act (Appendix 2)?

PART C.   AIDS IN THE WORKPLACE

1.   DISABILITY DISCRIMINATION: CONSTITUTIONAL LAW

When doctors treating gay men in New York and Los Angeles during the early 1980s first discovered a strange new disease that came to be known as AIDS (Acquired Immuno–Deficiency Syndrome), there was no comprehensive legal protection against employment discrimination directed at people with medical disabilities or diseases.

One obvious basis if such a claim arises in the public sector is constitutional law. The leading constitutional case on AIDS-related discrimination is *Glover v. Eastern Nebraska Community Office of Retardation (ENCOR)*, 867 F.2d 461 (8th Cir.1989), *cert. denied*, 493 U.S. 932 (1989). The court there enjoined a program adopted by the state of Nebraska which would have required state employees who provided services to the mentally disabled to submit to HIV testing. The Eighth Circuit adopted the findings of the district court that:

> [T]he risk of transmission of the AIDS virus from staff to client, assuming a staff member is infected with [the AIDS virus], in the ENCOR environment is extremely low, approaching zero. The medical evidence is undisputed that the disease is not contracted by casual contact. The risk of transmission of the disease to clients as a result of a client biting or scratching a staff member, and potentially drawing blood, is extraordinarily low, also approaching zero. The risk of transmission of the virus from staff to client due to the staff member

attending to a client's personal hygiene needs is zero. Further, there is absolutely no evidence of drug use or needle sharing at ENCOR, nor is there a problem of sexual abuse of clients by staff.

In short, the evidence in this case establishes that the risk of transmission of the [AIDS] virus at ENCOR is minuscule at best and [ENCOR'S policy] will have little, if any, effect in preventing the spread of [AIDS] or in protecting the clients. Further, from a medical viewpoint, this policy is not necessary to protect clients from any medical risks.

Id. at 461, *quoting Glover v. ENCOR*, 686 F.Supp. 243, 249 (D.Neb.1988). Based on these findings, the court concluded that the testing program was an unreasonable search and seizure violating the Fourth Amendment. *Id.* at 464.

Note that the Supreme Court has held that discrimination on the basis of disability does not trigger heightened equal protection scrutiny. *Cleburne v. Cleburne Living Center* (Chapter 1, Section 3[B][1]). In *Cleburne*, however, the Court invalidated a discrimination motivated only by prejudice against the mentally disabled.

2. THE REHABILITATION ACT

Only one federal anti-discrimination statute existed for disability-based claims in the early 1980s. Section 504 of the Rehabilitation Act of 1973, 29 U.S.C. § 794, protects people with disabilities from discrimination by the federal government and by entities which receive federal funds. It was used early in the epidemic to order children with HIV disease back into schools, to reinstate employees into jobs, to challenge the exclusion of individuals from various health care services, and to resist demands for individuals to undergo mandatory HIV antibody testing. The Fair Housing Amendments Act, which became law in March, 1989, extended federal non-discrimination protection for people with disabilities, for the first time, into the private sector. It prohibited private landlords and owners from discriminating against people with HIV disease in the sale or rental of dwellings.

Section 504 provides:

No otherwise qualified individual with handicaps * * * shall, solely by reason of his handicap, be excluded from participation in, be denied the benefits of, or be subjected to discrimination under any program or activity receiving Federal financial assistance * * *.

The term "handicap" includes a wide range of impairments—mobility, vision and hearing impairments, all types of physical diseases, drug and alcohol addiction, and mental impairments. The defining term for handicap is simply a "physical or mental impairment" that "substantially limits one or more * * * major life activities," 29 U.S.C. § 706(8)(B), such as walking, breathing, learning or working. 45 C.F.R.§ 84.3(j)(2)(i) (1987). The term also includes someone with a *record* of such an impairment and someone who is *perceived* as having such an impairment. 29 U.S.C. § 706(8)(B).

The fact that an individual has a handicap establishes the basic coverage for that person under § 504. In each case, however, the person must also be "otherwise qualified" for the particular position, service or benefit involved. See 29 U.S.C. § 794. This means that the person, in spite of his or her handicap, meets all of the essential requirements of the program or position in question. If a reasonable accommodation would enable the person to meet those requirements, the employer or other grantee of federal funds has an affirmative duty to make that accommodation. 45 C.F.R. § 84.3(k)(1) (1987).

As noted above, the definition of "handicap" in the statute refers generally to "physical or mental impairments." The text makes no distinction between contagious and non-contagious impairments. But that issue was raised in the case of Gene Arline, a teacher with tuberculosis who was fired because the school board was afraid that she might be contagious. In *School Board of Nassau County v. Arline*, 480 U.S. 273 (1987), the Supreme Court concluded that a contagious disease could constitute a handicap under § 504 under the basic definition of handicap in the law. *Id.* at 280–86. Although AIDS was not at issue in the facts of *Arline*, the case was litigated consciously in the shadow of AIDS, with attorneys on both sides using the example of AIDS to buttress their arguments.

The Supreme Court explained why it was rational for the statute to cover contagious diseases: while Congress might have been aware that a person with a contagious disease could pose health concerns in certain situations, it had already addressed that concern within the framework of § 504. Under the law, all individuals with handicaps were required to be "otherwise qualified" for the position or benefit they sought. In the case of a person with a contagious disease, the person would not be otherwise qualified if he or she "poses a significant risk of communicating an infectious disease to others in the workplace" and "if reasonable accommodation will not eliminate that risk." *Id.* at 287 n.16.

The more precise question in *Arline* was whether an employer could discriminate against an individual based on *fear* of contagiousness of the individual's impairment, as opposed to discrimination based on the actual physical effects of the impairment. Under the analysis put forward by the U.S. Department of Justice at the time, an employer could not discriminate against a person with HIV disease if the discrimination were based on the disabling effects of the disease, but an employer *could* discriminate against the person if the discrimination were based on the *fear* that the person could transmit the disease to others. The Justice Department *amicus* brief emphasized that such discrimination would not be unlawful regardless of how irrational or unreasonable the fear of contagion was. The Court ruled that the "contagious effects of a disease can [not] be meaningfully distinguished from the disease's physical effects on a claimant. * * * It would be unfair to allow an employer to seize upon the distinction between the effects of a disease on others and the effects of a disease on a patient and use that distinction to justify discriminatory treatment." *Id.* at 282.

3. THE AMERICANS WITH DISABILITIES ACT

Based on their success under § 504, AIDS advocates joined with the already-existing corps of disability rights advocates in Washington to urge Congress to extend the scope of disability civil rights laws, an effort which culminated in the enactment of the Americans with Disabilities Act of 1990 (the ADA). Most of the fundamental principles of how disability discrimination laws apply to AIDS, or HIV disease as it later became known (to include the full spectrum of the disease beginning with asymptomatic infection and ending with "full-blown" AIDS), were developed prior to the enactment of the ADA.

The ADA is patterned after § 504, and adopts its approach to disability-based discrimination. Because the ADA incorporated and updated then-existing law under § 504, its proponents could argue to a Congress uneasy about the politics of AIDS that it was making "no new law." ADA advocates drafted provisions that codified the Supreme Court's interpretation of § 504 in *Arline*. The primary impact of enacting the ADA was to, in effect, extend the scope of § 504 to cover all private sector employers, except those with fewer than 15 employees, a tremendous expansion in the reach of this branch of civil rights law. Remedies under the ADA mimic those available under Title VII.

The basic three-part definition of "disability" (a term the Congress substituted for "handicap") remains the same as under § 504: "(A) a physical or mental impairment that substantially limits one or more of the major life activities * * *; (B) a record of such an impairment; or (C) being regarded as having such an impairment." 42 U.S.C. § 12102(2). In the realm of employment,

> No covered entity shall discriminate against a qualified individual with a disability because of the disability of such individual in regard to job application procedures, the hiring, advancement, or discharge of employees, employee compensation, job training, and other terms, conditions and privileges of employment.

Id. § 12112(a). In turn, "qualified individual with a disability" is defined as:

> an individual with a disability who, with or without reasonable accommodation, can perform the essential functions of the employment position that such individual holds or desires. For purposes of this subchapter, [employment] consideration shall be given to the employer's judgment as to what functions of a job are essential, and if an employer has prepared a written description before advertising or interviewing applicants for the job, this description shall be considered evidence of the essential functions of the job.

Id. § 12111(8). Further, "reasonable accommodation" means

> (A) making existing facilities used by employees readily accessible to and usable by individuals with disabilities; and

(B) job restructuring, part-time or modified work schedules, reassignment to a vacant position, acquisition or modification of equipment or devices, appropriate adjustment or modifications of examinations, training materials or policies, the provision of qualified readers or interpreters, and other similar accommodations for individuals with disabilities.

Id. § 12111(9).

The statute also provides employers with a specific defense if:

* * * an alleged application of qualification standards, tests, or selection criteria that screen out or tend to screen out or otherwise deny a job or benefit to an individual with a disability has been shown to be job-related and consistent with business necessity, and such performance cannot be accomplished by reasonable accommodation. * * *

(b) The term "qualification standards" may include a requirement that an individual shall not pose a direct threat to the health or safety of other individuals in the workplace.

Id. § 12113. The influence of concerns about HIV disease is obvious in the language about "direct threat," a term that Congress defined as "a significant risk to the health or safety of others that cannot be eliminated by reasonable accommodation." *Id.* § 12111(3).

PROBLEM 10–5

THE ADA AND HOMOSEXUALITY

Although the ADA passed Congress with bipartisan support, and was signed into law by President Bush, some concern was expressed during the debate that it "rewarded bad behavior" by protecting persons with HIV disease. Consider the following remarks of Representative William Dannemeyer, Debate on the Passage of the Americans with Disabilities Act of 1990, 136 Cong. Rec. 2422 (May 17, 1990):

Mr. Speaker and Members, one of the major issues that needs to be debated by the Congress * * * is whether or not, as a matter of public policy, this Nation will say that included within the definition of a disabled person is somebody with a communicable disease * * *. With this bill, in the form that it is now to be considered by the House, if it is adopted, every HIV carrier in the country immediately comes within the definition of a disabled person. Why? Because they have a communicable disease. They are a carrier of a fatal virus that causes death.

Is that sound public policy? And since 70 percent of those people in this country who are HIV carriers are male homosexuals, we are going to witness an attempt or an utterance on the part of the homosexual community that, when this bill is passed, it will be identified by the homosexual community as their bill of rights.

To respond to this kind of concern, the ADA includes a provision specifying that "homosexuality and bisexuality are not impairments, and as such are not disabilities under this Act." 42 U.S.C. § 12211(a). (This provision was part of the bill that Congressman Dannemeyer was speaking against.)

The Dormouse in Alice in Wonderland argues that "I breathe when I sleep" does not mean the same thing as "I sleep when I breathe." Congressman Dannemeyer argued that 70% of the Americans with HIV are male homosexuals and then said that the ADA would be a bill of rights for the entire homosexual community. What would the Dormouse say to the Congressman?

Can it be argued that actions against gay people have a disparate impact on people with AIDS and that such actions are, therefore, prohibited by the ADA? What would the Congressman say to the Dormouse?

Consider the following examples:

1.   An employer announces that it will not hire any homosexuals (or, alternatively, any gay men) because they have a greater chance of having HIV disease. Valid under the ADA?

2.   A sero-negative gay man is fired by an employer who says that he wants no "diseased faggots in this workplace." The gay man sues under the ADA. What result?

3.   A sero-negative gay man is fired when it is discovered that he is gay. The employer has a policy against hiring lesbians, gay men and bisexuals; there is no mention of AIDS. The man sues under the ADA, asserting that its policy is invalid under the ADA because it has a disparate impact on the protected class of people with HIV disease. Result? Would it be different if the anti-gay policy applied only to gay men? For an argument that the ADA could be used in this way (thus confirming Rep. Dannemeyer's claim), see John Douglas, "HIV Disease and Disparate Impact under the Americans with Disabilities Act: A Federal Prohibition of Discrimination on the Basis of Sexual Orientation?," 16 *Berkeley J. Empl. & Lab.L.* 288 (1995).

Edwin C. Anderson v. Gus Mayer Boston Store of Delaware

U.S. District Court, Eastern District of Texas, 1996.
924 F.Supp. 763.

■ COBB, DISTRICT JUDGE. * * *

[Gus Mayer, a sole proprietorship owned by Randolph Ney, is a retail store in Beaumont specializing in ladies' fashion wear. David Anderson spent his entire adult working career, starting in 1982, in the employ of Gus Mayer until shortly before his death. Gus Mayer in the past had provided its employees with the opportunity to subscribe to a group health policy. Home Life Insurance Company (Home Life) began writing the group's coverage in 1989. As part of the employees' compensation, Gus Mayer paid fifty percent of the premiums charged the group with the participating employees paying the other fifty percent. Home Life adjusted premiums twice each year. Home Life raised its premium in response to expenses for treatment of Anderson's testicular cancer in 1988. He was diagnosed as HIV positive in 1991, a fact that became known to Home Life and Gus Mayer later that year.]

[In September 1992, Home Life announced a further premium increase of 30%, which some of Anderson's coworkers and Ney considered much too large for them to handle. Ney sought alternative coverage with John Alden Life Insurance Company ("JALIC"). The new carrier charged lower premiums but rejected Anderson's application for membership, the court found, because of his HIV status. Even after JALIC's decision to deny coverage only in Anderson's case, Gus Mayer decided to go ahead and switch group policies effective January 1, 1993. Gus Mayer made no timely effort to secure any alternative policies for Anderson either before or after this incident. Anderson left his position with Gus Mayer and filed a complaint with the EEOC and then a lawsuit charging discrimination in violation of the ADA. After he died, his parents were substituted as plaintiffs. Judge Cobb denied motions for summary judgment by both plaintiffs and defendant.]

The ADA requires covered entities to provide workers with disabilities with equal access to group health insurance plans, if any such plans exist. The ADA seems to make denying a disabled individual insurance of any kind because of that disability (or any proxy associated therewith) a violation of the Act. * * *

* * * Does an employer acquit all its ADA duties when it selects a group insurer that has refusal standards which effectively deny an employee an equal opportunity to obtain coverage due to the employee's disability-status? This Court finds that when a group insurer makes it a policy to refuse to extend coverage to an employee with a disability because of that disability, an employer violates the ADA by selecting that group insurer unless he makes provisions for the excluded individual to receive comparable health insurance in some other way. As with other provisions of the ADA, however, an employer may avail itself of the undue hardship defense upon appropriate proof. * * *

In the area of health insurance, two basic mandates underlie the entire ADA philosophical approach according to agency interpretations: First, employees with disabilities must be accorded equal access to whatever health insurance the employer provides to employees without disabilities; second, in employment decisions, employers may not take as a factor concerns about the impact of an individual's disability on the employer's health insurance plan. Gus Mayer with full knowledge of the probable exclusion of Anderson because of his AIDS-status still chose to apply to JALIC only. Anderson was not afforded equal access to JALIC coverage because of his disabilities, HIV and AIDS. JALIC categorically excluded individuals with AIDS from their plans, and it had no formal policy regarding HIV-positive individuals.

The fact that JALIC claims it had an independent reason (cancer) for declining Anderson is of no consequence, because equal access means *at a* *minimum* that an individual with a disability must have an *opportunity* to participate in a group plan. * * *

This court finds that when an employer changes group health providers to an insurer that would never consider covering one of the employees in the group because of that employee's disability (in this case, AIDS), the employer violates the ADA (because it has not provided equal access to insurance). The whole notion of equal access demands the employment of an *ex ante* perspective. Before applying to JALIC (*viz., ex ante*), Anderson had a zero percent chance at coverage *because* of his disability. In addition, Gus Mayer did not secure some alternative form of insurance for that employee with a disability.

Section 501(c) of the ADA explicitly allows some disability-based distinctions within insurance policies to be drawn by insurers.[a] However, total denial of group health coverage to an individual does not implicate risks. In other words, disability-based distinctions are only relevant when some coverage is extended to an individual with disabilities. No actuarial risk makes someone uninsurable. How does the fact that someone has AIDS affect one's chances of getting a broken leg? Even if positive correlations could be shown, JALIC has made no claim that it has conducted any such studies. The ADA puts the burden on those actors classifying risks to show both their rationality and permissibility.

. The EEOC Interim Guidance establishes a two step process when looking at alleged insurance discrimination: 1. Determine whether the challenged insurance term is a *Disability–Based Distinction*; 2. If and only if there is disability-based distinction, then determine whether *section 501(c)* of the ADA protects that disability-based distinction.

Here, Anderson was not subject to any disability-based distinctions in coverage. Instead, Anderson was denied *ANY and ALL* coverage whatsoever. It was not that coverage was being distributed unevenly; rather, Anderson had no coverage to be ratcheted down. He did not suffer from reduced coverage or caps on reimbursement; rather, because he had AIDS, Anderson was completely denied access to the group health insurance. The ADA requires that employees with disabilities must be afforded equal

a. [Eds.] Section 501(c) of the ADA reads as follows:

[Previous portions] of this Act shall not be construed to prohibit or restrict—

(1) an insurer, hospital or medical service company, health maintenance organization, or any agent, or entity that administers benefit plans, or similar organizations from underwriting risks, classifying risks, or administering such risks that are based on or not inconsistent with State law; or

(2) a person or organization covered by this chapter from establishing, spon-

soring, observing or administering the terms of a bona fide benefit plan that are based on underwriting risks, classifying risks, or administering such risks that are based on or not inconsistent with State law; or

(3) a person or organization covered by this chapter from establishing, sponsoring, observing or administering the terms of a bona fide benefit plan that is not subject to State laws that regulate insurance. Paragraphs (1), (2), and (3) shall not be used as a subterfuge to evade the purposes of [the anti-discrimination provisions] of this chapter.

access to whatever health insurance coverage the employer provides. In the area of group health insurance, the legislative history is clear:

> [W]ith respect to group health insurance coverage, an individual with a pre-existing condition may be denied coverage for that condition for the period specified in the policy but cannot be denied coverage for illnesses or injuries unrelated to the pre-existing condition.

For the reasons set forth above, section 501(c) does not apply to situations where an individual with a disability has been totally denied coverage of any kind. The EEOC found that David Anderson was not provided any insurance coverage whatsoever, and as such section 501(c) did not immunize Gus Mayer's actions. When complete denial of coverage is at issue, there simply are no disability-based distinctions to be considered. Section 501(c) does seem to state that it may be possible to provide certain coverage exclusions to individuals with disabilities if the risks of those disabilities so warrant and those risks are treated like other similar risks not associated with disabilities. The burden is a very heavy one on the employer, and that burden cannot be borne by an employer who completely denies coverage to an individual due to a disability.

In some situations, pre-existing conditions clauses, disability-based distinctions supported by legitimate cost data, and other risk-classifying devices may be permitted, but complete denial is a *per se* violation of the ADA's mandate that employers provide individuals with disabilities equal access to group health insurance.

The ADA explicitly recognizes that integrating disabled individuals into the workforce often will result in increased costs. Increased costs are thought to be the price we as a people must pay for equal dignity. There comes a point, however, where enormous expense involved in providing equal terms of employment to an otherwise qualified individual may result in an *undue burden* for a covered entity. The ADA takes account of these rare situations where an accommodation may be financially crippling by the operation of section 12112(b)(5)(A).

Whether an effort would be unduly burdensome depends upon the financial and structural resources of the covered entity. 42 U.S.C. § 12111(10)(B). The legislative history of the ADA recommends that the disabled person be consulted about what a reasonable accommodation might be to avoid employers overstating costs.

In the context of health insurance, the EEOC Interim Guidelines state that an employer must prove that coverage for a discrete group of disabilities would be so expensive as to cause the Employer's plan to become *financially insolvent*. The employer must also show that there is *no alternative* which would avoid the insolvency. This Court believes the question of undue hardship in the provision of David Anderson with equal access to health insurance to be a question for the fact-finder. As such, it is the basis of denying the Plaintiffs' Motion for Partial Summary Judgment.

NOTE ON THE ADA AND HEALTH BENEFITS FOR PEOPLE WITH AIDS

As the HIV epidemic persisted into the 1990s, and as medical discoveries allowed persons with the disease to live and work longer than had been possible in the 1980s, concern about the impact of HIV shifted more to the expense associated with long-term treatment. Fear of contagion gave way to fear of cost. Although protected by the ADA, employees with HIV disease continue to fear differential treatment. Do you think that occurred in the *Anderson* case? Is there a basis under the ADA to treat persons with HIV differently than persons with other expensive diseases, such as cancer? Should conditions be categorized according to cost? If so, would the coverage or non-coverage of certain conditions change with medical science? Note that, as with HIV disease, advances in treatment can mean greater expense, over a longer period of time.

*

CHAPTER 11

THE LAW'S CONSTRUCTION OF CONSENT

SECTION 1 Forcible Sex

SECTION 2 Sex by and With Minors

SECTION 3 Commercial Sex

It is commonly believed that "consent" is or should be the main arbiter of the legality of sexual activity. (Recall Jana Singer's argument [Chapter 9, Section 1] that family law is being "privatized," or left to private contracting. A similar impulse may be operating, perhaps incompletely, in the law of sexual activity.) A simple exercise may suggest that the matter is not so simple, or that the "consent" which validates sexual activity is not easily defined.[a]

Person A asks Person B to have intercourse, and B declines. The next day A offers B a diamond ring if B will have intercourse with A, and B accepts the ring and has sex with A. This may sound like the quintessential, and therefore legal, consensual sex, but the consent, and the legality, are not clear without further information about the context of this exchange. Consider nine elaborations on this scenario:

1. A and B are married to one another.

---

a. This exercise is adapted from William N. Eskridge, Jr., "The Many Faces of Consent," 37 *Wm. & Mary Law Rev.* 47, 49–51 (1995).

2. A is B's employer.

3. B earns a living by trading sex for valuables, and A is B's client.

4. A and B are brother and sister.

5. B is 16 years old, and A is 21 years old.

6. A is married to C.

7. B is mentally disabled.

8. A and B engage in oral sex (sodomy). (Variation: A and B are both women.)

9. A and B engage in sadomasochistic play, where A (the dominatrix) ties and whips B (the submissive) until welts form on various portions of B's body.

Next consider six elaborations on a scenario where A has intercourse with B over B's objections ("No! Please stop."):

1. A and B are strangers, and A pushes B against the wall and places a strong hand on B's throat during intercourse with B.

2. Same as 1, except add the following: A is a dominatrix, and B's protests are part of a bondage fantasy where B is ravaged by an overpowering prison guard.

3. A and B are strangers who meet at a bar; they go to A's residence and remove their clothing. After heavy petting, B objects to intercourse, but A persists over those objections.

4. Same as 3, except that A responds to B's objections with threats of bodily harm if B does not acquiesce in intercourse.

5. Same as 3, except that A and B have been dating for two years and have had intercourse 50 times during that period.

6. Same as 4, except that A and B are married.

Surely it will not be a surprise that each of the 15 examples above involves a different legal analysis. Whether there has been consent or whether apparent consent (or nonconsent) has legal significance depends upon context: the relationship of the participants, the status of each, and the nature of the desire or objection that is voiced by each. Is the type of sexual activity engaged in also relevant? This chapter will present descriptive and normative materials that bear on the law of sexual "consent." As you read the materials, consider what legal regulations strike you as sensible, what regulations should be abandoned entirely, and what regulations should be reformed. Consider, also, whether consent is really the ultimate issue in our increasingly "liberal" regime, and whether it should be. If not consent, what?

SECTION 1

FORCIBLE SEX

As the term is commonly used, "rape" connotes unconsented sexual intercourse. Rape law, therefore, is the focal point for any regulatory regime grounded upon consent. Yet rape is itself a contested concept. Its meaning has shifted, from only that sexual assault which is accompanied by physical injury or accomplished by use of weapons, to any sexual activity forced upon a person, often by someone she or he knows—a date, a spouse, a coworker, a family member.[b] Consider the social and legal change reflected in the following two definitions of "force":

> A man who handles a lady vigorously and with some force (against her will) is plainly guilty of an assault—of an indecent assault. But he does not have an intent to commit rape if his actions are taken in the hope or expectation of thereby awakening desire, and with the further intention of desisting if his approach does not arouse desire or lead to acquiescence but rather encounters continued resistance.

United States v. Bryant, 420 F.2d 1327, 1334 (D.C.Cir.1969).

> [The physical force element will be satisfied] if the defendant applies any amount of force against another person in the absence of what a reasonable person would believe to be affirmative and freely-given permission to the act of sexual penetration.

State ex rel. M.T.S., 609 A.2d 1266, 1277 (N.J.1992).

FBI data indicate that slightly more than 100,000 rapes—which the FBI defines as "carnal knowledge of a female forcibly and against her will" (including attempted rapes)—are reported to the police each year.[c] This number amounts to approximately 95 reported rapes per 100,000 females

---

b. Studies include Diana E.H. Russell, *Sexual Exploitation: Rape, Child Abuse, and Workplace Harassment* (1984); Mary Koss et al., "The Scope of Rape: Incidence and Prevalence of Sexual Aggression and Victimization in a National Sample of Higher Education Students," 55 *J. Consulting & Clinical Psychology* 162 (1987). On rape by spouses and boyfriends, see Julie Allison & Lawrence S. Wrightman, *Rape: The Misunderstood Crime* (1993); Susan Brownmiller, *Against Our Will: Men, Women, and Rape* (1975) Diana E.H. Russell, *Rape in Marriage* (1978); Robin

Warshaw, *I Never Called It Rape: The Ms. Report on Recognizing, Fighting, and Surviving Date and Acquaintance Rape* (1988). A popular account that has stirred debate is Katie Roiphe, *The Morning After: Sex, Fear, and Feminism on Campus* (1993), usefully reviewed by Wendy Kaminer, "What Is This Thing Called Rape?," *N.Y. Times*, Sept. 19, 1993, at G1.

c. U.S. Department of Justice, Federal Bureau of Investigation, *Crime in the United States 1994*, at 23 (1995).

12 years of age and over.[d] Data from the National Crime Victimization Study indicate that only 36 percent of rapes, 20 per cent of attempted rapes, and 41 per cent of sexual assaults were reported to law enforcement agencies; the same survey reported that two-thirds of rapes and sexual assaults were committed by someone acquainted with, known to or related to the victim.[e]

How should the law define "rape"?

PART A. THE LAW OF RAPE

Although unconsented touching can be the basis for a tort cause of action (assault or battery), American law has historically not criminalized sexual intercourse based solely on the absence of consent, without also a showing of force. In light of the following case, consider whether a victim's fear of harm is enough to justify a rape conviction, without evidence of direct force or explicit threats.

State v. Edward Rusk

Maryland Court of Appeals, 1981.
289 Md. 230, 424 A.2d 720.

■ MURPHY, CHIEF JUDGE.

Edward Rusk was found guilty by a jury in the Criminal Court of Baltimore (Karwacki, J. presiding) of second degree rape in violation of Maryland Code (1957, 1976 Repl. Vol., 1980 Cum.Supp.), Art. 27, § 463(a)(1), which provides in pertinent part:

"A person is guilty of rape in the second degree if the person engages in vaginal intercourse with another person:

(1) By force or threat of force against the will and without the consent of the other person; . . . ."

On appeal, the Court of Special Appeals, sitting en banc, reversed the conviction; it concluded by an 8–5 majority that in view of the prevailing law as set forth in *Hazel v. State*, 157 A.2d 922 (Md.1960), insufficient evidence of Rusk's guilt had been adduced at the trial to permit the case to go to the jury. * * *

At the trial, the 21–year-old prosecuting witness, Pat, testified that on the evening of September 21, 1977, she attended a high school alumnae meeting where she met a girl friend, Terry. After the meeting, Terry and Pat agreed to drive in their respective cars to Fells Point to have a few drinks. On the way, Pat stopped to telephone her mother, who was baby

---

d. U.S. Bureau of the Census, *Statistical Abstract of the United States: 1995*, at 203 (1995) (Table 315).

e. U.S. Department of Justice, "Criminal Victimization 1994," *Bureau of Justice Statistics Bulletin* 3, 8 (April 1996).

sitting for Pat's two-year-old son; she told her mother that she was going with Terry to Fells Point and would not be late in arriving home.

The women arrived in Fells Point about 9:45 p. m. They went to a bar where each had one drink. After staying approximately one hour, Pat and Terry walked several blocks to a second bar, where each of them had another drink. After about thirty minutes, they walked two blocks to a third bar known as E. J. Buggs. The bar was crowded and a band was playing in the back. Pat ordered another drink and as she and Terry were leaning against the wall, Rusk approached and said "hello" to Terry. Terry, who was then conversing with another individual, momentarily interrupted her conversation and said "Hi, Eddie." Rusk then began talking with Pat and during their conversation both of them acknowledged being separated from their respective spouses and having a child. Pat told Rusk that she had to go home because it was a week-night and she had to wake up with her baby early in the morning.

Rusk asked Pat the direction in which she was driving and after she responded, Rusk requested a ride to his apartment. Although Pat did not know Rusk, she thought that Terry knew him. She thereafter agreed to give him a ride. Pat cautioned Rusk on the way to the car that " 'I'm just giving a ride home, you know, as a friend, not anything to be, you know, thought of other than a ride;' " and he said, " 'Oh, okay.' " They left the bar between 12:00 and 12:20 a.m.

Pat testified that on the way to Rusk's apartment, they continued the general conversation that they had started in the bar. After a twenty-minute drive, they arrived at Rusk's apartment in the 3100 block of Guilford Avenue. Pat testified that she was totally unfamiliar with the neighborhood. She parked the car at the curb on the opposite side of the street from Rusk's apartment but left the engine running. Rusk asked Pat to come in, but she refused. He invited her again, and she again declined. She told Rusk that she could not go into his apartment even if she wanted to because she was separated from her husband and a detective could be observing her movements. Pat said that Rusk was fully aware that she did not want to accompany him to his room. Notwithstanding her repeated refusals, Pat testified that Rusk reached over and turned off the ignition to her car and took her car keys. He got out of the car, walked over to her side, opened the door and said, " 'Now, will you come up?' " Pat explained her subsequent actions:

> "At that point, because I was scared, because he had my car keys. I didn't know what to do. I was someplace I didn't even know where I was. It was in the city. I didn't know whether to run. I really didn't think at that point, what to do.

> "Now, I know that I should have blown the horn. I should have run. There were a million things I could have done. I was scared, at that point, and I didn't do any of them."

Pat testified that at this moment she feared that Rusk would rape her. She said: "[I]t was the way he looked at me, and said 'Come on up, come on up;' and when he took the keys, I knew that was wrong."

It was then about 1 a.m. Pat accompanied Rusk across the street into a totally dark house. She followed him up two flights of stairs. She neither saw nor heard anyone in the building. Once they ascended the stairs, Rusk unlocked the door to his one-room apartment, and turned on the light. According to Pat, he told her to sit down. She sat in a chair beside the bed. Rusk sat on the bed. After Rusk talked for a few minutes, he left the room for about one to five minutes. Pat remained seated in the chair. She made no noise and did not attempt to leave. She said that she did not notice a telephone in the room. When Rusk returned, he turned off the light and sat down on the bed. Pat asked if she could leave; she told him that she wanted to go home and "didn't want to come up." She said, " 'Now, [that] I came up, can I go?' " Rusk, who was still in possession of her car keys, said he wanted her to stay.

Rusk then asked Pat to get on the bed with him. He pulled her by the arms to the bed and began to undress her, removing her blouse and bra. He unzipped her slacks and she took them off after he told her to do so. Pat removed the rest of her clothing, and then removed Rusk's pants because "he asked me to do it." After they were both undressed Rusk started kissing Pat as she was lying on her back. Pat explained what happened next:

> "I was still begging him to please let, you know, let me leave. I said, 'you can get a lot of other girls down there, for what you want,' and he just kept saying, 'no'; and then I was really scared, because I can't describe, you know, what was said. It was more the look in his eyes; and I said, at that point—I didn't know what to say; and I said, 'If I do what you want, will you let me go without killing me?' Because I didn't know, at that point, what he was going to do; and I started to cry; and when I did, he put his hands on my throat, and started lightly to choke me; and I said, 'If I do what you want, will you let me go?' And he said, yes, and at that time, I proceeded to do what he wanted me to."

Pat testified that Rusk made her perform oral sex and then vaginal intercourse.

Immediately after the intercourse, Pat asked if she could leave. She testified that Rusk said, " 'Yes,' " after which she got up and got dressed and Rusk returned her car keys. She said that Rusk then "walked me to my car, and asked if he could see me again; and I said, 'Yes;' and he asked me for my telephone number; and I said, 'No, I'll see you down Fells Point sometime,' just so I could leave." Pat testified that she "had no intention of meeting him again." She asked him for directions out of the neighborhood and left. * * *

Rusk, the 31–year-old defendant, testified that he was in the Buggs Tavern for about thirty minutes when he noticed Pat standing at the bar. Rusk said: "She looked at me, and she smiled. I walked over and said, hi, and started talking to her." He did not remember either knowing or speaking to Terry. When Pat mentioned that she was about to leave, Rusk asked her if she wanted to go home with him. In response, Pat said that she would like to, but could not because she had her car. Rusk then suggested that they take her car. Pat agreed and they left the bar arm-in-arm.

Rusk testified that during the drive to her apartment, he discussed with Pat their similar marital situations and talked about their children. He said that Pat asked him if he was going to rape her. When he inquired why she was asking, Pat said that she had been raped once before. Rusk expressed his sympathy for her. Pat then asked him if he planned to beat her. He inquired why she was asking and Pat explained that her husband used to beat her. Rusk again expressed his sympathy. He testified that at no time did Pat express a fear that she was being followed by her separated husband.

According to Rusk, when they arrived in front of his apartment Pat parked the car and turned the engine off. They sat for several minutes "petting each other." Rusk denied switching off the ignition and removing the keys. He said that they walked to the apartment house and proceeded up the stairs to his room. Rusk testified that Pat came willingly to his room and that at no time did he make threatening facial expressions. Once inside his room, Rusk left Pat alone for several minutes while he used the bathroom down the hall. Upon his return, he switched the light on but immediately turned it off because Pat, who was seated in the dark in a chair next to the bed, complained it was too bright. Rusk said that he sat on the bed across from Pat and reached out

> "and started to put my arms around her, and started kissing her; and we fell back into the bed, and we were petting, kissing, and she stuck her hand down in my pants and started playing with me; and I undid her blouse, and took off her bra; and then I sat up and I said 'Let's take our clothes off;' and she said, 'Okay;' and I took my clothes off, and she took her clothes off; and then we proceeded to have intercourse."

Rusk explained that after the intercourse, Pat "got uptight."

> "Well, she started to cry. She said that she said, 'You guys are all alike,' she says, 'just out for,' you know, 'one thing.'

> "She started talking about—I don't know, she was crying and all. I tried to calm her down and all; and I said, 'What's the matter?' And she said, that she just wanted to leave; and I said, 'Well, okay;' and she walked out to the car. I walked out to the car. She got in the car and left."

Rusk denied placing his hands on Pat's throat or attempting to strangle her. He also denied using force or threats of force to get Pat to have intercourse with him. * * *

In argument before us on the merits of the case, the parties agreed that the issue was whether, in light of the principles of *Hazel*, there was evidence before the jury legally sufficient to prove beyond a reasonable doubt that the intercourse was "[b]y force or threat of force against the will and without the consent" of the victim in violation of Art. 27, § 463(a)(1). * * *

Hazel, which was decided in 1960, long before the enactment of § 463(a)(1), involved a prosecution for common law rape, there defined as "the act of a man having unlawful carnal knowledge of a female over the age of ten years by force without the consent and against the will of the victim." The evidence in that case disclosed that Hazel followed the prosecutrix into her home while she was unloading groceries from her car. He put his arm around her neck, said he had a gun, and threatened to shoot her baby if she moved. Although the prosecutrix never saw a gun, Hazel kept one hand in his pocket and repeatedly stated that he had a gun. He robbed the prosecutrix, tied her hands, gagged her, and took her into the cellar. The prosecutrix complied with Hazel's commands to lie on the floor and to raise her legs. Hazel proceeded to have intercourse with her while her hands were still tied. The victim testified that she did not struggle because she was afraid for her life. There was evidence that she told the police that Hazel did not use force at any time and was extremely gentle. Hazel claimed that the intercourse was consensual and that he never made any threats. The Court said that the issue before it was whether "the evidence was insufficient to sustain the conviction of rape because the conduct of the prosecutrix was such as to render her failure to resist consent in law." It was in the context of this evidentiary background that the Court set forth the principles of law which controlled the disposition of the case. It recognized that force and lack of consent are distinct elements of the crime of rape. It said:

> "Force is an essential element of the crime and to justify a conviction, the evidence must warrant a conclusion either that the victim resisted and her resistance was overcome by force or that she was prevented from resisting by threats to her safety. But no particular amount of force, either actual or constructive, is required to constitute rape. Necessarily, that fact must depend upon the prevailing circumstances. As in this case force may exist without violence. If the acts and threats of the defendant were reasonably calculated to create in the mind of the victim having regard to the circumstances in which she was placed a real apprehension, due to fear, of imminent bodily harm, serious enough to impair or overcome her will to resist, then such acts and threats are the equivalent of force."

As to the element of lack of consent, the Court said in *Hazel*:

> "[I]t is true, of course, that however reluctantly given, consent to the act at any time prior to penetration deprives the subsequent intercourse of its criminal character. There is, however, a wide difference between consent and a submission to the act. Consent may involve submission, but submission does not necessarily imply consent. Furthermore, submission to a compelling force, or as a result of being put in fear, is not consent."

The Court noted that lack of consent is generally established through proof of resistance or by proof that the victim failed to resist because of fear. The degree of fear necessary to obviate the need to prove resistance, and thereby establish lack of consent, was defined in the following manner:

"The kind of fear which would render resistance by a woman unnecessary to support a conviction of rape includes, but is not necessarily limited to, a fear of death or serious bodily harm, or a fear so extreme as to preclude resistance, or a fear which would well nigh render her mind incapable of continuing to resist, or a fear that so overpowers her that she does not dare resist."

Hazel thus made it clear that lack of consent could be established through proof that the victim submitted as a result of fear of imminent death or serious bodily harm. In addition, if the actions and conduct of the defendant were reasonably calculated to induce this fear in the victim's mind, then the element of force is present. *Hazel* recognized, therefore, that the same kind of evidence may be used in establishing both force and nonconsent, particularly when a threat rather than actual force is involved. * * *

Hazel did not expressly determine whether the victim's fear must be "reasonable." * * * While *Hazel* made it clear that the victim's fear had to be genuine, it did not pass upon whether a real but unreasonable fear of imminent death or serious bodily harm would suffice. The vast majority of jurisdictions have required that the victim's fear be reasonably grounded in order to obviate the need for either proof of actual force on the part of the assailant or physical resistance on the part of the victim.[3] We think that, generally, this is the correct standard. * * *

We think the reversal of Rusk's conviction by the Court of Special Appeals was in error for the fundamental reason so well expressed in the dissenting opinion by Judge Wilner when he observed that the majority had "trampled upon the first principle of appellate restraint . . . [because it had] substituted [its] own view of the evidence (and the inferences that may fairly be drawn from it) for that of the judge and jury . . . [and had thereby] improperly invaded the province allotted to those tribunals." In

---

3. See *State v. Reinhold*, 597 P.2d 532 ([Ariz.] 1979); *People v. Hunt*, 139 Cal.Rptr. 675 (1977); *State v. Dill*, 40 A.2d 443 ([Del.] 1944); *Arnold v. United States*, 358 A.2d 335 (D.C.App.1976); *Doyle v. State*, 22 So. 272 ([Fla.] 1897); *Curtis v. State*, 223 S.E.2d 721 ([Ga.] 1976); *People v. Murphy*, 260 N.E.2d 386 ([Ill.App.] 1970); *Carroll v. State*, 324 N.E.2d 809 ([Ind.] 1975); *Fields v. State*, 293 So.2d 430 (Miss.1974); *State v. Beck*, 368 S.W.2d 490 (Mo.1963); *Cascio v. State*, 25 N.W.2d 897 ([Neb.] 1947); *State v. Burns*, 214 S.E.2d 56 [N.C.], *cert. denied*, 423 U.S. 933 (1975); *State v. Verdone*, 337 A.2d 804 ([R.I.] 1975); *Brown v. State*, 576 S.W.2d 820 (Tex. Cr.App.1978); *Jones v. Com.*, 252 S.E.2d 370 ([Va.] 1979); *State v. Baker*, 192 P.2d 839 ([Wash.] 1948); *Brown v. State*, 581 P.2d 189 (Wyo.1978).

Some jurisdictions do not require that the victim's fear be reasonably grounded. See *Struggs v. State*, 372 So.2d 49 (Ala.Cr.App.), *cert. denied*, 444 U.S. 936 (1979); *Kirby v. State*, 59 So. 374 ([Ala. App.] 1912); *Dinkens v. State*, 546 P.2d 228 ([Nev.] 1976); citing *Hazel v. State*, supra; *State v. Herfel*, 182 N.W.2d 232 ([Wis.] 1971). See also *Salsman v. Com.*, 565 S.W.2d 638 (Ky.App.1978); *State v. Havens*, 264 N.W.2d 918 (S.D.1978).

view of the evidence adduced at the trial, the reasonableness of Pat's apprehension of fear was plainly a question of fact for the jury to determine. * * *

■ COLE, JUDGE, [joined by SMITH and DIGGES, JUDGES] dissenting. * * *

* * * It seems to me that whether the prosecutrix's fear is reasonable becomes a question only after the court determines that the defendant's conduct under the circumstances was reasonably calculated to give rise to a fear on her part to the extent that she was unable to resist. In other words, the fear must stem from his articulable conduct, and equally, if not more importantly, cannot be inconsistent with her own contemporaneous reaction to that conduct. The conduct of the defendant, in and of itself, must clearly indicate force or the threat of force such as to overpower the prosecutrix's ability to resist or will to resist. In my view, there is no evidence to support the majority's conclusion that the prosecutrix was forced to submit to sexual intercourse, certainly not fellatio. [Judge Cole analyzed 12 cases invoked in *Hazel*, prominently including the following.]

In *Selvage v. State*, 27 N.W.2d 636 (Neb.1947), an 18–year-old woman went to a dance with her brother and later decided to go to a cafe with the defendants and some other acquaintances. They drove to a ball park several blocks away where she and the defendant and another got out. The others in the car drove away. She and the two males walked about a block into the park; she refused their advances for intercourse. She claimed they threw her to the ground, held her while they took turns having sexual intercourse. While this was going on a car with its lights on drove up and the two young men hurried some distance away from her. She made no outcry, nor attempted to communicate with the people in this car. Later at a different place in the park, she claimed each had intercourse with her again. The three walked back to the cafe, drank coffee, and waited to get a car to take them to the city near her home. When they finally got a car, she testified the two repeated the acts of intercourse with her. She resisted but made no complaint to those riding in the front seat. When she got home she related to her parents what had happened.

The Supreme Court of Nebraska, in holding the evidence insufficient to convict for rape, said:

"Resistance or opposition by mere words is not enough; the resistance must be by acts, and must be reasonably proportionate to the strength and opportunities of the woman. She must resist the consummation of the act, and her resistance must not be a mere pretense, but must be in good faith, and must persist until the offense is consummated."
* * *

In each of the above 12 cases there was either physical violence or specific threatening words or conduct which were calculated to create a very real and specific fear of *immediate* physical injury to the victim if she did not comply, coupled with the apparent power to execute those threats in the event of non-submission.

While courts no longer require a female to resist to the utmost or to resist where resistance would be foolhardy, they do require her acquiescence in the act of intercourse to stem from fear generated by something of substance. She may not simply say, "I was really scared," and thereby transform consent or mere unwillingness into submission by force. These words do not transform a seducer into a rapist. She must follow the natural instinct of every proud female to resist, by more than mere words, the violation of her person by a stranger or an unwelcomed friend. She must make it plain that she regards such sexual acts as abhorrent and repugnant to her natural sense of pride. She must resist unless the defendant has objectively manifested his intent to use physical force to accomplish his purpose. The law regards rape as a crime of violence. The majority today attenuates this proposition. It declares the innocence of an at best distraught young woman. It does not demonstrate the defendant's guilt of the crime of rape. * * *

NOTES ON RUSK AND THE CHANGING LAW OF RAPE

1.   *Why Is There Any Requirement of Force? Was There a "Real" Rape in* Rusk? The narrow basis for the holding in *Rusk* was deference to the jury's determination of the complainant's and defendant's state of mind and actions. If the jury had acquitted, there would have been no appeal because of the rule against submitting a criminal defendant to double jeopardy. *Query*: Why is there any requirement of force in a rape prosecution? Why isn't it a crime for a person to persist in sexual advances after the other person has said, "Stop"? What stereotypes about men and women (and sex) underlie the law's refusal to go this far? Are they defensible?

Another query: What if there is a miscommunication, as defendant Rusk maintained in the Maryland case? What if A has sex with an unwilling B, but B does not explicitly indicate unwillingness (as by saying "stop" or "no"). Are there other signals that A should be charged with understanding? Does it make a difference if: (a) A and B have been dating and have had intercourse on prior occasions; (b) A is much bigger than B; or (c) A and B have been drinking heavily that evening? Should A be convicted of rape, usually a first or second degree felony, for a "mistake"? Who should bear the risk of such "mistakes"?

2.   *From the Common Law to the Model Penal Code, and Beyond.*[f] The common law required the rape complainant to resist "to the utmost," which seems today like the height of sexism. Several states modified the common law by specific statutory language. Most prominently, New York redefined rape to include sexual intercourse caused by the defendant's "forcible compulsion" of the complainant. Forcible compulsion, in turn, was premised upon the complainant's "earnest resistance" to the defendant's advances. This approach was followed by several state reform efforts

---

f.   Susan Estrich, *Real Rape* (1992) provides an excellent overview of the evolution of rape law.

in the 1970s (Hawaii, Kentucky, Utah), but was modified by New York in 1977 (replacing "earnest resistance" with "reasonable resistance") and finally abandoned in 1982.

The drafters of the Model Penal Code (MPC) in the 1950s criticized the New York as well as the common law approach, because of the focus on the actions and *mens rea* of the victim, rather than the actions and *mens rea* of the defendant (the traditional focus of criminal law). Section 213.1(1)(a) of the "official" 1962 draft of the MPC defined rape as sexual intercourse where the man "compels [the complainant] to submit by force or by threat of imminent death, serious bodily injury, extreme pain or kidnapping, to be inflicted on anyone."[g] Something like the MPC's approach, which focuses on the defendant's alleged force or threat rather than the complainant's alleged resistance, has been adopted in almost all the states.

Like the state law discussed in *Rusk*, the MPC has not been static; its sexual assault provisions have been revised to criminalize more conduct, and some states have gone further than the revised MPC. Utah, for example, defines rape, a first degree felony, as "sexual intercourse with another person without the victim's consent." Utah Code § 76–5–402 (1995). Consent is negated under Utah law if any of the following applies, *id*. § 76–5–406 (1996 Supp.):

(1) the complainant "expresses lack of consent through words or conduct";

(2) defendant overcomes the complainant's resistance through force or violence, **or** (3) concealment or surprise, **or** (4) threats of physical force, kidnapping or extortion;

(5) the complainant was "unconscious, unaware that the act is occurring, or physically unable to resist" **or** (6) suffers from a mental disease or defect rendering her or him incapable of appraising the nature of the act or resisting it, **or** (7) was tricked by the defendant into believing defendant was his or her spouse, **or** (8) was impaired by a substance administered by the defendant without the complainant's knowledge;

(9) the complainant was under 14 years old, **or** (10) was under 18 years old and the defendant was her or his parent, guardian, or person vested with a special legal trust over the complainant, **or** (11) was between 14 and 17 (inclusive) and the defendant was more than three years older and enticed or coerced the complainant to submit or participate in the sexual activity under -circumstances

g.   Section 213.1(1) also includes as rape sexual intercourse (b) when the actor has "substantially impaired" the female's judgment through alcohol or drugs, (c) the female is unconscious, or (d) the female is less than 10 years old. Rape is a second degree felony, unless the actors inflicts "serious bodily injury" on someone or kidnaps the female; then rape is a first degree felony.

Related provisions of the 1962 official draft include the crimes of "gross sexual imposition" (§ 213.1(2)), "deviate sexual intercourse by force or imposition" (§ 213.2), "corruption of minors and seduction" (§ 213.3), and "sexual assault" (§ 213.4).

not amounting to the force or threat required under subsection (2) or (4).

Rape aided or abetted by one or more persons, or rape accompanied by bodily injury, use or threat of a dangerous weapon, kidnapping, death, or serious bodily injury to be inflicted imminently on any person is aggravated sexual assault. *Id*. § 76–5–405.

Quaere: If the *Rusk* facts had arisen in Utah, and the seven judges had accepted the defendant's (and Judge Cole's) view of the facts, would a conviction have been justified by Utah law? Does § 76–5–406(1)'s view of consent create "negligent rape" as a felony in that state? Is this normatively desirable? After you read *Michael M.* (in Section 2[A] of this Chapter), consider whether or how the result would have been different if the prosecution had been brought under the Utah statute.

3. *Rape, Sodomy, and Compromise Verdicts.* The MPC's approach made proof of criminal liability for rape somewhat easier, while it simultaneously decriminalized sodomy unless it was "forcible." As of 1996, slightly more than half the states have followed up on the MPC's consent-based approach. Most states have taken a further step as well, combining rape and forcible sodomy laws into a unified law of "sexual assault." Texas, whose sexual offenses law is reproduced in Appendix 6 to this casebook, follows this approach. Consider the following thesis: sodomy laws, even laws prohibiting "consensual" sodomy, are now overwhelmingly used in prosecutions for male-female rape and adult-child sex.[h] Why would prosecutors tend to add a sodomy charge in those situations? For an example of the numerous compromise verdict cases in which a jury acquits of rape but convicts the defendant of sodomy, see *Post v. Oklahoma*, 715 P.2d 1105 (Okl.Crim.App.), *cert. denied*, 479 U.S. 890 (1986).

Recall that *Rusk* involved both vaginal and oral intercourse, the former a crime in Maryland only if forcible, the latter a crime in Maryland even if consensual. The Maryland Court of Appeals subsequently reinterpreted its sodomy law to be inapplicable to *heterosexual* sodomy in *Schochet v. State*, 580 A.2d 176 (Md.1990).

PROBLEM 11–1

DEFINING SEXUAL ASSAULT

You are a prosecutor in Texas. That state's sexual crimes law (as of 1996) is reproduced in Appendix 6 of this book. Would you seek a criminal conviction for the following conduct:

(a) A exposes his penis to B in a public park; B laughs and walks away.

(b) Same as (a), except B is upset by A's conduct;

h. See Larry Catá Backer, "Raping Sodomy and Sodomizing Rape: A Morality Tale About the Transformation of Modern Sodomy Jurisprudence," 21 *Am. J. Cr. L.* 27 (1993).

(c) A approaches B and compliments her appearance; B invites A to her room; B disrobes and takes off A's clothing; after heavy petting, A prepares to engage in cunnilingus with B; B says, "I don't like that." A engages in cunnilingus nonetheless, and B offers no apparent resistance.

(d) Same as (c), except that A and B are both women.

(e) A and B get drunk; once B is inebriated, A has sex with B, who neither invites nor protests the sexual activity.

(f) Same as (e), except that B is actually unconscious.

Martha Chamallas, Consent, Equality, and the Legal Control of Sexual Conduct

61 *Southern California Law Review* 777, 780–83, 814–19, 820–26, 830–33, 835–39, 840–42 (1988).*

I. THREE VIEWS OF SEXUAL CONDUCT

Contemporary law simultaneously exhibits three overarching views of sexual conduct. They can be roughly characterized as the traditional view, the liberal view, and the egalitarian view of sexual conduct. * * *

The traditional view is the familiar moralistic notion that the only sexual conduct that is acceptable is sex that occurs within marriage. The traditional view is historically linked to an older, fundamentally religious attitude toward sexual conduct which approves of sex only for the purpose of procreation. By tying sex to procreation, the traditional view functions to cement the relationship between biological parents and their children and to promote the family as the key social institution. When the traditional view is expressed in the law, the critical fact tends to be the status of the participants, rather than the purpose or nature of the sexual encounter. Legal regulation in the traditional mode regards nonmarital sexual activity, whether consensual or not, as properly subject to legal sanction. The traditionalist also tends to perceive the law as an important mechanism for expressing moral values and maintaining a morally decent society. Under the traditional mode of regulation, the law functions actively to enforce the moral code, and immoral activity is likely to be unlawful. The emphasis is on community standards, and individuals are expected to conform to communal norms.

In marked contrast to the traditional view, the most salient feature of the liberal view is the distinction it draws between morality and legality. Under this view, sexual conduct is quintessentially private conduct with which the law should not interfere. This conception of private sexual activity tolerates nonmarital sex in some circumstances. In place of marital status, the concept of consent emerges as the central demarcation line to separate lawful from unlawful sexual conduct. The liberal definition of consensual conduct in turn defines the sphere of protected private conduct.

The liberal view finds no warrant for legal intervention with consensual sex unless external harm to third parties can be proven. While not all forms of consensual sexual conduct between adults are affirmatively encouraged, the liberal ideology displays a greater tolerance for diversity among individuals than does the traditional view.

Because the egalitarian view is the newest to emerge, it is the most difficult of the three to characterize. Unlike the traditional view, the egalitarian conception of sexual conduct is not opposed to nonmarital sex. Instead, the fundamental animating concern is fostering equality between the sexes. The paramount goal of the egalitarian view is to afford women the power to form and maintain noncoercive sexual relationships, both within and outside of marriage. Perhaps the most important force behind the development of the egalitarian view has been the feminist critique of the liberal view. In particular, feminists have contended that the liberal notion of rights is inadequate to protect women against the coercive power exercised by men in society. Feminists theorize that the unequal status of women stems not only from biased governmental actions, but from the greater economic and social power exerted by men in the private sphere. Since liberalism's primary concern is with limiting governmental coercion, feminists charge that it is incapable of producing equality for women. Many recent legal reforms are thus based on a reassessment of the notions of consent and privacy that are central to the liberal attitude.

Like the traditional view, the egalitarian conception of sex tends to be moralistic and often calls for active legal intervention to regulate some forms of unacceptable sexual conduct. In this view, however, immoral sex is no longer associated with nonmarital sex or a person's status *per se*. Instead, for a feminist, immoral sex most often is synonymous with exploitive sex. The various legal reforms in the egalitarian mode represent a search for a refurbished notion of consent-a new conception of mutuality in sexual encounters that is capable of separating moral from exploitive sex. My tentative hypothesis is that moral sex is coming to be identified with sexual conduct in which both parties have as their objective only sexual pleasure or emotional intimacy, whether or not tied to procreation. Good sex, in the egalitarian view, is noninstrumental conduct. Sex used for more external purposes, such as financial gain, prestige, or power, is regarded as exploitive and immoral, regardless of whether the parties have engaged voluntarily in the encounter. * * *

II.   TRANSFORMING THE CONCEPT OF CONSENT IN THE EGALITARIAN MODE: THE TRIO OF UNACCEPTABLE INDUCEMENTS

The common thread that runs through the various legal developments just described is dissatisfaction with a narrow, behavior oriented definition of consent that equates consent with nonresistance. The feminist objection is that such a definition of consent is oblivious to the greater social and physical power of men. In the face of this inequality, women may not resist unfair inducements to male sexual initiatives, yet at the same time may not welcome those initiatives.

The feminist critique has prompted a refurbishment, but not an abandonment, of the concept of consent in the law of sex. Under the refurbished version of consent, consent is not considered freely given if secured through physical force, economic pressure, or deception. Consent secured by these inducements is no longer routinely treated as true consent—even if the woman conceivably could have avoided the sexual encounter by resisting.

In the view of some feminists, legal reforms that only refurbish, but do not displace, the concept of consent as a central feature of the law of sex may not be deep enough to effect substantial change. This radical critique of consent asserts that the social meaning of "consent" is inherently tied to a system of unequal sexual relationships in which the man actively initiates the sexual encounter and the woman is relegated to the more passive role of responding to initiatives. In the abstract, consent may be gender neutral. But as long as women do not in fact have the opportunity to initiate sexual relationships on equal terms with men, the concept of consent continues to suggest that women are appropriately the passive parties in sexual relationships.

This argument stresses the importance of rhetoric to our thinking and has considerable force. Thus, to avoid any connotation of inequality in sexual decision making, I will use the term "mutual," rather than "consensual" to denote the touchstone of acceptable sexual encounters under the refurbished concept of consent that I see emerging in the law.

Nonetheless, I am not seriously alarmed by the durability of consent rhetoric in the law. Whatever the law's language, its utility to women is likely to depend heavily on the presence of institutions responsive to women that exert pressure on the law. Rape crisis centers, shelters for battered women, and sensitivity training programs to counteract sexual harassment are some examples of female dominated institutions that were created to assure that changes in formal law of consent actually operate to benefit women. * * *

A.   PHYSICAL FORCE

The use or threat of physical force is universally condemned as an inducement to sex. If the recent drive to abolish the marital rape exemption is successful, the law on the books will criminalize virtually all forms of nonconsensual intercourse effected by physical force. In addition to criminal penalties, physically forced sex may now trigger civil liability as well. An employee who is compelled to have sex with her supervisor because he exerts physical force is likely to have a good claim for sexual harassment against her employer, and certainly has a tort action against the offending supervisor. Moreover, rape victims now have a better chance of recovering damages in third party actions against landlords, educational institutions, prisons, and other defendants who could have taken precautions to avoid the crime.

Despite the growing realization that physical force should not be used to induce submission, the formal legal rules governing rape are still not entirely free from a bias that accepts physical force as legitimate in some contexts. In addition to the continued vitality of the marital rape exemption in some jurisdictions, the intractably sexist nature of the legal concept of consent is most evident in cases involving the victim's revocation of consent. In three recent cases,[175] courts have held that a victim may not revoke consent if she initially consented to intercourse and penetration has already occurred. Two of these cases involve an allegation of rape by an acquaintance of the victim and, in each of the cases, the victim voluntarily accompanied the defendant to a bedroom. The victims testified that they had never given their consent to intercourse and that they were physically brutalized and raped. * * *

The rule restricting revocation of consent after penetration is unabashedly male oriented. The rule equates the harm of rape with penetration alone and ignores the loss of sexual freedom that occurs when a woman is forced to continue a sexual encounter against her will. The revocation rule seems to analogize rape to theft of property in which, once possession has been lawfully taken, it is too late to quarrel with the terms of the transaction. Access to a woman's vagina (euphemistically referred to as her "womanhood") is viewed as a valuable thing, separate and apart from the subjective desires and wishes of the woman herself.

* * * By refusing to give women the authority to stop unwanted intercourse, the revocation rule also reinforces the idea that, beyond a certain point in a sexual encounter, men are powerless to stop. The revocation rule places the blame on the woman who failed to exercise control sooner, and thereby diminishes sexual freedom for women in comparison to men. Albeit in a milder form than earlier evidentiary doctrines, the rule on revocation also communicates the message that sexually active women do not deserve plenary protection against nonconsensual sexual activity.

The most important issues regarding physically forced sex, however, are not issues of formal legal doctrine but instead concern the administration of the law. A de facto resistance requirement will still exist so long as police and prosecutors are reluctant to prosecute cases lacking tangible evidence of physical abuse. More importantly, when force is not actually applied but only threatened, there may be disagreement as to what types of behavior constitute an implicit threat of physical force. Some cases demand a special sensitivity to the particular predicament of the victim. For example, a teenage girl who is instructed by her uncle to engage in sexual acts may submit out of an amorphous fear of violence that stems as much from her uncle's superior status as from his precise words or actions. In such a case, the pressure exerted may be seen as arising either from an implicit threat of physical force or from a kind of deception that tricks the

---

175. *People v. Vela*, 218 Cal. Rptr. 161 (1985); *Battle v. State*, 414 A.2d 1266 ([Md.] 1980); *State v. Way*, 254 S.E.2d 760 ([N.C.] 1979). * * *

teenager into believing that her uncle has a legal or moral right to demand her compliance.

Finally, the laws against physically forced sex will not be effective unless victims also regard such force as unjustified and illegal. Recent studies indicate that both men and women still tolerate some kinds of physically forced sex, and continue to place blame on the victim rather than to assign sole responsibility to the aggressor. * * *

B.   ECONOMIC PRESSURE

The objection to economic pressure as an inducement to sex is neither as clear nor as pervasive in the law as the condemnation of physical force. Economic pressure is unlawful in some contexts but lawful in others. When the pressure is regarded as unlawful, it is labeled coercion; when the pressure is lawful, it is likely to be called a bargain.[191] Moreover, even coercive conduct that may not constitute a crime, may nevertheless subject the offender to a suit for damages or to some other noncriminal sanction, such as dismissal from employment.

Despite this complex pattern, it is probably accurate to declare that a man who tries to "buy" sex from an otherwise unwilling woman will most often violate some formal legal rule. * * * [T]he prohibition against economically coerced sex figures most prominently in sexual harassment suits. The normative theory underlying sexual harassment suits is that neither job benefits nor job detriments should be conditioned on sex. Even the female applicant who reluctantly agrees to have sex with the personnel director in order to get the job probably has a good sexual harassment claim. In the employment context, technical consent by a woman who is put to such an unfair choice is not regarded as effective consent.[193] It does not matter that her submission also produced a corresponding benefit. The law is willing to find sexual harassment from the existence of the improper inducement alone, because the personnel director abused his position to secure sex. Even if the applicant's choice to submit made sense given her own personal predicament, her acquiescence does not override the fact that the employment decision was unlawfully tainted by an impermissible consideration.

The presence of economic pressure outside the employment relationship, however, does not always vitiate consent. In the law of rape, for example, an important unanswered doctrinal question is whether submission effected by economic coercion constitutes legally effective consent.

191. The Model Penal Code characterizes the distinction between "coercion" and "bargain" as going to the "essential character of the threat." Coercion is described as overwhelming the will of the victim, while a bargain is viewed as an offer of "an unattractive choice to avoid some unwanted alternative." The comments recognize that it is "a task of surpassing subtlety" to differentiate the two in borderline cases. Model Penal Code § 213.1 commentary at 314.

193. The EEOC Guidelines prohibit unwelcome sexual advances whenever "submission to . . . such conduct by an individual is used as the basis for employment decisions affecting such individuals." Guidelines on Sexual Harassment, 29 C.F.R. § 1604.11(a)(2) (1982) * * *.

There are no reported cases of criminal prosecutions for sexual assault in which the compulsion used was of an economic nature. Moreover, in most jurisdictions, the paradigm case of sexual harassment in which the supervisor forces the employee to have sex with him to avoid dismissal is probably not criminally punishable as rape or sexual assault of a serious nature. These states characterize the employee's submission as consensual, unless the supervisor also threatens physical force.

There have been some initiatives to change the law of rape to encompass economically coerced sex. As of yet, however, no jurisdiction has passed a provision similar to the Swiss and Soviet criminal codes, that specifically punish persons who use their leverage as employers or supervisors to sexually exploit employees. Instead, the reforms that have been suggested in this country are more global in nature and attempt to outlaw all forms of unreasonable coercion, including psychological as well as economic coercion. For example, under the Model Penal Code, nonconsensual sexual intercourse resulting from coercion of a nonphysical nature may constitute the crime of gross sexual imposition, a third degree felony. In determining what is prohibited coercion for this offense, the test of the Model Penal Code is whether the threat made by the defendant "would prevent resistance by the woman of ordinary resolution." The commentary indicates that economic coercion is sufficient to satisfy the test and notes that if the defendant threatened to deprive the woman of a "valued" possession or caused her to lose her job, he would be guilty of the crime of gross sexual imposition. * * *

Proposals such as these to criminalize economically coerced sex are not likely to be adopted, in part because it is difficult to draft a precise statute that captures the many unacceptable forms of economic and psychological coercion without prohibiting what many perceive as less culpable conduct. The inadequacy of the Model Penal Code illustrates this problem.

The comments to the Model Penal Code, for example, attempt to draw the line between criminal coercion and noncriminal pressure by distinguishing between a bargain and coercion. The comments stress that it is not a crime for a man to induce submission from a woman as a result of a bargain, even if it is a bargain that she is no position to refuse. The commentary to the Model Penal Code gives the example of a wealthy man who threatens to withdraw economic support from his unemployed girlfriend, unless she agrees to continue their sexual relationship. The Code regards such pressure by the man as a legitimate offer of a bargain, rather than as coercion calculated to overcome the will of the girlfriend. If the man were the victim's employment supervisor, however, and threatened to have her fired if she refused to submit, the supervisor would be subject to criminal liability under the Code. What makes the first instance a "bargain" and the second instance "coercion" is not immediately apparent. The distinction might turn on the assumption that the girlfriend freely entered into the association with the man, knowingly exchanging sex for financial support, whereas the employee never bargained for sex as a condition of employment. Such a distinction would make it difficult to criminalize a case of sexual harassment in hiring where the person responsible for hiring made it clear that he would select only those applicants who agreed to engage in sex with him. If there were such knowledge of the sexual demands of the job, the compliant applicant might be said to have entered into a bargain. I suspect, however, that we would regard such a bargain as unduly coercive because most of us believe that sex should never be made a condition of employment. The above judgment, however, only raises the equally troubling question of whether sex should ever be made a condition of material support, even outside the employment context. * * *

[T]here is a reluctance to criminalize many of these privatized encounters. The unwillingness to prosecute the wealthy man who threatens to cut off his girlfriend, for instance, probably stems from two implicit judgments that underlie the notion of bargain: first, that the woman is to blame for getting herself in this predicament; second, that even if the man's tactics are objectionable, his conduct is not so outrageous as to warrant a loss of liberty. The tolerance of economic pressure in this context may reflect a belief that, in their personal lives, women have the freedom to choose whether to encumber their sexual relationships with material dependence. The belief is that although women may have to work, they do not have to be supported by their lovers. By so assuming, the criminal law saves itself a difficult case by case inquiry into consent. The refusal to regard economically coerced sex as rape allows men to continue to use their economic superiority to gain sexual advantage, provided that they use only their own resources (not their employer's) and target only those women who show some willingness to tie sex to financial gain. From the target's standpoint, however, the economic pressure may feel the same regardless of whether it is her employer or her lover who threatens economic harm if sex is denied them. * * *

C.   DECEPTION

It is debatable whether the law is at a point where deception is generally regarded as an impermissible inducement to sex. It might be claimed that the current legal prohibitions against deception in sexual relationships are exceptions to a more general rule that immunizes sexual encounters from charges of fraud. My reticence to pronounce any general tendency in the law stems principally from the scarcity of recent fraud cases. However, because the new tort claims for deception in sexual relationships may arise in typical, rather than only in extraordinary sexual encounters, they take on a special normative significance.

Similar to the approach taken in cases of economic coercion, there seems to be a greater willingness to impose civil sanctions for fraudulent sexual conduct, while saving criminal penalties for only the most egregious cases. The result is that the kind of consent that provides a defense to a criminal charge may not qualify as effective consent in a tort suit regarding the same conduct.

The criminal law recognizes only a very few instances of rape by fraud. The most consistently punished deceptive activity involves the administration of drugs or intoxicants to an unsuspecting victim in order to prevent her physical resistance to intercourse. These drug cases are the only rape by fraud cases that are likely to occur with any frequency. The prohibitions found in criminal codes against husband impersonation or other types of "fraud in the factum" are of little practical importance.

Significantly, the law of rape does not generally prohibit intercourse that results from fraudulent inducement, provided that the deceived party was aware that she was actually engaging in sexual intercourse. False promises of marriage, false representations of sterility, or false professions of love will not vitiate the deceived party's consent, even if the consenting party would never have agreed to the encounter if the truth were told. The law of rape in these cases requires only technical or apparent consent, even though it is the defendant who is solely responsible for the deception. The judgment here may be that the man who lies to get his way is less blameworthy than one who resorts to physical force or some forms of economic coercion. Correlatively, the woman who is deceived may be a less sympathetic victim. * * *

Perhaps the principal impediment to criminalizing rape by fraud is the desire to avoid the difficult task of choosing which lies will be treated as material and which will be dismissed as insignificant. There is a reluctance to judge the materiality of the deception solely from the victim's viewpoint, particularly when the sanction is criminal. A woman who consents to have sex with a man only because he falsely tells her that he is unmarried may well view the deception as material to her consent. So far, however, the criminal law continues to treat the woman's conduct as consensual, despite the material deception. * * *

* * * So far * * * the law has not placed an independent value on the sexual autonomy of plaintiffs and has only provided compensation to victims of deceit who also allege and prove serious physical injury. Even this limited coverage, however, makes the point that deceptive inducements to sex may be legally precarious. The fact that not all lies trigger legal liability does not undercut the legal recognition that some minimum standard of honesty in sexual relationships may be essential to effective consent.

III.   TOWARD AN EGALITARIAN IDEAL OF SEXUAL CONDUCT

Legal regulations concerning sex typically take the form of prohibitions and thus express a social judgment as to what kinds of sexual conduct are inappropriate. As the regulations affect more and more contexts, however, the negative image may evoke a positive image as well. Traditional sex regulations as I describe them fit a legal ideology that favors sex in marriage. Likewise, liberal sex regulations can be seen as expressing a legal ideology that favors consensual sex. We can thus expect to articulate another ideology of appropriate sex as legal regulations are increasingly reshaped under the feminist critique.

The positive ideal of sex that I infer from the legal developments described above is an ideal of sexual conduct based not just on consent, but on mutuality. Because egalitarian inroads into the law of sex are still new and incomplete, I do not mean to assert that the ideal which I shall describe is clearly defined or that it is the inevitable consequence of recent developments. However, it does appear that the concept of mutuality captures the ideas embodied in the feminist critique of both liberalism and traditionalism and provides a rationale for recent reforms. At this stage, the ideal I posit must be understood as a mixture of legal analysis, political advocacy, and philosophy.

An egalitarian ideal of mutuality is perhaps most clearly embodied in the current law of sexual harassment, which has moved beyond older notions of consent or voluntariness to a more victim oriented standard of appropriate sexual conduct. In the sexual harassment context, mutuality is determined whether the more passive target of sexual overtures actually welcomed the initiative. The welcome character of the initiative can in turn be determined by asking a hypothetical question—whether the target would have initiated the encounter if she had been given the choice. If we answer the question in the affirmative, there is some assurance of mutuality in the sexual encounter. The response of the target in such an encounter is more positive than, for example, an ambiguous decision not to resist. By redefining consent to mean welcomeness from the target's viewpoint, we can begin to incorporate the interests of women in the formulation of a legal standard. * * *

The following two examples demonstrate that the concept of mutuality, like its predecessor consent, is defined by limits that may differ depending on the context in which the sexual encounter takes place. Suppose, for example, that an applicant for a job is told that she must acquiesce in the sexual demands of the personnel director in order to get the job. If the job is more important to her than her sexual freedom, she might be pressured into submission. Although she would prefer to be hired without the sexual obligation, this is not quite the same as saying that she would not have initiated the encounter if she had been given a choice. In judging the welcomeness *vel non* of the exchange, the key question is whether we should consider the actual economic context. It may be that, if the target thought that sexual submission was the only way to get the job, she would have initiated the encounter. The real world connection between constrained choice in economic matters and relative lack of sexual freedom makes the notion of welcomeness—like the notion of consent—dependent on the particular set of options available in the concrete context. In the sexual harassment context, however, it appears that the law displays a willingness to presume unwelcomeness whenever sex is made a condition of employment. Only if it can be shown that the applicant in fact explicitly proposed the encounter, is the encounter likely to be viewed as welcome and outside the legal definition of harassment. In all other cases, we tend to regard any economic pressure exerted as unwarranted and thus try to ignore the impact of the economic pressure when we ask whether the victim actually welcomed the conduct.

The test for mutuality is likely to be altered when the pressure occurs outside the employment context, and arises from the threat to break off an intimate relationship. Take, for example, the situation of a teenage girl whose boyfriend threatens to stop seeing her unless they have sexual intercourse. Assume that she would prefer to keep the relationship without the sex. If she nevertheless gives in to the demands of her boyfriend, it is harder to classify the encounter as forced in the legal sense, at least as compared to the economically pressured sexual encounter occurring in the employment context. There is a greater inclination to particularize the incident and ask whether the girl's choice was voluntary, given the ultimatum of the boyfriend. We might, for example, ask whether she would have initiated the encounter knowing, even without his vocalizing it, that the offer was the only way to save the relationship. * * *

The egalitarian view of sex offered here differs in significant respects from both the traditional and liberal views of sexual conduct. Unlike the traditional view, the egalitarian view does not determine the acceptability of sexual encounters solely from the status of the parties. Exploitive sex can exist within a marriage when one spouse uses physical force or economic coercion to pressure the other to submit. To determine whether the encounter is moral from an egalitarian perspective requires an examination of each party's motivation. Moreover, these motivations must always be subject to reassessment to assure the continuing mutuality of the relationship. Compared to the static assessment of status under the traditional view, the assessment of motivation central to the egalitarian view is dynamic and, partly for this reason, tends to present particularly difficult problems of legal implementation.

The principal difference between the egalitarian view and the liberal view of acceptable sexual encounters centers on their differing understandings of the relationship between individual choice as manifested in sexual behavior and the broad goal of sexual freedom *per se*. Under the liberal view, the characterization of an encounter as sexual tends to relegate it to the private sphere and insulate it from legal regulation, absent strong evidence of physical coercion or harm to third parties. The maximization of individual choice in the liberal view necessarily maximizes freedom in society as a whole. Thus, for example, no convincing liberal argument can be made against prostitution because it is possible to view prostitution as expressing the sexual autonomy of the individual prostitute and the data are unpersuasive that prostitution causes harm to third parties.

The egalitarian perspective, in contrast, is more reluctant to equate individual choice with sexual freedom and is consciously directed toward expanding the choices actually available to women. For example, the egalitarian view does not conclude that because prostitutes initiate sexual encounters, prostitution necessarily furthers the sexual freedom of women. Because prostitution may be a choice of last economic resort for many women, the egalitarian is as likely to see it as the degrading artifact of sexual inequality as the expression of women's liberty. Insofar as genuine sexual freedom depends on sexual equality, full legal approval for prostitution may be appropriate only when resource equality between men and women is achieved. * * *

NOTES ON THE LAW'S MOVEMENT TOWARD A MUTUALITY APPROACH

A mutuality approach to the law of sexual assault would make the *Rusk* case easier. How far would a mutuality approach go? Would it support liability if the woman send signals of unwelcomeness that the man "negligently" ignored? Would mutuality theory support "strict liability" of the following sort: any unwelcome sexual contact would be criminal, but only a misdemeanor if nonforcible and negligent? Consider other implications of mutuality theory that have been showing up in the statutory and case law.

1. *Rape Within Marriage.* At common law, rape within marriage was an oxymoron, definitionally not possible: because the husband was effectively an absolute monarch within the family and the wife had few legal rights outside the household, the husband was entitled as a matter of law to have sex on demand, and indeed to force the wife to do virtually anything. The old common law even denied the wife a cause of action to prevent the husband from beating her. Nineteenth century common law and statutory reform recognized many legal rights for the wife (not to be beaten for example) but still enshrined marriage as a zone of sexual privacy within which "consent" was largely irrelevant; the 1962 official draft of the Model Penal Code, for example, perpetuated the exclusion of marital rape from the criminal law. Critics in the twentieth century attacked this "marital rape exemption," and the women's rights movement in the last 20 years has succeeded in superseding the common law exemption by statute in almost all the states. This would appear consistent with Chamallas' mutuality theory.

In many states, however, statutes still disallow rape prosecutions against husband-wife rape in some instances where the prosecution would be valid in the case of a nonmarried couple. This is the so-called "marital rape allowance."[i] Virginia law, for example, does not criminalize unconsented intercourse between husband and wife unless "(i) the spouses were living separate and apart, or (ii) the defendant caused serious physical injury to the spouse by the use of force or violence." Virginia Code § 18.2–61(B) (added in 1986). Chamallas would likely criticize Virginia's law as a holdover from the traditional regime.

---

i. On the marital rape allowance, see Diana E. Russell, *Rape in Marriage* (1990); Robin West, "Equality Theory, Marital Rape, and the Promise of the Fourteenth Amendment," 42 *Fla. L. Rev.* 45 (1990); Anne C. Dailey, "To Have and To Hold: The Marital Rape Exemption and the Fourteenth Amendment," *99 Harv. L. Rev. 1255* (1986) (student note); Jaye Sitton, "Old Wine in New Bottles: The "Marital" Rape Allowance," *72 N.C. L. Rev. 261* (1993) (student comment). On the evolution of the law's treatment of spousal abuse, see Reva B. Siegel, " 'The Rule of Love': Wife Beating as Prerogative and Privacy," 105 *Yale L.J.* 2117 (1996).

2. *Sex Between People in an Authority Relationship.* Wyoming law penalizes as rape in the second degree sexual intercourse when the "actor is in a position of authority over the victim and uses this position of authority to cause the victim to submit." Wyo. Stats. § 6–2–303(a)(vi) (1977). Such an actor is defined to include "parent, guardian, relative, household member, teacher, employer, custodian, or any other person who, by reason of his position, is able to exercise significant influence over a person." Id. § 6–2–301(a)(iv). How would mutuality theory judge this statute?

Under mutuality theory, should such a statute be interpreted to include intercourse between a boss and her or his secretary? A boss and his or her former secretary? A law professor and a student at the same law school but not in the professor's class? A clergy person and a member of the congregation? A psychotherapist and her or his patient? A doctor and his or her patient? A police officer and a citizen in her or his police district?

3. *Denial of Information as Force or Fraud.* When should a misrepresentation of fact invalidate consent? What about failure to provide information? See Chapter 12, Section 1, for a discussion of tort liability for failure to disclose having a sexually transmissible disease. What do you think of the following situation? Was there consent?

Thomas A. Neal and Jill LaGasse v. Mary Neal, 125 Idaho 617, 873 P.2d 871 (1994). "In January of 1990, defendant Thomas A. Neal filed for divorce after his wife became aware that he was having an extramarital affair. Mary Neal, his wife, counterclaimed for divorce and also asserted tort claims against Thomas Neal and Jill Lagasse. The gravamen of the claims against Thomas Neal and Jill Lagasse center upon allegations of an adulterous relationship between them."

Plaintiff sued for battery on the theory that her consent to sexual relations with her husband after his affair began was the product of fraud or misrepresentation, because she had not known of the affair.

"The district court concluded that Thomas Neal's failure to disclose the fact of his sexual relationship with LaGasse did not vitiate Mary Neal's consent to engage in sexual relations with him, such consent being measured at the time of the relations. We do not agree with the district court's reasoning. To accept that the consent, or lack thereof, must be measured by only those facts which are known to the parties at the time of the alleged battery would effectively destroy any exception for consent induced by fraud or deceit. Obviously if the fraud or deceit were known at the time of the occurrence, the 'consented to' act would never occur.

"Mary Neal's affidavit states that: '[I]f the undersigned had realized that her husband was having sexual intercourse with counterdefendant LaGasse, the undersigned would not have consented to sexual intercourse with counterdefendant Neal and to do so would have been offensive.' The district court opined that because the act was not actually offensive at the time it occurred, her later statements that it would have been offensive were ineffective. This reasoning ignores the possibility that Mary Neal may have engaged in a sexual act based upon a substantial mistake concerning the nature of the contact or the harm to be expected from it, and that she did not become aware of the offensiveness until well after the act had occurred. Mary Neal's affidavit at least raises a genuine issue of material fact as to whether there was indeed consent to the alleged act of battery.

"The district court also noted that Mary Neal's later sexual relations with her husband after becoming aware of his infidelity, extinguished any offensiveness or lack of consent. The fact that she may have consented to sexual relations on a later occasion cannot be said to negate, as a matter of law, an ineffective consent to prior sexual encounters. Again, her affidavit raises a question of fact regarding whether these prior sexual encounters were nonconsensual. This factual issue precluded the dismissal of the battery claim by the district court."

PROBLEM 11–2

SHOULD RAPE BE A HATE CRIME?

Is rape the quintessential hate crime against women? Consider the following provisions of the Violence Against Women Act (VAWA), 42 U.S.C. § 13981 (1994):

(c) Cause of action

A person (including a person who acts under color of any statute, ordinance, regulation, custom, or usage of any State) who commits a crime of violence motivated by gender and thus deprives another of the right [to be free from crimes of violence motivated by gender] shall be liable to the party injured, in an action for the recovery of compensatory and punitive damages, injunctive and declaratory relief, and such other relief as a court may deem appropriate.

(d) Definitions

For purposes of this section—

(1) the term "crime of violence motivated by gender" means a crime of violence committed because of gender or on the basis of gender, and due, at least in part, to an animus based on the victim's gender; and

(2) the term "crime of violence" means—

(A) an act or series of acts that would constitute a felony against the person or that would constitute a felony against property if the conduct presents a serious risk of physical injury to another, and that would come within the meaning of State or Federal offenses described in section 16 of title 18, [U.S.C], whether or not those acts have actually resulted in criminal charges, prosecution, or conviction and whether or not those acts were committed in the special maritime, territorial, or prison jurisdiction of the United States; and

(B) includes an act or series of acts that would constitute a felony described in subparagraph (A) but for the relationship between the person who takes such action and the individual against whom such action is taken.

How would one prove that a crime was "motivated by gender"? Should the law allow a rebuttable presumption that rape is *per se* gender motivated? What about male rape of other males? Return to the 15 examples at the beginning of this chapter and analyze whether each would support a cause of action under this statute.

A more fundamental issue has arisen in the early cases arising under this law. Defendants have challenged its constitutionality, asserting that creating a federal law right of action against private individuals for rape is beyond the power of Congress to legislate and must be left to the states. Defendants cite *United States v. Lopez*, 115 S.Ct. 1624 (1995), which struck down a federal criminal law prohibiting possession of a firearm within 1,000 feet of a school as beyond congressional authority to regulate under the commerce clause. The plaintiffs respond that violence against women affects women's movements and job possibilities, and therefore commerce. Plaintiffs also argue that Congress had an independent basis for enacting the law pursuant to its authority under section 5 of the Fourteenth Amendment.

The courts ruling on VAWA have split. VAWA was upheld in *Doe v. Doe*, 929 F.Supp. 608 (D.Conn.1996) and ruled unconstitutional in *Brzonkala v. Virginia Polytechnic and State University*, 935 F.Supp. 779 (W.D.Va. 1996). Both cases are on appeal. Note how the two jurisdictional bases are tied together by the relationship between the public/private (formerly the male/female) divide and conceptions of civil rights. Where should the conceptual boundary between public (affecting markets and therefore commerce) and private (purely individualized conduct) be drawn? Can the statute be independently supported by the Fourteenth Amendment? The relationship between the "jurisdictional" attacks on the VAWA and old legal immunities for male violence against women is explored in Reva B. Siegel, " 'The Rule of Love': Wife Beating as Prerogative and Privacy," 105 *Yale L.J.* 2117, 2196–2206 (1996).

PART B.   RACE AND DOUBLE-EDGED CONSTRUCTIONS OF "FORCE"

The construction of "consent" and "force" has operated differently for interracial sex.[j] Before the Civil War, the concept of rape had no legal

j. The account that follows draws from Derrick A. Bell, Jr., *Race, Racism, and American Law* (3d ed. 1992); John D'Emilio & Estelle Freedman, *Intimate Matters* 105–07 (1988); Jaquelyn Dowd Hall, " 'The Mind That Burns Within Each Body,' " in *Powers of Desire: The Politics of Sexuality* 328 (Ann Snitow et al. eds., 1983); A. Leon Higginbotham & Barbara K. Kopytoff, "Racial Purity and Interracial Sex in the Law of Colonial and Antebellum Virginia," 77 *Geo. L.J.* 1967 (1989); Herbert Hovenkamp, "Social Science and Segregation Before *Brown*," 1985 *Duke L.J.* 624; Hazel V. Carby, " 'On the Threshold of Woman's Era': Lynching, Empire and Sexuality in Black Feminist The-significance for slaves in most of the states sanctioning slavery. Because slaves were a form of property, the white master's insistence on sex with African women he "owned" was legally unproblematic, and some slaveowners coerced sex from slave women with complete impunity. Male slaves were punished severely for any kind of sex with white women, whether the sex was consensual under current usage or not, and there appear to have been few legal rules regulating sex between male and female slaves. Thus, there were no legal sanctions (beyond plantation rules and appeals to the master for protection) for slave women assaulted by slave men. Underlying the foregoing regulatory regime was a white sexualization of Africans as primitive, with exaggerated passions. Whites considered African–American women to be lustful and ceaselessly available, and black men to be dangerous predators.

Although the Civil War freed the slaves, established formal citizenship for the freed men and women, and assured them equal rights (including the right to validate their marriages), formal equality did little to alter patterns of interracial sex. In the short term, Reconstruction served to exacerbate old problems. Sharing southern views about African–American women, northern soldiers forced black women and girls to have sex with them and took black concubines. Southern men, in turn, vented their rage against freed slaves by sexually assaulting black women and lynching black men for alleged crimes against white female chastity. "During the Memphis race riot in 1866, whites attacked and killed black people, burned their homes, robbed and gang raped former slaves, raped several other black women at gunpoint, and attempted to rape a black child. In 1871, Harriet Smirl, wife of a black radical Republican in Columbia, South Carolina, told a congressional committee of her ordeal. Ku Klux Klan members had beaten her husband and later returned when she was alone in the house. They spit in her face, threw dirt in her eyes, told her to make her husband vote Democratic, and then gang raped her. When black men responded to these outrages and attempted to protect black women from the sexual assaults of white men, they became subject to physical attack themselves. In at least one case, a white sheriff authorized the public, sadistic beating of a black man who had tried to protect his wife's virtue." (D'Emilio & Freedman, *Intimate Matters* 105.) In short, sexuality became what D'Emilio and Freedman term a "weapon of terror" by which anxious white men responded to and sought to intimidate newly empowered blacks. As Hazel Carby describes it, whites "manipulate[d] sexual ideologies to justify political and economic subordination. * * * [W]hite men used their ownership of the body of the white female as a terrain on which to lynch the black male." (Carby, "Lynching, Empire and Sexuality," 270.)

Historians believe that the fear of racial mixture, outside of a system of white dominance, underlay the opposition to integration that so pervaded the South in the late nineteenth century (sources collected in Hovenkamp,

ory," 12 *Critical Inquiry* 262 (1985); Jennifer Wriggins, "Rape, Racism and the Law," 6 *Harv. Women's L.J.* 103 (1983).

"Social Science and Segregation"). Thus, the Jim Crow laws mandating segregation in the late nineteenth-century South rested upon a deep-seated fear that social mixing would lead to sexual mixing. As one southerner explained, "if we have intermarriage we shall degenerate; we shall become a race of mulattoes; we shall be another Mexico; we shall be ruled out from the family of white nations. Sir, it is a matter of life and death with the Southern people to keep their blood pure." (D'Emilio & Freedman, *Intimate Matters*, 106.) Hysteria about interracial mixing was the occasion for southern states to pass new laws to prevent interracial marriage during the 1860s; the term *miscegenation* first appeared in these laws. African–American political leaders resisted these efforts during Reconstruction, when they controlled or had substantial voice in state government, but their efforts were swept away after 1877, when the federal soldiers left the South.

During the Jim Crow era of the late nineteenth and early twentieth centuries, black men who married white women were persecuted, often through lynchings that were allowed or even encouraged by local law enforcement officials. At the same time, white men had sex, including forcible sex, with black women and were immune from legal sanction. "[I]n a patriarchal society, black men, as men, constituted a potential challenge to the established order. Laws were formulated primarily to exclude black men from adult male prerogatives in the public sphere, and lynching meshed with these legal mechanisms of exclusion. Black women represented a more ambiguous threat. They too were denied access to the politico-jural domain, but since they shared this exclusion with women in general, its maintenance engendered less anxiety and required less force. * * * Black women were sometimes executed by lynch mobs, but more routinely they served as targets of sexual assault.

"Most studies of racial violence have paid little attention to the particular suffering of women. Even rape has been seen less as an aspect of sexual oppression than as a transaction between white and black men. Certainly Claude Levi–Strauss's insight that men use women as verbs with which to communicate with one another (rape being a means of communicating defeat to the men of a conquered tribe) helps explain the extreme viciousness of sexual violence in the postemancipation era. Rape was in part a reaction to the effort of the freed man to assume the role of patriarch, able to provide for and protect his family. Nevertheless, as writers like Susan Griffin and Susan Brownmiller and others have made clear, rape is first and foremost a crime against women. Rape sent a message to black men, but more centrally, it expressed male sexual attitudes in a culture both racist and patriarchal." (Hall, " 'Mind That Burns,' " 331–32.)

African–American women served as a metaphorical counterpoint to the Victorians' idealization of the passionless woman, for the female descendants of slaves would never escape the taint, or allure, of white notions of animal carnality. Hence, white middle class efforts to protect women's chastity did not readily extend to the chastity of black women, and the protection of female purity took on particularly feverish dimensions when the feared rapist was a black man. The overwhelming majority of rapes were *intra*racial and the overwhelming majority of *inter*racial rapes were by white men against black women. Ida B. Wells in the 1880s, and Walter White of the NAACP and Jessie Daniel Ames of the Association of Southern Women for the Prevention of Lynching in the early twentieth century documented this reality, but their arguments fell on mostly deaf ears.

Jacqueline Dowd Hall describes the dramaturgy of a lynching in a way that shows the sex—as well as race—subordination instinct in the practice: "For whites, the archetypal lynching for rape can be seen as a dramatization of cultural themes, a story they told themselves about the social arrangements and psychological strivings that lay beneath the surface of everyday life. The story such rituals told about the place of white women in southern society was subtle, contradictory, and demeaning. The frail victim, leaning on the arms of her male relatives, might be brought to the scene of the crime, there to identify her assailant and witness his execution. This was a moment of humiliation. A woman who had just been raped, or who had been apprehended in a clandestine interracial affair, or whose male relatives were pretending that she had been raped, stood on display before the whole community. Here was the quintessential Woman as Victim: polluted, 'ruined for life,' the object of fantasy and secret contempt. Humiliation, however, mingled with heightened worth as she played for a moment the role of the Fair Maiden violated and avenged. For this privilege—if the alleged assault had in fact taken place—she might pay with suffering in the extreme. In any case, she would pay with a lifetime of subjugation to the men gathered in her behalf." (Hall, " 'Mind That Burns,' " 335.)

McQuirter v. State

Court of Appeals of Alabama, 1953.
36 Ala.App. 707, 63 So.2d 388.

■ PRICE, JUDGE.

Appellant, a Negro man, was found guilty of an attempt to commit an assault with intent to rape, under an indictment charging an assault with intent to rape. The jury assessed a fine of $500.

About 8:00 o'clock on the night of June 29, 1951, Mrs. Ted Allen, a white woman, with her two children and a neighbor's little girl, were drinking Coca–Cola at the "Tiny Diner" in Atmore. When they started in the direction of Mrs. Allen's home she noticed appellant sitting in the cab of a parked truck. As she passed the truck appellant said something unintelligible, opened the truck door and placed his foot on the running board.

Mrs. Allen testified appellant followed her down the street and when she reached Suell Lufkin's house she stopped. As she turned into the Lufkin house appellant was within two or three feet of her. She waited ten minutes for appellant to pass. When she proceeded on her way, appellant came toward her from behind a telephone pole. She told the children to run to Mr. Simmons' house and tell him to come and meet her. When appellant saw Mr. Simmons he turned and went back down the street to the intersection and leaned on a stop sign just across the street from Mrs. Allen's home. Mrs. Allen watched him at the sign from Mr. Simmons' porch for about thirty minutes, after which time he came back down the street and appellant went on home.

Mrs. Allen's testimony was corroborated by that of her young daughter. The daughter testified the appellant was within six feet of her mother as she approached the Lufkin house, and this witness said there was a while when she didn't see appellant at the intersection.

Mr. Lewis Simmons testified when the little girls ran up on his porch and said a Negro was after them, witness walked up the sidewalk to meet Mrs. Allen and saw appellant. Appellant went on down the street and stopped in front of Mrs. Allen's home and waited there approximately thirty minutes.

Mr. Clarence Bryars, a policeman in Atmore, testified that appellant stated after his arrest that he came to Atmore with the intention of getting him a white woman that night.

Mr. W. E. Strickland, Chief of Police of Atmore, testified that appellant stated in the Atmore jail he didn't know what was the matter with him; that he was drinking a little; that he and his partner had been to Pensacola; that his partner went to the "Front" to see a colored woman; that he didn't have any money and he sat in the truck and made up his mind he was going to get the first woman that came by and that this was the first woman that came by. He said he got out of the truck, came around the gas tank and watched the lady and when she started off he started off behind her; that he was going to carry her in the cotton patch and if she hollered he was going to kill her. He testified appellant made the same statement in the Brewton jail.

Mr. Norvelle Seals, Chief Deputy Sheriff, corroborated Mr. Strickland's testimony as to the statement by appellant at the Brewton jail.

Appellant, as a witness in his own behalf, testified he and Bill Page, another Negro, carried a load of junk-iron from Monroeville to Pensacola; on their way back to Monroeville they stopped in Atmore. They parked the truck near the "Tiny Diner" and rode to the "Front," the colored section, in a cab. Appellant came back to the truck around 8:00 o'clock and sat in the truck cab for about thirty minutes. He decided to go back to the "Front" to look for Bill Page. As he started up the street he saw the prosecutrix and her children. He turned around and waited until he decided they had gone, then he walked up the street toward the "Front." When he reached the intersection at the telegraph pole he decided he didn't want to go to the "Front" and sat around there a few minutes, then went on to the "Front" and stayed about 25 or 30 minutes, and came back to the truck.

He denied that he followed Mrs. Allen or made any gesture toward molesting her or the children. He denied making the statements testified to by the officers.

He testified he had never been arrested before and introduced testimony by two residents of Monroeville as to his good reputation for peace and quiet and for truth and veracity.

[On appeal, defendant challenged the sufficiency of the evidence.]

"'An attempt to commit an assault with intent to rape,' * * * means an attempt to rape which has not proceeded far enough to amount to an assault." *Burton v. State*, 62 So. 394, 396.

Under the authorities in this state, to justify a conviction for an attempt to commit an assault with intent to rape the jury must be satisfied beyond a reasonable doubt that defendant intended to have sexual intercourse with prosecutrix against her will, by force or by putting her in fear.

Intent is a question to be determined by the jury from the facts and circumstances adduced on the trial, and if there is evidence from which it may be inferred that at the time of the attempt defendant intended to gratify his lustful desires against the resistance of the female a jury question is presented.

In determining the question of intention the jury may consider social conditions and customs founded upon racial differences, such as that the prosecutrix was a white woman and defendant was a Negro man. *Pumphrey v. State*, 47 So. 156 [Ala.]; *Kelly v. State*, 56 So. 15 [Ala. App.].

After considering the evidence in this case we are of the opinion it was sufficient to warrant the submission of the question of defendant's guilt to the jury, and was ample to sustain the judgment of conviction. * * *

NOTES ON THE RACIALIZATION OF RAPE

1. *Burdens of Proof.* Note the law's asymmetry from the end of Reconstruction through the period after World War II. When a white man was accused of raping a white woman in the first half of this century, the law took her failure to risk life and limb to be "consent." When a white man was accused of raping a black woman, the law never intervened, and the woman "knew" better than to complain to the authorities, lest she be arrested for "corrupting" the white man with her "allure." The law rarely intervened when a black man raped a black woman, because people of color were essentially outside Jim Crow's protection. But when a black man was accused of raping a white woman, the presumptions were inverted. There was a strong presumption that a white woman would never consent to sex with an African–American man. See D. Carter, *Scottsboro: A Tragedy of the American South* (1979). *McQuirter* is an illustration of this presumption in action.

2. *Punishment to Fit the Crime.* A major concern of women's rights advocates has been the difficulty of obtaining convictions in cases of rape and, on occasion, of convincing courts in at least some cases that such convictions merited heavy sentences. From that perspective, it may seem somewhat paradoxical that until the 1970s, rape was a capital offense under the federal criminal code and in at least some states. Many feminists believed, however, that the threat of capital punishment worked to the benefit of the rape defendant, in that juries were repelled at the prospect of imposing death as a sanction, especially when the crime was not flagrantly brutal. So when a case challenging the constitutionality of imposing the death penalty for rape came before the Supreme Court, a number of feminist organizations filed an *amicus curiae* brief arguing that the death penalty created a barrier to proper law enforcement and constituted "a vestige of an ancient, patriarchal view of women as the property of men." The Court did in fact rule that the state could not impose death as a penalty for a crime that does not take human life. *Coker v. Georgia*, 433 U.S. 584 (1977).

The other side of the paradox, however, was the frequency with which death sentences were imposed for African–American men who were convicted of raping white women. Courtrooms, especially in the South, became the sites of "legal lynchings." Consider the complex construction of race and sexuality in *Wright v. State*, 190 S.E. 663 (Ga.1937), where a black man was accused of raping a white girl:

"The victim of defendant's alleged crime was between twelve and thirteen years of age at the time. The defendant was an employee of the park department of the City of Atlanta, at the Grant Park Zoo, and his duties consisted in feeding the wild animals. He had a key to the meat-house. * * *

"The injured female, together with other young children, was in the habit of playing in the park and around the zoo. There they made the acquaintance of the defendant, who was about fifty years of age. He got the female involved in this case to enter the meat-house with him, and there he would pat her legs and play with her private parts. On one occasion the girl lay down on a bench in the meat-house, and the defendant pulled up her dress, and, after feeling of her legs, tried to insert his penis in her privates, but failed. He got up, went to the sink near by, and discharged semen. On another occasion he evidently tried to have sexual intercourse with the girl, with both standing erect, and was unable to penetrate her privates, but nevertheless ejaculated on some iron pipes in the meat-house. The injured female testified to other occasions, and to an occasion on a certain day when the defendant succeeded in penetrating her privates with his penis. No effort was made by her to resist the defendant. A physician, who examined the female after the alleged rape, stated that her vagina would admit two of his fingers, and there were no tears; that that was an indication that she had had sexual intercourse, with that much opening; that it would take the male organs of a man to make such an opening; and that it was his opinion that the development of her private parts would admit the male organs of a man. The girl testified that a boy of nine years, two or three years before, had 'played with her.'

"* * * The discovery of the alleged crime was brought about by the fact that on one afternoon the girl accosted the defendant and urged that he buy from her some crochet work which her mother had given to her to sell. The defendant was in his automobile. She got in the automobile with him, sitting beside him, and he drove the automobile southeast of Atlanta towards Constitution. An automobile containing two county policemen approached and passed the defendant's automobile; and seeing what looked like to them someone duck down in defendant's car, they turned around and overtook the defendant's car, which had stopped, and the girl had got out of it. She appeared to be scared and trembling when they came up. After some questioning, she told the policemen that the defendant had patted her legs but did not do anything else.

"The police took the defendant and the girl to Lakewood Heights, telephoned for their lieutenant, and while awaiting his arrival one of the police stated to the girl that she had not told them the truth, and she replied 'about what?' This conversation was in the defendant's hearing. The policeman again said, 'You didn't tell me the truth.' The girl said 'Why?' The policeman then said, 'You didn't tell me the truth about this negro, did you?' The girl said 'What did he say?' The policeman replied, 'Never mind about what he said. I want to know what you have got to say about it.' Thereupon the girl stated: 'He said he had something to do with me, didn't he?' 'Well, he did. Last Friday.'

"* * * Several witnesses testified as to the previous good character of the defendant. Witnesses for the State testified as to his bad character, freshness with white girls, living with a negro woman not his wife, and the like. The defendant made a statement in which he protested his innocence, and denied going into the meat-house with the girl. Other witnesses corroborated the girl's testimony in this regard, and as to other circumstances. The jury returned a verdict finding the defendant guilty, and he was sentenced to death." The appeals court affirmed.

For a discussion of the complexities of an adult-child sexual interaction, see Section 2, *infra.*

3. *Invisible Woman: The Hill–Thomas Hearings.* The actor who historically has been least protected by the legal regime of consent has been the African–American woman. In a drama that galvanized the nation in 1991, Professor Anita Hill accused then-Judge (now Justice) Clarence Thomas of unwelcome sexual advances. What is your view of the following analysis of the cultural resonances of that event?

Kimberlé Crenshaw Williams, "Whose Life Is It Anyway? Feminist and Antiracist Appropriations of Anita Hill," in *Race-ing Justice, En–gendering Power* 402, 405–6, 414–5 (Toni Morrison editor, 1994). "The Thomas/Hill controversy presents a stark illustration of the problem as evidenced by the opposition between narratives of rape and of lynching. These tropes have come to symbolize the mutually exclusive claims that have been generated within both antiracist and feminist discourses about the centrality of sexuality to both race and gender domination. In feminist contexts, sexuality represents a central site of the oppression of women; rape and the rape trial are its dominant narrative trope. In antiracist discourses, sexuality is also a central site upon which the repression of blacks has been premised; the lynching narrative is embodied as its trope. (Neither narrative tends to acknowledge the legitimacy of the other; the reality of rape tends to be disregarded within the lynching narrative; the impact of racism is frequently marginalized within rape narratives.) Both these tropes figured prominently in this controversy, and it was in this sense that the debacle constituted a classic showdown between antiracism and feminism. * * * Anita Hill was of course cast in both narratives, but because one told a tale of sexism and the other told an opposing tale of racism, the simultaneity of Hill's race and gender was essentially denied. * * *

"White feminists have been reluctant to incorporate race into their narratives about gender, sex, and power. Their unwillingness to speak to the race-specific dimensions of black women's sexual disempowerment was compounded by their simultaneous failure to understand the ways that race may have contributed to Anita Hill's silence. Their attempt to explain why she remained silent spoke primarily to her career interests. Yet the other reasons why many black women have been reluctant to reveal experiences of sexual abuse—particularly by African–American men—remained unexamined. In fact, many black women fear that their stories might be used to reinforce stereotypes of black men as sexually threatening. * * * Content to rest their case on a raceless tale of gender subordination, white feminists missed an opportunity to span the chasm between feminism and antiracism. Indeed, feminists actually helped maintain the chasm by endorsing the framing of the event as a race versus a gender issue. * * * Identification by race or gender seemed to be an either/or proposition, and when it is experienced in that manner, black people, both men and women, have traditionally chosen race solidarity. Indeed, white feminist acquiescence to the either/or frame worked directly to Thomas's advantage: with Hill thus cast as simply a de-raced—that is, white—woman, Thomas was positioned to claim that he was the victim of racial discrimination with Hill as the perpetrator."

PART C.   SADOMASOCHISM: "CONSENSUAL VIOLENCE"?

All of the cases noted or excerpted in the earlier portion of this section are ones where the sexual contact was unwelcome from the perspective of the complainant. Correlatively, in all the cases, the conduct would have apparently been legal if the complainant had welcomed it. Consider the further case of sadomasochistic ("SM") sex, which is mutually desired coercive behavior, often with elaborate protocols for consent and for signaling the withdrawal of consent. Should this be illegal? The leading case is the following one from the British House of Lords.

Regina v. Anthony Brown et al.

United Kingdom, The House of Lords, 1993.
[1994] 1 AC 212, [1993] 2 All ER 75, [1993] 2 WLR 556.

[The appellants, a group of sado-masochists, willingly and enthusiastically participated in the commission of violent acts for the sexual pleasure engendered in the giving and receiving of pain. They pleaded not guilty on arraignment to counts charging various offenses under sections 20 and 47 of the Offenses against the Person Act 1861, relating to the infliction of wounds or actual bodily harm on genital and other areas of the body of the consenting victim. On a ruling by the trial judge that, in the particular circumstances, the prosecution did not have to prove lack of consent by the victim, the appellants were rearraigned, pleaded guilty, some to offenses under section 20 and all to offenses under section 47; and they were convicted. They appealed against conviction on the ground that the judge had erred in his rulings, in that the willing and enthusiastic consent of the victim to the acts on him prevented the prosecution from proving an essential element of the offence, whether charged under section 20 or section 47 of the Act of 1861. The Court of Appeal (Criminal Division) dismissed the appeal. A divided (3–2) panel of the House of Lords dismissed the appeal.]

■ LORD TEMPLEMAN. * * *

In some circumstances violence is not punishable under the criminal law. When no actual bodily harm is caused, the consent of the person affected precludes him from complaining. There can be no conviction for the summary offence of common assault if the victim has consented to the assault. Even when violence is intentionally inflicted and results in actual bodily harm, wounding or serious bodily harm the accused is entitled to be acquitted if the injury was a foreseeable incident of a lawful activity in which the person injured was participating. Surgery involves intentional violence resulting in actual or sometimes serious bodily harm but surgery is a lawful activity. Other activities carried on with consent by or on behalf of the injured person have been accepted as lawful notwithstanding that they involve actual bodily harm or may cause serious bodily harm. Ritual circumcision, tattooing, ear-piercing and violent sports including boxing are lawful activities.

In earlier days some other forms of violence were lawful and when they ceased to be lawful they were tolerated until well into the 19th century. Duelling and fighting were at first lawful and then tolerated provided the protagonists were voluntary participants. But where the results of these activities was the maiming of one of the participants, the defence of consent never availed the aggressor. A maim was bodily harm whereby a man was deprived of the use of any member of his body which he needed to use in order to fight but a bodily injury was not a maim merely because it was a disfigurement. The act of maim was unlawful because the King was deprived of the services of an able-bodied citizen for the defence of the realm. Violence which maimed was unlawful despite consent to the activity which produced the maiming. In these days there is no difference between maiming on the one hand and wounding or causing grievous bodily harm on the other hand except with regard to sentence. * * *

[In *Regina v. Coney*, 8 QBD 534 (1882), the court held that a prize-fight in public was unlawful notwithstanding the consent of the protagonists. *Rex v. Donovan*, [1934] 2 KB 498, held that a private beating of a girl of 17 for purposes of sexual gratification, allegedly with her consent, was unlawful. Bare-fisted fighting was held unlawful in *Attorney-General's Reference (No 6 of 1980)*, [1981] QB 715, where there was a risk of serious bodily harm.]

My Lords, the authorities dealing with the intentional infliction of bodily harm do not establish that consent is a defence to a charge under the Act of 1861. They establish that the courts have accepted that consent is a defence to the infliction of bodily harm in the course of some lawful activities. The question is whether the defence should be extended to the infliction of bodily harm in the course of sado-masochistic encounters. [His Lordship conceded that the issue is essentially one of public policy, because the legal authorities do not squarely address it.]

Counsel for some of the appellants argued that the defence of consent should be extended to the offence of occasioning actual bodily harm under section 47 of the Act of 1861 but should not be available to charges of serious wounding and the infliction of serious bodily harm under section 20. I do not consider that this solution is practicable. Sado-masochistic participants have no way of foretelling the degree of bodily harm which will result from their encounters. The differences between actual bodily harm and serious bodily harm cannot be satisfactorily applied by a jury in order to determine acquittal or conviction.

Counsel for the appellants argued that consent should provide a defence to charges under both section 20 and section 47 because, it was said, every person has a right to deal with his body as he pleases. I do not consider that this slogan provides a sufficient guide to the policy decision which must now be made. It is an offence for a person to abuse his own body and mind by taking drugs. Although the law is often broken, the criminal law restrains a practice which is regarded as dangerous and injurious to individuals and which if allowed and extended is harmful to society generally. In any event the appellants in this case did not mutilate their own bodies. They inflicted bodily harm on willing victims. Suicide is no longer an offence but a person who assists another to commit suicide is guilty of murder or manslaughter.

The assertion was made on behalf of the appellants that the sexual appetites of sadists and masochists can only be satisfied by the infliction of bodily harm and that the law should not punish the consensual achievement of sexual satisfaction. There was no evidence to support the assertion that sado-masochist activities are essential to the happiness of the appellants or any other participants but the argument would be acceptable if sado-masochism were only concerned with sex, as the appellants contend. In my opinion sado-masochism is not only concerned with sex. Sado-masochism is also concerned with violence. The evidence discloses that the practices of the appellants were unpredictably dangerous and degrading to body and mind and were developed with increasing barbarity and taught to persons whose consents were dubious or worthless.

A sadist draws pleasure from inflicting or watching cruelty. A masochist derives pleasure from his own pain or humiliation. The appellants are middle-aged men. The victims were youths some of whom were introduced to sado-masochism before they attained the age of 21. * * *

The evidence disclosed that drink and drugs were employed to obtain consent and increase enthusiasm. The victim was usually manacled so that the sadist could enjoy the thrill of power and the victim could enjoy the thrill of helplessness. The victim had no control over the harm which the sadist, also stimulated by drink and drugs, might inflict. In one case a victim was branded twice on the thigh and there was some doubt as to whether he consented to or protested against the second branding. The dangers involved in administering violence must have been appreciated by the appellants because, so it was said by their counsel, each victim was given a code word which he could pronounce when excessive harm or pain was caused. The efficiency of this precaution, when taken, depends on the circumstances and on the personalities involved. No one can feel the pain of another. The charges against the appellants were based on genital torture and violence to the buttocks, anus, penis, testicles and nipples. The victims were degraded and humiliated, sometimes beaten, sometimes wounded with instruments and sometimes branded. Bloodletting and the smearing of human blood produced excitement. There were obvious dangers of serious personal injury and blood infection. Prosecuting counsel informed the trial judge against the protests of defence counsel, that although the appellants had not contracted AIDS, two members of the group had died from AIDS and one other had contracted an HIV infection although not necessarily from the practices of the group. Some activities involved excrement. The assertion that the instruments employed by the sadists were clean and sterilized could not have removed the danger of infection, and the assertion that care was taken demonstrates the possibility of infection. Cruelty to human beings was on occasions supplemented by cruelty to animals in the form of bestiality. It is fortunate that there were no permanent injuries to a victim though no one knows the extent of harm inflicted in other cases. It is not surprising that a victim does not complain to the police when the complaint would involve him in giving details of acts in which he participated. Doctors of course are subject to a code of confidentiality.

In principle there is a difference between violence which is incidental and violence which is inflicted for the indulgence of cruelty. The violence of sado-masochistic encounters involves the indulgence of cruelty by sadists and the degradation of victims. Such violence is injurious to the participants and unpredictably dangerous. I am not prepared to invent a defence of consent for sado-masochistic encounters which breed and glorify cruelty and result in offenses under sections 47 and 20 of the Act of 1861. * * *

■ [LORD JAUNCEY OF TULLICHETTLE and LORD LOWRY concurred with this judgment in separate opinions.]

■ LORD MUSTILL: My Lords, this is a case about the criminal law of violence. In my opinion it should be a case about the criminal law of private sexual relations, if about anything at all. * * * [W]hatever the outsider might feel about the subject matter of the prosecutions—perhaps horror, amazement or incomprehension, perhaps sadness—very few could read even a summary of the other activities without disgust. The House has been spared the video tapes, which must have been horrible. If the criminality of sexual deviation is the true ground of these proceedings, one would have expected that these above all would have been the subject of attack. Yet the picture is quite different. * * *

* * * [T]he involvement of the Act of 1861 was adventitious. This impression is reinforced when one considers the title of the statute under which the appellants are charged, "Offenses against the Person." Conduct infringing [sections] 18, 20 and 47 of the 1861 Act comes before the Crown Courts every day. Typically it involves brutality, aggression and violence, of a kind far removed from the appellants' behavior which, however worthy of censure, involved no animosity, no aggression, no personal rancour on the part of the person inflicting the hurt towards the recipient and no protest by the recipient. In fact, quite the reverse. Of course we must give effect to the statute if its words capture what the appellants have done, but in deciding whether this is really so it is in my opinion legitimate to assume that the choice of the 1861 Act as the basis for the relevant counts in the indictment was made only because no other statute was found which could conceivably be brought to bear upon them. * * *

Throughout the argument of the appeal I was attracted by an analysis on the following lines. First, one would construct a continuous spectrum of the infliction of bodily harm, with killing at one end and a trifling touch at the other. Next, with the help of reported cases one would identify the point on this spectrum at which consent ordinarily ceases to be an answer to a prosecution for inflicting harm. This could be called "the critical level." It would soon become plain however that this analysis is too simple and that there are certain types of special situation to which the general rule does not apply. Thus, for example, surgical treatment which requires a degree of bodily invasion well on the upper side of the critical level will nevertheless be legitimate if performed in accordance with good medical practice and with the consent of the patient. Conversely, there will be cases in which even a moderate degree of harm cannot be legitimated by consent. Accordingly, the next stage in the analysis will be to identify those situations which have been identified as special by the decided cases, and to examine them to see whether the instant case either falls within one of them or is sufficiently close for an analogy to be valid. If the answer is negative, then the court will have to decide whether simply to apply the general law simply by deciding whether the bodily harm in the case under review is above or below the critical level, or to break new ground by recognising a new special situation to which the general law does not apply.

For all the intellectual neatness of this method I must recognise that it will not do, for it imposes on the reported cases and on the diversities of human life an order which they do not possess. Thus, when one comes to map out the spectrum of ordinary consensual physical harm, to which the special situations form exceptions, it is found that the task is almost impossible, since people do not ordinarily consent to the infliction of harm. In effect, either all or almost all the instances of the consensual infliction of violence are special. They have been in the past, and will continue to be in the future, the subject of special treatment by the law.

There are other objections to a general theory of consent and violence. Thus, for example, it is too simple to speak only of consent, for it comes in various sorts. Of these, four spring immediately to mind. First, there is an express agreement to the infliction of the injury which was in the event inflicted. Next, there is express agreement to the infliction of some harm, but not to that harm which in the event was actually caused. These two categories are matched by two more, in which the recipient expressly consents not to the infliction of harm, but to engagement in an activity which creates a risk of harm; again, either the harm which actually results, or to something less. These examples do not exhaust the categories, for corresponding with each are situations of frequent occurrence in practice where the consent is not express but implied. These numerous categories are not the fruit of academic over-elaboration, but are a reflection of real life. Yet they are scarcely touched on in the cases, which just do not bear the weight of any general theory of violence and consent. * * *

[Lord Mustill also rejected hostility, or "antagonism felt by the perpetrator toward the recipient" as the decisive factor, "although its presence or absence may be relevant when the court has to decide as a matter of policy how to react to a new situation."]

I thus see no alternative but to adopt a much narrower and more empirical approach, by looking at the situations in which the recipient consents or is deemed to consent to the infliction of violence upon him, to see whether the decided cases teach us how to react to this new challenge. I will take them in turn.

[His Lordship then examined a range of situations previously addressed by the law: (1) Euthanasia, the killing of someone with his or her consent, is illegal, as is duelling, consent to an activity running a high risk of death at the hand of another. (2) Maiming is likewise illegal, but the distinction between a maiming injury and one that is not is obsolete. (3) Prizefighting is also illegal, but (4) "contact" sports are not, unless the level of hurt is more "serious" than one would expect in the ordinary course of the game. (5) Surgery is lawful, as is (6) correction of a child or a prisoner by someone with lawful authority over the child or prisoner (e.g., a parent or a guard). (7) Dangerous pasttimes and religious mortification are lawful. (8) "Rough horseplay" is legal unless it goes "too far" in subjecting the injured to serious risk. See *Regina v. Jones*, [1886] 83 Cr. App. 375, which upheld the conviction for throwing children too far up in the air. (9) Ordinary fighting is illegal.]

The purpose of this long discussion has been to suggest that the decks are clear for the House to tackle completely anew the question whether the public interest requires [section] 47 of the 1861 Act to be interpreted as penalising an infliction of harm which is at the level of actual bodily harm, but not grievous bodily harm; which is inflicted in private (by which I mean that it is exposed to the view only of those who have chosen to view it); which takes place not only with the consent of the recipient but with his willing and glad co-operation; which is inflicted for the gratification of sexual desire, and not in a spirit of animosity or rage; and which is not engaged in for profit.

* * * When proposing that the conduct is not rightly so charged I do not invite your Lordships' House to endorse it as morally acceptable. Nor do I pronounce in favour of a libertarian doctrine specifically related to sexual matters. Nor in the least do I suggest that ethical pronouncements are meaningless, that there is no difference between right and wrong, that sadism is praiseworthy, or that new opinions on sexual morality are necessarily superior to the old, or anything else of the same kind. What I do say is that these are questions of private morality; that the standards by which they fall to be judged are not those of the criminal law; and that if these standards are to be upheld the individual must enforce them upon himself according to his own moral standards, or have them enforced against him by moral pressures exerted by whatever religious or other community to whose ethical ideals he responds. * * *

* * * In particular, if it were to be held that as a matter of law all infliction of bodily harm above the level of common assault is incapable of being legitimated by consent, except in special circumstances, then we would have to consider whether the public interest required the recognition of private sexual activities as being in a specially exempt category. This would be an altogether more difficult question and one which I would not be prepared to answer in favour of the appellants, not because I do not have my own opinions upon it but because I regard the task as one which the courts are not suited to perform, and which should be carried out, if at all, by Parliament after a thorough review of all the medical, social, moral and political issues, such as was performed by the Wolfenden Committee. * * *

[Lord Mustill reviewed the arguments in favor of criminalization.]

(1) Some of the practices obviously created a risk of genito-urinary infection, and others of septicaemia. These might indeed have been grave in former times, but the risk of serious harm must surely have been greatly reduced by modern medical science.

(2) The possibility that matters might get out of hand, with grave results. It has been acknowledged throughout the present proceedings that the appellants' activities were performed as a prearranged ritual, which at the same time enhanced their excitement and minimised the risk that the infliction of injury would go too far. Of course things might go wrong and really serious injury or death might ensue. If this happened, those responsible would be punished according to the ordinary law, in the same way as those who kill or injure in the course of more ordinary sexual activities are regularly punished. But to penalise the appellants' conduct even if the extreme consequences do not ensue, just because they might have done so would require an assessment of the degree of risk, and the balancing of this risk against the interests of individual freedom. * * *

(3) I would give the same answer to the suggestion that these activities involved a risk of accelerating the spread of auto-immune deficiency syndrome (AIDS), and that they should be brought within the 1861 Act in the interests of public health. The consequence would be strange, since what is currently the principal cause for the transmission of this scourge, namely consenting buggery between males, is now legal. Nevertheless, I would have been compelled to give this proposition the most anxious consideration if there had been any evidence to support it. But there is none, since the case for the Crown was advanced on an entirely different ground.

(4) There remains an argument to which I have given much greater weight. As the evidence in the present case has shown, there is a risk that strangers (and especially young strangers) may be drawn into these activities at an early age and will then become established in them for life. This is indeed a disturbing prospect, but I have come to the conclusion that it is not a sufficient ground for declaring these activities to be criminal under the 1861 Act. The element of the corruption of youth is already catered for by the existing legislation; and if there is a gap in it which needs to be filled the remedy surely lies in the hands of Parliament, not in the application of a statute which is aimed at other forms of wrongdoing. * * *

* * * The only question is whether these consensual private acts are offenses against the existing law of violence. To this question I return a negative response. * * *

■ [LORD SLYNN OF HADLEY also dissented from the Court's judgment in a separate opinion.]

NOTE ON THE "SPANNER CASE"

The prosecution of Anthony Brown and his colleagues was called the "Spanner case," after the code name given their investigation by Scotland Yard. The House of Lords decision provoked great criticism in the United Kingdom. *E.g.,* Bill Thompson, *Sadomasochism* (1994). In December, 1995, the European Court of Human Rights agreed to review the *Brown* decision. Article 7 of the European Convention on Human Rights prohibits retroactive criminal liability, and article 8 protects the right of privacy for members of citizen states. How should the European Court rule? A day later, Britain's Law Commission proposed decriminalizing consensual SM sexual activity.

PROBLEM 11–3

SADOMASOCHISTIC PRACTICES AND AMERICAN CRIMINAL LAW

Pat Califia's short story "Jessie"[k] commences with the winding down of a women's dance. The narrator, Liz, lover of "butch-looking women,"

---

k. "Jessie" is the first story in Pat Califia, *Macho Sluts: Erotic Fiction* 28–62 (1988). *Macho Sluts* was the item of litera- ture most often censored by Canadian Customs officials, according to evidence presented in the lawsuit filed by a lesbian and gay

passes up several opportunities to go home with women standing around. She has eyes only for the lean, leathered, electric Jessie, the bass guitarist for the band called "The Bitch." Jessie emerges from her dressing room. She claims Liz by threading her white silk scarf through a ring in Liz's throat collar. During the drive to Jessie's apartment, Liz recounts her initiation, years earlier, into lesbian bondage and discipline. They arrive at Jessie's apartment in a deserted warehouse district. "I felt a twinge of alarm," Liz narrates. "I hardly knew her. Anything could happen."

At the apartment, Jessie slaps Liz hard enough to redden her face, caresses her back and thighs, binds her hands together, and forces Liz's mouth onto her genitals. "I am going to possess you utterly for my own pleasure, make you completely and totally mine. Are you willing?" asks Jessie. "I've never wanted anything more," is the response. "That's the last time I'll ask for your permission or consent," replies Jessie.

Jessie ties Liz to her poster bed with hand and ankle restraints. Teasing Liz, Jessie displays her impressive array of whips and torture devices; she arouses Liz further by manipulating Liz's vagina with her fingers and threatening Liz's thighs with a lit candle. " 'Oh! No, no, no!' " cries Liz, the narrator. "The first rain of fire fell upon my skin. I struggled and cried for mercy. 'I can't stand this, I wept.' " " 'You have to,' she replies. Again and again she let the molten liquid sear me. She watched my face carefully, spacing each incident so as to give me time to catch my breath, doling out the pain with absolute precision."

"She bent her raven head and took my clitoris between her lips while she tormented my anus with the candle. I no longer thought about the future—coming, hurting, servicing her sweet, furry slit. I did not exist, except as a response to her touch. There was nothing else, no other reality, and no whim of my own will moved me." Jessie forces Liz to give her oral sex and then to bend over on the bed with her ass in the air. " 'Beat me,' I finally begged. She did not need a second invitation," and she whipped Liz's exposed buttocks with a doubled-up belt. Liz passes out and awakens the next afternoon in Jessie's arms.

If this scene occurred in the United Kingdom, it would appear to be criminal under the House of Lords opinion. What if the scene occurred in the state of Texas? What criminal laws, if any, could Jessie or Liz be charged with violating? (Recall the Texas statutes in Appendix 6.) Should any of their conduct be illegal? *Compare State v. Collier*, 372 N.W.2d 303 (Iowa App.1985). Consider the debate within feminist theory over the normative legitimacy of SM sexuality.

bookstore challenging the Customs practices. Janine Fuller & Stuart Blackley, *Restricted*   *Entry: Censorship on Trial* 57 (1995). See Chapter 6, Section 2.

Bat-Ami Bar On, Feminism and Sadomasochism: Self–Critical Notes

In *Against Sadomasochism* 75–76, 77–80.
Edited by Robin Ruth Linden et al., 1982.*

It is with an eye to the relational context of sexuality that the feminist opposition to sadomasochism has been articulated. The arguments of the feminist opposition focus on the nature of the practice of sadomasochism. The primary claim of this position is that the erotization of violence or domination, and of pain or powerlessness, is at the core of sadomasochism and, consequently, that the practice of sadomasochism embodies the same values as heterosexual practices of sexual domination in general and sexually violent practices like rape in particular. Thus, the feminist critics of sadomasochistic sexuality draw parallels between patriarchal sexuality, especially of the coercive kind, and the patriarchal sexual roles of dominance and submission that are assumed during the practice of sadomasochism. In this view, we are reminded that the feminist commitment to sexual liberation and to the struggle against sexual abuse is grounded in the rejection of patriarchal sexuality. Hence, it is argued that because of the nature of sadomasochistic roles, the practice of sadomasochism must be opposed by feminists. * * *

One statement appears repeatedly in feminist defenses of the practice of sadomasochism, usually as part of a definition of sadomasochism and before any defense argument is launched. Somewhat paraphrased, it explains that when a sadomasochistic encounter is entered consensually, the practice of sadomasochism does not resemble sexually violent practices like rape or heterosexual practices of sexual domination. In light of the feminist opposition to the practice of sadomasochism the statement can be understood as a response to the opposition's claims. * * *

However, there must be more to consent than formality if it is to have an impact on the nature of the practice of sadomasochism. In descriptions of sadomasochism the emphasis on the fantasy aspect of sexual encounters suggests that the participants understand that they are role playing and that these roles are governed by rules. The fundamental rule of the role playing assigns the control of a sadomasochistic encounter to the masochist, or to the person in the masochist role. The masochist is given the power to stop the sadist, or the person in the sadist role, and the sadist is under obligation to obey the masochist's command to discontinue whatever act is being performed. When one consents to participate in a sadomasochistic encounter, one is consenting to this rule, i.e., one accepts it as the rule that will govern their performance throughout the encounter.

Now if we look at the vindicators' appeal to consent, it should be obvious why consent is believed to determine the nature of the practice of sadomasochism. *The consent is to a rule of masochist control.* In light of this, the practice of sadomasochism does indeed appear not to violate the right to self-determination, as claimed by the feminist opposition. In

heterosexual practices of sexual domination and in sexually violent practices, the reins of control are in the hands of the dominant or violent party, not the powerless or victimized party. Hence, the right to determine what happens with and to one's body is violated in these practices. But the right to self-determination cannot be violated when the reins of control are in the hands of a person who plays the role of a powerless or victimized party.
* * *

The theory in which the feminist opposition is grounded may actually be inadequate to repudiate sadomasochism. But the opposition is not on the wrong track. The practice of sadomasochism embodies values that are or should be antithetical to feminism, even though sadomasochistic role playing may not be an exact replica of the roles of the sexes in patriarchy. Moreover, there is enough replication of patriarchal sexuality in sadomasochistic practices to make them suspect. Although the feminist opposition claims that sadomasochism replicates patriarchal *roles,* this view is incorrect: the replication is of *rules.*

The masochist control rule provides the masochist with the power to limit the behavior and authority of the sadist, and calls on the sadist to comply with the limitations set by the masochist. This is a negative power that cannot be held by an individual, as a member of an oppressed class, but which is held by the class as a whole. In a class situation this power stems from the dependence of the oppressors on the oppressed. This dependence secures the oppressed class against total destruction, although it does not secure *all* of its members against total destruction. And it secures none of its members treatment that is fair, enhancing of freedom and respectful of persons.

What kind of negative power is held by an oppressed class becomes more clear if we look at the situation of women under patriarchy. As an oppressed class, the physical existence of which is necessary for the reproduction of society both biologically and sociostructurally, women as a class have enough protection against annihilation. This is the same kind of protection that slaves have in a slave-based economy and which Jews in Nazi Germany *lacked* because they were considered utterly disposable. This protection does not extend very far though, because no individual woman is adequately protected against annihilation, nor against exploitation subjugation and humiliation. We are all potential victims of murder and actual victims of exploitation, subjugation and humiliation.

The individual woman's situation is replicated by the masochist or the person in the masochist's role. The masochist or person in the masochist role is the potential victim of murder and the actual victim of exploitation, subjugation and humiliation. As for women, the rules of sadomasochism limit the degree of exposure to the possibility of murder, and to actual exploitation, subjugation and humiliation. However, these rules do not change the essential quality of the experience.

The masochist-control rule, then, does no more than invest the power of the oppressed in the masochist. Indeed, the investment is rather formal. The masochist can expect compliance only insofar as the sadist is dependent on the masochist. The sadist dependence is community based. A sadist with a reputation for noncompliance with the masochist-control rule would probably be hard pressed to find a masochist in the sadomasochist community who would voluntarily enter into a sadomasochistic encounter. Moreover, such a sadist would probably be abandoned to the mercy of the larger society which up until now has not usually exhibited progressive tolerance toward sadomasochism.

In view of the dynamics that determine the relationship between sadists and masochists, there is little that is substantive about the consent of participants in sadomasochistic encounters. Sadomasochism is governed by the masochist-control rule not because feminist values prescribe the desirability of consent, but because of the overall dynamics which determine the situation. More than anything else, the consent of the participants is an expression of a mutual interest in sadomasochistic encounters

This mutual interest is in encounters in which violence or domination and pain or powerlessness are eroticized. Hence, these are encounters where the patriarchal idea of sexuality is played out. On this basis alone, interest in sadomasochism is not above criticism. Participation in sadomasochism exemplifies an interest in conduct that we are unlikely to partake in voluntarily in most ordinary situations, at least if what we are interested in is true liberation. There is no true liberation where there is abuse, humiliation and exploitation, not even when they occur in a context that is voluntary, chosen and of mutual interest.

Liberal ideology does not conceptualize liberation, including sexual liberation, as dependent on justice, freedom and the respect of persons. Insofar as the vindicators of sadomasochism are committed to liberalism, they would fail to see what is wrong with abuse, humiliation and exploitation if engaging in them is self-satisfying. Accordingly, they would see the denial of such satisfaction as repressive and oppressive. What is wrong with abusive, humiliating and exploitative conduct, whether toward oneself or others, is that it is contradictory to the ideals of respect of persons, freedom and justice. These ideals have been misconceptualized under liberalism to allow abuse, humiliation and exploitation.

As feminists, we have to go beyond the ideology of liberalism. If we are unlikely to choose to give and take abuse, to humiliate and be humiliated, to exploit and be exploited in ordinary encounters, then to affirm this behavior in our sexual relationships is possible only when we separate our sexuality from the rest of our lives and objectify it. The separation between our sexual lives and everything else that we do is patriarchal through and through. So is objectified sexuality.

Sadomasochistic sexuality presupposes and advocates fragmented modes of being and doing. These modes are so fragmented that different, indeed contradictory, rules are employed to govern the different fragments. This kind of fragmentation stands in polar opposition to feminist visions. Feminism is about reintegration into an holistic mode of being and doing. We must affirm our commitment to the integrity of our bodies and our selves, a commitment which the vindication of sadomasochistic sexuality renders hopelessly compromised.

Pat Califia, Feminism and Sadomasochism

In *Public Sex: The Culture of Radical Sex* 165, 167–73 (1994).*

Since there is so much confusion about what S/M is, I want to describe my own sexual specialties and the sadomasochistic subculture. I am basically a sadist. About 10 percent of the time, I take the other role (bottom, slave, masochist). This makes me atypical, since the majority of women and men involved in S/M prefer to play bottom. I enjoy leather sex, bondage, various forms of erotic torture, flagellation (whipping), verbal humiliation, fist-fucking, and water sports (playing with enemas and piss). I do not enjoy oral sex unless I am receiving it as a form of sexual service, which means my partner must be on her knees, on her back, or at least in a collar. I have non-S/M sex rarely, mostly for old times' sake, with vanilla friends to whom I want to stay close. My primary relationship is with a woman who enjoys being my slave. We enjoy tricking with other people and telling each other the best parts afterward.

Because sadomasochism is usually portrayed as a violent, dangerous activity, most people do not think there is a great deal of difference between a rapist and a bondage enthusiast. But sadomasochism is not a form of sexual assault. It is a consensual activity that involves polarized roles and intense sensations. An S/M scene is always preceded by a negotiation in which the top and bottom decide whether or not they will play, what activities are likely to occur, what activities will not occur, and about how long the scene will last. The bottom is usually given a *safe word* or *code action* she can use to stop the scene. This safe word allows the bottom to fantasize that the scene is not consensual and to protest verbally or resist physically without halting stimulation.

The key word to understanding S/M is *fantasy*. The roles, dialogue, fetish costumes, and sexual activity are part of a drama or ritual. The participants are enhancing their sexual pleasure, not damaging or imprisoning one another. A sadomasochist is well aware that a role adopted during a scene is not appropriate during other interactions and that a fantasy role is not the sum total of her being.

S/M relationships are usually egalitarian. Very few bottoms want full-time mistresses. In fact, masochists are known within the S/M community to be stubborn and aggressive. Tops often make nervous jokes about being slaves to the whims of their bottoms. After all, the top's pleasure is dependent on the bottom's willingness to play. This gives most sadists a mild to severe case of performance anxiety.

The S/M subculture is a theater in which sexual dramas can be acted out and appreciated. It also serves as a vehicle for passing on new fantasies, new equipment, warnings about police harassment, introductions to potential sex partners and friends, and safety information. Safety is a major concern of sadomasochists. A major part of the sadist's turn-on consists of deliberately altering the emotional or physical state of the bottom. Even a minor accident like a rope burn can upset the top enough to mar the scene. And of course a bottom can't relax and enjoy the sex if she doesn't completely trust her top. The S/M community makes some attempt to regulate itself by warning newcomers away from individuals who are inconsiderate, insensitive, prone to playing when they are intoxicated, or unsafe for other reasons. Unfortunately, the suppression of S/M isolates novice sadists and masochists from this body of information which can minimize danger and make playing more rewarding.

For some people outside the subculture, the fact that S/M is consensual makes it acceptable. They may not understand why people enjoy it, but they see that S/M people are not inhumane monsters. For other people, including many feminists, the fact that it is consensual makes it even more appalling. A woman who deliberately seeks out a sexual situation in which she can be helpless is a traitor in their eyes. Hasn't the women's movement been trying to persuade people for years that women are not naturally masochistic? Originally, this meant that women do not create their own second-class status, do not enjoy it, and are the victims of socially constructed discrimination, not biology. A sexual masochist probably doesn't want to be raped, battered, discriminated against in her job, or kept down by the system. Her desire to act out a specific sexual fantasy is very different from the pseudopsychiatric dictum that a woman's world is bound by housework, intercourse, and childbirth.

Some feminists object to the description of S/M as consensual. They believe that our society has conditioned all of us to accept inequities in power and hierarchical relationships. Therefore, S/M is simply a manifestation of the same system that dresses girls in pink and boys in blue; allows surplus value to accumulate in the coffers of capitalists while giving workers a minimum wage; and sends out cops and soldiers to keep down the disfranchised.

* * * Society shapes sexuality. We can make any decision about our sexual behavior we like, but our imagination and ability to carry out those decisions are limited by the surrounding culture. But I do not believe that sadomasochism is the result of institutionalized injustice to a greater extent than heterosexual marriage, lesbian bars, or gay male bathhouses. The S/M subculture is affected by sexism, racism, and other fallout from the system, but the dynamic between a top and a bottom is quite different from the dynamic between men and women, whites and blacks, or upper- and working-class people. That system is unjust because it assigns privileges based on race, gender, and social class. During an S/M encounter, roles are acquired and used in very different ways. The participants select particular roles that best express their sexual needs, how they feel about their particular partners, or which outfits are clean and ready to wear. The most significant reward for being a top or a bottom is sexual pleasure. If you

don't like being a top or a bottom, you switch your keys. Try doing that with your biological sex or your race or your socioeconomic status.

Some feminists still find S/M roles disturbing because they believe they are derived from genuinely oppressive situations. They accuse sadomasochism of being fascistic because of the symbolism employed to create an S/M ambiance. And some S/M people do enjoy fantasies that are more elaborate than a simple structure of top versus bottom. An S/M scene can be played out using the personae of guard and prisoner, cop and suspect, Nazi and Jew, white and black, straight man and queer, parent and child, priest and penitent, teacher and student, whore and client, etc.

However, no symbol has a single meaning. Meaning is derived from the context in which it is used. Not everyone who wears a swastika is a Nazi: not everyone who has a pair of handcuffs on his belt is a cop; and not everyone who wears a nun's habit is a Catholic. S/M is more a parody of the hidden sexual nature of fascism than it is a worship of or acquiescence to it.
* * *

S/M eroticism focuses on forbidden feelings or actions and searches for a way to obtain pleasure from them. It is the quintessence of nonreproductive sex. Those feminists who accuse sadomasochists of mocking the oppressed by playing with dominance and submission forget that *we* are oppressed. We suffer police harassment, violence in the street, and discrimination in housing and employment. We are not treated the way our system treats its collaborators and supporters.

The issue of pain is probably as difficult for non-S/M people to understand as polarized roles are. We tend to associate pain with illness or self-destruction. First of all, S/M does not necessarily involve pain. The exchange of power is more essential to S/M than intense sensation, punishment, or discipline. Second, pain is a subjective experience. Depending on the context, a certain sensation may frighten you, make you angry, urge you on, or get you hot. In many situations, people choose to endure pain or discomfort if the goal for which they are striving makes it worthwhile. Long-distance runners are not generally thought of as perverts, nor is Mother Theresa. The fact that our society disapproves of masochism while it lauds stressful athletic activity and religious martyrdom is an interesting demonstration of how sex has been made a "special case." We seem incapable of using the same reasoning and compassion we apply to nonsexual issues to formulate our positions on sexual issues.

S/M violates a taboo that preserves the mysticism of romantic sex because any pain involved is deliberate. Aroused human beings do not see, smell, hear, taste, or perceive pain as acutely as the nonaroused individual. Lots of people find bruises or scratches the morning after an exhilarating session of lovemaking and can't remember exactly how or when they got them. The sensations involved in S/M are not that different. But we're supposed to fall into bed and do it with our eyes closed. Good, enthusiastic sex is supposed to happen automatically between people who love each other. If the sex is less than stunning, we blame the quality of our partners' feelings for us. Planning a sexual encounter and using toys or equipment to produce specific feelings seems antithetical to romance.

What looks painful to an observer is probably being experienced as pleasure, heat, pressure, or a mixture of all these. A good top builds sensation slowly, alternates pain with pleasure, rewards endurance with more pleasure, and teaches the bottom to transcend her own limits. With enough preparation, care, and encouragement, people are capable of doing wonderful things. There is a special pride which results from doing something unique and extraordinary for your lover. The sadomasochist has a passion for making use of the entire body, every nerve fiber, and every wayward thought.

Recently, I have heard feminists use the term *fetishistic* as an epithet and a synonym for *objectifying*. Sadomasochists are often accused of substituting things for people, of loving the leather or rubber or spike heels more than the person who is wearing them. *Objectification* originally referred to the use of images of stereotypically feminine women to sell products like automobiles and cigarettes. It also referred to the sexual harassment of women and the notion that we should be available to provide men with sexual gratification without receiving pleasure in return and without the right to refuse to engage in sex. A concept which was originally used to attack the marketing campaigns of international corporations and the sexual repression of women is now being used to attack a sexual minority.

Fetish costumes are just as unacceptable to employers and advertising executives as women's wearing overalls and smoking cigars. Hardly instruments of the sexual repression of women, fetish costumes can provide the women who wear them with sexual pleasure and power. Even when a fetish costume exaggerates the masculine or feminine attributes of the wearer, it cannot properly be called sexist. Our society strives to make masculinity in men and femininity in women appear natural and biologically determined. Fetish costumes violate this rule by being too theatrical and deliberate. Since fetish costumes may also be used to transform the gender of the wearer, they are a further violation of sexist standards for sex-specific dress and conduct. * * *

Human sexuality is a complicated phenomenon. A cursory examination will not yield the entire significance of a sexual act. Fetishes have several qualities which make them erotically stimulating and unacceptable to the majority culture. Wearing leather, rubber, or a silk kimono distributes feeling over the entire skin. The isolated object may become a source of arousal. This challenges the identification of sex with the genitals. Fetishes draw all the senses into the sexual experience, especially the senses of smell and touch. Since they are often anachronistic or draw attention to erogenous zones, fetish costumes cannot be worn on the street. Fetishes are reserved for sexual use only, yet they are drawn from realms not traditionally associated with sexuality. Fetishism is the product of imagination and technology.

Sadomasochism is also accused of being a hostile or angry kind of sex, as opposed to the gentle and loving kind of sex that feminists should strive for. The women's movement has become increasingly pro-romantic love in the last decade. Lesbians are especially prone to this sentimental trend. Rather than being critical of the idea that one can find enough fulfillment in a relationship to justify one's existence, feminists are seeking membership in perfect, egalitarian couples. I question the value of this trend.

There is no concrete evidence that a sadomasochist's childhood contained any more corporal punishment, puritanism, or abuse than the childhoods of other people. There is also no evidence that we secretly fear and hate our partners. S/M relationships vary from no relationship at all (the S/M is experienced during fantasy or masturbation) to casual sex with many partners, to monogamous couples, and include all shades in between. There are many different ways to express affection or sexual interest. Vanilla people send flowers, poetry, or candy, or they exchange rings. An S/M person does all that and may also lick boots, wear a locked collar, or build her loved one a rack in the basement. There is little objective difference between a feminist who is offended by the fact that my lover kneels to me in public and a suburbanite who calls the cops because the gay boys next door are sunbathing in the nude. My sexual semiotics differ from the mainstream. So what? I didn't join the feminist movement to live inside a Hallmark greeting card.

Is there a single controversial sexual issue that the women's movement has not reacted to with a conservative, feminine horror of the outrageous and the rebellious? A movement that started out saying biology is *not* destiny is now trashing transsexuals and celebrating women's "natural" connection to the earth and living things. A movement that spawned children's liberation is now trashing boy-lovers and supporting the passage of draconian sex laws that assign heavier sentences for having sex with a minor than you'd get for armed robbery. A movement that developed an analysis of housework as unpaid labor and acknowledged that women usually trade sex for what they want because that's all they've got is now joining the vice squad to get prostitutes off the street. A movement whose early literature was often called obscene and was banned from circulation is now campaigning to get rid of pornography The only sex perverts this movement supports are lesbian mothers, and I suspect that's because of the current propaganda about women comprising the nurturing, healing force that will save the world from destructive male energy.

NOTES ON THE FEMINIST SM DEBATE

1. *The Analogy to Rape.* Recall Pat Califia's short story, "Jessie," described in Problem 11–3. Compare the scenario she describes to the rape in *State v. Rusk*. Is it different from a situation where the woman consents to petting but then says "no" as the petting becomes heavier? Does it make a difference that in date rape the discourse is dictated by the aggressor, while SM follows what Bar–On calls the "masochist control rule"? Is it relevant that Califia never mentions a "safe word" (a neutral word that will shut down the action immediately) in "Jessie"?

2. *The Rubin–MacKinnon Debate.* Notice the parallels between Bar–On's arguments and Catharine MacKinnon's views that sexuality is a tool of patriarchy (Chapter 3, Section 1[C]) and her anti-pornography arguments, which maintain that male-male porn (or SM) can be patriarchal and can hurt women (Chapter 6, Section 2). Similarly, Califia's arguments recall Gayle Rubin's views that sexuality is an independent good and that Americans need to accept the concept of "benign sexual variation" (Chapter 3, Section 1[C]). Is SM an appropriate context for the MacKinnon–Rubin debate?

3. *The Independent Issue of Criminalization.* Califia and Rubin would certainly oppose the House of Lords decision in *Brown*. Would Bar–On favor criminalization, as *Brown* held? Or should feminists favor other kinds of regulation for SM? Does MacKinnon's Indianapolis ordinance (Chapter 6, Section 2) represent an alternative approach?

SEX BY AND WITH MINORS

Most people believe that the law's regulation of sex with children is simple: there is an "age of consent," perhaps 16, and any sexual intercourse with a person under that age is illegal. This vision of the law serves a useful regulatory function (i.e., adults know that underage people are sexual "jailbait"), but it is multifariously erroneous. State law today defies easy characterization. Consider the following table as a starting point, and then consider further complexities raised in text. All of the descriptions are based upon the law in 1996.

MINOR CONSENT STATUTES:
U.S. STATES AND THE DISTRICT OF COLUMBIA

STATE	AGE	QUALIFICATIONS & EXCEPTIONS
Alabama	16	
Alaska	16	when actor in a position of authority
Arizona	18	
Arkansas	16	male must be 20 or older (18, if male in a position of authority)
Calif.	18	when actors not married
Colorado	15	partner must be at least 4 years older (18, if actor in a position of authority)
Conn.	16	partner must be more than 2 years older (18, if actor in a position of authority)
Delaware	16	12 if partner is less than 4 years older
D.C.	16	partner must be at least 4 years older, unless married; but fornication by unmarried people is a misdemeanor
Florida	18	minor must be of previously chaste character, unless chastity lost to same partner in past encounter
Georgia	16	if minor 14–15 and actor not more than 3 years older, actor may be punished for misdemeanor at court's discretion
Hawaii	14	
Idaho	16	
Illinois	18	partner must be 17 or older and in a position of authority
Indiana	14	defense if actor reasonably thought minor was 16 or older
Iowa	16	if actor 18 or older (if actor 16–17, minor cannot be more than 5 years younger)
Kansas	16	
Kentucky	16	

STATE	AGE	QUALIFICATIONS & EXCEPTIONS
Louisiana	17	(unmarried females) male must be over 17 and age difference greater than 2 years
Maine	16	partner must be 19 or older and at least 5 years older than minor (18, if actor in a position of authority)
Maryland	16	partner must be 21 or older
Mass.	16	(18, if minor "of chaste life")
Michigan	13	(16, if actor is member of same household, or blood relative, or in position of authority, or 5 or more years older than minor)
Minnesota	13	when actor more than 36 months older (16, if actor more than 48 months older, or in position of authority, or has significant relationship to minor)
Miss.	14	(18, if minor of previously chaste character, or if actor in a position of trust or authority)
Missouri	14	(17, if actor 21 or older)
Montana	16	
Nebraska	16	partner must be 19 or older
Nevada	16	partner must be 18 or older
N.H.	13	(16, if actor member of same household or blood relative; 18, if actor in position of authority)
N.J.	13	partner must be at least 4 years older (18, if actor blood relative or in position of authority)
New Mex.	13	(16, if actor in position of authority; 17, if actor at least 18 and 4 years older than minor)
New York	17	
N.C.	13	partner must be at least 12 and 4 years older than minor
N.D.	15	
Ohio	13	(16, if actor 18 or older)
Oklahoma	16	
Oregon	18	
Penn.	14	partner must be 18 or older
R.I.	16	if partner is 18 or older
S.C.	14	(16, when actor in position of authority)
S.D.	16	partner must be at least 3 years older
Tennessee	18	13 if partner is less than 4 years older
Texas	17	
Utah	16	
Vermont	16	unless couple married and act consensual (18, if minor entrusted to actor's care)
Virginia	13	
Wash.	18	if actor at least 60 months older, in a significant relationship to minor, and abuses supervisory position
W.V.	16	
Wisconsin	18	if minor under 15, incapable of consent as matter of law; if minor 15–17, incapacity to consent is rebuttable presumption
Wyoming	16	partner must be at least 4 years older

To begin with, in most states it is a misnomer to say that a minor can never "consent" to sex. In Pennsylvania, for example, it is "statutory rape" only if the actor is at least 18 years old and the minor is less than 14 years old. Not only can an adult have sex with a 15 year old, but a 15 year old can have sex with a 13 year old. And, of course, a 13 year old can have sex with another 13 year old. See also Tex. Penal Code tit. 5, § 22.011(a)(2), (e) [Appendix 6] (two children between 14 and 17 can "consent" to have sex with one another). Even in states that seem to prohibit any sexual activity by minors under an "age of consent," including California and New York, prosecutions usually do not occur when both parties are under age. (For a prominent counterexample, see *Michael M* below.)

Second, most states have penalties for any "sexual contact" (such as fondling) with persons under the specified ages. A few states regulate sexual use of objects (e.g., dildos) upon minors. Relatedly, many states have adopted a nuanced statutory scheme that penalizes by reference to both age and the type of sexual conduct (penetrative intercourse or nonpenetrative contact). For example, in Rhode Island penetrative sexual intercourse (i.e., vaginal, oral, and anal intercourse) with a person 14 years old or younger is first degree "child molestation sexual assault," a felony offering a sentence of 20 years to life in prison. R.I. Code § 11–37–8.1. It is second degree child molestation sexual assault if the defendant has nonpenetrative sexual contact with a person 14 years old or younger. *Id.* § 11–37–8.3. It is third degree sexual assault for a defendant older than age 18 to engage in penetrative sexual intercourse with a person between the ages of 14 and 16 years old. *Id.* § 11–37–6. It is hard to say what the precise "age of consent" actually is in Rhode Island, for a 15 year old can consent to sexual intercourse with an 18 year old but not someone older, and can consent to sexual contact by anyone else.

Third, in some states the age of the minor is an aggravating factor. In Tennessee rape is sexual penetration of the victim accompanied by coercion or fraud. Tenn. Code § 39–13–503. "Aggravated rape" is sexual penetration by an armed actor or by a group, by an actor causing bodily injury, or upon a victim under the age of 13. *Id.* § 39–13–502. "Statutory rape" is sexual penetration upon a victim at least 13 years old but younger than 18 years old by an actor 4 years or more older than the victim. *Id.* § 39–13–506.

Fourth, many states include special rules for situations where the adult is in a relation of trust or authority over the minor. In South Carolina, for example, "sexual battery" (defined to include vaginal, oral, and anal intercourse) against a person under the age of 11 years is first degree "criminal sexual conduct." S.C. Code § 16–3–655(1). If the minor is between 11 and 14 years old, sexual battery is second degree criminal sexual conduct. *Id.* § 16–3–655(2). Also second degree criminal sexual conduct is sexual battery with a minor between 14 and 16 if the actor is in a position of "familial, custodial, or official authority to coerce the victim to submit or is older than the victim." *Id.* § 16–3–655(3).

Fifth, virtually all of the state age of consent laws exempt married couples. That is, if an adult wants to marry a 15 year old person and can obtain parental consent (usually a prerequisite for underage marriages), the adult can have sex with that child.

Sixth, and perhaps only tangentially relevant, virtually all the states and the federal government have special regulations pertaining to the deployment of children in sexually oriented activities, including pornographic materials, massage parlors or prostitution operations, and live performances or sex shows.

PART A.   SEX BETWEEN MINORS

Virtually all the eighteenth and nineteenth century American statutes regulating sex with minors focused on girls. Indeed, these early "seduction" and "carnal knowledge" statutes worked from traditional ideas about girls and boys and sought to protect the chastity of girls from the rapacious desire of boys and men. The only regulation of sex with boys was sodomy laws, and in fact most reported nineteenth century sodomy cases involve sex between adults and children (both boys and girls). Use of neglect or "PINS" (person in need of supervision) statutes to control sexually wayward girls persisted until well into the twentieth century. See, *e.g., A. v. City of New York*, 335 N.Y.S.2d 33, 286 N.E.2d 432 (1972). After *Craig v. Boren* [Chapter 1, Section 3(A)], where the Supreme Court struck down a state law allowing girls to buy beer earlier than boys, one would think statutory sex discrimination seemingly so mired in stereotype would be invalid. Think again.

Michael M. v. Superior Court of Sonoma County

United States Supreme Court, 1981.
450 U.S. 464, 101 S.Ct. 1200, 67 L.Ed.2d 437.

■ JUSTICE REHNQUIST announced the judgment of the Court and delivered an opinion, in which THE CHIEF JUSTICE [BURGER], JUSTICE STEWART, and JUSTICE POWELL joined.

The question presented in this case is whether California's "statutory rape" law, § 261.5 of the Cal. Penal Code Ann. (West Supp. 1981), violates the Equal Protection Clause of the Fourteenth Amendment. Section 261.5 defines unlawful sexual intercourse as "an act of sexual intercourse accomplished with a female not the wife of the perpetrator, where the female is under the age of 18 years." The statute thus makes men alone criminally liable for the act of sexual intercourse.

In July 1978, a complaint was filed in the Municipal Court of Sonoma County, Cal., alleging that petitioner, then a 17 ½–year-old male, had had unlawful sexual intercourse with a female under the age of 18, in violation of § 261.5. The evidence, adduced at a preliminary hearing showed that at approximately midnight on June 3, 1978, petitioner and two friends approached Sharon, a 16 ½–year-old female, and her sister as they waited at a bus stop. Petitioner and Sharon, who had already been drinking, moved away from the others and began to kiss. After being struck in the face for rebuffing petitioner's initial advances, Sharon submitted to sexual intercourse with petitioner. Prior to trial, petitioner sought to set aside the information on both state and federal constitutional grounds, asserting that § 261.5 unlawfully discriminated on the basis of gender. [The California courts subjected the statutory discrimination to strict scrutiny and upheld it. The U.S. Supreme Court affirmed.]

* * * [T]he Court has had some difficulty in agreeing upon the proper approach and analysis in cases involving challenges to gender-based classifications. * * * Unlike the California Supreme Court, we have not held that gender-based classifications are "inherently suspect" and thus we do not apply so-called "strict scrutiny" to those classifications. Our cases have held, however, that the traditional minimum rationality test takes on a somewhat "sharper focus" when gender-based classifications are challenged. See *Craig v. Boren*, 429 U.S. 190, 210 n. * (1976) (Powell, J., concurring). In *Reed v. Reed*, 404 U.S. 71 (1971), for example, the Court stated that a gender-based classification will be upheld if it bears a "fair and substantial relationship" to legitimate state ends, while in *Craig v. Boren, supra*, 429 U.S. at 197, the Court restated the test to require the classification to bear a "substantial relationship" to "important governmental objectives."

Underlying these decisions is the principle that a legislature may not "make overbroad generalizations based on sex which are entirely unrelated to any differences between men and women or which demean the ability or social status of the affected class." *Parham v. Hughes*, 441 U.S. 347, 354 (1979) (plurality opinion of Stewart, J.). But * * * this Court has consistently upheld statutes where the gender classification is not invidious, but rather realistically reflects the fact that the sexes are not similarly situated in certain circumstances. *Parham v. Hughes, supra; Califano v. Webster*, 430 U.S. 313 (1977); *Schlesinger v. Ballard*, 419 U.S. 498 (1975); *Kahn v. Shevin*, 416 U.S. 351 (1974). As the Court has stated, a legislature may "provide for the special problems of women." *Weinberger v. Wiesenfeld*, 420 U.S. 636, 653 (1975). * * *

The justification for the statute offered by the State, and accepted by the Supreme Court of California, is that the legislature sought to prevent illegitimate teenage pregnancies. * * *

We are satisfied not only that the prevention of illegitimate pregnancy is at least one of the "purposes" of the statute, but also that the State has a strong interest in preventing such pregnancy. At the risk of stating the obvious, teenage pregnancies, which have increased dramatically over the last two decades, have significant social, medical, and economic consequences for both the mother and her child, and the State. Of particular concern to the State is that approximately half of all teenage pregnancies end in abortion. And of those children who are born, their illegitimacy makes them likely candidates to become wards of the State.* * *

The question thus boils down to whether a State may attack the problem of sexual intercourse and teenage pregnancy directly by prohibiting a male from having sexual intercourse with a minor female. We hold that such a statute is sufficiently related to the State's objectives to pass constitutional muster.

Because virtually all of the significant harmful and inescapably identifiable consequences of teenage pregnancy fall on the young female, a legislature acts well within its authority when it elects to punish only the participant who, by nature, suffers few of the consequences of his conduct. It is hardly unreasonable for a legislature acting to protect minor females to exclude them from punishment. Moreover, the risk of pregnancy itself constitutes a substantial deterrence to young females. No similar natural sanctions deter males. A criminal sanction imposed solely on males thus serves to roughly "equalize" the deterrents on the sexes. * * *

■ JUSTICE STEWART, concurring.

[Justice Stewart noted that aggressive sex by females was regulated in California: women could be prosecuted for molesting, annoying, or contributing to the delinquency of anyone under 18, Cal. Penal Code §§ 272, 647a; committing "any lewd or lascivious act," including consensual intercourse, with a child under 14, *id.* § 288; engaging in deviant sexual acts with anyone under 18, *id.* § 286(b)(1), 288a(b)(1); or aiding and abetting the violation of § 261.5 itself. According to statistics maintained by the California Department of Justice Bureau of Criminal Statistics, approximately 14% of the juveniles arrested for participation in acts made unlawful by § 261.5 between 1975 and 1979 were female. Thus, the issue is only whether the state can impose a single *additional* sanction against teen sexuality on a gender-specific basis.]

As the California Supreme Court's catalog shows, the pregnant unmarried female confronts problems more numerous and more severe than any faced by her male partner.[7] She alone endures the medical risks of pregnancy or abortion.[8] She suffers disproportionately the social, educational, and emotional consequences of pregnancy.[9] Recognizing this disproportion, California has attempted to protect teenage females by prohibiting males from participating in the act necessary for conception.[10] * * *

---

7. The court noted that from 1971 through 1976, 83.6% of the 4,860 children born to girls under 15 in California were illegitimate, as were 51% of those born to girls 15 to 17. The court also observed that while accounting for only 21% of California pregnancies in 1976, teenagers accounted for 34.7% of legal abortions.

8. There is also empirical evidence that sexual abuse of young females is a more serious problem than sexual abuse of young males. For example, a review of five studies found that 88% of sexually abused minors were female. Jaffe, Dynneson, & Ten Bensel, "Sexual Abuse of Children," 129 *Am. J. of Diseases of Children* 689, 690 (1975). * * *

9. Most teenage mothers do not finish high school and are disadvantaged economically thereafter. See Moore, "Teenage Childbirth and Welfare Dependency," 10 *Family Planning Perspectives* 233–235 (1978). The suicide rate for teenage mothers is seven times greater than that for teenage girls without children. F. Nye, School–Age Parenthood (Wash.State U.Ext.Bull. No. 667) 8 (1976). And 60% of adolescent mothers aged 15 to 17 are on welfare within two to five years of the birth of their children. Teenage Pregnancy, Everybody's Problem 3–4 (DHEW Publication (HSA) No. 77–5619).

10. Despite the increased availability of contraceptives and sex education, the pregnancy rates for young women are increasing.

■ JUSTICE BLACKMUN, concurring in the judgment. * * *

[Justice Blackmun argued that the state has greater discretion to adopt measures seeking to *prevent* pregnancies than to adopt measures regulating termination of unwanted pregnancies, even though both kinds of regulation implicate "substantial privacy rights in intimate affairs connected with procreation."]

I think, too, that it is only fair, with respect to this particular petitioner, to point out that his partner, Sharon, appears not to have been an unwilling participant in at least the initial stages of the intimacies that took place the night of June 3, 1978.* Petitioner's and Sharon's nonacquaintance with each other before the incident; their drinking; their withdrawal from the others of the group; their foreplay, in which she willingly participated and seems to have encouraged; and the closeness of their ages (a difference of only one year and 18 days) are factors that should make this case an unattractive one to prosecute at all, and especially to prosecute as a felony, rather than as a misdemeanor chargeable under § 261.5. But the State has chosen to prosecute in that manner, and the facts, I reluctantly conclude, may fit the crime.

■ JUSTICE BRENNAN, with whom JUSTICES WHITE and MARSHALL join, dissenting.

[Justice Brennan argued that California had presented no evidence that a gender-neutral statutory rape law, such as those adopted by 37 other states, would be less effective in preventing teenage sexual activity and

See Alan Guttmacher Institute, *11 Million Teenagers* 12 (1976). See generally C. Chilman, *Adolescent Sexuality in a Changing American Society* (NIH Pub.No.80–1426, 1980). * * *

* Sharon at the preliminary hearing testified as follows: * * *

"Q. [by the Deputy District Attorney]. Now, after you met the defendant, what happened?

"A. We walked down to the railroad tracks.

"Q. What happened at the railroad tracks?

"A. We were drinking at the railroad tracks and we walked over to this bush and he started kissing me and stuff, and I was kissing him back, too, at first. Then, I was telling him to stop * * * and I was telling him to slow down and stop. He said, 'okay, okay.' But then he just kept doing it. He just kept doing it and then my sister and two other guys came over to where we were and my sister said—told me to get up and come home.

[Sharon's sister and the others left Sharon and Michael alone again.] We was lying there and we were kissing each other, and then he asked me if I wanted to walk him over to the park; so we walked over to the park and we sat down on a bench and then he started kissing me again and we were laying on the bench. And he told me to take my pants off. "I said, 'No,' and I was trying to get up and he hit me back down on the bench and then I just said to myself, 'Forget it,' and I let him do what he wanted to do and he took my pants off and he was telling me to put my legs around him and stuff. * * *

"Q. How did he hit you?

"A. He slugged me in the face.

"Q. As a result of that, did you have any bruises or any kind of an injury?

"A. Yeah. * * *

"The Court: Did he hit you one time or did he hit you more than once?

"The Witness: He hit me about two or three times. * * *"

pregnancy than California's males-only law. He also argued that the law classically reflected gender stereotypes of the sort that had been fatal to statutes in *Craig* and other cases.]

* * * Until very recently, no California court or commentator had suggested that the purpose of California's statutory rape law was to protect young women from the risk of pregnancy. Indeed, the historical development of § 261.5 demonstrates that the law was initially enacted on the premise that young women, in contrast to young men, were to be deemed legally incapable of consenting to an act of sexual intercourse.[9] Because their chastity was considered particularly precious, those young women were felt to be uniquely in need of the State's protection. In contrast, young men were assumed to be capable of making such decisions for themselves; the law therefore did not offer them any special protection. * * *

■ JUSTICE STEVENS, dissenting. * * *

I think the plurality is quite correct in making the assumption that the joint act that this law seeks to prohibit creates a greater risk of harm for the female than for the male. But the plurality surely cannot believe that the risk of pregnancy confronted by the female—any more than the risk of venereal disease confronted by males as well as females—has provided an effective deterrent to voluntary female participation in the risk-creating conduct. Yet the plurality's decision seems to rest on the assumption that the California Legislature acted on the basis of that rather fanciful notion.

In my judgment, the fact that a class of persons is especially vulnerable to a risk that a statute is designed to avoid is a reason for making the statute applicable to that class. The argument that a special need for protection provides a rational explanation for an exemption is one I simply

---

9. California's statutory rape law had its origins in the *Statutes of Westminster* enacted during the reign of Edward I at the close of the 13th century (3 Edw. 1, ch. 13 (1275); 13 Edw. 1, ch. 34 (1285)). The age of consent at that time was 12 years, reduced to 10 years in 1576 (18 Eliz. 1, ch. 7, § 4). This statute was part of the common law brought to the United States. Thus, when the first California penal statute was enacted, it contained a provision (1850 Cal.Stats., ch. 99, § 47, p. 234) that proscribed sexual intercourse with females under the age of 10. In 1889, the California statute was amended to make the age of consent 14 (1889 Cal.Stats., ch. 191, § 1, p. 223). In 1897, the age was advanced to 16 (1897 Cal.Stats., ch. 139, § 1, p. 201). In 1913 it was fixed at 18, where it now remains (1913 Cal.Stats., ch. 122, § 1, p. 212). Because females generally have not reached puberty by the age of 10, it is inconceivable that a statute designed to prevent pregnancy would be directed at acts of sexual intercourse with females under that age. The only legislative history available, the draftsmen's notes to the Penal Code of 1872, supports the view that the purpose of California's statutory rape law was to protect those who were too young to give consent. The draftsmen explained that the "[statutory rape] provision embodies the well settled rule of the existing law; that a girl under ten years of age is incapable of giving any consent to an act of intercourse which can reduce it below the grade of rape." Code Commissioners' note, subd. 1, following Cal.Penal Code, p. 111 (1st ed. 1872). There was no mention whatever of pregnancy prevention. See also Note, "Forcible and Statutory Rape: An Exploration of the Operation and Objectives of the Consent Standard," 62 *Yale L.J.* 55, 74–76 (1952).

do not comprehend.[6]

In this case, the fact that a female confronts a greater risk of harm than a male is a reason for applying the prohibition to her—not a reason for granting her a license to use her own judgment on whether or not to assume the risk. Surely, if we examine the problem from the point of view of society's interest in preventing the risk-creating conduct from occurring at all, it is irrational to exempt 50% of the potential violators. And, if we view the government's interest as that of a *parens patriae* seeking to protect its subjects from harming themselves, the discrimination is actually perverse. Would a rational parent making rules for the conduct of twin children of opposite sex simultaneously forbid the son and authorize the daughter to engage in conduct that is especially harmful to the daughter? That is the effect of this statutory classification. * * *

NOTES ON STEREOTYPES AND STATUTORY RAPE LAWS

Justice Rehnquist's opinion in *Michael M.* has been overtaken by events: California has amended its statutory rape law to be gender neutral, and the Supreme Court in the VMI case (Chapter 1, Section 3[A]) has raised the constitutional bar for sex-based classifications, as now Chief Justice Rehnquist himself charged. (Does *VMI* essentially overrule *Michael M*?) Nonetheless, the discussion among the Justices explores issues that remain relevant.

1. *What Difference Does Sex Make?* Most feminists agreed with the dissent's charge that the Court was upholding a law that perpetuated gender stereotypes (boy aggressor, girl victim), contrary to *Craig. E.g.,* Wendy Webster Williams, "The Equality Crisis: Reflections on Culture, Courts, and Feminism," 7 *Women's Rts. L. Rptr.* 175 (Spring 1982), and Frances Olsen, "Statutory Rape: A Feminist Critique," 63 *Tex. L. Rev.* 387 (1987). Catharine MacKinnon, "Reflections on Sex Equality Under Law," 100 *Yale L.J.* 1281, 1305 (1991), faulted the plurality opinion for this reason but also faulted the dissent's greater concern "with avoiding the stereotyping attendant to the ideological message the law communicated than with changing the facts that make the stereotype largely true. In the interest of opposing facial distinctions and debunking the supposed myth of male sexual aggression, the fact that it is overwhelmingly girls who are sexually victimized by older males for reasons wholly unrelated to their capacity to become pregnant was completely obscured." Under feminist premises, how should *Michael M.* have been decided, if both the plurality and the dissent are misfocused?

6. A hypothetical racial classification will illustrate my point. Assume that skin pigmentation provides some measure of protection against cancer caused by exposure to certain chemicals in the atmosphere and, therefore, that white employees confront a greater risk than black employees in certain industrial settings. Would it be rational to require black employees to wear protective clothing but to exempt whites from that requirement? It seems to me that the greater risk of harm to white workers would be a reason for including them in the requirement—not for granting them an exemption.

2. *Rape and "Statutory Rape."* Note Justice Blackmun's observation that the intercourse in *Michael M.* was apparently consensual. Is that supported by the transcript material he quotes? One feature of statutory rape laws is that, like consensual sodomy laws, they provide prosecutors with an additional crime to charge rapists in cases where there may be a reasonable doubt of the victim's nonconsent. Is this a good feature of such laws? Or does it create too much prosecutorial discretion? Kristin Bumiller, "Rape as a Legal Symbol: An Essay on Sexual Violence and Racism," 42 *U. Miami L. Rev.* 75 (1987), argues that statutory rape improperly displaces inquiry from mutuality and consent and thereby obscures what should be the critical normative concern with any sex.

3. *What Should the Law Be?* How should the law treat sex with children? Draft or outline a statute and then apply it to the facts reported in the following problem.

PROBLEM 11–4

THE LAW AND CHILDREN'S SEXUAL EXPERIENCES

Felice Picano's *Ambidextrous: The Secret Lives of Children* (1985), a "memoir in the form of a novel," reminisces lustfully of the eleven-year-old author's sexual initiation by the skilled hands of Susan Flaherty, another eleven year old in a suburban basement. At age fourteen he had his first love affair, with Ricky Hersh, who introduced him to oral sex, public masturbation, and other violations of 1950s legal norms. Ricky himself had learned of gay sex from the "bj buddy" of his father, killed during the Korean War. Tony Warner had brought Ricky his father's footlocker, whose contents included pictures of his father and Tony engaged in oral sex. Ricky and the author spent langorous afternoons masturbating over these images and developed scenes of their own. Ricky considered the author his "bj buddy" but admitted that "someone older" had been his own initiation. An echo of that admission occurs a few pages later in the novel. The two fourteen year olds habitually engaged in shower-room sex after swimming practice. One afternoon, a nineteen-year-old guy caught them in the act but told them to go ahead with what they were doing. "I was about to say no, but the guy was already at the doorway, so Ricky immediately knelt in front of me to continue. As the man watched, he masturbated, coming all over Ricky's shoulder."

Has any illegal conduct occurred in this story? (Apply Texas law, Appendix 6.) Should any of the conduct be illegal?

PART B.   THE CRIMINALIZATION OF INTERGENERATIONAL SEX

As reflected in our chart of ages of sexual consent, sexual activity between a child and an adult is far more controversial than the same conduct between persons of similar ages. Notwithstanding this normative and legal disapproval, such activity is not uncommon, especially within the family. David Finklehor estimates that one of every five college students he surveyed was a victim of child abuse within the family; other estimates are more conservative, falling in the range of one in ten.[a]

Is the universal ban on adult-child sex justified by the resultant harm of such actions? On the one hand, a significant literature reports the trauma felt, especially by females, from childhood sexual experiences with adults, especially males.[b] On the other hand, a significant literature reports that many adult-child sexual encounters (typically fondling or oral sex and not vaginal or anal intercourse) are not necessarily harmful, especially if the adult is not a family member. Consider the following.

Claudia Konker, Rethinking Child Sexual Abuse: An Anthropological Perspective

62 *American Journal of Orthopsychiatry* 147–50 (1992).*

The American ideal of childhood sexual innocence often presumes that children and adolescents need legal protection from all sexual contact and, in some cases, from sexual information and contraception as well. Concern about sexual contact between adults and children generally pertains to its effects on the subsequent psychological health or moral development of the children.

It has been argued that teenage prostitution, criminal behavior, marital and sexual dysfunction, depression, and suicide can be traced to unresolved or repressed feelings about childhood sexual abuse. However, the evidence is far from conclusive. [Professor Ennew] found no reason to believe that sexual contact between an adult and child is inherently wrong or harmful:

> . . . a child's sexuality is in the process of development concurrent with physiological, psychological and emotional development it will be affected by all kinds of experience and much depends upon the context in which this occurs.[a]

American beliefs about childhood or child sexual abuse appear to be far from universal. When examined from an anthropological perspective, there are cultural differences in what is defined as appropriate adult sexual conduct, sexual maturity, and sexual pleasure. Further, what is considered

a. See David Finklehor, *Sexually Victimized Children* (1979); Glen A. Kercher & Merilyn McShane, "The Prevalence of Child Sexual Victimization in an Adult Sample of Texas Residents," 8 *Child Abuse & Neglect* 495–501 (1984) (11% of female respondents, 3% of male).

b. See *Incest as Child Abuse: Research and Implications* (Brenda J. Vander Mey & Ronald L. Neff eds., 1986); Susan Brownmiller, *Men, Women, and Rape* (1975); Elizabeth Janeway, "Incest: A Rational Look at the Oldest Taboo," *Ms. Magazine*, Nov. 1981, at 61–64, 81, 109.

* Copyright © 1992, American Orthopsychiatric Association. Reprinted by permission.

a. [Eds.] J. Ennew, *The Sexual Exploitation of Children* 59 (1986), building on the work of Finklehor, *e.g., Child Sexual Abuse: New Theory and Research* (1985).

"bad" sexual contact for children in one society may be regarded as "good" for proper child rearing and development in another.

In a variety of contemporary cultures it appears that adults may affectionately sniff, kiss, blow upon, fondle, and praise the genitals of young male and female children. Valued adult-child sexual contact routinely occurs as a part of initiation activities in at least 20 countries throughout the world. There are, for example, the ritualized practices of various indigenous groups in New Guinea. Although there are conscious cultural constraints on father-son incestuous relations, male children are sexually initiated by other adult males. Various adult initiation practices may include sexual insults and threats, fellatio, sodomy, urethral piercing and bloodletting, and older men rubbing semen on young boys. Also at initiation, Arapesh girls may have stinging nettles rubbed on their bodies and thrust up their vulvas. The ethnographic record contains many other such examples of normative adult/child sexual contact.

Many theorists agree that evolution from a state of nature into a state of culture arose from a group need to control sexual competition in order to promote cooperation for survival. The control of the sexual drive is unique among humans, whose mating and reproductive bonds are maintained via marriage and kinship, which are universally recognized as a basic organizing principle among humans.

In human relations, male behavior and female behavior represent unequal, differential system of rights, obligations, roles, and statuses. All are bound in a universal system of sexually derived, cultural categories. Cultural beliefs about children, childhood, marriage, and parenting are also based on unequal relational abstractions. Social categories serve as a symbolic idiom through which the sexual relationship between adults and the rest of society and culture is articulated.

What it means to be sexual or to experience sex—what it means to be a man, a woman, a male or a female child—varies significantly across and within cultural groups. There are sexual boundaries. As with adults, children are universally defined by sex and treated in accordance with their gender and future sexual roles. In the view of Cucchiari,

> At the heart of any gender system are notions of what constitutes appropriate sexual expression. This includes not only the mechanics of sexuality and the gender of one's erotic fancy, but the whole complex of objects, symbols, and fantasies that constitute normative or permissible eroticism.[b]

According to Freud, all human beings have a disposition toward "perversions" (unsocialized sexual thoughts and wishes) because they are a part of the human sexual instinct. It is now generally accepted that normative "socially permissible" gender-linked sexual behavior develops as

---

b. [Eds.] S. Cucchiari, "The Gender Revolution and the Transition from Bisexual Horde to Patrilocal Band: The Origins of Gender Hierarchy," in *Sexual Meanings: The Cultural Construction of Gender and Sexuality* 37–38 (Ortner & Whitehead eds. 1981).

children internalize the cultural norms and inhibitions that they encounter in their family origin.

Sexual arousal begins in infancy. Sexual awareness, self stimulation, and sexual curiosity are hallmarks of every young child's social awakening. Yet, since Freud's early writings, there has been little systematic research regarding normative childhood sexuality. The available data, however, tend to support Freud's theories. It has been found that children as young as three evidence interest in sexual reproduction and awareness of their gender identity. Between ages three and six, masturbation is common; children develop a clear sense of their sexual roles, and show gender-linked versions of adult behavior. By age five, children can relate erotic fantasies and become aroused in response to the stimuli of others.

Prior to the 1950's in America, Mohave Indian children of all ages received graphic and realistic sexual education, and many had complete sexual relations before the age of ten without parental or tribal disapproval. Among other American children, touching the genitals of their siblings and peers or their parents "is not uncommon on an 'incidental' basis even among [a nonclinical population of] 10–year olds." * * *

There is general agreement among anthropologists that the transition of human beings from "animals" to "people" is related to our mental ability to respond to symbolic distinctions as if they were real distinctions. In human populations, incest taboos—explicit and conscious cultural rules about whom to avoid sexually—are flexible and variable. Human incest taboos are not biological mandates, they are analytic categories. These abstract mental concepts are based on some cultural combination of marriage rules and factors of genealogical relatedness rather than on uniform restrictions on sexual behavior among family members.

Human reaction to the idea of sexually prohibited behavior may vary significantly, with responses ranging from a deeply internalized horror, to faint amusement, indifference, or social acceptance. For example, recent European research concluded that most Dutch parents and police react "rather calmly" to evidence of adult-child sexual infractions as they believe that "the majority of [child] sexual offenders are not severe criminals, but people who are unadjusted and very shy in establishing sexual relationships."[c]

Each culture has a right to define appropriate social conduct on its own terms. However, as Americans seek to cope with the problem of child sexual abuse, there is a tendency to deny that children are sexual beings with sexual feelings. Current legal, moral, and social welfare concerns about a national epidemic of child sexual abuse occur in the context of evolutionary literature and the ethnographic record, which indicate that adult-child sexual contact, even painful or eroticized sexual relations with young adolescents, may not lead to social and emotional pathology among the recipients. Child abuse, legal system, and mental health professionals might

---

c.   [Eds.] W.H. Wolters et al., "A Review of Cases of Sexually Exploited Children Re- ported to the Netherlands State Police," 9 *Child Abuse & Neglect* 571–74 (1985).

give greater consideration to the possibility that psychological damage resulting from adult-child sexual interaction may be related not simply to the physical contact per se, but to other family and interpersonal variables or to the stigmatization and punitive responses that can follow the disclosure of such behavior.

Nature demands reproduction and culture provides options. According to Scheper–Hughes and Stein, the recent focus on child sexual abuse as a paramount American social problem cannot be explained solely in terms of the phenomenon of child maltreatment itself. These anthropologists hold that:

> [Child abuse] functions as a generative metaphor, serving to displace other collective unconscious anxieties and contradictions in American society.... In this light, the identified, individualized, and *punished* child abusers function as one of our society's official symptom bearers for what is, in fact, normal pathology. It conceals that extent to which we are an abusive society.[d]

NOTES ON NORMATIVE THEORIES OF INTERGENERATIONAL SEX

Konker's essay normalizes intergenerational intimacy as a phenomenon that has few consequences for the minor, but thousands of people, mostly women, have painfully testified about the suffering that resulted from sexual abuse at the hands of adults. It remains unclear how much Konker's essay describes the situation, or how many persons have been painfully scarred by sex with adults when they were minors.

Nonetheless, as Konker suggests, empirical research does not support the conclusion that all adult-child sexual encounters are harmful to the child. Psychiatrist Larry Constantine defines "healthy sexual encounters with children" as

> ones (1) in which the child is sexually knowledgeable and fully comprehends the activity; (2) to which he or she freely consents on the basis of that comprehension; (3) that take place in a family and/or social setting that affirms such sexual experiences as appropriate, and (4) that (therefore) do not result in symptoms of dysfunction in the child or the family.

Larry L. Constantine, "The Effects of Early Sexual Experiences: A Review and Synthesis of Research," in *Children and Sex: New Findings, New Perspectives* 242 (Larry L. Constantine & Floyd M. Martinson eds., 1981). *Quaere:* Can a 12–year-old fully comprehend sexual activity? Freely consent? At what age could the existence of dysfunction be assumed?

1. *The Role of Gender.* Is the experience of adult-child sex different for girls than for boys? Sociologist Ken Plummer has written:

---

d. [Eds.] "Child Abuse and the Unconscious in American Popular Culture," in *Child Survival* 339, 341 (Scheper-Hughes ed. 1987).

Evidence suggests that boys are encouraged to break away from their mothers earlier than girls, and to establish patterns of behaviour that are more autonomous, assertive, active, aggressive and achievement oriented. This floods over into their construction of sexual meanings, whereby the boy is much more prone to organize sexuality around the satisfaction of his needs and to see himself as the active pursuer of sex. Many adult paedophiles say that boys actively seek out sex partners— perhaps this is partially a training ground for them to establish their prowess. * * * Girls by contrast often learn that their worlds are much more limited and compliant. * * * Often this sense of initial passivity and ultimate terrorism is caught in the adult male's (often the father's) sexual advances towards her. It is compounded by the violation of trust, and the harbouring of the act as a dreadful secret. Only recently have adult "survivors" of this rape been willing to speak out.

Ken Plummer, "Understanding Childhood Sexualities," in *Male Intergenerational Intimacy: Historical, Socio–Psychological, and Legal Perspectives* 241–42 (Theo Sandfort et al. eds., 1991). If Plummer is correct, could the law constitutionally regulate boys and girls differently under the doctrine of *Michael M.*?

2. *Incest.* Konker places all intergenerational sex into the same category. The social science literature treats adult-child sex within the family as substantially more harmful than sex between a child and an unrelated adult. The most frequent perpetrators of incest are fathers, either biological fathers or stepfathers. Most incestuous abuse is directed against girls. Some research indicates that incest is a highly gendered crime, in that reported violence by fathers against sons was almost always physical and not sexual, while 90 per cent of reported abuse toward daughters was sexual. Brenda J. VanderMey & Ronald L. Neff, *Incest as Child Abuse: Research and Applications* 49 (1986). If the law punishes incest more severely than physical abuse of children, is that underprotective of boys?

3. *Pedophiles as a Sexual Orientation Minority?* At the very same time when traditionalists were organizing to oppose gay rights with Anita Bryant's "Save the Children" campaign in Dade County, pedophiles were organizing as a sexual orientation minority within the gay movement. A conference on "Man/Boy Love and the Age of Consent" in December 1978 led to the formation of the North American Man/Boy Love Association (NAMBLA) in 1979. NAMBLA urged the gay rights movement to adhere to its early theme of sexual liberation and embrace its agenda of abolishing age of consent laws. Since then, there have been many intra-community debates over such issues as allowing NAMBLA to march in a gay pride parade. Is the gay community guilty of bias?

PART C. PROCEDURAL ISSUES IN CHILD SEX CASES

Interesting, and sometimes unique, issues of criminal and civil procedure are raised in cases involving child sexuality. The first two issues examined here, the tolling (i.e., delaying) of state statutes of limitations because of repressed memory and the defendant's right to cross-examine the child under the confrontation clause of the Sixth Amendment, are raised most often in incest cases, where a parent or other relative has engaged in sexual relations with a child. The third issue, entrapment, arises in connection with a federally sponsored child pornography ring.

Marlene Lemmerman v. Benjamin Fealk, 449 Mich. 56, 534 N.W.2d 695 (1995). Marlene Lemmerman alleged that she was sexually and physically abused by her father and aunt for approximately ten years, beginning in 1939, when she was three. As a coping mechanism, plaintiff claimed she developed a second personality who took her place during the abusive episodes. It is alleged that this personality dissociation repressed plaintiff's active memory of the abuse. Lemmerman recovered her memory of these episodes and allegedly got her father to confess to them and apologize to her before he died. She sued her father's estate for, *inter alia*, assault and battery and intentional infliction of emotional distress. The trial court dismissed the lawsuit because it was brought long after the period required by the statute of limitations for tort actions.

On appeal, Lemmerman argued that the statute of limitations should be tolled on either of two legal grounds: either because a reasonable victim could not have known about the tort until much later (the discovery rule) or because she was legally insane for that period and could claim the "insanity disability grace period." In an opinion by Justice Boyle, the Michigan Supreme Court rejected both arguments.

The primary purposes behind statutes of limitations are to encourage plaintiffs to pursue claims diligently and to protect defendants from having to defend against stale and fraudulent claims. These rules are not absolute, however. "When a plaintiff would otherwise be denied a reasonable opportunity to bring suit because of the latent nature of the injury or the inability to discover the causal connection between the injury and the defendant's breach of duty owed to the plaintiff, we have applied the discovery rule to prevent unjust results." Michigan has applied the discovery rule to toll the statute of limitations in claims involving injuries from toxic substances like asbestos and DES. Such substances were not known to be toxic when claimants were originally exposed to them or had toxic effects not known for years after exposure. In either event, the court found it only fair to give plaintiffs leeway time to discover their injuries.

"In those instances in which we have applied the common-law discovery rule to extend the statute of limitations, the dispute between parties has been based on evaluation of a factual, tangible consequence of action by the defendant, measured against an objective external standard. The presence of this external standard addresses the concern for reliable fact finding that is the underlying rationale for precluding untimely claims. Unlike the present claims, where liability must be determined solely by reference to one person's version of what happened as against another's, the factfinder's determination of liability is measured against an objective standard of care, such as the standard of care in the relevant profession or industry, at the time of the injury. Thus, despite the passage of time, an objective standard can be recreated for evaluation by the factfinder. In such contexts, confidence in the outcome does not hinge on whether a defendant remembered the particular operation resulting in the plaintiff's claim of malpractice, or whether the individuals who exposed product liability plaintiffs to latent injuries are still available to explain their decisions."

The Michigan Supreme Court believed that repressed memory claims are too "subjective" to fall under the rationale of the previous discovery rule cases. In its view, the risk of stale claims outweighed the injustice of cutting off possibly justified causes of action (in Lemmerman's case the abuser was of course deceased). In so holding, the court followed the large majority of other jurisdictions, *e.g.*, *Tyson v. Tyson*, 727 P.2d 226 (Wash. 1986). Like prior state courts, the Michigan court urged the state legislature to enact appropriate legislation. See, *e.g.*, Wash. Rev. Code § 4.16.340 (overriding *Tyson*). The court cited an emerging academic literature developing policy criteria that legislatures could consider when fashioning a rule.[c]

Pursuant to M.C.L. § 600.5851(1), a person who is entitled to bring a cause of action, but is insane when the claim accrues, is allowed a one-year grace period after the disability is removed to file suit, even though the limitation period for that action has run. Insanity is defined for purposes of the statute to mean "a condition of mental derangement such as to prevent the sufferer from comprehending rights he or she is otherwise bound to know." M.C.L. § 600.5851(2). Again following the lead of most other state courts, the Michigan Supreme Court rejected this as a justification for Lemmerman's delay. State courts have feared that such a broad application of the insanity disability period would "endanger precisely those policy goals advanced by statutes of limitation. The absence of verifiable evidence creates 'circumstances [that] would be unfavorable to a just examination and decision' and would increase the danger of the assertion of fraudulent or speculative 'claims.' "

Quaere: What troubled the courts in *Lemmerman* and related cases was the lack of scientific "objectivity" for efforts to retrieve repressed childhood memories of abuse. What power relations are being protected by this judicial move? Are courts insulated against charges of stodginess and unfairness by their repeated admonition that these issues should be resolved by the legislature, which has better factfinding capacities? If this area of inquiry became more "reliable" (whatever that means), should courts be open to rethinking this line of cases?

Maryland v. Sandra Ann Craig, 497 U.S. 836 (1990). Defendant Sandra Ann Craig, the owner and operator of a preschool program, was

---

c. See, *e.g.*, Ernsdorff & Loftus, "Let Sleeping Memories Lie? Words of Caution about Tolling the Statute of Limitations in Cases of Memory Repression," 84 *J.Crim.L. & Criminology* 129 (1993); Comment, "Adult Survivors of Childhood Sexual Abuse and the Statute of Limitations: The Need for Consis- tent Application of the Delayed Discovery Rule," 20 *Pepperdine L. Rev.* 1359 (1993); Note, "Easing Access to the Courts for Incest Victims: Toward an Equitable Application of the Delayed Discovery Rule," 100 *Yale L.J.* 2189 (1991).

charged with child abuse. At trial under Maryland law, the state invoked a statutory procedure allowing the judge to receive the child's testimony through one-way circuit television; the judge can order this procedure only if he or she finds that the child would be unable to present face-to-face testimony without disabling emotional distress. Defendant's counsel cross-examined the child in the separate room, but defendant herself was in the courtroom.

The confrontation clause of the Sixth Amendment provides that "[i]n all criminal prosecutions, the accused shall enjoy the right * * * to be confronted with the witnesses against him." Notwithstanding the apparent plain meaning of the confrontation clause, a divided (5–4) Supreme Court upheld this procedure. Justice O'Connor's opinion for the Court reasoned that the procedure did not compromise the "central concern" of the confrontation clause, "to ensure the reliability of the evidence against a criminal defendant by subjecting it to rigorous testing in the context of an adversary proceeding before the trier of fact." Although the clause reflects a constitutional presumption in favor of face-to-face "confrontation," that presumption can be sacrificed in the interest of public policy, so long as the core purpose of reliability is otherwise protected.

The Court's precise holding was that "where necessary to protect a child witness from trauma that would be caused by testifying in the physical presence of the defendant, at least where such trauma would impair the child's ability to communicate, the Confrontation Clause does not prohibit use of a procedure that, despite the absence of face-to-face confrontation, ensures the reliability of the evidence by subjecting it to rigorous adversarial testing and thereby preserves the essence of effective confrontation."

In dissent, Justice Scalia presented the following likely scenario: "A father whose young daughter has been given over to the exclusive custody of his estranged wife, or a mother whose young son has been taken into custody by the State's child welfare department, is sentenced to prison for sexual abuse on the basis of testimony by a child the parent has not seen or spoken to for many months; and the guilty verdict is rendered without giving the parent so much as the opportunity to sit in the presence of the child, and to ask, personally or through counsel, 'it is really not true, is it, that I—your father (or mother) whom you see before you—did these terrible things?' "

Quaere: What social script seems to underlie Justice Scalia's scenario? Are his concerns persuasive, or does Justice O'Connor fairly balance the complex factors involved in this case? Could the *Craig* rule be extended to cases involving rape, domestic violence, and forcible sodomy?

Keith Jacobson v. United States

United States Supreme Court, 1992.
503 U.S. 540, 112 S.Ct. 1535, 118 L.Ed.2d 174.

■ JUSTICE WHITE delivered the opinion of the Court.

On September 24, 1987, petitioner Keith Jacobson was indicted for violating a provision of the Child Protection Act of 1984 (Act), Pub.L. 98–

292, 98 Stat. 204, which criminalizes the knowing receipt through the mails of a "visual depiction [that] involves the use of a minor engaging in sexually explicit conduct...." 18 U.S.C. § 2252(a)(2)(A). * * *

In February 1984, petitioner, a 56-year-old veteran-turned-farmer who supported his elderly father in Nebraska, ordered two magazines and a brochure from a California adult bookstore. The magazines, entitled *Bare Boys I* and *Bare Boys II*, contained photographs of nude preteen and teenage boys. The contents of the magazines startled petitioner, who testified that he had expected to receive photographs of "young men 18 years or older." * * * The young men depicted in the magazines were not engaged in sexual activity, and petitioner's receipt of the magazines was legal under both federal and Nebraska law. Within three months, the law with respect to child pornography changed; Congress passed the Act illegalizing the receipt through the mails of sexually explicit depictions of children. In the very month that the new provision became law, postal inspectors found petitioner's name on the mailing list of the California bookstore that had mailed him *Bare Boys I* and *II*. There followed over the next 2 ½ years repeated efforts by two Government agencies, through five fictitious organizations and a bogus pen pal, to explore petitioner's willingness to break the new law by ordering sexually explicit photographs of children through the mail.

[The Post Office's campaign consisted of (1) solicitation of Jacobson to join the "American Hedonist Society" fabricated by the government, which Jacobson joined; (2) further solicitations to respond to a fictitious consumer research company, "Midlands Data Research," to which Jacobson responded, "I am interested in teenage sexuality. Please keep my name confidential" and to "Heartland Institute for a New Tomorrow" (HINT), which proclaimed that it was "an organization founded to protect and promote sexual freedom and freedom of choice" by seeking repeal of sexual activity and age of consent statutes, an effort with which Jacobson concurred; (3) a letter-writing campaign by an undercover investigator who testified as to his own [phony] interest in "kinky" videos, and to whom Jacobson responded, "As far as my likes are concerned, I like good looking young guys (in their late teens and early 20's) doing their thing together." As of 1987, Jacobson had faithfully responded to various made-up surveys but had not placed orders for child pornography with any of the phony government fronts.]

The Postal Service * * * continued its efforts in the Jacobson case, writing to petitioner as the "Far Eastern Trading Company Ltd." The letter began:

"As many of you know, much hysterical nonsense has appeared in the American media concerning 'pornography' and what must be done to stop it from coming across your borders. This brief letter does not allow us to give much comments; however, why is your government spending millions of dollars to exercise international censorship while tons of drugs, which makes yours the world's most crime ridden country, are passed through easily."

The letter went on to say:

"[W]e have devised a method of getting these to you without prying eyes of U.S. Customs seizing your mail.... After consultations with American solicitors, we have been advised that once we have posted our material through your system, it cannot be opened for any inspection without authorization of a judge."

The letter invited petitioner to send for more information. It also asked petitioner to sign an affirmation that he was "not a law enforcement officer or agent of the U.S. Government acting in an undercover capacity for the purpose of entrapping Far Eastern Trading Company, its agents or customers." Petitioner responded. A catalogue was sent, and petitioner ordered *Boys Who Love Boys*, a pornographic magazine depicting young boys engaged in various sexual activities. Petitioner was arrested after a controlled delivery of a photocopy of the magazine.

When petitioner was asked at trial why he placed such an order, he explained that the Government had succeeded in piquing his curiosity:

"Well, the statement was made of all the trouble and the hysteria over pornography and I wanted to see what the material was. It didn't describe the—I didn't know for sure what kind of sexual action they were referring to in the Canadian letter...."

In petitioner's home, the Government found the *Bare Boys* magazines and materials that the Government had sent to him in the course of its protracted investigation, but no other materials that would indicate that petitioner collected or was actively interested in child pornography. * * *

There can be no dispute about the evils of child pornography or the difficulties that laws and law enforcement have encountered in eliminating it. Likewise, there can be no dispute that the Government may use undercover agents to enforce the law. "It is well settled that the fact that officers or employees of the Government merely afford opportunities or facilities for the commission of the offense does not defeat the prosecution. Artifice and stratagem may be employed to catch those engaged in criminal enterprises." *Sorrells v. United States*, 287 U.S. 435, 441 (1932); *Sherman v. United States*, 356 U.S., at 372 (1958); *United States v. Russell*, 411 U.S. 423, 435–436 (1973).

In their zeal to enforce the law, however, Government agents may not originate a criminal design, implant in an innocent person's mind the disposition to commit a criminal act, and then induce commission of the crime so that the Government may prosecute. *Sorrells, supra*, at 442; *Sherman, supra*, at 372. Where the Government has induced an individual to break the law and the defense of entrapment is at issue, as it was in this case, the prosecution must prove beyond reasonable doubt that the defendant was disposed to commit the criminal act prior to first being approached by Government agents. *United States v. Whoie*, 925 F.2d 1481, 1483–1484 ([D.C.Cir.] 1991). * * *

* * * By the time petitioner finally placed his order, he had already been the target of 26 months of repeated mailings and communications from Government agents and fictitious organizations. Therefore, although he had become predisposed to break the law by May 1987, it is our view that the Government did not prove that this predisposition was independent and not the product of the attention that the Government had directed at petitioner since January 1985. * * *

* * * When the Government's quest for convictions leads to the apprehension of an otherwise law-abiding citizen who, if left to his own devices, likely would have never run afoul of the law, the courts should intervene. * * *

■ JUSTICE O'CONNOR, joined by THE CHIEF JUSTICE [REHNQUIST] and JUSTICES KENNEDY and SCALIA, dissenting. * * *

* * * The Court acknowledges that "[p]etitioner's responses to the many communications prior to the ultimate criminal act were . . . indicative of certain personal inclinations, including a predisposition to view photographs of preteen sex. . . ." If true, this should have settled the matter; Mr. Jacobson was predisposed to engage in the illegal conduct. Yet, the Court concludes, "petitioner's responses hardly support an inference that he would commit the crime of receiving child pornography through the mails."

The Court seems to add something new to the burden of proving predisposition. Not only must the Government show that a defendant was predisposed to engage in the illegal conduct, here, receiving photographs of minors engaged in sex, but also that the defendant was predisposed to break the law knowingly in order to do so. The statute violated here, however, does not require proof of specific intent to break the law; it requires only knowing receipt of visual depictions produced by using minors engaged in sexually explicit conduct. See 18 U.S.C. § 2252(a)(2). Under the Court's analysis, however, the Government must prove *more* to show predisposition than it need prove in order to convict.

The Court ignores the judgment of Congress that specific intent is not an element of the crime of receiving sexually explicit photographs of minors. The elements of predisposition should track the elements of the crime. The predisposition requirement is meant to eliminate the entrapment defense for those defendants who would have committed the crime anyway, even absent Government inducement. Because a defendant might very well be convicted of the crime here absent Government inducement even though he did not know his conduct was illegal, a specific intent requirement does little to distinguish between those who would commit the crime without the inducement and those who would not. In sum, although the fact that Mr. Jacobson's purchases of *Bare Boys I* and *Bare Boys II* were legal at the time may have some relevance to the question of predisposition, it is not, as the Court suggests, dispositive. * * *

NOTES ON *JACOBSON* AND THE USE OF STING OPERATIONS TO ENFORCE SEX LAWS

1. *Police Decoys and the Enforcement of Sex Laws.* The "victimless" nature of most morals laws means that there are usually no complainants. Thus, police enforcement depends on the use of undercover agents. Beginning in the nineteenth century, undercover police were sent into the streets to await solicitation by prostitutes, and by the early twentieth century they were cruising bait for male homosexuals. Often, the police would initiate contact with the suspect and would suggest illegal intercourse. It was not unusual in those days for the decoys to go through with the illegal intercourse, as exemplified by the Newport Naval Station decoys described in Chapter 2, Section 2(A)(2).

From the beginning of these decoy operations, middle class opinion was ambivalent about penalizing people for responding to covert police entreaties, and the prohibition of entrapment arose from such anxieties. Judges in New York and some federal courts (see *Sorrells*) enforced anti-entrapment rules before World War II. After the war, the California Supreme Court (under Chief Justice Roger Traynor) and the Warren Court (*Sherman*) gave such rules greater bite. Society's ambivalence about entrapment has grown weaker now that most sting operations are directed against drug dealers and, occasionally, corrupt public officials. Should *Jacobson* be read as an opinion which creates a two-tier law of entrapment, namely, the *Sherman* rule for drug dealers and a new stricter rule for sex crimes?

2. *The Constitutionality of the Statute?* Note the majority's fleeting invocation of *Stanley*. Can the state criminalize the *possession* of child porn? (Both *Jacobson* and *Stanley* reason on the assumption that the state can criminalize the *purchase as well as sale* of pornography, properly defined.)

Further query: The statute applies only if the customer "knowingly receives" through the mails a "visual depiction [that] involves the use of a minor engaging in sexually explicit conduct...." 18 U.S.C. § 2252(a)(2)(A). Does a customer have a valid defense if he can credibly claim that he had no specific knowledge that the performers in the film were under the age of 18 years old? The *Jacobson* dissent thought not, but for the law, see *United States v. X–Citement Video, Inc.*, 513 U.S. 64 (1994).

3. *The Social Construction of Pornography.* Yet another way to read *Jacobson* is a recoil against the government's "creating" prurient interest in the citizenry. Justice White seems to view Keith Jacobson as a man with a generalized taste for viewing nude young men. The government constructs Jacobson as a pedophile in three interlocking steps. First, the government creates a new crime of "possessing" magazines containing pictures of nude boys. Second, the government conducts a massive mail campaign to titillate Jacobson's interest in this freshly criminalized material, through both "political" exhortations for sexual liberty and "commercial" order forms. Third, the government pounces on Jacobson when he finally relents and orders some prohibited material.

This construction of the sex criminal goes one step beyond Foucault. Whereas Foucault focused on society's specification of increasingly detailed vices and sins as its mechanism for creating new classes of despised criminals, Justice White focuses on society's unflagging efforts to entice, even beg, these "new" criminals to act upon their desires. The "child" becomes increasingly an object of sexual speculation not only because of the creation of the new crime, but also because of the game the government conducts to ferret out the new criminals, and finally also because of the publicity surrounding the Supreme Court's dramatic reversal of Jacobson's conviction.

SECTION 3

COMMERCIAL SEX

Prostitution, an offer to engage in sexual activity for a fee, is an old profession. As a practice, its frequency has ebbed and flowed. Generally, prostitution flourishes most strongly in societies with high ratios of men to women; substantial urbanization and luxury time; and noncompanionate marriage.[a] Contemporary America (urban and lots of luxury time) has a great deal more prostitution than colonial America (rural and little luxury time), but probably much less than the towns of the frontier West (high male-to-female ratios and fewer companionate marriages) or than imperial Rome or China (urbanized and uninterested in companionate marriage).

Contemporary American culture offers greater variety of "sex work" than nineteenth century culture did. Sex work is no longer limited to conventional prostitution, where a customer engages in a transaction with a sex worker walking the streets or waiting in a bordello. Nor is it limited to transactions plus ongoing commercial "concubinage" arrangements, typically where a "kept woman" (or a "kept boy") is supported by a man, often a married man. Sex work now includes erotic dancing; performing in pornographic videos and movies; posing for photographs to be used in magazines and postcards; working in sexually provocative nightclubs; receiving calls as a dial-a-porn operator or jerk-off pal; providing "extra" services at adult massage parlors; and serving as a dominatrix (or dominator) for masochistic clients. Sex work is no longer performed exclusively by women selling sex to men. Increasingly, it is performed by transvestites and transsexuals selling sex to men, men selling sex to other men, and occasionally men selling sex to women. Still, there are few women as purchasers, and very few women selling sex to other women. What does this signify?

PART A. ANTI-PROSTITUTION LAWS

Prostitution and the public solicitation of prostitution have been criminal offenses in almost all states during the twentieth century, and most of the nineteenth century as well. Recall Chapter 2, Section 2(A)(1)'s discussion of the fervent anti-prostitution campaigns in most major American cities from the 1880s through the 1910s. During that period, anti-prostitu-

a. See Vern L. Bullough, *The History of Prostitution* (1964); John F. Decker, *Prostitution: Regulation and Control* (1979); Richard A. Posner, *Sex and Reason* 130–33 (1992); Richard Symanski, *The Immoral Landscape: Female Prostitution in Western Societies* (1981).

tion laws were extended to criminalize not just solicitation and sale on the part of the female prostitute, but also to criminalize (1) the running of "bawdy houses" and other places of illegal "assignation"; (2) the "promotion" of prostitution, by pimps and others, as well as compelling or enticing women and especially girls into the trade; and (3) the payment of a fee for sex by the customer. Interestingly, the last item, the expansion of anti-prostitution statutes to target "johns," was the slowest in coming and the most unevenly adopted. Anti-vice societies such as New York City's Committee of Fourteen (1906–30) agitated constantly—and without much success—for jailing customers as well as prostitutes.

At the national level, foreign prostitutes were formally excluded from entry into the United States, starting with the 1891 immigration law. More important, the Comstock Society, a national anti-vice organization, successfully lobbied for a federal anti-prostitution law, the so-called "White Slave Traffic Act," or the Mann Act. (Act of June 25, 1910, 36 Stat. 825, codified at 18 U.S.C. §§ 2421–2424.) That statute made it a federal criminal offense to "transport in interstate or foreign commerce * * * any woman or girl for the purpose of prostitution or debauchery, or for any other immoral purpose, or with the intent and purpose to induce, entice, or compel such woman or girl to become a prostitute or to give herself up to debauchery, or to engage in any other immoral practice." The Supreme Court in *Caminetti v. United States*, 242 U.S. 470 (1917) (excerpted in Chapter 2, Section 2[A][1]), applied the Mann Act to criminalize defendant's interstate transportation of his mistress, on the ground that extramarital "fornication" constituted an "immoral practice" under the statute (recall Problem 2–2). See *Cleveland v. United States*, 329 U.S. 14 (1946) (reaffirming *Caminetti*).

Prostitution laws changed very little from 1910 until 1970. Virtually all the states have revised their criminal codes in the quarter century since then, and most revised their anti-prostitution laws. Nevada repealed its anti-prostitution law, but most other states expanded their laws. Such laws were expanded to include nonvaginal intercourse (sodomy) and often also sexual contact for a fee, same-sex prostitution (including transvestite prostitution), and payment as well as receipt of a fee for sex (in those states that had not already embraced the customer in their statutes). Characteristic of the "new" anti-prostitution laws is the Texas law excerpted in Appendix 6. How do these expansions of the regulatory regime square with the conventional wisdom about the "liberalization" of sex laws since 1970?

Simultaneously with the "rights revolution" in constitutional law (see Preface on Constitutional Rights and Chapter 1), lawyers began challenging the criminalization of prostitution. Claims that such laws violated an individual's right to sexual privacy uniformly failed, on the ground that commercialization of sexual activity was a legitimate subject for state intervention. *United States v. Moses*, 339 A.2d 46 (D.C.App.1975). Also generally unsuccessful were sex discrimination challenges based on the policies of police agencies to enforce laws only against the (women) prostitutes, never against the (male) johns.

The People v. Superior Court of Alameda County

Supreme Court of California, 1977.
19 Cal.3d 338, 138 Cal.Rptr. 66, 562 P.2d 1315.

■ CLARK, JUSTICE. * * *

Defendants allege that the Oakland Police Department engages in the following practices which, defendants contend, manifest a policy of deliberate discrimination against women in enforcing section 647, subdivision (b).[1]

1. More men than women are employed as "decoys" for solicitation of acts of prostitution with the result that more female prostitutes than male customers are arrested for that crime.

2. In "trick" cases, the female prostitute, but not the male customer, is arrested even if his culpability is as great as, or greater than, hers. * * *

[3]. Female prostitutes are quarantined when arrested whereas their male customers are not so restrained.

[1] The record establishes that the Oakland Police Department does employ more men than women as decoys for solicitation of acts of prostitution and that, as a result of this practice, the department does arrest more female prostitutes than male customers for this crime. The critical question is whether the department adopted this practice—employing more men than women as decoys—with intent to discriminate against women. After a thorough evidentiary hearing into this matter of fact, the municipal court found that the practice was not adopted with such intent. It found, instead, that the practice is a consequence of the department's sexually unbiased policy of concentrating its enforcement effort on the "profiteer," rather than the customer of commercial vice. * * *

The subdivision of the Oakland Police Department having special responsibility for the enforcement of section 647, subdivision (b), is the vice control unit; this unit is also responsible for combatting illegal narcotics and gambling. For the purposes of this discussion, each of these criminal subcultures—prostitution, narcotics and gambling—may be thought of as pyramidal in structure. In narcotics, for example, the base of the pyramid is formed by users of illicit narcotics. The remainder of the structure is composed of providers of the contraband. The providers, from the major distributor at the apex of the triangle to the street dealer, are "profiteers" in the parlance of the vice control unit, i.e., they profit financially from the illicit commerce. An analogous structure can be perceived in prostitution. The customer forms the base of the triangle; the prostitute, male or female, constitutes the largest class of profiteers; and at the apex are the pimp, the panderer, and the bar, restaurant, hotel and motel proprietors who knowingly derive profit from the vicious trade.

---

1. Penal Code section 647 provides: "Every person who commits any of the following acts is guilty of disorderly conduct, a misdemeanor: * * * (b) Who solicits or who engages in any act of prostitution. As used in this subdivision, 'prostitution' includes any lewd act between persons for money or other consideration."

In order to most efficiently utilize its limited resources, the vice control unit concentrates on the profiteers in each vice with special emphasis on those at the apex of the illicit commerce. It is a matter of common knowledge of which we may take judicial notice that most law enforcement agencies—federal, state and local—endorse this approach with respect to narcotics. Although both parties to an illicit narcotics transaction break the law, as do both parties to an act of prostitution, no one seriously suggests that it is inappropriate for a law enforcement agency to concentrate on the profiteer and to carry out this policy by, among other things, using its undercover officers as decoys to arrest sellers rather than buyers. The record supports the municipal court's conclusion that the Oakland Police Department adopted a profiteer-oriented approach to prostitution in good faith and not as a smokescreen for deliberate discrimination against women.

In terms of personnel hours expended, 60 percent of the time allotted to prostitution is devoted to investigating pimps, panderers, and bar, restaurant, motel and hotel proprietors. Prostitutes, male and female, receive 30 percent of the unit's attention and customers are the subject of the remaining 10 percent. Because 95 percent of the pimps, etc., are male, as are 10 percent of the prostitutes and all of the customers, it is clear that the vice control unit devotes at least half of its resources to prosecuting men.

It is by no means certain that employing more male than female undercover officers as decoys for solicitation is the most efficient use of this limited resource in fighting prostitution. However, on the available evidence, the Oakland Police Department could in good faith come to this conclusion. Prostitutes, the municipal court found, average five customers per night; the average customer does not patronize prostitutes five times a year. Because of an effective grapevine, arrest of one prostitute by an undercover officer will deter others, at least for a time. Customers, on the other hand, are usually unknown to one another. Therefore, in the absence of widespread publicity, arrest of one customer will not deter others. Finally, using female decoys is twice as "expensive" as using males because an additional officer is required under current practice to ensure the female's safety. * * *

[2]   In trick cases, defendants allege, the Oakland Police Department arrests the woman, but not the man, even if his culpability is as great as, or greater than, hers.

In support of this allegation, defendants introduced evidence of six trick cases in which the woman was arrested for solicitation while the man was set free. In rebuttal, the People introduced evidence of four trick cases in which the man was arrested. Having judged the credibility of the witnesses, resolved any conflicts in their testimony, weighed the evidence and drawn factual conclusions, the municipal court found there was "absolutely no [sexual] discrimination whatsoever." [The court similarly dismissed plaintiffs' claims that prostitutes were placed under custodial arrest, whereas johns were released and told to appear in court.]

[3]   In the ordinary course of events, when weekends and holidays did not intervene, a female prostitute was tested for gonorrhea and syphilis the morning after her arrest. The result of the gonorrhea test was available the following morning. If the test was negative, she was released from quarantine. If the test was positive, she was given penicillin and then released from quarantine. In either case she was encouraged to return voluntarily to a clinic in a few days to obtain the result of the syphilis test. The procedure was the same for a male prostitute except that he was released from quarantine earlier because the test for gonorrhea in the male yields results more quickly. Customers were not quarantined. The quarantine procedure was discontinued on 21 April 1975 because of a significant decline in the gonorrhea infectivity rate among female prostitutes and because voluntary programs had become the preferred alternative among California public health officials.

The municipal court concluded that the previous practice—quarantining prostitutes while not so restraining their customers—was not a manifestation of a policy of deliberate discrimination against women by the Oakland Police Department. This conclusion was based on a finding that female prostitutes were more likely than their male customers to communicate venereal diseases. * * *

However, the most obvious ground for the trial court's conclusion that the quarantine procedure was not a manifestation of a policy of deliberate discrimination against women is, again, that male and female prostitutes were, essentially, treated alike under the program. The distinction was not between male and female, but between prostitute and customer. * * *

■ TOBRINER, ACTING CHIEF JUSTICE, dissenting. * * *

* * * I believe that the majority err in two respects. First, the majority mistakenly equate concentration of law enforcement efforts on sellers of illegal narcotics with the similar focus of enforcement procedures on the "profiteer" in prostitution transactions. In the case of narcotics transactions the Legislature itself has drawn a distinction between buyers and sellers, and has endorsed the policy of concentrating police resources on the apprehension of sellers. (See Health & Saf. Code, §§ 11350 [possession]; 11351 [possession for sale]; and 11352 [sale].)

But the Legislature specifically refused to draw such a distinction between prostitutes and their customers in defining the offense of solicitation. As the Court of Appeal noted in *Leffel v. Municipal Court* (1976) [126 Cal.Rptr. 773]; "The words 'every person ... who solicits ... any act of prostitution' are clear and unambiguous. 'Every' means 'each and all within the range of contemplated possibilities' (*Webster's New Internat. Dict.* [3d ed. 1961] Unabridged, p. 788.) ... Thus the ordinary meaning of the statute is that all persons, customers as well as prostitutes, who solicit an act of prostitution are guilty of disorderly conduct * * *."

Despite the clear legislative mandate to arrest and prosecute customers as well as prostitutes, the Oakland police have adopted an enforcement policy that directly contravenes the judgment of the Legislature. Although the police unquestionably may exercise discretion in the allocation of scarce resources, such discretion is not so unbridled as to permit the police to carve out invidious exceptions to a statutory prohibition, exceptions which the Legislature has specifically declined to enact. * * * [The state] may not enforce a facially fair solicitation statute as if it were directed only at women.

In addition to drawing an inappropriate analogy to the enforcement of drug laws, the majority err in accepting at face value the People's contention that the challenged "profiteer-oriented" enforcement policy bears no relation to traditional sex-based stereotypes but instead simply represents the most efficient means of reducing the incidence of prostitution.

From February 26, 1975, through April 22, 1975, the Oakland police were compelled by order of the Alameda County Superior Court to employ female decoys and to arrest male customers guilty of section 647, subdivision (b) violations. During this brief period of even-handed enforcement, the arrest of male customers, coupled with newspaper publicity surrounding the sex-neutral police procedures, resulted, according to the testimony of the senior vice squad officer, in a "devastating" reduction in observed levels of prostitution related offenses. Similar results have been achieved in other jurisdictions in which enforcement efforts have been directed at male customers as well as female prostitutes.

In light of the demonstrated success of an enforcement policy which encompasses both customers and prostitutes, I cannot accept the suggestion that the police department's resumption of its traditional enforcement policy, directed primarily at women, is explicable by reference to legitimate law enforcement objectives. Although the majority discern no discriminatory intent in the action of the Oakland police, I agree with the American Bar Association's section of Individual Rights and Responsibilities which has characterized such police practices as "one of the most direct forms of discrimination against women in this country today. In accordance with society's double standard of sexual morality, the woman who sells her body is punished criminally and stigmatized socially while her male customer ... is left unscathed." (ABA Section of Individual Rights and Responsibilities, Rep. to House of Delegates, Rep. No. 101B, p. 1 [1974].)

More than a half century ago, a New York court observed: "The men create the market, and the women who supply the demand pay the penalty. It is time this unfair discrimination and injustice should cease." (*People v. Edwards* [N.Y.Co.Ct.1920] 180 N.Y.S. 631, 634–635.) Hopefully, it will not be yet another half century before this discriminatory practice is eliminated. * * *

PROBLEM 11–5

FEDERAL CONSTITUTIONAL QUESTIONS ABOUT SEXUAL SOLICITATION LAWS

Federal equal protection law only targets "intentional" sex (or race) discrimination. Thus, if a law or policy does not deploy an explicit sex- or race-based classification and is challenged because of its "disparate" impact on women or people of color, it will not be subjected to heightened scrutiny unless the challengers can trace the disparate impact to a "discriminatory purpose." *Personnel Administrator v. Feeney*, 442 U.S. 256 (1979) (disparate impact on women), following *Washington v. Davis*, 426 U.S. 229 (1976) (disparate impact on blacks). Consider other constitutional bases for challenging such laws. Construct, for example, a First Amendment challenge to laws that criminalize "sexual solicitation," a public offer to have sex (usually written or applied only to sex for pay). Construct a privacy-based attack on laws that criminalize private sexual intercourse for pay. Apparently, neither challenge would succeed with the current Supreme Court. Why is that?

PART B.   SHOULD PROSTITUTION BE ILLEGAL?

Feminists have debated the politics of prostitution since the nineteenth century. For most of that period, there have been two primary "sides" in the debate: those who have argued that sex work should be decriminalized and treated as legitimate work, and those who have campaigned for the eradication of prostitution, viewing it as intrinsically an experience of subjugation. Gail Pheterson, a leading organizer in the prostitutes' rights movement, summarized this debate as "the tension between feminist struggle against male violence and feminist struggle for female self-determination."[b] Beginning in the 1970s and 1980s, new voices entered the public debate—those of sex workers themselves.[c]

Sex worker organizing began in 1973 with the formation in San Francisco of COYOTE—Call Off Your Old Tired Ethics. Other similar groups started in other large U.S. cities and in Europe. In 1985, the International Committee for Prostitute Rights (ICPR), based in Amsterdam, adopted a World Charter for Prostitutes' Rights at an international conference co-sponsored by the Dutch government. The ICPR demanded in part:

- Decriminalize all aspects of adult prostitution resulting from individual decision.

- Decriminalize prostitution and regulate third parties according to standard business codes.

- Enforce criminal laws against fraud, coercion, violence, child sexual abuse, child labor, rape and racism everywhere and across national boundaries, whether or not in the context of prostitution.

- Guarantee prostitutes all human rights and civil liberties, including the freedom of speech, travel, immigration, work, marriage and

b. Gail Pheterson (ed.), *A Vindication of the Rights of Whores* 19 (1989).

c. See Shannon Bell, *Reading, Writing and Rewriting the Prostitute Body* (1994), for an analysis of this evolution.

motherhood and the right to unemployment insurance, health insurance and housing.

- There should be no law which implies systematic zoning of prostitution. Prostitutes should have the freedom to choose their place of work and residence.

- All women and men should be educated to have periodical health screening for sexually transmitted diseases. Since health checks have historically been used to control and stigmatize prostitutes, and since adult prostitutes are generally even more aware of sexual health care than others, mandatory checks for prostitutes are unacceptable unless they are mandatory for all sexually active people.

The COYOTE–ICPR position is not the only voice of sex workers, however. Arguing that prostitution *is* sexual abuse, a group of former sex workers in Minneapolis formed WHISPER—Women Hurt In Systems of Prostitution Engaged in Revolt—in 1985. WHISPER seeks the abolition, rather than the reform, of prostitution. See Evolina Giobbe, "Confronting the Liberal Lies About Prostitution," in *The Sexual Liberals and the Assault on Feminism* (Dorchen Leidholdt & Janice G. Raymond, eds., 1989).

The feminist and the philosophical debate over the normative validity of how the law treats prostitution has intensified among intellectuals. Consider the following analysis by philosopher Debra Satz.

Debra Satz, Markets in Women's Sexual Labor

106 *Ethics* 63, 67–69, 70–72, 74, 77–79, 82–83 (October 1995).*

There is a widely shared intuition that markets are inappropriate for some kinds of human endeavor: that some things simply should not be bought and sold. * * * [M]any people believe that there is something about sexual and reproductive activities that makes their sale inappropriate. I have called the thesis supported by this intuition the asymmetry thesis. Those who hold the asymmetry thesis believe that markets in reproduction and sex are asymmetric to other labor markets. * * *

The Economic Approach

Economists generally frame their questions about the best way to distribute a good without reference to its intrinsic qualities. They tend to focus on the quantitative features of a good and not its qualities. Economists tend to endorse interference with a market in some good only when the results of that market are inefficient or have adverse effects on welfare.

* * * An economic approach to contracts will justify inalienability rules—rules which forbid individuals from entering into certain transactions—in cases where there are costly externalities to those transactions and in general where such transactions are inefficient. The economic

approach supports the asymmetry thesis when the net social costs of prostitution are greater than the net social costs incurred by the sale of other human capacities.

What are the costs of prostitution? In the first place, the parties to a commercial transaction share possible costs of disease and guilt. Prostitution also has costs to third parties; a man who frequents a prostitute dissipates financial resources which might otherwise be directed to his family; in a society which values intimate marriage infidelity costs a man's wife or companion in terms of mistrust and suffering (and therefore prostitution may sometimes lead to marital instability); and prostitutes often have diseases which can be spread to others. Perhaps the largest third-party costs to prostitution are "moralisms": many people find the practice morally offensive and are pained by its existence. * * *

The economic approach generates a contingent case for the asymmetry thesis, [but] I want to register three objections to this approach to justifying the asymmetry thesis.

First, and most obvious, both markets and contractual exchanges function within a regime of property rights and legal entitlements. The economic approach ignores the background system of distribution within which prostitution occurs. Some background systems, however, are unjust. How do we know whether prostitution itself is part of a morally acceptable system of property rights and entitlements?

Second, this type of approach seems disabled from making sense of distinctions between goods in cases where these distinctions do not seem to reflect mere differences in the net sum of costs and benefits. The sale of certain goods seems to many people simply unthinkable—human life, for example. While it may seem possible to justify prohibitions on slavery by appeal to costs and benefits (and even count moralisms in the sum), the problem is that such justification makes contingent an outcome which reasonable people do not hold contingently. It also makes little sense, phenomenologically, to describe the moral repugnance people feel toward slavery as "just a cost." * * *

Third, some goods seem to have a special status which requires that they be shielded from the market if their social meaning or role is to be preserved. The sale of citizenship rights or friendship does not simply produce costs and benefits: it transforms the nature of the goods sold. In this sense, the market is not a neutral mechanism of exchange: there are some goods whose sale transforms or destroys their initial meaning. * * *

The Essentialist Approach

Economists abstract from the qualities of goods they consider. By contrast essentialists hold that there is something intrinsic to the sphere of sex and intimacy that accounts for the distinction we mark between it and other types of labor. Prostitution is not wrong simply because it causes harm; prostitution constitutes a harm. Essentialists hold that there is some intrinsic property of sex which makes its commodification wrong. * * *

Some feminist critics of prostitution have argued that sexual and reproductive capacities are more crucially tied to the nature of our selves than to our other capacities. The sale of sex is taken to cut deeper into the self, to involve a more total alienation from the self. As Carole Pateman puts it "When a prostitute contracts out use of her body she is thus selling *herself* in a very real sense. Women's selves are involved in prostitution in a different manner from the involvement of the self in other occupations."[a] The realization of women's selfhood requires, on this view, that some of the capacities embodied in their persons, including their sexuality, remain "market-inalienable."

Consider an analogous strategy for accounting for the value of bodily integrity in terms of its relationship to our personhood. It seems right to say that a world in which the boundaries of our bodies were (more or less) secure would be a world in which our sense of self would be fundamentally shaken. Damage to, and violation of, our bodies affects us in a "deeper" way, a more significant way, than damage to our external property. Robbing my body of a kidney is a violation different in kind than robbing my house of a stereo, however expensive. Distributing kidneys from healthy people to sick people through a lottery is a far different act than using a lottery to distribute door prizes.

But this analogy can only be the first step in an argument in favor of treating either our organs or sexual capacities as market-inalienable. Most liberals think that individual sovereignty over mind and body is crucial for the exercise of fundamental liberties. Thus, in the absence of clear harms, most liberals would reject legal bans on voluntary sales or body parts or sexual capacities. Indeed, the usual justification of such bans is harm to self: such sales are presumed to be "desperate exchanges" that the individual herself would reasonably want to foreclose. American law blocks voluntary sales of individual organs and body parts but not sales of blood on the assumption that only the former sales are likely to be so harmful to the individual that given any reasonable alternative, she herself would refrain from such sales.

Whatever the plausibility of such a claim with respect to body parts, it is considerably weaker when applied to sex (or blood). There is no strong evidence that prostitution is, at least in the United States, a desperate exchange. In part this reflects the fact that the relationship people have with their sexual capacities is far more diverse than the relationship they have with their body parts. For some people, sexuality is a realm of ecstatic communion with another, for others it is little more than a sport or distraction. Some people will find consenting to be sexually used by another person enjoyable or adequately compensated by a wage. Even for the same person, sex can be the source of a range of experiences. * * *

* * * Margaret Radin raises a distinct worry about the effects of widespread prostitution on human flourishing.[b] Radin's argument stresses

---

a. [Eds.] Carole Pateman, *The Sexual Contract* (1988).

b. [Eds.] Margaret Radin, "Market Inalienability," 100 *Harv.L.Rev.* 1849 (1987).

that widespread sex markets would promote inferior forms of personhood. * * * For example, if the signs of affection and intimacy were frequently detached from their usual meaning, such signs might well become more ambiguous and easy to manipulate. The marks of an intimate relationship (physical intimacy, terms of endearment, etc.) would no longer signal the existence of intimacy. In that case, by obscuring the nature of sexual relationships, prostitution might undermine our ability to apply the criteria for coercion and informational failure. Individuals might more easily enter into damaging relationships and lead less fulfilling lives as a result.

Radin is committed to a form of perfectionism which rules out the social practice of prostitution as incompatible with the highest forms of human development and flourishing. But why should perfectionists condemn prostitution while tolerating practices such as monotonous assembly line work where human beings are often mere appendages to machines? Monotonous wage labor, moreover, is far more widespread than prostitution. Can a consistent perfectionist give reasons for differentiating sexual markets from other labor markets?

It is difficult to draw a line between our various capacities such that only sexual and reproductive capacities are essential to the flourishing self. * * *

The Egalitarian Approach

While the essentialists rightly call our attention to the different relation we have with our capacities and external things, they overstate the nature of the difference between our sexual capacities and our other capacities with respect to our personhood, flourishing, and dignity. They are also insufficiently attentive to the background conditions in which commercial sex exchanges take place. A third account of prostitution's wrongness stresses its causal relationship to gender inequality. [By gender inequality, Satz means both material inequality, *i.e.*, the lower incomes and assets and higher poverty for women, and status inequality, *i.e.*, negative stereotyping, victimization, and socio-political marginalization.]

* * * I do not think it is plausible to attribute to prostitution a direct causal role in income inequality between men and women. But I believe that it is plausible to maintain that prostitution makes an important and direct contribution to women's inferior social status. Prostitution shapes and is itself shaped by custom and culture, by cultural meanings about the importance of sex, about the nature of women's sexuality and male desire.

If prostitution is wrong it is because of its effects on how men perceive women and on how women perceive themselves. In our society, prostitution represents women as the sexual servants of men. It supports and embodies the widely held belief that men have strong sex drives which must be satisfied—largely through gaining access to some woman's body. * * *

My suggestion is that prostitution depicts an image of gender inequality, by constituting one class of women as inferior. Prostitution is a "theatre" of inequality—it displays for us a practice in which women are subordinated to men. This is especially the case where women are forcibly controlled by their (male) pimps. It follows from my conception of prostitution that it need not have such a negative effect when the prostitute is male. * * *

Suppose that we accept that gender inequality is a legitimate goal of social policy. The question is whether the current legal prohibition on prostitution in the United States promotes gender equality. The answer I think is that it clearly does not. The current legal policies in the United States arguably exacerbate the factors in virtue of which prostitution is wrong.

The current prohibition on prostitution renders the women who engage in the practice vulnerable. First, the participants in the practice seek assistance from pimps in lieu of the contractual and legal remedies which are denied them. Male pimps may protect women prostitutes from their customers and from the police, but the system of pimp-run prostitution has enormous negative effects on the women at the lowest rungs of prostitution. Second, prohibition of prostitution raises the dilemma of the "double bind": If we prevent prostitution without greater redistribution of income, wealth, and opportunities, we deprive poor women of one way—in some circumstances the only way—of improving their condition. Analogously, we do not solve the problem of homelessness by criminalizing it. * * *

NOTES ON WHETHER PROSTITUTION SHOULD BE LEGAL

1. *Prostitution and Rape: The Oddly Different Regulatory and Reformist Responses.* Martha Chamallas, "Consent, Equality, and the Control of Sexual Conduct," 61 *S. Cal. L. Rev.* 777, 826–28 (1988), notes the irony that economically coerced sex is not criminal in rape law, when the defendant would usually be a man, but it is criminal in prostitution law, when the defendant is usually a woman. Therefore, the rationale for regulating prostitution must be its "external effects," but as to those the evidence is very thin. She concludes: "This shaky legal foundation, coupled with the advocacy of decriminalization by important liberal organizations, should encourage reform of the laws banning prostitution. Yet there has been no significant change in prostitution laws in recent years." Feminists have not made anti-prostitution laws a target for reform, perhaps because so many of them see prostitution as usually or even intrinsically coercive to younger women.

2. *More from the Essentialist Critique of Prostitution.* Margaret Jane Radin, "Market Inalienability," 100 *Harv. L. Rev.* 1849 (1987), starts with preserving and engendering personhood as a central goal of law and society. She maintains that "[u]niversal commodification undermines personal identity by conceiving of personal attributes, relationships, and philosophical and moral commitments as monetizable and alienable from the self. A better view of personhood should understand many kinds of particulars— one's politics, work, religion, family, love, sexuality, friendships, altruism, experiences, wisdom, moral commitments, character, and personal attributes—as integral to the self. To understand any of these as monetizable or completely detachable from the person * * * is to do violence to our deepest understanding of what it is to be human." Is Satz' charge of perfectionism a valid one?

Radin further argues: "To conceive of something personal as fungible also assumes that persons cannot freely give of themselves to others. At best they can bestow commodities. At worst—in universal commodification—the gift is conceived of as a bargain. Conceiving of gifts as bargains not only conceives of what is personal as fungible, it also endorses the picture of persons as profit-maximizers. A better view of personhood should conceive of gifts not as disguised sales, but rather as expressions of the interrelationships between the self and others. To relinquish something to someone else by gift is to give of yourself. Such a gift takes place within a personal relationship with the recipient, or else it creates one. Commodification stresses separateness both between ourselves and our things and between ourselves and other people. To postulate personal interrelationship and communion requires us to postulate people who can yield personal things to other people and not have them instantly become fungible. Seen this way, gifts diminish separateness. This is why (to take an obvious example) people say that sex bought and paid for is not the same 'thing' as sex freely shared. Commodified sex leaves the parties as separate individuals and perhaps reinforces their separateness; they only engage in it if each individual considers it worthwhile. Noncommodified sex ideally diminishes separateness; it is conceived of as a union because it is ideally a sharing of selves."

3. *A Middle Way Between Criminalization and Legalization of Prostitution.* Radin also considers Satz' "double bind," that women's sexuality is demeaned or commodified without prostitution, so that criminalizing prostitution ends up depriving women of even the fruits of their labor. Radin argues that even in a world of gender inequality and incomplete commodification of women's sexuality, the ideal of market inalienability remains valuable. Complete commodification risks destroying whatever personhood remains for women in their sexuality.

"The issue thus becomes how to structure an incomplete commodification that takes account of our nonideal world, yet does not foreclose progress to a better world of more equal power (and less susceptibility to the domino effect of market rhetoric). I think we should now decriminalize the sale of sexual services in order to protect poor women from the degradation and danger either of the black market or of other occupations that seem to them less desirable. At the same time, in order to check the domino effect, we should prohibit the capitalist entrepreneurship that would operate to create an organized market in sexual services even though this step would pose enforcement difficulties. It would include, for example, banning brokerage (pimping) and recruitment. It might also include banning advertising. Trying to keep commodification of sexuality out of our discourse by banning advertising does have the double bind effect of failing to legitimate the sales we allow, and hence it may fail to alleviate significantly the social disapproval suffered by those who sell sexual services. It also adds 'information costs' to their 'product,' and thus fails to yield them as great a 'return' as would the full-blown market. But these nonideal effects must be borne if we really accept that extensive permeation of our discourse by commodification-talk would alter sexuality in a way that we are unwilling to countenance.'' Should these suggestions be adopted? How would Satz respond?

PART C. SEXUAL HARASSMENT IN A SEXUALIZED WORKPLACE

Marjorie Lee Thoreson, a*k*a Anneka DiLorenzo v. Penthouse International, Ltd. and Robert C. Guccione

New York Supreme Court, Appellate Division, 1st Department, 1992.
179 A.D.2d 29, 583 N.Y.S.2d 213.

■ RUBIN, JUSTICE.

[Plaintiff, a former Penthouse Magazine "Pet of the Year", was awarded $60,000 compensatory and $4 million punitive damages for alleged sexual discrimination under the New York Human Rights Law (Executive Law, art. 15).] The Trial Justice found that plaintiff was pressured into engaging in sexual activity with defendant Robert Guccione's business associates, specifically an 18–month liaison with a financial advisor and a single contact with an Italian furniture manufacturer. The court further concluded that plaintiff's compliance was an implicit condition of her employment which was terminated when she refused to participate in a promotional tour in Japan because she "was afraid what he was going to ask me to do on the tour" and "who he was going to ask me to sleep with next." The court commented, "[p]laintiff's testimony concerning these matters was contraverted [sic] only by defendant Guccione's blanket denial that the events took place. I do not believe him."

* * * We are not prepared to say that the totality of the circumstances, as perceived by the Trial Justice from the testimony, does not permit the conclusion that plaintiff was the victim of *quid pro quo* sexual harassment. While the dissenter's observation that plaintiff willingly embarked upon a career which exploited her sexuality is entirely accurate, it does not preclude the subsequent withdrawal of consent to exploitation, nor does it necessarily imply consent to sexual encounters of the type complained of. Even a wife, whose marital contract is deemed to imply consent to intimate physical contact, is free to withhold it (*People v. Liberta*, 474 N.E.2d 567 [N.Y.]).

Similarly, it cannot be said that the amount of the compensatory damages awarded by the Trial Justice is without foundation. Plaintiff testified that her experiences resulted in sufficient anguish to cause her to seek counselling from a psychotherapist. The Court of Appeals has emphasized that "medical treatment is not a precondition to recovery. Mental injury may be proved by the complainant's own testimony, corroborated by reference to the circumstances of the alleged misconduct" (*Matter of New York City Tr. Auth. v. State Div. of Human Rights*, 78 N.Y.2d 207, 216). As held in *Batavia Lodge No. 196, Loyal Order of Moose v. New York State Div. of Human Rights*, 35 N.Y.2d 143, 147, "due to the strong anti-discrimination policy spelled out by the Legislature of this State, an aggrieved individual need not produce the quantum and quality of evidence to prove compensatory damages he would have had to produce under an analogous provision, and this is particularly so where, as here, the discriminatory act is intentionally committed." * * *

[The court upheld plaintiff's compensatory damage award. The court overturned the punitive damages award, on the ground that the human rights law does not contemplate the award of such damages.]

[The concurring opinion of JUSTICE KASSAL agreed that the Human Rights Law carried with it no statutory authorization of punitive damages, but suggested that this would otherwise have been an appropriate case for them. The "sexual exploitation and harassment * * * subjected plaintiff to levels of humiliation and degradation that no civilized society should tolerate."]

■ JUSTICE WALLACH, (dissenting in part).

[Justice Wallach emphasized Thoreson's life history of sex work, starting as a topless dancer at age 16, after she had run away from home. She had acting aspirations and filmed several commercials, including one where she walked across a set partly nude. In 1973, she was photographed in semi-nude (topless) shots as Penthouse's "Pet of the Month," and plaintiff willingly entered into a sexual relationship with publisher Robert Guccione. Thoreson, then known under her stage name "Anneka de Lorenzo," was named "Pet of the Year" in 1975, which involved sizeable financial rewards, promotional travel, and acting lessons. Guccione arranged for her to have a minor role in the movie *Caligula*, co-produced by Guccione. Pressed by Guccione, Thoreson participated in the filming of two explicit lovemaking scenes, including a scene of sex between two women, for that movie. After filming a sequel, *Messalina, Messalina*, Thoreson lived apart from Guccione from August 1977 through September 1978.]

According to plaintiff, she returned to New York in September 1978 to live with Guccione and pursue her thespian career, enrolling at the Lee Strasberg Theatre Institute for acting lessons (one of her rewards for being Pet of the Year three years earlier). During this period following her return, in conversations over the course of about a month, Guccione broached the proposition that plaintiff have an affair with his financial adviser from London, in order to induce the latter to move to New York City permanently. The adviser, a longtime associate of Guccione, was married with a family, and made periodic trips to New York on defendants' business, often staying for as long as two weeks. Plaintiff was reluctant to engage in such an affair, but Guccione convinced her that it was important for the future of Penthouse, and furthermore, she supposedly owed him this favor in return for all he had done to enhance her career. At this point it does not appear that plaintiff considered the movie roles Guccione had secured for her to have been detrimental to her career.

Guccione's proposition with regard to the British financial adviser was initiated in early September 1978, and plaintiff ultimately agreed. The affair began in November and blossomed for a year and a half, during which plaintiff was lavishly entertained and showered with expensive gifts and intimate notes whenever the Briton came to town. She admitted that she fell in love with him. Meanwhile, Guccione put plaintiff back on the Penthouse payroll on October 16, 1978, on a $200 a week retainer, which was raised to $300 in December. In May 1980, plaintiff, assertedly feeling guilty about the possibility of breaking up her lover's family, terminated the affair. She evidently did not need Guccione's permission to do so. In fact, simultaneous with the breakup, plaintiff's weekly retainer was raised to $400.

Shortly thereafter, during the summer of 1980, plaintiff claims Guccione asked her to "date and sleep with a furniture manufacturer" from Milan. Guccione had been trying to secure a discount in furnishing a casino he was planning for Atlantic City (a project that never came to fruition), and he allegedly beseeched plaintiff to do this for him, again reminding her that she "owed him." The Italian manufacturer is never identified in the record. Indeed, the only details as to this purported rendezvous take up but a few lines of the 383 pages of plaintiff's direct testimony at trial:

"Q. Did you, in fact, have a meeting with the furniture man?

"A. Yes, I did.

"Q. Did you have relations with him?

"A. Yes, I did.

"Q. How many times?

"A. Once."

Caligula premiered in February 1980 to chilly notices and bombed at the box office. Anxious to exploit an overseas market for the film, Guccione arranged for plaintiff and her partner in the lesbian love scene to do a promotional tour in Japan, where there was apparently some popular interest in the movie and its stars. Having misgivings that her film career was now being tied so closely with her sexually explicit appearance in this movie, plaintiff decided not to go, and was fired.

In 1981, plaintiff commenced this action, alleging nine causes of action ranging from breach of contract in the delivery of promised remuneration, security and career advancement, to coercion, breach of promise, fraud and unjust enrichment, quantum meruit, emotional and vocational harm and degradation, and common law and statutory sexual harassment and discrimination. In a lengthy opinion, the trial court dismissed all causes of action except for unlawful sexual harassment and discrimination under the Human Rights Law (Executive Law § 296 [1] [a], § 297 [9]). Focusing exclusively on the two sexual liaisons supposedly "coerced" by Guccione (the 18–month affair with the British financial adviser, and the one-night stand with the unidentified Italian furniture manufacturer—neither of which, incidentally, is mentioned anywhere in the complaint), the trial court entered judgment for plaintiff in the sum of $4,060,000. Defendants alone have appealed.

It need hardly be emphasized that this case is all about sexuality. Whether it is about sexual discrimination is entirely another matter. Those terms are not synonymous. The gravamen of plaintiff's case before the trial court was that defendants breached their obligations under her talent management contract in failing to develop her career as a serious actress. This and all but one of her many other claims have been dismissed, and she does not cross-appeal from that determination. In this court she stands or falls entirely on her claim arising under the State statute interdicting employment discrimination, of which sexual harassment is a recognized category.

* * * What remains [of plaintiff's case] is a cause of action under the Human Rights Law that alleges that as a "condition of plaintiff's employment," she was required to "perform sexual favors for Guccione and for other employees and customers of Penthouse," including "aberrational sexual practices," all resulting from Guccione's "Svengali-like" hold over her. The denouement of plaintiff's relationship with defendants, according to the complaint, was her firing because of her "refusal to continue to perform such sexual favors during a scheduled trip to Tokyo with Guccione for the promotion of the movie 'Caligula'."

The statute (Executive Law § 296 [1][a]) defines as unlawful discriminatory practice an employer's refusal to hire or employ, his decision to bar or discharge from employment, his offer or denial of compensation or privilege in connection with employment, or his imposition of terms or conditions of employment, on the basis of sex. Admittedly, this plaintiff was *hired* on the basis of her sexuality; she was fired seven years later for her refusal to undertake an assigned promotional tour overseas, a legitimate condition of her management contract. The record is devoid of any of the crucially necessary evidence that her relationship with defendants was ever conditioned on *discriminatory* practices.

There is no evidence in the record before this court that plaintiff ever complained of her personal sexual relationship with Guccione; she admittedly loved him and willingly shared his bed. Nor is there a shred of evidence that she was expected to perform any "sexual favors" for anyone during the promotional tour to Japan. Nor is there any indication that she was ever asked to "perform sexual favors * * * for other employees and customers of Penthouse." The only evidence pointed to by the fact finder consisted of the two sexual liaisons with third parties at Guccione's request. In the first, plaintiff allegedly was to seduce the financial adviser into an adulterous relationship—hardly an "aberrational sexual practice," in light of her experience since the age of 16. Guccione's initial entreaty took place before plaintiff had even returned to the payroll from her year in Florida, so there is no evidence of coercion in the employment sphere; and plaintiff's compensation actually went up 33% after she broke off the 18–

month affair, so she was certainly not penalized for exercising her independence in terminating this relationship. The record is so devoid of details with regard to the second (one-night stand) affair that we may confidently conclude that little or no part of the large damage award rests upon that encounter. All we are left with is plaintiff's testimony that Guccione cajoled her with the assertion that she "owed him these favors." That is the sum and substance of his alleged "Svengali-like" hold over her, over the course of seven years.

The parties are in agreement that inasmuch as the Human Rights Law is so closely associated with title VII of the Civil Rights Act of 1964 (42 U.S.Code ch. 21, § 2000e *et seq.*, and particularly § 2000e–2), cases construing that Federal statute are controlling in interpreting discrimination under our State law. Clearly discernible in the prevailing case law are two varieties of actionable sexual harassment, each of which was urged by plaintiff, both at trial and on this appeal. The first is the *"quid pro quo,"* where continued employment and benefits are conditioned on the giving of sexual favors—stated simply, "sexual blackmail." The second is the offensive or "hostile environment," where the victim is subjected to demeaning acts or intimidation, such as in the form of insults and practical jokes, impinging on her character or ability to perform on the job. But in this class of case the sexual harassment must be so severe or pervasive as to alter the conditions of the victim's employment and to create an abusive working environment.

In order to determine whether the alleged sexual harassment at the work place is sufficiently severe and persistent as to affect seriously the well-being of the employee, the court must examine "the totality of the circumstances." This takes in a variety of subjective and objective factors, not the least of which is the background and experience of the employee, which would impact directly upon her reasonable expectations when entering the work environment. Also important is consideration of that work environment prior to plaintiff's arrival.

As to the environmental aspect, plaintiff is unconvincing with the suggestion that she was unaware of defendants' notoriety as a leading publisher in the sex industry in America. There is certainly no indication that the already sex-oriented atmosphere in this work environment suddenly became more pervasive after plaintiff appeared on the scene.

With regard to this employee's background and experience in sex-oriented activities, the evidence shows that plaintiff spent her formative working years in a sexually candid atmosphere. Before meeting defendants, she was no stranger to topless bars and to the silver screen, even in roles calling for her appearance in a state of undress. This is not to say that a worldly woman should be entitled to any less protection under the statute than one raised in sheltered circumstances. But background and character * * * are relevant, if not crucial, particularly where, as here, compensatory damages, based solely on emotional harm, are the basis of recovery. * * *

* * * One of the necessary elements of any claim of sexual harassment is the "unwelcomeness" of the sexual advances. The key language of the

surviving cause of action of the complaint alleges insistence on performance of sexual favors "for Guccione and for other employees and customers of Penthouse." But plaintiff admitted, in her testimony, that her on-again-off-again affair with Guccione was anything but unwelcome; she admitted falling in love with him, and willingly renewing her sleeping arrangements under his roof upon her returns from Italy and Florida. * * *

In sum, plaintiff actively sought out and pursued a career with a company known to be a veritable beacon of the sex industry. For seven years she rode the roller coaster of pleasure, fame and recognition. If ultimate fortune eluded her, that disappointment and frustration was nonetheless not actionable, as evidenced by the trial court's dismissal of the quantum meruit and breach of contract causes of action. That her acting career did not turn out the way she expected cannot be blamed on unsupported allegations of sexual discrimination, notwithstanding the character and actions of the defendants.

PROBLEM 11–6

SEX DISCRIMINATION IN A SEXUALIZED WORKPLACE: "HOOTERS"

The broad issue raised by *Thoreson* is whether the criteria for "sexual harassment" or "hostile work environment" should be different in a sexualized workplace. Consider a recent, controversial example: "Hooters," a chain of almost 200 restaurants (as of 1996) whose distinction is that the uniforms for its female waitstaff are skimpy shorts and tight white T-shirts. Although Hooters bills itself as a "family" restaurant, its sales pitch is decidedly sexual as well, targeting men with allusions to women's breasts and sexuality. The chain's dress code is consistent with that sales pitch.

In 1993, former waitresses in Minneapolis sued management for creating a work environment that invited male employees and customers to make sexual comments and gestures toward them. How would Satz, Radin, and Chamallas analyze this claim? For an analysis under feminist theory and Title VII, see Jeannie Sclafani Rhee, "Redressing for Success: The Liability of Hooters Restaurant for Customer Harassment of Waitresses," 20 *Harv. Women's L.J.* (1997).

CHAPTER 12

THE BODY: NEW FRONTIERS

SECTION 1   Aids: The Conflation of Sexuality and Disease

SECTION 2   Transgender Issues and the Law

SECTION 3   The Legal Regulation of Cross-Dressing

One way to think of the themes that recur in this book is to consider the body as a metaphor. The body itself has both a public and a private existence, and to some extent one can track the boundaries of those spheres in bodily terms. The body bespeaks public and private health, for example. It signifies the dynamics of what Foucault called "bio-power" and the processes of medicalization. It is the metaphorical terrain for contests between theories of causation that stress the "natural" or physical, and those that turn to social processes of causation and meaning. It is the stage upon which gender is performed, and the screen upon which identities are projected and from which they are broadcast.

In a sense, then, we have been focusing on the body all along. In this chapter, however, we turn consciously to this theme to examine three emerging clusters of issues in the field of sexuality, gender, and the law: AIDS as the issue in our time that most dramatically represents the conflation of sexuality and disease; the challenge posed by persons who are transgendered, *i.e.*, who seek hormonal or surgical change in anatomical sex to harmonize with their self-perceived gender; and the regulation of gender-normative dress, an issue that one might think of as trivial if it were not, apparently, so terrifying. Although we think of these as relatively new issues, each has generated a substantial body of law. Are they properly considered to be civil rights issues? Some advocate incorporating each into a rights or equality paradigm, and others insist that they are better understood as about health (physical or mental) or deviance.

The preceding chapters have been organized along doctrinal and theoretical themes. We structure this final chapter differently, grouping together a variety of legal issues (constitutional, employment, and family law, for example) as they relate to these three particular situations. We hope this chapter will serve as a set of case studies and a useful mechanism for drawing together and reviewing the themes of the book.

AIDS: THE CONFLATION OF SEXUALITY AND DISEASE

From the beginning, AIDS has been an overdetermined phenomenon: a sudden and frightening event with social, medical, cultural, and political causes and effects. The first cases of what is now known as Acquired Immune Deficiency Syndrome (AIDS) were identified in the U.S. in 1981.[a] From its earliest recognition, AIDS has been associated in the U.S. with homosexual men. Other, less formal, press accounts went so far as to refer to the disease as the "gay plague," the "gay cancer," or "gay-related immune deficiency" (GRID).

Domestically, this association between male homosexuality and AIDS remains true today, even though internationally the disease has been and is predominantly transmitted through heterosexual sexual contact. Indeed, heterosexually transmitted HIV infection is growing (both absolutely and relatively) in the U.S. In the Northeast, gay men no longer make up a majority of the new cases of AIDS. (See updated data accessible via the Internet at www.cdc.gov.)

This ongoing association between gay men and AIDS has led to many different outcomes, some logical, some irrational, and some profoundly revealing.

PROBLEM 12–1

THE PROCESS OF CLASSIFICATION

For counting purposes in the early years of the epidemic, the Centers for Disease Control (CDC) classified a bisexual man solely as gay, a gay drug user solely as gay, a gay hemophiliac solely as gay, and a gay blood transfusion recipient as gay. What assumptions about homosexuality and about epidemiology are revealed in this "statistical" decision? Is there a relationship between identity and disease? How might these statistical categories have affected attempts to identify the disease or to develop AIDS education and risk reduction activities? How might they have affected the political efforts and legal rights of gay men? Of others?

The current taxonomy used by CDC is much more complex, recognizing many possible epidemiological categories and combinations of catego-

---

a. "Kaposi's Sarcoma and Pneumocystis Pneumonia among Homosexual Men— New York and California," 30 *Morbidity &* *Mortality Weekly Rep. (MMWR)* 305 (June 3, 1981).

ries. In fact, the current categories do not include gay men at all, but rather "men who have sex with men." Why might the CDC have made this change? Is this category one of identity or solely one of conduct? Is the concept of a gay man relevant to AIDS at all? How could it not be?

The current taxonomy does not include a category of "women who have sex with women." To date, there have been no confirmed cases of transmission of HIV through lesbian sexual contact. There have been reports of HIV-infected lesbians who use drugs (who are classified as drug users) and of HIV-infected women who are bisexual (who are classified as heterosexual). What is implicit in this system of categorization?

PART A. THEORETICAL GROUNDINGS

Linda Singer, Bodies—Pleasures—Powers

1 *differences: A Journal of Feminist Cultural Studies* 45, 49–51, 53–54, 55–56 (1989).*

* * * The age of sexual epidemic demands a new sexual politics and, therefore, a rethinking of the relationship between bodies, pleasures, and powers beyond the call for liberation from repression. That is because, as Michel Foucault pointed out with a certain prescience, the power deployed in the construction and circulation of an epidemic, especially a sexual epidemic, functions primarily as a force of production and proliferation rather than as a movement of repression. The determination that a situation is epidemic is always, according to Foucault, a political determination (*The Birth of the Clinic 15*). Epidemics differ from diseases not in kind but in quantity. Hence the epidemic determination is in part a mathematical one, made by those with access to information and the authority to make and circulate such determinations. An epidemic emerges as a product of a socially authoritative discourse in light of which bodies will be mobilized, resources will be dispensed, and tactics of surveillance and regulation will appear to be justified. Foucault argues that a medicine of epidemic could only exist with supplementation by the police (*The Birth of the Clinic 15*). In this view, the construction of an epidemic situation has a strategic value in determining the configurations of what Foucault calls "bio-power," since the epidemic provides an occasion and a rationale for multiplying points of intervention into the lives of bodies and populations. For this reason, epidemics are always historically specific in a way that diseases are not, since the strategic imperatives motivating particular ways of coping with an epidemic always emerge as tactical responses to local utilities and circumstances. The construction of a sexual epidemic, as Foucault argues, provides an optimum site of intersection between individ-

ual bodies and populations. Hence sexual epidemic provides access to bodies and a series of codes for inscribing them, as well as providing a discourse of justification. When any phenomenon is represented as "epidemic," it has, by definition, reached a threshold that is quantitatively unacceptable. It is the capacity to make and circulate this determination, and to mobilize people in light of it, that constitutes the real political force of the discourse of sexual epidemic (Cindy Patton, *Sex and Germs: The Politics of AIDS* 51–66 [1985]). * * *

The history of the institutional responses to AIDS reveals how the politics of epidemics can work to solidify hegemonies. For years, gay activists and supporters lobbied for better funding for AIDS treatment and research, as the impact of the disease on their community increased. Such efforts went largely unrecognized and received little support from elected officials and health care professionals (Randy Shilts, *And the Band Played On* [1987]). It was not until the disease spread to other segments of the population and taxed health care resources that medical professionals began to speak of an epidemic. This indicates not only how power is operative in constructing epidemics but also how that construction can be used to organize attention, energy, and material support. * * *

The establishment of a connection between epidemic and transgression has allowed for the rapid transmission of the former to phenomena that are outside the sphere of disease. We are thus warned of the "epidemics" of teenage pregnancies, child molestation, abortion, pornography, and divorce. The use of this language marks all of these phenomena as targets for intervention because they have been designated as unacceptable, while at the same time reproducing the power that authorizes and justifies their deployment. According to this discourse, it is existing authority that is to be protected from the plague of transgressions. * * *

The limits of existing political discourse, as well as the urgency of the current situation, call for new forms of sexual political discourse, currency, and struggle. In this context, Foucault's work is especially helpful since his analysis of the proliferative operation of power supplements the limits of the repressive hypothesis, and offers the option of a strategic analysis which allows us to consider not only what is lost but also what is produced by the current organization of the sexual field which is itself a product of previous power deployments. This means that, counter to a logic which opposes erotic urgency and social utility or ghettoizes the sexual as some stable and invariable set of imperatives, Foucault's analysis demonstrates how the construction of each is dependent upon and made in light of the others, often, as in our age, with dire results which place our existence as a species in question. Part of the agenda for a sexual politics of epidemic will have to be a reconsideration of this "Faustian bargain," along with the generation of alternatives capable of mobilizing bodies sufficiently so as not to paralyze them in an economy of deprivation (Simon Watney, *Policing Desire* 123–35 [1987]). * * *

The underlying assumptions about the relationships among bodies, pleasures, and powers which make safe sex possible depend, at least indirectly, on Foucault's analysis and its destabilizing consequences. Safe sex presumes that pleasure and practice can be reorganized in response to overriding utilities and presumes, as well, the capacity of regimentary procedures to construct a body capable of taking pleasure in this new form of discipline. Unless bodies and pleasures are politically determined, they can not be redetermined, even in cases where that is what rational prudence would demand. The success of this strategy will thus depend not only on promulgating these techniques, but also on circulating a discourse that allows individuals to reconsider their bodies in a more liberatory and strategic way. What is new about the new sobriety is that its aesthetic of restraint is not represented in terms of a monastic economy of self-denial or obedience to some authoritative imperative, but is instead presented as a gesture of primary narcissism, a way of caring for and about oneself. Liberation, in this context, is relocated in an economy of intensification of control over one's body and one's position in sexual exchanges. * * *

Part of the change proffered by epidemic conditions is a shift in the relationship between knowledge and desire as they function in erotic situations. Specifically, knowledge of one's partner's physical condition and sexual history now becomes a prime object of concern. The erotic gaze is thus infected to some degree by the medical gaze which must learn to see sickness. The prudential aesthetic which characterizes the new sobriety creates specific forms of desire, like dating agencies, which promise matches with prescreened AIDS–free partners.

Failing such elaborate screening procedures, and given the limits of their reliability, the ideology of safe sex encourages a reorganization of the body away from the erotic priorities with which it has already been inscribed. Specifically, safe sex advocates indulgence in numerous forms of non-genital contact and the reengagement of parts of the body marginalized by an economy of genital primacy. It also entails a reconfiguration of bodies and their pleasures away from an ejaculatory teleology toward a more polymorphous decentered exchange, reviving and concretizing the critique of genital condensation begun over twenty years ago by sexual theorists like Marcuse and Firestone.

The new sobriety constructs a body well designed for the complexities of life in late capitalism, which requires a worker's body and a body of workers that are well-managed in the way a portfolio is well-managed, i.e., a body with flexible and diverse investments which maximize accumulated surplus as negotiable profits. The body constructed in the discourse of the new sobriety is inscribed with a discipline that is supposed to allow for more efficient functioning and control in both sex and work, in part, because this bodily regimen has been represented as an exercise in self-fulfillment and development which should be part of the well-managed enlightened life. * * *

Paula A. Treichler, AIDS, Homophobia and Biomedical Discourse: An Epidemic of Signification

1 *Cultural Studies* 263 (1987).*

An Epidemic of Signification

In multiple, fragmentary, and often contradictory ways we struggle to achieve some sort of understanding of AIDS, a reality that is frightening, widely publicized, and yet finally neither directly nor fully knowable. AIDS is no different in this respect from other linguistic constructions, which, in the commonsense view of language, are thought to transmit preexisting ideas and represent real-world entities and yet, in fact, do neither. For the nature of the relationship between language and reality is highly problematic; and *AIDS* is not merely an invented label, provided to us by science and scientific naming practices, for a clear-cut disease entity caused by a virus. Rather, the very nature of AIDS is constructed through language and in particular through the discourses of medicine and science; this construction is "true" or "real" only in certain specific ways—for example, insofar as it successfully guides research or facilitates clinical control over the illness. The name *AIDS* in part *constructs* the disease and helps make it intelligible. We cannot therefore look "through" language to determine what AIDS "really" is. Rather we must explore the site where such determinations *really* occur and intervene at the point where meaning is created: in language.

Of course, AIDS is a real disease syndrome, damaging and killing real human beings. Because of this, it is tempting—perhaps in some instances imperative—to view science and medicine as providing a discourse about AIDS closer to its "reality" than what we can provide ourselves. Yet the AIDS epidemic—with its genuine potential for global devastation—is simultaneously an epidemic of a transmissible lethal disease and an epidemic of meanings or signification. Both epidemics are equally crucial for us to understand, for, try as we may to treat AIDS as "an infectious disease" and nothing more, meanings continue to multiply wildly and at an extraordinary rate.[3] This epidemic of meanings is readily apparent in the chaotic assemblage of understandings of AIDS that by now exists. The mere enumeration of some of the ways AIDS has been characterized suggests its enormous power to generate meanings:

* Copyright © 1987 Routledge Press. Reprinted by permission.

3. The term *signification*, derived from the linguistic work of Ferdinand de Saussure, calls attention to the way in which language (or any other "signifying system") organizes rather than labels experience (or the world). Linking signifiers (phonetic segments or, more loosely, words) and signifieds (concepts, meanings) in ways that come to seem "natural" to us, language creates the illusion of "transparency," as though we could look through it to "facts" and "realities" that are unproblematic. Many scientists and physicians, even those sensitive to the complexities of AIDS, believe that "the facts" (or "science" or "reason") will resolve contradiction and supplant speculation; they express impatience with social interpretations, which they perceive as superfluous or incorrect. * * * The position of this essay is that signification processes are not the handmaidens of "the facts"; rather, "the facts" themselves arise out of the signifying practices of biomedical discourse.

1.   An irreversible, untreatable, and invariably fatal infectious disease that threatens to wipe out the whole world.

2.   A creation of the media, which has sensationalized a minor health problem for its own profit and pleasure.

3.   A creation of the state to legitimize widespread invasion of people's lives and sexual practices.

4.   A creation of biomedical scientists and the Centers for Disease Control to generate funding for their activities.

5.   A gay plague, probably emanating from San Francisco.

6.   The crucible in which the field of immunology will be tested.

7.   The most extraordinary medical chronicle of our times.

8.   A condemnation to celibacy or death.

9.   An Andromeda strain with the transmission efficiency of the common cold.

10.   An imperialist plot to destroy the Third World.   * * *

AIDS and Homophobia: Constructing the Text of the Gay Male Body

Whatever else it may be, AIDS is a story, or multiple stories, read to a surprising extent from a text that does not exist: the body of the male homosexual. It is a text people so want—need—to read that they have gone so far as to write it themselves. AIDS is a nexus where multiple meanings, stories, and discourses intersect and overlap, reinforce, and subvert one another. Yet clearly this mysterious male homosexual text has figured centrally in generating what I call here an epidemic of signification. Of course "the virus," with mysteries of its own, has been a crucial influence. But we may recall Camus's novel [*The Plague* (1947)]: "The word 'plague' . . . conjured up in the doctor's mind not only what science chose to put into it, but a whole series of fantastic possibilities utterly out of keeping" with the bourgeois town of Oran, where the plague struck. How could a disease so extraordinary as *plague* happen in a place so ordinary and dull? AIDS, initially striking people perceived as alien and exotic by scientists, physicians, journalists, and much of the US population, did not pose such a paradox. The "promiscuous" gay male body—early reports noted that AIDS "victims" reported having had as many as 1,000 sexual partners—made clear that even if AIDS turned out to be a sexually transmitted disease it would not be a commonplace one. * * *

It was widely believed in the gay community that the connection of AIDS to homosexuality delayed and problematized virtually every aspect of the country's response to the crisis. That the response *was* delayed and problematic is the conclusion of various investigators. Attempting to assess the degree to which prejudice, fear, or ignorance of homosexuality may have affected public policy and research efforts, Panem[a] concluded that

a.   [Eds.] Sandra Panem, "AIDS: Public Policy and Biomedical Research," 15 *Hastings Center Report* 24 (Aug. 1985).

homosexuality per se would not have deterred scientists from selecting interesting and rewarding research projects. But "the argument of ignorance appears to have more credibility." She quotes James Curran's 1984 judgment that policy, funding, and communication were all delayed because only people in New York and California had any real sense of crisis or comprehension of the gay male community. "Scientists avoid issues that relate to sex," he said, "and there is not much understanding of homosexuality." This was an understatement: according to Curran, many eminent scientists during this period rejected the possibility that AIDS was an infectious disease because they had no idea how a man could transmit an infectious agent to another man. * * *

It has been argued that the perceived *gayness* of AIDS was ultimately a crucial political factor in obtaining funding. Dennis Altman observes that the principle of providing adequate funding for AIDS research was institutionalized within the federal appropriations process as a result of the 1983 Congressional hearings chaired by Representatives Henry Waxman and Theodore Weiss, members of Congress representing large and visible gay communities.[b]

> Here one sees the effect of the mobilization and organization of gays ...; it is salutary to imagine the tardiness of the response had IV users and Haitians been the only victims of AIDS, had Republicans controlled the House of Representatives as well as the Senate (and hence chaired the relevant oversight and appropriations committees) or, indeed, had AIDS struck ten years earlier, before the existence of an organized gay movement, openly gay professionals who could testify before the relevant committees and openly gay congressional staff. * * *

So long as AIDS was seen as a battle for the body of the gay male—a battle linked to "sociological" factors at that—the biomedical establishment was not tremendously interested in it. The first professionals involved tended to be clinicians in the large urban hospitals where men with AIDS first turned up, epidemiologists * * * and scientists and clinicians who were gay themselves. Although from the beginning some saw the theoretical implications of AIDS, the possibility that AIDS was "merely" some unanticipated side-effect of gay male sexual practices (about which, as I've noted above, there was considerable ignorance) limited its appeal for basic scientists. But with the discovery that the agent associated with AIDS appeared to be a virus—indeed, a *novel retrovirus*—what had seemed predominantly a public health phenomenon (clinical and service-oriented) suddenly could be rewritten in terms of high theory and high science. The performance moved from off-off Broadway to the heart of the theater district and the price of the tickets went way up. Among other things, identifying the viral agent made possible the development of a "definitive test" for its presence; not only did this open new scientific avenues (for example, in enabling researchers to map precise relationships among di-

b. [Eds.] Dennis Altman, *AIDS in the Mind of America* 116–17 (1986).

verse AIDS and AIDS-like clinical manifestations), it also created opportunities for monetary rewards (for example, in revenue from patents on the testing kits). For these reasons, AIDS research became a highly competitive professional field. * * *

Reconstructing the AIDS Text: Rewriting the Body

There is now broad consensus that AIDS—"plague of the millennium," "health disaster of pandemic proportions"—is the greatest public health problem of our era. The epidemic of signification that surrounds AIDS is neither simple nor under control. AIDS exists at a point where many entrenched narratives intersect, each with its own problematic and context in which AIDS acquires meaning. It is extremely difficult to resist the lure, familiarity, and ubiquitousness of these discourses. The AIDS virus enters the cell and integrates with its genetic code, establishing a disinformation campaign at the highest level and ensuring that replication and dissemination will be systemic. We inherit a series of discursive dichotomies; the discourse of AIDS attaches itself to these other systems of difference and plays itself out there:

> self and not-self
>
> the one and the other
>
> homosexual and heterosexual
>
> homosexual and "the general population"
>
> active and passive, guilty and innocent, perpetrator and victim
>
> vice and virtue, us and them, anus and vagina
>
> sins of the parent and innocence of the child
>
> love and death, sex and death, sex and money, death and money
>
> science and not-science, knowledge and ignorance
>
> doctor and patient, expert and patient, doctor and expert
>
> addiction and abstention, contamination and cleanliness
>
> contagion and containment, life and death
>
> injection and reception, instrument and receptacle
>
> normal and abnormal, natural and alien
>
> prostitute and paragon, whore and wife
>
> safe sex and bad sex, safe sex and good sex
>
> First World and Third World, free world and iron curtain
>
> capitalists and communists
>
> certainty and uncertainty
>
> virus and victim, guest and host

As Christine Brooke–Rose demonstrates,[c] one must pay close attention to the way in which these apparently fundamental and natural semantic

---

c. [Eds.]   Christine   Brooke–Rose, "Woman as Semiotic Object," in *The Female* *Body in Western Culture: Contemporary Perspectives* 305–16 (Susan Rubin Suleiman ed. 1986).

oppositions are put to work. What is self and what is not-self? Who wears the white and who the black hat? (Or, in her discussion, perhaps, who wears the pants and who the skirt?) As Bryan Turner observes with regard to sexually transmitted diseases in general, the diseased are seen not as "victims" but as "agents" of biological disaster.[d] If Koch's postulates must be fulfilled to identify a given microbe with a given disease, perhaps it would be helpful, in rewriting the AIDS text, to take "Turner's postulates" into account: (1) disease is a language; (2) the body is a representation; and (3) medicine is a political practice.

There is little doubt that for some people the AIDS crisis lends force to their fear and hatred of gays; AIDS appears, for example, to be a significant factor in the increasing violence against them, and other homophobic acts in the US. But to talk of "homophobia" as though it were a simple and rather easily recognized phenomenon is impossible. When we review the various conceptions of the gay male body produced within scientific research by the signifier *AIDS*, we find a discourse rich in signification as to what AIDS "means." * * *

Repeated hints that the male body is sexually potent and adventurous suggest that homophobia in biomedical discourse might play out as a literal "fear of the same." The text constructed around the gay male body—the epidemic of signification so evident in the conceptions cited above and elsewhere in this essay—is driven in part by the need for constant flight from sites of potential identity and thus the successive construction of new oppositions that will barricade self from not-self. The homophobic meanings associated with AIDS continue to be layered into existing discourse: analysis demonstrates ways in which the AIDS virus is linguistically identified with those it strikes: the penis is "fragile," the urethra is "fragile," the virus is "fragile"; the African woman's body is "exotic," the virus is "exotic." The virus "penetrates" its victims; a carrier of death, it wears an "innocent" disguise. AIDS is "caused" by homosexuals; AIDS is "caused" by a virus. Homosexuality exists on a border between male and female, the virus between life and nonlife. This cross-cannibalization of language is unsurprising. What greater relief than to find a final refuge from the specter of gay sexuality where the language that has obsessively accumulated around the body can attach to its substitute: the virus. This is a signifier that can be embraced forever. * * *

Meanwhile on the home front monogamy is coming back into its own, along with abstention, the safest sex of all. The virus in itself—by whatever name—has come to represent the moment of truth for the sexual revolution: as though God has once again sent his only beloved son to save us from our high-risk behavior. Who would have thought He would take the form of a virus: a viral Terminator ready to die for our sins. * * *

d. [Eds.] Bryan A. Turner, *The Body and Society* 209, 221 (1984).

Harlon L. Dalton, AIDS in Blackface

118 *Daedalus* 205, 205–07, 213–17 (1989).*

My ambition in the pages that follow is to account for why we African–Americans have been reluctant to "own" the AIDS epidemic, to acknowledge the devastating toll it is taking on our communities, and to take responsibility for altering its course. By the end, I hope to convince you that what may appear to the uninitiated to be a crazy, self-defeating refusal to stand up and be counted is in fact sane, sensible, and determinedly self-protective. The black community's impulse to distance itself from the epidemic is less a response to AIDS, the medical phenomenon, than a reaction to the myriad social issues that surround the disease and give it its meaning. More fundamentally, it is the predictable outgrowth of the problematic relationship between the black community and the larger society, a relationship characterized by domination and subordination, mutual fear and mutual disrespect, a sense of otherness and a pervasive neglect that rarely feels benign.

If I am right, then there is a profound need to reorient the public health enterprise so that it can succeed in a multicultural society. Public health officials cannot simply wander uptown (or wherever the local black ghetto is situated), their expertise in one hand, their goodwill in the other, and expect to slay the disease dragon. They must first discern just who this particular public is and how it sees itself in relation to them. How does the black community see its own health needs, and how do they stack up against its other concerns? And, not least, just what has been the black community's prior experience in dealing with government do-gooders?

Answering these questions is not an impossible task, even in the midst of an epidemic. Consider, for example, the extent to which the relationship between the white gay community and the public health establishment changed in the mid–1980s. Much has been written about the latter's failure to intervene in a timely and sensitive way early on, when the AIDS epidemic might have been successfully contained. I do not quarrel with the explanations usually proffered for this failure—the health establishment's inability to identify with or care about the gay men who were viewed as the disease's principal targets, bureaucratic ineptitude and infighting, and an administration in Washington mindlessly committed to reducing social spending no matter what. I do, however, want to highlight an additional factor, the fact that initially most public health officials approached AIDS as solely a biomedical phenomenon and exhibited little comprehension of the many ways in which culture, politics, and disease intersect. Thus they failed to realize how much freight would attach to their well-intentioned attempts to safeguard the public's health and did not anticipate that both the gay community and the larger society would react in ways reflective of the social distance between the two.

The moment of truth arrived shortly after the Food and Drug Administration approved the first HIV antibody test for the screening of the nation's blood supply. Many health officials advocated that the test be used diagnostically as well, to determine whether persons in so-called high-risk groups had been exposed to the virus. The officials were surprised to discover that most gay organizations and AIDS support organizations took the opposite view and strongly recommended that gay men, including those who had engaged in high-risk activity, *not* take the test.

At first, the public health establishment saw this resistance as misguided, irresponsible, and self-destructive. In fairly short order, however (thanks largely to the efforts of "bridge" people who served, in effect, as bicultural interpreters), key officials began to see past the bare fact that their recommendations were being opposed, to the concerns underlying the gay community's opposition: that the test was not sufficiently accurate to be used for diagnostic purposes; that testing would produce needless mental anguish for many; that persons seeking the test might thereby open themselves to criminal liability by admitting to having engaged in sodomy or the use of illicit drugs; that testing would facilitate the quarantining of persons who tested positive; that absent strict confidentiality, testing would lead (at least for seropositives) to the loss of insurance, employment, and housing, and to social isolation and vilification as well. These concerns, the officials realized, were as much the lived reality of AIDS as helper-T cells and transmission routes.

It became apparent that to reach the gay community, public health officials had to learn to view the epidemic from the perspective of the gay community. Consequently, today even the most control-minded health officials take care to involve the gay community in decision making and emphasize the need for a high degree of test accuracy, for strict confidentiality, and for enhanced laws against discrimination. The moral of this story is plain. The public health establishment *can* take account of community differences if it has to. It *can* take account of the sociopolitical contexts in which it operates. It *can*, if pressed, recognize that its targets are, in an important sense, its teachers. * * *

[O]ne reason the black community has been slow in responding to AIDS is that many of us do not want to be associated with what is widely perceived as a gay disease. More than once I have heard of black parents readily volunteering, so as to forestall even more embarrassing speculation, that their HIV-infected children are addicts. Homophobia is not, of course, unique to the black community, but it takes on a particular character within the context of African–American history and culture.

First, let me distinguish between homophobia that is directed at whites and homophobia that is internal to the black community. As we seek to understand the former, it will be difficult, I suspect, to disentangle it from an animus based on race. That is to say, gay whites who encounter hostility from blacks may be the target of antigay sentiment, antiwhite sentiment, or both. Even the originators of the hostility may not know where one motivation ends and the other begins. Moreover, racial prejudice and homophobia may well activate or reinforce each other. It stands to reason that someone who is viewed as an "other" along one dimension will more easily be viewed as an "other" along a second and third. Internal homophobia does not suffer this complication, but it scarcely lacks complexity. Like most aspects of the African–American subculture, its roots are dual. The black community has doubtless been influenced by the larger society's attitudes toward sexual minorities even as its historical experience has produced a distinctive set of attitudes and practices. I would like to focus briefly on the latter.

In the manner in which homosexuality is spoken about, the black community differs markedly from the larger society. In our denunciation of homosexuality and of persons thought to be gay, blacks (including closeted gays) tend to be much more open and pointed than whites. Our verbal attacks seem tinged with cruelty and are usually delivered with an offhandedness that many white observers find unnerving. At the same time, there is, within the black community, an enormous gulf between talk and action, or for that matter, between talk and belief. What we say and what we think, or do, need not be congruent. In fact, a cruel tongue is often used to hide a tender heart. Bell Hooks tells of a "straight black male in a California community who acknowledged that though he often made jokes poking fun at gays or expressing contempt as a means of bonding in group settings, in his private life he was a central support person for a gay sister." "Such contradictory behavior," she adds, "seems pervasive in black communities."

On reflection, none of this is surprising. We, as a people, are given to verbal excesses, to hyperbole, to putdowns meant for sport rather than wounding. People of my generation and older grew up "playing the dozens," verbal horseplay that involved the most scandalous imaginable accusations about the families and acquaintances of the other participants. So long as you stayed within certain well-understood (albeit unwritten and unspoken) bounds of propriety, you could say vicious things without anybody thinking you really meant it. A similar dynamic attends verbal gay bashing. There is a common understanding of which nasty things are acceptable to say, and as long as one stays within the canon, one can claim an absence of malice.

There is, however, a key difference. In the dozens, the participants stand on equal footing; typically they alternate between the role of the slanderer and the role of the slanderized. In addition, there is no necessary relationship between the calumnies heaped on an individual and those heaped on her or his real-life position. In fact, one of the unwritten rules is that you tread lightly around areas of true vulnerability.

In practice, black communities across the country have knowingly and sometimes fully embraced their gay members. But the price has been high. In exchange for inclusion, gay men and lesbians have agreed to remain under wraps, to downplay, if not hide, their sexual orientation, to provide their families and friends with "deniability." So long as they do not put the community to the test, they are welcome. It is all right if everybody knows as long as nobody tells. That is more easily accomplished than you might imagine. For the most part, even the pillars of the black community are content to let its gay members be, and to live alongside them in mutual complicity. This is true even within the church. Indeed, it is a well-kept secret, or more precisely, it is well-denied knowledge, that gays are disproportionately represented within the ministry, including (and perhaps especially) the ministry of many of the more fundamental denominations.

This complex relationship works most successfully when gay men and lesbians are willing to carry on appearances, to live, in effect, straight lives. Many gay black men seek the ultimate cover and become ostentatiously involved with women. One noteworthy consequence of this phenomenon is that their female sexual partners may unknowingly be exposed to an increased risk of HIV infection.

What accounts for the way in which the black community has approached homosexuality—boisterous homophobic talk, tacit acceptance in practice, and a broad-based conspiracy of silence? I have a theory (and it is no more than that) that within the black community, internal homophobia has less to do with regulating sexual desire and affectional ties than with policing relations between the sexes. In this view, gay black men and lesbians are made to suffer because they are out of sync with a powerful cultural impulse to weaken black women and strengthen black men. They are, in a sense, caught in a sociocultural cross fire over which they have little control.

Among the many horrors of slavery is the havoc it wreaked on relations between black men and women. Slave couples were not allowed to form stable bonds, and those relationships that did develop were burdened in ways painful to recount. Men were torn away from their families, women were subjected to the slavemasters' bidding, and both were, on occasion, bred like animals. As a result, men were unable to provide for, much less protect, "their" women and women were unable to rely on their men. This emasculation of black men (when measured against traditional gender role expectations and concepts of male prerogative) bode ill for male-female relations in the postslavery era in the absence of a fundamental redefinition of gender. The near century of Jim Crow that followed—legalized discrimination backed up and surrounded by powerfully disintegrative social forces—simply added to the strain. Black people in general, black men in particular, were "kept in their place," routinely excluded from places that would bring them honor and respect or that would allow them to serve as family providers. While women could usually find employment as domestics, black men frequently drifted and did not, could not, come close to pulling their own weight.

For me, this reality is best captured by something that happened on the old Art Linkletter show during the 1950s, I believe. The show included a segment entitled "Kids Say the Darnedest Things," in which Linkletter interviewed children about whatever was on their minds. Somehow the word spread that on this particular day Linkletter would have a black kid on the show, a rare occurrence. Like hundreds of thousands of other black folk, I eagerly tuned in and watched with fascination and horror as this little kid, who looked a lot like me, answered the question "What do you want to be when you grow up?'' "I want to be a white man," he answered quickly and confidently. Linkletter gulped, paused, and then plunged ahead. "Why?" he asked. "Because," answered the kid, "my momma says that black men aren't worth shit!"

The network instantly broke for a commercial, and when the show returned, the little black kid had been whisked off the set, but no commercial break could stanch the psychic wound opened up in an entire community in that moment of childlike innocence. Black people talked about that show for months, amidst much handwringing and headshaking. Yet, despite the countless retellings and postmortems, the message implicit in the little boy's answer—that relations between black men and women had reached a parlous state—was never disrupted.

What does this have to do with homophobia? My suspicion is that openly gay men and lesbians evoke hostility in part because they have come to symbolize the strong female and the weak male that slavery and Jim Crow produced. More than even the mother quoted on the Linkletter show, lesbians are seen as standing for the proposition that "black men aren't worth shit." More than even the "no account" men who figure prominently in the repertoire of female blues singers, gay men symbolize the abandonment of black women. Thus, in the black community homosexuality carries more baggage than in the larger society. To address it successfully, we may have to take on such larger issues as the social construction of gender and the nature of male-female relations. * * *

NOTES ON SOCIAL MEANINGS OF AIDS

1. *A Foucauldian Approach.* In what ways has AIDS "multiplied the points of intervention" by the law "into the lives of bodies and populations"? Would you agree with Singer that these legal interventions "function[] primarily as a force of production and proliferation rather than as a movement of repression"? Why or why not? Which examples from case law and statutory law would support or undercut that statement?

2. *The Role of Law.* What are the implications for law of the "management" of the body that Singer describes? Does it signal a shift toward more neutral contractual terms of sexual discourse? If so, does the law of AIDS as it has actually evolved support her analysis? Consider that question as you read the remainder of this section (and recall the employment-related AIDS law of Chapter 10, Section 3).

Has the "epidemic of signification" that Treichler describes infected judicial texts? In reading the cases that follow, analyze each closely for its use of language, metaphor, and semantic oppositions. Think about how Singer and Treichler (and Foucault) would decide whether or when to use the word "epidemic." What would be the strategy behind using or not using that word? Assume that you are litigating an AIDS case, or clerking for a judge who will write an opinion in one. The tendency of most attorneys would probably be to rely heavily on the language of the scientific evidence presented in the case, but that is one of the sources of misinterpretations that Treichler and Singer challenge. How would you draft pleadings or other documents in such a way as to avoid the pitfalls they identify?

3. *Sexuality, Race, and Medicine.* Dalton argues that African–American gay men (and lesbians) are faced with a harsh choice between coming out and loyalty to their racial identity. How would this affect the design of government programs for services or safe sex education? Eliminating this identity conflict is one reason behind the widespread use of the term "men who have sex with men," rather than "gay men," in much of the recent AIDS literature.

Historian Allan Brandt describes an instance in which doctors literally invented a disease—*venereal insontium*, or venereal disease of the inno- cent—in order to avoid the discomfort of associating middle class women with syphilis. Allan M. Brandt, "A Historical Perspective," in *AIDS Law Today: A New Guide for the Public* 47 (1993). Compare this to the sorry tale of the Tuskegee experiment, in which African–American men infected with syphilis were denied treatment with penicillin in order to study the natural history of the disease. James H. Jones, *Bad Blood: The Tuskegee Syphilis Experiment* (1981). In both instances, a disease was so thoroughly racialized and sexualized that its very diagnosis depended on stereotype.

NOTE ON AIDS AND METAPHOR

"Rereading *Illness as Metaphor* [1978], I thought * * * " is the way Susan Sontag begins her important essay, *AIDS and Its Metaphors* (1988). Even more than most other illnesses, AIDS has been rich with metaphors, by which she means "giving the thing a name that belongs to something else."

Unlike other diseases, even cancer these days, AIDS is a disease "caused" by a "lifestyle" choice, and the shame of HIV infection is the shame impelled by sex negativity. Sontag says: "The unsafe behavior that produces AIDS is judged to be more than just weakness. It is indulgence, delinquency—addictions to chemicals that are illegal and to sex regarded as deviant," for "AIDS is understood as a disease not only of sexual excess but of perversity." Ralph Bolton, "AIDS and Promiscuity: Muddles in the Models of HIV Prevention," 14 *Medical Anthropology* 145 (1992), remarks on how obsessively the medical literature has associated HIV infection with number of sex partners, often explicitly using the term "promiscuity," even though the greater correlation is with unsafe sex practices and not number of partners.

Philosopher Georges Bataille earlier argued the connection between sex and death—sex as both a way to prolong life through the generation of new life in an infinite chain of being, and as a risk of life through the diseases and other costs of sex. *E.g., The Tears of Eros* (1988). AIDS connects sex and death in a more intimate way: one of the greatest pleasures of life becomes one of the greatest risks of death, especially among the young.

Consider some similarities between the metaphors associated with AIDS and those associated with homosexuality. As to the latter, Kenji Yoshino, "Suspect Symbols: The Literary Argument for Heightened Scrutiny for Gays," 96 *Colum.L.Rev.* 1753 (1996), points to the closet, the promiscuous body, and the pink triangle. People with AIDS (PWAs) are often closeted, for the reasons Sontag and Dalton identify. Yoshino reminds us that in the 1950s the homosexual closet was also considered a threatening "Trojan Horse," much the way PWAs are often seen today. Treichler recounts people's association of AIDS with the promiscuous (gay male) body. Finally, just as the pink triangle was used to mark threatening "perverts" in Nazi concentration camps, so William F. Buckley, Jr. once suggested tattooing the bodies of PWAs.

PART B.   PUBLIC HEALTH LAW

People v. Henrietta Adams and Peggy Madison

Supreme Court of Illinois, 1992.
149 Ill.2d 331, 173 Ill.Dec. 600, 597 N.E.2d 574.

■ MILLER, CHIEF JUSTICE.

In separate proceedings in the circuit court of Cook County, the defendants, Henrietta Adams and Peggy Madison, were convicted of prostitution. Pursuant to section 5–5–3(g) of the Unified Code of Corrections, the defendants were ordered to undergo medical testing to determine whether they were carriers of the human immunodeficiency virus (HIV), the cause of acquired immunodeficiency syndrome (AIDS). (Ill.Rev.Stat.1989, ch. 38, par. 1005–5–3(g).) Rather than submit to the court-ordered tests, the defendants filed motions challenging the constitutionality of section 5–5–3(g). Following a hearing, the trial judge determined that the testing procedure represented an illegal search and seizure and denied the defendants equal protection. Because the statute was declared unconstitutional, the State's appeal from that ruling lies directly to this court. For the reasons that follow, we reverse the judgment of the circuit court and remand these consolidated actions for further proceedings.

Section 5–5–3(g) of the Unified Code of Corrections provides as follows:

"Whenever a defendant is convicted of an offense under Sections 11–14 [prostitution], 11–15 [soliciting for a prostitute], 11–15.1 [soliciting for a juvenile prostitute], 11–16 [pandering], 11–17 [keeping a place of prostitution], 11–18 [patronizing a prostitute], 11–19 [pimping], 11–19.1 [juvenile pimping], 11–19.2 [exploitation of a child], 12–13 [criminal sexual assault], 12–14 [aggravated criminal sexual assault], 12–15 [criminal sexual abuse] or 12–16 [aggravated criminal sexual abuse] of the Criminal Code of 1961, the defendant shall undergo medical testing to determine whether the defendant has any sexually transmissible disease, including a test for infection with human immunodeficiency virus (HIV) or any other identified causative agent of acquired immunodeficiency syndrome (AIDS). Any such medical test shall be performed only by appropriately licensed medical practitioners and may include an analysis of any bodily fluids as well as an examination of the defendant's person. Except as otherwise provided by law, the results of such test shall be kept strictly confidential by all medical personnel involved in the testing and must be personally delivered in a sealed envelope to the judge of the court in which the conviction was entered for the judge's inspection in camera. Acting in accordance with the best interests of the victim and the public, the judge shall have the discretion to determine to whom, if anyone, the results of the testing may be revealed. The court shall order that the cost of any such test shall be paid by the county and may be taxed as costs against the convicted defendant." Ill. Rev. Stat. 1989, ch. 38, par. 1005-5-3(g).

[In this case, both defendants were convicted of prostitution.] * * * The defendants refused to submit to the HIV tests [which were imposed after conviction]. The parties submitted extensive memoranda on the issues, and an evidentiary hearing was held. At the hearing, the defendants presented the testimony of three expert witnesses, who questioned the utility of the testing requirement for persons convicted of prostitution. The witnesses were Dr. Renslow Sherer, chair of the Governor's Task Force on AIDS; Colleen Ahler, director of the AIDS program at Genesis House, a social services agency that works with women in prostitution; and Dr. John Raba, medical director at Cermak Health Services, which provides medical services to the Cook County Department of Corrections. These witnesses believed that mandatory HIV testing of sex offenders is ineffective and may even be counterproductive to the effort to stop the spread of AIDS, particularly among women in prostitution.

AIDS is a fatal illness for which there is no known cure. AIDS can be spread through the exchange of bodily fluids, as in sexual intercourse, in the sharing of needles by intravenous drug users, during pregnancy or childbirth, and through the donation of blood, organs, or semen. Section 5-5-3(g) does not specify a particular test to be used to determine whether the individual has HIV. The testimony introduced below, as well as the medical literature and the case law, however, refer to two tests that are used in combination to determine whether a person has been exposed to the causative virus. One is the enzyme-linked immunosorbent assay (ELISA). If the result of that test is positive, a second procedure, the Western Blot test, is then performed to confirm the initial result. The tests do not detect the virus itself but rather the presence of antibodies created by the body in response to the virus. The tests are considered to be reasonably accurate. Because there is a latency period of variable length, during which an individual does not immediately produce antibodies in response to exposure to HIV, a negative test does not necessarily mean that the person has not been exposed to the virus.

We note at the outset the scope of the issues before us. Although section 5-5-3(g) of the Unified Code of Corrections requires testing "to determine whether the defendant has any sexually transmissible disease," we are concerned here with only that portion of the statute specifically requiring testing for HIV. In addition, although conviction for any of a number of different offenses will trigger the testing requirement of section 5–5–3(g), the present defendants were charged with and found guilty of only one of the enumerated offenses, prostitution. Thus, the present cases involve only that portion of the statute requiring that persons convicted of prostitution undergo testing for HIV, and we limit our discussion accordingly. * * *

The challenged statute concerns matters lying at the heart of the State's police power. There are few, if any, interests more essential to a stable society than the health and safety of its members. Toward that end, the State has a compelling interest in protecting and promoting public health and, here, in adopting measures reasonably designed to prevent the spread of AIDS. "Upon the principle of self-defense, of paramount necessity, a community has the right to protect itself against an epidemic of disease which threatens the safety of its members." (*Jacobson v. Massachusetts* (1905), 197 U.S. 11, 27.) As we have noted, States enjoy broad discretion in devising means to protect and promote public health. Although these concerns do not immunize the challenged provision from constitutional scrutiny, they do indicate the broad sweep of the State's power in this area, and the compelling nature of that governmental interest.

The HIV testing statute is designed to serve a public health goal, rather than the ordinary needs of law enforcement. The manifest purpose of section 5–5–3(g) is to help control the spread of AIDS by identifying persons infected with the causative virus. The General Assembly has targeted at-risk groups, concentrating on sex offenders and, in companion legislation, illicit users of hypodermic syringes (see Ill.Rev.Stat.1989, ch. 38, par. 1005–5–3(h)). The results of the test are to remain confidential, subject to the discretion of the trial judge, who, "[a]cting in accordance with the best interests of the victim and the public," may authorize disclosure of the test results to others. (Ill.Rev.Stat.1989, ch. 38, par. 1005–5–3(g).) Once persons who are carriers of the virus have been identified, the victims of their conduct and the offenders themselves can receive necessary treatment, and, moreover, can adjust their conduct so that other members of the public do not also become exposed to HIV. In this way, the spread of AIDS through the community at large can be slowed, if not halted. We believe that the HIV testing requirement advances a special governmental need. See *Love v. Superior Court* (1990), 276 Cal. Rptr. 660, 664 (upholding California law requiring HIV testing of persons convicted of prostitution).

Having identified the important governmental purpose served by the statute, we must next balance that interest against the intrusion on personal freedom effected by the statute. The requirement of a warrant protects individual privacy "by assuring citizens subject to a search or seizure that such intrusions are not the random or arbitrary acts of government agents." [*Skinner v. Railway Executives' Ass'n,* 489 U.S. 602,

621–22 (1989).] In addition, the warrant requirement interposes between government and citizen the neutral judgment of a magistrate, charged with the independent assessment of the facts and circumstances assertedly justifying the particular intrusion. We do not believe that these purposes would be served by imposing here a separate requirement that the State secure a warrant before subjecting an individual to a test pursuant to the statute.

As the proceedings in these consolidated matters illustrate, an order directing a defendant to submit to testing under section 5–5–3(g) will customarily be entered by the presiding judge at the sentencing hearing, or at some other point following the defendant's conviction. The statute specifies the precise circumstances in which a test for HIV may be compelled. The testing requirement is automatically triggered upon a defendant's conviction for one of the offenses enumerated in the provision; in that case, the defendant must undergo testing for HIV, as well as for other sexually transmissible diseases. Beyond these limited circumstances, however, the statute contains no authority by which a judge may compel an individual to undergo a test for HIV. Thus, section 5–5–3(g) affords the court no discretion in determining whom to test. Under this statutory regimen, there would be nothing for the presiding judge, or other magistrate, to weigh if issuance of a warrant were to be required. The only discretionary function allowed by the statute lies in determining to whom the results of the test may be revealed. As the statute makes clear, however, that determination must be made by the court.

Even if a warrant is not required, probable cause, or some individualized suspicion, generally will be necessary to sustain the validity of a search or seizure challenged on fourth amendment grounds. But when the intrusion is minimal and an important governmental interest would be jeopardized by requiring individualized suspicion, a search may be deemed reasonable even though such suspicion is lacking.

When the challenged intrusion is intended to prevent the spread of a dangerous condition providing few articulable grounds for a search, other than categories of risk, and thus advances an important function that is related to administrative concerns of public health and safety, rather than to the concerns of criminal investigation, individualized suspicion may become less important. The aim of section 5–5–3(g) is not to ferret out evidence of misconduct but rather to provide reliable information concerning the HIV status of sex offenders, and possibly their victims. In view of this important public health mission, we consider that the State's interest in conducting suspicionless testing outweighs the individual's interest in requiring some degree of individualized suspicion.

The actual physical intrusion required by the HIV testing statute is relatively slight and poses no threat to the health or safety of the individual tested. The procedure involves the drawing of a sample of blood, and the test may be performed "only by appropriately licensed medical practitioners" (Ill.Rev.Stat.1989, ch. 38, par. 1005–5–3(g)). Such tests are performed safely and routinely many times during a person's life.

The test challenged in this case is a minor, routine laboratory procedure, and it poses no threat to the health or safety of the individual tested. As an additional circumstance reducing the impact of the intrusion on individual privacy interests, we note that the test results may be disclosed only to the person tested, and to others, as directed by the trial judge, and otherwise must remain confidential. Thus, we conclude that the intrusion mandated by section 5–5–3(g) is comparatively slight.

We recognize that the information obtained as the result of a positive HIV test may have a devastating impact on individuals who would prefer not to know their true status. In addition, persons with AIDS are often stigmatized and subject to social disapproval. These matters are indications of the seriousness of the AIDS problem. We do not agree with the defendants, however, that these consequences make the test more objectionable for fourth amendment purposes, for the focus of the fourth amendment inquiry must remain primarily on the actual physical intrusion caused by the search. Moreover, the statute at issue here requires that the test results remain confidential; they are subject to disclosure only upon court order.

The central focus of the defendants' challenge to the HIV testing statute is their argument that mandatory testing, even of high-risk groups, is not an effective means of combating the spread of AIDS. The defendants observe that many eminent public health authorities have declared their opposition to mandatory HIV testing. The defendants contend that mandatory testing is ineffective because the test results are not always accurate, whether through the variable latency of the virus, which can elude detection even though it is present in the body of the person tested, or through limitations on the sensitivity and specificity of the tests themselves. The defendants make the related argument that a negative test result might give the offender and the victim a false sense of security, causing them to believe mistakenly that they have not already been exposed to the virus. In addition, the defendants surmise that mandatory testing might even be counterproductive, particularly when it is used with groups such as women in prostitution. For example, defense witness Colleen Ahler testified that persons subject to mandatory testing might resent the physical and psychological intrusions produced by the test and thus choose not to voluntarily cooperate in further reducing the risk of spreading this disease. The defendants believe that voluntary testing and widespread public education are more effective measures of dealing with the AIDS problem.

Based on the evidence introduced in the circuit court, the defendants further assert that many of the sexual practices most frequently performed in prostitution do not involve activity having a high risk of HIV transmission. In addition, the defendants suggest that if a program of mandatory testing is going to be adopted, it should be limited to cases in which an offender has committed an act having some demonstrable risk of transmitting the disease. The defendants note that no sexual activity occurred in the present cases, and they conclude that their intended partners—undercover police officers—thus had no risk of exposure to the virus. * * *

The issue before us is not whether the State has chosen what all or even most experts would consider to be the best or most effective means of combating the disease, but whether the means chosen by the State can withstand constitutional scrutiny.

It is clear that unprotected sexual activity is a major means of transmitting AIDS. According to testimony presented in the court below, women in prostitution have on average 20 sexual encounters each week. Whether or not the statutory scheme provides the most effective means of dealing with the AIDS problem, we do not believe that its program of mandatory testing of certain groups of offenders is constitutionally infirm. * * *

The trial judge also found that the HIV testing requirement violates the equal protection clause of the Federal Constitution (U.S. Const. amend. XIV). The trial judge believed that the distinction recognized by the statute was not rationally related to a legitimate governmental interest. The defendants press the same contention here, relying on the Federal guarantee and its Illinois counterpart (Ill. Const.1970, art. I, § 2).

As a preliminary matter, we reject the alternative contention, made by the defendants and certain amici, that the statute creates a sex-based classification because of its impact on female offenders, and that it must therefore survive strict scrutiny under the Illinois Constitution's prohibition of sex-based discrimination (Ill. Const.1970, art. I, § 18; see *People v. Ellis* (1974), 311 N.E.2d 98). The statute draws no distinction between male and female offenders, and the defendants point to no evidence of an intent by the legislature to disadvantage female offenders. Accordingly, the additional claim of disparate impact must be rejected. See *Washington v. Davis* (1976), 426 U.S. 229, 240–42.

The defendants also argue that mandatory testing of certain groups of individuals is not an effective means of combating the spread of AIDS. To demonstrate that the testing statute will fail to achieve its avowed goal, or a legitimate governmental purpose, the defendants contend that the measure is both overinclusive and underinclusive in scope.

The defendants believe that the statute is overinclusive in scope because it includes within its scope offenses having no risk of AIDS transmission. For example, a person convicted of directing someone to a place of prostitution, which could be solicitation (Ill. Rev. Stat. 1989, ch. 38, par. 11–15), is subject to the statute's requirement. The defendants maintain that the statute is underinclusive in scope because it fails to require HIV testing for certain criminal and noncriminal conduct that is as likely to result in the transmission of AIDS as prostitution, the offense charged here. For example, the defendants point out that the statute omits from its testing requirement certain other offenses involving sexual misconduct, such as adultery, fornication, public indecency, sexual relations within families, and bigamy (Ill. Rev. Stat. 1989, ch. 38, pars. 11–7, 11–8, 11–9, 11–11, 11–12). In addition, the defendants observe that persons who engage in promiscuous noncriminal sexual activity are not subject to testing under the statute. The defendants contend that the extent to which the challenged statute is alternately overinclusive and underinclusive demonstrates the absence of any legitimate governmental purpose that would sustain it. * * *

The present statute does not impinge upon the exercise of a fundamental right or operate against a suspect class. Thus, under the standard of review appropriate here, the statute need not establish a perfect fit between the desired end and the means chosen to achieve that end.

In deciding which offenses to include in the statutory requirement and which ones to omit, the legislature may have considered the costs and utility of testing and might therefore have declined to impose the testing requirement with respect to those offenses for which the perceived need or danger was least. The evidence indicates that sexual activity is one of the primary means by which HIV is transmitted from one person to another. It was then appropriate for the legislature to include prostitution among the criminal offenses for which testing would be required. Such a requirement bears a rational relationship to the State interest in combating the spread of AIDS.

In sum, we conclude that the testing provision, as applied to the present defendants, does not deny them equal protection of the laws, under either the Federal or State Constitutions. * * *

City of New York v. New Saint Mark's Baths

Supreme Court of New York, 1986.
130 Misc.2d 911, 497 N.Y.S.2d 979.

■ JUSTICE RICHARD W. WALLACH:

This action by the health authorities of the City of New York is taken against defendant The New St. Marks Baths ("St. Marks") as a step to limit the spread of the disease known as AIDS (Acquired Immune Deficiency Syndrome). The parties are in agreement with respect to the deadly character of this disease and the dire threat that its spread, now in epidemic proportions, poses to the health and well-being of the community. * * *

Immediately relevant to this litigation are the scientific facts with respect to AIDS risk groups. During the five years in which the disease has been identified and studied, 73% of AIDS victims have consisted of sexually active homosexual and bi-sexual men with multiple partners. AIDS is not easily transmittable through casual body contact or transmission through air, water or food. Direct blood-to-blood or semen-to-blood contact is necessary to transmit the virus. Cases of AIDS among homosexual and bi-sexual males are associated with promiscuous sexual contact, anal intercourse and other sexual practices which may result in semen-to-blood or blood-to-blood contact.

According to medical evidence submitted by defendants (e.g. Fannin, M.D. aff.): "The riskiest conduct is thought to be that which allows the introduction of semen into the blood stream. Because anal intercourse may result in a tearing of internal tissues, that activity is considered high-risk for transmission."

Fellatio is also a high risk activity. As stated by the organizer of the AIDS Institute of the New York State Department of Health (Dickerman aff. ¶ 11):

> "Any direct contact with the semen of an infected person may increase the risk of AIDS transmission. The deposition of semen in areas likely to contain abrasions, open sores, and cuts and concurrent inflammatory processes which could result in the presence of susceptible lymphocytes increase the risk of AIDS transmission. Because the mouth represents such an area (the epithelial tissue in the mouth is more susceptible to injury than the epithelial tissue in the vagina), fellatio presents a high risk for the transmission of AIDS."

On October 25, 1985, the State Public Health Council, with the approval of the intervening New York State Commissioner of Health, adopted an emergency resolution adding a new regulation to the State Sanitary Code. This added regulation, Subpart 24–2 of the Sanitary Code (10 NYCRR 24–2), specifically authorized local officials, such as the City plaintiffs (City) here, to close any facilities "in which high risk sexual activity takes place." More specifically, in 10 NYCRR 24–2.2, the regulation provided:

> Prohibited Facilities: No establishment shall make facilities available for the purpose of sexual activities in which facilities high risk sexual activity takes place. Such facilities shall constitute a public nuisance dangerous to the public health.

In 10 NYCRR 24–2.1, the regulation furnished definitions:

> a.   "Establishment" shall mean any place in which entry, membership, goods or services are purchased.
>
> b.   "High Risk Sexual Activity" shall mean anal intercourse and fellatio.

The Public Health Council based this regulation on the Commissioner's "findings" that:

> Establishments including certain bars, clubs and bathhouses which are used as places for engaging in high risk sexual activities contribute to the propagation and spread of such AIDS-associated retro-viruses * * *

Appropriate public health intervention to discontinue such exposure at such establishments is essential to interrupting the epidemic among the people of the State of New York.

[In December 1985, the City moved to close the New St. Mark's Baths as a public health nuisance, citing the health risks at St. Mark's as defined in the state regulation. St. Marks and intervening patrons challenged the state regulation on the grounds that it was an invasion of defendants' patrons' rights to privacy and freedom of association under the United States Constitution.]

The City has submitted ample supporting proof that high risk sexual activity has been taking place at St. Marks on a continuous and regular basis. Following numerous on site visits by City inspectors, over 14 separate days, these investigators have submitted affidavits describing 49 acts of high risk sexual activity (consisting of 41 acts of fellatio involving 70 persons and 8 acts of anal intercourse involving 16 persons). This evidence of high risk sexual activity, all occurring either in public areas of St. Marks or in enclosed cubicles left visible to the observer without intrusion therein, demonstrates the inadequacy of self-regulatory procedures by the St. Marks attendant staff, and the futility of any less intrusive solution to the problem other than closure.

With a demonstrated death rate from AIDS during the first six months of 1985 of 1,248, plaintiffs and the intervening State officers have demonstrated a compelling state interest in acting to preserve the health of the population. Where such a compelling state interest is demonstrated even the constitutional rights of privacy and free association must give way provided, as here, it is also shown that the remedy adopted is the least intrusive reasonably available.

Furthermore, it is by no means clear that defendants' rights will, in actuality, be adversely affected in a constitutionally recognized sense by closure of St. Marks. The privacy protection of sexual activity conducted in a private home does not extend to commercial establishments simply because they provide an opportunity for intimate behavior or sexual release. * * *

* * * State police power has been upheld over claims of First Amendment rights of association where the nature of the assemblage is not for the advancement of beliefs and ideas but predominantly either for entertainment or gratification. A tangential impact upon association or expression is insufficient to obstruct the exercise of the State's police power to protect public health and safety.

To be sure, defendants and the intervening patrons challenge the soundness of the scientific judgments upon which the Health Council regulation is based, citing *inter alia* the observation of the City's former Commissioner of Health in a memorandum dated October 22, 1985 that "closure of bathhouses will contribute little if anything to the control of AIDS." Defendants particularly assail the regulation's inclusion of fellatio as a high risk sexual activity, and argue that enforced use of prophylactic sheaths would be a more appropriate regulatory response. They go further and argue that facilities such as St. Marks, which attempts to educate its patrons with written materials, signed pledges, and posted notices as to the advisability of safe sexual practices, provide a positive force in combatting AIDS, and a valuable communication link between public health authorities and the homosexual community. While these arguments and proposals may have varying degrees of merit, they overlook a fundamental principle of applicable law: "It is not for the courts to determine which scientific view is correct in ruling upon whether the police power has been properly exercised." The judicial function is exhausted with the discovery that the relation between means and end is not wholly vain and fanciful, an illusory pretense. Justification for plaintiffs' application here more than meets that test. * * *

NOTES ON AIDS AND PUBLIC HEALTH LAW

1. *Standard of Review.* What standard of review should the courts use in deciding challenges to the actions of public health officials? Are such actions held to the same lenient rational basis standard as other political or legislative decisions (unless they implicate a fundamental right or classify by suspect criteria)? Must they satisfy some higher threshold of medical or scientific correctness? Professor Scott Burris argues that AIDS law has produced the "rational medical basis" test, under which the courts apply "focused scrutiny" to public health actions that curtail individual liberties, asking, *inter alia,* whether the public health effectiveness of the measure outweighs their cost to individuals. Scott Burris, "Rationality Review and the Politics of Public Health," 34 *Villanova L. Rev.* 933 (1989). Was such a test used in the preceding two cases?

When experts in public health and medicine disagree, as they did in these cases, to what extent, if any, should such disagreement affect the tradition of deference to public officials? In these two cases, the actions of such officials were arguably violative of individual rights, but remember that medical expertise is also marshaled to support even more rights-negative positions. See, *e.g.,* the arguments presented by *amicus* Dallas Doctors Against AIDS in support of the Texas sodomy law, as described in *Baker v. Wade,* 106 F.R.D. 526, 530 (N.D.Tex.1985), *rev'd on other grounds,* 769 F.2d 289 (5th Cir.1985), *cert. denied,* 478 U.S. 1022 (1986).

2. *The Impact of Civil Rights Statutes on Public Health Law.* Reread the portions of § 504 of the Rehabilitation Act and the Americans with Disabilities Act that establish criteria for adverse actions in the employment context (Chapter 10, Section 3[B]–[C]). How does that standard compare with a rational basis, or a rational medical basis? Consider the following footnote to the Court's opinion in *School Board of Nassau County v. Arline,* 480 U.S. 273, 286 n.15 (1987) (holding that § 504 includes communicable conditions within the scope of "handicap," thus triggering anti-discrimination protections):

> [C]ourts may reasonably be expected normally to defer to the judgments of public health officials in determining whether an individual is otherwise qualified unless those judgments are medically unsupportable. Conforming employment decisions with medically reasonable judgments can hardly be thought to threaten the States' regulation of communicable diseases. Indeed, because the Act requires employers to respond rationally to those handicapped by a contagious disease, the Act will assist local health officials by helping remove an important obstacle to preventing the spread of infectious disease: the individual's reluctance to report his or her condition.

Professor Burris reads this footnote to establish "at a stroke * * * a substantive requirement of medical reasonableness in a class of decisions which, at least in theory, were previously subject only to a general test of hypothetical rationality." Do you agree?

3. *AIDS in the State Legislatures.* Thousands of AIDS-related bills were introduced in state legislatures during the 1980s, ranging from civil rights measures to provisions for mandatory testing and exclusions from certain workplaces. For a compilation of state statutes that specifically regulate AIDS, see Paul Barron, Sara J. Goldstein & Karen L. Wishnev, "State Statutes Dealing with HIV and AIDS: A Comprehensive State-by-State Summary," 5 *Law & Sexuality* 1 (1995). One general trend in the state legislatures was the modernization of many public health statutes with, for example, the incorporation of procedural due process provisions for isolation and quarantine. See, e.g., Fla. Stat. Ann. § 384.28; Minn. Stat. Ann. § 144.12. How would Foucault analyze this development?

PART C.   CRIMINAL AND CIVIL LIABILITY FOR SEXUAL TRANSMISSION

State of Oregon v. Timothy Alan Hinkhouse

Court of Appeals of Oregon, 1996.
139 Or.App. 446, 912 P.2d 921.

■ JUDGE LANDAU.

Defendant is infected with the human immunodeficiency virus (HIV). He was convicted of ten counts of attempted murder, ORS 163.115, and ten counts of attempted assault I, ORS 163.185, based on his conduct of engaging in unprotected sexual intercourse with a number of victims without disclosing his medical condition. On appeal, he argues that the convictions must be set aside, because the evidence is insufficient to establish that he intended to cause the death of or serious physical injury to any of his several victims. The state argues that the evidence is sufficient to support the convictions. We agree with the state and affirm.

[Hinkhouse learned that he was HIV-positive in 1989, the same year he began a sexual relationship with 15 year-old P.B., who later tested positive herself. On November 3, 1990, Hinkhouse told his probation officer, Bill Carroll, that he was HIV-positive. Carroll told him that if he passed the virus to another person, "he would be killing someone." Over the next several months, Carroll and defendant continued to have conversations about HIV and the need to take precautions to avoid transmitting the virus. In a telephone conversation in 1991, Carroll again cautioned defendant: "If you infect anyone, that is murder." Defendant said that he understood and agreed that he would take appropriate precautions. Nonetheless, in 1993, Hinkhouse entered into several sexual relationships where he refused to use a condom during sex and failed to disclose his HIV status.

In one relationship, with L.K., Hinkhouse had condomless sex over the objections of his partner and told her that he was HIV-negative; he also engaged in rough sex and anal intercourse with L.K. In another relationship, with M.S., Hinkhouse did wear condoms.]

At trial, Dr. Beers explained that HIV is transmitted through bodily fluids, including semen. He said that even nontraumatic sexual intercourse is an effective method of transmitting the disease and that more violent sex or anal sex increases the risk of transmission, because of the increased likelihood that tears in tissue break down the body's barriers to the virus. He explained that a person may be infected after a single sexual exposure.

Defendant's psychologist, Dr. Norman, testified that defendant had a long history of acting out sexually and that he suffered from attention deficit disorder. He opined that defendant understood how HIV is transmitted and that it is a fatal disease. Norman also testified that, although defendant had reportedly threatened in 1991 to "go out and spread" HIV, he did not lend much credence to such threats. According to Norman, defendant simply did not think about the consequences of his behavior.

The state's expert, Dr. Johnson, agreed that defendant suffers from attention deficit disorder. Johnson testified that defendant also suffers from a borderline personality disorder and is antisocial. He recounted that defendant had acknowledged that his parole officer had warned him not to infect other people, and that defendant had responded that "he was going to do whatever he wanted, whenever he wanted." Johnson also thought that it was significant that defendant agreed to use, and in fact used, condoms when having intercourse with a woman for whom he expressed affection, but he did not use condoms with the other women with whom he had sex. Johnson also reported a conversation with another of defendant's former sexual partners, who said that, although defendant had denied that he was HIV-positive, he said that if he were positive, he would spread the virus to other people. In Johnson's opinion, such statements, coupled with defendant's behavior, showed intentional, deliberate conduct. Particularly in the light of the pattern of systematically recruiting and exploiting multiple partners over a long period of time, Johnson said, he found no evidence to suggest that defendant was acting impulsively or without the intent to harm.

Defendant moved for a judgment of acquittal, which the trial court denied. On appeal, defendant argues that the trial court erred in denying his motion, because the evidence is insufficient to support convictions for either attempted murder or attempted assault. He argues that there is no evidence that he intended to cause death or serious bodily injury, only evidence that—at most—he acted in reckless disregard of the consequences of his conduct. The state contends that the evidence is sufficient to support the convictions on both sets of charges, based on the undisputed evidence that defendant concealed or lied about his HIV status, refused to wear condoms, and intentionally had unprotected sex with a number of women, while fully aware of the fact that he was exposing them to the virus.

* * * A person is guilty of attempting to commit a crime "when the person intentionally engages in conduct which constitutes a substantial

step toward commission of the crime." ORS 161.405(1). A person commits assault in the first degree when "the person intentionally causes serious physical injury to another by means of a deadly or dangerous weapon." ORS 163.185(1). A person commits attempted murder when he or she attempts, without justification or excuse, intentionally to cause the death of another human being. ORS 163.115; ORS 163.005. To act "intentionally" is to "act[] with a conscious objective to cause the result or to engage in the conduct so described." ORS 161.085(7).

Viewing the evidence in the light most favorable to the state, we conclude that there is sufficient evidence for a rational trier of fact to find that defendant intended to cause both physical injury and death. He knew that he was HIV-positive and that his condition was terminal. He knew that if he transmitted the virus to another person, that person eventually would die as well. He understood that having unprotected sex would expose his sexual partners to the virus and that a single sexual encounter could transmit the virus. He had been told, and he acknowledged, that having unprotected sex and transmitting the disease was "murder." He even signed an agreement that he would refrain from any unsupervised contact with women without the approval of his probation officer.

In spite of that awareness, defendant engaged in a persistent pattern of recruiting sexual partners over a period of many months. He consistently concealed or lied about his HIV status. He refused to wear condoms, or pretended to wear them, penetrating women without protection and against their protestations. He engaged in unprotected sex, including rough and violent intercourse, which increased the chances of passing the virus to his partners. He bragged about his sexual prowess, even after acknowledging his HIV status, and told at least one person that he intended to spread the disease to others by such conduct.

Defendant insists that he meant only to satisfy himself sexually, and that that is insufficient to prove intent to harm or to cause death. His conduct, however, demonstrates that his objective was more than mere sexual gratification. When he engaged in sexual intercourse with the woman he hoped to marry, he consistently wore condoms and made no attempt to conceal his HIV status. When he had sex with others, in contrast, he concealed or lied about his condition and refused any protection. Particularly in the light of the pattern of exploitation over a long period of time, a rational fact finder could conclude beyond a reasonable doubt that defendant did not act impulsively merely to satisfy his sexual desires, but instead acted deliberately to cause his victims serious bodily injury and death. The trial court did not err in denying defendant's motion for a judgment of acquittal.

Jane Doe and Infant Doe v. Earvin Johnson, Jr.

United States District Court, W.D.Michigan, 1993.
817 F.Supp. 1382.

■ DISTRICT JUDGE ENSLEN.

[Doe claimed that Johnson transmitted the HIV virus to her through unsafe sex and over her request that he use a condom. Because Johnson engaged in a "sexually active, promiscuous lifestyle," he should have warned her that he might have HIV or used a condom. Based upon these factual allegations, Doe sought relief on a variety of tort theories, characterized as the following counts in her complaint: (I) Negligence; (II) Breach of duty not to transmit HIV virus; (III) Battery; (IV) Fraud/Failure to warn (of HIV status); (V) Fraud/Failure to warn (of sexually active lifestyle); (VI) Strict liability; (VII) Loss of consortium (Infant Doe); and (VIII) intentional infliction of emotional distress. Johnson moved for dismissal of six of these counts (I, III–VI, and VIII) pursuant to Rule 12(b)(6) of the Federal Rules of Civil Procedure.]

Negligent Transmission (count I)

Fraud—Failure to Warn of HIV status (count IV)

Fraud—Failure to Warn of "Sexually Active Lifestyle" (count V)

In his motion to dismiss, defendant groups counts I, IV and V together for purposes of his first argument because he attacks each count on essentially the same ground: that defendant must have had "knowledge" of his HIV-positive status in order to have a duty under negligence or fraud (failure to warn) theories.

Count I of the Complaint alleges that defendant negligently breached a legal duty he owed to plaintiff Jane Doe not to transmit the HIV virus to her because he knew or should have known that he had the HIV virus. In order to state a claim for a cause of action arising from a tortious injury in the state of Michigan, such as that alleged by plaintiff Jane Doe in count I, a litigant must allege: (1) a legal duty owed by defendant to plaintiff; (2) a breach of that duty; (3) causation (proximate and causation in fact) between the breach of the duty and the injury; and (4) resultant damages.
* * *

[T]he common denominator in defendant's first argument addressing counts I, IV, and V is that he did not owe a duty to plaintiff Jane Doe. Specifically, Mr. Johnson argues that he cannot be held liable (did not have a "duty") under these counts unless he actually "knew that he was infected with the HIV virus." In his Reply Brief, however, defendant enhances his potential duty by arguing that he had a duty to plaintiff Jane Doe on these theories if she can show that (1) he "knew he was infected (with the HIV virus) or (2) knew he had symptoms (of the HIV virus)." Thus, defendant apparently concedes that actual knowledge of the disease is not absolutely necessary to have a "duty" to plaintiff Jane Doe for wrongful transmission of the HIV virus under negligence or fraud theories.

Plaintiffs, on the other hand, argue that they have stated a valid claim for transmission of the HIV virus under both negligence and fraud theories because either Mr. Johnson knew or "should have known" that he was infected with the HIV virus. Accordingly, since he allegedly knew or should have known that he was infected with the virus, he had a duty to refrain from having unprotected sexual relations with Ms. Doe. While not directly addressing the knowledge issue (e.g., at what level of "knowledge" does a duty "kick in"), plaintiffs appear to suggest that because defendant was "sexually active," "promiscuous" and engaged in sexual contact "with multiple partners," he "should have known" that he carried (or likely carried) the HIV virus. Thus, plaintiffs argue that the level of knowledge required in order to have a legal duty to another person is quite low—if one engages in "high risk" behavior, such as engaging in a great deal of unprotected sex with multiple partners, then that individual has sufficient knowledge that s/he may have the HIV virus. Accordingly, in such a case, plaintiffs argue that the potential tortfeasor has a duty under the law of negligence to act as a "reasonably prudent person under the circumstances" and presumably to not engage in unprotected sexual relations, or at least warn a potential partner of the possibility that s/he may have the HIV virus. * * *

Nonetheless, no matter how the issue is phrased, the Court believes that the key inquiry in this case is: at what level of knowledge of the HIV virus should a defendant foresee potential harm to a plaintiff such that s/he acquires a duty to act as a "reasonably prudent person," as well as to disclose his/her knowledge of the HIV virus to that plaintiff. Certainly, levels of knowledge of the HIV virus are wide-ranging. For example:

1) A defendant knows s/he has the HIV virus because s/he has been affirmatively diagnosed by a medical professional as having the disease;

2) A defendant knows that s/he has the HIV virus because s/he has specific knowledge of any particular fact, such as:

a) The defendant has experienced symptoms related to the HIV virus; or,

b) The defendant has come in contact with an individual, or several individuals, who have been diagnosed as having the HIV virus and defendant has engaged in conduct with such persons which results in a likelihood (or even a possibility) that s/he could have the disease because of such conduct;

3) A defendant has engaged in "high risk" conduct which may result in exposure to the HIV virus, such as a great deal of unprotected sexual contact with multiple partners; unprotected anal intercourse with multiple partners; shared needles with many individuals while using intravenous drugs; or several blood transfusions.

4) A defendant has engaged in conduct which may result in exposure to the HIV virus, such as unprotected sexual relations with one partner (who had unprotected sexual relations with at least one other person).

Thus, the Court must determine at what level of knowledge a defendant owes a legal duty to a plaintiff such that negligence and fraud causes of action can be maintained. Several courts and commentators have addressed this issue—all coming to slightly different conclusions. At the outset, I must note that it is clear to this Court causes of action based on negligent transmission of an infectious disease, as well as failure to disclose a disease (fraud) are cognizable under the law. *Earle v. Kuklo*, 98 A.2d 107 ([N.J.Super.] 1953) (tuberculosis); *Kliegel v. Aitken*, 69 N.W. 67 ([Wis.] 1896) (typhoid fever); *Smith v. Baker*, 20 F. 709 (S.D.N.Y.1884) (whooping cough); *Gilbert v. Hoffman*, 23 N.W. 632 ([Iowa] 1885) (smallpox); *Franklin v. Butcher*, 129 S.W. 428 ([Mo.App.] 1910) (smallpox); *Hendricks v. Butcher*, 129 S.W. 431 ([Mo.App.] 1910) (smallpox).

Moreover, it is clear to the Court that a plaintiff may maintain negligence and fraud claims based on wrongful transmission of venereal diseases, including genital herpes. *State v. Lankford*, 102 A. 63 ([Del.] 1917) (venereal disease); *Crowell v. Crowell*, 105 S.E. 206 ([N.C.] 1920) (venereal disease); *Kathleen K. v. Robert B.*, 198 Cal.Rptr. 273 ([Cal.App.] 1984) (herpes); *Long v. Adams*, 333 S.E.2d 852 ([Ga.App.] 1985) (herpes). * * *

Both parties agree that a defendant's actual knowledge that s/he is infected with an infectious disease is sufficient to establish a duty for purposes of negligence and fraud. * * *

Additionally, at least one court has held that where a defendant had knowledge of symptoms of an infectious disease, he was under a duty to warn the plaintiff of his symptoms—and the possibility that he may have the sexually transmitted disease. *M.M.D. v. B.L.G.*, 467 N.W.2d 645 (Minn. Ct.App.1991). * * *

Moreover, at least one court has indicated, in dicta, that a defendant may be under a duty to warn a plaintiff of the possibility that s/he may be infected with a sexually transmitted disease if s/he has knowledge that a prior sexual partner is infected with the HIV virus. See *C.A.U. v. R.L.*, 438 N.W.2d 441, 443 (Minn.Ct.App.1989). * * *

In balancing these factors, I find that a defendant owes a plaintiff a legal duty to, at the very least, disclose the fact that s/he may have the HIV virus, if: (1) the defendant has actual knowledge that s/he has the HIV virus; (2) the defendant has experienced symptoms associated with the HIV virus; or (3) the defendant has actual knowledge that a prior sex partner has been diagnosed as having the HIV virus. When an individual has knowledge that rises to the level of one of these three fact scenarios, the burden on that individual in revealing his or her HIV virus information is minimal when compared to the high risks of the disease. * * *

Thus, to the extent that plaintiffs' Complaint alleges (1) that Mr. Johnson had actual knowledge that he had the HIV virus on the evening of June 22, 1990 or morning of June 23, 1990; (2) that Mr. Johnson had experienced symptoms associated with the HIV virus prior to the evening of June 22, 1990 or morning of June 23, 1990; or (3) that Mr. Johnson had actual knowledge that a prior sex partner has been diagnosed as having the HIV virus prior to the evening of June 22, 1990 or morning of June 23, 1990, I find that it states a claim under Rule 12(b)(6). Accordingly, to this extent, defendant's motion to dismiss is denied.

Of course, one issue still remains in this motion with respect to counts I, IV and V: can a claim for wrongful transmission of the HIV virus on negligence or fraud theories survive a Rule 12(b)(6) motion on the sole basis that a defendant knows that s/he engaged in "high risk" activity, or knows that s/he is a member of a "high risk" group. For a number of reasons, I find that legal claims cannot be stated for wrongful transmission of the HIV virus on negligence or fraud theories on the sole basis that a defendant has engaged in "high risk" activity. Thus, without more, a defendant who has had unprotected sexual encounters with multiple partners does not have a legal duty to inform a plaintiff of his or her past sexual activity. I reached this decision based on the following legal, as well as policy, considerations:

I find that imposition of a duty to disclose a "high risk" lifestyle prior to sexual conduct, which theoretically puts a sex partner "at risk," would open a door better left closed. As was noted by the New York Supreme Court in the context of a claim for infliction of "AIDS-phobia":

> If this cause of action were permitted to continue, any party to a matrimonial action who alleged adultery would now have a separate tort action for damages for "AIDS-phobia" because unfortunately in this day and age any deviate from the marital nest could possibly result in exposure to AIDS. Certainly any claim that a spouse interacted with a prostitute would, under plaintiff's view, be grounds for damages separate from equitable distribution. Any person who had a blood transfusion within the last eight years would have to disclose this fact to their prospective or current spouse or risk a damages action for "AIDS-phobia" since such transfusion may have resulted in an exposure to the AIDS virus. The law can only be stretched so far.

Doe v. Doe, 519 N.Y.S.2d 595, 598 ([N.Y.Sup.Ct.] 1987).

Certainly, imposition of a duty to disclose one's "high risk" status raises a number of questions: as a matter of law, what is "high risk" activity? Who is in this "high risk" group? How should "high risk" be defined? Even if a workable definition of "high risk" were discovered, would a duty be imposed on non-high risk group members to disclose to every potential sex partner all prior sexual contacts with partners who were so-called "high risk" group members? Would the duty of disclosure encompass prior sexual contacts with others known to be "promiscuous" or "sexually active?" What are the equal protection implications of imposing such a standard on a class of people? What are the privacy implications of imposing such a standard on a class of people? Would the duty eventually extend to everyone who has had any sexual contact outside of a monogamous relationship? What type of theoretical exposure to the HIV virus, if any, would create a legal duty to be tested for the virus? Would the duty require doctors, nurses and other medical health professionals who come in contact with HIV infected patients to disclose this information to sexual partner?

Extending a duty to disclose the possibility, or fact, that one has engaged in "high risk" activity, which increases the odds of carrying and/or transmitting the HIV virus, is an extension I am unwilling to make. There is no duty, I find, to disclose "high risk" activity ... without more. * * *

Accordingly, for all of the reasons stated above, I hold that legal claims cannot be stated for wrongful transmission of the HIV virus on negligence or fraud theories on the sole basis that a defendant has engaged in "high risk" activity, or was a member of a "high risk" group. Thus, without more, a defendant who has had unprotected sexual encounters with multiple partners does not have a legal duty to inform a plaintiff of his or her past sexual activity. To the extent that defendant's motion addresses this issue, it is granted. Finding that count V of plaintiffs' Complaint only states a cause of action for fraud based on "high risk" activity, it will be dismissed.

Nonetheless, I find that the fact that one may have engaged in "high risk" activity is relevant to a claim for wrongful transmission of the HIV virus. Certainly, my ruling that a defendant owes a plaintiff a legal duty to, at the very least, disclose the fact that s/he may have the HIV virus, if one of the factors set forth [above] is present, allows room for inquiry into a defendant's past sexual and/or other "high risk" activity. For instance, a plaintiff will need to inquire whether any prior sex partners of a defendant have been diagnosed as having the HIV virus; when such diagnosis was made; when defendant learned of the diagnosis, etc.

As can be seen from my discussion above, there are many competing policy and legal issues in this case. Accordingly, I am willing—depending on the facts of a given case—to find that past "high risk" activity could be a relevant factor. That is, for purposes of summary judgment, if a plaintiff can show that a defendant engaged in "high risk" activity in conjunction with something else, then this Court would be willing to impose a lower requirement on the "something else." For instance, if defendant had unprotected sexual contact with multiple partners (as is alleged) and suffered symptoms related to the HIV virus that could be construed as "common maladies" (e.g., headaches, nondescript spots on body, weakness and fatigue, shingles, etc.), then this Court would find that defendant did in fact have a duty to act as a reasonable person under the circumstances, e.g., go to a medical professional, have an HIV virus test, refrain from sexual activity, warn sex partners, wear a condom during sexual contact, etc. I find that defendant's knowledge of his past "high risk" behavior may be relevant to this action.

Battery (count III)

Defendant argues that count III of plaintiffs' Complaint should be dismissed because plaintiffs have failed to state a claim for battery. Specifically, defendant argues that plaintiffs did not allege that he "intended to transmit the virus" to Ms. Doe, or believed that such transmission was "substantially certain" to occur. * * *

Battery is the willful and harmful or offensive touching of another person against their will. The Restatement of Torts states that where "[X] consents to sexual intercourse with [Y], who knows that [X] is ignorant of the fact that [Y] has a venereal disease, [Y] is subject to liability for battery." Restatement (Second) of Torts § 892B, illustration 5 (1985); see also *Kathleen K. v. Robert B.*, 198 Cal.Rptr. 273 ([Cal.App.] 1984). * * *

Defendant argues that plaintiffs have failed to state a claim because they did not state that defendant "intended to transmit," or knew with "substantial certainty" that he could transmit, the HIV virus to Ms. Doe. I disagree. Under Rule 12(b)(6) I must accept all allegations in the Complaint as true and construe these allegations "in the light most favorable to plaintiff[s]." In so doing, I find that plaintiffs have alleged a cause of action for the wrongful transmission of an infectious disease under a battery theory. Specifically, under the liberal Rule 12(b)(6) standard, I find that plaintiffs have alleged that defendant knew with "substantial certainty" that he could transmit the HIV virus to Ms. Doe. * * *

Strict Liability (count VI)

Count VI of plaintiffs' Complaint alleges that defendant is "strictly liable" for all harm suffered by Ms. Doe because his activity was "abnormally dangerous and ultrahazardous." * * *

The Restatement of Torts defines strict liability as:

(1) One who carries on an abnormally dangerous activity is subject to liability for harm to the person, land or chattels of another resulting from the activity, although he has exercised the utmost care to prevent the harm.

(2) This strict liability is limited to the kind of harm, the possibility of which makes the activity abnormally dangerous.

Restatement (Second) of Torts § 519.

Under the Restatement, the following factors must be considered in determining whether an activity is abnormally dangerous:

(a) existence of a high degree of risk of some harm to the person, land or chattels of other;

(b) likelihood that the harm that results from it will be great;

(c) inability to eliminate the risk by the exercise of reasonable care;

(d) extent to which the activity is not a matter of common usage;

(e) inappropriateness of the activity to the place where it is carried on; and

(f) extent to which its value to the community is outweighed by its dangerous attributes. * * *

For a number of reasons, I decline to extend the doctrine of strict liability to sexual activity. First, as stated above, Michigan courts have limited the scope of this doctrine to activities such as blasting, storing of inflammable liquids, etc. It seems unlikely to me that the Michigan courts would extend this doctrine to sexual activity.

Second, in applying the Restatement factors, it becomes clear that sexual activity, by definition, is not "abnormally" or "inherently" dangerous. Specifically, the risk associated with sexual activity can be dramatically reduced "by the exercise of reasonable care." Restatement (Second) of Torts § 520(c). For instance, the risk associated with sexual activity, spread of disease, can be reduced (although not completely eliminated) by use of a condom. Also, the Restatement suggests, and most cases have found, that in order to be abnormally dangerous, the activity must not be a matter of common usage. *Id.* § 520(d). Sexual activity is not an uncommon endeavor.
* * *

NOTES ON LEGAL REGULATION OF SEXUALLY TRANSMITTED DISEASE

1.   *Which Mens Rea Should Apply in Criminal Cases?* Under the Model Penal Code, one element of the crime of murder is that the killing be done either purposefully, knowingly or recklessly, under circumstances displaying "extreme indifference to the value of human life." Model Penal Code § 210.2(1)(b) (1996). Were Hinkhouse's actions sufficiently reckless to fall within the scope of attempted murder, as the court ruled? What if he had informed his partners of his HIV status and they had nonetheless engaged in sexual relations? Under the Model Penal Code's definition of murder, this fact would not have been relevant. Do you think it should be? Should it be relevant to a charge of assault? Note that under the law of both attempted murder and assault, actual transmission of HIV is not required. What would be the problems in imposing such a requirement?

2.   *Should Either Informing One's Partner or Using Precautions, or Both, Constitute a Defense?* Consider this argument:

> [N]either precautions nor disclosure *alone* should negate the offense. * * * [An HIV-infected person] has no right to defraud others into taking deadly sexual risks by remaining silent about his condition. Unless his sexual partners have been informed of an AIDS risk, it is not appropriate to view them as assuming the risk simply by having sex. * * * And even if the [person] believes he can shield his partner from risk by silently taking precautions, he should nonetheless disclose the truth and allow his partner to make the choice. * * * Even if the sexual partner is genuinely informed and is willing to forgo precautions, there is an important public interest in denying him or her that choice in order to contain the spread of the disease. Requiring use of available precautions notwithstanding a sexual partner's consent might also serve as useful insurance for situations in which the sexual partner may not wholly understand the situation to which he or she consents.

Kathleen A. Sullivan & Martha A. Field, "AIDS and the Coercive Power of the State," 23 *Harv. C.R.-C.L. L. Rev.* 139, 181–82 (1989). How would you draft a criminal law embodying what you believe should be the elements of and defenses to a crime of sexual transmission of disease? Would you limit it to HIV? In fact, many states have such statutes, some of which are HIV-specific. See, *e.g.*, Ill. Comp. Stat. Ann. ch. 720, § 5/12–16.2 (1996); Mich. Stat. Ann. § 333.5210(1) (1996).

Why shouldn't the state regulate even more directly, as by mandating the use of condoms by people who are infected with HIV? Would there be constitutional problems? Compare *Griswold* and *Eisenstadt* (Chapter 1, Section 1). Are they distinguishable?

3. *Should the State Abstain from Criminal Regulation in This Area?* One frequent debate has been whether the threat to liberty from the risk of incarceration and from the auxiliary processes in criminal law that allow the state to marshal its many powers of arrest, prosecution, surveillance, and investigation outweigh the gains to be realized by permitting any criminal law regulation of the sexual transmission of disease. Compare the judicial procedures in the *Hinkhouse* and *Johnson* cases. Was the criminal prosecution too draconian? Imagine a case with less damning facts. What if the theory of the prosecution was that a defendant was "reckless" because he knew himself to be a gay man who had engaged in unprotected sex? Would that provide the necessary *mens rea*? Is potential civil liability adequate to produce good behavior or punish the bad? Could it be more effective than criminal laws?

NOTE ON DESIGNING AN EFFECTIVE AIDS POLICY

The legal responses explored in this section—testing prostitutes, closing down bath houses, and imposing criminal or tort liability—are in your editors' opinion marginal responses, having virtually no actual effect on the spread of AIDS. (They might be justified on other grounds, perhaps.) An effective program should think bigger and be more systematic. There is a growing policy literature, drawing on the experience in other countries and within certain communities such as San Francisco.[b] (The following list is not an endorsement.)

- AIDS education in the public school system (see Chapter 7, Section 3[B]), with targeted public education programs for adults, including community-based programs;

- Condom distribution in the public school system and through public health authorities, perhaps even a state campaign to manufacture and distribute condoms to all citizens;

- Needle-exchange programs, as a large percentage of HIV infections occur because drug addicts share needles containing someone else's

---

b. See *AIDS in the Industrialized Democracies: Passions, Politics, and Policies* (David L. Karp & Ronald Bayer eds. 1992); Tomas J. Philipson & Richard A. Posner, *Private Choices and Public Health: The AIDS Epidemic in an Economic Perspective* (1993), critically reviewed by William N. Eskridge, Jr. & Brian D. Weimer, "The Economics Epidemic in an AIDS Perspective," 61 *U. Chi. L. Rev.* 733 (1994); Larry Gostin, "The Interconnected Epidemics of Drug Dependency and AIDS," 26 *Harv. C.R.-C.L. L. Rev.* 113 (1991).

infected blood;[c]

- Mandatory testing for HIV infection and required disclosure of HIV status; the ultimate version of this proposal leads to isolation of people with HIV;[d]

- Recognizing same-sex marriages and repealing state laws that criminalize same-sex intimacy;[e]

- Legalization of drugs and dispensation of drugs by the state through licensed stores that also instruct on safer sex techniques.

What cluster of policies do you think would be both useful and cost-effective? Should a different mix of policies be adopted for different communities?

c. See School of Public Health, Univ. Calif., Berkeley & Inst. for Health Policy Studies, Univ. Calif., San Francisco, *The Public Health Impact of Needle Exchange Programs in the United States and Abroad* (Sept. 1993); Lawrence O. Gostin et al., "Prevention of HIV/AIDS Among Injecting Drug Users," *J. Am. Med. Ass'n* (Dec. 1996).

d. The isolation policy is mainly associated with Cuba, but Sweden follows a less severe policy of mandatory testing and iso-lation. Benny Henriksson & Hasse Ytterberg, "Sweden: The Power of the Moral(istic) Left," in *AIDS in the Industrialized Democracies* 317.

e. Perhaps surprisingly, this is one of the points of agreement between Philipson & Posner's economic approach to the AIDS epidemic in *Public Choices and Private Health* 148, 179–80, and Eskridge & Weimer's critique in "Economics Epidemic," 768–69.

TRANSGENDER ISSUES AND THE LAW

The term "trans-sexual," first coined by physician D.O. Cauldwell in 1949, means a person who has an enduring, pervasive, and compelling desire to be a person of the opposite sex. Transsexuals are conventionally described as persons whose anatomic sex at birth differs from their "sexual identity," which is defined as the individual's subjective sense of which sex (gender?) he or she desires—and feels compelled—to be (perform?). For many such persons, the only satisfactory resolution of their situation is surgery to realign their genitalia and other anatomic characteristics to exist in harmony with their self-identification. Perhaps on no issue are the debates on whether such identity is inborn or culturally inscribed as acute as on the meaning of transsexualism. Recently, persons who express a need to change their sex or gender have started using the word "transgender" instead of "transsexual." By whatever term, tens of thousands of Americans have identified themselves as experiencing this disjunction between anatomy, self concept and social role. The response of the law to the realities of their lives has tested the limits of the definitions of sex and gender, disability and choice, disorder and cure.[a]

PART A. SEX DISCRIMINATION AND TRANS-SEXUAL/TRANSGENDER DISCRIMINATION

Q. What is Karen Ulane's gender?

A. Karen Ulane is a woman.

Q. Would you explain that?

Testimony at the trial of *Ulane v. Eastern Airlines, Inc.*, quoted in Richard Green, "Spelling 'Relief' for Transsexuals: Employment Discrimination and the Criteria of Sex," 4 *Yale L. & Policy Rev.* 125, 129 (1985).

---

a. Several recent books bring fresh perspectives to this issue. Transgender attorney Martine Rothblatt argues that our two-sex system should be replaced by a continuum of sex and gender, in *The Apartheid of Sex: A Manifesto on the Freedom of Gender* (1995). For an anthropological account of the process of changing sex/gender, see Anne Bolin, *In Search of Eve: Transsexual Rites of Passage* (1988). Bernice L. Hausman critically reviews the history of the medicalization of gender change in *Changing Sex: Transsexualism, Technology and the Idea of Gender* (1995).

Karen Frances Ulane v. Eastern Airlines, Inc.

U.S. Court of Appeals for the Seventh Circuit, 1984.
742 F.2d 1081, *cert. denied*, 471 U.S. 1017 (1985).

■ HARLINGTON WOOD, JR., CIRCUIT JUDGE.

Plaintiff, as Kenneth Ulane, was hired in 1968 as a pilot for defendant, Eastern Air Lines, Inc., but was fired as Karen Frances Ulane in 1981. Ulane filed a timely charge of sex discrimination with the Equal Employment Opportunity Commission, which subsequently issued a right to sue letter. This suit followed. Counts I and II allege that Ulane's discharge violated Title VII of the Civil Rights Act of 1964, 42 U.S.C. §§ 2000e—2000e–17 (1982): Count I alleges that Ulane was discriminated against as a female; Count II alleges that Ulane was discriminated against as a transsexual. The judge ruled in favor of Ulane on both counts after a bench trial. 581 F. Supp. 821. The court awarded her[2] reinstatement as a flying officer with full seniority and back pay, and attorneys' fees. * * *

Ulane became a licensed pilot in 1964, serving in the United States Army from that time until 1968 with a record of combat missions in Vietnam for which Ulane received the Air Medal with eight clusters. Upon discharge in 1968, Ulane began flying for Eastern. With Eastern, Ulane progressed from Second to First Officer, and also served as a flight instructor, logging over 8,000 flight hours.

Ulane was diagnosed a transsexual[3] in 1979. She explains that although embodied as a male, from early childhood she felt like a female.

---

2. Since Ulane considers herself to be female, and appears in public as female, we will use feminine pronouns in referring to her. [Eds: Contrast *Farmer v. Brennan, infra* page 1124, where the Supreme Court studiously avoided referring to Dee Farmer, a male-to-female transsexual, as either "he" or "she" and, instead, referred to Farmer as "petitioner" throughout the opinion.]

3. Transsexualism is a condition that exists when a physiologically normal person (i.e., not a hermaphrodite—a person whose sex is not clearly defined due to a congenital condition) experiences discomfort or discontent about nature's choice of his or her particular sex and prefers to be the other sex. This discomfort is generally accompanied by a desire to utilize hormonal, surgical, and civil procedures to allow the individual to live in his or her preferred sex role. The diagnosis is appropriate only if the discomfort has been continuous for at least two years, and is not due to another mental disorder, such as schizophrenia. See Testimony of Dr. Richard Green, expert witness for plaintiff, trial transcript for Sept. 26, 1983, 10:00 a.m., at 35–37; see generally American Psychiatric Association, *Diagnostic and Statistical Manual of Mental Disorders* § 302.50 (3d ed. 1980); Edgerton, Langman, Schmidt & Sheppe, "Psychological Considerations of Gender Reassignment Surgery," 9 *Clinics in Plastic Surgery* 355, 357 (1982); Comment, "The Law and Transsexualism: A Faltering Response to a Conceptual Dilemma," 7 *Conn. L. Rev.* 288, 288 n.1 (1975); Comment, "Transsexualism, Sex Reassignment Surgery, and the Law," 56 *Cornell L. Rev.* 963, 963 n.1 (1971). To be distinguished are homosexuals, who are sexually attracted to persons of the same sex, and transvestites, who are generally male heterosexuals who cross-dress, i.e., dress as females, for sexual arousal rather than social comfort; both homosexuals and transvestites are content with the sex into which they were born. See *Diagnostic and Statistical Manual of Mental Disorders* § 302.30; Wise & Meyer, "Transvestism: Previous Findings and New Areas for Inquiry," 6 *J. Sex & Marital Therapy* 116, 116–20 (1980); Comment, 7 *Conn. L. Rev.* at 292; Comment, 56 *Cornell L. Rev.* at 963 n.3.

Ulane first sought psychiatric and medical assistance in 1968 while in the military. Later, Ulane began taking female hormones as part of her treatment, and eventually developed breasts from the hormones. In 1980, she underwent "sex reassignment surgery." After the surgery, Illinois issued a revised birth certificate indicating Ulane was female, and the FAA certified her for flight status as a female. Ulane's own physician explained, however, that the operation would not create a biological female in the sense that Ulane would "have a uterus and ovaries and be able to bear babies." Ulane's chromosomes, all concede, are unaffected by the hormones and surgery. Ulane, however, claims that the lack of change in her chromosomes is irrelevant.[6] Eastern was not aware of Ulane's transsexuality, her hormone treatments, or her psychiatric counseling until she attempted to return to work after her reassignment surgery. Eastern knew Ulane only as one of its male pilots. * * *

The district judge first found under Count II that Eastern discharged Ulane because she was a transsexual, and that Title VII prohibits discrimination on this basis. While we do not condone discrimination in any form, we are constrained to hold that Title VII does not protect transsexuals, and that the district court's order on this count therefore must be reversed for lack of jurisdiction.

* * * Other courts have held that the term "sex" as used in the statute is not synonymous with "sexual preference." The district court recognized this, and agreed that homosexuals and transvestites do not enjoy Title VII protection, but distinguished transsexuals as persons who, unlike homosexuals and transvestites, have sexual identity problems; the judge agreed that the term "sex" does not comprehend "sexual preference," but held that it does comprehend "sexual identity." The district judge based this holding on his finding that "sex is not a cut-and-dried matter of chromosomes," but is in part a psychological question—a question of self-perception; and in part a social matter—a question of how society perceives the individual. The district judge further supported his broad view of Title VII's coverage by recognizing Title VII as a remedial statute to be liberally construed. He concluded that it is reasonable to hold that the statutory word "sex" literally and scientifically applies to transsexuals even if it does not apply to homosexuals or transvestites. We must disagree.

* * * While we recognize distinctions among homosexuals, transvestites, and transsexuals, we believe that the same reasons for holding that

---

6. Biologically, sex is defined by chromosomes, internal and external genitalia, hormones, and gonads. Chromosomal sex cannot be changed, and a uterus and ovaries cannot be constructed. This leads some in the medical profession to conclude that hormone treatments and sex reassignment surgery can alter the evident makeup of an individual, but cannot change the individual's innate sex. Others disagree, arguing that one must look beyond chromosomes when determining an individual's sex and consider factors such as psychological sex or assumed sex role. These individuals conclude that post-operative male-to-female transsexuals do in fact qualify as females and are not merely "facsimiles." E.g., Testimony of Dr. Richard Green, expert witness for plaintiff, trial transcript for Sept. 27, 1983, 10:35 a.m., at 226 & 252.

the first two groups do not enjoy Title VII coverage apply with equal force to deny protection for transsexuals.

It is a maxim of statutory construction that, unless otherwise defined, words should be given their ordinary, common meaning. The phrase in Title VII prohibiting discrimination based on sex, in its plain meaning, implies that it is unlawful to discriminate against women because they are women and against men because they are men. The words of Title VII do not outlaw discrimination against a person who has a sexual identity disorder, i.e., a person born with a male body who believes himself to be female, or a person born with a female body who believes herself to be male; a prohibition against discrimination based on an individual's sex is not synonymous with a prohibition against discrimination based on an individual's sexual identity disorder or discontent with the sex into which they were born. The dearth of legislative history on section 2000e–2(a)(1) strongly reinforces the view that that section means nothing more than its plain language implies.

When Congress enacted the Civil Rights Act of 1964 it was primarily concerned with race discrimination. "Sex as a basis of discrimination was added as a floor amendment one day before the House approved Title VII, without prior hearing or debate." *Holloway* [*v. Arthur Andersen and Co.,* 566 F.2d 659 (9th Cir.1977).]. This sex amendment was the gambit of a congressman seeking to scuttle adoption of the Civil Rights Act. The ploy failed and sex discrimination was abruptly added to the statute's prohibition against race discrimination.

The total lack of legislative history supporting the sex amendment coupled with the circumstances of the amendment's adoption clearly indicates that Congress never considered nor intended that this 1964 legislation apply to anything other than the traditional concept of sex. Had Congress intended more, surely the legislative history would have at least mentioned its intended broad coverage of homosexuals, transvestites, or transsexuals, and would no doubt have sparked an interesting debate. There is not the slightest suggestion in the legislative record to support an all-encompassing interpretation. * * *

* * * [I]f the term "sex" as it is used in Title VII is to mean more than biological male or biological female, the new definition must come from Congress.

The trial judge originally found only that Eastern had discriminated against Ulane under Count II as a transsexual. The judge subsequently amended his findings to hold that Ulane is also female and has been discriminated against on this basis. Even if we accept the district judge's holding that Ulane is female, he made no factual findings necessary to support his conclusion that Eastern discriminated against her on this basis. All the district judge said was that his previous "findings and conclusions concerning sexual discrimination against the plaintiff by Eastern Airlines, Inc. apply with equal force whether plaintiff be regarded as a transsexual or a female." This is insufficient to support a finding that Ulane was discriminated against because she is female since the district judge's previous findings all centered around his conclusion that Eastern did not want "[a] transsexual in the cockpit" (emphasis added).

Ulane is entitled to any personal belief about her sexual identity she desires. After the surgery, hormones, appearance changes, and a new Illinois birth certificate and FAA pilot's certificate, it may be that society, as the trial judge found, considers Ulane to be female. But even if one believes that a woman can be so easily created from what remains of a man, that does not decide this case. If Eastern had considered Ulane to be female and had discriminated against her because she was female (i.e., Eastern treated females less favorably than males), then the argument might be made that Title VII applied, cf. *Holloway* (although Title VII does not prohibit discrimination against transsexuals, "transsexuals claiming discrimination because of their sex, male or female, would clearly state a cause of action under Title VII") (dicta), but that is not this case. It is clear from the evidence that if Eastern did discriminate against Ulane, it was not because she is female, but because Ulane is a transsexual—a biological male who takes female hormones, cross-dresses, and has surgically altered parts of her body to make it appear to be female. * * *

NOTES ON THE MEANING OF "SEX DISCRIMINATION"

1. *Sex, Gender, Trans-sex, Transgender.* The *Ulane* court's interpretation of Title VII remains unchallenged by any subsequent court decision, although it has been soundly criticized. Most feminist scholars argue that the court read "sex" too narrowly, excluding the social trappings of masculinity and femininity commonly described as gender. Professor Valdes, for example, argues that although sex and gender are conceptually distinct, neither can exist in the culture or the law without the other. Ultimately, then, discrimination based "solely" on gender must necessarily also be discrimination based on sex. Francisco Valdes, "Queers, Sissies, Dykes and Tomboys: Deconstructing the Conflations of 'Sex,' 'Gender,' and 'Sexual Orientation' in Euro–American Law and Society," 83 *Calif. L. Rev.* 1 (1995). Professor Franke makes the more radical claim that gender determines sex, not the other way around. Only through a process of social construction do anatomic differences have meaning; in and of themselves, they are irrelevant. Katherine M. Franke, "The Central Mistake of Sex Discrimination Law: The Disaggregation of Sex from Gender," 144 *U. Penn. L. Rev.* 1 (1995). A distinctly different view is that of Professor Epstein, who objects to using the term "gender" because it connotes greater fluidity than "sex," which he believes to be fixed; he argues that prohibiting discrimination based on "gender" would outlaw practices and policies that appropriately differentiate. Richard A. Epstein, "Gender Is For Nouns," 41 *DePaul L. Rev.* 981 (1992). Taking yet another tack, sociologist Janice Raymond argues that transsexualism is itself trapped within the logic of gender, and constitutes an acquiescence to social stereotypes rather than a rejection of them. Janice G. Raymond, *The Transsexual Empire: The Making of the She–Male* (1994).

2. *The Relevance of the Ann Hopkins Case?* Think about the debate recounted by the previous note in light of *Hopkins v. Price Waterhouse* (Chapter 3, Section 2[B]; Chapter 10, Section 2[B]), where the Supreme Court recognized discrimination on the basis of gender characteristics as sex discrimination. Does *Hopkins* decisively reject the Epstein reading of Title VII? Does it rest upon or accept the Franke reading? Franke argues for "[a] more interesting and expansive reading of sex discrimination[:] * * * bias against the plaintiff because her gender (her inside core identity) did not match what others believed about her body (her outside or surface identity)—which is to say that a woman could have a biologically male body." Franke, "Central Mistake," 35. Would *Hopkins* reach that far? *Should* it?

3. *Theories Rejecting Sex Binarism.* How would the *Ulane* court have treated a "hermaphrodite" (Chapter 2, Section 3[A]), someone who had sex reassignment surgery to "correct" her outward genitals and hormone therapy to align all of the signals of "sex" in the same direction? Which "sex" is a person who has both male and female genitals? What "sex" is a person who has XXY chromosomes? Based on the materials on "intersexuals" in Chapter 2, Section 3[A], can it be maintained that there are just two sexes? Doesn't that support the Franke position?

If discrimination on the basis of "intersexual" characteristics is "sex" discrimination, why isn't it sex discrimination to discriminate against transsexuals, for whom the disconnect is emotional and not physical? How would the *Ulane* court respond to this logic?

4. *Europe Takes a Different View.* The European Court of Justice ruled in 1996 that a directive banning sex discrimination in employment must be interpreted to cover transsexuals. *P. v. S. and Cornwall County Council,* (Case C–13/94) [1996] 1 CEL 574. Plaintiff was fired by a British educational agency after giving notice of ongoing gender reassignment therapy and her intent to come to work as a woman. Defendants argued that there was no sex discrimination because female transsexuals were treated the same as male transsexuals. The Advocate General's analysis, adopted by the Court, stated in part:

> It is quite true that even if P. had been in the opposite situation, that is to say changing from female to male, it is possible that she would have been dismissed anyway. One fact, however, is not just possible, but certain: P. would not have been dismissed if she had remained a man.

> So how can it be claimed the discrimination on grounds of sex was not involved? How can it be denied that the cause of discrimination was precisely, and solely, sex? To my mind, where unfavourable treatment of a transsexual is related to (or rather is caused by) a change of sex, there is discrimination by reason of sex or on grounds of sex, if that is preferred. [Ed. note: the latter phrase is that of the applicable statute.] * * *

[F]or the purposes of this case, sex is important as a convention, a social parameter. The discrimination of which women are frequently the victim is not of course due to their physical characteristics, but rather to their role, to the image which society has of women. Hence the rationale for less favourable treatment is the social role which women are supposed to play * * * In the same way it must be recognised that the unfavourable treatment suffered by transsexuals is most often linked to a negative image, a moral judgement which has nothing to do with their abilities in the sphere of employment.

5. *Rewording Statutes.* The New York City's civil rights ordinance originally barred discrimination based on "sex," but was later amended to substitute the word "gender." Based on that change, one court has declared that it forbids discrimination against transsexuals. *Maffei v. Kolaeton Industry, Inc.*, 626 N.Y.S.2d 391 (N.Y.Sup.Ct.1995). The court had no evidence of what had prompted the legislators to substitute one word for the other. Relying on *Ulane*-style rulings, the New York court took at face value the reasoning that Congress intended the word "sex" in Title VII to refer to anatomic sex, because only "gender" referred to sexual identity, citing *Dobre v. National Railroad Passenger Corp.*, 850 F.Supp. 284, 286 (E.D.Pa.1993). The *Maffei* court concluded that the female-to-male plaintiff was protected against discrimination based on gender, in that he belonged to "a subgroup of men" who were transsexuals. *Id.* at 396.

Some legislatures have amended their civil rights statutes with the express purpose of adding protection for transsexuals. The San Francisco ordinance added the phrase "gender identity" to the list of prohibited bases for discrimination. San Francisco Admin. Code § 33–3301 *et seq.* The Minnesota statute included the phrase "having or being perceived as having a self image or identity not traditionally associated with one's biological maleness or femaleness" within its definition of "sexual orientation." Minn.Stat.Ann. § 363.01(45) (1996). These developments present a difficult strategic choice for advocates of equality for transgendered persons: Should one persist with arguments that existing statutes grant such protection, or should one seek new statutory language? The latter course would seem to concede the invalidity of the former.

6. *Confusions and Conflations.* Transsexualism is different from transvestism. The latter is defined as the desire of an individual to dress in the clothing of the opposite sex, but not to actually become a person of the opposite sex. (Note the assumptions buried in the phrase "opposite sex." Should we instead say "the other sex"? Or perhaps, "another sex"?) Sometimes the confusion of the two is due simply to ignorance or to prejudice. There are times, however, when the two do overlap. Part of the gender reassignment process involves transsexuals starting to dress everyday, at the workplace and elsewhere, in the clothes associated with the sex/gender they are about to assume. As we will see in the next section, courts sometimes distinguish between cross-dressing when done as part of this process and cross-dressing that is not medically prescribed. And courts sometimes assume that transsexualism amounts to the same thing as cross-dressing, and vice versa. Another confusion is between either transsexualism/transgender status or transvestism, and homosexuality. Courts often assume that either of the first two is a proxy for erotic attraction to persons of the same sex, but that is not necessarily the case.

In *Blackwell v. U. S. Department of the Treasury*, 830 F.2d 1183 (D.C.Cir.1987), the plaintiff alleged that he was both homosexual and a transvestite, and that the agency's refusal to rehire him was based on the handicap of transvestism. The trial court had ruled that although transvestism was a handicap, homosexuality was not; it found for the agency on the basis that defendant was denied a job because the interviewing officer perceived him to be gay, and did not realize that he was a transvestite. The Court of Appeals, in an opinion written by Judge (now Justice) Ruth Bader Ginsburg, vacated the lower court decision (while affirming the outcome) because "the liability of a government department under the [Rehabilitation] Act should not turn on the level of sophistication or ability to classify of the particular interviewing officer—in this case, on whether that officer knows that homosexuality and transvestism are not one and the same." *Id.* at 1184.

PROBLEM 12–2

EMPLOYMENT DISCRIMINATION AGAINST TRANSSEXUALS UNDER THE DISTRICT OF COLUMBIA HUMAN RIGHTS ACT

An employer in the District of Columbia fires a male-to-female transsexual from a secretarial job. The employer says to her face, "You are just too weird for this company. Everyone is freaking out!" The employee sues under the District's Human Rights Act [HRA, Appendix 2 to this book]. Will the District's courts find this to be sex discrimination? Sexual orientation discrimination? Some other kind of discrimination? See *Underwood v. Archer Management Services*, 857 F.Supp. 96 (D.D.C.1994).

Assume the District recognizes discrimination on the basis of sex-change to be actionable discrimination of some sort under the HRA. In the next case, the male-to-female employee is fired because female employees objected to her using the women's restroom, the employer made avoidance of the women's restroom a condition of her employment, and she violated that condition. Same result?

PART B.   THE MEDICALIZATION OF TRANSSEXUALISM

Jane Doe v. United States Postal Service

United States District Court for the District of Columbia, 1985.
37 F.E.P. Cases 1867, 1985 WL 9446.

■ JUDGE PRATT.

[In May 1983, the Postal Service offered Jane Doe, then a male, a temporary position as a clerk typist. Before starting work, Doe notified the appropriate personnel of her intention to undergo sex reassignment surgery to correct a medically diagnosed transsexual identity. The offer of employment was withdrawn. Alleging that she was discriminated against solely because of the intention to undergo the reassignment surgery, Doe sued the Post Office and specified officers for violating her rights under the Rehabilitation Act of 1973, 29 U.S.C. § 791 et seq., Title VII, and various common law and constitutional law doctrines. Judge Pratt dismissed the constitutional and Title VII claims but denied the government's motion to dismiss the Rehabilitation Act claim.]

The plaintiff alleges that she was handicapped by reason of her "medically and psychologically established need for gender reassignment surgery." In order to state a claim of handicap discrimination under the Rehabilitation Act, the plaintiff must allege that she is a handicapped person who was otherwise qualified for the position in question, and that her rejection was based solely on the handicap. The Rehabilitation Act defines a handicapped person as, "Any person who (i) has a physical or mental impairment which substantially limits one or more of such persons major life activities, (ii) has a record of such impairment, or (iii) is regarded as having such an impairment." 29 U.S.C. § 706(7)(B).

The defendants argue that transsexualism is not a physical or mental handicap subject to the protections of the Rehabilitation Act. Our task, at this point, is not to determine whether transsexualism in fact constitutes a physical or mental impairment for this plaintiff. Rather, we must examine the complaint and decide whether the "plaintiff can prove no set of facts in support of [her] claim." *Conley v. Gibson*, 355 U.S. 41, 45–6 (1957).

Under the applicable regulations, an "impairment" can be "any mental or psychological disorder, such as ... emotional or mental illness." 45 C.F.R. § 84.3(j)(2)(i)(B). The language of the Rehabilitation Act and of the accompanying regulations is broadly drafted, indicating a legislative intent not to limit the Act's coverage to traditionally recognized handicaps. See 45 C.F.R. 84 App. A § 3. For purposes of this motion, we find that the complaint adequately alleges the necessary "physical or mental impairment" to state a claim under the Rehabilitation Act.

Acknowledging that the plaintiff does allege "emotional and psychological disorders," the defendants focus on the requirement that the plaintiff allege an impairment which "substantially limits one or more of ... her major life activities." The regulations define the term "major life activities" as "functions such as caring for one's self, performing manual tasks, walking, seeing, hearing, speaking, breathing, and working." 45 C.F.R. § 84.3(j)(2)(ii). No definition is given to the term "substantially limits." Although these elements are not alleged with great specificity, we find that taken as a whole the complaint adequately alleges that at the time of the alleged discrimination the plaintiff's impairment substantially limited at least her major life activity of "working." The burden, of course, will be on the plaintiff to prove that her transsexualism actually is an impairment which substantially limits one or more of her major life activities, or otherwise brings her within the definition of handicapped persons. On this point, we do observe that the definition of handicapped person given in the Rehabilitation Act and 45 C.F.R. § 84.3(j) extends to those who are merely "regarded" by others as having an impairment which substantially limits major life activities. In particular, the regulations state that a handicapped person can be one who has a "physical or mental impairment that substantially limits major life activities only as a result of the attitudes of others toward such impairment." 45 C.F.R. § 84.3(j)(2)(iv). The questions of fact necessarily raised by defendants' arguments preclude our resolving the Rehabilitation Act claim on a motion to dismiss. * * *

NOTE ON THE APPLICATION OF DISABILITY DISCRIMINATION LAW

The *Doe* case settled when the Postal Service adopted a new policy recognizing transsexualism as a handicap. But cases like it (and *Blackwell, supra*) were short lived. In enacting the Americans with Disabilities Act in 1990, Congress insured that it would not be used to protect transsexuals from discrimination by explicitly excluding that condition as a recognized disability. 42 U.S.C. § 12208. Just to tidy up the law, Congress at the same time amended the Rehabilitation Act of 1973 (known as "Section 504") to also exclude transsexualism from coverage as a handicap under that statute. 29 U.S.C. § 706(8)(F)(i) (see Chapter 10, Section 2). Congress also excluded transvestism from both statutes at the same time.

Almost every state has its own law prohibiting discrimination based on disability, but few of them have taken up the question of whether transsexualism is covered. Washington state, Minnesota, and Oregon interpret their disability discrimination laws to include transsexualism. See *Doe v. Boeing Co., infra,* Section 3; Minn. Stat. Ann. § 363.01; announcement of Oregon Bureau of Labor and Industry, Oct. 9, 1996. How do you think the District of Columbia would interpret its Human Rights Act [Appendix 2] on this issue?

In contrast, the Iowa Supreme Court upheld the decision of the Iowa Civil Rights Commission that transsexualism was neither a physical nor a mental disability, nor was transsexualism a "perceived" handicap covered under the statute:

> Under the implementing rule, a physical impairment relates to an organic disorder of the body. No claim is made that a transsexual has an abnormal or unhealthy body. * * * A [transsexual] has a grave problem, but that problem does not necessarily constitute the kind of mental condition that the legislature intended to be treated as a substantial handicap to employment under the statute. * * * [T]rans-sexualism lacks the inherent propensity to limit major life activities * * * An adverse societal attitude does not mean that the transsexual is necessarily perceived as having a physical or mental impairment. Although a transsexual may have difficulty in obtaining and retaining employment, the commission could reasonably believe that difficulty is the result of discrimination based on societal beliefs that the transsex-

ual is undesirable, rather than from beliefs that the transsexual is impaired physically or mentally * * *

Sommers v. Iowa Civil Rights Commission, 337 N.W.2d 470, 476–77 (Iowa 1983). A federal district court construing the Pennsylvania statute followed the *Sommers* reasoning in denying protection under Pennsylvania's law in *Dobre v. National Railroad Passenger Corp. ("Amtrak")*, 850 F.Supp. 284, 288–90 (E.D.Pa.1993).

G.B. v. Jerome Lackner

California Court of Appeal, First District, Division 3, 1978.
80 Cal.App.3d 64, 145 Cal.Rptr. 555.

■ ABBE, ASSOCIATE JUSTICE.

In 1975, the appellant, hereinafter referred to as G. B., consulted Dr. John Brown, a plastic surgeon, who diagnosed him as suffering from gender identity dysphoria or transsexualism. Dr. Brown determined that it was medically necessary and reasonable to perform surgery, which would involve the removal of the male sex organs and construction of female genitalia.

Dr. Brown filed a treatment authorization request with the San Francisco Medi–Cal field office. The request was denied by Dr. Wayne Erdbrink, a Medi–Cal consultant who is an ophthalmologist. No examination of any kind was ever performed on G. B. by the Department of Health.

G. B. requested a hearing pursuant to Welfare and Institutions Code section 10950 and got it. It was held in San Francisco on October 28, 1975, before Lester Lisker, a referee for the Department of Health, who ordered the treatment authorization request be granted.

The order of the referee was reversed by the Director of the California Department of Health (hereinafter referred to as Director). His refusal to authorize Medi–Cal to pay for the proposed surgery is set forth in a document entitled "Decision of the Director" and was signed by Lee Helsel, Deputy Director. The decision reads, in part, as follows: "The proposed operation as described by the claimant's doctor is a description of a cosmetic operation that would change the appearance of the claimant's external genitalia. Inasmuch as the proposed operation is to be performed solely for that purpose, it must be considered a cosmetic operation that is not covered under the Medi–Cal Program."

At the hearing before the referee, G. B. presented evidence by Dr. W. A. Tennant, a psychologist, Dr. Richard Crews, a psychiatrist, Dr. Jack Leibman, a medical doctor whose specialty is internal medicine and is a consultant to the Stanford University gender dysphoria program, and Dr. John Brown, a physician specializing in surgery. Dr. Erdbrink, the ophthalmologist, appeared on behalf of the Department of Health and presented a Medi–Cal bulletin dated September 1974, which contained the following announcement: "All medical services directly related to the diagnostic workup, surgical procedure, hormonal therapy or psychiatric care involved in trans-sexual surgery are not payable under the Medi–Cal Program. Medi–Cal will, however, cover the medical complications of such medical care to the extent the complications are typical of those encountered in the general population, such as a recto-vaginal fistula following such trans-sexual surgery. Claims submitted for treatment of such complications must contain sufficient documentation to justify the medical need. . . . "

Dr. Leibman asserted that G. B. "must have this [gender change] surgery to alleviate her emotional problems, prevent them from exacerbation, and to rehabilitate her to the point where she can function as a normal person and participate fully in society."

Dr. Brown stated that G. B. "must have the requested surgery to treat her disorder and prevent further suffering, enable her to participate in normal living, and obtain steady employment."

Dr. Tennant concluded a discussion of this type of surgery as follows: "Denial of this valid medical treatment can lead to a further deterioration in the psychological health of the transsexual resulting in self-mutilating acts and in some cases suicide."

Dr. Richard Crews declared that, "As a general rule transsexuals have an improved psychological, social, and vocational adjustment after transsexual surgery. I believe this will prove to be the case for [G. B.]. Numerous attempts by way of therapy, pharmacology, behavioral and disciplinary approaches have generally been unavailing in treating the transsexual. Surgery is thus indicated for [G. B.] and I believe she would benefit significantly by it."

The reversal of the referee's decision by the Director was on the sole ground that the proposed surgery was cosmetic in that it would change the appearance of G. B.'s external genitalia and, therefore, was not covered under the Medi–Cal program. The Director's conclusion that castration and penectomy changes the appearance of male genitalia seems strained.

There is no dispute that G. B. is an adult male transsexual. Adult male transsexuals, such as G. B., are not transvestites nor homosexuals but are males who have irreversibly accepted a gender identification as female. (See generally, Stoller, *Sex and Gender* [1968]; Green & Money, *Transsexualism and Sex Reassignment* [1969] p. 268.) Medical experts agree that the etiology of transsexualism is unknown but that it occurs early in life and is a serious problem of gender role disorientation. (Benjamin, "Should Surgery be Performed on Transsexuals?," 25 *Am. J. Psychotherapy*, pp. 74–75.)
* * *

Dr. Brown, G. B.'s physician, states that surgery "is reasonable and necessary for the treatment of this mental disorder, an illness which, in the vast majority of cases, only surgery will cure. . . . Failure [to obtain the surgery] will inevitably lead to serious frustration and possible self-mutilation or suicide. Additionally, a preoperative transsexual, in my experience, is often unable to obtain employment due to employer's biases, the requirements of a physical examination prior to employment, or psychological instability resulting from the frustration at being trapped in the body of a person of the opposite sex."

John Hoopes, M.D., of the Gender Identity Clinic at the Johns Hopkins Medical Institute points out: "Over the years, psychiatrists have tried repeatedly to treat these people without surgery, and the conclusion is inescapable that psychotherapy has not so far solved the problem. The patients have no motivation for psychotherapy and do not want to change back to their biological sex. The high incidence of suicide and self-mutilation among these people testifies to the magnitude of the problem. If the mind cannot be changed to fit the body, then perhaps we should consider changing the body to fit the mind." (Green & Money, *Transsexualism and Sex Reassignment, supra,* at p. 268.)

The severity of the problem of transsexualism becomes obvious when one contemplates the reality of the male transsexual's desperate desire to have normally functioning male genitals removed because the male sex organs are a source of immense psychological distress. Transsexuals consider themselves members of the opposite sex cursed with the wrong sexual apparatus. * * *

The extent of Medi–Cal coverage is set forth in Welfare and Institutions Code section 14059 as follows: "Health care provided under this chapter may include diagnostic, preventive, corrective, and curative services and supplies essential thereto, provided by qualified medical and related personnel for conditions that cause suffering, endanger life, result in illness or infirmity, interfere with capacity for normal activity including employment, or for conditions which may develop into some significant handicap. [Para.] Medical care shall include, but is not limited to, other remedial care, not necessarily medical. Other remedial care shall include, without being limited to, treatment by prayer or healing by spiritual means in the practice of the religion of any church or religious denomination." * * *

Pursuant to this authority, the Director promulgated title 22, California Administrative Code, section 51305, subdivision (g), which reads: "Procedures for the treatment of defects for cosmetic purposes only are covered subject to prior authorization. Authorization for procedures primarily for purposes of correcting cosmetic defects may be granted only to: [Para.] (1) Complete the repair of serious disfigurement resulting from disease or trauma. [Para.] (2) Correct disfiguring defects which substantially interfere with opportunities for employment. These cases shall be referred to the California Department of Rehabilitation for consultation, evaluation or case management as provided in Section 51014. [Para.] (3) Provide necessary services to patients eligible for coverage by Crippled Children Services. These patients shall be referred to Crippled Children Services for case management as provided in Section 51013." * * *

The Department of Health has adopted a definition of cosmetic surgery which was approved by the California Medical Association. It defines cosmetic surgery as, "Surgery to alter the texture or configuration of the skin and its relationship with contiguous structures of any feature of the human body. [Para.] This alteration would be considered by the average prudent observer to be within the range of normal and acceptable appearance for the patient's age and ethnic background and by competent medical opinion to be without risk to the patient's physical or mental health. [Para.] It means only surgery which is sought by the patient for personal reasons and is not used to denote surgery which is needed to correct or improve physical features which may be functionally normal but which attracts undue attention or even ridicule by his peers, or which an average person would consider to be conspicuous, objectionable, abnormal or displeasing to others. [Para.] Operations performed to correct congenital anomalies, to remove tumors, or restore parts which were removed in treatment of a tumor or repair a deformity or scar resulting from injury, infection, or other disease process is obviously not cosmetic even though the appearance may be improved by the procedure.''

Surely, castration and penectomy cannot be considered surgical procedures to alter the texture and configuration of the skin and the skin's relationship with contiguous structures of the body. Male genitals have to be considered more than just skin, one would think.

The definition relied upon by the Director to establish that the surgery must be considered cosmetic requires that the alteration (of the skin) would be considered by the average prudent observer to be within the range of normal and acceptable appearance for the patient's age and ethnic background. The average prudent observer probably has no desire and will not observe what is under the skirts or trousers of either a pre-or postoperative transsexual. It is not a generally recognized characteristic of transsexuals to move about in public in the nude. Dr. Hoopes, previously quoted, states at page 268: "You would probably never recognize a transsexual as such if you met him casually, or even if you knew him well. I cannot state too emphatically how completely these people assume the role of the opposite sex. The male transsexual looks, dresses, and acts exactly like a woman, and the same is true for his female counterpart. They are not simply transvestites, people who receive pleasure from just wearing the clothes of the opposite sex; nor are they homosexuals, as commonly defined.''

It is clearly impossible to conclude that transsexual surgery is cosmetic surgery, even using the definition relied on by the Director. Drs. Leibman and Brown and Webster's dictionary define cosmetic as ''beautifying, pertaining to or making for beauty,'' that which tends ''to beautify or enhance the appearance of a person.''

The only evidence presented in this case was that the surgery was necessary and reasonable.

We conclude that the proposed surgery cannot be arbitrarily classified as cosmetic and inasmuch as this was the sole basis of the Director's decision, his decision must be set aside.

■ Scott, Acting P.J., dissenting.

* * * The majority today embarks upon a dangerous course of judicial intermeddling with the policy decisions of the Department of Health. If this

operation must be funded, Medi–Cal will be forced to authorize other surgical treatments as "cures" for neuroses. The Legislature has vested the Director with adequate discretion to determine the parameters of the Medi–Cal program. If the Legislature wishes the State of California to pay for transsexual operations, it may so provide. That is not a matter in which this court should become involved. * * *

No evidence was presented in the record that appellant's genitals were abnormal or unhealthy. In transsexual surgery, as in other kinds of cosmetic surgery, nothing is physically amiss with the function of the portion of the body which is altered. The surgery is performed in an effort to alleviate the patient's emotional distress which is caused by his subjective perception of his body. In the administrative record in the instant case, Dr. Leibman states that appellant must have the surgery to alleviate his "emotional" problems. Dr. Tennant describes transsexualism as "a complicated condition wherein an individual clearly anatomically of one sex, is uncomfortable in that social and sexual role, and firmly believes that he or she belongs to the other sex." Dr. Tennant characterizes the purpose of the operation as putting an end to mental suffering and psychological dysfunction. Dr. Crews defines a transsexual as "an individual who is otherwise psychologically competent but has a firm and substantial sexual and social role identification different from the biological anatomy." Dr. Crews states that surgery would be "advisable" for appellant "from a psychiatric standpoint."

Although appellant's psychological condition is admittedly more serious than the condition of most persons who request plastic surgery, this factor does not justify an appellate court in overruling the Director's determination that the surgery is cosmetic. The very nature of the operation described in the record, coupled with the total lack of evidence that appellant's genitals were diseased, damaged or deformed, provides substantial evidence to support the Director's determination that the operation is cosmetic. * * *

Another ground of the Director's decision, equally sufficient, standing alone, to uphold that decision, is the Director's determination that the proposed surgery is not "reasonable and necessary for the prevention, diagnosis or treatment of disease, illness or injury." As stated above, the Medi–Cal program will only pay for health care services which meet this standard. (Cal. Admin. Code, § 51303, subd.[a].) Again, giving proper consideration to the Director's interpretation of his own regulation, I would hold that substantial evidence supports the Director's conclusion that the proposed surgery does not qualify as a program benefit under section 51303, subdivision (a) of the California Administrative Code.

A quotation from the majority opinion illustrates the problem: "'If the mind cannot be changed to fit the body, then perhaps we should consider changing the body to fit the mind.' (Green & Money, *Transsexualism and Sex Reassignment*, p. 268.)" Transsexual surgery is vastly different from other types of surgery. Instead of treating the part of the person which is ill, that is, the mind, a transsexual operation surgically alters a normal, healthy part of the body to conform the appearance of that part, as nearly as is medically possible, to the patient's misperception of himself. If the Director has been charged by statute with making policy for the Medi–Cal program (Welf. & Inst. Code, § 14105), surely then the Director could reasonably conclude that this operation is not "reasonable and necessary for the prevention, diagnosis or treatment of disease, illness or injury," as those terms are used in the regulations of the Department of Health. * * *

NOTE ON TRANSSEXUALS' RIGHT TO TREATMENT UNDER FEDERAL AND STATE LAW

Indigent persons who qualify for health coverage under Medicaid are eligible for, *inter alia*, physician services and inpatient hospital services. 42 U.S.C. § 1396a(13)(B). Federal regulations provide that a state (which actually administers the joint federal-state Medicaid program) may not "arbitrarily deny or reduce the amount, duration or scope of such services to an otherwise eligible individual solely because of the diagnosis, type of illness, or condition." 42 C.F.R. § 440.230(c). Based on the language of the statute and the regulations, courts have generally accepted the claim for Medicaid coverage of transsexual surgery by persons who can substantiate their medical need for it. See, *e.g.*, *Pinneke v. Preisser*, 623 F.2d 546 (8th Cir.1980).

Traditionally, the law of contract has controlled the extent to which a private insurance policy will cover almost any treatment. In *Davidson v. Aetna Life & Casualty Ins. Co.*, 420 N.Y.S.2d 450 (N.Y.Sup.Ct.1979), an insurance company was ordered to pay for transsexual surgery on the ground that it did not fall within the contractual exclusion of cosmetic surgery. Most such contracts today specify that transsexual surgery is not covered.

Part C.   Public Law Issues Relevant to Transgendered Persons

M.T. v. J.T.

New Jersey Superior Court, Appellate Division, 1976.
140 N.J.Super. 77, 355 A.2d 204, *cert. denied*, 71 N.J. 345, 364 A.2d 1076 (1976).

■ Handler, J.A.D.

This appeal presents the portentous problem of how to tell the sex of a person for marital purposes. Involved is a post-operative transsexual, born a male but now claiming to be a female.

The case started inauspiciously enough when plaintiff M.T. filed a simple complaint in the Juvenile and Domestic Relations Court for support and maintenance. The legal issue sharpened dramatically when defendant J.T. interposed the defense that M.T. was a male and that their marriage was void. Following a hearing the trial judge determined that plaintiff was a female and that defendant was her husband, and there being no fraud, ordered defendant to pay plaintiff $50-a-week support. Notice of appeal was then filed by defendant.

A careful recapitulation of the testimony is appropriate. M.T. testified that she was born a male. While she knew that she had male sexual organs she did not know whether she also had female organs. As a youngster she did not participate in sports and at an early age became very interested in boys. At the age of 14 she began dressing in a feminine manner and later began dating men. She had no real adjustment to make because throughout her life she had always felt that she was a female.

Plaintiff first met defendant in 1964 and told him about her feelings about being a woman. Sometime after that she began to live with defendant. In 1970 she started to go to Dr. Charles L. Ihlenfeld to discuss the possibility of having an operation so that she could "be physically a woman." In 1971, upon the doctor's advice, she went to a surgeon who agreed to operate. In May of that year she underwent surgery for the removal of male sex organs and construction of a vagina. Defendant paid for the operation. Plaintiff then applied to the State of New York to have her birth certificate changed.

On August 11, 1972, over a year after the operation, plaintiff and defendant went through a ceremonial marriage in New York State and then moved to Hackensack. They lived as husband and wife and had intercourse. Defendant supported plaintiff for over two years when, in October 1974, he left their home. He has not supported plaintiff since.
* * *

[Dr. Ihlenfeld] first saw and examined plaintiff in September 1970 and took a medical history from her. She told him that she had always felt like a woman and was living like a woman. She wanted sex reassignment surgery as well as treatments and hormones so that she could end the conflict she was feeling, "confronted with a male body," in order to live her life completely as the woman she thought herself to be. Dr. Ihlenfeld diagnosed her as a transsexual. He knew of no way to alter her sense of her own feminine gender identity in order to agree with her male body, and the only treatment available to her was to alter the body to conform with her sense of psyche gender identity. That regimen consisted of hormone treatment and sex reassignment surgery. Dr. Ihlenfeld recommended such an operation and treated plaintiff both before and after it.

The examination of plaintiff before the operation showed that she had a penis, scrotum and testicles. After the operation she did not have those organs but had a vagina and labia which were "adequate for sexual intercourse" and could function as any female vagina, that is, for "traditional penile/vaginal intercourse." The "artificial vagina" constructed by such surgery was a cavity, the walls of which are lined initially by the skin of the penis, often later taking on the characteristics of normal vaginal mucosa; the vagina, though at a somewhat different angle, was not really different from a natural vagina in size, capacity and "the feeling of the walls around it." Plaintiff had no uterus or cervix, but her vagina had a "good cosmetic appearance" and was "the same as a normal female vagina after a hysterectomy." Dr. Ihlenfeld had seen plaintiff since the operation and she never complained to him that she had difficulty having intercourse. So far as he knew, no one had tested plaintiff to find out what chromosomes she had. He knew that plaintiff had had silicone injections in her breasts; he had treated her continuously with female hormones to demasculinize her body and to feminize it at the same time. In the doctor's opinion plaintiff was a female; he no longer considered plaintiff to be a male since she could not function as a male sexually either for purposes of "recreation or procreation."

Plaintiff also produced Charles Annicello, a psychologist who worked at the gender identity clinic of the Johns Hopkins University Hospital. He was qualified as an expert in transsexualism. This witness demonstrated through slides the various methods by which scientists define whether a person is male or female. The witness said that transsexualism represented only one sexual variant although it was not known whether its cause was chromosomal, gonadal or hormonal. Annicello expressed the opinion that if a person had a female psychic gender and underwent a sex reassignment operation, that person would be considered female although no person is "absolutely" male or female. * * *

The trial judge made careful findings of fact on this evidential record. He accepted the testimony concerning M.T.'s personal and medical history as related by her and her doctor. He noted that defendant knew of her condition and cooperated in her sex reassignment surgery. The parties married in New York and subsequently consummated their marriage by engaging in sexual intercourse. The judge also found that defendant later deserted plaintiff and failed to support her.

Drawing from the opinions of the experts the judge defined a transsexual as "an individual anatomically of one sex who firmly believes he belongs to the other sex." He enumerated the seven factors considered generally relevant to the determination of sex. According to the judge, a preoperative transsexual would appropriately be classified according to his anatomical sex. After a successful sex reassignment operation, however, "psychological sex and anatomical sex become consistent as to outward appearances." The judge ruled that plaintiff was of the female psychic gender all her life and that her anatomical change through surgery required the conclusion that she was a female at the time of the marriage ceremony. He stated:

> It is the opinion of the court that if the psychological choice of a person is medically sound, not a mere whim, and irreversible sex reassignment surgery has been performed, society has no right to prohibit the transsexual from leading a normal life. Are we to look upon this person as an exhibit in a circus side show? What harm has said person done to society? The entire area of transsexualism is repugnant to the nature of many persons within our society. However, this should not govern the legal acceptance of a fact. * * *

Defendant's basic and continuing contention is that the marriage between him and plaintiff was a nullity because plaintiff was a male at the time of the ceremony. We disagree with this position and affirm the decision of the lower court. * * *

* * * The historic assumption in the application of common law and statutory strictures relating to marriages is that only persons who can become "man and wife" have the capacity to enter marriage. The pertinent statutes relating to marriages and married persons do not contain any explicit references to a requirement that marriage must be between a man and a woman. Nevertheless that statutory condition must be extrapolated. It is so strongly and firmly implied from a full reading of the statutes that a different legislative intent, one which would sanction a marriage between persons of the same sex, cannot be fathomed.

The issue must then be confronted whether the marriage between a male and a postoperative transsexual, who has surgically changed her external sexual anatomy from male to female, is to be regarded as a lawful marriage between a man and a woman.

An English case, *Corbett v. Corbett*, 2 W.L.R. 1306, 2 All E.R. 33 (P.D.A. 1970) appears to be the only reported decision involving the validity of marriage of a true postoperative transsexual and a male person. The judge there held that the transsexual had failed to prove that she had changed her sex from male to female. * * * Based upon an assumed distinction between "sex" and "gender," the court held that "marriage is a relationship which depends on sex and not on gender." *Id*. at 1325. In addition, the judge was mindful that the marriage was unstable, brief and the sexual exchange between the parties—the husband was a transvestite— was ambivalent. He concluded on alternative grounds that the marriage had not been, and indeed could not be, consummated.

We cannot join the reasoning of the *Corbett* case. The evidence before this court teaches that there are several criteria or standards which may be relevant in determining the sex of an individual. It is true that the anatomical test, the genitalia of an individual, is unquestionably significant and probably in most instances indispensable. For example, sex classification of an individual at birth may as a practical matter rely upon this test. For other purposes, however, where sex differentiation is required or accepted, such as for public records, service in the branches of the armed forces, participation in certain regulated sports activities, eligibility for types of employment and the like, other tests in addition to genitalia may also be important. * * *

Our departure from the *Corbett* thesis is not a matter of semantics. It stems from a fundamentally different understanding of what is meant by "sex" for marital purposes. The English court apparently felt that sex and gender were disparate phenomena. In a given case there may, of course, be such a difference. A preoperative transsexual is an example of that kind of disharmony, and most experts would be satisfied that the individual should be classified according to biological criteria. The evidence and authority which we have examined, however, show that a person's sex or sexuality embraces an individual's gender, that is, one's self-image, the deep psychological or emotional sense of sexual identity and character. * * *

The English court believed, we feel incorrectly, that an anatomical change of genitalia in the case of a transsexual cannot "affect her true sex." Its conclusion was rooted in the premise that "true sex" was required to be ascertained even for marital purposes by biological criteria. In the case of a transsexual following surgery, however, according to the expert testimony presented here, the dual tests of anatomy and gender are more significant. On this evidential demonstration, therefore, we are impelled to the conclusion that for marital purposes if the anatomical or genital features of a genuine transsexual are made to conform to the person's gender, psyche or psychological sex, then identity by sex must be governed by the congruence of these standards.

Implicit in the reasoning underpinning our determination is the tacit but valid assumption of the lower court and the experts upon whom reliance was placed that for purposes of marriage under the circumstances of this case, it is the sexual capacity of the individual which must be scrutinized. Sexual capacity or sexuality in this frame of reference requires the coalescence of both the physical ability and the psychological and emotional orientation to engage in sexual intercourse as either a male or a female. * * *

In sum, it has been established that an individual suffering from the condition of transsexualism is one with a disparity between his or her genitalia or anatomical sex and his or her gender, that is, the individual's strong and consistent emotional and psychological sense of sexual being. A transsexual in a proper case can be treated medically by certain supportive measures and through surgery to remove and replace existing genitalia with sex organs which will coincide with the person's gender. If such sex reassignment surgery is successful and the postoperative transsexual is, by virtue of medical treatment, thereby possessed of the full capacity to function sexually as a male or female, as the case may be, we perceive no legal barrier, cognizable social taboo, or reason grounded in public policy to prevent that person's identification at least for purposes of marriage to the sex finally indicated. * * *

In this case the transsexual's gender and genitalia are no longer discordant; they have been harmonized through medical treatment. Plaintiff has become physically and psychologically unified and fully capable of sexual activity consistent with her reconciled sexual attributes of gender and anatomy. Consequently, plaintiff should be considered a member of the female sex for marital purposes. It follows that such an individual would have the capacity to enter into a valid marriage relationship with a person of the opposite sex and did do so here. In so ruling we do no more than give legal effect to a fait accompli, based upon medical judgment and action which are irreversible. Such recognition will promote the individual's quest for inner peace and personal happiness, while in no way disserving any societal interest, principle of public order or precept of morality. * * *

In re Elaine Frances Ladrach

Probate Court for Stark County, Ohio, 1987.
32 Ohio Misc.2d 6, 513 N.E.2d 828.

■ CLUNK, JUDGE.

The singular issue before the court is whether a post-operative male to female transsexual is permitted under Ohio law to marry a male. More simply stated, the issue is whether two individuals, biologically and legally of the same sex at birth, may contract to marry each other?

The sequence of events that resulted in the case at bar started inconspicuously with the filing of a Petition for Change of Name by Edward Franklin Ladrach on April 22, 1986. On the same day, the matter was heard by the court. (Hereafter, for purposes of clarity and notwithstanding the fact that the applicant contends to be a biological female, the court will refer to the applicant with masculine pronouns.) The petitioner presented himself in female dress and explained that he intended to undergo "transsexual surgery" later in the year and that at that time was undergoing psychotherapy and was taking female hormones. He further stated to the court that it was a prerequisite for the surgery that the transsexual person dress and act as a member of the opposite sex for an extended period of time prior to the surgery. Finally, the applicant asked the court to change his name to Elaine Frances Ladrach as a further outward manifestation of his desire to be recognized as a female person. * * *

The court believes that so long as there is no intent to defraud creditors or deceive others and the applicant has acted in good faith, then the petition should be granted. On this basis the court granted the requested name change.

The second contact with the Stark County Probate Court in this sequence of events occurred on or about September 22, 1986 when Elaine Frances Ladrach and his fiancé presented themselves to the marriage license bureau and filled out the information sheet for a marriage license.

The application indicated that Elaine had been married two previous times and that his previous spouses were of the female gender, and that both prior marriages had been terminated by divorce. The clerk at this point called the judge who then reviewed the unsigned application and also a signed letter by a physician that stated, "Elaine Frances Ladrach has undergone a gender transformation from male to female establishing a somatic gender to match that of her soul." The physician's letter further stated that he had performed the surgery on September 8, 1986. The judge then advised the applicants that he would review the matter and advise them of his decision.

A review of the marriage statute, R.C. 3101.01, led the court to conclude that the application must be denied and the applicants were so advised on or about September 26, 1986. The basis for the declination was that the statute specifically permits the marriage of "male persons" and "female persons" of certain ages and degrees of relationship to each other. The court advised Elaine that his birth certificate still showed him to be a male person and that Ohio law did not permit persons of the same gender to marry.

On November 4, 1986, Elaine Frances Ladrach filed an application for correction of birth record, stating that Item 4 which reads "Boy" should read "Girl." [This application was dismissed without prejudice, and, based on the pleadings as filed in that case, the court requested, and the parties agreed, to proceed on the issue of] whether a post-operative male to female transsexual is permitted under Ohio law to marry a male. * * *

The applicant testified that although he was born a male and was married twice, each time to a female, that he considered himself a female and had then demonstrated that fact by the change of name, cross-dressing and the submission to the recent medical surgical procedure that resulted in the removal of the penis and testicles and the creation of a vagina.

Robert Hamilton III, M.D., a Canton, Ohio physician specializing in obstetrics and gynecology, testified that he saw Elaine Frances Ladrach on December 15, 1986, for a physical examination to determine if he was of the female gender. Dr. Hamilton stated that Elaine had "normal female external genitalia" and that in his opinion "he would classify Elaine as a female." He further stated that he did not perform a pap smear or chromosomal test. When questioned by applicant's counsel as to whether a chromosomal test would show Elaine to be a female he replied "highly unlikely." * * *

Transsexualism's short legal history has not resulted in any definitive direction to the court. It would appear that only three states, Arizona, Louisiana and Illinois, have statutes that allow the birth record of a transsexual to be changed following sex reassignment surgery (also referred to as anatomical change of sex by surgery or sex alteration surgery). However, another twelve states have permitted a post-operative change of sex designation on birth records. Ohio is not one of the fifteen states. * * *

It is the position of this court that the Ohio correction of birth record statute, R.C. 3705.20, is strictly a "correction" type statute, which permits the probate court when presented with appropriate documentation to correct errors such as spelling of names, dates, race and sex, if in fact the original entry was in error. There was no error in the designation of Edward Franklin Ladrach as a "Boy" in the category of "sex" on his birth certificate, and for this reason the previously mentioned application for correction of birth record was dismissed by this court. * * *

It seems obvious to the court that if a state permits such a change of sex on the birth certificate of a post-operative transsexual, either by statute or administrative ruling, then a marriage license, if requested, must issue to such a person provided all other statutory requirements are fulfilled. * * *

After reviewing the reported cases, law review articles and the post-hearing brief of the applicant, this court concludes that there is no authority in Ohio for the issuance of a marriage license to consummate a marriage between a post-operative male to female transsexual person and a male person. [Judge Clunk distinguished *M.T. v. J.T.* on the ground that it involved the question of whether a husband had an ongoing support obligation after two years of marriage; the New Jersey court gave "no indication" whether it "would have ordered a marriage license to issue if the issue of transsexualism had been raised at the time of the marriage application."]

There was no evidence that applicant at birth had any physical characteristics other than those of a male and he was thus correctly designated "Boy" on his birth certificate. There also was no laboratory documentation that the applicant had other than male chromosomes. There has been nothing shown to this court to cause it to change the existing Ohio law. Therefore, the application of Elaine Frances Ladrach to obtain a marriage license as a female person is denied.

NOTE ON TRANSSEXUAL MARRIAGE AND CHILD CUSTODY LAW

One difference between the New Jersey and Ohio decisions is that the Ohio court had the opportunity to prevent a marriage from occurring—which it took—while the New Jersey court was faced with what it described as a *fait accompli*, in the form of a petition for post-separation support. A similar "make the best of it" dynamic is evident in custody decisions affecting transgendered persons. In *Christian v. Randall*, 516 P.2d 132 (Colo.App.1973), the court denied a father's attempt to regain custody from a former wife who had become a male, based on evidence that the children were doing well. See also *In re Custody of T.J.*, 1988 WL 8302 (Minn.App. 1988) (affirming award of custody to father diagnosed with gender dysphoria where evidence showed no adverse effect on child).

A radically different result obtained, however, in *Daly v. Daly*, 715 P.2d 56 (Nev.1986), where the Nevada Supreme Court, over a strong dissent, upheld a termination of parental rights of a father who had become a woman. There was evidence that their 10–year-old daughter was extremely upset by her father's becoming a woman; the girl told the court that she did not want to visit him. Although the evidence may have justified curtailing visitation, the court granted the mother's petition to terminate the father's parental rights, seemingly to assure the child that the visitation issue was "settled." In a parting shot, the court asserted that "[i]t was strictly Tim Daly's choice to discard his fatherhood." *Id.* at 59.

Dee Farmer v. Edward Brennan, Warden, et al.

Supreme Court of the United States, 1994.
511 U.S. 825, 114 S.Ct. 1970, 128 L.Ed.2d 811.

■ JUSTICE SOUTER delivered the opinion of the Court.

A prison official's "deliberate indifference" to a substantial risk of serious harm to an inmate violates the Eighth Amendment. See *Helling v. McKinney*, 113 S.Ct. 2475 (1993); *Wilson v. Seiter*, 501 U.S. 294 (1991); *Estelle v. Gamble*, 429 U.S. 97 (1976). This case requires us to define the term "deliberate indifference," as we do by requiring a showing that the official was subjectively aware of the risk.

The dispute before us stems from a civil suit brought by petitioner, Dee Farmer, alleging that respondents, federal prison officials, violated the Eighth Amendment by their deliberate indifference to petitioner's safety. Petitioner, who is serving a federal sentence for credit card fraud, has been diagnosed by medical personnel of the Bureau of Prisons as a transsexual, one who has "[a] rare psychiatric disorder in which a person feels persistently uncomfortable about his or her anatomical sex," and who typically seeks medical treatment, including hormonal therapy and surgery, to bring about a permanent sex change. American Medical Association, *Encyclopedia of Medicine* 1006 (1989); see also American Psychiatric Association, *Diagnostic and Statistical Manual of Mental Disorders* 74–75 (3d rev. ed. 1987). For several years before being convicted and sentenced in 1986 at the age of 18, petitioner, who is biologically male, wore women's clothing (as petitioner did at the 1986 trial), underwent estrogen therapy, received silicone breast implants, and submitted to unsuccessful "black market" testicle-removal surgery. Petitioner's precise appearance in prison is unclear from the record before us, but petitioner claims to have continued hormonal treatment while incarcerated by using drugs smuggled into prison, and apparently wears clothing in a feminine manner, as by displaying a shirt "off one shoulder," App. 112. The parties agree that petitioner "projects feminine characteristics." *Id.*, at 51, 74.

The practice of federal prison authorities is to incarcerate preoperative transsexuals with prisoners of like biological sex, and over time authorities housed petitioner in several federal facilities, sometimes in the general male prison population but more often in segregation. While there is no dispute that petitioner was segregated at least several times because of violations of prison rules, neither is it disputed that in at least one penitentiary petitioner was segregated because of safety concerns.

On March 9, 1989, petitioner was transferred for disciplinary reasons from the Federal Correctional Institution in Oxford, Wisconsin (FCI–Oxford), to the United States Penitentiary in Terre Haute, Indiana (USP–Terre Haute). Though the record before us is unclear about the security designations of the two prisons in 1989, penitentiaries are typically higher security facilities that house more troublesome prisoners than federal correctional institutes. See generally Federal Bureau of Prisons, *Facilities 1990*. After an initial stay in administrative segregation, petitioner was placed in the USP–Terre Haute general population. Petitioner voiced no objection to any prison official about the transfer to the penitentiary or to placement in its general population. Within two weeks, according to petitioner's allegations, petitioner was beaten and raped by another inmate in petitioner's cell. Several days later, after petitioner claims to have reported the incident, officials returned petitioner to segregation to await, according to respondents, a hearing about petitioner's HIV-positive status.

Acting without counsel, petitioner then filed a *Bivens* complaint, alleging a violation of the Eighth Amendment. See *Bivens v. Six Unknown Fed.*

Narcotics Agents, 403 U.S. 388 (1971). As defendants, petitioner named respondents: the warden of USP–Terre Haute and the Director of the Bureau of Prisons (sued only in their official capacities); the warden of FCI–Oxford and a case manager there; and the director of the Bureau of Prisons North Central Region Office and an official in that office (sued in their official and personal capacities). As later amended, the complaint alleged that respondents either transferred petitioner to USP–Terre Haute or placed petitioner in its general population despite knowledge that the penitentiary had a violent environment and a history of inmate assaults, and despite knowledge that petitioner, as a transsexual who "projects feminine characteristics," would be particularly vulnerable to sexual attack by some USP–Terre Haute inmates. This allegedly amounted to a deliberately indifferent failure to protect petitioner's safety, and thus to a violation of petitioner's Eighth Amendment rights. Petitioner sought compensatory and punitive damages, and an injunction barring future confinement in any penitentiary, including USP–Terre Haute. * * *

We reject petitioner's invitation to adopt an objective test for deliberate indifference. We hold instead that a prison official cannot be found liable under the Eighth Amendment for denying an inmate humane conditions of confinement unless the official knows of and disregards an excessive risk to inmate health or safety; the official must both be aware of facts from which the inference could be drawn that a substantial risk of serious harm exists, and he must also draw the inference. This approach comports best with the text of the Amendment as our cases have interpreted it. The Eighth Amendment does not outlaw cruel and unusual "conditions"; it outlaws cruel and unusual "punishments." An act or omission unaccompanied by knowledge of a significant risk of harm might well be something society wishes to discourage, and if harm does result society might well wish to assure compensation. The common law reflects such concerns when it imposes tort liability on a purely objective basis. But an official's failure to alleviate a significant risk that he should have perceived but did not, while no cause for commendation, cannot under our cases be condemned as the infliction of punishment. * * *

We are no[t] persuaded by petitioner's argument that, without an objective test for deliberate indifference, prison officials will be free to ignore obvious dangers to inmates. Under the test we adopt today, an Eighth Amendment claimant need not show that a prison official acted or failed to act believing that harm actually would befall an inmate; it is enough that the official acted or failed to act despite his knowledge of a substantial risk of serious harm. We doubt that a subjective approach will present prison officials with any serious motivation "to take refuge in the zone between 'ignorance of obvious risks' and 'actual knowledge of risks.' " Brief for Petitioner 27. Whether a prison official had the requisite knowledge of a substantial risk is a question of fact subject to demonstration in the usual ways, including inference from circumstantial evidence, and a factfinder may conclude that a prison official knew of a substantial risk from the very fact that the risk was obvious. For example, if an Eighth Amendment plaintiff presents evidence showing that a substantial risk of inmate attacks was "longstanding, pervasive, well-documented, or expressly noted by prison officials in the past, and the circumstances suggest that the defendant-official being sued had been exposed to information concerning the risk and thus 'must have known' about it, then such evidence could be sufficient to permit a trier of fact to find that the defendant-official had actual knowledge of the risk." Brief for Respondents 22.

Nor may a prison official escape liability for deliberate indifference by showing that, while he was aware of an obvious, substantial risk to inmate safety, he did not know that the complainant was especially likely to be assaulted by the specific prisoner who eventually committed the assault. The question under the Eighth Amendment is whether prison officials, acting with deliberate indifference, exposed a prisoner to a sufficiently substantial "risk of serious damage to his future health," *Helling*, 113 S.Ct., at 2481, and it does not matter whether the risk comes from a single source or multiple sources, any more than it matters whether a prisoner faces an excessive risk of attack for reasons personal to him or because all prisoners in his situation face such a risk. * * *

Because, however, prison officials who lacked knowledge of a risk cannot be said to have inflicted punishment, it remains open to the officials to prove that they were unaware even of an obvious risk to inmate health or safety. That a trier of fact may infer knowledge from the obvious, in other words, does not mean that it must do so. Prison officials charged with deliberate indifference might show, for example, that they did not know of the underlying facts indicating a sufficiently substantial danger and that they were therefore unaware of a danger, or that they knew the underlying facts but believed (albeit unsoundly) that the risk to which the facts gave rise was insubstantial or nonexistent.

In addition, prison officials who actually knew of a substantial risk to inmate health or safety may be found free from liability if they responded reasonably to the risk, even if the harm ultimately was not averted. A prison official's duty under the Eighth Amendment is to ensure "reasonable safety," *Helling*, 113 S.Ct., at 2481, a standard that incorporates due regard for prison officials' "unenviable task of keeping dangerous men in safe custody under humane conditions." *Spain v. Procunier*, 600 F.2d 189, 193 (C.A.9 1979) (Kennedy, J.). Whether one puts it in terms of duty or deliberate indifference, prison officials who act reasonably cannot be found liable under the Cruel and Unusual Punishments Clause. * * *

In a suit such as petitioner's, insofar as it seeks injunctive relief to prevent a substantial risk of serious injury from ripening into actual harm, "the subjective factor, deliberate indifference, should be determined in light of the prison authorities' current attitudes and conduct," *Helling*, 113 S.Ct., at 2477: their attitudes and conduct at the time suit is brought and persisting thereafter. An inmate seeking an injunction on the ground that there is "a contemporary violation of a nature likely to continue," *United States v. Oregon Medical Society*, 343 U.S. 326, 333 (1952), must adequately plead such a violation; to survive summary judgment, he must come forward with evidence from which it can be inferred that the defendant-officials were at the time suit was filed, and are at the time of summary judgment, knowingly and unreasonably disregarding an objectively intolerable risk of harm, and that they will continue to do so; and finally to establish eligibility for an injunction, the inmate must demonstrate the continuance of that disregard during the remainder of the litigation and into the future. In so doing, the inmate may rely, in the district court's discretion, on developments that postdate the pleadings and pretrial motions, as the defendants may rely on such developments to establish that the inmate is not entitled to an injunction. If the court finds the Eighth Amendment's subjective and objective requirements satisfied, it may grant appropriate injunctive relief. * * *

[Under the Eighth Amendment standard adopted by the Court, summary judgment for the defendants was inappropriate. The trial court had merely cited Farmer's failure to complain, but Justice Souter ruled that other evidence could establish a subjective knowledge of Farmer's risk.] [P]etitioner pointed to respondents' admission that petitioner is a "nonviolent" transsexual who, because of petitioner's "youth and feminine appearance" is "likely to experience a great deal of sexual pressure" in prison. App. 50–51, 73–74. And petitioner recounted a statement by one of the respondents, then warden of the penitentiary in Lewisburg, Pennsylvania, who told petitioner that there was "a high probability that [petitioner] could not safely function at USP–Lewisburg," id., at 109, an incident confirmed in a published District Court opinion. * * *

■ JUSTICE THOMAS, concurring in the judgment.

Prisons are necessarily dangerous places; they house society's most antisocial and violent people in close proximity with one another. Regrettably, "[s]ome level of brutality and sexual aggression among [prisoners] is inevitable no matter what the guards do ... unless all prisoners are locked in their cells 24 hours a day and sedated." *McGill v. Duckworth*, 944 F.2d 344, 348 (C.A.7 1991). Today, in an attempt to rectify such unfortunate conditions, the Court further refines the "National Code of Prison Regulation," otherwise known as the Cruel and Unusual Punishments Clause. *Hudson v. McMillian*, 112 S.Ct. 995, 1001 (1992) (Thomas, J., dissenting). * * *

Even though the Court takes a step in the right direction by adopting a restrictive definition of deliberate indifference, I cannot join the Court's opinion. For the reasons expressed more fully in my dissenting opinions in *Hudson* and *Helling*, I remain unwilling to subscribe to the view, adopted by *ipse dixit* in *Estelle*, that the Eighth Amendment regulates prison conditions not imposed as part of a sentence. Indeed, "[w]ere the issue squarely presented, ... I might vote to overrule *Estelle*." *Helling*, 113 S.Ct., at 2485 (Thomas, J., dissenting). Nonetheless, the issue is not squarely presented in this case. Respondents have not asked us to revisit *Estelle*, and no one has briefed or argued the question. In addition to these prudential concerns, stare decisis counsels hesitation in overruling dubious precedents. For these reasons, I concur in the Court's judgment. * * *

THE LEGAL REGULATION OF CROSS-DRESSING

Marjorie Garber, Vested Interests: Cross–Dressing and Cultural Anxiety 10–13, 16–17 (1992). Shakespeare scholar Marjorie Garber argues that cross-dressing in western culture is both pervasive and under constant pressure to conform to the prevailing gender binarism. For Garber, however, "one of the most important aspects of cross-dressing is the way in which it offers a challenge to easy notions of binarity, putting into question the categories of 'female' and 'male,' whether they are considered essential or constructed, biological or cultural. The current popularity of cross-dressing as a theme in art and criticism represents, I think, an undertheorized recognition of the necessary critique of binary thinking, whether particularized as male and female, black and white, yes and no, Republican and Democrat, self and other, or in any other way."

Cross-dressing, Garber maintains, undermines binary thinking by putting into play a "third" way of articulation. She invokes the following parallels. The "Third World" was originally conceived as the battleground arena between the United States and the Communist bloc; in classical drama, the "third actor" was added by Sophocles to open up the drama constrained by the binary opposition between a protagonist and antagonist. In Lacanian psychology, the "Symbolic" is the third dimension, which is neither unmediated reality nor dyadic complementarity (mirror imagery), but is instead the world with which the subject interacts only through immersion in cultural languages, customs, and codes.

"All three of these examples—the Third World, the third actor, and the Symbolic—involve moving from a structure of complementarity to a contextualization, in which what once stood as an exclusive dual relation becomes an element in a larger chain. * * * This interruption, this disruptive act of putting into question, is * * * precisely the place, and the role, of the transvestite." Specifically, Garber maintains that cross-dressing becomes an index of what she calls a "category crisis," that is, "a failure of definitional distinction, a borderline that becomes permeable, that permits of border crossings from one (apparently distinct) category to another: black/white, Jew/Christian, noble/bourgeois, master/servant, master/slave. The binarism male/female * * * is itself put in question or under erasure in transvestism, and a transvestite figure, or a transvestite mode, will always function as a sign of overdetermination—a mechanism of displacement from one blurred category to another. An analogy here might be the so-called 'tagged' gene that shows up in a genetic chain, indicating the presence of some otherwise hidden condition. It is not the gene itself, but its presence, that marks the trouble spot, indicating the likelihood of a crisis somewhere, elsewhere." Thus Garber argues that cross-dressing does not always or necessarily signal a gender crisis; it may be a marker for something else.

PART A.   WHEN CLOTHES MAKE A MAN: A HISTORY OF AMERICAN REGULATION OF CROSS DRESSING[a]

St. Louis in 1864 adopted Ordinance No. 5421, article II, § 2, which among other things prohibited cross dressing:

> Whoever shall, in this city, appear in any public place in a state of nudity, or in a dress not belonging to his or her sex, or in an indecent or lewd dress; or shall make an indecent exposure of his or her person, or be guilty of an indecent or lewd act or behavior; or shall exhibit, sell or offer to sell, any indecent or lewd book, picture or other thing; or shall exhibit or perform any indecent, immoral, or lewd play or other representation, shall be deemed guilty of a misdemeanor.

A similar regulation was adopted in 1866 by San Francisco as one of that city's early "General Orders." Chicago's and Nashville's 1881 Codes contained a like provision, and anti-cross-dressing rules were adopted by Minneapolis in 1877, Oakland in 1879, San José in 1882, and by Cedar Rapids, Iowa; Columbia, Missouri; Kansas City, Missouri; Memphis, Tennessee; Newark, New Jersey; Santa Barbara, California; and other cities around the turn of the century.

No state law specifically targeted cross-dressing per se, but "disguise" laws were sometimes applied to cross dressers. A New York statute of 1845 defined as an unlawful vagrant "[a] person who, having his face painted, discolored, covered, or concealed, or being otherwise disguised, in a manner calculated to prevent his being identified, appears in a road or public highway." New York Laws 1845, ch. 3, § 6, recodified in the 1881 Code of Criminal Procedure as § 887(7). California in 1873 adopted a law prohibiting the concealment of one's identity by wearing a masque or disguise. California Laws 1873–74, ch. 614, p. 426, § 15, codified as California Penal Code § 185. Other states and municipalities had similar anti-disguise regulations. Anecdotal evidence as well as police records establish that these laws were invoked by police to arrest cross-dressing women and men.

Who was prosecuted under these laws? At whom were they aimed? The earliest laws focusing on cross dressing may have been responses in part to the first wave of the women's movement. The image of women wearing trousers signified a broader claim for participation in the workforce outside

---

a. The material that follows is taken from Nan D. Hunter, "Gender Disguise and the Law" (draft 1990) and William N. Eskridge, Jr., "The Legal Construction of the Homosexual: American Regulation of Same–Sex Intimacy, 1880–1946," *Iowa L. Rev.* (forthcoming 1997).

the home and for personal mobility.[b] Relatedly, the cross-dressing and disguise statutes may have had a common origin in preventing fraud and deceit. The mutual object of such laws in the nineteenth century were "gender fraud" cases: women who sought to "pass" as men (Hunter 1–5). This practice had begun much earlier, but nineteenth century America saw many publicized examples. With increasing urbanization, the attention of the state came to focus on cross dressing as a signal of gender deviance, often expressed in statutes prohibiting vagrancy, public lewdness, or indecency.

Born in 1849, Jeanne Bonnet was the most notorious cross dresser in the West.[c] As a teenager in San Francisco, she organized gangs of boy thieves, and in the 1870s organized a gang of female prostitutes who renounced men and supported themselves through petty theft and shoplifting. According to one account, she was arrested 20 times for "wearing male attire." She reportedly went to jail for some of the arrests because she refused to pay the fine. "The police might arrest me as often as they wish— I will never discard male attire as long as I live." Bonnet was assassinated in 1876, probably by an enraged male pimp, while visiting her lover, former prostitute Blanche Buneau.

Not all cross dressers were treated as roughly as Bonnet. When in 1897 Elvira Mugarrieta, a/k/a Babe Bean, was detained by police in Stockton, California, for dressing as a man, the authorities were surprisingly tolerant of this gender-bending eccentric. Persuaded that she did not violate the state masquerade law because she conspired to commit no crime nor deceit, Babe Bean was allowed to dress as she wished and was hired as a correspondent for a local newspaper. Other "Girls of Stockton" protested, observing: "There used to be a law against females dressing like the human male being, but it seems not to apply to Babe Bean. If Babe Bean is a girl, and continues to dress in boys' clothing, the rest of us ought to have the same privilege, and we are going to do it."[d] Dozens of women as well as men came to Bean's defense. Mugarrieta fought in the Spanish–American War as Jack Bean and lived in San Francisco for almost 36 years as Jack Garland, a woman who completely submerged her identity under male attire.

After 1900, however, the urban middle class was no longer so bemused by gender bending. Whereas Babe Bean could dress as a male with little

---

b. Elizabeth Cady Stanton wrote in 1869: "When we have a voice in the legislature we shall dress as we please, and if, by concealing our sex we find that we, too, can roam up and down the earth in safety, we shall keep our womanhood a profound secret." Quoted in Louis Sullivan, *From Female to Male: The Life of Jack Bee Garland* 2 (1990). Stockton, California assertedly had a law prohibiting cross dressing for precisely this reason, but the law was repealed by the 1890s. *Id.* at 64.

c. See San Francisco Lesbian and Gay History Project, "'She Even Chewed Tobacco': A Pictorial Narrative of Passing Women in America," in *Hidden from History: Reclaiming the Gay & Lesbian Past* 183, 188–190 (Martin Duberman, Martha Vicinus and George Chauncey, Jr., editors, 1989).

d. Quoted in Sullivan, *From Female to Male* 62–63.

harassment in 1890s Stockton, Jack Garland felt compelled to carry on a complete charade in post–1900 San Francisco, which was one of the few cities to have an ordinance directed specifically and exclusively against cross dressing, adopted in June 1903. By the turn of the century, gender inappropriateness was no longer just a curiosity—it was widely considered a dangerous sickness (Chapter 2, Section 2[A][2]).

In the next generation, cross dressing became increasingly associated with various forms of both gender and sexual deviance. Magnus Hirschfeld, in *Die Transvetitien* (1910), described people who had strong sexual urgings to dress in attire of the opposite sex. Although Hirschfeld carefully distinguished between transvestism (erotic stimulation from cross dressing) and homosexuality (erotic attraction to a person of the same sex), the American sexologists followed Krafft–Ebing in thinking the two phenomena related. Carroll Smith–Rosenberg and other feminist historians have documented the association between dressing as men and the demands of young women (straight as well as gay) for greater personal freedom at the beginning of the twentieth century (Chapter 2, Section 2).

Municipal ordinances prohibiting cross dressing grew like weeds in a vacant lot in the twentieth century. Cities as different as Los Angeles, Dallas and Houston, Detroit, Miami and Miami Beach, and Cincinnati and Columbus adopted laws making it illegal to appear in attire not of one's sex. Police records substantiating how many people were arrested for violating such ordinances are extremely difficult to locate, and existing ones may be incomplete. We do know that in St. Louis, for example, approximately half a dozen people a year (including males and females in roughly equal numbers) were arrested for "appearing in dress not belonging to [his] sex" between 1887 and 1920, after which such arrests disappear from the records. Anecdotal evidence suggests that these laws were often used to harass butch lesbians and gay female impersonators well after 1920.

PART B.   THE STATE'S INTEREST IN GENDER NORMATIVE DRESS

People of the State of New York v. Mauricio Archibald

Supreme Court, Appellate Term, First Department, 1968.
58 Misc.2d 862, 296 N.Y.S.2d 834, *affirmed* 27 N.Y.2d 504, 312 N.Y.S.2d 678, 260 N.E.2d 871 (1970).

■ PER CURIAM.

The defendant was convicted, after a trial, of the offense of vagrancy (Code Crim. Pro., § 887, subd. 7—impersonating a female). The statute provides that one is a vagrant "who * * * [has] his face painted, discolored, covered or concealed, or being otherwise disguised, in a manner calculated to prevent his being identified."

At trial the officer testified that, while patrolling a subway station platform at 4:00 a.m., he observed three people engaged in a loud conversation. The officer testified that after he passed the group, "the defendant turned around and over the right shoulder winked at me with his eye and again turned around and continued walking away from me * * *." The officer spoke briefly to the defendant and when asked whether he was a boy or girl, the defendant replied "I am a girl." The testimony further indicated that the defendant was wearing a white evening dress, high heel shoes, blonde wig, female undergarments, and facial makeup.

The defendant admittedly appeared in a public subway station dressed in female attire and concealed his true gender. In doing so, the defendant was in violation of subdivision 7 of section 887 which forbids a disguise "in a manner calculated to conceal his being identified."

It is not true, as the defendant contends, that in order to sustain a conviction under this section, the People must establish that the defendant was a vagrant without visible means of support; that element need not be proven within the purview of subdivision 7 of section 887. * * *

An additional element which defendant seeks to introduce into this section is that the People must prove a specific intention of employing the disguise to commit some illegal act. * * * The unequivocal wording of the statute does not require a showing of criminal intent, nor is it to be employed therein. * * *

Judgment of conviction affirmed.

■ JUDGE MARKOWITZ, dissenting.

This conviction is predicated solely upon the appellant's attire, *viz.*, female clothing and makeup. He was neither disorderly, abusive, nor otherwise conducting himself in an unlawful manner. Nor can it be seriously questioned that he was on the subway platform incident to traveling home from a masquerade party. Nevertheless, he was convicted of violating subdivision 7 of section 887 of the Code of Criminal Procedure. The history of this section, however, leads to the conclusion that his conviction was error and that this case is not within the purview of the vagrancy laws.

The prototype of subdivision 7 of section 887 was enacted into law by chapter 3 of the Laws of 1845 entitled "An Act to prevent persons appearing disguised and armed." * * * As indicated therein the original section was enacted as part of an over-all policy aimed at ending the anti-rent riots, an armed insurrection by farmers in the Hudson Valley. The rioting had reached such intensity that a state of insurrection had been declared. This particular statute was addressed to a specific group of insurrectionists who, while disguised as "Indians," murdered law enforcement officers attempting to serve writs upon the farmers. The "Indians" were in fact farmers, who as part of their costumes, wore women's calico dresses to further conceal their identities. The only connection this section had with men attired in female clothing was the fact that the attire was used in furtherance of a scheme of murder and insurrection. Indeed, males dressed in female attire for purposes other than discussed above were not even considered by the Legislature adopting the section. It thus would appear that the appellant's conduct herein was neither within the meaning of the section nor within the contemplation of the Legislature which first enacted the statute.

Notwithstanding the legislative history and circumstances surrounding the enactment of the original law, it is urged by the majority that this conviction be affirmed on the strength of cases decided by this court, particularly *People v. Gillespi* and *People v. Johnson*, both affirmed 15 N.Y.2d 529, by a divided court. However, the facts disclose that reliance and emphasis in those cases were placed upon the recidivism of the defendants combined with the nature of their conduct.

The section in its present form is aimed at discouraging overt homosexuality in public places which is offensive to public morality. In addition to a deterrent to sexual aberration, it is also addressed to crime detection and prevention of criminal activity. These areas are within the province of legislative controls. In practice, the section has been strictly confined to these narrow limits. While *Gillespi* and *Johnson* were deemed to be within the section's narrow scope, it is clear that the instant appellant's conduct herein was not. In contrast to *Gillespi* and *Johnson*, appellant testified that the only reason he was dressed in women's clothing was to attend a masquerade party where he had been drinking; that he had never been arrested; that he was gainfully employed; that he had visible means of support; and that he did not make a habit of dressing in female attire. By no stretch of the imagination could he be considered to be within any of the categories encompassed by the section as construed.

* * * "Mere masquerading is not sufficient; and I cannot conceive that our Legislature, in the exercise of its police power, intended to declare such an act [masquerading] *malum prohibitum*, i.e., criminal in itself without proof of specific criminal intent." [*People v. Luechini*, 136 N.Y.S. 319, 320 (1912).]

If appellant's conviction was correct then circus clowns, strangely attired "hippies," flowing-haired "yippies" and every person who would indulge in the Halloween tradition of "Trick or Treat" ipso facto may be targets for criminal sanctions as vagrants. Today women are wearing their hair increasingly shorter, and men are wearing their hair increasingly longer. Facial makeup, hair dyeing and cosmetic treatment are no longer the exclusive province of women. Men's and women's clothing styles are becoming increasingly similar. Thus, carrying the majority view to its logical conclusion, a young man or woman could possibly be convicted under this section as a vagrant merely for venturing into the street in his or her normal attire, which is otherwise acceptable in society today. * * *

It is clear from the above that behavior of the appellant herein is not the type of conduct ever intended by the Legislature to be subject to the limitations of the vagrancy statute. Therefore, as applied to appellant, the statute in question constitutes an overreaching, an invalid exercise of the State's police power. * * *

City of Chicago v. Wallace Wilson and Kim Kimberley

Illinois Supreme Court, 1978.
75 Ill.2d 525, 27 Ill.Dec. 458, 389 N.E.2d 522.

■ THOMAS J. MORAN, JUSTICE.

Defendants were arrested on February 18, 1974, minutes after they emerged from a restaurant where they had had breakfast. Defendant Wilson was wearing a black, knee-length dress, a fur coat, nylon stockings and a black wig. Defendant Kimberley had a bouffant hair style and was wearing a pants suit, high-heeled shoes and cosmetic makeup. Defendants were taken to the police station and were required to pose for pictures in various stages of undress. Both defendants were wearing brassieres and garter belts; both had male genitals. * * *

At trial, the defendants testified that they were transsexuals, and were, at the time of their arrests, undergoing psychiatric therapy in preparation for a sex reassignment operation. As part of this therapy, both defendants stated, they were required to wear female clothing and to adopt a female life-style. Kimberley stated that he had explained this to the police at the time of his arrest. Both defendants said they had been transsexuals all of their lives and thought of themselves as females. [Both were convicted and fined $100 each.]

Section 192–8 of the Code provides:

"Any person who shall appear in a public place * * * in a dress not belonging to his or her sex, with intent to conceal his or her sex, * * * shall be fined not less than twenty dollars nor more than five hundred dollars for each offense." * * *

In *Kelley v. Johnson* (1976), 425 U.S. 238, the Supreme Court was confronted with the question of whether one's choice of appearance was constitutionally protected from governmental infringement. At issue was an order promulgated by petitioner, the commissioner of police for Suffolk County, New York, which order established hair-grooming standards for male members of the police force. The court acknowledged that the due process clause of the fourteenth amendment "affords not only a procedural guarantee against deprivation of 'liberty,' but likewise protects substantive aspects of liberty against unconstitutional restrictions by the State." (425 U.S. 238, 244.) The court observed, however, that its prior cases offered little, if any, guidance on whether the citizenry at large has some sort of liberty interest in matters of personal appearance. It assumed for purposes of its opinion that such did exist.

In determining the scope of that interest and the justification that would warrant its infringement, the court distinguished claims asserted by individuals of a uniformed police department from claims by the citizenry at large, noting that the distinction was "highly significant." (425 U.S. 238, 245.) The court held that, in the context of the case before it, the burden rested with the respondent police officer to demonstrate that there was no rational connection between the regulation and the police department's legitimate function of promoting safety of persons and property. After analyzing the need for uniformity and discipline within the ranks of the police department, the court concluded that the challenged order was rationally related to two legitimate objectives: first, "to make police officers readily recognizable to the members of the public," and second, to foster the "espirit de corps which such similarity is felt to inculcate within the police force itself." (425 U.S. 238, 248.) Mr. Justice Powell, who specially concurred, noted that "[w]hen the State has an interest in regulating one's personal appearance * * * there must be a weighing of the degree of infringement of the individual's liberty interest against the need for the regulation." 425 U.S. 238, 249. * * *

Even though one's choice of appearance is not considered a "fundamental" right (*Richards v. Thurston* (1st Cir.1970), 424 F.2d 1281, 1284–85), the State is not relieved from showing some justification for its intrusion. As *Kelley* suggests, the degree of protection to be accorded an individual's choice of appearance is dependent upon the context in which the right is asserted. It is, therefore, incumbent upon the court to analyze both the circumstances under which the right is asserted and the reasons which the State offers for its intrusion.

In this court, the city has asserted four reasons for the total ban against cross-dressing in public: (1) to protect citizens from being misled or defrauded; (2) to aid in the description and detection of criminals; (3) to prevent crimes in washrooms; and (4) to prevent inherently antisocial conduct which is contrary to the accepted norms of our society. The record, however, contains no evidence to support these reasons.

If we assume that the ordinance is, in part, directed toward curbing criminal activity, the city has failed to demonstrate any justification for infringing upon the defendants' choice of public dress under the circumstances of this case.

Both defendants testified that they are transsexuals and were, at the time of their arrest, undergoing psychiatric therapy in preparation for a sex-reassignment operation. * * * Neither of the defendants was engaged in deviate sexual conduct or any other criminal activity. Absent evidence to the contrary, we cannot assume that individuals who cross-dress for purposes of therapy are prone to commit crimes.

The city's fourth reason (as noted above) for prohibiting the defendants' choice of public dress is apparently directed at protecting the public morals. In its brief, however, the city has not articulated the manner in which the ordinance is designed to protect the public morals. It is presumably believed that cross-dressing in public is offensive to the general public's aesthetic preference. There is no evidence, however, that cross-dressing, when done as a part of a preoperative therapy program or otherwise, is, in and of itself, harmful to society. In this case, the aesthetic preference of society must be balanced against the individual's well-being.

Through the enactment of section 17(1)(d) of the Vital Records Act (Ill. Rev.Stat. 1977, ch. 111 ½, par. 73–17(1)(d)), which authorizes the issuance of a new certificate of birth following sex-reassignment surgery, the legislature has implicitly recognized the necessity and validity of such surgery. It would be inconsistent to permit sex-reassignment surgery yet, at the same time, impede the necessary therapy in preparation for such surgery. Individuals contemplating such surgery should, in consultation with their doctors, be entitled to pursue the therapy necessary to insure the correctness of their decision.

Inasmuch as the city has offered no evidence to substantiate its reasons for infringing on the defendants' choice of dress under the circumstances of this case, we do not find the ordinance invalid on its face; however, we do find that section 192–8 as applied to the defendants is an unconstitutional infringement of their liberty interest. The judgments of the appellate court and the circuit court are reversed and the cause is remanded to the circuit court with directions to dismiss.

City of Columbus v. John H. Rogers

Ohio Supreme Court, 1975.
41 Ohio St.2d 161, 324 N.E.2d 563.

■ C. William O'Neill, Chief Justice.

Section 2343.04 of the Columbus City Codes reads:

"No person shall appear upon any public street or other public place in a state of nudity or in a dress not belonging to his or her sex, or in an indecent or lewd dress."

Appellant states as a proposition of law that Section 2343.04 '* * * is unconstitutionally vague on its face on the grounds it fails to give fair notice of the conduct forbidden by the ordinance and fails to provide guidelines to law enforcement officials charged with its enforcement.' * * *

In holding a Cincinnati ordinance prohibiting prowling unconstitutional in *Cincinnati v. Taylor* (1973), 303 N.E.2d 886, it was said in the course of the opinion,

"Section 901–P10 is unconstitutionally void for vagueness, because it does not provide adequate standards by which activity can be determined as legal or illegal.

"The standard is inadequate '* * * to give a person of ordinary intelligence fair notice that his contemplated conduct is forbidden by the statute. The underlying principle is that no man shall be held criminally responsible for conduct which he could not reasonable understand to be proscribed.' *United States v. Harriss* (1954), 347 U.S. 612, 617.

"The ordinance is also inadequate in providing guidelines for law enforcement officials charged with its enforcement. Such boundless discretion granted by the ordinance encourages arbitrary and capricious enforcement of the law. * * *"

The rationale underlying the "void for vagueness" doctrine was expressed in *Columbus v. Thompson* (1971), 266 N.E.2d 571, wherein it was stated:

"Basic to any penal enactment is the requirement that it be sufficiently clear in defining the activity proscribed, and that it contain 'ascertainable standards of guilt.' *Winters v. New York* (1948), 333 U.S. 507, 515.

"The purpose of such a requirement is, as stated in *Connally v. General Construction Co.* (1926), 269 U.S. 385, 391, '* * * to inform those who are subject to it what conduct on their part will render them liable to its penalties * * *. And a statute which either forbids or requires the doing of an act in terms so vague that men of common intelligence must necessarily guess at its meaning and differ as to its application, violates the first essential of due process of law.' " * * *

Appellant was convicted for violating the provision of the ordinance prohibiting public appearance by any person '* * * in a dress not belonging to his or her sex.' The determinative issue is whether the quoted language of the ordinance gives 'a person of ordinary intelligence fair notice that his contemplated conduct is forbidden,' or whether that language is so vague 'that men of common intelligence must necessarily guess at its meaning and differ as to its application.'

Modes of dress for both men and women are historically subject to changes in fashion. At the present time, clothing is sold for both sexes which is so similar in appearance that "a person of ordinary intelligence" might not be able to identify it as male or female dress. In addition, it is not uncommon today for individuals to purposely, but innocently, wear apparel which is intended for wear by those of the opposite sex.

Once it is recognized that present-day dress may not be capable of being characterized as being intended for male or female wear by a "person of ordinary intelligence," the constitutional defect in the ordinance becomes apparent.

The defect is that the terms of the ordinance, "dress not belonging to his or her sex," when considered in the light of contemporary dress habits, make it "so vague that men of common intelligence must necessarily guess at its meaning and differ as to its application." Therefore, Section 2343.04 of the Columbus City Codes violates the due process clause of the Fourteenth Amendment to the United States Constitution.

Section 2343.04 "* * * is also inadequate in providing guidelines for law enforcement officials charged with its enforcement." This infirmity is of special significance in relation to the ordinance here which makes "* * * criminal activities which by modern standards are normally innocent." *Papachristou v. Jacksonville* (1972), 405 U.S. 156, 163. * * *

NOTES ON THE DECLINE AND FALL OF CROSS–DRESSING STATUTES

1. *The Chronology.* The cases from *Archibald* to *Wilson/Rogers* suggest that cross-dressing laws were still being enforced in the 1960s and 1970s, a fact confirmed by newspaper reports and oral evidence. But the laws fell into disfavor in the 1970s and 1980s, when judges invalidated them right and left and the political process showed no interest in reviving them. In a classic example of "first in, last out," St. Louis' ordinance against cross-dressing remained on the books and enforced until 1986, when a federal court ruled both it and the law against lewd behavior invalid on vagueness grounds. *D.C. and M.S. v. City of St. Louis,* 795 F.2d 652 (8th Cir.1986).

2. *The Constitutional Theories.* Note the different theories deployed by the courts in *Wilson* and *Rogers*: equal protection violation based on "personal appearance" and a due process violation based on the law's vagueness. Does anything turn on which theory is better? Does a comparison of *Wilson* and *Rogers* help debunk the canard that equal protection theories are "forward-looking" and progressive, while due process theories are "backward-looking" and traditionalist? Note, also, the absence of theory: none of the judges found the cross-dressing ordinances to be sex discrimination. Is that a worthless argument?

3. *Cross–Dress for Success: The Social Context.* Recall Garber's thesis. Early enforcement of cross-dressing laws reflected a crisis in gender roles, as women insisted on equality with men, including the right to wear pants. By 1920, however, the category crisis was one of sexuality: cross-dressing signified sexual "perversion" or "deviation." By 1980, that particular crisis may have ebbed. This ebbing is reflected in the cases, as is another feature.

The law that was applied in *Archibald* was not nearly as clear as the one held too vague in *Rogers*. What changed was not principles of due process, but dress customs themselves, as Chief Justice O'Neill's opinion makes clear. The hippies' gender rebellion, women's liberation, and gay pride—all developments of the 1960s and 1970s—paved the way for unisex clothing and took some of the sting out of cross-dressing. Is Garber, perhaps, wrong that cross-dressing still reflects category crisis? Has the subject become a popular object of academic discourse at the very point when it has lost most of its capacity to shock? Consider the following problem, though.

PROBLEM 12–3

CONTEXT, CROSS–DRESSING, AND CONDUCT UNBECOMING

You are a Navy judge. A sailor is brought before you on charges of bringing discredit to the Navy, a violation of Article 134 of the Uniform Code of Military Justice. Last month, he was named "sailor of the month" for his role in supervising entertainment on base, and in that capacity has organized several musical performances in which men have played the roles of women. An elderly retired admiral attended the most recent production and remarked that it was "the best service drag I've seen since World War II." Moreover, like you, the sailor has been part of numerous instances of the "King Neptune ceremony," a time-honored sea-faring tradition. In that ceremony, each time a ship crosses the Equator, those aboard who have crossed before dress as Neptune, and those who have never crossed previously are made to dress and act in ways said to amuse the god of the sea. Cross dressing is a typical part of the ceremony. The sailor is now being prosecuted, based on evidence that he was seen on several occasions in and around his (off-base) apartment dressed in a wig and women's clothes. There is no evidence as to his sexual orientation, nor as to any sexual conduct. His attorney moves to dismiss the charge on the ground that there is no Navy regulation barring cross-dressing. What result? For real-life comparisons, see *United States v. Guerrero*, 33 M.J. 295 (Ct.Mil.App.1991), and *United States v. Davis*, 26 M.J. 445 (Ct.Mil.App.1988).

PART C. CROSS-DRESSING ON THE JOB AND IN THE FAMILY

Jane Doe v. Boeing Co.

Washington Supreme Court, 1993.
121 Wash.2d 8, 846 P.2d 531.

■ GUY, JUSTICE.

[Jane Doe was hired as a Boeing engineer in 1978. At the time of hire, Doe was a biological male and presented herself as such on her application for employment. In 1984, after years of struggling with her sexual identity, Doe concluded that she was a transsexual, and in 1985 notified Boeing of her desire to have sex reassignment surgery. This necessitated living for one year as a female. Boeing informed Doe that while Doe was an anatomical male, she could not use the women's rest rooms or dress in "feminine" attire, but she could dress as a female and use the women's rest rooms after completion of her sex reassignment surgery.]

While Doe was an anatomical male, Boeing permitted Doe to wear either male clothing or unisex clothing. Unisex clothing included blouses, sweaters, slacks, flat shoes, nylon stockings, earrings, lipstick, foundation, and clear nail polish. Doe was instructed not to wear obviously feminine clothing such as dresses, skirts, or frilly blouses. Boeing applied its unwritten dress policy to all employees, which included eight other transsexuals who had expressed a desire to have sex reassignment surgery while working for Boeing. Both Doe's psychologist and treating physician testified that what Doe was allowed to wear at Boeing was sufficiently feminine for Doe to qualify for sex reassignment surgery.

Between June and late September 1985, Boeing management received approximately a dozen anonymous complaints regarding Doe's attire and use of the women's rest rooms. On October 25, 1985, following the receipt of a complaint about Doe using the women's rest room, Boeing issued Doe a written disciplinary warning. The warning reiterated Boeing's position on acceptable attire and rest room use and stated that Doe's failure to comply with Boeing's directives by November 1, 1985, would result in further corrective action, including termination. During this "grace" period, Doe's compliance with Boeing's "acceptable attire" directive was to be monitored each day by Doe's direct supervisor. Doe was told that her attire would be deemed unacceptable when, in the supervisor's opinion, her dress would be likely to cause a complaint were Doe to use a men's rest room at a Boeing facility. No single article of clothing would be dispositive. Doe's overall appearance was to be assessed.

Doe's transsexualism did not interfere with her ability to perform her job duties as a software engineer at Boeing. There was no measurable decline in either her work group's performance or in Doe's own job performance. There was no testimony to indicate that Boeing's dress restrictions hindered Doe's professional development.

On November 4, 1985, the first day Doe worked after the grace period, Doe wore attire that her supervisor considered acceptable. Doe responded that she was disappointed that her attire was acceptable, and that she would "push it" the next day. By "push it", Doe testified that she meant she would wear more extreme feminine attire. The next day, Doe came to work wearing similar attire, but she included as part of her outfit a strand of pink pearls which she refused to remove. This outfit was similar to one she had been told during the grace period was unacceptable in that the addition of the pink pearls changed Doe's look from unisex to "excessively" feminine. Doe was subsequently terminated from her position at Boeing as a result of her willful violation of Boeing's directives.

[Doe filed a handicap discrimination action against Boeing pursuant to RCW 49.60, Washington's Law Against Discrimination (hereafter Act). The parties agreed to bifurcated proceedings and to a nonjury trial on the issue of liability. The trial court held that Doe was "temporarily handicapped" under its construction of WAC 162–22–040. The trial court further concluded that Boeing's actions reasonably accommodated Doe's condition and, thus, ruled in favor of Boeing on liability. The intermediate appeals court reversed and ordered judgment for Doe. The Washington Supreme Court reversed and reinstated the trial court's judgment dismissing the case.]

This case presents two issues for review. First, is Jane Doe's gender dysphoria a "handicap" under RCW 49.60.180? We hold that Doe's gender dysphoria is not a handicap under the Act. The definition of "handicap" for enforcement purposes in unfair practice cases under RCW 49.60.180, as defined in WAC 162–22–040, requires factual findings of both (1) the presence of an abnormal condition, and (2) employer discrimination against the plaintiff because of that condition. While gender dysphoria is an abnormal condition, we hold that Doe was not "handicapped" by her gender dysphoria because Boeing did not discharge her because of that condition.

Second, did Boeing have to provide Doe's preferred accommodation under RCW 49.60.180? We hold that the scope of an employer's duty to reasonably accommodate an employee's abnormal condition is limited to those steps necessary to enable the employee to perform his or her job. We hold that Boeing's actions met this standard and did not discriminate against Doe by reason of her abnormal condition. * * *

Inasmuch as Boeing did not discharge Doe based on her abnormal condition but on her refusal to conform with directives on acceptable attire, we must turn our attention to whether Boeing discriminated against Doe by failing to reasonably accommodate her condition of gender dysphoria.

The Legislature intended the Act to prohibit discrimination in employment against individuals who suffer an abnormal physical, mental, or sensory "handicap." Laws of 1973, 1st Ex. Sess., ch. 214, § 1, p. 1648; see generally RCW 49.60.010, .030(1)(a). We recognize that employers have an affirmative obligation to reasonably accommodate the sensory, mental, or physical limitations of such employees unless the employer can demonstrate that the accommodation would impose an undue hardship on the conduct of the employer's business. WAC 162–22–080. The issue before us is whether Boeing had a duty to accommodate Doe's preferred manner of dress prior to her sex reassignment surgery. We hold that the scope of an employer's duty to accommodate an employee's condition is limited to those steps reasonably necessary to enable the employee to perform his or her job.

Doe contends that Boeing's dress code failed to accommodate her condition and, thus, was discriminatory. We disagree. The record substantially supports the trial court's findings that Boeing reasonably accommodated Doe in the matter of dress by allowing her to wear unisex clothing at work. Despite this accommodation, Doe determined unilaterally, and without medical confirmation, that she needed to dress as a woman at her place of employment in order to qualify for sex reassignment surgery. Our review of the record is limited to determining whether substantial evidence exists to support the trial court's findings of fact. We find substantial support for the trial court's finding that Doe had no medical need to dress as a woman at work in order to qualify for her surgery.

[P]laintiff's experts declined to state that any particular degree of feminine dress was required in order for plaintiff to fulfill any presurgical requirements. In fact, the evidence was uncontradicted that the unisex dress permitted by Boeing ... would not have precluded plaintiff from meeting the Benjamin Standards presurgical requirement of living in the social role of a woman. Finding of fact 39. * * *

* * * The trial court found that Boeing's policy on accommodation of transsexuals was developed with input from Boeing's legal, medical, personnel and labor relations departments. The Boeing medical department consulted with outside experts in the field and reviewed the literature on transsexualism. The trial court also held that Boeing has a legitimate business purpose in defining what is acceptable attire and in balancing the needs of its work force as a whole with those of Doe. The record supports the trial court's findings of fact and conclusions of law that Boeing developed and reasonably enforced a dress policy which balanced its legitimate business needs with those of its employees.

Doe further argues that, as a gender dysphoric, her perceived needs should have been accommodated. We disagree. The Act does not require an employer to offer the employee the precise accommodation he or she requests. Her perceived need to dress more completely as a woman did not impact her job performance. Both the trial court and the Court of Appeals found that Doe's condition had no measurable effect on either Doe's job performance or her work group's performance. That is not to say that Doe did not have emotional turmoil over the changes that were taking place in her life, but that turmoil did not prevent her from performing her work satisfactorily. Based on the record, there was no need for any further action by Boeing to facilitate Doe in the performance of job-related tasks.

Doe also argues that Boeing failed to accommodate her unique condition because its dress policy was uniformly applied. The Court of Appeals agreed, stating that "identical treatment may be the source of discrimination in the case of a handicapped employee, while different treatment, necessary to accommodate a handicap, can eliminate discrimination." We stated in [*Holland v. Boeing Co.*, 583 P.2d 621 (1978)], however, that identical treatment may be a source of discrimination "only when the work environment fails to take into account the unique characteristics of the handicapped person." While Boeing's dress code was uniformly applied, such generically applied work rules are not discriminatory per se unless they affect an employee's ability to perform his or her job. In Doe's case, "different" treatment was not required to accommodate her condition because her condition did not affect her ability to perform her job. * * *

The concept of "reasonable" accommodation is linked to necessity. The employer's duty to accommodate is appropriately limited to removing sensory, mental or physical impediments to the employee's ability to perform his or her job. Doe's gender dysphoria did not impede her ability to perform her engineering duties. Therefore, Boeing had no duty to provide any further accommodation to Doe beyond what it provided for all employees. * * *

NOTES ON EMPLOYMENT NONDISCRIMINATION AND DRESS CODES

1. *The Jurisprudence of Hair Lengths and Dress Codes.* In a series of cases in the 1970s, plaintiffs challenged employer rules that required men to cut their hair to much shorter lengths than was required for female employees, and required women to wear skirts while men could wear pants (or vice versa). Such challenges, on grounds of sex discrimination, were universally rejected unless the court found that the form of dress was demeaning for one sex. Courts ruled that employers could establish reasonable dress and grooming codes, so long as both male and female employees had to comply with the rules, even if the rules were somewhat different for the different sexes. *See, e.g., Carroll v. Talman Federal Savings & Loan Ass'n*, 604 F.2d 1028 (7th Cir.1979), *cert. denied*, 445 U.S. 929 (1980); *Willingham v. Macon Telegraph Publishing Co.*, 507 F.2d 1084 (5th Cir. 1975).

2. *Personal Appearance Discrimination?* The District of Columbia's Human Rights Act [Appendix 2] and the employment discrimination ordinances of many other cities prohibit discrimination on the basis of "personal appearance." Would courts in those jurisdictions have afforded relief to Jane Doe? Reconsider your answer to Problem 12–2 in light of this argument.

3. *What Is the Category Crisis in Jane Doe's Case?* Was Boeing or its employees threatened by a man *dressed as a woman?* Or of a *man* dressed as a woman, and using the women's rest room? Recall how the shower room is the situs of arguments against gays in the military (Chapter 4, Section 3). The rest room may be the situs of arguments against transvestites in the workplace. Would it be sexual harassment for an employer to allow men to use women's rest rooms?

In re Karin T. v. Michael T.

Family Court, Monroe County, 1985.
127 Misc.2d 14, 484 N.Y.S.2d 780.

■ LEONARD E. MAAS, JUDGE.

The Department of Social Services of Erie County, New York, brings this proceeding against the respondent, Michael T., pursuant to the Uniform Support of Dependents Act (Domestic Relations Law art 3–A). The Department, as assignee of Karin T., seeks support from the respondent for the benefit of two children, David T., born October 8, 1980, and Falin T., born January 17, 1983. Petitioner further alleges that the respondent, Michael T., is the father of the dependent children.

To this rather routine-appearing petition, the respondent has filed an answer which sets forth as an affirmative defense the following: "2. That the respondent is a female and she is not the father of the said children. That the children were artificially inseminated." * * *

Respondent was born on August 16, 1948, and is denominated a female named Marlene A. T. In her 20's she became increasingly unhappy with her feminine identity and attempted to change that identity and to live like a man. In pursuance thereof, she changed her name from Marlene to Michael, dressed in men's clothing and obtained employment which she regarded as "men's work." At some time prior to May of 1977, the respondent and Karin T. commenced a relationship. In May of 1977, Karin T. and Michael T., also known as Marlene T., obtained a marriage license in the Village of Spencerport in the County of Monroe. At that time, no birth certificate was requested of either party and a marriage license was issued. Subsequently, Karin T. and the respondent participated in a marriage ceremony which was performed by a minister in the Town of Parma, County of Monroe. This was evidenced by a certificate of marriage executed by said minister.

Thereafter, two children were born by means of artificial insemination. The physician, prior to engaging in the procedure, had both parties execute an agreement, a copy of which is annexed hereto and made a part hereof.

David T. was born October 8, 1980, and Falin T. was born January 17, 1983, as a result of the artificial insemination performed by the physician.

Subsequent to the birth of the second child in 1983, the parties separated and the respondent moved to the Monroe County area and is employed in Monroe County.

Although some question has been raised as to whether or not by means of medical procedures the respondent has indeed become a transsexual, this court would be without jurisdiction to determine that fact and for the purposes of this proceeding only, finds that the respondent is indeed a female.

During the period of 1977 through 1983, it would appear that Karin T. and the respondent lived together in the same household and both contributed to the support of the family and to the children who are the subjects of this proceeding.

The court has been further informed that there is presently pending in the Supreme Court of Erie County, State of New York, an action between Karin T. and the respondent to declare the "marriage" of 1977 null and void.

Family Court being of limited jurisdiction lacks the power to determine all of the rights and obligations which the factual web created by these parties presents. However, this court does have jurisdiction to determine whether or not this respondent is responsible for the support of these children.

Neither counsel for the parties nor the court has found any authority similar to the fact situation in this case. This is a case of first impression and its resolution will carry the court through uncharted legal waters. As a general rule only biological or adoptive parents are liable for the support of children. Where extraordinary circumstances require, courts have held nonparents responsible for the support of children.

It is conceded that the children involved in this proceeding were born only after the respondent affixed her name to the agreement indicating she was the husband. The agreement stated in part:

"a.   That such child or children so produced are his own legitimate child or children and are the heirs of his body, and

"b.   That he hereby completely waives forever any right which he might have to disclaim such child or children as his own." * * *

* * * The contract entered into by this respondent with the mother and the doctor must inure to the benefit of these children. Ordinarily, children are unable to enforce the provisions of an agreement between parents. However, under extraordinary circumstances courts have permitted this to be done.

* * * [C]ertainly the document which was signed by the respondent and by which these children were brought into the world gives rise to a situation which must provide these two children with remedies. To hold otherwise would allow this respondent to completely abrogate her responsi-

bilities for the support of the children involved and would allow her to benefit from her own fraudulent acts which induced their birth no more so than if she were indeed the natural father of these children. Of course, the respondent was free to engage and live in any lifestyle which she felt appropriate. However, by her course of conduct in this case which brought into the world two innocent children she should not be allowed to benefit from those acts to the detriment of these children and of the public generally.

As an additional defense, the respondent maintains that only a parent is liable for the support of children as set forth in Domestic Relations Law article 3–A. (See, Domestic Relations Law § 32.) She avers that by reason of the fact that she is female, she biologically could not be the parent of these children nor has she formally adopted them.

The term "parent" is not defined in said statute except in biological terms and the court has found no authority to the contrary. *Ballantine's Law Dictionary* 911 (3d ed.) defines "parent" as "[the] father or mother". In *Black's Law Dictionary* 1003 (5th ed. 1979) "parent" is defined as "[one] who procreates, begets, or brings forth offspring." The actions of this respondent in executing the agreement above-referred to certainly brought forth these offspring as if done biologically. The contract and the equitable estoppel which prevail in this case prevent the respondent from asserting her lack of responsibility by reason of lack of parenthood. This court finds that under the unique facts in this case, respondent is indeed a "parent" to whom such responsibility attaches.

The respondent is chargeable with the support of these children and this case is referred to the hearing examiner to determine the level of such support. Whatever may be the rights and/or remedies of the respondent and the mother of these children concerning custody, visitation, inheritance rights and any others are left to another forum at another time. * * *

NOTE ON RIGHTS OF CROSS–DRESSING PARENTS

This interesting case is made easier by the convergence of the contract and moral responsibility on the result: protect the children. As to the issues reserved by the court—child custody and visitation—the answers are not so easy. Should a parent's cross-dressing be considered in child custody and visitation? A number of courts have refused to overturn a trial court's determination that a cross-dressing parent (in each case the father) should retain the custody and/or visitation rights initially established in the divorce decree, where there was no credible proof of harm to the child. See, e.g., *Mayfield v. Mayfield*, 1996 WL 489043 (Ohio App. 5th Dist.1996); *P.L.W. v. T.R.W.*, 890 S.W.2d 688 (Mo.App.1994). An appellate court also left undisturbed, however, a trial court's decision not to expand a father's visitation rights to include overnight visits, because of his cross-dressing. *B. v. B.*, 585 N.Y.S.2d 65 (N.Y.App.Div.1992). There are surely many unreported cases to the same effect. Upon what evidence could such a judgment rest? Is there any more basis for discriminating against cross-dressing heterosexual parents than for discriminating against lesbian and gay parents (Chapter 9, Section 3[A])? Less basis?

APPENDICES

APPENDIX 1

INDIVIDUAL RIGHTS PROVISIONS FROM THE AMENDMENTS TO THE CONSTITUTION OF THE UNITED STATES

Amendment I [1791]

Congress shall make no law respecting an establishment of religion, or prohibiting the free exercise thereof; or abridging the freedom of speech, or of the press; or the right of the people peaceably to assemble, and to petition the Government for a redress of grievances.

Amendment II [1791]

A well regulated Militia, being necessary to the security of a free State, the right of the people to keep and bear Arms, shall not be infringed.

Amendment III [1791]

No Soldier shall, in time of peace be quartered in any house, without the consent of the Owner, nor in time of war, but in a manner to be prescribed by law.

Amendment IV [1791]

The right of the people to be secure in their persons, houses, papers, and effects, against unreasonable searches and seizures, shall not be violated, and no Warrants shall issue, but upon probable cause, supported by Oath or affirmation, and particularly describing the place to be searched, and the persons or things to be seized.

Amendment V [1791]

No person shall be held to answer for a capital, or otherwise infamous crime, unless on a presentment or indictment of a Grand Jury, except in cases arising in the land or naval forces, or in the Militia, when in actual service in time of War or public danger; nor shall any person be subject for the same offence to be twice put in jeopardy of life or limb; nor shall be compelled in any criminal case to be a witness against himself, nor be deprived of life, liberty, or property, without due process of law; nor shall private property be taken for public use, without just compensation.

Amendment VI [1791]

In all criminal prosecutions, the accused shall enjoy the right to a speedy and public trial, by an impartial jury of the State and district wherein the crime shall have been committed, which district shall have been previously ascertained by law, and to be informed of the nature and cause of the accusation; to be confronted with the witnesses against him; to have compulsory process for obtaining witnesses in his favor, and to have the Assistance of Counsel for his defence.

Amendment VII [1791]

In Suits at common law, where the value in controversy shall exceed twenty dollars, the right of trial by jury shall be preserved, and no fact tried by a jury, shall be otherwise re-examined in any Court of the United States, than according to the rules of the common law.

Amendment VIII [1791]

Excessive bail shall not be required, nor excessive fines imposed, nor cruel and unusual punishments inflicted.

Amendment IX [1791]

The enumeration in the Constitution, of certain rights, shall not be construed to deny or disparage others retained by the people.

Amendment X [1791]

The powers not delegated to the United States by the Constitution, nor prohibited by it to the States, are reserved to the States respectively, or to the people.

* * *

Amendment XIII [1865]

Section 1. Neither slavery nor involuntary servitude, except as a punishment for crime whereof the party shall have been duly convicted, shall exist within the United States, or any place subject to their jurisdiction.

Section 2. Congress shall have power to enforce this article by appropriate legislation.

Amendment XIV [1868]

Section 1. All persons born or naturalized in the United States, and subject to the jurisdiction thereof, are citizens of the United States and of the State wherein they reside. No State shall make or enforce any law which shall abridge the privileges or immunities of citizens of the United States; nor shall any State deprive any person of life, liberty, or property, without due process of law; nor deny to any person within its jurisdiction the equal protection of the laws.

* * *

Section 5. The Congress shall have power to enforce, by appropriate legislation, the provisions of this article.

Amendment XV [1870]

Section 1.   The right of citizens of the United States to vote shall not be denied or abridged by the United States or by any State on account of race, color, or previous condition of servitude.

Section 2.   The Congress shall have power to enforce this article by appropriate legislation.

* * *

Amendment XIX [1920]

[1]   The right of citizens of the United States to vote shall not be denied or abridged by the United States or by any State on account of sex.

[2]   Congress shall have power to enforce this article by appropriate legislation.

* * *

*

APPENDIX 2

THE DISTRICT OF COLUMBIA HUMAN RIGHTS ACT (EXCERPTS)

Subchapter I

§ 1–2501 Intent of Council.

It is the intent of the Council of the District of Columbia, in enacting this chapter, to secure an end in the District of Columbia to discrimination for any reason other than that of individual merit, including, but not limited to, discrimination by reason of race, color, religion, national origin, sex, age, marital status, personal appearance, sexual orientation, family responsibilities, matriculation, political affiliation, physical handicap, source of income, and place of residence or business.

§ 1–2502 Definitions.

The following words and terms when used in this chapter have the following meanings: * * *

(2) "Age" means 18 years of age or older except that, in a case of employment, age shall be defined as 18 to 65 years of age, unless otherwise prohibited by law. * * *

(4) "Commission" means the District of Columbia Commission on Human Rights, as established by Commissioner's Order No. 71–224, dated July 8, 1971. * * *

(8) "Educational institution" means any public or private institution including an academy, college, elementary or secondary school, extension course, kindergarten, nursery, school system or university; and a business, nursing, professional, secretarial, technical, or vocational school; and includes an agent of an educational institution. * * *

(10) "Employer" means any person who, for compensation, employs an individual, except for the employer's parent, spouse, children or domestic servants, engaged in work in and about the employer's household; any person acting in the interest of such employer, directly or indirectly; and any professional association. * * *

(15) "Labor organization" means any organization, agency, employee representation committee, group, association, or plan in which employees participate directly or indirectly; and which exists for the purpose, in whole or in part, of dealing with employers, or any agent thereof, concerning grievances, labor disputes, wages, rates of pay, hours, or other terms, conditions, or privileges of employment; and any conference, general com-

mittee, joint or system board, or joint council, which is subordinate to a national or international organization. * * *

(17) "Marital status" means the state of being married, single, divorced, separated, or widowed and the usual conditions associated therewith, including pregnancy or parenthood. * * *

(21) "Person" means any individual, firm, partnership, mutual company, joint-stock company, corporation, association, organization, unincorporated organization, labor union, government agency, incorporated society, statutory or common-law trust, estate, executor, administrator, receiver, trustee, conservator, liquidator, trustee in bankruptcy, committee, assignee, officer, employee, principal or agent, legal or personal representative, real estate broker or salesman or any agent or representative of any of the foregoing.

(22) "Personal appearance" means the outward appearance of any person, irrespective of sex, with regard to bodily condition or characteristics, manner or style of dress, and manner or style of personal grooming, including, but not limited to, hair style and beards. It shall not relate, however, to the requirement of cleanliness, uniforms, or prescribed standards, when uniformly applied for admittance to a public accommodation, or when uniformly applied to a class of employees for a reasonable business purpose; or when such bodily conditions or characteristics, style or manner of dress or personal grooming presents a danger to the health, welfare or safety of any individual.

(23) "Physical handicap" means a bodily or mental disablement which may be the result of injury, illness or congenital condition for which reasonable accommodation can be made.

(24) "Place of public accommodation" means all places included in the meaning of such terms as inns, taverns, road houses, hotels, motels, whether conducted for the entertainment of transient guests or for the accommodation of those seeking health, recreation or rest; restaurants or eating houses, or any place where food is sold for consumption on the premises; buffets, saloons, barrooms, or any store, park or enclosure where spirituous or malt liquors are sold; ice cream parlors, confectionaries, soda fountains and all stores where ice cream, ice and fruit preparation or their derivatives, or where beverages of any kind are retailed for consumption on the premises; wholesale and retail stores, and establishments dealing with goods or services of any kind, including, but not limited to, the credit facilities thereof; banks, savings and loan associations, establishments of mortgage bankers and brokers, all other financial institutions, and credit information bureaus; insurance companies and establishments of insurance policy brokers; dispensaries, clinics, hospitals, bath-houses, swimming pools, laundries and all other cleaning establishments; barber shops, beauty parlors, theatres, motion picture houses, airdromes, roof gardens, music halls, race courses, skating rinks, amusement and recreation parks, trailer camps, resort camps, fairs, bowling alleys, golf courses, gymnasiums, shooting galleries, billiards and pool parlors; garages, all public conveyances operated on land or water or in the air, as well as the stations and

terminals thereof; travel or tour advisory services, agencies or bureaus; public halls and public elevators of buildings and structures, occupied by 2 or more tenants, or by the owner and 1 or more tenants. Such term shall not include any institution, club, or place of accommodation which is in its nature distinctly private except, that any such institution, club or place of accommodation shall be subject to the provisions of § 1–2531. A place of accommodation, institution, or club shall not be considered in its nature distinctly private if the place of accommodation, institution, or club:

(A) Has 350 or more members;

(B) Serves meals on a regular basis; and

(C) Regularly receives payment for dues, fees, use of space, facilities, services, meals, or beverages directly or indirectly from or on behalf of nonmembers for the furtherance of trade or business. * * *

(28) "Sexual orientation" means male or female homosexuality, heterosexuality and bisexuality, by preference or practice.

(29) "Source of income" means the point, the cause, or the form of the origination, or transmittal of gains of property accruing to a person in a stated period of time; including, but not limited to, money and property secured from any occupation, profession or activity, from any contract, agreement or settlement, from federal payments, court-ordered payments, from payments received as gifts, bequests, annuities, life insurance policies and compensation for illness or injury, except in a case where conflict of interest may exist. * * *

(31) "Unlawful discriminatory practice" means those discriminatory practices which are so specified in subchapter II of this chapter.

Subchapter II

§ 1–2511 Equal opportunities.

Every individual shall have an equal opportunity to participate fully in the economic, cultural and intellectual life of the District and to have an equal opportunity to participate in all aspects of life, including, but not limited to, in employment, in places of public accommodation, resort or amusement, in educational institutions, in public service, and in housing and commercial space accommodations.

§ 1–2512 Unlawful discriminatory practices in employment.

(a) General.—It shall be an unlawful discriminatory practice to do any of the following acts, wholly or partially for a discriminatory reason based upon the race, color, religion, national origin, sex, age, marital status, personal appearance, sexual orientation, family responsibilities, physical handicap, matriculation, or political affiliation of any individual:

(1) To fail or refuse to hire, or to discharge, any individual; or otherwise to discriminate against any individual, with respect to his compensation, terms, conditions, or privileges of employment, including promotion; or to limit, segregate, or classify his employees in any way which

would deprive or tend to deprive any individual of employment opportunities, or otherwise adversely affect his status as an employee;

(2) To fail or refuse to refer for employment, or to classify or refer for employment, any individual, or otherwise to discriminate against, any individual; or

(3) To exclude or to expel from its membership, or otherwise to discriminate against, any individual; or to limit, segregate, or classify its membership; or to classify, or fail, or refuse to refer for employment any individual in any way, which would deprive such individual of employment opportunities, or would limit such employment opportunities, or otherwise adversely affect his status as an employee or as an applicant for employment; or

(4) (A) To discriminate against any individual in admission to or the employment in, any program established to provide apprenticeship or other training or retraining, including an on-the-job training program;

(B) To print or publish, or cause to be printed or published, any notice or advertisement, or use any publication form, relating to employment by such an employer, or to membership in, or any classification or referral for employment by such a labor organization, or to any classification or referral for employment by such an employment agency, unlawfully indicating any preference, limitation, specification, or distinction, based on the race, color, religion, national origin, sex, age, marital status, personal appearance, sexual orientation, family responsibilities, matriculation, physical handicap, or political affiliation of any individual.

(b) Subterfuge.—It shall further be an unlawful discriminatory practice to do any of the above said acts for any reason that would not have been asserted but for, wholly or partially, a discriminatory reason based on the race, color, religion, national origin, sex, age, marital status, personal appearance, sexual orientation, family responsibilities, matriculation, physical handicap, or political affiliation of any individual.

(c) Accommodation for religious observance.—(1) It shall further be an unlawful discriminatory practice for an employer to refuse to make a reasonable accommodation for an employee's religious observance by permitting the employee to make up work time lost due to such observance, unless such an accommodation would cause the employer undue hardship. An accommodation would cause an employer undue hardship when it would cause the employer to incur more than de minimis costs.

(2) Such an accommodation may be made by permitting the employee to work:

(A) During the employee's scheduled lunch time or other work breaks;

(B) Before or after the employee's usual working hours;

(C) Outside of the employer's normal business hours;

(D) During the employee's paid vacation days;

(E) During another employee's working hours as part of a voluntary swap with such other employee; or

(F) In any other manner that is mutually agreeable to the employer and employee.

(3) When an employee's request for a particular form of accommodation would cause undue hardship to the employer, the employer shall reasonably accommodate the employee in a manner that does not cause undue hardship to the employer. Where other means of accommodation would cause undue hardship to the employer, an employee shall have the option of taking leave without pay if granting leave without pay would not cause undue hardship to the employer.

(4) An employee shall notify the employer of the need for an accommodation at least 10 working days prior to the day or days for which the accommodation is needed, unless the need for the accommodation cannot reasonably be foreseen.

(5) In any proceeding brought under this section, the employer shall have the burden of establishing that it would be unable reasonably to accommodate an employee's religious observance without incurring an undue hardship, provided, however, that in the case of an employer that employs more than 5 but fewer than 15 full-time employees, or where accommodation of an employee's observance of a religious practice would require the employee to take more than 3 consecutive days off from work, the employee shall have the burden of establishing that the employer could reasonably accommodate the employee's religious observance without incurring an undue hardship; and provided further, that it shall be considered an undue hardship if an employer would be required to pay any additional compensation to an employee by reason of an accommodation for an employee's religious observance. The mere assumption that other employees with the same religious beliefs might also request accommodation shall not be considered evidence of undue hardship. An employer that employs 5 or fewer full-time employees shall be exempt from the provisions of this subsection.

§ 1–2519 Unlawful discriminatory practices in public accommodations.

(a) General.—It shall be an unlawful discriminatory practice to do any of the following acts, wholly or partially for a discriminatory reason based on the race, color, religion, national origin, sex, age, marital status, personal appearance, sexual orientation, family responsibilities, physical handicap, matriculation, political affiliation, source of income, or place of residence or business of any individual:

(1) To deny, directly or indirectly, any person the full and equal enjoyment of the goods, services, facilities, privileges, advantages, and accommodations of any place of public accommodations;

(2) To print, circulate, post, or mail, or otherwise cause, directly or indirectly, to be published a statement, advertisement, or sign which

indicates that the full and equal enjoyment of the goods, services, facilities, privileges, advantages, and accommodations of a place of public accommodation will be unlawfully refused, withheld from or denied an individual; or that an individual's patronage of, or presence at, a place of public accommodation is objectional, unwelcome, unacceptable, or undesirable.

(b) Subterfuge.—It is further unlawful to do any of the above said acts for any reason that would not have been asserted but for, wholly or partially, a discriminatory reason based on the race, color, religion, national origin, sex, age, marital status, personal appearance, sexual orientation, family responsibilities, physical handicap, matriculation, political affiliation, source of income, or place of residence or business of any individual.

§ 1–2520 Unlawful discriminatory practices in educational institutions.

It is an unlawful discriminatory practice, subject to the exemptions in § 1–2503(b), for an educational institution:

(1) To deny, restrict, or to abridge or condition the use of, or access to, any of its facilities and services to any person otherwise qualified, wholly or partially, for a discriminatory reason, based upon the race, color, religion, national origin, sex, age, marital status, personal appearance, sexual orientation, family responsibilities, political affiliation, source of income or physical handicap of any individual; or

(2) To make or use a written or oral inquiry, or form of application for admission, that elicits or attempts to elicit information, or to make or keep a record, concerning the race, color, religion, or national origin of an applicant for admission, except as permitted by regulations of the Office.

(3) Notwithstanding any other provision of the laws of the District of Columbia, it shall not be an unlawful discriminatory practice in the District of Columbia for any educational institution that is affiliated with a religious organization or closely associated with the tenets of a religious organization to deny, restrict, abridge, or condition—

(A) the use of any fund, service, facility, or benefit; or

(B) the granting of any endorsement, approval, or recognition,

to any person or persons that are organized for, or engaged in, promoting, encouraging, or condoning any homosexual act, lifestyle, orientation, or belief.

§ 1–2526 Aiding or abetting.

It shall be an unlawful discriminatory practice for any person to aid, abet, invite, compel, or coerce the doing of any of the acts forbidden under the provisions of this chapter or to attempt to do so.

§ 1–2531 Compliance with chapter prerequisite for licenses.

All permits, licenses, franchises, benefits, exemptions, or advantages issued by or on behalf of the government of the District of Columbia, shall specifically require and be conditioned upon full compliance with the provisions of this chapter; and shall further specify that the failure or refusal to comply with any provision of this chapter shall be a proper basis for revocation of such permit, license, franchise, benefit, exemption, or advantage.

§ 1–2532 Discriminatory effects of practices.

Any practice which has the effect or consequence of violating any of the provisions of this chapter shall be deemed to be an unlawful discriminatory practice.

§ 1–2556 Private cause of action.

(a) Any person claiming to be aggrieved by an unlawful discriminatory practice shall have a cause of action in any court of competent jurisdiction for damages and such other remedies as may be appropriate, unless such person has filed a complaint hereunder: Provided, that where the Office has dismissed such complaint on the grounds of administrative convenience, or where the complainant has withdrawn a complaint, such person shall maintain all rights to bring suit as if no complaint had been filed. No person who maintains, in a court of competent jurisdiction, any action based upon an act which would be an unlawful discriminatory practice under this chapter may file the same complaint with the Office.

(b) The court may grant such relief as it deems appropriate, including but not limited to, such relief as is provided in § 1–2553(a).

* * *

*

APPENDIX 3

WISCONSIN FAIR EMPLOYMENT ACT (EXCERPTS)

111.31 Declaration of policy

(1) The legislature finds that the practice of unfair discrimination in employment against properly qualified individuals by reason of their age, race, creed, color, handicap, marital status, sex, national origin, ancestry, sexual orientation, arrest record, conviction record, membership in the national guard, state defense force or any other reserve component of the military forces of the United States or this state or use or nonuse of lawful products off the employer's premises during nonworking hours substantially and adversely affects the general welfare of the state. Employers, labor organizations, employment agencies and licensing agencies that deny employment opportunities and discriminate in employment against properly qualified individuals solely because of their age, race, creed, color, handicap, marital status, sex, national origin, ancestry, sexual orientation, arrest record, conviction record, membership in the national guard, state defense force or any other reserve component of the military forces of the United States or this state or use or nonuse of lawful products off the employer's premises during nonworking hours deprive those individuals of the earnings that are necessary to maintain a just and decent standard of living.

(2) It is the intent of the legislature to protect by law the rights of all individuals to obtain gainful employment and to enjoy privileges free from employment discrimination because of age, race, creed, color, handicap, marital status, sex, national origin, ancestry, sexual orientation, arrest record, conviction record, membership in the national guard, state defense force or any other reserve component of the military forces of the United States or this state or use or nonuse of lawful products off the employer's premises during nonworking hours, and to encourage the full, nondiscriminatory utilization of the productive resources of the state to the benefit of the state, the family and all the people of the state. It is the intent of the legislature in promulgating this subchapter to encourage employers to evaluate an employe or applicant for employment based upon the employe's or applicant's individual qualifications rather than upon a particular class to which the individual may belong.

(3) In the interpretation and application of this subchapter, and otherwise, it is declared to be the public policy of the state to encourage and foster to the fullest extent practicable the employment of all properly qualified individuals regardless of age, race, creed, color, handicap, marital status, sex, national origin, ancestry, sexual orientation, arrest record, conviction record, membership in the national guard, state defense force or

any other reserve component of the military forces of the United States or this state or use or nonuse of lawful products off the employer's premises during nonworking hours. Nothing in this subsection requires an affirmative action program to correct an imbalance in the work force. This subchapter shall be liberally construed for the accomplishment of this purpose.

(4) The practice of requiring employees or prospective employees to submit to a test administered by means of a lie detector, as defined in § 111.37 (1) (b), is unfair, the practice of requesting employees and prospective employees to submit to such a test without providing safeguards for the test subjects is unfair, and the use of improper tests and testing procedures causes injury to the employees and prospective employees.

(5) The legislature finds that the prohibition of discrimination on the basis of creed under § 111.337 is a matter of statewide concern, requiring uniform enforcement at state, county and municipal levels.

111.32   Definitions

When used in this subchapter: * * *

(2) "Commission" means the labor and industry review commission. * * *

(4) "Department" means the department of industry, labor and job development.

(5) "Employe" does not include any individual employed by his or her parents, spouse or child.

(6) (a) "Employer" means the state and each agency of the state and, except as provided in par. (b), any other person engaging in any activity, enterprise or business employing at least one individual. In this subsection, "agency" means an office, department, independent agency, authority, institution, association, society or other body in state government created or authorized to be created by the constitution or any law, including the legislature and the courts.

(b) "Employer" does not include a social club or fraternal society under ch. 188 with respect to a particular job for which the club or society seeks to employ or employs a member, if the particular job is advertised only within the membership.

(7) "Employment agency" means any person, including this state, who regularly undertakes to procure employees or opportunities for employment for any other person.

(8) "Handicapped individual" means an individual who:

(a) Has a physical or mental impairment which makes achievement unusually difficult or limits the capacity to work;

(b) Has a record of such an impairment; or

(c) Is perceived as having such an impairment.

(9) "Labor organization" means:

(a) Any organization, agency or employe representation committee, group, association or plan in which employees participate and which exists for the purpose, in whole or in part, of dealing with employers concerning grievances, labor disputes, wages, rates of pay, hours or other terms or conditions of employment; or

(b) Any conference, general committee, joint or system board or joint council which is subordinate to a national or international committee, group, association or plan under par. (a).

(13) "Sexual harassment" means unwelcome sexual advances, unwelcome requests for sexual favors, unwelcome physical contact of a sexual nature or unwelcome verbal or physical conduct of a sexual nature. "Sexual harassment" includes conduct directed by a person at another person of the same or opposite gender. "Unwelcome verbal or physical conduct of a sexual nature" includes but is not limited to the deliberate, repeated making of unsolicited gestures or comments of a sexual nature; the deliberate, repeated display of offensive sexually graphic materials which is not necessary for business purposes; or deliberate verbal or physical contact of a sexual nature, whether or not repeated, that is sufficiently severe to interfere substantially with an employe's work performance or to create an intimidating, hostile or offensive work environment.

(13m) "Sexual orientation" means having a preference for heterosexuality, homosexuality or bisexuality, having a history of such a preference or being identified with such a preference.

111.321 Prohibited bases of discrimination

Subject to §§ 111.33 to 111.36, no employer, labor organization, employment agency, licensing agency or other person may engage in any act of employment discrimination as specified in § 111.322 against any individual on the basis of age, race, creed, color, handicap, marital status, sex, national origin, ancestry, arrest record, conviction record, membership in the national guard, state defense force or any reserve component of the military forces of the United States or this state or use or nonuse of lawful products off the employer's premises during nonworking hours.

111.322 Discriminatory actions prohibited

Subject to §§ 111.33 to 111.36, it is an act of employment discrimination to do any of the following:

(1) To refuse to hire, employ, admit or license any individual, to bar or terminate from employment or labor organization membership any individual, or to discriminate against any individual in promotion, compensation or in terms, conditions or privileges of employment or labor organization membership because of any basis enumerated in § 111.321.

(2) To print or circulate or cause to be printed or circulated any statement, advertisement or publication, or to use any form of application for employment or to make any inquiry in connection with prospective

employment, which implies or expresses any limitation, specification or discrimination with respect to an individual or any intent to make such limitation, specification or discrimination because of any basis enumerated in § 111.321.

(2m) To discharge or otherwise discriminate against any individual because of any of the following:

(a) The individual files a complaint or attempts to enforce any right under § 103.02, 103.10, 103.13, 103.28, 103.32, 103.455, 103.50, 104.12, 109.03 or 109.07 or §§ 101.58 to 101.599 or 103.64 to 103.82.

(b) The individual testifies or assists in any action or proceeding held under or to enforce any right under § 103.02, 103.10, 103.13, 103.28, 103.32, 103.455, 103.50, 104.12, 109.03 or 109.07 or §§ 101.58 to 101.599 or 103.64 to 103.82. * * *

(3) To discharge or otherwise discriminate against any individual because he or she has opposed any discriminatory practice under this subchapter or because he or she has made a complaint, testified or assisted in any proceeding under this subchapter.

111.325   Unlawful to discriminate

It is unlawful for any employer, labor organization, licensing agency or person to discriminate against any employe or any applicant for employment or licensing.

111.36   Sex, sexual orientation; exceptions and special cases

(1) Employment discrimination because of sex includes, but is not limited to, any of the following actions by any employer, labor organization, employment agency, licensing agency or other person:

(a) Discriminating against any individual in promotion, compensation paid for equal or substantially similar work, or in terms, conditions or privileges of employment or licensing on the basis of sex where sex is not a bona fide occupational qualification.

(b) Engaging in sexual harassment; or implicitly or explicitly making or permitting acquiescence in or submission to sexual harassment a term or condition of employment; or making or permitting acquiescence in, submission to or rejection of sexual harassment the basis or any part of the basis for any employment decision affecting an employe, other than an employment decision that is disciplinary action against an employe for engaging in sexual harassment in violation of this paragraph; or permitting sexual harassment to have the effect of substantially interfering with an employe's work performance or of creating an intimidating, hostile or offensive work environment. Under this paragraph, substantial interference with an employe's work performance or creation of an intimidating, hostile or offensive work environment is established when the conduct is such that a reasonable person under the same circumstances as the employe would consider the conduct sufficiently pervasive to interfere substantially with the person's work performance or to create an intimidating, hostile or offensive work environment.

(br) Engaging in harassment that consists of unwelcome verbal or physical conduct directed at another individual because of that individual's gender, other than the conduct described in par. (b), and that has the purpose or effect of creating an intimidating, hostile or offensive work environment or has the purpose or effect of substantially interfering with that individual's work performance. * * *

(c) Discriminating against any woman on the basis of pregnancy, childbirth, maternity leave or related medical conditions by engaging in any of the actions prohibited under § 111.322, including, but not limited to, actions concerning fringe benefit programs covering illnesses and disability.

(d) 1. For any employer, labor organization, licensing agency or employment agency or other person to refuse to hire, employ, admit or license, or to bar or terminate from employment, membership or licensure any individual, or to discriminate against an individual in promotion, compensation or in terms, conditions or privileges of employment because of the individual's sexual orientation; or

2. For any employer, labor organization, licensing agency or employment agency or other person to discharge or otherwise discriminate against any person because he or she has opposed any discriminatory practices under this paragraph or because he or she has made a complaint, testified or assisted in any proceeding under this paragraph.

(2) For the purposes of this subchapter, sex is a bona fide occupational qualification if all of the members of one sex are physically incapable of performing the essential duties required by a job, or if the essence of the employer's business operation would be undermined if employees were not hired exclusively from one sex.

(3) For purposes of sexual harassment claims under subparagraph (1)(b), an employer, labor organization, employment agency or licensing agency is presumed liable for an act of sexual harassment by that employer, labor organization, employment agency or licensing agency or by any of its employees or members, if the act occurs while the complaining employe is at his or her place of employment or is performing duties relating to his or her employment, if the complaining employe informs the employer, labor organization, employment agency or licensing agency of the act, and if the employer, labor organization, employment agency or licensing agency fails to take appropriate action within a reasonable time.

* * *

*

THE PROPOSED EMPLOYMENT NON-DISCRIMINATION ACT (ENDA)

A Bill

To prohibit employment discrimination on the basis of sexual orientation.

Be it enacted by the Senate and House of Representatives of the United States of America in Congress assembled,

SEC. 1.   SHORT TITLE.

This Act may be cited as the "Employment Non-Discrimination Act of 1996".

SEC. 2.   DISCRIMINATION PROHIBITED.

A covered entity, in connection with employment or employment opportunities, shall not-

(1) subject an individual to different standards or treatment on the basis of sexual orientation;

(2) discriminate against an individual based on the sexual orientation of persons with whom such individual is believed to associate or to have associated; or

(3) otherwise discriminate against an individual on the basis of sexual orientation.

SEC. 3.   BENEFITS.

This Act does not apply to the provision of employee benefits to an individual for the benefit of his or her partner.

SEC. 4.   NO DISPARATE IMPACT.

The fact that an employment practice has a disparate impact, as the term "disparate impact" is used in section 703(k) of the Civil Rights Act of 1964 (42 U.S.C. 2000e–2(k), on the basis of sexual orientation does not establish a prima facie violation of this Act.

SEC. 5.   QUOTAS AND PREFERENTIAL TREATMENT PROHIB-ITED.

(a) QUOTAS.—A covered entity shall not adopt or implement a quota on the basis of sexual orientation.

(b) PREFERENTIAL TREATMENT.—A covered entity shall not give preferential treatment to an individual on the basis of sexual orientation.

SEC. 6.   RELIGIOUS EXEMPTION.

(a) IN GENERAL.—Except as provided in subsection (b), this Act shall not apply to religious organizations.

(b) FOR–PROFIT ACTIVITIES.—This Act shall apply with respect to employment and employment opportunities that relate to any employment position that pertains solely to a religious organization's for-profit activities subject to taxation under section 511(a) of the Internal Revenue Code of 1986 as in effect on the date of the enactment of this Act.

SEC. 7.   NONAPPLICATION TO MEMBERS OF THE ARMED FORCES; VETERANS' PREFERENCES.

(a) ARMED FORCES.—(1) For purposes of this Act, the term "employment or employment opportunities" does not apply to the relationship between the United States and members of the Armed Forces.

(2) As used in paragraph (1), the term "Armed Forces" means the Army, Navy, Air Force, Marine Corps, and Coast Guard.

(b) VETERANS' PREFERENCES.—This Act does not repeal or modify any Federal, State, territorial, or local law creating special rights or preferences for veterans.

SEC. 8.   ENFORCEMENT.

(a) ENFORCEMENT POWERS.—With respect to the administration and enforcement of this Act in the case of a claim alleged by an individual for a violation of this Act—

(1) the Commission shall have the same powers as the Commission has to administer and enforce title VII of the Civil Rights Act of 1964 (42 U.S.C. 2000e et seq.); * * *

[The bill sets out enforcement powers under statutes pertaining to Congressional employees.]

(4) the Attorney General of the United States shall have the same powers as the Attorney General has to administer and enforce title VII of the Civil Rights Act of 1964 * * * and

(5) the courts of the United States shall have the same jurisdiction and powers as such courts have to enforce title VII of the Civil Rights Act of 1964 * * *.

(b) PROCEDURES AND REMEDIES.—The procedures and remedies applicable to a claim alleged by an individual for a violation of this Act are as follows:

(1) the procedures and remedies applicable for a violation of title VII of the Civil Rights Act of 1964 (43 U.S.C. 2000e et seq.) in the case of a claim alleged by such individual for a violation of such title, * * *

[The bill sets forth procedures and remedies established in the Governmental Employee Rights Act of 1991, 2 U.S.C. § 1202 et seq., and the Congressional Accountability Act of 1995, 109 Stat. 3, for Congressional employees.]

SEC. 9.   STATE AND FEDERAL IMMUNITY.

(a) STATE IMMUNITY.—A state shall not be immune under the eleventh article of amendment to the Constitution of the United States from an action in a Federal court of competent jurisdiction for a violation of this Act. In an action against a State for a violation of this Act, remedies (including remedies at law and in equity) are available for the violation to the same extent as such remedies are available in an action against any public or private entity other than a State.

(b) LIABILITY OF THE UNITED STATES.—The United States shall be liable for all remedies (excluding punitive damages) under this Act to the same extent as a private person and shall be liable to the same extent as a nonpublic party for interest to compensate for delay in payment.

SEC. 10.   ATTORNEYS' FEES.

In any action or administrative proceeding commenced pursuant to this Act, the court or the Commission, in its discretion, may allow the prevailing party, other than the United States, a reasonable attorney's fee, including expert fees and other litigation expenses, and costs. The United States shall be liable for the foregoing the same as a private person.

SEC. 11.   RETALIATION AND COERCION PROHIBITED.

(a) RETALIATION.—A covered entity shall not discriminate against an individual because such individual opposed any act or practice prohibited by this Act or because such individual made a charge, assisted, testified, or participated in any manner in an investigation, proceeding, or hearing under this Act.

(b) COERCION.—A person shall not coerce, intimidate, threaten, or interfere with any individual in the exercise or enjoyment of, or on account of his or her having exercised, enjoyed, assisted, or encouraged the exercise or enjoyment of, any right granted or protected by this Act.

SEC. 12.   POSTING NOTICES.

A covered entity shall post notices for employees, applicants for employment, and members describing the applicable provisions of this Act in the manner prescribed by, and subject to the penalty provided under, section 711 of the Civil Rights Act of 1964 (42 U.S.C. 2000e–10).

SEC. 13.   REGULATIONS.

The Commission shall have authority to issue regulations to carry out this Act.

SEC. 14.   RELATIONSHIP TO OTHER LAWS.

This Act shall not invalidate or limit the rights, remedies, or procedures available to an individual claiming discrimination prohibited under any other Federal law or any law of a State or political subdivision of a State.

SEC. 15.   SEVERABILITY.

If any provision of this Act, or the application of such provision to any person or circumstance, is held to be invalid, the remainder of this Act and the application of such provision to other persons or circumstances shall not be affected thereby.

SEC. 16.   EFFECTIVE DATE.

This Act shall take effect 60 days after the date of the enactment of this Act and shall not apply to conduct occurring before such effective date.

SEC. 17.   DEFINITIONS.

As used in this Act:

(1) The term "Commission" means the Equal Employment Opportunity Commission.

(2) The term "covered entity" means an employer, employment agency, labor organization, joint labor management committee, an entity to which section 717(a) of the Civil Rights Act of 1964 (42 U.S.C. 2000e (e)) applies, an employing authority of the House of Representatives, an employing office of the Senate, or an instrumentality of the Congress.

(3) The term "employer" has the meaning given such term in section 701 (b) of the Civil Rights Act of 1964 (42 U.S.C. 2000e(b)).

(4) The term "employment agency" has the meaning given such term in section 701(e) of the Civil Rights Act of 1964 (42 U.S.C. 2000e(e)).

(5) The term "employment or employment opportunities" includes job application procedures, hiring, advancement, discharge, compensation, job training, or any other term, condition, or privilege of employment.

(6) The term "instrumentalities of the Congress" has the meaning given such term in section 117(b)(4) of the Civil Rights Act of 1991 (2 U.S.C. 601(b)(4)).

(7) The term "labor organization" has the meaning given such term in section 701(d) of the Civil Rights Act of 1964 (42 U.S.C. 2000e(d)).

(8) The term "person" has the meaning given such term in section 701(a) of the Civil Rights Act of 1964 (42 U.S.C. 2000e(a)).

(9) The term "religious organization" means—

(A) A religious corporation, association, or society; or

(B) a college, school, university, or other educational institution, not otherwise a religious organization, if-

> (i) it is in whole or substantial part controlled, managed, owned, or supported by a religious corporation, association, or society; or

> (ii) its curriculum is directed toward the propagation of a particular religion.

(10) The term "Senate employee" has the meaning given such term in section 301(e) of the Civil Rights Act of 1991 (2 U.S.C. 1201(e)).

(11) The term "sexual orientation" means homosexuality, bisexuality or heterosexuality, whether such orientation is real or perceived.

(12) The term "State" has the meaning given such term in section 701(i) of the Civil Rights Act of 1964 (42 U.S.C. 2000e(i)).

*

ORDINANCE No. 22

An Ordinance of the City of West Hollywood Establishing Regulations Governing the Creation, Termination and Effect of Domestic Partnerships

21 February 1985.

THE CITY COUNCIL OF THE CITY OF WEST HOLLYWOOD DOES ORDAIN AS FOLLOWS:

Section 1. Definition of a Domestic Partnership

A. A domestic partnership shall exist between two persons if the following is true:

(1) The persons are not related by blood closer than would bar marriage in the State of California;

(2) Neither person is married or related by marriage;

(3) The persons share the common necessities of life;

(4) The persons are eighteen (18) years old or older;

(5) The persons are competent to enter a contract;

(6) The persons declare that they are each other's sole domestic partner;

(7) The persons are responsible for each other's welfare;

(8) The persons agree to notify the City of any change in the status of their domestic partnership;

(9) Neither person has declared that he or she has a different domestic partner;

(10) The persons file a statement of domestic partnership as set forth in Section 2 of this ordinance.

Section 2. Statement of Domestic Partnership

A. *Contents*

Domestic partners may make an official record of their domestic partnership by completing, signing and submitting to the City Clerk a statement of domestic partnership. Persons submitting a statement of domestic partnership must declare under penalty of perjury:

(1) The persons are not related by blood closer than would bar marriage in the State of California;

(2) Neither person is married or related by marriage;

(3) The persons share the common necessities of life;

(4) The persons are eighteen (18) years old or older;

(5) The persons are competent to enter a contract;

(6) The persons declare that they are each other's sole domestic partner;

(7) The persons are responsible for each other's welfare;

(8) The persons agree to notify the City of any change in the status of their domestic partnership;

(9) Neither person has declared that he or she has a different domestic partner.

The domestic partnership statement shall include the date on which the persons become each other's domestic partners and the address or addresses of both partners.

B.   *Amendment of Domestic Partnership Statement.*

Partners may amend this statement at any time in order to change an address by filing a new statement.

C.   *Termination of Domestic Partnership.*

Any member of a domestic partnership may terminate the domestic partnership by filing a termination statement with the City Clerk. The person filing the termination statement must declare under penalty of perjury: (1) The domestic partnership is terminated and (2) A copy of the termination statement has been mailed to the other domestic partner.

D.   *New Statements of Domestic Partnership.*

No person who has filed an affidavit of domestic partnership may file another statement of domestic partnership until six (6) months after a statement of termination of a previous partnership has been filed with the City Clerk.

[We omit Sections 3 and 4, which are recordkeeping provisions.]

Section 5.   Civil Actions.

Any person defrauded by a false statement contained in a statement of domestic partnership[,] termination statement or amendment statement may bring a civil action for fraud to recover his or her losses.

[We omit Section 6, which renders the Uniform Partnership Act inapplicable to domestic partners.]

Section 7.   Visitation Rights.

All health care facilities including but not limited to hospitals, convalescent facilities or other longterm care facilities shall allow a domestic partner of a patient to visit the patient unless no visitors are allowed.

Section 8.   Jail Visitation.

All City jails shall allow an inmate's domestic partner to visit the inmate unless:

(1) No visitors are allowed, or

(2) The authority in charge of the jail decides that the particular visitor is a threat to the security of the facility.

Section 9. Forms.

The following forms shall be sufficient proof of the creation or termination of domestic partnership:

A. *STATEMENT OF DOMESTIC PARTNERSHIP*

We, the undersigned, do declare that:

(1) We are not related by blood;

(2) Neither of us is married, nor are we related by marriage;

(3) We share the common necessities of life;

(4) We are each other's domestic partner, and we have been each other's domestic partner since _____ .

(5) We are the sole domestic partner of each other;

(6) We are both over 18 years of age;

(7) We are responsible for each other's welfare;

(8) We agree to notify the City of any change in the status of our domestic partnership arrangement.

I declare under penalty of perjury under the laws of the State of California that the statements above are true and correct.

Executed on _____, 19__, at _____, California.

Signed: _____

Print: _____

Address: _____

_____

Telephone Number: _____

Signed: _____

Print: _____

Address: _____

_____

Telephone Number: _____

B. *STATEMENT TERMINATING DOMESTIC PARTNERSHIP*

I declare under penalty of perjury under the laws of the State of California that the statements above are true and correct.

Executed on _____, 19__, at _____, California.

Signed: _____

Print: _____

Address: _____

_____

Telephone Number: _____

*

Texas Sex Crime Statutes

VERNON'S TEXAS STATUTES AND CODES ANNOTATED PENAL CODE
TITLE 5. OFFENSES AGAINST THE PERSON
CHAPTER 21. SEXUAL OFFENSES * * *

Section 21.06. *Homosexual Conduct*

(a) A person commits an offense if he engages in deviate sexual intercourse with another individual of the same sex.

(b) An offense under this section is a Class C misdemeanor.

Section 21.07. *Public Lewdness*

(a) A person commits an offense if he knowingly engages in any of the following acts in a public place or, if not in a public place, he is reckless about whether another is present who will be offended or alarmed by his:

(1) act of sexual intercourse;

(2) act of deviate sexual intercourse;

(3) act of sexual contact; or

(4) act involving contact between the person's mouth or genitals and the anus or genitals of an animal or fowl.

(b) An offense under this section is a Class A misdemeanor.

Section 21.08. *Indecent Exposure*

(a) A person commits an offense if he exposes his anus or any part of his genitals with intent to arouse or gratify the sexual desire of any person, and he is reckless about whether another is present who will be offended or alarmed by his act.

(b) An offense under this section is a Class B misdemeanor.

Section 21.11. *Indecency With a Child*

(a) A person commits an offense if, with a child younger than 17 years and not his spouse, whether the child is of the same or opposite sex, he:

(1) engages in sexual contact with the child; or

(2) exposes his anus or any part of his genitals, knowing the child is present, with intent to arouse or gratify the sexual desire of any person.

(b) It is an affirmative defense to prosecution under this section that the actor:

(1) was not more than three years older than the victim and of the opposite sex; and

(2) did not use duress, force, or a threat against the victim at the time of the offense.

(c) An offense under Subsection (a)(1) is a felony of the second degree and an offense under Subsection (a)(2) is a felony of the third degree.

CHAPTER 22. ASSAULTIVE OFFENSES

Section 22.01. Assault

(a) A person commits an offense if the person:

(1) intentionally, knowingly, or recklessly causes bodily injury to another, including the person's spouse;

(2) intentionally or knowingly threatens another with imminent bodily injury, including the person's spouse; or

(3) intentionally or knowingly causes physical contact with another when the person knows or should reasonably believe that the other will regard the contact as offensive or provocative.

(b) An offense under Subsection (a)(1) is a Class A misdemeanor * * *.

(c) An offense under Subsection (a)(2) or (3) is a Class C misdemeanor * * *.

[We have omitted provisions added in 1995 that relate to assaults on "public servants."]

Section 22.011. Sexual Assault

(a) A person commits an offense if the person:

(1) intentionally or knowingly:

(A) causes the penetration of the anus or female sexual organ of another person by any means, without that person's consent;

(B) causes the penetration of the mouth of another person by the sexual organ of the actor, without that person's consent; or

(C) causes the sexual organ of another person, without that person's consent, to contact or penetrate the mouth, anus, or sexual organ of another person, including the actor; or

(2) intentionally or knowingly:

(A) causes the penetration of the anus or female sexual organ of a child by any means;

(B) causes the penetration of the mouth of a child by the sexual organ of the actor;

(C) causes the sexual organ of a child to contact or penetrate the mouth, anus, or sexual organ of another person, including the actor; or

(D) causes the anus of a child to contact the mouth, anus, or sexual organ of another person, including the actor.

(b) A sexual assault under Subsection (a)(1) is without the consent of the other person if:

(1) the actor compels the other person to submit or participate by the use of physical force or violence;

(2) the actor compels the other person to submit or participate by threatening to use force or violence against the other person, and the other person believes that the actor has the present ability to execute the threat;

(3) the other person has not consented and the actor knows the other person is unconscious or physically unable to resist;

(4) the actor knows that as a result of mental disease or defect the other person is at the time of the sexual assault incapable either of appraising the nature of the act or of resisting it;

(5) the other person has not consented and the actor knows the other person is unaware that the sexual assault is occurring;

(6) the actor has intentionally impaired the other person's power to appraise or control the other person's conduct by administering any substance without the other person's knowledge;

(7) the actor compels the other person to submit or participate by threatening to use force or violence against any person, and the other person believes that the actor has the ability to execute the threat; or

(8) the actor is a public servant who coerces the other person to submit or participate;

(9) the actor is a mental health services provider who causes the other person, who is a patient or former patient of the actor, to submit or participate by exploiting the other person's emotional dependency on the actor; or

(10) the actor is a clergyman who causes the other person to submit or participate by exploiting the other person's emotional dependency on the clergyman in the clergyman's professional character as spiritual adviser.

(c) In this section:

(1) "Child" means a person younger than 17 years of age who is not the spouse of the actor.

(2) "Spouse" means a person who is legally married to another.

(d) It is a defense to prosecution under Subsection (a)(2) that the conduct consisted of medical care for the child and did not include any contact between the anus or sexual organ of the child and the mouth, anus, or sexual organ of the actor or a third party.

(e) It is an affirmative defense to prosecution under Subsection (a)(2) that the actor was not more than three years older than the victim, and the victim was a child of 14 years of age or older.

(f) An offense under this section is a felony of the second degree. * * *

Section 22.06.   *Consent as Defense to Assaultive Conduct*

The victim's effective consent or the actor's reasonable belief that the victim consented to the actor's conduct is a defense to prosecution under Section 22.01 (Assault), 22.02 (Aggravated Assault), or 22.05 (Deadly Conduct) if:

(1) the conduct did not threaten or inflict serious bodily injury; or

(2) the victim knew the conduct was a risk of:

(A) his occupation;

(B) recognized medical treatment; or

(C) a scientific experiment conducted by recognized methods. * * *

TITLE 9.   OFFENSES AGAINST PUBLIC ORDER AND DECENCY

CHAPTER 42.   DISORDERLY CONDUCT AND RELATED OFFENSES

Section 42.01.   *Disorderly Conduct*

(a) A person commits an offense if he intentionally or knowingly:

(1) uses abusive, indecent, profane, or vulgar language in a public place, and the language by its very utterance tends to incite an immediate breach of the peace;

(2) makes an offensive gesture or display in a public place, and the gesture or display tends to incite an immediate breach of the peace;

(3) creates, by chemical means, a noxious and unreasonable odor in a public place;

(4) abuses or threatens a person in a public place in an obviously offensive manner;

(5) makes unreasonable noise in a public place other than a sport shooting range, as defined by Section 250.001, Local Government Code, or in or near a private residence that he has no right to occupy;

(6) fights with another in a public place;

(7) enters on the property of another and for a lewd or unlawful purpose looks into a dwelling on the property through any window or other opening in the dwelling;

(8) while on the premises of a hotel or comparable establishment, for a lewd or unlawful purpose looks into a guest room not his own through a window or other opening in the room;

(9) discharges a firearm in a public place other than a public road or a sport shooting range, as defined by Section 250.001, Local Government Code;

(10) displays a firearm or other deadly weapon in a public place in a manner calculated to alarm;

(11) discharges a firearm on or across a public road; or

(12) exposes his anus or genitals in a public place and is reckless about whether another may be present who will be offended or alarmed by his act.

(b) It is a defense to prosecution under Subsection (a)(4) that the actor had significant provocation for his abusive or threatening conduct.

(c) For purposes of this section:

(1) an act is deemed to occur in a public place or near a private residence if it produces its offensive or proscribed consequences in the public place or near a private residence; * * *

(d) An offense under this section is a Class C misdemeanor unless committed under Subsection (a)(9) or (a)(10), in which event it is a Class B misdemeanor. * * *

CHAPTER 43. PUBLIC INDECENCY
SUBCHAPTER A. PROSTITUTION

Section 43.01. *Definitions*

In this subchapter:

(1) "Deviate sexual intercourse" means any contact between the genitals of one person and the mouth or anus of another person.

(2) "Prostitution" means the offense defined in Section 43.02.

(3) "Sexual contact" means any touching of the anus, breast, or any part of the genitals of another person with intent to arouse or gratify the sexual desire of any person.

(4) "Sexual conduct" includes deviate sexual intercourse, sexual contact, and sexual intercourse.

(5) "Sexual intercourse" means any penetration of the female sex organ by the male sex organ.

Section 43.02. *Prostitution*

(a) A person commits an offense if he knowingly:

(1) offers to engage, agrees to engage, or engages in sexual conduct for a fee; or

(2) solicits another in a public place to engage with him in sexual conduct for hire.

(b) An offense is established under Subsection (a)(1) whether the actor is to receive or pay a fee. An offense is established under Subsection (a)(2) whether the actor solicits a person to hire him or offers to hire the person solicited.

(c) An offense under this section is a Class B misdemeanor, unless the actor has been convicted previously under this section, in which event it is a Class A misdemeanor.

Section 43.03.   Promotion of Prostitution

(a) A person commits an offense if, acting other than as a prostitute receiving compensation for personally rendered prostitution services, he or she knowingly:

(1) receives money or other property pursuant to an agreement to participate in the proceeds of prostitution; or

(2) solicits another to engage in sexual conduct with another person for compensation.

(b) An offense under this section is a Class A misdemeanor.

Section 43.04.   Aggravated Promotion of Prostitution

(a) A person commits an offense if he knowingly owns, invests in, finances, controls, supervises, or manages a prostitution enterprise that uses two or more prostitutes.

(b) An offense under this section is a felony of the third degree.

Section 43.05.   Compelling Prostitution

(a) A person commits an offense if he knowingly:

(1) causes another by force, threat, or fraud to commit prostitution; or

(2) causes by any means a person younger than 17 years to commit prostitution.

(b) An offense under this section is a felony of the second degree.

* * *

SUBCHAPTER B. OBSCENITY

Section 43.21. Definitions

(a) In this subchapter:

(1) "Obscene" means material or a performance that:

(A) the average person, applying contemporary community standards, would find that taken as a whole appeals to the prurient interest in sex;

(B) depicts or describes:

(i) patently offensive representations or descriptions of ultimate sexual acts, normal or perverted, actual or simulated, including sexual intercourse, sodomy, and sexual bestiality; or

(ii) patently offensive representations or descriptions of masturbation, excretory functions, sadism, masochism, lewd exhibition of the genitals, the male or female genitals in a state of sexual stimulation or arousal, covered male genitals in a discernibly turgid state or a device designed and marketed as useful primarily for stimulation of the human genital organs; and

(C) taken as a whole, lacks serious literary, artistic, political, and scientific value.

(2) "Material" means anything tangible that is capable of being used or adapted to arouse interest, whether through the medium of reading,observation, sound, or in any other manner, but does not include an actual three dimensional obscene device.

(3) "Performance" means a play, motion picture, dance, or other exhibition performed before an audience.

(4) "Patently offensive" means so offensive on its face as to affront current community standards of decency.

(5) "Promote" means to manufacture, issue, sell, give, provide, lend, mail, deliver, transfer, transmit, publish, distribute, circulate, disseminate, present, exhibit, or advertise, or to offer or agree to do the same.

(6) "Wholesale promote" means to manufacture, issue, sell, provide, mail, deliver, transfer, transmit, publish, distribute, circulate, disseminate, or to offer or agree to do the same for purpose of resale.

(7) "Obscene device" means a device including a dildo or artificial vagina, designed or marketed as useful primarily for the stimulation of human genital organs.

(b) If any of the depictions or descriptions of sexual conduct described in this section are declared by a court of competent jurisdiction to be unlawfully included herein, this declaration shall not invalidate this section as to other patently offensive sexual conduct included herein.

Section 43.22. *Obscene Display or Distribution*

(a) A person commits an offense if he intentionally or knowingly displays or distributes an obscene photograph, drawing, or similar visual representation or other obscene material and is reckless about whether a person is present who will be offended or alarmed by the display or distribution.

(b) An offense under this section is a Class C misdemeanor.

Section 43.23. Obscenity

(a) A person commits an offense if, knowing its content and character, he wholesale promotes or possesses with intent to wholesale promote any obscene material or obscene device.

(b) An offense under Subsection (a) is a state jail felony.

(c) A person commits an offense if, knowing its content and character, he:

(1) promotes or possesses with intent to promote any obscene material or obscene device; or

(2) produces, presents, or directs an obscene performance or participates in a portion thereof that is obscene or that contributes to its obscenity.

(d) An offense under Subsection (c) is a Class A misdemeanor.

(e) A person who promotes or wholesale promotes obscene material or an obscene device or possesses the same with intent to promote or wholesale promote it in the course of his business is presumed to do so with knowledge of its content and character.

(f) A person who possesses six or more obscene devices or identical or similar obscene articles is presumed to possess them with intent to promote the same.

(g) It is an affirmative defense to prosecution under this section that the person who possesses or promotes material or a device proscribed by this section does so for a bona fide medical, psychiatric, judicial, legislative, or law enforcement purpose.

Section 43.24. Sale, Distribution, or Display of Harmful Material to Minor

(a) For purposes of this section:

(1) "Minor" means an individual younger than 18 years.

(2) "Harmful material" means material whose dominant theme taken as a whole:

(A) appeals to the prurient interest of a minor, in sex, nudity, or excretion;

(B) is patently offensive to prevailing standards in the adult community as a whole with respect to what is suitable for minors; and

(C) is utterly without redeeming social value for minors.

(b) A person commits an offense if, knowing that the material is harmful:

(1) and knowing the person is a minor, he sells, distributes, exhibits, or possesses for sale, distribution, or exhibition to a minor harmful material;

(2) he displays harmful material and is reckless about whether a minor is present who will be offended or alarmed by the display; or

(3) he hires, employs, or uses a minor to do or accomplish or assist in doing or accomplishing any of the acts prohibited in Subsection (b)(1) or (b)(2).

(c) It is a defense to prosecution under this section that:

(1) the sale, distribution, or exhibition was by a person having scientific, educational, governmental, or other similar justification; or

(2) the sale, distribution, or exhibition was to a minor who was accompanied by a consenting parent, guardian, or spouse.

(d) An offense under this section is a Class A misdemeanor unless it is committed under Subsection (b)(3) in which event it is a felony of the third degree.

Section 43.25. *Sexual Performance by a Child*

(a) In this section:

(1) "Sexual performance" means any performance or part thereof that includes sexual conduct by a child younger than 18 years of age.

(2) "Sexual conduct" means actual or simulated sexual intercourse, deviate sexual intercourse, sexual bestiality, masturbation, sado-masochistic abuse, or lewd exhibition of the genitals.

(3) "Performance" means any play, motion picture, photograph, dance, or other visual representation that can be exhibited before an audience of one or more persons.

(4) "Produce" with respect to a sexual performance includes any conduct that directly contributes to the creation or manufacture of the sexual performance.

(5) "Promote" means to procure, manufacture, issue, sell, give, provide, lend, mail, deliver, transfer, transmit, publish, distribute, circulate, disseminate, present, exhibit, or advertise or to offer or agree to do any of the above.

(6) "Simulated" means the explicit depiction of sexual conduct that creates the appearance of actual sexual conduct and during which a person engaging in the conduct exhibits any uncovered portion of the breasts, genitals, or buttocks.

(7) "Deviate sexual intercourse" has the meaning defined by Section 43.01.

(b) A person commits an offense if, knowing the character and content thereof, he employs, authorizes, or induces a child younger than 18 years of age to engage in sexual conduct or a sexual performance. A parent or legal guardian or custodian of a child younger than 18 years of age commits an offense if he consents to the participation by the child in a sexual performance.

(c) An offense under Subsection (b) is a felony of the second degree.

(d) A person commits an offense if, knowing the character and content of the material, he produces, directs, or promotes a performance that includes sexual conduct by a child younger than 18 years of age.

(e) An offense under Subsection (d) is a felony of the third degree.

(f) It is an affirmative defense to a prosecution under this section that:

(1) the defendant, in good faith, reasonably believed that the child who engaged in the sexual conduct was 18 years of age or older;

(2) the defendant was the spouse of the child at the time of the offense;

(3) the conduct was for a bona fide educational, medical, psychological, psychiatric, judicial, law enforcement, or legislative purpose; or

(4) the defendant is not more than two years older than the child.

(g) When it becomes necessary for the purposes of this section or Section 43.26 to determine whether a child who participated in sexual conduct was younger than 18 years of age, the court or jury may make this determination by any of the following methods:

(1) personal inspection of the child;

(2) inspection of the photograph or motion picture that shows the child engaging in the sexual performance;

(3) oral testimony by a witness to the sexual performance as to the age of the child based on the child's appearance at the time;

(4) expert medical testimony based on the appearance of the child engaging in the sexual performance; or

(5) any other method authorized by law or by the rules of evidence at common law.

Section 43.251. *Employment Harmful to Children*

(a) In this section:

(1) "Child" means a person younger than 18 years of age.

(2) "Massage" has the meaning assigned to the term "massage therapy" by Section 1, Chapter 752, Acts of the 69th Legislature, Regular Session, 1985 (Article 4512k, Vernon's Texas Civil Statutes).

(3) "Massage establishment" has the meaning assigned by Section 1, Chapter 752, Acts of the 69th Legislature, Regular Session, 1985 (Article 4512k, Vernon's Texas Civil Statutes).

(4) "Nude" means a child who is:

(A) entirely unclothed; or

(B) clothed in a manner that leaves uncovered or visible through less than fully opaque clothing any portion of the breasts below the top of the areola of the breasts, if the child is female, or any portion of the genitals or buttocks.

(5) "Sexually oriented commercial activity" means a massage establishment, nude studio, modeling studio, love parlor, or other similar

commercial enterprise the primary business of which is the offering of a service that is intended to provide sexual stimulation or sexual gratification to the customer.

(6) "Topless" means a female child clothed in a manner that leaves uncovered or visible through less than fully opaque clothing any portion of her breasts below the top of the areola.

(b) A person commits an offense if the person employs, authorizes, or induces a child to work:

(1) in a sexually oriented commercial activity; or

(2) in any place of business permitting, requesting, or requiring a child to work nude or topless.

(c) An offense under this section is a Class A misdemeanor.

Section 43.26.   *Possession or Promotion of Child Pornography*

(a) A person commits an offense if:

(1) the person knowingly or intentionally possesses material containing a film image that visually depicts a child younger than 18 years of age at the time the film image of the child was made who is engaging in sexual conduct; and

(2) the person knows that the material depicts the child as described by Subdivision (1).

(b) In this section:

(1) "Film image" includes a photograph, slide, negative, film, or videotape, or a reproduction of any of these.

(2) "Sexual conduct" has the meaning assigned by Section 43.25.

(3) "Promote" has the meaning assigned by Section 43.25.

(c) The affirmative defenses provided by Section 43.25(f) also apply to a prosecution under this section.

(d) An offense under this section is a felony of the third degree.

(e) A person commits an offense if:

(1) the person knowingly or intentionally promotes or possesses with intent to promote material described by Subsection (a)(1); and

(2) the person knows that the material depicts the child as described by Subsection (a)(1).

(f) A person who possesses six or more identical film images depicting a child as described by Subsection (a)(1) is presumed to possess the film images with the intent to promote the material.

(g) An offense under Subsection (e) is a felony of the third degree.

* * *

*

TOPICS INDEX

References are to pages

ABORTION, 30–36, 63–64, 233
education, 660
historical background, 30, 35–36, 164
parental consent and notification, 190–201
sex equality, and, 34–36, 196
speech about, 579–581, 653

ACADEMIC FREEDOM, 620–630, 632–638
See also Education
schools versus teachers, 621–625, 632–638
sexual harassment and, 632–638

ACQUIRED IMMUNO-DEFICIENCY SYNDROME (AIDS)
See also Americans with Disabilities Act
adoption and child custody, 843–844
defamation and outing, 485–490
disease and epidemic as a social construction, 661, 1065, 1069–1073, 1079
employment discrimination, 958–967
immigration exclusion, 189
policy responses,
bathhouse closing, 1086–1089
child custody, 843–844
condom distribution, 1100
criminalization, 753, 1090, 1099–1100
education,
federal public health, 676, 680
secondary schools, 654, 666, 1100
mandatory testing, 1080, 1101
needle exchange programs, 1100
tort claims, 1092
prostitution and, 1080
race issues, 1074–1077

ADOPTION, 660, 770, 786–787, 827, 841–868
lesbian and gay, 786–787, 841–848
second-parent, 861–868
surrogacy, 775–778
transracial, 867–868, 848

ADULTERY, 1, 37, 55, 233, 740, 742, 745, 828–831

AFFIRMATIVE ACTION, 871

AFRICAN-AMERICANS
See Critical Race Theory; Race and Sexuality

AID TO FAMILIES WITH DEPENDENT CHILDREN (AFDC)
see Welfare Benefits

AMERICAN PSYCHIATRIC ASSOCIATION, 185–187, 197–198, 252

AMERICANS WITH DISABILITIES ACT (ADA), 961–967, 1111
AIDS, HIV infection, and, 963–967
homosexuality and, 962–963
exclusion of transsexuals, 1111

ARMED FORCES
See Military

ARTIFICIAL INSEMINATION 848–861
surrogacy and, 774–781

BILL OF RIGHTS
See also Due Process Clause; First Amendment; Privacy
criminal procedure, preface, 1147–1148
due process (including equal protection), preface, 16, 34–36, 73–92, 92–131, 877–879, 1147–1149
privacy, preface, 2, 6–37, 40–72, 119, 951–952, 1147–1148

BIRTH CONTROL
general, 31–37, 233, 652
minors and, 29–30, 653, 667, 671–672
race and, 6–7

BISEXUALITY, 225, 301–304, 313, 701

CHILD CUSTODY AND VISITATION, 828–841
adultery, 828–831
AIDS, 835
race, 831–832
sexual orientation, 832–841
empirical and psychological evidence, 846–848
parent-daughter disputes, 837–841
spousal disputes, 832–837

CHILD SEXUAL ABUSE, 150–151, 171–172, 274–278, 525–532, 847, 1021–1043
See also Statutory Rape
intergenerational sex as, 1030–1035
pornography as, 525–532, 1038–1041

1187

CHRISTIANITY, 136, 229–230, 233, 242–244, 251, 263, 455–463, 685, 697, 703, 714–715

CIVIL RIGHTS ACT OF 1964, TITLE VII
See Employment Discrimination

COHABITATION OUTSIDE OF MARRIAGE
contractual obligations, 766, 781–786
    same-sex relationships, 784–785
legitimacy of nonmarital children, 765–766
new legal categories, 791
privacy right preface,
third-party obligations, 785–786, 787–788

COLLEGES AND UNIVERSITIES, 81–92, 696
See also Education

CONSUMERISM, 770–771
commercial sex, 1044–1062
critique of commodification, 771, 775–780, 1052–1054, 1055–1056
sex reassignment surgery, 212–213
surrogacy, 774–781, 849–853

COMSTOCK LAWS, 2, 3, 37, 154–155

CONSENT, SEXUAL
    See also Rape
assault, 971, 993
authority figures, 993, 1057
coercion,
    economic, 537, 551, 986
    physical, 537, 551, 984
    psychological, 537, 551, 988
critique of, 250, 982–1015, 1051–1055
fraud and misrepresentation, 551, 988
history of, 307–308
minors and, 274–280, 1021–1030
sadomasochism, 549, 1003–1020
sodomy, 37–72

CRIMINAL LAWS REGULATING SEXUALITY AND GENDER DEVIANCE 1–2, appendix 6
adultery, 1, 37, 55
bigamy (polygamy), 1, 824–826
child molestation and pornography, 1, 524–532, 533, 549–550, 1038–1042, 1183–1185 (Texas)
cross–dressing and masquerade, 1, 1130, 1136–1139
disorderly conduct, 166–167, 1178–1179 (Texas)
fornication, 1, 55
incest, 1, 823–824
indecent conduct with minor, 1175 (Texas)
indecent exposure, 167, 1175 (Texas)
loitering, 166
obscenity, 1, 508–516, 1180–1183 (Texas)
prostitution, 153–155, 1044–1045, 1179–1180 (Texas)
public health, 1086–1089, 1090
public indecency and lewdness, 1, 37, 167, 1131, 1175 (Texas)
rape (sexual assault), 1, 980, 1023, 1176–1178 (Texas)

CRIMINAL LAWS REGULATING SEXUALITY AND GENDER DEVIANCE—Cont'd
sex with minors, 1021–1038, 1131, 1176–1178 (Texas)
sexual psychopath laws, 172–174
sodomy, 1, 37–72, 118, 366–372, 485, 745, 750, 1005–1010, 1019–1020, 1175 (Texas)
solicitation, 44, 167, 1042–1043, 1055–1057, 1080, 1179–1180 (Texas)
vagrancy, including lewd vagrancy, 167, 627, 1132

CRITICAL RACE THEORY
    See also Race and Sexuality
censorship (Kimberlé Crenshaw), 567–573
hate speech (Mari Matsuda), 491–495
intersections of race and sex (Kimberlé Crenshaw), 567–573
    lynching (Jacqueline Dowd Hall), 998
    rape, 995–1002
    workplace harassment (Crenshaw), 911–912, 1002–1003
intersections of race and sexual orientation,
    AIDS (Harlon Dalton), 1074–1078
    history (Tomàs Almaquer), 245
    military policies, 321–341, 388, 397
segregation and manhood (Kenneth Karst), 321–341

CROSS-DRESSING
child custody and visitation, 1144–1146
criminalization, 2, 1130–1136
employment discrimination, 1137–1144
sexual perversion and, 164–168
transsexualism and, 1135–1137, 1140–1143

DISPARATE IMPACT (TITLE VII), 282–287, 631, 898–937
ADA and AIDS, 1089

DISPARATE TREATMENT (TITLE VII), 733, 898–937, 1104

DIVORCE, 607, 772–774
See also Marriage

DEFENSE OF MARRIAGE ACT (DOMA), 816–817

DOMESTIC PARTNERSHIP, 763, 781–794, 795–868, appendix 5

DUE PROCESS CLAUSE
equal protection,
    race, 320, 334–336, 1148
    sex, 320, 346–357
    sexual orientation, 320, 374–384, 638
privacy rights, 6, 8–37, 40–72, 117, 1147–1148
vagueness, 39–40, 512, 573

ECONOMIC THEORY
Chicago school theory (Richard Posner), 228, 238–244, 246, 779, 1051–53
feminist theory (Carol Rose, Debra Satz), 248, 826, 1051–1052

ECONOMIC THEORY—Cont'd
Marxist theory (John D'Emilio, Eleanor Leacock), 228, 234–238, 246, 795

EDUCATION, 595–681
abortion, 579–581, 653, 655, 656, 660
AIDS and other sexually transmitted diseases,
    educational need, 662–665
    religion and, 686, 693
    sexual harassment and AIDS education, 652, 673
    state laws (survey), 675, 686
    theory, 662–663
athletic teams, sex discrimination, homophobia, 644
gender equity, 644–651
libraries and censorship, 610–618
"no promotion of homosexuality" policies,
    federal, 676–681
    state, 426–430, 673
pregnancy and family planning advice, 579–581, 654–662
prom night, 598–602
sex education, 620, 652–656, 666, 686
sex segregation,
    all-male schools, 81–90, 646–649
    all-female schools, 645, 650
sexual harassment in schools, 630–644
    claim for relief, 631–632, 639
    males against females, 630, 632, 639
    straights against gays, 638
speech (general), 426–430, 597, 621
student organizations,
    high school, 602, 609–610
    university, 443–453, 455–462, 696
teachers and sexuality,
    bisexuality, 301–304
    homosexuality, 426–430, 625–629
    sexual speech, 632
    sexually harassing speech, 630–632
    variations, 629–630
theories of, 595–596, 606–609, 663–666

EMPLOYMENT DISCRIMINATION
    See also Americans with Disabilities Act; Disparate Impact; Disparate Treatment
disability, 958–967
dress, 1140–1144
gender, 282–287, 913–918, 938–948
gender dysphoria, 913–918, 1103–1111, 1142
marital status, 957–958
sex, 876–880
    state and federal discrimination,
        armed forces (combat exclusion), 74–78, 319, 342–365
        pregnancy, 81
        veterans' preferences, 879–880
    laws protecting against private sex discrimination,
        District of Columbia Human Rights Act, 444–453, 1151–1157, appendix 2

EMPLOYMENT DISCRIMINATION—Cont'd
sex—Cont'd
    laws protecting against private sex discrimination—Cont'd
        Civil Rights Act of 1964, Title VII, pp. 89, 92, 736, 879, 898–948
        history, 898–900
        pregnancy, 896–897, 900–913
        sexual harassment, hostile workplace, 919–937
        Wisconsin Fair Employment Act 956, appendix 3
sexual orientation, 880, 913–918
    state and federal anti-gay discrimination,
        armed forces, 109–117, 319, 366–407, 434–436
        federal civil service, 174–175, 746, 880–896
        federal security clearances, 891
        state employees, 124–131, 426–429, 628, 726, 745
        teachers, 175, 625, 627–628, 725
    laws protecting against private anti-gay discrimination, 948–958
        District of Columbia Human Rights Act, 444–453, appendix 2
        Employment Non-Discrimination Act, 949–950, appendix 3
        listing state laws, 949 notes
        Title VII, failure to cover, 914–917, 926–930
transsexualism,
    federal law, 1103–1106
    state law, 1109, 1111

ENTRAPMENT, 1038–1042

EQUAL ACCESS ACT, 609

EQUAL EDUCATIONAL OPPORTUNITY ACT OF 1974, pp. 646–647

EQUAL PROTECTION CLAUSE
age discrimination, 92
disability discrimination, 92–93
general, 24–30
intimate association discrimination, 124–131, 1147–1149
race discrimination, preface, 320, 704, 723, 1148–1149
sex discrimination, preface, 34–36, 73–92, 320, 346, 501, 503–504, 536, 552, 636, 646, 649, 877, 897, 1148–1149
sexual orientation discrimination, 92–131, 320, 638, 701, 726–727

EQUAL RIGHTS AMENDMENT
State constitutions, preface (listing states)
U. S. Constitution (proposed), preface, 78, 122, 345

ESSENTIALISM, 267–268, 270–271, 273, 296–300, 548, 1052–1055

FAMILY AND MEDICAL LEAVE ACT, 906

FEMALE GENITAL MUTILATION, 756–760

FEMINIST THEORY
See also Marriage; Queer Theory; Rape; Social Construction Theory; Surrogate Motherhood
Foucauldian feminism (Judith Butler, Vicki Bell), 228, 271–274, 277–282
liberal feminism (Wendy Webster Williams, Jana Singer), 765–773, 780
mutuality feminism (Martha Chamallas), 982–1015
radical feminism,
marriage critics (Carole Pateman, Paula Ettelbrick), 795, 817–818
regulatory (Bat–Ami Bar On, Catharine MacKinnon), 228, 249–250, 534–542, 1012–1015, 1029
prosex (Gayle Rubin, Pat Califia), 228, 250–259, 1015–1019
rational choice feminism (Carol Rose), 248

FIRST AMENDMENT
See also Free Exercise Clause; Free Speech Clause; Freedom of Association; Outing
exclusions, preface (general survey),
defamation and libel, 479–489, 509, 529, 554
hate speech, 491–506, 561, 638
obscenity, 6, 20–21, 508–520, 632, 637, 678
forums, preface (general survey),
adult theatres, 519–524
colleges and universities, 419, 443, 445–462, 481–484, 495, 531, 551, 632, 696
internet, 594
libraries, 610, 618
movies, 517
music lyrics, 564
newspapers, 463–472, 473–478, 508, 607, 626
radio and television, 463–472, 583–593, 626
secondary schools, 597–598, 606–610, 618, 621, 624
sex education and reproductive rights materials, 531, 544, 579–581
general theory and introduction, preface, 411, 509, 514–517
identity expression, 426–429, 430, 435–436, 441–443, 443–453, 455–462
rights of,
association, 415–419, 609
marching, 438–441
privacy, 463, 472–479
publication, 411–413, 515–516, 714
religious freedom, 443–453, 455–462, 686, 693–696, 713

FIRST AMENDMENT—Cont'd
rights of—Cont'd
sexual expression, 516, 519, 553, 602, 935–937
speech, 433, 491–506, 512, 553, 573, 602, 681
sodomy laws inconsistent with, 434–436

FORNICATION, 1, 26–27, 37, 55, 233, 742, 745

FOUCAULDIAN THEORY, 57–61, 69, 257–258, 524, 1043
See also Social Constructionist Theory

FREE EXERCISE CLAUSE, 445, 683–687, 693–696
See also First Amendment

FREE SPEECH CLAUSE, 6, 20–21, 445, 516, 620, 700
See also First Amendment

FREEDOM OF ASSOCIATION, 124–131, 415–419, 704, 711
See also First Amendment

FREUDIAN THEORY, 70–72, 141–152, 171, 272, 277, 291
See also Sexologists

GENDER
history, 162–166, 245, 321–331, 683
science and, 138–140, 208–210
sexual orientation, relation to, 260, 753
theory of, 90–92, 123–124, 249–261, 280–282, 296–300

GENETICS, 217–219

HATE SPEECH, 491–506, 561

HERMAPHRODITES, 204–209, 211–212

HUMAN IMMUNO-DEFICIENCY VIRUS (HIV)
See Acquired Immuno–Deficiency Syndrome (AIDS)

ILLEGITIMACY, 307

IMMIGRATION LAW
asylum for refugees, 755–761
exclusions from entry,
HIV disease, 189
prostitution, 155–156, 739
psychopathic personality, 175–189
"good moral character" requirement for citizenship, 739–743

INCEST, 1, 210, 274–278, 823–824

INDECENCY, 1, 37, 583–594, 1175, 1179

INITIATIVES AND REFERENDA
anti-civil rights, 684, 715, 723–724
anti-gay, 93–108, 715–716, 725–738
Colorado's Amendment, 2 93–106, 726–736
discourse of equivalents (Jane Schacter), 733–738

INITIATIVES AND REFERENDA—Cont'd
anti-gay—Cont'd
  Oregon's Ballot Measure 9, 726, 729

INTERGENERATIONAL SEX
See Minors, Sex With

INTERNATIONAL AND COMPARATIVE LAW
asylum, 755–756
hate speech, 561
obscenity law and pornography regulation, 555–560
privacy right to sexual intimacy, 752
sex and sexual orientation discrimination, 747–748, 751–756
transgender discrimination, 761

JUDAISM, 124–131, 292–296, 703

LIBERTARIAN THEORY (John Stuart Mill), 246–248

MANN ACT OF 1910, pp. 156–162, 1045

MARITAL STATUS DISCRIMINATION
employment benefits and sexual orientation discrimination, 124–131
religious reasons and free exercise, 695
statutory protections,
  California Fair Housing Act, 695, 723
  District of Columbia Human Rights Act, appendix 2
  Wisconsin Fair Employment Act, 957–958, appendix 3

MARKETS, ROLE OF, 235–239

MARRIAGE, 763–868
alimony, 772–773
constitutional right, 795–807
decline of, 763, 771, 795
hermaphrodites and, 211–212
history of, 241–244, 763
incestuous, 210, 823–824
limits imposed by the state, and legal challenges thereto,
  age, 822
  consanguinity, 823–824
  disease, 769
  imprisonment, 806–807
  mental disability, 769
  number, 824–826
  poverty preface, 769
  race preface, 795–799
  sex preface, 799–805, 807–822
  support obligations preface, 805–806
minors, with, 768, 822
natural law theory of, 230–232
polygamy, 107, 768, 822, 824–826
privatization of (Jana Singer),
  contract rights of cohabitants, 766–767
  contractual variation of marital obligations, 767
  individuation of the spouses, 768
  no-fault divorce, 769
  rights of nonmarital children, 765–766

MARRIAGE—Cont'd
privatization of (Jana Singer)—Cont'd
  single mothers, pauperized by, 772–774
rights and benefits of (list), 793–794
same-sex marriage, 764, 799–805, 807–822
sex and, 11–15, 18, 21, 29–30, 765
transsexuals' marriage, 1117–1124

MARXIST THEORY, 234–238, 246, 249, 259, 795

MEDICALIZATION, 6, 8, 19, 33, 368–371, 1109–1117

MILITARY
judicial deference to preface, 334–336, 346–359, 374–384
discriminations according to,
  age, 390
  cross–dressing, 1139–1140
  disabilities, 390
  height, 390
  race, 319, 321–341
  religion preface,
  sex, 74–78, 342–365, 390
  sexual orientation, 109–117 176, 310–313, 366–407, 434–436
  speech about sexual orientation, 388, 433
  weight, 390
manhood, 321–331
sexual harassment, 384–388
unit cohesion and morale, 388–407

MINORS, SEX BY AND WITH, 1021–1043
procedural issues, 1035–1036
  confrontation of (minor) accuser, 1037–1038
  entrapment, 1038–1042
  statute of limitations (suppression of memory), 1036–1037
statutory rape laws, 1021–1023 (list), 1176–1177 (Texas)
  constitutionality, 1024–1029
  intergenerational sex, 1030–1031, 1175
  penalties, 1176–1177
  sex between minors, 1024
theory and critique,
  anthropological perspective, 1031–1035
  feminist critique of intergenerational sex, 278, 1029
  foucault defense of intergenerational sex, 278–279, 1043
  other normative theories, 1034

MISCEGENATION, 120–121, 122–123, 795–799

MODEL PENAL CODE AND SODOMY REFORM, 37–39, 980

NATURAL LAW THEORY, 229–234

OUTING, 463–490

OBSCENITY, 1, 20–21, 413–414, 508–520, 526, 1180
See also First Amendment; Indecency

PEDOPHILIA
See Minors, Sex with

POLYGAMY, 107, 161–162, 247–248, 703, 732, 739, 756, 760, 824–826
same-sex marriage and, 825

PORNOGRAPHY
See also Obscenity
child, 525–532
electronic, 594
feminist debate over, 525, 533–549
gay pornography, 547, 561–562, 581
race issues, 567–576

PREGNANCY, 6–7, 3–37, 81, 607, 654, 896–897, 900–913
See also Employment Discrimination

PRISONS preface, 314–316, 1124–1130

PRIVACY, 2, 6–37, 40–72, 119, 233, 316–318, 472–479, 628
compulsory HIV testing and, 1080

PROSTITUTION, 1, 37, 44, 153–162, 307–308, 1044–1062
and AIDS, 1080

PUBLIC ACCOMMODATIONS, 437–438, 438–442, 707, 723

PUBLIC-PRIVATE DICHOTOMY, 18–19, 43–44, 92, 474–477, 518–519, 521–525, 582–583, 744, 752, 1072, 1096

QUEER THEORY
See also Social Construction Theory
deconstructive theory (Eve Sedgwick, Janet Halley), 66–71, 228, 289–300, 304–305, 313, 629
identity theory (Nan Hunter, William Eskridge, Jr.), 429–430, 434, 453, 476
pro-sex feminism (Gayle Rubin, Pat Califia, Duggan–Hunter–Vance), 228, 250–259, 1015–1019

RACE AND SEXUALITY
See also Critical Race Theory
adoption, 867–868, 848
AIDS, 1074–1076, 1078–1079
armed forces segregation, 321–341
censorship,
    library books, 610–617
    rap music, 564–573
child custody, 831–832
Hill–Thomas, 1002–1003
initiatives and referenda, 723–725
rape law, 995–1002, 1019, 1077–1078

RAPE, 1, 274–277, 279–280, 463–472, 759, 971–976
hate crime, 994
marital exemption, 992
Model Penal Code, 979–981, 987
race and, 995–1002, 1019, 1077–1078

REHABILITATION ACT OF 1973 (SECTION 504), 959–960, 1111

RELIGION, 229, 252, 292–296, 515, 656–657, 684–685, 695–697, 713–715
See also Christianity; Free Exercise Clause; Judaism; Religious Freedom Restoration Act

RELIGIOUS FREEDOM RESTORATION ACT, 684, 693–694

SADOMASOCHISM, 257, 549, 581–582, 1003, 1010–1011, 1020
See also Feminist Theory

SECURITY CLEARANCES, 891

SEX DISCRIMINATION
See also Equal Protection Clause; Sexual Harassment
abortion as, 34–36
gender stereotyping as, 74–78, 90–93, 260, 282–287, 647, 1103–1106
hostile school environment as, 639
pregnancy discrimination as, 81
sexual harassment as, 636, 638, 1062
sexual orientation discrimination as, 92–131, 260, 384–388, 638, 642
state discrimination, 78–92, 647, 1049, 1085

SEXOLOGISTS
early sexologists (Richard von Krafft–Ebing, Havelock Ellis), 136–141, 168, 175, 184
empiricists and post-Freudians (Alfred Kinsey, Evelyn Hooker), 145–148, 175, 179, 256, 595
Freudians and their critics,
    American Freudians (Sandor Rado, Irving Bieber), 144–145, 171, 184
    anti-clinicians (Thomas Szasz, Michel Foucault), 151–152
    feminist critics (Nancy Chodorow), 148–151
    Sigmund Freud's thought, 141–145, 171
gender issues,
    binarism (Krafft–Ebing), 138–140
    social construction of gender (John Money), 208–210
homosexuality,
    genetic theory (Dean Hamer), 217–219
    hormonal studies, 216–217
    hypothalamus theory (Simon LeVay), 214–216
    psychopathic disease theory (Sandor Rado), 145
law and sexology,
    censorship, 168–170
    cross-dressing ordinances, 1130–1132
    "hard-wired" homosexuality and arguments for gay rights (Edward Stein), 219–225
    immigration exclusion for psychopathic personality (rise and fall), 175–189
    sexual psychopath laws, 172–174
sex binarism issues,

Sexologists—Cont'd

sex binarism issues—Cont'd

   chromosomal anomalies (John Money), 203–207

   hermaphroditism (John Money), 204–209, 211–212

   intersexes (Anne Fausto–Sterling), 203

Sexual Harassment, 608, 630–632, 636–639, 673, 919–937

within sexualized workplace, 1057–1062

Sexual Orientation Discrimination

adoption and foster parenting, 786–787, 841–848

child custody and visitation, 832–841

employment, 124–131, 1104–1105

   state and federal anti-gay discrimination,

      federal armed forces, 109, 319, 366–407

      federal civil service, 880–895

      federal security clearances, 891

      state civil service, 949 note

      state teachers, 625–628, 731

   laws protecting against private antigay discrimination, 93–108

      District of Columbia Human Rights Act, 444–453, 696

      Employment Non–Discrimination Act, appendix 4

      state laws listed, 949 note

equal protection claims (general), 92–124

immigration, 761

initiatives repealing pro-gay laws, 725–726

marriage, 120, 799–817

military exclusion, 109, 319, 366–407

naturalization, 742–743

public education policies against "promoting" homosexuality, 426–429, 655, 666

sodomy laws, 37–72, 108, 742, 750

surro-gay arrangements, 849–853

Sexually Transmitted Diseases (STDs), 652, 654, 657

Social Construction Theory

basic theory (Michel Foucault, Janet Halley), 262–267, 268–271

examples,

   binarism of sex and gender (Anne Fausto–Sterling, Katharine Franke), 90–91, 203–204, 1106–1108, 1129

   child sex taboos (Claudia Konker), 1031

   compulsory heterosexuality (Adrienne Rich)

   disease and epidemics (Linda Singer, Paula Treichler), 1066–1069

   dress codes (Marjorie Garber), 1129–1130

   gender stereotypes (Nancy Chodorow, Mary Anne Case)

   homophobia (Jane Schacter), 733

   hostile or discouraging workplaces (Vicki Schultz)

   incest taboos (Foucault, Vicki Bell), 274–280

Social Construction Theory—Cont'd

examples—Cont'd

   pornography (David Cole), 521–525

   privacy (Jed Rubenfeld), 316–318

   race and sexuality (Kimberlé Crenshaw, Harlon Dalton), 567, 1074–1078

   religion (Robert Cover), 709

   sexual orientation (Mary McIntosh), 262

   sexual psychopathy (Thomas Szasz), 151–152

feminism and (Judith Butler, Vicki Bell), 271–282

law as an agent (Janet Halley, Ellen Ross, Rayna Rapp), 306–309

Sodomy Laws

constitutionality, 37–72, 118

   federal preface, 40–72

   state, 37–72, 731, 745, 750, 1175

history, 1, 37–72, 167, 981

lists of sodomy laws, 38–39 notes

   currently applicable to consensual sodomy, 38 note

   only applicable to consensual sodomy if homosexual, 38–39 notes

normative critique, 56

   double bind for gay people (Janet Halley), 57

   homophobia (Kendall Thomas), 66–71

   importance of intimacy (Michael Sandel), 71–72

Speech-Conduct Distinction, 425, 518–525

Status-Conduct Debate, 57–61, 101–102, 106, 108–119, 383–384, 628, 699, 738

Statutory Rape

See also Minors, Sex with

Sterilization, preface

Surrogacy Contracts, 774–781

feminist debate,

   best interests of the child (Susan Okin), 780

   connections between mother and child (Robin West), 779–780

   exploitation of women (Carole Pateman), 779

   gender stereotyping (Debra Satz), 780–781

   market inalienability (Margaret Radin), 776–778, 779

   women's exploitation of their bodies (Carmel Shalev and Lori Andrews)

gestational surrogacy, 778, 781 note

statutes prohibiting or regulating (list), 778

surro-gay arrangements (Marla Hollandsworth), 781, 849–853

Title VII, Civil Rights Act of 1964

See Employment Discrimination

TRANSGENDER, TRANSSEXUALS, 79, 1102–1119
child custody and visitation, 1124
defined, 1102–1103, 1110–1119
marriage, 1117–1124
medicalization, 212–213, 1109–1117
workplace discrimination, 1103–1107, 1111

TRANSVESTISM
See Cross–Dressing

UNITED STATES
as a party in litigation, 74, 81, 109, 158, 179,
    310, 348, 374, 403, 404, 411, 508, 573,
    585

UNITED STATES—Cont'd
policy positions of, 8, 174, 175–178, 186–189,
    338–346, 357–359, 366–373, 400–403,
    573–579

VAGUENESS, preface, 39–40, 162, 512, 573

VIOLENCE
against gay men and lesbians, 108, 638, 760
against women, 759, 994–995

VIOLENCE AGAINST WOMEN ACT, 994–995

WELFARE BENEFITS, 772

WORKPLACE DISCRIMINATION
See Employment Discrimination

†